Debrett's People of Kent

LEEDS CASTLE
Photograph by W R Davies, Spectrum Colour Library

Debrett's People of Kent

Edited by
Julie West

Executive Editor
Patricia Ellis

Series Co-ordinator
Michelle Jacques

Published by

DEBRETT'S PEERAGE LIMITED

73/77 Britannia Road · PO Box 357 · London · SW6 2JY

ISBN 1 870520 01 7

Debrett's People of Kent
Published by Debrett's Peerage Limited
73/77 Britannia Road · PO Box 357 · London · SW6 2JY

Printed in England

Computer typesetting prepared by Morton Computer Services Limited, Scarborough, Yorks.

Printed and bound by BPCC Wheatons Ltd, Marsh Barton, Exeter

CONTENTS

G506 DNV

FOREWORD

It is with great pleasure that I welcome *Debrett's People of Kent*, the first in a new series of county biographical reference books to be published by Debrett's.

Debrett's People of Kent is a very welcome addition to all those local books that already adorn our bookshelves. It is unique in its aims and achievements for the very reason that it is so much more than just a reference book. It contains a mine of useful information on such matters as correct forms of style and address and I note with interest the inclusion of four articles reflecting different aspects of Kent, past and present.

As Lord Lieutenant I am especially pleased that Debrett's has chosen Kent with which to begin its new county series, and I am sure that the books to follow will be met with equal praise.

Robin Leigh-Pemberton

INTRODUCTION

Debrett's People of Kent is the first in a new series of county books and, like *Debrett's People of Today*, it contains the biographies of many eminent contemporary men and women. We have selected some 2,500 Men and Maids of Kent, Kentish Men and Maids, and people involved with the county who come from without its boundaries. All have made a significant contribution to British society as a whole or feature prominently in the local life of the county.

The introductory pages of the book give an abundance of useful information, from brief biographies of members of the Royal Family, to correct forms of address. There is also a Foreword by Robin Leigh-Pemberton, the Lord Lieutenant of Kent, to whom we would like to extend our grateful thanks. In addition, there are four informative articles about various aspects of the county. Our senior editor, David Williamson, has written an intriguing piece entitled The Honour of Kent which traces the history of the Dukedom of Kent; Peter Battrick from The National Trust tells about The Attractions of Kent to both the local and visitor alike; E W Swanton, the well known cricket writer, has written a short history of cricket in Kent, and Alan Bignell, author of 'Hopping Down in Kent' as well as numerous other local books, provides us with a fascinating account of hop farming in Kent dating back to the middle ages.

The third section of the book contains useful commercial and professional listings of businesses and services from both in and around the county.

Finally, it only remains for me to thank all those who have helped to produce *Debrett's People of Kent*, and in particular, Patricia Ellis, Michelle Jacques, Charles Kidd and David Williamson for their valuable guidance. We look forward to producing the next books in the series.

JULIE WEST

THE COUNTY ARMS OF KENT

HERALDIC DESCRIPTION

Arms– Gules a Horse forcene Argent.

Crest– Issuant from a Mural Crown proper three masts rigged with courses set and topsails furled proper flying from each mast head a pennon Argent charged with a Cross Gules.

Supporters– On either side a Sea Lion Or gorged with a Collar Gules pendent therefrom an escutcheon the dexter of the Arms of the See of Canterbury and the sinister of the Arms of the Cinque Port.

Motto– Invicta

AN EXPLANATION OF THE COMPONENT PARTS OF THE ARMORIAL BEARINGS

Shield– The white horse rampant on a red field has for many years been the badge of Kent and tradition ascribes it to Horsa, a leader of the first Saxon settlement in England, in the Isle of Thanet. The horse is modelled on an old depiction in the Maidstone Museum and is considered to be among the best existing examples of the Kentish Wild Horse.

Crest– The crest is composed of a mural coronet with three masts and sails rising therefrom. The coronet commemorates the fact that for four hundred years Kent was a kingdom. Its mural form is symbolic of the many fortified castles and towns in the County and the masts and sails are emblems of its intimate connexion with the Navy, the Mercantile Marine and Sea Fisheries.

Supporters– The sea-lions which support the shield are symbolic of the support which Kentish seamen have given to the sea-power of England through the centuries and the fact that the long coast-line of Kent is part of the frontier of England.

From the collar of one sea-lion is suspended a shield from the Arms of the Cinque Ports, which for about two hundred years supplied the whole fighting navy of England, and continued to provide a large proportion for much longer. Four of the Cinque Ports are in Kent.

From the collar of the other sea-lion is suspended a shield from the Arms of the Archbishopric of Canterbury, the See of St. Augustine who landed in Kent A.D. 597, and the primary See of the English Church.

Motto– The word "Invicta", meaning "unconquered" or "untamed", is honoured by long usage, and possibly owes its origin to the defence put up by the community of Kent against William the Conqueror. An extract from "A Topographie or Survey of the County of Kent" by Richard Kilburne, 1659, reads:-

> "... For the ancient valour of the people of this County, they claime, and are allowed the front in Battailes. And they onely of all *England* obtleyned and reteyne the name of UNCONQUERED: For (as if all the antient English valour were remaining in them) they only resisted King *William* the Conquerour, when all other Counties submitted) and (capitulating with him) reserved to themselves and their posterity, their antient Customes and Liberties."

The motto is borne upon a ribbon approximating as nearly as possible to the time-honoured Kentish Grey, a colour of significance in the days of the weaving industy in Kent.

Helmet and Mantling– The helmet and mantling are included in conformity with heraldic practice in cases where a crest is displayed. The mantling is of red and white in conformity with the livery colours shown on the shield.

The Armorial bearings were granted to Kent County Council on 17th October 1933 and re-confirmed to the new County Council on reorganisation on 16th April 1975.

Reproduced courtesy of Kent County Council

THE HONOUR OF KENT

THEIR ROYAL HIGHNESSES THE DUKE AND DUCHESS OF KENT
Photograph by Norman Parkinson, Camera Press London

From the 5th to the 8th centuries AD, Kent was one of the foremost kingdoms of the Saxon Heptarchy. The Oiscings, the dynasty founded by Hengest and named from his son Oisc, were the first to accept christianity when King Ethelbert and all his court rejected the pagan gods and received baptism from Pope Gregory's missionary St Augustine (destined to become the first Archbishop of Canterbury) in 597. Thereafter the royal house produced many saints of both sexes before the kingdom was absorbed into the larger entity of Wessex. King Egbert of Wessex (802-839), under whom this took place, was almost certainly the son of a Kentish Princess and consequently the blood of Hengest and Ethelbert flows today in that of HM Queen Elizabeth II.

In 1067 William the Conqueror rewarded his redoubtable half-brother Odo, Bishop of Bayeux, who had accompanied him at the Battle of Hastings, by creating him Earl of Kent and Warden of Dover Castle with a grant of some 200 manors in the county. The powerful and warlike Bishop had a long career in the course of which he attempted to acquire many more Kentish manors and eventually became so corrupted by his greed that William was obliged to deprive him of the Earldom and imprison him in Normandy, only ordering his release when on his deathbed in 1087. Odo returned to England with his nephew William Rufus and almost immediately resumed his old pursuits, intriguing and plundering, until Rufus banished him from the country. He now sought favour with his eldest nephew, Robert, Duke of Normandy, and left with him to take part in the Crusade, but death overtook him at Palermo in February 1097 and he was buried in the Cathedral there. The Earldom of Kent was claimed without success by his full nephew, William, Count of Mortain; but 130 years were to elapse before Kent again became a peerage honour.

In February 1226/7, King Henry III, eight days after attaining his majority, granted the county of Kent to his Justiciar, Hubert de Burgh, the most powerful man in the kingdom. Hubert died 12 May 1243, but as the remainder to the Earldom of Kent had been limited to his issue by his third wife Margaret, daughter of William the Lion, King of Scots, of whom there was none surviving, it became extinct.

Almost another 80 years passed by until 28 July 1321, when King Edward II conferred the Earldom of Kent on his half-brother, Edmund of Woodstock, the youngest son of King Edward I, by girding him with the sword and granting him the sum of £30 per annum from the revenues of the county as well as several farms and hundreds of land to hold for life. Edmund had already been summoned to Parliament on his 19th birthday (5 August 1320), whereby he is held to have become Lord Woodstock. Poor Edmund eventually became a victim of the times, being caught up in the intrigues and skirmishes with Queen Isabel, Mortimer and Prince Edward which finally led to the deposition of Edward II. Edmund supported his nephew King Edward III but later in an inexplicable change of face after being convinced that Edward II was still alive, began plotting for his half-brother's restoration, was arrested, charged with high treason, condemned and executed as a traitor at Winchester 19 March 1330.

The Earldom of Kent was restored on petition the following December to Edmund's son, also Edmund, it being stated that "he should not lose the title of Earl, his father having been at all times good and loyal although deceived by wicked men." The little boy did not live very long to enjoy his honour, dying 5 October 1331, aged about five. He was succeeded as Earl of Kent and Lord Woodstock by his brother John, who in his turn died childless in 1352 and was succeeded by his only sister Joan, the famous "Fair Maid of Kent," described by Froissart as "the most beautiful lady in the whole realm of England, and the most amorous." Joan's chequered matrimonial career was the scandal of her day. At a tender age she became the child bride of Sir Thomas de Holand, who left soon after to participate in the French wars of King Edward III. While he was distinguishing himself at Crecy, Joan contracted a marriage with William Montagu, Earl of Salisbury, with whom she was apparently infatuated. Thomas petitioned Pope Clement VI, who after ordering an investigation into the matter which took two years to complete, finally ordered Joan to return to her lawful husband, which she did. During the whole of this period Joan remained at court and was reputed to have become the mistress of her cousin the King. The traditional story of her dropping her garter at a ball and the King retrieving it with the words "Honi soit qui mal y pense" ("evil to him who thinks ill of it") and subsequently founding the order of the Garter is probably based on truth and belongs to this period of Joan's life. Thomas de Holand, who was a founder member of the Order, died in Normandy in December 1360 and the following October his widow married Edward, Prince of Wales (known to history as "The Black Prince"), the son of her reputed one time lover the King. He was her junior by nearly two years and died before his father in 1376. The following year their only surviving son succeeded his grandfather as King Richard II and Joan, as the King's mother, became the first lady in the land retaining that position until Richard's marriage in 1382. In the preceding year she had been on a pilgrimage to Canterbury when her carriage was surrounded by a threatening mob of Wat Tyler's Kentish insurgents and she was so frightened that she ordered her entourage to drive back to London without a single halt. The "Fair Maid" died at Wallingford Castle, Berkshire, in August 1385 and was succeeded by her son Thomas de Holand, who became 5th Earl of Kent. He died in 1397 and was succeeded by his son, also Thomas, as 6th Earl. Later in the same year Thomas was created Duke of Surrey by his half-uncle the King, but after Richard's downfall in 1399 he fell foul of the Lancastrians and was finally captured and beheaded at Cirencester in January 1400. The Dukedom of Surrey became extinct but the Earldom of Kent passed to Thomas's brother Edmund, the last Earl of his family, who died without legitimate issue in 1408.

The Earldom of Kent was revived in 1461 in favour of William Neville, a son of the Earl of Westmorland, but again became extinct on his death in 1463. It was revived again in 1465 for Edmund

Grey, Lord Grey of Ruthin, a kinsman of the Holands. The Earldom was to remain with the Grey family for the best part of three centuries. They never resided in the county and took no interest in its affairs, although Anthony, the 11th Earl, died suddenly on the bowling green at Tonbridge in August 1702. His son and successor, Henry, 12th Earl, having played a prominent role in Tory politics was created Marquess of Kent in 1706 and Duke of Kent in 1710 by Queen Anne. Unfortunately his sons all died before him and on his death in June 1740, the Dukedom, Marquessate and Earldom of Kent became extinct.

In 1799 Kent became a Royal Dukedom when King George III created his fourth son, Prince Edward, Duke of Kent and of Strathearn and Earl of Dublin. Although this Dukedom became extinct on the Prince's death in 1820, he is remembered as the father of Queen Victoria, who, rather curiously, reduced Kent to an Earldom again when she conferred it on her second son Prince Alfred with the Earldom of Ulster and Dukedom of Edinburgh in 1866. Prince Alfred, who became reigning Duke of Saxe-Coburg and Gotha in succession to his paternal uncle, died before his mother in 1900 and as his only son had predeceased him, the peerage honours became extinct once again.

On 12 October 1934 King George V created his fourth son, Prince George, Duke of Kent, Earl of St Andrews and Baron Downpatrick. The creation was made a little over a month before the Prince's very popular marriage to Princess Marina of Greece and Denmark was due to take place and the new young Duke and Duchess soon emerged as what would today be termed "trendsetters' with an adoring following. Unfortunately, the Second World War came all too soon and Prince George tragically lost his life in a flying accident while on active service in August 1942, leaving his widow with three young children. The elder son, Prince Edward, succeeded his father as 2nd Duke of Kent and has spent his whole life in devoted public service, ably supported by his charming Duchess, the former Miss Katharine Worsley, whom he married in 1961.

DAVID WILLIAMSON

THE 14th CENTURY MOATED CASTLE IN SCOTNEY CASTLE GARDEN
D Sellman/The National Trust

THE ATTRACTIONS OF KENT

For too many Kent is just on the road to somewhere else, a county to pass through on the way to or from the Continent. They are the unfortunate ones; for those who live here or who bother to glance to one side as they race past, it is a place to explore and return to again and again, to enjoy the diversity it offers in everything. From the White Cliffs to the wooded Weald, from sturdy Martello Towers to the majesty of Leeds Castle, from tranquil village green to bustling city market, there really is something for everyone.

Kent offers many faces to the discerning viewer. The world knows the White Cliffs of Dover, where the North Downs finally meet the sea. Behind the coast lies a fertile plain, the "Garden of England". Slowly the undulations increase until suddenly there are steep hills, sharp corners, far-reaching vistas. You are in the Kentish Weald, heartland of the early iron industry where the once impenetrable forest was slowly felled to provide charcoal for the furnaces, and timber for ships and dwellings, many of which still survive to form the weather-boarded face of the wealden village; Biddenden, home of the "Maydes", Siamese twins Eliza and Mary Chalkhurst who lived here around 1100; Goudhurst, huddling around the hilltop church; Cranbrook, once the centre of the clothmaking industry, and Tenterden where the age of steam lives on in the form of the Kent and East Sussex Railway. The chalk downlands and rich soils of the North, the rolling wooded hills of the centre give way to the flat, windswept marshes of the South East. Romney Marsh offers a unique landscape, dotted with sheep and fascinating churches, and reeking of a history built on smuggling. Dungeness, and the lonely marshes of the Swale Estuary to the North, are a bird-watchers' paradise. A diverse landscape indeed.

While the coastal marshes remain isolated and sparsely populated, much of North Kent today falls heavily under the shadow of Greater London. The influence of the capital has always been there and the county can still proudly live up to its age-old label of the "Garden of England", with agriculture crowding round the outer edges of suburbia. The county town of Maidstone is set amongst some of England's most scenic and fertile countryside. Orchards and hopfields surround the town, and the area also provides most of London's fruit and vegetables. As agriculture changes so does the face of Kent. Demand for English hops has declined, but the white-cowled oasthouses remain to entrance visitors – now mostly as homes rather than work places. Faversham, however, on the Swale, remains one of the last brewing centres in the country, while Whitbread's Hop Farm, at Beltring, is a reminder of just how the brewing industry used to affect the country people of Kent, many of whom can still remember the "invasions" of the East Enders at harvest time each year, bringing a new language and lifestyle. Orchards still abound, smothering the countryside with billowing spring blossoms.

A garden indeed. Blessed with a soft climate, Kent has sired many a fruit, the cherries Kentish Bigarreau and Kentish Red, the nut Kentish Cob, and plums, apples and pears. Today an ancient fruit has returned, the grape. Perhaps introduced before the Romans, and certainly popular in medieval monasteries, Kentish and England's vineyards languished until the second half of this century. Now there are vineyard tours and tastings of wines that are winning gold medals against the best that Europe can offer. And while the subject is food, don't forget Whitstable's Oyster Festival every July and August.

The climate that created the "Garden of England" has also produced some of the finest gardens in England. Spring is early, marked by the azaleas, camellias and rhododendrons of Emmetts and Riverhill House Gardens, near Sevenoaks. Connoisseurs aim first for Sissinghurst Castle Garden, with its exquisite collection of "open air living rooms", created just 50 years ago by Vita Sackville-West and Harold Nicolson. A garden worthy of its international fame, from the Spring bulbs of the Lime Walk, through the heavy scents of rambling Bourbon and Damask roses of high summer, to the dramatic late summer colours of the Cottage Garden. Roses abound, not just in the grand gardens but around every cottage door, creating an atmosphere of romance that is nowhere better reflected than at Scotney Castle, Lamberhurst. Here the garden, nestling around the ruins of a small 14th century moated castle in the unspoilt valley of the River Bewl, abounds with azaleas, water-lilies and wisteria, secluded corners and panoramas of delight.

There are castles all over and around the county. Kent for thousands of years has been the chosen landing place for invaders; the Romans landed here, as did Hengist and Horsa. The French ravaged the coast in the 13th and 14th centuries, while Napoleon looked fondly across the Channel in the early 19th century, as did Hitler in the 20th century. To protect their conquest the Romans built their own defences; at Dover, the castle, with its magnificent keep added by Henry II, dominates the hilltop above the town. Of the original Cinque Ports, set up by Edward I's Charter of 1278 granting privileges in return for providing ships for the King's fleet to defend the realm, four were in Kent; Dover, Sandwich, Hythe and Romney, only Hastings lay outside the county, but only Dover remains a flourishing port. In Napoleonic times the castle defences were brought up to date with a cunning system of spiral staircases, grenade shafts for blowing up trapped troops and remotely controlled doors for taking prisoners. It was the threat of Napoleonic invasion that brought about the rash of Martello Towers around the coast. One can visit No. 24 at Dymchurch. It was from above the White Cliffs that the great guns of two world wars bombarded the French Channel ports. Remains of gun emplacements can be seen right round "Hell-Fire Corner" from the Dover Patrol Memorial to Lydden Spout Battery.

The "loveliest castle in the world" was how Lord Caenarfon christened Leeds castle, near Maidstone. Whether it is or not is in the eye of the beholder, but this is a fairytale castle, dating from the 9th century, built on two small islands in a lake surrounded by 500 acres of superb parkland, laid out by "Capability" Brown. Such a fine setting made it a favoured retreat of medieval Queens of England.

An English Queen spent her childhood here in Kent, at Hever Castle, Edenbridge. Here was the scene of courtship between Henry VIII and Anne Boleyn. This beautiful moated 13th century castle is set in magnificent gardens where the couple can still be imagined, walking, enjoying the maze, formal Italian Garden, topiary and a Rhododendron Walk. Henry VIII is closely associated, too, with Knole, around which has grown Sevenoaks. More of a village than a house, Knole has 7 courtyards, 52 staircases and 365 rooms, using some artistic licence, and is correspondingly known as a "calendar house". Intimately linked with the Sackville family, Knole's appearance is in fact owed to Thomas Bouchier, Archbishop of Canterbury. It was a later Archbishop, Cranmer, who, wisely recognising a hint from Henry VIII, made a gift of the house to the King, and it remained in royal hands until 1566 when Elizabeth I presented it to her cousin, Thomas Sackville, subject to lease. In 1603 Sackville bought the freehold and, although now owned by The National Trust, the family has lived there ever since.

"Good Queen Bess" is also closely associated with Penshurst Place, home of the Sidney family from 1552. Sir Philip Sidney's brilliant life at Elizabeth's court was cut off in its prime before the walls of Zutphen, in the Low Countries. His heroic death in 1586 is remembered in the shape of his helmet which holds pride of place in the breathtaking Great Hall, itself perfectly preserved from 1341.

There are no such close family associations at Ightham Mote, a few miles east of Knole; its exquisite beauty has been held in many hands. This moated manor house is hidden down narrow leafy lanes and the apparently harmonious construction has in fact developed over 300 years. With its two chapels, a heavily beamed Great Hall where a skeleton literally was found in a walled-up cupboard, cobbled courtyard with huge Victorian dog kennel, plus such a magical location, this is a hidden gem on the Sevenoaks Ridge.

While Ightham Mote spans the last 500 years of Kent's history, Chartwell, near Westerham, brings it almost right up to date. The home of Sir Winston Churchill from 1924 to the end of his life, the house is much as it was when he lived there, his wartime study at its heart. It was the wonderful views across the Weald that appealed to Churchill as much as the house, and much of the atmosphere of Chartwell is in the garden and the orchard he planted. The Golden Rose Walk was planted by the Churchill children to mark their parents Golden Wedding Anniversary in 1958, and around the whole garden is the wall Sir Winston helped to build in his "Wilderness Years." Many of Churchill's paintings are on view, both in the house and in the garden studio.

The history of Kent is totally entwined with that of Canterbury, the city and its cathedral being at the heart of its mercantile and religious life. It was Chaucer who so mischievously documented

THE GARDEN AT CHARTWELL
D Sellman/The National Trust

the medieval pilgrims' travels to the city. The path they followed, now known as the Pilgrims Way, started life in the Iron Age or earlier as the major trade route between Salisbury Plain and the ports to the continent. Thomas à'Beckett's jewel encrusted tomb in the Cathedral was destroyed by Thomas Cromwell's men, who removed 26 cartloads of booty for their master, but the old walled town speaks of not just its own and Kent's, but England's history at every corner.

The maritime history of England, too, is an extension of that of Kent, particularly in the cases of the towns along the Thames and the Medway. Nelson joined his first ship at Gillingham, Drake began his career on the Medway, and the Georgian dockyard at Chatham has been restored as an evocative working museum. Further west is Rochester, a city that captivated Charles Dickens and to which he refers in his works. It also boasts a rich Norman heritage; its castle is one of the finest Norman military buildings in Britain and only Canterbury in the whole of England can claim an older cathedral.

Rochester and Canterbury are today busy, bustling centres, now extended far beyond the old city walls, for Kent does not just have its roots set deep in the history of England, it looks hard to the future. Modern Ashford is one of the country's fastest growing business centres, soon to have a major continental rail passenger and freight interchange. Dover remains the premier port for cross-channel shipping, a link set to become more permanent and tangible when the Channel Tunnel, leaving from under Shakespeare Cliff, is finally opened. Tunbridge Wells mixes old and new with the recently restored Pantiles shopping centre. The county looks forward with enthusiasm, but in most cases without totally taking its eyes from the best of that which has gone before.

Kent offers so much to see and enjoy to anyone caring to take the time to share its history, to smell the blossom, to watch a game of cricket on a village green. There will be further temptations to rush, blinkered, as the motorways are extended, as the railway to London is improved, the Tunnel opened. All good for business, but offering even less opportunity to get to know the real Kent. The discerning traveller will bide a while, travel quiet lanes, stay in a weather-boarded inn or a tile-hung farmhouse surrounded by orchards, and then he will begin to know all that Kent really has to offer.

PETER BATTRICK

CRICKET BRED IN KENTISH SOIL

The medieval beginnings of cricket are shrouded in the mists of the Weald. What is however certain is that the game evolved in the forest clearings of Kent and Sussex. It was well established in the mid-17th century when a man was charged at Maidstone with selling beer at a match without a licence – which suggests a crowd. It was written of this period that "every cottage in the cricket-playing districts in Kent had a well-greased bat either kept in the bacon-rack or hung up behind the kitchen door."

The game took stronger root when during the Commonwealth the nobility and gentry forsook London for their estates and took to playing with the villagers in their employ. Hence came patronage and matches for stake-money.

The Sackvilles of Knole were early on the scene, and (jumping ahead) we find that in the first of all matches of which the full score has been preserved – when Kent beat England by one wicket on the Artillery Ground in London in 1744 – John, 7th Lord played under the captaincy of Val Romney, his father's gardener. It was no doubt on evidence such as this that the historian, Trevelyan, wrote that if the French aristocracy had played cricket with their servants there would have been no Revolution.

"England" in this context meant the southern counties. In due course the game drifted north, with strongholds among the piece-workers of Nottingham and Sheffield, and thence across the Pennines. Overseas, the Navy and Army planted cricket in the far-flung colonies. In the mid-19th century English professionals were taking missionary teams to Australia. By now teams from the West Indian territories visited one another. In 1878 the first Australian tourists came to England, and down to Kent, where it all began.

By now the first days of Kent's glory were behind them when England and Kent played one another frequently and with honours even. "The good old Kent XI" of Alfred Mynn, Fuller Pilch and Felix were acclaimed The First Champions. The Canterbury Week was instituted in 1842, and at once became, as it is today a century and a half later, the chief focus – flagship if you like – of Kent cricket.

It says enough of the breadth of interest throughout the county that Kent XIs have hosted matches on no fewer than 32 grounds, from the metropolitan centres, Blackheath, Beckenham and Catford Bridge down through Dartford, Sevenoaks, Tonbridge, Maidstone and Canterbury to Folkestone and Dover.

Though there had been an earlier club centred on Maidstone the present Kent CCC dates from 1870. For many years it revolved around the formidable figure of the 4th Lord Harris, who was captain from 1875 for 15 years (the same length of tenure as Colin Cowdrey) and at one stage was concurrently Captain, Chairman and President. He led England in the first-ever Test at home in 1880, and went on playing club cricket, when not engaged in serving the Queen-Emperor in India or being involved in high affairs of state at home, almost until his death aged 81 in 1932. Lord Harris guided the affairs both of MCC and Kent all his long life, a benevolent though outwardly formidable despot, who exerted a stronger influence on the game than anyone since. By a few he is still remembered with mingled awe and affection 60 years later.

Kent's fortunes in the last century depended upon which amateurs could make themselves available. Four victories over the Australians in two decades is evidence of their strength at best. Equally they were too inconsistent to challenge the strongest counties, Notts, Surrey and Yorkshire.

The turning-point came with the foundation in 1897 at Tonbridge of the training-ground for young professionals presided over by Captain William McCanlis, and called the Tonbridge Nursery. R L Arrowsmith, the historian of Kent cricket, wrote that although McCanlis "no doubt inculcated those basic principles of cricket that never alter" he thought that "he achieved more by what he was than by what he said. They were all so anxious to please him – that was the great secret."

The transformation in Kent's affairs was almost immediate. By the onset of the first World War in 1914 the county had won the first four of its seven Championships, were runners-up once and third

Photographs Courtesy of Kent County Cricket Club

four times. In this period the Nursery had produced a dozen cricketers good enough, either then or subsequently, to win Kent caps: Blythe, Fielder, Woolley, Hardinge, Freeman (all of whom played for England), Humphreys, Seymour, Fairservice, Hubble, Preston, Jennings and Collins – plus several who had successful careers with other counties.

On permanent loan to Kent from the Marsham family is a handsome cuttings book covering fully the events of 1906 under the leadership of Cloudesley Marsham. It includes literally hundreds of letters and telegrams of congratulation from a remarkable cross-section of Kent life showing how all sorts and conditions of men were united in support for the County XI. The senders range in the social scale from the Viceroy of India to inhabitants of the Poplar Workhouse!

In the first 35 summers after the Nursery began operations Kent never finished below half-way in the Championship. Unfortunately there was no successor in the McCanlis mould. In the 1920s Gerry Weigall had two spells in charge, first at Tonbridge and, when the Nursery moved, at Canterbury. An immortal character, he was too idiosyncratic to succeed. Most of his swans turned out to be geese – though, to his eternal credit, he at first glance induced Leslie Ames of Elham to take up wicket-keeping, to complement his budding skill as a batsman.

Amateurs, of course, still had an important part to play and there was seldom a lack of them right up to the abolition of the distinction in 1962. When Kent won its first Championship in 1906 the first five in the batting averages were amateurs. They never had quite such a preponderance again, if only because that summer saw the arrival of one, Frank Edward Woolley, prince of players, the Pride of Kent, of whose first season *Wisden* with the studied moderation of the times wrote that "the colt Woolley deserves more than passing notice." The cricket-writers of those days knew better than to encourage swollen heads. Not indeed that that was likely in Frank's case. Superb all-rounder that he was, and as commanding a left-hand batsman as ever graced the stage he was in private life a modest, quiet fellow. Only Sir Jack Hobbs narrowly defeated his aggregate of 58,959 in addition to which he took 2,068 wickets and made more than a thousand catches.

By the first war then Kent's position among what were generally known as the Big Six was assured: Surrey, Kent and Middlesex in the south; Yorkshire, Lancashire and Notts on the river Trent and to the north. Between the wars the county never had the resources in the faster bowling techniques to add to the four titles. Yet they were always popular as the fastest scoring side in England, and they nearly always finished close behind the leaders; twice runners-up in the 1930s, they finished third three years running. Moreover in "Tich" Freeman they had a phenomenally successful bowler of the leg-break and googly-type. If there is one statistic which completely baffles modern cricketers it is that in eight successive summers he took 200 wickets, in four of them (1928-31) the bag was 1,122! Only Wilfred Rhodes finished ahead of his aggregate of 3,776.

Kent's only prolonged spell in the shadows occurred after the Second World War when for 15 years they languished near the foot of the Championship. Revival came in the latter years of M C Cowdrey's captaincy. With Leslie Ames beside him as Secretary-Manager Colin brought off the Championship in the Club's Centenary Year of 1970. These were golden times for Kent with ten awards in the four competitions within twelve years.

There have been near-misses since then, and some not so near. As I write, players, members and followers all over the county are hungry for a return to the days of glory which ended with the winning of the Championship in 1978. There has been a distinct levelling of resources among the seventeen counties since then, but Kent's fortunes will rise again, for sure. How splendid it would be if the process were to begin in 1991!

E W SWANTON

THE WHITBREAD HOP FARM, BELTRING
Photograph Courtesy of Syndication International Library

KENT'S "WICKED WEED": THE HISTORY OF HOP FARMING IN KENT

You need only stand in a Kentish hop garden and experience the dizzying perspectives of the bines and the narcotic aroma of the papery hop cones to understand something of the almost mystic significance hops have for that most favoured county.

Kent and hops have become almost synonymous during the last six hundred years, although hops have been growing in Britain certainly since Roman times and possibly long before that. We know the Romans ate bine shoots as a delicacy, akin to asparagus, and they may have brought their Mediterranean hops with them as they spread across Western Europe.

But at the time of the Norman Conquest, English hops were weeds growing wild in the hedgerows and in one sense it was sheep that brought the cultivation of hops to England.

During the 13th century, English wool was as good as any in the world but English technology and skill needed to turn it into fine woollen goods was less distinguished. So, in the 14th century, Edward III had the idea of encouraging Flemish weavers to come and settle in England and give a boost to this country's woollen industry.

Although many of the Flemish weavers found England very much to their liking, they did not take as readily to the thick, sweet ale that was their host country's favourite tipple. They much preferred the lighter, clearer Continental beer with its bitter taste imparted by hops, which were also used to clarify it.

So they began to grow their own hops here, in their gardens at first, much as we would grow runner beans today, for the beer they brewed themselves. It was not long, however, before beer gained a much wider popularity despite protests by ale-quaffing traditionalists that the well-known soporific quality of hops made men lazy. Efforts were even made to ban "this wicked weed" from the brewing process, but popular demand was too strong and soon hops were being cultivated in many English counties.

Hops like a strong, well-drained soil and shelter from climatic extremes. Both East Kent and The Weald suited them very well and both claim to have had the first commercial hop gardens.

But hops also demand of their growers a heavy investment of cash and care during the three or four years it takes the plants to become established and start yielding any returns.

For centuries, hops were grown on poles, usually of ash, larch or chestnut and whether a farmer planted his own coppices or bought the hundreds of poles he needed from someone else, they represented a major outlay.

Hops, too, are prone to attack by disease and pests and before the days of chemical sprays it was by no means certain that a grower would not find a flourishing hop garden ravaged almost overnight and the return he looked for lost for another three or four years at least.

One of the main reasons why Kent became the premier hop county of England was because it had, as well as the right natural conditions, some of the most prosperous farmers in the country who for centuries had flourished by supplying an ever-growing market in London with eagerly sought-after crops of all kinds, and who could afford the heavy investment hops demanded.

Until the 16th century, The Weald was the industrial centre of England. Its towns and villages rang with the clamour of the ironfounders who produced the guns that armed the great wooden warships of the day. But then fears began to be voiced that if the ironfounders did not stop burning the dwindling Wealden forest trees to fuel their furnaces, there would soon be no timber left to build the ships that carried the cannons.

The argument had nothing to do with "green" issues. It was a conflict between the ironmasters and the ship builders and it was the ship builders who won. Other sources of fuel were available in the coal fields of the North but once the timber was gone there could be no more heart-of-oak navy.

At about the same time as The Weald fell silent and industry gave way to agriculture, the Industrial Revolution was bloating the populations of the cities, including London, and the demand for beer – a safer and certainly more palatable alternative to the public water supply – led to the establishment of major commercial breweries to replace old home-brewing habits.

Quite suddenly, the demand for hops increased, too.

The combination of the right natural conditions, good road and water communications with London, and farmers who could afford the necessary investment, soon established Kent as undisputed king of the hop-growing counties, producing more than half of the entire national crop. Just a few hundred acres of Kent hop gardens in 1700 had become about 46,000 acres by 1875.

In the early days of hop cultivation it was usual for the bines to be grown on little mounds or hills, three or four plants forming the corners of a triangle or a square on each hill. Each plant had its own pole, different varieties needing different lengths of pole. The hills were in rows, variously spaced according to the variety of hops being grown.

In a garden of six-foot plants, the hills would be six feet apart, three poles to every hill, 1,210 hills to the acre. Seven-foot plants would be grown on four poles to the hill, 889 hills to the acre. As time went by, different arrangements of poles were introduced, some encouraging the bines to grow diagonally rather than vertically. That made the bines grow longer, so that they carried more hops, but it required two poles for each bine and was, therefore, more expensive.

It was only in the 1930s that poles gave way on many farms to the American innovation of a continuous web of coarse coir string threaded from metal spikes in the ground to hooks on a network of overhead wire supported from a cage of permanent poles round the whole garden. The mounds became much less pronounced, although each group of bines is still known as a hill, even today.

For harvesting, instead of the bines being cut near the bottom and the poles, with the hops still on them, pulled out of the ground and carried to the pickers, the pickers moved steadily through the "sets" (a given number of hills) pulling on each string as they came to it until it broke, bringing down the bine in order that the hops could be picked off it into bins or baskets.

Now, the strings are cut by men or women riding on a tractor-propelled platform and taken by trailer directly to the hop picking machines that are, generally, housed in a large purpose-built shed in or near the farm yard.

Before the machines came, harvesting the hops demanded plenty of seasonal labour and just as London consumed much of the beer made with Kentish hops, so London also provided much of the labour needed to pick them.

From the 16th century onwards, large numbers of Londoners trekked into West Kent each September for the annual "hopping down in Kent". East Kent relied more for its casual labour on gipsies and people from Canterbury and the Medway Towns.

Many of the "hoppers" relied upon the extra income to clothe themselves and their families for the coming winter and for many of them it was the only holiday they ever had. They enjoyed it determinedly, some of them returning to the same farm year after year, all through their lives.

But after 1945, as living standards in London and elsewhere continued to improve, it became increasingly difficult for the Kent farmers to recruit pickers in the numbers they needed. They were forced to bring in another American innovation, the hop picking machines. Once the machines were installed, hand pickers were no longer needed and within a few years – certainly by the 1960s – the old style hand-picking of hops had pursued this spiral of cause and effect into history. Although hop gardens still provide a large number of jobs for casual workers (often students now) it is only a tiny fraction of the hundreds of thousands that were needed in the 19th and early 20th centuries.

Kent is still the premier hop county of Britain, although the total acreage of hops is far less now than it used to be. As major capital renewals such as machinery, wire and poles become necessary, many smaller growers are deciding enough is enough and turning their hop gardens over to more profitable crops.

Some experts predict that within another ten years the fifty or sixty farmers still growing hops in Kent will have dwindled to perhaps four or five specialists. Less beer is being drunk and the development of hop extracts and concentrates means fewer hops are needed anyway.

Many of the more popular lagers are brewed in Britain under foreign licences that specify the use of imported hops.

It was the Continental taste for beer that gave Kent its hop gardens and, ironically, it is the Continental taste for lager that is taking them away again.

ALAN BIGNELL

HOP PICKERS AT CRANBROOK, 1906

HOP PICKERS ARRIVING AT PADDOCK WOOD, 1945

Photographs Courtesy of Kent Messenger

THE ROYAL FAMILY

For full details see *Debrett's Peerage and Baronetage*

HER MAJESTY THE QUEEN, Elizabeth Alexandra Mary; style in the United Kingdom: Elizabeth II, by the Grace of God, of the United Kingdom of Great Britain and Northern Ireland and of Her Other Realms and Territories Queen, Head of the Commonwealth, Defender of the Faith; crowned at Westminster Abbey 2 June 1953; celebrated her Silver Jubilee 1977; er da of His Majesty King George VI (d 6 Feb 1952) and of Lady Elizabeth Angela Marguerite Bowes-Lyon (HM Queen Elizabeth The Queen Mother, *qv*), da of 14 Earl of Strathmore and Kinghorne; *b* 21 April 1926; *m* 20 Nov 1947, HRH The Prince Philip, Duke of Edinburgh, KG, KT, OM, GBE, PC, *qv*; 3 s, 1 da (*see below*); *Heir* s, HRH The Prince of Wales, *qv*; Lord High Adm of the United Kingdom; Col-in-Chief: Life Guards, Blues and Royals (Royal Horse Gds and 1 Dragoons), Royal Scots Dragoon Gds (Carabiniers and Greys), 16/5 Queen's Royal Lancers, Royal Tank Regt, RE, Grenadier Gds, Coldstream Gds, Scots Gds, Irish Gds, Welsh Gds, Royal Welch Fus, Queen's Lancashire Regt, Argyll and Sutherland Highlanders (Princess Louise's), Royal Green Jackets, RAOC, Queen's Own Mercian Yeo, Duke of Lancaster's Own Yeo, Corps of Royal Mil Police, Corps of Royal Canadian Engrs, Canadian Forces Mil Engrs Branch, King's Own Calgary Regt, Royal 22e Regt, Govr-Gen's Foot Gds, Canadian Grenadier Gds, Le Regiment de la Chaudière, Royal New Brunswick Regt, 48 Highlanders of Canada, Argyll and Sutherland Highlanders of Canada (Princess Louise's), Royal Canadian Ordnance Corps, Malawi Rifles; Capt-Gen: RA, HAC, Combined Cadet Force, Royal Canadian Artillery, Royal Malta Artillery; Air Cdre-in-Chief: RAuxAF, RAF Regt, Royal Observer Corps, Royal Canadian Air Force Aux; Hon Air Cdre RAF Marham, Cmdt-in-Chief RAF Coll Cranwell, Hon Cmmr Royal Canadian Mounted Police, Master of the Merchant Navy and Fishing Fleets, Head Civil Defence Corps and Nat Hosp Service Reserve; Sovereign of all British Orders of Knighthood, Order of Merit, Royal Order of Victoria and Albert, Order of Crown of India, Order of Companions of Honour, Distinguished Service Order, Imperial Service Order, Order of Canada; Sovereign Head of Order of Hosp of St John of Jerusalem, Order of Australia, The Queen's Service Order of NZ; patron Royal Coll of Physicians Edinburgh and Victoria League for Cwlth Friendship; FRS 1947; Residences: Buckingham Palace, London SW1A 1AA; Windsor Castle, Berkshire; Balmoral Castle, Aberdeenshire; Sandringham House, Norfolk

EDINBURGH, HRH The Duke of; HRH The Prince Philip; KG (1947), KT (1952), OM (1968), GBE (mil 1953), PC (1951, Canada 1957); cr Baron Greenwich, of Greenwich, Co London, Earl of Merioneth, and Duke of Edinburgh (UK 1947); naturalized a British subject and adopted surname of Mountbatten 1947; granted title, style and attribute of Royal Highness 1947; granted style and titular dignity of a Prince of UK 1957; only s of HRH Prince Andrew of Greece and Denmark, GCVO (d 1944), and HRH Princess (Victoria) Alice Elizabeth Julia Marie, RRC (d 1969), da of 1 Marquess of Milford Haven; *b* 10 June 1921; *Educ* Cheam Sch, Salem, Baden, Gordonstoun, RNC Dartmouth; *m* 20 Nov 1947, HM Queen Elizabeth II, *qv*; 3 s, 1 da; 1939-45 War, Mediterranean Fleet (Home Waters) and with British Pacific Fleet in SE Asia and Pacific (despatches, Greek War Cross; 1939-45, Atlantic, Africa, Burma (with Pacific rosette), and Italy Stars; War Medal 1939-45 (with oak leaf) and French Croix de Guerre (with Palm); a personal ADC to HM King George VI 1948; Field Marshal; Capt-Gen RM; Col-in-Chief: Queen's Royal Irish Hussars, Duke of Edinburgh's Royal Regt (Berks and Wilts), Queen's Own Highlanders (Seaforth and Camerons), REME, Intelligence Corps, Army Cadet Force, Royal Canadian Regt, Seaforth Highlanders of Canada, Cameron Highlanders of Ottawa, Queen's Own Cameron Highlanders of Canada, Royal Canadian Army Cadets; Col Grenadier Gds; Hon Col: Edinburgh and Heriot-Watt Univs OTC, Trinidad and Tobago Regt; *Navy:* Adm of the Fleet; Sea Cadet Corps, Royal Canadian Sea Cadets; Marshal of the RAF; Air Cdre-in-Chief: ATC, Royal Canadian Air Cadets; Hon Air Cdre RAF Kinloss; Cmdt-in-Ch and Extra Master Merchant Navy;

memb cncl Duchy of Cornwall 1952-, Ranger of Windsor Great Park 1952-, Lord High Steward of Plymouth 1960-; chllr of univs: Salford 1967-71, Wales 1948-, Edinburgh 1952-, Cambridge 1977-; master bench Inner Temple 1954-, elder bro Trinity House 1952, (master 1969-; hon bro Hull 1953-);pres: Amateur Athletic Bd 1952-, Cwlth Games Fedn 1955-, Br Sportsman's Club 1958-, Central Cncl of Physical Recreation 1951-, City & Guilds of London Inst 1951-, ESU of Cwlth 1952-, Guards' Polo Club 1955-, RAS of Cwlth 1958-, Royal Household Cricket Club 1953-, Royal Merchant Navy Sch 1952-, RSA 1952-, World Wild Life Fund British Nat Appeal 1961-; third pres Int Wild Life Fund 1981-; Royal pres Soc of Friends of St George's and Descendants of KGs 1948-; patron and trustee Duke of Edinburgh's Award, chm Duke of Edinburgh's Ctee for Queen's Awards to Industry 1965-; patron UK branch Soc d'Entr'aide of Legion of Honour; Adm and Cdre Royal Yacht Sqdn 1961-68; Adm of Yacht Clubs: House of Lords, Royal Motor, Royal Southern, Bar, Dart, Royal Gibraltar, RNSA, Royal Yacht Club of Victoria (Australia) and of Great Navy State of Nebraska USA; King George VI Coronation Medal 1937, Queen Elizabeth II Coronation Medal 1953; Grand Master and First or Princ Kt of Order of British Empire 1953; FRS 1951

HM QUEEN ELIZABETH THE QUEEN MOTHER; Lady Elizabeth Angela Marguerite, *née* Bowes-Lyon; Lady of the Order of the Garter (1936), Lady of the Order of the Thistle (1937), CI (1931), GCVO (1937), GBE (1927); da of 14 Earl of Strathmore and Kinghorne, KG, KT, GCVO, TD, JP, DL (d 1944) and Nina Cecilia, GCVO (d 1938), da of Rev Charles William Frederick Cavendish-Bentinck (gs of 3 Duke of Portland, who was twice Prime Minister during King George III's reign); *b* 4 Aug 1900: *m* 26 April 1923, HM King George VI (d 6 Feb 1952); 2 da (HM The Queen and HRH The Princess Margaret, *qqv);* Col-in-Chief: 1 Queen's Dragoon Gds, The Queen's Own Hussars, 9/12 Royal Lancers (Prince of Wales's), King's Regt, Royal Anglian Regt, Light Inf, The Black Watch (Royal Highland Regt), RAMC, The Black Watch (Royal Highland Regt) of Canada, The Toronto Scottish Regt, Canadian Forces Medical Services; Hol Col: Royal Yeo, London Scottish (Gordon Highlanders) (TA), Univ of London Contingent OTC; Cmdt-in-Chief: WRNS, WRAC, RAF Central Flying Sch, WRAF, Nursing Corps and Divs St John Ambulance Bde; hon member of Lloyd's; pres British Red Cross Soc 1937-52, since when dep pres; pres Royal Highland and Agric Soc 1963-64; Gold Albert Medal of RSA 1952; Grand Master Royal Victorian Order 1937; pres Univ Coll of Rhodesia and Nyasaland 1957-70, chllr London Univ 1955-81, first chllr Dundee Univ 1967; bencher Middle Temple 1944 (tres 1949); hon fellow London Univ, and of King's Coll London; FRS; appointed Lord Warden and Admiral of the Cinque Ports and Constable of Dover Castle (the first woman to hold this office) 1978; received Royal Victorian Chain 1937; Grand Cross of Legion of Honour; GCStJ; *Residences:* Clarence House, London SW1A 1BA; Royal Lodge, Windsor Great Park, Berks; Birkhall, Ballater, Aberdeenshire; Castle of Mey, Caithness-shire

WALES, HRH The Prince of; HRH The Prince Charles Philip Arthur George; KG (1958, invested and installed 1968), KT (1977), GCB and Great Master of Order of the Bath (1975), AK, QSO, PC 1977; cr Prince of Wales and Earl of Chester 1958 (invested 1969); also Duke of Cornwall and Rothesay, Earl of Carrick and Baron of Renfrew, Lord of the Isles and Great Steward of Scotland; eldest s and h of HM Queen Elizabeth II, *qv*; *b* 14 Nov 1948; *Educ* Cheam Sch, Gordonstoun, Geelong GS Australia, Trinity Coll Cambridge (MA, Polo Half-Blue), Univ Coll of Wales, Aberystwyth; Bar of Gray's Inn 1974 (hon bencher 1975); *m* 29 July 1981, Lady Diana Spencer (*see* Wales, HRH The Princess of); 2s (*see below*); *Heir*, HRH Prince William of Wales, *qv*; Col-in-Chief: The Royal Regt of Wales (24/41 Foot) 1960-, The Cheshire Regt 1977-, The Gordon Highlanders 1977-, Lord Strathcona's Horse (Royal Canadian) Regt 1977-, The Parachute Regt 1977-, The Royal Regt of Canada 1977-, 2 King Edward VII Own Goorkhas 1977-, The Royal Winnipeg Rifles 1977-; personal ADC to HM 1973-; Col Welsh Guards 1974-; Cdr RN 1976-, Wing Cdr RAF 1976-; Hon Air Cdre RAF Brawdy 1977-; Col-in-Chief Air Reserves Gp of Air Cmd in Canada 1977-, pres: Soc of Friends of St George's and Descendants of KG's 1975-,

United World Colls 1978-, The Prince's Trust 1975-; Cdre Royal Thames Yacht Club 1974-, High Steward Royal Borough of Windsor and Maidenhead 1974-; chm: Queen's Silver Jubilee Trust 1978-, The Prince of Wales' Ctee for Wales 1971-; chllr The Univ of Wales 1976-, memb bd Cwlth Devpt Corpn 1979-; patron: The Press Club, Transglobe Expedition, Welsh National Opera, Royal Sch for the Blind, Mary Rose Trust; author of: The Old Man of Lochnagar, A Vision of Britain; Coronation Medal 1953, Queen's Silver Jubilee Medal 1977; *Residences:* Kensington Palace, London W8 4PU; Highgrove House, Doughton, Tetbury, Glos GL8 8TG

WALES, HRH The Princess of; Lady Diana Frances, *née* Spencer; 3 da of 8 Earl Spencer, LVO, DL and (first wife) Hon Mrs Shand Kydd; *b* 1 July 1961; *Educ* Riddlesworth Hall, West Heath, Switzerland; *m* 29 July 1981, HRH The Prince of Wales, *qv*; 2 s *(see below)*; former kindergarten teacher

WALES, HRH Prince William of; Prince William Arthur Philip Louis; s and h of HRH The Prince of Wales, *qv*; *b* 21 June 1982

WALES, HRH Prince Henry (Harry) of; Prince Henry Charles Albert David; yr s of HRH The Prince of Wales, *qv*; *b* 15 Sept 1984

YORK, HRH The Duke of; HRH The Prince Andrew Albert Christian Edward; CVO (1979); *cr* Baron Killyleagh, Earl of Inverness, and Duke of York (UK 1986); 2 s of HM The Queen; *b* 19 Feb 1960; *Educ* Gordonstoun, Lakefield Coll Sch Ontario, RNC Dartmouth; Lieut RN, served S Atlantic Campaign 1982 as helicopter pilot HMS *Invincible*; personal ADC to HM The Queen 1984; *m* 23 July 1986, Sarah Margaret Ferguson (*see* York, HRH The Duchess of); 2 da (*see below*) *Residence:* Buckingham Palace, London SW1A 1AA

YORK, HRH The Duchess of; Sarah Margaret, *née* Ferguson; da of Maj Ronald Ivor Ferguson, The Life Guards, and his 1 w, Susan Mary, *née* Wright (now Mrs Hector Barrantes); *b* 15 Oct 1959; *Educ* Hurst Lodge Sunningdale, Queen's Secretarial Coll London; *m* 23 July 1986, HRH The Duke of York, *qv; 2 da (see below)*

YORK, HRH Princess Beatrice of; Princess Beatrice Elizabeth Mary; er da of HRH The Duke of York; *b* 8 Aug 1988

YORK, HRH Princess Eugenie of; Princess Eugenie Victoria Helena; yr da of HRH The Duke of York; *b* 23 March 1990

HRH The Prince Edward Antony Richard Louis; CVO (1989); 3 and yst s of HM The Queen; *b* 10 March 1964; *Educ* Gordonstoun, Jesus Coll Cambridge; former house tutor and jr master Wanganui Collegiate Sch NZ; 2 Lieut RM 1983; *Residence:* Buckingham Palace, London SW1A 1AA

HRH THE PRINCESS ROYAL; HRH The Princess Anne Elizabeth Alice Louise; GCVO (1974); declared Princess Royal 13 June 1987; o da of HM The Queen; *b* 15 Aug 1950; *Educ* Benenden; *m* 14 Nov 1973, Capt Mark Anthony Peter Phillips, CVO, ADC (P); 1 s, 1 da (*see below*); Col-in-Chief: 14/20 King's Hussars, Worcs and Sherwood Foresters Regt (29/45 Foot) and 8 Canadian Hussars (Princess Louise's), Royal Corps of Signals, Canadian Forces Communications and Electronics Branch, Grey and Simcoe Foresters Militia; Ch Cmdt WRNS, Hon Air Cdre RAF Lyneham; pres: Save The Children Fund, British Acad of Film and Television Arts, WRNS Benevolent Trust, Windsor Horse Trials, Royals Sch for Daughters of Offrs of RN and RM (Haslemere); patron: Assoc of WRNS, Communications and Electronics Assoc, Riding for the Disabled Assoc, Jersey Wildlife Trust, R Corps of Signals Assoc, Royal Corps of Signals Instn, Breast Cancer Research Trust, Save the Children Action Group, Army and RA Hunter Trials, Gloucester and N Avon Fedn of Young Farmers' Clubs, Horse of the Year Ball, Benenden Ball; vice-patron British Show Jumping Assoc; Cmdt-in-Ch St John Ambulance and Nursing Cadets; chllr London Univ 1981-; *Residence:* Gatcombe Park, Minchinhampton, Stroud, Glos GL6 9AT

PHILLIPS, Peter Mark Andrew; s of HRH The Princess Royal, *qv*; *b* 15 Nov 1977

PHILLIPS, Zara Anne Elizabeth; da of HRH The Princess Royal, *qv*; *b* 15 May 1981

SNOWDON, HRH The Princess Margaret, Countess of; HRH The Princess Margaret Rose; CI (1947), GCVO (1953); yr da of His late Majesty King George VI and Lady Elizabeth Angela Marguerite Bowes-Lyon (HM Queen Elizabeth The Queen Mother, *qv*); *b* 21 Aug 1930; *m* 6 May 1960 (m dis 1978), 1 Earl of Snowdon, GCVO; 1 s, 1 da (*see below*); Col-in-Chief: Royal Highland Fus (Princess Margaret's Own Glasgow and Ayrshire Regt), 15/19 King's Royal Hussars, Princess Louise Fus, Highland Fus of Canada, QARANC; Dep Col-in-Chief Royal Anglian Regt, Hon Air Cdre RAF Coningsby, chllr Univ of Keele; pres: Barnado's Scottish Children's League, Victoria League, Sunshine Homes and Schs for Blind Children (Royal Nat Inst for the Blind), Royal Ballet, NSPCC (and Royal Scottish Soc), Dockland Settlements, Friends of the Elderly and Gentlefolk's Help, Invalid Children's Aid Assoc (also chm cncl), Sadler's Wells Fndn, English Folk Dance and Song Soc, Horder Centres for Arthritics, Girl Guides Assoc, RASE; patron: Princess Margaret Rose Hosp Edinburgh, Royal Coll of Nursing, Nat Cncl of Nurses of UK, London Festival Ballet, Tenovus (Inst of Cancer Research); bencher Lincoln's Inn and tres 1967; Grand Pres of St John Ambulance Assoc and Bde, hon memb and patron of Grand Antiquity Soc of Glasgow; CStJ; *Residence* Kensington Palace, London W8 4PU

LINLEY, Viscount; David Albert Charles Armstrong-Jones; s of HRH The Princess Margaret and s and h of 1 Earl of Snowdon; *b* 3 Nov 1961; *Educ* Bedales, John Makepeace Sch of Woodcraft, Beaminster, Dorset.

ARMSTRONG-JONES, Lady Sarah Frances Elizabeth; da of HRH The Princess Margaret and 1 Earl of Snowdon ; *b* 1 May 1964; *Educ* Bedales.

GLOUCESTER, HRH 2 Duke of; HRH Prince Richard Alexander Walter George; GCVO (1974); also Earl of Ulster and Baron Culloden (both UK 1928); 2 but only surv s of HRH the late Prince Henry, 1 Duke of Gloucester (d 1974, 3 s of King George V) and HRH Princess Alice, Duchess of Gloucester, *qv*; *b* 26 Aug 1944; *Educ* Eton, Magdalene Coll Cambridge (MA, Dip Arch); *m* 8 July 1972, Birgitte Eva, GCVO (1989), DStJ (Col-in-Ch Royal Army Educational Corps; pres: London Region WRVS, Royal Alexander and Albert Sch, Cambridge House; patron: Asthma Research Cncl, Bobath Centre), da of Asger Preben Wissing Henriksen, lawyer, of Odense, Denmark, and his 1 w, Vivian, da of late Waldemar Oswald Van Deurs, whose name she assumed; 1 s, 2 da (*see below*); *Heir* s, Earl of Ulster, *qv*; *Career* RIBA, FSA, FRSA; Col-in-Chief: The Gloucestershire Regt 1975-, Royal Pioneer Corps 1977-; Hon Col Royal Monmouthshire RE (Militia) 1977-; pres: Inst of Advanced Motorists 1971-, Cancer Research Campaign 1973-, Nat Assoc of Boys' Clubs 1974-, British Consultants Bureau 1978-, E England Agric Soc 1979-; vice-pres British Leprosy Relief Assoc 1971-; patron: ASH 1974-, Victorian Soc 1976-, Bulldog Manpower Services 1976; ranger of Epping Forest 1975-; Grand Prior Order of St John of Jerusalem 1975-; KStJ; *Residences* Kensington Palace, London W8 4PU; Barnwell Manor, Peterborough, Cambs PE8 5PJ

ULSTER, Earl of; Alexander Patrick Gregers Richard; s and h of HRH 2 Duke of Gloucester, GCVO, *qv*; *b* 24 Oct 1974

WINDSOR, Lady Davina Elizabeth Alice Benedikte; er da of HRH 2 Duke of Gloucester, GCVO, *qv*; *b* 19 Nov 1977

WINDSOR, Lady Rose Victoria Birgitte Louise; yr da of HRH 2 Duke of Gloucester, GCVO, *qv*; *b* 1 March 1980

GLOUCESTER, HRH Princess Alice, Duchess of; Lady Alice Christabel, *née* Montagu Douglas Scott; GCB (1975), CI (1937), GCVO (1948), GBE (1937); 3 da of 7 Duke of Buccleuch and Queensberry, KT, GCVO, JP (d 1935), and Lady Margaret Alice, *née* Bridgeman (d 1954), 2 da of 4 Earl of Bradford; *b* 25 Dec 1901; *Educ* St James's Sch W Malvern, Paris; *m* 6 Nov 1935, HRH The Prince Henry William Frederick Albert, KG, KT, KP, GCB, GCMG, GCVO, 1 Duke of Gloucester (d 10 June

1974, 3 s of King George V); 1 s (*see above*) and 1 s decd (HRH Prince William, who was killed in an aeroplane accident 28 Aug 1972); Air Chief Marshal WRAF; Col-in-Chief: KOSB, Royal Hussars, RCT; Dep Col-in-Chief Royal Anglian Regt; memb cncl British Red Cross Soc; Dep Cmdt-in-C Nursing Corps and Divs of St John Ambulance Bde 1937-; GCStJ; *Residences* Kensington Palace, London W8 4PU; Barnwell Manor, Peterborough, Cambs PE8 5PJ

KENT, HRH 2 Duke of; Prince Edward George Nicholas Paul Patrick; KG (1985), GCMG (1967), GCVO (1960); also Earl of St Andrews and Baron Downpatrick (both UK 1934); er s of HRH 1 Duke of Kent, KG, KT, GCMG, GCVO, PC (killed on active service 25 Aug 1942, 4 s of King George V), and HRH Princess Marina, CI, GCVO, GBE (d 27 Aug 1968), yst da of HRH late Prince Nicholas of Greece and Denmark; *b* 9 Oct 1935; *Educ* Eton, Switzerland, RMA Sandhurst; *m* 8 June 1961, Katharine Lucy Mary, GCVO (1977) (Controller-Cmdt WRAC and Hon Maj-Gen; Col-in-Chief Army Catering Corps, Hon Col Yorks Volunteers TAVR, chllr Leeds Univ), only da of late Sir William Arthington Worsley, 4 Bt; 2 s, 1 da (*see below*); Maj-Gen (ret) Royal Scots Dragoon Gds; Col-in-Chief: Royal Regt of Fusiliers, Devonshire and Dorset Regt; Col Scots Gds, personal ADC to HM 1966-, GSO II E Cmd 1966-68, company instr RMA Sandhurst 1968-70, cmd C Sqdn Royal Scots Greys 1970-71; Grand Master United Grand Lodge Freemasons of England and Grand Master Order of St Michael and St George; pres: Wellington Coll, Cwlth War Graves Cmmn. Scout Assoc, Technician Educn Cncl; vice-chm British Overseas Trade Bd 1976-; chllr Surrey Univ 1977-; dir British Insulated Callender's Cables 1981-; FRS 1990; *Residences* York House, St James's Palace, London SW1A 1BQ; Anmer Hall, King's Lynn, Norfolk PE31 6RW

ST ANDREWS, Earl of; George Philip Nicholas Windsor; er s, and h of HRH 2 Duke of Kent, KG, GCMG, GCVO, *qv*; *b* 26 June 1962; *Educ* Eton, and Downing Coll Camb; *m* 9 Jan 1988, Sylvana, da of Max Tomaselli and formerly wife of John Paul Jones; 1 s (Edward Edmund Maximilian George, Lord Downpatrick *b* 2 Dec 1988)

WINDSOR, Lord Nicholas Charles Edward Jonathan; 2 s of HRH 2 Duke of Kent, KG, GCMG, GCVO, *qv*; *b* 25 July 1970

WINDSOR, Lady Helen Marina Lucy; da of HRH 2 Duke of Kent, KG, GCMG, GCVO, *qv*; b 28 April 1964

KENT, HRH Prince Michael of; HRH Prince Michael George Charles Franklin; 2 s of HRH 1 Duke of Kent (killed on active service 1942); *b* 4 July 1942; *Educ* Eton, RMA Sandhurst; *m* 30 June 1978, Baroness Marie Christine Agnes Hedwig Ida, da of late Baron Günther Hubertus von Reibnitz, and formerly wife of Thomas Troubridge, yr bro of Sir Peter Troubridge, 6 Bt; 1 s, 1 da (*see below*); Maj Royal Hussars to 1981; foreign attaché liaison sec MOD 1968-70, UN Force Cyprus 1971, Defence Intelligence Service 1974-76, Army Recruiting Directorate 1976-78, GSO Defence 1974-76, Army Recruiting Directorate 1976-78, GSO Defence Intelligence Staff 1978-81; pres: British Bobsleigh Assoc 1977-, Soc of Genealogists, Inst of Motor Industry 1978-, Royal Patriotic Fund Corpn 1980-, Soldiers', Sailors' and Airmen's Families Assoc 1982-; Cwlth pres Royal Lifesaving Soc; memb: RAC British Motor Sports Cncl, British Olympic Assoc 1977-, HAC; *Residences* Kensington Palace, London W8 4PU; Nether Lypiatt Manor, Stroud, Glos GL6 7LS

WINDSOR, Lord Frederick Michael George David Louis; o s of HRH Prince Michael of Kent, *qv*; *b* 6 April 1979

WINDSOR, Lady Gabriella (Ella) Marina Alexandra Ophelia; o da of HRH Prince Michael of Kent, *qv*; *b* 23 April 1981

HRH Princess Alexandra, the Hon Lady Ogilvy; HRH Princess Alexandra Helen Elizabeth Olga Christabel; GCVO (1960); da of HRH 1 Duke of Kent (killed on active service 1942); *b* 25 Dec 1936; *Educ* Heathfield, Paris; *m* 24 April 1963, Hon Sir Angus Ogilvy, KCVO, 2 s of 12 Earl of Airlie, KT, GCVO, MC; 1 s, 1 da (*see below*); Col-in-Chief: 17/21 Lancers, Queen's Own Rifles of Canada, The King's Own Border Regt, The Canadian Scottish Regt (Princess Mary's); Dep Col-in-Chief LI, Dep Hon Col-Royal Yeo TAVR, Air Chief Cmdt Princess Mary's RAF Nursing Service; Hon Cmdt-Gen: Royal Hong Kong Police Force, Royal Hong

Kong Aux Police Force; pres: Royal Commonwealth Soc for the Blind, Children's Country Holidays Fund, Queen Alexandra's House Assoc, Star and Garter Home for Disabled Sailors, Soldiers and Airmen, Alexandra Rose Day, British Sch at Rome, Royal Humane Soc; vice-pres British Red Cross Soc; patron Queen Alexandra's Royal Naval Nursing Service; chllr: Lancaster Univ 1964-, Univ of Mauritius 1974-, Hon FRCPS, Hon FRCOG, Hon FFA RCS; *Residences* Thatched House Lodge, Richmond Park, Surrey; 22 Friary Court, St James's Palace, London SW1A 1BQ

OGILVY, James Robert Bruce; o s of HRH Princess Alexandra, *qv*, and Hon Sir Angus Ogilvy, KCVO; *b* 29 Feb 1964; *Educ* Eton; *m* 30 July 1988, Julia Caroline, eldest da of Charles Frederick Melville Rawlinson

MOWATT, Mrs Paul; Marina Victoria Alexandra; *née* Ogilvy; o da of HRH Princess Alexandra, *qv*, and Hon Sir Angus Ogilvy, KCVO; *b* 31 July 1966; *m* 2 Feb 1990, Paul J Mowatt, s of David Mowatt; 1 da (Zenouska *b* 26 May 1990)

THE ORDER OF SUCCESSION

The first twenty-five persons in line of succession to the throne

HRH The Prince of Wales

HRH Prince William of Wales

HRH Prince Henry of Wales

HRH The Duke of York

HRH Princess Beatrice of York

HRH Princess Eugenie of York

HRH The Prince Edward

HRH The Princess Royal

Peter Phillips

Zara Phillips

HRH The Princess Margaret, Countess of Snowdon

Viscount Linley

Lady Sarah Armstrong-Jones

HRH The Duke of Gloucester

Earl of Ulster

Lady Davina Windsor

Lady Rose Windsor

HRH The Duke of Kent
(NB Earl of St Andrews would be next in line but for his marriage to a Roman Catholic. His rights are, however, transmitted to his son who follows.)

Lord Downpatrick

Lord Nicholas Windsor

Lady Helen Windsor
(NB HRH Prince Michael of Kent would be next in line but for his marriage to a Roman Catholic. His rights are, however, transmitted to his two children who follow)

Lord Frederick Windsor

Lady Gabriella Windsor

HRH Princess Alexandra, the Hon Lady Ogilvy

James Ogilvy

THE ROYAL HOUSEHOLDS

THE QUEEN'S HOUSEHOLD

Lord Chamberlain, The Earl of Airlie, KT, GCVO, PC
Lord Steward, The Viscount Ridley, TD
Master of the Horse, The Earl of Westmorland, KCVO
Mistress of the Robes, The Duchess of Grafton, GCVO
Lords in Waiting, Lt-Col the Lord Charteris of Amisfield, GCB, GCVO, OBE, QSO, PC (Permanent); The Lord Maclean, KT, GCVO, KBE (Permanent); The Lord Somerleyton; The Viscount Boyne; The Viscount Long; The Viscount Ullswater; The Lord Reay; The Earl of Strathmore and Kinghorne; The Viscount Astor
Captain, Gentlemen at Arms, The Lord Denham, PC
Captain, Yeoman of the Guard, The Viscount Davidson
Treasurer of the Household, Alastair Goodlad, MP
Comptroller of the Household, Sir George Young, Bt
Vice-Chamberlain of the Household, David Lightbown, MP
Ladies of the Bedchamber, The Countess of Airlie, CVO; The Lady Farnham
Extra Ladies of the Bedchamber, The Countess of Cromer, CVO; The Marchioness of Abergavenny, DCVO
Women of the Bedchamber, The Hon Mary Morrison, DCVO; The Lady Susan Hussey, DCVO: Mrs John Dugdale, DCVO; The Lady Elton
Extra Women of the Bedchamber, Mrs John Woodroffe, CVO; The Lady Rose Baring, DCVO; Mrs Michael Wall, DCVO; Lady Abel Smith, DCVO; Mrs Robert de Pass
Equerries, Lt- Col Blair Stewart-Wilson, CVO; Sqdn Ldr David Walker, RAF
Temporary Equerry, Capt the Hon Richard Margesson
Private Secretary, The Rt Hon Sir Robert Fellowes, KCVO, CB
Deputy Private Secretary, Sir Kenneth Scott, KCVO, CMG
Assistant Private Secretary, Robin Janvrin, LVO
Chief Clerk, Mrs Graham Coulson, MVO
Press Secretary, Charles Anson
Deputy Press Secretary, John Haslam, LVO
Assistant Press Secretaries, Richard Arbiter; Geoffrey Crawford
Deputy Keeper and Deputy Treasurer, John Parsons
Defence Services Secretary, Rear Adm David Allen, CBE
Keeper of the Privy Purse and Treasurer to The Queen, Major Sir Shane Blewitt, KCVO
Chief Accountant and Paymaster, Frank Mintram, CVO
Personnel Officer, Gordon Franklin, CVO
High Almoner, The Bishop of St Albans (The Rt Rev John Taylor, MA)
Secretary, Royal Almonry, Peter Wright, CVO
Master of the Household, Rear Admiral Sir Paul Greening, KCVO
Deputy Master of the Household, Lt-Col Blair Stewart-Wilson, CVO
Chief Clerk, Michael Jephson, MVO
Comptroller, Lord Chamberlain's Office, Lt-Col George West, CVO
Assistant Comptroller, LCO, Lt-Col Malcolm Ross, OBE
Secretary, LCO, John Titman, CVO
Marshal of the Diplomatic Corps, Lt-Gen Sir John Richards, KCB
Vice-Marshal of the Diplomatic Corps, Roger Hervey, CMG
Assistant Marshals of the Diplomatic Corps, Stanley Martin, LVO; Clive Almond, OBE
Secretary, Central Chancery of the Orders of Knighthood, Lt-Col Malcolm Ross, OBE
Crown Equerry, Lt-Col Seymour Gilbart-Denham
Superintendent, Royal Mews, Major Albert Smith, MBE
Master of The Queen's Music, Malcolm Williamson, CBE, AO
Poet Laureate, Edward Hughes, OBE
Gentlemen at Arms: Lieutenant, Major David Jamieson, VC, CVO
Clerk of the Cheque and Adjutant, Major Thomas St Aubyn
Yeomen of the Guard: Lieutenant, Colonel Alan Pemberton, CVO, MBE
Clerk of the Cheque and Adjutant, Col Greville Tufnell

Clerk of the Closet, The Bishop of Chelmsford (The Rt Rev John Waine, BA)
Deputy Clerk of the Closet, The Rev Canon Anthony Caesar, LVO, MA, MusB, FRCO
Dean of the Chapels Royal, The Bishop of London, PC (The Rt Rev and Rt Hon Graham Leonard)
Sub-Dean of the Chapels Royal, The Rev Canon Anthony Caesar, LVO, MA, MusB, FRCO
Head of the Medical Household and Physician, Dr Anthony Dawson, MD, FRCP
Apothecary to The Queen, Dr Nigel Southward, LVO, MA, MB BChir, MRCP
Serjeant Surgeon, William Slack, MCh, FRCS
Windsor Castle: Constable and Governor, Admiral Sir David Hallifax, KCB, KBE
Superintendent, Major Barrie Eastwood, MBE
Director of the Royal Collection and Surveyor of the Queen's Works of Art, Sir Geoffrey de Bellaigue, KCVO, FSA
Surveyor of The Queen's Pictures, Christopher Lloyd
Librarian, Royal Library, Oliver Everett, LVO
Heralds and Pursuivants, see HER MAJESTY'S OFFICERS OF ARMS

HOUSEHOLD OF QUEEN ELIZABETH THE QUEEN MOTHER

Apothecary to the Household, Dr Nigel Southward, LVO, MA, MB BChir, MRCP
Clerk Comptroller to the Household, Malcolm Blanch, LVO
Comptroller, Captain Sir Alastair Aird, KCVO
Equerries, Lt-Col Sir Martin Gilliat, GCVO, MBE; Major Sir Ralph Anstruther, Bt, KCVO, MC; Major Raymond Seymour, LVO
Temporary Equerry, Captain Giles Bassett
Mistress of the Robes, Vacant
Ladies of the Bedchamber, The Dowager Viscountess Hambleden, GCVO; The Lady Grimthorpe, CVO
Women of the Bedchamber, The Dowager Lady Fermoy, DCVO, OBE; Mrs Patrick Campbell-Preston, DCVO; The Lady Elizabeth Basset, CVO; The Lady Angela Oswald
Lord Chamberlain, The Earl of Dalhousie, KT, GCVO, GBE, MC
Page of Honour, Viscount Lumley
Press Secretary, Major John Griffin, CVO
Private Secretary, Lt-Col Sir Martin Gilliat, GCVO, MBE
Apothecary to the Household at Royal Lodge, Windsor, Dr John Briscoe, MA, MB BChir, MRCGP, DObst, RCOG
Treasurer, Major Sir Ralph Anstruther, Bt, KCVO, MC

HOUSEHOLD OF THE PRINCE PHILIP, DUKE OF EDINBURGH

Chief Clerk and Accountant to the Household, Vernon Jewell, MVO
Equerry, Major Sir Guy Acland, Bt, RHA
Temporary Equerries, Capt Michael Hutchings; Capt Alastair Rogers, RN
Private Secretary and Treasurer, Brian McGrath, CVO

HOUSEHOLD OF THE PRINCE AND PRINCESS OF WALES

Apothecary to the Household, Dr Michael Linnett, OBE, MB BS, FRCGP
Equerry to The Prince of Wales, Cdr Alastair Watson, RN
Equerry to The Princess of Wales, Sqdn Ldr David Barton, RAF
Temporary Equerry to The Prince of Wales, Capt Rupert Cockcroft
Lady in Waiting, Miss Anne Beckwith-Smith, LVO
Extra Ladies in Waiting, Mrs George West; Viscountess Campden; Mrs Max Pike; Miss Alexandra Loyd; The Hon Mrs Vivian Baring; Mrs James Lonsdale (temporary)
Private Secretary and Treasurer to The Prince and Princess of Wales, Sir John Riddell, Bt
Assistant Private Secretary to The Prince of Wales, Peter Westmacott
Comptroller to The Prince of Wales, Cdr Richard Aylard, RN
Assistant Private Secretary to The Princess of Wales, Lt Cdr Patrick Jephson, RN

HOUSEHOLD OF THE DUKE AND DUCHESS OF YORK

Ladies in Waiting, Mrs John Spooner; Mrs John Floyd
Extra Ladies in Waiting (temporary), Miss Lucy Manners; Mrs Harry Cotterell

Equerry, Capt Alexander Buchanan-Baillie-Hamilton, The Black Watch

Private Secretary and Treasurer, Capt Neil Blair, RN

Comptroller and Assistant Private Secretary, Miss Lynn White.

HOUSEHOLD OF THE PRINCE EDWARD

Private Secretary and Equerry, Lt-Col Sean O'Dwyer, Irish Guards

HOUSEHOLD OF THE PRINCESS ROYAL

Ladies in Waiting, Mrs Richard Carew Pole, LVO; Mrs Andrew Feilden, LVO; The Hon Mrs Legge-Bourke LVO; Mrs Malcolm Wallace; Mrs Timothy Holderness-Roddam; Mrs Charles Ritchie

Extra Ladies in Waiting, Miss Victoria Legge-Bourke, LVO; Mrs Malcolm Innes, LVO; The Countess of Lichfield

Private Secretary, Lt-Col Peter Gibbs, LVO

Assistant Private Secretary, The Hon Mrs Louloudis

HOUSEHOLD OF THE PRINCESS MARGARET, COUNTESS OF SNOWDON

Apothecary to the Household, Dr Nigel Southward, LVO, MA, MB BChir, MRCP

Comptroller, Major the Lord Napier and Ettrick, CVO

Equerry, Major the Lord Napier and Ettrick, CVO

Extra Ladies in Waiting, The Lady Elizabeth Cavendish, LVO; Lady Aird, LVO; Mrs Robin Benson, LVO; The Hon Mrs Wills, LVO; Mrs Jane Stevens; The Lady Juliet Townsend, LVO; The Lady Glenconner; The Hon Mrs Whitehead, LVO; The Countess Alexander of Tunis; Mrs Charles Vyvyan

Personal Secretary, Miss Muriel Murray Brown, CVO

Private Secretary, Major the Lord Napier and Ettrick, CVO

HOUSEHOLD OF PRINCESS ALICE, DUCHESS OF GLOUCESTER

Apothecary to the Household, Dr Nigel Southward, LVO, MA, MB BChir, MRCP

Clerk Comptroller, Mrs Gordon Franklin

Comptroller, Maj Nicholas Barne

Equerry, Maj Nicholas Barne

Extra Equerry, Lt-Col Sir Simon Bland, KCVO

Ladies in Waiting, Dame Jean Maxwell-Scott, DCVO; Mrs Michael Harvey

Private Secretary, Maj Nicholas Barne

HOUSEHOLD OF THE DUKE AND DUCHESS OF GLOUCESTER

Apothecary to the Household, Dr Nigel Southward, LVO, MA, MB BChir, MRCP

Clerk Comptroller, Mrs Gordon Franklin

Comptroller, Maj Nicholas Barne

Equerry, Maj Nicholas Barne

Extra Equerry, Lt-Col Sir Simon Bland, KCVO

Ladies in Waiting, Mrs Michael Wigley, LVO; Mrs Euan McCorquodale; Mrs Howard Page; The Lady Camoys (temporary)

Extra Lady in Waiting, Miss Jennifer Thomson

Assistant Private Secretary to the Duchess of Gloucester, Miss Suzanne Marland

Private Secretary, Maj Nicholas Barne

HOUSEHOLD OF THE DUKE AND DUCHESS OF KENT

Apothecary to the Household, Dr Nigel Southward, LVO, MA, MB BChir, MRCP

Clerk Comptroller, Mrs Antigoni Christodoulou

Temporary Equerry, Capt the Hon Christopher Knollys

Ladies in Waiting, Mrs Alan Henderson, CVO; Mrs David Napier, LVO

Extra Lady in Waiting, Mrs Peter Wilmot-Sitwell

Private Secretary, Andrew Palmer, CMG, CVO

HOUSEHOLD OF PRINCE AND PRINCESS MICHAEL OF KENT

Ladies in Waiting, The Hon Mrs Leatham; Miss Anne Frost

Personal Secretary to Prince Michael of Kent, Miss Caroline Sherrington

Personal Secretary to Princess Michael of Kent, Mrs Julian Fellowes

HOUSEHOLD OF PRINCESS ALEXANDRA, THE HON LADY OGILVY

Extra Equerry, Major Peter Clarke, CVO

Lady in Waiting, The Lady Mary Mumford, CVO

Extra Ladies in Waiting, Mrs Peter Afia; The Lady Mary Colman; The Hon Lady Rowley

Private Secretary and Extra Lady in Waiting, Miss Mona Mitchell, CVO

THE QUEEN'S HOUSEHOLD IN SCOTLAND

Hereditary Lord High Constable, The Earl of Erroll
Hereditary Master of the Household, The Duke of Argyll
Hereditary Standard Bearer for Scotland, The Earl of Dundee
Hereditary Bearer of the National Flag of Scotland, The Earl of Lauderdale
Hereditary Keepers:-
Holyrood, The Duke of Hamilton and Brandon
Falkland, Ninian Crichton-Stuart
Stirling, The Earl of Mar and Kellie
Dunstaffnage, The Duke of Argyll
Dunconnel, Sir Fitzroy Maclean, Bt, CBE
Keeper of Dumbarton Castle, Brig A S Pearson, CB, DSO, OBE, MC, TD
Governor of Edinburgh Castle, Lt-Gen Sir John MacMillan, KCB
Dean of the Order of the Thistle, The Very Rev Gilleasbuig Macmillan, MA, BD
Dean of the Chapel Royal, Very Rev Prof R A S Barbour, MC, MA, DD
Physicians in Scotland, Dr Peter Brunt, MD, FRCP; Dr Alexander Muir, MD, FRCPEdin
Surgeons in Scotland, Jetmund Engeset, ChM, FRCS; Ian Macleod, BSc, MD, ChB, FRCS
Apothecary to the Household at Balmoral, Dr Douglas Glass, MB ChB
Apothecary to the Household at the Palace of Holyrood, Dr Henry Gebbie, MB ChB, MRCGP
Royal Company of Archers:
Capt-Gen and Gold Stick for Scotland, Col the Lord Clydesmuir, KT, CB, MBE, TD
Adjutant, Major the Hon Lachlan Maclean
Heralds and Pursuivants, see HER MAJESTY'S OFFICERS OF ARMS

HER MAJESTY'S OFFICERS OF ARMS

ENGLAND
College of Arms, Queen Victoria Street, London EC4 4BT

EARL MARSHAL
His Grace the Duke of Norfolk, KG, GCVO, CB, CBE, MC

KINGS OF ARMS
Garter–Sir (Alexander) Colin Cole, KCVO, TD, FSA
Clarenceux–Sir Anthony Richard Wagner, KCB, KCVO, DLitt, FSA
Norroy and Ulster–John Philip Brooke Brooke-Little, CVO, FSA

HERALDS
York (and Registrar)–Conrad Marshall John Fisher Swan, CVO, PhD, FSA
Chester–David Hubert Boothby Chesshyre, LVO, FSA
Windsor–Theobald David Mathew
Lancaster–Peter Llewellyn Gwynn-Jones
Somerset–Thomas Woodcock
Richmond–Patric Laurence Dickinson

PURSUIVANTS
Portcullis–Peter Brotherton Spurrier
Bluemantle–Terence David McCarthy
Rouge Croix–Henry Edgar Paston-Bedingfeld
Rouge Dragon–Timothy Hugh Stewart Duke

HERALDS EXTRAORDINARY
Norfolk–George Drewry Squibb, LVO, QC, FSA
Wales–Major Francis Jones, CVO, TD, FSA, DL
New Zealand–Phillippe Patrick O'Shea
Surrey (and Earl Marshal's Secretary)–Sir Walter John George Verco, KCVO
Beaumont–Francis Sedley Andrus, LVO
Arundel–Rodney Onslow Dennys, CVO, OBE, FSA
Maltravers–John Martin Robinson, DPhil, FSA

SCOTLAND
Court of the Lord Lyon , HM New Register House, Edinburgh

THE RT HON THE LORD LYON KING OF ARMS
Sir Malcolm Rognvald Innes of Edingight, KCVO, WS, FSA Scot

HERALDS
Albany–John Alexander Spens, RD, WS
Rothesay–Sir Crispin Agnew of Lochnaw, Bt
Ross–Charles John Burnett, FSA Scot

PURSUIVANTS
Kintyre–John Charles Grossmith George,FSA Scot
Unicorn–Alastair Lorne Campbell of Airds, yr, FSA Scot

PURSUIVANTS OF EARLS (Not forming part of Her Majesty's Household)
Pursuivants to the Earl of Erroll and the Countess of Mar
Slains–Peter Drummond-Murray of Mastrick (Pursuivant to the Earl of Erroll)
Garioch–David Gordon Allen d'Aldecamb Lumsden of Cushnie (Pursuivant to the Countess of Mar)

GENERAL TABLE OF PRECEDENCE IN ENGLAND AND WALES

The Queen
The Duke of Edinburgh
The Prince of Wales
The Sovereign's younger sons
The Sovereign's grandsons (according to the seniority of their fathers)
The Sovereign's cousins (according to the seniority of their fathers)
Archbishop of Canterbury
Lord High Chancellor
Archbishop of York
The Prime Minister
Lord High Treasurer (no such office exists at present)
Lord President of the Council
The Speaker of the House of Commons
Lord Privy Seal
Ambassadors and High Commissioners

Above all Peers of their own degree:
- Lord Great Chamberlain
- Lord High Constable (no such office exists at present)
- Earl Marshal
- Lord High Admiral (office held by HM The Queen)
- Lord Steward of the Household
- Lord Chamberlain of the Household

Master of the Horse
Dukes of England
Dukes of Scotland (none created since 1707)
Dukes of Great Britain (1707–1801)
Dukes of Ireland (created before 1801)
Dukes of the United Kingdom (created since 1801)
Eldest sons of Dukes of the Blood Royal (when they are not brothers, grandsons, uncles, or nephews of the reigning sovereign)
Marquesses of England
——— Scotland (none created after 1707)
——— Great Britain (1707–1801)
——— Ireland (created before 1801)
——— the United Kingdom (created since 1801)
Eldest sons of Dukes
Earls of England (anterior to 1707)
Earls of Scotland (none created after 1707)
Earls of Great Britain (1707–1801)
Earls of Ireland (created before 1801)
Earls of the United Kingdom (created since 1801)
Younger sons of Dukes of the Blood Royal (when they are not brothers, grandsons, uncles or nephews of the reigning sovereign)
Eldest sons of Marquesses
Younger sons of Dukes
Viscounts of England
——— Scotland (anterior to 1707)
——— Great Britain (1707–1801)
——— Ireland (anterior to 1801)
——— the United Kingdom (created since 1801)
Eldest sons of Earls
Younger sons of Marquesses
Bishop of London
——— Durham
——— Winchester
English Diocesan Bishops (according to date of consecration)
Bishops Suffragan (according to date of consecration)
Secretaries of State (if barons)
Barons of England
Barons of Scotland (none created since 1707)
——— Great Britain (1707–1801)
——— Ireland (anterior to 1801)
——— the United Kingdom (created since 1801)
Lords of Appeal in Ordinary
Commissioners of the Great Seal (those persons who execute the office of Lord High Chancellor when it happens to be vacant)
Treasurer of the Household
Comptroller of the Household
Vice-Chamberlain of the Household
Secretaries of State (when not barons)
Eldest sons of Viscounts
Younger sons of Earls
Eldest sons of Barons
Knights of the Garter
Privy Councillors
Chancellor of the Exchequer
——— Duchy of Lancaster

Lord Chief Justice
Master of the Rolls
President of the Family Division
The Vice-Chancellor of the Chancery Division
Lord Justices of Appeal, ranking according to date of appointment
Judges of the High Court of Justice, ranking according to date of appointment
Vice-Chancellor of the County Palatine of Lancaster
Younger sons of Viscounts
____________ Barons
Younger sons of Life Peers
Baronets
Knights of the Thistle
Knights Grand Cross of the Bath
Knights Grand Commanders of the Star of India
Knights Grand Cross of St Michael and St George
Knights Grand Commanders of the Order of the Indian Empire
Knights Grand Cross of the Royal Victorian Order
Knights Grand Cross of the Order of the British Empire
Knights Commanders of the Bath
Knights Commanders of the Star of India
Knights Commanders of St Michael and St George
Knights Commanders of the Order of the Indian Empire
Knights Commanders of the Royal Victorian Order
Knights Commanders of the Order of the British Empire
Knights Bachelor
Official Referees of the Supreme Court of Judicature
Circuit Judges
County Court Judges of England and Wales
Masters in Chancery
Master of Court of Protection
Companions of the Bath
Companions of the Star of India
Companions of St Michael and St George
Companions of the Indian Empire
Commanders of the Royal Victorian Order
Commanders of the Order of the British Empire
Companions of the Distinguished Service Order
Lieutenants of the Royal Victorian Order
Officers of the Order of the British Empire
Companions of the Imperial Service Order
Eldest sons of the younger sons of Peers
Eldest sons of Baronets
Eldest sons of Knights of the Garter
Eldest sons of Knights, according to the precedence of their fathers
Members of the Royal Victorian Order
Members of the Order of the British Empire
Younger sons of Baronets
Younger sons of Knights
Esquires
Gentlemen

RELATIVE RANK AND PRECEDENCE IN THE NAVY, ARMY AND AIR FORCE

Admiral of the Fleet	Field Marshal	Marshal of the RAF
Admiral	General	Air Chief Marshal
Vice Admiral	Lieutenant-General	Air Marshal
Rear Admiral	Major-General	Air Vice-Marshal
Commodore	Brigadier	Air Commodore
Captain	Colonel	Group Captain
Commander	Lieutenant-Colonel	Wing Commander
Lieutenant Commander	Major	Squadron Leader
Lieutenant	Captain	Flight Lieutenant
Sub Lieutenant	Lieutenant	Flying Officer
Commissioned Officers from Warrant Rank	Second Lieutenant	Pilot Officer

PRECEDENCE AMONG LADIES.

The daughter of a peer does not lose her own rank should she marry a person not a peer, but if she marries a peer her title and precedence are merged in his, *e.g.*, if the daughter of a duke marries a baron, she takes the rank of a baroness. Maids of Honour* to the Queen Regnant, the Queen Consort, or the Queen Dowager, who are not the daughters of peers, are styled Honourable for life. The widow of a peer, baronet or knight who re-marries does not retain any title or precedence acquired from her previous husband, but may do so only by courtesy. A dowager peeress or the widow of a baronet, while a widow, takes precedence of the wife of the living holder of the title. The divorced wife of a peer or baronet derives no rank or precedence from her former husband but unless she remarries usually retains the title with her christian or forename prefixed (e.g. Mary, Lady Jones). Official rank and precedence is not communicable to the wife, but the wife of a lord mayor has precedence derived from her husband's office.

The Queen
The Queen Mother
The Princess of Wales
The Duchess of York
The Princess Royal
Sister of the Sovereign
Granddaughters of the Sovereign
Wives of the Sovereign's uncles
Wives of the Sovereign's cousins
Cousin of the Sovereign
The Prime Minister
Duchesses of England
——— Scotland
——— Great Britain
——— Ireland
——— the United Kingdom
Wives of the eldest sons of Dukes of the Blood Royal
Marchionesses (in the same order as the Duchesses)
Wives of the eldest sons of Dukes
Daughters of Dukes (while unmarried, or when married to commoners)
Countesses (in the same order as the Duchesses)
Wives of the younger sons of Dukes of the Blood Royal
Wives of the eldest sons of Marquesses
Daughters of Marquesses (while unmarried or when married to commoners)
Wives of the younger sons of Dukes
Viscountesses (in the same order as the Duchesses)
Wives of the elder sons of Earls
Daughters of Earls (while unmarried, or when married to commoners)
Wives of younger sons of Marquesses
Baronesses (in the same order as the Duchesses)
Wives of the eldest sons of Viscounts
Daughters of Viscounts (while unmarried or when married to a commoner)
Wives of the younger sons of Earls
Wives of the eldest sons of Barons
Daughters of Barons (if unmarried, or when married to a commoner)
Maids of Honour
Wives of Knights of the Garter
Privy Councillors (Women)
Wives of the younger sons of Viscounts
Wives of the younger sons of Barons
Daughters of Lords of Appeal
Wives of the sons of Legal Life Peers
Wives of Baronets (according to the dates of creation of titles held by their husbands)
Wives of Knights of the Thistle
Dames Grand Cross of St Michael and St George
Dames Grand Cross of the Royal Victorian Order
Dames Grand Cross of the Order of the British Empire
Wives of Knights Grand Cross of the Bath
Wives of Knights Grand Commanders of the Star of India
Wives of Knights Grand Cross of St Michael and St George
Wives of Knights Grand Commanders of the Indian Empire
Wives of Knights Grand Cross of the Royal Victorian Order
Wives of Knights Grand Cross of the Order of the British Empire
Dames Commanders of the Bath
Dames Commanders of St Michael and St George
Dames Commanders of the Royal Victorian Order

Dames Commanders of the Order of the British Empire
Wives of Knights Commanders of the Bath
Wives of Knights Commanders of the Star of India
Wives of Knights Commanders of St Michael and St George
Wives of Knights Commanders of the Indian Empire
Wives of Knights Commanders of the Royal Victorian Order
Wives of Knights Commanders of the Order of the British Empire
Wives of Knights Bachelor
Commanders of St Michael and St George
Commanders of the Royal Victorian Order
Commanders of the Order of the British Empire
Wives of Commanders and Companions of the Orders of the Bath, the Star of India, St Michael and St George, Indian Empire, Royal Victorian Order, and the British Empire
Wives of Companions of the Distinguished Service Order
Lieutenants of the Royal Victorian Order
Officers of the Order of the British Empire
Wives of Lieutenants of the Royal Victorian Order
Wives of Officers of the Order of the British Empire
Companions of the Imperial Service Order
Wives of Companions of the Imperial Service Order
Wives of the eldest sons of the younger sons of Peers
Daughters of the younger sons of Peers
Wives of the eldest sons of Baronets
Daughters of Baronets
Wives of the eldest sons of Knights of the Garter
Wives of the eldest sons of Knights Bachelor
Daughters of Knights Bachelor
Members of the Royal Victorian Order
Members of the Order of the British Empire
Wives of members of the Royal Victorian Order
Wives of members of the Order of the British Empire
Wives of the younger sons of Baronets
Wives of the younger sons of Knights
Wives of Esquires
Wives of Gentlemen

*No Maids of Honour have been appointed since the reign of King George V and it must be assumed that the dignity has now lapsed and seems unlikely to be revived.

GENERAL TABLE OF PRECEDENCE IN SCOTLAND

GENTLEMEN

The Duke of Edinburgh*
Lord High Commissioner to the General Assembly of the Church of Scotland (during sitting of General Assembly)
Duke of Rothesay (The Prince of Wales)
Sovereign's Younger Sons
Sovereign's Grandsons
Sovereign's Cousins
Lord-Lieutenants of Counties†
Lord Provosts of Cities being *ex-officio* Lord-Lieutenants of Counties of Cities†
Sheriffs Principal†
Lord Chancellor of Great Britain
Moderator of General Assembly of Church of Scotland (during office)
The Prime Minister (if male)
Keeper of the Great Seal of Scotland (the Secretary for Scotland) (if a Peer)
Keeper of the Privy Seal of Scotland (if a Peer)
Hereditary High Constable of Scotland
Hereditary Master of the Household in Scotland
Dukes (as in English Table)
Eldest sons of Dukes of the Blood Royal
Marquesses (as in English Table)
Eldest sons of Dukes
Earls (as in English Table)
Younger sons of Dukes of the Blood Royal
Eldest sons of Marquesses
Younger sons of Dukes
Keeper of the Great Seal (the Secretary for Scotland) (if not a Peer)
Keeper of the Privy Seal (if not a Peer)
Lord Justice-General
Lord Clerk Register
Lord Advocate
Lord Justice-Clerk
Viscounts (as in English Table)
Eldest sons of Earls
Younger sons of Marquesses
Barons or Lords of Parliament (Scotland) (as in English Table)
Eldest sons of Viscounts
Younger sons of Earls
Eldest sons of Barons or Lords of Parliament
Knights of the Garter
Knights of the Thistle
Privy Counsellors
Senators of the College of Justice (Lords of Session), including Chairman of Scottish Land Court
Younger sons of Viscounts
Younger sons of Barons or Lords of Parliament
Baronets
Knights Grand Cross and Knights Grand Commanders of Orders (as in English Table)
Knights Commanders of Orders (as in English Table)
Solicitor-General for Scotland
Lord Lyon King of Arms
Sheriffs Principal (when not within own county)††
Knights Bachelor
Sheriffs
Companions of the Bath
Thence as in English Table

Lord-Lieutenants of Counties and of Counties of Cities during their term of office and with the limits of their jurisdiction have precedence before the Sheriffs Principal having concurrent jurisdiction.

GENERAL TABLE OF PRECEDENCE IN SCOTLAND

LADIES

The Queen
The Queen Mother
Duchess of Rothesay (The Princess of Wales)
Sovereign's Daughter
Sovereign's Sister
Sovereign's Granddaughters
Wives of Sovereign's Uncles
Wives of Dukes of the Blood Royal
Wives of Princes of the Blood Royal
Sovereign's Cousin
The Prime Minister (if female)
Duchesses (as in English Table)
Wives of the eldest sons of Dukes of the Blood Royal
Marchionesses (as in English Table)
Wives of eldest sons of Dukes
Daughters of Dukes
Wives of younger sons of Dukes of the Blood Royal
Wives of eldest sons of Marquesses
Daughters of Marquesses
Wives of younger sons of Dukes
Countesses (as in English Table)
Viscountesses (as in English Table)
Wives of eldest sons of Earls
Daughters of Earls
Wives of younger sons of Marquesses
Baronesses, or Ladies of Parliament (Scotland) (as in English Table)
Wives of eldest sons of Viscounts
Daughters of Viscounts
Wives of younger sons of Earls
Wives of eldest sons of Barons or Lords of Parliament
Daughters of Barons or Lords of Parliament
Wives of Knights of the Garter
Wives of Knights of the Thistle
Privy Counsellors (women)
Wives of youngers sons of Viscounts
Wives of younger sons of Barons
Wives of Baronets
Dames Grand Cross of Orders (as in English Table)
Wives of Knights Grand Cross and Knights Grand Commanders of Orders (as in English Table)
Dames Commanders of Orders (as in English Tables)
Wives of Knights Commanders of Orders (as in English Tables)
Wives of Knights Bachelor and Wives of Senators of the College of Justice (Lords of Session) including the wife of the Chairman of the Scottish Land Court**
Companions of the Order of the Bath
Thence as in English Table

* By Royal Warrant dated 18 September 1952, it was declared that HRH the Duke of Edinburgh was henceforth to have Precedence next to HM the Queen, thus having place before the Lord High Commissioner.

** Taking precedence among themselves according to the dates of their husbands' creation as Knights or appointment as Senators of the College of Justice, respectively.

† During term of office, and within their respective Counties, Cities, and Sheriffdoms.

†† In Scotland Sheriffs exercise judicial functions.

POSITION OF LETTERS AFTER THE NAME

The abbreviations 'Bt' or 'Bart' (for a Baronet) and 'Esq', if applicable, precede all other letters.

The series of other letters are grouped either by regulations or by custom as follows:

1. Orders and Decorations conferred by the Crown.
2. Appointments in the following order, Privy Counsellor, Aide de Camp to Her Majesty, Honorary Physician to The Queen, Honorary Surgeon to The Queen, Honorary Dental Surgeon to The Queen, Honorary Nursing Sister to The Queen, and Honorary Chaplain to The Queen, viz. PC, ADC, QHP, QHS, QHDS, QHNS and QHC.
3. Queen's Counsel, Justice of the Peace and Deputy Lieutenant, viz. QC, JP and DL.
4. University Degrees.
5. (a) Religious Orders.
   (b) Medical Qualifications.
6. (a) Fellowships of Learned Societies,
   (b) Royal Academicians and Associates,
   (c) Fellowships, Memberships, etc., of Professional Institutions, Associations, etc.,
   (d) Writers to the Signet.
7. Member of Parliament, viz. MP.
8. Membership of one of the Armed Forces, such as RN or RAF.

The following notes are given for guidance.

It is important to keep the group order, even if the individual series of letters in Groups 4, 5 and 6 present difficulties. For further details see the appropriate section.

The nature of the correspondence determines which series of letters should normally be included under Groups 4, 5 and 6. For instance, when writing a professional letter to a doctor of medicine one would normally add more medical qualifications than in a social letter.

On a formal list all the appropriate letters are usually included after each name.

Those who have letters signifying Crown Honours and Awards are usually given only the principal letters in Groups 3, 4 and 5 (e.g. MD, FRCS, FRS).

A peer who is a junior officer in the Armed Forces, is not usually addressed by his Service rank in social correspondence, unless he so wishes, or a letter is forwarded to him at a Service address or club.

1. ORDERS AND DECORATIONS

All the appropriate letters are obligatory in correspondence and lists. The order is laid down for Knights, Dames and others.

They are addressed according to their rank, with the appropriate letters after their name in order of precedence. The use of all these letters is obligatory, e.g John Brown, Esq, CBE, MVO, TD.

The recipient is allowed to use the appropriate letters for the Order from the date of announcement in the 'London Gazette'.

Those promoted within the same Order of Chivalry do not continue to show the letters of the lower class of that Order, e.g. if Brigadier John Smith, OBE, is promoted to CBE he is addressed as Brigadier John Smith, CBE, the OBE being dropped.

Precedence of letters

The full list of honours and awards in order of precedence *of letters* is given below. A baronet has the letters Bt or Bart immediately after the name, and before any letters which signify honours.

It should be noted the VC and GC have precedence of *all* letters signifying Orders (including Knightly grades therein), Decorations and Medals.

The Order of Merit (OM) and Companion of Honour (CH) are important honours which bestow no title on the holder. The letters OM follow GCB, and CH follow GBE.

Some people prefer PC after KG since that is its correct position in order of precedence.

Victoria Cross	VC
George Cross	GC
Knight of the Garter	KG
Knight of the Thistle	KT
Knight/Dame Grand Cross of the Order of the Bath	GCB
Order of Merit	OM
Knight Grand Commander of the Star of India	GCSI
Knight/Dame Grand Cross of the Order of St Michael and St George	GCMG
Knight Grand Commander of the Indian Empire	GCIE
Knight/Dame Grand Cross of the Royal Victorian Order	GCVO
Knight/Dame Grand Cross of the British Empire	GBE
Companion of Honour	CH
Knight Commander of the Bath	KCB
Dame Commander of the Bath	DCB
Knight Commander of the Star of India	KCSI
Knight Commander of St Michael and St George	KCMG
Dame Commander of St Michael and St George	DCMG
Knight Commander of the Indian Empire	KCIE
Knight Commander of the Royal Victorian Order	KCVO
Dame Commander of the Royal Victorian Order	DCVO
Knight Commander of the British Empire	KBE
Dame Commander of the British Empire	DBE
Companion of the Order of the Bath	CB
Companion of the Order of the Star of India	CSI
Companion of the Order of St Michael and St George	CMG
Companion of the Order of the Indian Empire	CIE
Commander of the Royal Victorian Order	CVO
Commander of the Order of the British Empire	CBE
Distinguished Service Order	DSO
Lieutenant of the Royal Victorian Order	LVO
Officer of the Order of the British Empire	OBE
Imperial Service Order	ISO
Member of the Royal Victorian Order	MVO
Member of the Order of the British Empire	MBE
Indian Order of Merit (Military)	IOM
Royal Red Cross	RRC
Distinguished Service Cross	DSC
Military Cross	MC
Distinguished Flying Cross	DFC
Air Force Cross	AFC
Associate, Royal Red Cross	ARRC
Order of British India	OBI
Distinguished Conduct Medal	DCM
Conspicuous Gallantry Medal	CGM
George Medal	GM
Distinguished Conduct Medal of the Royal West African Frontier Force and the King's African Rifles	DCM
Indian Distinguished Service Medal	IDSM
Distinguished Service Medal	DSM
Military Medal	MM
Distinguished Flying Medal	DFM
Air Force Medal	AFM
Medal for Saving Life at Sea	SGM
Indian Order of Merit (Civil)	IOM
Colonial Police Medal for Gallantry	CPM
Queen's Gallantry Medal	QGM
British Empire Medal	BEM
King's Police Medal	KPM
King's Police and Fire Service Medal	KPFSM
Queen's Police Medal	QPM
Queen's Fire Service Medal	QFSM
Colonial Police Medal for Meritorious Service	CPM
Meritorious Service Medal	MSM
Army Emergency Reserve Decoration	ERD
Volunteer Officer's Decoration	VD
Territorial Decoration	TD
Efficiency Decoration	ED
Decoration for Officers of the Royal Naval Reserve	RD
Decoration for Officers of the Royal Naval Volunteer Reserve	VRD
Air Efficiency Award	AE
Canadian Forces Decoration	CD

ORDER OF CANADA

The formation of the Order of Canada was announced in 1967.

The Order, of which the Queen is Sovereign, is divided into the following grades according to its last revised constitution:

CC Companion of the Order of Canada, with precedence after VC and GC before all other letters.

OC Officer of the Order of Canada, with precedence after CC.

CM Member of the Order of Canada, with precedence after OC.

The Cross of Valour, The Star of Courage and The Medal of Bravery have no letters.

ORDER OF AUSTRALIA

The Order of Australia was established in 1975.

The Order, of which The Queen is Sovereign, consists of a General Division and a Military Division and is divided into the following classes:

AK Knight of the Order of Australia, with precedence after the Order of Merit.

AD Dame of Order of Australia, with the same precedence as Knight of the Order of Australia.

AC Companion of the Order of Australia, with precedence after Knight Grand Cross of the Order of the British Empire.

AO Officer of the Order of Australia, with precedence after the Knight Bachelor.

AM Member of the Order of Australia, with precedence after the Distinguished Service Order.

OAM Medal of the Order of Australia, with precedence after the Royal Red Cross (2nd class).

THE QUEEN'S SERVICE ORDER OF NEW ZEALAND

This order was established in 1975. The Order, of which The Queen is Sovereign, is divided into two parts, for Community Service and for Public Services.

There are two divisions:

QSO Companions of The Queen's Service Order, with precedence after Officer of the Order of the British Empire.

QSM The Queen's Service Medal, with precedence after Queen's Gallantry Medal, and before British Empire Medal.

2. PRIVY COUNSELLORS AND APPOINTMENTS TO THE QUEEN

For peers the letters PC are obligatory. For other Privy Counsellors, 'Rt Hon' before the name is sufficient identification. As the other appointments to the Crown (QHP, QHS, etc.) are held for a limited period only, they are not always used by recipients.

3. UNIVERSITY DEGREES

Doctorates in the faculties of Divinity and Medicine (DD, MD) and Masters degrees in the latter (eg MS) are given in all correspondence. Other divinity degrees (eg BD) are sometimes included.

Other degrees in medicine (e.g. MB BS) are sometimes included, especially in professional correspondence, but if one progresses in the same degree only the higher is given.

Doctorates in other faculties are sometimes given, especially if the correspondence concerns the particular profession or subject (e.g. LLD, DSc). Alternatively, except for surgeons, the envelope may be addressed as 'Doctor' before his name, without giving his (or her) degrees.

Other degrees are seldom, and MA and BA never, used in social correspondence, but they are generally included in a formal list.

4. (a) RELIGIOUS ORDERS

Letters for members of religious communities, when used, should be included, e.g. SJ. Some Members of the Order of St. Benedict do not normally use the letters OSB as the prefix of 'Dom' or 'Dame' is held to be a sufficient identification.

(b) MEDICAL QUALIFICATIONS

Fellowships are given in all correspondence (e.g. FRCP, FRCS)

Other qualifications are sometimes given, especially those which are the highest held. They are usually included when writing professionally.

When all letters signifying qualifications are included, as for example in a nominal list, they should appear in the following order.

(*Note:* Fellows and Members of each category precede the next category):

Medicine
Surgery (except MRCS)
Obstetrics, Gynaecology and other specialities
Qualifying diplomas (e.g. MRCS, LRCP)
Other diplomas (e.g. DPH, DObst, RCOG)

In practice, a maximum of three series of letters including MD (see Group 3 above) is usually sufficient in ordinary correspondence (e.g. MD, MS, FRCS).

5. (a) FELLOWSHIPS OF LEARNED SOCIETIES

Fellowships fall into two categories:
(a) honorific, i.e. nomination by election,
(b) nomination by subscription.

Normally only honorific fellowships are used in social correspondence (e.g. FRS, FBA). Fellowships by subscription are generally restricted to correspondence concerning the same field of interest, e.g. a writer to a Fellow of the Zoological Society on the subject of zoology will include FZS after the name.

There is no recognized order for placing these letters. Strictly speaking, they should be arranged according to the date of foundation or incorporation of the societies concerned, but some hold that those with a Royal Charter should precede others.

In practice the following is usually adhered to:

(1) Where one society is indisputably of greater importance than another, the letters may be placed in that order; or alternatively the fellowship of the junior society may be omitted.
(2) If such precedence cannot be determined, the letters may be placed in order of conferment. Where this is not known, they may be placed in alphabetical order.
(3) Where a fellow is pre-eminent in a particular subject, his fellowship of a society connected with this interest may either be placed first, or his other fellowships omitted.

The following are some of the principal learned societies, with their dates of incorporation:

Fellow of The Royal Society	FRS	1662
Fellow of The Society of Antiquaries	FSA	1707
Fellow of The Royal Society of Edinburgh	FRSE	1783
Fellow of The Royal Society of Literature	FRSL	1823
Fellow of The British Academy	FBA	1901

Presidents of some societies have special letters to signify their appointment, e.g. The President of the Royal Society has PRS after his name, but these letters are only used within the particular society.

The Royal Society of Literature bestows an award limited to ten recipients, the Companion of Literature. The letters CLitt are placed before the Fellowship.

(b) ROYAL ACADEMY OF ARTS, THE ROYAL SCOTTISH ACADEMY, ETC.

It is not suggested that Royal Academicians yield in precedence to fellows of learned societies. In practice the two lists do not coincide.

The President and Past Presidents are indicated as follows:

President of the Royal Academy	PRA
Past President of the Royal Academy	PPRA
President of the Royal Scottish Academy	PRSA
Past President of the Royal Scottish Academy	PPRSA

Royal Academicians and Associates are included as follows:

Royal Academician	RA
Royal Scottish Academician	RSA
Associate of the Royal Academy	ARA
Associate of the Royal Scottish Academy	ARSA

Similarly with other Academies, e.g. President Royal Hibernian Academy (PRHA) and Academicians (RHA).

Honorary Academicians and Associates do not normally use the relevant letters.

(c) FELLOWSHIPS AND MEMBERSHIPS OF PROFESSIONAL INSTITUTIONS, ASSOCIATIONS, ETC.

These letters are usually restricted to correspondence concerning the particular profession.

It is not suggested that professional societies as such yield precedence to learned societies, but in point of fact the two groups do not coincide to any great extent. Most of the senior learned societies which elect fellows are senior in age and importance to the professional. Those whose fellowships are by subscription are generally only used in the particular field of interest. For example, if Mr. John Smith is a Chartered Engineer and a Fellow of the Royal Historical Society, he would normally be described professionally as John Smith, Esq, CEng, FIMechE. When corresponding on historical subjects he is normally described as John Smith, Esq, FR HistS. If both series of letters are placed after his name, it is usual to place first those which concern the particular function or subject.

As there is no recognized order for placing qualifications awarded by different bodies, a recipient usually places these letters on headed paper, business cards, etc. in order of importance to his particular profession.

The Engineering Council

The Engineering Council was granted a Royal Charter in 1981. The object of the Council is to advance the education and training of engineers and technologists, and to promote the science and practice of engineering for the public benefit. The Engineering Council accredits engineering academic courses and training programmes in the UK and registers qualified engineers.

There are 47 Professional Engineering Institutions which are nominated bodies of The Engineering Council and which work closely with the Council in the qualification and registration areas. Of these 47 Professional Institutions, 17 are chartered. The Engineering Council, through its Board for Engineers' Registration, determines the standards and criteria for the education, training and levels of experience by which Chartered Engineers, Incorporated Engineers and Engineering Technicians may be registered, enabling them to use the designatory letters CEng, IEng, and EngTech respectively. Chartered Engineers must be in membership of a nominated Chartered Engineering Institution, or an institution affiliated body.

The designatory letters CEng, denoting Chartered Engineer, follow immediately after an individual's name and decorations and are followed in turn by the letters F (Fellow) or M (Member) identifying him with the particular institution(s) to which he belongs. Thus J Smith, Esq, OBE, CEng, FICE, MIMechE, is a Chartered Engineer who is a Fellow of the Institution of Civil Engineers and a Member of the Institution of Mechanical Engineers.

The nominated bodies which are also Chartered Engineering Institutions are: Royal Aeronautical Society, Institution of Civil Engineers, Institution of Chemical Engineers, Institution of Electrical Engineers, Institute of Energy, Institution of Gas Engineers, Institute of Marine Engineers, Institution of Mechanical Engineers, Institute of Metals, Institution of Mining Engineers, Institution of Mining and Metallurgy, Royal Institution of Naval Architects, Institution of Production Engineers, Institution of Structural Engineers, Institute of Measurement and Control, Chartered Institution of Building Services Engineers and the British Computer Society (The BCS is subject to a transitional period).

Chartered Societies of the Land

Three chartered societies of the land, viz.:

The Royal Institution of Chartered Surveyors
The Chartered Land Agents' Society
The Chartered Auctioneers' and Estate Agents' Institute

united in June 1970 to become the Royal Institution of Chartered Surveyors. Fellows and Professional Associates respectively have the letters FRICS and ARICS.

Incorporated Society of Valuers and Auctioneers

The Incorporated Society of Auctioneers and Landed Property Agents united in April 1968 with The Valuers Institution to form The Incorporated Society of Valuers and Auctioneers, with the letters FSVA and ASVA.

(d) WRITERS TO THE SIGNET

It is customary for the letters WS to follow the name after University degrees and those which signify Fellowship or Membership of a Society or Institution, despite the fact that the WS Society (an ancient Society of Solicitors in Scotland) is frequently considerably older than many Institutions. This is a way of indicating the profession. It is not customary for the letters WS to be used socially.

6. APPOINTMENTS

The letters MP are always shown for a Member of Parliament.

The letters QC are always shown for a Queen's Counsel including a County Court Judge, but not High Court Judge.

The letters JP for a Justice of the Peace and DL for a Deputy Lieutenant may be included *in that order.* In practice they are often omitted for a peer, or for one with several honours and awards.

Note: There is no official abbreviation for Lord-Lieutenant, HM Lieutenant or a Vice-Lieutenant.

7. MEMBERSHIP OF ONE OF THE ARMED FORCES

Royal Navy.—The letters 'RN' (or 'Royal Navy', which this Service prefers) are placed after the names of serving officers of and below the rank of Captain. They are also placed after the names of retired Captains, Commanders, and Lieutenant-Commanders where they are prefixed by Naval rank. The letters RNR are likewise used by officers of the Royal Naval Reserve.

Army.—The appropriate letters which signify a Regiment or Corps may be placed after the name for officers on the active list of and below the rank of Lieutenant-Colonel, but are often omitted in social correspondence. These letters are not used for retired officers.

Corps have letter abbreviations (e.g. RE, RAMC, RAOC, RAPC). Most regiments are written in full.

Royal Air Force.—The letters RAF are placed after serving and retired officers, except for Marshals of The Royal Air Force. Officers above the rank of Group Captain do not often use these letters. Similarly with RAFVR.

Royal Marines.—The letters 'RM' (or 'Royal Marines' which some officers prefer) are placed after the names of serving and retired officers of and below the rank of Lieutenant-Colonel. Similarly RMR (Royal Marines Reserve).

FORMS OF ADDRESSING PERSONS OF TITLE

Ecclesiastical and Services prefixes of rank are written before other titles. A High Officer of State or an official holding an important office, should be addressed by his official title when the communication refers to official business.

Eldest Sons of Dukes, Marquesses, and Earls bearing courtesy titles should not be styled "The Rt. Hon." or "The" unless they themselves are Peers or Members of the Privy Council.

Formal conclusions to letters to Peers. The style "I am, my Lord, Your obedient servant" may be used (as applicable), but "Yours faithfully" and "Yours truly" are now more customarily adopted, except for letters to Members of the Royal Family. After the Lambeth Conference 1968 under the guidance of the Archbishop of Canterbury, a simplified form of address for the Clergy of the Church of England was announced.

Commanders, Companions, Officers or Members of any Order and recipients of Decorations and Medals are addressed according to their rank and are entitled to place the recognised initials after their names in the following order:—VC, GC, OM, VA, CI, CH, CB, CSI, CMG, CIE, CVO, CBE, DSO, LVO, (4th class), OBE, QSO, ISO, MVO (5th class), MBE, RRC, DSC, MC, DFC, AFC, ARRC, DCM, CGM, GM, DSM, MM, DFM, AFM, SGM, CPM (for Gallantry), QGM, BEM, KPM, KPFSM, QPM, QFSM, CPM (for Meritorious Service), ERD, TD, ED, RD, VRD, AE, CD.

Succession to hereditary titles. By custom those who have succeeded to peerages and baronetcies are not so addressed until after their predecessor's funeral.

New honours. Knights and Dames of Orders of Chivalry may use their style of "Sir" and "Dame" and the appropriate letters after their names, and Knights Bachelor their style of "Sir" immediately their honours have been announced. Other recipients of honours may also use the appropriate letters. Peers may use their titles after the patent of creation has passed the Great Seal, when their respective Peerage titles will be announced. Full details of forms of address are included in DEBRETT'S CORRECT FORM.

Air Efficiency Award.—The Air Efficiency Award, introduced in 1942 to recognize meritorious Service in the Royal Auxiliary Air Force and the RAFVR, since 1975 officers including retired officers who have received the Award may place AE after their names.

Albert Medal.—In Oct. 1971, The Queen approved the exchange by which holders of the Albert Medal (AM) receive the George Cross. *See* George Cross.

Ambassador (British).—LETTERS.—*Superscription.* (When in the country to which he is accredited only). "His Excellency [preceding all other ranks and titles], HM Ambassador to ____ ." *Commencement,* "Sir" or socially according to rank. *Conclusion,* "I have the honour to be Sir, Your Excellency's obedient servant." PERSONAL ADDRESS, "Your Excellency."

Ambassador's Wife. She is not entitled to the style "Her Excellency" and is referred to and addressed by name or conversationally as the Ambassadress.

Archbishop.—LETTERS.—*Superscription,* "The Most Rev The Lord Archbishop of ____," *Commencement,* "Dear Archbishop." PERSONAL ADDRESS, "Your Grace" or "Archbishop." On retirement from office he reverts to the style of Bishop.

Archbishop's Wife.—As the wife of an Esquire.

Archdeacon.—LETTERS.—*Superscription,* "The Venerable the Archdeacon of [Ely]." *Commencement,* "Dear Archdeacon." The prefix of the Venerable is not retained after retirement unless the title of Archdeacon Emeritus has been conferred.

Baron.—LETTERS.—*Superscription,* "The Right Hon the Lord ____ " or socially "The Lord ____." *Commencement,* "My Lord" or socially "Dear Lord ____." PERSONAL ADDRESS, "My Lord."

Baroness.—LETTERS.—*Superscription*, if a Baroness in her own right "The Right Hon the Baroness ____." or socially "The Baroness ____," or "The Right Hon the Lady ." or "The Lady ____." If the wife of a Baron "The Right Hon the Lady ____," or socially "The Lady ____." *Commencement*, "Madam" or socially "Dear Lady ____." PERSONAL ADDRESS, "Madam." [See also Baron's Widow.]

***If a Baroness in her own right marry a commoner and has issue, the children have the same rank and are addressed as if their father were a Baron.

Baronet.—LETTERS.—*Superscription*, "Sir [Charles] ____ Bt." (The abbreviation "Bart." is also sometimes used). *Commencement*, "Sir." PERSONAL ADDRESS, "Sir" or socially "Dear Sir [Charles]".

Baronet's Widow.—*Same as Baronet's Wife* if present baronet is unmarried. For widows where present incumbent of the title is married ["Dowager"]. As to re-marriage, see "Widows."

Baronet's Wife.—LETTERS.—*Superscription*, if the daughter (i) of a commoner. "Lady ____"; (ii) of a Baron or a Viscount, "The Hon Lady ____"; (iii) of an Earl, a Marquess, or a Duke, "The Lady [Emily] ____." *Commencement*, "Madam.", or socially, "Dear Lady ____." PERSONAL ADDRESS, "Madam."

Baron's Daughter.—LETTERS.—*Superscription*, if married (i) to an esquire, "The Hon Mrs ____"; (ii) to a knight, or a baronet, "The Hon Lady ____"; (iii) to the son of a Baron, or Viscount, or to the younger son of an Earl, "The Hon Mrs ____," or if her husband has a married brother. "The Hon Mrs [William] ____"; (iv) to the younger son of a Marquess or a Duke, "The Lady [Henry] ____." If unmarried, "The Hon [Mary] ____"; (v) to the eldest son of a Duke, Marquess, or Earl by his courtesy title. [*See* also under "Duke's Daughter."] *Commencement*, "Madam." PERSONAL ADDRESS, "Madam," or socially if married to an esquire, "Dear Mrs ____," or according to her husband's rank if a Peer.

Baron's Son.—LETTERS.—*Superscription*, "The Hon [John] ____." *Commencement*, "Sir." PERSONAL ADDRESS, "Sir." or socially "Dear Mr ____." See also "Master of ____."

Baron's Son's Widow.—*Same as Baron's Son's Wife* so long as she remains a widow. As to re-marriage, see "Widows."

Baron's Son's Wife.—LETTERS.—*Superscription*, "The Hon Mrs [Edward] ____," but if the daughter (i) of a Viscount or Baron "The Hon Mrs ____," (ii) of an Earl, a Marquess, or a Duke, "The Lady [Ellen]." [*See* also under "Duke's Daughter." *Commencement*, "Madam," or socially, if her father an esquire "Dear Mrs ____" or according to her father's rank, if a Peer. PERSONAL ADDRESS, "Madam."

Baron's Widow.—*Same as Baroness* if present Baron is unmarried. For widows where present incumbent of title is married [see "Dowager"]. As to re-marriage, see "Widows."

Bishop (Diocesan).—LETTERS.—*Superscription*, "The Rt Rev the Lord Bishop of ____," *Commencement*, "Dear Bishop."

Bishop (Commonwealth, Church Overseas, Irish, Scottish Episcopal, Suffragan and Welsh).—LETTERS.—*Superscription*, "The Right Rev the Bishop of ____." Exceptions, The Bishop of Meath (Premier Bishop of Ireland), and the Primus of Scotland, who are styled "Most Rev" *Commencement*, "Dear Bishop."

(Bishop retired).—Letters commence "Dear Bishop," and are addressed "The Right Rev [John Smith], DD."

Bishop's Wife.—As wife of Esquire.

Cabinet Ministers.—Are Invariably Privy Counsellors, which see.

Canon.—LETTERS.—*Superscription*, "The Rev Canon [John Smith]." *Commencement*, "Dear Canon, " or "Dear Canon [Smith]." On retirement from office he reverts to the style of other clergy unless he has been appointed a Canon Emeritus.

Chairman of Scottish Land Court, as for Lord of Session.

Circuit Judge.—See "Judge, Circuit."

Clergy.—Letters.—*Superscription*, "The Rev John ____." *Commencement*, "Dear Mr (Smith)" or "Dear Father Smith." Personal Address, "Sir." The Reverend precedes any title: The Rev the Hon. It is *incorrect* to write "The Hon and Rev" or "The Rev *Mr.*" Christian name or initials should always be shown.

Consuls [British].—Letters.—*Superscription*, " ____, Esq, HM ['Consul-General,' 'Consul,' or 'Vice-Consul,' as the case may be] ____," In other respects as an Esquire.

Countess.—Letters.—*Superscription*, "The Rt Hon the Countess of ____," or socially "The Countess of ____," In other respects, as Baroness. [See also "Earl's Widow."] *Commencement*, formally "Madam," socially "Dear Lady ____." If a Countess in her own right marries a gentleman of lesser degree than herself, and has issue, the children would have same rank and are addressed as if their father were an Earl.

Dames of Orders of Chivalry prefix "Dame" to their Christian names, adding the initials "GCB," "GCMG," "GCVO," "GBE" "DCB," "DCMG." "DCVO," or "DBE," as the case may be, after the surname. *Commencement*, formally "Madam" or socially "Dear Dame Edith ____" or "Dear Dame Edith." Personal Address, "Dame Edith."

Dean.—Letters.—*Superscription*, "The Very Rev the Dean of ____." *Commencement*, "Dear Dean." Personal Address, "Sir." The prefix of "The Very Rev" is not retained on retirement.

Degrees.—Those with doctorates of any faculty may be addressed by the appropriate abbreviations after their names, following those of orders, decorations and medals conferred by the Crown. DD should always be included. Masters' and bachelors' degrees are not used in social correspondence. The order of letters signifying doctorates and degrees depends on the individual university which confers them.

Deputy Lieutenant.—The letters DL are usually put after name. They follow JP.

Divorced Ladies. When a lady is divorced she loses any precedence which she gained by marriage. With regard to divorced Peeresses, the College of Arms, acting on an opinion of the Lord Chancellor, has long held that such persons cannot claim the privileges or status of Peeresses which they derived from their husbands. Divorced Peeresses are not summoned to a Coronation as Peeresses. The above remarks apply to ladies who have divorced their husbands as well as to those who have been divorced.
The correct style and description of divorced ladies who have not remarried, nor have taken steps to resume their maiden name with the prefix of Mrs, is as follows:

The former wife of a Peer or courtesy Peer,—Mary, Viscountess ____.

The former wife of a Baronet or Knight,—Mary, Lady ____.

The divorced wife of an "Honourable,"—The Hon Mrs John ____, or alternatively she may prefer to be known as Mrs Mary ____.

The divorced wife of a younger son of a Duke or Marquess,—The Lady John ____,

The divorced wife of an untitled gentleman,—Mrs Mary ____ initials.

Dowager Lady is addressed according to her rank. Immediately a peer, or a baronet, marries, the widow of the previous incumbent of the title becomes "The Dowager"; but if there is more than one widow living of previous incumbents of a title, use must be made of the Christian name as a distinction, since the style of Dowager belongs to the senior of the widows for her lifetime. This prefix, however, is very much less used than formerly, use of the Christian name generally being preferred. In such cases ladies are addressed as The Right Hon [Mary], Countess of ____"; or socially as "[Mary], Countess of ____," etc., etc., if a peeress; or, as Ellen, Lady ____," if a Baronet's widow.

Duchess.—LETTERS.—*Superscription*, "Her Grace the Duchess of ____," or socially "The Duchess of ____." *Commencement*, formally "Madam," or socially "Dear Duchess of ____" or "Dear Duchess." PERSONAL ADDRESS, "Your Grace." [See also "Duke's Widow," and for "Duchess of the Blood Royal" *see* "Princess."]

Duke.—LETTERS.—*Superscription*, "His Grace the Duke of ____" or socially "The Duke of ____." The very formal style of "The Most Noble" is now rarely used. *Commencement*, "My Lord Duke," "Dear Duke of ____," or [more usual] "Dear Duke." PERSONAL ADDRESS, "Your Grace." [For "Duke of the Blood Royal" *see* "Prince."]

Duke's Daughter.—LETTERS.—*Superscription*, "The Lady [Henrietta] ____." *Commencement*, "Madam," or socially "Dear Lady Henrietta ____" or "Dear Lady Henrietta." PERSONAL ADDRESS, "Madam."

*** If the daughter of a Duke, a Marquess, or an Earl marries a Peer she is addressed according to the rank of her husband. If she marries the eldest son of a Duke, Marquess or Earl she is known by her husband's courtesy title, but if the daughter of a *Duke* or *Marquess* marries the eldest son of an Earl she is sometimes addressed by the courtesy title of her husband, but she may revert to the style of Lady [Mary] Stavordale, i.e. her own title, followed by her husband's courtesy title. His surname must never be used. This form is invariably used by such ladies after divorce.

Duke's Eldest Son, assumes by courtesy a secondary title of his father, and is addressed personally as if he were a Peer without 'The Most Hon' or 'The Rt Hon' *Superscription*, "Marquess of ____" (or as title adopted may be).

Duke's Eldest Son's Daughter is by courtesy addressed as if her father were a Peer.

Duke's Eldest Son's Eldest Son assumes by courtesy the third title of his grandfather, and is addressed personally as if he were a peer provided such courtesy title is the title of a Peerage vested in his grandfather. *Superscription*, "Earl of ____" or "Lord ____" (or as title adopted may be).

Duke's Eldest Son's Younger Son is by courtesy addressed as if his father were a Peer.

Duke's Eldest Son's Widow, *Same as Duke's Eldest Sons's Wife* so long as she remains a widow. As to re-marriage, *see* "Widows."

Duke's Eldest Son's Wife is known by his courtesy title, and is addressed personally as a peeress without 'The Most Hon' or 'The Rt Hon'.

Duke's Widow, *same as Duchess* if present Duke is unmarried. For widows where present incumbent of title is married [*see* "Dowager"]. As to re-marriage, *see* "Widows."

Duke's Younger Son.—LETTERS.—*Superscription*, "The Lord [Robert] ____." *Commencement*, formally "My Lord," or socially "Dear Lord Robert ____," or "Dear Lord Robert." PERSONAL ADDRESS, "My Lord."

Duke's Younger Son's Widow, *same as Duke's Younger Son's Wife.* As to re-marriage, *see* "Widows."

Duke's Younger Son's Wife.—LETTERS.—*Superscription*, "The Lady [Thomas] ____." *Commencement*, "Madam," or socially "Dear Lady Thomas ____," or "Dear Lady Thomas."

Earl.—LETTERS.—*Superscription*, "The Right Hon the Earl of ____," or socially "The Earl of ____." In other respects as Baron.

Earl's Daughter, *same as Duke's Daughter.*

Earl's Eldest Son bears by courtesy a lesser (usually the second) title of his father, and is addressed as if he were a Peer but without 'The Rt Hon'. *Superscription*, "Viscount ____."

Earl's Eldest Son's Daughter is by courtesy addressed as if her father were a Peer.

Earl's Eldest Son's Son is by courtesy addressed as if his father were a Peer. [If a Scottish Earldom, the eldest may be addressed as "The Master of ____." *See* Master.]

Earl's Eldest Son's Widow, *same as eldest son's Wife* so long as she remains a widow. As to re-marriage, *see* "Widows."

Earl's Eldest Son's Wife is usually known by his courtesy title (for exception see under "Duke's Daughter"), and is addressed personally as if a Peeress but without 'The Rt Hon'.

Earl's Widow, *same as Countess if* present Earl is unmarried. For widows where present incumbent of the title is married [*see* "Dowager"].

Earl's Wife.—*See* "Countess."

Earl's Younger Son, *same as Baron's Son.*

Earl's Younger Son's Widow, *same as Baron's Son's Wife.*

Earl's Younger Son's Wife, *same as Baron's Son's Wife.*

Edward Medal.—In Oct. 1971, The Queen approved the exchange by which holders of the Edward Medal (EM) receive the George Cross. (see George Cross).

Esquire.—LETTERS.—*Superscription,* "[Edward] ____, Esq." *Commencement,* "Sir." PERSONAL ADDRESS, "Sir."

Esquire's Widow, *same as Esquire's Wife.* She continues to use her late husband's christian name unless she re-marries, e.g. Mrs John Smith *not* Mrs Mary Smith.

Esquire's Wife.—*Superscription.* "Mrs [Egerton]," or "Mrs [John Egerton]." The former style is applicable if she is the wife of the head of the family, provided that there is no senior widow living, who retains the style for life or until re-marriage. —LETTERS.— *Commencement,* "Madam." PERSONAL ADDRESS, "Madam."

Fire Service Medals.—See Police Medals.

George Cross. The letters GC take precedence after VC, and before all other honours and decorations.

Governor of a Country within the British Commonwealth is styled "His Excellency" [preceding all other ranks and titles] while actually administering a Government and within its boundary (also an officer administering in his absence). If the Governor has not been knighted he is styled "His Excellency Mr John Smith." Esquire should not be used with HE.

Governor-General.—The style of His Excellency precedes all other titles and ranks, and is used while actually administering a Government and within the territory administered. —LETTERS.—*Superscription,* "His Excellency [Sir John] ____, Governor-General of ____" (also an officer administering in his absence). In other respects as for Governor.

Governor-General's Wife.—The style of "Her Excellency" has, since 1924, been confined to the wives of the Govs-Gen of Countries of the Commonwealth within the country administered by her husband.

Governor's Wife.—She is not accorded the style of "Her Excellency."

Grandchildren of Peers.—If the eldest son of a peer predeceases his father and the grandson succeeds to the peerage held by his grandfather, a Royal Warrant is necessary (when such succession has eventuated) to grant to his younger brothers and his sisters, the "rank, title, place, pre-eminence, and precedence" which would have been due to them if their father had survived to inherit the Peerage.

High Commissioner.—*Superscription,* His Excellency [preceding all other ranks, and titles] the High Commissioner for ____." Otherwise as for an Ambassador.

"Honourable" in Commonwealth Countries. The title of "Honourable" is borne *for life* by all Members of the Queen's Privy Council in Canada, Members of the Canadian Senate and Premiers and Lieutenant-Governors of Canadian Provinces, and of the Executive Councils of the Commonwealth of Australia and of the States of Victoria and Tasmania. In Canada the title of "Honourable" is borne *during office* by the following categories of Judges in Canada—Judges of Supreme and Exchequer Courts of Canada the Chief Justices and Judges of the Supreme Courts of Ontario, Nova Scotia, New Brunswick, Alberta and Newfoundland, the Court of Queens's Bench and the Superior Court of Quebec, the Court of Appeal and the Court of Queen's Bench of Manitoba and Saskatchewan, the Court of Appeal and the Supreme Court of British Columbia, the Supreme Court of Judicature of Prince Edward Island, and the Territorial Courts of NW Territories and Yukon Territory. They are eligible to be personally recommended by the Governor-General for Her Majesty's permission to retain the title on retirement. Also in Commonwealth countries all Members of Executive Councils, all Members of Legislative Councils (other than Legislative Councils of Provinces of Canada), and by the Speaker of the Lower House of the Legislatures. It is also used locally by Members of the Executive and Legislative Councils of territories not possessing Responsible Government. The following in Commonwealth Countries are eligible to be recommended to retain the title of "Honourable" on retirement. Executive Councillors who have served for at least three years as Ministers or one year as Prime Minister; Presidents of Senates and Legislative Councils and Speakers of Legislative Assemblies on quitting office after having served three years in their respective offices: Senators and Members of the Legislative Councils on retirement or resignation after a continuous service of not less than ten years.

[*See* also Judges in Commonwealth and Overseas Territories]

Invitations. When sent jointly to married couples at their home address, the envelope should always be addressed to the wife.

Judge of City of London Court, as for Circuit Judge.

Judge in Commonwealth and Overseas Territories.—The title of "The Right Honourable" is borne for life by the Chief Justice of Canada. The title of "Honourable" during tenure of office is borne by Chief Justices and Judges of the High Court of Australia, and the Supreme Courts of New South Wales, Vic, Queensland, S Aust, W Aust, Tasmania, NZ, and the Judges of the Supreme and Exchequer Courts, and the Chief Justices and Judges of certain other Courts in the provinces of Canada; also such Chief Justices and Judges of those Courts as may be specially permitted to bear it after retirement. *Superscription,* "The Hon the Chief Justice," or "The Hon Mr Justice ____." Judges of the Supreme Courts in Commonwealth Countries are styled "The Honourable."

Judge, Circuit.—For the various appointments see Table of General Precedence. – LETTERS. – *Superscription,* "His Honour Judge ____." PERSONAL ADDRESS—"Sir", but when on the Bench, "Your Honour." The prefix of "His Honour," but not "Judge," is retained after retirement from office, but personal address as "Judge" or "Judge Brown" may be continued unofficially in retirement.

Judge of High Court.—LETTERS.—*Superscription,* (official) "The Hon Mr Justice ____." (private) "Sir John ____." *Commencement,* "Sir." PERSONAL ADDRESS, "Sir," but when on the Bench, "My Lord," or, "Your Lordship." *See also* "Lord Chief Justice of England," "Master of the Rolls," "Lord Justice of Appeal," and "Lord of Appeal in Ordinary."

Judges of High Court, Ladies.—LETTERS. —*Superscription,* (official) "The Hon Mrs Justice ____" (private) "Dame Mary Smith ____," *Commencement,* "Madam." PERSONAL ADDRESS, "Madam," but when on the Bench "My Lady" or "Your Ladyship."

Justice of the Peace.—PERSONAL ADDRESS.—When on the Bench, "Your Worship," and in other respects as an Esquire. The letters JP are usually put after name.

Knight Bachelor.—LETTERS.—*Superscription*, "Sir [George] ____." In other respects same as Baronet. The letters KB should *not* be used.

Knight's Wife, *same as Baronet's Wife*. The wife of a clergyman of the Church of England who receives a Knighthood of an Order of Chivalry but consequently not the accolade, retains the style of "Mrs ____."

Knight of an Order of Chivalry, *same as Knight Bachelor*, but adding to the superscription the recognised letters of the Order, such as "GCB," or "KCB". Clergymen of the Church of England and Honorary Knights do not receive the accolade, and consequently are addressed by the letters of the Orders but not the prefix "Sir."

Knight's Widow, *same as Knight's Wife* so long as she remains a widow. As to re-marriage, *see* "Widows."

Lady (untitled). *See* Esquire's wife and widow. Of unmarried daughters, the eldest of the senior generation is styled "Miss [Egerton]." A younger daughter is addressed as "Miss [Helen Egerton]."

Lady Mayoress. *See* "Lord Mayor's Wife."

Lieutenant-Governor.—Isle of Man, Jersey and Guernsey, as for Governor. The style of a Lt-Gov of a Canadian Province is "*The Hon*" (borne for life).

Life Peer.—He is addressed as for an hereditary peer.—*See* "Baron."

Life Peer's Son.—*See* "Baron's son."

Life Peer's Daughter.—*See* "Baron's daughter."

Life Peeress. *See* "Baroness."

Life Peeress in her own right. She is addressed as for an hereditary peeress. *See* "Baroness."

Lord, in Peerage of Scotland.—*See* "Baron."

Lord Advocate.—LETTERS.—*Superscription*, "The Rt Hon the Lord Advocate," or, "The Rt Hon [George] ____." In other respects as an esquire. [The prefix of Rt Hon is not retained after retirement from office, unless a Member of the Privy Council.]

Lord Chancellor.—LETTERS.—*Superscription*, "The Rt Hon the Lord High Chancellor." In other respects as a peer according to his rank.

Lord Chief Justice.—LETTERS.—*Superscription*, "The Lord Chief Justice of England," or "To the Right Hon Lord ____, Lord Chief Justice of England." In other respects as a Judge, except when of noble rank, when he is addressed according to his degree.

Lord High Commissioner to General Assembly of Church of Scotland.—LETTERS.—*Superscription*, "To His Grace the Lord High Commissioner." *Commencement*, "Your Grace." PERSONAL ADDRESS, "Your Grace."

Lord Justice-Clerk.—LETTERS. —*Superscription*, "The Rt Hon the Lord Justice-Clerk" (if a Privy Counsellor), otherwise "The Hon the Lord Justice-Clerk". *Commencement*, "Dear Lord Justice-Clerk." PERSONAL ADDRESS, Addressed for all purposes by their appointments and not by the Judicial Titles with which they take their seats on the bench.

Lord Justice-General.—LETTERS.—*Superscription*, "The Rt Hon the Lord Justice-General". *Commencement*, "Dear Lord Justice-General." PERSONAL ADDRESS, *See* Lord Justice-Clerk.

Lord Justice of Appeal.—LETTERS.—*Superscription*, "The Right Hon Lord Justice ," or "To the Right Hon Sir [Robert] ____." In other respects as a Judge of High Court.

Lord Mayor.—LETTERS.— The Lord Mayors of London, York, Belfast, and Cardiff have the privilege of being styled "The Rt Hon"; and permission to use this style has also been granted to the Lord Mayors of Sydney

(NSW), Melbourne (Vic), Adelaide (S Aust), Perth (W Aust.), Brisbane (Queensland), and Hobart (Tasmania). *Superscription*, "The Rt Hon the Lord Mayor of ____." or "[Henry ____,] The Rt Hon Lord Mayor of ____," [The prefix of Right Hon is not retained after retirement from office. [*See also* "Lord Provost."]. *Commencement*, "My Lord," or less formally, "Dear Lord Mayor." *Superscription* for other Lord Mayors "The Right Worshipful the Lord Mayor of ____."

Lord Mayor's Wife or Lady Mayoress.—Letters.—*Superscription*, "The Lady Mayoress." In other respects as Knight's or Esquire's wife.

Lord of Appeal-in-Ordinary.—*See Baron.*

Lord of Session, Scottish.—Letters.—*Superscription*, "The Hon Lord ____." In other respects as a Baron, but children have no courtesy styles. *See* also Lord Justice Clerk and Lord Justice General.

Lord of Session's Wife or Widow.—Letters.—*Superscription*, "Lady ____." In other respects as Baron's wife.

Lord Provost.—Letters.—*Superscription*, The Lord Provosts of Edinburgh and Glasgow are addressed as "The Rt Hon the Lord Provost," while in office. The prefix may be placed before the name of the holder in the case of the Lord Provost of Edinburgh. In other respects as a Baron. The Lord Provost of Perth, Dundee and Aberdeen are styled "The Lord Provosts of ____."

Lord Provost's Wife. Same as the wife of an Esquire. The style of Lady Provost is incorrect.

Marchioness.—Letters.—*Superscription*, "The Most Hon the Marchioness of ____," or socially, "The Marchioness of ____." In other respects as Baroness. [*See also* "Marquess's Widow."]

Marquess.—Letters.—*Superscription*, "The Most Hon the Marquess of ____," or less formally, "The Marquess of ____." In other respects as Baron.

Marquess's Daughter, *same as Duke's Daughter.*

Marquess's Eldest Son, *same as Duke's Eldest Son. Superscription*, "Earl of ____" (or as title adopted may be).

Marquess's Eldest Son's Daughter is by courtesy addressed as if her father were a peer.

Marquess's Eldest Son's Eldest Son, *same as Duke's Eldest Son. Superscription*, "Viscount ____" (or as title adopted may be).

Marquess's Eldest Son's Younger Son is by courtesy addressed as if his father were a Peer, viz. "The Hon ____."

Marquess's Eldest Son's Widow, *same as Duke's Eldest Son's Widow.*

Marquess's Eldest Son's Wife is known by his courtesy title, and is addressed personally as a peeress without 'The Rt Hon'.

Marquess's Widow, *same as Marchioness*, if present Marquess is unmarried. For widows where present incumbent of title is married [see "Dowager"]. As to re-marriage see "Widows."

Marquess's Younger Son, *same as Duke's Younger Son.*

Marquess's Younger Son's Widow, *same as Duke's Younger Son's Wife*, As to re-marriage, see "Widows."

Marquess's Younger Son's Wife, *same as Duke's Younger Son's Wife.*

Master.—This title is borne in the *Peerage of Scotland* by the heir apparent or presumptive of a Peer. It is also used *by courtesy* by the eldest son of a Peer by courtesy. In the case of the heir apparent, "Master" is normally used by the eldest son of a Viscount and Lord, as the heirs of the senior grades of the Peerage normally use a courtesy title. He is styled "The Master of ____" (the appropriate title will be found under the Peerage article). If the heir be a woman, she is officially designated "The Mistress of ____" but this title is seldom used. A Master's wife is styled "The Hon Mrs [Donald Campbell"] or according to her husband's rank.

Master of the Rolls.—Letters .—*Superscription*, "The Right Hon the Master of the Rolls," or "The Right Hon ____," according to *Commencement*, as "Judge." Personal Address, "Sir," but when on the Bench, "My Lord," or "Your Lordship."

Mayor (whether man or woman).—LETTERS.—*Superscription*, (if Mayor of a City), "The Right Worshipful the Mayor of ____", (if a Mayor of a Borough or Town Mayor), "The Worshipful the Mayor of ____." *Commencement*, "Sir (or Madam)." In other respects as an Esquire or an Esquire's wife. The form "Dear Mr Mayor" may be used for a man or woman.

Members of the Executive and Legislative Councils.—See Honourable in Commonwealth Countries.

Members of Parliament.—According to rank, but adding the initials "MP" after title or name and honours.

Military Officers.—See "Naval, Military, and Air Force Officers."

Minister of the Crown.—If a Privy Counsellor, see that section, otherwise see Member of Parliament or Grade of Peerage. The social form of "Dear Secretary of State," or "Dear Minister" may be used if the matter concerns the Department.

Moderator of the General Assembly of Church of Scotland. By Order in Council the Moderator has precedence in Scotland and at Court functions immediately after Bishops of the Church of England, and while in office is addressed as "Rt Rev" Former Moderators, "Very Rev."

Naval, Military, and Air Force Officers.—Professional rank should always precede any titles, *e.g.*, "Adm (the Right Hon) the Earl of ____," "Gen the (Right Hon) Lord ," "Air-Marshal Sir ____," but Lieutenants in the Army, Flying Officers and Pilot Officers in the Air Force are addressed by their social and not their professional rank, *e.g.*, "The Hon Benjamin ____, Irish Guards," "George ____, Esq., 11th Hussars," or "William ____, Esq., RAF."

Peers and Peeresses by courtesy. —As commoners they are not addressed as "Rt Hon" or "The" but "Viscount [Brown]" or appropriate title.

Police and Fire Service Medals. The letters KPM, KPFSM, QPM, QFSM and CPM are now placed after the name. If the Colonial Police Medal were awarded for gallantry the letters CPM are placed before BEM, and if for meritorious service after QFSM (see paragraph 4 at beginning of section).

Prebendary.—As for Canon, but substituting the word Prebendary for Canon.

Prime Minister, The.—See Privy Counsellors. The social form of "Dear (Mr.) Prime Minister" may be used if the matter concerns his office.

Prince.—LETTERS.—*Superscription*, (i) the son of a Sovereign "His Royal Highness The Prince [Edward]": (ii) other Princes "His Royal Highness Prince [Michael of Kent]"; (iii) Duke "His Royal Highness The Duke of [Gloucester]." *Commencement*, "Sir," *Conclusion*, "I have the honour to be, Sir. Your Royal Highness's most humble and obedient servant." PERSONAL ADDRESS, "Your Royal Highness," and henceforward as "Sir." [*See also* Royal Family.]

Princess.—LETTERS.—*Superscription*, (i) the daughter of a Sovereign "Her Royal Highness The Princess [Royal]"; (ii) other Princesses "Her Royal Highness Princess [Alexandra], the Hon Lady Ogilvy"; (iii) Duchess "Her Royal Highness the Duchess of [Kent]." *Commencement*, "Madam." *Conclusion*, "I have the honour to be, Madam, Your Royal Highness's most humble and obedient servant." PERSONAL ADDRESS, "Your Royal Highness," and henceforward as "Ma'am." [*See also* Royal Family.]

Privy Counsellors, also spelt PRIVY COUNCILLORS. — LETTERS. — *Superscription*, "The Right Hon ____," but if a peer then as such, followed by the letters "PC," *after* all Orders and Decorations. *Commencement, &c.*, according to the rank of the individual. Privy Counsellors of Northern Ireland, which are no longer created, are entitled to the prefix of Right Hon and are included in this section. Members of the Privy Council of Canada are entitled to the style of "Hon" for life. *Commencement*, as for Esquire or appropriate rank.

Privy Counsellors, Wives of.—They enjoy no special style or precedence as such.

Provost.—As for Dean, but substituting the word Provost for Dean.

Provost (Scotland).—LETTERS.—*Superscription*, "The Provost of ____ ." *Commencement*, "Dear Provost." PERSONAL ADDRESS, "Provost."

Queen Mother.—LETTERS.—*Superscription*, for formal and state documents, "Her Gracious Majesty Queen Elizabeth The Queen Mother," otherwise "Her Majesty Queen Elizabeth The Queen Mother." *Commencement*, as for the Queen Regnant. *Conclusion*, "I have the honour to remain, Madam, Your Majesty's most humble and obedient servant." PERSONAL ADDRESS, as for the Queen Regnant.

Queen Regnant.—LETTERS.—*Superscription*, for formal and state documents. "The Queen's Most Excellent Majesty." otherwise "Her Majesty The Queen," *Commencement*, "Madam," or "May it please your Majesty." *Conclusion*, "I have the honour to remain Madam, Your Majesty's most humble and obedient servant." PERSONAL ADDRESS, "Your Majesty," and henceforth as "Ma'am."

Queen's Counsel.—LETTERS.—*Superscription*, " ____ Esq, QC." In other respects as an Esquire. The letters are used after the name by Circuit Judges, but not by High Court Judges.

Rt Honourable.—This prefix is borne by Privy Counsellors of Great Britain and Northern Ireland, the Governor General of Canada, and Prime Minister and Chief Justice of Canada *for life*; by Earls, Viscounts and Barons: (except peers by courtesy) their wives and widows; and certain Lord Mayors (see Lord Mayors), and Provosts of Edinburgh and Glasgow (see Lord Provosts).

Royal Dukes. —See "Prince."

Royal Family.—On 11 Dec 1917, it was ordained that "The children of any Sovereign of the United Kingdom and the children of the sons of any such Sovereign and the eldest living son of the eldest son of the Prince of Wales, shall have and at all times hold and enjoy the style, title, or attribute of Royal Highness with their titular dignity of Prince or Princess prefixed to their respective Christian names, or with their other titles of honour; and that the grandchildren of the sons of any such Sovereign in the direct male line (save only the eldest living son of the eldest son of the Prince of Wales) shall have the style and title enjoyed by the children of Dukes." [*See* also "Queen Regnant," "Queen Mother." "Prince," and "Princess."]

Rural Deans. No special form of address.

Secretary of State. See "Minister of the Crown" and "Privy Counsellors."

Sheriff.—LETTERS.—*Superscription*, "Sheriff." PERSONAL ADDRESS, Addressed on the bench as "My Lord" or "My Lady" and formally and socially as "Sheriff ____ ."

Sheriff Principal.—LETTERS.—*Superscription*, "Sheriff Principal ___." *Commencement*, "Sheriff Principal." PERSONAL ADDRESS, Addressed on the bench as "My Lord" or "My Lady", and formally and socially as "Sheriff ____ ."

Sovereign, The.—See "Queen Regnant."

Titles just announced.—See paragraph at commencement of this section.

Trinity House, Elder Brethren of are entitled to be called "Captain," with precedence after Naval Captains.

Victoria Cross.—The letters VC take precedence of all other honours and decorations.

Viscount.—LETTERS.—*Superscription*, "The Right Hon the Viscount ____," or socially "The Viscount ____." In other respects as Baron.

Viscountess.—LETTERS.—*Superscription*, "The Right Hon the Viscountess ____." or socially, "The Viscountess." In other respects as Baroness and Baron's widow. [See also "Viscount's Widow"].

Viscount's Son, and his Wife or Widow *same as Baron's.*

Viscount's Daughter, *same as Baron's.*

Viscount's Widow, *same as Viscountess* if present Viscount is unmarried. For widows where present incumbent of title is married [see "Dowager"]. As to re-marriage, see "Widows."

Wales, Prince of. See "Prince" and "Royal Family."

Widows.—A Widow who re-marries *loses* any title or precedence she gained by her previous marriage, and is not recognised as having any claim to bear the title of her deceased husband, *e.g.:* at a coronation or other State ceremonial, the widow of a peer would not be summoned as a peeress if she had subsequently married a commoner; and, if having espoused a peer of lesser degree than her former husband, she would only be recognised by the rank acquired by her last marriage. [*See also* Esquire's Widow.]

LONDON CLUBS

American	95 Piccadilly, W1	071-499 2303
Army and Navy	36 Pall Mall, SW1	071-930 9721
Anglo-Belgian	60 Knightsbridge, SW1	071-235 2121
Arts	40 Dover Street, W1	071-499 8581
Athenaeum	107 Pall Mall, SW1	071-930 4843
Beefsteak	9 Irving Street, WC2	071-930 5722
Boodle's	28 St James's Street, SW1	071-930 7166
Brooks's	St James's Street, SW1	071-499 0072
Buck's	18 Clifford Street, W1	071-734 6896
Caledonian	9 Halkin Street, SW1	071-235 5162
Canning	42 Half Moon Street, W1	071-499 5163
Carlton	69 St James's Street, SW1	071-493 1168
Cavalry and Guards'	127 Piccadilly, W1	071-499 1261
City of London	19 Old Broad Street, EC2	071-588 7991
East India, Devonshire, Sports and Public Schools	16 St James's Square, SW1	071-930 1000
Eccentric	9 Ryder Street, SW1	071-930 6133
Farmers	3 Whitehall Court, SW1	071-930 3557
Flyfishers'	24a Old Burlington Street, W1	071-629 6776
Garrick	15 Garrick Street, WC2	071-836 1737
Gresham	15 Abchurch Lane, EC4	071-629 7231
Hurlingham	Ranelagh Gardens, SW6	071-736 8411
Lansdowne	9 Fitzmaurice Place, Berkeley Square, W1	071-629 7200
MCC (Marylebone Cricket Club)	Lord's Cricket Ground, NW8	071-286 3649
National Liberal	1 Whitehall Place, SW1	071-930 9871
Naval and Military	94 Piccadilly, W1	071-499 5163
New Cavendish	44 Great Cumberland Place, W1	071-262 5536
Oriental	Stratford House, Stratford Place, W1	071-629 5126
Portland	42 Half Moon Street, W1	071-499 1523
Pratt's	14 Park Place, SW1	071-493 0397
Queen's	Palliser Road, W14	071-385 3421
Reform	104 Pall Mall, SW1	071-930 9374
Royal Air Force	128 Piccadilly, W1	071-499 3456
Royal Automobile	89-91 Pall Mall, SW1	071-930 2345
Royal Ocean Racing	20 St James's Place, SW1	071-493 2248
Royal Over-Seas League	Over-Seas House, St James's Street, SW1	071-408 0214
Royal Thames Yacht	60 Knightsbridge, SW1	071-235 2121
St Stephen's	34 Queen Anne's Gate, SW1	071-222 1382
Savile	69 Brook Street, W1	071-629 5462
Ski Club of Great Britain	118 Eaton Square, SW1	071-235 4711
Travellers'	106 Pall Mall, W1	071-930 8688
Turf	5 Carlton House Terrace, SW1	071-930 8555
United Oxford & Cambridge University	71 Pall Mall, SW1	071-930 4152
University Women's	2 Audley Square, South Audley Street, W1	071-499 6478
White's	37 St James's Street, SW1	071-493 6671

CLUBS OUTSIDE LONDON

Caledonian	32 Abercromby Place, Edinburgh 3	031 557 2675
Jockey	High Street, Newmarket	0638 663101
Kildare St and University	17 St Stephen's Green, Dublin 2	0001 76 65 23
Ladies Club	29 Queensferry Road, Edinburgh 2	031 225 8002
Leander	Henley-on-Thames	04912 3665
Manchester	50 Spring Gardens, Manchester	061 834 7678
New	86 Princess Street, Edinburgh 2	031 226 4881
Northern Counties	Hood Street, Newcastle-upon-Tyne	0632 326611
Puffin's	c/o Martin's, 70 Rose Street North, Edinburgh	031 225 3106
Royal and Ancient	St Andrews	0334 72112
Royal Irish Automobile	34 Glasgow Street, Dublin 2	001 77 06 68
Royal Scottish Automobile	11 Blythswood Square, Glasgow 2	041 221 3850
Royal Yacht Squadron	Cowes, Isle of Wight	0983 292743
Stephen's Green	9 St Stephen's Green North, Dublin	0001 77 47 44
Ulster	48 High Street, Belfast	0232 230355
Ulster Reform	4 Royal Avenue, Belfast	0232 23411
Western	32 Royal Exchange Square, Glasgow 1	041 221 2016
Yorkshire	17 Museum Street, York	0904 24116

A READER'S GUIDE

The editors would like to point out the following features of a standard entry in *Debrett's People of Kent*

Bracketed forenames indicate name(s) not used by the entrant, the first forename following a bracketed forename is the one commonly used by the entrant.

Well-known colleges and schools are listed without the word college or school.

Children are listed with the names of sons in order of birth first and followed by daughters in order of birth, in accordance with generally accepted genealogical practice.

Careers are set out in chronological order with military service listed first (where applicable), followed by professional career, followed by public career and finally by awards, foreign orders and decorations and fellowships.

Clubs within London are listed without the word London; where membership of a club outside London occurs the location of the club follows in brackets.

Style indicates the preferred style to be used in addressing correspondence to an entrant.

A list of abbreviations used in this publication can be found at the back of the book.

Please also note that entrants addresses, home or otherwise, have not been published where this has been requested and that some individuals have preferred not to appear in *Debrett's People of Kent.*

LISTINGS

Commercial and Professional Listings appear at the back of the book. Such listings have not been restricted to Kent based organisations alone but also include services provided in the surrounding home counties and London.

DISCLAIMER

Debrett's make every effort to check and update the information contained in this publication.

Any errors or omissions which remain are unintentional, and no liability of any kind is accepted by the publisher or distributor in respect of them. Such errors or omissions should be drawn to Debrett's attention for correction in future editions.

A

ABRAMS, Drummond Ernest; s of Reginald Frank Abrams, and Winnifred Edith, *née* Stripp; *b* 9 Oct 1933; *Educ* Tonbridge; *m* 1, (m dis 1965); 1 da (Susan Jennifer b 5 April 1962); m 2, 17 Sept 1966, Edna, *née* Van Den Bergh; 1 s (Alexander John Drummond b 25 Oct 1970), 1 da (Juliette Kirsten Annabel b 21 July 1968); *Career* qualified CA 1957; ptnr Spain Brothers & Co 1961- (joined 1950); pres S Eastern Soc of CAs 1985-86; chm: Communications Directorate ICAEW (elected to Cncl 1985), Great Weald Enterprise Agency; *Recreations* theatre and astronomy; *Style*— Drummond E Abrams, Esq; Spain Brothers & Co, 16 Lonsdale Gardens, Tunbridge Wells, Kent TN1 1NU (☎ 0892 546546, fax 0892 511334)

ABSOLON, Philip Andrew; s of Rev Canon Peter Chambers Absolon, of The Vicarage, 2 Waltham Rd, Gillingham, and Joan Mary, *née* James; gggs of John Absolon the Victorian water-colour artist; *b* 24 Nov 1960; *Educ* Epsom Coll of Art (Dip Fine Art); *Career* poet; worked with Medway Poets; artist; exhibitions incl: Epsom Coll of Art 1982, Rochester Adult Educn Centre 1986 and 1987, Chatham Art Centre 1988, Gillingham Adult Educn Centre 1989, Hazelmere Art Gallery 1989; involved in work of Medway Arts Centre; *Style*— Philip Absolon, Esq; The Vicarage, 2 Waltham Rd, Gillingham, Kent ME8 6XQ (☎ 0634 31690)

ADAMS, Prof John Norman; s of Vincent Smith Adams, of Lintz Green, Rowlands Gill, Tyne and Wear, and Elsie Adams (d 1964); *b* 24 Dec 1939; *Educ* Newcastle upon Tyne Royal GS, Univ of Durham; *Career* admitted slr 1965; private practice 1965-70, lectr Univ of Sheffield 1971-79, prof of commercial law Univ of Kent 1987- (sr lectr 1979-87), called to the Bar Inner Temple 1984; visiting prof: Univ of Maryland, Nat Law Centre Washington DC, Notre Dame Law Sch Univ of Paris; memb Br Literary and Artistic Copy Right Assoc; *Books* Bibliography of 18th Century Legal Literature (1982), Merchandising Intellectual Property (1987), Understanding Contract Law (1987), Commercial Hiring and Leasing (1989), Franchising (3 edn, 1990); *Recreations* music, walking; *Clubs* Savage, Lansdowne; *Style*— Prof John Adams; University of Kent, Keynes College, Canterbury CT2 7NP (☎ 0227 764000, fax 0227 459025)

ADAMS, Rev Peter Anthony; s of William Norman Adams, of 9 Western Court, Cheltenham, Glos, and Olive Mona, *née* Williams ; *b* 10 Jan 1948; *Educ* King's Sch Glos, King's Coll London (BD, MTh, AKC), St Augustine's Coll Canterbury; *Career* ordained deacon Canterbury 1972, hon asst chaplain St Paul's Athens, Curate Ashford Kent 1973-79, ordained priest 1974; priest i/c: Holy Trinity Ramsgate 1979-86, St George-the-Martyr Ramsgate 1984-86; rector Holy Trinity and St George Ramsgate 1986-; chm govrs Holy Trinity C of E (Aided) Sch Ramsgate, govr St George's Sch Broadstairs; chaplain to: E Kent Branch RE Assoc, Royal Br Legion; memb: Liturgical Advsy Ctee Diocese of Canterbury, Diocesan Advsy Ctee; *Recreations* swimming, reading; *Style*— The Rev Peter Adams; The Rectory, Winterstoke Way, Ramsgate, Kent CT11 8AG (☎ 0843 593593)

ADAMS, Richard Borlase; CBE (1982); s of James Elwin Cokayne Adams (d 1961), and Susan Mercer, *née* Porter (d 1985); *b* 9 Sept 1921; *Educ* Winchester, Trinity Coll Oxford; *m* 1951, Susan Elizabeth, da of Col Ronald Streeter Lambert, MC (d 1976); 2 s (Christopher, Jeremy), 1 da (Jill); *Career* served WWII with Rifle Bde ME and Italy; chm: Islay Kerr & Co Ltd Singapore 1963-66, British India Steam Navigation Co Ltd 1970-84 (dir 1966, md 1969); P & OSN Co: dir 1970-, dep md 1974, md 1979-84, chief exec 1981-84; dir Clerical Medical and General Life Assurance Soc 1975-88; chm Kent Assoc for the Disabled 1986-; *Recreations* gardening, tennis, golf; *Clubs* Oriental; *Style*— Richard Adams, Esq, CBE; Beacon House, Bethersden, Ashford, Kent TN26 3AE (☎ 023 382 247)

ADAMS, William George; s of Charles Alfred Adams (d 1963), of Chatham, Kent, and Alice Violet, *née* Fry (d 1919); *b* 30 Sept 1913; *m* 30 Oct 1934, Florence Rose, da of Samson Robert Burford (d 1938), of Chatham; 2 s (William Frederick b 1935, Brian Samson b 1937 d 1951), 2 da (Mavis Florence b 1946, Rosemary b 1953); *Career* haulage contractor and coal factor 1926-88, gen merchant 1989-; memb Medway C of C; *Recreations* all sports; *Style*— William Adams, Esq; 40 Green St, Gillingham, Kent ME7 5TJ (☎ 0634 574790, bus 0634 52273)

ADAMS, William Horace; s of David Horace Adams (d 1965), and Patience, *née* Dixon (d 1963); *b* 15 Aug 1925; *Educ* Stamford Sch, Oakham Sch; *m* 1947, Joan, da of James Pugh (d 1960); 2 s, 2 da; *Career* chartered surveyor; chm: RICS Continental Euro Branch 1981, Waterglade International Holdings plc 1987-; pres: Br Chapter Int Real Est Fndn (FIABCI) 1982-83, Arbitration and Conciliation Cncl FIABCI 1982-90; dir Property Intelligence Ltd 1984-; conslt: Security Pacific National Bank 1984-90, Privatbanken (now Vaibank) 1985-, Bankers Trust Co 1990-, and others; Freeman City of London, Liveryman Worshipful Co of Gardeners; *Recreations* golf; *Clubs* RAC; *Style*— William H Adams, Esq; Westering, 17 Coombe Rd, Otford, Sevenoaks, Kent TN14 5RG (☎ 09592 2565); 15 Les Mesnils du Golf, Evian le Bains, Haute Savoie, France; Waterglade International Holdings plc, Waterglade House, 5/7 Ireland Yard, London EC4V 5DQ (☎ 071 248 8301)

ADAMSON, Dr Donald; JP (City of London 1983); s of Donald Adamson (d 1982), of Brookfield Lymm, Cheshire, and Hannah Mary, *née* Booth; *b* 30 March 1939; *Educ* Manchester GS, Magdalen Coll Oxford, Univ of Paris (MA, MLitt, DPhil); *m* 24 Sept 1966, Helen Freda, da of Frederick Percival Griffiths (d 1970), of Mossley Hill, Liverpool; 2 s (Richard Henry b 17 Jan 1970, John Daniel b 21 April 1971); *Career* author and historian; visiting fell Wolfson Coll Cambridge; judge Museum of the Year Awards 1979-83, memb exec ctee Nat Heritage 1980; memb Cambridge Soc (Kent Branch); Liveryman Worshipful Co of Haberdashers 1976; FSA 1979, FRSL 1983, FIL 1989; Lord of the Manor of Dodmore; Chevalier Ordre des Palmes Académiques France 1986; *Books* The Genesis of Le Cousin Pons (1966), Dusty Heritage (1971), The House of Nell Gwyn (jtly, 1974), A Rescue Policy for Museums (1980), Balzac Illusions Perdues (1981), Les Romantiques français devant la Peinture espagnole (1985), two translations of Balzac novels; *Recreations* paintings, T S Eliot, gastronomy, water sports; *Clubs* Beefsteak, City Livery; *Style*— Dr Donald Adamson, JP; Dodmore House, The Street, Meopham, Kent DA13 OAJ; Topple Cottage, Polperro, Cornwall PL13 2RS; 171 Clifford's Inn, London EC4A 1BY (car tel: 0836 659418)

ADJAYE, Dr Nellie Turbyne; da of Dr Joseph Samuel Annan, of Ghana, and Elizabeth Aba Annan, of Ghana; *b* 22 Jan 1946; *Educ* Wesley Girls HS Ghana, E Anglian Sch for Girls Bury St Edmunds, The Royal Free Hosp Med Sch Univ of London (MB BS, MRCP, MSc); *m* 22 May 1976, Dr Robert Egbert Adjaye, s of Robert E K Adjaye, of Ghana; *Career* sr house offr in paediatric neurology Hosp for Sick Children Gt Ormond St London 1977-78, paediatric registrar N Middx and St Anns Hosp London 1979-81, lectr and sr registrar in community paediatrics St Mary's Hosp Med Sch London 1981-87, conslt in community paediatrics Maidstone Health Authy 1987-; author of papers on: Factors Affecting Immunisation Uptake, Measles Immunisation, Chicken Pox Isolation and School Health, Neonatal Screening for Sickle Cell Disease; hon med advsr Nat Sickle Cell Soc, past sec Med Women's Fedn (London Assoc), supporter Women of Kent charity activities; memb: BPA, BMA; *Recreations* gardening, Cho Kwando, (martial arts). photography, swimming, travel; *Clubs* Weslsy Girls' HS Old Girls Assoc; *Style*— Dr Nellie Adjaye; Kits Coty Ward, Preston Hall Hospital, London Rd, Maidstone, Kent ME20 7NJ (☎ 0662 710161 ext 3061)

ADKINSON, Keith; s of (Henry) Bernard Adkinson, and Elsie May, *née* Edmonds; *b* 25 Dec 1949; *Educ* Ashford GS; *Career* elected SLD cnclr Maidstone North Ward Maidstone Borough Cncl 1988-; memb Maidstone - Beauvais Twinning Assoc; *Recreations* travel, languages, photography, philately, gardening; *Style*— Keith Adkinson, Esq; 34 John St, Maidstone, Kent ME14 2SQ (☎ 0622 678515); Commercial Union Assurance Co plc, Brenchley House, Week St, Maidstone, Kent ME14 2SQ (☎ 0622 671355, fax 0622 673261)

AGARWAL, Dr Gopal Chandra; s of Bisheshwar P Agarwal (d 1944), and Kailash, *née* Devi; *b* 13 Dec 1934; *Educ* K G Med Coll Lucknow India (MB BS), Med Coll Kanpur India (DMRE), Univ of Liverpool (DTM & H); *m* 22 June 1960, Dr Vasantika Agarwal, da of Nihal Chand Shastri (d 1960); 1 s (Sanjoy K b 3 Nov 1962), 1 da (Seema b 21 Oct 1966); *Career* house surgn St Bart's Hosp Rochester 1966-68, house physician Wilson Hosp Mitcham Surrey 1969-72, registrar All Saints Hosp Chatham Kent 1973, GP 1974-; *Recreations* gardening, walking, driving, swimming; *Style*— Dr Gopal Argawal; 11 The Shades, Strood, Kent ME2 2UD (☎ 0634 710145); Health Centre, Gun Lane,

Strood, Kent ME2 4UL (☎ 0634 717755)

AGARWAL, Dr Sanjay K; s of Dr Gopal C Agarwal, of 11 The Shades, Strood, Kent, and Dr Vasantika Agarwal; *b* 3 Nov 1962; *Educ* Sir Joseph Williamson's Mathematical Sch Rochester, St George's Hosp Med Sch London (MB BS); *Career* house surgn Epsom Dist Hosp 1986-87, house physician and gynaecologist St James' Hosp Balham 1987-88, house surgn St George's Hosp 1988-89, res Duke Univ Med Center Durham N C USA 1989-; *Recreations* driving, photography, sports, computing; *Style—* Dr Sanjay Agarwal; 11 The Shades, Strood, Kent ME2 2UD (☎ 0634 710145); Duke University Medical Center, Durham, N C 27710, USA

AGGETT, Ms Valerie (Mrs John Grenier); da of James William Cocksey (d 1986); *b* 15 Dec 1950; *Educ* Bury GS, Univ of Durham (BA), Coll of Law Guildford; *m* 1 (m dis), Mr Aggett; m 2, 1981, John Allan Grenier, s of Rev George Arthur Grenier (d 1973); 1 step s, 1 step da; *Career* slr; princ and md The HLT Group Ltd 1976- (Queen's Award for Export 1982); *Recreations* motor cruising, tennis, interior design, fashion; *Clubs* RAC, Reform, Queens; *Style—* Ms Valerie Aggett; The HLT Group Ltd, 200 Greyhound Rd, London W14 9RY (☎ 071 385 3377); Plovers, Ruck Lane, Horsmonden, Kent

AIKMAN, Anthony Robert; s of William Robert Aikman (d 1982), and Marjorie Roberta Amanda, *née* MacMillan; *b* 3 Feb 1942; *Educ* Westminster, Univ Coll of N Wales Bangor (BSc); *Career* forestry offr: Kent, Africa; freelance journalist: Central and S America, Italy; scriptwriter of radio short stories Rome; dir: Hollywood movie The Genesis Children, Outward Bound Centre Italy, Melanesian Mission Solomon Isles; explorations incl: Sahara by motorbike, S China Seas, S American headwaters, Empty Quarter of Arabia, Masai tribes; memb: Soc of Authors, Tibet Soc, The Euro Movement; *Books* The Caves of Segada (1986), The Eye of Itza (1987), The Brokers of Doom (1988), Treehouses (1989); *Recreations* skiing, sailing, riding, amateur dramatics; *Clubs* Royal Cinq Ports Yacht; *Style—* Anthony Aikman, Esq; St Margaret's Bay, nr Dover, Kent CT15 6DD (☎ 0304 852277)

AISHER, Jack Edward; DL (Kent); s of Owen Aisher (d 1963), and Emily, *née* Willis (d 1958); *b* 22 April 1910; *Educ* Maidstone GS; *m* 14 Sept 1933, Eileen Elsie, da of Sidney Squires (d 1965); 3 s (Trevor Jack b 1935, Peter Anthony b 1938 d 1987, Michael John b 1942); *Career* Capt RE 1940-45; Marley plc: joined 1926, dir 1946, vice chm 1978, chm 1982-87, non exec dir 1987-; pres: Dover-Deal Cons Assoc, Deal-Walmer Men of Kent and Kentish Men; memb: Bd Govrs Sevenoaks Sch, Cncl Univ Kent at Canterbury; Hon DCL Univ of Kent; *Recreations* golf; *Clubs* Royal Cinque Ports, Royal St Georges, Royal and Ancient; *Style—* Jack Aisher, Esq, DL; The Chart House, The Beach, Walmer, Deal, Kent CT14 7HJ; Marley plc, London Rd, Riverhead, Sevenoaks, Kent

AITKEN, Jonathan William Patrick; MP (C) South Thanet 1983-; s of Sir William Aitken, KBE, MP (d 1964), and Hon Lady Aitken, MBE, JP; is gn of 1 Baron Beaverbrook and gs of 1 Baron Rugby; bro of Maria Aitken, the actress; *b* 30 Aug 1942; *Educ* Eton, ChCh Oxford; *m* 1979, Lolicia Olivera (economist), da of O A Azucki, of Zürich; 1 s (William b 7 Sept 1982), twin da (Victoria, Alexandra b 14 June 1980); *Career* private sec to Selwyn Lloyd 1964-66, foreign corr Evening Standard 1966-71, md Slater Walker (ME) 1973-75, MP (C) Thanet E 1974-1983, fndr and chm Aitken Hume Int 1979-, temp chief exec TV-AM Mar-Apr 1983; *Books* A Short Walk on the Campus (1966), The Young Meteors (1967), Land of Fortune: A Study of the New Australia (1971), Officially Secret (1971); *Clubs* Beefsteak, Turf, Pratt's; *Style—* Jonathan Aitken, Esq, MP; 8 Lord North St, London SW1

ALBERY, Ian Bronson; s of Sir Donald Arthur Rolleston Albery (d 1988), and Ruby Gilchrist, *née* Macgilchrist (d 1956); Ian Albery is the fifth generation in the theatre and both f (Sir Donald Albery) and gf (Sir Bronson Albery) as well as step ggf (Sir Charles Wyndham) were all knighted for servs to the theatre; *b* 21 Sept 1936; *Educ* Stowe, Lycée de Briançon France; *m* 1, 1966 (m dis 1985), Barbara Yuling, *née* Lee; 2 s (Wyndham b 1968, Bronson b 1971); 1 da (Caitlin b 1985), by Jenny Beavan; *Career* Soc of W End Theatre: exec 1965-, pres 1977-79, vice pres 1979-82; tstee Theatres Tst 1977-, memb Drama and Dance Panel Br Cncl 1978-88, dep chm London Festival Ballet Ltd 1984-90, dir Ticketmaster Ltd 1985-, chm and md Donmar Ltd 1986-; prodr or co-prodr of over 50 West End prodns; prodr and md Theatre of Comedy Co Ltd 1987-90, Wyndham Ltd 1987-; *Clubs* Garrick; *Style—* Ian B Albery, Esq; Raspit Hill, Coach Rd, Ivy Hatch, Kent TN15 0PE; Donmar Ltd, Donmar House, 54 Cavell St, Whitechapel, London E1 2HP (☎ 071 790 9937, fax 071 790 6634, telex 264892)

ALCHIN, Hon Mrs (Juliet Alers); da of 2 Baron Hankey, KCMG, KCVO; *b* 15 Oct 1931; *m* 1957, Peter John Wrensted Alchin, only s of His Hon Judge Gordon Alchin, AFC (d 1947), of Duffields, Medmenham, Bucks; 1 s (Gordon David b 1961), 2 da (Vanessa Frances b 1962, Chloe Sylvia b 1965); *Career* tech offr for visually handicapped Kent Social Servs 1979-; *Recreations* music, painting, sailing, walking; *Style—* The Hon Mrs Alchin; Parkstone, Clenches Farm Rd, Sevenoaks, Kent (☎ 0732 457 188)

ALCHIN, Peter John Wrensted; s of His Hon Judge Gordon Alchin (d 1947), of Medmenham, nr Marlow, Bucks, and Sylvia, *née* Wrensted (d 1939); *b* 25 July 1928; *Educ* Tonbridge, Hertford Coll Oxford (MA); *m* 23 Feb 1957, Hon Juliet, da of 2 Baron Hankey, KCMG, CMG, KCVD; 1 s (Gordon b 1960), 2 da (Vanessa b 1961, Chloe b 1963); *Career* Nat Serv cmmnd 2 Lt York and Lancaster Regt 1947-49; called to the Bar Middle Temple 1951; practising S Eastern circuit until 1960, legal advsr and co sec in indust (incl 3 years with Turner and Newall Ltd) 1960-70; admitted slr 1970; slr Supreme Court, currently ptnr Stephenson Harwood; chm Footpaths Ctee Sevenoaks Soc, elected Kent Jt Consultative Ctee 1988; Freeman Worshipful Co of Skinners 1947-, memb Worshipful Co of Slrs; *Recreations* painting, music, walking, sailing; *Clubs* Little Ship; *Style—* Peter Alchin, Esq; 1 St Paul's Churchyard, London EC4 (☎ 071 329 4422, fax 071 606 0822, telex 886789)

ALDINGTON, 1 Baron (UK 1962) Toby Austin Richard William Low; KCMG (1957), CBE (1945, MBE 1944), DSO (1941), TD and Clasp (1950), PC (1954), DL (Kent 1973); 1 Baron (UK 1962); s of Col Stuart Low, DSO (d on active serv 1942; s of Sir Austin Low, CIE, JP), and Hon Gwen Atkin, da of Baron Atkin, PC (Life Peer, d 1944); *b* 25 May 1914; *Educ* Winchester, New Coll Oxford (BA, MA); *m* 10 April 1947, (Felicité Anne) Araminta, er da of Sir Harold Alfred MacMichael, GCMG, DSO (d 1969), and former w of Capt Paul Humphrey Armytage Bowman; 1 s (Charles b 1948), 2 da (Jane b 1949, Ann b 1956); *Heir* s, Hon Charles Low; *Career* served WWII KRRC 1939-45, Brig BGS5 Corps 1944-45; barr Middle Temple 1939; MP (C) Blackpool N 1945-62, Parly Sec MOS 1951-54, min of state BOT 1954-57, dep chm Cons Pty Orgn 1959-63; chm: House of Lords' Select Ctee on Overseas Trade 1984-85, Sub Ctee A House of Lords' Euro Communities Ctee 1989-; chm: Ctee of Mgmnt Inst of Neurology 1961-78, Grindlays Bank 1964-76, Port of London Authy 1971-77, BBC Gen Advsy Cncl 1971-79, Sun Alliance & London Insurance 1971-85, National Nuclear Corporation 1973-80, Westland plc 1978-85, Leeds Castle Fndn 1984-; dep chm GEC 1964-84 (chm 1963-68); dir: Lloyds Bank 1967-85, Citicorp (USA) 1969-83; pres Cons Assoc Ashford Div, tstee Brain Res Tst 1973-, warden Winchester Coll 1979-87, hon fell New Coll Oxford 1976; *Recreations* gardening, golf; *Clubs* Carlton, Beefsteak, Royal St George's Golf, Rye Golf, Royal and Ancient Golf; *Style—* The Rt Hon the Lord Aldington, KCMG, CBE, DSO, TD, PC, DL; Knoll Farm, Aldington, Ashford, Kent TN25 7BY (☎ 0233 720292); Leeds Castle, Maidstone, Kent ME17 1PL (☎ 0622 765400, fax 0622 35616)

ALEXANDER, Prof Albert Geoffrey; s of William Francis Alexander (d 1969), of Kingston upon Hull, and Muriel Katherine, *née* Boreham (d 1989); *b* 22 Sept 1932; *Educ* Bridlington Sch, UCH Dental Sch Univ of London (BDS, MDS, LDSRCS, FDSRCS); *m* 2 June 1956, (Dorothy) Constance, da of Harry Johnson (d 1980), of Orpington; 1 da (Susan Elizabeth b 1959); *Career* Nat Serv Capt RADC 1956-58; dental house surgn UCH 1955-56, lectr in conservative dentistry UCH Med Sch 1960-62, sr lectr conservation and periodontics UCL Dental Sch, prof of conservative dentistry Univ of London 1972 (reader 1969), appointed to chair of conservative dentistry UCL Sch of Med 1976, dean UCL Sch of Dentistry 1977-(vice dean 1974-77); fell: UCL 1986, Int Coll of Dentists; memb: Gen Dental Cncl, Senate Univ of London, Cncl at UCL; memb: BDA, Br Soc for Dental Res, Br Soc for Restorative Dentistry, Fedn Dentaire Internationale; *Books* The Prevention of Periodontal Disease (1971), Self Assessment Manual No 3 - Clinical Dentistry (1978), A Companion to Dental Studies (volumes 2 and 3, 1988); *Recreations* photography; *Style—* Prof Albert Alexander

ALEXANDER, Anthony Ernest; s of Henry Gustav Alexander (d 1986), and Alice, *née* Polackova; *b* 7 Oct 1945; *Educ* St Paul's, Downing Coll Cambridge (MA); *m* 6 July 1969, Ilana, da of Maurice Raphael Setton, of Jerusalem, Israel; 1 s (Daniel b 17 Sept 1974), 1 da (Sharon b 10 May 1973); *Career* ptnr: Herbert Oppenheimer, Nathan & Vandyk 1973-88 (sr ptnr 1988), Denton Hall Burgin & Warrens 1988-; Freeman Worshipful Co of Slrs 1988; memb: Law Soc 1971, The Pilgrims; *Books* England-Legal Aspects of Alien Acquisition of Real Property (contrib); *Recreations* music and classical studies; *Style—* Anthony Alexander, Esq; Colebrook, Merlewood Drive, Chislehurst, Kent BR7 5LQ (☎ 081 467 1669, fax 081 295 1151); Denton Hall Burgin & Warrens, Five Chancery Lane, Clifford's Inn, London EC4A 1GU (☎ 071 242 1212, fax 071 404 0087, car tel 0860 375 698, telex 263567/262738 BURGIN G)

ALEXANDER, Richard; s and h of Sir Charles G Alexander, 2 Bt, and his 1 w, Mary, da of Stanley Richardson; *b* 1 Sept 1947; *Educ* Bishop's Stortford Coll; *m* 1971, Lesley Jane, da of Frederick William Jordan, of Orpington; 2 s (Edward Samuel b 1974, James Gundry b 1977); *Career* pub rels offr and ed House Magazine Furness Withy Group; Freeman City of London, Liveryman Worshipful Co of Merchant Taylors'; MIPR; *Style—* Richard Alexander, Esq; Wealden Hall, Pilgrims Way, Detling, nr Maidstone, Kent ME14 3JY; Furness Withy Group, Furness House, 53 Brighton Rd, Redhill, Surrey RH1 6YL

ALEXANDER, Dr William David; s of Rev Hugh Crighton Alexander, of Oakington, Cambridge, and Monica Alexander, *née* Hill; *b* 9 June 1945; *Educ* Clifton, St Thomas's Hosp Med Sch London (MB BS), MRCP,; *m* 12 June 1968, Dr Dorothy Hanson Crawford, da of Sir Theo Crawford, of Langton Green, Tunbridge Wells, Kent; 2 s (Danny b 1970, Theo b 1973); *Career* conslt physician and dir Diabetes Unit Queen Mary's Hosp Sidcup and Bexley Health Authy 1978-; author of various reports and papers on diabetes related topics; chm: Queen Mary's Hosp Med Staff and Exec Ctees 1983-85, SE Thames Diabetes Physicians Gp 1984-88; govr Chislehurst and Sidcup GS 1984-86, hon sec Med Advsy Ctee and med advsr Br Diabetic Assoc 1984-89, conslt memb Dist Mgmnt Bd 1988-; FRCP 1989, FRSPB; memb: BMA, BDA, EASD; *Recreations* taxidermy, Bexley borough choir, beekeeping; *Clubs* Chislehurst Golf; *Style*— Dr William Alexander; Yeomans Hall, 27 Halfway St, Sidcup, Kent DA15 8LQ (☎ 081 302 2678); Diabetes Unit, Queen Mary's Hospital, Sidcup, Kent (☎ 081 302 2678)

ALI, (Syed) Moazzam; s of Syed Wajid Ali (d 1943), of Lahore, and (Syeda) Rashida Wajid Ali, *née* Sardar Ali (d 1974); *b* 15 Aug 1937; *Educ* Central Model Sch Lahore Pakistan, Univ of Punjab Pakistan (BDS); *m* 23 March 1967, Mary Ruth, da of James Dunning Barbour, of Langham, Colchester, Essex; 2 s (Vajid b 1979, Yusef b 1982), 3 da (Manzy b 1968, Muna b 1969, Masuma b 1974); *Career* house surgn W Pakistan Dental Hosp Lahore: oral surgery 1958, prosthetics 1958-59; pt/t gen practice Lahore 1959-62, dental offr dental unit Muslim Masjid Hosp Lahore 1960-62; gen practice: London 1965-66, Ramsgate 1966-, Birchington on Sea 1984-; memb: Isle of Thanet Philatelic Soc, Rotary Club Ramsgate, Broadstairs CC; *Recreations* philately, photography, gardening; *Style*— Moazzam Ali, Esq; 28 Park Ave, Broadstairs, Kent CT10 2EY (☎ 0843 67699); 131 High St, Ramsgate, Kent CT11 9UA (☎ 0843 592423, 0843 42306)

ALI, Dr (Mohammad) Shaukat; s of Shahamat Ali (d 1973), and Hashena Begum; *b* 1 June 1939; *Educ* Kasba High English Sch, Dhaka Govt Coll, Univ Med Coll Dhaka (MB BS), Univ of Liverpool (DTM & H); *m* 30 Sept 1962, Hasina, da of Yakub Ali Bhuiyan, of Chittagong, Bangladesh; 2 s (Sanwar b 1965, Shahrar b 1969), 2 da (Sherlia b 1967, Shabrina b 1977); *Career* registrar in gen med Professorial Unit Chittagong Med Coll Hosp 1964-65, sr registrar in geriatric and gen med KCH 1971-74, conslt physician in geriatric and gen med Greenwich Dist Hosp 1974-; author of various articles; actively involved with: BMA, Overseas Doctors Assoc UK, Bangladesh Med Assoc UK (past pres); currently chm Dist Div of Med; memb BMA 1966, MRCP (Lord) 1973, FRCPI 1984 (MRCPI 1971), FRCP (Glas) 1984, FRCPE 1984; *Books* British Medical Journal (contrib, 1978); *Recreations* photography, gardening, cooking and entertaining; *Clubs* West Kent Medico-Chirurgical Soc; *Style*— Dr Shaukat Ali; Greenwich District Hospital, Vanbrugh Hill, London SE10 9HE (☎ 081 858 8141)

ALLEN, Colin Mervyn Gordon; CBE (1978); s of Cecil Gordon Allen (d 1980), of 1 Roundmoor Close, Saltford, Bristol and Gwendoline Louise Allen, *née* Hutchinson (d 1974); *b* 17 April 1929; *Educ* King Edwards' Sch Bath, Open Univ (BA), Univ of London (MA); *m* 1953, Patricia Mary, da of William Thomas Seddon (d 1943); 2 s (Timothy, Mark), 1 da (Claire); *Career* gen mangr Covent Garden Market Authy 1967-89; pres: Assoc of Wholesale Markets within Int Union of Local Authys 1972-78, Inst of Purchasing and Supply 1982-83; *Style*— Colin Allen, Esq, CBE; 10 Whitecroft Way, Beckenham, Kent BR3 3AG; Covent House, Covent Garden Market, London SW8 5NX (☎ 071 720 2211)

ALLEN, Hon Mrs (Francesca Nicola); *née* Sternberg; *née* Sternberg; da of Baron Plurenden (Life Peer; d 1978), and Baroness Plurenden, *qv*; *b* 1962; *m* 7 Oct 1989, Douglas G Allen, eldest s of B G Allen, of Scott City, Kansas, USA; *Style*— The Hon Mrs Allen; Plurenden Manor, High Halden, Kent

ALLEN, (Ethel Maud) Mary; da of Arthur Frederick Willard (d 1946), of London, and Sarah Maud, *née* Chenery (d 1975); *b* 9 April 1924; *Educ* Birkbeck Coll London, Royal Free Hosp Med Sch (MB BS); *m* 14 Sept 1957, John Norman Allen, s of Alfred John Allen (d 1946), of London; 1 s (Graham Robin b 1959), 1 da (Ruth Lydia b 1960); *Career* HO 1962-64, ACMO 1964-66, SCMO 1966-71, PMO 1971-86, med advsr Kent CC Adoption and Fostering Agency 1986-; DObstRCOG 1964, MFCM 1974; BPA 1978; *Recreations* reading, music, crosswords, walking; *Style*— Mrs E Mary Allen; Mylkehouse, Sissinghurst, Kent TN17 2JN (☎ 0580 712803); Health Authorities, Springfield, Maidstone (☎ 0622 671411)

ALLEN, Robert Egerton (Bob); s of Thomas Simpson Allen (d 1935), of Langley Hall, Macclesfield, and Vera, *née* Ross-Clunis (d 1975); *b* 16 Dec 1927; *Educ* Pretoria Boys HS, SACS Cape Town SA; *m* 27 Feb 1954, Helen Elizabeth Sutherland, da of Howard Summers Clark (d 1962), of Victoria, BC, Canada; 2 s (John b 1959, Peter b 1961); *Career* ACF Queens Own Cape Town Highlanders 1946-52; photo engraver 1945-68, manufacturers agent 1968-; memb: East Peckham Parish Cncl 1969- (chm 1987-89), Tonbridge and Malling Borough Cncl (Ind) 1976-; Mayor Tonbridge and Malling 1986-87; fndr memb: East Peckham Residents Assoc 1963, East Peckham Historical Soc 1967, East Peckham Rugby Club (and pres) 1977-88; treas sec and chm Mgmnt Ctee East Peckham Playing Field Assoc; *Recreations* walking, classical music, photography; *Style*— Bob Allen, Esq; 94 Snoll Hatch Rd, East Peckham, Tonbridge, Kent (☎ 0622 571554)

ALLINGHAM, John Parry; s of John Parry Allingham, of Dover, and Rosemary Anne Simmons, *née* Kennedy; *b* 24 Oct 1962; *Educ* Dover GS, London Hosp Med Coll; *m* 16 July 1988, Carol Ann, da of Henry Vinall, of Ramsey, Cambridgeshire; 1 s (William Parry b 1 June 1990), 1 da (Grace Elizabeth b 6 Dec 1988); *Career* Capt RAMC, regtl MO 49 Field Regt RA 1989-90; house physician Harlow Essex 1987, house surgn Queen Elizabeth Mil Hosp 1988, casualty offr Ashford Kent 1988; memb BMA; *Recreations* running, playing soccer; *Style*— John Allingham, Esq

ALLINGHAM, Prof Michael; s of Cdr Henry Peter Allingham, of Longparish, Hampshire, and Patricia Gould, *née* Penrose; *b* 29 Oct 1943; *Educ* Lancing, Univ of Edinburgh (MA, PhD); *m* Jane, *née* Fenn; 1 s (Daniel Matthew Edward b 1972), 1 da (Chloe Sascha Jane b 1976); *Career* lectr: Univ of Edinburgh 1967-69, Univ of Essex 1969-71, Univ of Bristol 1973-74, LSE 1974-77; asst prof Northwestern Univ 1971-72, assoc prof Univ of Pennsylvania 1972-73, prof economic theory Univ of Kent 1977-; chm Allingham Anderson Asset Allocation Ltd; assoc ed Journal of Economics; tres C of E Children's Soc; *Books* Equilibrium and Disequilibrium (1973), General Equilibrium (1975), Value (1983), Unconscious Contracts (1987), Theory of Markets (1989); *Style*— Prof Michael Allingham; Eliot College, University of Kent, Canterbury, Kent CT2 7NS (☎ 0227 764000, fax 0227 459025, telex 965449)

ALUWIHARE, Nedra Priyanti; s of Tikiri Bandara Aluwihare, and Manel Kamini Kannangara; *b* 14 Feb 1963; *Educ* Blackheath HS, Royal Free Hosp Med Sch (MB BS); *Career* sr house offr Pathology Dept Addenbrook Hosp Cambridge 1988-; *Style*— Nedra Aluwihare, Esq; 3 Hoblands End, Chislehurst, Kent BR7 6HH (☎ 081 3004979); Addenbrook Hospital, Cambridge (☎ 0223 24515 ext 3175)

AMBIKAPATHY, Parameswaraiyer; s of Subramanyaiyer Parameswaraiyer (d 1972), and Subramanyaiyer Saraswathyamma; *b* 28 Dec 1942; *Educ* Sri Lanka (MB BS); *m* 1 July 1974, Jayalakshmi Ambikapathy, da of Subramanyaiyer Srinivasan (d 1988); 2 c (Sujidra b 1975, Subadra b 1978); *Career* med offr of health Kandy Dist Ceylon 1972-75, lectr Faculty of Med Univ of Ceylon 1975-83, med offr in obstetrics and gynaecology UK 1980-84, GP 1984-; memb: Hindu Centre London, Br Tamil Assoc, Br Assoc Young Musicians; life memb: Bharatya Vidya Bhavan (Inst of Indian Culture), Britannia Hindu Temple Tst London, Red Cross Soc; memb: BMA, RCGP, Med Protection Soc; *Recreations* music, Hindu philosophy and science; *Style*— Parameswaraiyer Ambikapathy, Esq; Crockenhill Vale Surgery, Eynsford Rd, Crockenhill, Swanley, Kent BR8 8JT (☎ 0322 67447)

AMES-LEWIS, Rev Richard; s of William Edmund Ames Lewis, OBE (d 1988), of Watermans, Ewhurst Green, Robertsbridge, E Sussex, and Mary Elizabeth, *née* Ashbee; *b* 12 Jan 1945; *Educ* St Pauls Sch London, Emmanuel Coll Cambridge (BA, Dip Arch, MA), Westcott House Cambridge; *m* 22 July 1967, Katharine Mary, da of David Maurice Graham, of 9 Vine Rd, Barnes, London; 1 s (Jonathan b 1974), 2 da (Eleanor b 1970, Caroline b 1972); *Career* architect in private practice 1969-76; ordained Rochester Cathedral: deacon 1978, priest 1979; asst curate parish of St Mark Bromley 1978-81, assoc vicar of Edenbridge and Crockham Hill 1981-84, vicar of Edenbridge and priest i/c Crockham Hill 1984-; *Recreations* chamber music, gardening; *Style*— The Rev Richard Ames-Lewis; The Vicarage, Mill Hill, Edenbridge, Kent TN8 5DA (☎ 0732 862258)

AMNER, Dennis Edward; s of Albert Clifford Amner (d 1961), of Woolwich, and Rose Selina, *née* Wright (d 1988); *b* 5 March 1937; *Educ* Shooters Hill GS, Woolwich Poly; *m* 15 June 1968, Irmgard, da of Franz Strasser (d 1970), of Aschach/Donau, Austria; *Career* Lance Sgt RAPC; surveyor; Thomas & Edge Ltd 1952-65, RC Amner Welling Kent 1965-73, princ in private practice 1973-; memb Nat Tst; FFS 1976, FCSI 1977, ACIOB 1955, MBIM 1975, FRSH 1977; *Recreations* Latin ballroom and flamenco dancing, languages, motoring holidays, walking, music, reading; *Style*— Dennis E Amner, Esq; Incorporated Surveyor, 41 Hillcrest Rd, Orpington, Kent BR6 9AN (☎ 0689 20613)

AMNER, Ronald Clifford; s of Albert George Amner (d 1968), of Kidbrooke, Lane, Eltham, London, and Rosina, *née* Wright (d 1987); *b* 4 Sept 1926; *Educ* St Margaret's Plumstead, Ancona Road GS, Woolwich Poly, Coll of Estate Mgmnt; *m* 2 Sept 1950, Betty Joyce, da of George Harold Elliott (d 1973), of Bexleyheath, Kent; 2 da (Brenda Jill, Janet Shirley); *Career* served Royal Fusiliers 1944, SAS training Swindon, transfd to RASC then NAAFI, i/c road tport Shiabah Persian Gulf; apprentice bricklayer ST Blackler Ltd Plumstead (later mangr); sr BLMC surveyor: RW Bowman, Bovis Group (and estimator); surveyor private practice 1961-; Lord of the Manor North Cray Kent; memb: Royal Soc of Health 1959, Chartered Inst of Building 1968, Party Wall Surveyors Club 1988; FFAS 1957, Inst of Bldg Estimators 1959; *Recreations* golf; *Clubs* Shooter's Hill Golf; *Style*— Ronald Amner, Esq; 9 Buckingham Ave, Welling, Kent DA16 2LY (☎ 081 304 1545)

ANASTASI, George; s of Michael Anastasi, and Paraskevou, *née* Mattheou; *b* 20 Oct 1941; *Educ* The Quintin Sch London, Goldsmiths Coll London; *m* 19 Dec 1964, Maureen Gillian Gloria, da of Alfred Charles Adams (d 1959); 1 s (Robert Matthew b 23 Nov 1979); *Career* asst vice pres Deltec Trading Co Ltd London 1969-73; mangr: First Boston Corp London 1973-74, Williams & Glyn's Bank Ltd London 1974-78; dir Donaldson Lufkin & Jenrette London 1978-80, exec mangr Arab Int Fin Ltd London 1980-83, dir Svenska Int plc London 1983-; *Style*— George Anastasi, Esq; 7 Clarendon Way, Chislehurst, Kent (☎ 0689 20112); Svenska House, 3-5 Newgate St, London EC1A 7DA

(☎ 071 329 4467, fax 071 329 0036/7, telex 894716)

ANDERSON, Albert Alfred James; OBE (1980); s of Frank Alfred Anderson (d 1963), of Oare, Faversham, Kent, and Alice Morley, *née* Cock (d 1978); *b* 15 April 1909; *m* 26 Dec 1931, Alice Rhoda, da of Hermanus Bertram Rupert Alphonso de Leur (ka 1915), of Strood, Kent; 2 s (John Malcolm b 1939 d 1961, Roger Frank b 1942), 1 da (Margaret (Mrs MacInnes) b 1933); *Career* Cdr V Co 13 Bn, Royal W Kent HG, Maj 1941-46; chm and fndr The Kent Art Printers Ltd, chm World Sporting Publications Ltd; cncllr Rochester City Cncl 1936-58 (alderman 1952); chm: Kent Mayors' Assoc 1975-76, 1980-81 and 1988-89 (fndr memb), Kent Rating Valuation Panel 1976-81, Rochester and Chatham Cons Assoc 1973-76, tstees Baynards Charity 1980-; pres: Medway Mentally Handicapped Soc 1963-, Rochester and Chatham Parly Constituency 1976-83, Medway Parly Constituency 1983-; pres Medway C of C 1964-68; hon life pres Medway & Gillingham C of C; govr Sir Joseph Williamson Maths Sch Rochester; Home Office ind memb: Canterbury Prison Parole Review Ctee 1973-82, Ladies Cookham Wood Borstal Prison Parole Review Ctee 1977-83; Mayor of Rochester, Constable of the Castle, Adm of the River Medway, JP 1951-53; Freeman: City of London 1953, City of Rochester Minnesota USA 1952; Liveryman Worshipful Co of Stationers and Newspaper Makers 1953; *Recreations* golf, voluntary charitable and public work; *Clubs* City Livery, St Stephens, Castle (Rochester); *Style*— Albert Anderson, Esq, OBE; Satis Court, Esplanade, Rochester, Kent ME1 1QE (☎ 0634 42933); Kent Art Printers Ltd, 344 High St, Rochester, Kent ME1 1DT (☎ 0634 44352, fax 0634 42114)

ANDERSON, David St Kevin; s of Frederick St Kevin Anderson (d 1982), of Worthing, and Eileen Celia, *née* Warwick; *b* 4 Oct 1927; *Educ* Clayesmore Sch Dorset; *m* 26 June 1959, Mary Isabella Ivory, da of late William Garnett Ivory, of East Grinstead; 1 s (Nigel St Kevin b 24 May 1960), 1 da (Rosanagh Jane b 6 May 1962); *Career* Lance Corpl RM 1945-46, Lt 1 Bn Royal Fusiliers BAOR 1946-48; Calico Printers Assoc Ltd 1948-50, WA Beardsell & Co Ltd India 1950-56, Dexion Ltd 1956-70, Gravity Randall Ltd 1970-75 and 1984-87, WC Youngman Ltd 1975-84, Frank Odell Ltd 1987-88, conslt NR Associates 1989-; chm Cowden Parish Cncl; memb ctee Cowden and Dist Royal Br Legion; Liveryman Worshipful Co of Vintners 1956; *Recreations* photography, gardening, foreign travel, appreciation of fine wine; *Style*— David Anderson, Esq; Medway House, Cowden, Edenbridge, Kent TN8 7JQ (☎ 0342 850578)

ANDERSON, Prof Michael John; s of Ronald Arthur Anderson (d 1981), of Llantwit Major, and Dorothy Alma Anderson; *b* 4 June 1937; *Educ* Taunton Sch, Univ of Bristol (BA); *m* 29 Dec 1973, Alessandra Pierangela Lucia, da of dott Girolamo di Gregorio (d 1983), of Bisceglie, Italy; 2 da (Silvia b 1977, Marina b 1980); *Career* The Welch Regt 1956-58; mangr New Theatre Cardiff 1963-64, lectr in drama Univ of Bristol 1964-78; prof of drama: Univ Coll of North Wales Bangor 1978-90 (chm Standing Ctee of Drama Dept 1979-82), Univ of Kent 1990-; memb Welsh Arts Cncl 1985-90 (chm Drama Ctee), joint Sec Gen Int Federation for Theatre Res 1989-; FRSA; *Books* Classical Drama and its Influence (ed, 1965), Anger and Detachment: A Study of Osborne, Arden and Pinter (1979); *Recreations* travel, films; *Clubs* Royal Commonwealth Soc, Circolo Unione Bisceglie (Italy); *Style*— Prof Michael Anderson; 28 Nunnery Fields, Canterbury (☎ 0227 464578); Darwin College, The University, Canterbury (☎ 0227 764000)

ANDERSON, Dr (John Stewart) Nicholas; s of Brig Thomas Stephen James Anderson, CBE, TD (d 1969), and Elizabeth Johnson, *née* Baird; *b* 19 Dec 1946; *Educ* Wellington, Selwyn Coll Cambridge, Guys Hosp (MA, MB BChir, DObstRCOG); *m* 31 July 1971, Grete, da of Henning Koefoed (d 1951); 2 s (Thomas George Nicholas b 1975, Richard Mark Joakim b 1979), 1 da (Anne-Marie b 1973); *Career* house offr Guys Hosp 1971; GP Paddock Wood 1975; MRCGP; *Recreations* golf; *Clubs* Hawks, Elvers, Royal Ashdown Forest Golf; *Style*— Dr Nicholas Anderson; Mascalls Pound Cottage, Maidstone Rd, Paddock Wood, Kent TN12 6LT (☎ 0892 832043); Woodlands Health Centre, Allington Rd, Paddock Wood, Kent TN12 6AR (☎ 0892 833331)

ANDREW, Nigel Carmichael; s of Roger Carmichael Andrew, of Cambridge, and Joan May, *née* Alexander; *b* 27 Nov 1951; *Educ* Mill Hill Sch, The London Hosp Med Coll, Moorfields Eye Hosp; *Career* opthalmic surgn; memb Apothecaries Soc of London; *Recreations* squash, tennis, clay and game shooting; *Clubs* Kent and Canterbury; *Style*— Nigel Andrew, Esq; Cornerways, Stodmarsh, Canterbury, Kent CT3 4BD (☎ 0227 721256); Kent and Canterbury Hospital, Ethelbert Rd, Canterbury, Kent CT1 3NG (☎ 0227 766877)

ANDREWS, Nicholas Anthony Stuart; s of Gordon Leslie Andrews (d 1981), of Feltwell, Norfolk, and Beatrice Maud, *née* Jones; *b* 11 Nov 1947; *Educ* St Audrey's Sch Hatfield, Mid-Herts Coll, NW London Poly; *m* 4 March 1972, Sarah Denison, da of Geoffrey John Hubert Denison Collins, of Herne Bay, Kent; 1 s (Alastair Robert Crawford b 1976), 1 da (Hannah Rachael Crawford b 1974); *Career* slr's managing clerk: Trower Still and Keeling Lincoln's Inn to 1973, Lee Bolton and Lee Canterbury 1973-82, Furley Page Fielding and Barton Canterbury 1982-; clerk: tstees Hosp of St Thomas Eastbridge Canterbury, Bekesbourne with Patrixbourne Parish Cncl; reader Parish of Wingham with Elmstone Preston and Stourmouth; *Recreations* fly fishing, motoring; *Clubs* Kent and Canterbury; *Style*— Nicholas Andrews, Esq; Ashwood Farmhouse, Mill Lane, Preston-next-Wingham, Kent (☎ 0227 722395); Garth Cottage, Great Edstone, Kirkbymoorside, N Yorks

ANDREWS, Richard Christian; s of Leslie Andrews (d 1963), of Tunbridge Wells, and Kathline, *née* Lawson (d 1931); *b* 21 Jan 1929; *Educ* Judd Sch Tonbridge; *m* 1, Monica Mary Clifton (d 1960); m 2 (m dis) Barbara Beastal; 3 s (Ivan, Timothy, David); *Career* Nat Serv RAF; process operator BP 1949-82, bee farmer; Strood RDC 1963-74 (chm 1970-71), City of Rochester upon Medway 1976- (Mayor 1986-87); chm Local Branch RNLI 1971-81; memb: Rochester Rotary, NFU; *Recreations* sailing, wood carving; *Style*— Richard Andrews, Esq; 27 Hoo Common, Chattenden, Rochester, Kent ME3 8LT (☎ 0889 252892)

ANDREWS, Dr Vivienne Elizabeth; da of Harry Andrews (d 1985), of London, and Elizabeth Margaret, *née* Byatt; *b* 19 Oct 1951; *Educ* St George's Hosp Med Sch (MB BS, MRCPath); *m* 2 Sept 1978, Dilwyn Allen Morgan, s of George Thomas Morgan, of Sittingbourne; 1 s (Malcolm Edward b 2 March 1989); *Career* conslt haematologist Dartford and Gravesham DHA 1984-; memb: Save the Children Fund, Amnesty Int; memb Br Soc Haematology; *Recreations* flying; *Clubs* Civlair Flying; *Style*— Dr Vivienne Andrews

ANDRUS, (Francis) Sedley; LVO (1982); s of late Brig-Gen Thomas Alchin Andrus, CMG, JP (d 1959), and Alice Loveday, *née* Parr (d 1984); b on first anniversary of d of gf Adm Alfred Arthur Chase Parr, sometime naval ADC to Queen Victoria; *b* 26 Feb 1915; *Educ* Wellington, St Peter's Coll Oxford (MA); *Career* Bluemantle Pursuivant of Arms 1970-72, Lancaster Herald of Arms 1972-82, Beaumont Herald of Arms Extraordinary 1982-; landowner; *Style*— Sedley Andrus, Esq, LVO; College of Arms, Queen Victoria St, London EC4V 4BT (☎ 071 248 2762); 8 Oakwood Rise, Longfield, Kent DA3 7PA (☎ 047 47 5424)

ANGEL, Richard Reeve; s of Edward Reeve Angel (d 1988), of Cranford, Northants, and Hope Aldrich Cleaveland Angel (d 1981); *b* 4 Aug 1928; *Educ* Oundle, Univ of Edinburgh; *m* 1951, Margaret Vivien, da of William Warren (d 1956), of Taunton, Somerset; 2 da; *Career* dir: Reeve Angel International 1959-74, Whatman Reeve Angel plc 1974-90, Whatman plc 1990-; pres Br Laboratory Ware Assoc 1970-72; *Recreations* reading, golf; *Style*— Richard Angel, Esq; Spring Walk, Nevill Court, Tunbridge Wells, Kent (☎ 0892 20592); Whatman plc, Springfield Mill, Maidstone, Kent ME14 2LE (☎ 0622 692022)

ANKRETT, Dr Vivienne Owen; da of Raymond Ankrett, and Eithwen Doreen, *née* Owen; *b* 10 Sept 1957; *Educ* WNSM (MB BCH), RCGP (MRCGP), RCOG (DRCOG); *m* 2 July 1983, Dr Ian Williams, s of Theophilus Williams; 1 s (David James b 1987), 1 da (Kirsty Emma b 1988); *Career* received RCGP award Welsh Cncl 1986, regularly published articles in leading med jls; *Books* BMA Complete Family Health Encyclopedia (1990); *Style*— Dr Vivienne Ankrett; 59 Longmeads, Rusthall, Tunbridge Wells, Kent TN3 0AU (☎ 0892 541444); Medical Centre, Greggswood Rd, Tunbridge Wells, Kent (☎ 0892 541444)

ANNIS, Philip Geoffrey Walter; s of Walter Annis, of Bleak House, Windermere, Cumbria, and Lilian Alice, *née* Norris; *b* 7 Feb 1936; *Educ* Sale Co GS Sale Cheshire, Kelsick GS Ambleside Westmorland, Univ of Manchester (BA); *m* 15 June 1967, Olive Winifred, da of Edward Walter Scarlett, OBE, of Ilford, Essex; 1 s (Edward Philip b 30 April 1970); *Career* Nat Serv 2 Lt RA 1957-59, actg Flt Lt RAFVR (T) 1960-62, TA 1961-67, RA (TA); inspr grade 3 Bd of Inland Revenue 1959-62; Nat Maritime Museum: joined 1962, co-ordinator of museum servs 1971-79, dep dir 1979-86; mangr of regtl history project RA Inst 1986-; FSA 1973, FRHistS 1975; Cdr of the Order of the Lion of Finland 1987; *Books* Naval Swords (1970), Swords for Sea Service (with Cdr W E May, 1970); *Recreations* gardening, walking, reading; *Style*— Philip Annis, Esq; Royal Artillery Institution, Old Royal Military Academy, Woolwich, London SE18 4DN (☎ 081 854 2242 ext 5613)

ANSON, James William; CBE (1969); s of Lt-Col George Frank Wemyss Anson, OBE (d 1942); *b* 9 Jan 1915; *Educ* Fettes, Gonville and Caius Coll Cambridge (BA); *m* 1940, Barbara Mary, da of late Gordon Peace, OBE; 1 s, 1 da; *Career* served WWII as Maj 2 Royal Sikhs in Iraq, Persia, Syria, Palestine, Egypt, Western Desert, Italy and Greece, GHQ MEF Cairo; chm and md Mackinnon Mackenzie & Co (agents for P&O Steam Navigation Co in India) 1964-69 (joined 1937), tstee Port of Bombay 1965-69, pres Bombay C of C and Indust 1967-68, dep pres Associated Cs of C of India 1967-68, gen mangr Overseas Containers Ltd 1970-77; hon sec Br Italian Soc 1977; Cavaliere of the Order Al Merito della Republica Italiana 1982; *Recreations* golf, gardening, formerly cricket and rugby football; *Clubs* MCC, Royal St George's (Sandwich), Hawks (Cambridge); *Style*— James Anson, Esq, CBE; Courtlands, Pilgrim's Way, Wrotham, Kent (☎ 0732 822400)

ANTHONY, Dr Donald William James (Don); s of George Anthony, of Sidcup, Kent, and Annie Eva Starkey (d 1962); *b* 6 Nov 1928; *Educ* Loughborough Univ of Sci and Technol (Dip Phys Ed), Univ of London (Dip Health Ed), Univ of Leicester (MEd, PhD); *m* 6 June 1958, Jadwiga, da of Wladeslaw Rzeszowski (d 1942); 1 s (Anthony Marek Louis b 14 July 1964); *Career* asst lectr physical educn Univ of Manchester 1954-56, lectr

Loughborough Univ of Technol 1956-59, princ lectr Avery Hill Coll 1959-85; author of several articles and books, journalist, broadcaster and organiser of several sports film festivals; holder of English hammer throwing record and AAA champion 1953, memb Br Olympic hammer throwing team 1956; memb Br Olympic Ctee (chm BOA Educn Ctee), fndr and pres English Volleyball Assoc, advsr IOC Olympic Solidarity, sports admin, conslt to govt and commercial cos; memb NATFHE; *Books* Know the Game Volleyball (1948), Keeping Fit for All Ages (1962), Success in Volleyball (1962), The PE Teacher's A-Z (1970), How to Keep Fit (1972), A Strategy for British Sport (1980), Field Athletics (1982), Olympic English (1986), Britain and the Olympic Games (1986); *Recreations* tennis, reading, walking; *Style*— Dr Don Anthony

ANTHONY, Ronald Desmond; s of William Arthur Anthony (d 1987), and Olive Francis, *née* Buck (d 1986); *b* 21 Nov 1925; *Educ* Sidcup and Chistlehurst GS, Imperial Coll of Sci and Technol (BSc, ACGI); *m* Betty Margaret, da of Walter Frederick Newton Croft (d 1971); 4 da (Frances b 1951, Jennifer b 1953, Rebecca b 1957, Sarah b 1958); *Career* served RCS 1943-48; Vickers Armstrongs (Supermarine) 1950-57, Nuclear Power Plant Co 1957-60, inspr of nuclear installations 1960-85, HSE 1974-85, head Safety Policy Div 1977-80 (bd memb 1977-85), chief inspr of nuclear installations 1980-85, engrg conslt 1985-; pres BNES 1987-89, FIMechE, FINucE, MRAeS; *Recreations* golf; *Style*— Ronald Anthony, Esq; 3 Mereside, Orpington, Kent BR6 8ET

ANWYL, Doris Evelyn; da of Richard Thomas Anwyl (d 1938), and Amy Elizabeth *née* Bottle (d 1952); *b* 23 Sept 1912; *Educ* Rosedean Private Sch Thornton Heath, Croydon HS, Croydon Sch of Art (City and Guilds Certs), Sutton Sch of Art (City and Guilds Teachers Cert); *Career* teacher of crafts: Southern Coll of Art Portsmouth 1934-38, Guildford and Sutton Schs of Art (pt/t) 1938-41, Sutton Sch of Art 1941-49, Benenden Sch For Girls 1949-72, ret; voluntary teacher of embroidered collage to disabled membs of Tenterden Day Centre 1981- (organised prodn of hanging to celebrate Silver Jubilee of Kent Assoc for the Disabled 1986); memb Kent Assoc for the Disabled, life memb Tenterden Tst, fndr memb E Kent Branch of Embroiderers' Guild 1970; ctee memb: Tenterden Museum, Tenterden Residents Assoc; Freeman: City of London 1933, Worshipful Co of Fishmongers' 1933; fell Soc of Designer Craftsmen; *Recreations* gardening; *Style*— Doris Anwyl

APPLEYARD, Dr (William) James; s of Edward Rollo Appleyard (d 1937), and Maud Oliver, *née* Marshall (d 1979); *b* 25 Oct 1935; *Educ* Canford, Exeter Coll Oxford, Guy's Hops Med Sch (MA, BM BCh, MRCS, DRCOG); *m* 25 Jan 1964, Elizabeth Anne, da of Peter Read-Ward; 1 s (Richard James b 1966), 2 da (Lisa Jane b 1968, Suzanne Mary b 1970); *Career* paedriatric res Univ of Louisville Kentucky USA 1964-65, sr house offr Hosp for Sick Children Gt Ormond St 1967, Dyers Co res fell St Thomas's Hosp London 1968-69, sr paediatric registrar Guy's Hosp London 1969-71, conslt paediatrician Canterbury Thanet Health Dist 1971-, assoc prof of paediatrics UK St Georges Univ Sch of Med Granada WI 1985; author of: res papers on problems of newborn infants in Archives Diseases of Childhood, a study of the needs of multiply handicapped children; Univ of London rep on Kent AHA 1973-78, treas BPA 1983-88, chm Sr Hosp Conf 1983-86; memb: CMC 1983-93, Info Advsy Gp to Dept of Health 1985-, cncl RCP 1988; dep chm Rep Body of BMA 1989-90, patron The Dyspraxia Tst; FRCP; *Recreations* lawn tennis, photography; *Clubs* Athenaeum, The Penn; *Style*— Dr James Appleyard; Kent and Canterbury Hospital, Children's Dept, Ethelbert Rd, Canterbury, Kent CT1 3NG (☎ 0227 766877)

APPS, Harold Edwin Martin; s of Charles Apps (d 1946), of Tenterden, Kent, and Margery, *née* Martin (d 1987); *Educ* Ashford GS; *Career* ROC 1944-45 (aux reservists 1947-73); family firm 1946-54; mangr Alfred Goslett London 1956-58 (asst mangr 1954-56), md H Bookman and Co Tenterden 1960-69 (dir 1958-60), chief cashier Lloyds plc Hythe 1969-87; cncllr: Tenterden Rural DC 1964-73 (Chm Environmental Health Ctee 1968-72), High Halden Parish Cncl 1964- (vice chm 1974-78); Ashford Borough Cncl 1973-: vice chm Housing Ctee 1974-77, chm Housing Mgmnt 1974-77, dep Mayor 1978-79, Mayor 1979-80, dep ldr 1981-87, chm Dist Plans 1983-87, vice chm personnel 1987-88, chm Environmental Health Ctee 1988- (chm 1977-78, vice chm 1987-88); pres: Tenterden Rotary Club 1965-66 (memb 1962-69), High Halden Cons Assoc, High Halden Horticultural Soc; govr: High Halden C of E Primary Sch 1969- (vice chm 1973-), Homewood Secdy Sch Tenterden 1969-; asst treas Ashford Cons Assoc 1988-; memb: Home/Water and Southern Home Safety Cncl 1987-, Nat Cncl Inland Tport 1987-, Dungeness Power Station Liaison Ctee 1988-, Community Health Cncl 1988-, St Mary's Parochial Church Cncl, High Halden Memb Hall Ctee; *Recreations* cricket, gardening; *Style*— Harold Apps, Esq; 2 Mill Gardens, High Halden, Ashford, Kent TN26 3LY (☎ 0233 850 698)

ARBUTHNOT, Sir John Sinclair-Wemyss; 1 Bt (UK 1964), of Kittybrewster, Aberdeen; MBE (1944), TD (1951); s of Maj Kenneth Wyndham Arbuthnot, the Seaforth Highlanders (ka Second Battle of Ypres 1915; ggs of George Arbuthnot, JP, first of Elderslie, himself a yr bro of Sir William Arbuthnot, 1 Bt, of Edinburgh); *b* 11 Feb 1912; *Educ* Eton, Trinity Coll Cambridge (MA); *m* 3 July 1943, (Margaret) Jean, yr da of (Alexander) Gordon Duff (d 1978); 2 s (William Reierson, James Norwich), 3 da (Elizabeth Mary b 27 May 1947, Louise Victoria (Mrs Lancaster) b 26 Oct 1954, Alison Jane b 9 April 1957); *Heir* s, William Reierson Arbuthnot; *Career* dir and chm of Tea Cos 1934-75; MP (C) Dover 1950-64; PPS to: Min of Pensions 1952-55, Min of Health 1956-57; chm of ctees and temp chm of House of Commons 1958-64; jt hon sec of Assoc of Br C of C 1953-59, vice pres Tstee Savings Banks Assoc 1962-75, chm Folkestone and Dist Water Co 1971-87; memb Church Assembly and Gen Synod of C of E 1955-75, cmmr Second Church Estates 1962-64, church cmmr for E 1962-77, tstee Lambeth Palace Library 1964-77; KASG; *Recreations* gardening; *Clubs* Carlton; *Style*— Sir John Arbuthnot, Bt, MBE, TD; Poulton Manor, Ash, Canterbury, Kent CT3 2HW (☎ 0304 812516)

ARMITAGE, John Patrick; s of Rev Cyril Moxon Armitage, MVO (d 1966), of St Bride's Rectory, Fleet St, London, and Eva, *née* Brinsmead; *b* 17 March 1935; *Educ* Marlborough; *m* 1, 28 Aug 1965 (m dis 1973), Marah Helen, *née* Douglas; 1 s (Edward b 8 Dec 1967); m 2, 14 Oct 1984, Nicola Caroline, da of Larry Gaines, of Crosstrees, Saltwood, Kent; *Career* Nat Serv cmmnd 2 Lt E Yorks Regt UK, Malaya, Germany 1954-56; sales exec Noel Gay Music Co Ltd 1956-59, dir Ogilvy & Mather Ltd 1971-85 (account exec 1959-71); chm: Primary Contact Ltd 1985-, Ogilvy & Mather Focus Ltd 1988-; memb Mark Soc; *Recreations* golf; *Clubs* Littlestone Rye, Royal and Ancient; *Style*— John Armitage, Esq; Ludwell House, Charing, Kent (☎ 023 371 2469)

ARMSTRONG, Prof (Walter) Alan; s of Walter Henry Armstrong (d 1985), of Healaugh, Yorkshire, and Elsie, *née* Carter; *b* 25 Dec 1936; *Educ* Tradcaster GS Yorkshire, Univ of Birmingham (BA, PhD); *m* 11 Aug 1962, Heather Ruth Ann, da of Jonathan David Davies, of Saltash, Cornwall; 1 s (Jonathan Alan b 1971), 1 da (Alison Jane b 1968); *Career* Nat Serv RAF 1955-57; asst lectr then lectr economic and social hist Univ of Nottingham 1962-68; lectr hist Univ of Warwick 1968-69; Univ of Kent at Canterbury: lectr economic and social hist 1969-73, sr lectr 1973-75, reader in social and demographic history 1975-83, prof economic and social hist 1983-; parish cncllr Adisham 1970-80; FRHist Soc; *Books* Stability and Change in an English Country Town - A Social Study of York 1801-51 (1974), Farmworkers - A Social and Economic History 1770-1970 (1988); *Style*— Prof Alan Armstrong; Woodside, 166 The Street, Adisham, Canterbury, Kent (☎ 0304 840691); Eliot College, University of Kent, Canterbury, Kent (☎ 0227 764000)

ARMSTRONG, Jim Taylor; s of William Armstrong, of Perth, Scotland, and Magdelaine Elizabeth, *née* Taylor; *b* 12 Feb 1951; *Educ* Perth Acad, Sir John Deanes GS, Sunderland Poly (BSc), Univ of Bradford (MPharm); *Career* pre-registration pharmacist Park Pharmacy Maidenhead 1972-73, pharmacy mangr Selles Chemists Hull 1973-75, staff pharmacist Castle Hill Hosp Humberside 1975-79, dist pharmacist Medway Health Authy 1979-; Lib Democrat cncllr City of Rochester upon Medway 1987-, former chm Medway Br Royal Pharmaceutical Soc; MRPharmS, MIPharmM; *Recreations* golf, snooker, walking, reading, Open Univ; *Clubs* Roffen; *Style*— Jim Armstrong, Esq; 2 Bleakwood Rd, Walderslade, Chatham, Kent ME5 0NF (☎ 061 660081); Pharmacy (☎ 0634 407311 ext 5318, fax 0634 407311 ext 5316)

ARMSTRONG, Michael; MBE (1984); s of Ronald Armstrong, of IOM, and Mary, *née* Boon; *b* 21 May 1934; *Educ* Hanley Castle Worcs, Newton Abbot GS Devon, Univ of London (LLB); *m* 6 June 1964, Sandra Margaret, da of Alexander George Shave (d 1952), of Hildenborough; 3 da (Rebecca b 18 May 1965, Bridget b 14 Aug 1967, Charlotte b 15 Sept 1971); *Career* Lt RA 1987-89; slr 1956-; NP 1965-; farmer 1974-; clerk to Cmmr of Income Tax 1981-; cncllr Kent CC 1977-85 (chm Property Supplies and Servs Ctee 1981-85); chm: Tonbridge Round Table 1965-66 (memb 1962-74), Round Table Area 16 1968-69; memb: Cons Assoc Tonbridge and Malling 1971- (variously treas, vice chm, chm and pres), Tonbridge Rotary Club 1974- (pres 1986-87), Kent Kent Co St John Ambulance Cncl 1978-90, SE Area Cons Gen Purposes Ctee 1986-89; pres: Tunbridge Wells Tonbridge and Dist Law Soc 1985-86, Kent Law Soc 1987-88; chm Tonbridge Abbeyfield Soc; memb: Law Soc 1959, NFU 1974; *Recreations* farming, gardening; *Style*— Michael Armstrong, Esq, MBE; Durham's Farm, Egg Pie Lane, Hildenborough, Kent TN11 8PE (☎ 0732 833241, fax 0732 838121); 180 High St, Tonbridge, Kent TN9 1BD (☎ 0732 770660, fax 0732 362452)

ARNOLD, David John; s of Capt Eric John Arnold, and Yvonne Mae, *née* Stewart (d 1956); *b* 3 Feb 1949; *Educ* Duke of Yorks Royal Mil Sch, Guy's Hosp Dental Sch (LDS, RCS); *m* 25 Sept 1971, Margaret Helen Bernadette (Peggy), da of Peter Loye, of Isleworth, Middlesex; 2 s (David Mark b 25 Dec 1974, Martin Peter b 8 July 1976), 1 da (Laura Frances b 2 Feb 1980); *Career* princ dental surgn Maidstone 1974-; memb: Bearsted Round Table 1975- (chm 1984-85), Ctee Maidstone Rugby Club 1983-, Maidstone Volleyball Team 1987-; *Recreations* rugby, golf, squash, tennis, volleyball; *Clubs* Bearsted Golf; *Style*— David Arnold, Esq; The Dell, Avery Lane, Otham, Maidstone, Kent (☎ 0622 861298); 42 College Rd, Maidstone, Kent (☎ 0622 52340, 0622 672702)

ARNOLD, Jacques Arnold; MP (C) Gravesham 1987-; s of Samuel Arnold (d 1985), and Eugenie, *née* Patentine; *b* 27 Aug 1947; *Educ* sch in Brazil, LSE;

m 22 May 1976, Patricia Anne, da of Dennis Maunder, of Windsor, Berks; 1 s (David Samuel b 1984), 2 da (Hazel Jane b 1979, Philippa Rachel b 1981); *Career* asst gp rep Midland Bank Brazil 1976-78, regnl dir Thomas Cook Group 1978-84, asst trade fin dir Midland Bank 1984-85, dir American Express Europe Ltd 1985-87; currently: memb Educn Sci and Arts Select Ctee, sec Br Latin American Parly Gp; C cncllr Oundle 1981-85; *Style*— Jacques A Arnold, Esq, MP; Fairlawn, 243 London Rd, West Malling, Kent ME19 5AD (☎ 0732 848573); House of Commons, London SW1A 0AA (☎ 071 219 4150)

ARNOLD, Dr Kim Gordon; s of Peter Gordon Arnold, of Eastbourne, Sussex, and Patricia, *née* Platt; *b* 13 Feb 1948; *Educ* Eltham Coll, St Thomas's Hosp Med Sch (MRCP); *m* 12 July 1975, Brenda Mary, da of Aubrey Leonard Michell (d 1988), of London; 3 s (Nicholas John b 9 Sept 1979, Richard James b 1 Nov 1981, Jonathan b 24 Oct 1983); *Career* Conslt physician geriatric med Bloomsbury Health Authy; hon sr lectr geriatric med: UCL Med Sch, Middlesex Med Sch; periods of secondment to Health Advsy Serv; memb Br Geriatric Soc; *Recreations* computing, walking, camping; *Style*— Dr Kim Arnold; 2 Romney Drive, Sundridge Ave, Bromley, Kent BR1 2TE (☎ 081 466 1775); St Pancras Hosp, 4 St Pancras Way, London NW1 (☎ 071 387 4411, ext 372)

ARNOTT, Dr Neil David; s of Dr James Arnott, of Ide Hill, Sevenoaks, Kent, and Barbara Stella Marcia, *née* Edwards; *b* 2 Dec 1949; *Educ* Tonbridge, St Thomas' Hosp Univ of London (MB BS); *m* 18 June 1971, Sarah Anne, da of Rev Canon Norman James Mantle, of Tunbridge Wells; 2 s (David Edward b 18 July 1976, Matthew James b 24 May 1979), 2 da (Katie Helen (twin) b 18 July 1976, Lucy Victoria b 21 July 1981); *Career* house offr St Thomas Hosp 1972-73, sr house offr St Mary's Hosp and Salisbury Hosp; GP Sevenoaks 1980- (Saskatchewan Canada 1976-80), police surgn Sevenoaks 1980-, sch med offr Sevenoaks Sch 1987-; MO: St John's Ambulance, Freshfields, Sevenoaks Fire Station; memb: BMA, Canadian Med Soc; DRCOG 1975, LMCC 1977, MRCGP 1980; *Recreations* squash, tennis, sailing; *Clubs* Knole Park Golf; *Style*— Dr Neil Arnott; Guzzlers Wood, Ide Hill, Sevenoaks, Kent TN14 6JT (☎ 0732 75221); Amhurst Medical Centre, Sevenoaks, Kent TN13 2JO (☎ 0732 459255)

ASHENDEN, Rev Gavin Roy Pelham; s of Michael Roy Edward Ashenden, of Merton Park, London, and Doreen Barker, *née* Simpson; *b* 3 June 1954; *Educ* King's Sch Canterbury, Univ of Bristol (LLB), Oakhill Theol Coll (CNAA, BA), Heythrop Coll Univ of London (MTh); *m* 27 June 1975, Marjory Janet, da of Wing Cdr Henry Dow, RCAF (d 1973); 1 s (Thomas Benedict Frances b 1985), 1 da (Hannah Alison Naomi b 1983); *Career* curate St James Bermondsey 1980-82, team vicar St Antony's Hamsey Green Sanderstead 1982-89, univ chaplain and lectr Univ of Sussex 1989-; memb Keston Coll Cncl, dir Aid to Russian Christians; *Books* Guidebook to the Spiritual Life (ed Toon, 1987); *Recreations* squash, flautist; *Style*— The Rev Gavin Ashenden; 112 Beaconsfield Villas, Brighton, E Sussex BN1 6HE; Keston College, Heathfield Rd, Keston, Kent; The Meeting House, Sussex University BN1 9QN (☎ 0273 606755)

ASHFIELD, Dr Robert James; s of Edward James Ashfield (d 1938), of Tunbridge Wells, and Florence Maude, *née* Morgan (d 1965); *b* 28 July 1911; *Educ* Tonbridge, RCM (DMus); *m* 18 Aug 1947, Mary Elizabeth Ashfield, JP, *née* Lee; 2 da (Francis Rhoda b 1949, Sally Elizabeth b 1952); *Career* RASC 1941-46; organist: St John's Smith Square London 1933-41, Southwell Cathedral 1946-56, Rochester Cathedral 1956-77, conductor Rochester Choral Soc 1956-77, prof RCM 1957-81; fndr and chm Medway Concert Soc 1988-; hon assoc RCM; FRCO; *Recreations* composing church and organ music; *Style*— Dr Robert Ashfield; 2 Grange Way, Rochester, Kent ME1 3DU (☎ 0634 841508)

ASHFORD, Ronald; s of Russell Sutcliffe Ashford (d 1960), of Hilltop, Powntley Copse, Alton, Hants, and Dorothy, *née* Shorland (d 1963); *b* 24 Aug 1932; *Educ* St Edwards Sch Oxford, De Havilland Aeronautical Tech Sch; *m* 18 June 1955, Francoise Louisa Gabrielle, da of Camille Genestal Du Chaumeil (d 1978), of Le Havre, France; 2 s (Mark b 1959, Peter b 1961); *Career* PO RAF 1956-58; flt test engr De Havilland Aircraft Co 1953-56, flt test engr and sr aerodynamicist De Havilland Aircraft Co/Hawker Siddeley Aviation 1958-68, design surveyor Air Registration Bd 1968-72; CAA: design surveyor 1972-82, head Flt Dept 1982-83, dir gen airworthiness 1983-87, head of operational safety 1987-88, gp dir of safety 1988-, bd memb 1988-; memb Exec Bd Euro Jt Aviation Authys; Freeman Guild of Air Pilots and Air Navigators 1990; CEng 1970, FRAeS 1983, FIMechE 1986; *Recreations* walking, gardening, light aircraft flying; *Style*— Ronald Ashford, Esq; Chartcote, Goodley Stock Rd, Crockham Hill, Edenbridge, Kent TN8 6TA (☎ 0732 866252); Aviation House, Gatwick Airport, West Sussex RH6 0YR (☎ 0293 573078, telex 878753, fax 0293 573997)

ASHMORE, Vice Adm Sir Peter William Beckwith; KCB (1972, CB 1968), KCVO (1980, MVO (4 Class) 1948), DSC (1942); s of late Vice Adm Leslie Haliburton Ashmore, CB, DSO (d 1974), and late Tamara Vasilievna Schutt, of Petrograd; yr bro of Adm of the Fleet Sir Edward Ashmore; *b* 4 Feb 1921; *Educ* Yardley Court, RNC Dartmouth; *m* 1952, Patricia Moray, da of late Adm Sir Henry Tritton Buller, GCVO, CB (d 1960), and Lady Hermione, *née* Stuart, da of 17 Earl of Moray; 1 s, 3 da; *Career* midshipman RN 1939, served WWII (despatches), Lt 1941, Equerry to HM The King 1946-1948, Cdr 1951, Capt 1957, Rear Adm 1966, COS to CIC Western Fleet and NATO CIC E Atlantic 1967-69, Vice Adm 1969, Chief Allied Staff NATO Naval HQ S Europe 1970-72; Master of HM's HM's Household 1973-86, ret; extra equerry to HM The Queen 1952; *Recreations* golf, tennis, fishing; *Style*— Vice Adm Sir Peter Ashmore, KCB, KCVO, DSC

ASHTON-BOSTOCK, David Ashton; s of Cdr John Bostock, DSC, RN; additional surname and arms assumed by Royal Licence 1953, at the wish of his great-uncle Samuel Ashton-Yates; *b* 17 Feb 1933; *Educ* Wellington, Maidstone Coll of Art, Byam Shaw Art Sch; *m* 1965 (m dis 1983), Victoria Rosamond, da of Capt Richard White, DSO, RN; 1 s (decd), 1 da; *Career* interior designer; vice pres Alexandra Rose Day, chm Ridley Art Soc, memb Cncl Interior Decorators and Designers Assoc; memb of Lloyd's; *Recreations* painting, gardening, genealogy; *Style*— David Ashton-Bostock, Esq; Danes Bottom Place, Wormshill, Sittingbourne, Kent (☎ 062 784 476); 28 Sutherland St, London SW1 (☎ 071 834 1696); Ashton-Bostock Interior Decorations, 21 Charlwood St, London SW1 (☎ 071 828 3656)

ASKEW, Stephen James Thomas; s of Arthur James Hammond Askew, of Longfield, Kent, and Margaret Mary, *née* Faulkner; *b* 16 June 1954; *Educ* Chislehurst and Sidcup GS for Boys, South Bank Poly; *m* 29 Oct 1977, Hilary Anne, da of Graham Newham Timm (d 1976); 2 s (James Graham b 9 May 1983, Thomas Owen b 29 Nov 1984), 2 da (Louise Margaret b 23 April 1980, Clare Isobel b 30 Jan 1982); *Career* CA; audit trainee (articled clerk) P D Leake & Co (now Pannel Kerr Forster) Chartered Accountants 1973-78, Creasey Son & Wickenden 1979-83, ptnr Waring & Partners 1984- (joined 1973); memb Broadstair's Round Table 1985-; memb ICAEW 1981; *Recreations* water sports; *Style*— Stephen Askew, Esq; Three Chimneys, Westcliffe Gardens, Westbrook, Kent CT9 5DT (☎ 0843 223753); Waring & Partners, Roper Yard, Roper Rd, Canterbury, Kent CT2 7EX (☎ 0227 766666k, fax 0227 766667)

ASLAM, Dr Toqeer; s of Mohammed Aslam, of Pakistan, and Zahida, *née* Naseem; *b* 17 Aug 1957; *Educ* Univ of Bristol (MB ChB); *Career* gen med Royal Devon and Exeter Hosp 1981-82, gen surgery Bristol Royal Infirmary 1982, accident and emergency orthopaedics surgery and paediatrics Maidstone Hosp 1982-85, obstetrics and gynaecology All Saints Hosp Chatham 1985-86, sch and child health serv Medway Health Authy 1986-87, GP Walderslade 1987-; fndr: Wishing Well Charity (now pres), Maidstone Hospice Project 1983; loaned Wishing Well name to Gt Ormond St Childrens Hosp for its redevpt appeal (Wishing Well Appeal) 1987, fndr and proprietor Welcome House Residential Care Homes for the recovering mentally ill Medway and Swale; *Style*— Dr Toqeer Aslam; 53 First Ave, Gillingham, Kent ME7 2LH (☎ 0634 571861); Princes Park Medical Centre, Dove Close, Walderslade, Chatham, Kent (☎ 0634 201272)

ASPINALL, John Victor; s of late Col Robert Aspinall, and Mary Grace, *née* Horn, later Lady Osborne (d 1987); *b* 11 June 1926; *Educ* Rugby (asked to leave), Jesus Coll Oxford (sent down); *m* 1, 1956 (m dis 1966), Jane Gordon Hastings; 1 s, 1 da; m 2, 1966 (m dis 1972), Belinda Musker; m 3, 1972, Lady Sarah Marguerite Curzon; 1 s; *Career* WWII, Royal Marine 1943-45; fndr: Howletts Zoo Park 1958, Clermont Club 1962, Port Lympne Zoo Park 1973, Aspinall's Club 1978, Aspinall Curzon Club 1984; *Books* Best of Friends (1976); *Style*— John Aspinall, Esq; Howletts, Canterbury, Kent; Port Lympne, Lympne, Kent; 1 Lyall St, London SW1; Noordhoek Manor, Cape Town 7985, SA; 64 Sloane St, London SW1 (☎ 071 235 2768, fax 071 235 4701)

ASPINALL, (Harry) Michael; s of Leonard Aspinall (d 1969), of Tunbridge Wells, Kent, and Eva, *née* Whitworth; *b* 22 Nov 1926; *Educ* Sutton Valence; *m* 12 Jan 1952, (Joan) Avril, da of Maj Lancelot Kaye Machattie Powell, MC (d 1936), of Adelaide, S Aust; 1 s (Mark Christopher Leonard b 20 Aug 1957), 1 da (Rebecca Carol (Mrs Bayley) b 18 July 1953); *Career* admitted slr 1948; ptnr Snell and Co 1954, NP 1958, sr ptnr Thomson Snell and Passmore 1986-90; local dir Sun Alliance Insurance Gp, chm Abbeyfield Tunbridge Wells Soc Ltd; pres Tunbridge Wells Tonbridge and District Law Soc 1969; *Recreations* wide interests in arts and crafts subjects, travel, reading, food and wine; *Clubs* Royal Ocean Racing, Ski Club of GB, MCC; *Style*— Michael Aspinall, Esq; Courthopes, Whiligh, Wadhurst, East Sussex TN5 7JU (☎ 0892 88 2492); Thomson Snell & Passmore, 3 Lonsdale Gardens, Tunbridge Wells, Kent TN1 1NX (☎ 0892 510000, fax 0892 49884, telex 95194)

ASTBURY, Michael Henry Richardson; s of John Astbury, OBE (d 1968), and Joyce Elsie, *née* Richardson (d 1978); *b* 3 May 1929; *Educ* Edinburgh Acad, Perse Sch Cambridge, St Catharine's Coll Cambridge (MA); *m* 31 March 1959, Margaret, da of Leslie Arthur Hammond (d 1981); 2 s (Peter John Hammond b 5 June 1960, Jonathan Robert Hammond b 27 June 1962); *Career* Nat Serv RAEC 1947-49 (Greece, Egypt); called to the Bar Middle Temple 1953; asst sec Manchester Ship Canal Co 1954-57, sec Employers Fedn of Ceylon 1961-63 (dep sec 1957-61), prosecuting slr DTI 1963-67, dep sec Gen Cncl of the Senate of the Inns of Court and the Bar 1967-77, sec Inc

Soc of Valuers and Auctioneers 1977-89; chm Kent Family Health Servs Authy Med Servs Ctee (and dep chm Jt Servs Ctee), tstee S Bromley Hospiscare; sec Kentish Cobnuts Assoc; memb: Panel of Reference Secs MMC, St Peters PCC Ightham Kent; Freeman: City of London, Worshipful Co of Glovers; MCIArb; *Books* Halsburys' Laws of England (contrib, 4 edn), Butterworths Encyclopaedia of Forms and Precedents (advsy ed, 5 edn); *Recreations* sailing, gardening, reading; *Clubs* MCC; *Style*— Michael Astbury, Esq; The Coach House, Oldbury, Ightham, nr Sevenoaks, Kent (☎ 0732 884163)

ASTOR OF HEVER, Irene, Lady; Lady Irene Violet Freesia Janet Augusta; da of Field Marshal 1 Earl Haig, KT, GCB, DM, GCVO, KCIE (d 1928); *b* 7 Oct 1919; *m* 4 Oct 1945, 2 Baron Astor of Hever (d 1984); 2 s, 3 da; *Career* hon life memb BRCS (holder of Queen's Badge of Honour, chm and pres Kent Branch 1976-82), patron Kent Co Royal Br Legion Women's Section, pres Kent Agric Soc 1981 and 1982, vice pres RNIB, vice patron Nat Asthma Campaign; CStJ; *Style*— The Rt Hon Irene, Lady Astor of Hever; Holly Tree House, French St, Westerham, Kent TN16 1PW (☎ 0959 62141); 11 Lyall St, Eaton Sq, London SW1X 8DH (☎ 071 235 4755)

ASTOR OF HEVER, Rt Hon the Lord John Jacob Astor; 3 Baron (UK 1956); s of 2 Baron Astor of Hever by his w, Lady Irene Haig, da of 1 Earl Haig, KT, GCB, OM, GCVO, KCIE; *b* 16 June 1946; *Educ* Eton; *m* 1, 1970 (m dis 1990), Fiona Diana Lennox, da of Capt Roger Harvey, JP, DL, Scots Gds, and Diana (da of Sir Harry Mainwaring, 5 and last Bt, by his w Generis, eld da of Sir Richard Williams-Bulkeley, 12 Bt, KCB, VD, JP, and Lady Magdalen Yorke, da of 5 Earl of Hardwicke); 3 da (Hon Camilla Fiona b 1974, Hon Tania Jentie b 1978, Hon Violet Magdalene b 1980); m 2, 5 May 1990, Hon Elizabeth, da of Viscount Mackintosh of Halifax, OBE, BEM; *Heir* bro Hon Philip Douglas Paul Astor; *Career* formerly Lt LG served Malaysia, Hong Kong, NI; md: Terres Blanches Services Sarl 1975-77, Valberg Plaza Sarl 1977-82, Honon et Cie 1982-; pres: Astor Enterprises Inc 1983-, Astor France Sarl 1990-; chm: Cncl of St John Kent; *Clubs* White's, Cavalry and Guards'; *Style*— The Rt Hon the Lord Astor of Hever; Frenchstreet House, Frenchstreet, Westerham, Kent TN16 1PW (☎ 0959 62783)

ATHERTON, Brig Maurice Alan; CBE (1981), JP (Kent 1982), DL (Kent 1984); s of Rev Harold Atherton (d 1975), of Sheffield, and Beatrice, *née* Shaw (d 1958); *b* 9 Oct 1926; *Educ* St John's Sch Leatherhead, Staff Coll Camberley; *m* 28 Aug 1954, Guendolene Mary (Wendi), da of Col James Bryan Upton, MBE, TD, JP, DL (d 1976), of Hotham, York; 1 s (James Patrick b 7 Sept 1966), 1 da (Christine Wendy b 6 March 1965); *Career* cmmnd E Yorks regt 1946; serv in Egypt, Sudan, Malaysia, Germany, Austria, Hong Kong, Ghanam college chief instructor RMA Sandhurst 1964-67; Cdr: 1 Green Howards 1967-69, Dover Shorncliffe Garrison 1976-81; Dep Constable Dover Castle 1976-81, magistrate dover Bench 1982-; HS Kent 1983-84; county pres: Royal Br Legion 1982-, Men of the Trees 1985-; chm: Kent Ctee Army Benevolent Fund 1984-, Maurice House Broadstairs, Diocesan Property Ctee; *Recreations* shooting, gardening, skiing; *Clubs* Army and Navy, Lansdowne; *Style*— Brig M A Atherton, CBE, JP, DL; Digges Place, Barham, Canterbury, Kent CT4 6PJ (☎ 0227 831420)

ATKIN, Roger Dean; s of (Arthur) James Atkin, of Herne Bay, Kent, and Acie, *née* Dean; *b* 2 April 1939; *Educ* Herne Bay Sch; *m* 21 May 1969, Wendy Anne, da of Sqdn Ldr Alexander Thomas Stewart, DFC, AFC; 2 s (Stewart Dean b 15 April 1971, Alister Graham b 22 August 1973); *Career* signals RAF served UK and W Germany 1959-61; underwriting memb Lloyd's 1980, fndr Atkin Raggett Ltd (Lloyd's broker), dir Edgar Hamilton (Marine) Ltd; memb Herne Bay UDC 1967-69, chm SE Area Young Cons 1969-70; Freeman City of London 1969; Liveryman: Worshipful Co of Cooks 1972, Worshipful Co of Insurers 1986; MIEx 1975; *Clubs* Royal Over-Seas League, City Livery, Canterbury; *Style*— Roger D Atkin, Esq; Herne Brow, Pigeon Lane, Herne, Herne Bay, Kent CT6 7ES (☎ 0227 374 423); Edgar Hamilton Group, Lloyd's of London, London EC3

ATTENBOROUGH, Michael Francis; s of (Ralph) John Attenborough, CBE, of Chislehurst, Kent, and (Edith) Barbara, *née* Sandle; *b* 21 Oct 1939; *Educ* Rugby, Trinity Coll Oxford (MA); *m* 7 March 1970, Carol Finlay, da of Dr George Alexander Sharp, of Bishops Stortford, Herts; 1 s (Thomas Julian b 23 May 1972), 1 da (Sophie Jane b 24 Feb 1975); *Career* Hodder & Stoughton Publishers 1962- (publishing dir 1980-); memb Worshipful Co of Haberdashers 1961; *Recreations* golf, cricket; *Clubs* Garrick, Band of Brothers, Royal St George's, Royal and Ancient; *Style*— Michael Attenborough, Esq; 17 Parkgate, Blackheath, London SE3; Hodder & Stoughton Publishers, 47 Bedford Square, London WC1 3DP (☎ 071 636 9851, fax 071 631 5248, telex 885887)

ATTENBOROUGH, Philip John; s of John Attenborough, CBE, of Chislehurst, Kent, and Barbara, *née* Sandle (d 1988); *b* 3 June 1936; *Educ* Rugby, Trinity Coll Oxford; *m* 28 Sept 1963, Rosemary, da of Dr Brian Littler, CB, of High Barnet, Herts; 1 s (Timothy b 28 June 1967), 1 da (Clare b 3 April 1965); *Career* chm: Hodder & Stoughton Ltd, Hodder & Stoughton Holdings Ltd 1975-, The Lancet Ltd 1977-; pres Publishers Assoc 1983-85, dir Book Tokens Ltd 1985-; chm Br Cncl Publishers Advsy Ctee 1989-; govr Judd Sch Tonbridge 1987-; *Recreations* trout fishing, watching cricket, playing tennis and golf; *Clubs* Garrick, MCC, Kent CCC, Rye Golf; *Style*— Philip Attenborough, Esq; Colhanger, Seal Chart, Sevenoaks, Kent TN15 0EJ (☎ 0732 61516); Hodder & Stoughton Ltd, Mill Rd, Dunton Green, Sevenoaks, Kent TN13 2YA (☎ 0732 460134, fax 0732 460134)

ATTLEE, Hon Mrs (Rosemary); 2 da of late 1 Baron Elton; *b* 22 Jan 1925; *m* 1, 1946 (m dis 1955), William, er s of William Yates, of Appleby, Westmorland; 1 s (decd), 2 da; m 2, 1955, David Charles Attlee, s of Wilfrid Henry Waller Attlee (d 1962); 1 s, 1 da; *Style*— The Hon Mrs Attlee; Great Woodland Farm, Lyminge, Folkestone, Kent

ATTWOOD, Marion Marguerite; da of Eric Victor Jordan (d 1980), of Canterbury, and Florence, *née* Wilkinson; *b* 5 Sept 1934; *Educ* Br Forces Sch Jamaica W1; *m* 10 July 1954, Maj Arthur Henry Thomas Attwood, s of Robert Hugh Mann Attwood (d 1962), of Mablethorpe, Lincs; 3 s (Paul b 1955, Neil b 1957, Douglas b 1965); *Career* chiropodist 1979-; memb (Cons) Canterbury City Cncl 1983- (chm Environment Special Ctee 1990); pres Canterbury Gateway Club for Mentally Handicapped, vice pres Hettie Barber Handicap Club Canterbury; exec memb: Canterbury Volunteer Bureau, Canterbury Age Concern; tstee: Adkinson Cooper Almshouse, Municipal Charities Canterbury, Maynard and Cotton Hosp Charity; memb Br Chiropody Assoc; *Recreations* reading, gardening, siamese cats; *Style*— Mrs Marion Attwood; 25 Lesley Ave, Canterbury, Kent (☎ 0227 765265)

ATTWOOD, Dr Paul Robert Arthur; s of Maj Arthur Henry Thomas Attwood, and Marion Marguerite Attwood; *b* 20 Feb 1955; *Educ* Richmond Sch Yorkshire, Southampton Med Sch (MB BS, DObst RCOG); *m* 16 July 1983, Sally Cathryn, da of (Ronald) Kevin Kemp, of Teynham, Kent; 2 da (Cathryn Megan b 20 Nov 1985, Sophie Louise b 28 March 1988); *Career* house surgn Queen Alexandra's Hosp Portsmouth 1979-80, house physician Weymouth and Dist Hosp 1980; William Harvey Hosp Ashford: sr house offr accident and emergency 1980-81, GP vocational trg scheme 1981-84, clinical asst accident and emergency Margate Hosp 1985-; memb: St John's Ambulance 1981-82, Ramsgate Round Table 1985-; memb BMA; *Style*— Dr Paul Attwood; 1 Wickham Ave, Ramsgate, Kent CT11 8AY (☎ 0843 593420)

AUDLEY, 25 Baron (E 1312-13); Richard Michael Thomas Souter; s of Sir Charles Alexander Souter, KCIE, CSI, and Charlotte Dorothy Jesson (sis of Thomas Tuchet-Jesson, f of 23 Baron and the 23 Baron's sis who as Baroness Audley was 24 holder of that title; Charlotte and Thomas were children of Charlotte, da of John Thicknesse-Tuchet, bro of 21 Baron Audley, by her husb Thomas Jesson); suc cous 1973; *b* 31 May 1914; *Educ* Uppingham; *m* 1941, Pauline, da of Dallas Louis Eskell; 3 da; *Heir* all 3 da as coheiresses presumptive: Hon Mrs Carey Mackinnon, Hon Mrs Michael Carrington, Hon Amanda Souter, *qqv*; *Career* Capt RA WW II; dir Graham Miller & Co, ret 1982; fell Chartered Inst of Loss Adjusters; *Recreations* shooting, gardening; *Style*— The Rt Hon The Lord Audley; Friendly Green, Cowden, nr Edenbridge, Kent (☎ 034 286 850682)

AUSTEN-SMITH, Air Marshal Sir Roy David; KBE (1979), CB (1975), DFC (1953); s of D Austen Smith, of Kingsdown, Kent; *b* 28 June 1924; *Educ* Hurstpierpoint; *m* 1951, Patricia Ann, *née* Alderson; 2 s; *Career* RAF, served WWII, Cdr Br Forces Cyprus, AOC Air HQ Cyprus and Admin Sovereign Base Areas Cyprus 1976-78; head Br Def Staff Washington and Def Attaché 1978-81, ret; Gentleman Usher to HM The Queen 1982-; *Style*— Air Marshal Sir Roy Austen-Smith, KBE, CB, DFC; c/o National Westminster Bank, Swanley, Kent

AUSTIN, David Colin (Dave); s of Harry William Austin, of Leicester, and Elsie May, *née* Payne; *b* 15 Feb 1958; *Educ* Kingswood Comp Sch Corby Northants, Open Univ; *Career* Police Constable in Northants 1976, dubbing projectionist Mercury Studiosound 1978, tech operator BBC Radio Networks 1981, freelance broadcaster i/c Drivetime and Out & About BBC Radio Kent 1988-; *Recreations* radio controlled model aeroplanes, cake decorating, photography; *Clubs* Medway Model Flying; *Style*— Dave Austin, Esq

AUSTIN, Jonathan; s of John Jaques Austin, of Islington, and Constance Mary, *née* Williams; *b* 15 Aug 1946; *Educ* Brentwood Sch Essex, Sevenoaks Sch, Univ of York (BA); *m* 12 April 1969, Virginia, da of John Burdett Branston (d 1968), of Leicester; 3 da (Emma b 7 June 1972, Lucy b 12 Aug 1974, Rebecca b 28 July 1978); *Career* admitted slr 1971; articled Messrs Tuckett Williams & Kew Bristol 1968-70, ptnr with Boys & Maughan Margate 1972-; memb: Slrs Benevolent Assoc, Legal Aid Practitioners Gp; hon educn and trg offr Kent Law Soc, past pres Isle of Thanet Law Soc; past memb: Legal Aid Ctee Area 2, Rotary Club of Westgate and Birchington; past chm Margate Round Table; memb Law Soc, ACIArb; *Books* Waterlows 'Photoforms' Licensing Precedents (1989); *Recreations* amateur dramatics, family; *Clubs* Wig and Pen; *Style*— Jonathan Austin, Esq; India House, Hawley St, Margate, Kent CT9 1PZ (☎ 0843 220288, fax 0843 299475)

AUSTIN, Juliet Leathes; da of Bernard Oliver Leathes Prior, of Norwich, Norfolk, and Ann, *née* Godfrey (d 1972); *b* 22 April 1944; *Educ* Downe House, Univ of Birmingham (BA); *m* 10 Feb 1968, Anthony James Kirkpatrick Austin, s of James George Rex Austin, of Victoria Island, BC, Canada; 1 da (Elizabeth Marjorie b 6 June 1971); *Career* teacher City of Birmingham Educn

Authy, library clerk House of Commons, housemistress Downe House, headmistress Combe Bank; memb Exec Ctee and Professional Ctee Girl's Schs Assoc (regnl chm 1988-90); *Recreations* sailing, singing, walking, reading; *Style*— Mrs Juliet Austin; Little Brenchleys, 1 Rectory Lane, Harrietsham, Kent (☎ 0622 850490); The Convent, Combe Bank, Sundridge, Sevenoaks, Kent TN14 6AE (☎ 0959 62508)

AUSTIN-COOPER, Richard Arthur; o s of Capt Adolphus Richard Cooper, of Ditton, Kent, and Doris Rosina, *née* Wallen; see Burke's Irish Family Records under Cooper (co Tipperary); *b* 21 Feb 1932; *Educ* Wellingborough GS, Inst of Bankers (Dip); *m* 1, 28 March 1953 (m dis 1963), Sylvia Anne Shirley Berringer; m 2, 28 Sept 1963 (m dis 1974), Valerie Georgina, da of Henry Drage, of Tottenham, London; 1 s (Matthew b 1969), 1 da (Samantha b 1967); m 3, 1986, Rosemary Swasland, *née* Gillespie; *Career* served RA Intelligence Corps 21 SAS Regt, Hon Artillery Co; dep head Stocks & Shares Dept Banque de Paris et des Pays Bas 1969-74, mangr Banking Div Brook St Bureau of Mayfair Ltd 1974-77, chief custodian and London registrar of Canadian Imperial Bank of Commerce 1975-78, personnel offr Deutsche Bank AG London Branch 1978-85, sr mangr and head of personnel Deutsche Bank Capital Markets Ltd; fndr fell Inst of Heraldic and Genealogical Studies; memb Bd of Mgmnt: Barbican YMCA, City of London Central Markets Coal Corn and Rates, Leadenhall Market, Billingsgate Market, music mgmnt ctees 1978-81, Court of Common Cncl for Cripplegate Ward 1978-81, City of London TAVR Assoc, Mgmnt Ctee Barbican Sch of Music and Drama (and mature student), Irish Peers Assoc; govr: City of London Sch for Girls 1979-80, City of London Freemens Sch 1980-81, Lansbury Adult Educn Inst 1979-82, Sheriffs and Recorders Fund at the Old Bailey 1979-; represented the City of London Corpn on the Gtr London Arts Cncl 1979-80, Freedom of the City of London 1964; last tstee City of London Imp Vols 1980-81; prizes for athletics, operatic singing (tenor), painting; FCIB, FRSA, FRSAIre, MBIM, FSA (Scot); *Recreations* genealogical research, tenor concerts, sketching; *Clubs* Special Forces, SAS Old Comrades, Intelligence Corps Old Comrades; *Style*— Richard Austin-Cooper, Esq; Forge Cottage, Dunn St, Bredhurst, Kent ME7 3LX (☎ 0634 378024); Deutsche Bank Capital Markets Ltd, 150 Leadenhall St, London EC3V 4RJ (☎ 071 283 0933)

B

BACKLEY, Steven James; s of John Backley, and Pauline, *née* Hogg; *b* 12 Feb 1969; *Educ* Bexley and Erith Tech HS, Loughborough Univ of Technol; *Career* javelin thrower; holder of world jr record in 1989, finished third in overall athletics Grand Prix to Said Aouita and Roger Kingdom 1989, UK record holder 85.90m set in Barcelona 1989, England Rep Cwlth Games Auckland NZ 1990; *Recreations* athletics; *Clubs* Cambridge Harriers (Bexley); *Style*— Steven Backley, Esq; 22 Beechway, Bexley, Kent D45 3DG (☎ 081 303 4405)

BACON, Sir Sidney Charles; CB (1971); s of Charles Bacon; *b* 11 Feb 1919; *Educ* Woolwich Poly, London Univ (BSc Eng); *Career* md Royal Ordnance Factories and dep chm bd 1972-79, ret; memb Cncl City and Guilds of London Inst 1983-; FEng 1979, FIMechE, FIProd E; kt 1977; *Style*— Sir Sidney Bacon, CB; 228 Erith Rd, Bexley Heath, Kent DA7 6HP

BADCOCK, Maj-Gen John Michael Watson; CB (1976), MBE (1969), DL (Kent 1980); s of late R D Badcock, MC, JP; *b* 10 Nov 1922; *Educ* Sherborne, Worcester Coll Oxford; *m* 1948, Gillian Pauline, *née* Attfield; 1 s, 2 da; *Career* enlisted in ranks (Army) 1941, cmmnd RCS 1942; war serv 1945-47: UK, BAOR, Ceylon; serv 1947-68: UK, Persian Gulf, BAOR, Cyprus; Cdr 2 Inf Bde and dep Constable Dover Castle 1968-71, dep mil sec 1971-72, Manning dir (Army) 1972-74, def advsr and head Br Def Liaison Staff Canberra 1974-77, ret; Col Cmdt RCS 1974-80 and 1982-, Hon Col 31 Hon Col 31 (London) Signal Regt (Vol) 1978-83, chm SE TA & VRA 1979-85; Master of Signals 1982-90; *Recreations* rugby, football, cricket, hockey; *Clubs* Army and Navy; *Style*— Maj-Gen John Badcock, CB, MBE, DL; c/o RHQ Royal Signals, 56 Regency St, London SW1P 4AD

BADDELEY, Mark David; s of late Mark Baddeley (d 1930), gs of Sir John Baddeley, 1 Bt, and hp of kinsman Sir John Wolsey Baddeley, 4 Bt; *b* 12 May 1921; *Educ* Cliftonville Coll; *Style*— Mark Baddeley, Esq; Woodberry, George V Ave, Margate, Kent

BAIN SMITH, Lady Corisande; da of 8 Earl of Tankerville (d 1971), of Chillingham, Northumberland and Violet, Countess of Tankerville, JP, *née* Pallin; *b* 10 April 1938; *Educ* St James West Malvern, Univ of Oxford; *m* 1963, Lt Cdr Timothy Bain Smith, CPA, RN, s of Lt-Col George Stewart Bain Smith, GC (d 1972); 2 s (James b 1964, Charles b 1966); *Style*— Lady Corisande Bain Smith; Wickens Manor, Charing, Kent

BAINS, Malcolm Arnold; JP (Norfolk Island), DL (Kent 1976); s of Herbert Bains, of Newcastle-upon-Tyne; *b* 12 Sept 1921; *Educ* Hymers Coll, Univ of Durham (LLB); *m* 1, 1942 (m dis 1961), Winifred Agnes Davies; 3 s; m 2, 1968, Margaret Hunter; *Career* slr; clerk of Kent CC and clerk to Lieutenancy of Kent 1970-74; fell ANU and advsr to NSW govt Aust 1977-78; chm Local Govt Review Bd of Victoria 1978-79; head Norfolk Island Public Serv 1979-82; JP (Norfolk Island); FRSA; *Publications* The 'Bains' Report on Local Authority Mgmnt (1973); *Style*— Malcolm Bains Esq, JP, DL; Somers Cottage, Lamer St, Meopham, Kent; PO Box 244, Norfolk Island, via Australia 2899

BAKER, Alfred Joseph; s of William Ahern Baker (d 1967), of Tottenham, and Katherine, *née* O'Sullivan (d 1954); *b* 8 Jan 1927; *Educ* Trent Park Trg Coll (Cert Ed), Univ of London (BSc, Dip Ed), Open Univ (BA); *m* 16 Aug 1965, Dr Hildegard Hermine Maria Baker, da of Dr Ludwig Starmayr Hofrat (d 1978), of Linz, Austria; 2 s (Stephen William Ludwig b 19 Aug 1966, Thomas Alfred b 19 March 1968), 1 da (Katharine Margaret b 7 June 1972); *Career* Br Army 1945-48; serv: Egypt, Palestine, Iraq and Greece; manual worker 1941-45, clerk HM Inspector of Taxes 1948-49, clerical offr COI 1948-55, exec offr Prison Cmmn 1955, asst teacher The Modern Sch Colney 1957-61; head Dept of English: Clarendon Secdy Sch 1961-64, Mtendere Secdy Sch Dedza Malawi 1965-67, Sandown Court Secdy Sch Tunbridge Wells 1968-85; Tunbridge Wells Borough Cncl: cncllr 1984-, cncl rep SE region Ctee, Nat Housing and Town Planning Cncl, ldr Lib Democratic Gp; ldr Tunbridge Wells SLDP; govr: St Augustine's Primary Sch, St Barnabus' Primary Sch; active memb St Augustine's Parish; memb: Trinity Drama Club Tunbridge Wells, Oast Theatre Tonbridge; *Recreations* acting, travel, literature, directing plays; *Style*— Alfred Baker, Esq; 6 Henley Close, Tunbridge Wells, Kent TN2 3RJ (☎ 0892 31578)

BAKER, Paul Kenneth Hay; s of George Kenneth Baker (d 1976), of Beckenham, and Margaret Elizabeth Hay, *née* Greenaway; *b* 20 Feb 1948; *Educ* Eastbourne Coll; *Career* mangr Deloitte Haskins & Sells CAs 1967-78, dir accounting servs RAC 1978-83, fin dir Deinhard & Co Ltd Wine Shippers 1983-, gp fin controller W J Manton Holdings Ltd 1989-90, fin mangr The King's Sch Canterbury 1990-; memb: Croydon Dist Soc of CAs, Ctee London Philharmonic Soc; chm and former treas Crystal Palace FC Vice Presidents' Club; FCA 1979 (ACA 1972), FBIM 1980; *Clubs* Croydon Dining (former pres and sec), Kent CCC, Croydon Cons, Croham Hurst GC, Royal Automobile; *Style*— Paul Baker, Esq

BAKER, His Hon Judge Paul Vivian; QC (1972); s of Vivian Cyril Baker (d 1976), of Haywards Heath, Sussex, and Maud Lydia, *née* Jiggins (d 1979); *b* 27 March 1923; *Educ* City of London Sch, Univ Coll Oxford (MA, BCL); *m* 2 Jan 1957, Stella Paterson, da of William Eadie (d 1941), of Edinburgh; 1 s (Ian David b 1958), 1 da (Alison Joyce b 1960); *Career* RAF 1941-46, navigator and wireless operator, Flt Lt; called to the Bar, Lincoln's Inn 1950; bencher Lincoln's Inn 1972, circuit Judge 1983; Law Quarterly Review: asst ed 1960-70, ed 1971-87; *Books* Snell's Principles of Equity (co-ed edns 24-29, 1954-90); *Recreations* music, gardening; *Clubs* Athenaeum, Authors; *Style*— His Hon Judge Paul Baker, QC; 9 Old Square, Lincoln's Inn, London WC2A 3SR (☎ 071 242 2633)

BAKER, Richard William Shelmerdine; s of Lt-Col Charles Bradbeer Baker (d 1979), and Vera Margaret, *née* Shelmerdine; *b* 17 Jan 1933; *Educ* Buxton Coll; *m* 1 (m dis 1975), Teresa Mary Elizabeth, *née* Smith; 1 s (David b 22 Feb 1960), 1 da (Lisa b 31 July 1962); m 2, 30 May 1975, Vanda, da of Percy William Macey (d 1989); *Career* Nat Serv 1951-53, cmmnd 2 Lt, transfd AER 1953, Lt 1954, Actg Capt 1960; mgmnt post Marks and Spencer 1954-60, sales dir and gp md Barbour Index Ltd 1972-79, sr vice pres and gen mangr Sun Life Assurance Co of Canada (rep 1960-72, memb Sr Advsy Cncl for Int Ops), md Sun Life of Canada (UK) Ltd; chm: Sun Life of Canada Unit Managers Ltd, Sun Life of Canada Home Loans Ltd; dir Life Assurance and Unit Trust Regulatory Orgn; pres GB Wheelchair Basketball Assoc; MIOD; *Recreations* horse racing, golf, tennis, cricket, collecting antiques; *Clubs* Canada, East India, MCC; *Style*— Richard Baker, Esq; Wissenden House Oast, Bethersden, Kent TN26 3EL (☎ 023 382 352); Fisher House, Hillside Park, Sunningdale, Berks SL5 9RP (☎ 0990 22664); Sun Life of Canada, Basing View, Basingstoke, Hants RG21 2DZ (☎ 0256 841414, fax 0256 460067, car tel 0831 414 385, telex 858654)

BAKER, Wei Mei; *b* 2 May 1949; *Educ* Malaysian schs; *m* 1975, Stephen Andrew Baker; *Career* fin dir Leopold Joseph & Sons Ltd 1985-, non exec dir RLJ Finance Ltd 1986-, chm International Banking Information Systems User Group 1988-; *Style*— Mrs Wei Baker; Hobbits Oast, Goodnestone, Faversham, Kent (☎ 0795 532 555); 31-45 Gresham St, London EC2V 7EA (☎ 071 588 2323, fax 071 726 0105, telex 886454-5)

BAKER WHITE, Robin John; s of Col John Baker White, TD (d 1988), of Street End, Canterbury, and Irene, *née* Graham (d 1981); *b* 1 Oct 1932; *Educ* Blundell's; *m* 19 Oct 1957, Diane Mary, da of Sidney Ling (d 1972), of Victoria, BC, Canada; 1 s (John Mark b 1960), 1 da (Nicola Gai (Mrs Betteridge) b 1961); *Career* Nat Serv cmmnd 15/19 Kings Royal Hussars 1952-53, served Leics Yeo TA 1953-57; farm mangr T A Saul Beds 1952-62, inherited family estate 1988; dir Grain Harvesters Ltd Wingham 1984-; chm and treas local Cons Assoc 1968-88, tstee Canterbury Cons Assoc 1981-; memb: Ctee Kent CCC 1985-90, Agric Land Tbnl SE Area 1986-, Kent CLA Cncl 1989 (Ctee 1982-), SE Countryside Forum; chm Canterbury Industl Consultative Cncl 1988-; *Recreations* politics and current affairs, foreign travel, shooting, gardening, watching cricket; *Clubs* MCC, Farmers, Kent CCC, Band of Brothers; *Style*— Robin Baker White, Esq; Street End Place, Street End, Canterbury, Kent (☎ 022770 225)

BALASUNDARAM, Dr Leela; da of Shankar Govind Naravane, and Sharada, *née* Dongre; *b* 8 Dec 1926; *Educ* D M Madan HS Jamshedpur India, Bombay DFP Bombay (MB BS), Univ of London (DA); *m* 4 May 1955, Dr Venkataramanan Balasundaram, s of S Venkataramanan (d 1988), of Vasant Vihar, New Delhi; 2 s (Vikram b 3 Nov 1956, Arjun b 1 June 1958); *Career* gynaecological and med sr house offr JJ and St Georges Hosp Bombay 1950-53, surgical gynaecological and obstetric sr house offr Hastings Gp of Hosps

1953-54; anaesthesia sr house offr: Hastings and Durham 1959-60, Dartford 1970-71; GP Dartford 1973- (initially dealt mainly with non-English speaking immigrant ethnic minority women, involved with population Temple Hill Estate Dartford since 1980); memb: BMA, Hindu Cultural Soc, Hindu Centre Maharashira Mandal; *Recreations* gardening, music, tennis; *Style—* Dr Leela Balasundaram; 8 Priory Hill, Dartford, Kent DA1 2BH (☎ 0322 78027)

BALCHIN, Robert George Alexander; s of Leonard George Balchin (d 1968), and Elizabeth, *née* Skelton; the Balchin family settled in Surrey c1190, Sir Roger de Balchen owning lands in both Normandy and Surrey, Adm Sir John Balchin (1669-1744) was Governor of Greenwich RN Hosp; *b* 31 July 1942; *Educ* Bec Sch, Univ of London, Univ of Hull (MEd, Adv DipEd); *m* 1970, Jennifer, da of Bernard Kevin Kinlay (d 1975), of Cape Town; 2 s (Alexander b 1975, Thomas (twin) b 1975); *Career* asst master Chinthurst Sch 1964-68, head English Dept Ewell Sch 1968-69, dir Hill Sch Westerham Kent 1980 (headmaster 1972-80), DG St John Ambulance 1984-90; chm Campaign for a Gen Teaching Cncl 1981-84; memb: Surrey CC 1981-85, Centre for Policy Studies 1982-; treas E Surrey Cons Assoc 1982-85, dep area treas Cons Pty 1983-86, vice chm Cons Pty SE Area 1986-90, conslt dir Cons Central Office 1988-, Cons treas SE England 1990-; chm: Grant-Maintained Sch Tst 1989-, Choice in Education 1989-, Pardoc-Blacker Publishing Ltd 1989-; Liveryman Goldsmiths Co 1987 (Freeman 1987); Hon DPhil Northland Open Univ Canada 1985; Hon FCP 1987, Hon FHS 1987; Commander's Cross (Pro Merito Melitensi SMOM) 1987; KStJ 1984; *Books* Emergency Aid in Schools (1984), New Money (1985), Choosing a State School (jtly, 1989); *Recreations* restoration of elderly house; *Clubs* Athenaeum, Carlton, St Stephen's Constitutional; *Style—* Robert Balchin, Esq; New Place, Lingfield, Surrey RH7 6EF (☎ 0342 834543); 7 Ashley Court, Westminster, London SW1P 1EN; 239-245 Vauxhall Bridge Rd, London SW1V 1EJ (☎ 071 828 9855); The Hill, Pilgrims Way, Westerham, Kent (☎ 0959 93391)

BALCON, Jonathan Michael Henry; TD (1965); s of Sir Michael Balcon (d 1977), film prodr, and Aileen Freda, *née* Leatherman; *b* 7 Dec 1931; *Educ* Eton, Gonville and Caius Coll Cambridge; *m* 1 Oct 1955, Hon Sarah Patricia Mills, da of 5 Baron Hillingdon (d 1982); 3 da (Deborah b 1956, Sarah-Clair b 1957, Henrietta b 1960); *Career* TA 1951-67, City of London Yeo (Rough Riders) 1951-62 (cmmnd 1956), Inns of Court and City Yeo 1962-67 (Maj 1966 cmdg B Sqdn); underwriting agent at Lloyds, dir C I de Rougemont & Co Ltd, chm Michael Balcon Productions Ltd; Kent Special Constabulary 1967- (Cmdt C Div); pres Sevenoaks Combined Div St John Ambulance, memb Kent Ctee SE TAVRA (chm Recruiting Kent 1983-87); Queen's Jubilee Medal, Special Constabulary Long Service Medal and Bar; *Recreations* shooting; *Clubs* City of London; *Style—* Jonathan Balcon, Esq, TD; The Grey House, Seal, Sevenoaks, Kent (☎ 0732 61592/61819); C I de Rougemont & Co Ltd, 71-74 Mark Lane, London EC3 (☎ 071 481 9277)

BALCON, Hon Mrs (Sarah Patricia); *née* Mills; da of 5 Baron Hillingdon, MC, TD; *b* 1933; *Educ* Westonbirt; *m* 1955, Jonathan Michael Henry Balcon, TD, o s of late Sir Michael Balcon; 3 da (Deborah b 1956, Sarah Clair b 1957, Henrietta b 1960); *Career* tstee Harrison Zoological Museum, vice pres Kent Girl Guide Assoc; *Recreations* travelling, paleontology, fine arts; *Style—* The Hon Mrs Balcon; The Grey House, Seal, Sevenoaks, Kent (☎ 0732 61592)

BALDWIN, Christopher William Kennard; s of Peter Godfrey Kennard Baldwin (d 1979), of Lindsay Hill, Antigua, W Indies, and Joan Lillian, *née* Burgess-Driver; *b* 26 Dec 1945; *Educ* Skinners Sch; *m* 5 March 1984, Emma Margaret, da of Lt-Col Humphrey Crossman, JP, DL, of Cheswick House, Berwick upon Tweed, Northumberland, and Lady Rose Crossman, o da of Field Marshal 1 Earl Alexander of Tunis, KG, GCB, OM, GCMG, CSI, DSO, MC, PC (d 1969); 1 s (John Lindsay Alexander b 23 Jan 1989); *Career* landowner Bedgebury Estate Kent; capt Br Bobsleigh Team, Br Bobsleigh Champion (Cervinia 1974, St Moritz 1976); chm Kent Co Ctee Game Conservancy Tst 1987-; *Recreations* shooting, skiing, fishing; *Style—* Christopher Baldwin, Esq; Twyssenden Manor, Bedgebury, Goudhurst, Kent

BALDWIN, Michael; s of Harold Jesse Baldwin (d 1989), of Luss Cottage, Meopham, Kent, and Elizabeth Aimee, *née* Crittenden (d 1968); *b* 1 May 1930; *Educ* Gravesend Co GS, St Edmund Hall Oxford (BA); *m* 1, 22 May 1954 (m dis 1979), Jean Margaret, da of Richard Bruce (d 1974), of Sheffield; 2 s (Matthew James b 1959, Adam Richard b 1961); m 2, 1987, Gillian, *née* Beale; 1 s (Joel St John b 1988); *Career* cmmnd TA 415 Coast Regt RA 1954; asst master St Clement Danes GS 1955-59, princ lectr and head of English and drama Whitelands Coll Putney 1967-79 (lectr 1959, sr lectr 1961); presenter and scriptwriter BBC schs progs 1963-67: Adventures in English, Listening and Writing; presenter and writer Thames TV's Writer's Workshop 1970-79; winner of: Rediffusion Prize at Br Screen Awards 1970, Cholmondley Award for Poetry 1984; memb: Advsy Panel Daily Mirror (now W H Smith) Children as Writers/Young Writers Annual Competition 1954-, Ctee Nat Assoc of Sch Magazines 1964-67; Arvon Fndn: memb Cncl of Mgmnt 1968-, vice chm 1975-, chm Arvon at Lumb Bank 1980-88; involved in Poetry Soc/W H Smith Poets in Schools Scheme 1970-; FRSL 1985; *Books* incl: The Silent Mirror (1951), Grandad with Snails (1960, 1963), Poems by Children (ed, 1962), In Step with a Goat (1962), Miraclejack (1963), Sebastian (1966), There's a War On! (1970), The Way to Write Poetry (1982), The River and the Downs (1984), The Way to Write Short Stories (1986), Exit Wounds (1987, 1988), Holofernes (1988, 1989); *Clubs* Crime Writer's, Groucho's, Colony Room; *Style—* Michael Baldwin, Esq; 35 Gilbert Rd, Bromley, Kent BR1 3QP (☎ 081 4607147)

BALL, Denis William; MBE (1971); s of William Charles Thomas Ball, of 17 Warburton Close, Park Lane, Eastbourne, Sussex, and Dora Adelaide, *née* Smith; *b* 20 Oct 1928; *Educ* Tonbridge, BNC Oxford (MA); *m* 5 Aug 1972, Marja Tellervo (d 1987), da of Osmo Lumijarvi, of Sontula 42, Toijala, Finland; 2 s (Christian b 1975, Robin b 1976), 1 da (Sasha b 1981); *Career* served RN 1947-49, RNR 1953-85 (Lt Cdr 1958-); housemaster The King's Sch Canterbury 1954-72 (asst master 1953-72), headmaster Kelly Coll Tavistock 1972-85; dir: Western Bloodstock Ltd 1986-, James Wilkes plc 1987, Perkins Foods plc 1987-; conslt Throgmorton Redbridge Properties Ltd 1990-; Investment Management Ltd 1987-88; memb: Squash Rackets for Oxford Univ, Kent Real Tennis for Jesters, MCC, HMC 1972-85, HMA 1972-85; tstee Tavistock Sch 1972-85, vice chm of Govrs St Michael's Sch Tavistock 1974-; memb: Ickham PCC 1986- (treas 1990-), Johnson Club 1987-; *Recreations* Elizabethan history, cryptography, literary and mathematical puzzles, cricket, real tennis, golf; *Clubs* East India, Devonshire, Sports and Public Schools, MCC; *Style—* Denis Ball, Esq, MBE; Ickham Hall, Ickham, nr Canterbury, Kent

BALSTON, His Hon Judge Antony Francis; s of Cdr Edward Francis Balston, DSO, RN, of Oast House, Crowhurst, Battle, E Sussex, and Diana Beatrice Louise, *née* Ferrers; *b* 18 Jan 1939; *Educ* Downside, Christ's Coll Cambridge (MA); *m* 13 Aug 1966, Anne Marie Judith, da of Gerald Anthony Ball, MBE (d 1971); 2 s (James Edward Leopold b 1967, Andrew Timothy Edmund b 1969), 1 da (Alexandra Sarah Louise b 1972); *Career* Nat Serv RN 1957-59; admitted slr 1966; ptnr Herington Willings & Penry Davey of Hastings 1966-85, rec 1980, hon rec of Hastings 1984, circuit judge 1985; *Recreations* gardening; *Style—* His Hon Judge Balston; The Law Courts, Barker Rd, Maidstone, Kent (☎ 0622 754966)

BAMJI, Dr Andrew Nariman; s of Dr Nariman Sorabji Bamji (d 1978), of Highgate, London, and Joan Elizabeth, *née* Jermyn; *b* 14 Aug 1950; *Educ* Highgate Sch, Middx Hosp Med Sch Univ of London (MB BS); *m* 10 June 1978, Elizabeth Mary, da of Raymond William Millard, of Bridgwater, Somerset; 1 s (Nicholas b 1985), 1 da (Alexandra b 1981); *Career* conslt in rheumatology and rehabilitation: Brook General Hosp, Dreadnought Seamans Hosp 1983-89, Queen Mary's Hosp Sidcup, Erith and Dist Hosp 1983-; dir Elmstead Yr Disabled Unit QMH Sidcup 1985-, Chelsfield Park Hosp 1987-, clinical tutor and dir of med educn Frognal Centre for Med Studies 1990-; memb: Br Soc for Rheumatology, Med Disability Soc; chm SE Thames RHA Working Pty on Brain Injury Rehabilitation 1989-90; memb BMA, FRCP; *Books* Atlas of Clinical Rheumatology (eds Dieppe, Bacon, Bamji, Watt, 1986); *Recreations* wine, French holidays, gardening, antiques, pianola; *Style—* Dr Andrew Bamji; Queen Mary's Hospital, Frognal Ave, Sidcup, Kent DA14 6LT (☎ 081 302 2678, fax 081 308 0457)

BAMPTON, Deborah Ellen; s of Albert Richard Bampton, of 68 Castlefields, Istead Rise, Meopham, Kent, and Ann Ceila, *née* Johnson; *b* 7 Oct 1961; *Career* capt England Women's Football Team, player mangr Millwall Lionesses; *Style—* Miss Deborah Bampton; 46 Rider Close, Parish Gate Drive, Blackfen, Kent DA15 8TZ (☎ 081 859 5837)

BANCROFT, Brig Donald Royle Jackson; OBE (1961); s of Maj Peter Henson Bancroft (d 1969), and Florence Adolphine, *née* Jackson (d 1962); *b* 18 July 1916; *Educ* RMA Sandhurst; *m* 1, (m dis), Phyllis Catherine, *née* Angas (d 1977); m 2, 8 May 1948, Elizabeth Ann Rosetta, da of Maj Lawrence Lee Bazeley Angas, MC (d 1972), of S Aust, London and NY; 1 s (Richard Lee b 23 Nov 1950), 1 da (Catherine Clare Elizabeth b 3 March 1949); *Career* cmmnd KSLI 1936; WWII: France and Burma (depatches), Korea (despatches), E Africa (despatches); cmd KSLI 1953-56, cmd 149 Inf Bde 1962-65; def attaché and Cdr Cwlth Mission Korea 1966-68, ret 1968; farmer 1968-, breeder of Sussex Cattle and Blonde d'Acquitaine; pres Kilndown Br Legion, vice pres Bewl Flyfishers; *Recreations* shooting, fishing; *Clubs* Naval and Military; *Style—* Brig Donald Bancroft, OBE; Chicks Farm, Kilndown, Cranbrook, Kent (☎ 0892 890 396); Flat 19, 34 Sloane Court West, London SW3 (☎ 071 730 1058)

BANKS, Frank David; s of Samuel Banks, and Elizabeth Banks; *b* 11 April 1933; *Educ* Liverpool Collegiate Sch, Carnegie Mellon Univ; *m* 1, 1955, Catherine Jacob; 1 s, 2 da; m 2, 1967, Sonia Gay Coleman; 1 da; *Career* chm H Berkeley (Hldgs) Ltd, dir Constructors John Brown Ltd 1974-; FCA; *Style—* Frank Banks, Esq; Town House, Ightham, Sevenoaks, Kent TN15 9HH

BARBER, Colin Thomas; s of Frank Barber, OBE, of Folkestone, Kent, and Lilian Barber, MBE; *b* 8 Feb 1948; *Educ* Haileybury, Kingston Coll of Advanced Technol, Univ of London (BSc); *m* 9 June 1973, Diana Elizabeth, da of Peter Parkyn (d 1987), of SA; *Career* dir: Scac UK Ltd, Socomar Ltd, F Barber Properties Ltd; memb ICA 1972; FICA 1979; *Recreations* gardening, spectating amateur dramatics, tennis, bridge, watching rugby union and

American football; *Clubs* Old Haileyburian RFC, Bidborough Tennis, Leigh Tennis, The Club, The Danish, CGA, Bidborough Gardening Assoc, Bidborough Amateur Dramatic Soc, Tonbridge East Theatre, IOD; *Style*— Colin T Barber, Esq; Bidborough Close, Frank's Hollow Rd, Bidborough, Kent TN3 0UD; Unit 6, Colnestate, Old Bath Rd, Colnbrook, Bucks SU3 0NJ (☎ 0753 683530); c/o Scac UK Ltd, 9 Fairway, Green Lane, Hounslow, Middlesex TW4 6BU

BARBER, Frank; s of Sidney Barber, and Florence, *née* Seath; *b* 5 July 1923; *Educ* W Norwood Central Sch; *m* Dec 1945, Gertrude Kathleen, *née* Carson; 2 s (John b 1951, Alan b 1947 decd), 1 da (Ann b 1948); *Career* WWII Fl Lt RAFVR 1942-46; Lloyd's 1939-, underwriter Frank Barber & Others 1962-81, ptnr Morgan Fentiman & Barber 1968-; memb: Ctee of Lloyds (1977-80, 1981-85, 1987), Cncl of Lloyds (1983-85, 1987); chm Lloyd's Underwriters Non Marine Assoc 1972; dep chm: Br Insurers Euro Ctee 1983, Lloyd's 1983-84; *Recreations* music, walking, sailing; *Clubs* Royal Dart Yacht, Lloyd's Yacht; *Style*— Frank Barber, Esq; Godden House, Godden Green, Sevenoaks, Kent TN15 0HP (☎ 0732 61170); Morgan Fentiman & Barber, Lloyd's, London (☎ 071 327 3744, fax 071 623 8233)

BARBER, John David; s of Capt Frank Barber, OBE, of Folkestone, and Lilian Barber, *née* Graham, MBE; *b* 18 Oct 1949; *Educ* Haileybury and Imperial Serv Coll, Coll of St Mark and St John, Univ of Exeter (BEd); *m* July 1983, Christine Margaret, da of late George Faulkner, of Tunbridge Wells; 1 step s (Nicholas Dominic Baylis), 1 step da (Paula Michelle Baylis); *Career* house parent Dr Barnardo's Homes 1970-74; Yardley Court Prep Sch: asst master 1974-77, housemaster and sr master 1977-81, headmaster 1982-; dist rep IAPS Cncl 1987-89 (memb 1983-), chm IAPS Tennis Ctee 1990-, sec Yardley Court Assoc Tst; life memb: Br Moroccan Soc, Haileybury Soc; memb: Nat Tst, Eng Heritage, ISIS, NAHT, CGA, Tonbridge Civic Soc, Oast Theatre, Bidborough Amateur Dramatic Soc, Tonbridge Rotary, Pembury Hosp League of Friends, Tonbridge Parish Church, Assoc of Coll of Preceptors; *Recreations* matters educational, tennis, reading, philately, French and France, bridge, geography; *Clubs* Haileybury Old Boys Rugby; *Style*— John Barber, Esq; Yardley Court School, Somerhill, Tonbridge, Kent TN11 0NJ (☎ 0732 352124)

BARBROOK, Dr Alexander Thomas; s of Alexander John Barbrook (d 1982), and Evelyn Elizabeth Anne Barbrook (d 1986); *b* 20 Aug 1927; *Educ* Canton HS Cardiff, Univ Coll of Wales Cardiff (BA); *m* 1, 12 Aug 1955 (m dis 1978), Marie Patricia, da of Flt Lt Leonard Craven, RAF (d 1960); 1 s (Richard Alexander b 21 June 1956), 1 da (Helen Marie b 16 Aug 1960); m 2, 17 Aug 1981, Margaret Ann Clucas, da of Arthur Read, of Wolverhampton; *Career* asst lectr Univ of Nottingham 1954-56, princ Educnl Centres of York and S Wales 1956-61, lectr in politics Loughborough Univ 1961-66; Univ of Kent: lectr and sr lectr Bd of Politics and Govt 1967-75; dir Sch of Continuing Educn 1975-, memb Universities Cncl for Adult and Continuing Educn; FRSA 1981; *Books* God Save the Commonwealth: An Electoral History of Massachusetts (1972), Patterns of Political Behaviour (1976), Power and Protest in American Life (with C Bolt, 1980); *Recreations* music, travel, food and wine, arts; *Clubs* Reform; *Style*— Dr Alexander Barbrook; 4 Church Hill, Chilham, Canterbury, Kent CT4 8DA (☎ 0227 730472); School of Continuing Education, The University, Canterbury, Kent CT2 7NZ (☎ 0227 764000 ext 3502, fax 0227 458745)

BARHAM, David George Wilfrid; JP (Kent 1961), DL (Kent 1976); s of Harold Arthur Barham (d 1978), of Rolvenden, Kent, and Edith Dulcie Brown, *née* Taylor (d 1988); *b* 6 Oct 1926; *Educ* Malvern, RAC Cirencester (Dip Estate Mgmnt); *m* 28 Oct 1955, Catherine Margaret, da of Col Rixon Bucknall, MBE (d 1975), of Rotherfield, Sussex; 3 s (William b 1958, Edward b 1962, Robert b 1965), 1 da (Jennifer b 1957); *Career* Lt RHG 1944-48; farmer, land agent in private practice; general cmmr Taxation 1960-; former chm Kent Branch CLA, memb Kent CC for Tenterden 1959-69; chm: Kent TAVRA Assoc 1975-81, Kent Ctee COSIRA (now Rural Devpt Cmmn) 1982-89; High Sheriff of Kent 1974-75; FRICS; *Recreations* gardening, country pursuits; *Clubs* Army and Navy, RAC; *Style*— D G W Barham, Esq, JP, DL

BARKER, Hon Adam Campbell; s of Baroness Trumpington of Sandwich (Jean, *née* Campbell-Harris) (Life Baroness), and William Alan Barker, of Sandwich, Kent (d 1988); *b* 31 Aug 1955; *Educ* The Kings Sch Canterbury, Queens' Coll Cambridge (MA); *m* 1985, Elizabeth Mary, da of Eric Marsden, OBE; 1 s (Christopher Adam b 1989), 1 da (Virginia Giverny b 1987); *Career* lawyer; assoc Webster & Sheffield NY 1980-; barr 12 King's Bench Walk London 1978-80; *Recreations* golf, tennis, horse racing, bridge; *Clubs* Oxford and Cambridge, Royal St George's (Sandwich), Hurlingham, Pilgrims; *Style*— The Hon Adam Barker; Rose Cottage, 54 King St, Sandwich, Kent CT13 9BL (☎ 0304 617256); 169 East 90th Street 9, NY 10128, USA (☎ 010 212 369 0723); 19th Floor, 237 Park Ave, NY 10020, USA (☎ 010 212 808 6128)

BARKER, Richard Philip; s of Philip Watson Barker (d 1971), and Helen May, *née* Latham (d 1957); *b* 17 July 1939; *Educ* Repton, Trinity Coll Cambridge (MA), Univ of Bristol (Cert Ed); *m* 30 July 1966, Imogen Margaret, da of Sir Ronald Montague Joseph Harris, KCVO, CB, of Slyfield Farmhouse, Stoke D'Abernon, Surrey; 2 s (Jolyon b 1967, Thorold b 1971), 1 da (Rosalind b 1969); *Career* asst master: Bedales Sch 1963-65, Marlborough 1967-81; dir A Level Business Studies Project 1966-75, lectr Inst of Educn London 1974-75, headmaster Sevenoaks Sch 1981-; memb various ctees HMC; Understanding Business (series ed, 1975-); *Recreations* fishing, sailing, beekeeping, educational matters; *Clubs* RSA; *Style*— Richard Barker, Esq; Sevenoaks School, Sevenoaks, Kent TN13 1HU (☎ 0732 455133, fax 0732 456143)

BARKER, Prof Theodore Cardwell; s of Norman Humphrey Barker (d 1973), and Louie Nettleton, *née* Cardwell (d 1970); *b* 19 July 1923; *Educ* Cowley Sch St Helens, Jesus Coll Oxford (MA), Univ of Manchester (PhD); *m* 2 Aug 1955, Joy Marie, da of Ernest Pierce (d 1974); *Career* prof of econ and social history Univ of Kent at Canterbury 1964-76 (fndr memb), subsequently prof of econ history Univ of London (now emeritus); Int Hist Congress 1990- (chm Br Nat Ctee 1976-, memb Central Bureau 1980-90); memb Econs Bd and chm History Bd CNAA 1976-80; chm: Mgmnt Ctee Inst of Hist Res Univ of London 1977-88, Athlone Press Ctee; pres: Econ History Soc 1986-89 (hon sec 1960-86), sometime cncl memb Royal Hist Soc; FRHistS 1963; *Books* A Merseyside Town in the Industrial Revolution (with J R Harris, 1954), The Girdlers' Company (1957), Pilkington Brothers and the Glass Industry (1960), Business History (with R H Campbell, Peter Mathias and B S Yamey, 1960), A History of London Transport (with Michael Robbins, volume I 1963, volume II 1976), The Carpenters' Company (with B W E Alford, 1968), An Economic History of Transport in England (with C I Savage, 1974), A History of British Pewter (with M J Hatcher, 1974), The Long March of Everyman (ed, 1974), The Glassmakers (1977), The Transport Contractors of Rye (1982), The Economic and Social Effects of the Spread of Motor Vehicles (ed, 1987), An Illustrated History of London Transport (1990), The Dietary Surveys of Dr Edward Smith (with D J Oddy and John Yudkin); *Recreations* walking, driving, trying to think; *Clubs* Reform; *Style*— Prof Theodore Barker

BARLAS, Dr John Alexander; TD (1967); s of Ernest Douglas Montague Barlas (d 1952), and Elena Georgina Matilda, *née* Kenyon (d 1954); *b* 21 Aug 1921; *Educ* Felsted, St Thomas's Hosp Univ of London (MB BS, MRCS, MRCGP, LRCP); *m* 30 Oct 1948, Pamela Honor, da of John Keith Finlayson Coutanche (d 1951); 2 da ((Honor) Jane b 23 Aug 1950, Shena Rozel b 11 June 1954); *Career* Capt RAMC 1944, RMO Royal W African Frontier Force 1944-46, Capt RAMC (TA) 1954, RMO 4/5 Bn Royal W Kent Regt (TA) 1954, Maj RAMC (TA); house physician paediatrics St Helier Hosp Carshalton 1944, supernumeracy registrar paediatrics St Thomas's Hosp 1946, sr house offr Putney Hosp 1947; GP: Eastbourne 1948, Tonbridge 1950-81, Sevenoaks 1981-87; admty surgn and agent Tonbridge area 1954-81, clinical asst Geriatric Dept Pembury Hosp 1954-87; clerk Shipbourne Parish Cncl 1986-, memb Tonbridge Cncl of Social Serv 1988-, chm and tstee High Hilden Old People's Home; memb BMA; *Recreations* riding, fishing, travelling; *Style*— Dr John Barlas, TD; Higlers, Shipbourne, Kent

BARNARD, Derek Ernest; s of George Alfred Barnard, of Gillingham, Kent, and Kathleen Teresa, *née* Murphy; *b* 6 Oct 1944; *Educ* Gillingham Tech HS, St Lukes Coll Exeter, Birkbeck Coll London (CertEd, BSc, MSc, DipGeog); *m* 22 Aug 1970, Sheila Maureen, da of Frederick George Hammond, of Larkfield, Kent; 1 s (Ian b 1979), 2 da (Alison b 1975, Helen b 1983); *Career* Tunbridge Wells GS for Boys: dep headteacher 1980-88, headteacher 1988-; treas Crowborough CC 1981-; *Books* Index To Wisden Cricketers Almanack (1985); *Recreations* cricket, soccer, collecting antiquarian books; *Clubs* Royal Over-Seas League; *Style*— Derek Barnard, Esq; 150 Southridge Rise, Crowborough, East Sussex TN6 1LL (☎ 0892 653024); Tunbridge Wells Grammar School for Boys, St John's Rd, Tunbridge Wells, Kent TN4 9XB (☎ 0892 29551)

BARNES, Sir Denis Charles; KCB (1967, CB 1964); s of Frederick Charles Barnes (d 1944); *b* 15 Dec 1914; *Educ* Hulme GS Manchester, Merton Coll Oxford; *m* 1938, Patricia, da of Col Charles Murray Abercrombie, CMG, CBE (d 1933), of Prestbury, Cheshire; *Career* entered Home Civil Service 1938, dep sec Miny of Labour 1964-66, perm sec 1966-73, chm MSC 1973-75; dir: Glynwed Ltd, General Accident Fire & Life Assurance Corporation 1976-85; pres Manpower Soc 1976-, perm sec Dept of Employment 1968-73; FIPM; *Clubs* Savile; *Style*— Sir Denis Barnes, KCB; The Old Inn, 30 The Street, Wittersham, Kent (☎ 079 77 528)

BARNES, (Anthony) John (Lane); s of Lt-Col Cyril Lane Barnes, MC, MBE (d 1976), of Plymouth, Devon, and Joan Lewis, *née* Gibson; *b* 9 April 1937; *Educ* Plymouth Coll, Gonville and Caius Coll Cambridge (MA); *m* 2 Jan 1965, Mary Leonora, da of Leonard Burton Parkes (d 1964), of Walsall, Staffs; 1 s (David b 4 Oct 1966), 2 da (Eleanor b 4 June 1968, Charlotte b 28 Sept 1972); *Career* Nat Serv RN 1956-58, cmmnd Midshipman 1956, Sub Lt 1957; Drosier fellowship Gonville and Caius Coll Cambridge 1961-64, asst lectr in political sci Dept of Govt LSE 1964-65, lectr in political sci LSE 1965-, archives fell Churchill Coll Cambridge 1990; memb Advsy Cncl Inst of Contemporary Br History, sr vice chm Fedn of Univ Cons and Unionist Assocs 1961-62; Cons parly candidate Walsall N 1964-70, gen elections; served on Cons Pty Policy Gp on: Machinery of Govt 1964-65 and 1978-79,

Regnl and Local Govt 1966-68; memb Cncl of Navy Records Soc 1967-70, alderman Greenwich Borough Cncl 1968-73, memb Cons Nat Advsy Ctee on Educn 1969-85, chm SE Area Advsy Ctee on Educn 1971-74, vice chm Sevenoaks Cons Assoc 1971-74; Kent CC: memb 1973-89, vice chm Educn Ctee 1973-77 and 1987-89, chm Educn Ctee 1977-82, chm Libraries Sub Ctee 1984-85, vice chm 1985-87, chm Schs Sub Ctee 1987-89; memb: Cncl and Court Univ of Kent 1977-82, SE Thames RHA 1984-, Bishop's Cncl Diocese of Rochester 1987-, Cncl of Nat Academic Awards 1988-; chm Rochester Diocesan Bd of Educn 1987- (memb 1981-87); author of numerous articles on political subjects in both academic and gen jls, hist advsr on documentaries for both BBC and ITV; *Books* Baldmin A Biography (with R K Middlemas, 1969), Contemporary History in Europe (contrib, 1969), The Decade of Disillusion (contrib, 1972), The Leo Amery Diaries Volume One 1896-1929 (co-ed D J Nicholson, 1980), Ruling Performance (contrib, 1988), Contemporary History Practice and Method (contrib, 1988), The Empire at Bay The Diaries of L S Amery Volume Two (co-ed D J Nicholson, 1988), Blackwells Biographical Dictionary of Twentieth Century British History (contrib, 1990); *Recreations* cricket, listening to music; *Style—* John Barnes, Esq; Furnace Farm, Furnace Lane, Lamberhurst, Kent TN3 8LE (☎ 0892 890788); London School of Economics, Houghton St, London WC2A 2AE (☎ 071 405 7686, fax 071 242 0392)

BARNES, John Norman; s of Norman Henry Barnes, of Poole, Dorset, and Helen Alberta, *née* Stocker; *b* 16 March 1942; *Educ* Hatfield Coll; *m* 17 April 1971, Patricia Dorothy, da of Capt Alan Lloyd Hagger (d 1985); 2 da (Nicola Louise Patricia, Amy Jane Elizabeth); *Career* nuclear scientist; res offr Nuclear Electric plc 1969-, radiation safety advsr Central Radiochemical Lab Gravesend; cncllr (Cons) Gravesend Borough Cncl: Housing and Enviromental Health Ctee, Recreation and Amenities Ctee, Leisure Devpt Ctee, Engrg and Planning Ctee, Fin and Admin Ctee; sch govr Istead Rise Infants and Juniors; memb: Gravesham Cons Assoc, Soc of Radiological Protection; MSRP; *Recreations* sportsboat driver/owner; *Clubs* Kent Boat and Ski; *Style—* John Barnes, Esq; Nuclear Electric plc, Canal Rd, Gravesend, Kent DA13 9LB (☎ 0474 532165, fax 0474 532134, telex 965512); 31 Worcester Close, Istead Rise, Gravesend, Kent DA13 9LB

BARNETT, Christopher Robin; s of Harold Earnest Barnett, of Portsmouth, and Nora Lily Barnett; *b* 18 March 1944; *Educ* Sri Lanka and Singapore, Open Univ (BA); *m* 20 Jan 1967, Gloria Rosetta, da of John Rowe (d 1987), of Milton Keynes; 1 s (Matthew b 1973), 2 da (Hannah b 1976, Rebecca b 1977); *Career* asst dir Housing Devpt Corp Milton Keynes 1973-82, sr asst dir Milton Keynes Borough Cncl 1982-85, dir Health and Housing Dover Dist Cncl; memb: Rotary Club Dover, Temple Ewell PCC; ASVA 1976, FIH 1979; *Recreations* running, French travel, wine, sailing; *Style—* Christopher Barnett, Esq; Dover District Council, Honeywood Rd, Dover, Kent (☎ 0304 821199, fax 0304 824917)

BARNETT, Hon Mrs (Kathleen Irene Mary); *née* Hennessy; da of 1 Baron Windlesham, OBE (d 1953); *b* 1914; *Educ* private; *m* 1947, Wilfred Ernest Barnett, 3 s of Ernest Barnett, of Chesterfield, Derbyshire; 2 s (Robin George, Nicholas James); *Style—* The Hon Mrs W Barnett; Pullington Cottage, Benenden, Cranbrook, Kent (☎ 0580 240435)

BARRATT, Oliver Chester; s of John Chester Barratt, and Shiela Vivian, *née* Power; *b* 2 May 1962; *Educ* Sevenoaks Sch, Falmouth Sch of Art (BA); *m* 7 April 1990, Tabitha, da of Peter Saunders; *Career* art tutor CARE for Mentally Handicapped Adults 1986, Henry Moore sculpture fell Canterbury Sch of Art 1990; regular sculpture exhibitions in London and Kent 1986-90; *Style—* Oliver Barratt, Esq; 1 Oldbury Hall Cottage, Ightham, Kent TN15 9DD (☎ 0732 885907)

BARRATT, (Francis) Russell; CB (1975); s of Frederick Russell Barratt (d 1957); *b* 16 Nov 1924; *Educ* Durban HS, Clifton, Univ Coll Oxford; *m* 1, 1949 (m dis 1978), Janet Mary, *née* Sherborne; 3 s; m 2, 1979, Josephine Norah Harrison, da of Brig D McCririck (d 1947); *Career* dep sec HM Treasy; *Recreations* reading, music, golf; *Style—* Russell Barratt, Esq, CB; Little Paddocks, Smallhythe Rd, Tenterden, Kent TN30 7LY (☎ 058 06 3734)

BARRY, Sir (Lawrence) Edward Anthony Tress; 5 Bt (UK 1899), of St Leonard's Hill, Clewer, Berks, and Keiss Castle, Wick, Caithness-shire; Baron de Barry of Portugal, Lord of the Manors of Ockwells and Lillibrooke, Berks; s of Maj Sir Rupert Barry, 4 Bt, MBE (d 1977); *b* 1 Nov 1939; *Educ* Haileybury; *m* 1968 (m dis 1990), Fenella, da of Hilda Hoult, of Knutsford, Cheshire; 1 s, 1 da; *Heir* s, William Rupert Philip Tress Barry b 13 Dec 1973; *Career* former Capt Gren Gds; *Style—* Sir Edward Barry, Bt; 3 Sunnyside Cottages, Warehorne Rd, Hamstreet, Kent (☎ 023 373 2454)

BARRY, Sheila, Lady; Sheila Georgina Veronica; da of Maj George Joseph Francis White, MBE, of Longacre, Andover Rd, Winchester; *m* 12 May 1951, as his 2 w, Maj Sir Rupert Barry, 4 Bt, MBE (d 1977); 3 s (Timothy b 1952, Nicholas b 1957, Jonathan b 1960), 2 da (Tara b 1954, Xandra b 1962); *Style—* Sheila, Lady Barry; Brisley Rise, Willesborough Lees, Ashford, Kent

BARSTOW, Clive; s of Alfred Barstow (d 1982), of Meltham, Huddersfield, and Marjorie Betty, *née* Wright; *b* 2 Feb 1956; *Educ* Huddersfield Sch of Art, Gloucestershire Coll of Art and Design (BA), Chelsea Sch of Art (MA); *m* 15 July 1978, Josephine, da of Eugeniusz Jozwik, of Skegness, Lincolnshire; 1 s (Rory b 10 May 1987); *Career* artist; exhibitions incl: New Contemporaries (ICA London), Third Seoul Int Print Bienalle (Korea) 1981, Mappin Gallery (Sheffield) 1982, Royal Soc of Painters & Etchers 1989, Aspex Gallery (Portsmouth) 1983; works in collections of: Nat Museum Modern Art Korea, Graves Gallery Sheffield, Br Cncl, DOE; lectr: Brighton Poly, Newcastle Poly, Sheffield Poly, Sunderland Poly, Kingston Poly, Maidstone Coll of Art, Cardiff Coll of Art, Hull Coll of Art, Gloucestershire Coll of Art; sr lectr in art & design Middlesex Poly; *Recreations* football, tennis; *Clubs* Sutton Valence Football, Sutton Valence Tennis; *Style—* Clive Barstow, Esq; Middlesex Polytechnic, Cat Hill, Barnet, Hertfordshire EN4 8HT (☎ 081 368 1299)

BARTLEET, Rt Rev David Henry; *see*: Tonbridge, Bishop of

BARTON, Dr Claire Melanie; da of Lt Cdr David Ivan Barton, RN (d 1977), and Heather Mary Barton; *b* 28 March 1960; *Educ* Edgehill Coll Bideford, Clare Coll Cambridge (MA, MB BChir), St Thomas's Hosp Med Sch London (MRCP); *Career* house physician St Thomas Hosp 1984, house surgn Kingston Gen Hosp 1985; sr house offr: Osler Chest Unit Churchill Hosp Oxford, Cardiology and Gen Med John Radcliffe Gen Hosp Oxford 1986; jr res fell Royal Marsden Hosp Surrey 1987, res fell and post grad student in tumour pathology Royal Marsden Hosp Fulham Rd London; res fell and hon registrar Cancer Res Campaign Clinical Trials Unit Queen Elizabeth Hosp Birmingham 1988, res fell and sr registrar Med Oncology Hammersmith Hosp London 1989-; memb BMA; *Recreations* tennis, badminton, theatre, film, lit; *Style—* Dr Claire Barton; 11 Old Orchard Lane, Leybourne, Kent ME19 94H (☎ 0732 848982); Hammersmith Hospital, Dept of Clinical Oncology, Du Cane Rd, London W12 (☎ 081 743 2030, fax 081 743 8766)

BARTON, Dr David Garbutt; s of James Richard Barton (d 1983), of York, and Marion Joyce, *née* Garbutt; *b* 29 Jan 1937; *Educ* St Peters Sch York, Emmanuel Coll Cambridge, Univ Coll Hosp Med Sch Univ of London (MA, MB BChir, MRCS, LRCS, DCH, DObstRCOG, FPCert); *m* 2 April 1961, Bernice Ann, da of George Birnie Banton, of Wallasey; 2 s (Sebastian b 1963, Hugo b 1968); *Career* 2 Lt 5 W Yorks Regt (TA) 1958, Lt 1960, resigned 1962; GP Herne Bay Kent 1968-; co surgn St John Ambulance Kent, memb St John Cncl for Kent; Freeman City of London 1977, Liveryman Worshipful Soc of Apothecaries 1977; FRCS (Ed) 1969, FRCGP 1976; OStJ 1990; *Books* Child Care in General Practice (contrib 2 edn, 1982); *Recreations* theatre, ballet, opera, memb Glyndbourne; *Clubs* BMA London, Kent and Canterbury, Kent CCC; *Style—* Dr David Barton; 64 Western Esplanade, Herne Bay, Kent CT6 8DN; Lower Chitty Farm, Chislet, nr Canterbury, Kent; St Annes Surgery, Herne Bay, Kent (☎ 0227 366 945)

BARTON, (Malcolm) Peter Speight; s of Michael Hugh Barton, of Brockenhurst, Hants, and Diana Blanche, *née* Taylor; *b* 26 March 1937; *Educ* St Edward's Sch Oxford, Magdalen Coll Oxford (BA); *m* 7 Sept 1963, Julia Margaret, da of Hon James Louis Lindsay, *qv*; 2 s (Henry (Harry) b 1967, Christopher b 1970), 1 da (Fenella b 1965); *Career* Nat Serv 2 Lt Oxford and Bucks LI (later 1 Greenjackets) 1955-56, Capt London Rifle Bde Rangers TA 1960-63; admitted slr 1964; ptnr Travers Smith Braithwaite 1967-86; memb Stock Exchange 1986; md Shearson Lehman Hutton Inc 1986-; memb: Law Soc, Int Bar Assoc; *Recreations* walking, shooting, skiing; *Clubs* City Law; Primrose Hill, Hawkhurst, Kent (☎ 058075 2132); 29 Campden Street, London W8 (☎ 01 229 4006); Shearson Lehman Hutton Inc, 1 Broadgate, London EC2M 7HA (☎ 01 260 2931 & 01 601 0011)

BARWICK, David John; JP; s of Richard Robert Oliver Barwick, OBE (d 1982), and Phylis Mary, *née* Goodban; *b* 10 Sept 1932; *Educ* St Lawrence Coll Ramsgate; *m* 4 Oct 1958, Gillian Cowell, da of Gerald Cowell Williams (d 1985); 3 s (Richard b 1960, Jonathan b 1961, Jeremy b 1963), 1 da (Susan); *Career* builder; md RJB (Plant) Ltd 1974-90, chm R J Barwick & Sons Ltd 1982-90 (dir 1960-87, md 1975-90); pres Southern Region Bldg Employers Confedn 1984; FBIM, FCIOB; *Recreations* golf, gardening; *Clubs* Royal Cinque Ports Golf, IOD; *Style—* David J Barwick, Esq, JP; Overglen, St Clare Rd, Walmer, Deal, Kent CT14 7QB (☎ 0304 374897); Coombe Valley Rd, Dover, Kent CT17 0UJ (☎ 0304 203716, fax 0304 240293)

BASDEN, Rev Father Christopher David; s of James R Basden, of Kerens Ave, Elkins, W Va, USA, and Bernadette Joan Mary, *née* Glencross; *b* 19 Dec 1952; *Educ* Salesian Coll Beirut Lebanon, Georgetown Univ Washington DC USA (BA), St John's Seminary Wonersh Surrey (Cert in Theology); *Career* ordained to catholic priesthood at Jesuit Church Wimbledon by the Most Rev William Barden Archbishop of Isphahan of the Latins 1979; priest: St Teresa's Ashford 1980-83, St Stephen's Welling 1983-90, St Francis Maidstone 1990-; co-ordinating chaplain: St Catherine's and St Columbia's Schs Bexleyheath 1985-90, St Simon Stock Sch Maidstone 1990-; *Recreations* pilgrimage, recusant history, education; *Style—* The Rev Father Christopher Basden; Grove House, Week St, Maidstone, Kent ME14 1RH (☎ 0622 756217)

BASU, Himansu Kumar; s of Sudhangsu Kumar Basu, of Calcutta, and Rajlaxmi, *née* Ghosh (d 1950); *b* 10 April 1934; *Educ* Univ of Calcutta (MB BS), Univ of Liverpool (PhD), MRCOG; *m* 1 May 1976, Lynda Ann, da of Ronald Sanders, of Rochester, Kent; 1 s (Christopher Kumar b 1984), 1 da

(Maya Louise b 1979); *Career* lectr in obstetrics and gynaecology Univ of Liverpool 1965-72, conslt obstetrician and gynaecologist Dartford and Gravesend Health Authy 1972-; RCOG: memb Cncl 1977-83 and 1988-, memb Fin and Exec Ctee 1980-83, memb Examinations Ctee 1981-84; RSM Section of Obstetrics and Gynaecology: memb Cncl 1979-88, hon sec 1983-84, vice pres 1985-88; memb: Osprey's Gynaecological Soc, SE Gynaecological Soc (sec 1976-82, vice pres 1983-86, treas 1987-); examiner: MBChB, DRCOG, MRCOG 1984-; pres Rotary Club of Northfleet 1989-90 (memb 1980-); FRCS 1963, FRCOG 1984; *Recreations* travel, photography, good food; *Style*— Himansu Basu, Esq; Glengarry, Woodlands Lane, Shorne, Gravesend, Kent DA12 3HH (☎ 0474 82 2294); Fawkham Manor Hospital, Manor Lane, Fawkham, Kent DA3 8ND (☎ 0474 879900, fax 0474 879827)

BASU, Dr Ranendra Nath; s of Bimal Chandra Bose (d 1972), of Allahabad, India, and Champak, *née* Sircar; *b* 15 July 1941; *Educ* Allahabad Univ India (BSc), Calcutta Univ (MB BS), Delhi (MD), London (MRCPath); *m* 1, 31 Oct 1965 (m dis 1977), Shubhra Datta, da of Kumud Nath Datta (d 1968), of Calcutta, India; 1 s (Alok b 1968), 1 da (Puja b 1973); m 2, 18 Feb 1978, Susan Alberta; *Career* registrar in pathology St George's Hosp London 1975-78, sr registrar histopathology and cytopathology Charling Cross Hosp London 1978-84, conslt pathologist i/c cytopathology Tunbridge Wells Health Dist 1985-; memb: Int Acad of Cytology, Br Div Int Acad of Pathology; *Recreations* fly-fishing, photography, gardening, travel; *Clubs* Camera (London); *Style*— Dr Ranendra Basu; Leywoods, 38 Glenmore Park, Tunbridge Wells, Kent TN2 5NZ (☎ 0892 547486); Pembury Hospital, Pembury, Tunbridge Wells, Kent (☎ 0892 823535)

BATEMAN, Barry Richard James; *b* 21 June 1945; *Educ* Univ of Exeter (BA); *m* Christine; 1 s (James b 1980); *Career* res dir Hoare Govett 1972-75 (investmt analyst 1967-72), mktg dir Datastream 1975-81, sr mktg dir Fidelity International Management Ltd 1981-86, md Fidelity Investment Services Ltd 1986-; memb Soc of Investmt Analysts; *Recreations* photography, music, E Type Jaguars, writing; *Clubs* Jaguar Drivers; *Style*— Barry Bateman, Esq; High Trees, Pine Coombe, Shirley Hills, Croydon, Surrey CR0 5HS (☎ 081 656 8638); Fidelity Investment Services Ltd, Oakhill House, 130 Tonbridge Rd, Hildenborough, Tonbridge, Kent TN11 9DZ (☎ 0732 361 144, fax 0732 832 792, telex 957 344 FIMLO)

BATEMAN, Col Giles Barthrop; OBE (1982); s of Sqn Ldr Anthony Edward Barthrop Bateman (d 1970), and Dorothea May Pryce, *née* Aspinall (d 1973); *b* 10 Jan 1939; *Educ* Sutton Valence, Staff Coll Nat Def Coll; *m* 31 Dec 1966, Susan Jennifer (Sue), da of Robert Ben Chalcraft, of Greenford, Middlesex; 2 s (Noel Christopher Barthrop b 1969, Alexander James Barthrop (Alex) b 1972); *Career* cmmnd Queen's Own Royal W Kent Regt 1958; regtl and staff posts incl: England and Cyprus 1958, Kenya 1961, Br Guiana 1964, Singapore 1965-67, Bahrain 1968, NI 1969 and 1975, Aust 1976-78; Sch of Serv Intelligence 1982-85, MOD def intelligence and gen staff posts 1985-90; *Recreations* gardening, music, books; *Clubs* Royal Cwlth Soc; *Style*— Col Giles Bateman, OBE; c/o Lloyds Bank, Hawkhurst, Kent; MOD, Main Building, Whitehall Ave, London SW1 (☎ 071 218 6789)

BATES, John; s of William James Bates, and Ethel, *née* Young; *b* 9 Nov 1930; *Educ* Portchester Secdy Sch, Purbrook Park HS, King's Coll London, Open Univ (BA); *m* 8 Aug 1959, Marita Joan, da of Ronald Richard Powell; 3 da (Sarah Jane b 1962, Rebekah Joan b 1964, Judith Anna b 1966); *Career* Nat Serv RA 1948-50; asst teacher: Portsea Boys Secdy 1953-55, Bridgemary Mixed Secdy 1955-60; head of dept Swanmore Mixed Secdy 1960-68; dep head: Herne Bay Mixed Secdy 1968-71, Sorothy Stringer Mixed Secdy 1971-75; head Archers Court Secdy 1975-; lay preacher Methodist church 1953-; ldr Hampshire Methodist Church Youth Club; fell London Coll of Theology 1953, memb NAHT 1975; *Style*— John Bates, Esq; Archers Court School, Whitfield, Dover, Kent CT16 2EG

BATES, Maj-Gen Sir (Edward) John (Hunter); KBE (1969, OBE 1952), CB (1965), MC (1944); s of Ernest Bates (d 1954), of Bournemouth; *b* 5 Dec 1911; *Educ* Wellington, Corpus Christi Coll Cambridge (MA); *m* 1947, Sheila Ann, da of Maj Herbert Norman (d 1962), of Victoria, BC, Canada; 2 s, 2 da; *Career* dir RA WO 1961-64, Cmdt RMCS 1964-67, Col Cmdt RA 1966-76, dir Royal Def Acad 1967-69, Special Cmmr Duke of York's Royal Mil Sch 1972-; personnel dir Thomson Regional Newspapers 1969-78; master Worshipful Co of Haberdashers 1978-79; *Recreations* fishing, shooting; *Clubs* Army and Navy, Rye Golf; *Style*— Maj-Gen Sir John Bates, KBE, CB, MC; Chaffenden, Frensham Rd, Rolvenden Layne, Cranbrook, Kent TN17 4NP (☎ 0580 241 536)

BATES, Dr Rosalind Eva; da of Kennedy Cameron, of Cumbria, and Eva Killen, *née* Fleming; *b* 16 Jan 1943; *Educ* Victoria Coll Belfast, Queens Univ Belfast (MB BCh, BAO), Univ of London (DPM, MRCPsych); *m* 9 July 1966, (William) Terence Gardner Bates, s of W E Bates (d 1974), of Belfast and Slough; 2 da (Clare Winifred Fleming b 1969, Marion Louise Cameron b 1971); *Career* sr registar Bethlem Royal and Maudsley Hosps 1980-82, conslt psychiatrist Bromley Health Authy 1982-; memb: Br Inst of Mental Handicap, Br Neuropsychiatric Assoc; *Recreations* contemporary literature, theatre, classical music, learning foreign languages; *Clubs* Cwlth Tst; *Style*— Dr Rosalind Bates; Bassetts Centre, Starts Hill Rd, Farnborough, Kent BR6 7WF (☎ 0689 53388)

BATEUP, John Brian; s of John Maynard Bateup (d 1971), of Horsmonden, Kent, and Dorothy Nellie, *née* Rose; *b* 22 Aug 1949; *Educ* The Judd Sch Tonbridge Kent; *m* 5 Jan 1974, Christine Anne, da of Rev William Preston, of Horsmonden, Kent; 3 s (Matthew b 1983, Timothy b 1986, Andrew b 1989), 2 da (Helen b 1975, Anne b 1977); *Career* actuary; md: Reliance Mutual Insurance Society Ltd 1982-, The British Life Office Ltd, Reliance Fire and Accident Insurance Corporation Ltd, Reliance Unit Managers Ltd, Reliance Pension Scheme Trustee Ltd; FIA; *Recreations* sport, especially table-tennis; *Clubs* IOD, Actuarial Dining; *Style*— John B Bateup, Esq; Reliance House, Tunbridge Wells, Kent TN4 8BL (☎ 0892 510033, fax 0892 510676)

BATTERBURY, His Hon Judge Paul Tracy Shepherd; TD 1972 (and 2 bars 1978 and 1984), DL (Greater London 1986), rep DL (London Borough of Housing 1989-); s of Hugh Basil John Batterbury (d 1986), of Sidcup, and Inez, *née* Shepherd; *b* 25 Jan 1934; *Educ* St Olaves GS, Univ of Bristol (LLB); *m* 11 April 1962, Sheila Margaret, da of John Arthur Watson, of Eltham; 1 s (Simon b 1963), 1 da (Sarah b 1967); *Career* RAF 1952-55, Maj RA (TA) 1959-85; called to the Bar Inner Temple 1959; dep circuit judge 1975-79, recorder 1979-83, circuit judge 1983-; memb Sidcup and Chislehurst UDC 1960-62, memb Greenwich Borough Cncl 1968-71 (chm Housing Ctee 1970-71), tstee St Olaves Prep Sch New Eltham 1969-, fndr chm Gallipoli Meml Lectures 1985, vice pres SE London St John Ambulance 1988-; *Recreations* walking, caravanning; *Clubs* Civil Service; *Style*— His Hon Judge Batterbury, TD, DL; 5 Paper Buildings, Temple, London EC4 (☎ 071 583 9275)

BATTRICK, Capt Michael Christopher; s of Cdr David Leonard Battrick, RD, of Durban, SA, and Mary, *née* Elliot-Brown; *b* 3 Feb 1946; *Educ* Plympton GS Plymouth, Plymouth Sch of Navigation, Univ of Southampton Sch of Maritime Studies (Master Mariner); *m* 6 July 1968, Rosalind Alexandra, da of Michael Geoffrey Charles Thomas, of Folkestone; 1 s (Charles David b 22 Sept 1978), 3 da (Sarah Jane b 28 Sept 1967, Catherine Leah b 20 March 1971, Rebecca Moray b 3 Jan 1973); *Career* cadet MN 1962-66, navigating offr Shell Tankers 1966-73; master: ARC Marine Southampton 1973, P&O Southern Ferries 1974-75; Trinity House Pilot Poole 1975-79, Trinity House London Dist 1988, first class PLA; sec London Dist UK Pilots' Assoc 1981- (Poole Dist 1975-79), govr Folkestone Sch for Girls 1984- (Alderney Middle Sch Dorset 1975-79), dist cncllr Shepway 1987-, charter tstee town of Folkestone 1987-; MNI 1975-85; *Recreations* caravanning, badminton, gardening, computing; *Clubs* Caravan, Goodwin Sands Potholing; *Style*— Capt Michael Battrick; 7 Broadfield Rd, Folkestone, Kent CT20 2JT (☎ 0303 55808); Pilotage Department, Port of London Authority, Alexandra House, Royal Terrace Pier, Gravesend, Kent DA12 2BD (☎ 0474 567716)

BATTRICK, Peter John; s of Lt Cdr John Victor Battrick, RNR, of Keswick, Cumbria, and Elizabeth Margaret, *née* Brindle; *b* 16 March 1953; *Educ* Queen Elizabeth GS Blackburn, Univ of Lancaster (BA), St Martin's Coll (PGCE); *m* 7 Aug 1976, Karen Elizabeth, da of John Walsh, of Blackburn, Lancashire; *Career* teacher: Mount Pleasant HS Salisbury Rholdesia 1975-76, King Edward VII Sch Lytham 1977-85; regnl pub affrs mangr for Kent and E Sussex Nat Tst 1989- (asst info offr for Cumbria and Lancs 1986-88); memb: Lancashire CC 1960-, Wadhurst CC 1990-; *Recreations* cricket, walking, gardening, good books; *Style*— Peter Battrick, Esq; The National Trust, Scotney Castle, Lamberhurst, Tunbridge Wells, Kent TN3 8JN (☎ 0892 890651)

BAXTER, Cncllr Keith Dennis; s of Dennis Baxter, of 116 Hambledon Rd, Waterlooville, Portsmouth, Hampshire, and Doris Georgina, *née* Hall; *b* 23 May 1951; *Educ* Purbrook Park Co GS; *m* 4 Aug 1973, Elaine Joy, da of Ronald Albert Sydney Bunn, of 19 Claydon Ave, Southsea, Portsmouth, Hampshire; 2 da (Rebecca Louise b 4 April 1978, Emma Jane b 24 July 1981); *Career* Zurich Insurance Co: trainee Portsmouth 1969, asst claims supt 1973, claims supt 1975, asst mangr 1981, mangr Maidstone Branch 1988; elected Maidstone Borough Cncl 1986; chm: E Area Planning Ctee 1987, Planning and Transportation Ctee 1988, Local Plan Gp 1988, Car Parking Policy Gp 1988; memb: Mid Kent Chartered INSU Inst, Maidstone SLDP; memb Soc of FCII 1986 (ACII 1972, FCII 1973); *Recreations* reading, politics, sports; *Style*— Cncllr Keith Baxter; 12 The Maltings, Grove Green, Maidstone, Kent ME14 5UF (☎ 0622 37189); Zurich Insurance Co, Chaucer House, Knightrider St, Maidstone, Kent ME15 6LD (☎ 0622 764526)

BAYLY, Clifford John; s of Paul William Bayly (d 1979), of London, and Dorothy, *née* Cooper (d 1939); *b* 19 May 1927; *Educ* St Martin's Sch of Art, Camberwell Sch of Art (NDD) ; *m* 28 Aug 1951, Jean Audrey, da of William Samuel Alfred Oddell (d 1986); 2 s (Martin Paul b 1956, Patrick William b 1962), 1 da (Caroline Joanna (Mrs Davies) b 1954); *Career* artist; illustrator numerous children's books 1960-82, head graphic design Maidstone Coll of Art 1961-81; work incl: series of Alignment paintings Royal Acad 1981-86, five one-man shows Aust 1984-87, regular exhibitor London and Kent, major landscape triptych for Winchester Hosp Mgmnt Ctee 1988, exhibitor Weald of

Kent Preservation Soc and Nat Art Collection Fund; vice chm Local Environmental and Amenity Soc 1982-84, pres Weald of Kent Art Gp; MSIA 1960-70, assoc memb Soc of Painters in Watercolours 1981, memb RWS 1983 (vice pres 1987); *Books* Painting Boats and Harbours (1982), Painting Towns and Buildings (1983); *Recreations* travel, sailing, history; *Style—* Clifford Bayly, Esq; The Stables, Oaks Farm, High St, Staplehurst, Kent TN12 0BH (☎ 0580 891302)

BEADLE, Geoffrey Richard Munro; s of Richard Frederick William Beadle (d 1964), of Birchington, Kent, and Lily May-Ena, *née* Green (d 1975); *b* 23 March 1929; *Educ* Chatham House GS Ramsgate, Balliol Coll Oxford (BA, MA); *m* 11 Aug 1966, Cosette Helene May, da of Septimus Frederick Oswald Harris, of Lee-on-the-Solent, Hants; 1 da (Philippa Helen b 1969); *Career* Gunner Nat Serv RA 1951, 2 Lt 58 Med Regt RA 1952-53, discharged HAC (TA) 1953-57; admitted slr 1957; asst slr Pearless de Rougemont & Co E Grinstead 1957-58, sr ptnr Boys & Maughan Margate and Canterbury 1989 (joined 1958, ptnr 1961); pres Rotary Club Sandwich 1964-65 (vice pres 1963-64), musical dir Dover Choral Soc 1967-88, churchwarden Kingston nr Canterbury 1974-81; *Recreations* singing, choir training, golf, reading; *Clubs* United Oxford and Cambridge Univ; *Style—* Geoffrey Beadle, Esq; 14 New Dover Rd, Canterbury, Kent CT1 3AP (☎ 0227 459817); Messrs Boys & Maughan, 1 St Margarets St, Canterbury, Kent CT1 2TT (☎ 0227 464481, fax 0227 762311)

BEALE, Dr John Daniel; s of Thomas Beale (d 1959), of Cefn Cribwr, Glamorgan, and Hannah Margaret, *née* Rees (d 1955); *b* 24 July 1937; *Educ* Bridgend GS, St Mary's Hosp Univ of London (MB BS, MRCGP); *m* 16 Sept 1962, (Elizabeth) Yolande, da of Rev Trevor Omri Jenkins, of Ramsgate; 2 s (Gideon b 1963, Jonathan b 1964), 2 da (Hannah b 1966, Rachel b 1969); *Career* paediatric house physician Children's Dept St Mary's Hosp Paddington Green 1962-63, casualty offr Hampstead Gen Hosp 1963, asst MOH Bournemouth 1963-64, princ in gen practice Church Village Glamorgan 1965-71, ptnr Grange Road Surgery Ramsgate 1971-; med advsr: Stelrad Ramsgate, Modern Jet Support Servs Manston Airport, Euro Missionary Fellowship; church elder; MFHom; *Recreations* walking, bird watching; *Style—* Dr John Beale; 21 Royal Espanade, Ramsgate, Kent CT11 0HA (☎ 0843 595054); The Grange Medical Centre, Westcliffe Rd, Ramsgate, Kent CT11 9LJ (☎ 0843 595051)

BEALE, Richard Walter; s of Vernon Herbert Tress Beale, of Parsonage Farm, Brenchley, Kent, and Mary Elizabeth, *née* Symes (d 1982); *b* 19 July 1949; *Educ* Temple Grove Preparatory Sch Uckfield Sussex, Brighton Coll Sussex, Hadlow Agric Coll Tonbridge Kent; *m* 12 Oct 1974, Melanie Sheila, da of Malcolm Frank Sanderson, of Summer Hill, Smallhythe, Tenterden, Kent; 1 s (James Malcolm Tress b 1978), 2 da (Alice Helen Mary b 1980, Celia Elisabeth Charlotte b 1985); *Career* farmer and landowner 1969-81, formed Dartel Holdings 1981, joined Bd of Egerton Trust plc, md Denehurst Homes The General Housebuilding Subsidiary; memb NFU Kent; *Recreations* cricket, shooting; *Clubs* Castle Hill Cricket, Tonbridge Rugby; *Style—* Richard Beale, Esq; 189 Forest Rd, Tunbridge Wells, Kent (☎ 0892 30887); Denehurst Homes Ltd, 7 Lonsdale Gardens, Tunbridge Wells, Kent (☎ 0892 515684)

BEAN, Hugh Cecil; CBE (1970); s of Cecil Walter Claude Bean, MBE (d 1975), and Gertrude Alice, *née* Chapman (d 1982); *b* 22 Sept 1929; *Educ* Beckenham GS, RCM; *m* 16 April 1963, Mary Dorothy, da of Henry Unwin Harrow (d 1981); 1 da (Fiona b 8 May 1969); *Career* Grenadier Gds 1949-51; prof of violin RCM 1954, ldr Philharmonia Orch 1956-67, assoc ldr BBC Symphony Orch 1967-69, ldr LSO 1969-71; memb Music Gp of London 1951-88; recordings: Elgar Violin Concerto (EMI), Vivaldi's Seasons (Decca), numerous works of chamber music for various cos; memb Royal Philharmonic Soc; FRCM 1968; *Recreations* model aircraft, steam railways, record collecting; *Style—* Hugh Bean, Esq, CBE; 30 Stone Park Ave, Beckenham, Kent BR3 3LX (☎ 081 650 8774)

BEARCROFT, (Joseph) Peter; s of Arthur William Bearcroft (d 1975), of 17 Filey Rd, Scarborough, and Elizabeth Jane, *née* McKinley (d 1982); *b* 15 July 1923; *Educ* St Mary's GS, Hummersknott nr Darlington, Queensland Univ Brisbane Aust, Balliol Coll Oxford (MA); *m* 14 June 1952, Dr Rosalind Irene Bearcroft, da of Albert Victor Chamberlain, MBE (d 1978); 1 s (Philip b 13 March 1964), 2 da (Charlotte b 5 June 1962, Emma b 19 May 1968); *Career* flying cadet Fleet Air Arm 1942, flying trg with US Navy 1943-44, Sub Lt RNVR, flying control offr Fleet Air Army HQ for the Normandy Landings 1944, TAMY I and MONAB 5 Aust SE Asia Cmd 1945, demob Lt RNVR 1946; jr commercial asst ICI Ltd Distribution Centre Billingham, trainee Manchester Assurance Co Ltd 1949, trainee tech asst Howards & Sons (Ilford) Ltd; Horlicks Ltd 1950-63: mgmnt trainee market res offr, asst to co sec, head Mktg Div; dir Pristine Products Ltd and Airwick Ltd; BR Bd 1963-83: dir of mktg (HQ) 1963-65, freight mktg and sales mangr, chief freight mangr Western Region (Paddington) HQ, freight mktg advsr (HQ) 1978-83, ret 1983; business cnsllr DTI and Dept of Employment 1983-86, currently private industl mktg conslt and business advsr; underwriting memb Lloyds 1981; fndr chm: Railway Mktg Soc 1971-83, Tport and Distribution Gp Inst of Mktg (memb Nat Cncl); memb Ctee for Terotechnol with DTI 1973-78; fndr memb SDP 1981; memb Catholic Union, prov pres Caterian Assoc 1990; Freeman City of London, Liveryman Worshipful Co of Marketors 1976; FCIT, FCIM, fell Inst of Logistics and Physical Distribution Mgmnt; *Recreations* swimming, golf, reading, travelling; *Clubs* MCC, Cricketers; *Style—* Peter Bearcroft, Esq; Barming Place, Maidstone, Kent ME16 9ED (☎ 0622 727844)

BEARCROFT, Dr Rosalind Irene; da of Victor Albert Chamberlain, MBE (d 1978), of Cardiff, and Irene Mary Chamberlain, *née* Price; *b* 16 May 1926; *Educ* Howell's Sch, Univ of Wales (BSc), Somerville Coll Oxford (BA, MA), UCH (MB BS, DPM); *m* 14 June 1952, (Joseph) Peter Bearcroft, s of Arthur William Bearcroft (d 1975), of Scarborough; 1 s (Philip b 1964), 2 da (Charlotte b 1962, Emma b 1968); *Career* held jr hosp Dr appts in London and Wales, sr registrar St Ebba's Hosp Epsom Surrey; conslt psychiatrist: Maidstone Hosp, Kent and Sussex Hosp Tunbridge Wells; conslt in child and family psychiatry Tunbridge Wells; chm: Regnl Speciality Sub Ctee on Child and Adolescent Psychiatry Met RHA (SE), Tunbridge Wells Health Dist Div of Psychiatry; rep on: Kent Police Advsy Ctee for Maidstone Health Dist, Kent Child Protection Ctee for RCPsych Speciality Sub Ctee on Psychiatry SE Thames RHA; memb: Cncl Catholic Union (memb Issues Ctee), Guild of Catholic Drs, Conslt and Specialists Assoc; vice pres and fndr memb Parenthood; memb BMA, FRCPsych; *Recreations* travelling, swimming, reading, gardening; *Style—* Dr Rosalind Bearcroft; Barming Place, Maidstone, Kent ME16 9ED (☎ 0622 727844/0831 231831)

BEAUMONT, Adrian Geoffrey John; s of Walter John Beaumont, of Hayes, Middx, and Doris Kathleen, *née* Hurkett; *b* 16 Sept 1949; *Educ* Bishopshalt Sch Hillingdon, St Lukes Coll Exeter; *m* 11 May 1979, Linda Ellen, da of John Dale (d 1963), of Denham, Buckinghamshire; 2 s (David John b 1983, Richard Adrian b 1986); *Career* teacher Harlington Sch Hillingdon 1971-79, dep head of sci Whitmore HS Harrow 1979-87, head of sci Canterbury HS 1987-, asst in trg of novice and experienced teachers Christ Church Coll Canterbury, introduced educnl bdcasting by Satelite in Kent via the Olympus Satelite 1988, gave lecture at NASA and US Dept of Commerce Third Int Satelite Direct Bdcast Servs Users Conf 1988; fndr of links between Canterbury HS and: Unionville HS Pa USA 1987, Secdy Sch Number 8 Vladimir USSR 1989; worked on construction of space observatory at Canterbury HS opened by Apollo 15 Lunar Module Pilot Col James B Irwin and featured on BBC's Blue Peter 1990, organiser of Col Irwin's UK Tour 1990, invited by US Vice Pres to be UK rep at First Int Space Camp Huntsville Alabama 1990, graduated from US Space Camp Aug 1990, team ldr on design and construction of experimental payload to be flown on Soviet Space Station Mir and operated by first Br astronaut Juno Mission 1991, active in establishing links between schs and indust and schs and the community; memb: Cultural Ctee Canterbury Three Towns Assoc, Ctee E Kent Radio Soc, Assoc for Sci Educn, Inst of Advanced Motorists; *Publications* Report of the Proceedings - Third International Satelite Direct Broadcasters Services Users Conference (contrib, 1988); *Recreations* amateur radio (call sign G7FWF), reading; *Style—* Adrian Beaumont, Esq; 18 Richmond Gardens, Canterbury, Kent (☎ 0227 470796); The Canterbury High School, Knight Ave, Canterbury, Kent CT2 8QA (☎ 0227 463971, fax 0227 762801)

BEAVAN, Alan Gordon; OBE (1985); s of Maj William Gordon Beavan, MC (d 1981), of Wokingham, and Marie Helene, *née* Ganteaume (d 1983); *b* 27 Nov 1925; *Educ* St Illtyd's Coll Cardiff; *m* 4 Sept 1954, (Nora) Jeanne, da of William John White (d 1954), of Cardiff; *Career* marine engr 1946-57; asst mangr Mountstuart Dry Docks Ltd Cardiff 1957-61; marine supt: Thomas Watson (Shipping) Ltd Rochester 1961-71, British Dredging Ltd 1971-82, tech mangr RMC E Coast Aggregates Ltd 1982-89; chm: SE Eng Section Inst of Marine Engrs 1970-72, Rochester and Chatham Cons Assoc 1976-79, Mid Kent Cons Assoc 1983-86; cncllr Rochester upon Medway City Cncl 1987, memb Bd of Govrs of three local schs; CEng, FIMarE 1978; *Recreations* philately, horticulture; *Clubs* St Stephen's; *Style—* Alan Beavan, Esq, OBE; 55 The Ridgeway, Chatham, Kent ME4 6PB (☎ 0634 846136)

BEBBINGTON, Dr Paul Ernest; s of Dr Ernest Bebbington, of Stepps, Glasgow, and Dorothy Isobel Mackinlay (d 1989); *b* 18 May 1945; *Educ* Nottingham HS, Jesus Coll Cambridge (BA, MA, MB BChir, MPhil, MRCP, MPCPsych, PhD); *m* 11 July 1970, Pamela Margaret, da of Frederick William Fox, of Newport, Gwent; 1 s (Magnus William Paul b 1976); *Career* scientific staff MRC Social Psychiatry Unit 1977, hon conslt psychiatrist Maudsley Hosp 1980, hon reader social and epidemiological psychiatry Inst of Psychiatry 1990 (hon sr lectr 1980), asst dir Social and Community Psychiatry Unit; Cambridge Athletics Blue 1967; hon sec Res Ctee Mental Health Fndn 1983-87; memb Exec Ctee Social Community and Rehabilitation Section RCPsych; *Books* What is a Case? (ed, 1981), Psychiatric Disorders in the Elderly (ed, 1985), Manual of Practical Psychiatry (1985), Living with Mental Illness (1987), Schizophrenia: The Major Issues (ed, 1988), Working in Partnership (1990); *Recreations* athletics; *Clubs* Hawks; *Style—* Dr Paul Bebbington; Institute of Psychiatry, MRC Social & Community Psychiatry Unit, De Crespigny Park, London SE5 8AF (☎ 071 7035411, fax 071 7030458)

BECKETT, Allan Harry; MBE; s of George William Harry Beckett, MM (d 1949), of Belvedere, Kent, and Emma Louise, *née* Stokes (d 1983); *b* 4 March 1914; *Educ* E Ham Secdy Sch, Univ of London (BSc); *m* 25 June 1949, Ida Gwladys, da of Kenbryd Morris James, DCM (d 1983), of Keston, Kent; 2 s (Michael b 1950, Timothy b 1953), 1 da (Sian b 1957); *Career* RE 1940, 142 OCTU 1940, cmmnd 2 Lt 1941, Capt 1942, Staff Maj 1942, tech advsr in field 21 Army RE 1944, seconded to BAOR 1945; engrg asst: A J Bridle 1934-35, HM Office of Works 1935-37; bridge designer Br Steelwork Assoc 1937-38, asst site engr Woolwich Arsenal Chief Architects Dept 1938-39; sr engr Sir Bruce White Wolfe Barry and Ptnrs Conslting Engrs 1946 (ptnr 1957-, sr ptnr 1983-); FICE, MIConsE; *Publications* numerous tech papers on engrg; *Recreations* sailing; *Clubs* St Stephens and Erith Yacht; *Style—* Allan Beckett, Esq, MBE; Thistledown, Wood Way, Farnborough Park, Kent; 83 Abbey St, Faversham, Kent (☎ 0689 52193); 270 Vauxhall Bridge Rd, Westminster, London SW1V 1BB (☎ 071 233 6423, fax 071 834 7265)

BEDDARD, Lt-Col Jonathan Patrick Owen; MBE (1981); s of Terence Elliot Beddard (d 1966), and Ursula Mary Howard Beddard, BEM, *née*, Gurney-Richards (d 1985); *b* 17 March 1944; *Educ* Cheam Sch, Eton; *m* 4 Dec 1979, Felicity Victoria, da of Lt-Col Granville Reginald Arthur Brooking, of Sussex; 1 s (Henry Terence b 1981), 1 da (Genevieve Daisy b 1984); *Career* served Far E, Ops in Borneo 1963-64, Instr Jungle Warfare Sch 1967-69, Loan Serv Fiji 1972-74, Staff Coll Camberley 1977, Ops NI 1969/71/ 81, BAOR 1970-72 and 1982-85, CO 2 Bn Royal Green Jackets 1983-85, MOD 1985-87; dir London Portfolio Services Ltd; Freeman City of London, Liveryman Worshipful Co of Skinners; *Recreations* fencing, subaqua, diving; *Clubs* Epee, British Sub Aqua (instr), Landsdowne; *Style—* Lt-Col Jonathan Beddard, MBE; Barnfield House, Hawkhurst, Kent TN18 4PX (☎ 05805 2388); C Hare and Co, 37 Fleet St, London EC4; London Portfolio Services, 52 Grosvenor Gardens, London W1A 0AU

BEEBY, (Douglas) Ian; s of Sidney Douglas Beeby, of Sedlecombe, E Sussex, and Phyllis, *née* Banner (d 1972); *b* 10 May 1940; *Educ* Bromsgrove GS, Downing Coll Cambridge (MA, MChir), St Thomas's Hosp Med Sch London (MB BChir); *m* 13 Dec 1963, Gillian Wendy, da of George David Foster, of Birstall, W Yorks; 3 s (Timothy Ian b 23 Oct 1964, Jonathan Charles b 25 Aug 1966, John Benjamin b 16 Aug 1970); *Career* house surgn Birmingham Accident Hosp 1967-68, sr house surgn Kingston upon Thames 1968-69, surgical registrar United Sheffield Hosps then Portsmouth 1969-72, Vandervell res fell Inst of Cancer Res 1973-74, sr surgical registrar St George's and Royal Marsden Hosps 1975-80, conslt surgn Medway Health Dist 1980-, sr conslt surgn 1990-; author of pubns in professional jls; fndr memb Pancreatic Soc of GB and I 1975-; memb: Br Assoc of Surgical Oncology 1978-, Local Exec Ctee of BMA 1982-88, Medway Health Authy 1985-89; fell Assoc of Surgns of GB and I 1985-, FRCS; *Recreations* good food, skiing, tennis, swimming, theatre; *Clubs* Castle; *Style—* Ian Beeby, Esq; Malt House, 28 St Margaret's St, Rochester, Kent ME1 1TU (☎ 0634 811601); St Bartholomews Hospital, Rochester, Kent ME1 1DS (☎ 0634 402030 ext 4203); BUPA Alexandra Hospital, Walderslade ME5 9PG (☎ 0634 687166)

BEECH, Jeremy Wilson; s of Ivor Wilson Beech (d 1981), and Elsie May Beech (d 1956); *b* 2 June 1949; *Educ* Danemark Sch Winchester, Fire Serv Coll; *m* 14 Oct 1989, Joanna Mary, da of Ronald Pringle; *Career* fire offr; jr ranks 1965-73, intermediate operational cmd 1973-81, divnl cdr Essex Fire Bde 1981-83, asst chief offr London Fire Bde 1983-86, dep chief offr Gloucestershire Fire Bde 1986-88, chief fire offr Kent 1988-; int speaker on: the Channel tunnel, int disasters, search and rescue ops; memb: Inter-Governmental Channel Tunnel Safety Authy, Fire Servs Examinations Bd of Assessors, Instn of Fire Engrs, Cncl of the Cwlth and Overseas Fire Servs Assoc, Cncl for the Order of St John; UK chm Jt Anglo French Rescue and Public Safety Working Gp, chm Number 5 Dist Chief and Asst Fire Offrs Assoc; *Recreations* music, photography, gardening; *Clubs* Guild of Firefighters; *Style—* Jeremy Beech, Esq; Kent Fire Brigade Headquarters, The Godlands, Tovil, Maidstone, Kent ME15 6XB (☎ 0622 692121, fax 0622 691503)

BEEK, Rev Canon Michael Peter; s of Frederick William Beek, CBE (d 1967), and Edna Annie, *née* West (d 1985); *b* 9 April 1927; *Educ* Whitgift Sch, Emmanuel Coll Cambridge (BA, MA), Lincoln Theol Coll (GOE); *m* 2 June 1951, Pamela Jean, da of Allan William Webster (d 1978); 1 s (Christopher b 1952), 2 da (Valerie b 1954, Elizabeth b 1959); *Career* RASC 1945-48; curate St Barnabas Mitcham 1952-55, priest i/c St Thomas Ensbury Park Bournemouth 1955-58, vicar Higham with Merston Kent 1958-66; rector Gravesend Kent 1966-74, rural dean Gravesend 1970-74, hon canon Rochester 1973, rector Speldhurst Kent 1974-83, rural dean Tunbridge Wells 1974-83, vicar Bromley 1983-; chm: NSPCC Thameside Branch 1966-73, Cncl of Social Responsibility for Dioceses of Canterbury & Rochester 1976-83; vice chm Bromley NSPCC 1987-; *Recreations* walking, travel, music; *Style—* The Rev Canon Michael Beek; The Vicarage, 9 St Paul's Square, Bromley, Kent BR2 0XH (☎ 081 4606275)

BEESON, Very Rev Trevor Randall; s of Arthur William Beeson (d 1979), and Matilda Beeson (d 1980); *b* 2 March 1926; *Educ* King's Coll London, St Boniface Coll Warminster (MA); *m* 1950, Josephine Grace, da of Ernest Joseph Cope (d 1974); 2 da (Jean, Catherine); *Career* dean of Winchester 1987-; FKC; *Books* The Church of England in Crisis (1973), Discretion and Valour (1974), A Vision of Hope (1984); *Recreations* gardening, cricket; *Style—* The Very Rev the Dean of Winchester; The Deanery, Winchester SO23 9LS; Grove House, Church St, St Clements, Sandwich, Kent

BEETHAM, Marshal of the RAF Sir Michael James; GCB (1978, KCB 1976), CBE (1967), DFC (1944), AFC (1960), DL (Norfolk 1988); s of Maj George Beetham, MC (d 1953), and Eva Vivian, *née* Adam (d 1978); *b* 17 May 1923; *Educ* St Marylebone GS; *m* 3 Nov 1956, Patricia Elizabeth, da of Henry Lane, of Christchurch, NZ; 1 s (Alexander Michael b 14 Aug 1961), 1 da (Lucinda Mary b 7 March 1958); *Career* RAF 1941-, CAS 1977-82, Air ADC to HM The Queen 1977-82, hon Air Cdre 2620 Sqdn (Co of Norfolk) RAuxAF; dir: Brixton Estate plc 1983-, GEC Avionics Ltd 1984- (chm 1986-90); chm Tstees RAF Museum 1983-, pres Bomber Command Assoc 1985-; FRAeS 1982; *Recreations* golf; *Clubs* RAF, Royal W Norfolk Golf; *Style—* Marshal of the RAF Sir Michael Beetham, GCB, CBE, DFC, AFC; GEC Avionics Ltd, Airport Works, Rochester, Kent ME1 2XX (☎ 0634 816223, fax 0634 832490)

BELHAVEN AND STENTON, 13 Lord (S 1647); Robert Anthony Carmichael Hamilton; s of 12 Lord Belhaven and Stenton (d 1961); *b* 27 Feb 1927; *Educ* Eton; *m* 1, 1952 (m dis 1973), (Elizabeth) Ann, da of late Col Arthur Moseley, DSO, of NSW; 1 s, 1 da; m 2, 1973 (m dis 1986), Rosemary, da of Sir Herbert Williams, 1 Bt, MP (d 1954), sis of Sir Robin Williams, Bt, and formerly w of Sir Ian Mactaggart, 3 Bt; 1 adopted da; m 3, 1986, Malgorzata Maria, da of Tadeusz Pobog Hruzik-Mazurkiewicz, of Krakow, Poland; 1 da (Alexandra Maria b 1987); *Heir* s, Master of Belhaven; *Career* Army 1945-48, cmmnd Cameronians 1947; farmer 1950-72, cook 1972-80; sits as Cons Peer in House of Lords; *Recreations* writing children's stories, growing vegetables; *Clubs* Army and Navy; *Style—* The Rt Hon the Lord Belhaven and Stenton; 16 Broadwater Down, Tunbridge Wells, Kent

BELL, Rev Adrian Christopher; s of Capt Frank Bell (d 1988), of Luton, Beds, and Mary, *née* Broom; *b* 11 Feb 1948; *Educ* Luton GS, King's Coll London (AKC), St Augustine's Coll Canterbury; *m* 23 Sept 1971, Marian Catherine, da of Charles Smith, of 644 East Bank Rd, Sheffield; 2 s (Nicholas b 1983, James b 1984); *Career* curate: St Aidan with St Luke Sheffield 1971-74, Willesborough with Hinxhill Canterbury 1974-78; vicar: Hollingbourne, Leeds, Hucking, Broomfield 1978-84, Herne Bay 1984-; chaplain: Leeds Castle 1978-84, Royal Br Legion & Ex-Serviceman's Club, Herne Bay Blind Club, Arthritis Care Herne Bay, Herne Bay Rotary Club; chm: Herne Bay Umbrella, Herne Bay Town Show, Herne Bay Vol Bureau; govr Herne Bay Co Primary Sch; *Books* Vicarage Cookbook (1989); *Recreations* cooking, swimming, chinese porcelain collecting; *Style—* The Rev Adrian Bell; The Vicarage, 38 Beltinge Rd, Herne Bay, Kent CT6 6BU (☎ 0227 37490); The Parish Office, Underdown Rd, Herne Bay, Kent CT6 5BU (☎ 0227 366640)

BELL, Cncllr Henry (Harry); s of Edward William Bell (d 1961), and Elizabeth Mary, *née* Richards (d 1966); *b* 2 Jan 1919; *Educ* Colfes GS; *m* 21 June 1941, Barbara Gladys May, da of John McGregor Laing (d 1960), of Ladywell; 1 s (Stuart Henry b 9 Feb 1953); *Career* RA 1937; served WWII RQMS 1939-46, Iceland, France, Belguim, Holland, Germany (despatches 1944); gp gen mangr Ford Main Dealers Dartford 1955-80, mangr HAM Garages Group 1981-87; borough cncllr Dartford, parish cncllr Stone, chm Dartford Cons Assoc 1985-88, chm Dartford and Gravesham CHC; sch govr, memb Kent CC Elderly Ctee and Mentally Handicapped Ctee; *Clubs* Dunkirk Veterans, R A Assoc, Dartford Conservatives; *Style—* Cncllr Harry Bell

BELL, Rear Adm John Anthony; CB (1977); s of Mathew Bell (d 1948), of Dundee, and Mary Ann Ellen, *née* Goss (d 1979); *b* 25 Nov 1924; *Educ* St Ignatius Coll, Univ Coll of S Wales (BA, BSc, LLB); *m* 1946, (Eileen) Joan, da of Daniel Woodman (d 1934); 3 da; *Career* RM 1943-45, RAN 1948-52, SACLANT USA 1961-64, dir Naval MET 1973-75, Rear Adm 1975, dir Naval Educn 1975-79; called to the Bar Gray's Inn 1970; educn sec BBC 1979-83; vice pres United Servs Catholic Assoc 1979-, chm Kent Ecumenical Cmmn 1982-; pres Kent Area RN Assoc 1982-, vice pres RN Assoc 1983-; dep chm Police Complaints Bd 1983-; KSG 1983; *Recreations* swimming, travel, France; *Style—* Rear Adm John Bell, CB; The Beild, Conifer Ave, Hartley, Kent DA3 8BX (☎ 047 47 2485)

BELL, William Edwin; CBE (1980); s of Cuthbert Edwin Bell (d 1961), and Winifred Mary, *née* Simpson; *b* 4 Aug 1926; *Educ* Univ of Birmingham, Royal Sch of Mines; *m* 1952, Angela Josephine, da of Flt Lt E Vaughan, MC (d 1931); 2 s, 2 da; *Career* exec Royal Dutch/Shell Gp, dir Shell International 1980-84, non-exec dir Costain Gp plc, chm Enterprise Oil plc 1984-; CBIM, FInstPet; *Recreations* golf, sailing (yacht 'Bel Esprit'); *Clubs* Chichester Yacht, Nevill Golf; *Style—* William Bell, Esq, CBE; Fordcombe Manor, nr Tunbridge Wells, Kent

BELLINGHAM, Prof Alastair John; s of Stanley Herbert Bellingham, of Ewell, Surrey, and Sybil Mary, *née* Milne; *b* 27 March 1938; *Educ* Tiffin Boys' Sch, Kingston upon Thames, UCH Med Sch London; *m* 24 May 1963,

(Valerie) Jill, da of Kenenth Morford (d 1971); 3 s (James R b 24 April 1964, Richard K b 14 April 1969, Paul T b 25 Feb 1973); *Career* Mackenzie-Mackinnon Streafield fell RCP 1968-69, res fell Univ of Washington USA 1969-70, sr lectr haematology UCH Med Sch London 1971-74; prof of haematology: Univ of Liverpool 1974-84, Kings Coll London 1984-; former sec Br Soc for Haematology 1984-87, cncl memb Royal Coll Pathology 1987-; FRCP 1976, FRCPath 1986; *Recreations* photography, oenology, viticulture, claret tasting; *Style*— Prof Alastair Bellingham; 13 Barnmead Rd, Beckenham, Kent BR3 1JF (☎ 081 778 0730); Dept of Haematological Medicine, Kings College School of Medicine & Dentistry, Bessemer Rd, London SE5 9RS (☎ 071 326 3080)

BENDALL, Peter Stanley; s of Stanley Bendall (d 1989), of Barn Elms, Woodside, Polegate Rd, East Sussex, and Cora, *née* Crosby (d 1985); *b* 5 Nov 1951; *Educ* Sevenoaks Sch, Univ of Warwick (BA); *m* 5 May 1983, Lynda Mary, da of Herbert Anthony Humphreys, of 3 Parrock Ave, Gravesend, Kent; 1 s (Alastair Robert Charles b 18 April 1984), 2 da (Elizabeth Kathleen b 25 Feb 1976, Louise Mary b 20 Jan 1978); *Career* CA; ptnrs asst McCabe and Ford 1978-80, fin controller Filtrasol Ltd 1980-82, ptnrs asst Mitchell and Co 1982-84, princ Peter S Bendall; FCA 1982 (ACA 1977); *Recreations* swimming, rugby football; *Style*— Peter Bendall, Esq; Two Shoes, Tollgate Place, Headcorn, Ashford, Kent TN27 9SU (☎ 0233 890157); Town Hall Chambers, Town Hall, Tenderden, Kent (☎ 058 06 5658)

BENFIELD, Charles Nettleton; s of George Nettleton Benfield (d 1956), of Maidstone, Kent, and Alice Maud, *née* Hewbry; *b* 10 Sept 1923; *Educ* Maidstone GS; *m* Daphne Mildred, da of Bertram William Richardson (d 1966), of Barming, Kent; 1 s (John Nettleton b 21 Dec 1965); *Career* War Serv RCS 1941-46; funeral dir 1950, master builder 1960-; memb: Malling DC 1960, Tonbridge and Malling Borough Cncl 1973, Wateringbury Parish Cncl 1956; churchwarden Wateringbury Church 1967-73 (cncl memb 1951), pres Wateringbury FC; *Recreations* cricket, motor sport; *Style*— Charles Benfield, Esq; Grandsden, Tonbridge Rd, Wateringbury, Kent (☎ 0622 812257); 242 Tonbridge Rd, Wateringbury, Maidstone, Kent (☎ 0622 812257)

BENN, (Edward) Glanvill; s of Sir Ernest Benn, Bt, CBE (d 1954), and Gwendolen Dorothy Benn, JP, *née* Andrews; *b* 31 Dec 1905; *Educ* Harrow, Clare Coll Cambridge; *m* 4 Jun 1931, (Beatrice) Catherine Benn, MBE, da of Claude Newbald (d 1943), of Wallington, Surrey; 1 s (James b 1944), 1 da (Elizabeth b 1936); *Career* MOI 1939, 2 Lt E Surrey Regt 1940, Adj 11 Bn E Surrey Regt 1941-42, Staff Coll Camberley 1943, Bde Maj 138 Bde Italy 1944, GSO2 Land Forces Adriatic 1945 (despatches); office boy NY Times 1925; dir: Ernest Benn Ltd publishers 1928-75, Benn Bros Ltd publishers 1928-75 (chm 1945-75), Exchange Telegraph Co Ltd 1961-72 (chm 1969-72); tstee Advertising Benevolent Soc 1951-71 (cncl memb 1937-61, chm Fin Ctee 1950-60), chm Advertising Advsy Ctee ITA 1959-63, hon treas Cwlth Press Union 1967-77 (hon life memb 1975), appeals chm Newspaper Press Fund 1971, pres Periodical Publishers Assoc 1976-77; Liveryman Worshipful Co of Stationers and Newspaper Makers 1935 (Master 1977-78); *Clubs* Reform, Aldeburgh Golf; *Style*— Glanvill Benn, Esq; Crescent Cottage, Aldeburgh, Suffolk IP15 5HW; Benn Bros plc, Sovereign Way, Tonbridge, Kent

BENN, Sir (James) Jonathan; 4 Bt (UK 1914), of The Old Knoll, Metropolitan Borough of Lewisham; s of Sir John Andrews Benn, 3 Bt (d 1984), and Hon Ursula Lady Benn, da of 1 Baron Hankey; *b* 27 July 1933; *Educ* Harrow, Clare Coll Cambridge; *m* 2 July 1960, Jennifer Mary, eld da of Dr Wilfred Vivian Howells, OBE (d 1987), of The Ferns, Clun, Shropshire; 1 s, 1 da (Juliet b 1966); *Heir* s, Robert Ernest Benn; *Career* dir Reedpack Ltd; chm and chief exec Reed Paper and Bd (UK) Ltd, chm J & J Maybank Ltd; pres Br Paper and Bd Industries Fedn 1985-87; *Style*— Sir Jonathan Benn, Bt; Fielden Lodge, Tonbridge Road, Ightham, nr Sevenoaks, Kent TN15 9AN

BENNETT, (Frederick Onslow) Alexander Godwyn; TD; s of Alfred Bennett, of Sulhamstead, Berks, and Marjorie Muir Bremner; *b* 21 Dec 1913; *Educ* Winchester, Trinity Coll Cambridge; *m* 18 Nov 1942, Rosemary, er da of Sir Malcolm Perks, 2 Bt; 1 s, 4 da; *Career* served WWII, cmmnd 8 RB (TA) 1939, Lt-Col 9901 SHAEF 21 Army Gp (despatches twice), US Bronze Star; joined Whitbread and Co 1935; chm: Whitbread and Co Ltd 1972-77, Whitbread Investment Co Ltd 1977-88; chm Brewers Soc 1970-72; pres Kent CCC 1983; Master Worshipful Co of Brewers 1965; *Clubs* MCC; *Style*— Alexander Bennett, Esq, TD; Grove House, Selling, Faversham, Kent (☎ 0227 752250)

BENNETT, John Richard; s of Sgt John Philip Bennett (ka 1945), of Erith, Kent, and Joyce, *née* Auckland (who m 2 1947, Eric Henry Rushbrook); *b* 27 March 1945; *Educ* Brockley GS, Pembroke Coll Oxford (MA); *m* 24 July 1971, (Frances) Ann, *née* Dunn; 1 da (Joanne Amelia b 1974); *Career* GLC: admin offr 1966-69, mgmnt advsr 1970-74, dist housing mangr 1974-78; trg offr Dexion Ltd 1969-70; Gravesham Borough Cncl: borough housing offr 1978-85, borough housing and health offr 1985-88, dir of housing and environmental health 1988-; memb: Cncl Inst of Housing 1987-, Hostels Sub Ctee Gravesend Churches HA; dir PATH (LA) 1989-, tstee Charities of Henry Pinnock 1987-; memb BIM; *Recreations* badminton, skiing, reading, climatology; *Clubs* Old Brockleians Soc, Oxford Union, The Royal Institution; *Style*— John Bennett, Esq; Gravesham Borough Council, Civic Centre, Windmill St, Gravesend, Kent DA12 1AU (☎ 0474 564422, fax 0474 337453)

BENNETT, Nicholas John Hick; s of Capt Claude Bennett (d 1980), of 1 Langham Close, Westbrook, Margate, Kent, and Daphne Kerven, *née* Holliday; *b* 14 Aug 1940; *Educ* Wellington House Sch Westgate, The King's Sch Canterbury; *m* 23 March 1968, Judith Anne, da of Hugh Norman Mockett, of 92 Pierremont Ave, Broadstairs, Kent; 2 s (Andrew James Hick b 1970, Giles Alexander b 1976), 1 da (Helen Judith b 1972); *Career* admitted slr 1962; ptnr Boys and Maughan Slrs Margate 1965-81, princ Nicholas Bennett and Co Slrs Sandwich 1981-; fndr pres Rotary Club of Thanet, former pres Thanet Squash Rackets Club; former chm: Margate Round Table, Kent Round Table; memb Ctee Sandwich Sports and Leisure Centre; Liveryman Worshipful Co of Basketmakers; memb Law Soc 1962; *Recreations* golf, music, cricket; *Clubs* MCC, City Livery; *Style*— Nicholas Bennett, Esq; North Goodwin House, Cliff Promenade, Broadstairs, Kent CT10 3QY; Nicholas Bennett & Co, 21 Market St, Sandwich, Kent CT13 9DA (☎ 0304 617988, fax 0304 612464)

BENNETT, Rodney Keith; s of George Henry Bennett, and Helena Winifred Florence; *b* 11 March 1946; *Educ* Upbury Manor Secdy Sch, Mid-Kent Coll; *m* 14 June 1975, Dorothy Jean, da of George Buttle Lake (d 1970); 1 da (Julie b 14 June 1977); *Career* MOD: weapons fitter 1966-69, mechanical fitter 1974-78, civilian instructional offr 1978-79; services mangr and fire offr Allders of Chatham 1979-; MIPlantE 1981, FEng; *Recreations* photography, cycling; *Style*— Rodney Bennett, Esq; Allders, 220-246 High St, Chatham, Kent ME4 4NJ (☎ 0634 407377)

BENSON, Clifford George; s of George Benson, of 112 Blackshots Lane, Grays, Essex, and Doris Lilian, *née* Jennings; *b* 17 Nov 1946; *Educ* RCM; *m* 1 Sept 1973, Dilys Morgan, da of Robert Davies, of Craig Wen, Bwlch-y-Gwynt Rd, Llysfaen, nr Colwyn Bay, Clwyd; 2 da (Sarah b 22 July 1975, Emily b 8 Aug 1977); *Career* concert pianist; first prize with Levon Chilingirian on violin BBC Beethoven Duo Competition 1969, Royal Festival Hall debut playing Rachmaninov 3 Piano Concerto 1970, first prize with Levon Chilingirian Int Duo Competition Munich 1971, recital with Thea King and Peter Pears Aldeburgh Festival 1975, performed Constant Lambert Piano Concerto 1975, world premiere of Richard Rodney Bennet's Three Romantic Pieces for BBC Pebble Mill Howard Ferguson 80th birthday concert 1988; performed solo piano recitals and concertos world-wide incl: Canada, Middle and Far East, USA, Czechoslovakia, Europe; regular broadcaster BBC Radio 3; recordings with: Deutsche Grammophon, CBS, Hyperion, Chandos, CRD; compositions incl: Three Pieces for Piano 1983, Mozart goes to Town (piano duet) 1985, Au Revoir Sylvie 1988; memb ctee Tonbridge Music Club; life memb RCM Student's Union, memb ISM; *Style*— Clifford Benson, Esq

BENSON, Mark; s of Frank Edward Benson, and Judith Ann, *née* Harrison; *b* 6 July 1958; *Educ* Sutton Valence; *m* 20 Sept 1986, Sarah Patricia, da of Lawrence John Watts; 2s (Lawrence Mark Edward b 16 Oct 1987, Edward Robert b 23 June 1989); *Career* Kent CCC: joined 1978, capped 1981, benefit match 1991, capt 1991; played for England (21 & 30 v India in Birmingham) 1986; *Style*— Mark Benson, Esq; Kent County Cricket Club, St Lawrence Ground, Old Dover Rd, Canterbury, Kent CT1 3NZ (☎ 0227 456 886, fax 0227 762168)

BERKELEY, Frederic George; s of Dr Augustus Frederic Millard Berkeley (d 1952), of Kennington, and Anna Louisa, *née* Inniss (d 1954); *b* 21 Dec 1919; *Educ* Elstree Sch, Aldenham, Pembroke Coll Cambridge (MA); *m* 1; 1 s, 1 da (1 da decd), 1 step s; m 2, 1988, Helen Kathleen Lucy; 1 step s, 1 step da; *Career* served WWII, Maj Normandy (wounded); slr, ptnr Lewis and Lewis 1951-70, vice chm and chm Legal Aid Area Ctee 1964-70, Master of Supreme Court 1971, chief Master of Supreme Court Taxing Office 1988-; gen ed Butterworths Costs Serv; *Recreations* reading, gardening, travel, writing; *Style*— Frederic Berkeley, Esq; The Royal Courts of Justice, The Strand, London WC2A 2LL (☎ 071 936 6227); 10 Dover House, Abbey Park, Beckenham, Kent BR3 1QB

BERKELEY, Hugh Rowland Comyns; s of Rowland Frank Brackenbury Berkeley, of Little Heronden, High St, Hawkhurst, Kent, and Margaret, *née* Kelleher; *b* 22 July 1938; *Educ* St George's Coll Weybridge Surrey, Neuchatel Business Sch Neuchatel Switzerland; *m* 30 June 1962, Cherry, da of Lt Cdr Humphrey Cleveland Hookway, DSC; 2 s (Robert b 11 Sept 1964, Neil b 17 May 1966), 1 da (Theresa b 10 March 1969); *Career* aviation broker Stewart Smith Lloyds of London 1959 (CT Bowring 1958), ptnr Berkeley Haulage & Co 1961; md: Berkeley Invicta Ltd 1977, D & H Holdings 1984; FInstD 1980, FBIM 1981, AInstM 1981; *Recreations* rugby, flying, skiing; *Clubs* Tonbridge Rugby; *Style*— Hugh Berkeley, Esq; Ethnam, Ethnam Lane, Sandhurst, Kent TN18 5PS (☎ 0580 850217); 191 Bravington Rd, Maida Vale, London; D & H Holdings Ltd, Maidstone Rd, Matfield, Tonbridge, Kent TN12 7JN (☎ 089272 2202, fax 089272 3507, telex 95539 BERK G, car tel 0836 553707)

BERNADT, Dr Morris William; s of Himan Bernadt, of Cape Town, SA, and Jean, *née* Alkin; *b* 8 Sept 1946; *Educ* Rondebosch Boys' HS Cape Town, Univ of Cape Town Med Sch (MB BCh); *m* 20 Dec 1970, Ann Penelope, da of Ben-zion Beinart (d 1979); 1 s (Jeremy Martin b 1978), 1 da (Gillian Clare Belinda b 1981); *Career* hosp trainee and res worker St Bart's Hosp and Med Sch 1973-76, sr registrar and clinical lectr Maudsley Hosp and Inst of Psychiatry 1977-81, conslt psychiatrist Bromley Health Authy and hon sr lectr King's Coll Hosp Sch of Med and Dentistry 1982-; author of twenty scientific papers and articles; Bromley rep to Regnl Psychiatry Speciality Sub Ctee, med advsr to Bromley Alcohol Advsy Serv; *Books* Handbook of Addiction Behaviour (contrib, 1990); *Recreations* jogging, piano playing, chess; *Clubs* Streatham Chess; *Style—* Dr Morris Bernadt; Beckenham Hospital, Croydon Rd, Beckenham, Kent BR3 3QL (☎ 081 650 0125)

BERRIMAN, Sir David; s of late Algernon Edward Berriman, OBE and late Enid Kathleen, *née* Sutcliffe; *b* 20 May 1928; *Educ* Winchester, New Coll Oxford (MA), Harvard Business Sch (PMD course); *m* 1, 1955 (m dis 1969), Margaret Lloyd, *née* Owen; 2 s; m 2, 1971, Shirley Elizabeth, *née* Wright; *Career* Citibank 1952-56, Ford Motor Co UK 1956-60, AEI Hotpoint 1960-63, United Leasing Corp 1963-; dir: Morgan Grenfell Holdings (formerly Morgan Grenfell) 1963-73, Guinness Mahon 1973-87, Cable and Wireless plc 1975-88, Bahrein Telecom Co 1982-88, Britannia Building Society 1983-, British Screen Finance Ltd 1985-, Videotron Corp Ltd 1989-, Sky Television plc (formerly Satellite plc) (chm 1981-85), East European Development Ltd 1990-, Kent Community Housing Trust 1990-; chm: Bunzl Textile Holdings Ltd 1978-88, Alban Communications Ltd 1983-90, NE Thames Regnl Health Authy 1984-90; dep chm The Nat Film and TV Sch 1989- (dir 1977-), memb Br Screen Advsy Cncl (formerly Interim Action Ctee on Future of Br Film Indust), former memb Govt Ctee on Harland and Wolff Diversification; chm of govrs MacIntyre (for the Mentally Handicapped); govr Utd Med and Dental Schs of St Thomas' and Guy's Hosps 1982-84; FCIB, CBIM; kt 1990; *Books* XYZ Case; *Recreations* golf, tennis; *Clubs* RAC, Royal St George's Golf; *Style—* Sir David Berriman; Britannia Building Society, Newtown House, Leek, Staffs ST13 5RG

BERRIMAN, John Robert Lloyd; s of Sir David Berriman, of Plaxtol, Kent, and Margaret Lloyd, *née* Owen; *b* 14 July 1956; *Educ* Marlborough; *m* 15 Aug 1981, Lindsey Kathryn Ann, da of Bryan Augustin McSwiney; *Career* qualified CA 1979; ptnr Coopers & Lybrand Deloitte 1987-(joined 1975); govr The MacIntyre Fndn, fndr memb and memb Mgmnt Ctee MacIntyre Housing Assoc (currently treas); FCA 1990; *Recreations* lawn tennis, golf, music; *Clubs* RAC, Queen's, The Lawn Tennis Assoc; *Style—* John Berriman, Esq; Avenue Cottage, Seal Chart, nr Sevenoaks, Kent TN15 OHA (☎ 0732 62288); Plumtree Court, London EC4A 4HT (☎ 071 583 5000)

BERRY, Anthony Arthur; s of Francis Berry (d 1936), of London, and Amy Marie Freeman (d 1966); family have been wine merchants in Exeter and 3 St James's St London since 1700s; *b* 16 March 1915; *Educ* Charterhouse, Trinity Hall Cambridge (BA); *m* 1953, Sonia Alice, da of Sir Harold Graham-Hodgson, KCVO (d 1960); 1 s (Simon), 1 da (Victoria); *Career* wine merchant; chm Berry Bros and Rudd Ltd 1965-85 (dir 1946-); chm Wine Trade Benevolent Soc 1968, cellarer Saintsbury Club 1978-; Master Vintners Co 1980-81; *Recreations* golf, walking; *Clubs* Boodle's, Royal St George's Golf, Royal Wimbledon Golf, Saintsbury, Bath and County; *Style—* Anthony Berry, Esq; 4 Cavendish Crescent, Bath BA1 2UG (☎ 0225 422669); Windy Peak, St Margaret's Bay, Kent CT15 6DT (☎ 0304 952413)

BERRY, Dr (Anne) Caroline; da of Charles Rushton Elliott (d 1989), of Jersey, CI, and Evelyn Anne *née* Le Cornu (d 1986); *b* 1 April 1937; *Educ* Bedgebury Park Sch, The Middlesex Hosp London (MB BS, PhD); *m* 13 June 1958, (Robert James) Sam; 1 s (Andrew b 1963), 2 da (Alison b 1963, Susan b 1965); *Career* conslt clinical geneticist Guys Hosp 1979-; MRCP 1987; *Books* Rites of Life: Christians & Biomedical Decision Making (1987); *Style—* Dr Caroline Berry; SE Thames Regional Genetics Centre, Guys Hospital, London SE1 9RT (☎ 071 955 4648)

BERRY, Maurice Walter Lewis; s of Maj Stanley Coe Berry (d 1975), of Brenley, Faversham, and Anne Jane Barbara, *née* Thomas (d 1976); *b* 20 July 1915; *Educ* The Leys Sch Cambridge; *m* 18 Sept 1940, (Mary) Pamela, da of Capt Frank Shires, of Gernhill, Fixby, Huddersfield; 2 s (Nigel b 1948, Julian b 1950), 1 da (Amanda Wilmington b 1946); *Career* TA 1939, E Kent Yeo 97 Field Regt RA, War Serv W Kent Yeo 143 Field Regt RA; awarded: 1939/45 Star, France and Germany Star, Defence Medal, Victory Medal; hop and fruit grower and gen farmer; memb: Faversham Horticultural Soc, Blean Beagles, Wildfowl Tst (and breeder), Kent Branch CLA; *Recreations* shooting, wildfowl breeding, gardening; *Clubs* Farmers, Kent and Canterbury, Faversham Farmers; *Style—* Maurice Berry, Esq; Brenley, Faversham, Kent ME13 GLY (☎ 0227 751318); Gushmere Court Farm, Selling, Faversham (☎ 0227 752205)

BERRY, Prof Robert James; s of Albert Edward James Berry (d 1952), of Preston, Lancs, and Nellie, *née* Hodgson (d 1956); *b* 26 Oct 1934; *Educ* Shrewsbury, Gonville and Caius Coll Cambridge (BA, MA), Univ Coll London (PhD, DSc); *m* 13 Jun 1958, Anne Caroline, da of Charles Rushton Elliott; 1 s (Andrew b 11 July 1963), 2 da (Alison (twin) b 11 July 1963, Susan b 26 June 1965); *Career* lectr Royal Free Hosp of Med 1962-78 (reader, prof), prof of genetics UCL 1978-; govr Monkton Coombe Sch 1979-; memb: Gen Synod of C of E 1970-90, Cncl NERC 1981-87; pres: Linnean Soc 1982-85, British Ecological Soc 1987-89, Euro Ecological Fedn 1990-; treas Mammal Soc 1981-87, vice pres Zoological Soc of London 1988-90, memb Human Fertilization and Embryology Authy 1990-; tstee Nat Museums and Galleries on Merseyside; FIBiol 1974, FRSE 1981; *Publications* Teach Yourself Genetics (1965, 3 edn 1977), Adam and the Ape (1975), Natural History of Shetland (jtly, 1980), Neo Darwinison (1982), Free to be Different (jtly 1984), Natural History of Orkney (1985), God and Evolution (1988), Evolution, Ecology and Environment Stress (1989); ed: Biol of the House Mouse (1981), Evolution in the Galapagos (1984), Encyclopaedia of Animal Evolution (1986), Nature, Natural History and Ecology (1987); *Recreations* walking, resting; *Style—* Prof Robert Berry, FRSE; Quarfseter, Sackville Close, Sevenoaks, Kent TN13 3QD; Department of Biology, Medawar Building, University College London, Gower St, London WC1E 6BT (☎ 071 380 7170, fax 071 380 7026)

BERTRAM, John Alexander; s of Maj David Craig Bertram, GM, TD, of 19 Eastgate Rd, Tenterden, Kent, and Phyllis Mary, *née* Mead (d 1986); *b* 2 March 1934; *Educ* Forest Sch, Dover Coll, Univ of London (LLB), Sch of Law; *m* 4 april 1950 (m dis), (Elizabeth) Sarah, da of Hugh Gwilym Hughes (d 1984), of Tunbridge Wells, Kent; 1 s (Mark b 1966), 1 da (Jane b 1963); *Career* RASC 1957-59, 2 Lt 1958; admitted slr 1957; ptnr Thomson Snell and Passmore Solicitors 1964-, pres Tunbridge Wells Tonbridge and Dist Law Soc 1984; memb Law Soc 1957; *Recreations* travel, reading; *Clubs* Army and Navy; *Style—* John Bertram, Esq; The Coach House, Cabbage Stalk Lane, Tunbridge Wells, Kent (☎ 0892 35699); Thomson Snell & Passmore, Lyons East St, Tonbridge, Kent TN9 1HL (☎ 0732 771411, fax 0732 770445, telex 957263 TWSP TON G)

BEST, Dr Richard Myles; s of Godfrey Myles Best (d 1950), of Birchinston, Kent, and Elsie Marion Stacey, *née* Lydall (d 1979); *b* 16 May 1925; *Educ* Friends Sch Saffron Walden, Univ of London (MB BS); *m* 1, Richenda, *née* Dowse (d 1965); 3 s (Philip William b 17 Dec 1960, Roger Anthony b 21 July 1963, Jonathan Richard (twin) b 21 July 1963); m 2, 26 Oct 1974, Veronicam, da of Joseph Shaw, BEM, of Salford; 2 da (Emma Jane Louise b 5 May 1970, Rachel Anne b 30 April 1976); *Career* GP Queensborough 1963-89, ret; *Recreations* fell walking, music, literature, cricket; *Style—* Dr Richard Best; Mill House, High St, Queenborough, Kent ME11 5AQ (☎ 0795 580506)

BEST-SHAW, Sir John Michael Robert; 10 Bt (E 1665), of Eltham, Kent; s of Cdr Sir John Best-Shaw, 9 Bt, RN (d 1984), and Elizabeth Mary Theodora, eld da of late Sir Robert Heywood Hughes, 12 Bt of East Bergholt; *b* 28 Sept 1924; *Educ* Lancing, Hertford Coll Oxford (MA), Univ of London (CertEd); *m* 1960, Jane, da of Alexander Guthrie; 2 s (Thomas b 1965, Samuel b 1971), 1 da (Lucy b 1961), and 1 child decd; *Heir* s, Thomas Joshua, *qv*; *Career* late Capt Queen's Own Royal W Kent Regt, served WW II NW Europe; with Fedn Malaya Police 1950-58, church work 1959-71, teaching 1972-82, social work 1982-; *Recreations* gardening, writing; *Clubs* Royal Cwlth Soc; *Style—* Sir John Best-Shaw, Bt; The Stone House, Boxley, Maidstone, Kent ME14 3DJ (☎ 0622 757524)

BEST-SHAW, Thomas Joshua; s and h of Sir John Michael Robert Best-Shaw, 10 Bt, *qv*; *b* 7 March 1965; *Educ* Maidstone GS, Univ of Reading (BSc); *Style—* Thomas Best-Shaw, Esq; c/o The Stone House, Boxley, Maidstone, Kent

BETT, Michael; CBE (1990); s of Arthur Bett, OBE, and Nina, *née* Daniells; *b* 18 Jan 1935; *Educ* Aldenham, Pembroke Coll Cambridge (MA); *m* 3 Oct 1959, Christine Angela Bett, JP, da of Maj Horace Reid, JP; 1 s (Timothy Mark b 1961), 2 da (Sally Maria b 1963, Lucy Ann b 1965); *Career* dir Industl Rels Engrg Employers Fedn 1970-72; personnel dir: GEC 1972-77, BBC 1977-81, BT 1981-85; md LCS div, md BT UK 1985-91, vice chm British Telecom plc 1990-; former memb: Pay Bd, May Ctee of Inquiry into UK Prison Serv, Ctee of Inquiry into Water Dispute 1983, Griffiths Inquiry into NHS Mgmnt, Armed Forces Pay Review Body, Manpower Servs Cmmn, Cncl Cranfield Inst of Technol; memb cncl: Inst of Manpower Studies, Int Mgmnt Centre Buckingham; vice pres Royal TV Soc, dir Eng Shakespeare Co; chm: Nurses Pay Review Body, Mgmnt Ctee Bromley CABX; DBA (honoris causa IMCB), CBIM, FIPM, FRSA; *Style—* Michael Bett, Esq, CBE; Colets Well, The Green, Otford, Sevenoaks, Kent

BETTS, William Reuben; s of William Louis Betts (d 1961), and Doris, *née* Pumfrey (d 1977); *b* 27 June 1924; *Educ* St John's Sch Leatherhead Surrey; *m* 24 May 1950, Barbara Nellie, da of James George Wilkin (d 1941); 1 da (Rosemary Frances); *Career* chartered surveyor; sr ptnr Burrows & Day Chartered Surveyors 1977-85; Kent County Agric Soc: vice chm 1971-84, hon life govr 1984-; chartered memb Weald of Kent Round Table 1957- (fndr memb Lagos, Nigeria 1963); pres: Central Assoc Agricultural Valuers (Kent) 1977-79, Ashford Cattle Show; chm Kent branch RICS 1980; assoc Chartered Auctioneers and Estate Agents Inst 1948, FRICS; *Recreations* beekeeping, DIY; *Clubs* Elwick (Ashford); *Style—* William R Betts, Esq; Ilex Cottage, Bramble Lane, Wye, Ashford, Kent TN25 5EH (☎ 0233 812693)

BEVAN, John Stuart; s of Frank Oakland Bevan, of Stour Row, Dorset, and

Ruth Mary, *née* Sadler; *b* 19 Nov 1935; *Educ* Eggar's GS, Jesus Coll Oxford (MA), St Bart's Hosp Med Coll (MSc); *m* 30 July 1960, Patricia Vera Beatrice, da of Alfred Charles William Joyce, of Shillingstone, Dorset; 2 s (David b 16 Nov 1961, Robin b 14 Aug 1966), 2 da (Elizabeth b 19 Dec 1962, Sally b 22 March 1965); *Career* Harefield Hosp (Pathology Lab) 1954-56, physicist UKAEA 1960-62, lectr and sr lectr S Bank Poly (previously Borough Poly) 1962-73, dir of educn ILEA 1979-82 (asst then sr asst educn offr 1973-76, dep educn offr 1977-79), sec NAB 1982-88, dir Educn Servs LRB 1989-; dep co cmmr and chm Nat Activities Bd Kent Scout Assoc; memb exec ctees: ATTI 1968-73 (pres 1972-73), NUT 1970-73, AEO 1977-82 (chm 1981-82); hon fell: S Bank Poly 1988, Westminster Coll Oxford 1990; Hon DUniv Surrey 1990; FInstP 1972; *Books* The Space Environment (jtly, 1969); *Recreations* scouting, mountaineering; *Style—* John Bevan, Esq; 4 Woodland Way, Bidborough, Tunbridge Wells, Kent TN4 0UX (☎ 0892 27461); LRB, Globe House, Temple Place, London WC2 3HP (☎ 071 633 1698)

BEVAN, Brig Timothy David Vaughan (Tim); s of Maj D J V Bevan, TD (d 1986), and Hon Hilary Evelyn, *née* Pakington; *b* 20 Aug 1939; *Educ* Abberley Hall, Shrewsbury; *m* 1, 1964 (m dis 1988), Jill Sarah Murrell; 1 s (Simon David Vaughan b 16 Sept 1970), 1 da (Charlotte Hilary Vaughan b 19 April 1968); m 2, Penelope Edyth McCloy, da of Douglas Lavers, of Auckland, NZ; *Career* CO 2 LI Brig 1979-81, Cmd I5 Inf Bde 1987-90; *Recreations* theatre, history, painting; *Clubs* Army and Navy; *Style—* Brig Tim Bevan; Lloyds Bank Ltd, 16 Cheriton High St, Folkestone, Kent CT19 4EU

BEVINS, Kenneth Milton; CBE (1973), TD (1951); s of John Milton Bevins (d 1928), of Liverpool, and Grace Eveline Bevins, bro of Rt Hon John Reginald Bevins; *b* 2 Nov 1918; *Educ* Liverpool Collegiate Sch; *m* 1, 1940, Joan Harding (d 1969); 2 da; m 2, 1971, Diana, da of late Godfrey J Sellers, of Keighley; *Career* WWII: 136 Field Regt RA incl with 14 Army Burma 1943-46, Maj RA (TA); Royal Insurance Co: sec 1957, gen mangr 1963, dep chief gen mangr 1966, chief gen mangr 1970-80, dir 1970-89; dir Fire Protection Assoc 1963-77 (chm 1966-68), dir Trade Indemnity Co 1970-80 (chm 1975-80), chm Br Insur Assoc 1971-73, Mutual & Federal Insurance Co Ltd 1971-80, dir British Aerospace 1980-87; memb: Jt Fire Res Orgn Steering Ctee 1966-68, Home Sec's Standing Ctee on Crime Prevention 1967-73, exec ctee City Communications Centre 1976-80, Bd British Aerospace 1980-81, Govt Ctee to review Export Credit Ctee Dept 1983-84; *Recreations* travel, gardening, reading, photography, paintings, handiwork; *Clubs* Army and Navy, Oriental; *Style—* Kenneth Bevins, Esq, CBE, TD; Linton, The Drive, Sevenoaks, Kent TN13 3AF (☎ 0732 456909)

BIGHAM, Hon (Ralph) John; s of 2 Viscount Mersey, PC (d 1956); *b* 3 Aug 1913; *Educ* Eton; *m* 1954, Cicely Ruth (d 1986), yst da of Percy Johnson, of Douglas, IOM; *Career* OStJ; *Style—* The Hon John Bigham

BIGNELL, Alan Walter; s of Frank Bignell (d 1954), of Tonbridge, and Elizabeth Lucy, *née* Colegate (d 1990); *b* 15 June 1928; *Educ* Sussex Rd Secdy Sch Tonbridge, Tunbridge Wells Tech Inst; *m* 16 June 1951, Audrey Moreen, da of William Ewart Talbot Gray (d 1980), of Whitstable, Kent; 2 s (Brian b 1954, Eric b 1955), 1 da (Judith b 1956); *Career* Kent Messenger: reporter 1957, local govt specialist 1969; former chm Kent Dist Inst of Journalists, Kent Journalist of the Year 1989, memb Soc of Authors; *Books* Kent Villages (1975), Hopping Down In Kent (1977), Kent Lore (1983), Kent Village Book (1986), Tales Of Old Kent (1986), Kent Surrey & Sussex (1988), Kent Headlines (1989); *Recreations* reading, Kent history, gardening; *Style—* Alan Bignell, Esq; 8 Woodleas, Barming, Maidstone, Kent ME16 9JL (☎ 0622 728146); Kent Messenger, New Hythe Lane, Larkfield, Maidstone, Kent ME20 6SG (☎ 0622 717880)

BILLOT, Hugh Edward; s of Capt Ernest John Billot, and Daisy, *née* Morgan; *b* 21 Nov 1941; *Educ* Penarth Co GS, Univ of Wales Inst of Sci and Technol (BA), Univ of Bradford (MSc); *m* 20 Sept 1967, Lesley Margaret, da of Barry Alexander Phillips, of Fryarne Park, Stelling Minis, Kent; 1 s (Matthew), 1 da (Charlotte); *Career* personnel mgmnt: GKN Sankey Ltd 1964-73, Pilkington Bros Ltd St Helens Lancs 1973-76; industl rels mangr 1976-84, personnel dir Sheerness Steel Co plc Kent 1986-; dir: Swale Enterprise Agency, Steel Training Ltd; chm: Kent Employer Network, Euro Coal and Steel Community Housing Ctee; memb: Ctee Sheppey Industs Assoc, UK Housing Ctee, CBI Kent Employers Gp; FIPM 1988, MInstD 1988 (MBIM 1977); *Recreations* golf, dog walking; *Clubs* Tudor Park Golf and Country; *Style—* Hugh Billot, Esq; Randolph's Leap, Charing, Kent (☎ 023 371 3075); Datchet House, West Parade, Hythe, Kent (☎ 0303 238101); Sheerness Steel Co plc, Sheerness, Kent (☎ 0795 663333, fax 0795 662147, car tel 0860 365 421, telex 965022 & 965764)

BINDER, Alan Naismith; OBE (1974); s of Frederick John Binder (d 1961), of Hampshire, and Kathleen Mary, *née* Darker (d 1967); *b* 4 Aug 1931; *Educ* Bedford Sch, Magdalen Coll Oxford (MA); *m* 1958, Gillian Patricia, da of George Francis Wilson, of Sussex; 1 s (Jonathan b 1962), 2 da (Jennifer b 1958, Stephanie b 1959); *Career* dir Shell International Petroleum Co Ltd 1984, pres Shell International Trading Co 1987; *Recreations* tennis, skiing, reading, music; *Clubs* Carlton, Leander, MCC; *Style—* Alan Binder, Esq, OBE; Old Place, Speldhurst, Kent TN3 0PA (☎ 089 286 3227); Shell Centre, London SE1 7NA (☎ 071 934 5878)

BINNING, Kenneth George Henry; CMG (1976); s of Henry Binning (d 1976), of Wivenhoe, Essex, and Hilda, *née* Powell (d 1987); *b* 5 Jan 1928; *Educ* Bristol GS, Balliol Coll Oxford (MA); *m* 28 Feb 1953, Pamela Dorothy, da of Alfred Edward Pronger (d 1963), of Streatham, London; 3 s (Simon Kenneth b 1955, Julian Charles b 1957, Marcus Adam b 1963), 1 da (Susanna Clare b 1960); *Career* Nat Serv Capt RAEC 1950-52; HM Treasy 1952-59 (private sec to Fin Sec 1956), UK AEA 1959-65, seconded Miny of Technol 1965-67 (1969-), asst dir Progs Analysis Unit 1967-69, dir gen Concorde Prog (UK) 1973-76, set up Invest in Br Bureau 1976-80, govt dir BSC 1980-82, dir Govt Rels NEI plc 1983-; *Recreations* music, gardening; *Clubs* Reform; *Style—* Kenneth Binning, Esq, CMG; 12 Kemerton Road, Beckenham, Kent BR3 2NJ (☎ 081 650 0273); NEI plc, Tavistock House East, Woburn Walk, Burton St, London WC1 (☎ 071 387 9393)

BINNS, Malcolm; s of Douglas Priestley Binns (d 1988), of Keighley, Yorkshire, and May, *née* Walker; *b* 29 Jan 1936; *Educ* Bradford GS, RCM; *Career* prof RCM 1961-65; concert pianist: London debut 1959, debut Promenade Concerts 1960, regular performances at Proms 1962-, Royal Festival Hall debut 1961, has appeared in London Philharmonic seasons 1962-; soloist with all major Br orchs, over 30 recordings, first complete recording of Beethoven Piano Sonatas on original instruments, played Far E and toured with Scot Nat Orch and Limbourg Orch 1987-88; ARCM; *Recreations* gardening; *Style—* Malcolm Binns, Esq; c/o Ibbs and Tillett, 18B Pindock Mews, London W9 2PY (☎ 071 286 7526)

BIRCH, Linda (Mrs Pitt); da of Richard George Milner Birch (d 1969), and Elizabeth, *née* Lindop; *b* 1 July 1947; *Educ* Folkestone Sch for Girls, Folkestone Sch of Art; *m* 29 July 1981, Rev Trevor Pitt, s of Arthur Edwin Pitt (d 1990); *Career* freelance illustrator of children's books with over 80 published to date, worked for BBC TV's Jackanory prog and BT's telemessage cards; tutor in adult educn at Canterbury and lectr in schs and colls; exhibitions incl: RWS, Children's Books of the Year Exhibition 1988; MSIAD; *Recreations* reading, painting; *Style—* Miss Linda Birch; The Vicarage, Elham, Canterbury, Kent CT4 6TT (☎ 0303 840219); The Studio, Parsonage Farm, Craft Workshops, North Elham, Canterbury, Kent (☎ 0303 840369)

BIRCH, Dr Raymond George; s of George Birch (d 1929), of Station St, Sittingbourne, and Bertha Shilling, *née* Jarvis (d 1961); *b* 6 May 1915; *Educ* Kings Sch Rochester, Bart's (MRCS, MRCGP, LRCP); *m* 5 Aug 1940, Diana June, *née* Finnie; 2 da (Susan Geraldine b 1940, Diana Kathryn Redfern b 1943); *Career* Maj HG 1940-45; GP Sittingbourne 1940-79; med offr: BRCS 1946 (Badge of Hon 1976 and 1986), Portland Cement Mills 1950-79, Kent Co Agricultural Soc (hon); hon chief surgn Br Fire Servs Assoc 1952-; pres: Gore Court Cricket and Hockey Club 1971-89, Sittingbourne Soc; *Recreations* archaeology, farming, hockey, cricket; *Clubs* Farmers, Whitehall Court; *Style—* Dr Raymond Birch; Downsells, Bredgar, Sittingbourne, Kent ME9 8AP (☎ 062884264)

BIRKMYRE, Sir Henry; 2 Bt (UK 1921), of Dalmunzie, Co Perth; s of Sir Archibald Birkmyre, 1 Bt, CBE (d 1935); *b* 24 March 1898; *Educ* Wellington; *m* 1922, Doris Gertrude, da of Col Herbert Austen Smith, CIE (d 1949); 1 s, 1 da; *Heir* s, Archibald Birkmyre; *Career* serv WWI with RFA in France; former co dir; *Recreations* golf; *Clubs* Rye Golf, Cooden Beach Golf; *Style—* Sir Henry Birkmyre, Bt; Tudor Rest, 2 Calverley Park Gardens, Tunbridge Wells, Kent TN1 2DX

BIRMINGHAM, Prof David Bevis; s of Walter Barr Birmingham, of Shaftesbury, and Norah, *née* Langford, of St Vincent, WI; *b* 6 June 1938; *Educ* Collége Henchoz Switzerland, Univ Coll of Ghana (BA), Univ of London (PhD); *m* 17 Feb 1962, Elizabeth Jane, da of Christopher Beech Taylor (d 1984); 2 s (Robert b 2 July 1964, Stephen b 26 May 1971); *Career* prof of modern hist Univ of Kent 1980-; past pres African Studies Assoc of the UK; *Books* The Portugese Conquest of Angola (1965), Trade and Conflict in Angola (1966), Pre-Colonial African Trade (1970), Central Africa to 1870 (1981), History of Central Africa (2 vols, 1983), Nkrumah (1990); *Style—* Prof David Birmingham; University of Kent, Canterbury, Kent CT2 7NS (☎ 0227 764000)

BISHOP, Dr (Arthur) Clive; s of Charles Henry Bishop (d 1966), of Newcastle, Staffs, and Hilda, *née* Clowes; *b* 9 July 1930; *Educ* Wolstanton Co GS Newcastle, King's Coll London (BSc, PhD); *m* 8 Sept 1962, Helen, da of Joseph Benninson (d 1983), of Stoke-on-Trent; 1 da (Anne b 1965); *Career* Nat Serv Educn Branch RAF 1955-57; geologist HM Geological Survey Edinburgh 1954-58, lectr in geology Queen Mary Coll London 1958-69; Br Natural History Museum: princ sci offr 1969-72, keeper of mineralogy 1975-89 (dep keeper 1972-74, dep dir 1982-89); fell King's Coll London 1985, Membre d'Honneur La Societe Jersiase 1983; memb GA (pres 1978-80), life memb Mineralogical Soc (pres 1978-80); FGS; *Books* An Outline of Crystal Morphology (1967), Country Life Guide to Minerals, Rocks and Fossils (with W R Hamilton and A R Woolley, 1974); *Recreations* drawing and painting; *Style—* Dr Clive Bishop; 4 Viewfield Rd, Bexley, Kent DA5 3EE (☎ 081 302 9602)

BISHOP, John Michael; s of Lt Wilfred Charles John Michael Bishop (d 1988), of Whitstable, Kent, and Margery Bains, *née* Emmerson; *b* 1 March 1947; *Educ* Kent Coll Canterbury, LSE (LLB); *m* 12 Aug 1982, Laurie Marie, da of Lyman Charles Harris (d 1980), of Virginia Beach, Virginia, USA; 2 da (Heather Virginia, Lucy Cecilia); *Career* Kent and Co of London Yeo (TA) 1965-67; head barr of chambers at 7 Stone Buildings Lincolns Inn 1986, head of chambers at 31 Watling St Canterbury Kent 1988-; memb Hon Soc Middle Temple Lincoln's Inn; *Recreations* photography, antiquarian books; *Style—* John Bishop, Esq; Greenfields, Pean Hill, Whitstable, Kent

BISHOP, Thomas (Tim) Frederick; s of Frederick Stanley Bishop (d 1970), and Edith Gertrude, *née* Pore (d 1968); *b* 4 April 1937; *Educ* St Olaves and St Saviors GS London, Timaru Boys HS New Zealand, Canterbury Coll, Univ of New Zealand; *m* 13 march 1959, Jennifer Clare, da of Darcley Francis Hocking (d 1963); 1 s (Tristram b 1961), 1 da (Charlotte b 1959); *Career* nat dir Arthur Young McClelland Moores and Co 1977-82 (ptnr 1975); chm: Spicer and Pegler Assoc 1987 (md 1983-87), Spicer and Oppenheim Consultants 1987 (chm of UK Conslting Operations 1988); *Recreations* tstee Rye art gallery; *Style—* Tim Bishop, Esq; Spicer and Oppenheim, 13 Bruton St, London (☎ 071 480 7766)

BISSILL, Raymond Norman; s of Herbert Cyril Bissill (d 1973), of Chestfield, Whitstable, Kent, and Evelyn Violet, *née* Sydney; *b* 14 Oct 1938; *Educ* Chatham GS for Boys, Medway Coll of Technol (Dip Bldg); *m* 7 Feb 1975, Sally Ann, da of Maj Roy Albert Smith, MBE (ret), of Whitstable, Kent; 2 s (Adam b 1976, James b 1977), 1 da (Abigail b 1974); *Career* chm and md: Abbey Grove Securities Ltd, R Bailey and Co Ltd, Errill Securities Ltd, Bailey Builders Ltd; pres The Canterbury and Dist Bldg Employees Confedn 1979-81, chm The E Kent Jt Consultative Ctee of Bldg 1987-88; FID, FCIOB; *Recreations* squash, skiing, windsurfing; *Clubs* Kent and Canterbury, Whitstable Yacht; *Style—* Raymond N Bissill, Esq; Penraevon, Chestfield Rd, Chestfield, Whitstable, Kent; R Bailey and Co Ltd, Malvern House, Broad St, Canterbury, Kent

BLACK, Thomas Charteris; s of John Sutherland Charteris Black (d 1967), and Gertrude Margaret, *née* Stout (d 1976); *b* 12 Sept 1914; *Educ* Univ Coll Sch Frognall London, Sch of Pharmacy London (MPharmS); *m* 28 March 1942, (Violet) Lorna, da of Brig-Gen William Denman Croft, CB, DMG, DSO (d 1968), of Mawnan Smith, Cornwall; 1 s (Peter b 1952), 2 da (Jane b 1943, Susan b 1945); *Career* HG 1940-41: Cdr No 1 Platoon, No 3 Co, 1 Co of London Bn, Cdr Buckingham Palace Detachment of Kings Gd 1941; seaman RN Patrol Serv 1941-42, cmmnd Fighter Direction Offr 1942; RNVR: Sub Lt HMS Victorians RNVR 1942-43, Lt HMS Ukussa 1944, Lt HMS Valiant 1944, Lt HMS Boxer 1945, Lt Cdr HMS Glory 1945-46; Menley & James Ltd: factory worker 1930-33, office mangr 1933-39, manufactured Stilboestrol 1938-39, mktg mangr 1939-41 and 1946-49, mktg dir 1949-56; mangr of commercial devpt Pfizers Ltd 1957-59, mktg mangr Miles Ltd 1959-67, vice pres of int ops Miles Inc USA 1969-79 (mktg dir Ames Div 1967-69); sec local Royal Br Legion, treas local Cons Assoc; Liveryman Worshipful Soc Apothecaries 1951, Freeman City of London 1952; FRSA 1951, FRPharmS 1977 (MPharmS 1938); *Recreations* bowls, walking; *Style—* Thomas Black, Esq; Michaelmas, Convent Close, St Margarets-at-Cliffe, Dover, Kent CT15 6JD (☎ 0304 853142)

BLACKFORD, Sqdn Ldr Peter Fitzgerald; s of Joseph Blackford (d 1959), and Sheila, *née* O'Halligan (d 1952); *b* 22 Nov 1920; *Educ* Tonbridge, RAF Coll Cranwell; *m* 23 July 1943, Sheila, da of Lt-Col Henry Joseph Higgs (d 1936), of Notts; 4 s (Timothy b 1945, Christopher b 1948, Jeremy b 1952, Patrick b 1954); *Career* reg RAF offr 1938-57, wartime ops in UK and Europe, ret as Sqdn Ldr 1957; subsequently worked as personnel mangr in several cos incl Wellcome Foundation 1969-82; *Recreations* gardening; *Style—* Sqdn Ldr Peter F Blackford; Shode House, Dux Lane, Plaxtol, nr Sevenoaks, Kent

BLACKLEDGE, Michael Glyn; s of Edward John Blackledge (d 1981), of Bromley, Kent, and Winifred May, *née* Hemsley; *b* 24 Oct 1954; *Educ* Colfe's GS Lee London, South Bank Poly (Dip Estate Mgmnt), Garnett Coll (Cert Ed); *m* 21 Aug 1976, Janet May, da of Edward Arthur Connell, of Beckenham, Kent; 2 s (Jonathan b 1984, Alexander b 1990); *Career* surveyor Thames Water Authy 1974-78; valuer: City of Westminster 1978-79, London Borough of Croydon 1979-81; sr lectr: Vauxhall Coll of Bld and Further Educn 1981-88, Thames Poly 1988-89; sr surveyor King & Co 1989-, tutor Coll of Estate Mgmnt 1989-; Freeman City of London, memb Worshipful Co of Feltmakers; ARICS 1978; *Recreations* writing, golf, soccer, wargaming and computing; *Style—* Michael Blackledge, Esq; King & Company Chartered Surveyors, 7 Stratford Place, London W1N 9AE (☎ 071 493 4933, telex 885485, fax 071 409 0469 071 409 0676)

BLAGG, Dr Thomas Frederick Colston; s of Lt-Col Thomas Colston Blagg (d 1983), of Brunsell Hall, Car-Colston, Notts, and Loys Willis, *née* Cope (d 1989); *b* 10 Aug 1942; *Educ* Oakham, Keble Coll Oxford (BA, MA), Inst of Archaeology Univ of London (PhD); *Career* admitted slr 1967; in practice 1967-70, freelance archaeologist 1970-78, memb educn serv Br Museum 1978; lectr in archaeology Univ of Kent 1978-; FSA 1983; *Books* The Roman Riverside Wall and Monumental Arch in London (jtly, 1980), Papers in Iberian Archaeology (jtly, 1984), Military and Civilian in Roman Britain (jtly, 1984); *Recreations* travel (wine and ruins), shooting, London; *Style—* Dr Thomas Blagg, FSA; Rutherford College, The University, Canterbury, Kent CT2 7NX (☎ 0227 764000)

BLAKE, Lt-Col Eugene Percival Thomas (Hugh); s of William Blake (d 1957), of Kingsbury, London, and Mary, *née* Cahill (d 1963); *b* 4 Jan 1926; *Educ* Kingsbury Co GS; *m* 2 Feb 1950, Mary, da of Michael Gregan (d 1955), of Ennis, Co Clare, Eire; 2 s (Peter b 1951, Derek b 1953); *Career* Royal Fus 1943-55 (Private, 2 Lt, Lt, Capt), attached Indian Army 1 Gurkha Rifles 1945-47; RAOC: joined 1955, Capt, Maj, Lt-Col 1970-81; asst dir ordnance servs E Midland Dist 1970-73, OIC tech servs Central Ordnance Depot Donnington 1973-75, Cdr RAOC troops W Dortmund 1975-77, perm pres courts martial 1 Armoured Div 1977-81; memb SE Kent Community Health Cncl 1986-90, vice chm Tenterden Residents Assoc 1986-87; dep ldr Ashford Borough Cncl 1990 (memb 1983-, chm Personnel Sub Ctee 1987); *Recreations* clay pigeon shooting, pistol shooting, sailing; *Style—* Lt-Col Hugh Blake; 25 Knockwood Rd, Tenterden, Kent TN30 7AP (☎ 05806 2003)

BLAKE, Philip Haslewood; s of Robert Frederick Blake (d 1944), of Belfast, and Josephine Anne Isabella, *née* Sloss (d 1962); descended from all the sons of Edward III who left issue, all the like Magna Carta Barons, Sir Thomas More and William Haslewood, executor of Lord Nelson; Lordship of Barham Kent in family since 1597; *b* 3 May 1907; *Educ* Campbell Coll Belfast, RCM London; *Career* sub ed Northern Whig Belfast 1927-30, info offr Br Pavilion NY World's Fair 1939-40, temp admin offr Br Info Services NY, set up Govt Exhibition Serv in USA 1940-43, ed British Topography Encyclopedia Britannica 1943-44; conductor Belfast Concerts for Sch Children and ENSA Orch 1944-45, music advsr ENSA in BLA 1945, PRO i/c visual publicity Min of Town and Country Planning 1946-48, Inland Revenue 1949-51; press offr: Fedn of Civil Engrg Contractors 1952-60, Royal Mint 1960-61; Soc of Genealogists: fndr Res Dept and first dir 1961-62, genealogist 1963-; memb: Cncl Br Record Soc 1949-, Kent Arch Soc 1982- (chm Records Ctee), Cncl Irish Genealogical Res Soc 1986-87 (fell and dir of res 1987); fndr: Assoc of Genealogists and Record Agents (AGRA) 1968, Kent Record Collections 1985; author of many articles in learned journals; *Books* History of Federation of Civil Engineering Contractors (1960), Canterbury Cathedral, Christ Church Gate (1965); *Recreations* chess, vintage cars; *Style—* Philip Blake, Esq; 5 Watkin Rd, Folkestone, Kent CT19 5EP (☎ 0303 41739)

BLAKEBROUGH, Howard; s of William Kenneth Blakebrough, of Halifax, Yorks, and Amy, *née* Blenard; *b* 21 May 1944; *Educ* Heath GS Halifax, Univ of Manchester (BSc); *m* 9 March 1968, Valerie Jean, da of Leslie Malcolm Golton, of Seaford, Sussex; 1 s (Simon Kevin b 5 March 1970), 1 da (Helen Claire b 3 May 1972); *Career* prodn mangr Lever Bros (Port Sunlight) Ltd 1966-71, factory mangr Bowyers (Wiltshire) Ltd 1971-77; W A Turner Ltd: prodn dir 1977-81, md 1981-; ctee memb Br Meat Mfrs Assoc; bd dir: Weald and W Kent Regnl C of C, Royal Tunbridge Wells C of C; *Recreations* water polo, bridge, badminton, running; *Style—* Howard Blakebrough, Esq; Pashley House, Pashley Rd, Ticehurst, Wadhurst, E Sussex TN5 7HE (☎ 0580 200013); W A Turner Ltd, Broadwater Lane, Tunbridge Wells, Kent TN2 5RD (☎ 0892 515215, fax 0892 510028)

BLAKEY, (Charles) Conrad; RD (1977), JP (1971); s of George Bernard Blakey, of White Lodge, Old Golf Links, Cliff Rd, Hythe, Kent, and Marie Blakey; *b* 20 Aug 1941; *Educ* William B Barbour Acad, Paisley GS, HMS Conway; *m* 18 Sept 1971, Celia, da of Sir Robert J Sainsbury; 2 s (Simon b 1973, Michael b 1975); *Career* RNR: Midshipman 1959, Lt 1964, Lt Cdr 1971; dep chm Martello Textile Co Ltd 1976; chm: Folkestone and District Sports Centre Ltd 1984, Cantab Ltd 1987 (dir 1986); dir Kentstone Properties plc 1990-; dep chm Kent Probation Ctee; memb: SE Kent DHA, Bd HM Prison Canterbury (resigned 1987); *Recreations* golf, rugby, cricket, opera; *Clubs* Rye Golf, Naval & Military, Kent CCC; *Style—* Conrad Blakey, Esq, RD, JP; White Lodge, Old Golf Links, Cliff Rd, Hythe, Kent CT21 5XN (☎ 0303 66019); Martello Textile Co Ltd, 216 Dover Rd, Folkestone, Kent CT19 6SJ (☎ 0303 57587, fax 0303 58477, car tel 0836 250973, telex 965474 MARTEX)

BLAND, Lt-Col Sir Simon Claud Michael; KCVO (1982, CVO 1973, MVO 1967); s of Sir (George) Nevile Maltby Bland, KCMG, KCVO (d 1972), and Portia Christabel Irene, *née* Ottley (d 1968); *b* 4 Dec 1923; *Educ* Eton; *m* 1954, Olivia Beatrice, da of late Maj William Blackett, of Arbigland, Dumfries; 1 s, 3 da; *Career* WWII Scots Gds (served Italy), Br Jt Servs Mission Washington DC 1948-49, 2 Bn Scots Gds Malaya 1949-51, asst mil advsr UK High Cmmn Karachi 1959-60; comptroller and asst private sec to: HRH late Duke of Gloucester 1961-74, HRH late Prince William 1968-72; comptroller private sec and equerry to HRH Princess Alice, Duchess of Gloucester and to TRH the Duke and Duchess of Gloucester 1972-89 (extra equerry 1989-); conslt Operation Raleigh Industrial Metals Services Ltd; dir West End branch Commercial Union; pres: Friends of Edenbridge Hosp, Edenbridge Div St John Ambulance Bde, Edenbridge Players, Lingfield and Area Branch riding for the Disabled; vice pres Edenbridge Town Band; cncl memb: Distressed

Gentlefolk's Aid Assoc, The Coll of St Barnabas; tstee: Grant Maintained Sch Tst; KStJ 1987 (CStJ 1978); *Recreations* shooting; *Clubs* Buck's; *Style—* Lt-Col Sir Simon Bland, KCVO; Gabriel's Manor, Edenbridge, Kent (☎ 0732 862340)

BLAZEY, Cncllr Montague Ian; s of Alfred Hurrell Blazey (d 1959), of Beckenham, and Violet Catherine, *née* Petrie; *b* 21 May 1928; *Educ* St Dunstans' Coll Catford, King Henry VIII Sch Coventry; *m* 30 July 1955, Maureen Tyrell, da of Albert John Creedy, MBE (d 1969), of Beckenham; 2 s (Iain Andrew David b 1962, Bruce Gordon Phillip b 1968), 2 da (Karen Elisabeth Fiona b 1958, Morag Jenifer Hurrell b 1960); *Career* Sun Alliance Insurance Group: underwriter 1952-60, sr underwriter 1960-74, gp liaison supt 1974-81, asst property insur mangr 1981-83, property insur mangr 1983-89, ret 1989; consult Economic Insurance Co Ltd 1989-; London Borough of Bromley: cncllr 1968-, chm Social Servs Ctee 1976- (exec 1978), dep Mayor 1976-77, Mayor 1978-79; chm: Govrs Cator Park Sch For Girls 1975-, Bromley Dist Scout Cncl 1980-, Govrs St Christopher's Sch 1987-, Bromley DHA 1989-; *Recreations* travel, reading, music; *Style—* Cncllr Montague Blazey; Dachsthorn, 17 Park Ave, West Wickham, Kent BR4 9JU (☎ 081 777 7234); District Headquarters, Farnborough Hospital, Farnborough Common, Orpington, Kent BR6 8ND (☎ 0689 62422, fax 0689 62423)

BLEASE, Harry; MBE (1985); s of Percy Blease, of Lymm, Cheshire (d 1972), and Charlotte Jane, *née* Jones (d 1961); *b* 5 Nov 1917; *Educ* Sale Cheshire; *m* 15 Sept 1945, Joan Mabel, da of George William Guy Andrews, of Chatham (d 1958); 1 da (Margaret Jean b 1950); *Career* writer RN 1940, cmmnd 1949, Lt Cdr 1962, ret 1967; administrator Sea Cadet HQ London 1967-69, pt/t sec RN and RM Children's Tst 1969-84, pt/t administrator Pembroke House (home for aged sailors) Gillingham 1970-82; memb Cncl Offrs' Pension Soc 1969-86; cncllr Gillingham Borough Cncl 1970-90, tstee Medway Mission to Seamen Tst 1975-, Mayor of Gillingham 1976-77 and 1981-82, hon treas Medway Ctee King George's Fund for Sailors 1976-84 (chm 1984-), tstee King George V Homes for the Aged Gillingham 1979-; chm of govrs: Byron CP Sch Gillingham 1977-88, Napier CP Sch Gillingham 1982-88; chm Japanese Link Ctee 1982-, memb Cncl SE Area Sanctuary Housing Assoc 1984-88, dep govr Hosp of Sir John Hawkins Knight Chatham 1985-, chm Kent Mayor's Assoc 1986-87, memb Kent Consumer Consultative Ctee Southern Water Region 1986-89; *Recreations* gardening, philately; *Style—* Harry Blease, Esq, MBE; 261 Napier Rd, Gillingham, Kent ME7 4LY (☎ 0634 51223)

BLIGH, Lady Harriet Esme Ghislaine; da of 9 Earl of Darnley (d 1955); *b* 27 April 1949; *Educ* Cobham Hall, Somerville Coll Oxford; *Style—* Lady Harriet Bligh; Meadow House, Cobham, nr Gravesend, Kent DA12 3BZ (☎ 0474 814 210)

BLOOMFIELD, Barry Cambray; s of Clifford Wilson Bloomfield (d 1981), and Eileen Elizabeth Bloomfield (d 1953); *b* 1 June 1931; *Educ* East Ham GS, Univ Coll Exeter (BA), Birkbeck Coll London (MA); *m* 29 Dec 1958, Valerie Jean, da of George Philpot (d 1964); *Career* Nat Serv 1952-54; asst Nat Central Library 1955, librarian Coll of St Mark & St John 1956-61, asst librarian LSE 1961-63, librarian Sch of Oriental and African Studies 1972-78 (dep librarian 1963-72), dir India Office Library & Records FCO 1978-82, keeper Dept of Oriental Manuscripts and Printed Books 1983-85 (dir collection devpt), Br Library 1985; hon memb Darwin Coll Univ of Kent 1982-; fell Library Assoc 1965; memb: cncl Britain-Burma Soc 1979-, VP Bibliographical Soc 1979-, cncl Royal Asiatic Soc 1980-84, cncl Br Assoc for Cemeteries in S Asia 1980-, Exec Ctee Friends of the Nat Libraries 1981-, Bibliographical Soc, Oxford Bibliographical Soc, Cambridge Bibliographical Soc; *Books* W H Auden: a bibliography (2 edn, with E Mendelson, 1972), An Author Index to Selected British Little Magazines (1976), Philip Larkin: a bibliography (1979), Middle East Studies and Librarianship (1980); *Recreations* reading, music; *Clubs* Cwlth Tst, Civil Serv; *Style—* Barry Bloomfield, Esq; British Library, 14 Store Street, London, WC1E 7DG (☎ 071 323 7637)

BLOW, Stanley; OBE (1984), DL (Kent 1979); s of Jack Blow (d 1976), of 11 Helenslea Ave, Golders Green, London, and Lily, *née* Robinstein (d 1981) ; *b* 6 June 1924; *Educ* Wessex Gardens London; *m* 24 Nov 1947, Constance Elizabeth, da of Andrew Goodrich (d 1951), of 37 Cholmley Gardens, W Hampstead, London; 1 da (Anne (Mrs Budd) b 16 Aug 1953); *Career* Corpl Home Guard 1940-45; joined M Blow (fruit growers and merchants) 1938, ptnr S Blow (Matfield) 1949, merged with Matfield Fruit Supplies Ltd 1983, dir Paddock Wood Distribution Centre 1973-85; contested: Parly elections (Lib) 1964-70, Euro Parly election (Lib) W Kent and E Surrey 1979; pres: Tunbridge Wells St John Ambulance Cadets, Tunbridge Wells Orpheus Male Voice Choir, Mid-Kent Social and Lib Democrats, Kent Playing Fields Assoc; Freeman City of London, Liveryman Farmers Co 1968, Liveryman Fletchers Co 1984; SBStJ 1985; *Books* Act Imaginatively (1987); *Recreations* history, reading, golf, gardens; *Clubs* MCC, Kent CC, Hoppers Tie; *Style—* Stanley Blow, Esq, OBE, DL; Cotuams Hall, Hollingbourne, Maidstone, Kent ME17 1TP; 6 Sackville Gardens, Hove, Sussex (☎ 0622 880464)

BLUCK, Duncan Robert Yorke; CBE (1990, OBE 1984); s of Thomas Edward Bluck, and Ida Bluck; *b* 19 March 1927; *m* 1952, Stella Wardaw, *née* Murdoch; 1 s, 3 da; *Career* chm: Cathay Pacific Airways 1980-84 (dir 1970-, md 1971-84), Swire Pacific Ltd 1980-84 (dir 1970-), John Swire & Sons (HK) Ltd 1980-84 (dir 1970-84), Hong Kong Aircraft Engineering Co Ltd 1980-86, Br Tourist Authy 1984-90, English Tourist Bd 1984-90, Kent Econ Devpt Bd 1985-; dir Hong Kong and Shaighai Bank Corp 1980-84; JP Hong Kong 1976-84; chm English Schs Fndn (Hong Kong) 1976-84, memb Court Univ of Kent; *Recreations* sailing, swimming, tennis; *Clubs* Brooks's; *Style—* Duncan Bluck, Esq, CBE; Elfords, Hawkhurst, Kent TN18 4RP (☎ 0580 752153); John Swire & Sons Ltd, Swire House, 59 Buckingham Gate, London SW1E 6AJ (☎ 071 834 7717)

BLUETT, David Frederick; s of Frederick Dawson Bluett (d 1977), of 6 Fairleas Court, Courtdown Rd, Beckenham, Kent, and Muriel Emma, *née* Fells (d 1982); *b* 5 Dec 1937; *Educ* Cranleigh; *m* (m dis), Gillian Lalage, da of Richard Travis Harris; 2 s (James Edward Nutcombe b 3 Oct 1974, Charles Piers b 28 June 1978); *Career* CCF Artillery Section Cranleigh Sch 1951-55, HAC 1955-56, Nat Serv RA 1956-58, cmmnd 1957, Kent Yeo 1958-63; Royal Insurance Co 1955-56; chm: Bluett Smith & Co Ltd (and subsids of family co) 1972 (joined 1959, md 1968), Sunset Cleaning Group 1975-89, subsids of TKM plc 1980-83, Saunders Abbott 1987; Old Cranleighan RFC: former Capt, sec, chm and vice pres; former chm Old Cranleighan Soc, former Capt Old Cranleighans Golf Soc; involved with St Christopher's Hospice; Liveryman: Worshipful Co of Skinners 1968 (Freeman 1961), Worshipful Co of Carmen 1979 (memb court); FInstD 1960; *Recreations* tennis, golf, previously squash and rugby; *Clubs* City Livery, E India, RAC, IOD, HAC, Royal Cinque Ports, Old Cranleighan, Tower Ward, Offrs Dining (Kent), County of London Yeo; *Style—* David Bluett, Esq; Fairfield, Furze Hill, Kingwood, Tadworth, Surrey KT20 6HB (☎ 07373 51867); Bluett House, 189-195 High St, Beckenham, Kent BR3 1BA (☎ 081 658 2222, 081 658 0915, fax 081 650 1017, car 0860 300748, telex 946254)

BLUNDELL, Keith John; s of John Blundell (d 1945), and Bessie, *née* Jenner (d 1974); *b* 7 Jan 1936; *Educ* Maidstone GS, Medway Coll of Art; *m* 24 Sept 1960, Joan Ann, da of Albert Groves (d 1970); 1 s (John b 1963), 2 da (Karen b 1965, Kristin b 1969); *Career* architect; project architect Poltock and Associates 1960-72, dir Chapman and Hanson 1982- (sr architect 1972-82); MRIBA 1970; *Recreations* jazz musician; *Style—* Keith Blundell, Esq; Navarac, Stockett Lane, Coxheath, Maidstone, Kent ME17 4PS (☎ 0622 745347); Chapman and Hanson, 29 Widmore Rd, Bromley, Kent BR1 1RT (☎ 081 460 8834, 081 460 8838)

BLYTON, Carey; s of Hanley Harrison Blyton, and Florence Maud, *née* Pullen; *b* 1932; *Educ* Beckenham GS Kent, UCL, Trinity Coll of Music London (BMus), Royal Danish Acad of Music Copenhagen; *m* Mary Josephine Mills; 2 s (Matthew James, Daniel Carey); *Career* music ed: Mills Music Ltd 1958-63, Faber & Faber Ltd (now Faber Music Ltd) 1964-74; music lectr 1963-; prof of harmony conterpoint and orchestration Trinity Coll of Music London 1963-73, visiting prof of composition for film TV and radio Guildhall Sch of Music and Drama London 1972-83; short story writer and nonsense poet; composer; piano music incl: Six Epigrams (1951), Three Impressions (1963-64); madrigals and partsongs incl: What Then is Love (1956), The Silly Flea (1962), In Lighter Mood (1972), A Nursery Song Suite (1985); song cycles incl: The Poetry of Dress (1956), Prayers from the Ark (1964-65); voice and chamber ensemble: Moresques (1952), The Maiden Deceived (1982); music for schs: Mixed Bag (1962-63), Sweeney Todd the Barber (1977), Dracula! (1983), Frankenstein! (1987); chamber music: Scherzo (1949), For the Delight of Shiva (1986); music for saxophone quartet incl: In Memoriam Scott Fitzgerald (1971), Suite Carolina (1984); music for brass: Eilgut-Galopp (1980), Sweet and Sour Rag (1983), Pasticheries (1987); music for orchestra: Cinque Port (1957-58), The Birds of the Air (1971), Overture: The Hobbit (1967); *Books* The Faber Book of Nursery Songs (1968), Bananas in Pyjamas (1972), Noah & the Unicorns (1979); *Recreations* keeping tropical fish, reading; *Clubs* The Aborigine; *Style—* Carey Blyton, Esq; 55 Goldsel Rd, Swanley, Kent BR8 8HA (☎ 0322 64380)

BODYCOMBE, Peter Douglas; s of Kenneth Alfred Bodycombe, of London, and Violet Alice, *née* Albon; *b* 29 Sept 1941; *Educ* Alleyns Sch; *m* 10 Aug 1963, Brenda Patricia, da of Albert Joseph Simco (d 1989); 1 s (Andrew David b 23 Feb 1969), 1 da (Kim Lesley b 5 March 1967); *Career* stockbroker's clerk Phillips & Drew 1958-65; National Westminster Bank plc: joined Norwich 1965, asst mangr Canterbury 1979, various managerial positions 1979-87, mangr Faversham 1988, sr mangr Maidstone 1990; memb: Ctee Chartered Inst of Bankers, NFU, Maidstone C of C; AIB; *Recreations* gardening, photography, walking; *Clubs* Kent & Canterbury Cons; *Style—* Peter Bodycombe, Esq; National Westminster Bank plc, PO Box 4, 3 High St, Maidstone, Kent ME14 5RZ (☎ 0622 758401)

BOGGIA, Cncllr William George (Bill); s of Arthur George Boggia (d 1984), of Faversham, and Eva, *née* Maberlet; *b* 27 Sept 1929; *Educ* Rochester Tech, Kent Farm Inst Hadlow Coll; *m* 17 Sept 1960, Alfreda Sylvia, da of Alfred Scatter Kite (d 1965); 1 s (Arthur Graham b 15 May 1963), 1 da (Clare Louise b 3 Aug 1961); *Career* former poultry farmer; dir Coast and Country Caravans Ltd 1966-; cncllr Rural Dist of Swale 1967-74, borough cncllr Swale East Down Ward, exec memb Swale Relate, fndr chm Canterbury Poultry Farmers Gp, sec Village Hall Ctee, chm of various Swale RDC Ctees, dep Mayor 1982-84, Mayor 1984-85; FBIM, FInstSMM; *Recreations* country sports; *Style—* Cncllr Bill Boggia; Boughton House, Graveney, Faversham, Kent (☎ 0795 531000); Coast and Country Caravans Ltd, Cleve Hill, Graveney, Faversham, Kent

BOLLAND, Sir Edwin; KCMG (1981, CMG 1971); s of George Bolland, of Moerly, Yorks; *b* 20 Oct 1922; *Educ* Morley GS, Univ Coll Oxford; *m* 1948, Winifred, da of William Mellor, of Moerly, Yorks; 1 s, 3 da; *Career* joined FO 1947, head Far Eastern Dept 1965-67, cnsllr Washington 1967-71, ambass Bulgaria 1973-76, head Br delgn to negotiate MBFR 1976-80, ambass Belgrade 1980-82; *Style—* Sir Edwin Bolland, KCMG; Lord's Spring Cottage, Godden Green, Sevenoaks, Kent

BOLT, Prof Christine Anne; da of William Eastwood Jackson (d 1970), and Vera, *née* Stuttard; *b* 10 Aug 1940; *Educ* Bolton Sch Lancs, Westfield Coll London (BA), UCL (PhD); *m* 18 Aug 1962, Ian Geoffrey Bolt; *Career* Univ of Kent at Canterbury 1966-: prof of American history 1984, pro vice chllr 1988-; visiting asst prof of history Wayne State Univ Detroit 1969-70, visiting assoc prof of history Northern Illinois Univ 1970-71; Br Acad and Newberry Library Fellowship, Huntington Library Fellowship, Huntington-Hayes Fndn grant, Leverhulme Tst Fund Fellowship, Wolfson Fndn Fellowship, Leverhulme Tst Fund grant; govr Bromley HS 1985-88, academic tstee Kennedy Meml Tst; *Books* The Anti-Slavery Movement and Reconstruction (1969), Victorian Attitudes to Race (1971), A History of the USA (1974), Power and Protest in American Life (co-author with A T Barbrook, 1980), Anti-Slavery, Religion and Reform (co-ed S Drescher, 1980), American Indian Policy and American Reform (1987); *Style—* Prof Christine Bolt; University of Kent, Eliot College, Canterbury, Kent CT2 7NS (☎ 0227 764000)

BOMPAS, Donald George; CMG (1966); s of Rev Edward Anstie Bompas (d 1956), of London; *b* 20 Nov 1920; *Educ* Merchant Taylors', Oriel Coll Oxford; *m* 1946, Freda Vice, da of Fred Milner Smithyman (d 1969), of Malawi; 1 s, 1 da; *Career* formerly with Overseas Audit Serv; auditor-gen: Malaya 1960-63, Malaysia 1963-66; sec: Guy's Hosp Med and Dental Schs 1969-82, United Med and Dental Schs of Guy's and St Thomas's Hosps 1984-86; managing exec: Philip & Pauline Harris Charitable Tst 1986-; Liveryman Worshipful Co of Merchant Taylors' 1951; Hon JMN (Malaya) 1961; *Clubs* Royal Cwlth Soc; *Style—* Donald Bompas, Esq, CMG; 8 Birchwood Rd, Petts Wood, Kent (☎ 0689 821661)

BOND, Denis; s of Alfred Thomas Bond, of Worthing, Sussex, and Alice Margaret, *née* Simpson; *b* 22 Nov 1946; *Educ* Sedgehill Comp Sch Catford London, Rose Bruford Coll of Speech and Drama Sidcup Kent; *Career* actor; reg TV work 1970-85 incl: Beryl's Lot, No appointment Necessary, Juliet Bravo, Ain't Half Hot Mum, Kenny Everett Shows, Dick Emery Shows; children's TV scriptwriter from 1980 incl: Pipkins, The Munch Bunch, Rainbow, Let's Pretend; *Books* Freddy, The Naughtiest Mouse in the World (1981), The Munch Bunch (12 books and 3 annuals, 1982-85), Dagon (9 books, 1983), Around the World with Willy Fog (4 books, 1985), The Time Lords of Tolemac (1986), The Slave Traders of Ganox (1987), Rough Mix (1988), Soap (1989), The Dragon Who Couldn't Help Breathing Fire (1990), Remix (1990), Yell! (1990); *Recreations* pop music, reading, teaching Spanish; *Style—* Denis Bond, Esq; c/o The Sharland Organisation, 9 Marlborough Crescent, Bedford Park, London W4 1HE (☎ 081 742 1919)

BONE, Dr David Harbord; s of late Wilfred Bone, and Rose, *née* Harbord (d 1987); *b* 7 June 1916; *Educ* Hymens Coll Hull Yorks, St Bart's Hosp Med Sch London (LRCP); *Career* appointed Flying Offr med branch of RAF Vol Res 1942, served in France and Holland, MO RAF station Biggin Hill Kent; casualty offr Queen Mary's Hosp for the E End Stratford London; MRCS; *Books* The Bees of Westerham (1952), The Bees of Swanland (1957), A Lenten Pie (1960), Narrow Days (1966); *Recreations* med matters, the countryside, photography, writing poetry, printing and publishing own books, collecting books, bee-keeping, film-making; *Style—* Dr David Bone; Lees Court, Canterbury Rd, Charing, nr Ashford, Kent TN27 0EX (☎ 0233 712938)

BOORMAN, Edwin Roy Pratt; s of Henry Roy Pratt Boorman, of St Augustine's Priory, Bilsington, Ashford, Kent, and Enid Margaret Ashby, *née* Starke; *b* 7 Nov 1935; *Educ* Rydal Sch, Queens' Coll Cambridge (MA); *m* 1 (m dis 1982), Merilyn Ruth Petit; 4 da (Geraldine Ruth b 1966, Cecilia Anne b 1968, Imogen May b 1971, Nicola Helen b 1972); m 2, 22 OCt 1983, Janine Mary, da of William Craske, of Penenden Heath, Maidstone, Kent; 1 s (Henry Edwin Pratt b 1984); *Career* Nat Serv RA 1954-56; ed South Eastern Gazette 1960-62, ed Kent Messenger 1962-65 (trg 1959-60); Kent Messenger Ltd: md 1965-74, gp md 1975-86, chm and chief exec 1986-; dep cncllr Newspaper Soc, fin dir Royal Br Legion Industs, chm Kent Assoc of Boys' Clubs, govr Sutton Valence Sch, tax cmmnr Maidstone 2 Dist Kent; ct asst Worshipful Co of Stationers and Newspaper Makers; *Recreations* sailing (Yacht Messenger); *Clubs* Ocean Cruising, Medway Yacht; *Style—* Edwin Boorman, Esq; Redhill Farm, 339 Redhill, Wateringbury, Kent ME18 5LB (☎ 0622 812227); Kent Messenger Limited, Messenger House, New Hythe Lane, Larkfield, Maidstone, Kent ME20 6SG (☎ 0622 717880, fax 0622 719637)

BOORMAN, Edwin Roy Pratt; s of Henry Roy Pratt Boorman, *qv*; *b* 7 Nov 1935; *Educ* Rydal Sch, Queens' Coll Cambridge (MA); *m* 1, (m dis 1982), Merrilyn Ruth Pettit; 4 da; 2 1983, Janine Mary, da of William Craske, of Penenden Heath, Maidstone; 1 s; *Career* chm Kent Messenger Ltd 1986- (md 1965); *Recreations* sailing, yacht Messenger; *Clubs* Ocean Cruising, Medway Yacht; *Style—* Edwin Boorman, Esq; Redhill Farm, 339 Redhill, Wateringbury, Kent; Kent Messenger, Messenger House, New Hythe Lane, Larkfield, Kent ME20 6SG (☎ 77880)

BOORMAN, Henry Roy Pratt; CBE (1966, MBE 1945); s of Barham Pratt Boorman, JP, of Cedars, Maidstone (d 1928), and Elizabeth Rogers (d 1932); *b* 21 Sept 1900; *Educ* Leys Sch Cambridge, Queens' Coll Cambridge (BA, MA); *m* 1, 1933, Enid Margaret, da of Edgar E Starke; 1 s (Edwin Roy Pratt, *qv*); m 2, 1947, Evelyn Mary, da of Frederick G Clinch; 1 da (Mary Elizabeth); *Career* Dep County Welfare Offr 1941; Maj 1944 (served N Europe); Kent Messenger: journalist 1922-28, ed and proprietor 1928-52, chm 1952-82, pres 1982-; ed Journal Kent 1931-62 (for which awarded Sir Edward Hardy Gold Medal by Assoc of Men of Kent and Kentish Men 1964); pres Newspaper Soc 1960-61; Kent CC 1933-46, Mayor of Maidstone 1962-63, Alderman Maidstone 1964-70, JP 1962-63, DL Kent 1968-82; tenor bell given to Canterbury Cathedral in H Boorman's name by Kent Messenger 1980; awarded Medal of Honour American Biographical Inst; FJI 1936; *Books* Merry America; *Recreations* travel; *Clubs* Royal Cwlth Soc; *Style—* Henry Boorman, Esq, CBE; St Augustine's Priory, Bilsington, Ashford, Kent TN25 7AU (☎ 023 372 252)

BOOTH, Rev Canon David Herbert; MBE (1944); s of Robert Booth (d 1941), of Milborne St Andrews, and Clara Annette, *née* Harvey; *b* 26 Jan 1907; *Educ* Bedford Sch, Pembroke Coll Cambridge (MA); *m* 2 May 1942, Diana Mary, da of Lt-Col William Wheaton Chard, MC (d 1953), of Brighton; 2 s (Peter b 1947, David b 1951), 1 da (Bridget b 1952); *Career* WWII RNVR 1939-45, served Chaplain HMS Orion, HMS Collingwood, advanced pty Western Desert, 30 AV RM; asst curate Hampton Parish Church 1932-34, chaplain Tonbridge Sch 1935-39, rector of Stepney 1945-53, vicar of Brighton 1953-59, archdeacon of Lewes 1959-71, provost Shoreham Coll 1977- (headmaster 1972-77); chaplain to HM The Queen 1975-77; memb local educn ctees; govr: Brighton Coll, Haileybury Coll; fndr and pres Nat Schools Jumping Championship 1963-; *Style—* The Rev Canon David Booth, MBE; Courtyard Cottage, School Rd, Charing, Ashford, Kent TN27 (☎ 023371 3349)

BOREHAM, Sir (Arthur) John; KCB (1980); 3 s of Ven Frederick Boreham (d 1966), Archdeacon of Cornwall and Chaplain to the Queen, and Caroline Mildred, *née* Slater (d 1943); *b* 30 July 1925; *Educ* Marlborough, Trinity Coll Oxford; *m* 1948, Heather, o da of Harold Edwin Horth (d 1952); 3 s (Stephen b 1949, Jonathan b 1951, Simon b 1955), 1 da (Deborah b 1959); *Career* served RAF Flt Lt 1943-46; dir Central Statistical Office and head Govt Statistics 1978-85; visiting fell Nuffield Coll Oxford 1979-88; pres Inst of Statisticians 1984-, conslt to CARICOM 1989-90, chm Weald of Kent Breast Cancer Tst; FIS; *Recreations* music, golf; *Clubs* Knole Park Golf; *Style—* Sir John Boreham, KCB; Pipers Croft, Brittains Lane, Sevenoaks, Kent TN13 2NG (☎ 0732 454678)

BORNER, Dr (Gertrude) Margaret; da of Frederick William Child (d 1957), of Torquay, and Lucy Hannah, *née* Pratt (d 1951); *b* 24 Nov 1916; *Educ* Leeds Girls HS, Univ of Leeds (MB ChB, DRCOG); *m* 25 Sept 1946, Ronald Stewart Borner, OBE, VRD, s of Cdr Ernest Stuart Borner (d 1953); 1 s (John Stuart b 11 July 1947); *Career* Capt RAMC served UK, India and Egypt 1942-46; GP 1940-41; med offr: Kent CC Clinics, Family Planning Assoc Clinics; chm Faversham United Municipal Charities 1979-83 (tstee 1962-), govr Queen Elizabeth Sch Faversham 1965-86; memb BMA 1940-76; *Recreations* gardening, languages; *Clubs* Farmers; *Style—* Dr Margaret Borner; Mindon, Ashford Rd, Faversham, Kent (☎ 0795 532021)

BORNER, Ronald Stewart; OBE (1958), VRD (1947); s of Cdr Ernest Stuart Borner (d 1953), of Mindon, Ashford Rd, Faversham, and Emily, *née* Fisher (d 1954); *b* 18 Feb 1913; *Educ* The Abbey Sch Beckenham, Haileybury; *m* 25 Sept 1946, Dr (Gertrude) Margaret Borner, da of Frederic Child (d 1957), of Torquay; 1 s (John Stuart b 1947); *Career* London Div RNVR (later RNR) 1934-61: joined as Sub Lt, Cdr 1939-45, French Fleet UK and E Indies Fleet in Greece and France; Peat Marwick Mitchell 1936-39, bursar Taunton Sch 1946; sec: Chartered Land Agents Soc 1947-57, Chartered Auctioneers and Estate Agents Inst (and sec various ctees and benevolent fund) 1957-70; dir of admin Savill's 1970-80, conslt 1980-82; govr Coll of Estate Mgmnt 1953-72; memb: Bd of Studies in Estate Mgmnt Univ of London 1957-70, Cncl Old Haileyburians Soc 1961-64; Cncl Int Real Estate Fedn 1961-76, vice pres: Faversham Bde St Johns Ambulance 1964-80, Royal Star and Garter Home for Disabled Sailors Soldiers and Airmen 1984- (govr 1971-84, chm Fin Ctee 1979-84); appointed by Dept of Enviroment as chm of Ctee on Use of Valuers in the Pub Serv 1972-73, chm Friends of Faversham Cottage Hosp 1977-80 (memb Ctee 1972-88, hon sec 1972-77); Liveryman Worshipful Co of Farmers 1959 (Master 1972-73); FCA, ACMA; *Recreations* cricket, all sport; *Clubs*

MCC, Farmers; *Style*— Ronald Borner, Esq, OBE, VRD; Mindon, Ashford Rd, Faversham, Kent ME13 8XJ (☎ 0795 532021)

BOSANQUET, David Graham; s of Prof Robert Carr Bosanquet (d 1935), of Alnwick, Northumberland, and Ellen Sophia, *née* Hodgkin (d 1965); *b* 8 Oct 1916; *Educ* Winchester, Trinity Coll Cambridge (MA, LLM); *m* 23 Aug 1941, Camilla, da of Sir Harry Ralph Ricardo (d 1974), of Woodside, Graffham, Sussex; 1 s (Robin b 1944), 2 da (Joanna b 1946, Annabel b 1950); *Career* Maj RA 1940-46, served NW Europe; slr; dir: Fitzwilliam (Peterborough) Properties 1968-, Provincial Insurance plc 1970-86, Provincial Group plc 1986-90; conslt Currey & Co 1987- (ptnr 1951-87); *Recreations* gardening, painting, amateur dramatics; *Clubs* United Oxford and Cambridge Univ; *Style*— David Bosanquet, Esq; Wyndside, Church Rd, Ryarsh, West Malling, Kent (☎ 0732 842351); 18 Montagu Square, London (☎ 071 935 0119); 21 Buckingham Gate, London SW1 (☎ 071 828 4091, fax 071 828 5049)

BOSCAWEN, Hon Evelyn Arthur Hugh; s and h of 9 Viscount Falmouth; *b* 13 May 1955; *Educ* Eton, RAC Cirencester; *m* 1977, Lucia Caroline, da of Ralph Vivian-Neal, of Poundisford Park, Somerset; 1 s (b 1979), 1 da (b 1982); *Career* farmer; dir Goonvean & Rostowrack China Clay Co 1979-; local dir Sun Alliance; *Recreations* shooting, sailing; *Style*— The Hon Evelyn Boscawen; c/o Tregothnan Estate Office, Truro, Cornwall (☎ 087 252 310)

BOSCAWEN, Hon Nicholas John; 2 s of 9 Viscount Falmouth; *b* 14 Jan 1957; *Educ* Eton, RAC Cirencester; *m* 6 July 1985, Virginia M R, yr da of Robin Beare, of Scraggs Farm, Cowden, Kent; *Career* land agent Cluttons 1980-85, institutional stockbroker Sheppards 1985-87, dir The Invisible Chef 1988-; ARICS; *Recreations* shooting, fishing, skiing, sailing, gardening; *Clubs* Annabels; *Style*— The Hon Nicholas Boscawen; Peckham Place, Peckham Bush, Tonbridge, Kent TN12 5NA (☎ 0732 851 975, 0860 200 318)

BOSTOCK, James Edward; s of William George Bostock (d 1948), and Amy, *née* Titley (d 1976); *b* 11 June 1917; *Educ* Borden GS Sittingbourne, Medway Sch of Art, RCA London; *m* 20 Dec 1939, Gwladys Irene, *née* Griffiths; 3 s (Philip b 1946, Michael b 1950, Christopher b 1959); *Career* Durham LI and RCS 1940-46; sr lectr Ealing Sch of Art 1946-60, head of dip studies Stoke on Trent Coll of Art 1960-65, vice princ West of England Coll of Art 1965-70, academic devpt offr Bristol Poly 1970-78; has exhibited water colours engravings etchings and drawings worldwide; one-man shows in: Margate, Broadstairs, Deal, Folkestone, Canterbury; memb: Soc of Wood Engravers 1950, E Kent Art Soc, Ramsgate Arts Soc; hon ret fell Royal Soc of Painter - Etchers 1947; ARCA; *Books* Roman Lettering for Students (1959), Woodengraved Illustrations to Poems of Edward Thomas (1988); *Style*— James Bostock, Esq; 80 Lindenthorpe Rd, Broadstairs, Kent CT10 1DB (☎ 0843 69782)

BOSTON, David Merrick; OBE (1976); s of Dr Hugh Merrick Boston (d 1980), of 86 Crane St, Salisbury, Wilts, and Jessie Mary, *née* Ingham (d 1979); *b* 15 May 1931; *Educ* Bishop Wordworth's Sch Salisbury Wilts, Selwyn Coll Cambridge (BA, MA), Univ of Cape Town; *m* 12 Aug 1961, Catharine Mary, da of Rev Prof E G S Parrinder, of Orpington, Kent; 1 s (Peter b 1966), 2 da (Janet b 1963, Andrea b 1969); *Career* Nat Serv 1950-51, Adj Marine Craft Trg Sch RAF Calshot, Flying Offr RAFRO 1951-55; Field Survey South African Inst of Race Relations 1955, keeper of ethnology (formerly special offr) Liverpool Museums 1956-62, asst keeper Dept of Ethnography Br Museum 1962-65, dir (formerly curator) Horniman Museum and Library 1965-; visiting scientist: Nat Museum of Man Ottawa 1970, Japan Fndn Tokyo 1986; chm Br Nat Ctee of the Int Cncl of Museums 1976-80, hon sec Royal Anthropological Inst 1985-88 (vice pres 1972-75 and 1977-80), vice chm Int Ctee for Museums and Ethnography 1989-; vice pres Dulwich Decorative and Fine Arts Soc, tstee Photographers' Gallery; FMA, FRAI, FRAS, FRGS; Ordenom Jugoslavenske Zastave sa zlatnom zvezdom na ogrlici (Yugoslavia) 1981; *Books* Pre-Columbian Pottery of the Americas (1980); *Recreations* travel; *Style*— David Boston, Esq, OBE; 10 Oakleigh Park Ave, Chislehurst, Kent (☎ 081 467 1049); Horniman Museum, London Rd, Forest Hill, London SE23 (☎ 081 699 1872/2339)

BOTTLE, Prof Robert Thomas; s of Edward James Bottle (d 1949), of Dial House, Harrietsham, Kent, and Hilda, *née* Tupper (d 1967); *b* 11 Feb 1929; *Educ* Ashford GS, Univ of London (BSc), Univ of Birmingham (PhD); *m* 7 Aug 1960, Margaret Joan, da of Samuel Horace Pilling (d 1989), of Wigan, Lancs; 1 s ((Robert) Alex b 1971), 2 da (Janet Margaret b 1961, Vanessa Anne b 1963); *Career* res assoc Indiana Univ 1954-55, sr res chemist Dunlop Res Centre 1955-56; lectr physical chemistry: Liverpool Coll of Technol 1956-60, Univ of Bradford 1960-71; prof sch library sci Syracuse Univ 1968-70, lectr librarianship Univ of Strathclyde 1972-73; City Univ: dir Centre Info Sci 1973-83, prof info sci 1979-; memb Cncl Inst Info Scientists 1973-79, 1982-88 and 1990-; cncllr Harrietsham Parish Cncl 1976- (chm 1976-78, vice chm 1978-79 and 1987-), chm Noise Pollution Sub-Ctee N Downs Rail Concern 1988-; FLA 1973, fell Inst Info Sci 1977; *Books* Use of Chemical Literature (3 edn, 1979), Use of Biological Literature (2 edn, 1971), Gratis Controlled Circulation Journals for the Chemical and Allied Industs (1970); *Recreations* gardening, village life, bridge; *Style*— Prof Robert Bottle; Dial House, East St, Harrietsham, Maidstone, Kent ME17 1HJ (☎ 0622 859622); Department of Information Science, City University, Northampton Square, London EC1V 0HB (☎ 071 253 4399, fax 071 250 0837)

BOUCHER, Dr Barbara Joan; da of Dr P L Boucher, of Ripley, Surrey, and Helena R, *née* Delacy (d 1966); *b* 28 Dec 1932; *Educ* London Hosp Med Coll Univ of London (BSc, MB BS, MD); *m* 14 Feb 1961, Prof Robert Donald Cohen, s of Dr H H Cohen (d 1988), of Plymouth, Devon; 1 s (Martin Arthur Boucher b 1966), 1 da (Susan Lucinda (Dr Legg) b 1963); *Career* 1958-70: trg posts, registrar, sr registrar; conslt physician The Royal London Hosp 1970-, sr lectr Med Unit The Royal London Hosp Med Coll; author of various papers on human metabolism and disease incl studies on diabetes and hormonal disorders; memb: RSM, Med Res Soc, Br Diabetic Assoc, Soc for Endocrinology; pres London Hosp and Coll Music Soc; FCRP; *Books* Tests in Diabetes (jtly), The Metabolic and Molecular Basis of Acquired Disease (contrib, 1990); *Recreations* reading, gardening, riding, choral singing; *Style*— Dr Barbara Boucher; The Royal London Hospital, London E1 1BB (☎ 071 377 7000, 2262 or 2263, fax 071 377 7293)

BOULDEN, Peter Gorham; s of George Loftus Boulden (d 1975), of Aldington, Kent, and Alice Ann, *née* Franks (d 1979); *b* 14 Dec 1918; *Educ* Victoria Rd Central Sch, South Central Sch Ashford; *m* 17 Jan 1944, Lauré Veronique, da of Bendict Laurent Brun (d 1953), of Fribourg, Switzerland and Folkestone, Kent; 1 s (Martin b 1956), 3 da (Christine b 1946, Yvonne b 1949, Virginia b 1959); *Career* War Serv Aux Unit 1940-45; sr ptnr GL Boulden and Sons Farmers; dir: Kent Woolgrowers Ashford Ltd, Romney Marsh Viners Ltd; chm E Ashford RDC 1970-74 (memb 1953-74); Ashford Borough Cncl: memb 1974-, chm 1974, Mayor 1975 and 1986, ldr of cncl 1981-84, currently vice chm Planning Ctee 1988-; chm: Parish Cncl, local playing field assoc; former chm Aldington Detention Centre, former churchwarden Aldington Church, sch govr, vice pres local FC, memb NFU; *Style*— Peter Boulden, Esq; The Manor, The Avenue, Aldington, Ashford, Kent TN25 7EG

BOULIS, Dr Zoser; s of Fouad Boulis (d 1976), and Irene Grais, *née* Wassif; *b* 1 Jan 1944; *Educ* Secdy Sch Khartoum Sudan, LRCP, MRCS; *m* 21 July 1974, Afaf, da of Hanna Ayoub Girgis; 1 s (Michael b 9 April 1975), 1 da (Sandra Anne b 23 April 1976); *Career* sr house offr gen surgery The Royal Marsden Hosp Fulham London, registrar gen surgery Barking Hosp Essex, sr registrar radiology The Royal Free Hosp Hampstead London; conslt radiology: Bromley Health Authy (Farnborough, Bromley and Beckenham Hosps), The Sloane Hosp, Chelsfield Park Hosp; memb BMA, FRCS 1972 (Edinburgh 1973, Glasgow 1974), FRCR 1985; *Recreations* travelling abroad, music; *Style*— Dr Zoser Boulis; Farnborough Hospital, Ultrasound Department, Farnborough Common, Orpington, Kent BR6 8ND (☎ 0689 53333 ext 471/498)

BOULT, Lt-Col Peter Walter Swinton; TD; s of Maj Peter Swinton Boult, MC (d 1955), of New Bunnee, Hoylake, Cheshire, and Rose Cawston, *née* Pattisson (d 1948); *b* 13 Sept 1919; *Educ* Shrewsbury; *m* 11 June 1949, (Elizabeth) Jane, da of Sir Frank Samuel Alexander, 1 Bt (d 1959); 2 s (Nigel b 1952 d 1984, Geoffrey b 1955), 2 da (Rosanne b 1950, Alison b 1953); *Career* WWII cmmnd 2 Lt RA (TA) 1939, served 149 RHA Regt Western Desert, instr RA OCTU Cairo, served 102 Regt Northumberland Hussars, instr Gunnery Sch of Artillery Salisbury Plain 1944, demob 1946; cmd Lt-Col 290 (City of London) FD Regt RA (TA) 1955-57; articled to CAs Liverpool 1937-39, produce merchant and dir of cos trading in London Commodity Exchange 1946-64; dir: Symbol Biscuits Ltd (subsid of J Lyons & Co Ltd) 1964-68, Metlex Industries (chm 1980-82); dir of other cos within IS plc; pres Hardware Mfrs Assoc 1977-79, cncl memb CBI 1973-82 (chm Surrey area 1977-81), cncl chm Nat Artillery Assoc 1969-80, dep chm TA Sports Bd 1970-79; Liveryman: Worshipful Co of Distillers 1958, Worshipful Co of Tallow Chandlers 1960 (Warden 1987); *Recreations* watching sport, bridge, golf, golf course design; *Clubs* MCC, Aldeburgh Golf, Chislehurst Golf, Band of Brothers, Kent CCC; *Style*— Lt-Col Peter W S Boult, TD; Wellwood, Watts Lane, Chislehurst, Kent BR7 5PJ (☎ 081 467 3216)

BOURDEAUX, Rev Canon Michael Alan; s of Richard Edward Bourdeaux, and Lillian Myra, née Blair; *b* 19 March 1934; *Educ* Truro Sch, St Edmund Hall Oxford (MA, BD), Moscow State Univ; *m* 1, 1960, Gillian Mary, *née* Davies (d 1978); 1 s (Mark), 1 da (Karen); m 2, 1979, Lorna Elizabeth, da of John Waterton, of Birch House, Preston, St Mary, Sudbury, Suffolk; 1 s (Adrian), 1 da (Lara); *Career* ordained: deacon 1960, priest 1961; res assoc Centre de Recherches Geneva Switzerland 1965-68, London res fell Univ of London 1968-70, visiting prof St Bernard's Seminary Rochester NY 1969, res fell Royal Inst of Int Affairs 1970-72, Kathryn C Davis prof of slavic studies Wellesley Mass 1981, Templeton Prize 1984, sr assoc memb St Anthony's Coll Oxford and visiting fell St Edmund Hall Oxford 1989-90, Hon Canon Rochester Cathedral 1990; memb Philharmonia Chorus 1961-, fndr and gen dir Keston Coll 1969-, memb Br Tennis Umpires Assoc 1974-; *Books* Opium of the People (1965, 2 edn 1977), Religious Ferment in Russia (1968), Patriarch and Prophets (1970, 2 edn 1975), Faith on Trial in Russia (1971), Land of Crosses (1979), Risen Indeed (1983), Ten Growing Soviet Churches (1987), Gorbachov, Glasnost and the Gospel (1990); *Clubs* Athenaeum; *Style*— The

Rev Canon Michael Bourdeaux; Bishopsdown, 34 Lubbock Rd, Chislehurst, Kent BR7 5JJ (☎ 081 467 3550); Keston College, Heathfield Rd, Keston, Kent BR2 6BA (☎ 0689 50116, telex KESCOL 897684)

BOURKE, Dr Margaret Elizabeth; da of Timothy Bourke, of Bexleyheath, and Freda Elizabeth, *née* Foster; *b* 28 March 1959; *Educ* St Joseph's GS Abbey Wood, Univ of Southampton (BSc, BMed), MRCP; *Career* house offr Southampton and Portsmouth 1987-88; sr house offr: Whittington Hosp, Brompton Hosp, Hammersmith Hosp 1988-89; registrar: Whittington Hosp, UCH, Middlesex Hosp 1989-; memb: BMA, Med Women's Fedn; *Recreations* horse riding, skiing, windsurfing, theatre; *Style*— Dr Margaret Bourke; 32 Freta Rd, Bexleyheath, Kent DA6 2NY (☎ 081 3038271); Whittington Hospital, Highgate Hill, London N19 5NF (☎ 071 272 3070)

BOWDEN, John Robert; s of Arthur Frederick Bowden, of Kemsing, Sevenoaks, Kent, and Gwenda, *née* Pallant; *b* 29 May 1956; *Educ* Yardley Court Tonbridge, Harrow, Univ of Bristol; *m* 20 Jan 1979, Patricia Mary, da of Harry Crossley Cowsill, of Little Compton, Glos; 1 da (Faye Elizabeth b 31 Jan 1987); *Career* admitted slr 1982; Chancellor & Ridley Bexleyheath: articled clerk 1977-82, asst slr 1982-84, ptnr 1984-89; ptnr Chancellors 1989-; treas Bexley and Dartford Law Soc; memb Law Soc; *Recreations* restoring cars, photography, clay pigeon shooting; *Style*— John Bowden, Esq; Dee Banks, Ironstones, Langton Green, Tunbridge Wells, Kent TN3 0YD (☎ 0892 548636); Chancellors, 246A Broadway, Bexleyheath, Kent DA6 8BB (☎ 081 303 0077, fax 081 304 4023)

BOWMER, Jenny; da of Roy Bowmer, of Strood, Kent, and Pamela Dorathy, *née* Frost; *b* 7 Feb 1959; *Educ* Chapter Secdy Sch For Girls, Brighton Poly (BA); *Career* artist; gp exhibitions incl: Dark Caves Light Vision (Brighton Gallery of Fine Art) 1988, West End Studio Gp Show (Chatham Historic Dockyard) 1990, solo shows incl Current Works (Medway Arts Centre) 1989; led creative workshops for Gillingham and Ashford cncls and youth serv etc 1988-; art tutor for artability Freedom Centre Sheerness 1989-, art tutor Maidstone Care in the Community Project 1989-, sculpture tutor Gravesend Adult Educn Centre 1990; project devpt worker Arts in Medway Gillingham 1990- (project worker 1988- 90); *Recreations* studio time, drinking red wine; *Style*— Ms Jenny Bowmer; West End Studios, 116A High St, Chatham, Kent

BOWYER, Barry Robert; s of Flt Lt Frederick George Bowyer, of Purley, Surrey (d 1955), and Norah Margaret, *née* Bownick (d 1966); *b* 31 July 1936; *Educ* Glenwood Sch Surrey; *m* 15 Dec 1962, Gillian Margaret, da of Walter Henry Mann, of Suffolk (d 1948); 3 s (Christopher St John b 1964, Jonathan James b 1967, Robert Alexander b 1969); *Career* RAF 1956-59; tech advsr Electronics Indust 1959-63, publishing and advertising accounts mangr 1963-67; chm chief exec and fndr: Bowyer Design Consultancy Ltd, Bowyer Design Advertising 1978, Bowyer Design PR 1980; govr John Mayne Sch, memb Cons Pty, memb Biddenden Ward Ashford Borough Cncl; *Recreations* vintage cars, painting sculpture, travel; *Clubs* Naval and Military, Bentley Drivers, Aston Martin Owners; *Style*— Barry Bowyer, Esq; Tollgate House, Biddenden, Kent (☎ 0580 291830, 0580 291560, fax 0580 292080)

BOYCE, Rev John Frederick; s of Flt Lt Victor Leonard Boyce, of Rustington, Sussex, and Helen Madeline Boyce (d 1970); *b* 20 July 1933; *Educ* Bromley GS, London Coll of Divinity (Assoc of London Coll of Divinity); *m* 31 May 1958, Shirley Ann, da of John Bertram Wilson Armstrong, OBE, of Seaford, Sussex; 1 s (Mark), 1 da (Helen); *Career* Southwark Cathedral: deacon of Anglican Church 1957, ordained priest of the church 1958; curate: Earlsfield London 1957-60, Westerham Kent 1960-63, Farnborough Kent 1963-66; vicar Sutton at Hone Kent 1966-73, priest i/c Chiddingstone Kent 1973-74, rector Chiddingstone and Causeway 1974-84, ldr Chiddingstone Gp of Parishes 1980-83, vicar of Brenchley 1984-; dep chm Mangrs Barnardo's Knotley Community Home with Educn (fndn mangr), chm of Govrs Brenchley and Matfield C of E Aided Primary Sch (fndn govr); *Recreations* narrow gauge railway models, photography, gardening; *Clubs* 009 Soc; *Style*— The Rev John Boyce; 8 Broadoak, Brenchley, Tonbridge, Kent (☎ 089 272 2140)

BOYLE, Lady Georgina Susan; da of 9 Earl of Shannon; *b* 7 Feb 1961; *Career* artist, watercolourist; *Style*— Lady Georgina Boyle; Brandfold Barn Cottage, Goudhurst, Kent TN17 1JJ

BRABOURNE, 7 Baron (UK 1880); John Ulick Knatchbull; 16 Bt (E 1641); s of 5 Baron Brabourne, GCSI, GCIE, MC, JP, MP (d 1939, sometime viceroy and actg govr-gen India) by his w, Lady Doreen Browne (Dowager Lady Brabourne, d 1979, da of 6 Marquess of Sligo); suc er bro, 6 Baron (d 1943, shot by the Germans after escaping from a prison train in Italy and recaptured); *b* 9 Nov 1924; *Educ* Eton, BNC Oxford; *m* 1946, Lady Patricia Edwina Victoria Mountbatten (Countess Mountbatten of Burma, *qv*), da of 1 Earl Mountbatten of Burma; 4 s (and 1 s decd), 2 da; *Heir* s, Lord Romsey; *Career* dir: Thames TV plc, Mersham Productions Ltd; prod/co-prod feature films: Harry Black and the Tiger (1958), Sink the Bismarck (1960), HMS Defiant (1961), Othello (1966), Romeo and Juliet (1966), The Mikado (1967), Up the Junction (1968), The Dance of Death (1969), The Tales of Beatrix Potter (1971), Murder on the Orient Express (1974), Death on the Nile (1978), Stories from a Flying Trunk (1979), The Mirror Crack'd (1980), Evil Under the Sun (1982), A Passage to India (1984), Little Dorrit (1987); TV prods: The Life and Times of Lord Mountbatten (1968), Royal Family (1969, memb Advsy Ctee), Romantic Versus Classic Art (1973), The National Gallery - A Private View (1974), A Much Maligned Monarch (1976), Royal Heritage (1977, memb Advsy Ctee), Leontyne (1988); chm: Br Cncl Advsy Ctee on Film TV and Video, Cncl Caldecott Community, Govrs of Norton Knatchbull Sch; govr: Gordonstoun, Nat Film Sch, Wye Coll, United World Coll of the Atlantic; tstee: BAFTA, Sci Museum, Nat Museum of Photography; dep pro chllr Univ of Kent; pres Kent Tst for Nature Conservation; memb: Br Screen Advsy Cncl, Br Film and TV Prodrs Assoc; vice pres Royal Soc of Nature Conservation; *Style*— The Rt Hon the Lord Brabourne; Newhouse, Mersham, Ashford, Kent TN25 6NQ (☎ 0233 623466); 39/41 Montpelier Walk, London SW7 1JH (☎ 071 589 8829)

BRADBURY, Surgn Vice Adm Sir Eric Blackburn; KBE (1971), CB (1968); s of late A B Bradbury, of Orchard House, Maze, Co Antrim; *b* 2 March 1911; *Educ* Royal Belfast Academical Instn, Queen's Univ Belfast; *m* 1939, Elizabeth Constance, da of late J G Austin, of Armagh; 3 da; *Career* RN Med Serv 1934, Surgn Capt 1959, MO i/c RN Hosp Haslar 1966, Surg Rear Adm 1966, Surgn Vice Adm 1969, Med DG of the Navy 1969-72; chm Tunbridge Wells DHA 1981-84; Hon LLD Queen's Univ Belfast; FRCS 1972; CStJ, former QHP; *Style*— Surgn Vice Adm Sir Eric Bradbury, KBE, CB; The Gate House, Nevill Park, Tunbridge Wells, Kent TN4 8NN (☎ 0892 27661)

BRADBURY, Jennifer Kathleen; da of Frederick Clarke (d 1948), of Hammersmith, London, and Winfred Maud, *née* Wheeler (d 1987); *b* 2 Oct 1946; *Educ* Godolphin and Latymer GS for Girls Hammersmith, Open Univ; *m* 5 July 1969 (m dis 1978); 1 s (Jason Richard b 11 March 1972), 1 da (Wendy Louise b 23 Feb 1974); *Career* PA to dir of Res Inst 1980-86, PA to canon of Windsor at St George's Chapel Windsor Castle 1986-87, area mangr E Kent Barnardos 1987-; voluntary work: RSPCA (10 years involvement), WWF (5 years involvment); MICFM; *Recreations* study of ecology and conservation, reading; *Style*— Mrs Jennifer Bradbury; Valley View, Church Lane, Waltham, Canterbury, Kent (☎ 022 770 473, 022 770 603)

BRADFORD, Prof Henry Francis; s of Henry Bradford, and Rose Bradford; *b* 8 March 1938; *Educ* Dartford GS, UCL, Univ of Birmingham, Inst of Psychiatry London; *m* 28 March 1964, Helen, da of Benjamin Caplan (d Nov 1985); 1 s (Daniel Benjamin Alexander b 24 Aug 1969), 1 da (Sonya Helen b 25 Jan 1968); *Career* Imperial Coll London: lectr in biochemistry 1968-, reader in biochemistry 1975-, prof of neurochemistry 1979-, dir of undergraduate studies 1988-; ed The Journal of Neurochemistry 1973-81; silver jubilee lectr Indian Inst of Chemical Biology Calcutta 1982, Sandoz lectr Inst of Neurology London 1985 (1976), guest lectr Int Soc for Neurochemistry Japan 1985, Harold Chaffer Meml lectr Univ of Otago NZ 1987; gen ed The Biochemist 1988-; author of about 250 scientific papers, ed 3 vols of scientific reviews; chm MRC Epilepsy Res Coordinating Ctee 1978-88 (memb Neuroscience Ctee and Bd 1973-82), scientific advsr Brian Res Tst 1985-90, hon archivist The UK Biochemical Soc 1988- (hon sec 1973-81); bronze medal for contrib to neurochemistry Univ of Okayama Japan 1985; memb: UK Biochemical Soc, Int Soc Neurochemistry, Brain Res Assoc; *Books* Chemical Neurobiology (1985); *Recreations* natural history, music; *Style*— Prof Henry Bradford; 5 Scotts Ave, Shortlands, Bromley, Kent BR2 0LG (☎ 081 464 4615); Department of Biochemistry, Imperial College, South Kensington, London SW7 2AZ (☎ 071 589 5111, telex 261503, fax 071 584 7596)

BRADLEY, (David) John; s of David John Bradley (d 1954), of 33 Priestfields, Rochester, Kent, and Dorothy Frances Mary *née* Black (d 1948); *b* 22 Aug 1924; *Educ* Rochester Cathedral Choir Sch, Kings Sch Rochester; *Career* RN 1942-46; dir Thomas Watson (Shipping) Ltd; consul for Sweden; tstee: Watts Charity (Rochester), Shaferbury Homes and Arethusa; cncl memb and former chm Friends of Rochester Cathedral, govr Sir John Hawkins Hosp, chm Lord Chancellor's Advsy Ctee; Freeman City of London 1971, memb Worshipful Co of Watermen & Lightermen; FICS 1965 (memb 1948), FInstFF; Knight Order of Vasa (Sweden 1965), Knight First Class Order of Polar Star (Sweden 1981); *Recreations* sailing, farming, fruit growing; *Clubs* Castle (Rochester), Danish; *Style*— John Bradley, Esq; Buck Hole Farm, High Halstow, Rochester, Kent ME3 8SE (☎ 0634 250 895); 252 High St, Rochester, Kent ME1 1HZ (☎ 0634 44632, telex 96109)

BRADLEY, Joseph Clyde; s of Joseph Richard Bradley, and Ada Beatrice Bradley; *b* 21 May 1940; *Educ* Gt Yarmouth GS, UCL (BA, BSc); *m* 1962, Ute Brunhilde; 1 s (Martin b 1968), 1 da (Karen b 1971); *Career* Unilever 1961-72; Nationwide Building Soc: gen mangr 1972-81, chief exec 1981-, md 1982-87; md Prudential Property Services 1988-; FICMA, FInstM, FRSA; *Recreations* music, chess, kayaking, cycling; *Style*— Joseph Bradley, Esq; Ravelston, 80 St Georges Rd West, Bickley, Bromley, Kent; Prudential Property Services Ltd, Winchmore House, 15 Fetter Lane, London EC4 1JJ (☎ 071 430 0176)

BRAGG, (Henry) John; *b* 28 Nov 1929; *Educ* Torquay GS, Chelsea Coll Univ of London (Dip Pharmaceutical Chemistry); *m* 1, 14 Aug 1954, Jean (d 1969); 1 s (Nicholas b 12 June 1960), 2 da (Catherine b 20 July 1958, Elizabeth b 26 March 1963); m 2, 26 Oct 1972, Anthea, da of late K E Shelley, QC; *Career* pharmaceutical devpt Glaxo Laboratories 1952-55, dir and gen mangr euro chemicals business Pfizer Ltd 1955-70; md Calor Group (Imperial Continental Gas Assoc) 1970-85 (formerly dep chm i/c LPG distribution, oil exploration N Sea, tport, agric interests), currently non exec dir Advanced Petroleum Technol Ltd (mfrg oil well drilling bits and related equipment); memb Sandwich Town Cncl 1985-, Mayor of Sandwich 1989-90, memb ctee Sandwich Soc; fell Royal Pharmaceutical Soc 1950, FCIT, FInstD; *Recreations* golf, hunting, skiing; *Clubs* Royal St George's Golf; *Style*— John Bragg, Esq; Hideway House, St George's Rd, Sandwich, Kent CT13 9LE (☎ 0304 612364); Canterbury and Thanet Health Authority, Regency Buildings, 3 Royal Crescent, Ramsgate, Kent CT11 9PF (☎ 0843 594592, fax 0843 592400)

BRAGGE, Nicolas William; s of Norman Hugh Bragge, of The Towers, Brabourne, nr Ashford, Kent, and Nicolette Hilda, *née* Simms (d 1989); *b* 13 Dec 1948; *Educ* S Kent Coll of Technol Ashford, Holborn Coll of Law Univ of London (LLB), Inns of Court Sch of Law; *m* 23 Dec 1974, Pamela Elizabeth, da of Ronald Gordon Brett; 3 s (Thomas Hereward b 1976, Christopher Joseph b 1980, Alasdair Charles b 1986); *Career* called to the Bar Inner Temple 1972; in practice at Patent Bar 1973-, examiner of the Supreme Court 1978-88; pt/t chm Social Security Appeal Tbnls 1990-; author of various articles on legal and hist subjects; memb Br Gp AIPPI; Freeman City of London 1969, Liveryman Worshipful Co of Cutlers 1974; *Recreations* family; *Clubs* City Livery; *Style*— Nicolas Bragge, Esq; New Court, Temple, London EC4Y 9BE (☎ 071 353 1769/8719, fax 071 583 5885); The Towers, Brabourne, nr Ashford, Kent

BRAITHWAITE-YOUNG, Rev Donald Cecil; s of Henry James Young (d 1949), and Amelia, *née* Braithwaite (d 1929); *b* 26 Aug 1906; *Educ* Streatham GS, King's Coll London, St Johns Seminary Guildford; *Career* cmmnd chaplain RAF 1944-62; ordained RC priest 1938; curate at: Brighton, Anerley, Chatham; parish priest Goudhurst, ret 1982; Knight Commander of Equestrian Order of the Holy Sepulchre, hon conventual chaplain of SMO of St John of Jerusalem Rhodes and Malta; *Recreations* bridge, reading, travel; *Clubs* RAF, Piccadilly; *Style*— The Rev Donald Braithwaite-Young; Vine Cottage, Headcorn, Kent TN27 9SB (☎ 0622 890776)

BRAMLEY, Noël Charles; s of Ronald George Bramley, of Toronto, Canada, and Cecilie Mary, *née* Smith; *b* 26 Jan 1948; *Educ* Winston Churchill Collegiate Inst Toronto, Ryerson Poly Inst Toronto (Dip Hotel and Restaurant Admin); *m* 24 Sep 1977, Carol Joyce, da of Denis John Charles Gilchrist, of Strood, Kent; 2 da (Gemma b 1979, Melissa b 1981); *Career* Royal Canadian Ordnance Corps (Reserves) 1966-1970; md John Lane (Ship Stores) Ltd 1971 (joined 1970); fndr: Bramley Ferry Supplies Ltd 1980, Bramley Vintners Ltd 1986 (chm and md), Medway Bond & Storage Co Ltd 1988 (chm and md); Freeman City of London 1971, Liveryman Worshipful Co of Butchers 1971; MInstM 1974, MBIM 1981; *Recreations* tennis, skiing, wines, reading, farming; *Clubs* The Castle (Rochester), Wellington; *Style*— Noël Bramley, Esq; The Old Vicarage, Oare, Faversham, Kent ME13 0QB (☎ 0795 532342); Duke of Clarence Trading Centre, Sheerness, Kent ME12 1RN (☎ 0795 580001, fax 0795 580002, car tel 0836242411, telex 966203 LEBRAM G)

BRANNAN, Keith William; s of Harold William Brannan, of Hythe, and Dorothy, *née* Woodward; *b* 17 March 1947; *Educ* Whitgift Trinity Sch Croydon, Canterbury Coll of Art Sch of Architecture (Dip Arch); *m* 20 Oct 1973, Ann, da of Thomas Mason, of Bethersden; 1 s (Duncan Paul b 26 Aug 1975), 1 da (Alison Kay b 26 Feb 1978); *Career* architect's asst British Railways Board Architects Dept 1968-69, architect Tucker Joyce Laws of Tunbridge Wells 1971-75, fndr Mason Brannan Design Partnership 1975-; parish cncllr 1979-; chm: Bethersden PTA 1983-88, Bethersden Parish Cncl 1988-90; *Recreations* Bethersden Tennis (former chm); *Style*— Keith Brannan, Esq; Mason Brannan Design, Bethersden, Ashford, Kent TN26 3EL (☎ 0233 82536)

BRASINGTON, John Vincent; s of Baily George Brasington (d 1984), of East Grinstead, Sussex, and Anne, *née* Tuite (d 1988); *b* 5 April 1935; *Educ* Maidstone GS, Barnstaple GS; *m* 27 July 1963, Mary, da of Thomas Idwal Jones (d 1958), of Anglesea; 1 s (Damian b 1964), 1 da (Helen b 1967); *Career* short serv cmmn RAF 1957-60; articled clerk 1951-56, admitted slr 1957; Church Bruce Hawkes Brasington and Phillips (formerly Church Bruce and Hawkes): asst slr, ptnr 1962-, sr ptnr; chm Catholic Children's Soc: Arundel & Brighton, Portsmouth, Southwark; memb Law Soc; Knight of the Equestrian Order of the Holy Sepulchre of Jerusalem; *Recreations* golf, swimming; *Style*— John Brasington, Esq; Badgers Rake, Pear Tree Lane, Shorne, Gravesend, Kent DA12 3JS (☎ 047 482 2510); 51/54 Windmill St, Gravesend, Kent (☎ 0474 560361, fax 0474 328315)

BRAZIER, Julian William Hendy; MP (C) Canterbury 1987-; s of Lt-Col Peter Hendy Brazier, and Patricia Audrey Helen, *née* Stubbs, ggd of Bishop Stubbs of Oxford noted lectr and author of the Constitutional History of England; *b* 24 July 1953; *Educ* Dragon Sch Oxford, Wellington, BNC Oxford (MA), London Business Sch; *m* 21 July 1984, Katharine Elizabeth, da of Brig Patrick Blagden, CBE; 2 s (twins); *Career* SSLC with RE and Capt TA; Charter Consolidated Ltd 1975-84, H B Maynard Management Consultants 1984-87; *Recreations* cross country running, science, philosophy; *Style*— Julian W H Brazier, Esq, MP; c/o House of Commons, London SW1A 0AA

BRENTON, Annabel Louisa; da of Alan Harry Robson, of Curlew Cottage, Sharrington, Norfolk, and Eileen Marie, *née* Hayward; *b* 17 Oct 1958; *Educ* Loughton Co HS, Univ of London (LLB, AKC), Univ of Oxford (BCL); *m* 29 Aug 1981, Timothy Deane Brenton, *qv*, s of Cdr Ronald William Brenton, MBE (d 1982); 1 da (Louisa Elizabeth b 8 April 1990); *Career* admitted slr 1984; ptnr Messrs Withers 1988-; memb Law Soc; *Recreations* golf, gardening, needlepoint; *Clubs* Fakenham Golf; *Style*— Mrs Annabel Brenton; 20 Essex St, London WC2R 3AL (☎ 071 836 8400)

BRENTON, Timothy Deane; s of Cdr Ronald William Brenton, MBE (d 1982), and Peggy Cecilia Deane, *née* Biggs; *b* 4 Nov 1957; *Educ* King's Sch Rochester, Britannia RNC, Univ of Bristol (LLB); *m* 29 Aug 1981, Annabel Louisa, *qv*, da of Alan Harry Robson, of Curlew Cottage, Sharrington, Norfolk; 1 da (Louisa Elizabeth b 8 April 1990); *Career* RN 1975-79; lectr in law King's Coll London 1980; called to the Bar Middle Temple 1981; *Recreations* golf, windsurfing, fishing; *Clubs* Fakenham Golf; *Style*— Timothy Brenton, Esq; 2 Essex Court, Temple, London EC4 (☎ 071 583 8381, fax 071 353 0998, telex 8812528 ADROIT G)

BRETT, Rev Canon Peter Graham Cecil; s of Cecil Brett, of Woburn Sands, Bucks, and Doris, *née* Robinson; *b* 16 June 1935; *Educ* Bedford Mod Sch, Emmanuel Coll Cambridge (MA); *m* 19 Aug 1961, Gillian Mary, da of Dr George Field Bramley (d 1981), of Cheltenham; 3 s (Benedict Peter Bramley b 1963, Thomas Justin Edward b 1969, Daniel James Matthew b 1971), 1 da (Anna Mary Caroline b 1965); *Career* Nat Serv 2 Lt Beds and Herts Regt 1954-56; asst curate: Tewkesbury Abbey 1961-64, St Peter's Bournemouth 1964-66; chaplain Univ and Hatfield Colls Univ of Durham 1966-72, rural dean Houghton-Le-Spring Co Durham 1981-83 (rector 1972-83), canon residentiary of Canterbury Cathedral 1983-; prior St John's Hosp Canterbury 1987-; memb: Euro Cathedrals Assoc, Int Common on Monuments and Sites UK, Assoc of Leading Visitor Attractions, Cncl of The Canterbury Soc; govr: Christ Church Coll Canterbury, Simon Langton Schs Canterbury, The Kings Sch Canterbury; rotarian; *Recreations* wood-carving, continental travel, islands, monasticism; *Style*— The Rev Canon Peter Brett; 22 The Precincts, Canterbury, Kent CT1 2EP (☎ 0227 459757); Cathedral House, 11 The Precincts, Canterbury CT1 2EH (☎ 0227 762862, fax 0227 762897)

BREWER, Malcolm Alexander; s of George Henry Brewer (d 1988), of London, and Elizabeth, *née* Cowan; *b* 27 April 1947; *Educ* Buckingham Gate Secdy Modern Sch; *m* 17 July 1971, Maria Stephania, da of Frank Kulczycki (d 1974), of London; 1 s (Paul George John b 1975), 1 da (Julia Helen b 1977); *Career* area housing mangr London Borough of Hackney 1987, neighbourhood housing mangr London Borough of Lambeth 1989; Lab Pty Cities of London and Westminster Constituencies: treas 1966-70, agent for Alf Dubs in gen election 1970; Dartford Borough Cncl: cncllr for Princes Ward 1976-87 (voluntarily stepped down), chm controlling Lab Gp 1978-81, chm Housing Ctee 1979-82, sec to Lab Oppn Gp 1981-86, oppn housing spokesman 1982-86; press offr Dartford Constituency Lab Pty 1976-87; *Recreations* politics; *Style*— Malcolm Brewer, Esq; 48 Clarendon Gardens, Dartford, Kent DA2 6EZ (☎ 0322 227013); London Borough of Lambeth, 55 Union Grove, London SW8 (☎ 071 627 1695)

BRICE, Edward St John; er s of W Brice, OBE, TD, DL, of Highover Hoo, Rochester; *b* 15 Feb 1936; *Educ* Tonbridge, Clare Coll Cambridge (MA); *m* 1960, Elizabeth, da of G Grieve; 1 s, 1 da; *Career* farmer; Lloyd's underwriter; memb Kent CC 1977, High Sheriff Kent 1980-81, chm Kent Co Agric Soc 1984-; Master Worshipful Co of Skinners 1990; *Recreations* golf, tennis; *Clubs* Royal and Ancient, Royal St George's Golf, MCC; *Style*— Edward Brice, Esq; Hoo Lodge, Hoo, Rochester, Kent (☎ 0634 251078)

BRIDGE, Very Rev Antony Cyprian (Tony); s of Cdr Cyprian Dunscomb Charles Bridge, RN (d 1938), and Gladys, *née* Steel (d 1969); *b* 5 Sept 1914; *Educ* Marlborough, Royal Acad Sch of Art; *m* 10 May 1937, Brenda Lois, da of Dr Raymond Streatfeild; 1 s (Cyprian b 1955), 2 da (Victoria b 1944, Charlotte b 1946); *Career* served WWII, demobbed Maj 1945; artist and painter; ordained: deacon 1955, priest 1956; curate Hythe Kent 1955-58, vicar Christ Church Lancaster Gate London 1958-68, dean of Guildford 1968-86, dean emeritus 1986-; FSA 1980; *Books* Images of God (1960), Theodora: Portrait in a Byzantine Landscape (1978), The Crusades (1980), Suleiman the Magnificent (1983), One Man's Advent (1985), Richard the Lionheart (1989); *Recreations* bird watching; *Style*— The Very Rev Tony Bridge, FSA; 34 London Rd, Deal, Kent CT14 9TE (☎ 0304 366792)

BRIGHOUSE, Mary Irene Alice; da of Ingram Arthur Barrett (d 1985), and Irene, *née* Arbasini Bovary, Contessa Della Torre dei Torti; *b* 24 Sept 1936; *Educ* Barker Coll Buenos Aires, Inmaculee Conception Coll Buenos Aires, Univ of Buenos Aires (LLB); *m* 22 Nov 1959, David John Brighouse, s of John Brighouse (d 1969); 2 s (Ronald b 1970, Alexander b 1976), 1 da (Marina b 1966); *Career* consular and visa offr Buenos Aires Br Embassy 1958-72, teacher St Joseph's Convent Sch Cliffe; annual exhibitor of paintings Harrods Buenos Aires Art Gallery 1958-72, parish cncl clerk Cliffe 1987, charity worker with Br Community abroad, govr St Helen's Sch Gravesend; memb: Br Community Cncl Soc of Br Artists Buenos Aires 1958-72, Ecumenical Ctee for Christian Unity Strood, local conservation socs in Kent; life memb St Andrew's Soc of the River Plate; *Recreations* music, painting, country walks; *Style*— Mrs Mary Brighouse; Ferndale, 8 Station Rd, Cliffe, nr Rochester, Kent (☎ 0634 221823)

BRIGHT, Barry William; s of Richard John Bright, of Gravesend, and Hannah Bell, *née* Rainey; *b* 27 June 1947; *Educ* St George's C of E Gravesend; *m* 18 May 1974, Marilyn Christina, da of Marshall Albert Marsh (d 1986); 2 s (Mark William Richard b 1982, Paul Martin James b 1985); *Career* co sec; chm Kent Co FA 1983- (cncl memb 1972-), Kent rep FA Cncl 1984-, former chm N Kent Sunday Football League; *Recreations* sport, philately; *Style*— Barry W Bright, Esq; The Briars, Gold St, Cobham, nr Gravesend, Kent DA12 3AA (☎ 0474 814501); Gillingham Football Club Co Ltd, Redfern Ave, Gillingham, Kent ME7 4DD (☎ 0634 51854)

BRIGHT, Michael John; s of John Thomas Bright (d 1984), and Alice Hearne; *b* 10 Aug 1944; *Educ* Bromley GS Kent; *m* 15 July 1967, Catherine Ellen, da of Clifford Brown; 1 s (James Michael b 1972), 1 da (Victoria Jane b 1970); *Career* chief exec and md New Scotland Insurance Group plc, dep chm Independent Insurance Co Ltd 1988- (chief exec and md 1987-); dir and gen mangr Lombard Elizabethan Insurance Co plc (subsequently Lombard Continental Insurance plc) 1982-87; Orion Insurance Co Ltd 1967-82 (gp asst gen mangr 1980); memb Lloyds of London; memb The Worshipful Co of Insurers, Freeman City of London; ACII; *Recreations* gardening, reading, holidays; *Clubs* Marylebone Cricket (memb); *Style*— Michael J Bright, Esq; The Oasts, Biddenden Rd, Smarden, Kent (☎ 0233 77289); Independent Insurance Co Ltd, 12th Floor, Fountain House, 130 Fenchurch St, London EC3M 5AU (☎ 071 623 8877, fax 071 283 8275)

BRINE, Roger Ernest William; s of Ernest Albert Brine, of Bexhill-on-sea, E Sussex, and Ivy, *née* Funnell; *b* 13 Nov 1943; *Educ* Purley GS; *m* 12 May 1973, Monica, da of Erich Bredenbrucher (d 1945), of Herdecke, Germany; 1 s (Martin b 1974), 1 da (Katharine b 1977); *Career* admitted slr 1969; ptnr: Vallis and Struthers 1971-78, Amhurst Brown Colombotti 1988-; memb: Law Soc, City of Westminster Law Soc, Soc for Computers and Law, Sevenoaks Round Table 1974-84; *Recreations* reading, swimming; *Style*— Roger Brine, Esq; 2 Duke St, St James's, London SW1Y 6BJ (☎ 071 930 2366, telex 261857, fax 071 930 2250)

BRITTAIN-CATLIN, Timothy John; s of John Edward Jocelyn Brittain-Catlin (d 1987), of Woolage Green, Kent, and Jennifer, *née* Manasseh (now Lady Balfour of Burleigh); *b* 5 July 1961; *Educ* Westminster, Trinity Coll Cambridge (MA), UCL (Dip Arch); *Career* architect; specialist in renovation and conversion of historic bldgs, architectural book critic of The World of Interiors; co-fndr SDP Nat Student Orgn 1981; fndr SDP Student Orgn at: Univ of Cambridge 1981, UCL 1984; FRSA 1987, MRIBA 1988; *Style*— Timothy Brittain-Catlin, Esq; 28 Liverpool Lawn, Ramsgate, Kent CT11 9HJ (☎ 0843 580048)

BROCK, Baroness; Chrissie Palmer; *née* Jones; da of John Alfred Jones, of Leeds; *b* 1 June 1903; *Educ* Leeds Girls' HS, Royal Sch Needlework; *m* 1979, as his 2 w, Baron Brock (d 1980); 2 step da; *Career* private sec; *Style*— The Rt Hon the Lady Brock; 39 Chancellor House, Tunbridge Wells, Kent TN4 0BT

BROCKLEHURST, Ben Gilbert; s of Ernest Brocklehurst (d 1935), and Kathleen Brocklehurst (d 1965); *b* 18 Feb 1922; *Educ* Bradfield Coll; *m* 1, March 1947 (m dis 1957), Mary; m 2, June 1962, Belinda, da of William S Bristowe; 3 s, 1 da; *Career* 10 Devon Regt 1940, Maj 16 FF Rifles Indian Army 1942, Lt-Col 4/12 FF Regt LA 1946 served Burma; dairy farmer Berks 1947; joined Advertisement Dept Country Life 1957, advertisement mangr Tothill Press 1961, advertisement dir Mercury House Pubns (md 24 Magazines Mercury House 1970), proprietor The Cricketer 1972, fndr Cricketer Holidays; co cricketer: Somerset 2 XI 1951, Somerset 1XI 1952-54 (capt 1953 and 1954); *Recreations* cricket, golf, tennis, squash; *Clubs* Naval and Military, Piccadilly, MCC, Free Foresters, IZ; *Style*— Ben Brocklehurst, Esq; Beech Hanger, Ashurst, nr Tunbridge Wells, Kent (☎ 089274 0256)

BROMFIELD, Frederick Victor; s of Frederick Gerald Thomas Bromfield (d 1975), of Peckham, London, and Zena Thora Palfrey, *née* Baines; *b* 25 Aug 1942; *Educ* Camberwell Sch of Art (NDD); *m* 1, 8 Oct 1967 (m dis 1977), Susan Mary, da of David Hall, of Peterborough, Cambs; 1 s (Dominic b 28 June 1969), 1 da (Melanie b 12 March 1968); m 2, 30 July 1977, Elizabeth Jean Yeaman, da of Andrew McKenzie Watson (d 1983), of Salisbury, Wiltshire; 3 da (Felicia b 20 June 1979, Amy b 19 April 1982, Emily b 30 June 1983); *Career* artist; major works: The Faerie Queene 1974, series on theme of bats 1976-79, Elegy 1984, series on theme of Mr Punch 1988-89; art tutor Bromley Adult Educn Serv 1979-; *Recreations* music appreciation, reading; *Style*— Frederick Bromfield, Esq; 178 Kings Rd, Biggin Hill, Westerham, Kent TN16 3NJ (☎ 0959 75307)

BROMLEY, Archdeacon of; *see*: Francis, Ven Edward Reginald

BROOKER, Dr Arthur Edward William; s of Edward John Brooker (d 1963), of London, and Mary Harriett, *née* Fuller (d 1953); *b* 12 Dec 1912; *Educ* Roan Sch Greenwich, Univ of London St Bartholomew's Hosp Med Coll (MRCS, LRCP, MB BS, MD); *m* 14 Nov 1942, Kathleen Elma, da of George Alexander Raw (d 1973), of IOW; 2 s (John b 1946, Stephen b 1956), 1 da (Catherine b 1950); *Career* Capt RAMC 1939-45; jr scholarship St Bartholomew's Hosp Med Coll 1932, extern-intern St Bartholomew's Hosp 1938, sr med registrar RPMS 1946-47, asst Med Professorial Unit Royal Hosp Sheffield 1947-48, GP princ Cliftonville 1948-76, locum conslt rheumatology S E Thames RHA 1976-85, examining MO DHSS 1978-87, occasional ship's surgn for various shipping lines; sometime memb Kent Local Med Ctee, life memb Assoc of Men of Kent and Kentish Men, veteran memb Royal Temple YC, memb Br Soc for Rheumatology 1958-; Freeman City of London 1970, Liveryman Worshipful Soc of Apothecaries 1970; life memb BMA 1937, FRCGP 1970; *Books* Cervical Spondylosis (thesis in two volumes, 1963), Cervical Spondylosis - A Clinical Study with Comparative Radiology (jtly, in Brain, 1965); *Recreations* photography and videography, motoring, sailing; *Clubs* Royal Temple Yacht; *Style*— Dr Arthur Brooker; Six Elms, Lanthorne Rd, Broadstairs, Kent CT10 3NA (☎ 0843 68741)

BROOKS, Lawrence; s of Capt Edward Albert Brooks (d 1966), of Broadlands, Sussex, and Madge Vera Brooks (d 1984); *b* 4 Oct 1946; *Educ* Allhallows Sch; *m* 5 May 1979, Elaine Frances, da of Donald Hamblett, of Beauworth Park, Maidstone, Kent; 2 da (Annabel Elise b 1980, Georgina Clair b 1985); *Career* admitted slr 1971; ptnr Whitehead Monckton 1974; chm SE Rent Assessment Panel 1986; memb Law Soc 1971; *Recreations* sailing, skiing; *Clubs* Ski Club of GB, Hastings and St Leonards Sailing; *Style*— Lawrence Brooks, Esq; Chaidhurst Oast, Chainhurst Marden, Kent; Whitehead Monckton & Co, 72 King St, Maidstone, Kent (☎ 0622 690077, fax 0622 690050, telex 966477 WHITE G)

BROWN, Allen Roger; MVO (1980); s of Arthur William Brown (d 1970), of Maidstone, Kent, and Cicie, *née* Rogers (d 1937); *b* 29 Dec 1934; *m* 24 March 1956, Brenda, da of John Thomas Breakwell (d 1974), of Birmingham; 2 s (Mark b 1960, Richard (twin) b 1960), 1 da (Judy Catherine b 1956); *Career* Nat Serv RN 1953-65; diplomat; Br Embassy postings: Brussels 1967-69, Benghazi 1969-71, Kuwait 1973-75, Berne 1978-81, Amman 1981-85, Baghdad first sec commercial 1987-; Middle E Centre for Arab Studies Lebanon 1971-73; *Recreations* good husbandry; *Style*— Allen Brown, Esq, MVO; c/o Foreign and Commonwealth Office (Baghdad), King Charles St, London SW1

BROWN, Andrew Edwin; s of Edwin Charles Brown, of Gillingham, Kent, and Kathleen, *née* Worrell; *b* 22 Aug 1945; *Educ* Sir Joseph Williamson's Mathematical Sch Rochester, Guy's Hosp Dental and Med Sch Univ of London (BDS, MB BS); *m* 31 May 1969, Joan Elizabeth, da of Frank Phillips, of Huddersfield, Yorks; 1 s (Simon Charles b 1978), 2 da (Rachel Claire b 1972, Helen Louise b 1974); *Career* conslt maxillofacial surgn Queen Victoria Hosp E Grinstead and Medway and Maidstone Health Authys 1981-; fell in dental surgery RCSEng; FRCSEd; *Recreations* graphic art, philately, travel, DIY; *Style*— Andrew Brown, Esq; Speedwell House, North Pole Rd, Barming, Maidstone, Kent ME16 9HH (☎ 0622 726789); The Somerfield Hospital, London Rd, Maidstone, Kent ME16 0DU (☎ 0622 686581)

BROWN, (Brian) David; s of Thomas Brown, of Sidcup, Kent, and Eleanor, *née* Dinning; *b* 26 June 1935; *Educ* Erith Tech Coll, Univ of Durham (BSc); *m* 12 Nov 1960, Margaret Terry, da of late Robert Docherty; 1 s (Richard David b 16 March 1970), 1 da (Katharine Elizabeth b 19 May 1972); *Career* divnl head Power Div APC 1965-68, chief engr Power Div BNDC 1968-71; BBE: assoc dir 1971-80, engrg dir 1980-85, ops dir 1985-86; engrg dir Transmanche Link 1986-90; tech advsr to TML Bd 1990-; CEng, FIMechE, FIMarE, FINucE, memb IOD; *Recreations* swimming, walking, gardening; *Clubs* Balfour Beatty Sports; *Style*— David Brown, Esq; Transmanche Link, Shearway House, Shearway Rd, Folkestone, Kent CT19 4QU (☎ 0303 278978, fax 0303 2790801)

BROWN, Prof Fred; s of Fred Brown (d 1982), of Burnley, Lancs, and Jane Ellen, *née* Fielding (d 1975); *b* 31 Jan 1925; *Educ* Burnley GS, Univ of Manchester (BSc, MSc, PhD); *m* 1 May 1948, Audrey Alice, da of Ernest Doherty (d 1954); 2 s (Roger b 21 Nov 1949, David b 17 Oct 1953); *Career* asst lectr in chemistry Univ of Manchester 1946-48, lectr Univ of Bristol 1948-50, sr sci offr Hannah Dairy Res Inst 1950-53, sr sci offr Christie Hosp Manchester 1953-55; Animal Virus Res Inst Pirbright: sr sci offr 1955-58, princ scientific offr 1958-64, sr princ scientific offr 1964-71, dep chief scientific offr 1971-83, dep dir 1980-83; head Virology Dept Wellcome Biotechnology 1983-; memb Soc for Gen Microbiology, vice pres Inst of Biology 1988-90; FRS 1981; *Recreations* fell walking, watching cricket and association football; *Style*— Prof Fred Brown, FRS; Syndal, Glaziers Lane, Normandy, Guildford, Surrey GU3 2DF (☎ 0483 811107)

BROWN, Heather; da of Thomas Reginald Johnson, of Budleigh Salterton, Devon, and Dorothy, *née* Wakefield; *b* 15 March 1942; *Educ* Clifton HS for Girls Bristol, Univ of Bristol (BSc); *m* 18 Sept 1965, Peter John Brown, s of Walter John Brown (d 1951), of Beckenham, Kent; *Career* graduate programmer IBM (UK) Laboratories Hursley 1963-65, res asst Mathematical Laboratory Univ of Cambridge 1965-68; Univ of Kent Computing Laboratory:

graduate demonstrator 1968-70, lectr in computer sci 1970-85, reader in computer sci and head of Academic Div 1985-; visiting res assoc Stanford Univ California USA 1980, memb Ed Bd Electronic Publishing Origination Dissemination and Design (EP-odd) 1987-; memb prog ctee for several int confs incl: EP 88 Int Conf of Electronic Publishing, Document Manipulation and Typography Nice 1988, Doc Proc 88 ACM Conf on Document Processing Systems Santa Fe 1988, EP90 Int Conf on Electronic Publishing, Document Manipulation and Typography Washington DC 1990; memb: ctees BSI 1984-89, Ctee Br Computer Soc 1984-89 (chm specialist gp in electronic publishing 1984-86), Ctee Conf of Profs of Computor Sci; conf chm EP86 Int Conf on Text Processing and Document Manipulation 1986; FBCS 1986; *Recreations* walking, gardening, bird watching; *Style*— Mrs Heather Brown; Computing Laboratory, The University of Kent, Canterbury, Kent CT2 7NF (☎ 0227 764000)

BROWN, Ian James Morris; s of Bruce Beveridge Brown (d 1957), of Alloa, Scotland, and Eileen Frances, *née* Carnegie (d 1986); *b* 28 Feb 1945; *Educ* Dollar Acad, Univ of Edinburgh (MA, DipEd, MLitt); *m* 8 June 1968, Judith Ellen, da of George Woodall Sidaway, of Adelaide; 1 s (Joshua b 1977), 1 da (Emily b 1972); *Career* playwright 1967-; sch teacher 1967-69 and 1970-71; lectr in drama: Dunfermline Coll Edinburgh 1971-76, Br Cncl Edinburgh and Istanbul 1976-78; princ lectr Crewe and Alsager Coll 1978-86 (seconded as sec Cork Enquiry into Professional Theatre 1985-86); drama dir Arts Cncl of GB 1986-; *plays incl*: Mother Earth 1970, The Bacchae 1972, Positively the Last Final Farewell Performance (ballet scenario) 1972, Carnegie 1973, Rune (choral work) 1973, The Knife 1973, Rabelais 1973, The Fork 1976, New Reekie 1977, Mary 1977, Runners 1978, Mary Queen and the Loch Tower 1979, Pottersville 1982, Joker in the Pack 1983, Beatrice 1989; *Recreations* theatre, sport, travel; *Style*— I J M Brown, Esq; Arts Council, 14 Gt Peter St, London SW1P 3NQ (☎ 071 333 0100)

BROWN, Jackie; da of Peter Wyatt Brown, of Southchurch, Southend, and Rosemary Ann, *née* Gunnel (d 1986); *b* 8 April 1958; *Educ* King John Sch Thundersley Essex, Southend Tech Coll, Preston Poly (BA); *m* 29 Sept 1984, Simon Philip Wilkinson, s of Peter Charlton Wilkinson, of Leigh on Sea, Essex; 2 da (Elizabeth Mary Joyce b 15 Jan 1985, Rosemary Alice Nuillag b 23 Dec 1989); *Career* artist; one person exhibition (LYC Museum & Art Gallery Cumbria) 1982, Views and Horizons (Yorkshire Sculpture Park) 1983, Mud Sticks & Stones (residency Riverside Country Park) Gillingham 1989, Wall Connections (Morley Gallery London) 1989; work in private collections, involved in Pre-Art course at Canterbury Tech Coll; *Style*— Ms Jackie Brown

BROWN, John Henry; s of John Brown (d 1966), and Emily Maria, *née* Whitewood; *b* 14 Sept 1929; *m* 5 June 1960, Sheila May, da of Albert Herbert Sargent, of Maidstone; 1 s (Jonathan b 28 Aug 1970), 1 da (Jane b 4 Jan 1964); *Career* at photographic studio John's Studio London 1956-80; Breakthrough Tst London 1980-84, admin post Hi Centre Maidstone 1985-88, chief exec Hi Kent Assoc Maidstone 1989- ; fndr Eng Deaf Chess Assoc; *Recreations* chess; *Style*— John Brown, Esq; 28 Normanhurst Rd, Borough Green, Sevenoaks, Kent TN15 8HU (☎ 0732 884539); Hi Kent Association, Marsham St, Maidstone, Kent ME14 1HH (☎ 0622 691151, fax 0622 672436)

BROWN, Keith John; JP (1979); s of Frederick Charles Brown, and Doris Lilian, *née* French; *b* 21 June 1949; *Educ* Forest Hill Sch, City and East London Coll, Univ of London; *Career* ocularist: Moorfields Eye Hosp 1970, Kent Co Ophthalmic and Aural Hosp Maidstone 1973, Kent and Sussex Hosp Tunbridge Well 1975; private practice ownership: Brown Poole & Ptnrs Tunbridge Wells 1972, Brown and Gimpel Southborough 1979; ind private practice: Southborough, Maidstone, W Malling 1981; consIt oculist: Keelers (Cromwell Hosp) 1984, Trotters Edinburgh 1986, Dolland and Aitchison Gp 1987, Chaucer Hosp Canterbury 1988; chm Lib Democrat Pty Cranbrook and Dist; Freeman: City of London, Worshipful Co of Spectacle Makers; fndr fell Br Assoc Dispensing Opticians 1986; *Recreations* cooking, walking, shooting; *Clubs* Nat Lib; *Style*— Keith Brown, Esq, JP; Linnet House, Hawkhurst, Kent (☎ 0580 753 668); 23-27 Swan St, West Malling, Kent (☎ 0732 848 384); 100 London Rd, Southborough, Tunbridge Wells, Kent (☎ 0892 31004, telex prestel MBX 580 211167)

BROWN, Dr Percy Edgar; s of Noel Alfred Brown (d 1956), of Broadstone, Dorset, and Dorcas Alice Float, *née* Young; *b* 30 Sept 1923; *Educ* Berkhamsted Sch for Boys, Guy's Hosp (MB BS, MRCP, MRCGP); *m* 23 Dec 1946, Patricia Margery, da of John Reginald Forbes Williams (d 1974), of Gravesend, Kent; 2 s (Michael Palliser b 1951, Paul b 1964), 3 da (Penelope Janette b 1949, Priscilla Elizabeth b 1956, Patricia Margaret b 1959); *Career* res med offr Gravesend and N Kent Hosp 1946-47, med offr RAF Med Servs Germany 1947-49, GP Gravesend Kent 1949-85, sr med offr HM Prison Med Serv 1985-; memb: Inst of Psycho-Sexual Med, Nat Assoc of Family Planning Drs; *Recreations* travel in third world investigating health care systems; *Clubs* Gravesend Pudden; *Style*— Dr Percy Brown; HMP Maidstone, County Rd, Maidstone, Kent ME14 1UZ (☎ 0474 356861)

BROWN, Peter John; s of Walter John Brown (d 1951), of Beckenham, Kent, and Marjorie Winifred, *née* Johnson; *b* 30 July 1939; *Educ* Sutton Valence, Clare Coll Cambridge (BA, PhD), Univ of N Carolina (MSc); *m* 18 Sept 1965, Heather, da of Thomas Reginald Johnson, of Budleigh Salterton, Devon; *Career* IBM (UK) Laboratories Hursley Park 1963-65; Univ of Kent at Canterbury 1968-: lectr in computer sci, reader, prof 1976-; visiting scientist UFRJ Rio de Janeiro Brazil 1979, visiting prof Stanford Univ California USA 1980, Erskine fell Univ of Canterbury NZ 1987; awards: Hartree premium IEE 1983, BCS Tech Award 1988; memb ctees in BCS and SERC, govr Southbank Poly 1982-84; FBCS 1970, FRSA 1980; *Books* Macro Processors and Techiques for Software Portability (1974), Software Portability (ed, 1977), Writing Interctive Compilers and Interpreters (1979), Pascal from BASIC (1982), Starting with UNIX (1984), Introduction to PC/IX and PC Xenix (with P Szilard and S Weeks, 1985), Software Engineering (ed jtly, 1986); *Recreations* playing 5-a-side football, gardening, bird watching; *Style*— Peter Brown, Esq; Computing Laboratory, The University, Canterbury, Kent CT2 7NF (☎ 0227 764000)

BROWN, Timothy Frank (Tim); s of Frank Steel Brown, of The Furrows, Borstal, Rochester, Kent, and Katherine Mary, *née* Osenton; *b* 7 Nov 1944; *Educ* Sir Joseph Williamson's Mathematical Sch; *m* 1 July 1967, Kathleen Patricia, da of Frederick Geoffrey Smith (d 1975); 2 s (Matthew Philip b 1975, Michael James b 1980), 2 da (Karen Patricia b 1971, Amy Clare b 1978); *Career* CA; Larking & Larking 1963-68, Deloitte's 1968-69, md UBS Philips & Drew (joined 1969); FCA 1968, ATII 1969; *Style*— Tim Brown, Esq; Angley Lake, Cranbrook, Kent TN17 2PR (☎ 0580 714248); UBS Phillips & Drew, 100 Liverpool St, London (☎ 071 901 3333)

BROWNE, Henry Buxton; s of Richard Buxton Browne (d 1922), of Durban, SA, and Mary Hill Ryrie (d 1949); kinsman of Barons Brocket, Croft and Denman; *b* 28 Oct 1919; *Educ* private sch; *m* 4 April 1953, Enid Dorothy, da of George Cuthbert Jarvis (d 1965), of Petts Wood, Kent; *Career* served 1940-46 RA, RAOC and REME in UK, France and Germany; FCA; *Recreations* golf, genealogical research; *Clubs* Chislehurst Golf; *Style*— H Buxton Browne, Esq; 1 Moorlands, Wilderness Rd, Chislehurst, Kent BR7 5HB

BRUCE, Clive Ian; s of Reginald Bruce (d 1982), and (Sarah) Eileen, *née* Brown; *b* 19 Jan 1941; *Educ* Rossall Sch Fleetwood, Univ of Liverpool (BSc); *m* 31 Aug 1968, Christina Dryhurst, da of Trevor Beech Jones, of Tyldesley, Lancs; 2 da (Linda b 1971, Catherine b 1973); *Career* investmt mangr Refuge Aussurance plc (joined 1963); cncllr: Eccles Borough Cncl 1969-72, Ash cum Ridley Parish Cncl 1979-87, Sevenoaks DC 1987-; vice chm Housing Sub Ctee 1990-; chm of govrs New Ash Green Middle Sch 1982-; AIA 1972, AMSIA; *Style*— Clive Bruce, Esq; 11 Spring Cross, New Ash Green, Longfield, Kent DA3 8QG (☎ 0474 874177); Refuge Assurance plc, 66 Gresham St, London EC2V 7PQ (☎ 071 600 0339, fax 071 606 3842)

BRUCE-LOCKHART, Alexander John (Sandy); s of Col John MacGregor Bruce-Lockhart, CB, CMG, OBE, of Rye, Sussex; *b* 4 May 1942; *Educ* Dragon Sch Oxford, Sedbergh, RAC; *m* 12 March 1966, Tess, da of Edward Pressland (d 1985); 2 s (Mark Alexander b May 1968, Simon David b 4 July 1973), 1 da (Tash Emma b 3 Jan 1970); *Career* farmer Headcorn 1967- (Rhodesia, now Zimbabwe 1963-66); chm Maidstone Cons Assoc, memb Kent CC; *Style*— Sandy Bruce-Lockhart, Esq; Upper Boy Court Farm, Headcorn, Kent TN27 9LA (☎ 0622 890651)

BRUNNARIUS, Lesley Jane; da of Martin Brunnarius, and Mary Christina, *née* Holman; *b* 15 Aug 1963; *Educ* Oakmeeds Comp Sch Burgess Hill, Haywards Heath Sixth Form Coll, Worthing Art Coll, Canterbury Art Coll (BA), Royal Acad of Art London; *Career* painter; exhibitions incl: Kent Art & Design (Maidstone) 1985, 1985 Spirit of London Competition (The Mall) 1985 and Royal Festival Hall (London) 1986, 1986/87 Spirit of London Competition Royal Festival Hall, Young Artists SE Maidstone 1989, Rye Art Gallery 1990; One Woman Show Tunbridge Wells 1989, GLC Spirit of London Painting Prize; *Recreations* walking, cycling, maintaining self sufficient garden; *Style*— Miss Lesley Brunnarius; Stable Cottage, Shirley Hall, Leggs Lane, Langton Green, nr Tunbridge Wells, Kent TN3 0RQ (☎ 0892 863752)

BRYANT, Jonathan Nicholas; JP (Tunbridge Wells and Cranbrook 1979); s of Basil Stuart Bryant (d 1976), and Margaret Ethel, *née* Black (d 1987); *b* 12 July 1944; *Educ* Cheltenham, Southbank Poly; *m* 4 June 1966, Sandra Anne, da of Alexander William Kendrick (d 1984); 2 s (Nicholas Stuart b 1966, Rupert Charles Stuart b 1972), 1 da (Jane Alexandra b 1967); *Career* chm and md Brymor Ltd and Bryant Corporation plc 1969-; tax cmmr 1978-; Master Worshipful Co of Curriers 1983-84; *Recreations* family, reading, walking and village organisations; *Style*— Jonathan Bryant, Esq, JP; Greenwood, Frant, Tunbridge Wells, Kent TN3 9DR (☎ 089 275 462); Brymor Ltd, Tonbridge Rd, E Peckham, Tonbridge, Kent TN3 9DR (☎ 0622 871384)

BUCKINGHAM, Maria (Janice Irene Bunce); da of Albert George Morgan Bunce (d 1971), of 27 Chatsworth Ave, Bromley, Kent, and Irene Beatrice, *née* Coxhead (d 1971); *b* 8 March 1937; *Educ* Bromley Co GS for Girls, Birbeck Coll London (BSc); *m* 5 April 1958 (m dis 1972), Joseph Stephen Henry Collins, s of late Joseph Collins, of 63, Oakhurst Grove, London; 2 s (Stephen Richard b 1959, Robert Charles b 1960); *Career* computer programmer OCL 1979-84, computer systems designer GLC 1984-86, computer systems mangr Davy McKee 1986-88, photographer running own studio 1988-; author of: treatise on Fossilised Turtles in Palaeontology 1971, article on old brick Tudor Chimney Stacks in Kent Life 1988; official photographer to Bromley C of C (memb Exec Ctee), sec London Region of Master Photographers Assoc, memb London Portrait Gp; former FGS/ Licentiate Master Photographers Assoc, memb BIPP; *Recreations* walking, running, dancing (folk and historical), singing, crafts and history (especially costume); *Style*— Mrs Maria Buckingham; 10 Bevercote Walk, Upper Belvedere, Kent DA17 5RB (☎ 03224 63489); Photography by Maria Studio, 224A High St, Bromley, Kent BR1 1PQ (☎ 081 313 0235)

BUCKLEY, Graham Michael; s of Alfred Thomas Buckley, of Staplehurst, Kent, and Gladys May, *née* Wackett; *b* 12 Aug 1942; *Educ* Hampton GS, Southwest HS Minneapolis USA, LSE (BSc); *m* 17 Aug 1963 (m dis); 2 da (Caroline Fiona b 1965, Alexandra Catherine b 1967); *Career* sales mangr Procter & Gamble Ltd, brands mangr Mars Ltd, gen mangr National Carbonising Co, sales dir Yardley of London, md Bacchante Ltd, dep chm Spong Holdings plc, pres Design Style Products, md and chief exec Alfred Reader & Co Ltd; *Recreations* sailing and photography, travel and skiing; *Style*— Graham Buckley, Esq; Salden Lodge, Burgh Hill, Etchingham, East Sussex TM19 7PE (☎ 058025 285); Alfred Reader & Co Ltd, Imuicta Works, Teston, Maidstone, Kent ME18 5AW (☎ 0622 812230, fax 0622 814224)

BUCKWELL, Prof Allan Edgar; s of George Alfred Donald Buckwell, of Timsbury, Avon, and Jessie Ethel Neave (d 1989); *b* 10 April 1947; *Educ* Gillingham GS, Univ of London (BSc), Univ of Manchester (MA); *m* 1, (m dis 1990); 2 s (Andrew Simon b 1967, Timothy James b 1971); *Career* lectr Univ of Newcastle upon Tyne 1973-84, prof agric econs Univ of London 1984-; memb: Agric Econs Soc, Euro Assoc of Agric Economists; *Books* Costs of the Common Agricultural Policy (with D R Harley, K Parton and K J Thompson, 1982), Chinese Grain Economy and Policy (with Cheng Liang Yu, 1990); *Style*— Prof Allan Buckwell; 57 Oxenturn Rd, Wye, Ashford, Kent TN25 5AY (☎ 0233 813106); Department of Agricultural Economics, Wye College, University of London, Wye, Ashford, Kent TN25 5AH (☎ 0233 812401, fax 0233 813320)

BUDD, Bernard Wilfred; s of Rev William Robert Arscott Budd (d 1955), of Elham, and Florence Daisy, *née* Hewson (d 1970); *b* 18 Dec 1912; *Educ* Cardiff HS, W Leeds HS, Pembroke Coll Cambridge (MA); *m* 29 April 1944, Margaret Alison (Meg), da of Rt Hon E Leslie Burgin, MP, of Harpenden, Herts; 2 s (Colin b 1945, Robert Andrew b 1952); *Career* Indian Civil Serv 1935-47, Pakistan Admin Serv 1947-51, called to the Bar 1952, appointed QC 1969, ret 1982; Lib Parly Candidate Folkstone 1974 and 1979 (Dover 1964 and 1966), chm Assoc of Lib Lawyers 1978-82, vice pres Int Assoc for the Protection of Industl Property (Br Gp), lay preacher Methodist Church; *Recreations* bird watching, hill walking, gardening; *Clubs* United Oxford and Cambridge, Nat Lib; *Style*— Bernard Budd, Esq, QC; Highlands, Elham, Canterbury, Kent CT4 6UG (☎ 0303 840350)

BUDD, Margaret Alison (Meg); MBE; da of Rt Hon (Edward) Leslie Burgin, MP (d 1945), of Harpenden, Herts, and Dorothy Theresa, *née* Cooper (d 1975); *b* 8 Dec 1914; *Educ* St George's Sch Harpenden, Girton Coll Cambridge (BA); *m* 29 April 1944, Bernard Wilfred Budd, QC, s of Rev William Robert Arscott Budd, of Elham, Canterbury; 2 s (Colin Richard b 1945, Robert Andrew Budd b 1952); *Career* Women's Lib Fedn: former pres, former Euro liason offr, former int liason offr; memb and former pres Shepway SLD, memb Canterbury and Dist Assoc of Graduate Women, Methodist lay preacher; *Clubs* Nat Lib; *Style*— Mrs Meg Budd, MBE; Highlands, Elham, Canterbury, Kent CT4 6UG (☎ 0303 840350)

BULGIN, Sally Ann; da of Ernest Arthur Bulgin, of Barham, Kent, and Patricia Joy, *née* Aldrich; *b* 8 Nov 1957; *Educ* Highworth Sch for Girls Ashford, Univ of Reading, Courtauld Inst Univ of London; *Career* ed The Artist (incorporating Art and Artists Magazine) 1985-; memb Assoc of Int Art Critics; *Recreations* Kent county badminton player, squash, running, most sports; *Style*— Ms Sally Bulgin; Caxton House, 63-65 High St, Tenterden, Kent TN30 6BD (☎ 05806 3673)

BULLEN, Dr William Alexander; s of Francis Lisle Bullen, and Amelia, *née* Morgan; *b* 22 Sept 1918; *Educ* Merchant Taylors', London Hosp Med Coll (MRCS, LRCP, MRCGP); *m* 1, 1942 (m dis 1956), Phyllis, da of George Leeson; 3 da (Susan b 1943, Penelope b 1944, Virginia b 1950); m 2, 1956 (m dis 1983), Mary, da of Leigh Crutchley; m 3, 10 June 1983, Rosalind Margaret, da of Lawrence Reginald Gates; *Career* WWII cmmnd RTR (SR) 1939, resigned Maj 1946; med dir Boehringer-Pfizer 1957-62; pres: Pfizer Canada 1962-64, GM Pfizer Consumer Options UK 1964-66; chm Coty (England) 1965-66, md Scribbans Kemp 1966-67; chm: Thos Borthwick & Sons plc 1975-81 (md 1967-77), Whitburgh Investments 1976-80; Président Boucherie Bernard Paris 1977-81; memb Canterbury Wine Growers, assoc memb English Vineyards Assoc; Freeman City of London 1975, Liveryman Worshipful Co of Butchers 1975; FBIM 1976; *Recreations* sailing, music, viticulture; *Clubs* Royal Thames Yacht; *Style*— Dr William Bullen

BULLOCK, John; s of Robert Arthur Bullock (d 1960), of London, and Doris Edith Jane, *née* Thomas; *b* 12 July 1933; *Educ* Latymer Upper Sch; *m* 3 Sept 1960, Ruth Jennifer, da of Vernon William Bullock (d 1979), of Coulsdon, Surrey; 3 s (Mark b 1965 d 1982, Alastair b 1967, Robert b 1969); *Career* cmmnd RAF 1956-58; Smallfield Fitzhugh Tillet & Co 1949-56 and 1958-61; Robson Morrow: joined 1961, ptnr 1965-70 (Robson Morrow merged with Deloitte Haskins & Sells), ptnr i/c Deloitte Haskins & Sells Management Consultants 1971-79; Deloitte Haskins & Sells: managing ptnr 1979-85, dep sr ptnr 1984-85, sr ptnr 1985-90; vice chm Deloitte Haskins & Sells International 1985-89, chm Deloitte Europe 1985-89, dep chm Coopers & Lybrand Deloitte (jt sr ptnr), chm Coopers & Lybrand Europe 1990-; pt/t memb UK Energy Authy; Liveryman Worshipful Co of Chartered Accountants 1989; FCA, FCMA, FIMC; *Recreations* opera, theatre, ballet, skiing, sailing, tennis; *Clubs* Gresham; *Style*— John Bullock, Esq; Coopers & Lybrand Deloitte, 128 Queen Victoria St, London EC4P 4JX (☎ 071 248 3913, fax 071 248 3623, telex 894941)

BULMER, Dr John Nelson; s of Gordon Nelson Bulmer, of 29 Sprotbrough Rd, Doncaster, S Yorks, and Carmen Muntyan, *née* Blanco Pando; *b* 22 July 1952; *Educ* Percy Jackson GS Doncaster, Queens' Coll Cambridge, St Thomas's Hosp London; *m* 24 July 1982, Rachel Ann, da of Robert Auld, of 57 Nursery Drive, Banbury, Oxon; 1 s (Robbie Jon b 16 May 1986); *Career* conslt anaesthetist: SE Kent DHA, Buckland Hosp Dover (with clinical responsibility for intensive care in The High Dependency Unit); FFA, RCS 1980; *Recreations* fencing, bonsai, music, motorcycling; *Clubs* Deal Fencing, Lute Soc; *Style*— Dr John Bulmer; Pinecroft, Downs Rd, East Studdal, nr Dover, Kent CT15 5DA (☎ 0304 373518); Buckland Hospital, Coombe Valley Rd, Dover, Kent (☎ 0304 201624)

BUNDY, Dr Allan Graeme; s of Walter Ernest Bundy (d 1974), of 7 Hampstead Hill Gardens, London, and Ivy Moore, *née* Ward (d 1984); *b* 9 April 1929; *Educ* Lower Sch John Lyon Harrow, St George's Hosp Med Sch, Kings Coll London (MB BS, DTM&H, DObstRCOG); *m* 21 Oct 1967, Phillis Eldeca Margaretta, da of John Benjamin Isaacs (d 1970), of Guyana; 3 s (Andrew b 30 March 1962, Christopher Graeme b 7 April 1968, Richard Allan b 30 Sept 1970), 1 da (Ruth Eldeca 13 May 1969); *Career* Nat Serv Royal Signals and RAMC 1947-49; various appts held St George's Hosp and Whipps Cross Hosp 1959, med offr Sierra Leone Devpt Co at Hosps in Pepel, Marampa, Tonkolili 1960-64, appt in obstetrics Bedford Gen Hosp 1964, med offr Matthews Ridge Guyana (special interest malariology) 1965, med offr in obstetrics Windsor Hosp Gp 1966, med offr Mackenzie Hosp Guyana 1967-71, in practice Uranium City Canada and pt/t Grande Cache Alberta (incl flying doctor work) 1971-79, GP Health Centre Dover and dep police surgn 1979-; CIH; memb: RSM, Royal Soc for Tropical Med; *Recreations* horticulture, music, sheep farming; *Style*— Dr Allan Bundy; Chilton Farm Cottage, Alkham, Dover, Kent (☎ 0304 825481); The Health Centre, Dover, Kent (☎ 0304 202525)

BURDEN, Mary Elizabeth; da of Corpl Henry Francis Burden, of Bepton, Midhurst, W Sussex, and Diana Mary, *née* Ellis; *b* 5 Oct 1946; *Educ* Midhurst Secdy Sch, St Loye's Sch of Occupational Therapy; *Career* occupational therapist; basic grade Royal Sussex Co Hosp Brighton 1968-69, sr Netherne Hosp Coulsdon Surrey 1973-75 (basic grade 1969-73), locum Coonac Rehabilitation Centre Melbourne Aust 1975-76, sr Acre Day Hosp Worthing Sussex 1976-77, head Bexley Hosp Kent 1979-83 (dep head 1977-79), dist occupational therapist Bexley Health Dist Kent 1983-; co-tutor Christian Listeners, memb Br Assoc Occupational Therapists 1968-; *Recreations* country dancing, amateur dramatics, walking; *Style*— Miss Mary Burden; Bexley Hospital, The Mansion Occupational Therapy Department, Bexley, Kent (☎ 0322 526282 ext 2263)

BURGESS, Dr Colin Gordon; s of Ernest Arthur Walter Burgess (d 1976), of Henfield, Sussex, and Evie, *née* Evans (d 1983); *b* 2 Feb 1940; *Educ* Epsom Coll, South Bank Poly (BSc, PhD); *m* 10 Aug 1963, Rosalind Ann, da of Sydney George Gray (d 1964), of 6 Springhead Rd, North Fleet, Kent; 1 s (Alastair Mark b 5 May 1973), 1 da (Claire Louise b 11 Dec 1969); *Career* tech mangr Castrol Plastics Ltd 1966-69, export mangr Cray Valley Products (Coates Inks Ltd) 1969-72, tech dir Swan Plastics 1972-76, md Kent Chemical Co 1980- (commercial and tech dir 1977-80), chm Ian Young Aerosols Ltd 1988; Freeman City of London 1981, Liveryman Worshipful Co of Horners 1981; FRSC, MPI, FInstDir; *Style*— Dr Colin Burgess; Kent Chemical Co, George House, Bridewell Lane, Tenterden, Kent TN3 9DL (☎ 05806 4244, fax 05806 5652, telex 95508)

BURNETT, (Ernest) John; s of Ernest Burnett, MBE, of Staplehurst Manor, Staplehurst, Kent, and Norah Agnes, *née* Davis (d 1982); *b* 7 Oct 1931; *Educ* Liverpool Collegiate Sch, Colfe's GS; *m* 17 Dec 1955, Anne, da of Walter Hazell (d 1946), of IOW; 2 s (Jonathan b 1959, David b 1963), 1 da (Brigitte b 1956); *Career* CA 1955; ptnr Victor Stewart & Co 1959-69, princ John Burnett & Co (later John Burnett McMahon & Co) 1969-; cncllr Maidstone Borough 1972-84; Freeman City of London, memb Court of Assts Worshipful Co of Bowyers; FCA, FCCA, ATII; *Recreations* philosophy, restoration of Elizabethan timbered house; *Style*— John Burnett, Esq; Chequers, High St, Headcorn, Ashford, Kent TN27 9NE (☎ 0622 890 052); 103 Newgate St, London EC1A 7AP (☎ 071 606 4861, fax 071 606 4862)

BURRETT, John Arthur; s of Albert Arthur Burrett, of Melbourne, Aust, and Gladys, *née* Green; *b* 23 Oct 1947; *Educ* Eliot Coll Univ of Kent (BA); *m* 17 Aug 1979, Jennifer Ann; *Career* cmmnd RAOC 1970, ret 1974; called to the Bar Middle Temple 1979; dir: Canterbury Chambers Ltd, Manston Aviation Ltd; *Recreations* private pilot; *Clubs* Thanet Flying; *Style*— John Burrett, Esq; The Canterbury Chambers Ltd, Watling St, Canterbury, Kent CT1 2UD (☎ 0227 456865, fax 0227 456890)

BURRINGTON, Ernest; s of Harold Burrington (d 1978), of Chadderton, Lancs, and Laura, *née* Slater; *b* 13 Dec 1926; *m* 5 Jan 1950, Nancy, da of Fred Crossley (d 1988), of Lees, Oldham; 1 s (Peter), 1 da (Jill); *Career* Army 1943-47; reporter and sub ed Oldham Chronicle 1947-49 (reporter 1941-43), sub ed Bristol Evening World 1950; Daily Herald: sub ed Manchester 1950, night ed 1955, London night ed 1957; asst ed IPC Sun 1965 (night ed 1964), asst ed and night ed News International Sun 1969, dep night ed Daily Mirror 1970, assoc ed Sunday People 1972 (dep ed 1971), ed The People 1985-88 and 1989-90, md Mirror Group Newspapers 1990 (dep chm and asst publisher 1988); dir: MGN Magazine and Newsday Ltd 1989-, Sygma Photo Agency Paris 1990-, The European Ltd 1990-, IQ Newsgraphics Ltd 1990-; chm Syndication International 1989-; memb: Int Press Inst, Foreign Press Assoc; tstee: Int Inst of Child Studies, Youthscan; *Recreations* travel, tennis, bridge; *Style*— Ernest Burrington, Esq; Mirror Group Newspapers, Holborn Circus, London EC4A 1AR (☎ 071 822 2599, fax 071 882 2144, telex 896713)

BURROWS, Reginald Arthur; CMG (1964); s of Arthur Richard Burrows (d 1947), and Nellie Gertrude, *née* Oxley (d 1963); f was first dir of programmes of BBC in 1923, subsequently sec gen The Int Bdcasting Union Geneva; *b* 31 Aug 1918; *Educ* Mill Hill Sch, St Catharine's Coll Cambridge (MA); *m* 1952, Jenny Louisa Henriette (d 1985), da of Maurice Campiche, of Lausanne, Switzerland; 1 s (Stephen), 1 da (Susan); *Career* served WWII RAF in Europe, SE Asia, Wing Cdr, cmmnd 13 Sqdn; Dip Serv 1947-78: France, Pakistan (twice), Iran, Vietnam, Netherlands, Turkey; asst under sec of state 1976-78; *Recreations* skiing, tennis, mountain walking; *Style*— Reginald Burrows, Esq, CMG; 9 Summer Court, Summer Hill, Hambledown, Canterbury, Kent, CT2 8NP (☎ 0227 457394)

BURY, Rev Nicholas Ayles Stillingfleet; s of Maj Johm (Bill) Bury, MC (d 1983), of Westgate on Sea, and Joan, *née* Bacon; *b* 8 Jan 1943; *Educ* King's Sch Canterbury, Queens' Coll Cambridge (MA), Univ of Oxford (DipEd); *m* July 1971, Jennifer Anne Newbold, da of Dr John Loudon, of Cranleigh, Surrey; 2 s (Barney, Sam), 1 da (Corinne); *Career* curate Liverpool Parish Church 1968-71, chaplain ChCh Oxford 1971-75; vicar: St Mary's Shephall Herts 1975-84; St Peter in Thanet Kent 1984-; Hon MA Univ of Oxford; *Recreations* golf; *Style*— The Rev Nicholas Bury; St Peter's Vicarage, St Peter's, Broadstairs, Kent (☎ 0843 62728)

BUSBY, (Thomas Samuel) Charles; CBE (1977 OBE 1971), AE (1946), DL (Kent 1981); s of Thomas William Busby (d 1974), and his w Alice, *née* Feaver (d 1972); *b* 28 July 1919; *Educ* Cranbrook Sch Kent; *m* 1949, Diana Daun, da of William Cruickshank Dalgarno (d 1954); *Career* joined 500 Sqdn (Co Kent) AAF 1939, served Coastal Cmd Sqdns as Flt Lt (demobilised 1946); FSVA incorporated surveyor, auctioneer and estate agent (ret 1984); chm Royal Br Legion Village and Industries 1965-, life vice pres Kent Br Legion 1967- (vice chm 1952, chm 1962-67), vice chm Central Kent Hosp Mgmnt Ctee 1970-72 (memb 1964), chm Preston Hosp Ctee 1970-74, Maidstone Health Authy 1984-88; memb: Cncl Br Cwlth Ex-Services League 1971-, Maidstone and Dist Hosp Mgmnt Ctee 1972-74, Kent Family Practitioner Ctee 1974-75; nat chm Royal Br Legion 1975-78 (nat vice chm 1972-75), chm Brith Memb Cncl World Veterans Fedn 1977- (lay memb med advsy ctee), pres SE Area Royal Br Legion 1986; *Recreations* gardening, rugby football and cricket; *Clubs* RAF, Royal Overseas League; *Style*— Charles Busby, Esq, CBE, AE, DL; Willow Cottage, Benenden, Cranbrook, Kent TN17 4DB (☎ 0580 240466)

BUTCHER, Michael Joseph Edward; s of Edward Harry Butcher (d 1985), of France, and Margaret Enid, *née* Camp; *b* 9 Aug 1951; *Educ* Haylards Heath GS, Univ of Keele (BA); *Career* called to the Bar Grays Inn 1975; memb Legal Dept ESSO UK plc and Exxon USA 1976-88, legal dir and sec Eurotunnel Group 1989 (legal advsr 1988); *Recreations* chess, cinema, reading, skiing; *Style*— Michael Butcher, Esq; Eurotunnel, Victoria Plaza, 111 Buckingham Palace Rd, London SW1W 0ST (☎ 071 834 7575)

BUTLER, Prof John Richard; s of Henry Ernest Butler (d 1957), of London, and Hilda Dorothy, *née* Reed; *b* 29 April 1942; *Educ* Mill Hill Sch, Univ of Nottingham (BA, MA), Univ of Kent (PhD); *m* 7 Sep 1963, Gillian Muriel, da of Harold Kempthorne (d 1972), of Worthing, Sussex; 1 s (Mark Richard b 1965); *Career* res assoc Univ of Manchester 1965-69; Univ of Kent at Canterbury: res fell 1969-84, prof 1984-; memb: Chaucer Housing Assoc Canterbury 1970-80, Mental Health Review Tbnl 1973-, Canterbury and Thanet Community Health Cncl 1974-78, Soc for Social Med (hon sec 1978-83, chm 1987-89), Maidstone Health Authy 1983-; chm of govrs Kent Coll Canterbury 1976-81, lay preacher Methodist Church 1985-; *Books* Who Goes Home? (1970), Family Doctors and Public Policy (1973), How Many Patients? (1980), Health and Health Services (1984), Too Many Patients? (1987), Child Health Surveillance (1989); *Recreations* amateur dramatics, listening to music, tennis, supporting Arsenal; *Style*— Prof John Butler; University of Kent at Canterbury, George Allen Wing, Canterbury, Kent CT2 7NF (☎ 0227 764000 ext 3672)

BUTT, Geoffrey Frank; s of Frank Thomas Woodman Butt (d 1946), of Exeter, and Dorothy Rosamond, *née* Graseman (d 1968); *b* 5 May 1943; *Educ* Royal Masonic Sch Bushey, Univ of Reading (BA); *m* 8 July 1972, Lee Anne, da of Frederick Arthur Davey, of Exmouth; 2 s (David b 1973, Richard b 1976), 1 da (Anne (twin) b 1976); *Career* joined Office Slr for Customs and Excise 1971 (qualified slr, sr legal asst 1974, asst slr 1982, princ asst slr 1986); memb Law Soc 1970; *Recreations* family life, gardening, classical music, literature and art; *Style*— Geoffrey Butt, Esq; Office of the Solicitor for the Customs and Excise, New King's Beam House, 22 Upper Ground, London SE1 9PJ (☎ 071 382 5126)

BYERS, Jean Marina; da of John Pollard (d 1950), of Accrington, Lancashire, and Janet Erskine, *née* Kelly; *b* 27 Aug 1934; *Educ* Accrington HS for Girls, Univ of Manchester (BSc), Homerton Coll Cambridge; *m* 27 April 1957 (m dis 1979), Eric Byers, s of Sydney Byers, of Cockermouth; 1 s (Graham b 15 Feb 1961), 1 da (Helen (Mrs Harrison-Hall) b 15 Dec 1958); *Career* head teacher: Barton Court GS for Girls Canterbury 1980-87, Highworth Sch for Girls Ashford 1988-; pres: Canterbury Ladies Circle 1975-76, Soroptimist Int of Canterbury 1988-89; Nat Assoc of Head Teachers: pres Canterbury Dist 1983-85, pres Kent Branch 1986-87, nat cncl memb for Kent Bexley Bromley and Havering 1988-; *Recreations* travel, music; *Style*— Mrs Jean Byers; Highworth School for Girls, Quantock Drive, Ashford, Kent TN24 8UD (☎ 0233 624910)

C

CADELL, Vice Adm Sir John Frederick; s of Henry Dunlop Mallock Cadell (d 1936), of York, and Elizabeth, *née* Vandyke (d 1989), of Faversham; *b* 6 Dec 1929; *Educ* BRNC Dartmouth, RNC Greenwich; *m* 15 Feb 1958, Jaquetta Bridget, da of Paterick Gould Nolan (d 1968); 1 s (Charles Henry b 1965), 2 da (Caroline Elizabeth b 1959, Alexandra Jane b 1961); *Career* Capt 3 Frigate Sqdn 1975, DG Naval Personal Servs 1980, COS to Cdr Naval Forces South 1982; dist and gen mangr Canterbury and Thanet Authy 1986; *Recreations* skiing, tennis, chess; *Style*— Vice Adm Sir John Cadell; Great Mongeham House, nr Deal, Kent CT14 0HD (☎ 0304 373658); Canterbury and Thanet Health Authority, Regency Buildings, Ramsgate, Kent CT11 9PF (☎ 0843 594592)

CAIN, Peter Michael; s of Terence James Cain, of Newmarket, Suffolk, and Queenie Audrey Christina, *née* Llanelly; *b* 24 Aug 1943; *Educ* Newmarket GS; *m* 26 Aug 1978, Jayne Stewart, da of Kenneth Ian Murray (d 1987), of Storrington, W Sussex; *Career* chief accountant Northwick Park Hosp 1970-72, asst treas Newcastle Health Authy 1972-74; SE Kent Health Authy: treas 1974-85, dir of resources 1985-; nat cncllr Healthcare Financial Mgmnt Assoc; treas: SE Kent RSPB Membs Gp, E Ashford Rural Tst, Folkestone and Dist 41 Club; *Recreations* birdwatching, dogwalking; *Style*— Peter Cain, Esq; SE Kent Health Authority, Asheton, Radnor Park West, Folkestone, Kent CT19 5HL (☎ 0303 850202)

CAIRNS, Hon (Hugh) Andrew David; yr s of 5 Earl Cairns, GCVO, CB (d 1989); *b* 27 Aug 1942; *Educ* Wellington, Trinity Coll Dublin (BA); *m* 1966, (Celia) Elizabeth Mary, da of Lt-Col Francis Cecil Leonard Bell, DSO, MC, TD, of Cross Glades, Chiddingfold, Surrey; 1 s, 1 da; *Career* banker; regnl dir Barclays Bank plc; dir United Services Tstee; *Recreations* shooting, fishing, golf; *Clubs* Pratt's, Royal St George's Golf; *Style*— The Hon Andrew Cairns; Knowle Hill Farm, Ulcombe, nr Maidstone, Kent (☎ 0622 850240)

CAIRNS, Hon Mrs Andrew Cairns (Cecilia) Elizabeth Mary; da of Lt-Col Francis Cecil Leonard Bell, DSO, MC, TD, of Cross Glades, Chiddingfold, Surrey, and Mary Wynne, *née* Jacob; *b* 14 Sept 1943; *Educ* Priors Field Godalming Surrey, Trinity Coll Dublin (BA); *m* 22 Oct 1966, Hon (Hugh) Andrew David, s of Rear Adm The Earl Cairns, KCVO (d 1989); 1 s (Bertie b 28 Jan 1972), 1 da (Katherine b 27 June 1974); *Career* admitted slr 1978; sr legal asst Charity Commission 1972-78, ptnr Jaques and Lewis 1984-90 (asst slr 1979-84); specialist in charity law; memb Wills and Equity Ctee Law Soc; *Books* Charities: Law and Practice (1988); *Recreations* gardening, fishing; *Style*— The Hon Mrs Andrew Cairns; Knowle Hill Farm, Ulcombe, Maidstone, Kent ME17 1ES (☎ 0622 850240)

CAIRNS, Hon Hugh Sebastian Frederick; s and h of Viscount Garmoyle and gs of 5 Earl Cairns; *b* 26 March 1965; *Educ* Eton; *Style*— The Hon Hugh Cairns

CALCUTT, Christopher Geoffrey Sparks; s of Patrick Ivor Calcutt, of Shropshire, and Dorothy Joan, *née* Le Lacheur (d 1976); *b* 14 Dec 1950; *Educ* Cheam, Sherborne, Univ of Exeter (BSc); *m* 14 April 1984, Nicola Jane, da of Robert Campbell Thornton, of Ayrshire; 1 s (Edward Tom b 1987), 1 da (Eleanor Joan b 1985); *Career* dir Calcutt & Sons Ltd 1969-; chartered surveyor; ptnr Strutt & Parker 1985-; memb: MENSA 1968-, Exec Ctee Folkestone and Hythe Cons Assoc, Fundraising Ctee Canterbury Umbrella, PRO Kent Branch RICS; chm Elmsted and Stelling Ward of Cons Assoc; ARICS, FInstD 1987; *Clubs* Kent and Canterbury; *Style*— Christopher Calcutt, Esq; Dundas Farm, Elmsted, Ashford, Kent TN25 5JW (☎ 0233 75293); Strutt & Parker, 2 St Margarets St, Canterbury, Kent CT1 2TP (☎ 0227 451123)

CALDERWOOD, Richard Johnston; s of Alistair Lawton Calderwood, DFC, AFC, of Aulaways, Zimbabwe, and Inex Annandale, *née* Johnston; *b* 18 April 1946; *Educ* St Stephen's Coll Bulaways Rhodesia; *m* 10 Sept 1976, Susan Elizabeth, da of David Basil Jones (d 1988), of Sevenoaks, Kent; 3 s (Alistair b 1977, William b 1978, Peter b 1982); *Career* articled clerk Coopers & Lybrand London, chief accountant and head of Corp Fin Standard Merchant Bank of Rhodesia 1973-76, owner of professional CA firm 1983-; FCA (ACA 1970); *Recreations* sailing, flying; *Style*— Richard Calderwood, Esq; c/o Roper Yard, Roper Rd, Canterbury, Kent CT2 7EX (☎ 0227 766666, fax 0227 766667)

CALDIN, Prof Edward Francis Hussey; s of Edward Caldin (d 1951), and Agnes Mary, *née* Hussey (d 1948); *b* 5 Aug 1914; *Educ* Wimbledon Coll, St Paul's, Queen's Coll Oxford (MA, DPhil, DSc); *m* 17 April 1944, Mary, da of Joseph Francis Parker (d 1960); 2 s (Hugh Peter b 1946, (Peter) Giles b 1948); *Career* jr res fell Queen's Coll Oxford 1939-45, Armaments Res Dept MOS 1941-45; Univ of Leeds: lectr 1945-54, sr lectr 1954-64, reader 1964-65; Univ of Kent at Canterbury: reader 1965-66, prof of physical chemistry 1966-79, emeritus prof 1979-; author of approximately 100 papers on chemistry and philosophy of science; memb: RSC, Br Soc for the History of Sci, Br Soc for the Philosophy of Sci, Newman Assoc; *Books* The Power and Limits of Science (1949), Science and Christian Apologetic (1953), Chemical Thermodynamics (1958), The Structure of Chemistry (1961), Fast Reactions in Solution (1964), Proton-Transfer Reactions (co-ed V Gold, 1975); *Style*— Prof Edward Caldin; Chemical Laboratory, University of Kent, Canterbury, Kent CT2 7NH (☎ 0227 764000)

CALLER, Cnclr Colin William; s of Victor George Caller, of Gravesend, Kent, and Emma Alice Mabel, *née* Lown; *b* 30 July 1954; *Educ* Gordon Secdy Modern Sch; *m* 4 Oct 1975, Sylvia Dawn Lita, da of Fredrick Thomas Skeates (d 1970), of Gravesend; 2 s (Kevin Colin b 1976, Gary Anthony b 1977); *Career* BR: joined 1973, driver's asst 1974-76, train driver 1976-; local union rep ASLEF 1984- (memb 1974-), memb Lab Party 1984-, borough cncllr Gravesham 1987-; memb: Housing and Environmental Health Ctee 1987-, Leisure Servs Ctee 1987-, Fin and Admin Sub Ctee 1989-; *Recreations* visiting historical buildings, going out with family; *Style*— Cnclr Colin Caller; 4 Kenia Walk, Gravesend, Kent DA12 4HN (☎ 0474 568809)

CALLOW, (Lynda) Jasmine; da of Lionel Frederick Gresham (d 1986), of Bradford, W Yorks, and Dinah, *née* Franklyn; *b* 11 Feb 1954; *Educ* Maidstone GS; *m* 28 Aug 1983, Leo Joseph Callow, s of late Leo Callow, of Eire; 1 s (Alexander Leo b 1989); *Career* registered gen nurse St Bart's Hosp London 1972-76, registered midwife King's Coll Hosp London 1977-79, head of Midwifery Servs Maidstone Health Authy 1986-89; *Recreations* dressmaking, interior design, travel; *Style*— Mrs Jasmine Callow; Wilton Cottage, 31 The Street, Kennington, Ashford, Kent TN24 9HB (☎ 0233 622439); Maidstone Hospital, Hermitage Lane, Maidstone, Kent (☎ 0622 729000)

CALVER, Dr Gary Dennis; s of Geoffrey James Calver (d 1987), of Gt Yarmouth, and Monica Jean, *née* Sharman; *b* 13 June 1957; *Educ* Gt Yarmouth GS, Guy's Hosp Univ of London (MB BS, MRCGP); *m* 26 March 1983, Sarah Mary Teresa, da of John Twigg (d 1963); 2 s (James b 1985, George b 1987); *Career* jr doctor Utd Norwich Hosps, GP 1987-; memb Geriatric Planning Team (SE Kent), winner Benjamin Gooch Prize 1986; DObstRCOG, Dip Geriatric Med RCP; *Recreations* squash, golf; *Style*— Dr Gary Calver; 180 Sandgate Rd, Folkestone, Kent CT20 2HN (☎ 0303 221133)

CALVOCORESSI, Maj Ion Melville; MBE (1945), MC (1942); s of Matthew John Calvocoressi, and Agnes Hermione, da of late Judge Robert Melville, of Sussex and Salop; *b* 12 April 1919; *Educ* Eton, Magdalen Coll Oxford (MA); *m* 1947, Katherine, da of Capt Edward Coverley Kennedy, RN (ka 1939, ggs of Hon Robert Kennedy, bro of 1 Marquess of Ailsa and 3 s of 11 Earl of Cassillis), and Rosalind, da of Sir Ludovic Grant, 11 Bt; 3 s, 1 da; *Career* Scots Gds 1939-46: ME, Sicily, Italy, SE Asia 1941-45, ADC, GOC 8 Army 1944, Mil Asst; CGS ALFSEA 1945; memb London Stock Exchange 1949; High Sheriff Kent 1978-79; *Recreations* cricket, gardening; *Clubs* Cavalry and Guards, City of London, Pratt's, MCC, Kent CCC; *Style*— Maj Ion Calvocoressi, MBE, MC; Court Lodge, Westerham, Kent (☎ 0959 63358)

CAMBRIDGE, Alan John; s of Thomas David Cambridge (d 1969), and Winifred Elizabeth, *née* Jarret (d 1970); *b* 1 July 1925; *Educ* Beckenham GS; *m* 1947, Thelma, da of Francis Elliot (d 1960); 3 s, 1 da; *Career* RAF 1943-47, Flt Sgt rear gunner, 150 Sqdn Bomber Cmd; War Pensions Office and MPNI 1948-55; Cwlth Rels Office: joined 1955, Madras 1956-58, Kuala Lumpur 1959-62, Rhodesia and Nyasaland 1962-65; HM Dip Serv 1965, 1 sec UN Dept FCO 1966-69, del UN Gen Assembly 1968, 1 sec Prague 1969, 1 sec (consular aid) Suva 1970-72, consul Milan 1972-74, asst head Info Dept FCO 1974-78, 1 sec (info) Ankara 1978-81, asst head then head Migration and Visa Dept FCO 1981-85, ret 1985; assessor FCO 1985-; *Recreations* photography, tennis, swimming; *Clubs* Civil Service; *Style*— Alan Cambridge,

Esq; 9 The Ferns, Carlton Rd, Tunbridge Wells, Kent TN1 2JT (☎ 0892 31223): Foreign and Commonwealth Office, King Charles St, London SW1

CAMERON, Prof (James) Malcolm; s of James Cameron, and Doris Winifred Mary, *née* Robertson; *b* 29 April 1930; *Educ* The HS of Glasgow, Univ of Glasgow; *m* 23 July 1956, Primrose, *née* McKerrell; 1 da (Maureen b 1963); *Career* hon conslt London Hosp 1967-, dir Dept of Forensic Med London Hosp Med Coll 1970-; hon conslt in forensic med to: Army at Home 1971-, RN 1972-, RAF 1990-; prof of forensic med Univ of London at The London Hosp Med Coll 1973-, Ver Heyden de Lancey reader in forensic med Cncl of Legal Educn Gray's Inn 1978-; sec gen Br Acad of Forensic Scis 1970-85 (pres 1978), pres Br Assoc in Forensic Med 1985-87; MO Amateur Swimming Fedn of GB 1981-, pres Beckenham Swimming Club 1983-84 (hon MO 1977-), hon med advsr Amateur Swimming Assoc 1985-, vice pres Assoc of Prevention of Addiction 1985-, memb Med Commission of Fedn Int de Natation Amateur 1987-, chm and hon sec Med Ctee Ligue Européene de Natation 1990-, pres Kent Co Amateur Swimming Assoc 1989 (hon med advsr 1981-); memb: Med Advsy Commission of BOA, Drug Abuse Advsy Gp of Sports Cncl, Faculty of Int Soc for Prevention of Introgenic Complications, NW Kent Medico-Chirurgical Soc; *Books* Practical Forensic Medicine (2 edn with Camps, 1971), Forensic Dentistry (with Sims, 1973), Atlas of the Battered Child (with Rae, 1975); *Clubs* Savage, Royal Naval Med, Scribes; *Style*— Prof Malcolm Cameron; The London Hospital Medical College, Turner St, London E1 2AD (☎ 071 377 7621/2)

CAMERON, Sheila Morag Clark; QC (1983); da of Sir James Clark Cameron, CBE, TD, of 62 Haven Green Court, Ealing, London, and Lady Irene Maud, *née* Ferguson (d 1986); *b* 22 March 1934; *Educ* Commonwealth Lodge Sch Purley Surrey, St Hugh's Coll Oxford (MA); *m* 3 Dec 1960, Gerard Charles Ryan; 2 s (Andrew b 21 Aug 1965, Nicholas b 6 Dec 1967); *Career* called to the Bar Middle Temple 1957; Harmsworth law scholar 1958, pt/t lectr law Univ of Southampton 1960-64, pt/t tutor Cncl of Legal Educn, rec Crown Court, bencher Middle Temple 1988; memb: Bar Cncl 1967-70, Cncl on Tbnls 1986-90; boundary Cmmn for England 1989-; chllr Diocese of Chelmsford 1969; memb: Cncl Wycombe Abbey Sch 1972-76, Legal Advsy Cmmn Gen Synod C of E 1975; vicar Gen Province of Canterbury 1983; *Style*— Miss Sheila Cameron, QC; 2 Harcourt Buildings, Temple, London EC4Y 9DB (☎ 071 353 8415, fax 071 353 7622)

CAMPBELL, Agnes, Lady; Agnes Louise; da of late William Henry Gerhardi; *m* 1, Victor Vsevolod Watson, MBE; m 2, 1941, as his 3 wife Sir Ian Vincent Hamilton Campbell, 7 Bt, CB (d 1978); 1 s; *Style*— Agnes, Lady Campbell; Barcaldine Castle, Ledaig, Argyllshire; White Rose, Hawkhurst, Kent

CAMPBELL, Hon Alastair Colin Leckie; s (by 1 m) and h of 3 Baron Colgrain; *b* 16 Sept 1951; *Educ* Eton, Trinity Coll Cambridge; *m* 1979, Annabel Rose, da of Hon Robin Hugh Warrender (s of 1 Baron Bruntisfield, MC); 2 s (Thomas Colin Donald b 9 Feb 1984, Nicholas Robin b 12 Dec 1986); *Style*— The Hon Alastair Campbell; The Stables, Everlands, Sevenoaks, Kent

CAMPBELL, Hon Neil Donald; DSC (1945); yst s of 2 Baron Colgrain (d 1973); *b* 24 Aug 1922; *Educ* RNC Dartmouth; *m* 1951, Angela Louise Vereker, da of Rt Hon Sir Ronald Hibbert Cross, 1 Bt, KCMG, KCVO; 2 s (and 1 s decd), 1 da; *Career* late Lt RN, ret 1947; dir: Geo & R Dewhurst 1947-56, James Capel 1956-77; *Style*— The Hon Neil Campbell; Yorks Hill Farm, Ide Hill, Sevenoaks, Kent

CAMPBELL, Hon Robert (Robin) Dudley; 2 s of late 2 Baron Colgrain (d 1973); *b* 6 July 1921; *Educ* Eton, Trinity Coll Cambridge; *m* 1, 1954 (m dis 1978), Cecilia Barbara, da of late Cdr Alexander Leslie, RN; 2 da; m 2, 1983, Mrs Muriel Anne Kendal, da of George Tuson, RN (ka 1941), of Loughborough, Leics; *Career* late Scots Gds; dep chm and dir C E Coates & Co 1981-, md Baltic Investments (London) Ltd; *Style*— The Hon Robin Campbell; Sharp's Place, Boughbeech, Edenbridge, Kent

CAMPOLINI, John Christopher; JP; s of Guerino Campolini (d 1987), of London, and Evelyn, *née* Valente (d 1978); *b* 2 Aug 1946; *Educ* St Joseph's Coll Beulah Hill London; *m* 15 Sept 1968, Anita Rita, da of Ciro Muscio, of London; 1 s (Mark John b 22 March 1971), 1 da (Nicola Maria b 1 March 1974); *Career* md: Coldstream (Engineering) Ltd, James Fortune Associates Ltd; memb: Knights of St Columba, Catenian Assoc; Freeman City of London; *Recreations* amateur radio, cultivation of cacti, music; *Style*— John Campolini, Esq, JP; 12 Fellbrigg Rd, London SE22 9HH (☎ 081 693 6200, fax 081 693 6137)

CANDY, Thomas Frank; s of Frank Patrick Candy, and Jacqueline Honoreen, *née* Vroome; *b* 18 Dec 1955; *Educ* Eastbourne Coll, Univ of Surrey; *Career* banker; dir Eurobond Dept Hambros Bank Ltd; *Recreations* tennis, squash, windsurfing, skiing; *Clubs* Queen's; *Style*— Thomas Candy, Esq; Fairlawn, Parkfield, Sevenoaks, Kent; Hambros Bank Ltd, 41 Tower Hill, London (☎ 071 480 5000)

CANHAM, (Bryan Frederick) Peter; MC (1943); s of Frederick William Canham (d 1961), and Emma Louisa, *née* Martin (d 1971); *b* 11 April 1920; *Educ* Trinity Co Sch; *m* 1944, Rita Gwendoline, *née* Huggett, 1 s (Richard); *Career* Capt 1 RTR, N Africa, Italy, NW Europe 1939-46; controller S Europe and N Africa Shell Int Petroleum 1956-60; fin dir: Shell Co Philippines and assoc cos 1960-63, Shell Co Malaysia and assoc cos 1963-68, div head loans directorate dir gen XVIII EEC 1973-76 (dir investmt and loans 1976-80); chm Eurofi (UK) Ltd 1980-; FCIS (ACIS); *Style*— Peter Canham, Esq, MC; The Old Laundry, Penshurst, Kent (☎ 0892 870 239); The Cottage, Stedhamhall, nr Midhurst, W Sussex (☎ 073081 2947); Eurofi plc, Guildgate House, Newbury Berks (☎ 0635 31900)

CANNEY, Ronald Lindsay; s of late James Robertson Campbell Canney, of Cambridge, and Violet, *née* Newton (d 1976); *b* 17 Jan 1916; *Educ* Oundle, Univ of Cambridge (MA, MB MChir), Wurzburg Germany, LRCP; *m* 26 June 1943, Kathleen Joan (Judy), da of Alfred Cotter (d 1970), of Bangor, NI; 1 s (Peter Julian Campbell b 1944), 1 da (Elizabeth Lindsay b 1947); *Career* Surgn Lt RNVR; med appts: Guy's Royal Cancer Hosp, Gt Ormond St Hosp; conslt surgn: Kent and Canterbury Hosp, Isle of Thanet Hosp 1947; ret 1981; memb: Nat Tst, Kent Naturalist Tst, Cncl Preservation Rural Eng, Nat Art Collection Fund, Canterbury Soc, Monday Club, Freedom Assoc, Kent CCC, Band of Brothers; memb BMA, Fell Assoc of Surgns GB and Ireland, FRCS, FRSM, FRICS; *Recreations* fly-fishing, shooting, gardening, golf; *Clubs* Royal St George's Golf (Sandwich); *Style*— Ronald Canney, Esq; The Red House, Petham, nr Canterbury CT4 5QN (☎ 022 770242)

CANTERBURY, Archdeacon of; Archdeacon of; *see*: Till, Ven Michael Stanley

CANTERBURY, 102 Archbishop of; Most Rev and Rt Hon Robert Alexander Kennedy Runcie; MC (1945), PC (1980); Primate of all England and Metropolitan; patron of 179 livings, Archdeaconries of Canterbury and Maidstone (each of which is endowed with a canonry), and 6 Cathedral Preacherships; province (contains 29 sees) founded by St Augustine (under Ethelbert King of Kent) 597; s of Robert Dalziel Runcie (d 1945), of Crosby, Merseyside, and Ann Edna, *née* Benson (d 1949); *b* 2 Oct 1921; *Educ* Merchant Taylors', BNC Oxford (MA), Westcott House Cambridge (Dip Theol); *m* 5 Sept 1957, (Angela) Rosalind, da of J W Cecil Turner, MC (d 1968), of Cambridge; 1 s (James b 1959), 1 da (Rebecca b 1961); *Career* served WWII Scots Gds, tank offr Normandy, Baltic, PA to Br Rep Italy/ Yugoslavia Boundary Cmmn 1945-46; ordained 1949, curate All Saints Gosforth 1950-52, chaplain and vice princ Westcott House Cambridge 1953-56, dean Trinity Hall Cambridge 1956-60, princ Cuddesdon Theol Coll 1960-70, bishop St Albans 1970-80; Anglican chm Anglican-Orthodox Joint Doctrinal Cmmn 1973-; pres: Church Army, C of E Children's Soc, Royal Sch of Church Music, Churches Cncl for Health and Healing, BCC, Help the Hospices, Corpn of the Sons of the Clergy; hon memb Canterbury Rotary Club 1981-; Freeman City of: London, Canterbury, St Albans; Freeman: Worshipful of Merchant Taylors, Worshipful Co of Grocers, Worshipful Co of Butchers; Hon DD: Univ of Oxford 1980, Univ Cambridge 1981, Univ of the South Sewanee 1981, St Andrew's Univ 1989, New Raday Coll Budapest 1987, Univ of South Carolina 1987, Yale Univ 1989; Hon DLitt: Univ of Keele 1981, Rikkyo Univ Tokyo 1987; Hon DCL Univ of Kent 1982, Hon LittD Univ of Liverpool 1983; Cross of the Order of the Holy Sepulchre 1986, Order of St Vladimin Class II 1975; *Books* Cathedral and City: St Albans Ancient and Modern (ed, 1978), Windows onto God (1983), Seasons of the Spirit (1983), One Light for One World (1988), Theology, University and the Modern World (1988), Authority in Crisis? (1988), The Unity We Seek (1989); *Recreations* opera, reading history and novels, owning Berkshire pigs; *Clubs* Athenaeum, Cavalry and Guards; *Style*— The Most Rev and Rt Hon the Lord Archbishop of Canterbury,MC; Lambeth Palace, London SE1 7JU (☎ 071 928 8282, fax 071 261 9836); The Old Palace, Canterbury, Kent

CANTOR, Dr Timothy Jefferson; s of Dr Jack Cantor, of Faversham, Kent and Kathleen Maud, *née* Wallach; *b* 9 Jan 1951; *Educ* King's Sch Canterbury, Middlesex Hosp Med Sch Univ of London (MB BS, MRCOG, MRCGP); *Career* house surgn Middlesex Hosp London 1974-75, house physician Leicester Royal Infirmary 1975; sr house offr in obstetrics and gynaecology: Bristol 1975-77, Nottingham 1977-78; res sr house offr in urology Nottingham City Hosp 1978-79, GP trainee Nottingham 1979-81, ptnr Thornhills Med Gp Larkfield 1981-; memb: BMA, Assoc For Gen Practice Maternity Care; *Recreations* classical music, squash, windsurfing, skiing; *Clubs* Harvey's Squash (Maidstone); *Style*— Dr Timothy Cantor; 24 Bridgewater Place, Leybourne, West Halling, Kent ME19 5QS (☎ 0732 842790); Thornhills Medical Group, 732 London Rd, Larkfield, Maidstone, Kent ME20 6BG (☎ 0732 843900)

CAPON, Cncllr Christopher John; s of Charles John Capon (d 1988), of Hythe, and Kathleen, *née* Reilly (d 1971); *b* 27 May 1937; *Educ* Blockhill Park Secdy Sch; *m* 12 Oct 1963 (m dis 1983), Gillian, *née* Downs; 1 da (Nicola b 9 Nov 1964); *Career* Nat Serv RAMC 1955-57, left as Corpl; mangr Co-op 1957-64 (joined 1952), postman 1964-87; footballer: Hythe Town, Hythe Albion, Hythe Stragglers; Churchill Fellowship (to study USA postal system) 1971, speaker Cinque Ports 1972-73, Mayor of Hythe 1972-74 (cncllr 1967-), panel memb Industl Tribunals 1973-76, co cncllr 1977-, vice chm Shepway DC 1990- (memb 1974); *Style*— Cncllr Christopher Capon; Cambridge Villa, 16

Seabrook Rd, Hythe, Kent CT21 5NA (☎ 0303 268095)

CARDINAL, Prof Roger; s of Thomas Cardinal, of Folkestone, and Ada Eliza, *née* Melbourne (d 1989); *b* 27 Feb 1940; *Educ* St Dunstan's Coll Catford, Univ of Cambridge (BA, MA, PhD); *m* 19 July 1965, Agnes, da of Josef Meyer (d 1979); 2 s (Daniel b 1966, Felix b 1974); *Career* asst prof Univ of Manitoba Canada 1965-67, lectr Univ of Warwick 1967-68; Univ of Kent at Canterbury: lectr in French 1968-76, sr lectr in French 1976-81, reader in comparative literary studies 1981-87, prof of literary & visual studies 1987-; visiting assoc prof Univ of Toronto Canada 1976-77; *Books* Outsider Art (1972), German Romantics (1975), Figures of Reality (1981), Expressionism (1984), The Landscape Vision of Paul Nash (1989); *Recreations* playing piano, windowgazing, gliding; *Style*— Prof Roger Cardinal; Keynes College, University of Kent at Canterbury, Canterbury, Kent CT2 7NP (☎ 0227 764000, fax 0227 459025)

CARPENTER, Robert David Evans; s of Ernest Henry Carpenter (d 1973), of Reading, and Muriel Carpenter; *b* 22 Jan 1940; *Educ* Mill Hill; *m* 16 Sept 1967, Gloria, *née* Faith Davies, da of Gordon Stuart Clarke (d 1980); 1 s (James Nicholas b 9 June 1970), 1 da (Caroline Claire b 18 Dec 1972); *Career* ptnr Montagu Loebl Stanley & Co 1979-85 (joined 1968), dir investmt res Kitcat & Aitken 1985-90, dir Carr Kitcat & Aitken 1990-; AIB 1962; *Recreations* squash; *Style*— Robert Carpenter, Esq; 86 Manor Way, Beckenham, Kent BR3 3LR (☎ 081 650 0358); Carr Kitcat & Aitken, 1 London Bridge, London SE1 9TJ (☎ 071 378 7050, fax 071 403 0755, telex 8956121)

CARR, (Charles) Richard; TD; s of Charles Walter Henry Carr (d 1977), of Smarden, Kent, and Martha Corinna, *née* Copeland (d 1984); *b* 8 Oct 1927; *Educ* Sherborne; *m* 12 Sept 1957, Jane Frances, da of Gp Capt Freke William Wiseman-Clarke, CBE (d 1977), of Belgrave Mews South, London; 1 s (Edward b 1964), 2 da (Sally b 1958, Lucinda b 1961); *Career* Maj 21 SAS (Artist Rifles) TA 1948-62; dir Joseph Sandell & Co Ltd 1957 (joined 1952), md Sandell Smythe & Drayson Ltd 1968 (joined 1964), dep chm Sandell Perkins plc 1983-88 (chm 1970-83), dir Travis Perkins plc 1988-89, ret 1989; non exec dir Kent Opera 1978-89; memb: Tenterden Kent CC 1981-, Kent TA & VRA 1981-; chm: Kent Police Authy 1981-, Timber R & D Assoc 1982-84, Ashford Constituency Cons Assoc 1983-86, fin and group Ctee SE Arts Assoc 1983-; pres Timber Trade Fedn 1987-89; Sr Warden Worshipful Co of Builders' Merchants (Master Elect), Freeman City of London; *Clubs* Naval and Military, Band of Brothers; *Style*— Richard Carr, Esq, TD; The Cloth Hall, Biddenden, Ashford, Kent TN27 8AG (☎ 0580 291334)

CARSON, Dr Sally Jane; da of Roy Ernest Carson, of 97 Baston Rd, Hayes, and Patricia Alice Charlotte Carson; *b* 19 April 1964; *Educ* Langley Park Sch for Girls Beckenham, Kings Coll Sch of Med and Dentistry Univ of London (MB BS); *Career* house physician Maidstone Hosp 1987-88, house surgn Farnborough 1988-89; sr house offr: Orpington Hosp 1988-89, on gp vocational trg scheme William Harvey Hosp Ashford 1989-; *Recreations* badminton, food and wine, gardening; *Style*— Dr Sally Carson; The Granary, Hothfield Manor, Church Lane, Hothfield, Ashford, Kent TN26 1EL (☎ 0233 626901); William Harvey Hospital, Kennington Rd, Willesborough, Ashford, Kent TN24 0LZ (☎ 0233 633331)

CARTER-CLOUT, Derrick Gilbert; s of Leslie Douglas Carter-Clout (d 1969), of 20 Saffrons Court, Compton Place Rd, Eastbourne, Sussex, and Hilda Elizabeth, *née* Kendall; *b* 13 Aug 1920; *Educ* Cranleigh, Sch of Bldg Brixton; *m* 1, 8 April 1945 (m dis), Joyce Elizabeth (d 1975), da of Percy Welford Davidson (d 1961), of Cloverlands, Birthwaite Rd, Windermere; 1 s (Anthony b 1948), 1 da (Catherine b 1946); m 2, 1964, Joan Dane, da of George Robert Gummery (d 1929); *Career* HAC 1938, RE OCTU 1939, cmmnd 2 Lt RE 1940, India Royal Bombay Sappers and Miners 1940, Maj RBS Malaya 9 India Div 1941, India Co Cmd 1941, invalided out of serv 1944; jt pres G & S Allgood Ltd (Architectural Ironmongers) 1980- (propentor 1947, md 1948-80); pres Execs Assoc of GB 1979-84 (dir 1967-69, chm 1969-70), chm Local Cons Branch Ashford Kent 1984, ctee memb E Ashford Rural Tst; cncl memb City Livery Club 1988; Freeman Worshipful Co of Ironmongers 1979, memb Guild of Freeman City of London 1984 (Freeman 1960); FFB; *Recreations* golf; *Clubs* Ashford Golf, City Livery, Rugger, Wellington, IOD, Henley Royal Regatta; *Style*— Derrick Carter-Clout, Esq; The Grange, Mersham, nr Ashford, Kent (☎ 023 3720314); Flat 30, Silsoe House, 50 Park Village East, London NW1 (☎ 071 388 0645); G & S Allgood Ltd, Carterville House, Euston Rd, London NW1 (☎ 071 387 9951, fax 071 380 1232, telex 261817)

CARTWRIGHT, Christopher Egerton; s of Herbert Edward Cartwright (d 1978), and Ruth, *née* Collins; *b* 19 Oct 1944; *Educ* Kings Sch Worcester, Univ of Bristol; *m* 30 Dec 1967, Susan Lois, da of Anthony John Mindham, of Brighton, Sussex; 1 s (James Egerton b 1971), 1 da (Sarah Elizabeth b 1974); *Career* stockbroker; formerly ptnr and dir Wood MacKenzie & Co, Paribas Ltd; memb Stock Exchange, ACA 1969; *Recreations* gardening, microcomputing, angling, guitar; *Clubs* Chiselhurst Golf; *Style*— Christopher Cartwright, Esq; Hostye Farm, Cudham Lane North, Cudham, Kent TN14 7QT (☎ 0959 73163, car tel 0831 201 663); Paribas Ltd, 33 Wigmore St, London W1H 0BN (☎ 071 355 2000)

CARVER, (Edmond) Robin; MBE (1989); s of Felix Edmond Carver, OBE (d 1973), of Farnham, Surrey, and Ruth Margaret, *née* Fishwick; *b* 23 Jan 1930; *Educ* St Andrews Coll SA, Bradfield Coll; *m* 17 May 1958, June Rosemary, da of Reginald Maw (d 1936); 1 s (Jeremy Reginald b 14 Aug 1962), 1 da (Amanda Helen b 25 Nov 1964); *Career* Ottoman Bank: Jordan, Iraq, Israel, Egypt, Cyprus; personnel mangr Shell International Petroleum Co Ltd 1956-70, pub affrs mangr Shell Research Ltd 1970-86; cncllr Canterbury City Cncl, Mayor Canterbury 1979, pres Disabled Drivers' Assoc Kent Branch; chm: Canterbury Branch Men of Kent and Kentish Men, Kent Ctee for Employment of Disabled People; memb Chamber of Trade Cncl Canterbury; *Recreations* watching cricket, gardening, travel; *Clubs* Kent CC, Purchasers; *Style*— Robin Carver, Esq, MBE; Eastfields, High St, Fordwich, Canterbury CT2 0BW (☎ 0227 710933)

CASSIDY, Sean Henry Dermot; s of Capt Dr Patrick Francis Cassidy, RAMC (d 1987), and Mary Archman, *née* McDermott; *b* 7 Oct 1953; *Educ* Whitefriars Sch Cheltenham, Stockwell Coll of Educn Bromley Kent (Cert Ed); *Career* master gen subjects and house tutor Dulwich Coll Prep Sch Cranbrook Kent 1976-80; headmaster: Merton Court Prep Sch Sidcup Kent 1980-83, Harenc Prep Sch Foots Cray Kent 1983-; vice pres Chislehurst and Sidcup Divs St John Ambulance 1984-, chm Friends of St John Ambulance 1983-85, cncllr London Borough of Bexley 1985-88, tstee Bexley Archaeological Gp; memb: Mgmnt Ctee Chislehurst and Sidcup Housing Assoc 1990-, Old Bexley and Sidcup Cons Assoc, Ind Schs Assoc Inc, Coll of Preceptors; fund raiser: Br Heart Fndn, Childrens Liver Disease Fndn; *Recreations* organising and leading adventure holidays for young people, fishing, music, photography; *Clubs* Old Bexley and Sidcup Cons, Sidcup and Foots Cray Utd Servs; *Style*— Sean Cassidy, Esq; Church House, 167 Rectory Lane, Foots Cray, Sidcup, Kent DA14 5BU (☎ 081 309 0619)

CASSWELL, Hon Mrs (Helen Jennifer Frances); *née* Annesley; yst da of 14 Viscount Valentia, MC; *b* 13 Oct 1935; *m* 1957, Simon FitzRoy Casswell, yst s of His Hon Joshua David Casswell, QC (d 1963); 1 s, 2 da; *Style*— The Hon Mrs Casswell; The Limes Farm, Smarden, nr Ashford, Kent

CATTELL, George Harold Bernard; s of Harold William Kingston Cattell (d 1955); *b* 23 March 1920; *Educ* Royal GS Colchester, Staff Coll Camberley, Royal Mil Coll of Sci; *m* 1951, Agnes Jean, da of Brig John Hardy (d 1969); 3 s (Jonathan, Jeremy, Simon), 1 da (Sarah); *Career* served with RA Maj; asst dir London Engrg Employers Fedn 1958-60, with Rootes Group and Chrysler Organisation 1960-68 (former dir of manufacturing UK Chrysler), dir of Manpower and Productivity Servs Dept of Employment and Productivity 1968-70, DG NFU 1970-78, chief exec (former gp md) FMC Group plc (meat wholesalers) 1978-, chief exec NFU Holdings Ltd 1978-84; FBIM, FRSA; *Recreations* tennis, fishing; *Clubs* IOD; *Style*— George Cattell, Esq; Little Cheveney, Yalding, Kent (☎ 365)

CATTRALL, Peter Jeremy; s of Ralph W Cattrall, of Westwood, Old Green Road, Cliftonville, Margate, Kent, and Sally, *née* Lunn; *b* 8 Jan 1947; *Educ* Kings Sch Canterbury, Trinity Coll Oxford (MA); *m* 26 April 1975, Amanda Jane Maria, da of Maj Gen W N J Withall, CB, of Wiltshire; 1 s (Charles David b 1 March 1980), 1 da (Sarah Louise b 21 Sept 1982); *Career* sch master Holmewood House Kent; admitted slr 1974; asst slr Knocker and Foskett Kent 1974-77, slr to Esso UK plc (formerly Esso Petroleum Co Ltd) 1977-88; memb: Kent Co Squash Side, Beckenham CC, IBA, Oxford Union; memb Law Soc; *Recreations* cricket, squash, golf, tennis, swimming, cycling, reading, music, current affairs; *Clubs* Utd Oxford and Cambridge Univ, MCC, Rye Golf, Free Foresters, I Zingari, Arabs, Jesters, Band of Brothers, Harlequins, Vincents; *Style*— Peter Cattrall, Esq; 21 Whitmore Road, Beckenham, Kent (☎ 071 658 7265, 071 245 2150)

CAUKILL, David; s of Philip Caukill, of 90 Exford Rd, Lee, London, and Mary Mattingly, *née* Hore; *b* 27 April 1954; *Educ* Brockley County GS, Univ of Bath (BSc); *m* 3 Sept 1983 (m dis 1989), Nicola Jane, da of Christopher Hugh Folland; *Career* admitted ptnr Arthur Andersen & Co 1988 (audit sr 1978-81, mangr 1981-88); ACA 1979; *Recreations* sailing, golf, music; *Clubs* Langley Park Golf, Ikoyi 1938; *Style*— David Caukill, Esq; 18 Grange Drive, Chislehurst, Kent BR7 5ES (☎ 081 467 1524); Arthur Andersen & Co, 1 Surrey St, London WC2 R2PS

CAVALIERO, Roderick; s of Eric Cavaliero (d 1961), and Valerie de Vesci, *née* Logan (d 1975); *b* 21 March 1928; *Educ* Tonbridge, Hertford Coll Oxford (BA); *m* 31 Aug 1957, Mary, da of John McDonnell (d 1981); 1 s (Rohan b 1963), 4 da (Louisa b 1958, Annamaria b 1960, Rosalind b 1967, Juliana b 1969); *Career* Br Cncl offr 1958-88: rep Brazil 1967-70, controller personnel and staff recruitment 1970-75, rep Italy 1975-77, asst DG 1977-82, dep DG 1982-88; chm Educn and Trg Export Ctee 1979-88, pres Br Educnl Equipment Assoc 1988-; tstee: Charles Wallace India Tst 1982-, St George's Eng Sch Rome 1982-, Br Sch at Rome, Centre for Br Teachers, Keats-Shelley Meml Assoc, Christian Orgns Res and Trg; *Books* Olympia and the Angel (1958), The Last of the Crusaders (1960); *Recreations* gardening, reading, writing; *Style*— Roderick Cavaliero, Esq; 10 Lansdowne Rd, Tunbridge Wells, Kent TN1 2NJ (☎ 0892 33452)

CAVELL, Martin; s of Alfred William Cavell (d 1950), of 377 Singlewell Rd, Gravesend, and Ethel Lily Mary, *née* Martin (d 1963); *b* 24 April 1928; *Educ* Gravesend GS for Boys, Rochester Sch of Art; *m* 2 April 1956, Hazel Doreen, da of Charles George William Farmer (d 1959), of 70 Woodford Ave, Gravesend; 1 s (Martin David b 1960), 1 da (Susan (Mrs Hill) b 1957); *Career* started own architectural practice 1958; cmmns incl: Mid Kent Golf Clubhouse Gravesend 1964, Shorne Village Hall 1976, Alms Houses Gravesend; memb: Old Gravesendians RFC, Gravesend Rowing Club; ARIBA; *Recreations* rugby, rowing, skiing; *Style—* Martin Cavell, Esq; The Brindles, Pear Tree Lane, Shorne, Gravesend, Kent DA12 3JS (☎ 047 482 2951); 23 Wrotham Rd, Gravesend, Kent DA11 OPA (☎ 0474 352781, fax 0474 535297)

CAVENDISH-TRIBE, Hon Mrs (Winifred); *née* Cavendish; 3 and yst da of 6 Baron Waterpark (d 1948), and his 2 w, May (d 1969), da of William Ernest Burbidge; *b* 1 June 1909; *Educ* St Monica's Priory Dorset; *m* 13 Dec 1929, Capt Albert Frank Tribe, who later assumed additional surname of Cavendish (d 1962), 4 s of late Lt Cdr Arthur Ernest Tribe, RNR; 1 s; *Style—* The Hon Mrs Cavendish-Tribe; Saxons Beech Hill, Bridge, nr Canterbury, Kent

CHADWICK, Dr Derek James; s of Dennis Edmund Chadwick (d 1955), of Barnsley, and Ida, *née* Kay (d 1979); *b* 9 Feb 1948; *Educ* St Joseph's Coll Blackpool, Keble Coll Oxford (BA, BSc, MA, D Phil); *m* 20 Dec 1980, Susan, da of Hugh Alistair Reid, OBE (d 1983), of Liverpool; 2s (Andrew b 1984, Mark b 1986); *Career* ICI fell Univ of Cambridge 1972-73, prize fell Magdalen Coll Oxford 1973-77, Royal Soc Euro Exchange fell ETH Zurich 1975-77, Univ of Liverpool 1977-88 (lectr, sr lectr, reader); dir Ciba Foundation London 1988-; author of many papers in chemistry jls; *Books* contrib to: Aromatic and Heteroaromatic Chemistry (1979), Comprehensive Heterocyclic Chemistry (1984), The Research and Academic Users' Guide to the IBM PC (1988); *Recreations* music, skiing, gardening; *Style—* Dr Derek Chadwick; 4 Bromley Ave, Bromley, Kent BR1 4BQ (☎ 081 460 3332); The Ciba Foundation, 41 Portland Place, London W1N 4BN (☎ 071 636 9456, fax 071 436 2840)

CHADWICK, Peter; s of Kenneth Fred Chadwick (d 1985), and Grace Jean, *née* Holden; *b* 19 Aug 1946; *Educ* St Pauls, Churchill Coll Cambridge (BA, MA); *m* 27 Oct 1971, Diana Kathryn Lillian, da of Frank Richard Stanford Kellett, of Northampton; 1 da (Lindsey Nichola b 1974); *Career* CA; princ Dept of Indust 1977-79, ptnr Peat Marwick Mitchell & Co 1982, currently managing ptnr Kent practice Peat Marwick McLintock; FCA 1979 (ACA 1970); *Style—* Peter Chadwick, Esq; The Old Rectory, Little Chart, Ashford, Kent TN27 0QH; Peat Marwick McLintock, Barham Court, Teston, Maidstone, Kent ME18 5BZ (☎ 0622 814814, fax 0622 814888)

CHAKRAVARTY, Saroj Kanti; s of Prakash Chandra Chakravarty (d 1981), of Uttarpara, W Bengal, India, and Prafulla Prova, *née* Roy (d 1986); *b* 1 Feb 1934; *Educ* Bengal Acad Rangoon Burma, Scottish Church Coll Calcutta India, Univ of Calcutta (BA); *m* 26 Jan 1973, Mandira, da of Narendra Kumar Kusary (d 1969), of Darjeeling, India; 1 s (Devkumar b 11 April 1976); *Career* gp mgmnt accountant Ralph Hilton Tport Servs Ltd London 1969-74, gp bd dir and co sec James McNaughton Paper Gp Ltd Erith Kent 1974-; assoc memb Inst of Chartered Secs and Admins; *Recreations* golf, writing occasional articles for newspapers in India; *Clubs* Cherry Lodge Golf, (Biggin Hill); *Style—* Saroj Chakravarty, Esq; Mrinal, 55 The Avenue, Beckenham, Kent BR3 2EE; James McNaughton Paper Group Ltd, Jaymac House, Church Manor Way, Erith, Kent (☎ 081 7111, fax 081 311 4162, telex 8812613)

CHAMBERLIN, Richard Alexander; s of John Alexander Chamberlin, MC, of Lenham, Kent, and Kathleen Mary, *née* Fraser (d 1990); *b* 1 July 1951; *Educ* The Kings Sch Canterbury, Jesus Coll Cambridge (BA); *m* 1977, Mary-Angela, da of Norman William Stoakes Franks, of Folkestone, Kent; 2 da (Zoe b 1977, Naomi b 1979); *Career* articled Clerk Wedlake Bell 1973-75; admitted slr 1975; ptnr Freshfields 1981 (joined 1976); memb Worshipful Co of Solicitors; memb Law Soc; *Recreations* archaeology, sailing; *Clubs* Leander, Kent Archaeological Soc, Cambridge Soc (Kent Branch); *Style—* Richard Chamberlin, Esq; Whitefriars, 65 Fleet St, London EC4Y 1HT (☎ 071 936 4000)

CHANDLER, Godfrey John; *b* 4 July 1925; *Educ* Clarks Coll London; *m* 1948, Audrey Haydee; 3 s (Timothy b 1952, Graham b 1953, Henry b 1960), 1 da (Susan b 1949); *Career* ptnr Cazenove & Co 1957-85; dir: Globe Investment Trust plc 1980-90, Strata Investment Trust plc 1985-90, Stratton Investment Trust plc 1986-90, Lloyds Development Capital Ltd 1986-90, Halifax Building Soc (London Bd) 1981-87; dep chm W H Smith Group 1982-88; hon fell Darwin Coll Cambridge, visiting fell Henley Coll of Mgmnt; *Recreations* gardening, chess; *Clubs* City of London; *Style—* Godfrey Chandler, Esq; Stormont Court, Godden Green, Sevenoaks, Kent TN15 OJS (☎ 0732 61505)

CHANDLER, James John; s of George John Chandler (d 1974), of Bromley, Kent, and Lilian May, *née* Martin; *b* 22 March 1947; *Educ* Haberdashers' Aske's, Brixton Sch of Bldg (pt/t); *m* 27 May 1972 (m dis 1989), Iris Fay, da of Ronald Debenham, of London; 2 s (Paul James, Jonathan Mark); *Career* quantity surveyor Matthew Hall Engineering Ltd 1966-69 (trainee 1963-66); R Durtnell & Sons Ltd Brasted Kent: quantity surveyor 1969-71, chief quantity surveyor 1971-74, dep contracts dir 1974-76, contracts dir 1976-85, md 1985-; dir: Durtnell Ltd, RG Champion Ltd, R Durtnell & Sons (Canada) Ltd; md Peter C Chackett Ltd; former: chm S Lewisham Young Cons, chm Cage Green Ward Tonbridge and Malling Cons Assoc, vice chm S Lewisham Cons Assoc (appts at ward level), govr Cage Green Co Primary Sch; govr Slade Co Primary Sch Tonbridge; cncllr Tonbridge and Malling Borough Cncl 1976-84 (chm Recreation and Amenities Ctee 1977-80, ldr of Cncl and chm Policy and Resources Ctee 1980-84); memb of various ctees Co and Dist Parish Liaison Ctees; AIQS (prizewinner); FRICS 1985 (ARICS 1983); *Recreations* gardening, football, reading, eating out, theatre, cinema; *Style—* James Chandler, Esq; R Durtnell & Sons Ltd, Rectory Lane, Brasted, Westerham, Kent (☎ 0959 64105, fax 0959 64756)

CHANDLER, Rev Dr Michael John; s of John Godfrey Chandler (d 1989), of Deal, Kent, and Ena Doris, *née* Holdstock (d 1954); *b* 27 May 1945; *Educ* Lincoln Theol Coll, King's Coll London (PhD), Univ of London Dip in Theology, Lambeth Dip in Theology (STh); *m* 16 July 1966, Janet Mary, da of Walter Raines (d 1980), of Canterbury, Kent; 1 s (Timothy b 1969), 1 da (Deborah b 1971); *Career* curate: St Dunstan's Canterbury 1972-75, St John's Margate 1975-78; vicar: Newington 1978-88, with Bobbing and Iwade 1978-80, with Hartlip and Stockbury 1980-88; rural dean of Sittingbourne 1984-88, rector St Stephen's Canterbury 1988-; chaplain to High Sheriff of Kent 1988-89, diocesan sec SPCK 1988-; Canterbury Diocesan: memb Synod 1980-, memb Bd of Educn 1980-88, memb Bd of Ministry 1984-88, memb Pastoral Ctee 1988-; memb Archbishop's Cncl 1988-, chm Canterbury Christian Aid 1988-90; *Recreations* bee keeping, reading, walking; *Style—* The Rev Dr Michael Chandler; The Rectory, St Stephen's Green, Canterbury, Kent CT2 7JU (☎ 0227 65391)

CHANDLER, Prof Tony John; s of Harold William Chandler (d 1975), and Florence Ellen, *née* Moore (d 1970); *b* 7 Nov 1928; *Educ* Alderman Newton GS Leicester, King's Coll London (BSc, DipEd, MSc, PhD, MA); *m* 4 Sept 1954, Margaret Joyce; 1 s (Adrian Mark b 1960), 1 da (Kathryn Anne (Mrs Peneycad) b 1957); *Career* Nat Serv 1 Lt RAF 1950-52; prof: UCL 1969-73 (lectr 1956-65, reader 1965-69), Univ of Manchester 1973-77; master of Birkbeck Coll London 1977-79 (lectr 1952-56); author numerous articles in meteorological and geographical jls; vice pres RMS 1973-75 (sec 1969-73); memb: NERC, Ctee of Experts on Major Hazards Health and Safety Exec, Royal Cmmn on Environmental Pollution 1973-77, Royal Soc Study Gp on Pollution in the Atmosphere 1974-77, Standing Ctee on Energy and the Environment 1978; *Books* The Climate of London (1965), Modern Meteorology and Climatology (1972 and 1981); *Recreations* clockmaking and collecting, reading, travel, music; *Style—* Prof Tony Chandler; Charnwood, 44 Knoll Rise, Orpington, Kent BR6 0EL (☎ 0689 32880); Department of Geography, University College London, 26 Bedford Way, London WC1H 0AP (☎ 071 387 7050, fax 071 380 7565)

CHAPMAN, Roy John; s of William George Chapman (d 1978), of Kettering, and Frances Harriet, *née* Yeomans (d 1981); *b* 30 Nov 1936; *Educ* Kettering GS, St Catharine's Coll Cambridge (MA); *m* 23 Sept 1961, Janet Gibbeson, da of Roy Gibbeson Taylor (d 1955) of Worthing; 2 s (William b 1962, Henry b 1972), 1 da (Lucy b 1964); *Career* CA; Arthur Andersen & Co 1958-: ptnr 1970-, managing ptnr London 1984-, managing ptnr UK 1989-; memb Advsy Cncl London Enterprise Agency 1985-88; FCA, FIMC, CBIM, FBPICS; *Recreations* cricket, walking, opera, literature, idling; *Clubs* United Oxford and Cambridge Univ, Hawks, MCC; *Style—* Roy Chapman, Esq; Arthur Andersen & Co, 1 Surrey Street, London WC2 (☎ 071 836 1200, fax 071 831 1133, telex 8812 711)

CHAPPLE, Hon Barry Joseph; yr s of Baron Chapple (Life Peer), *qv*; *b* 1951; *Educ* Hawes Down Comprehensive Sch; *m* 1980, Angela Christine, da of Kenneth R Medgett; *Style—* The Hon Barry Chapple; c/o The Rt Hon Lord Chapple, EETPU, Hayes Court, West Common Road, Bromley BR2 7AU

CHAPPLE, Baron (Life Peer UK 1985), of Hoxton, Greater London; Francis Joseph Chapple (Frank); s of Frank Chapple, of Shoreditch, and his w, Emily, da of Joseph Rook, of Hoxton; *b* 1921,Aug; *Educ* Elementary Sch; *m* 1944, Joan Jeanette, da of James Nicholls; 2 s (Hon Roger Francis b 1947, Hon Barry Joseph b 1951); *Career* electrician; memb TUC Gen Council 1971, gen sec EEPTU 1966-84; dir: National Nuclear Corporation 1980-, Southern Water Authority 1983-, Inner City Enterprises 1983-; chm TUC 1982-83; memb NEDC; *Style—* The Rt Hon Lord Chapple; EETPU, Hayes Court, West Common Rd, Bromley, Kent

CHAPPLE, Hon Roger Francis; er s of Baron Chapple (Life Peer), *qv*; *b* 1947; *Educ* Brooke House Comprehensive Sch; *m* 1969, Susan Audrey, da of Charles F W Brown; 2 s (David b 1974, Robin b 1981), 1 da (Rachel b 1972); *Style—* The Hon Roger Chapple; c/o The Rt Hon Lord Chapple, EETPU, Hayes Court, West Common Road, Bromley BR2 7AU

CHAPUT DE SAINTONGE, Dr (David) Mark; s of Lt-Col Rolland Alfred Aime, CMG (d 1989), and Barbara, *née* Watts; *b* 1 Oct 1942; *Educ* Whitgift Sch Croydon, London Hosp Med Coll (BSc, PhD, MB BS); *m* 15 Dec 1973, Gail Nicola, da of Norman Mason (d 1985); 3 s (Luke b 1976, Daniel b 1978, Edward b 1980); *Career* sr house offr Med Unit Nottingham Gen Hosp 1968-

69, sr lectr in clinical pharmacology and therapeutics London Hosp Med Coll 1973- (lectr 1969); conslt physician in gen med: Bethnal Green Hosp 1976-79, London Hosp 1976-; sr lectr in clinical pharmacology Bart's 1981-; numerous scientific papers on clinical trials and med judgement; assoc Center Res on Judgement Policy at Inst Cognitive Sci Univ of Colorado 1984-, memb Ed Bd British Journal Clinical Pharmacology 1983-89, dep ed Drug and Therapeutics Bulletin 1986-90; FRCP 1986; *Books* Current Problems in Clinical Trials (with Prof D W Vere, 1984); *Recreations* pottery, shooting; *Style—* Dr Mark Chaput de Saintonge

CHENEY, Donald Harvey; s of Arthur Stanley Cheney (d 1975), and Jessie Cheney (d 1986); *b* 16 Jan 1931; *Educ* Eggars GS Alton Hants, Harrow Weald Co GS Middx, Regent St Poly Sch of Architecture (Dip Arch); *m* 13 Feb 1956, Gillian Evelyn Florence Frances Cheney, JP, da of Guy Holman Tatum (d 1969); 3 da (Frances b 1956, Fiona (Mrs Ford) b 1960, Claire b 1968); *Career* qualified as architect 1955; in practice: NZ 1956-62, S Coast of England 1963-(ptnr 1970-); cncl memb RIBA 1983, external examiner Canterbury Sch of Architecture 1982-87, memb Franco Br Union of Architects 1977-; chm Hythe Venetian Fete 1978-86, Hythe town cncllr 1981-86; Freeman City of London 1983; memb: Worshipful Co of Arbitrators 1983, Worshipful Co of Architects 1985; MRIBA 1956, assoc memb NZ Inst of Architects 1956, CIArb 1976; *Recreations* sailing, photography; *Clubs* Royal Cinque Ports YC, St John House; *Style—* Donald Cheney, Esq; Crosstrees, North Rd, Hythe, Kent (☎ 0303 68720); La Lande Du Burgos, Guehenno 56, France; The Tramway Stables, Rampart Rd, Hythe, Kent CT21 5BG (☎ 0303 260 515, fax 0303 68214, car tel 0860 729 904)

CHESHIRE, Frank Joseph; s of Harold Cheshire (d 1960), of Bradford, Yorks, and Norah Wilkinson (d 1967), of Bradford; *b* 20 May 1923; *Educ* St Bede's GS Bradford; *m* 31 Dec 1955, Pamela Margaret, da of Jack Albert Sargeant (d 1973), of Romford, Essex; 4 s (Paul Francis b 1 Dec 1956, John Harold (twin) b 1 Dec 1956, Mark Edward b 28 April 1958, Ian Philip b 9 Jan 1961); *Career* RAF 1942-46: Bomber Cmd Pathfinder Force pilot, Capt 1944-45; supervisory fin analyst Ford Motor Co Dagenham 1951-59, gp accountant aeronautical equipment Plessey Co 1959-63, budget mangr Associated Television Ltd 1963-64, cost control mangr ITT (Europe) Inc 1964-68; fin controller World-Wide Product Group ITT Inc: Consumer 1968-71, Electrical Electronic & Semiconductor Mfrg & Distribution 1972-80; dist cncllr Thanet Kent 1982-87, co cncllr Margate East Div Kent 1985-89; assoc memb Chartered Inst Mgmnt Accountants; *Recreations* golf, tennis, skiing, mild epicurianism; *Clubs* North Foreland Golf; *Style—* Frank Cheshire, Esq; Vinway, 36 Princes Gardens, Cliftonville, Kent CT9 3AR (☎ 0843 220044)

CHESSELLS, (Arthur David) Tim; s of Brig Arthur Edgar Chessells, and Carmel Mary, *née* McGinnis; *b* 15 June 1941; *Educ* Stonyhurst; *m* 20 Aug 1966, Katharine, da of Dick Goodwin Penshurst; 2 s (Patrick, Richard), 2 da (Nicola, Phoebe); *Career* Arthur Young: ptnr 1972-, managing ptnr Bristol 1972-76, London 1976-86, head of consltg practice 1986-89; dir: Odgers & Co Ltd 1989-, various private cos; memb Kent AHA (chm fin panel 1979-82), vice chm Tunbridge Wells Health Authy 1982-88, memb SE Thames RHA 1988-90, chm NE Thames RHA 1990-; memb of Cncl St Christopher's Hospice 1989-, tstee Kent Community Housing Tst 1990-, auditor Kent CC 1984-89; FCA; *Recreations* gardening, shooting; *Clubs* Carlton; *Style—* Tim Chessells, Esq; North East Thames Regional Health Authority, 40 Eastbourne Terrace London W2 3QR (☎ 071 262 8011)

CHESWICK, Julian Blake; s of Herbert Julian Cheswick (d 1987), of Chichester, and Doris Valentine, *née* Chapman (d 1980); *b* 5 July 1935; *Educ* City of London Sch, Croydon Tech Coll (DMS, DIPM); *m* 1, 27 April 1957 (m dis 1967), Celia Violet, da of Francis Rowland Jenkins, of Virginia Water, Surrey; m 2, 24 Aug 1967, Christine Margaret Bruce, da of William Henry Stevens (d 1963); 2 da (Amy b 1971, Belinda b 1975); *Career* NCO in CRMP 1954-56; apprentice engr 1951-54, various prodn and mktg appts 1957-72, admin controller MCL Group Tunbridge Wells 1972-82, ptnr Catercraft (catering contractors) 1984-; memb Sevenoaks Cons Assoc, former chm and pres Otford Branch Cons Assoc; Sevenoaks DC 1987-: memb Main Ctees on Leisure and District Serv Bd, chm Community Servs and Grants Sub Ctee, Sevenoaks dist rep for Sports Cncl and Arts Cncl; Freeman City of London 1964, memb Worshipful Co of Coopers; APIM 1980; *Recreations* art, photography, food and wine; *Style—* Julian Cheswick, Esq; The Firs, Rye Lane, Otford, Sevenoaks, Kent TN14 5JF (☎ 09592 3652)

CHILD-VILLIERS, (Edward) John Mansel; s of Sqdn Ldr Hon Edward Mansel Child-Villiers (d 1980), and Mary Barbara Emma Torrens, *née* Frampton; *b* 29 April 1935; *Educ* Harrow; *m* 2 June 1958, Celia Elinor Vadyn, da of Cyril Hall Green (d 1973) (see Debrett's Peerage, Blake Bt); 2 s (Alexander b 1961, Roderick b 1963); *Career* memb Lloyd's 1962-; literary executor 18 Baron Dunsany 1966-; *Recreations* Bordeaux wines; *Style—* John Child-Villiers, Esq; Stable House, Mystole, Canterbury, Kent CT4 7DB (☎ 0227 738729)

CHILDISH, William Charley (Billy); s of late Reginald John Childish, and June Doreen, *née* Lewis; *b* 1 Dec 1959; *Educ* Walderslade Secdy Sch Chatham, Medway Coll of Design; *m* 1 Dec 1983, Sheila Betty, *née* Clark; *Career* co-fndr: Phyroid Press (with Sexton Ming) 1978, Hangman Books (with Jack Ketch) 1982; singer with Pop Rivets 1977-80; singer and guitarist with: The Milkshakes 1981-84, Thee Mighty Caesars 1985-88, Thee Headcoats 1989-90; poetry readings at: Cambridge Lit Festival 1982, Lancaster Lit Festival 1988- (also Oslo, Barcelona, Amsterdam, Hamburg, New York); painting exhibition Barcelona and Hamburg 1989; appeared on over 45 long playing records, over 20 collections of poetry published 1980-; fndr memb The Medway Poets; *Books* To The Quick (1988), The Girl in the Tree (1988), Admissions to Strangers (1989), The Deathly Flight of Angels (1990); *Clubs* WOAH; *Style—* Billy Childish, Esq

CHILDS, Virginia Elizabeth; JP (1986); da of Lt Cdr David Armine Howarth, of Blackboys, Sussex, and Nanette Russell McLean, *née* Smith; *b* 8 Aug 1949; *Educ* Walthamstow Hall Sevenoaks; *m* 1 June 1974, Michael Antony, s of Harold Frederick Childs (d 1968), of Sevenoaks, Kent; 2 s (Daniel David Howarth b 1976, Gregory Michael b 1978); *Career* design conslt ME 1982-84, author Biography of Lady Hester Stanhope (1989); *Recreations* sailing, squash, gardening; *Style—* Mrs Virginia Childs, JP; Longwood, Langton Rd, Langton Green, Tumbridge Wells, Kent; Deer Park, Treope Manor Estate, Port Isaac, Cornwall (☎ 0892 28252)

CHIPPS, Trevor Stanley; s of Harold Stanley Chipps (d 1967), of Sutton, Surrey, and Laura, *née* Butler (d 1983); *b* 1 Jan 1934; *Educ* Sutton GS Surrey, Law Soc Sch of Law London; *m* 4 Aug 1958, Stephanie Georgina, da of George Kimberley Perkins (d 1973), of Tunbridge Wells; 3 s (Richard Stanley George b 4 Oct 1962, Jonathan Stephen Trevor b 15 April 1964, Benjamin Francis James b 23 June 1968); *Career* admitted slr 1958; ptnr Trevor Stanley Chipps, Cmmr of Oaths 1964, NP 1972; borough cncllr Maidstone 1965-68, parish clerk 1984-86, memb: Kent Law Soc 1960, Prov Notaries Soc 1972; Freeman City of London; memb of Court of Assts Worshipful Co of Gold and Silver Wyre Drawers; memb Law Soc 1958; *Recreations* travel, music, opera, drama and many other interests; *Style—* Trevor Chipps, Esq; Fir Tree Oast, Chart Sutton, Maidstone, Kent; Old Stone Court, 34a Lower Stone St, Maidstone, Kent (☎ 0622 686662, fax 0622 690832)

CHONG, Dr Sonny Kwang Fook; s of Eugene Ngiap Lye Chong, of Malacca, Malaysia, and Anna Kim Neo, *née* Choo; *b* 18 Oct 1949; *Educ* St Francis Institution and HS Malacca, Faculty of Med Univ of Malaya (MMed, MSc, MD); *m* 20 April 1974, Valerie Yee May, da of Yang Seong Teck (d 1964); 2 s (Christopher b 12 April 1985, Mervyn b 15 Nov 1988), 2 da (Natalie b 27 July 1978, Natasha b 5 July 1983); *Career* paediatric registrar Westminster Childrens Hosp London 1980, CIRCA fell in paedatric gastroenterology St Barts Hosp and hon sr registrar Queen Elizabeth Hosp for Children London 1981, lectr in child health Kings Coll Hosp and Med Sch 1984, conslt paediatrician Gravesend and N Kent Hosp 1988-; visiting prof: Children's Hosp Pittsburgh 1988, Riley Children's Hosp Indianapolis 1989; conslt paediatrician to the Royal Brunei Family; asst hon gen sec Int Acad of Paediatrics and Trans disciplinary Educn and Int Coll of Paediatrics 1985-86; memb Br Paediatric Gastroenterology Soc 1985, Br Soc Immunology 1988-, Br Paediatric Assoc 1982-; Malaysian Br Cwlth fencing team memb 1970-; MRCP 1977; *Recreations* fencing, badminton, classical guitar; *Style—* Dr Sonny Chong; Gravesend & North Kent Hospital, Bath St, Gravesend, Kent DA11 0DG (☎ 0474 564333)

CHURCH, Dr (William) Edward; s of William Edward Church, and Laura Anne, *née* Sloper; *b* 2 July 1917; *Educ* Denstone Coll, Trinity Coll Cambridge (MA, MB BChir), St Thomas' Hosp (MRCP); *m* 21 March 1942, Enid Marjorie, da of William Henry Wallace; 4 s (William Edward b 11 Aug 1943, Richard Charles Wallace b 26 April 1946, Thomas Sloper b 8 Nov 1948, Robert John b 29 July 1950); *Career* Capt RAMC, MO 3 Parachute Bde on D Day, POW in Germany; memb: Kent Archaeological Soc, Essex Archaeological Soc, Harleain Soc, Kent Family History Soc, Monumental Brass Soc; cncllr Inst of Heraldic and Genealogical Studies; fell Soc of Genealogy, FSG; *Books* Fordwich the Lost Port (contrib with son T S Church chapter entitled The Lukyn Family, 1975); *Recreations* cricket and rugby football; *Clubs* Univ Vandals, Harlequins, St Thomas' Hospital and Ashford FC; *Style—* Dr Edward Church; Mannering House, Bethersden, nr Ashford, Kent TN26 3DJ (☎ 023 382 277)

CLAGUE, Andrew Charlesworth; s of John Charlesworth Clague, of Canterbury, and Margaret Elsie, *née* Musgrave; *b* 15 May 1951; *Educ* La Sainte Union Convent Herne Bay, St Edmunds Sch Canterbury, Canterbury Coll of Art (DipArch); *m* 23 June 1973, Alison Francesca, da of Dennis Arthur Land, of London; 2 s (James Charlesworth b 26 June 1980, Nicholas Charlesworth b 6 Nov 1986), 2 da (Anna Genevieve b 6 Sept 1978, Isabel Lucy b 6 Nov 1984); *Career* John C Clague 1975, ptnr John Clague & Partners, sr ptnr Clague 1987-; chm: Canterbury and Dist Branch RIBA, RIBA Regnl Practice Ctee, Canterbury and Dist Round Table; sec St Edmunds Soc, treas Canterbury Conservation Advsy Ctee; *Recreations* windsurfing, sailing, swimming, children; *Clubs* Kent and Canterbury, Canterbury Rotary, Men of Kent, Chamber of Trade, Canterbury Soc; *Style—* Andrew Clague, Esq; 1 Blackfriars St, Canterbury, Kent CT1 2AP (☎ 0227

761113); 62 Burgate, Canterbury, Kent CT1 2HJ (☎ 0227 762060, fax 0227 762149)

CLAPHAM, His Hon Brian Ralph; s of late Isaac Bleazard Clapham, and Laura Alice, *née* Meech; *b* 1 July 1913; *Educ* Tonbridge, Wadham Coll Oxford, UCL, Open Univ; *m* 1961, (Renata) Margaret, da of Dr Rudolph Pius Warburg; 2 s; *Career* called to the Bar 1936; Parly candidate (Lab): Tonbridge 1950, Billericay 1951 and 1955, Chelmsford 1959; circuit judge 1974-85; govr West Kent Coll; memb Tonbridge and later Southborough Urban DCs 1947-74 (chm Tonbridge Urban DC 1959-60), Freeman City of London; FCIArb; *Recreations* walking and talking; *Style—* His Hon Brian Clapham; Crown Court, Maidstone, Kent

CLARABUT, Cdr Guy Stewart Chetwode; DSO (1943), DSC (1945), JP (1963); s of Gen Reginald Blaxland Clarabut, CB, CBE (d 1976), and Mary Stewart, *née* Gill (later Mrs Wilder, d 1972); *b* 19 Sept 1919; *Educ* Cheltenham; *m* 4 Feb 1942, Stella Joyce, da of Capt William David Strachan-Smith, RN (d 1975); 1 s (Richard Ian b 1950), 1 da (Sarah Gaye b 1943); *Career* entered RN 1937, midshipman RN 1938, sub Lt in destroyer Moutrose 1940; served in submarines: Thrasher, Traveller, Stygian, Sentinel, Alcide and Thermopylae (all 1940); Naval Staff Course 1950, requested ret 1955; London and Rochester Trading Co 1955; Crescent Shipping: md 1962-82, chm and md 1966-82; dir proprietor to Hays Wharf 1964-82, chm Nat Assoc of Warehouse Keepers 1965, chm Bowker and King 1970-82; Medway Port Authy: dir 1970-86, vice chm 1973-86; chm Humphrey and Grey 1972-82, pilotage cmmr 1974-87; Gen Cmmr of Tax 1970-, sr warden Rochester Bridge 1984 (asst 1974-88); memb Worshipful Co Shipwrights 1962, Freeman City of London 1961; *Recreations* sailing, skiing, golf; *Clubs* Royal Ocean Racing, RAC, Medway Yacht; *Style—* Cdr Guy Clarabut, DSO, DSC, JP, RN; Wyebank, Bowesden Lane, Shorne, Gravesend, Kent (☎ 0474 822253)

CLARE, Prof Anthony Ward; *née* Blackwood; s of Bernard J Clare, of 29 Albany Rd, Ranelagh, Dublin 6, and Mary Agnes, *née* Dunne; *b* 24 Dec 1942; *Educ* Gonzaga Coll Dublin, Univ Coll Dublin (MB BCh, BAO, MD), Univ of London (MPhil); *m* 4 Oct 1966, Jane Carmel, da of Gabriel Sarsfield Hogan (d 1989), of Shelbourne Rd, Dublin 4; 3s (Simon John b 1970, Peter Tobias b 1975, Sebastian Patrick b 1985), 4 da (Rachel Judith b 1967, Eleanor Ruth b 1971, Sophie Carolyn b 1978, Justine Chiara b 1982); *Career* intern St Joseph Hosp Syracuse NY 1966-67; registrar: St Patrick's Hosp Dublin 1967-69, Bethlem Royal and Maudsley Hosps London 1970-72; dep dir Gen Practice Res Unit Inst of Psychiatry 1979-82 (sr registrar and res worker 1973-78), prof and head Dept of Psychological Med St Bart's Hosp Med Coll 1982-88, med dir St Patrick's Hosp Dublin and prof of clinical psychiatry Trin Coll Dublin 1989- ; memb Health Educn Authy, chm Centre Ctee King Edward's Hosp Fund for London; numerous broadcasts incl: Let's Talk About Me, In The Psychiatrist's Chair (BBC 1982), Stop The Week; FRCPI 1983, FRCPsych 1986; *Books* Psychiatry in Dissent (1976, 2 edn 1980), Let's Talk About Me (1981), In the Psychiatrist's Chair (1984), Lovelaw (1986); *Recreations* tennis, opera, family life; *Style—* Prof Anthony W Clare; 87 Coper's Cope Rd, Beckenham, Kent BR3 1NR (☎ 01 650 1784); Delville, Lucan, Co Dublin, Republic of Ireland (☎ 0001 264782); St Patrick's Hospital, James's Street, Dublin 8, Republic of Ireland (☎ 0001 775423)

CLARK, Hon Alan Kenneth McKenzie; MP (C) Plymouth Sutton Feb 1974-; s of Baron Clark, OM, CH, KCB (Life Peer, d 1983) and 1 w Elizabeth, *née* Martin (d 1976); *b* 13 April 1928; *Educ* Eton, ChCh Oxford; *m* 1958, Caroline Jane, da of Col Leslie Brindley Bream Beuttler (and ggda of Hon George Ogilvie-Grant, 6 s of 6 Earl of Seafield); 2 s (James, Andrew); *Career* served Household Cavalry Trg Regt 1946 and RAuxAF 1952-54; barr Inner Temple; mil historian; memb: Inst Strategic Studies, Royal United Services Inst for Def Studies; vice chm Parly Def Ctee, memb Parly Home Affrs Ctee; under sec of state for Employment (responsibilities incl legislation on trade union's political levy) 1983-86, min for Trade 1986-89, min for Def Procurement 1989-; *Clubs* Brooks's, Pratt's; *Style—* The Hon Alan Clark, MP; Saltwood Castle, Kent CT21 4QU (☎ 0303 267190)

CLARK, Rev David Gordon; s of Hugh Gordon Clark (d 1966), of Longmynd, Links Ave, Felixstowe, Suffolk, and Caroline Keeling, *née* Roberts (d 1983); *b* 23 Aug 1929; *Educ* Gresham's, Clare Coll Cambridge (MA); *m* 4 Jan 1964, Alison, da of Robert James Lathbury (d 1984), of Longham Wood, Lakestreet, Mayfield, Sussex; 2 c (Hilary b 1965, Jonathan Gordon b 1967); *Career* vicar St John the Evangelist Walthamstow 1960-69; rector: Stansted with Fairseat 1969-82, Stansted with Fairseat and Vigo 1982-; garden opened for Nat Gardens Scheme 1981-; memb: RHS, Hardy Plant Soc; pres Stansted Hort and Homecraft Soc; *Recreations* gardening in Kent, planting trees in Dorset, singing; *Clubs* Old Greshamian; *Style—* The Rev David Clark; The Rectory, Fairseat, Sevenoaks, Kent TN15 7LT (☎ 0732 822494)

CLARK, Derek John; s of Robert Clark (d 1970), of Eastbourne, and Florence Mary, *née* Wise (d 1960); *b* 17 June 1929; *Educ* Selhurst GS, SE London Tech Coll 1956-59; *m* 21 March 1949, Edna Doris, da of Alfred Coome (d 1966), of Croydon; 1 s (Paul Wesley b 1949), 1 da (Laura Alison b 1955); *Career* Nat Serv RAF 1948-49; asst sec (later comptroller) RICS 1966-70, dir of admin Inst of Cost Mgmnt Accountants 1970-82, sec Inst of Structural Engrs 1982-; FCIS 1982; *Recreations* squash, athletics; *Style—* Derek Clark, Esq; 7 Elvington Green, Hayesford Park, Bromley, Kent BR2 9DE (☎ 081 460 9055); The Institute of Structural Engineers, 11 Upper Belgrave St, London SW1X 8BH (☎ 071 235 4535)

CLARK, James Henry Mullin; TD (1946); s of Arthur Torwerth Clark (d 1954), of Cardiff, and Gladys Mary, *née* Mullin (d 1962); *b* 21 March 1913; *Educ* City of Cardiff HS; *m* 1 March 1941 Hilda Margaret (d 1985), da of Claud Percival Hailey (d 1938), of Llandaff; 1 s (John b 1946), 1 da (Carolyn b 1948); *Career* cmmnd TD RA 1936; War Serv with RA: UK 1939-41, W Desert 1942-43, Italy 1943-45; CA; Coopers & Lybrand 1946-49, Mobil Oil Group 1949-76, Sedgwick Group 1976-79; tstee and hon treas Beckenham Parochial Charities, memb Rochester Diocesan Synod, churchwarden St Paul's Church Beckenham; hereditary Freeman City of Cardiff; fell ICAEW 1937, FInstPet 1953; *Recreations* golf, reading, travel; *Clubs* Beckenham Probus; *Style—* James Clark, Esq, TD; 67 Southend Rd, Beckenham, Kent (☎ 081 650 1908)

CLARK, Michael John; s of Kenneth Alfred Clark, of Queensdale, Harare, Zimbabwe, and Constance Adelaide, *née* White; *b* 9 June 1942; *Educ* Allan Wilson Zimbabwe, Inst Credit and Financial Mgmnt SA, Chartered Inst Secs; *m* 1 (m dis 1978), Elizabeth Helen; 2 s (Michael b 1973, Robert b 1974); m 2, 20 March 1979, Joyce Elizabeth, da of Francis John Geeves (d 1966); *Career* returned to Eng from Zimbabwe 1978, gen mangr Barker Hammond 1979, currently fin dir to all cos in Sw Bligh Electrical Gp (co sec 1982); *Recreations* golf; *Clubs* St Augustine's Golf, Chestfield Golf; *Style—* Michael Clark, Esq; 16 Canterbury Rd West, Cliffsend, Ramsgate, Kent CT12 5DY (☎ 0843 594500); Bligh Holdings Ltd, 1-2 North Lane, Canterbury, Kent CT2 7EA (☎ 0227 456931, fax 0227 472940)

CLARKE, Anthony Peter; QC (1979); s of Harry Alston Clarke (d 1979), and Isobel, *née* Kay; *b* 13 May 1943; *Educ* Oakham Sch, King's Coll Cambridge; *m* 7 Sept 1968, Rosemary, da of K W Adam, of Barnham, Sussex; 2 s (Ben b 7 Jan 1972, Thomas b 20 June 1973), 1 da (Sally b 3 June 1977); *Career* called to the Bar Middle Temple 1965; arbitrator: Lloyds, ICC; rec, wreck cmmr; Membre de la Chambre Arbitrale Maritime; *Recreations* tennis, golf, holidays; *Style—* Anthony Clarke, Esq, QC; Lewes Heath, Horsmonden, Kent TN12 8EE (☎ 0892 723783); 2 Essex Court, Temple, London EC4Y 9AP (☎ 071 583 8381, fax 071 353 0998, telex 8812528 ADROIT)

CLARKE, Barrie James; s of James Clarke (d 1984), of 138 Reedshaw Bank, Offerton, Stockport, Cheshire, and Ellen, *née* Gaffey; *b* 25 May 1944; *Educ* St Michael's Sch Stockport; *Career* Lab Pty: trainee agent 1968, asst agent to Alf Morris, MP (Wythenshawe constituency) 1968, asst agent to Sir Harold Wilson, KG, FRS, MP, PM (Huyton constituency) 1969, agent and organiser Gravesend constituency 1970-74, nat youth offr 1974-76, nat political educn offr 1976-86, nat trg and legal offr 1986-87, trg conslt 1987-; civilian attached to Br Mil Hosp (RAMC) Hannover W Germany Br Army of the Rhine; gen involvement Lab Pty; co cncllr representing Luton and Wayfield (Medway NE) area of Chatham Kent 1981-; memb APEX; *Books* The Reasonable Agenda (critique of Lab Pty structure); *Recreations* sailing, driving; *Clubs* Dartford WMC; *Style—* Barrie Clarke, Esq; 126 Knights Manor Way, Dartford, Kent DA1 5SP (☎ 0322 94434); Kent County Council, County Hall, Maidstone, Kent (☎ 0622 671411)

CLARKE, Dr David Robert; *b* 14 April 1945; *Educ* Aldenham, Middx Hosp Univ of London (MB BS, DA, DObstRCOG, MRCGP); *m* 23 Sept 1972, Carole Andrea, *née* Livesey; 1 s (Hugo David Lee b 27 Nov 1980), 1 da (Poppy Anna Lee b 7 April 1979); *Career* house physician Harefield Hosp 1970; Middx Hosp: house surgn orthopaedics 1970, casualty offr 1971, anaesthetist 1973; house surgn Barnet Gen Hosp 1971, res med offr King Edward VII Hosp for Offrs London 1972, house surgn obstetrics and gynaecology Central Middx Hosp 1974, trainee GP Croydon Surrey 1975, community med offr Croydon AHA 1976, princ in gen practice Med Centre Sittingbourne 1977-; *Recreations* golf, tennis, shooting, sailing; *Clubs* Faversham Golf, Aldeburgh Yacht; *Style—* Dr David Clarke; Hartlip House, Hartlip, Sittingbourne, Kent ME9 7TL; The Med Centre, 32 London Rd, Sittingbourne, Kent ME10 1ND (☎ 0795 472109)

CLARKE, Graham Arthur; s of Maurice William Mason Clarke, of Tenterden, Kent, and Hilda Mary, *née* Spencer; *b* 27 Feb 1941; *Educ* Beckenham and Penge GS, Beckenham Sch of Art, RCA; *m* Wendy Elizabeth, da of Capt Raymond Douglas Hudd (d 1987), of Boughton Monchelsea, Kent; 1 s (Jason Samuel b 1965), 3 da (Abigail Lucy b 1968, Emily Miranda b 1972, Matilda Amy b 1981); *Career* artist and writer; works in collections of: V & A, The Tate Gallery, Nat libraries of Scotland Ireland and Wales, Bodleian Oxford, Fitzwilliam Cambridge, Nat Library Congress USA; Biography of Graham Clarke by Clare Sydney 1985; memb Governing Body Kent Inst Art and Design, fndr chm PEDIFUND, presented the painting Dance For Peace a gift to Peace Museum Hiroshima Japan 1989; *Books* Gout de Grenouille (1981), Graham Clarke's History of England (1987), Graham Clarke's Grand Tour (1989), Joe Carpenter and Son (An English Nativity) (1990); *Style—* Graham Clarke, Esq; White Cottage, Green Lane, Boughton Monchelsea, Maidstone, Kent ME17 4LF (☎ 0622 743938)

CLARKE, John Neil; s of George Philip Clarke (d 1969); *b* 7 Aug 1934; *Educ* Rugby, King's Coll London (LLB); *m* 1958, Sonia Heather, *née* Beckett; 3 s; *Career* chm: Johnson Matthey plc 1984-89, Molins plc 1989-, Genchem Holdings Ltd 1989-; FCA; *Clubs* MCC, Royal W Norfolk Golf, Addington Golf; *Style*— J Neil Clarke Esq; High Willows, 18 Park Ave, Farnborough Park, Kent BR6 8LL (☎ 0689 51651); The Cottage, Hall Lane, Thornham, Norfolk (☎ 048 526 269); 35 Ely Place, London EC1N 6TD

CLARKE, William; *b* 13 June 1908; *Educ* Secdy Educn Barnes London; *m* 1, 1932, Hilda Primrose, *née* Brum (d 1933); m 2, 26 Dec 1940, Elsa May, da of Francis George Amos (d 1968); 1 s (William Boris b 16 Oct 1941), 1 da (Lesley b 27 Oct 1944); *Career* Regular Army RAMC 1933-44 (med discharge), Orderly Room Sgt; clerk: Harrods Advertising Dept 1923-28, Gaumont British Picture Corporation 1928-31; shopkeeper 1931-33, chief clerk Middx TA Assoc and similar clerical posts until ret 1973; lectr London and Home Counties to Townswomen's Guilds and Women's Insts on off beat London and the Brontë sisters until moving to Kent 1975; poems published in: TLS, Poetry Review, Punch, Pick of Punch, Countryman, Country Life, Tribune, The Lady; poems broadcast by Radio Kent and Egyptian State Radio; *Books* Shades of Khaki and Other Poems (1976), The Brontës Were Here (biography, 1977), An Anthology From X Review (contrib, 1988), More Poems From The Second World War (contrib, 1989); *Recreations* walking, reading, listening to classical music; *Style*— William Clarke, Esq

CLARKSON, Gerald Dawson; QFSM (1983); s of Alexander Dickie Clarkson (d 1986), of St Mary Cray Kent, and Agnes Tierney, *née* Price; *b* 4 June 1936; *Educ* Westminster Tech Coll, Poly of Central London (BA); *m* 21 March 1959, Rose Lilian, da of Thomas Montague Hodgson (d 1971), of Clapham; 1 s (Nicholas b 1963), 1 da (Penelope b 1965); *Career* Nat Serv RE 1959-61; London Fire Brigade: joined 1961, station offr 1969, asst divnl offr 1972, divnl offr 1974, dep asst chief offr 1979, asst chief offr 1980, awarded Fire Serv Long Serv and Good Conduct Medal 1981, dep chief offr and chief exec 1987; Good Conduct Medal 1981, offr brother OStJ 1989; memb Central Fire Brigades Advsy Cncl 1980, advsr to Assoc of Met Authys 1987, vice pres Cwlth and Overseas Fire Serv Assoc 1989 (pres 1990), memb Fedn Br Fire Orgns 1989 (chm 1990), dir NFPA USA 1990; Freeman City of London 1983, fndr Master of the Guild of Firefighters; FBIM 1978, FIMS 1979, FRSH 1987, hon fell IFE 1989-; *Recreations* music, sailing, fishing; *Clubs* The East India; *Style*— Gerald Clarkson, Esq, QFSM; Oldfield Lodge, Oldfield Rd, Bickley, Bromley, Kent BR1 2LE (☎ 081 467 4106); London Fire & Civil Defence Authority, London Fire Brigade Headquarters, 8 Albert Embankment, London SE1 7SD (☎ 071 587 4000, telex 918200, fax 071 587 4169, car 0836 245964)

CLAY, John Martin; s of Sir Henry Clay (d 1954), and 1 w Gladys, *née* Priestman; *b* 20 Aug 1927; *Educ* Eton, Magdalen Coll Oxford; *m* 1952, Susan Jennifer, da of Lt-Gen Sir Euan Miller, KCB, KBE, DSO, MC (d 1985); 4 s; *Career* chm Johnson and Firth Brown Ltd; former dir Bank of England, dir Hambros plc; *Recreations* sailing; *Clubs* Medway Yacht; *Style*— John Clay, Esq; 41 Tower Hill, London EC3

CLAYDEN, Dr Graham Stuart; s of Colin Stewart Clayden (d 1985), of Bournemouth, and Amy Joyce, *née* Burrough; *b* 8 Jan 1947; *Educ* Bournemouth Sch, Univ of London (MD); *m* 25 Aug 1970, Christine, da of Reginald Thomas Steele (d 1980); 1 s (Jonathan Stuart b 1972), 1 da (Anna Francesca b 1974); *Career* sr registrar in paediatrics Hosp for Sick Children Gt Ormond St 1977, sr lectr and hon conslt in paediatrics St Thomas' Hosp 1977-89, reader in paediatrics and hon conslt UMDS 1989-; bd memb Dartmouth House Centre, academic bd memb Br Paediatric Assoc, founding govr Br Paediatric Computer and Info Gp; MRCP 1972, FRCP 1984; *Books* Treatment and Prognosis in Paediatrics (1988), Catechism in Paediatrics (1987); *Recreations* choral singing, bassoon; *Style*— Dr Graham Clayden; Paediatric Unit, United Medical and Dental Schools of Guy's and St Thomas's Hospitals, Lambeth Palace Rd, London SE1 7EH (☎ 071 928 9292, ext 3046)

CLAYTON, Anthony Styles (Tony); s of Peter Stuart Clayton, and Brenda Burton, *née* Whittaker; *b* 4 Feb 1949; *Educ* Lawrence Sheriff Sch Rugby, Rugby, Univ of Sussex (BSc, MA); *m* 5 April 1975, Gillian Margaret (Gill), da of Stanley Arthur Bruton (d 1987), of Marlow, Bucks; 1 s (James b 1981), 1 da (Rebecca b 1983); *Career* secondment to Br Gas 1972; Br Steel: planning dir London 1973-79, commercial mgmnt 1979-83; mgmnt advice and trg dir Strategic Planning Inst 1983-; Friends of the Earth, Cycling Campaign Organiser, past chm West Kent SDP, memb SLDP SE Regnl Policy GP; town cnclr Sevenoaks 1987, dist cnclr Sevenoaks 1987, SLD memb Sevenoaks DC; *Recreations* cycling; *Clubs* Nat Lib; *Style*— Tony CLayton, Esq; 75 Bayham Rd, Sevenoaks, Kent TN13 3XB (☎ 0732 451087); Strategic Planning Institute, 56 Haymarket, London SW1Y 4RM (☎ 071 930 5055, fax 071 839 5392)

CLAYTON, John Robert; s of Robert Guest Clayton (d 1980), of Burnley, and Margaret Alice, *née* James; *b* 8 Nov 1939; *Educ* Queen Elizabeth's GS Blackburn, Univ of Manchester (BSc); *m* 10 April 1965, Norma Mary, da of David Edward Jones, of Cardiff; 1 s (David b 2 Dec 1969), 1 da (Helen b 12 Sept 1966); *Career* asst chief engr Stevenage Development Corporation 1972-78, head engrg servs London Borough of Richmond-upon-Thames 1978-85, dir Planning and Tech Servs Dover DC 1985-; past pres Amwell Rotary Club, memb Dover Rotary Club; MIHT 1962, MICE 1965, FIHT 1983, FICE 1984, MBIM 1984; *Recreations* walking, swimming, studying people; *Style*— John Clayton, Esq; 1 Bramley Gdns, Whitfield, Dover CT16 3EU (☎ 0304 820294); Dover District Council, Honeywood Rd, Whitfield CT16 3EU (☎ 0304 821199)

CLEGG-HILL, Hon Mrs Frederic; Alice Dorothy; yr da of Rear Adm Cuthbert Godfrey Chapman, MVO (d 1931), and Hon Dorothy Beatrix Wynn, da of 3 Baron Newborough; *b* 21 Sept 1910; *m* 18 Nov 1938, Maj Hon Frederic Raymond Clegg-Hill (ka 1945), yr s of 6 Viscount Hill (d 1957); 1 s (Peter David Raymond Charles, *qv*); *Style*— The Hon Mrs Frederic Clegg-Hill; The Old Forge, Stone in Oxney, nr Tenterden, Kent

CLEGG-HILL, Peter David Raymond Charles; s of Maj Hon Frederic Raymond Clegg-Hill (ka 1945), 2 s of 6 Viscount Hill, and Hon Mrs Frederic Clegg-Hill, *qv*; hp to Viscountcy of cous, 8 Viscount Hill; *b* 17 Oct 1945, (posthumous); *Educ* Tabley House Sch; *m* 1973, Sharon Ruth Deane, of NZ; 2 s (Paul b 1979, Michael Charles David b 1988), 5 da (Catherine b 1974, Jennifer b 1976, Susan b 1980, Rachel b 1984, Mellisa b 1986); *Career* farmer; *Style*— Peter Clegg-Hill, Esq; The Old Forge, Stone-in-Oxney, Tenterden, Kent

CLEMENCE, (John) Alistair; TD (1972); s of L A Clemence (d 1978), of Bexhill on Sea, and Helen, *née* Gillies (d 1982); *b* 17 May 1937; *Educ* Tonbridge; *m* 8 April 1967, Heather May Kerr, da of Canon C J Offer (d 1964), of Ightham, Kent; 3 s (William b 1969, James b 1970, Jonathan b 1973); *Career* Nat Serv Seaforth Highlanders 1956-58, 2 Lt 1957; London Scottish Regt TA 1959-72, Lt 1959, Capt 1963, Maj 1970; Regtl Col 1989, Dep Hon Col 1/51 Highland Vols 1989, regtl treas 1973-89; CA; ptnr Finnie & Co (formerly L A Clemence & Co) 1966-, dir Alfred Knight Ltd (piano mfrs); Liveryman Worshipful Co of Skinners 1969; FCA, FInstD, FBIM; *Recreations* gardening; *Clubs* Army and Navy; *Style*— J A Clemence, Esq, TD; Bassetts, Mill Lane, Hildenborough, Kent TN11 9LX; 46 Church Ave, Beckenham, Kent BR3 1DT (☎ 081 658 7911)

CLEMENT, Dr Michele Ingrid; da of Maj Joseph Cyril Clement (d 1984), and Joyce Mona Clement; *b* 18 Sept 1951; *Educ* Queenswood Sch, UCL (BSc), UCH (MB BS); *m* 30 May 1981, Timothy Henry Corn, s of Harold Henry Corn (d 1985); 2 s (Edward Harry b 1983, Charles Joseph b 1985); *Career* house post UCH; jr med posts: King's Coll Hosp 1977-78, UCH 1978-79; dermatology trg: St John's Hosp 1980, King's Coll Hosp 1980-87; appointed conslt dermatologist Bromley Health Authy 1987; MRCP 1978; *Books* Topical Steroids for Skin Disorders (1987); *Style*— Dr Michele Clement; Dermatology Department, Farnborough Hospital, Farnborough Common, Orpington, Kent BR6 8ND (☎ 0689 63333 ext 295)

CLEOBURY, Nicholas Randall; s of Dr John Frank Cleobury, of Croft House, Street End, Lower Hardes, Canterbury, Kent, and Brenda Julie, *née* Randall; *b* 23 June 1950; *Educ* King's Sch Worcester, Worcester Coll Oxford (MA); *m* 4 Nov 1978, Heather Noelle, da of Noel Kay (d 1981), of 8 Station Rd, Upper Poppleton, York; 1 s (Simon Randall b 23 Oct 1979), 1 da (Sophie Noelle b 12 Dec 1981); *Career* asst organist: Chichester Cathedral 1971-72, Christ Church Oxford 1972-76; chorus master Glyndebourne Opera 1977-79, asst dir BBC Singers 1978-80, princ conductor of opera RAM 1981-87, dir Aquarius 1983-; 1980-: int conductor working throughout UK, Europe and Scandinavia, regular TV and BBC Radio and Prom appearances, numerous commercial recordings; princ guest conductor Gävle Orch (Sweden) 1989-, princ conductor city of Cambridge Orchestral Assoc 1990-; FRCO 1968; hon RAM 1985; *Recreations* cricket, reading, walking, food, wine; *Clubs* Savage; *Style*— Nicholas Cleobury, Esq; China Cottage, Church Lane, Petham, Canterbury, Kent CT4 5RD (☎ 0227 70 584, fax 0227 70 827)

CLIFFORD, Brian David; s of Lt W D Clifford (d 1978), and Doris Septima, *née* Magnay; *b* 15 July 1942; *Educ* Downhills Central Sch London; *m* 1, 5 Nov 1965 (m dis), Jenny Margaret, da of Morgan Goronwy Rees (d 1980); 2 s (Samuel William b 29 May 1966, Benjamin Luke b 24 Oct 1968); m 2, 22 Oct 1977, Linda Mary, *née* Stearns; *Career* picture ed Womans Mirror Magazine 1961-62, dep picture ed Sunday Mirror 1962-65, exec picture ed Sun Newspaper 1965-66, night picture ed Daily Mail 1966-67, prodr Yorkshire TV 1968; BBC TV: script writer TV News 1969, stills mangr 1969-73, sales mangr Photographs 1973-79, ed Picture Publicity 1979-86, chief asst Info Div 1986-87, dep head Info Div 1987-88, head of Info Servs 1988-; Tottenham Schoolboys footballer 1956-57, head chorister St Philip's Church 1955-57; rugby coach Cranbrook RFC 1979-, memb Mgmnt Ctee Biddenden CC 1980; memb NUJ; *Recreations* horse breeding, photography, watching Tottenham Hotspur; *Style*— Brian Clifford, Esq; Mount House, Sissinghurst Castle, Cranbrook, Kent TN17 2AB (☎ 0580 713668)

CLIFFORD, Edwin Francis; JP (1958); s of James Clifford (d 1952), of Maidstone, and Lilian Mary, *née* Elliston; *b* 19 Sept 1921; *Educ* Maidstone GS; *m* 22 April 1950, Evelyn, da of Herbert Bourne (d 1963), of Maidstone; 1 s (Paul b 1952), 1 da (Jane b 1960); *Career* chm James Clifford & Son Ltd 1966- (dir 1949-) (family firm founded in Maidstone 1747); dep chm Maidstone magistrates 1972-; chm: Edmett Swain and Hanson Charity, Cutbush and Corrall Charity 1980-; tstee: Cobtree Charity, Maidstone Relief in Need Charity, Bentlif Wing Maidstone Museum; vice chm St Faith's Parochial Church Cncl Maidstone, patronage tstee St Luke's Church Maidstone; *Recreations* history, travel, chess; *Style*— Edwin Clifford, Esq, JP; James Clifford & Son Ltd, Westree Works, Hart St, Maidstone, Kent (☎ 0622 690202)

CLIFT, Robert John; s of Alfred Whittier Clift, of Balsall Common, Coventry, and Edna Joyce, *née* Guest; *b* 1 Aug 1962; *Educ* Bablake Sch Coventry, Univ of Nottingham (BA); *m* 26 Sept 1987, Helen Claire, da of William Henry Beck, of Sidcup, Kent; *Career* hockey player; Champions' Trophy: bronze medallist Karachi 1984, silver medallist Perth 1985; World Cup silver medallist London 1986, Euro Cup silver medallist Moscow 1987, Olympic Games gold medallist Seoul 1988; 118 caps England and GB; ACIB; *Recreations* golf, hockey; *Clubs* East Grinstead; *Style*— Robert Clift, Esq; Midland Bank plc, 70 Pall Mall, London SW1 (☎ 071 930 9353, fax 071 976 1008)

CLOSE, Peter Alwen; s of Lt-Col Richard Alwen Close, of 12 Back Lane, Cerne Abbas, Dorset, and Marjorie Anne Close; *b* 1 June 1943; *Educ* Haileybury, ISC, Gonville and Caius Coll Cambridge (MA); *m* 27 Aug 1966, Carole Lynne, da of Kenneth Guy Douglas Evans; 3 da (Sarah Louise b 1967, Georgina Anne b 1969, (Alison) Gail b 1976); *Career* headmaster: Hardye's Sch Dorchester Dorset 1981-87, Cranbrook Sch 1987-; cricket blue Univ of Cambridge 1965, Dorset Co CC 1961-67 (capped 1961); *Recreations* golf, skiing, cricket, travel, languages; *Clubs* Quidnuncs; *Style*— Peter Close, Esq; Cranbrook School, Cranbrook, Kent TN17 3JD (☎ 0580 712554)

CLOWES, Col Sir Henry Nelson; KCVO (1981, CVO 1977), DSO (1945), OBE (1953); yr s of Maj Ernest William Clowes, DSO (d 1951), of Bradley Hall, Ashbourne, Derbys, by his w Blanche, da of Rear Adm Hon Algernon Littleton, who was 2 s of 2 Baron Hatherton; the Admiral's w was Lady Margaret Needham, sis of 2 Earl of Kilmorey; *b* 21 Oct 1911; *Educ* Eton, Sandhurst; *m* 1941, Diana Katharine, MBE, da of Maj Basil Kerr, DSC (d 1957; himself ggs of 6 Marquess of Lothian by his 2 w, who was Lady Harriet Scott, da of 3 Duke of Buccleuch); 1 s (Capt Andrew Henry Clowes, Scots Gds (ret 1967), sometime Equerry to HRH The (1) Duke of Gloucester, m 1967, Georgiana, da of Richard Cavendish, of Holker Hall, Cumbria); *Career* served Scots Gds 1931-57 (cmd 2 Bn then 1 Bn, Lt-Col cmdg 1954-57, ret 1957); Lt Hon Corps Gentlemen at Arms 1976-81 (joined 1961, Clerk of the Cheque and Adj 1966, Standard Bearer 1973-76); *Recreations* gardening, shooting, fishing, travel; *Clubs* Cavalry and Guards, Shikar, Pratt's; *Style*— Colonel Sir Henry Clowes, KCVO, DSO, OBE; 57 Perrymead St, London SW6 3SN (☎ 01 736 7901)

CLOWES, Lady Rose; *née* Nevill; 3 and yst da of 5 Marquess of Abergavenny; *b* 15 July 1950; *m* 8 March 1990, George Mark Somerset Clowes, er s of Archibald Somerset Clowes, of Ashlands, Billesdon, Leics; *Style*— The Lady Rose Clowes; c/o The Most Hon the Marquess of Abergavenny, KG, OBE, Eridge Park, Tunbridge Wells, Kent, TN3 9JT

CLUTTON, (Bernard Geoffrey) Owen; s of Maj Arthur Hennry Clutton, MC (d 1979), and Joyce, *née* Worthington; *b* 3 March 1951; *Educ* St Aidens Coll Grahamstown, Univ of the Witwatersrand (BA, LLB), Univ of Oxford (BCL); *m* 12 Oct 1979, Rosemary Elizabeth, da of Geoffrey Thomas Skett; 1 s (William Henry b 28 March 1988); *Career* admitted slr 1980; ptnr Macfarlanes 1984-; President's Certificate Nat Playing Fields Assoc; Liveryman Worshipful Co of Slrs; memb Law Soc, ATII; *Style*— Owen Clutton, Esq; Macfarlanes, 10 Norwich St, London EC4A 1BD (☎ 071 831 9222, telex 296381, fax 071 831 9607)

COBB, Lt-Col Angela Vera; MBE, TD, DL; da of Brig John Morley Stebbings, MC, TD (d 1966), of Ramsgate, and Doris Percy, *née* Chalmer (d 1947); *b* 11 Feb 1920; *Educ* Convent of the Assumption Ramsgate, St Georges Sch Ascot Berks; *m* 4 July 1945, (Francis) David Cecil Cobb, s of Francis Cecil Cobb (d 1936), of Margate; 1 da (Carolyn Frances b 15 July 1948); *Career* served ATS 1939-46, fndr ATS Band 1941, cmd until 1946, served TA ATS WRAC 1947-63; co cncllr 1961-77; memb: AHA, FPC, Br Legion; *Recreations* golf, bridge, shooting; *Clubs* Royal Temple Yacht, Naval and Military, In and Out; *Style*— Lt-Col Angela Cobb, MBE, TD, DL

COBBETT, John Richard; s of Hugh Ronald Cobbett (d 1981), of Bristol, and Winifred Florence, *née* Howlett (d 1969); *b* 2 Aug 1947; *Educ* Cotham GS Bristol; *m* 22 Feb 1975, Elizabeth Patricia, da of William Hibbert Hartle (d 1972), of Berkhamsted; 3 da (Merewyn Jane b 21 Feb 1977, Anna Noel b 7 Dec 1978, Victoria Marjorie b 23 Feb 1982); *Career* accountant Smiths Industries plc London 1976-84, fin dir Hobourn Engineering Ltd Rochester 1987-89 (chief accountant 1984-87), fin mangr Calor Engineering Ltd 1989-; chm Bd Govrs Hollingbourne Co Primary Sch, memb Ctee Hollingbourne Action Gp to re-route Channel Tunnel High Speed Rail Link, FCMA, ACIS, AInstM; *Recreations* house restoration, family, camping, sailing; *Clubs* William Cobbett Soc; *Style*— John Cobbett, Esq; Foxgrove House, Hollingbourne, nr Maidstone, Kent ME17 1TR (☎ 0622 880543); Calor Engineering Ltd, Maidstone Rd, Platt, Sevenoaks, Kent TN15 8JN (☎ 0732 883144, fax 0732 882910)

COCKCROFT, William Lonsdale (Bill); JP (Maidstone 1988); s of William Lonsdale Denys Cockcroft, of Tonbridge, and Olive Maud, *née* Stubbings; *b* 28 April 1948; *Educ* Judd Sch Tonbridge, South Bank Poly; *m* 8 Dec 1973, Dorothy Pamela (Dottie), da of Sidney George French (d 1982), of Hadlow; 2 s (Michael b 1976, David b 1978), 1 da (Sophie b 1983); *Career* Sawyer & Fisher (chartered quantity surveyors): joined 1965, assoc 1975, ptnr 1980; scout co cmmr 1986, memb Scout Assoc Nat Exec 1988; ARICS 1975, FRICS 1981, MBIM 1985; *Recreations* sailing, scouting; *Style*— Bill Cockcroft, Esq, JP; 8 Mountsfield Close, Maidstone, Kent ME16 0EZ (☎ 0622 672717); Sawyer & Fisher, Cornwallis House, Pudding Lane, Maidstone, Kent (☎ 0622 679532, fax 0622 679536, car phone 0836 231748)

COCKETT, Geoffrey Howard; s of William Cockett (d 1970), of Southampton, and Edith Gertrude, *née* Dinham (d 1957); *b* 18 March 1926; *Educ* King Edward VI Sch Southampton, Univ of Southampton (BSc); *m* 1951, Elizabeth Mary Florence, da of Stanley Frederick Bagshaw (d 1970), of Orpington; 2 da (Juliet, Jenny-Sarah); *Career* chartered physicist; res scientist: Royal Aircraft Establishment 1948-52, Armament Res Establishment 1952-67, Henley Mgmnt Coll 1968; supt Physics Res Chem Def Establishment 1968-71, supt Optics and Surveillance System RARDE 1971-76, head Applied Physics Gp 1976-83; dep dir (systems) and chief scientific offr RARDE 1983-86, conslt scientist MOD Whitehall 1987-; memb Orpington Sports Club, vice pres Old Edwardians Assoc 1990; FInstP; *Recreations* opera, photography, under gardening; *Style*— Geoffrey Cockett, Esq; RARDE, Fort Halstead, Sevenoaks, Kent TN14 7BP

COCKING, Dr (John) Brian; s of Gilbert Cocking (d 1967), of Morecambe, and Doris, *née* Bell (d 1979); *b* 24 Sept 1936; *Educ* Royal GS Lancaster, Emmanuel Coll Cambridge (MA, MB BChir), Middx Hosp Med Sch London; *m* 17 Feb 1962, Rosemary Elisabeth, da of Stanley Richard Burnett, of Thanet; 2 s (Alexander John b 27 July 1971, Edward Michael b 16 March 1975), 1 da (Fiona Elisabeth b 15 Jan 1964); *Career* house physician Middx Hosp London 1961-62, house surgn Royal Sussex Co Hosp Brighton 1962, house physician Central Middx Hosp London 1962-63, sr house physician United Sheffield Hosps 1964, med registrar and sr med registrar United Sheffield Hosps and Northern Gen Hosp Sheffield 1964-73, conslt physician and gastroenterologist Thanet Dist Gen Hosp Margate 1973-, author of numerous published articles on gastrointestinal topics; chm SE Thames Regnl Med Advsy Ctee, conslt memb Canterbury and Thanet DHA Dist Med Advsy Gp; FRCP; *Recreations* sailing, hillwalking, squash; *Clubs* Leander (Henley on Thames), Minnis Bay Sailing, Thanet Squash Rackets; *Style*— Dr Brian Cocking; Foreland View, 68 Fitzroy Ave, Kingsgate, Broadstairs, Kent CT10 3LT (☎ 0843 68400); Thanet District General Hospital, St Peter's Rd, Margate, Kent CT9 4AN (☎ 0843 225544)

COCKS, Dr Leonard Robert Morrison (Robin); TD (1979); s of Ralph Morrison Cocks (d 1970), and Lucille Mary, *née* Blackler; *b* 17 June 1938; *Educ* Felsted, Hertford Coll Oxford (BA, MA, DPhil, DSc); *m* 31 Aug 1962, Elaine Margaret, da of Canon J B Sturdy; 1 s (Mark b 1964), 2 da (Zoe b 1967, Julia b 1970); *Career* 2 Lt RA 1957-59, active serv Malaya; scientist Nat History Museum 1965, keeper of palaeontology, cmmr Int Cmmn on Zoological Nomenclature 1980-; sec Geological Soc 1985-89, pres Palaeontological Assoc 1986-88; FGS; *Books* The Evolving Earth (1981), contrib to over 80 articles in sci jls on geology and palaeontology; *Style*— Dr Robin Cocks, TD; 12 Winchester Park, Bromley BR2 OPY; Natural History Museum, Cromwell Rd, London SW7 5BD (☎ 071 938 8845)

COHEN, Christopher David Arthur; s of His Hon Judge Nathaniel Arthur Jim Cohen, *qv* of Crockham Hill, Edenbridge, Kent, and Judith Alexandra Grace Luard (d 1974); *b* 23 June 1928; *Educ* Rugby; *m* 18 Sept 1954, Judith Mary Pyne; 2 s (Peter b 1961, Michael b 1961), 1 da (Virginia b 1959); *Career* Nat Serv 1946-48; articled clerk 1948, admitted slr 1954; ptnr Holman Fenwick and Willan 1961-89, slr Staff Pension Fund; memb Law Soc; Freeman City of London, Liveryman Worshipful Co of Slrs; *Style*— Christopher Cohen, Esq; The Farmhouse, Winkhurst Green, Ide Hill, Kent (☎ 073 275 257)

COHEN, His Hon Judge Nathaniel Arthur (Jim); JP (Surrey 1958); 2 s of Sir Benjamin Arthur Cohen, KC (d 1942), and Margaret Abigail, *née* Cohen; *b* 19 Jan 1898; *Educ* Rugby, CCC Oxford; *m* 1, 1927 (m dis), Judith Alexandra Grace, da of Capt Sandford William Luard; 2 s (Christopher, *qv*, Jeremy); m 2, 1936, Joyce, da of Harvey Collingridge, of Woking, Surrey; *Career* called to the Bar 1923, circuit judge 1955-70; *Style*— His Hon Judge Cohen, JP; Bay Tree Cottage, Crockham Hill, Edenbridge, Kent

COHEN, Prof Robert Donald; *b* 11 Oct 1933; *Educ* Clifton, Trinity Coll Cambridge (MA, MD); *m* 14 Feb 1961, Barbara Joan, *née* Boucher; 1 s (Martin b 1966), 1 da (Susan b 1963); *Career* The London Hosp Med Coll Univ of London: prof of metabolic med 1974-82, prof of med 1982-; chm: DHSS Computer R & D Ctee 1976-80, Special Advsy Ctee in Gen Internal Med 1985-90, Jt Ctee on Higher Med Trg 1985-90; memb: GMC 1988-, Cncl Imperial Cancer Res Fund 1989-; FRCP 1971; *Books* Clinical and Biochemical Aspects of Lactic Acidosis (with H F Woods, 1976); *Recreations* water colour painting, sailing; *Style*— Prof Robert Cohen; Medical Unit, The Royal London Hospital, Whitechapel Rd, London E1 1BB (☎ 071 377 77110, fax 071 377 7677)

COHN-SHERBOK, Rabbi Dr Dan; s of Dr Bernard Cohn-Sherbok, of Denver, Colorado, USA, and Ruth, *née* Goldstein; *b* 1 Feb 1945; *Educ* Williams Coll (BA), Hebrew Union Coll (BHL, MA), Univ of Cambridge (MLitt, PhD); *m* 18 Dec 1976, Lavinia Charlotte, *qv* da of Graham Douglas Heath (d 1969); *Career* rabbi in US Aust Eng and SA 1971-74, lectr in theology Univ of Kent 1975-; gen ed Studies in Jewish Theology (Edwin Mellen Press); memb: Editorial Bd Modern Theology and Religion Today, Exec Ctee Soc of Old Testament Study; dir Centre for Study of Religion and Soc Univ of Kent, reg broadcaster with Radio Kent; *Books* The Jews of Canterbury (1985), Exploring Reality (ed, 1986), On Earth as It Is in Heaven: Jews, Christians and Liberation Theology (1987), The Jewish Heritage (1989), Holocaust Theology (1990), Jewish Petitionary Prayer: A Theological Exploration (1990), The Canterbury Papers; Religion and Modern Society (ed, 1990), The Salman Rushdie Affair in Inter-Religious Perspective (ed, 1990), Issues in Contemporary Judaism (1990), Tradition and Unity: Sermons Published in Honour of Robert Runcie (ed, 1990), Rabbinic Perspectives on the New Testament (1990); *Recreations* keeping cats, conversation; *Clubs* Athenaeum; *Style*— Rabbi Dr Dan Cohn-Sherbok; Rutherford College, University of Kent, Canterbury, Kent (☎ 0227 764000)

COHN-SHERBOK, Lavinia Charlotte; da of Graham Douglas Heath (d 1969), and Margery Joan, *née* Small; *b* 7 April 1952; *Educ* Benenden Sch, Girton Coll Cambridge (MA), Homerton Coll Cambridge (PGCE), Univ of Kent at Canterbury (MA); *m* 18 Dec 1976, Dan Cohn-Sherbok, *qv*, s of Bernard Sherbok, of Denver, Colorado, USA; *Career* head of religious studies: South Hampstead HS 1974-76, Highsted Sch Sittingbourne 1976-78; head of gen studies and girls' tutor King's Sch Canterbury 1980-87, princ West Heath Sch Sevenoaks 1988-; memb: Ctee The Canterbury Soc, St Mary's Kippington PCC; govr: Ashford Sch, Northbourne Park Sch; FRSA; *Recreations* keeping cats, taking Open University courses; *Clubs* Lansdowne, The English Speaking Union; *Style*— Mrs Lavinia Cohn-Sherbok; West Heath School, Sevenoaks, Kent TN13 1SR (☎ 0732 452541)

COLCHESTER, Dr Alan Charles Francis; s of John Sparrow Colchester (d 1981), of E Chiltington, Sussex, and Norah Diana Taylor, *née* Pengelley; *b* 4 Oct 1947; *Educ* Haileybury, BNC Oxford (BA), UCH London (BM, BCh), Univ of London (PhD, MRCP); *m* 17 Aug 1974, Nicola Jane, da of Edward Rocksborough Smith (d 1989), of Briantspuddle, Dorset; 1 s (Rupert b 1984), 2 da (Nancy b 1979, Emily b 1981); *Career* res med offr RAF Inst of Aviation Med Farnborough 1978-81, registrar in neurology The London Hosp 1982-83, sr registrar in neurology Atkinson Morley's and St George's Hosps London 1983-87, conslt neurologist SE Kent and Maidstone 1987-, sr lectr in neurology Guy's Hosp London 1987-, res into cerebal circulation, computer vision and med image analysis; *Recreations* music, natural history, inventing; *Style*— Dr Alan Colchester; The Old Rectory, Stowting, nr Ashford, Kent TN25 6BE (☎ 0303 862474); Guy's Hosp, St Thomas's St, London SE1 9RT (☎ 071 955 4162, fax 071 955 4532)

COLDWELL, John Walter; s of Bernard Victor Coldwell (d 1980), and Patricia Victoria, *née* French; *b* 10 April 1950; *Educ* Sir Joseph Williamson's Mathematical Sch Rochester, Sittingbourne Coll of Educn (CertEd); *m* 19 April 1982, Rosemary Margaret, da of Ronald John (d 1978); 2 s (Marius Andreas Ronald b 1978, Gabriel Bernard b 1983); *Career* writer; co-ordinator Salford Poem Swop Scheme, writer in schs W H Smith; *Books* Hoo Me Sir? (1988), More Lasting Than A Fish Supper (1988), The Motorway to Nowhere (1988), Daleks on Ramsay Street (1988), Beast in the Bedroom (1989) The Bees Knees (1990); *Recreations* reading, wildlife, gardening, foreign travel; *Style*— John Coldwell, Esq

COLE, Graham; *b* 26 Aug 1946; *Educ* Univ of Exeter (BA); *Career* CA; ptnr corp fin Deloitte Haskins & Sells; Freeman City of London; FCA, assoc memb BR Assoc Hotel Accountants; *Recreations* shooting, collecting antiquarian maps; *Clubs* Les Ambassadeurs; *Style*— Graham Cole, Esq; Deloitte Haskins & Sells, Hillgate House, 26 Old Bailey, London EC4M 7PL (☎ 071 248 3913, fax 071 236 2367, telex 8955899

COLE, Graham John; s of Maurice Richard Cole, of Gravesend, and Molly Iolene, *née* Jury; *b* 20 March 1953; *Educ* Gravesend Sch for Boys, Univ of East Anglia (BA); *m* 20 Feb 1982, Renita Janine, da of Arthur Stanger (d 1975); *Career* dep ed Kent Evening Post 1981-82, managing ed Gulf Mirror Bahrain 1983-84, dep ed Kent Messenger 1985-89, ed Kent Evening Post 1990-; memb Guild of Br Newspaper Eds; *Recreations* cricket, television and reading memoranda; *Clubs* Kent CCC; *Style*— Graham Cole, Esq; Kent Evening Post, Messenger House, Larkfield, Maidstone, Kent ME20 6SE (☎ 0622 717880)

COLE, Robert Henry; s of Henry George (d 1960), and Anne Elizabeth, *née* Simmonds; *b* 5 May 1934; *Educ* Wilson's London, Ruskin Coll Oxford; *m* 26 April 1958, Pamela Jean, da of Stanley Arthur Figg (d 1960), of London; *Career* gp trg offr Kelihers London 1967-72 (corrector of the press 1955-66), servs mangr British Printing and Communication Corporation 1973-86, press servs mangr Maxwell Communication Corporation plc 1987-; memb Governing Cncl Printers Charitable Corpn; Freeman City of London 1957, life memb Guild of Freemen of the City of London 1957; Liveryman: Worshipful Co of Stationers 1971, Worshipful Co of Makers of Playing Cards 1979; MBIM 1969, MITD 1969, FRSA 1970, MIOP 1971, MIIM 1979; *Recreations* walking, reading; *Style*— Robert H Cole, Esq; 11 Sheridan Crescent, Chislehurst, Kent BR7 5RZ (☎ 081 467 9939); Maxwell Communication Corporation plc, Holborn Circus, London EC1P 1DQ, (☎ 071 377 4731, fax 071 353 0360, telex 888804)

COLE, William Charles; s of Albert William Cole (d 1989), of West Wickham, Kent, and Rosina, *née* Garratt; *b* 13 Jan 1946; *Educ* St Joseph's Coll; *m* 9 Sept 1972, Sally Freda, da of Frederick James Still (d 1988), of Croydon, Surrey; 2 da (Emma b 6 Dec 1974, Hannah b 27 Dec 1977); *Career* CA 1970-73, stockjobber Stocken and Lazarus 1983-87, merged with Akroyd and Smithers PLC 1977 and Warburg Securities 1987, fin and admin dir Oliff & Ptnrs PLC 1987-; memb: The Stock Exchange 1981, TSA 1988; FCA 1970; *Recreations* golf, tennis, swimming; *Clubs* RAC, Cherry Lodge Golf; *Style*— William Cole, Esq; The White House, 15 Park Ave, Farnborough Park, Orpington, Kent BR6 8LJ (☎ 0689 51833); Oliff & Ptnrs PLC, Saddlers House, Gutter Lane, Cheapside, London EC2 6BR (☎ 071 374 0191, telex 919325, fax 071 374 2063, car 0860 211876)

COLGRAIN, 3 Baron (UK 1946); David Colin Campbell; s of 2 Baron Colgrain, MC (d 1973), and Margaret Emily (Madge), *née* Carver (d 1989); *b* 24 April 1920; *Educ* Eton, Trinity Coll Cambridge; *m* 1, 20 June 1945 (m dis 1964), Veronica Margaret, da of late Lt-Col William Leckie Webster, RAMC; 1 s, 1 da; m 2, 1973, Mrs Sheila McLeod Hudson; *Heir* s, Hon Alastair Campbell; *Career* served WWII, Lt 9 Lancers, UK and ME (wounded Alamein 1942); exec Grindlays Bank: India and Pakistan 1945-48, London 1949; Antony Gibbs & Sons Ltd and successive cos 1949-83 (dir 1954-83, ret 1983); chm Alexander & Berendt Ltd 1967-; *Recreations* music, farming, forestry; *Clubs* Cavalry and Guards'; *Style*— The Rt Hon the Lord Colgrain; Bushes Farm, Weald, Sevenoaks, Kent (☎ 0732 463279)

COLLACOTT, Peter Barrie; s of Dr Ralph Albert Collacott, of 1 Fordview Close, Great Glen, Leicester, and Ruby Hilda, *née* Nash; *b* 19 June 1944; *Educ* King's Sch Rochester; *m* 4 Sept 1971, Frances Rosamond, da of Lt Cdr Edward Clarence Hibbard, of 585 Maidstone Rd, Blue Bell Hill, Rochester, Kent; 2 s (Nicholas Peter b 1973, Piers Dominic b 1978), 2 da (Esther Rosamond b 1976, Hannah Kate b 1985); *Career* CA; articled clerk Jackson Pixley 1963-68, sr auditor Price Waterhouse 1968-71; accountant: Keyser Ullmann Ltd 1971-75, NM Rothschild & Sons Ltd 1976-79, Miny of Overseas Devpt (and sec) 1977-79; auditor gen Govt of Tonga 1979-80, fin dir NM Rothschild Asset Mgmnt Ltd 1985- (fin controller 1980-85); dir: NM Rothschild Fund Management Ltd, NM Rothschild Asset Management (CI) Ltd (non exec); FICA 1968; *Recreations* cricket, squash, tennis; *Style*— Peter Collacott, Esq; Chart Cottage, Seal Chart, Sevenoaks, Kent; Five Arrows House, St Swithins Lane, London EC4N 8NR (☎ 071 280 5000, fax 071 929 1643, telex 888031)

COLLETT-WHITE, Rev Thomas Charles; s of Brig Harold Edwin Collett-White, DSO, RA, of The Mill House, Great Henny, nr Sudbury, Suffolk, and Patience Winifred Collett-White, JP; *b* 13 Aug 1936; *Educ* Wellington, Trinity Coll Cambridge (MA); *m* 31 July 1965, Jennifer Anne, da of Rev Frederick Arthur Gadd, of Hampton, New Brunswick, Canada; 1 s (Michael b 21 March 1968), 2 da (Nicola b 20 June 1966, Charlotte b 1 May 1973); *Career* Nat Serv 2 Lt RA 1954-56; asst curate: St Marks Gillingham Kent 1962-66, All Saints Normanton Yorks 1966-69; vicar: St Augustines Highbury London 1969-76, St Marks Gillingham 1979-; rector St Johns Huntingdon Quebec Canada 1976-79; chaplain: Medway Hosp 1979-85, Gillingham Branch Br Legion; involved with churches in Poland; *Recreations* skiing, poetry, tennis; *Style*— The Rev Thomas Collett-White; St Marks Vicarage, Canterbury St, Gillingham, Kent

COLLEY, Graham David; s of Raymond Nigel Colley (d 1972), and Margaret Siriol, *née* Lewis; *b* 19 June 1953; *Educ* Nottingham HS, UCW Aberystwyth (LLB), Coll of Europe Bruges Belgium (Cert De Hautes Etudes Europeennes), Coll of Law Chester; *m* 3 June 1978, Rose Edith, *qv*, da of James Milham, of Brighton; 1 da (Eleanor Anne Claire b 17 Jan 1986); *Career* ptnr Graham and Rose Colley Solicitors Kennington London and Chatham Kent; memb Lib Democrats, parly candidate Lib Alliance Mid-Kent 1987-, currently co cncllr for Medway S (Weedswood and Horsted); *Recreations* family; *Clubs* National Liberal Club; *Style*— Graham Colley, Esq; 284 High St, Chatham, Kent ME4 4BP (☎ 0634 812234, fax 0634 849690, page 081 884 3344 - A7605)

COLLEY, Rose Edith; da of James Milham, of Brighton, W Sussex, and Violet, *née* Harris; *b* 4 March 1954; *Educ* Ellington Secdy Sch for Girls Ramsgate, Clarendon House GS Ramsgate, UCW Aberystwyth (BSc), Garnet Coll London (CertEd); *m* 3 June 1978, Graham David Colley, *qv*, s of Dr Nigel Colley (d 1973), of Nottingham; 1 da (Eleanor Anne Claire b 17 Jan 1986); *Career* slr; ptnr Graham & Rose Colley Solicitors London; memb: London Borough of Southwark 1984-, ILEA 1988-90; *Recreations* politics, reading, classical music; *Style*— Ms Rose Colley; 3 Hayles St, London SE11 4SU (☎ 071 735 2466); 13 Maidstone Rd, Lenham, Kent; Graham & Rose Colley Solicitors, 284 High St, Chatham, Kent ME4 4BP (☎ 0634 812234, fax 0634 849690)

COLLIER, Kenneth John; s of William Thomas Collier (d 1977), of Blackwood, Kent, and Phyllis Collier, *née* Jones; *b* 5 May 1932; *Educ* The Lewis Sch Pengham Glam, UCW Swansea (BA, Dip Ed); *m* 4 Sept 1954, Margaret Joy, da of William Oswald William (d 1968), of Gwent; 2 s (Simon William b 1963, William James Cledan 1971), 1 da (Jane Elizabeth b 1963); *Career* RAF 1953-55; teacher: Herne Bay Secdy Sch 1953-60, Sir William Nottage Sch Whitstable 1960-62, College du Leman Geneva Switzerland 1962-63, Herne Bay Secdy Sch 1963-66; dep head Walmer Secdy Sch 1966-71, teacher ODA Kagumo Teacher Trg Coll Kenya 1971-74, head Castlemount HS 1974; *Recreations* drama, music, bridge, fly fishing, snooker; *Style*— Kenneth Collier, Esq; King's Court, Kingsdown Park, Tankerton, Whitstable, Kent CT5 2DF; Castlemount High School, Laureston Place, Dover, Kent CT16 1QT (☎ 0304 206572)

COLLIER, Paulette Marianne; da of John Collier, of Westbrook, nr Margate, and Elizabeth, *née* Knowles; *b* 17 Oct 1960; *Educ* Ursuline Convent Westgate On Sea, Medway Coll of Design, Humberside Coll of Higher Educn (BA); *Career* printmaker exhibiting as Paulette; works exhibited in selected gp shows incl: Spirit of London (Royal Festival Hall) 1985, Print '86 (Barbican) 1986, Miniature Print Biennial (Silvermine Guild Galleries Connecticut and John Szoke Gallery New York) 1987, Fourth Annual Int Exhibition of Miniature Art (Del Bello Gallery Toronto Canada) 1989, Entively Intaglio (Royal Festival Hall) 1989, 10th Mini Print Int (Taller Galeria Fort Cadaques) 1990; asst coordinator Etching Workshop Kew Studio 1984-, printmaking lectr Brixton Coll 1988-, p/t printmaking and illustration lectr Stourbridge Coll of Art and Technol 1988-; *Recreations* contemporary dance, swimming, softball; *Style*— Ms Paulette Collier; c/o Kew Studio, 270 Sandycombe Rd, Kew (☎ 071 582 8071)

COLLIER, Shirley Diane; da of William Faux, of Bexley, Kent, and Dora Esther, *née* Marks (d 1974); *b* 28 Oct 1936; *Educ* James Allen's Girls Sch E Dulwich, Pitmarns' Coll, City Univ (CPE); *m* 14 June 1958, Raymond George Collier, s of George Albert Collier (d 1965), of Margate, Kent; 1 s (Peter Jeremy b 1 Jan 1964), 1 da (Jeanette Elizabeth b 25 April 1959); *Career* court asst Bromley Magistrates' Court 1974, sr court clerk Croyden Magistrates' Court 1979; called to the Bar Middle Temple 1984, legal asst Slrs Dep Met Police 1985; Crown Prosecution Serv: crown prosecutor 1986, sr crown prosecutor 1988-; *Recreations* gardening, tennis, dog breeding (labrador); *Clubs* Crelsfield Park Lawn Tennis; *Style*— Mrs Shirley Collier; 6 Beech Rd, World's End Lane, Chelsfield, Orpington, Kent BR6 6BD (☎ 0689 57952); CPS, 6 Floor Marlowe House, 109 Station Rd, Sidcup, Kent (☎ 081 302 7824)

COLLINS, Alan John Charles; s of Charles Albert Collins (d 1987), of Rayleigh, Essex, and Lilian Maud, *née* Williamson (d 1960); *b* 23 Nov 1942; *Educ* Royal Liberty Sch, Essex; *m* 7 March 1970, Cleusa, da of Pedro Luiz Calgaro (d 1984), of Sao Paulo, Brazil; 1 s (Robert b 1972), 1 da (Lisa b 1976); *Career* elected memb Lloyds 1976, chm and chief exec PSM Holdings Ltd 1986-, chm and chief exec PS Mosse and Ptnrs Ltd (Lloyd's Brokers) 1988- (dir 1971, md 1979); *Recreations* tennis, skiing; *Clubs* Connaught, Slim Jim's; *Style*— Alan Collins, Esq; 69 Downs Hill, Beckenham, Kent BR3 2HD (☎ 081 6589868)

COLLINS, Richard Edward Charles; s of Sqdn Ldr Edward C G Collins, of Westgate, Kent, and Jessie, *née* Charles; *b* 9 Jan 1943; *Educ* Chigwell Sch, St George's Hosp Med Sch Univ of London (MB BS); *m* 23 Oct 1971, Valerie Margaret, da of Joseph Celba (d 1968); 3 da (Emma Elizabeth b 1977, Katherine Jane b 1978, Louise Alexandra b 1981); *Career* res fell Harvard Med Sch 1974-75, conslt surgn Kent and Canterbury Hosp 1976-, regnl advsr SE Thames for RCS 1989, chm Med Advsy Ctee Chaucer Hosp 1985-; numerous conribs to med lit; hon med offr Kent CCC; FRCS, FACS; *Style*— Richard Collins, Esq; Seatonden, Ickham, Canterbury, Kent CT3 1SL (☎ 0227 721033); Kent and Canterbury Hospital, Ethelbert Rd, Canterbury, Kent CT1 3NG; Chaucer Hospital, Canterbury, Kent (☎ 0227 766877, 0227 455466)

COLLINS, Vere; s of L G A Collins (d 1947), of Ingles, Folkestone, and Ruth, *née* Seymour (d 1959); *b* 20 Jan 1917; *Educ* Eton, Jesus Coll Cambridge; *m* 5 June 1952, Marian Dorothy, da of Brig R W Andrews, DSO, MC (d 1976), of St Johns Cottage, Winterslow, Salisbury; 1 s (Jonathan Ferdinando b 12 April 1955), 1 da (Julia b June 1952); *Career* served Capt The Buffs Regt 1939-45; md JH & J Wine Merchants, dir Corney & Barrow Wine Merchants; former cmmr Inland Revenue and memb Kent Valuation Panel; memb Kent 2 XI 1938, pres Kent CCC 1980-81; tstee and past pres Huggens Coll Northfleet; memb: MCC I Zingari, Free Foresters Band of Brothers; Liveryman Worshipful Co of Vintners; *Recreations* shooting; *Clubs* Army and Navy; *Style*— Vere Collins, Esq

COLTHURST, Sir Richard La Touche; 9 Bt (I 1744), of Ardrum, Inniscarra, Co Cork; s of Sir Richard St John Jefferyes Colthurst, 8 Bt (d 1955), and Denis Maida Hanmer, *née* West (d 1965); *b* 14 Aug 1928; *Educ* Harrow, Peterhouse Cambridge; *m* 24 Oct 1953, Janet Georgina, da of Leonard Almroth Wilson-Wright (d 1971), of Coolcarrigan, Co Kildare; 3 s (Charles b 1955, James b 1957, Henry b 1959), 1 da (Georgina b 1961); *Heir* s, Charles St John Colthurst; *Career* underwriting memb of Lloyd's; Freeman City of London, Liveryman Worshipful Co of Grocers; *Recreations* cricket, gardening, forestry; *Clubs* City University, MCC; *Style*— Sir Richard La T Colthurst, Bt

COLVILLE, Hon (Charles) Anthony; 2 s of 3 Viscount Colville of Culross (ka 1945), of Kinneff, Kincardineshire, Scotland, and Kathleen Myrtle Colville, OBE, *née* Gale (d 1986); *b* 5 Aug 1935; *Educ* Rugby, Magdalen Coll Oxford (BA); *m* 2 Oct 1965, Katherine, da of Humphrey John Sankey (d 1945), of Kinangop, Kenya; 2 s (Robert Quintin Oxnam b 1971, Charles Alexander b 1974); *Career* Sub Lt RNVR; HM Overseas Civil Serv Kenya 1958-64; articled Clifford-Turner and Co 1966-69, admitted slr 1969, ptnr The Buss Murton Partnership 1972-; memb Slrs Benevolent Assoc, chm Tunbridge Wells Branch Br Diabetic Assoc; memb Law Soc; *Recreations* history, music; *Style*— The Hon C A Colville; Rydes, Nevill Court, Tunbridge Wells, Kent TN4 8NL (☎ 0892 542514); The Buss Murton Partnership, The Priory, Tunbridge Wells, Kent TN1 1JJ (☎ 0892 510222, fax 0892 510333)

COLVIN, Dr Brian Trevor; s of Clifford James Leslie Colvin (d 1990), of Sevenoaks, and Ivy Emmeline, *née* Goodchild; *b* 17 Jan 1946; *Educ* Sevenoaks Sch, Clare Coll Cambridge (BA, BChir, MA, MB), London Hosp Med Coll; *m* 21 Aug 1971, Kathryn Frances, da of Ernest Osborne (d 1966); *Career* sr lectr haematology and conslt haematologist: Royal London Hosp and Med Coll 1977-, St Peter's Hosp Gp and Inst of Urology 1977-86; med post grad sub dean London Hosp Med Coll 1987- (sr clinical tutor 1985-87), conslt advsr Acute Unit Royal London Hosp 1988-; memb Standing Ctee of Membs RCP 1973-77, chm NE Thames Regnl Assoc of Haematologists 1981-84, memb Med Advsy Gp Haemophilia Soc 1982-, ctee memb Br Soc for Haematology 1983-86, examiner RCPath 1984-, sec Haemostasis and Thrombosis Sub Ctee 1986-, cncl memb Pathology Section of RSM 1989-; memb BMA, FRCPath 1988 (MRCPath 1976), FRCP 1990 (MRCP 1972), FRSM 1989; various papers, articles and contribns to books incl Haematology Pocket Consultant (with A C Newland, 1988); *Recreations* foreign travel, opera, cricket; *Clubs* Marylebone CC; *Style*— Dr Brian Colvin; Department of Haematology, Royal London Hospital, Whitechapel Rd, London E1 1BB (☎ 071 377 7455)

COMPIGNE-ROGERS, Robin Christopher; s of Maj Leslie Robert Sidney Rogers, CPM (mangr rubber plantation in Malaya 1927-64), and Patricia Dorothy Madeleine, *née* Compigné-Stone; *b* 12 March 1941; *Educ* Taunton Sch Somerset, Royal Tunbridge Wells Coll of Art; *m* 1, 18 March 1967 (m dis); 1 s (Julian Simon Compigné b 1969), 1 da (Samantha Compigné b 1968); m 2, Sara Phillips, *née* Dawson-Walker; 1 da (Katherine Sheila Compigné b 1981); *Career* trainee rubber planter 1960-61, mgmnt trainee P & O Lines London 1961-1962, mercantile asst Mackinnon Mackenzie Hong Kong and Singapore 1962-1969, dep shipping mangr P & O Agents Durban SA 1969-1970, admin mangr SA and Namibia Western Bank Johannesburg 1970-1971, special projects mangr Freemans Mail Order Co 1971-1973, md Robinstudio 1979-1983; heraldic artist and calligrapher 1979-; fndr memb Most Honourable Company of Armigers 1987 (armorist and Kent representative 1987, registrar 1988); fell Huguenot Soc of GB and Ireland; memb: Heraldry Soc, Royal Tunbridge Wells C of C; *Recreations* music, oil painting, family history and genealogy, rugby fanatic; *Style*— Robin Compigné-Rogers, Esq; 17 Westwell Ct, Tenterden, Kent TN30 6TS (☎ 05806 2203)

CONNELL, Edward Arthur; s of Edward Connell (d 1950), of London, and Mary Ann, *née* Gadsby; *b* 26 Oct 1919; *Educ* Camberwell Sch of Arts and Crafts, London Coll of Printing; *m* 21 Aug 1949, May, da of Percy Godfrey Sims (d 1952), of London; 1 da (Janet May (Mrs Blackledge) b 1956); *Career* RAC 1940, W/Cpl 1944, demob 1946, discharged from Army Res on med grounds 1952; lectr Camberwell Sch of Arts and Crafts 1946-60; Colour Printing Co: mangr 1948-53, dir 1953-70, md 1970-75, chm 1975-84, ret; memb: Beckenham Cons Assoc, Bromley Art Soc, RSPB; City & Guilds of London Silver Medal 1946; Freeman: City of London 1967, Worshipful Co of Feltmakers 1975; memb Inst of Printing 1950-85; *Recreations* oil painting, gardening, motoring; *Clubs* United Wards, Guild of Freemen; *Style*— Edward Connell, Esq; 41 Kenwood Drive, Beckenham, Kent BR3 2QY (☎ 01 650 9324)

CONYBEARE, Martin Edward; s of Ernest Thomas Conybeare, CBE (d 1979), and Marjorie Deacon, *née* Blaikley; *b* 9 March 1940; *Educ* Tonbridge Sch, Guy's Hosp Med Sch (MB BS); *m* 24 July 1965, Virginia Catherine, da of James Conwy Morgan, CMG; 1 s (Edmund b 1972), 2 da (Catherine b 1966, Lucia b 1969); *Career* conslt orthopaedic surgn Canterbury and Thanet Health Authy 1979; former chm Canterbury and Thanet Dist Med Advsy Ctee, sec and cncl memb Orthopaedic Section RSM; FRCS; *Recreations* music, hill walking, rough gardening; *Style*— Martin Conybeare, Esq; 74 London Rd, Canterbury, Kent CT2 8LS (☎ 0227 454097); Kent and Canterbury Hosp, Ethelbert Rd, Canterbury, Kent

CONYNGHAM, 7 Marquess (I 1816); Frederick William Henry Francis Conyngham; also (sits as) Baron Minster (UK 1821), Earl Conyngham (I

1781), Baron Conyngham (I 1781), Viscount Conyngham (I 1789), Viscount Mount Charles (I 1797), Earl of Mount Charles and Viscount Slane (I 1816); patron of one living; s of 6 Marquess Conyngham (d 1974), by 2 w Antoinette Winifred, *née* Thompson (d 1966); *b* 13 March 1924; *Educ* Eton; *m* 1, 29 April 1950 (m dis 1970), Eileen Wren, o da of Capt Clement Wren Newsam; 3 s; m 2, 1971, Elizabeth Ann, yr da of late Frederick Molyneux Hughes, of Fareham, Hants, and formerly w of David Sutherland Rudd; m 3, 1980, Daphne Georgina Adelaide (d 24 Nov 1986), eld da of R C Armour, and formerly w of C P V Walker; m 4, 29 May 1987, (Emma Christianne) Annabelle, o da of (Denys) Martin Agnew, of Grosvener Court, Grove Road, East Cliffe, Bournemouth; *Heir* s, Earl of Mount Charles; *Career* late Capt Irish Gds; *Style*— The Most Hon The Marquess Conyngham; Bifrons, nr Canterbury, Kent; Myrtle Hill, Ramsey, Isle of Man

CONYNGHAM, Lord Frederick William Patrick; 3 s of 7th Marquess Conyngham, *qv*, by his 1 w, Eileen; *b* 23 March 1959; *Style*— The Lord Frederick Conyngham

COOK, Audrey Rosa; da of William Charles Cook, of Langton Green, and Jessie Kate Ellen, *née* Tacchi; *b* 9 Jan 1927; *Educ* Chatham GS, Tonbridge GS, Tunbridge Wells Sch of Art, Bretton Hall Yorkshire; *Career* still life oil painter; one man exhibitions at: Sevenoaks, Tonbridge, Tunbridge Wells, Oxted, Tewkesbury; paintings exhibited at: The David Curzon Gallery, The Bowmoore Gallery, The Hurlingham Gallery; memb: Mensa, St Mary's parish church Westerham; *Recreations* sculpture, ceramics; *Style*— Miss Audrey Cook; 4 Streatfeild House, Granville Rd, Westerham, Kent TN16 1RT (☎ 0959 62324)

COOK, Kenneth Anthony; s of Walter Cook (d 1953), and Marion Grace Berry, *née* Lovell (d 1988); *b* 11 March 1933; *Educ* Haberdashers Askes; *m* 5 July 1952, (Jeanne) Sylvia, da of Thomas Harris; 4 s (Martin b 1960, Ian b 1961, Simon b 1964, Brian b 1967); *Career* Pannell Kerr Forster 1954-63, ptnr Judkins CA's 1963-; FCA, FCIS, ATII, FBIM; *Recreations* swimming; *Clubs* Farmers, Castle (Rochester); *Style*— Kenneth Cook, Esq; Newnham Court, Detling, Maidstone, Kent ME14 3ER (☎ 0622 37948); 16 Star Hill, Rochester, Kent ME1 1UU (☎ 0634 830321, fax 0634 830969, telex 9401 6714 JUDKE, car tel 0836 213163)

COOKE, Rear Adm Anthony John; CB (1980); s of Rear Adm John Ernest Cooke, CB (d 1980), and Kathleen Mary, *née* Haward (d 1976); *b* 21 Sept 1927; *Educ* St Edward's Sch Oxford; *m* 1951, Margaret Anne, da of Frederick Charles Hynard; 2 s, 3 da; *Career* RN 1945, Cdre in Cmd Clyde Submarine Base 1973-75, Rear Adm 1976, sr naval memb directing staff RCDS 1975-78, Adm Pres RNC Greenwich 1978-80; Freeman City of London, Liveryman Shipwrights' Co; priv sec to Lord Mayor of London 1981-; *Recreations* philately; *Clubs* City Livery; *Style*— Rear Admiral Anthony Cooke, CB; Chalkhurst, Eynsford, Kent (☎ Farningham 862789)

COOKE, His Honour Judge; (Richard) Kenneth; OBE (1945); s of Richard Cooke, and Beatrice Mary; *b* 17 March 1917; *Educ* Sebright Sch Wolverley, Birmingham U; *m* 1945, Gwendoline Mary Black; *Career* slr 1939, practising 1945-52, clerk to Justices 1952-70, metropolitan stipendiary magistrate 1970, recorder of the Crown Court 1972-1980, circuit judge (SE) 1980-; memb Lord Chllr's Advsy Ctee on Trg of Magistrates 1979-; hon dep chm Magistrates Assoc 1981-82 (chm Legal Ctee 1980-); licensed reader Rochester Diocese 1970-; pres SW London Branch Magistrates Assoc 1984-; *Style*— His Honour Judge Cooke, OBE; 8 St Paul's Square, Church Rd, Bromley, Kent (☎ 01 464 6761)

COOKE, Raymond Edgar; OBE; s of late Edgar Jonathan Cooke; *b* 14 Feb 1925; *Educ* Univ of London; *m* 1948 (m dis 1968), Marjorie Evelyn; 1 s, 1 da; m 2, 1987, Jennifer, da of Léon J Goossens CBE (d 1988); *Career* former designs engr BBC; tech dir Wharfedale Wireless Works Ltd 1955-61; fndr and md KEF Electronics Ltd 1961-88 (now life pres); FRSA, FBKSTS, FAES; *Style*— Raymond Cooke Esq, OBE; Kingswood Lodge, Nevill Park, Tunbridge Wells, Kent (☎ 0892 31843; office: 0622 672261, fax 0662 50653, telex Kefel G 96140)

COOMBE, Donald Howard; JP (1973); *b* 21 Oct 1927; *Educ* Northbrook C of E Sch Lee, Roan Sch Greenwich, Univ of The World (MA); *m* 5 June 1948, Betty Joyce, da of George William Adie (d 1938); 2 s (Richard Howard b 25 April 1953, David b 8 Oct 1958); *Career* RN 1942-47, hon cmmn to adm Texas Navy 1976; chm: RTC Ltd Lloyds Brokers 1971-, Portcullis Insurance Services Ltd 1985-; memb Lloyds 1974; fndr chm: Coombe Tst Fund, Coombe Holiday Tst Fund; chm Victoria Wellesley Tst (all registered charities for Needy Children), dep pres Thanet Red Cross, former cmmr Scouts Assoc; hon attorney-gen N Carolina, chm of bench 1982, cmmr Income Tax 1978-85; Freeman: City of London 1970, City of Dallas Texas 1976; Liveryman Worshipful Co of Poulters 1978; Order of St George Sweden 1974; *Recreations* charity fundraising, social work, boxing; *Clubs* National Sporting, Wig & Pen; *Style*— Donald H Coombe, Esq, JP; Sunarise, Beckenham Place Park, Kent BR3 2BN (☎ 081 658 2714, fax 081 663 3932); 7 Lovat Lane, London EC3R 8DT (☎ 071 283 7367, fax 071 283 3593)

COOPER, Rt Hon Sir Frank; GCB (1979, KCB 1974, CB 1970), CMG (1961), PC (1983); s of late Valentine H Cooper, of 37 The Square, Fairfield, Manchester; *b* 2 Dec 1922; *Educ* Manchester GS, Pembroke Coll Oxford (hon fell 1976); *m* 1948, Peggie, da of F J Claxton; 2 s, 1 da; *Career* pilot RAF 1941-46; joined Civil Serv 1948, dep under sec of state MOD 1968-70, dep sec CSD 1970-73, perm under sec of state NI Office 1973-76, perm under sec of state MOD 1976-82, ret 1982; dir: Babcock 1983-89, Morgan Crucible 1983-, N M Rothschild and Sons 1983-; chm High Integrity Systems 1986-; memb Cncl King's Coll London 1983-89 (fell 1987); chm: Kings Coll Med and Dental Sch 1984-89, Imperial Coll 1988- (fell 1988); visitor Loughborough Univ 1988-; chm: Cranbrook Sch 1984 (govr 1982), Liddell Hart Tstees 1986-, Inst of Contemperary Br History 1986-; vice pres Army Records Soc 1989 (vice chm 1986-88), memb Advsy Cncl on Public Records 1989-; *Clubs* Athenaeum, Naval and Military, RAF; *Style*— The Rt Hon Sir Frank Cooper, GCB, CMG; Delafield, 34 Camden Park Rd, Chislehurst, Kent BR7 5HG

COOPER, Reginald David (Reg); s of Albert Reginald Cooper, of Oxford, and Florence Maria, *née* Titcomb; *b* 23 June 1934; *Educ* City of Oxford HS for Boys; *m* 2 April 1955, Audrey Elizabeth, da of Edward Henry Downs (d 1951), of Oxford; 1 s (Andrew David b 15 Jan 1958), 1 da (Annette Elizabeth b 7 Nov 1961); *Career* Nat Serv RAF fighter control 1953-55; nat parts mangr Volkswagen GB Ltd 1972-73, commercial dir Nexus International Holdings Ltd 1981-84, distribution and purchasing dir Micro Business Systems Terminals Ltd 1984-86, md Port Ramsgate Ltd 1986-; memb: Nat Tst, RSPB, RHS; *Recreations* golf, photography, music (listening only), gardening, visiting beauty spots/stately homes; *Clubs* Kingswood Golf, Epsom Sports, Royal Temple Yacht; *Style*— Reg Cooper, Esq; The Little House, 2a Ridgeway, Epsom, Surrey KT19 8LB (☎ 0372 742158); Port Ramsgate Ltd, Ramsgate, Kent CT11 8RP (☎ 0843 587661, fax 0843 589570)

COOPER, (Hulbert) Rodney; s of Hulbert Francis Cooper (d 1959), of Bromley, Kent, and Dorothy Amy Burtt (d 1966); *b* 11 April 1933; *Educ* Bromley GS, Univ of London (BSc), Ravensbourne Coll of Art & Design, Central Sch of Art, RNC Greenwich; *m* 7 Oct 1961, (Mary) Anne, da of Aubrey George Eames (d 1962), of Bromley, Kent; 1 s (Matthew b 1963), 1 da (Nancy b 1967); *Career* Lt RN 1957-60 served HMS Ocean; port educn offr Chatham; sci advsr Br Pavilion Brussels World Fair 1956, res chemist A Wander Ltd 1960-63, designer Sir Basil Spence and Ptnrs 1963-70; Bldg Design Ptnrship 1970-: assoc 1973-80, ptnr 1980-84, sr ptnr 1984- (responsible for interior, graphic and prod design); external examiner: Univ of Wales Architectural Sch, Middx Poly; lectr Ravensbourne Coll of Design; FCSD 1975; *Books* The Trade Report (1988), Specification (3 edn, 1989), contrib to architectural and design jls; *Recreations* cine photography, clarinet, tennis, driving fast cars, making people laugh; *Style*— Rodney Cooper, Esq; Building Design Partnership, PO Box 4WD, 16 Gresse St, London W1A 4WD (☎ 071 631 4733, fax 071 631 0393, telex 25322)

COPELAND, Sonia Constance Josephine (Mrs Harry Bloom); da of Dr F J Copeland, of Rustington, Sussex, and Betty Constance Josephine, *née* Walker; *b* 5 Nov 1941; *Educ* Godolphin Sch, Worthing Tech Coll, Univ of Madrid, Open Univ; *m* 24 March 1967, Harry Bloom (the novelist) (d 1981), s of late Jack Bloom; 1 s (Orlando Bloom b 13 Jan 1977), 1 da (Samantha Bloom b 16 Jan 1975); *Career* journalist Worthing Herald, asst ed Guidepost Madrid, Vogue, Central Office of Info, asst ed FO Pubns, fndr FUSS (magazine of Univ of Kent), fndr and dir Concorde Int Summer Schs (Canterbury) 1972, fndr and sole dir Champion Int (golf and english sports courses) 1987; memb: St Mary's Bredin Church, Canterbury Ladies Speakers Club, NUJ 1959-69; author of numerous articles; *Recreations* golf, music, reading, children; *Clubs* Chestfield Golf; *Style*— Ms Sonia Copeland; Virgilia House, 12 St Thomas' Hill, Canterbury, Kent; The Old Forge, 81 Old Dover Rd, Canterbury, Kent (☎ 0227 456292); Concorde Int, Hawkes Lane, Canterbury, Kent (☎ 0227 65537)

COPLEY, Antony Robert Hanchett; s of Alan H Copley, of Barnes House, 22 The Ave, Radlett, Herts, and Iris, *née* Pohlman; *b* 1 July 1937; *Educ* Gresham's, Worcester Coll Oxford (BA), St Antony's Coll Oxford (MA, MPhil); *Career* lectr Univ Coll of N Wales 1963-67; Univ of Kent 1967-: lectr then sr lectr then reader in modern history; visiting academic Jawaharlal Nehru Univ monsoon semester 1973, visiting fell Univ of Ibadan 1974-75, visiting lectr Nankai Univ 1988; res ed (UK) Indo-British Review: A Journal of History; former sr awarder Oxford Local Delegacy of Examinations; memb Exec Ctee Gandhi Fndn; friend: Canterbury Festival, Deal Music Festival, Stour Music Festival; FRHistS, FRAS; *Books* The Political Career of C Rajagopalachari 1937-54 (1978), Gandhi: Against The Tide (1987), Sexual Moralities in France 1780-1980 (1990); *Recreations* walking, broadly cultural, travel; *Style*— Antony Copley, Esq; Rutherford College, The University, Canterbury, Kent CT2 7NX (☎ 0227 764000 ext 3448)

CORLESS, James; s of Thomas Corless (d 1974), and Jessica, *née* Turner (d 1984); *b* 6 Oct 1942; *Educ* Ashton-under-Lyne Tech Sch, Heginbottom Sch of Art, Goldsmiths Coll London (NDD, DipAD); *m* 1, (m dis 1982) Carole Anne; 2s (Simeon Thomas b 1968, Vaughan Lee b 1971); m2, 26 Sept 1983, Kim Denise, da of Derek Brian Moule, of London; 2s (Dorian Victor Frederick b 1984, Christian James b 1988), 1da (Jessica Victoria Ann b 1985); *Career* sch teacher ILEA 1963-65, seconded to Whitechapel Gallery to organise educnl exhibitions; head of Art Dept: Abbeywood Sch 1970-71, Friern Sch For Girls 1971-74; cmmnd works incl: 13 sculptured bronze trophies for HM Royal Naval Submarine Fleet HMS Dolphin, large relief sculpture For Status Quo, text art work and tech advice For Know How Book of Paint & Print; opened Blackheath Gallery 1975; advsr and supplier of art works to: Bank of Credit & Commerce, Arthur Anderson, Tate & Lyle, Tunnel Refineries, Priest Marion Property, Lloyds Bank, Johnson & Higgins; chm Central Residents Assoc 1975-85, chm and Fndr Blackheath Village Traders Assoc 1984-88; *Recreations* opera, music, sport, gardening, reading, cooking; *Style*— James Corless, Esq; Blackheath Gallery, 34A Tranquil Vale, Blackheath, London SE3 OAX (☎ 081 852 1802, mobile 0831 439 456)

CORMACK, Lady Miranda Maxwell; *née* Fyfe; da of 1 and last Earl of Kilmuir, PC, GCVO (d 1967); *b* 13 Dec 1938; *m* 2 April 1960, Michael Ormiston Cormack, er s of late H M Cormack, of Bookham, Newton Valence, Hants; 2 s, 1 da; *Career* teacher; *Style*— The Lady Miranda Cormack; 31 White Hart Wood, Sevenoaks, Kent TN13 1RS (☎ 0732 457230)

CORNISH, Dr Derek Charles; s of Charles Richard Cornish (d 1932), of London, and Hilda Grace, *née* King (d 1986); *b* 30 Dec 1929; *Educ* Latymer's Sch Edmonton, Birkbeck Coll London (BSc, PhD); *m* 1, 18 Aug 1956, Kathleen Mary (d 1985), da of John Baden Thomas (d 1978), of Southfields; 2 s (Iain Charles Andrew b 1960, Richard John Edmund b 1962), 1 da (Sara Louise Clare b 1958); m 2, 21 Nov 1987, Susan Lougher Iredale, da of Arthur Austin Williams, of Bromyard, Herefordshire; *Career* Nat Serv LAC aircraft radar asst 1948-50; laboratory asst: Royal Mint Refinery (NM Rothschild and Co) 1950, Scribbans-Kemp (London) Ltd 1950-53; res asst Scribbans-Kemp (Research and Development) Ltd 1953-56; p/t lectr Goldsmith's Coll London and NW Kent Coll of Technol 1956-59; Br Scientific Instrument Res Assoc (later renamed Sira Ltd): sr scientist 1957-67, head of Materials Section 1967-68; Sira Inst: head of Materials and Processes Gp 1968-71, laboratory mangr Industl Instrumentation Div 1971-79, business mangr Industl Instrumentation Div 1979-81; Sira Ltd: exec dir 1980-, dir Technol Servs Div 1981-87, dep md 1987-; Sira Safety Services Ltd: non-exec dir 1981-, chm 1987-; co sec SIREP International Instrument Users' Assoc 1982-, non-exec dir Sira Certification Serv 1988-, non-exec chm Sira Communications Ltd 1989-, dir Growmead Ltd 1989-; memb: DTI Instrumentation Projects Ctee 1974-88, Norfolk and Norwich Archaeological Soc 1979-, Norfolk Record Soc 1979-, Physical Tech Sub Ctee Nat Measurement Accreditation Serv 1981-, BSI Ctee 1986-; Inst of Measurement and Control: memb 1977-80, fell 1980-, vice pres 1986-88, pres 1989; chm govrs Bullers Wood Sch for Girls Chislehurst 1980- (govr 1978-), sr memb Instrument Soc of America 1983-; Freeman City of London 1987, Liveryman Worshipful Co of Scientific Instrument Makers 1987; CChem, FRSC 1977; *Books* The Mechanism of Glass Polishing (1961), Sampling Systems for Process Analysers (jtly,1981); *Recreations* photography, philately, gardening, genealogy, travel, narrow boating; *Style*— Dr Derek Cornish; Sira Ltd, South Hill, Chislehurst, Kent BR7 5EH (☎ 081 467 2636, fax 081 467 6515)

CORNISH, Robert Charles; s of David Charles Cornish, of Harrow, Middlesex, and Eileen Mollie, *née* Weare; *b* 31 Dec 1962; *Educ* Stanmore Coll, Watford Sch of Art and Design, Canterbury Coll of Art and Design (BA), RCA (MA); *Career* contrib to art exhibitions 1984-89: Spring Show London, The Double Elephant Barbican Centre, Kent Art and Design Maidstone, The Symmondsbury Gallery Dorset, 150 years of Print making at RCA; winner The Stowells of Chelsea Trophy Royal Acad; fndr The First Edition Studios 1987-, intaglio printer and editioner of Artists Prints 1987-, sessional lectr in fine art various colls 1987-; memb Printmakers Cncl; *Recreations* fishing, walking, cycling, restoring old cars; *Style*— Robert Cornish, Esq; Stable Cottage, Shirley Hall, Leggs Lane, Langton Green, Tunbridge Wells, Kent TN3 0RQ (☎ 0892 863752); First Edition Studios, Shirley Hall, Leggs Lane, Langton Green, Kent TN3 0RQ (☎ 0892 863752)

CORNWALLIS, 3 Baron (UK 1927); Fiennes Neil Wykeham Cornwallis; OBE (1963), DL (Kent 1976); only s of 2 Baron Cornwallis, KBE, KCVO, MC, JP, DL (d 1982) by his 1 w, Cecily (d 1943), da of Sir James Heron Walker, 3 Bt; *b* 29 June 1921; *Educ* Eton; *m* 1, 17 Oct 1942 (m dis 1948), Judith, o da of Lt-Col Geoffrey Lacy Scott, TD; 1 s, 1 da (decd); m 2, 1 June 1951, Agnes Jean, yr da of Capt Henderson Russell Landale; 1 s, 3 da; *Heir* s (by 1 w), Hon Jeremy Cornwallis; *Career* serv WWII Lt Coldstream Gds (1941-44, then invalided); pres: Br Agric Contractors Assoc 1952-54, Nat Assoc Agric Contractors 1957-63 and 1986-; dir Planet Building Society 1968- (chm 1971-75); chm: Magnet and Planet Building Society 1975-77, Town and Country Building Society 1977-81 (dir 1975-), CBI Smaller Firms Cncl 1974-82 (chm 1979-82), Apples and Pears Ltd 1989-; memb Bd of Tstees Chevening Estate 1979-; rep of Horticultural Co-operatives in EEC 1975-86; vice pres Fedn of Agric Co-operatives 1984-86; chm: FAC Fruit Forum 1972-89, Kingdom Quality Assur Scheme 1986-89; Pro Frand Master (Freemasons) United Grand Lodge 1982- (prev Dep Grand Master); FIHort; *Recreations* fishing; *Clubs* Brooks's, Farmers', Pratt's; *Style*— The Rt Hon the Lord Cornwallis, OBE, DL; Ruck Farm, Horsmonden, Tonbridge, Kent TN12 8DT (☎ 089 272 2267); Dundurn House, St Fillans, Crieff, Perthshire (☎ 076 485 252); 25B Queens' Gate Mews, London SW7 5QL (☎ 071 589 1167)

COSEDGE, Andrew John; s of David Ernest Cosedge, of Bexleyheath, Kent, and Edna Amy Mary, *née* Cull; *b* 13 Jan 1949; *Educ* Christ's Hosp, Univ of Exeter (LLB); *m* 14 June 1986, Denise Hazel, da of Anthony Raymond Teasdale, of Sutton Coldfield; *Career* called to the Bar Inner Temple 1972; chm Old Blues RFC; *Recreations* rugby; *Clubs* Old Blues RFC; *Style*— Andrew Cosedge, Esq; 17 Sevenoaks Rd, Borough Green, Kent TN15 8AX (☎ 0732 884456); 3 Stone Buildings, Lincoln's Inn, London WC2A 3XL (☎ 071 242 4937, fax 071 405 3896)

COTTELL, Michael Norman Tizard; OBE (1988); s of Norman James Cottell (d 1973), of Southampton, and Eileen Claire Cottell; *b* 25 July 1931; *Educ* Peter Symonds Sch Winchester, Univ Coll Southampton, Univ of Birmingham; *m* 1 June 1957, Joan Florence, da of Edward Clarence Dolton (d 1973), of Winchester; 2 s (Paul, Robert); *Career* Nat Serv RE 1951-53, Suez Crisis 1956; highway engr 1948-67: Hampshire, Gloucestershire, Berkshire, Northamptonshire; asst to co surveyor Suffolk CC 1967-73, dep co surveyor E Sussex CC 1973-76; co surveyor: Northamptonshire 1976-84, Kent 1984-; fell of Engrg 1990; FICE 1958 (MICE), FIHT 1954, MBIM 1971; *Recreations* swimming, sailing, music, theatre; *Clubs* RAC; *Style*— Michael Cottell, Esq, OBE; Springfield, Maidstone, Kent ME14 2LQ (☎ 0622 671411)

COTTRELL, Bryce Arthur Murray; s of Brig Arthur Foulkes Baglietto Cottrell, DSO, OBE (d 1962), of Boughton Lees, Ashford, Kent, and Mary Barbara, *née* Nicoll (d 1986); *b* 16 Sept 1931; *Educ* Charterhouse, CCC Oxford (MA); *m* 1955, Jeane Dolores, da of R P Monk (d 1942), of Coventry; 2 s, 2 da; *Career* memb Stock Exchange 1958, chm Phillips and Drew Stockbrokers 1985-88 (ptnr 1963-85); funding dir CCC Oxford 1990-, govr St Leonards Mayfield Sch; CBIM; *Recreations* railways, spectator sports, paintings; *Clubs* City of London; *Style*— Bryce Cottrell, Esq; Boscobel House, Bourne Lane, Tonbridge, Kent TN9 1LG (☎ 0732 353 959)

COTTRELL, Henry Claude; s of Henry Cottrell (d 1953); *b* 13 June 1921; *Educ* Lawrence Sheriff Sch Rugby; *m* 1949, Audrey, da of Thomas Hannah (d 1936); 1 s; *Career* served WWII RAF; actuary; sr ptnr Phillips and Drew stockbrokers 1972-78; dir: AMEV Ltd, Caffyns plc; chm Watts Blake Bearne and Co plc; Liveryman: Worshipful Co of Glass Sellers (Master 1977-78), Worshipful Co of Actuaries (Master 1981-82); receiver gen Order of St John 1981-86, OStJ 1979, KStJ 1981; *Recreations* fly-fishing; *Clubs* City Livery; *Style*— Henry Cottrell, Esq; Whitecraigs, Parkfield, Sevenoaks, Kent TN15 0HX (☎ 0732 61228)

COUCH, John Albert; s of Albert John Couch (d 1982), of 1 Norfolk Rd, Romford, Essex, and Violet Emily, *née* Stebbings (d 1953); *b* 24 Sept 1933; *Educ* Thomas Calton Sch Dulwich; *m* 26 June 1954, Maureen Pamela, da of Frederick Lawrence Couling (d 1943), of 28 Kelvington Rd, London; 1 s (Nicholas John b 6 Feb 1961); *Career* Nat Serv RAF 1952-54; Syrett & Sons (Slrs) London 1951-62; Pattinson & Brewer (Slrs) London: articled clerk 1962, admitted slr 1973, ptnr 1973, opened Chatham office 1978-; specialist in medico legal claims for industl diseases and employment law, pt/t chm Industl Tbnls 1987-88; co-author Occupational Bladder Cancer - A Guide for Clinicians for British Journal of Urology; memb: Law Soc, Kent Law Soc; *Recreations* photography, swimming, life saving; *Clubs* Wig and Pen; *Style*— John Couch, Esq; Keepers Cottage, High St, Seal, Sevenoaks, Kent TN15 0AG (☎ 0732 62957); Pattinson & Brewer, 8-12 New Rd, Chatham, Kent ME4 4QR (☎ 0634 830080, fax 0634 830813); 30 Great James St, London WC1N 3HA

COUCHMAN, James Randall; MP (Cons) Gillingham 1983-; s of Stanley Randall Couchman, and Alison Margaret Couchman; *b* 11 Feb 1942; *Educ* Cranleigh Sch, King's Coll Newcastle upon Tyne; *m* 1967, Barbara Jean, da of Max Heilbrun (d 1956); 1 s, 1 da; *Career* memb Bexley Borough Cncl 1974-82, chm Bexley Social Servs 1975-78 and 1980-82, parly candidate (Cons) Chester le Street 1979, dir Chiswick Caterers Ltd 1980-, chm Bexley Health Authy 1981-83, PPS and former sec of state for Social Security 1984-; former posts incl: chllr Duchy of Lancaster, min for health; *Style*— James Couchman, Esq, MP; House of Commons, London SW1

COUCHMAN, Martin; s of Frederick Alfred James Couchman (d 1970), of Halstead, Kent, and Pamela Mary, *née* Argent; *b* 28 Sept 1947; *Educ* Sutton Valence, Exeter Coll Oxford (BA); *m* 29 Oct 1983, Carolyn Mary Constance, da of Victor Frow Roberts (d 1987), of Childer Thornton, Cheshire; 2 s (Edmund b 1985, William b 1987), 1 da (Annie b 1989); *Career* bldg indust 1970-77; NEDO: indust advsr 1977-84, head of admin 1984-87, on secondment as UK dir of Euro Year of the Environment 1987-88, sec to NEDC 1988-; *Recreations* amateur dramatics, Anglo-Saxon history, armchair archaeology; *Style*— Martin Couchman, Esq

COULL, Maj-Gen John Taylor; s of John Sandeman Coull (d 1970), of Aberdeen, and Ethel Marjory, *née* Taylor; *b* 4 March 1934; *Educ* Robert Gordon's Coll Aberdeen, Univ of Aberdeen (MB, ChB); *m* 27 Dec 1958, Mildred, da of Francis Thomson Macfarlane, of Bickley, Bromley; 3 s (Stephen John b 1960, Gordon David b 1962, Andrew Thomson b 1965); *Career* cmmnd RAMC 1960; conslt: gen surgery 1969, orthopaedic surgery 1972; advsr on orthopaedic surgery MOD 1977-86, conslt surgn BAOR 1986-

88, dir of surgery and conslt surgn to the Army 1988-, conslt surgn Royal Hosp Chelsea; author of articles on hip dislocation amputation and fracture fixation; contrib: Field Surgery Pocket Book, Rob Smith Surgery; FRCS, FBOA (memb Cncl 1985-87),FRSM; *Recreations* house maintenance, woodwork, gardening; *Clubs* RSM; *Style—* Maj-Gen John Coull; Ministry of Defence, First Avenue House, High Holborn, London WC1V 6HE (☎ 071 430 5825)

COULMAN, Michael Raymond; s of Col Edward Raymond Coulman, OBE, TD (d 1956), of Bracken Cottage, Newtown, Newbury, Berks, and Margaret Annie, *née* Stow (d 1984); *b* 28 Oct 1932; *Educ* Winchester, Trinity Coll Oxford (BA, MA); *m* 1, 23 July 1969, Jacqueline (d 1980), da of Anthony Cuthbert Morris Marsham (d 1975), of West Malling, Kent; 1 s (Robert b 1973), 1 da (Camilla b 1977); m 2, 9 April 1981, Patricia Margaret, da of Hon Edward Carson (d 1987), of Hastings, Sussex; 3 step da (Lucy Fife-Jamieson b 1972, Georgina b 1976, Sophie b 1976); *Career* 2 Lt KRRC 1951-53; with Anglo American Corp SA; stockbroker; ptnr Sheppards 1968-85 (then taken over by BAII), dir Personal Financial Management Tunbridge Wells Kent 1989-; *Recreations* golf; *Clubs* MCC, I Zingari, Tennis and Racquets Assoc, Rye Golf; *Style—* Michael Coulman, Esq; Bainden Farmhouse, Horsmonden, Tonbridge, Kent (☎ 089 272 2528); Personal Financial Management, Tunbridge Wells, Kent (☎ 0892 510 510)

COULSON, Richard Lewis Harrison; s of Lewis John Harrison Coulson (d 1966), of Rochester, and Muriel Beatrice, *née* Phillips; *b* 5 Oct 1950; *Educ* King's Sch Rochester, N London Poly (ALA); *m* 11 Aug 1976, Patricia Mary, da of Frederick Rodwell, of Maidstone; 1 da (Lisa b 7 June 1981); *Career* various posts Arts & Libraries Dept Kent CC 1974-86, dir Coulsons children's book specialists 1986-88, lectr and reviewer in children's lit 1986-, lectr and researcher in genealogy 1986-; dir: Firmstart Medway 1988-90, Training Group Medway 1989-90; area fin and info mangr Social Servs Dept Kent CC 1990-; memb Advsy Bd Kent Educnl Guidance 1988-, exec memb Medway Cncl for Voluntary Serv 1988-, vice chm Kent Forum on Special Needs Housing 1988-; chm: N Downs Housing Assoc 1989-, Medway & N Kent Relate 1989-90, Old Roffensian Soc 1989-; co-ordinator Medway Info Network 1989-90, fndr memb and co-ordinator Medway Debt Forum 1989-90; *Books* A Chronology of Strood (co-author, 1983), A Chronology of Herne Bay (1984), The Library Limerick (co-ed, 1986), A History of King's School Rochester (1989); *Recreations* family life and local historical research; *Style—* Richard Coulson, Esq; Social Services Department, Kent County Council, Compass Centre South, Chatham Maritime, Chatham, Kent ME4 4YH (☎ 0634 880404, fax 0634 881200)

COUNSELL, Dr Garth Forrest; s of Rev Harry Counsell (d 1966), and Elizabeth, *née* George; *b* 25 Aug 1934; *Educ* Crewkerne Sch Somerset, Univ of Bristol (MB ChB, DCH), DObstRCOG, MRCGP; *m* 14 March 1959, Patricia Jean, da of Sidney Thomas, of Trowbridge Wilts; 1 s (Richard Garth b 10 April 1960); *Career* house physician and casualty offr Southmead Hosp Bristol 1957, paediatric and obstetric house offr Odstock Hosp Salisbury 1958, asst in gen practice Ashurst New Forrest 1959; GP and hosp med offr: Faversham Kent 1960-75, Folkestone Kent 1975-; trainer in gen practice 1979-; designed with others Faversham Health Centre and large new gp practice premises in Folkestone; organist Faversham Methodist Church 1960-75; memb Br Geriatic Soc; memb BMA; *Recreations* organs, church, theatre; *Style—* Dr Garth Counsell; 17 Bybrook Field, Sandgate, Folkestone, Kent CT20 3BQ; 2 Downs Rd, Folkestone, Kent (☎ 0303 48691)

COUSENS, James Royall (Roy); s of Henry William Royall Cousens (d 1950), of Nottingham, and Lillias Ethel Cousens (d 1981); *b* 9 Feb 1930; *Educ* Peoples Coll Nottingham; *m* 5 Aug 1961, Simone, da of Oscar Charles Joseph Baeghe (d 1974), of France; 1 da (Laura Jane); *Career* Nat Serv RE 1951-53; architect; assoc Ley Colbeck & Ptnrs London 1969-83, own practice 1983-; FRIBA 1969 (ARIBA 1960); *Recreations* golf; *Clubs* Lamberhurst Golf; *Style—* Roy Cousens, Esq; 63 Yew Tree Rd, Tunbridge Wells, Kent TN4 0BG (☎ 0892 25340)

COVA, Bruce Charles; MBE (1982); s of Ceserino Cova, and Maude Doris, *née* Longman; *b* 17 Oct 1944; *Educ* Kingston GS, SE London Tech Coll, NALGO Correspondance Inst (Dip Municipal Admin), Ealing Tech Coll (Dip Mgmnt Studies); *m* 1, 25 March 1967 (m dis 1983), Valerie Ann, da of Frederick James Hunt (d 1963); 1 s (Matthew b 19 Sept 1970), 1 da (Antonia b 15 March 1973); m 2, 30 May 1986, Sara Anne, da of Barry Lovell; 1 da (Holly b 13 Sept 1989); *Career* various local govt appts 1961-79; London Borough of Hammersmith and Fulham: dir environmental servs 1979-85, dir social servs 1985-87; chief exec Sevenoaks DC 1987-; memb Inst Environmental Health Offrs 1965; FBIM 1982; *Recreations* riding, fishing; *Style—* Bruce Cova, Esq, MBE; Sevenoaks District Council, Council Offices, Argyle Rd, Sevenoaks, Kent (☎ 0732 741222, fax 0732 740693)

COWDREY, Christopher Stuart; s of Michael Colin Cowdrey, CBE, and Penelope Susan, *née* Chiesman; *b* 20 Oct 1957; *Educ* Wellesley House Broadstairs, Tonbridge; *m* 1 Jan 1989, Christel Margareta, da of Carl-Johan Arne Holst-Sande; *Career* cricketer; debut in Kent 2 XI 1972, capt of Young England to W Indies 1976, capped 1979, England debut in Bombay 1984, played all 5 Test Matches v India 1984-85, took a wicket with 4 ball in Test cricket bowling Kapil Dev, England capt v W Indies at Headingley 1988, capt of Kent 1985-90 (over 300 first class matches, over 12000 runs, over 200 wickets, 8 man of the match awards), played 3 one day Internationals for England, scored century in first innings in Benson and Hedges competition (as did father); *Books* Good Enough? (autobiography, with Jonathan Smith, 1986), What's Your Sport (with David Lemmon, 1988); *Recreations* golf; *Clubs* Royal St George's Golf, Kent CCC, Marlebone CC; *Style—* Christopher Cowdrey, Esq; Kent County Cricket Club, St Lawrence Ground, Old Dover Rd, Canterbury, Kent (☎ 0227 456886)

COWELL, Roger Housden; s of Ernest Frederick Cowell; *b* 3 Sept 1939; *Educ* King's Sch Rochester; *m* 1963, Margaret Anne, *née* Hillier; 1 s, 1 da; *Career* md Ace Filtration Ltd, dir Climavent SA Paris; CEng; *Recreations* squash, gardening, horology; *Clubs* Rumford; *Style—* Roger Cowell, Esq; Rooks Drift, Southfleet, Kent (☎ 047 483 2660); Airflow Works, Seymour Rd, Northfleet, Kent DA11 7BW (☎ 0474 325666, fax 0474 333132)

COWIE, James Strachan; s of Peter Cowie (d 1957), of Aberdeen, and Agnes, *née* Strachan (d 1972); *b* 7 Feb 1926; *Educ* Robert Gordons Coll Aberdeen, Univ of Aberdeen (MA), Magdalene Coll Cambridge; *m* 13 Sept 1952, Sheila, da of Edwin Mackay (d 1938), of Aberdeen; 2 s (Peter b 1958, Nigel b 1962); *Career* RAF 1944-48; admin offr HM Colonial Serv and Overseas Civil Serv N Rhodesia and Zambia 1953-65, bursar Cranbrook Sch Kent 1965-66; Univ of Kent at Canterbury 1966-: admin offr, asst registrar, sr asst registrar, head Office for Undergrad Recruitment Servs; memb: Supervisory Gp Rhodesia/Zimbabwe Independence Elections 1980, Cncl of Mgmnt UCCA; *Recreations* wine, flying light aircraft, travel; *Style—* James Cowie, Esq; The Registry, University of Kent, Canterbury, Kent CT2 7NZ (☎ 0227 764000, fax 0227 452196)

COX, Andrew John; s of Ronald Herbert Samuel Cox, of Stourbridge, W Midlands, and Shirley Ann, *née* Easlea (d 1972); *b* 23 Nov 1956; *Educ* Lawrence Sheriff Sch, Rugby, Univ Coll Cardiff (BSc); *m* 18 Aug 1986, Madedeine, da of Leonard Joseph Woodward (d 1983), of Beckenham, Kent; 2 s (Samuel Joseph b 16 Sept 1988, Jacob Alexander b 8 Sept 1990); *Career* CA; auditor Touche Ross & Co 1978-82, fin controller Westar Oil (UK) Ltd 1982-86, mgmnt conslt Price Waterhouse 1986- (seconded to Dept of Energy 1987-88); ACA 1982; *Recreations* canals, gardening, reading; *Style—* Andrew Cox, Esq; 21 Roedean Close, Orpington, Kent BR6 9WB (☎ 0689 71978); Price Waterhouse, 1 London Bridge, London SE1 9QL (☎ 071 939 3000)

COX, Charles Clifton; s of Cecil Clifton Cox (d 1933), of Cambridge, and Elizabeth, *née* Hall (d 1918); *b* 4 Sept 1913; *Educ* Perse Sch Cambridge; *m* 5 April 1939, Joan Denby, *née* Pamplin; 1 da (Valerie Joan Clifton (Mrs Hale) b 18 Sept 1946); *Career* cmmnd Beds Yeo TA 1937, 1 Bn Cambs Regt RA, transferred REME, ret Lt-Col 1945; trained Hawker Siddeley, Rootes Group 1943-49, sales dir Egertons (Ipswich) Ltd 1949-58, Martin Walter Group 1958-78 (ret as dir 1978); cncllr Canterbury DC (ctee memb: Policy, Planning Estates (vice chm), Works Servs, Housing Review Bd); memb: Canterbury Soc Exec Ctee, Canterbury Conservation Advsy Ctee, Oaten Hill Soc; sch govr and chm, tstee 4 charitable tsts, chm Fin and Gen Purposes Ctee Prince of Wales Youth Club, pres Spring Lane Community Assoc; memb Ct of Univ of Kent at Canterbury; Freeman City of Cambridge; *Recreations* rugby union football (for Cambs), golf, squash, walking, gardening, vintage cars; *Clubs* Conservative; *Style—* Charles Cox, Esq; Council Offices, Military Rd, Canterbury, Kent (☎ 0227 763763, fax 0227 763727)

COX, (Henry) Peter Berridge; s of Capt Henry Berridge Cox, RN (d 1949), of Folkestone, and Mary Millicent Venables, *née* Palin (d 1973); *b* 18 Dec 1916; *Educ* Lancing; *m* 29 June 1940, Mona Maragaret Muir, da of Daniel Maclean (d 1959), of Capetown, SA; 1 s (Andrew Peter Berridge b 1946), 2 da (Rosemary Anne Berridge (Mrs Fox) b 1941, Valerie Margaret Berridge (Mrs Yorke) b 1946); *Career* War Serv discharged Maj 1939-46; CA; ret as sec Industrial and Commercial Finance Corp 1947-57, chief accountant and sec British Enka 1958-61, vice chm Louis Dreyfus and Co Ltd 1968-72; dir: Ship Mortgage Finance Corp 1962-68, Burier Markes Ltd 1968-72, Shipowners Mutual Strike Assoc of Bermuda 1968-80; non-exec dir Northern Star Insurance 1969-89, gp shipping advsr Barclays Bank 1973-79; advsr: Civil and Marine Ltd 1969-89, British Shipbuilders 1980-82; local cncllr Sidcup and Chislehurst 1952-55; FCA; *Recreations* golf, bridge, reading; *Style—* Peter Cox, Esq; 1 Avonhurst, Camden Park Rd, Chislehurst, Kent BR7 5HQ (☎ 081 467 3803)

COX, Dr Stuart James; JP (Kent 1981); s of Edward James Cox, of London, and Winifred Irene Amy, *née* Sawyer (d 1988); *b* 1 April 1923; *Educ* Selhurst GS, The Queen's Univ of Belfast (MB BCh, BAO); *m* 1, 26 Aug 1944, Eithne Lilian (d 1977), da of William Foreman (d 1948), of Barrow-in-Furness; 1 s (Robert b 3 Dec 1945), 1 da (Amanda b 22 Nov 1950); m 2, 24 Nov 1979, Peggy Rosaline, da of Edward Moore, JP (d 1931), of Dartford, Kent; *Career* RAF 1941-46 Flt Lt, pilot 65 Fighter Sqdn; princ gen med practioner 1953-80; Kent CC: memb 1967-, dep leader 1973-77, vice chm 1977-79 and 1988-, chm 1979-81, chm Social Servs Ctee 1986-89; chm: Kent Police Authy 1973-77, Medway Health Authy 1981-86, Kent Ambulance Ctee 1981-86, Fire and

Emergency Planning Ctee 1989-; govr Police Staff Coll 1977-81; memb Cncl: Univ of Kent at Canterbury, Kent Agric Soc (and life govr); memb Bd Age Concern Eng, warden Rochester Bridge Tst, steward Rochester Cathedral; life memb: Kent Playing Field Assoc, RAF Assoc, City of Rochester Soc; pres: Gillingham Cons Assoc, Medway YC (and past cdre); fndn govr: Rochester Mathematical Soc, Rochester GS for Girls; memb: Medway Postgrad Med Soc, William Harvey Soc of London, BMA; memb Worshipful Soc of Apothecaries 1981, Freeman City of London 1983; *Recreations* sailing, golf, shooting, music; *Clubs* Medway Yacht, Castle (Rochester); *Style—* Dr Stuart Cox, JP; 29 Berengrave Lane, Rainham, Kent (☎ 0634 366775)

COX, Timothy John Lomas; TD (1971); s of Arthur Cox (d 1979), of Lower Willingdon, Sussex, and Winifred Mabel, *née* Lomas-Smith (d 1975); *b* 9 March 1939; *Educ* King's Sch Rochester; *m* 5 Sept 1970, Julia Rosemary, da of Henry Francis Workman (d 1988), of Grantown on Spey, Morayshire; 1 s (Adrian b 1974), 1 da (Rosemary b 1976); *Career* cmmnd 2 Lt RA TA 1959, (actg Maj 1970-), central vol HQ RA 1973-89 (Maj 1975-89); admitted slr 1962; ptnr Oswald Hickson Collier & Co 1966-; memb various professional and mil assocs; Freeman City of London 1983, Freeman and Liveryman Worshipful Co of Painter Stainers; *Recreations* photography, scuba diving, country pursuits; *Style—* Timothy Cox, Esq, TD; Messrs Oswald Hickson Collier & Co, Essex House, Essex St, The Strand, London WC2R 3AQ (☎ 071 836 8333, fax 071 240 2236)

COX-FREEMAN, Laurie; *Educ* Winterbourne Sch, Selhurst Sch; 3 children; *Career* navigator RAF Coastal Cmd 1944-47; trainee J Walter Thompson Advertising Agency 1947-52; Service Advertising: account exec 1952, dir 1960, md 1962; Horniblow Cox-Freeman Advertising: founded 1965, sold out 1980; dir FCB Advertising USA 1980-89, chm and chief exec Park Advertising & Marketing Ltd 1980-89, formed LCF & Ptnrs 1989-; govr Folkestone Sch for Girls, memb Steering Ctee Friends of the League at the William Harvey Hosp Ashford; *Style—* Laurie Cox-Freeman, Esq; Sea Purse, St Margaret's Bay, nr Dover, Kent (☎ 0304 852682)

COXON, Dr Robert David Alexander (Sandy); s of Robert Victor Coxon (d 1980), of Juniper House, Lincombe Lane, Boars Hill, Oxford, and Dr Mary Wynne Coxon, *née* Bowen; *b* 16 Jan 1950; *Educ* Dragon Sch Oxford, Magdalen Coll Sch Oxford, Guy's Hosp Med Sch London (MRCS, LRCP); *m* 12 Jan 1980, Bridget Susan, da of Raymond Potten, of 55 Bulkington Ave, Worthing, W Sussex; 1 s (Christopher b 1984), 1 da (Helen b 1982); *Career* house surgn St Luke's Hosp Guildford 1974-75, physician St Helen's Hosp Hastings 1975, Hastings Gen Practice Vocational Trg Scheme 1976-79 (appts incl SHO in St Helens Royal E Sussex and Buchanan Hosp Hastings, GP Thanet Rye E Sussex and Hastings), princ in gen practice Dymchurch and N Rowney 1979-; appointed Doctor Nuclear Protectorate Durgeness B Power Station 1985-; memb: Kent Local Med Ctee 1984-, Med Exec Ctee SE Kent AHA 1982-; chm GP Div Med Exec Ctee 1985-88; govr Dymchurch Primary Sch, memb SS Peter Paul Dymchurch PCC; Freeman City of London 1983; *Recreations* ocean cruising, mountaineering, skiing, running vintage cars; *Clubs* Humber Register; *Style—* Dr Sandy Coxon; Barn House, Tartane Lane, Dymchurch, Romney Marsh, Kent TN29 0LJ; 9 Orgarswick Ave, Dymchurch, Kent; Church Lane, Surgery, New Romney, Romney Marsh, Kent (☎ 0303 872245)

CRABTREE, Derek; s of Robert Crabtree (d 1987), of Canterbury, and Ethel, *née* Hollows (d 1962); *b* 25 May 1932; *Educ* Rochdale GS, Univ Coll Leicester (BSc), Nuffield Coll Oxford, Princeton Univ; *m* 4 Aug 1962, (Anne) Christiane, da of Dr Jürgen Müller (d 1945), of Königsberg, Germany; 1 s (Michael Jürgen b 1966), 1 da (Catherine Anne b 1968); *Career* procter visiting fell Princeton Univ 1955-56, asst lectr then lectr Univ of Exeter 1956-67 (acting head Dept Pub Admin Nigerian Coll 1960, visiting lectr Univ of Oregon 1963-64), lectr then sr lectr Univ of Kent 1967-, master of Keynes Coll Univ of Kent 1973-; memb and sometime chm Bd of Visitors HM Prison Canterbury 1976-87; memb: Canterbury Rotary Club 1980-, Cncl of Friends of Canterbury Cathedral 1984-; govr The Kings Sch Rochester 1987-; *Books* Keynes and the Bloomsbury Group (co-ed A P Thirlwall, 1978); *Recreations* walking, architecture, recorded music; *Clubs* Rotary; *Style—* Derek Crabtree, Esq; 53 Hackington Rd, Tyler Hill, Canterbury, Kent CT2 9NE (☎ 0227 471503); Keynes College, University of Kent at Canterbury, Canterbury, Kent CT2 7NP (☎ 0227 764000)

CRAMPTON, Prof Richard John; s of John Donald Crampton (d 1988), and Norah, *née* Haden; *b* 23 Nov 1940; *Educ* Queen Elizabeth's GS Hartlebury Worcs, Solihull Sch, Trinity Coll Dublin (MA), Sch of Slavonic and E Euro Studies Univ of London (PhD); *m* 10 July 1965, Celia Primrose Mary, da of Dermot Marshall Harriss (d 1943); 2 s (William G Richard b 1969, Benjamin T David b 1972); *Career* Univ of Kent: lectr 1967-78, sr lectr 1978-88, prof E Euro history 1988-; *Books* The Hollow Détente (1981), Bulgaria 1878-1918: A History (1983), A Short History of Modern Bulgaria (1987), Bulgaria: World Bibliographic Series (1989); *Recreations* reading, listening to music, eating and drinking, bird watching; *Style—* Prof Richard Crampton; 1 Ravenscourt Rd, Rough Common, Canterbury, Kent CT2 9DH (☎ 0227 760847); Rutherford College, The University, Canterbury, Kent CT2 7NX (☎ 0227 764000 ext 3401, fax 0227 459025)

CRAPPER, Rodney Reginald Owen; s of Reginald Crapper (d 1978), of Zimbabwe, and Alma Florence, *née* Owen; *b* 16 Aug 1933; *Educ* Jeppe HS Johannesburg SA, Witwatersrand Tech Coll Johannesburg; *m* 1 Dec 1962, Annette Lilian Elizabeth, da of Leslie Robert Browning (d 1977), of Durban, SA; 2 da (Deborah Alison b 1967, Samantha Lee b 1968); *Career* professional ice skater 1956-59, customer serv engr 1960-; memb Canterbury City Cncl 1987-; chm Govrs Frank Montgomery Secdy Sch, ward chm Cons Assoc, chm Sturry Bypass Action Gp, tstee Canterbury and Whitstable Railway Museum Tst; *Recreations* badminton, sailing, countryside; *Style—* Rodney Crapper, Esq

CRAWFORD, Maj-Gen Ian Campbell; CBE (1982); *b* 17 June 1932; *Educ* Dumfries Acad, Univ of Edinburgh (MB ChB); *m* 4 April 1959, Phyllis Mary; 1 s (Niall b 1967), 1 da (Fiona b 1960); *Career* conslt physician (Cardiology) Queen Elizabeth Mil Hosp Woolwich 1977-83 and 1985-90; dir Army Med and consltg physician to Army; FRCPE 1972, FRCP 1986; *Style—* Maj-Gen Ian C Crawford, CBE; The Arbour, Bobbing, Kent (☎ 0795 842292); Queen Elizabeth Military Hospital, Woolwich, London SE18 (☎ 081 856 5533)

CRAWFORD, Sir Theodore (Theo); s of Theodore Crawford (d 1925), and Sarah, *née* Mansfield (d 1958); *b* 23 Dec 1911; *Educ* St Peter's Sch York, Glasgow Acad, Univ of Glasgow (BSc, MB ChB, MD); *m* 1, 1938, Margaret Donald (d 1973), da of Dr George Green, DSC; 2 s, 3 da; m 2, 1974, Priscilla Leathley, da of Guy Leathley Chater (d 1974); *Career* served RAMC 1941-45, UK, France, Belgium and Germany, Maj; dir of pathological servs St George's Hosp and Med Sch 1946-77, prof of pathology Univ of London 1948-77, now emeritus; hon sec Cancer Res Campaign 1967-70 (chm Sci Ctee 1955-67); pres RCPath 1969-72, conslt advsr in pathology Dept of Health 1969-78; Hon LLD Univ of Glasgow 1979; FRCP (Glasgow 1962), FRCPath 1963, FRCP (London) 1964; kt 1973; *Books* Modern Trends in Pathology (ed, 1967), The Pathology of Ischaemic Heart Disease (1977); *Recreations* gardening, music, walking; *Clubs* Sloane; *Style—* Sir Theo Crawford; 9 Asher Reeds, Langton Green, Tunbridge Wells, Kent TN3 0AL (☎ 089 286 3341)

CRAWFURD, Dr (Anthony) Raymond; s of Kenneth Crawfurd, of Uplands, Stoke Poges, Bucks, and Mary Isabel, *née* Jarrett; *b* 14 Jan 1942; *Educ* Winchester, Magdalen Coll Oxford (MA, BM BCh), King's Coll Hosp Med Sch (DCH, LMSSA, DRCOG, MRCP); *m* 4 Oct 1969, Dr Dorothy Mair, da of Rev David Charles Elijah Rowlands (d 1975), of Treorchy, Rhondda, Glamorgan; 1 s (James b 1974), 1 da (Kate b 1971); *Career* house physician and sr house offr: King's Coll Hosp, Royal Liverpool Children's Hosp, Alder Hey Hosp, Kent and Canterbury Hosp 1967-70; sr ptnr Crawfurd & Partners 1989- (joined 1970); hon med offr Amateur Fencing Assoc; memb: BOA Med Ctee, Commission Medicale Fedn Internationale d'escrime; chm: Tenterden Day Centre, Kent Co Amateur Fencing Union; govr Tenterden Co Primary Sch; Liveryman Worshipful Soc of Apothecaries 1967, Freeman City of London; *Recreations* fencing, skiing, heraldry; *Style—* Dr Raymond Crawfurd; Seymour House, Shoreham Lane, St Michaels, Tenterden, Kent (☎ 05806 2967); Ivy Court, Tenterden, Kent TN30 6RB (☎ 05806 3666)

CREW, Edward Michael; s of Joseph Edwin Crew, of Gloucester, and Cecilia May, *née* Davis; *b* 13 Jan 1946; *Educ* Haberdashers' Aske's, RCDS; *m* 17 June 1967, Gillian, da of Edward Frederick John Glover, of Birchington; 1 s (Duncan Edward b 1971), 1 da (Lynne Gillian b 1969); *Career* Chief Supt SE London Traffic Div Met Police 1982-84 (joined 1965), Dep Chief Constable Kent Co Constabulary 1989- (Asst Chief Constable 1984-89); cncl memb; OStJ; *Recreations* good food, walking, gardening, travel; *Style—* Edward Crew, Esq; Deputy Chief Constables Ofice, Maidstone, Kent ME15 9BZ (☎ 0622 690690, fax 0622 690511)

CRITCHLEY, Philip; CB (1990); s of Henry Stephen Critchley (d 1980), of Cumbria, and Edith Adela, *née* Currie (d 1980); *b* 31 Jan 1931; *Educ* Manchester GS, Balliol Coll Oxford (MA); *m* 1962, Stella Ann, da of Frederick John Barnes, of Kent; 2 s (Conrad b 1965, Brian b 1966), 1 da (Rachel b 1971); *Career* Nat Serv Intelligence Corps 1953-55, Corpl BAOR; civil servant; under sec DOE, dir of network mgmnt and maintenance (highways) Dept of Tport; memb: Ashford Youth Theatre, Local Philosophy Gp; *Recreations* tree conservation; *Clubs* Blackheath Harriers, Oxford Union; *Style—* Philip Critchley, Esq, CB; Redstone House, Maidstone Rd, Ashford, Kent TN25 4NP (☎ 0233 621037); US/DMNAM, Department of Transport, 2 Monck St, London SW1P 3EB (☎ 071 276 2830)

CRITTENDEN, Keith; s of Corpl Albert Thomas Crittenden (d 1957), and Norah Edith, *née* Taylor; *Educ* Snodland Secdy Sch, Maidstone Tech Sch; *m* 12 Oct 1983, Lynette Ann, da of Alec William Smith, of Gloucester, Orchard Drive, Weavering, Maidstone, Kent; 2 s (Daryl Mark b 29 Oct 1964, Russell Stephen b 19 June 1969); *Career* Bailey Garages (Kent) Ltd: vehicle sales mangr 1973-81, co gp dir 1981-; fndr fell Inst Sales Mgmnt 1984; *Recreations* golf, photography, travel; *Clubs* Tudor Park Golf and Country, Choughs Golfing; *Style—* Keith Crittenden, Esq; Bailey Garages (Kent) Ltd, Ashford Rd, Harrietsham, Kent ME17 1BQ (☎ 0622 859363)

CROFT, His Hon Judge; David Legh; QC (1982); s of Alan Croft (d 1965), of Dore, Sheffield, and Doreen Mary, *née* Mitchell; *b* 14 Aug 1937; *Educ* Haileybury, Univ of Nottingham (LLB); *m* 27 July 1963, Susan Mary, da of

George Richard Winnington Bagnall (d 1982), of Wickham, nr Newbury, Berks; 2 s (Rupert Legh b 1966, Jocelyn Harry b 1968); *Career* called to the Bar Middle Temple 1960; QC 1982, rec 1985, circuit judge 1987; *Recreations* cooking; *Style*— His Hon Judge Croft, QC

CROFT, Maj Sir John Archibald Radcliffe; 5 Bt (UK 1818), of Cowling Hall, Yorks; s of Tom Radcliffe Croft, OBE (d 1964, s of 2 Bt); suc cous 1979; *b* 27 March 1910; *Educ* King's Sch Canterbury; *m* 26 Sept 1953, Lucy Elizabeth, da of late Maj William Dallas Loney Jupp, OBE; 1 s; *Heir* s, Thomas Croft; *Career* Maj W Yorks Regt (ret); *Recreations* shooting, fishing, golf; *Clubs* Army and Navy; *Style*— Maj Sir John Croft, Bt; The Barn House, Rayham Farm, Whitstable, Kent (☎ 0227 277816)

CROLLA, Hon Mrs ((Susan Patricia) Rose); *née* Cornwallis; 3 da of 3 Baron Cornwallis, OBE, DL (by his 2 w); *b* 30 March 1963; *m* 4 July 1986, Scott Simon Crolla, s of Romano Crolla, of Albert Court, London; *Style*— The Hon Mrs Crolla; Ruck Farm, Horsmonden, Tonbridge, Kent TN12 8DT

CROMPTON, Barbara Janet; da of Edward Crompton (d 1961), of Hexham, Northumberland, and Edith Margaret, *née* Seddon; *b* 17 May 1945; *Educ* Queen Elizabeth GS Hexham Northumberland, Univ of Newcastle Upon Tyne (BSc); *Career* physics teacher Kangar W Malaysia with VSO 1968, asst teacher of physics Queen Elizabeth HS Windermere 1969-74, dep head St Anne's Sch 1987-90 (head of physics and housemistress 1974-87), headmistress Kent Coll Pembury; school teacher fell commoner Sidney Sussex Coll Cambridge 1986; MInstP 1984; *Recreations* windsurfing, sailing, photography, camping; *Style*— Miss Barbara Crompton; Kent College, Pembury, Tunbridge Wells, Kent TN2 4AX (☎ 0892 822006)

CRONIN, John Walton; s of John Cronin (d 1952), and Alice Cronin (d 1944); *b* 14 Oct 1915; *Educ* Xaverian Coll Manchester, Univ of Manchester, Cadet Coll Bangalore; *m* 1947, Mrs Eileen Veronica Bale, da of Michael Roy Rector (d 1959); 1 da (Sheelagh), 1 step s (Peter Bale); *Career* WWII 1940-46, Maj Indian Army DAQMG; res magistrate and acting high court judge, advsy cmmr to govr on detained persons N Rhodesia 1955-65, stipendiary and circuit magistrate Grand Bahama 1965-71, chm Industl Tribunals 1972-88; co dir Kent St John Ambulance 1974-78; OStJ 1977; *Clubs* Royal Cwlth Soc; *Style*— John Cronin, Esq; 6 Chelsea Court, Hythe, Kent (☎ 0303 267879)

CROOK, 2 Baron (UK 1947), of Carshalton, Co Surrey; Douglas Edwin Crook; o s of 1 Baron Crook (d 1989), and Ida Gertrude Catherine, *née* Haddon (d 1985); *b* 19 Nov 1926; *Educ* Whitgift Middle Sch Croydon, Imperial Coll London (BSc, DIC); *m* 15 Feb 1954, Ellenor, da of Robert Rouse (d 1962), of Sunderland; 1 s (Hon Robert Douglas Edwin b 29 May 1955), 1 da (Hon Catherine Hilary (Hon Mrs (Christopher John) Ramsdale) b 22 May 1960); *Heir* s, Hon Robert Douglas Edwin Crook; *Career* MICE; ACGI; *Style*— The Rt Hon Lord Crook; Ridgehill Barn, Etchinghill, Folkestone, Kent CT18 8BP (☎ 0303 863 353)

CROOKENDEN, Lt-Gen Sir Napier; KCB (1970, CB 1966), DSO (1945), OBE (1954), DL (Kent 1979); 2 s of Col Arthur Crookenden, CBE, DSO (d 1962), and Dorothy, *née* Rowlandson; *b* 31 Aug 1915; *Educ* Wellington, RMC Sandhurst; *m* 3 Aug 1948, Hon Patricia Nassau, da of 2 Baron Kindersley, CBE, MC; 2 s, 2 da, *qv*; *Career* Cheshire Regt 1935, cmd 9 Para Bir 1944-46 and 16 Para Bn 1960-61, dir Land/Air Warfare 1964-66, Comdt Royal Mil Coll of Science 1958-59, Col The Cheshire Regt 1969-71, GOCiC Western Cmd 1969-72, Col Cmdt Prince of Wales Div 1971-74; dir: Lloyds Bank Ltd SE Regnl Bd 1973-86, Flextech Ltd 1973-86; tstee Imperial War Museum 1973-83, chm SSAFA 1974-85, Lt HM Tower of London 1975-81; *Books* Drop Zone Normandy (1976), Airborne at War (1978), Battle of the Bulge 1944 (1980); *Clubs* Army and Navy; *Style*— Lt-Gen Sir Napier Crookenden, KCB, DSO, OBE, DL; Twin Firs, Four Elms, Edenbridge, Kent TN8 6PL (☎ 073 270 229)

CROOKENDEN, Hon Lady (Patricia Nassau); *née* Kindersley; er da of 2 Baron Kindersley, CBE, MC (d 1976); *b* 5 Aug 1922; *m* 3 Aug 1948, Lt-Gen Sir Napier Crookenden, KCB, DSO, OBE, *qv*; 2 s, 2 da; *Style*— The Hon Lady Crookenden; Twin Firs, Four Elms, Edenbridge, Kent TN8 6PL

CROPPER, Ralph; s of Charles William Cropper, and Florence, *née* Betts; *b* 6 June 1913; *Educ* LSE (BA, MSc); *m* 25 May 1935, Irene Amy; 4 c; *Career* sr exec offr Road Haulage Assoc until 1949, ind tport consit in road tport 1949-; md: Conquers Transport Ltd 1952-82, Transport Counsellors Ltd 1956-80; former vice pres Deptford Cons Assoc; chm: Movement for London 1982-, Copers Cope Res Assoc; memb: SE Gas Consultative Ctee for 25 years (chm some of its ctees), industl tbnls for 15 years; Freeman City of London, Liveryman Worshipful Co of Carmen; FCIT, FREconS; *Clubs* City Livery; *Style*— Ralph Cropper, Esq; Dunbar, Beckenham Place Park, Beckenham, Kent (☎ 081 650 1546)

CROSLAND, Prof Maurice Pierre; s of David Crosland, and Berthe, *née* Mispoulet; *b* 19 March 1931; *Educ* Stationers Sch, Univ of London (BSc, MSc, PhD); *m* 22 April 1957, Joan Mary, da of William Cooley; 3 s (Peter b 1959, Michael b 1962, Paul b 1966), 1 da (Margaret b 1964); *Career* visiting prof: Univ of California Berkeley 1967, Cornell Univ NY 1967-68; reader in history of sci Univ of Leeds 1969-74 (lectr 1963), visiting prof Univ of Pennsylvania 1971, prof of history of sci and dir of Unit for the History Philosophy and Social Rels of Sci Univ of Kent Canterbury 1974-; hon ed British Journal for History of Science 1965-71, pres Br Soc for the History of Sci 1974-76, memb Int Acad of History of Sci 1976-; Dexter award American Chem Soc 1984; *Books* The Societ of Arcueil. A view of French Science at the Time of Napoleon I (1967), Historical Studies in the Language of Chemistry (2 edn, 1978), Science in France in the Revolutionary Era Described by Thomas Bugge (1969), The Science of Matter. A Historical Survey (1971), The Emergence of Science in Western Europe (1975), Gay-Lussac, Scientist and Bourgeois (1978); *Recreations* walking, classical music, continental travel, cycling; *Style*— Prof Maurice Crosland; Unit for History of Science, Physics Building, University of Kent, Canterbury, Kent CT2 7NR (☎ 0227 764000)

CROSSMAN, David; s of Henry William Crossman (d 1966), and Gertrude Edith Mary, *née* Glasscock; *b* 12 Jan 1947; *Educ* Belmont Sch Tottenham, City Coll for Further Educn London; *m* ;1 s (Tom Dow-Smith b 1972); *Career* professional TV prodr and dir 1974-; credits incl: The London Programme 1977, A Question of Sex 1978, The Cannon and Ball Show 1979-81, Metal Mickey 1980-81, A Week in Politics 1982, Chips Comic 1983, The Pocket Money Programme 1984-85, The Editors 1990; individual memb IPPA, memb Dir Guild of GB; *Recreations* photography, motoring, fatherhood; *Style*— David Crossman, Esq; Flat One, 58 Wickham Rd, Beckenham, Kent BR3 2RQ (☎ 081 658 2012); Dareks Production House (fax 081 658 2012)

CROUCH, Sir David Lance; s of Charles Littler Stanley Crouch (d 1966), of Northwood, Middx, and Rosalie Kate, *née* Croom (d 1972); *b* 23 June 1919; *Educ* Univ Coll Sch; *m* 5 July 1947, Margaret Maplesden, da of Maj Sydney Maplesden Noakes, DSO, of Shorne, Kent; 1 s (Patrick b 19 May 1954), 1 da (Vanessa b 11 Oct 1951); *Career* served RA 1939-46, Maj, attached RAF 1944-45, service in N Africa, Europe, Burma; dir Westminster Communications Group Ltd; contested (C) W Leeds 1959, MP (C) Canterbury 1966-87; memb: SE Thames RHA 1970-84, cncl Univ of Kent at Canterbury 1971, MRC 1984-87; chm: The Kent Soc 1987-, The Theatres Tst 1987-; govr Kent Inst of Art and Design 1988-, tstee Crisis at Christmas; Hon DCL Univ of Kent at Canterbury 1987; FRSA; kt 1987; *Books* A Canterbury Tale (1987); *Recreations* golf, painting; *Clubs* Athenaeum, MCC; *Style*— Sir David Crouch; The Oast House, Fisher St, Badlesmere, Faversham, Kent (☎ 0227 730528)

CROUCH, Patrick Seymour Maplesden; s of Sir David Crouch, and Margaret, *née* Noakes; *b* 1954; *Educ* Radley, Sir John Cass Sch of Art, St Martins Coll of Art; *m* 6 Oct 1979, (Carol) Anne, da of Peter Marsh; 1 da (Catherine Diana); *Career* sculptor; student and asst to Edward Bainbridge-Copnall, MBE and Tony Gray 1970-73; teacher of sculpture: adult educn Kent 1982-87, Canterbury Coll 1988-, The John Makepeace Sch of Craftsmen 1988-, Saint Martin's Coll of Art 1988-, Kent Inst of Art and Design 1988-; exhibitions incl: Royal Acad, New Metropole (Folkstone), Mall Galleries (London), Contemporary Art Fair (Bath), Trinity Arts Centre (Tunbridge Wells), Sculpture at Marygate (York) 1985, Eastern Rooms (Rye), Kingsgate Workshop Gallery (London), Chelsea Farmers Market, Christopher Hull Gallery (London), Festival of London Sculpture Show Alexandra Palace 1988, Sculpture at Canterbury 1989-90, Sculpture Installation at the Harbour Yard Chelsea Harbour (London); artist in residence: Tunbridge Wells 1983, Sevenoaks Festival 1985, Sculpture for the Garden (Harlow Car Gardens Harrogate) 1986; jury memb IPV Centenary Exhibition of Children's Art Budapest ; *Recreations* formula 1 motor racing, cricket; *Style*— Patrick Crouch, Esq; 58 St Martins Hill, Canterbury, Kent CT1 1PS (☎ 0227 455648)

CROWSON, Richard Borman; CMG (1986); s of Clarence Borman Crowson (d 1980), of Gainsborough, and Cecilia May, *née* Ramsden (d 1973); *b* 23 July 1929; *Educ* Queen Elizabeth's GS Gainsborough, Downing Coll Cambridge (MA); *m* 1, 29 Feb 1960 (m dis 1974), Sylvia, *née* Cavalier; 1 s (Anthony b 26 Feb 1961), 1 da (Hilary b 3 March 1964); m 2, 21 May 1983, Judith Elaine, da of Marion Earl Clark, of Lincoln, Nebraska, USA; 1 step s (David b 5 Aug 1967); *Career* HM Colonial Serv Uganda 1955-62, FO 1962-63, 1 Sec (Commercial) Br Embassy Tokoyo 1963-68, dep high cmmr Barbados 1968-70, FCO 1970-74, cnsllr (Commercial and Aid) Br Embassy Jakarta 1975-77, cnsllr (Hong Kong Affairs) Br Embassy Washington (also accredited in Ottawa) 1977-82, cnsllr Br Embassy Berne 1983-85, Br high cmmr Mauritius and concurrently HM Ambass Fed Islamic Repub of the Comoros 1985-89; FCIS 1962; *Recreations* music, theatre; *Clubs* Royal Cwlth Soc; *Style*— Richard Crowson, Esq, CMG; 67 Crofton Rd, Orpington, Kent (☎ 0689 891320)

CROXFORD, Peter Michael; s of Sqdn Ldr Kenneth Herbert Croxford (d 1986), and Enid Agnes, *née* Walton (d 1988); *b* 31 July 1937; *Educ* Portsmouth GS; *m* 2 March 1966, Brenda Margaret, da of George Alfred Winsor, ISM, of Hither Green; 1 s (Bradley Peter b 1972), 2 da (Helen Enid b 1967, Claire Rosalind b 1969), 1 step s (John George b 1957), 2 step da (Susan Margaret b 1959, Gillian Dorothy b 1961); *Career* md The News Shopper 1976-; dir: South London Guardian 1987-, Reed Southern Newspapers 1988-; *Recreations* reading, travel, sports; *Clubs* MCC,

Middleton Sports; *Style—* Peter Croxford, Esq; 74 Elm Grove, Orpington, Kent BR6 0AD (☎ 0689 32612); Mega House, Crestview Drive, Petts Wood, Orpington, Kent BR5 1BT (☎ 0689 36211, fax 0689 891479)

CROXON, Derrick Gwynn; s of Charles William Croxon (d 1968) of Maidstone, Kent; *b* 10 Jan 1923; *Educ* King's Sch Rochester, UCL; *m* 1947, Rachel Ann, da of late William Griffith Thomas; 2 da; *Career* Capt RE, Major RASC Italy; chem engineer/gen mgmnt trainee Reed International 1949; Kimberly-Clark Ltd: works dir 1954, md 1961-83, ret as conslt; *Recreations* tennis, sailing, beekeeping; *Clubs* Medway Yacht; *Style—* Derrick Croxon, Esq; Somerfield Rd, Maidstone, Kent (☎ 0622 58161)

CRUMP, Cynthia Dorothy; da of Ivor Edward Alexander Welch (d 1972), and Anni, *née* Jones; *b* 17 Dec 1938; *Educ* Lady Margaret HS Cardiff, UCW Aberystwyth (BA, CertEd); *m* 11 Aug 1962, Maj Howard Crump, s of Alfred Crump (d 1983); 2 s (Gareth Neil b 1963, Ian Stuart b 1964); *Career* teacher: Malaysia and Hong Kong 1960-70, Folkestone Harrogate and Quainton 1970-80; headmistress: Ripple Co Primary Sch Deal, Deal Parochial CEP; exec memb NAHT for S Kent, memb Local Panel for Secdy Selection; *Recreations* gardening, walking, reading, crosswords; *Style—* Mrs Cynthia Crump; Deal Parochial CEP (aided) School, London Rd, Deal, Kent CT14 9TA (☎ 0304 374464)

CRUSH, Harvey Michael; s of George Stanley Crush (d 1970), of Chislehurst, Kent, and Alison Isabel, *née* Lang; *b* 12 April 1939; *Educ* Chigwell Sch Essex; *m* 1, 21 Aug 1965 (m dis 1982), Diana, da of Frederick Joseph Bassett (d 1965), of Coulsdon, Surrey; 1 s (Nicholas b 1 Dec 1967), 1 da (Emily b 21 May 1971); m 2, 9 Dec 1982, Margaret Rose (Maggie), da of Nicholas Dixson (d 1986); *Career* admitted slr 1963; ptnr Norton Rose 1968-, dir TOSG Trust Fund Ltd 1970-; memb Supreme Court Rule Ctee 1984-88; vice pres City of London Law Soc 1989-, hon slr Assoc of Br Aviation Conslts; hon life memb Sevenoaks and Dist Motor Club (chm 1968-71); Liveryman: Worshipful Co of Slrs 1982 (memb Court of Assts 1987-), Worshipful Co of Farriers 1984; MRAeS 1980; memb Law Soc; *Recreations* travel, flying, motor sport; *Style—* Harvey Crush, Esq; Kempson House, Camomile St, London EC3A 7AN (☎ 071 283 2434, fax 071 588 1181)

CULLEN, John Gavin; s of Gavin Hunter Cullen (d 1964), and Alice Mary, *née* Grieve (d 1966); *b* 30 April 1936; *Educ* Robert Gordon's Coll Aberdeen, RCM, Christ's Coll Cambridge (MA, organ scholar); *m* 9 April 1966, Mary Elaine, da of Ven Thomas Berkeley Randolph (Archdeacon of Hereford and Canon of Hereford Cathedral, d 1987); 2 s (Christopher b 1967, Jonathan b 1974), 1 da (Alison b 1969); *Career* organist and master of choristers St Andrew's Cathedral Aberdeen 1961-63, dir of music Abingdon Sch Oxford 1964-67, dir of music and organist Tonbridge Sch Kent 1967-, conductor and musical dir Tonbridge Philharmonic Soc 1967-; composer of several compositions for choir and organ; chm: educn section ISM 1979-80, Public and Prep Schs Music Ctee 1980-85; examiner The Assoc Bd of Royal Schools of Music, vice pres The Curwen Inst; FRCO, ARCM, memb Incorp Soc of Musicians; *Recreations* smallholding, family and friends, golf; *Style—* John Cullen, Esq; The Old Farm House, Golden Green, Tonbridge, Kent (☎ 0732 850 739); Tonbridge School, Kent (☎ 0732 365555)

CUMMING, (John) Alan; CBE (1983); s of John Cumming; *b* 6 March 1932; *Educ* George Watson's Coll Edinburgh; *m* 1958, Isobel Beaumont, *née* Sked; 3 s; *Career* Woolwich Building Society: chief exec 1969-86, dir 1978-, exec vice chm 1986-; chm: Bldg Soc Assoc 1981-83, Cavendish Wates First Assured plc, Woolwich Homes Ltd; pres Euro Community Mortgage Fedn 1984-87, chm Thamesmead Town, chm Utd Reformed Church Tst, pres Int Union of Housing Fin Institutions 1990-; dir: Value and Income Tst plc; dir: Nat Kidney Res Fndn; *Recreations* bridge, golf; *Clubs* Caledonian; *Style—* Alan Cumming, Esq, CBE; 8 Prince Consort Drive, Chislehurst, Kent (☎ 081 467 8382); Woolwich Building Society, Corporate Headquarters, Watling St, Bexleyheath, Kent DA6 7RR (☎ 081 854 2400)

CUMMING, John Stuart; s of Stuart F M Cumming, MC, FFA (d 1961); *b* 18 March 1928; *Educ* Marlborough, CCC Cambridge; *m* 1956, Iseult Margaret, da of late Carl W Mercer; 1 s, 3 da; *Career* Lt RAOC; dir Hambros Bank Ltd 1977-88; dir Br Merchant Banking and Securities Houses Assoc 1989-; vice chm of govrs Rose Hill Sch Tunbridge Wells; MICAS; *Recreations* travel, gardening, opera; *Clubs* Sloane; *Style—* John Cumming Esq; Cheyne House, Langton Green, Tunbridge Wells, Kent TN3 0HP (☎ 0892 862066, office 071 796 3606)

CUNNINGHAM, John Roderick; s of John Cunningham (d 1952), of Kent, and Millicent, *née* Seal (d 1929); *b* 13 May 1926; *Educ* Beckenham Sch Kent, Queen's Univ Belfast NI (BSc); *m* 1964, Monica Rachel, da of Cedric Robert Seymour George (d 1964), of Horley, Surrey; 1 s (Roderick b 1965), 2 da (Meryl b 1955 (from previous marriage), Clare b 1970); *Career* dir Coutts and Co 1980-87, chm Nikko Bank plc 1987-; memb Bd of Govrs of Cordwainers Coll, chm City Branch Royal Soc of St George; vice chm: City Branch IOD, Tonbridge Cons Assoc; Master Worshipful Co of Loriners 1984; FCIB, FRSA; *Recreations* gardening in Southern Spain, City of London activities; *Clubs* IOD, Overseas Bankers, City Livery; *Style—* John R Cunningham, Esq; Oak Lodge, 126 Pembury Road, Tonbridge, Kent TN9 2JJ; The Nikko Bank (UK) plc, 17 Godliman Street, London EC4V 5BD (☎ 071 528 7070)

CURD, Sylvia Margaret; da of William Henry Smith (d 1936), of Court Lodge, Eltham, and Harriet Jane, *née* Tooley (d 1959); *b* 25 July 1923; *Educ* Forest Hill Sch for Girls, Roan Sch; *m* 23 Sept 1940, Leonard Walter Curd (d 1976), s of Charles Percival Curd (d 1941), of Ladywell, London; 2 s (David Leonard b 18 March 1945, Thomas Guy b 2 Dec 1952), 2 da (Sylvia Anne b 1 March 1943, Mary Pamela (twin) b 2 Dec 1952); *Career* antiques dealer; memb: NADFAS, Nat Arts Collection Fund, Weald of Kent Preservation Soc, Nat Tst, Goudhurst Drama Gp, Friends of St Mary's; *Recreations* painting, spinning, music, reading, travel; *Clubs* Drama; *Style—* Mrs Sylvia Curd; Old Saddlers, Church Rd, Goudhurst, Kent TN17 1BH (☎ 0580 211458)

CURRY, Rev Anthony Bruce; s of Arthur Samuel Curry (d 1974), and Gladys Hilda Curry (d 1966); *b* 17 Jan 1931; *Educ* Canterbury Cathedral Choir Sch, The King's Sch Canterbury, St Edmund Hall Oxford (MA), Wells Theol Coll; *m* 26 March 1955, (Ada Lettitia) Anne, da of Henry Jackson (d 1978), of Cardiff; 3 da (Gillian b 1956, Susan b 1959, Diana b 1965); *Career* asst curate All Saints Perry St Gravesend 1955-56, chaplain and music asst King's Sch Canterbury 1956-61, rector of Penshurst 1961-76, dir of Music Kelly Coll Tavistock and asst priest St Andrews Calstock 1976-85, rector of Brasted 1985-; examiner Royal Schs of Music 1980-; author of various articles on Influence of Lutheran Theology on J S Bach's Passion 1977; fndr: Penshurst Choral Soc and Orch 1963-, Becket Tst Penshurst 1974, Kelly Orch 1976-, Kelly Choral Soc 1976-; organ advsr Rochester Diocese 1971-76, reformed St Martins Singers and Players Brasted 1985-, music festival adjudicator, organist Bach recitals in France and Kent; responsible for twinning of Edenbridge and Mont-Saint-Aignan 1974; ARCO 1949; Médaille D'Honneur Mont-Saint-Aignan (France) 1986; *Recreations* chamber music, French language and culture, motoring; *Style—* The Rev Anthony Curry; The Rectory, Brasted, Westerham, Kent TN16 1NH (☎ 0959 63491); L'Ecurie, Montceau-Echarnant, 21360 Bligny-Sur-Ouche, France

CURTIS, Ken E; s of James Curtis (d 1932), and Rosina, *née* Hartley-Beaton (d 1975); *b* 8 May 1919; *Educ* Eldon Sch, Hornsey Sch of Art, Instituto del Arte Florence Italy; *m* 21 June 1947, Anne, da of James Scully (d 1966); 1 s (Glenn b 14 Feb 1953), 1 da (Kim b 6 Oct 1956); *Career* WWII RCSTA Royal Mountain Regt and Med Regts 1939-46 (despatches Italy 1944); advertising agent Dorland Advertising (subsid) 1933-39, gen mangr Scientific Publicity 1946-48, md Skingle of the Strand and We Design It Ltd 1948-68; dir: (jt) SF Partners 1968-80, (account) Smedley McAlpine 1980-87, Leberl Advertising 1987-; memb RA Comrades Assoc; Freeman City of London 1961, Liveryman Worshipful Co of Carmen 1961; MIPA; Polish Order of Merit (War Serv Polish Army in Italy 1944); *Recreations* writing, wildlife; *Clubs* City Livery, World Trade Centre; *Style—* Ken Curtis, Esq; 35 Brabourne Rise, Park Langley, Beckenham BR3 2SQ; Leberl Advertising, 7 Brooks Court, Kirtling St, London SW8 5BX (☎ 071 720 1966)

CUTHBERT, Cncllr Colin Spencer; s of Spencer Arthur Cuthbert (d 1927), of Cliftonville, and Norah Edith, *née* Dening (d 1971); *b* 2 Oct 1922; *Educ* Chatham House GS Ramsgate; *m* 24 Feb 1945, Barbara, da of John Nicholls (d 1982), of Merthyr Tydfil, S Wales; 3 da (Susan b 21 Nov 1947, Julia b 18 Aug 1951, Anne b 13 Aug 1954); *Career* War Serv Flt Sgt RAF and RAAF served Europe; md SA Cuthbert & Co Ltd; magistrate Margate Bench 1967-77, former memb Margate Borough Cncl, dep ldr Thanet Dist Cncl; memb various local music socs and choirs, former memb London Chamber Singers; *Recreations* music, ham radio, travel, people; *Style—* Cncllr Colin Cuthbert; 37 Laleham Rd, Margate, Kent; 14 Church St, Penyslassen, Merthyr Tydfil (☎ 0843 227061); 278/280 Northdown Rd, Margate, Kent (☎ 0843 220125)

CUTTING, Dr John Charles; s of Dr Charles Latham Cutting of Bath, and Frances Cutting (d 1946); *b* 31 Oct 1946; *Educ* Hymers Coll Hull, Guy's Hosp (MB BS, MD, MPhil); *m* 1, (m dis 1981), Elizabeth Ann, *née* Murgatroyd; 2 s (Roger Kenneth b 21 July 1975, Graham John b 4 Oct 1977; m 2, 22 Sept 1984, Rosemary Catherine Anne, da of Ralph Ivor Charlish (d 1982); *Career* sr lectr KCH 1979-83, conslt psychiatrist Bethlem Royal and Maudsley Hosps London 1983-; memb ed bd Journal of Neurology, Neurosurgery and Pschiatry; FRSM 1973, memb assoc BR Neurologists 1982; *Books* The Psychology of Schizophrenia (1985), The Clinical Roots of the Schizophrenia Concept (with M Shepherd, 1987); *Recreations* reading, gardening, tennis, bridge; *Style—* Dr John Cutting; Mill Wood, Wall Hill, Forest Row, E Sussex RH18 5EG (☎ 034 2823335)

D

D'AVIGDOR-GOLDSMID, Lady; Rosemary Margaret; eldest da of Lt-Col Rice Iltyd Charles Nicholl, TD (d 1950); *b* 22 July 1910; *m* 1, 29 Oct 1931 (m dis 1934), Sir Peter Horlick, 3 Bt (d 1958); m 2, 23 Feb 1940, Maj Sir Henry Joseph d'Avigdor-Goldsmid, 2 Bt, DSO, MC, TD (d 1976); 2 da (1 decd); *Recreations* horse racing; *Style—* Lady d'Avigdor-Goldsmid; The Old Laundry, Tudeley, nr Tonbridge, Kent TN11 0NT (☎ 0732 352314); 2 Eaton Mansions, Cliveden Place, London SW1 (☎ 071 730 3034)

DABESTANI, Dr Mehdi; s of Amrollah Dabestani, of Bombay, India, and Nawrasteh Dabestani; *b* 23 June 1945; *Educ* Grant Med Coll Bombay, Univ of Bombay (MB BS); *m* 21 July 1978, Fereshteh, da of Hassan Rezaei, of Shiraz, Iran; 2 s (Mehran b 1979, Farhad b 1980); *Career* Nat Serv army med offr Iran 1978-79; employed in various hosps, GP 1983-; sec Spiritual Assembly of Baha'is of Gillingham; memb: GMC 1975, MDU 1976, BMA 1976; *Recreations* swimming, chess, backgammon, computers; *Style—* Dr Mehdi Dabestani; 222a Hempstead Rd, Hempstead, Gillingham, Kent ME7 3QG (☎ 0634 35264); Walderslade Medical Centre, Princes Ave, Chatham, Kent ME5 7PQ (☎ 0634 682611)

DAFTER, Raymond Maurice (Ray); s of Maurice Henry Dafter, of Swindon, Wilts, and Dorothy Joan, *née* Vincent; *b* 22 April 1944; *Educ* Marlborough GS, The Coll Swindon, Harvard Univ; *m* 25 Sept 1965, Christine, da of William Charles Richard Franklin (d 1976), of Swindon, Wilts; 2 da (Yvonne Louise b 5 May 1968, Claire Rachel b 13 Dec 1970); *Career* journalist: Evening Advertiser Swindon 1961-64, Evening Post Bristol 1964-70, Financial Times London 1970-83; central dir Public and Overseas Relations Electricity Cncl London 1983-88, dep chief exec and head of consultancy Valin Pollen Ltd 1988-90, corp affairs dir Enterprise Oil plc 1990-; cncl memb Br Inst of Energy Econ; FInstPet 1978, MIPR 1988; *Books* Running Out of Fuel (1978), Scraping the Barrel (1980), Winning More Oil (1982); *Recreations* sailing, music, flying, walking; *Style—* Ray Dafter, Esq; Wolsey Oast, Claygate Rd, Laddingford, Kent (☎ 089 273 376)

DAGGER, John Frederick Hannay; s of Richard Leslie Dagger, (d 1973), of Newcastle upon Tyne, and Iris, *née* Hannay (d 1973); *b* 13 July 1927; *Educ* Uppingham; *m* 19 June 1948, Patricia Anne, da of Charles Edward Thompson (d 1979), of Sheffield; 1 s (Richard b 1950), 1 da (Sarah b 1953); *Career* Capt Coldstream Gds 1945-52 (Malaya 1948-50); tea planter S India 1952-56, Hopfactors (UK) Ltd 1957 (dir 1963-86); genealogist; memb AGRA 1984; *Recreations* walking, looking up old relatives; *Style—* John Dagger, Esq; Oak House, Horsmonden, Tonbridge, Kent TN12 8LP (☎ 0892 722272)

DAKERS, Michael John; s of William Geoffrey Dakers, and Dorothy Irene, *née* Groombridge; *b* 21 June 1944; *Educ* Dover Coll, Coll of Law, Notts Coll of Technol; *m* 7 June 1969, Jennifer Anne, da of Glyn Lewis Coxon (d 1987), of Roughclose, Fairy Lane, Sale, Cheshire; 1 s (Oliver Jevon b 31 Dec 1971), 1 da (Lorna Anne b 19 Aug 1970); *Career* admitted slr 1967; ptnr Basset & Boucher 1969-85, sr ptnr Dakers Green Brett 1985-; legal memb Town Planning Inst 1975 (legal asst 1970), cmmr of oaths 1970-71, hon pub rels offr Kent Law Soc 1974-86, pres Rochester Chatham and Gillingham Law Soc 1987; City of Rochester Round Table: memb 1970-85, chm 1973-74, sec 1980-81; memb Rochester Rotary Club 1977-87; govr Dover Coll 1984-; chm: Firmstart Medway 1988-, Medway Sports Cncl 1986-89-, Medway Rugby Football Club 1986-88-; memb Law Soc 1967; *Recreations* rugby, squash, travel, building dry stone walls; *Clubs* Castle Maidstone (Rochester), Roffen; *Style—* Michael Dakers, Esq; The Old Bellhouse, Lower Warren Rd, Aylesford, Kent; Dakers Green Brett, 125 High St, Strood, Kent ME2 4TJ (☎ 0634 290929, fax 0634 290398)

DANCE, Cncllr Edwin William Francis; s of Francis George Dance (d 1943), of Spencers Wood, Reading, and Elsie Ada, *née* Rays (d 1965); *b* 10 Sept 1933; *Educ* Reading Sch, Univ of Reading (BSc); *m* 22 Sept 1962, Jennifer Hilda, da of Charles Rayfield (d 1979), of Bexley, Kent; 1 da (Angela Mary (Mrs Collard) b 1964); *Career* asst tech offr Miny of Agric 1957, farmer 1958-82, area mangr Kent CC Key Scheme 1983-; memb: Westerham Parish Cncl 1977-, Sevenoaks Dist Cncl 1978-; chm Tunbridge Wells Community Heath Cncl 1988- (memb 1982-); memb Cons Party; chm: Gravesend Young Conservatives 1961-63, Crockham Hill Primary Sch Parent Teachers Assoc 1964-65, Crockham Hill Bonfire Soc 1973-82, Crockham Hill Jubilee Ctee 1976-77, Playing Fields Ctee 1978-85, Edenbridge British Week 1980, Edenbridge NFU 1979-81; memb Kent Co Exec, vice chm Party Ctee, sch govr 1979-88; memb: Kent Playfields Assoc Exec 1981-, Nat Playfields Cncl 1981-, Edenbridge CAB Mgmnt Ctee, Kent Fire Liason Ctee; *Recreations* model and preserved railways, local history, touring; *Clubs* Farmers (past memb); *Style—* Cncllr Edwin Dance; 35 Ash Rd, Westerham, Kent TN16 1EJ (☎ 0959 63151); Varo House, Dartford, Kent (☎ 0322 92427, 0322 72987, 0322 75891)

DANIEL, Ian Roger; s of Colin Vernon George Raynor Daniel, of Upchurch, Kent, and Doris Edith, *née* Tress; *b* 20 Sept 1947; *Educ* Sir Joseph Williamson's Maths Sch Rochester, Barking Regnl Coll; *m* 17 Aug 1978, Angela Mary, da of Stanley Charles Lacy (d 1980); 2 da (Nicola Daniel b 1970, Sarah Daniel b 1971); *Career* fin controller Southern Europe Measurex International Systems Ltd 1976-81, fin dir and co sec Deacon Contracting Group Ltd 1981-; CIMA, MIOD; *Recreations* golf, cricket, badminton; *Clubs* Sheerness Golf, Milstead Cricket, Gore Court Badminton; *Style—* Ian Daniel, Esq; Black Brooms, 114 Oak Lane, Upchurch, Sittingbourne, Kent (☎ 0634 34538); Deacon Contracting Group Ltd, Buckingham House, Longfield Rd, Tunbridge Wells, Kent (☎ 0892 39211, fax 0892 36361, car phone 0836 239633)

DANIELS, Christopher Cyril; s of Douglas Archibald Daniels, OBE (d 1954), of Deal, Kent, and Phyllis Everett, *née* Gattie; *b* 29 Dec 1935; *Educ* Sir Roger Manwoods Sch Sandwich Kent, Univ of Bonn; *m* 31 Dec 1980, Jeanette Collyer Hamlin, *née* Pallett; 1 s (John Collyer Hamlin b 1966), 1 da (Helen Rosemary b 1968), both children by previous marriage; *Career* Capt Army Legal Serv 1960-61; dep town clerk Deal 1963-64, former sr ptnr Kingsford Arrowsmith & Wightwick Canterbury, clerk to Gen Cmmnrs of Income Tax 1976-; clerk to Charity of William Barrow Borden Kent 1976-, currently conslt Robinson & Allfree & Kingsfords; memb: Rotary Club of Canterbury, Nat Ctee Assoc of Clerks to Gen Cmmnrs of Income Tax, Assoc of Men of Kent and Kentish Men; tstee Kent and Canterbury Club; memb Law Soc; *Recreations* walking, swimming; *Clubs* Royal Cwlth Tst, Kent and Canterbury Club; *Style—* Christopher Daniels, Esq; Mandalay House, Pierpoint Rd, Whitstable, Kent CT5 4NW; 16 Watling St, Canterbury, Kent (☎ 0227 762247)

DARBY, Rev Michael Barwick; s of Lewis Barwick Darby (d 1979), of Ramsgate, and Georgina Elizabeth Rita, *née* Stannard (d 1961); *b* 18 Feb 1934; *Educ* Chatham House Ramsgate, Univ Coll of St David Lampeter (BA), Trinity Coll Bristol; *m* 31 March 1962, Dorothy Joyce, da of William James Johnson (d 1976), of Ramsgate; 1 s (Andrew b 30 Nov 1971), 2 da (Nicola b 12 June 1965, Philippa b 14 March 1970); *Career* Nat Serv RAF; curate: St Andrew's Thornhill Square London 1963-66, St John's W Ealing London 1966-68; vicar: St Mary's Broomfleet Yorkshire 1968-73, Emmanuel Paddington London 1973-78; chaplain: The Good Shepherd Ahwaz Iran 1978-79, Christ Church Rio de Janeiro Brazil 1980-83; vicar St Faith's Maidstone 1984-; chm: Paddington Christian Cncl Community Work Ctee 1975-77, Paddington Christian Cncl 1977; memb: London Rent Assessment Panel 1977, Br Security Ctee in Ahwaz 1978-79; hon chaplain: Mission to Seaman Rio de Janeiro 1980-83, Maidstone ATC 1986-; *Recreations* filling in forms, walking, reading, railways, photograph, local church history; *Clubs* Rotary (Maidstone); *Style—* The Rev Michael Darby; St Faith's Vicarage, Moncktons Lane, Maidstone, Kent ME14 2PY (☎ 0622 51079); 20 Liverpool Lawn, Ramsgate, Kent

DARDRY-SMITH, Francis Alan; s of Basil Herbert Dardry-Smith, and Kathleen Emily Jean, *née* Pugh; *b* 20 March 1949; *Educ* Highfields Rochester Kent; *m* 21 May 1977, Jacqueline Yvonne, da of Charles Hugh Brace, of Torren House, Woolwich, London; 1 s (Simon Christopher b 1978), 1 da (Alison Clare b 1981); *Career* mangr Ronald Bampton 1975-81, princ ptnr Dardry-Smith estate agents surveyors and auctioners 1981-86; md: Fernfen Assoc, Second Nature Gift Shops, Second Nature Garden Designs; sales dir Oakhaven Gp of Cos, dir Kentish Property Centres; Lord of the Manor of Bavent and of Courston Hall; memb: Assoc of Men of Kent and Kentish Man (longstanding), Woodland Tst; FNAEA; *Recreations* golf, squash, village and country life, nature conservation; *Style—* Francis Dardry-Smith, Esq; Little

Barn, The Lees, Challock, Kent (☎ 023 374 433); Palace Gallery, Market Place, Charing, Kent (☎ 023 371 3587)

DART, Philip John; s of Wilfrid Stanley Dart, of Torquay, and Irene Jean, *née* Crews; *b* 8 July 1956; *Educ* Audley Park Sch Torquay, S Devon Tech Coll, Univ of Hull (BA); *m* 2 Nov 1985, Claudia Peta Kathleen, da of Peter Leaf; 1 s (Joseph b 1989), 1 da (Jessica b 1987); *Career* dir B Co 1979-80, artistic dir Channel Theatre Co 1986- (assoc dir 1980-86), freelance theatre dir; *Books* The Mysteries at Canterbury Cathedral (co-adapter, 1986); *Recreations* swimming, collecting 1930's memorabilia; *Style*— Philip Dart, Esq; Channel Theatre Co, Granville Theatre, Victoria Parade, Ramsgate, Kent CT11 8DG (☎ 0843 588280, 588260)

DAVIES, David Cyril; s of D T Davies, and Mrs G Davies, JP; *b* 7 Oct 1925; *Educ* Lewis Sch Pengam, UCW Aberystwyth (LLB); *m* 1952, Joan Rogers; 2 children; *Career* headmaster Crown Woods Sch 1971-84; *Style*— David Davies, Esq; 9 Plaxtol Close, Bromley, Kent (☎ 071 464 4187)

DAVIES, Hon David Daniel; yr s of Baron Davies of Penrhys (Life Peer); *b* 1944; *m* 1969, Cheryl, da of Thomas Herbert, of Tylorstown, Rhondda; 1s; *Style*— The Hon David Davies

DAVIES, Elidir Leslie Wish; s of late Rev Thomas John Landy Davies, and Hetty Boucher, *née* Wish; *b* 3 Jan 1907; *Educ* Colchester Sch, Bartlett Sch of Architecture, Univ of London; *m* 1, Vera, *née* Goodwin (d 1974); m 2, 1976, Kathleen Burke-Collis; *Career* chartered architect Elidir L W Davies and Partners; FRIBA, FRSA; *Clubs* Garrick; *Style*— Elidir Davies, Esq; Burnswood, Groombridge, Kent

DAVIES, Gordon Lionel; s of William Colin Davies (d 1956), of Sevenoaks, and Florence May, *née* Sellick (d 1966); *b* 14 April 1926; *Educ* Sevenoaks Sch, Camberwell Sch of Art, RCA (ARCA); *Career* botanical illustrator and author of occasional articles for House & Garden magazine 1948-70; designer of fabrics and wallpaper; maker of porcelain and terra cotta figures; large scale murals painted at: Wye Coll Kent, Wolfson Coll Cambridge, Braxted Park Essex, Chandos Chapel Whitchurch, and in France Switzerland and USA; paintings and drawings shown regularly at Royal Acad Summer Exhibition 1953-, reg one man shows in London and Kent 1976-; chm Hastingleigh Parish Cncl 1970- (memb 1967-); *Books* Working with Acrylics (1984); *Recreations* gardening, music, travel; *Style*— Gordon Davies, Esq; South View, Hastingleigh, Ashford, Kent TN25 5HU (☎ 023 375 264)

DAVIES, Brig (David) Hugh; MC (1944); s of David John Davies, JP (d 1938), of Carmarthen, Dyfed, Wales, and Catherine Jane, *née* Philipps (d 1963); *b* 17 Aug 1918; *Educ* Cathedral Sch Hereford, RMC Sandhurst; *m* 20 March 1943, Audrey, da of Jesse James Smith (d 1954), of Tenterden, Kent; 1 da (Jane Caroline (Mrs Cookson) b 15 Nov 1945); *Career* cmmnd KORR 1938, active serv Palestine 1938-39 (wounded), WWII serv 107 Regt RAC (Adj, Sqdn Ldr, Actg CO), Holland (wounded 1944), Staff Coll Haifa Palestine 1945, GS02 1 Div and Actg GS01 Palestine 1946-48, transferred 7 QOH, Adj 1948-49 (despatches 1949), DAAG AG 17 WO 1949-51, Sqdn Ldr and 2 i/c 7 Hussars 1951-53, instr Staff Coll Camberley 1956-58, CO 1958-61 asst dir plans Jt Planning Staff MOD 1961-63, Cdr 5 Inf Bde Gp 1963-65, Col QOH 1964-72, Brig RAC HQ Western Cmd 1966-68; chm: Rose Smith & Co (Fuel) Ltd 1978-84 (non exec dir 1968-75), Kent Royal Br Legion; pres Ashford Valley Foxhounds, Rolvenden and Tenterden branches Royal Br Legion; treas Rolvenden Cons Assoc; Hon Freeman Carmarthen 1950; *Recreations* hunting, fishing; *Clubs* Cavalry and Guards, Army and Navy; *Style*— Brig Hugh Davies, MC; Barton Wood, Rolveden, Cranbrook, Kent (☎ 0580 241 294)

DAVIES, Philippa June; da of Godfrey William Frederick Goodman (Bill) (d 1969), of Rosemount Cottage, Chislehurst, Kent, and Rhona Joyce, *née* Tallack; *b* 7 June 1946; *Educ* Farringtons Sch Chislehurst Kent, Guy's, London Sch of Physiotherapy; *m* 24 June 1967, John Howard (Jake) Davies, s of Charles Ronald Davies, TD, JP, DL (d 1975), of Blackburn, Lancs; 1 s (William b 2 May 1973), 2 da (Fenella b 20 May 1969, Annabel b 15 Jan 1971); *Career* chartered physiotherapist; Ashford Hosp 1977-87, Kent and Canterbury Hosp 1982-88, i/c Sports Injury Clinic Univ of Kent 1986-, own private practice 1988, physiotherapist to Combined Univs Cricket Team 1988-90; PRO E Kent Branch of Chartered Soc of Physiotherapy, past govr of Simon Langton GSs Canterbury, fndr and hon sec The Betjeman Soc; squash coach (co player 1976-78), winner Outer Kent League plate 1976 and 1977, runner up Intercity Nat Squash Competition 1987, donor of Philippa Davies Trophy to be competed for by teams of girls from Kent clubs; author various articles on physiotherapy for Kentish Gazette; *Recreations* walking, talking, calligraphy, tennis, squash, golf, book collector, dolls house collector; *Clubs* Canterbury Lawn Tennis, Kent Soc, Betjeman Soc, Kent SRA, Old Farringtonians Assoc, Faversham NADFAS; *Style*— Mrs Philippa Davies; Haleswood, 2 The Crescent, St Stephens, Canterbury, Kent CT2 7AG (☎ 0227 454200); The Sports Injury Clinic, The University of Kent, Canterbury, Kent CT2 7HZ (☎ 0227 764000)

DAVIES, Ronald Vickers; s of Percy Horatio Alderman Davies (d 1972), of Rochester, and Evelyn Lucy, *née* Salt; *b* 19 Dec 1932; *Educ* Troy Town Secdy Sch Rochester, GSM (Assoc GSM), The Coll of Preceptors; *m* 10 Aug 1967, Gladys, da of William Cornelius Dennord, of 11 Lancelot Ave, Strood, Kent; 1 s (Edward Dennord b 22 July 1969); *Career* teacher Borstal Manor Co Primary Sch 1962-70, headmaster St Mary's Co Primary Sch 1978- (dep headmaster 1970-78); hon local rep of Assoc Bd of Royal Schs of Music, treas Medway Towns Schs Music Assoc, dir Medway Heritage Centre; Assoc Coll of Preceptors 1976; *Recreations* singing, reading, gardening; *Style*— Ronald Davies, Esq; 193 Wilson Ave, Rochester, Kent (☎ 0634 403500); St Mary's County Primary School, Gun Lane, Strood, Kent (☎ 0634 717115)

DAVIES, Lady Venetia Constance Kathleen Luz; *née* Hay; da of 14 Earl of Kinnoull; *b* 1929; *m* 1953, Maj Joseph Trevor Davies; 2 da (Nicola b 1957, Sally b 1960); *Style*— The Lady Venetia Davies; 14 Old School Court, Grimston Gardens, Folkestone, Kent CT20 2UA

DAVIS, Lady Alison Elizabeth; yst da of 1 Earl Attlee (d 1967); *b* 14 April 1930; *m* 8 March 1952, Richard Lionel Lance Davis, s of late Maj Arthur Owen Lance Davis, of Hinckley, Leics; 3 da (Jennifer (Mrs Lochen) b 1953, Tessa (Dr Dormon) b 1955, Belinda (Mrs Johnston) b 1957); *Style*— The Lady Alison Davis; Westcott, 8 Beacon Rise, Sevenoaks, Kent TN13 2NJ

DAVIS, Chloë Marion; *née* Pound; OBE (1975); da of Richard Henry Pound; *b* 15 Feb 1909; *m* 1928, Edward Thomas Davis; 1 s; *Career* memb Consumer Consultative Ctee EEC 1973-76, Cncl on Tribunals 1970-79, Consumer Standards Advsy Ctee of Br Standards Instn 1965-78 (chm 1970-73); chm Consumer Affrs Gp of Nat Organisations 1973-; *Style*— Mrs Edward Davis OBE; Auberville Cottage, 246 Dover Rd, Walmer, Kent

DAVIS, Rev Clinton Ernest Newman; s of Stanley Ernest Davis (d 1989), of Fairlight, Hastings, E Sussex, and Muriel Rosemary, *née* Sawyer; *b* 19 Nov 1946; *Educ* Chislehurst and Sidcup GS for Boys, Maidstone Tech Coll, Coll of Law Guildford, Wycliffe Hall Oxford; *m* 23 Dec 1972, Nancy Margaret, da of Donald Ivor Litten, of Saltwood, Hythe, Kent; 2 s (Rupert Clinton Newman b 1974, Edward Gabriel Anastasius b 1975), 1 da (Sophie Joy Elizabeth b 1982); *Career* admitted slr 1971; articled 1966-71, asst slr Wellers Bromley 1971-73, asst prosecuting slr Kent CC 1973-78; ordained priest by Archbishop of Canterbury 1981 (deacon 1980); asst curate: Holy Trinity Margate 1980-84, St Lawrence-in-Thanet (with special responsibility for St Mary the Virgin Cliffsend) 1984-87 and St Catherine Manston 1985-87; officiating chaplain RAF Manston 1987, vicar of Sandgate 1987-; chaplain: St Mary's Hosp Etchinghill 1987-, 2nd Sandgate Scouts Gp, Royal Br Legion Sandgate Branch; vocations advsr for Archdeaconry of Canterbury 1988-; vice chm governing body Sandgate Co Primary Sch; *Recreations* family, law, music, gardening, education; *Style*— The Rev Clinton Davis; The Vicarage, 10 Meadowbrook, Sandgate, Folkestone, Kent CT20 3NY (☎ 0303 48675)

DAVIS, David Osmond; s of Wing Cdr John Osmond Davis (d 1975), of Espinette, Fordcombe, Kent, and Gwendoline Adelaide, *née* Rolles (d 1975); *b* 17 Oct 1935; *Educ* Sevenoaks Sch; *m* 3 Oct 1959, Sylvia, da of Harry Clarke (d 1988), of The Royal Hosp, Chelsea; 1 s (Mark Osmond b 31 Aug 1960), 1 da (Heidi Gail Osmond b 10 Oct 1964); *Career* Nat Serv fighter control RAF 1956; Osmond Davis & Co Ltd: joined 1956, co sec 1958, dir 1963, chm and md 1975; chm Kent and E Sussex Region Corpn of Insur Brokers 1978, vice pres Br Insur and Investmt Brokers Assoc 1989- (regnl chm 1979); gen cmmnr Income Tax Sevenoaks Div Kent, chm of govrs Tonbridge GS for Girls; memb: Tonbridge Rotary Club (pres 1981-82); memb Tonbridge and Malling Borough Cncl Hildenborough Ward 1973-87: chm cncl 1978-79, chm Planning and Transportation Ctee, ldr cncl; Freeman Tonbridge and Malling Borough Cncl 1987; ACII; *Recreations* countryside matters, beekeeping, conservation; *Clubs* Royal Automobile; *Style*— David Osmond Davis, Esq; Barley Corn, Vines Lane, Hildenborough, Tonbridge, Kent TN11 9LT (☎ 0732 832544); Osmond Davis & Co Ltd, Minerva House, Bordyke, Tonbridge, Kent TN9 1NP (☎ 0732 366611)

DAVIS, Gillian Ann; da of Leslie William Palmer (d 1987), of Bearsted, Kent, and Margery Florence, *née* Chapman; *b* 3 Dec 1941; *Educ* Chislehurst Sidcup Girls GS, Battersea Coll of Technol (BSc); *m* 3 April 1965, Leonard George Davis, s of George Charles Davis (d 1988), of Chislehurst, Kent; 1 s (Gavin George b 1969), 1 da (Tina Ann b 1967); *Career* system analyst IBM 1963-66, L Messel Stockbrokers 1966-67, dir and co sec Glensound Electronics Ltd 1978-; treas Medway and Maidstone Gp Coeliac Soc UK; *Recreations* dress making, reading; *Style*— Mrs Gillian Davis; Glensound Electronics Ltd, Brooks Place, Maidstone, Kent ME14 1HE (☎ 0622 753662, fax 0622 762330)

DAVIS, Ivor John Guest; CB (1983); s of Thomas Henry Davis (d 1963); *b* 11 Dec 1925; *Educ* Devonport HS, Univ of London (external BSc); *m* 1954, Mary Eleanor, da of Robert Porter Thompson (d 1974); 2 c; *Career* comptroller-gen patents trade marks and designs Patent Office 1978-85; pres Admin Cncl Euro Patent Office 1981-84; dir Common Law Inst of Intellectual Property 1986; *Recreations* music, gardening; *Style*— Ivor Davis, Esq, CB; 5 Birch Close, Eynsford, Dartford, Kent (☎ 0322 862725)

DAVIS, Kenneth Joseph; s of Kenneth Sydney Joseph Davis, of North Weald, Essex, and Dorothy May Addison, *née* Briggs; *b* 19 March 1948; *Educ* Mark Hall Sch Harlow Essex, City of Portsmouth Coll of Educn and Univ of Southampton (BEd), Wolverhampton Poly (DMS), London Inst of Educn (MA); *m* 5 Sept 1970, Susan Mary, da of late George Cavell Thompson, of

Harlow, Essex; 1 s (Simon Kenneth George b 23 Jan 1979); *Career* computor operator and programmer London 1966-67, teacher Walsall W Midlands 1973-78 (Hants 1971-73), professional asst E Sussex CC 1978-80; Kent CC: asst educn offr 1980-83, divnl educn offr 1983-86, area educn offr 1986-; former memb: Maidstone Round Table, Chatham Round Table; chm Medway and Gillingham Young Enterprise Bd, memb Soc of Educn Offrs 1980; MBIM 1988; *Recreations* sailing; *Clubs* Bewl Sailing; *Style*— Kenneth Davis, Esq; North Kent Area Education Office, Mountbatton House, Military Rd, Chatham, Kent ME4 4JE (☎ 0634 407300)

DAVIS, Leonard George; s of George Davis (d 1988), of Chislehurst, Kent, and Winifred Mary, *née* Heywood (d 1960); *b* 9 March 1938; *Educ* Chislehurst and Sidcup Co Gs, Imperial Coll London (BSc); *m* 3 April 1965, Gillian Ann, da of Leslie William Palmer (d 1987), of Bearsted, Kent; 1 s (Gavin George b 1969), 1 da (Tina Ann b 1967); *Career* Designs Dept BBC 1959-66, fndr Glen Sound Services 1966-, chm and md Glensound Electronics Ltd 1978-; memb: Audio Engrg Soc Inc, Sound and Communications Industs Fedn, Old Centralians; assoc Inst of Broadcast Sound, ACGI; *Recreations* squash, furniture making; *Clubs* Harvey's Squash and Social; *Style*— Leonard Davis, Esq; Glensound Electronics Ltd, Brooks Place, Maidstone, Kent ME14 1HE (☎ 0622 753662, fax 0622 762330)

DAVIS, Michael Edward; s of Capt Raymond Norris Davis, of Sevenoaks, Kent, and Margaret, *née* Pierce; *b* 14 Aug 1951; *Educ* Sevenoaks Sch, Univ of London (BA); *m* 17 Aug 1974, Helen Frances, da of William Podmore, OBE JP, of Consall Hall, Wetley Rocks, Stoke on Trent, Staffs; 1 s (Paul Michael William b 4 July 1983), 1 da (Laura Helen Margaret b 6 Feb 1986); *Career* admitted slr 1977; ptnr Herbert Smith 1986- (joined 1975); Freeman Worshipful Co of Slrs; memb: Law Soc, Int Bar Assoc, Acad of Exports, Soc of Construction Law; *Recreations* horse riding, water skiing, travel, landscaping, rugby football; *Style*— Michael Davis, Esq; Herbert Smith, Watling House, 35 Cannon St, London EC4M 5SD (☎ 071 489 8000, fax 071 329 0426)

DAVIS, Michael Gerard; s of John Michael Davis (d 1972), of The Ridgeway, Wimbledon, London, and Helen, *née* Burke (d 1973); *b* 15 Sept 1924; *Educ* Wimbledon Coll, St John's Coll Cambridge; *m* 15 April 1958, (Mary) Carmel, da of Jeremiah John O'Sullivan (d 1961), of Greystones, Co Wicklow, Ireland; 2 s (Paul Michael b 6 Jan 1962, Michael Joseph b 3 May 1964); *Career* Flt Lt RAF 1943-47; asst treas Imperial Chemical Industries plc London 1960-65, fin dir ICI Europa Ltd Brussels Belgium 1969-80; memb SE Kent DHA, hon treas E Kent Hospice Project; FCA 1955 (ACA 1950); *Recreations* golf; *Clubs* Royal Cinque Ports Golf (Deal); *Style*— Michael Davis, Esq; Whitewalls, Granville Rd, St Margaret's Bay, Dover, Kent CT15 6DR (☎ 0304 852871)

DAWES, George Edwyn; s of George William Dawes, of Burnt Oak, Orlestone, nr Ashford, Kent, and Jill Margaret, *née* Davidson; *b* 24 March 1958; *Educ* Kings Sch Canterbury, Univ of Bristol (BA); *Career* Heathcote Ball & Co Leicester 1980-88 (co mangr 1983-88), mangr Phillips Son & Neale (Folkstone Branch) 1990-; friend of NSPCC; memb: Prehistoric Soc, BASC, The Game Conservancy; ARICS; *Recreations* shooting, squash, tennis, cricket, reading; *Clubs* Shepway Stragglers Cricket, Pluckley Cricket, The Orlestone Gp; *Style*— George Dawes, Esq; Phillips, 11 Bayle Parade, Folkestone, Kent CT20 1SQ (☎ 0303 45555)

DAY, Sir Derek Malcolm; KCMG (1984, CMG 1973); s of Alan W Day (d 1968), and Gladys, *née* Portlock (d 1974); *b* 29 Nov 1927; *Educ* Hurstpierpoint Coll, St Catharine's Coll Cambridge (MA); *m* 1955, Sheila, da of George Nott (d 1955), of Newnhan Bridge, Worcs; 3 s (William, Richard, Nicholas), 1 da (Katharine); *Career* HM Foreign Serv 1951: 3 sec Br Embasssy Tel Aviv 1953-56, private sec to ambass Rome 1956-59, 2 then 1 sec FO 1959-62, 1 sec HM Embassy Washington 1962-66, 1 sec FO 1966-67, asst private sec to Sec of State for Foreign Affrs 1967-68, head of Personnel Ops Dept FCO 1969-72, cnsllr Br High Cmmn Nicosia 1972-75, HM ambass to Ethiopia 1975-78, asst under sec FCO 1979, dep under sec of state FCO 1980, chief clerk 1982-84, Br high cmmr Ottawa 1984; dir Monenco Ltd Canada; cncl memb Canada-UK C of C, cmmr Cwlth War Graves Cmmn, vice chm BRCS, chm and govr Hurstpierpoint Coll, govr Bethany Sch; *Clubs* Hawks (Cambridge), United Oxford and Cambridge; *Style*— Sir Derek Day, KCMG; Etchinghill, Goudhurst, Kent

DAY, Frank Mercer; s of Mercer Day (d 1966), of Marden, and Ada, *née* Boorman (d 1974); *b* 8 June 1909; *Educ* Rose Hill Sch Tunbridge Wells; *m* 1 June 1940, Barbara Evelyn, da of Walter Merricks, of Icklesham, Sussex; 2 s (Roger b 1943, Colin b 1946), 3 da (Josephine b 1942, Heather b 1948, Daphne (twin) b 1948); *Career* farmer and horticulturalist; pres Kent CCC 1976; memb Lloyds, NFU, CLO; *Recreations* cricket, bowls, hockey; *Clubs* Kent Co Cricket, Marden Bowls, Marden Cricket, Marden Russetts Hockey; *Style*— Frank Day, Esq

DAY, Rev George Chester; s of Stanley George Day, of New Malden, and Edith Mary, *née* Biss; *b* 22 Sept 1945; *Educ* Kingston GS, Univ of Exeter (BA), Clifton Theol Coll, Univ of London (BD); *m* 16 Aug 1969, Elaine Hilda, da of Cyril Victor Quinnell, of Tonbridge; 1 s (Mark b 1972), 1 da (Katharine b 1975); *Career* ordained deacon 1971, ordained priest 1972, curate St Lawrence Morden i/c Emmanuel Church 1975-81 (St John with St Stephen Reading 1971-75), vocation and miny sec Church Pastorial Aid Soc 1981-85, vicar St Barnabas Church St Paul's Cray 1986-; *Recreations* gardening, mountain walking; *Style*— The Rev George Day; The Vicarage, Rushet Rd, St Paul's Cray, Orpington, Kent BR5 2PU (☎ 0689 21353)

DAY, (Edward) Peter; s of John Day (d 1968), of West Farleigh, Maidstone, and Florrie Julia Levett Tassell (d 1972); *b* 14 Oct 1912; *Educ* Maidstone GS, Sutton Valence; *m* 1, 6 June 1936, Eileen Mary (d 1981), da of Ernest John Parker; 1 s (John Peter b 6 July 1938); m 2, 10 July 1982, Shirley Maureen Day; *Career* farmer; special Constable 1936-62; JP Tonbridge and Malling 1962-82 (chm of Bench 1976-82); chm: Maidstone Round Table 1933-51, Maidstone Branch NFU 1944-45 (memb 1930-), Hops Ctee NFU 1949-76 (memb 1948-), Kent Branch NFU 1955-56, Legal Ctee Kent NFU 1966-83 (memb 1956-90), Bd of Visitors Maidstone Prison 1974-75 (memb 1965-75), Kent Magistrates Assoc 1976-78 (memb 1974-82), West Farleigh Parish Cncl 1957- (memb 1946-); churchwarden West Farleigh PCC 1951-82 (treas 1940-82), memb Governing Body East Malling Res Station 1954-87, ctee memb ARC Res Ctee; *Recreations* rugby, cricket, golf, hunting, shooting; *Style*— Peter Day, Esq; Green Oaks, Charlton Lane, W Farleigh, Maidstone, Kent ME15 0PA (☎ 0622 812296); Tutsham Farm, W Farleigh, Maidstone, Kent (☎ 0622 812532)

de BENE, John William; s of Reginald Burton de Bene (d 1988), and Anthea Mary, *née* Halliday, of Cranbrook, Kent; *b* 5 April 1945; *Educ* Univ of Birmingham (MB ChB); *m* Jill Elizabeth; 2 da (Jessica b 27 April 1977, Harriet b 27 June 1978); *Career* Capt TA Med Corps Rhodesian Govt; princ in gen practice Maidstone 1973-90; unit gen mangr: Maternal and Child Health Unit Maidstone Health Authy 1985-, Acute, Elderly and Physically Handicapped Health Unit Maidstone Health Authy 1988-; memb BMA; *Recreations* music, theatre, opera; *Style*— John de Bene, Esq; 8 Wytherling Close, Bearsted Park, Maidstone, Kent (☎ 0622 35186); Maidstone Hospital, Post Grad Centre, Hermitage Lane, Barming, Maidstone, Kent ME16 9QQ (☎ 0622 729000 x 4752); The Surgery (☎ 0622 52345)

de COURCY, Molly Elizabeth; da of Sidney Havelock Buley (d 1957), of Herts, and Elfie Mary, *née* Stockbridge (d 1965); *b* 31 Oct 1931; *Educ* St Mary's Convent Cambridge, Univ of Reading (BSc, DipEd); *m* 17 April 1954, Alan Victor de Courcy, s of James Victor de Courcy, of Surrey; 2 s (Bruce b 27 April 1956, Ian b 16 May 1958), 1 da (Sally b 9 Dec 1962); *Career* biology teacher Ely HS and Simon Langton GS for Girls; field offr duke of Edinburgh Award Scheme, pres Dial Kent, pres Canterbury and Thanet Multiple Sclerosis Soc, exec Kent Rural Community Cncl; memb Riverside Youth Club, E Kent Art Soc, Canterbury Festival and Theatre Tst; chm children and families sub ctee Kent CC Social Servs, memb Canterbury and Thanet DHA, chm of govrs St Nicholas Special Sch; govr: SLGS, Parkside Primary Sch, SLBS; chm Ashford Sch for Girls; *Recreations* long distance walking, painting, cooking, travel; *Style*— Mrs Molly de Courcy; Badgers Hill, Chilham, Canterbury, Kent (☎ 0227 730315), Kent County Council, County Hall, Maidstone, Kent (☎ 0227 730315)

DE DARANYI, Hon Mrs (Kirstie Elisabeth); *née* Forbes-Sempill; da of 19 Lord Sempill, AFC (d 1965), and his 2 w, Cecilia Alice, *née* Dunbar-Kilburn (d 1984); *b* 9 Aug 1944; *m* 1, 1968 (m dis 1989), John Michael Forbes-Cable (who assumed the additional surname of Forbes by Deed Poll 1968); 2 s (William Richard Craigievar b 1970, Malcolm Dunbar Craigievar b 1972); m 2, 17 Feb 1990, Bela P de Daranyi, 2 s of late Bela de Daranyi and late Countess Margit Daranyi-Haller de Hallerkeo, of Budapest, Hungary; *Style*— The Hon Mrs de Daranyi; Wingham Barton Manor, Westmarsh, nr Canterbury, Kent CT3 2LW

DE FRESNES, (Christopher) Ian; eldest s of 12 Baron de Fresnes (French title); *b* 8 May 1942; *Educ* Ampleforth, Glasgow Sch of Art; *m* 1, 1969 (dis 1971), Elvira Maria, da of Wing Cdr Marcel Pustelniak; 1 s (Robert b 1970); m 2, 1973, Angela, da of Lt-Col Denys Ainsworth Yates; 1 s (Rawdon b 1974) 1 da (Nicola b 1975); *Style*— Ian de Fresnes, Esq; Elm Tree House, High Halden, Ashford, Kent TN26 3BP

DE GELSEY, Alexander Henry Marie; CBE (1989); s of Baron Henry de Gelsey (d 1963), and Marguerite, *née* Lieser (d 1965); *b* 24 June 1924; *Educ* RC Univ Sch Budapest, Trinity Coll Cambridge; *m* 5 Feb 1969, Romy, da of Frederick Edgar Cairns (d 1972), of Oxford; 1 da (Annabel b 1975); *Career* chm Sericol Int Ltd 1955-, memb SE Thams RHA 1984-88, chm E Kent Enterprise Agency 1985-; memb: Kent Econ Devpt Bd 1986-, Kent Investments Ltd 1986-, Southern Bd BR 1988-, Special Health Authy 1989-, Governing Cncl Univ of Kent 1989-; govr: Cobham Hall Sch, W Heath Sch; hon consul gen of the Republic of Hungary 1990-; *Recreations* shooting, boating, travelling, walking; *Style*— Alexander de Gelsey, Esq, CBE; 22 South Terrace, London SW7 2TD (☎ 071 581 2541, fax 071 584 4156); Boughton Church House, Faversham, Kent ME13 9NB (☎ 0227 751202, fax 0227 750962)

DE L'ISLE, Lord William Philip Sidney; 9 Bt (UK 1806 & 1818), of Castle Goring, Sussex, and 7 Bt of Penshurst Place, Kent, respectively, VC (1944), KG (1968), GCMG (1961), GCVO (1963), PC (1951); 1 Viscount (UK 1956), also Baron De L'Isle and Dudley (UK 1835); s of 5 Baron De L'Isle and Dudley, JP (d 1945), and Winifred (d 1959), da of Roland Yorke Bevan and Hon Agneta, da of 10 Lord Kinnaird; *b* 23 May 1909; *Educ* Eton, Magdalene Coll Cambridge; *m* 1, 8 June 1940, Hon Jacqueline Corinne Yvonne Vereker (d 1962), o da of Field Marshal 6 Viscount Gort (I) and 1 Viscount Gort of Hamsterley (UK 1946), VC, GCB, CBE, DSO, MVO, MC (d 1946); 1 s, 4 da (Hon Elizabeth (Hon Mrs Abel Smith) b 1941, Hon Catherine (Hon Mrs Villiers) b 1942, Hon Anne (Hon Mrs Harries) b 1947, Hon Lucy (Hon Mrs Willoughby) b 1953); m 2, 24 March 1966, Margaret, da of Maj-Gen Thomas Shoubridge, CB, CMG, DSO, and wid of 3 Baron Glanusk, DSO; *Heir* s, Maj the Hon Philip John Algernon Sidney, MBE, b 21 April 1945; *Career* served Grenadier Guards Reserve 1929 and WWII; Barclays Bank 1936-39; sits as Cons peer in House of Lords; MP (C) Chelsea 1944-45, parly sec Miny of Pensions 1945, sec of state for Air 1951-55, govr gen of Aust 1961- 65; former dir various public cos incl: Lloyds Bank plc, British Match Co plc, Schweppes plc, Phoenix Assurance plc (chm 1966-79), Manufacturers Hanover Trust plc, Continental Insurance Co of New York plc; dir No 1 Poultry Ltd Palmerston; pres: Freedom Assoc 1984- (chm 1975-84), SE England Tourist Bd; chm Winston Churchill Memorial Tst, dep pres Victoria Cross and George Cross Assoc; former tstee: British Museum, Nat Portrait Gallery, RAF Museum, Royal Armouries Museum; hon bencher Gray's Inn 1982; hon memb Grocers' Co 1987; Hon LLD: Univ of Sydney, Hampden Sydney Coll Virginia; hon fell: Magdalene Coll Cambridge, Australian Inst of Architecture; hon FRIBA; FCA 1934; KStJ; *Recreations* painting, gardening, shooting; *Clubs* White's; *Style*— The Rt Hon Viscount De L'Isle, VC, KG, GCMG, GCVO, PC; Penshurst Place, Tonbridge, Kent (☎ 0892 870223); Glanusk Park, Crickhowell, Brecon

DE LA BEDOYERE, Comtesse Michael; Charlotte; *née* Halbik; *b* 24 Nov 1931; *Educ* The Old Palace Mayfield Sussex; *m* 1961, as his 2 w, Comte Michael de la Bédoyère, sometime ed Catholic Herald and gs through his f of Alexis Huchet, Marquis de la Bédoyère (who m 1869 Hon Mildred Greville-Nugent, da of 1 Baron Greville); Charles Huchet de la Bédoyère was cr Comte 1710 and was Procureur-Général of the Bretagne Parlement, while another Huchet was cr Comte 1815 by Napoleon; Bertrand Huchet, Seigneur de la Huchetais and Sec of State to Jean V, Duke of Brittany, m c 1420 Jeanne de la Bédoyère, Dame de la Bédoyère; Comte Michael was gs through his mother of Dr A Thorold, sometime Bishop of Winchester; 2 c; *Career* md Search Press Ltd, Burns & Oates Ltd (publishers to the Holy See 1842-); *Recreations* gardening, swimming, photography; *Clubs* Hurlingham; *Style*— Comtesse Michael de la Bédoyère; Spey House, Mayfield, E Sussex; Wellwood, North Farm Rd, Tunbridge Wells, Kent TN2 3DR (☎ 0892 510850)

DE LA BERE, Adrian; s of Sir Rupert De la Bère, 1 Bt (d 1978); hp of bro, Sir Cameron De la Bère, 2 Bt; *b* 17 Sept 1939; *Style*— Adrian De la Bère Esq

de SMITH, (Catherine) Joan; da of Louis Benjamin Natley (d 1955), of London, and Hettie, *née* Emanuel (d 1954); *b* 27 Dec 1925; *Educ* Henrietta Barnett Sch Hampstead, LSE; *m* 5 May 1946 (m dis 1965), Prof Stanley Alexander de Smith (d 1974), s of Joseph de Smith (d 1962), of London; 2 s (Michael John b 1951, Nicholas Mark b 1958), 2 da (Jane Catherine b 1947, Anna Margaret b 1949); *Career* sr operational res scientist SIGMA 1963-67, md William Key & Ptnrs 1967-70, dir EAL 1970-73, chm and md: Joan de Smith & Ptnrs Ltd 1974-85, Joan de Smith Systems Ltd 1979-85; memb Cane Hill Hosp Ctee 1953-63, chm Kent FPC 1985-90, bd memb Dental Practice Bd 1985-; FSS 1950, MBCS 1965, FORS 1965, MRSM 1986; *Recreations* competitive bridge, writing; *Clubs* RSM; *Style*— Ms Joan de Smith; Tunbridge Wells, Kent (☎ 0892 514450)

DE STACPOOLE, 6 Duke (Papal title, conferred 1831 by Gregory XVI); George Geoffrey Robert Edward de Stacpoole; also Count Stacpoole (French cr of Louis XVIII 1818) and Marquis de Stacpoole (Papal title conferred by Leo XII 1826); s of 5 Duke, JP (d 1965); The Stacpooles have resided in Ireland from the twelfth century, the family name is taken from a feudal lordship in Pembrokeshire; *b* 21 June 1917; *Educ* Downside; *m* 15 July 1947, Dorothy Anne, o da of late Richard Edmund Dease, of Rath House, Co Leix; 2 s (George Richard b 1948, David Henry Oliver b 1951), 1 da (Valerie Brigid Dorothy (Mrs Jeremy Richardson) b 1950); *Career* Maj late Royal Ulster Rifles, served WWII; *Style*— Major the Duke de Stacpoole; Hempsted Corner Cottage, Benenden, Cranbrook, Kent TN17 4ET (☎ 0580 240634)

DEAN, Hon Mrs (Jenefer); *née* Mills; da of 5 Baron Hillingdon (by 1 m); *b* 6 April 1935; *m* 7 April 1962, His Hon Joseph Jolyon Dean, *qv*, s of Basil Dean, CBE (d 1978); 1 s (Ptolemy Hugo b 1967), 2 da (Antigone Lucy b 1963, Tacita Charlotte b 1965); *Career* previous involvement with Br Red Cross and Ashford CAB (currently mangr); *Style*— The Hon Mrs Dean; The Hall, West Brabourne, Ashford, Kent

DEAN, His Hon Joseph Jolyon; s of Basil Dean, CBE (d 1978), and Esther Bagger, *née* Van Gruisen, formerly Dean (d 1983); *b* 26 April 1921; *Educ* Harrow, Univ of Oxford (MA); *m* 7 April 1962, Hon Jenefer, *née* Mills, *qv*, da of 5 Baron Hillingdon MC (d 1982), of the Tod House, Seal, Kent; 1 s, 2 da; *Career* Mil Serv RA 1941-46, Capt 51 Highland Div, Western Desert, Sicily, Normandy, Holland, Germany; barr 1947, bencher Middle Temple 1972, circuit judge 1976 (ret 1987); chm E Ashford Rural Tst 1988; *Books* Hatred Ridicule or Contempt, A Book of Libel Cases (1953); *Clubs* Army and Navy; *Style*— His Hon Joseph Dean; The Hall, West Brabourne, Ashford, Kent

DEAN, (Cecil) Roy; s of Arthur Dean (d 1989), of Herts, and Flora Clare Dean (d 1980); *b* 18 Feb 1927; *Educ* Watford GS, London Coll of Printing and Graphic Arts (dip), Coll for the Distributive Trades (MIPR); *m* 1954, Heather, da of Sydney Sturtridge (d 1981); 3 s (Jonathan, Nicholas, Charles); *Career* RAF India and Pakistan 1945-48, COI 1948-58; writer and broadcaster, author of numerous pamphlets and articles on int affrs, BBC radio series The Poetry of Popular Song; HM Dip Serv: Colombo 1958-62, Vancouver 1962-64, Lagos 1964-68, FCO 1968-71 and 1973-76, Houston 1971-73, dir Arts Control and Disarmament Res Unit 1976-83, dep Br high cmmr Accra Ghana 1983-86, ret; memb UN Sec-Gen's Expert Gp on Disarmament Insts 1980-81; tstee Urbanaid 1986,; *Recreations* crosswords (Times Nat Champion 1970 and 1979), light verse, songwriting; *Style*— Roy Dean, Esq; 14 Blyth Rd, Bromley, Kent BR1 3RX (☎ 081 460 8159)

DEAN, Trudy; da of Arthur Vivian Helmer, of 91 East St, Long Buckby, Northampton, and Kathleen, *née* O'Leary; *b* 16 Oct 1946; *Educ* Bilston Girls' HS, QMC London (BA), Senate House Univ of London (DipEd); *m* 1 Aug 1970, John Richard Dean, s of Norman Clifford Dean, of 24 Allerton Grange Drive, Leeds, Yorkshire; 1 s (Gregg Anthony b 22 July 1974), 1 da (Elizabeth Hazel b 1 May 1972); *Career* teacher Highbury Hill HS for Girls; ctee memb Malling Age Concern, parish cncllr West Malling, co cnclr Kent (Democrat); *Recreations* literature, theatre, music; *Style*— Mrs Trudy Dean; 49 Offham Rd, West Malling, Kent ME19 6RB (☎ 843119)

DEBENHAM, Michael George Scott; s of Archibald Ian Scott Debenham, DFC, of Bowerland Farm, Bowerland Lane, Lingfield, Surrey, and Daphne Joann, *née* Godber; *b* 12 Oct 1943; *Educ* Haileybury, ISC, Univ of St Andrews (BSc); *m* July 1966 (m dis 1980), Janine Elizabeth, da of Anthony Davies, of Crockham Hill, Edenbridge, Kent; 3 da (Sarah b 14 April 1968, Anna b 27 March 1970, Tessa b 11 April 1974); m 2, 6 March 1981, Roberta, da of Luigi Courir, of Genova, Italy; *Career* Br Inspecting Engineer Ltd: dir (Material Control Ltd) 1971, dir 1976, dir (Internat Ltd) 1976, dir (Pipelines Ltd) 1982, md 1987, dir (Hldgs Uk Ltd) 1987; memb Tandridge PCC 1976-77; Liveryman Worshipful Co of Taylors; MIHT 1968, MICE 1971, CEng 1971, AWeldI 1985, FIQA 1986; *Recreations* tennis, squash, gardening; *Style*— Michael Debenham, Esq; British Inspecting Engineers Ltd, Bank of America House, Elmfield Rd, Bromley, Kent (☎ 081 464 3434, fax 081 290 0701, telex 919 572)

DEEDES, Baron (Life Peer UK 1986), of Aldington, Co Kent; William Francis; MC (1944), PC (1962), DL (Kent 1962); s of Herbert William Deedes, JP, of Saltwood Castle (which was sold 1925) and Sandling Park (which was sold 1897), and Melesina Gladys, JP, 2 da of Philip Chenevix Trench, gs of Richard Chenevix Trench, yr bro of 1 Baron Ashtown; *b* 1 June 1913; *Educ* Harrow; *m* 1942, Evelyn Hilary, da of Clive Branfoot, of Stonegrave, Yorks; 1 s (Hon Jeremy Wyndham b 1943) and 1 s decd (Julius Brook b 1947 d 1970), 3 da (Hon Juliet Evelyn Mary b 1948, Hon Victoria Frances Jill (Hon Mrs Southey) b 1950, Hon Lucy Rose (Hon Mrs Crispin Money-Coutts) b 1955); *Career* served WWII Maj KRRC (TA); ed The Daily Telegraph 1974-85; memb Historic Bldgs Cncl England 1958-62, MP (C) Ashford 1950-74, min without portfolio 1962-64, parly under sec Home Office 1955-57, parly sec Miny Housing and Local Govt 1954-55; *Clubs* Carlton, Beefsteak, Royal and Ancient; *Style*— The Rt Hon Lord Deedes, MC, PC, DL; New Hayters, Aldington, Kent (☎ 023 372 269)

DEERE, Col Edward George; GSM (NI, 1947); s of Sydney Charles Deere, of Newton Aycliffe, Co Durham, and Rose Mary, *née* Bennett (d 1981); *b* 4 Sept 1942; *Educ* Duke of York's Royal Mil Sch Dover, Guy's Hosp London (BDS); *m* 27 Feb 1965, Angela Mary, da of John Holmes (d 1989), of Shoreham-by-sea, Sussex; 1 s (Robert Edward John b 1966), 1 da (Harriet Mary Rose b 1970); *Career* cmmnd 2 Lt RADC 1961, Capt 1964, Maj 1969, Lt-Col 1977, Col 1987; sr specialist dental offr BMH Iserlohn W Germany 1975, sr registrar in oral surgery Charing Cross Hosp 1978; conslt dental offr: BMH Munster W Germany 1979, BMH Iserlohn W Germany 1980, Queen Elisabeth Mil Hosp Woolwich 1982, BMH Munster W Germany 1985, 22 Field Hosp RAMC 1988; specialist orthodontic private practice Horsham 1989-; FDSRCS 1973, FDSRCSEd 1973, D'ORTH RCS 1975; *Recreations* photography, golf, computing, gardening; *Clubs* RSM; *Style*— Col Edward Deere; 9 Bonar Place, Chislehurst, Kent BR7 5RJ (☎ 081 4671377)

DEIGHTON, (Mary) Elizabeth Anne; da of Baron Uthwatt, PC (Life Baron, d 1949), of London and Sandwich, and Lady Uthwatt, OBE, *née* Meeres (d 1950); *b* 27 May 1921; *Educ* St Helens Sch Northwood, LSE (BSc), St Anne's Coll Oxford (MA); *m* 3 April 1947, Herbert Stanley Deighton, s of Stanley Deighton (d 1958), of Sussex; 1s (Mark Andrew Thomas b 1953), 2 da (Anne Felicity b 1949, Jane Elizabeth b 1952); *Career* served WAAF 1940-45; res asst Asa Briggs and OUP 1949-51, fndr and dir Bear Lane Gallery

(Oxford) 1957, conslt Editions Alecto 1963-66, conslt and mangr Studio International 1967-70; private art conslt; lectr in USA for Mellon Fndn 1966, staff tutor and lectr Open Univ 1971-85, dir of studies Canterbury Branch Univ of 3 Age 1985-87, sometime Arts Cncl lectr on touring exhibitions 1986; author of various published articles; memb: Gen Cncl Museum of Modern Art Oxford, various local orgns; *Books* Looking into Paintings (ed, 1985); *Recreations* painting, gardening, music; *Clubs* Oxford and Cambridge; *Style*— Mrs Elizabeth Deighton; White Friars, Sandwich, Kent CT13 9AB (☎ 0304 612278)

DENISON-PENDER, Hon Emma Charlotte; e da of 3 Baron Pender; *b* 1 Feb 1964; *Style*— The Hon Emma Denison-Pender

DENISON-PENDER, Hon Mary Anne Louise; yr da of 3 Baron Pender; *b* 17 Nov 1965; *Style*— The Hon Mary Anne Denison-Pender

DENISON-PENDER, Hon Robin Charles; yr s of 2 Baron Pender, CBE (d 1965) and bro of 3 Baron; *b* 7 Sept 1935; *Educ* Eton; *m* 7 May 1966, Clare Nell, only da of Lt-Col James Currie Thomson, MBE, TD, JP, DL, of Stable Court, Walkern, Herts; 2 s, 1 da; *Career* late 2 Lt 11 Hussars 1954-56; memb London Stock Exchange; vice pres Royal Albert Hall 1970-83, chm The Knole Club 1985-; *Recreations* golf, gardening, tennis; *Clubs* White's; *Style*— The Hon Robin Denison-Pender; Jessups, Mark Beech, Edenbridge, Kent TN8 5NR (☎ 0342 850684)

DENNEY, Dr Ronald Colin; s of Alfred Edward Henry Denney, of Romford, Essex, and Ada Lilian, *née* Griffiths; *b* 27 June 1936; *Educ* SE Essex Co Tech Sch, SE Essex Tech Coll (BSc), Sir John Cass Coll (PhD), Duke Univ North Carolina; *m* 2 March 1963, Jacqueliine, da of Norman Eric Reddy (d 1974), of Redhill, Surrey; 1 s (Graham Paul b 6 April 1969), 1 da (Fiona Claire b 25 Feb 1973); *Career* lectr Enfield Coll of Technol 1962-65, sr res chemist Hopkin & Williams Ltd 1967-68; Thames Poly London: lectr 1968-72, sr lectr 1972-89, princ lectr 1983-89, reader in organoanalytical chemistry 1989-; author of sixty scientific papers; Cons Pty parly cand: Poplar 1970, Basildon 1974; pres Sevenoaks Cons Assoc 1989- (chm 1979-82), co-opted memb Kent Educn Ctee 1989-; *Books* incl: This Dirty World (1971), Alcohol and Accidents (1986), King Oak of Sevenoaks (a children's story, 1989); *Recreations* reading, writing, running; *Clubs* Blackheath Harriers; *Style*— Dr Ronald C Denney; School of Biological and Chemical Sciences, Thames Polytechnic, Wellington St, Woolwich, London SE18 6PF (☎ 081 316 8340, fax 081 316 8305)

DENNING, (Charles Henry) David; s of late Lt-Gen Sir Reginald Denning, KCVO, KBE, CB, of Delmonden Grange, Hawkhurst, Kent, and Lady Eileen Violet Denning, OBE, *née* Currie; *b* 1 May 1933; *Educ* Winchester; *m* 21 June 1958, Patricia Margaret, da of Cdr Nigel Loftus Henry Fane (d 1974); 2 s (James Henry b 1959, Guy William b 1962), 2 da (Sophia Jane b 1964, Venetia Mary b 1966); *Career* cmmnd 11 Hussars 1952, demob 1954, Territorial Offr City of London Yeo 1954-57; underwriting memb Lloyds 1960-; dir: B W Noble Ltd Insurance Brokers 1968-74, C T Bowring Insurance Ltd 1973-74; md The Copenhagen Reinsurance Co UK Ltd 1974-; dep chm Reinsurance Offices Assoc 1987- (memb Exec Ctee); *Recreations* shooting, farming; *Clubs* The Gresham; *Style*— David Denning, Esq; Bewl Bridge Farm, Lamberhurst, Kent TN3 8JJ (☎ 0892 890876)

DENNISON, Dr Jacqueline Ann; da of Hugh John Langford, of Folkestone, Kent, and Mary Elizabeth Catherine, *née* Horn; *b* 19 Oct 1954; *Educ* Folkestone GS for Girls, Univ of London (MB BS); *m* 17 July 1976, Colin Keith Dennison, s of Tom Dennison, of Purley, Surrey; 2 s (Stephen Gareth b 1983, Philip James b 1984); *Career* sr house offr West Kent Hosp 1979-81, princ in gen med practice Maidstone 1981-; *Recreations* literature, theatre; *Style*— Dr Jacqueline Dennison; 50 College Rd, Maidstone, Kent ME15 6SA (☎ 0622 752345)

DENNY, Charles Alistair Maurice; s and h of Sir Alistair Denny, 3 Bt; *b* 7 Oct 1950; *Educ* Wellington, Univ of Edinburgh; *m* 1981, Belinda (Linda), yr da of J P McDonald, of Dublin; 1 s (Patrick Charles Alistair b 1985), 1 da (Georgina Mary b 1989); *Recreations* golf, gardening; *Clubs* Royal and Ancient Golf, St Andrews; *Style*— Charles Denny, Esq

DENNY, Jonathan Molesworth; s of Maj Noel Nigel Molesworth Denny, MC, of Wokingham, Berkshire, and Margaret Louise, *née* Fulcher; *b* 28 Aug 1953; *Educ* Charterhouse, Univ of Southampton (LLB); *m* 20 May 1978, Annette Clare, da of Peter Raymond Underwood Easteal (d 1986), of Upper Coomera, Queensland, Aust; 2 s (Timothy Peter Noel b 1985, James Rupert Simon b 1990), 1 da (Charlotte Lois Clare b 1983); *Career* admitted slr 1977; managing ptnr Cripps Harries Hall 1990- (ptnr 1982-90); memb Law Soc; *Recreations* cricket, tennis, skiing, viticulture; *Style*— Jonathan Denny, Esq; Meadow Lodge, Merriments Lane, Hurst Green, East Sussex TN19 7RD (☎ 058 086 241); Cripps Harries Hall, 84 Calverley Rd, Tunbridge Wells, Kent TN1 2UP (☎ 0892 515121, fax 0892 515444)

DENNY, Ronald Mackinnon; s of Frank Herbert Denny (d 1947), of Enfield, Middx, and Gladys Amy, *née* Mackinnon (d 1976); *b* 23 Dec 1920; *Educ* Edmonton GS, RAF Coll, Univ of London (Dip TS), Univ of Kent (MA), Univ of Birmingham; *m* 14 Feb 1945, Gwenllian Audrey Caroline, da of Brinley Richard Cound (d 1948), of Burryport, S Wales; 2 da (Diane Meryl b 1948, Sally Shan b 1953); *Career* RAFVR 1939, cmmnd Pilot Offr Tech Radar Branch 1943, Offr i/c Flt Lt Airborne Radar Honiley 1944-46, demob 1946 Flt Lt; asst airport mangr Heathrow Airport 1953-56; seconded to: NATO Paris 1958-60, Chateauroux France 1960-64; controller Eastern Rd Construction Unit 1968-73, asst sec Dept of Tport 1974-80, dep DG Br Property Fedn 1981-87, mgmnt conslt 1988-, chm Bain Clarkson Property Insurance Ltd 1989-; AAA Champion 120 yards high hurdles Middx and Southern Counties 1939; chm Farningham Parish Cncl 1989-, govr Authony Roper Primary Sch 1989-; FBIM 1971, FIHT 1980, MCIT 1981, Hon Fell Architectural Assoc 1981; *Recreations* travel, gardening; *Clubs* RAF; *Style*— Ronald Denny, Esq; Maplescombe Oasts, Farningham, Kent DA4 0JY (☎ 0322 864 363); 35 Catherine Place, London SW1E 6DY (☎ 071 828 0111, fax 071 834 3442)

DENT, Rev Dr Christopher Mattinson; s of Rev Arthur Joseph Dent (d 1988), of Burcot, Worcs, and Gwendoline Muriel, *née* Hillier; *b* 21 May 1946; *Educ* Richard Hale Sch Hertford, Pocklington Sch, King's Coll London (BA, MTh, AKC), Jesus Coll Cambridge (MA), New Coll Oxford (MA, DPhil), Westcott House Cambridge; *m* 17 March 1984, Vanessa Maud, da of Henry John Linney (d 1978), of Hove, Sussex; 1 s (Jonathan b 1987), 1 da (Elizabeth b 1990); *Career* curate of Chelsea 1972-76; New Coll Oxford: asst chaplain 1976-79, fell dean of divinity and chaplain 1979-84; vicar of Hollingbourne and Hucking with Leeds and Broomfield 1984-, asst warden (dir of trg) Canterbury Diocesan Assoc of Readers 1987-90; chm Govrs Leeds and Broomfield C of E Primary Sch; *Books* Protestant Reformers in Elizabethan Oxford (1983); *Recreations* history, archaeology, music; *Style*— The Rev Dr Christopher Dent; Hollingbourne Vicarage, Maidstone, Kent ME17 1UJ (☎ 0622 880243)

DENT, Hon Rosamond Mary (Sister Ancilla, OSB); da of William Herbert Shelley Dent, MC, and 19 Baroness Furnivall (d 1969, when the Barony became abeyant between Sister Ancilla and Hon Mrs Bence); co-heiress to Barony, renounced right in favour of sister; *b* 3 June 1933; *Educ* Holy Child Convent Mayfield; *Style*— Sister Ancilla, OSB; Minster Abbey, Minster, nr Ramsgate, Kent

DERMOTT, William; CB (1984); s of William Dermott, and Mary Dermott; *b* 27 March 1924; *Educ* Univ of Durham (MSc); *m* 1946, Winifred Joan Tinney; 1 s, 1 da; *Career* agric scientist Univ of Durham and Wye Coll Univ of London 1943-46, MAFF 1976- (sr SG specialist and dep chief sci specialist 1971-76), head of Agric Sci Serv, pres Br Soc of Soil Sci 1981-82, actg DG ADAS 1983-84; *Style*— William Dermott, Esq, CB; 22 Chequers Park, Wye, Ashford, Kent TN25 5BB (☎ 0233 812694)

DEVAS, Michael Campbell; MC (1945); only s of Geoffrey Charles Devas, MC (d 1971; whose mother was Edith, da of Lt-Col Hon Walter Campbell, 3 s of 1 Earl Cawdor), by his w Joan (d 1975), great niece of Rt Hon Sir Henry Campbell-Bannerman, the Liberal PM (1906-08); *b* 6 June 1924; *Educ* Eton; *m* 1, 28 June 1952 (m dis 1966), Patience Merryday, da of late Sir Albert Gerald Stern, KBE, CMG (d 1966); 1 s, 1 da; m 2, 12 Oct 1967, Gillian Barbara, da of late Col H M P Hewett, of The Court House, Chipping Warden, nr Banbury, and formerly w of Charles Arthur Smith-Bingham; 1 s; *Career* banker; chm Colonial Mutual Life Assurance (London Bd) 1982-, joined M Samuel & Co Ltd 1947, dir 1960; dir Kleinwort Benson Ltd 1965-86 (ret), chm Kleinwort Charter Investment Trust plc, dir Dover Corporation (USA); *Recreations* sailing, skiing; *Clubs* White's, Royal Yacht Sqdn; *Style*— Michael Devas, Esq, MC; Hunton Court, Maidstone, Kent (☎ 06272 307); 24 Lugdate Hill, London EC4P 4BD

DEVERALL, Philip Brook; s of William James Deverall, of 7 Blue Waters Drive, Lyme Regis, Dorset, and Marion, *née* Brook (d 1983); *b* 30 April 1937; *Educ* Lymm GS Cheshire, UCL (MB BS); *m* 10 June 1961, Ann Beaumont, da of Frank Henry Drury (d 1961); 2 s (Stephen Charles b 16 July 1962, James Joseph b 6 Feb 1976), 1 da (Helen Catherine b 10 Feb 1965); *Career* house physician and surgn UCH London 1960-61, sr house surgn Barnet Hosp 1961-63, cardio vascular fell Univ of Alabama USA 1968-70, conslt heart surgn Leeds Hosp 1970-77 (registrar in surgery 1963-65, sr registrar 1965-68), conslt heart surgn Guy's 1977; author of several scientific articles and chapters in books; memb: Br Cardiac Soc, American Heart Assoc, Soc of Thoracic Surgns, Soc of Thoracic Surgns USA; hon memb Soc of Cardiovascular Surgns of Asia 1987; *Recreations* travel, theatre, music; *Style*— Philip Deverall, Esq; 3 Northfield Close, Bromley, Kent BR1 2WZ (☎ 081 467 5418); Flat 11, 22 Park Crescent, London W1N 3PD (☎ 071 636 0641); 21 Upper Wimpole St, London W1M 7TA (☎ 071 935 2847, telex 266549 PBDEV G)

DEVEREUX, Robert Charles Debohun; s of Herbert Morris Devereux (d 1949), and Fanny Rosemary Devereux (d 1980); *b* 15 Dec 1928; *Educ* Repton, Univ of Cambridge (MA); *m* 23 Oct 1954, Anna-Mary, da of Henry Edmund Theoderic Vale (d 1969); 1 s (Charles b 3 June 1956), 2 da (Christina b 13 April 1958, Jane b 12 June 1961); *Career* Nat Serv RE 1947-49 Egypt; Wellcome plc: joined 1953, chief engr 1958, gen prodn mangr 1964-69, ops dir 1972-; memb Chem Industs Assoc Trade Affrs Bd 1959-69, pres NW Kent Post Grad Med Centre 1972-77; CEng, MIMechE, FBIM; *Recreations* reading, gardening; *Clubs* RAC; *Style*— Robert Devereux, Esq; Wellcome plc, Temple Hill, Dartford, Kent DA1 5AH (☎ 0322 223488, fax 0322

228564)

DEVLIN, Hon Matthew; 4 and yst s of Baron Devlin, PC (Life Peer); *b* 8 June 1946; *Educ* Winchester, New Coll Oxford; *m* 25 July 1969, Rosemary Joan Boutcher, 3 da of Lt-Col E C Van der Kiste, of The Old Rectory, Durrington, Wilts; 2 s (William b 17 March 1972, Edward b 21 April 1975), 2 da (Beatrice b 16 May 1970, Mary b 10 Jan 1977); *Career* banker Citibank NA; *Style*— The Hon Matthew Devlin; Ruffway, Platt Common, St Mary's Platt, Sevenoaks, Kent (☎ 0732 885380)

DEVLIN, Hon Timothy; 3 s of Baron Devlin, PC (Life Peer); *b* 28 July 1944; *Educ* Winchester, Univ Coll Oxford; *m* 31 Jan 1967, Angela, er da of A J G Laramy; 2 s (Sebastian b 1973, Fabian b 1975), 2 da (Miranda b 1969, Esmeralda b 1971); *Career* journalist; former news ed TES, reporter The Times 1971-73 (educ corr 1973-77), nat dir ISIS 1977-84, PR dir IOD 1984-86, assoc dir Charles Barker Traverse-Healy 1986-89, fndr Tim Devlin Enterprises (PR consultancy); *Style*— The Hon Timothy Devlin; Ramsons, Maidstone Rd, Staplehurst, Kent TN12 0RD (☎ 0580 893176)

DEVONSHIRE, Michael Norman; TD (1969); s of Maj Norman George Devonshire (d 1983), of Tunbridge Wells, and Edith, *née* Skinner (d 1965); *b* 23 May 1930; *Educ* The Kings Sch Canterbury; *m* 31 March 1962, Jessie Margaret, da of Meirion Roberts (d 1974), of Tywyn Merioneth; *Career* 2 Lt RA 1953-55, TA 1956-69, Queen's Own Royal West Kent Regt, Queen's Regt; admitted slr 1953; Master of Supreme Court (Taxing Office) 1979, rec Crown Court 1987; dist cmmr Tonbridge Scouts 1969-74, pres London Slrs Litigation Assoc 1974-76, cdre Boughbeach Sailing Club 1976-79, memb Rotary Club of the Pantiles Tunbridge Wells, treas SE Regnl Assoc RYA, memb Cncl RYA 1978-; *Books* Taxation of Contentious Costs (1979); *Recreations* sailing; *Style*— Michael Devonshire, Esq, TD; 17 Chestnut Ave, Southborough, Tunbridge Wells, Kent TN4 OBS (☎ 0892 28672); Royal Courts of Justice, The Strand, London WC2 (☎ 071 936 6526)

DEWS, Peter; s of John Dews (d 1961), and Edna, *née* Bloomfield (d 1976); *b* 26 Sept 1929; *Educ* Queen Elizabeth GS Wakefield, Univ Coll Oxford (BA, MA); *m* 1960, Ann, da of Arthur Stanley Rhodes (d 1982); *Career* schoolmaster 1952-54; BBC dir sound and TV 1954-64; dir: Ravinia Festival Chicago 1964 and 1971, Birmingham Rep Theatre 1966-72, Hadrian VII Birmingham 1967, London 1968, NY 1969, Chichester Festival Theatre 1978-80, Stratford Ontario 1984 (1973, 1981); awarded: Antoinette Perry (Tony) Award Broadway 1969, Guild of TV Drama Prodrs and Dirs award for best drama prodn An Age of Kings 1960; Hon DLitt Univ of Bradford; *Style*— Peter Dews, Esq; 29 Water St, Deal, Kent CT14 6DJ (☎ 0304 368937)

DIBBLE, (Lucy) Grace; da of Thomas George Dibble (d 1952), and Rhoda Maria Anne, *née* Hatton (d 1946); *b* 3 Oct 1902; *Educ* Bearsted Nat Sch, Maidstone Girls' GS, Homerton Coll Cambridge (Dip, BA); *Career* exchange teacher Gen Wolfe Sch Winnipeg Canada; teacher trg: St Mary's Poona India, UMC and WTTC and RTTC W Nigeria; teacher: St Philip's and Southborough Maidstone, Ede GS Nigeria, Dane Court GS Broadstairs; pres Thanet Branch UNA; memb: Isle of Thanet Geographical Assoc, Broadstairs Cncl of Churches Ctee, Women's World Day of Prayer Ctee, Thanet Natural History Soc, St Peter's & Broadstairs Hort Soc, Holy Trinity Church Broadstairs PCC, WRVS (ret); WVS Long Serv Medal (and bar), Rotary Club of Broadstairs Community Award 1981; *Books* Return Tickets (vol I & II 1968), More Return Tickets (1979), Return Tickets to Southern Europe (1980), Return Tickets to Scandinavia (1982), Return Tickets to Yugoslavia (1986), Return Tickets to Here and There (1988), No Return Tickets (1989); *Recreations* gardening, photography, travel; *Clubs* PLR; *Style*— Miss Grace Dibble; St Christopher's, 1 Dumpton Park Drive, Broadstairs, Kent CT10 1RE (☎ 0843 63905)

DIBLEY, Kathleen; s of George Edward Dibley, MC (d 1945), of Lamberhurst, Kent, and Stella Winifred Agenes, *née* Dwyer (d 1976); *Educ* private tutoring, Bexley Coll; *Career* journalist Fleet Street Features Serv 1953-57, press offr Josiah Wedgwood & Sons Ltd 1953-57, publicity dir William Whiteley of Bayswater 1958-65, dir of PR Osbourne Peacock Public Relations 1965-70, head of PR Arthur Sanderson & Sons Ltd 1970-75, freelance interior designer 1975-, PR conslt and journalist 1975-; currently ed: Home Textiles and Furnishings Review, The Polio Bulletin; chm Darent Cray Nat Tst Assoc 1980-86, vol lectr Nat Tst, tstee Abraham and Sarah Fndn, PR conslt New Horizons Tst, memb Soc of Industl Designers; Fell Inst of Journalists, MIPR; *Books* Short Short Stories (1973), The Dyers (1975); *Recreations* travel, music, painting, needlework, art; *Style*— Miss Kathleen Dibley; 126 Radnor Ave, Bexleyheath, Kent DA16 2BY (☎ 081 304 3166, fax 081 304 3166)

DICK, (Elizabeth) Frances; da of Jonathan Hutchinson (d 1972), of Haslemere, Surrey, and Ellen Frances, *née* Seymour; *b* 18 May 1931; *Educ* Sidcot Sch Winscombe Avon, Radcliffe Infirmary Oxford (SRN); *m* 20 Dec 1952, Gavin Colquhoun Dick, *qv*, s of John Dick (d 1949) of Hamilton, Lanarkshire; 2 da (Helen Frances b 1953, Catherine Penelope b 1956); *Career* staff nurse Sevenoaks Hosp 1954-55 1958-60 and 1967, pre-sch playgroup owner and supervisor 1968-; dist cncllr for Sevenoaks Weald and Underriver 1979-; Sevenoaks DC: chm Leisure Ctee 1986-87 and 1990-, vice chm 1987-88, chm 1988-89; vice chm and chm Sevenoaks Cons Womens Ctee 1974-80, vice chm SE Area Cons Womens Ctee 1980-83, vice pres Sevenoaks Cons Assoc 1983- (memb 1966, vice chm 1980-83), vice chm and chm Tunbridge Wells Community Health Cncl 1986-88, sch govr of 3 schs; chm: govrs Oak Bank Sch, Mgmnt Ctee Sevenoaks Day Nursery 1986-; *Style*— Mrs Frances Dick; Fell Cottage, Bayley's Hill, Sevenoaks, Kent TN14 6HS (☎ 0732 453704)

DICK, Gavin Colquhoun; s of John Dick (d 1949), of Motherwell, Lanarkshire, and Catherina MacAuslan, *née* Henderson (d 1983); *b* 6 Sept 1928; *Educ* Hamilton Acad, Univ of Glasgow (MA), Balliol Coll Oxford (MA), SOAS, Univ of London (Cert); *m* 20 Dec 1952, (Elizabeth) Frances, *qv*, da of Jonathan hutchinson (d 1972), of Haslemere, Surrey; 2 da (Helen b 1953, Catherine b 1956); *Career* Lt 3 RTR 1952-54; Civil Serv DTI (formerly Bd of Trade): asst princ 1954-58, princ 1958-67, UK trade cmmr Wellington NZ 1961-64, asst sec 1967-75, jt sec Review Ctee on Overseas Rep 1968-69, under sec 1975-84, govr Coll of Air Trg Hamble 1975-80; bd memb English Ests 1982-84, conslt Office of Telecoms 1984-87, conslt Radio Communications Div 1987-89; vice chm Mobile Radio Trg Tst 1990-; *Recreations* linguistics; *Clubs* United Oxford and Cambridge University; *Style*— Gavin Dick, Esq; Fell Cottage, Bayley's Hill, Sevenoaks, Kent TN14 6HS (☎ 0732 453704)

DICKENS, Michael Charles; s of late Arnold Dickens, of Northampton, and Winifred Agnes, *née* Crick; *b* 13 May 1941; *Educ* Wycliffe Coll; *m* 1, 22 March 1969 (m dis 1976), Sheila Fay, *née* Bugden; 1 s (Charles Arnold Grant John b 26 Jan 1970); m 2, 14 Nov 1988, Barbara Anne, da of Robert Raymond Wills, of Canterbury; *Career* md The Butterfly Farm Ltd 1959-83; mangr: Bournes Estate Agency 1967-90, Kings Estate Agency Ashford 1990-; FREntS, Assoc of Nat Assoc of Estate Agents; *Books* The World of Butterflies (1972), The World of Moths (1973); *Recreations* study of lepidoptera, collector of books on lepidoptera, conservation, the countryside, music, reading, walking, cars, cooking, photography, antiques, touring; *Style*— Michael Dickens, Esq; 37 Tally Ho Rd, Shadoxhurst, Ashford, Kent TN26 1HL (☎ 0233 620667); Kings Estate Agents, 10-12 Middle Row, Ashford, Kent TN24 8SQ (☎ 0233 646411)

DICKETTS, Robert Anstey Ivor; s of (Walter Arthur) Charles Dicketts (d 1956), and Judith Rose, *née* Kelman; *b* 31 Aug 1944; *Educ* Dover Coll; *m* 2 March 1974, Priscilla Susan, da of Dr Stephen Falkland (d 1986); 1 s (Oliver Simon b 31 May 1979); *Career* CA; articled Messrs Blackburns Robson & Coates 1964-69, mangr Crick and Bussell 1969-71, ptnr Lee Dicketts & Co 1972-; vice pres SE Soc of CAs 1990-91 (ctee memb 1984-); FCA; *Recreations* golf, amateur dramatics, cooking, tennis, wine, reading; *Clubs* IOD, Lamberhurst Golf; *Style*— Robert Dicketts, Esq; Rosemary Cottage, Wards Lane, Wadhurst, East Sussex TN5 6HN (☎ 0892 883603); Lee Dicketts & Co, York House, 37 High St, Seal, Sevenoaks, Kent TN15 0AW (☎ 0732 62655, fax 0732 63121)

DIGNAN, Maj-Gen Albert Patrick; CB (1978), MBE (1952); s of Joseph William Dignan (d 1964), and Rosetta Weir (d 1978); *b* 25 July 1920; *Educ* Christian Brothers Sch Dublin, Trinity Coll Dublin (MA, MD); *m* 1952, Eileen, da of James John White (d 1956); 2 s, 1 da; *Career* Brig and Consltg Surgn FARELF 1969-71, sr conslt surgeon and asst prof of mil surgery Queen Alexandra Mil Hosp Millbank 1972-73, dir Army surgery and consltg surgn to the Army 1973-78, QHS 1974-78, hon conslt surgn Royal Hosp Chelsea, hon conslt oncology and radiotherapy Westminster Hosp 1975-78, conslt in accident and emergency med Ealing Hosp 1978-79; fell Assoc of Surgns of GB and Ireland, FRCS, FRCSI, FRSM; *Recreations* gardening, golf; *Style*— Maj-Gen Albert Dignan, CB, MBE; 37 Queens Rd, Beckenham, Kent (☎ 081 658 7690)

DIMOND, Bronwyn Vivienne Sylvia; da of Arnold Hill-Evans (d 1967), and Patricia Davison, *née* Downes; *b* 9 Aug 1944; *Educ* Rugby HS for Girls, Univ of London (Dip Nursing); *m* 1, Gary Windsor Roberts; m 2, Dr Aubrey Hugh (Kim) Dimond; 1 da (Helen Sarah Hill Roberts); *Career* Maj QARANC (V) 308 Evac Hosp; qualified SRN; staff nurse United Sheffield Hosps and Sheffield Royal Infirmary 1964, theatre sister Utd Sheffield Hosps and Children's Hosp 1964-68, theatre supt Duchess of Kent Children's Orthopaedic Hosp Hong Kong 1968-71, head of biology Greengates Int Sch Mexico City 1971-74, theatre sister Royal Surrey Co Hosp 1974-75, nursing offr St Luke's Hosp Guildford 1975-76, sr nursing offr (I) res W Surrey and N Hants Dist 1976-77, area nurse Serv Planning Surrey AHA 1977-80, actg dist nursing offr N Surrey Health Dist 1979-80, regnl nurse res and Serv Planning Oxford RHA 1980-81, chief nursing offr Portsmouth and SE Hants Health Authy 1981-83, Nursing Div Regnl Liaison Serv Planning DHSS 1983-86, unit gen mangr Acute Servs Dartford and Gravesham Health Authy 1990- (unit gen mangr Priority Care Servs 1987-90); *Recreations* equitation; *Style*— Mrs Bronwyn Dimond; Meadow Bank, 5 Hasteds, Hollingbourne, Kent ME17 1UQ (☎ 0622 880510); Dartford & Gravesham Health Authority, Unit General Manager, Acute Services, Joyce Green Hospital, Dartford, Kent

DIWAKAR, Dr Kethavan Narayanswamy; s of Kethavan Narayanswamy (d 1962), of Bangalore, India, and Savitramma, *née* Naidu (d 1957); *b* 29 May

1932; *Educ* Univ of Mysore India (BSc, MB BS), Royal Coll of Physicians and Surgns London (DMRD, MRCR); *m* 27 April 1966, Shantha, da of Judge N Sandur (d 1961), of Madras, India; 2 s (Vinod b 15 April 1967, Previn b 17 Dec 1970); *Career* registar and sr registar in radiology Royal Infirmary Glasgow 1966-73; Medway Hosp Gillingham: conslt in radiology 1973-, head of Dept of Radiology 1975-; Medway Health Authy rep on Radiology Specialty Ctee SE Thames RHA 1975-; memb BMA; *Recreations* world travel, gardening, good food and wine, fine ceramic and procelain figurine art collection; *Style—* Dr Kethavan Diwakar; 11 Pear Tree Lane, Hempstead, Gillingham, Kent ME7 3PS (☎ 0634 365148); Medway Hospital, Department of Radiology, Gillingham, Kent ME7 5NY (☎ 0634 830000, ext 3310)

DIXEY, Michael Paul; s of Paul Arthur Groser Dixey, of Little Easton, Great Dunmow, Essex, and Mary Margaret Baring, *née* Garrod; *b* 18 Jan 1942; *Educ* Stowe, Univ of Bristol (BSc); *m* 8 Aug 1964, Margaret Ann, da of George Wardell; 4 da (Catherine b 1966, Julia b 1968, Louise b 1970, Anna (twin) b 1970); *Career* GEC Ltd 1966-70, PA Managment Consultants Ltd 1970-78, Fisher Controls Ltd 1978-82, dir Thermal Conversions Ltd 1982-86, sr conslt PE International Ltd 1986-; treas Invicta E Kent Athletic Club, observer Canterbury Festival, friend Canterbury Archaeological Soc, Lib Democrat cncllr Harbledown Ward Canterbury City Cncl 1987; CEng 1973, MIMechE 1973, MIMC 1977; *Recreations* squash, politics, vernacular architecture; *Clubs* Canterbury Squash Rackets, Invicta E Kent Athletic; *Style—* Michael Dixey, Esq; Linden House, Linden Grove, Canterbury, Kent CT2 8AB (☎ 0227 456626); P-E International, Park House, Wick Rd, Egham, Surrey TW20 0HW (☎ 0784 434411, fax 0784 471405, telex 933783)

DIXON, Bryan; s of John Dixon (d 1964), of Keswick, Cumbria, and Margaret, *née* Hind (d 1952); *b* 10 Oct 1933; *Educ* Keswick Sch, Univ of Sheffield (BL); *m* 1 Nov 1958, Beryl, da of Thomas Gabbott (d 1965), of Blackburn, Lancs; 1 s (Andrew b 20 April 1964), 1 da (Fiona b 12 Dec 1965); *Career* inspr weights and measures Warrington City Borough 1959-62, sr inspr weights and measures Cheshire CC 1962-68, co trading standards offr Kent CC 1984- (dep chief inspr weights and measures 1969-84); advsr to foreign states on trading standards matters; fell Inst Trading Standards Admin; *Recreations* foreign travel, walking, gardening; *Style—* Bryan Dixon, Esq; 2 Sandy Mount, Bearsted, Maidstone, Kent; Kent County Council, Room 41, Springfield, Maidstone, Kent ME14 2LS (☎ 0622 671411 ext 2301, fax 0622 761730)

DOBB, Erlam Stanley; CB (1963), TD; s of Arthur Erlam Dobb (d 1957); *b* 16 Aug 1910; *Educ* Ruthin Sch, Univ Coll of N Wales; *m* 1937, Margaret, da of Percy Williams (d 1955), of Colwyn Bay; *Career* Royal Welsh Fus Maj TA; asst and land cmmr Miny of Agric Fisheries and Foods 1935-47, Agric Land Serv 1947-71 (dir 1959-70), dir-gen ADAS 1973-75; govr Royal Agric Coll 1960-75, chm Thomas Phillips Price Tstees 1971-83 (tstee and memb 1984), memb Agric Res Cncl 1973-75; *Clubs* Farmer's; *Style—* Erlam Dobb, Esq, CB, TD; Churchgate, Westerham, Kent (☎ 0959 62294)

DOBBY, David Lloyd; s of William Lloyd Dobby, of Walmer, Deal, Kent, and Susan Kathleen, *née* Jobson (d 1986); *b* 6 April 1936; *Educ* St Dunstan's Coll Catford, Regent St Poly (Dip Arch); *m* 17 March 1967, Lesley Madeline, da of Frederick William Herron, of Walmer, Deal, Kent; 2 da (Anna b 19 March 1969, Liz b 27 July 1971); *Career* architect 1965; CWS 1957-59, Ronald Ward & Ptnrs 1959-61, Raymond Spratley & Ptnrs 1961-63, Douglas Marriott & Ptnrs 1963-65, James Munce Partnership 1965-68, Rush & Tompkins Group 1968-73; ptnr private practice 1973-86: John Floydd Partnership, Dobby Foard & Ptnrs, DY Davies Dobby Foard; dir practice DY Davies plc 1986-88, md Sargent & Potiriadis 1988-89; mgmnt conslt Practice and Quality Assurance 1990-; House of the Year Design Award 1970 and 1972; designs incl: First Bush Bank W Africa, theme park Florida, new railway village Ashford Kent, Rush & Tompkins HQ offices Sidcup, Chatham House Duke of York St St James; parish cncllr 1978-86; treas local ballet sch 1980-85, memb Dover Girls GS PTA 1980-86; Freeman City of London 1981, Liveryman Worshipful Co of Joiners and Ceilers 1981; MRIBA 1965, LicIQA 1990 ; *Recreations* golf, reading; *Clubs* Royal Cinque Ports, East India, Folio Soc; *Style—* David Dobby, Esq; 10 Jarvist Place, Kingsdown, nr Deal, Kent CT14 8AL (☎ 0304 373331)

DOBSON, Mark Christopher; s of Bryan Peter Dobson, and Yvonne Mary, *née* Tutt; *b* 24 Oct 1967; *Educ* Simon Langton GS For Boys Canterbury; *Career* professional cricketer with Kent CCC; 8 first class appearances to date, first class debut v Essex in Southend 1989, played for Kent v Aust touring team 1989 (scored 33 in second innings); winter tours: Durban 1988, Cape Town 1989 and 1990; *Recreations* football, Chelsea FC, fitness; *Clubs* Kent CCC, The Mote CC, Beverley CC, Green Point CC (Cape Town SA); *Style—* Mark Dobson, Esq; Kent County Cricket Club, St Lawrence Ground, Old Dover Rd, Canterbury CT1 3NZ (☎ 0227 456886, fax 0227 762168)

DOBSON, Nigel Hewitt; s of George Hewitt Dobson (d 1984), of Beckenham, Kent, and Ethel Grace, *née* Boxshall; *b* 13 Aug 1949; *Educ* St Dunstans Coll; *Career* Whinney Murray & Co (now Ernst & Young) 1968-: Ernst & Ernst St Louis Missouri 1974-75, corporate advsy servs dir Whinney Murray 1976-, seconded corporate fin dept Midland Bank 1978-80, ptnr corporate reconstruction 1981-; FCA (ACA 1972); *Recreations* sailing, gardening, reading; *Style—* Nigel Dobson, Esq; 5 Samuel Court, 44 Kelsey Park Ave, Beckenham, Kent BR3 2UN (☎ 081 658 3115); Minnis Bay, Birchington, Kent; Ernst & Young, Becket House, 1 Lambeth Palace Rd, London SE1 7EU (☎ 071 928 2000)

DOBSON, Susan Angela (Sue); da of Arthur George Henshaw, and Nellie, *née* Flower (d 1978); *b* 31 Jan 1946; *Educ* Holy Family Convent, Assumption Convent Ramsgate, Ursuline Convent Westgate on Sea, NE London Poly (BA, Dip HE); *m* 1966 (m dis 1974), Michael Dobson; *Career* fashion, cookery and beauty ed Femina 1965-69, contributing ed Fair Lady 1969-71; ed: SA Inst of Race Rels 1972, Wedding Day and First Home 1978-81, Successful Slimming 1981, Woman & Home 1982-; *Books* The Wedding Day Book (1981, 1989); *Recreations* travel, books, photography, theatre, music, exploring countryside around home in Kent; *Style—* Ms Sue Dobson; IPC Magazines, Kings Reach Tower, Stamford St, London SE1 9LS (☎ 071 261 5423)

DODD, William Atherton; CMG (1983); s of Frederick Dodd (d 1979) of Mayfield, Newton Lane, Chester, and Sarah, *née* Atherton (d 1976); *b* 5 Feb 1923; *Educ* City GS Chester, Christs Coll Cambridge (MA, Cert Ed); *m* 10 Aug 1949, Marjorie, da of Maj Reginald Charles Penfold, MC (d 1970), of Reckerby, Queens Park, Chester; 2 da (Patricia b 1954, Janet b 1957); *Career* WW11 Capt 8 Gurkha Rifles 1942-45; sr history master Ipswich Sch 1947-52, educn offr Miny of Educn Tanganyika/Tanzania 1952-65, under sec ODM 1980-83 (advsr 1970-77, educn advsr 1978-83), conslt Univ of London Inst of Educn 1983- (lectr 1965-70) chm Sir Christopher Cox Meml Fund, UK rep UNESCO Exec Bd 1983-85; *Books* Primary School Inspection in New Countries (1968), Society Schools and Progress in Tanzania (with J Cameron, 1970), Teacher at Work (1970); *Recreations* walking, music, watching cricket; *Clubs* MCC, Kent CR, Sevenoaks Vine; *Style—* William Dodd, Esq, CMG; 20 Bayham Rd, Sevenoaks, Kent TN13 3XD (☎ 0732 454238); Inst of Education, Univ of London, 20 Bedford Way, London WC1H 0AL (☎ 071 636 1500 ext 734)

DOE, Howard Francis; s of Canon Francis Harold Doe, of The Rectory, Fittleworth, W Sussex, and Dorothy Eugenia, *née* Howard; *b* 29 Oct 1943; *Educ* Highgate Sch; *m* 6 March 1965, Lesley Myra, da of William Edmund Farthing (d 1985), of Winchmore Hill, London; 3 s (Martin Howard b 1973, Neville Francis b 1975, Rupert William Christopher b 1983); *Career* sec Peabody Tst 1977- (asst sec 1971-77); Gillingham Borough Cncl: cncllr 1972-, chm Leisure Servs Ctee 1976-88, chm Health and Housing Ctee 1988-90; dir and ctee memb Sir Oswald Stoll Fndn, dir and exec ctee memb N London Hospice Gp 1983-, chm of govrs Park Wood Primary Schs Gillingham 1988-; FCIS 1974, FFA 1977, FInst AM 1987; *Recreations* swimming, studying philosophy; *Style—* Howard Doe, Esq; The Warren, 21 Style Close, Gillingham, Kent ME8 9LS (☎ 0634 366419); Peabody Trust, 207 Waterloo Rd, London SE1 8XW (☎ 071 928 7811, fax 071 261 9187)

DOLDING, Derek Alfred Frank; s of Alfred Isaac Dolding, of Belvedere, Kent, and Beatrice Phyllis, *née* Green; *b* 6 Aug 1932; *Educ* Colfe's GS Lewisham; *m* 2 April 1955 (m dis 1984), Jean, da of William Everett, of Leagrave, Bedfordshire; 2 s (Peter Alfred b 1 Jan 1956, Mark Andrew b 21 July 1963), 3 da (June Marie b 5 July 1957, Pauline Anne b 24 Aug 1958, Sandra Jane b 30 March 1962); *Career* local govt 1948-52, insur 1952-60, proprietor and conservationist Eng Wildlife Park 1982-86, insur 1987-; former ldr Thanet DC 1980-82, co cncllr Margate W Div Kent 1982-; *Recreations* sub-aqua diver, amateur naturalist, conservation; *Style—* Derek Dolding, Esq; 12 Kingfisher Close, Garlinge, nr Margate, Kent

DOLE, John Anthony; s of Thomas Stephen Dole (d 1974), of Faversahm, Kent, and Winifred Muriel, *née* Henderson; *b* 14 Oct 1929; *Educ* Berkhamsted Sch; *m* 1952, Patricia Ivy, da of Victor Clements, of Kent; 2 s (Nicholas, Marcus); *Career* admin The Sports Cncl 1972-75, dir Sr Staff Mgmnt DOE and Tport 1978-82, controller of the Crown Suppliers 1982-86, controller and chief exec HM Stationery Office 1987-89, ret; *Recreations* writing, philately; *Style—* John Dole, Esq

DONAGHY, Roger; s of George Gerald Donaghy (d 1989), and Florence, *née* Thompson; *b* 10 Feb 1940; *Educ* Portadown Tech Coll, Univ of Adelaide; *m* 17 Nov 1962, Rachael, da of Joseph Watson, of Portadown, Co Armagh, NI; 1 da (Nina Dianne b 1968); *Career* reporter and feature writer Portadown Times 1955-61, feature writer Advocate Newspapers Tasmania 1961-63, TV reporter and industl corr Aust Broadcasting Corp Adelaide 1961-65; BBC World Serv News 1966-; journalist, duty ed, newsroom ed; FDR memb Rotary Club of Danson; *Recreations* golf, travel, reading, photography; *Style—* Roger Donaghy, Esq; 41 Bean Rd, Bexleyheath, Kent (☎ 081 303 5109); BBC, Bush House, Strand, London WC2 (☎ 071 240 3456)

DORMER, Philip Godfrey; s of Harold Frank Dormer (d 1958), of Ashford, Kent, and Doris Louise, *née* Butler (d 1957); *b* 26 July 1923; *Educ* Mosely GS Birmingham, Birmingham Central Tech Coll, London Foot Hosp; *m* 10 Nov 1943, Joan Muriel, da of George Ernest Hall, of Ashford, Kent; 1 da (Janet Mary); *Career* War Serv RN 1942-46; chiropodist; private practice 1949-; industl chiropodist: Energen Foods Ashford (formerly Rank Hovis McDougall) 1954-66, Marks & Spencer plc Ashford 1966-86; Contractual chirpodist NHS;

former jt sec E Kent branch Soc of Chiropodists, former chm Kent State Registered Chiropodists Gp; memb: Soc of Chiropodists 1949, RIPH & H 1949; *Books* Eastwell the 'Royal' Village (2 edn 1988); *Recreations* local history, writing, gardening; *Style*— Philip Dormer, Esq; Fir Tree Cottage, Lenacre St, Eastwell, Ashford, Kent (☎ 0233 620 423)

DOUBLEDAY, Garth Leslie; JP 1956 (chm Sittingbourne Bench for 8 years), DL 1965; s of Sir Leslie Doubleday, of Sittingbourne (d 1975), and Nora, *née* Foster (d 1975); *b* 13 July 1913; *Educ* Charterhouse, Clare Coll Cambridge (MA); *m* 28 Nov 1946, May Alison, da of Frank Hann, of Tenby (d 1966); 3 s (Edmund b 1949, Oliver b 1952, Frank b 1952), 3 da (Veronica b 1948, Clare b 1950, Joanna b 1954); *Career* WWII Lt Col RA in ME; dir family farming business, Gen Cmmr of Income Tax 1970-88, High Sheriff of Kent 1976-77, govr and treas Wye Coll, memb Kent Police Authy (vice chm 1979-83); Master Worshipful Co of Fruiterers 1968; *Recreations* racing, foreign travel; *Clubs* Farmers, MCC; *Style*— Garth Doubleday, Esq, JP, DL; Rodmersham House, nr Sittingbourne, Kent (☎ 0795 23545)

DOUGLAS, Lord Gawain Archibald Francis; s of 11 Marquess of Queensberry (d 1954), by his 3 w (*qv* Mimi, Marchioness of Queensberry); *b* 23 May 1948; *Educ* Downside, Royal Acad of Music (LRAM); *m* 1971, Nicolette, da of Col Frank Eustace (d 1976), of Hong Kong; 1 s (Jamie b 1975), 5 da (Dalziel b 1971, Elizabeth b 1974, Natasha b 1976, Margarita b 1978, Mary-Anne b 1981); *Career* former prof of pianoforte Blackheath Conservatoire of Music, music prof Kent Rural Music Sch Canterbury, concert recitalist, accompanist and duettist in company with wife; *Recreations* tennis, swimming, writing short stories and poems, books; *Clubs* Polish Hearth; *Style*— The Lord Gawain Douglas; 2 Archery Sq, Walmer, Deal, Kent (☎ 0304 375813)

DOUGLAS, James Murray; CBE (1985); da of Herbert Douglas (d 1968), and Amy Crawford Murray (d 1976); *b* 26 Sept 1925; *Educ* Morrisons Acad Crieff, Univ of Aberdeen (MA), Balliol Coll Oxford (BA); *m* 1950, Julie, da of Hermann Kemmner (d 1969); 1 s (Michael b 1952), 1 da (Kathleen b 1954); *Career* RAF Fl Lt 1944-47; entered Civil Serv 1950, Treasy 1960-63, asst sec Miny Housing and Local Govt 1964, sec Royal Cmmn on Local Govt 1966-69, dir-gen CLA 1970-90; vice-pres Confedn of Euro Agric 1971-88, chm Enviroment Ctee 1988-90; wrote various articles on local govt and landowning; sec Euro Landowning Orgns Gp 1972-87; memb: Econ devpt Ctee for Agric 1972-90, Cncl CBI 1986-89, NW Kent Branch Oxford Univ Soc, N Kent Decorative and Fine Arts Soc; *Publications* various articles on local govt and landowning; *Recreations* golf, music, reading, films, theatre; *Clubs* Utd Oxford & Cambridge Univ, Chislehurst Golf; *Style*— James Douglas, Esq, CBE; 1 Oldfield Close, Bickley, Kent (☎ 081 467 3213)

DOUGLAS, Rev Robert Vernon; s of Rev Robert Henry Douglas (d 1970), of Tunbridge Wells, Kent, and Edith Joy, *née* Williams (d 1980); *b* 25 March 1924; *Educ* Haileybury, Pembroke Coll Cambridge (MA), Wells Theol Coll; *m* 25 June 1955, Sylvia May, *née* Holgate, da of Charles Lindsay Holgate (d 1987), of Borough Green, Sevenoaks, Kent; 2 s (Jeremy Charles Lindsay b 29 Sept 1960, Stephen Robert Lindsay b 27 April 1966); *Career* Sub Lt RNVR 1941-45; ordained deacon 1950, priested 1951; vicar: St Philip and St James Chatham 1955-66, St Mary's Platt 1980-; rector St James North Cray 1966-80; chaplain: Chatha ATC, Sea Cadet Corps Ruxley, TOCH Chatham, Royal Br Legion at North Cray and St Mary's Platt; *Style*— The Rev Robert Douglas; The Vicarage, St Mary's Platt, Sevenoaks, Kent (☎ 0732 885482)

DOVE, Leonard Ernest; CBE (1969); s of Alfred Dove (d 1955); *b* 10 Feb 1913; *Educ* Wilson's GS Camberwell; *m* 1938, Florence May, da of William Humphrey Shipley (d 1942); 1 s (and 1 s decd), 2 da; *Career* accountant and comptroller Gen Bd of Customs and Excise 1963-73; hon treas Methodist Church (overseas div) 1972-84, memb Kent Environmental Cncl 1983-; *Style*— Leonard Dove, Esq, CBE; 23 Stambourne Way, West Wickham, Kent BR4 9NE (☎ 081 777 5213)

DOVER, Bishop of 1980-; Rt Rev Richard Henry McPhail Third; s of Henry McPhail Third (d 1952), of Reigate, and Marjorie Caroline, *née* Richardson (d 1982); *b* 29 Sept 1927; *Educ* Alleyne's Sch Dulwich, Reigate GS, Emmanuel Coll Cambridge (MA), Lincoln Theoligical Coll; *m* 4 June 1966, (Constance) Helen, da of The Late Rev William George Illinworth, of Lyminge; 2 da (Christine b 1967, Hilary b 1969); *Career* ordained: deacon at Southwark 1952, priest at Southwark 1953; curate St Andrew Mottingham and All Saints Sanderstead 1952-55, i/c St Edmund Riddlesdown 1955-59; vicar: Sheerness 1959-67, Orpington 1967-76; rural dean of Orpington 1973-76, hon canon Rochester Cathedral 1974-76, bishop of: Maidstone 1976-80, Dover (with responsibility for diocesan affrs) 1980-; *Recreations* music, walking; *Style*— The Rt Rev The Bishop of Dover; Upway, St Martins House, Canterbury, Kent CT1 1PR (☎ 0227 464537); Diocesan House, Lady Wooton's Green, Canterbury, Kent CT1 1NQ (☎ 0227 459382)

DOWDING, Muriel, Baroness; Muriel; da of late John Albino; *Educ* Walthamstow Hall Sevenoaks, Convent of the Holy Child Sussex; *m* 1, 1935, Maxwell Whiting, RAF (ka 1944); 1 s; m 2, 25 Sept 1951, as his 2 w, Air Chief Marshal 1 Baron Dowding, GCB, GCVO, CMG (d 1970); *Career* vice pres RSPCA 1981-83; pres Nat Anti-Vivisection Soc, tstee Ferne Animal Sanctuary, pres Nat Animal Rescue Kennels, hon treas Int Assoc Against Painful Experiments on Animals, founder and chm Beauty Without Cruelty 1959, resigned 1981; *Books* Beauty not the Beast (1980); *Recreations* theosophy, spiritualism, astrology, all occult subjects; *Style*— The Rt Hon Muriel, Lady Dowding; Ashurst Lodge, Speldhust Rd, Langton Green, Tunbridge Wells, Kent TH3 0JF

DOWNES, David George; s of Rev Canon George Sidney John Downes (d 1969), and Lilian Elizabeth, *née* Osborne (d 1967); *b* 26 Nov 1929; *Educ* St John's Sch Leatherhead, Jesus Coll Cambridge; *m* 9 April 1953, Margaret Dorothea, da of Edward Charles Percy Curzon (d 1955); 1 s (John Stephen Curzon b 1957), 1 da (Sarah Elizabeth Jane Curzon b 1960); *Career* admitted slr 1956; chm Kent Rural Community Cncl, pres Kent Assoc of Parish Cncls; *Style*— David Downes, Esq; Cape House, Ash, Canterbury, Kent CT3 2HJ (☎ 0304 812427)

DOWNS, Donald Alexander Primrose; s of David Alexander Downs (d 1969), of Westerham, Kent, and Harriet Helsdon, *née* Plumbly (d 1935); *b* 22 May 1924; *Educ* Sevenoaks, The Polytechnic (Dip Arch), NAC (Cert); *Career* Lt 3 Carabiniers (Prince of Wales's Dragoon Gds) 1944-47, served Burma; architect 1955-84: Pite Son & Fairweather, Raglan Squire & Ptnrs, PSA DOE; ed Journal of the Flyfishers Club 1975-80; contrib to: Flyfishers Journal, Salmon and Trout Assoc Magazine, Trout and Salmon Magazine, Journal of the Flydressers Guild; pres The Fly Dressers Guild, sec Assoc of Professional Game Angling Instrs, examiner Nat Anglers Cncl; Friend of Save The Children 1988; ARIBA 1955, APGAI 1974; *Books* with John Veniard: Fly-tying Problems and their Answers (1970), Fly-tying Development Progress (1972), Modern Fly-tying Techniques (1973); *Recreations* angling, beagling, writing verse, cartooning; *Clubs* The Flyfishers; *Style*— Donald Downs, Esq; The Mead, Hosey, Westerham, Kent TN16 1TA

DOYLE, John Howard; s of Eric Doyle (d 1976), of Holling Bourne House, nr Maidstone, Kent, and Frances Thompson, *née* McLaine; *b* 15 Feb 1928; *Educ* Sherborne; *m* 1, 19 Oct 1956 (m dis 1977), Caroline Knapp-Fisher; 2 s (Charles Alexander Hastings b 1 May 1962, Christopher John Francis b 3 Jan 1971), 3 da (Serena Mary b 7 Jan 1958, Anna b and d 1973, Emma Louise b 11 Aug 1975); m 2, 10 Aug 1978, Elizabeth Eileen, da of Bernard Rickatson-Hatt, of London; *Career* dir: CF Doyle Ltd 1955-, Thomas Seager Ltd (and chm) 1962-86, Unipress Inc Tampa Florida USA 1984-, Westonworks Faversham; painter; exhibitions incl: Royal Acad 1965 (debut), Spinks & Sons St James 1982 1986 and 1990, Catto Gallery Hampstead 1988; memb Hollingbourne RDC 1954-56; memb Diocesan Advsy Ctee for Diocese of Canterbury 1977-84, chm Romney Marsh Historic Churches Tst 1980-88 (pres 1989); Freeman City of London 1966, memb Worshipful Co of Haberdashers, hon memb Worshipful Co of Painter-Stainers; RWS 1986 (Assoc 1978); *Books* An Artist's Journey Down the Thames (1988); *Recreations* golf, shooting, gardening; *Clubs* The Arts, Rye Golf; *Style*— John Doyle, Esq; Church Farm, Warehorne, Ashford, Kent TN26 2LP (☎ 023 373 2204)

DOYLE, Sir Reginald Derek Henry; CBE (1980); s of John Henry Doyle (d 1966), and Elsie, *née* Palmer; *b* 13 June 1929; *Educ* Aston Commercial Coll; *m* 12 Dec 1953, June Magretta, da of Bertram Stringer (d 1940); 2 da (Amanda Jayne b 3 May 1959, Wendy Louise b 13 March 1963); *Career* RN 1947-54; Fire Serv 1954-84: chief fire offr Worcestershire, Hereford and Worcester 1974 and Kent 1977, fire serv inspectorate 1984-, currently HM Chief Inspr of Fire Services; memb Rotary Club Kent; memb Guild of Fire Fighters; CBIM 1989, FIFireE 1973; *Recreations* badminton, shooting, swimming; *Style*— Sir Reginald Doyle, CBE; Home Office, Queen Annes St, London SW1H 9AT (☎ 071 273 3561)

DRAYSON, Rachel; JP (Buckinghamshire 1969); da of Stephen Spencer Jenkyns, MC (d 1956), of Winchester, and Lorna, *née* Jaques (d 1958); *b* 1 Oct 1922; *Educ* Burton HS for Girls, Godolphin Sch Salisbury; *m* 24 Aug 1943, Robert Quested Drayson, *qv*, s of Frederick Louis Drayson (d 1963), of Ramsgate; 1 s (Nicholas b 8 May 1953), 2 da (Gillian b 13 May 1944, Elizabeth b 29 July 1946); *Career* WRNS Portsmouth Cmd 1941-44, leading WREN 1942; Mothers' Union: memb 1944, served on Central Cncl 1974-77; sec of PCC St Nicholas Church Sandhurst, involved in Meals on Wheels Serv, cncl memb Wadhurst Coll; transfd to Norfolk Cmmn 1979, serv on Norwich City Bench 1980-84, supplemental on Kent Cmmn 1984; *Style*— Mrs Rachel Drayson, JP; Three Gables, Linkhill, Sandhurst, Cranbrook, Kent TN18 5PQ

DRAYSON, Robert Quested; DSC (1943); s of Frederick Louis Drayson (d 1963), of Kent, and Elsie Mabel, *née* West (d 1971); *b* 5 June 1919; *Educ* St Lawrence Coll Ramsgate, Downing Coll Cambridge (BA, MA); *m* 1943, Rachel, da of Stephen Spencer Jenkyns (d 1956); 1 s (Nicholas), 2 da (Gillian, Elizabeth); *Career* RNVR 1939-46, Lt in cmd HM Motor Torpedo Boats; asst master and housemaster St Lawrence Coll 1947-50, asst master Felsted 1950-55; headmaster: Reed's Sch Cobham 1955-63, Stowe 1964-79; appointed lay reader 1979, res lay chaplain to Bishop of Norwich 1979-84; govr: Parkside 1958-63, Beachborough 1965-79, Bilton Grange 1966-79, Beechwood Park 1967-79, Monkton Combe Sch 1976-85, St Lawrence Coll 1976-, Felixstowe Coll 1981-84; chm of Govrs Riddlesworth Hall Sch 1980-84;

memb: HMC Ctee 1973-75 (chm Midland Div 1975), Gen Cncl S American Missionary Soc (chm Selection Ctee 1980-), Allied Schs Cncl 1980-, Cncl McAlpine Educn Endowments Ltd 1982-, Ctee Ind Schs' Travel Assoc 1982-, Cncl Martyr's Meml & C of E Tst 1983-; elected to Band of Brothers 1987; FRSA; *Recreations* hockey (Cambridge Blue 1946-47), Kent XI (capt 1947-56, Final Eng trial 1950), watching cricket, golf, walking; *Clubs* Hawks (Cambridge); *Style—* Robert Drayson, Esq, DSC; Three Gables, Linkhill, Sandhurst, Cranbrook, Kent TN18 5PQ (☎ 0580 850447)

DUCK, Roger James; s of Percy William Duck (d 1960), of Shenfield, Essex, and Rosina Ethel, *née* Tarling; *b* 13 Nov 1927; *Educ* Brentwood Sch, Univ of Kent (BA); *m* 26 March 1955, Dorothy Margaret, da of Frederick George Henry Clark (d 1954), of Brentwood; 1 s (Simon b 1964); *Career* admitted slr 1953; dep town clerk Hove 1966-73, chief exec The Dartford Borough (formerly Dist) Cncl 1973-88, author of published articles and lectr on Admin Comparisons Between Britain And France; chm: Brentwood Round Table 1960-61, Brighton and Hove 41 Club 1973-74; Soc of Local Authy Chief Execs: memb Exec Cncl 1985-88, chm SE Branch 1986-87; AIL 1981 (memb Mgmnt Ctee of Indust and Commerce Div 1987-, chm 1990; *Recreations* French life and culture; *Style—* Roger Duck, Esq

DUCROTOY, (Christine) Athalie; da of James Thomas Albert Rawlings, of Puhoi, NZ, and Reneé, *née* Moulton; *b* 13 March 1942; *Educ* Ethelburgers Convent Deal, Ruawai Coll Northland NZ; *m* (Maxsim) René, s of Philibert Olivier Julefy Ducrotoy (d 1955), of Mombasa, Kenya; 4 s (Richard Antony Sullivan, Michael Andrew Sullivan, James Nicholas Hartley Sullivan, Marcel Maxsim), 3 da (Simone Antonia Odette Sullivan, Melanie Avena Louisa Sullivan, Chantal Maria); *Career* chiropodist; tropical nurse NZ, S Pacific and Brazil; ed Leopold Stokowski Society London soc magazine; sec New Hebrides Red Cross S Pacific 1972-74; memb: Br Cncl New Hebrides 1973-74, Br Chiropody Assoc, Brazilian Soc; Freeman City of London 1983; *Recreations* genealogy; *Clubs* Guild of Freemen; *Style—* Mrs Athalie Ducrotoy; Primrose Cottage, St Margarets-At-Cliffe, Kent; 12 Market St, Deal, Kent

DUFFETT, Peter Lionel; s of Rev George Henry Duffett (d 1983), and Iris Kathleen, *née* Yerbury; *b* 19 Oct 1941; *Educ* Royal Liberty Sch Romford, Royal Latin Sch Buckingham, ChCh Oxford; *m* 28 April 1964, Anita Lilian, da of Frederick Edward East, of Hythe, Kent; 2 s (Richard Stephen b 1965, Ian Peter b 1969), 1 da (Jane Alison b 1967); *Career* called to the Bar Middle Temple 1980 (non practising); dir and actuary Welfare Insur Co Ltd 1973; Prudential Assur Co Ltd: asst gen mangr SA Branch 1978, orgn and methods mangr London 1980; NRG London Reinsurance Co Ltd: actuary 1986, gen mangr (life) and actuary 1989-; deacon Folkestone Baptist Church 1972-75, magistrate Folkestone and Hythe PSD 1972-75; Liveryman Worshipful Co of Actuaries 1986; FIA, FCII, FCCA; *Recreations* art appreciation, pottering; *Style—* Peter Duffett, Esq; NRG London Reinsurance Co Ltd, Fountain House, 130 Fenchurch St, London EC3P 3BD (☎ 071 626 3851, fax 071 623 1628)

DUKE, Maj Gen Sir Gerald William; KBE (1966, OBE 1943), CB (1962), DSO (1945), DL (Kent 1970); s of Lt-Col A A G Duke (d 1950), and Irene, *née* Colbeck (d 1965); *b* 12 Nov 1910; *Educ* Dover Coll, RMA Woolwich, Jesus Coll Cambridge (BA); *m* 3 April 1946, Mary Elizabeth, *née* Burn (d 1979); 1 s (Peter b 1947), 1 da (Susan b 1948); *Career* reg army offr RE 1931-65, served in Egypt, Palestine, W Desert, Sicily, Italy, NW Europe, Malaya, Baor; co dir: Peter Lind 1965-69, Brixton Estate plc 1971-81; govr Dover Coll 1961-, vice pres the Hockey Assoc 1965-, chm SSAFA Kent 1973-84, pres Scout Assoc Kent 1974-86; *Books* The History of the Royal Engineer Yacht Club (1982); *Recreations* sailing, golf; *Clubs* Royal Ocean Racing, Rye Golf; *Style—* Maj Gen Sir Gerald Duke, KBE, CB, DSO, DL; Little Barnfield, Hawkhurst, Kent TN18 4PX

DUNCAN, Alan James; s of George Edmund Duncan, of Norwich, Norfolk, and Lillian May Duncan; *b* 21 Oct 1932; *Educ* City of Norwich Sch for Boys, Norwich City Coll, Cambridge Coll of Technol; *m* 1 March 1958, Jean Audrey, da of Henry Frederick Hill, of Lowestoft, Suffolk; 2 s (Andrew b 1961, John b 1969), 1 da (Linda b 1958); *Career* Nat Serv RAF 1951-53; sr tech asst Co-op Wholesale Society 1953-58; Batchelors Foods Ltd: laboratory chemist 1958-62, factory chemist and quality controller 1962-66, process devpt mangr 1966-81; md Enterprise Ashford Ltd 1987- (dir 1982-87); memb: Industl Div Ctee Ashford C of C and Indust, BT North Downs and Weald Dist Consumer Liaison Panel; CChem, MRIC 1980, MIFST 1976; *Recreations* walking, history; *Clubs* Elwick (Ashford), Ashford Business; *Style—* Alan Duncan, Esq; Enterprise Ashford Ltd, Enterprise Centre, Old Railway Works, Newtown Rd, Ashford, Kent TN24 OPD (☎ 0322 630307)

DUNGATE, Desmond William (Bill); s of Percy James Dungate (d 1964), of Gravesend, Kent, and Emily, *née* Kitley (d 1958); *b* 18 Jan 1924; *Educ* Gravesend GS; *m* 19 Sept 1953, Audrey Margaret, da of George Thomas Chubb (d 1967), of Gravesend; 2 s (Paul Anthony b 1959, Peter Leslie b 1966), 1 da (Mary b 1956); *Career* Air Crew Cadet RAF 1943-47; Swanscombe UDC 1940-50, Valuation Office Inland Revenue 1950-65; chief rent offr: Bromley 1965-75, Kent 1975-87; clerk Burham Parish Cncl 1986-, honoursman Rating and Valuation Assoc, fndr memb and former chm Inst of Rent Offrs; assoc Rating and Valuation Assoc 1951-86, hon fell Inst of Rent Offrs 1988- (fell 1966-87); *Books* Service Charges - A New Approach to Depreciation (1986); *Clubs* Nalgo Gravesend Cricket (pres); *Style—* Bill Dungate, Esq; 90 Poplar Grove, Maidstone, Kent ME16 0AL (☎ 0622 755099)

DUNLOP, Rear Adm Colin Charles Harrison; CB (1972), CBE (1963), DL (Kent 1976-); s of Rear Adm Samuel Harrison Dunlop, CB (d 1950), of Guildford, Surrey, and Hilda Dunlop (d 1965); *b* 4 March 1918; *Educ* Marlborough, Royal Navy Staff Coll; *m* 29 Jan 1941, Moyra Patricia O'Brien, da of John Albert Gorges (d 1967), of Perth, Australia; 3 s (Angus Patrick Harrison b 1943, Robin Charles O'Brien b 1945 d 1946, Christopher Graham Harrison b 1947); *Career* joined RN 1935, WWII served HMS Kent, Valiant Diadem and Orion, later served HMS Theseus and Sheffield, sec to 1 Sea Lord 1960-63, cmd HMS Pembroke 1964-66, dir Def Policy (A) 1968-69, promoted to Rear Adm 1969, Cdr Br Naval Staff Washington 1969-71, Flag Offr Medway 1971-74, ret 1974; dir gen: Cable TV Assoc, Nat TV Rental Assoc 1974-83; ret; memb co ctee SSAFA 1986-, chm of govrs Sir John Hawkins Hosp Chatham 1984-; *Recreations* cricket, country pursuits; *Clubs* Army and Navy, MCC, IZingari, Band of Brothers, Free Foresters; *Style—* Rear Adm Colin Dunlop, CB, CBE, DL; Chanceford Farm, Sand Lane, Frittenden, nr Cranbrook, Kent (☎ 0580 80242)

DUNLOP, Graeme Dermott Stuart; s of Maj-Gen Dermott Dunlop, CB, CBE (d 1980), of Hildenborough, Kent, and Ethel Whitson, *née* Scott; *b* 25 June 1942; *m* 10 March 1972, Annette Brigid, da of Joseph Flynn (d 1969), of Bexleyheath, Kent; 1 s (Michael b 1977), 2 da (Caroline b 1973, Clare b 1978); *Career* md: North Sea Ferries 1979-87, P&O European Ferries Ltd 1987-; *Recreations* squash, tennis; *Clubs* MCC, Hurlingham; *Style—* Graeme Dunlop, Esq; Sandyhurst House, Sandyhurst Lane, Ashford, Kent TN25 4NX (☎ 0233 642244); P&O European Ferries Ltd, Channel House, Channel View Rd, Dover, Kent CT17 9TJ (☎ 0304 223203, fax 0304 223433)

DUNN, Angus Henry; s of Col Henry George Mountfort Dunn (d 1969), and Catherine Mary (d 1986); *b* 30 Dec 1944; *Educ* Marlborough, King's Coll Cambridge (MA); Pennsylvania Univ; *m* 1973, Carolyn Jane, da of Alan Bartlett, of The Oast, High Tilt, Cranbrook, Kent; 2 s (Thomas b 1974, James b 1977), 1 da (Eliza b 1983); *Career* HM Diplomatic Service 1968-73; FCO, (Kuala Lumpur, Bonn); joined Morgan Grenfell & Co Ltd 1972-, dir 1978-, exec dep chm Morgan Grenfell (Asia) Ltd Singapore 1983-85; dir Julianas Hldgs plc 1983-85; *Books* Export Finance (co-author, 1986); *Recreations* riding, sailing; *Clubs* Royal Thames Yacht; *Style—* Angus Dunn, Esq; Dower House, Oxon Hoath, Tonbridge, Kent

DUNN, Janet Elizabeth; da of Denis Wall (d 1983), of Dulwich and Sidcup, and Betty Louise, *née* Baker; *b* 5 July 1952; *Educ* Charles Edward Brooke Sch Camberwell, King's Coll London (BD), Southlands Coll Wimbledon (PGCE); *m* 3 April 1976, Robert John Dunn, MP, s of Robert Dunn (d 1986), of Swinton, Manchester; 2 s (Alexander b 1982, Oliver b 1983); *Career* dep headmistress James Allen's Girls Sch 1974-81 (head of Religious Educn Dept 1979-81); co cncllr Dartford W Div, sec to Cons Gp Kent CC, patron CWCC Dartford Cons Assoc; chm: Dartford & Gravesend Police Advsy Ctee, Bd of Govrs Milestone Special Sch Dartford; vice-chm Christian Solidarity Int (UK), Supporter SOS Children's Villages; *Recreations* travel, antiques, enjoying our children; *Style—* Mrs Janet Dunn; The Rookery, Green St Green, Dartford, Kent DA2 8DP; Kent County Council, County Hall, Maidstone, Kent ME14 1XQ (☎ 0622 671411 x 4373, fax 0622 59905)

DUNN, Robert John; MP (C) Dartford 1979-; s of Robert Dunn (d 1986); *b* 14 July 1946; *Educ* State Schs; *m* 1976, Janet Elizabeth, da of Denis Wall (d 1983); 2 s; *Career* former sr buyer with Sainsbury's; contested (C) Eccles 1974 (vice pres Eccles Cons Assoc 1974-); jt sec Cons Backbench Educn Ctee 1980-82, advsr to Prof Assoc of Teachers 1982-83; pps: DES to 1982, Cecil Parkinson (chm Cons Pty) 1982-83, under-sec of state DES 1983-88, chm Con Back Bench Soc Security Ctee 1988-, memb 1922 ctee 1988-; pres Dartford YCs 1976-; *Clubs* Carlton; *Style—* Robert Dunn, Esq, MP; House of Commons, SW1 (☎ 071 219 5209)

DUNN, (George) Roger; s of George Dunn, and Marjorie Rose, *née* Brown; *b* 10 Jan 1936; *Educ* Tettenhall Coll, Univ of Bristol (BSc); *m* 22 Aug 1970, (Patricia) Jane, da of Frank J R Law (d 1972), of Churchill, Worcs; 3 da (Sarah b 1972, Claudia b 1975, Juliet b 1977); *Career* Tube Investmts 1958-67, AIC Ltd 1967-75, chm and md Arcontrol Ltd 1975-; memb: SE Regnl Cncl of CBI, Engrg Cncl Regnl Orgn, ct Bristol Univ; chm GAMBICA Ctee (for mfrg electrical switchgear and centl gear assemblies); FIEE, MIMechE, FInstD; *Recreations* swimming, playing the flute, private flying; *Style—* Roger Dunn, Esq; Ancontrol Ltd, Borough Green, Kent TN15 8RD (☎ 0732 883151, fax 0732 885982, telex 95580)

DUSSEK, Julian Eric; s of Lt-Cdr Eric Albert Dussek, of Plaxtol, Kent, and Ivy Marion, *née* Wynne; *b* 12 April 1944; *Educ* St Lawrence Coll Ramsgate, Univ of London (MB BS); *m* 6 Sept 1969, (Margot) Vanessa Tryce, da of Lt-Cdr Edward Guy Tryce Morgan (d 1964); 1 s (John b 1976), 1 da (Nicola b 1973); *Career* conslt thoracic surgn: The Brook Regnl Cardiothoracic Unit

1981-89, Guys Hosp 1981-, Brighton Health Authy 1981-, St Thomas Hosp 1989-; author of contribs to books on cardiothoracic and oesophageal surgery; chm Plaxtol Parish Cncl, sec Soc of Cardiothoracic Surgns of GB; FRCS 1974; *Recreations* cooking and the history of eating; *Style*— Julian Dussek, Esq; Tebolds, The Street, Plaxtol, Sevenoaks, Kent TN15 0QJ (☎ 0732 810489); The Cardiothoracic Unit, Guys Hospital, London SE1 9RT (☎ 01 955 4322)

DYKE, Cncllr William Graham; s of William John Dyke, (d 1969), of Northfleet, and Emily Edith, *née* Slater (d 1973); *b* 17 Aug 1927; *Educ* Gravesend GS for Boys; *m* 1, 1948 (m dis 1975), Muriel Irene; 2 s (Peter Graham b 1949, Martin Ian b 1953); m 2, 1978, Dorothy (d 1981); m 3, 28 Nov 1982, Constance Leta, da of Alfred George Guy Holland (d 1967), of Gravesend; *Career* building mangr, building conslt Building Estimating Surveying Services 1984-; memb Gravesend Borough Cncl 1965, chm Highways Works and Servs Ctee Gravesend Borough Cncl (rep Woodlands Ward 1973); memb: Gravesend Lions Club, Cons Pty; life memb Northfleet Traders Assoc, govr Southfields Sch; *Recreations* public service; *Style*— Cncllr William Dyke; Cleveland, 68 Windsor Rd, Gravesend, Kent DA12 5BN (☎ 0474 362201)

E

EADES, Caroline Annabelle; da of Henry Southwell Eades, and Marguerite Elsie Virginia, *née* Marshall; *b* 13 Dec 1949; *Educ* George Dixon Girls GS Birmingham, Univ of Bristol (LLB), Coll of Law Guildford; *Career* admitted slr 1974; articled Norwich Co Borough Cncl 1972-74, asst slr Cambs CC 1974-80, sr slr Northumberland CC 1980-87, sr slr Kent CC 1989-; force slr Kent Constabulary 1989-, memb: Channel Tunnel Cooperation in Criminal Justice Sub Ctee, Kent Police Crown Prosecution Serv and Courts Liaison Ctee, Law Soc Local Govt Gp, Gp of Slrs to Chief Constables, Kent Law Soc, Maidstone Film Soc, Law Soc; *Recreations* music, writing letters to The Times, travel; *Clubs* Royal Overseas League; *Style—* Ms Caroline Eades; Kent Constabulary Headquarters, Sutton Rd, Maidstone, Kent (☎ 0622 690690, fax 0622 687827)

EADY, David; QC (1983); s of Thomas William Eady (d 1978), and Kate, *née* Day; *b* 24 March 1943; *Educ* Brentwood Sch, Trinity Coll Cambridge (MA, LLB); *m* 1974, Catherine Hermione, yr da of Joseph Thomas Wiltshire, of Little Clarendon, North Rd, Bathwick, Bath; 1 s (James b 1977), 1 da (Caroline b 1975); *Career* called to the Bar Middle Temple 1966; rec 1986, memb Home Office ctee on privacy and related matters (The Calcutt Ctee) 1989-90; *Books* The Law of Contempt (jtly, with A J Arlidge, QC); *Recreations* music, watching Kent cricket at Canterbury; *Style—* David Eady, Esq, QC; Goodshill Ho, Tenterden, Kent TN30 6UN (☎ 058 06 3644); 1 Brick Ct, Temple, London EC4Y 9BY (☎ 071 353 8845)

EADY, Hon Georgina Mary Rose Swinfen; da of 3 Baron Swinfen, JP; *b* 1 Feb 1964; *Educ* Christ's Hospital Girls' Sch, Simon Langton Girls' Sch; *Career* sec to Charles M Hale (md) Donaldson Lufkin & Jenrette Securities Corp; *Recreations* opera, ballet, riding; *Style—* The Hon Georgina Eady; Dene House, Wingham, Canterbury, Kent CT3 1NV

EAGER, Robert Donald; s of Donald George Eager, of Littlehampton, W Sussex, and Genevieve Elizabeth, *née* Barbour; *b* 11 Dec 1950; *Educ* Brighton Hove and Sussex GS, Univ of Kent (BSc), Univ of Essex (MSc); *m* 24 Nov 1979, Christina Jane, da of Arthur William Howard Middleton, of Sudbury, Suffolk; *Career* sr lectr in computing Univ of Kent 1987- (lectr 1979-87); memb Cncl of Kent soc; MBCS 1987, memb Assoc for Computing Machinery (USA); *Books* Introduction fo PC DOS (as Bob Eager 1985), Fundamentals of Operating Systems (4 edn with A M Lister 1988); *Recreations* theatre, music, photography, amateur radio; *Style—* Robert Eager, Esq; Univ of Kent, Computing Lab, Canterbury, Kent CT2 7NF (☎ 0227 764000 ext 7589, fax 0227 762811)

EAGLES, Lt-Col (Charles Edward) James; LVO (1988); s of Maj Charles Edward Campbell Eagles, DSO, RMLI (ka 1918), and Esmé Beatrice, *née* Field (d 1965); *b* 14 May 1918; *Educ* Marlborough; *m* 1941, Priscilla May Nicolette, da of Brig Arthur Cottrell, DSO, OBE (d 1962), of Boughton Aluph Cottage, Ashford, Kent; 1 s (Anthony), 3 da (Susan, Jane, Mary); *Career* RM 1936-65; Civil Serv, MOD 1965-83; HM Body Gd of Hon Corps of Gentlemen-at-Arms: memb 1967-88, Harbinger 1981-86, Standard Bearer 1986-88; *Recreations* shooting; *Clubs* Army and Navy; *Style—* Lt-Col James Eagles, LVO, RM; Fallowfield, Westwell, Ashford, Kent (☎ 0233 712552)

EALHAM, Alan George Ernest; s of Stuart Alan Ealham, of Ashford, Kent, and Olive May, *née* Butler; *b* 30 Aug 1944; *Educ* South Secdy Sch Ashford, Folkstone Tech Coll; *m* 14 Sept 1968, Susan Patricia (Sue), da of Ronald Patrick Barton; 1 s (Mark Alan b 27 Aug 1969), 1 da (Loise Clare b 4 March 1971); *Career* played cricket Kent 2nd XI 1962; Kent CCC: joined playing staff 1966, played 1967-68 (Kent's most successful era winning 13 trophies and finals), capt 1978-80 (winning B&H Cup and Championship 1978), ret 1982, rejoined 1988 as 2nd XI captain and coach; 306 first class games, over 10,000 first class runs, 4,000 one day runs, highest score 153 v Worcester, Canterbury; 12th man for Eng on 4 occasions, Kent Co organiser for Kwik Cricket (Primary Schs); *Recreations* golf, club cricket; *Clubs* Ashford; *Style—* Alan Ealham, Esq; 20 Woodside, Dunkirk, nr Faversham, Kent ME13 9NY (☎ 0795 750631); Kent County Cricket Club, St Lawrence Ground, Canterbury, Kent (☎ 0227 456886)

EDDLESTON, Prof Adrian Leonard William Francis; s of Rev William Eddleston, of 25 Springfields, Colyford, Colyton, Devon, and Kathleen Brenda, *née* Jarman; *b* 2 Feb 1940; *Educ* Queen Elizabeth's GS Blackburn, St Peter's Coll Oxford (MA, BM BCh, DM), Guy's Hosp; *m* 10 Sept 1966, Hilary Kay, da of Kenneth Radford (ka 1942); 3 s (Stephen b 1969, Andrew b 1972, Paul b 1974), 1 da (Carolyn b 1968); *Career* conslt physician King's Coll Hosp 1976-, vice dean King's Coll Sch of Med and Dentistry 1987- (prof liver immunology 1982-, sub dean curriculum 1984-89); memb Camberwell Health Authy 1986-; sec Euro Assoc Study of Liver 1982-84, euro rep Cncl Int Assoc for Study of Liver 1984-88; FRCP 1974, memb Assoc Physicians GB and Ireland 1974; *Books* Immunology of Liver Disease (1979); *Recreations* electronics, computing, model aircraft, music; *Style—* Prof Adrian Eddleston; Liver Unit, King's College School of Medicine and Dentistry, Denmark Hill, London SE5 9RS (☎ 071 326 3066, fax 071 274 7246)

EDELEANU, Dr Ion-Dan; s of Ion Edeleanu (d 1966), and Marie, *née* Costa Foru (d 1980); *b* 14 June 1925; *Educ* Morrison Acad, Bedford Sch, Christ's Coll Cambridge, London Hosp (MA, MB BChir); *m* 5 Dec 1953, Doreen, da of Robert Hughes (d 1972), of Bala N Wales; 1 s (Hugh Robert b 30 Dec 1955), 1 da (Mary Louise b 18 Oct 1958); *Career* Nat Serv RAMC 1951-52; GP; house surgn and house physician London Hosp 1950, asst in Gen Practice Lincoln 1953-59, princ in gen practice Gravesend 1959, sr ptnr Seven Docton; former sch govr Northfleet Sch, former pres Rotary Club of Northfleet, prov ground offr Province of E Kent, vice pres Gravesend Rugby Club, memb CPRE; FRSM; memb: BMA, Br Soc of Med and Dental Hypnosis; *Recreations* gardening, squash; *Clubs* Rotary; *Style—* Dr Ion-Dan Edeleanu; Haydown, Great Buckland, Luddesdowne, Gravesend, Kent DA13 0XF (☎ 0474 814329); 65a Perry St, Gravesend, Kent (☎ 0474 356661)

EDGLEY, Peter Hiron; s of Leslie Charles Edgley, of Sevenoaks, and Queenie Winifred, *née* Keene (d 1979); *b* 17 Feb 1935; *Educ* Charterhouse; *m* 11 Feb 1956, Dorothy Ellen, da of Donald Harry Henley, of Elham; 3 s (Martyn Peter Henley b 15 April 1957, Simon Richard Leslie b 13 Aug 1958, Nicholal Paul Hiron b 21 July 1962); *Career* Nat Serv 2Lt 1 Bn The Buffs 1953-55, served in Kenya; md CH Peacock Ltd Watford 1963-66, dir Merritt and Hatcher Ltd 1965-68, exec dir E Westminster Press Planning Div 1969-76, vice chm F J Parsons Ltd 1973-74; md: Middlesex Co Press 1976-79, South Eastern Newspapers 1979-83; dir and dep md Kent Messenger Ltd 1980- (jt md 1985-89, dep chm 1990); chm: Watford Master Printers 1963, Kent and Downes Newspaper Publishers Assoc 1974 and 1988-90, Brough Green CC 1970-76, Kent CCC 1988-; vice pres Street End CC 1990; *Recreations* sport, gardening; *Clubs* Kent County Cricket, Hoppers; *Style—* Peter Edgley, Esq; Wise Follies, The Square, Elham, Nr Canterbury, Kent CT4 6TJ (☎ 0303 840498); Kent Messenger Ltd, 9 St George's Place, Canterbury, Kent CT1 1UU (☎ 0227 768181, fax 0227 762415)

EDGSON WRIGHT, Paul; s of Hugh Edgson Wright, MM (d 1979), of Folkestone, Kent, and Diana Christine, *née* Smith; *b* 3 March 1935; *Educ* Marlborough; *m* 11 June 1960, Gillian Elspeth, da of Sidney Leonard Shaw, of Santiago, Chile; 2 s (Mark b 1963, (Andrew) Peter b 1967), 1 da (Kathryn b 1961); *Career* articled Barton Mayhew & Co CAs 1953-59, Riddell Stead Graham & Hutchinson CAs Montreal PQ Canada 1959-61, Stanhay (Ashford) Ltd Gp 1961-72 (taken over by Hestair plc 1971) (appointed fin dir and co sec 1970), chm Stanhay (Autos) Ltd 1972-76, gp chief accountant MacBlast gp of cos 1976-77, Rothman Pantall & Co CAs 1978-84, formed Shaws CAs (reg insolvency practitioner) specialising in insolvency and investigations 1985; FCA; *Recreations* shooting, fishing, sailing, ornithology; *Style—* Paul Edgson Wright, Esq; Clareville House, 26/27 Oxendon St, London SW1Y 4EP (☎ 071 930 2217, telex 893715 ROTHCO G, fax 071 930-9849)

EDWARDES, Diana Cook; da of Frederick Armand Rimer (d 1982), and Gladys Elizabeth, *née* Borthwick (d 1964); *b* 10 March 1927; *Educ* American Acad of Dramatic Art NY, RAM (LRAM), Univ of London (BEd); *m* 15 July 1948, Paul Lionel Joseph Edwardes (d 1987), s of Capt Hugh Edwardes (d 1974); 1 s (Simon Richard b 1954), 2 da (Jane Emily b 1949, Pamela Michele b 1957); *Career* actress then theatre dir 1946-63, fndr memb Young Vic Theatre; dir: West Kent Youth Theatre (fndr 1965), own theatre touring and repertory cos; head of English Tunbridge Wells GS for Girls 1973-; memb Guild of Adjudicators; *Books* Ideas in Action (1979); *Recreations* family, friends, walking; *Style—* Mrs Diana Edwardes; East House, Nuttree Green, Shipbourne, Kent TN11 9QA, (☎ 0732 833569)

EDWARDS, David Michael; s of Denis Arthur Edwards, of London, and Maude, *née* Cruse; *b* 4 Dec 1947; *Educ* Tulse Hill, London Coll of Printing; *m* 1968, and Christine Nancy, da of John Carzana, of Kent; 2 s (Justin b 1979, Julian b 1981); *Career* publishing Print Buying; chm Paperback Production Gp 1981-82; chm Book Production Gp 1986-87, dir Macdonald & Co Ltd 1981-82; dir (fndr) Century Publishing Co Ltd 1982-85; dir Century Hutchinson Publishing Gp Ltd 1985-; *Recreations* golf, tennis, photography; *Clubs* Played Soccer Corinthian Casuals AFC (1st team) 1966-68; *Style*— David Edwards; 50 Barnfield Wood Rd, Beckenham, Kent BR3 2SU; Brookmount House, 62-65 Chandos Place, London WC2N 4NW (telex 261212 LIT LDNG, fax 01-836 1409)

EDWARDS, Gareth Paul; s of Gwilym Arwyn Edwards (d 1974), of Bromley, Kent, and Margaret Jean, *née* Macrow; *b* 11 June 1957; *Educ* The Leys Sch Cambridge, Kings Coll London (LLB); *m* 11 July 1981, Carol Lesley, da of Leslie James Hewson, LAC, African Star, Defence Medal, Imperial Service Medal (d 1977), of Harborne, Birmingham; *Career* admitted slr 1981; articles Stephenson Harwood London 1979-81, ptnr Clarkson Wright & Jakes 1984 (joined 1981); memb Bromley Family Practitioner Ctee, hon sec Bromley Hockey Club; memb Law Soc 1981; *Recreations* hockey, cricket, skiing; *Clubs* Bromley Hockey, Flying Wickets Cricket; *Style*— Gareth Edwards, Esq; Clarkson Wright & Jakes, Valiant House, 12 Knoll Rise, Orpington, Kent BR6 0PG (☎ 0689 76121, fax 0689 78537)

EDWARDS, John Coates; CMG; s of Herbert John Edwards, and Doris May Edwards; *b* 25 Nov 1934; *Educ* Skinners' Sch Tunbridge Wells, BNC Oxford; *m* 1959, Mary, *née* Harris; 1 s, 1 da; *Career* HM Dip Serv; head: British Devpt Div in the Caribbean 1978-81, West Indian and Atlantic Dept FCO 1981-84; dep high cmmr Br High Cmmn Nairobi Kenya 1984-88, Br high cmmr Maserv Lesotho 1988-; *Clubs* Royal Cwlth Soc, Multaiga Country Club (Nairobi); *Style*— John Edwards, Esq, CMG; Fairways, Ightham, Sevenoaks, Kent (☎ 0732 883556); Foreign and Commonwealth Office, King Charles St, London SW1

EDWARDS, Kathryn Helen; da of Kenneth Henry Edwards, of Caergwrle, Wrexham, Clwyd, and Joan, *née* Pritchard; *b* 1 May 1967; *Educ* Castell Alun HS Hope Wrexham, Wrexham Coll of Art, Maidstone Coll of Art (BA); *Career* self-employed photographer 1989-; sculptor; awarded purchase prize by SE Arts Assoc for sculpture Noiseless Immersion 1989; exhibitions incl: SE Open (Maidstone Gallery) 1989, Kathryn Edwards-Sculpture and Photographs (Maidstone Library Gallery) 1990; *Recreations* theatre, phrenology, travel; *Style*— Miss Kathryn Edwards; 45 Old Tovil Rd, Maidstone, Kent ME15 6PR (☎ 0622 751877)

EDWARDS, Nigel Llewellyn; s of Meirion Edwards, Sunbury on Thames, Middx, and Vida Mabel, *née* Jenkins; *b* 7 Oct 1952; *Educ* King's Sch Gutersloh, Llandoveny Coll, Univ of Birmingham (LLB); *m* 9 July 1977, Marilyn Frances (Lyn), da of Lt Ronald Edward Price, RN (d 1981), of Shepperton, Middx; 2 da (Louise b 17 June 1980, Megan b 8 Dec 1984); *Career* admitted slr 1977; articled Culross Lipkin & Co 1975-77 (asst slr 1977-78), asst slr Landau & Scanlan 1978-79, ptnr Neville Brabon 1981-83 (asst slr 1979-81), estab Nigel Edwards & Company 1983; memb Rotaract 1975-80, chm Bearsted Round Table 1988-89 (memb 1981-); memb: Law Soc, Kent Law Soc; *Recreations* squash, tennis, skiing, golf; *Style*— Nigel Edwards, Esq; Little Milgate, Otham Lane, Bearsted, Maidstone, Kent MH5 8SJ (☎ 0622 37171); White Cottage, Ashford Rd, Maidstone, Kent ME14 5DA (☎ 0622 690575, fax 0622 691354)

EDWARDS, Norman John; s of Ernest Edwards, MBE, and Maude Mary Edwards; *b* 18 Oct 1920; *Educ* Eltham Coll; *m* 14 June 1952, (Isabelle) Margaret Doff, da of Edmond Compton; 1 s (Andrew b 1956), 2 da (Rosalyn b 1954, Gay b 1958); *Career* RE 1940-46, Bengal Sappers and Miners Indian Army 1942-46; ptnr Bernard Thorpe & Ptnrs 1958-85; govr Eltham Coll (chm Walthamstow Hall 1975-85); memb Worshipful Co of Paviors; memb RICS 1948; *Recreations* gardening, sailing; *Clubs* Oriental, City Livery; *Style*— Norman Edwards, Esq; Westfield, Holbrook Lane, Chislenvest, Kent (☎ 01 467 3458)

EDWARDS, Peter Wallace; s of Wallace Edward Edwards (d 1972), of Stockbury, Maidstone, and Anne, *née* Partington (d 1986); *b* 8 March 1940; *Educ* Maidstone GS; *m* 24 Dec 1966, Susan Edwards, da of Raymond Percy Martin, of Cornwall; 3 s (Karl Warren b 1967, Dominic Paul b 1969, Toby Martin b 1975); *Career* asst ed Bermuda Sun 1964-65, dep ed Kent Evening Post 1970-73, ed Kent Messenger 1973-78, ptnr Edwards Harvey Assoc and ed and proprietor The Maidstone Star 1979-; memb: Cncl and Mgmnt Ctee Maidstone Hospice Appeal, Maidstone Crime Prevention Panel, Police Advsy Ctee; vice pres Maidstone United FC; *Recreations* sports, American football; *Style*— Peter Edwards, Esq; The Maidstone Press Centre, Bank St, Maidstone, Kent ME14 1PZ (☎ 0622 674177, fax 0622 690053)

EGAN, Patrick Valentine Martin; s of Eric Egan; *b* 17 July 1930; *Educ* Downside; *m* 1953, Mary Theresa, da of Frederick Hinds Coleman (d 1960); 3 da; *Career* Signals Instr RA Far E 1949-50; exec dir Unilever plc and Unilever NV 1978-; nominated memb Cncl Lloyds of London, non-exec dir Fisons plc; *Recreations* riding, hunting, gardening; *Style*— Patrick Egan Esq; Whiteways, Sissinghurst, Cranbrook, Kent (☎ 0580 713201)

ELEY, Dr Barry Michael; s of Horace Henry Eley (d 1971), and Ena Maud, *née* Cast (d 1975); *b* 6 March 1940; *Educ* St Olave's & St Saviours GS, The London Hosp Dental Sch (BDS, LDS, RCS); *m* 1 June 1963, Julie Christina, da of Arthur William Rumbold; 1 s (Peter John b 10 Dec 1965), 1 da (Esther Jane b 12 March 1968); *Career* house surgn London Hosp Med Sch 1963; Kings Coll Hosp Dental Sch: asst lectr and registrar 1963-65, lectr in cons dentistry 1965-74, sr lectr periodontology 1974-80; Kings Coll Sch of Med and Dentistry: sr lectr and conslt 1980-89, head Periodontal Dept 1980-, dir Sch of Dental Hygiene 1980-, read and conslt periodontology: author over 55 scientific papers; FDS, RCS 1972; memb: BDA, BSP, BSDR, RMS ; *Books* Amalgam Tattoos (1982), Outline of Periodontics (with J D Mason, 2 edn 1989); *Recreations* badminton, golf, listening to music, walking, astronomy; *Style*— Dr Barry Eley; 10 Grosvenor Rd, Petts Wood, Orpington, Kent BR5 1QU

ELGAR, David Charles; s of Frank Edward Elgar, of Wingham, and Ethel Mary Elgar, JP, *née* Dee (d 1983); *b* 24 June 1947; *Educ* Selwyn House Broadstairs, Tonbridge Coll of Estate Mgmnt, Univ of London (BSc), Wye Coll London (post grad Dip); *m* 31 July 1971, Jane Anne, da of Maurice Edwin Turner, of Ash; 1 s (John Charles b 6 April 1981), 1 da (Caroline Joan b 31 March 1978); *Career* asst Burrows and Co Ashford 1970-73, sr ptnr Charles Elgar and Sons 1985- (ptnr 1973-); appointed to Lord Chllr's Panel of Agric Arbitrators 1987; treas and memb Wingham Parochial Church Cncl 1976-, chm Wingham Parish Cncl 1983-87 (memb 1976-87); RICS: prof assoc 1972, fell 1978, chm Jr Branch 1980-81, chm Kent Branch 1987-88, hon sec Rural Practice Div 1988-, memb Gen Cncl 1988-; fell Central Assoc of Agric Valuers 1974, sr vice pres Kent Valuers Club; *Recreations* gardening, walking, watching cricket; *Clubs* Kent and Canterbury, Canterbury Farmers, London Farmers; *Style*— David Elgar, Esq; The Oasthouse, Hearts Delight, Wingham, Canterbury, Kent CT3 1EP (☎ 0227 720531); Charles Elgar and Sons, 41 High St, Wingham, Canterbury, Kent CT3 1AB (☎ 0227 720557, fax 0227 728330)

ELLINGWORTH, Lady Amanda Patricia Victoria; *née* Knatchbull; da of 7 Baron Brabourne and Countess Mountbatten of Burma; *b* 26 June 1957; *Educ* Gordonstoun, Kent Univ, Peking Univ, Goldsmith Coll London; *m* 31 Oct 1987, Charles V Ellingworth, er s of William Ellingworth, of Laughton, Leics; *Career* social worker; *Style*— The Lady Amanda Ellingworth; Newhouse, Mersham, Ashford, Kent TN25 6NQ

ELLIOT, Prof Harry; CBE (1975); s of Thomas Elliot (d 1961), of Weary Hall Style, Mealsgate, Cumbria, and Hannah Elizabeth, *née* Littleton (d 1928); *b* 28 June 1920; *Educ* Allhallows Sch, Nelson Sch, Univ of Manchester (BSc, MSc, PhD); *m* 27 May 1943, Betty, da of Henry Leyman (d 1974), of Doddiscombsleigh, Devon; 1 s (Brian b 1944), 1 da (Jean b 1948); *Career* WWII 1941-46; PO Tech (SIGS) RAFVR, served Coastal Cmd incl liason duties with USAAF and USN, demob Flt Lt 1946; lectr physics Univ of Manchester 1948-53; Imperial Coll: sr lectr 1953-60, prof 1960-80, sr res fell 1981-90, emeritus prof; Holweck Prize and Medal of Inst of Physics and French Physical Soc; author of numerous papers and articles published in learned jls; memb SRC; ARCS Imperial Coll 1961; chm: Astronomy Space and Radio Bd 1971-77, Cncl Royal Soc 1978, Euro Space Agency; FRS 1973, FWAAS 1983, FRAS 1984; *Recreations* painting, gardening, military history; *Style*— Prof Harry Elliot, CBE; Broadwater Down, Tunbridge Wells TN2 5PE

ELLIOTT, Ian Rodney; s of John Archibald Elliott (d 1975), of Exeter, and Florence Mary; *b* 27 April 1940; *Educ* King's Norton GS Birmingham; *m* 14 Aug 1970 (m dis 1988), Yolande Francesca Yvette, da of Dr Keith Leonard McNeilly; 2 da (Michelle Yolande b 7 June 1971, Sophie-Louise b 31 Oct 1972); *Career* sales rep Cadbury Bros Ltd 1956-66; Purnell and Sons Ltd: sales rep, area sales mangr, field sales mangr, asst sales mangr, sales mangr; Mam Inn Play Ltd mktg exec 1982-, Pearce Signs Kent gen mangr 1982-, Pearce Signs Southern Ltd sales mangr; memb Chartered Inst Mktg; *Recreations* tennis, family and friends, food and wine; *Clubs* Canterbury Lawn Tennis; *Style*— Ian Elliott, Esq; Leascroft, The Drive, Chestfield, Kent CT5 3NW (☎ 022 779 2670); Pearce Signs Southern Ltd, Elizabeth Works, Margate Rd, Broadstairs, Kent CT10 2PU (☎ 0843 64075, fax 0843 860854)

ELLIOTT, Michael Alwyn; s of William Alwyn Edwards and Mrs Jill Elliott, *née* Thornton; assumed stepfather's name; *b* 15 July 1936; *Educ* Raynes Park GS, Insead; *m* 1962, Caroline Margaret, da of John Edward McCarthy; 2 s (Gregory, Dominic), 1 da (Sophie); *Career* dir Kimberly Clark Ltd 1977-79, gen admin Nat Theatre 1979-85, dir admin Denton Hall Burgin & Warrens (slrs) 1985-88, business conslt 1988-; *Recreations* theatre, golf; *Style*— Michael Elliott, Esq; 149 Forest Rd, Tunbridge Wells, Kent TN2 5EX

ELLIS, Andrew Steven; OBE (1984); s of Peter Vernon Ellis, and Kathleen, *née* Dawe; *b* 19 May 1952; *Educ* St Dunstan's Coll Catford, Trinity Coll Cambridge (BA), Univ of Newcastle (MSc), Newcastle Poly (BA Law); *m* 13 Jul 1975(m dis 1987), Patricia Ann Stevens, da of William Skinner; *Career* proprietor Andrew Ellis (printing and duplicating services) 1973-81, election organiser 1981-85, sec gen Lib Pty 1985-86; chief exec SLD 1988-89; consultant in pub affairs governmental relations and political orgn 1989-; vice chm Lib Pty 1980-86; contested (Lib) Newcastle upon Tyne Central (1974, 1976 by election, 1979), Boothferry (1983); ldr Lib Gp Tyne and Wear CC 1977-81; *Books* Algebraic Structure (with Terence Treeby, 1971), Let Every Englishman's Home be his Castle (1978); *Clubs* Nat Liberal; *Style—* Andrew Ellis, Esq, OBE; 19 Hayle Rd, Maidstone, Kent ME15 6PD (☎ 0622 678 443)

ELLIS, Hugh David Stacey; s of Hugh Gwilym Ellis, CBE (d 1984), and Sheila Mildred Kathleen Wallis *née* Lovell (d 1979); *b* 3 Sept 1940; *Educ* Westminster, King Alfreds, Royal Naval College; *m* 1961 Tessa Jane, da of Colin Westin Robertson, of Sevenoaks, Kent; 1 s (Hugh Guy Jocelyn), 1 da (Charlotte Francis); *Career* fin mangr GEC plc 1968-71, fin dir Delta Metal Electrical (Hldgs) Ltd 1971-77, md Haw Par Bros Int Ltd 1977-83; Inchcape plc: dir SE Asia 1984-87, dir planning and devpt 1987-; *Recreations* reading, music, photography, squash, gardening; *Style—* Hugh Ellis, Esq; Woodsden Cottage, Water Lane, Hawkhurst, Kent; Inchcape plc, St Janes's House, 23 King St, London SW1Y 6QY (☎ 071 321 0110, fax 071 321 0604)

ELLISON, Prof Arthur James; s of Lawrence Joseph Ellison, of Birmingham (d 1978), and Elsie Beatrice Ellison; *b* 15 Jan 1920; *Educ* Solihull Sch, Univ of London (BSc, DSc); *m* 1, 1952, Marjorie (d 1955), da of Walter Cresswell, of Sheffield; m 2, 1963, Marian Elizabeth, da of John Gordon Gumbrell, of London (d 1976); 1 s, 1 da; *Career* design engr Higgs Motors Ltd 1938-43, tech asst Royal Aircraft Estab 1943-46, design engr Br Thomson-Houston Co Ltd 1947-58 (graduate apprentice 1946); lectr and sr lectr Queen Mary Coll Univ of London 1958-72, hon prof Nat Univ of Engrg Lima Peru 1968, prof of electrical and electronic engrg and head of dept City Univ London 1972-85 (prof emeritus 1985-), author of numerous papers and volumes on engrg and psychical res; fndr and chm Int Conf on Electrical Machines 1974-85 (pres of honour), pres Soc for Psychical Res 1976-79 and 1981-84; *Books* The Reality of the Paranormal (1988); *Recreations* reading, meditation, parapsychology and travel; *Clubs* Athenaeum; *Style—* Prof Arthur Ellison; 10 Foxgrove Ave, Beckenham, Kent BR3 2BA (☎ 081 650 3801); The City University, Northampton Sq, London EC1V 0HB (☎ 071 253 4399)

ELLS, Eric John; s of Eric Edwin Ells (d 1975); *b* 6 April 1929; *Educ* Blackfen Central; *m* 1952, Amelia Florence, *née* Baulch; 1 s, 2 da; *Career* dir: Sungkai Hldgs (Australia) Ltd, Lloyds Ave Registrars Ltd (chm), Rowe Evans (Indonesia) Ltd, Rowe Evans Investments plc, RW Securities Ltd, Supara Investments Ltd, Sungkai Hldgs Ltd, WJ & H Thompson (Rubber) Ltd; alternate: Bertam Hldgs plc, Lendu Hldgs plc; *Recreations* travel; *Style—* Eric Ells, Esq; 10 Hurstwood Drive, Bickley, Bromley, Kent BR1 2JF (☎ 081 4676456)

ELSEY, Karl William; s of William John Elsey, of Swansea, and Gladys Doreen Elsey; *b* 20 Nov 1958; *Educ* Bishop Gore GS Swansea; *m* 10 June 1988, Theresa Jane, da of Edward Charles Baker, of Rainham, Kent; *Career* professional footballer with Maidstone United; formerly with: Queens Park Rangers, Newport Co, Cardiff City, Gillingham, Reading; *Style—* Karl Elsey, Esq; Maidstone United Football Club, Bowerdene House, 1 Bower Terrace, Maidstone, Kent ME16 8RY (☎ 0622 754403, fax 0622 685803)

ELSTON, John David; s of Lt-Col John William Elston (d 1984), and Alwyn, *née* Fawbert; *b* 2 Aug 1946; *Educ* Norwich Sch, Richmond Sch Yorks, Univ of Newcastle upon Tyne (BA); *m* 27 Sept 1980, Victoria Ann Harding (Vicky), da of Victor William Brown, of 41 Cherry Post Crescent, Etobicoke, Toronto, Canada; 2 s (James b 1982, Henry b 1988), 1 da (Georgina b 1986); *Career* sr exec James Capel & Co 1985- (joined 1973); FCA 1979; *Recreations* squash, tennis, bridge; *Style—* John Elston, Esq; The Dene, 9 Kippington Rd, Sevenoaks, Kent TN13 2LH (☎ 0732 457087); James Capel & Co, James Capel House, PO Box 551, 6 Bevis Marks, London EC3A 7TQ (☎ 071 621 0011, fax 071 621 0496, telex 888866 JC LDN G)

ELWES, Jeremy Vernon; CBE (1984); s of Eric Vincent Elwes (d 1985), of Sevenoaks, Kent, and Dorothea, *née* Bilton; *b* 29 May 1937; *Educ* Wirral GS, Bromley GS, City of London Coll (ACIS); *m* 1963, Phyllis Marion, da of George Herbert Harding Relf, of Halstead, Sevenoaks, Kent; 1 s (Jonathan b 1969); *Career* chartered sec; dir Sevenoaks Constitutional Club Co Ltd 1977-; chm Cons Political Centre Nat Advsy Ctee 1981-84, personnel dir Reed Business Publishing Ltd 1982-; chm: Sutton Entetrprise Agency Ltd and SE Area Provincial Cncl 1986-90; memb Cons Pty Nat Union Exec Ctee 1974-, memb and judge Int Wine and Spirits Competition Ltd 1983-, prospective chm St Helier NHS Tst, chm Walthamstow Hall 1984- (govr 1977-), govr Eltham Coll 1977, memb Gp Ctee Gen Cncl Cons Gp for Europe 1990 (1985-89, memb 1977-); Chevalier Ordre des Chevaliers Bretvins (Baillage de GB, Maitre des Ceremonies 1984-88, Chancelier 1986-); *Recreations* wine, food, reading, golf; *Clubs* Carlton, St Stephen's Constitutional, Edenbridge Golf and Country; *Style—* Jeremy Elwes, Esq, CBE; Crispian Cottage, Weald Rd, Sevenoaks, Kent TN13 1QQ (☎ 0732 454208); Reed Business Publishing Group, Quadrant House, The Quandrant, Sutton, Surrey SM2 5AS (☎ 081 661 3019, telex 892084 REEDBP G, fax 081 661 8948)

EMERSON, Robert Daniel; s of Ambrose Emerson (d 1954), of Vennes, Lausanne, Switzerland, and Olive Lillian, *née* Thompson (d 1986); *b* 27 July 1929; *Educ* Haileybury, Gonville and Caius Coll Cambridge (MA); *m* 19 Nov 1965, Sally Ann d'Esterre, da of T W V Taylor, of Kinsale, Co Cork; 1 s (Daniel Paul Ambrose b 1971), 1 da (Harriet Joanna b 1968); *Career* Nat Serv 1947-49, cmmnd RA, served 26 H Field Regt RA Malaya; dir Int Div The Economist Intelligence Unit Ltd 1956-66, various appts Morgan Crucible Group 1967-83, dir of various major subsids Thomas Tilling plc 1978-83, md Kent Econ Devpt Bd 1984-; ACA 1956, FCA 1966; *Recreations* skiing, reading, theatre, country pursuits; *Clubs* Reform, Hurlingham, Kinsale Yacht; *Style—* Robert Emerson, Esq; Meadow House, Stockbury, Kent ME9 7UN (☎ 0795 844076); KEDB, Brenchley House, Week St, Maidstone, Kent

EMERTON, Dame Audrey Caroline; DBE (1989); da of George William Emerton (d 1971), of Tunbridge Wells, and Lily Harriet, *née* Squirrell; *b* 10 Sept 1935; *Educ* Tunbridge Wells GS, Battersea Coll of Technol; *Career* SRN; sr tutor St George's Hosp London 1968, princ nursing offr teaching Bromley HMC 1968-70, chief nursing offr Tunbridge Wells and Leybourne HMC 1970-73, regnl nursing offr SE Thames RHA 1973-; chief nursing offr St John Ambulance Bde 1988- (co nursing offr 1970-84, co cmmr 1984-88); chm: Eng Nat Bd for Nurses Midwives and Health Visitors 1983-85, UK Central Cncl Nursing Midwives and Health Visitors 1985-; Hon DCL Univ of Kent 1989; memb: Royal Coll Nursing, RSM; FRSA; *Style—* Dame Audrey Emerton, DBE; The Corner House, 2 Carlton Rd, Tunbridge Wells, Kent TN1 2JS (☎ 0892 27923); South East Thames RHA, Thrift House, Collington Ave, Bexhill, E Sussex TN39 3NQ (☎ 0424 730073)

ENGLAND, Colin Philip; s of Harry Richard England, of Langton Green, Tunbridge Wells, Kent, and Edith Francis, *née* Martin; *b* 4 Feb 1937; *Educ* Open Univ (BA, Dip Municipal Admin), Associate Chartered Institute of Secretaries and Administrators; *m* 28 Sept 1963, Christine Elaine, da of Reginald George Henry Paskins Twitchen (d 1974), of Bexleyheath; 1 s (Neil David b 12 Nov 1966), 1 da (Joanne Caroline b 26 May 1975); *Career* chief exec (UK) Money Concepts 1988-; dir: Genesis (UK) Ltd Hldgs, Genesis (Fin Servs), Genesis (Recruitment Servs), Genesis (Business Servs); govr Ravensbourne Sch for Girls Bromley Kent; Freeman City of London, Liveryman Worshipful Co of Masons; ACISA 1984; *Style—* Colin England, Esq; 36 The Chase, Bromley, Kent BR1 3DF (☎ 01 464 0563); 37 Spring St, London W2 1JA (☎ 01 706 4084, fax 01 706 4083)

ENGLISH, Cncllr Eileen Grace; da of Ernest Henry Iveson (d 1965), of Tottenham, London, and Grace, *née* Voller (d 1975); *b* 22 Jan 1939; *Educ* Tottenham Co Sch, Univ of Exeter (BA, Cert Ed); *m* 30 Dec 1961, Geoffrey James, s of Sir John English, MBE (d 1973), of Yeovil, Somerset; 2 s (John b 25 Nov 1964, Stephen b 14 April 1967); *Career* asst teacher Southend HS for Girls Essex 1961-63, lectr S Kent Coll of Technol Ashford Kent 1972-; fndr memb local SDP, elected memb Ashford Borough Cncl 1987 (candidate 1983), memb Liberal Democrats 1988; fndr memb Pluckley Pantomime Gp, memb Pluckley Gardening Soc, former sec Pluckley Parochial Church Cncl, former memb Pluckley Women's Inst; memb: HA, Royal Archaelogical Inst; *Recreations* gardening, knitting, cooking, amateur dramatics, cycling; *Style—* Cncllr Eileen English; Coopers Cottage, Forge Hill, Pluckley, Ashford, Kent (☎ 0233 84276); South Kent College of Technology, Jemmett Rd, Ashford, Kent (☎ 0233 624513)

EPSOM, Dr Joseph Edward; s of Joseph Edward Epsom, of Loughton, Essex (d 1952), and Mary, *née* Woods (d 1971); *b* 8 Aug 1919; *Educ* St Ignatius Coll, QMC London, London Hosp Med Coll, LRCP, DPH and DIH Royal Colls of Surgns and Physicians; *m* 2 July 1945, Barbara, da of Henry Swarbrick, of Bradford, Yorks (d 1966); 7 s (Michael b 18 June 1947, Richard b 5 March 1950, Joseph b 8 March 1951, Henry b 16 Nov 1955, Paul b 15 Oct 1956, John b 27 March 1958, Philip b 15 July 1962), 3 da (Susan b 9 April 1946, Ruth b 17 Jan 1949, Barbara b 11 Jan 1953); *Career* Capt RAMC/RASC 1940-46, OC 47 Port and Beach Detachment 21 Army Gp in Normandy France Belgium Holland Germany; house physician and emergency offr London Hosp 1950, asst princ gen practice 1950-53, registrar Radcliffe Infirmary United Oxford Hosps 1953-54, asst MOH Met Borough of Stepney 1954-56, dep MOH Tottenham Borough Cncl 1956-60; MOH: Met Borough of Bermondsey 1960-65, London Borough of Southwark 1965-74; hon conslt community physician Guy's Hosp, princ sch MO Southwark; chm London Food Ctee 1970-74, fndr City of London Med Res Fund, memb of the Court Leet Kings Manor Southwark, hon fell Assoc Port Health Authys; Liveryman Worshipful Co of Loriners 1973; memb of Faculty of Community Med, fell Soc of Community Med; MRCS, FRSH; *Books* Community Screening London Boro Southwark (1970), Modern Trends in Oncology (contrib 1974); *Recreations* sailing; *Clubs* City Livery, Livery Yacht, Cruising Assoc, Royal Cinque Ports Yacht Dover; *Style—* Dr Joseph Epsom

ERIAN, John; s of Dr Habib Erian (d 1976), of Cairo, and Aida, *née* Mitry; *b* 12 Aug 1948; *Educ* St Georges Coll, Ain-Shams Med Univ Cairo (MB, BCh); *m* 7 July 1973, Jennifer, da of Norman Frank Felton, of 2 Oakes Ave, Hanworth, Middlx TW13 5JD; 2 s (Michael b 1974, Gehanne b 1976), 1 da (Simonne b 1977); *Career* conslt obstetrician and gynaecologist; W Cumberland Hosp 1975-79, St George's Hosp 1979-82, Queen Charlotte's Hosp and Chelsea Hosp for Women 1982-83, St Thomas Hosp 1983, Guy's Hosp 1983-85, Farnborough Hosp Kent 1985-; fndr of Bromley Dist

Colposcopy Serv and Endocrine Unit and gift treatment Orpington Lions Club, pioneered yag laser surgery in UK as an alternative to hysterectomy: MRCOG 1981; *Recreations* tennis, tabel tennis, swimming, theatre, music; *Style*— John Erian, Esq; Farnborough Hospital, Farnborough Common, Locksbottom, Orpington, Kent (☎ 0689 53333 car 0836 580007)

EUSTACE, Hon Mrs (Dorothy Anne); yr da of 1 and last Baron Percy of Newcastle (d 1958), and Stella Katherine, *née* Drummond; *b* 21 Sept 1926; *Educ* Univ of Durham (MB BS); *m* 23 March 1957, Maj Thomas Robert Hales Eustace, o s of late Louis Charles Moss Eustace, of The Cliff, Mousehole, Penzance, Cornwall; 1 s (James b 1960), 2 da (Alicia b 1958, Katherine b 1965); *Style*— The Hon Mrs Eustace; Glebe House, Boughton Aluph, Ashford, Kent

EVANS, Hon Mrs (Cicili Carol); *née* Paget; yst da of 1 and last Baron Queenborough, GBE (d 1949) (by 2 w), gs of 1 Marquess of Anglesey; *b* 18 April 1928; *m* 10 Dec 1949, Capt Robert Victor John Evans, Welsh Guards, s of late Brig John Meredith Jones Evans, *qv*, CBE, MC, of Wishanger, Churt, Farnham, Surrey; 2 s, 1 da; *Style*— The Hon Mrs Evans; Gainsford House, Cowden, Kent TN8 7JD

EVANS, Georgina Ellen; da of Frederick James Westlake (d 1985), of 189 Coast Rd, Pevensey Bay, Sussex, and Joan Margaret, *née* Graves (d 1986); *b* 21 Dec 1950; *Educ* Stockwell Manor Comp; *m* 21 March 1981, Terence George Evans, s of George Albert William Evans, of 209 Coast Rd, Pevensey Bay, Sussex; 1 s (Bradley b 1982), 1 da (Georgina b 1981); *Career* accountant Hagley Knight & Co 1971-75, dep accountant Kings Coll Hosp Med Sch 1975-81, accountant Armour Lock & Safe Co 1981-; FCA 1981; *Recreations* reading, walking, cooking, redecoration, gardening; *Style*— Mrs Georgina Evans; 20 Whitmore Rd, Beckenham, Kent; Armour Cock & Safe Co, 209 Stockwell Rd, Brixton, London SW9 (☎ 071 733 4537)

EVANS, (Ieuan) Lynn; s of Rev Thomas John Evans (d 1973), of Ealing Green, London, and Jenny, *née* Lloyd-Williams (d 1958); *b* 15 July 1927; *Educ* Bradford GS, Haverfordwest GS, St Marys Hosp Med Sch (MB BS); *m* 6 June 1956, Menna, da of Rev Evan James (d 1966), of Porthcawl; 1 s (Rowland b 1961), 1 da (Siân b 1963); *Career* Nat Serv jr surgical specialist RAMC Queen Alexandra's Mil Hosp 1951-53; conslt surgn: Lewisham & St John's Hosp 1965-87, Guys Hosp 1982-84; surgical tutor Guys Hosp Med Sch 1970-87; hon conslt surgn: St Lukes Hosp for the Clergy 1983-87, Royal Soc of Musicians of GB; cncl memb: Assoc of Surgns of GB & Ireland, section of surgery RSM, Med Soc of London, Harveian Soc; pres W Kent Medico-Chirurgical Soc; elder Utd Reformed Church; Freeman: Worshipful Soc of Apothecaries of London, City of London 1975; FRCS 1954; *Recreations* skiing, gardening, travel; *Style*— Lynn Evans, Esq; 34 Birchwood Rd, Petts Wood, Orpington, Kent

EVANS, Prof Michael Charles Whitmore; s of Allen Whitmore Evans, of London, and Doris, *née* Smith; *b* 24 Sept 1940; *Educ* King Edwards Sch Birmingham, Univ of Sheffield (BSc, PhD); *m* 28 Dec 1963, Christine Stella, da of John Marshall (d 1985); 2 s (Peter Whitmore b 1967, Nicholas John b 1969); *Career* assoc specialist Dept of Cell Physiology Univ of California Berkeley 1964-66, lectr in botany kings Coll London 1966-73, prof in plant chemistry UCL 1982- (reader 1973-82); contrib numerous papers in scientific jnls; chm Plant Scis and Microbiology Sub-Ctee 1987- (memb 1985-), Biological Sci Ctee memb SERC1987-; *Recreations* birdwatching, gardening; *Style*— Prof Michael Evans; Dept of Biology, Darwin Building, University College London, Gower St, London WC1E 6BT (☎ 01 380 7312, fax 01 380 7026)

EVANS, (Haydn) Michael; s of John Robert Evans (d 1953), of Dyfed, and Ethel Phyllis; *b* 22 Sept 1942; *Educ* Llandovery Coll, Univ of Loughborough; *m* 2 April 1966 (m dis 1990), Patricia Margaret; 1 s (Marcus Haydn b 6 Nov 1971), 1 da (Lora Joanne b 5 March 1967); *Career* mktg exec Hoechst Chemicals Ltd 1963-65; dir: Whatman Scientific Ltd 1972- (joined 1965), British Labware Ltd 1988-; pres: Fedn of Euro Distributors of Scientific Laboratory Prods 1986-84, Br Laboratory Ware Assoc 1990; FBIM 1982; *Recreations* woodland preservation; *Style*— Michael Evans, Esq; Whatman Scientific Ltd, Springfield Mill, Maidstone, Kent ME14 2LE (☎ 0622 692022)

EVANS, Ven Patrick Alexander Sidney; *b* 28 Jan 1943; *Educ* Clifton, Lincoln Theol Coll; *m* 3 c; *Career* curate: Lyonsdown 1973-76, Royston 1976-78; vicar: Gt Gaddesden (and diocesan stewardship advsr) 1978-82, Tenterden with Smallhythe 1982-89; rural dean W Charing 1988-89, archdeacon of Maidstone and diocesan dir of ordinands 1989-; *Style*— The Ven the Archdeacon of Maidstone; Archdeacon's House, Charing, Ashford, Kent TN27 0LU (☎ 023 3712294)

EVANS, Capt Robert Victor John; DL (1986); s of Brig J M J Evans, CBE, MC (d 1957), *see Burkes Landed Gentry 18th Edn, Vol iii, Evans of Broomhall*, of Wishanger, Churt, Surrey, and Camilla, *née* Clifford (d 1971); *b* 27 Dec 1921; *Educ* RNC Dartmouth; *m* 10 Dec 1949, Hon Cicili Carol Paget, *qv*, da of Baron Queenborough, GBE, JP (d 1949), of Camfield Place, Hatfield, Herts; 2 s (John Almeric b 13 Sept 1950, Michael Hugh b 11 Nov 1956), 2 da (Camilla Carol b 22 Jan 1952 d 1963, Patricia Antonietta b 18 July 1959); *Career* served WWII 2 Armoured Bn Welsh Gds, cmmnd Welsh Gds 1941, regular cmmn 1946, ret 1953; memb London Stock Exchange 1960-78; pres: Westerham Branch Royal Br Legion, Assoc of Men of Kent and Kentish Men 1983-; memb: Nat Appeals Ctee Cancer Res Campaign 1960- (vice chm 1969-84, chm 1984-), Shrievalty Cncl 1984-; High Sheriff Kent 1982-83, chm Sevenoaks and Dist Crime Prevention Panel 1987-90; *Clubs* Cavalry and Guards; *Style*— Capt Robert Evans, DL; Gainsford House, Cowden, Kent TN8 7JD (☎ 0342 850587)

EVANS, Rev Stanley Munro; s of William Stanley Evans (d 1953), of Minster-in-Sheppey, and Annabella, *née* Munro (d 1978); *b* 21 April 1930; *Educ* Borden GS Sittingbourne, King's Coll London (AKC), Warminster; *m* 13 Oct 1979, Marie Jean, da of William Shaw Carmichael (d 1946), of Margate; *Career* Nat Serv RAF 1948-50; ordained: deacon 1954, priest 1955; asst curate St Laurence in Thanet 1957-63 (St Oswald Norbury 1954-57); priest i/c: St Christopher Newington 1957-63, Bicknor and Huckinge 1969-71; vicar St Saviour Westgate on Sea 1972- (Bredgar (with Bicknor and Huckinge from 1971) 1963-72); memb Kent Co Assoc of Change Ringers 1944- (chm 1971-74, vice pres 1974-), govr Bredgar C of E Primary Sch 1963-72 (chm 1967-72), chm of govrs St Saviour's C of E Primary Sch Westgate on Sea 1972-; chaplain to: the Mayor of Margate 1979-80 and 1990-, Royal Br Legion 1972-, St Mildred of Thanet Chapter of the Guild of Servants of the Sanctuary 1989-; memb: RBL Housing Assoc's House Ctee for Ralph Grimshaw and Countess Mountbatten Courts Westgate on Sea 1980-, Canterbury Diocesan Publicity Ctee 1965-68, Sittingbourne Cncl for Church Social Work 1963-72 (vice chm 1970-72), Ctee Sittingbourne Cncl of Churches 1968-72 (vice chm 1971-72), Canterbury Diocesan Synod 1970-72, 1979-88; *Recreations* music, bellringing, walking, swimming, reading, gardening, travel; *Style*— The Rev Stanley Evans; The Vicarage, Thanet Rd, Westgate on Sea, Kent CT8 8PB (☎ 0843 31869)

EVERARD, Frederick Michael; s of Frederick Alfred John Beatty Everard, CBE (d 1988), of Fawkham, Kent, and Penelope Baker Everard, JP, *née* Wall (d 1976); *b* 5 June 1948; *Educ* Oundle, City of London Poly (BA); *m* 1 April 1978, Pamela Elizabeth, da of John William George Reader (d 1977), of Gravesend, Kent; 4 da (Sarah Louise, Victoria Jane, Caroline Rebecca, Edwina Violet); *Career* chm FT Everard & Sons Ltd (dir 1974-), jt md Short Sea Europe plc 1989-; memb Br Waterways Bd 1983-88, vice pres GCBS 1990-; treas RINA 1987-90; memb: Port Users' Consultative Ctee, Lloyd's Register of Shipping Gen Ctee; vice chm Nat Waterways Tport Assoc; past pres Assoc of Master Lightermen & Barge Owners; Prime Warden Worshipful Co of Shipwrights 1989-90; *Recreations* music, jogging, tennis, golf; *Style*— Frederick Everard, Esq; F T Everard & Sons Ltd, The Wharf, Greenhithe, Kent DA9 9NW (☎ 0322 842345, fax 0322 843422)

F

FABER, Sir Richard Stanley; KCVO (1980), CMG (1977); er s of Sir Geoffrey Cust Faber (d 1961), and Enid Eleanor, da of Sir Henry Erle Richards, KCSI, KC; bro of Thomas Erle Faber; *b* 6 Dec 1924; *Educ* Westminster, ChCh Oxford (MA); *Career* served RNVR 1943-46; entered HM Dip Serv 1950; served: Baghdad, Paris, Abidjan, Washington; cnsllr: The Hague 1969-73, Cairo 1973-75; asst under sec of state FCO 1975-77, ambass Algiers 1977-81, ret; *Books* Beaconsfield and Bolingbroke (1961), The Vision and the Need: Late Victorian Imperialist Aims (1966), Proper Stations: Class in Victorian Fiction (1971), French and English (1975), The Brave Courtier (Sir William Temple) (1983), High Road to England (1985), Young England (1987); *Clubs* Travellers'; *Style—* Sir Richard Faber, KCVO, CMG

FAGG, Timothy Peter; s of Joseph Thomas Fagg, MBE, of Tile Lodge, Sandyhurst Lane, Ashford, Kent, and Jean Stella, *née* Linsdell; *b* 9 April 1951; *Educ* Wellington House Westgate, King's Sch Canterbury, Trinity Coll Cambridge (MA); *m* 23 Aug 1980, Helen Margaret, da of William Charles Todd (d 1986), of Moffat, Dumfrieshire; 2 s (Joseph William b 31 March 1984, Thomas Charles b 19 Jan 1986), 1 da (Katy Helen b 11 June 1982); *Career* admitted slr 1976; McKenna & Co 1973-76; actor 1976-80, repertory seasons Westcliffe Folkestone; ptnr Kingsford Flower & Pain 1982- (slr 1980-82); chm area 16 Kent Round Table 1988-89, vice chm Ashford Age Concern 1988-, sec Kent Soc RFU Referees 1988-, memb Ctee SE Gp RFU 1988-; memb: Law Soc 1975, Equity 1978; *Recreations* rugby (referee), squash, golf, amateur dramatics; *Style—* Timothy Fagg, Esq; Hollis Barn, Egerton, Kent TN27 9BD; Kingsford Flower & Pain, 2 Elwick Rd, Ashford, Kent (☎ 0233 624545, fax 0233 645486)

FAGGE, John Christopher; s and h of Sir John Fagge, *qv*, 11 Bt; *b* 30 April 1942; *Style—* John Fagge, Esq

FAGGE, Sir John William Frederick; 11 Bt (E 1660); s of William Archibald Theodore Fagge, *qv* (d 1924), 4 s of 8 Bt, and Nellie, *née* Wise (d 1924); suc unc, Sir John Harry Lee Fagge, 10 Bt, 1940; *b* 25 Sept 1910; *m* 11 May 1940, Ivy Gertrude, da of William Edward Frier, of Newington, Kent; 1 s, 1 da; *Heir* s, John Christopher Fagge; *Career* farmer; *Style—* Sir John Fagge, Bt; 26 The Mall, Faversham, Kent

FALLA, Paul Stephen; s of late Brig Norris Stephen Falla, CMG, DSO, of Wellington, New Zealand, and Audrey Frances, *née* Stock; *b* 25 Oct 1913; *Educ* Wellington and Christ's Coll NZ, Balliol Coll Oxford; *m* 1958, Elizabeth Mary, *née* Shearer; 1 da; *Career* HM Foreign Service 1936-67, cnsllr (FO, FCO) 1950-67 (dep dir of Res 1958-67); editor Oxford English-Russian Dictionary published 1984; Scott Moncrieff Prize for translation from French 1972 and 1981, Schlegel-Tieck Prize for translation from German 1983; translated about 45 books from various languages on politics, history, art; FIL, fell Inst of Translation and Interpreting; *Recreations* reading (history, politics, philosophy, belles-lettres), studying languages; *Clubs* Travellers'; *Style—* P S Falla, Esq; 63 Freelands Rd, Bromley, Kent BR1 3HZ (☎ 01 460 4995)

FALLAW, Elizabeth; da of Brian Fife Fallaw, of Newcastle upon Tyne, and Ella, *née* Cairns; *b* 30 July 1939; *Educ* Harrogate Coll, Durham Univ; *m* 10 Feb 1968, Peter Graham Bloom, s of Stanley Charles Edward Bloom (d 1985), of Smarden, Kent; *Career* trg in market res Proctor & Gamble, Lintas advertising agency 1972-82 (joined bd 1979), gp account dir Dolrand advertising agency 1982-88, ptnr Sellers Marchant 1988-; memb: NABS Cncl 1981-, St James Egerton PCC 1984-; church warden 1987-; memb MRS 1967, MIPA 1977; *Recreations* riding, village life, collecting wine; *Clubs* Women's Advertising of London (pres 1982-83); *Style—* Ms Elizabeth Fallaw; Luckhurst House, Pluckley, nr Ashford, Kent TN27 0SN (☎ 023 384 540); Sellers Marchant Associates, 64 Mount Ephraim, Tunbridge Wells, TN4 8BG (☎ 0892 544069, fax 0892 515556)

FALLON, Ivan Gregory; s of Padraic Joseph Fallon (d 1974), and Dorothea, *née* Maher (d 1985); *b* 26 June 1944; *Educ* St Peter's Coll, Wexford, Trinity Coll Dublin (BBS); *m* 14 Jan 1967, Susan Mary, da of Dr Robert Francis Lurring, of Kidderminster; 1 s (Padraic Robert b 1974), 2 da (Tania Helen b 1967, Lara Catherine b 1970); *Career* Irish Times 1964-66, Thomson Provincial Newspapers 1966-67, Daily Mirror 1967-68, Sunday Telegraph 1968-84, city ed Sunday Telegraph 1979-84, dep ed Sunday Times 1984-; govr: United Med and Dental Sch Guy's and St Thomas's Hosps, Univ of Buckingham; tstee: Project Tst 1984, Generation Tst, Guy's Hosp; pres Trinity Coll Dublin Business Alumni London Chapter; FRSA 1989; *Books* Delorean: The Rise and Fall of a Dream Maker (with James Srodes, 1983), Takeovers (with James Srodes, 1987), The Brothers: The Rise of Saatchi and Saatchi (1988); *Recreations* squash, tennis; *Clubs* Beefsteak, RAC; *Style—* Ivan Fallon, Esq; The Sunday Times, 1 Pennington St, Wapping, London (☎ 071 782 5000)

FALLON, Dr James Aikman; s of Michael Fallon, of Edinburgh, and Doreen Moya, *née* Millen; *b* 1 Nov 1934; *Educ* St Aloysius Coll Glasgow, Univ of Glasgow (MA, PhD); *m* 8 Aug 1959, Isabella Mackintosh, da of Hugh Richardson (d 1952), of Causewayhead, Stirling; 7 da (Anne b 1960, Dorothy b 1961, Monica b 1962, Teresa b 1963 d 1984, Barbara b 1967, Julia b 1970, Christina b 1979); *Career* Nat Serv 5 Royal Inniskilling Dragoon Gds War Office Staff 1956-58; teacher Holyrood Sr Secdy Sch Glasgow 1959-64, dep rector St Joseph's Acad Kilmarnock 1970-73 (princ history teacher 1964-70), rector St Mungo's HS Falkirk 1973-79, headmaster Sacred Heart Sch Tunbridge Wells 1979-; chm Duke of Edinburgh's Award Panel; *Books* Scottish Mercenaries in the Service of Denmark and Sweden 1626-32 (Thesis 1972); *Recreations* yachting, Munro climbing, golf, 16th and 17th century European history, heraldry; *Clubs* Bewl Valley Sailing; *Style—* Dr James Fallon; Stuart House, 12 Pembury Rd, Tunbridge Wells, Kent TN2 3QD (☎ 0892 27224); Sacred Heart School, Pembury Rd, Tunbridge Wells, Kent TN2 3QD (☎ 0892 29193)

FAREBROTHER, Dr Martin John Brice; s of John Robert Fareborther, of 22 Copse Hill, Purley, Surrey, and Stella Kathleen, *née* Brice; *b* 7 March 1942; *Educ* Reigate GS, Queen's Coll Cambridge (MB BChir, MA, MD), Guy's Hosp Med Sch; *m* 19 March 1966, (Lesley) Ann, da of Lesley George Fox, of Newcastle under Lyme; 5 da (Katharine b 1970, Joanna b 1972, Rebecca b 1979, Alice b 1981, Helen b 1981 (twin)); *Career* house surgn Guy's Hosp 1967, house physician Royal Sussex Co Hosp Brighton 1968, jr med registrar Guy's Hosp 1969-70, sr house physician Brompton Hosp 1970, registrar in respiratory med City Hosp Edinburgh 1970-72, sr registrar in med Newcastle upon Tyne Hosps 1973-76, conslt physician gen and respiratory med Medway Health Dist and sr lectr in med St Thomas' Hosp Med Sch 1976-, unit gen mangr (acute servs) Medway Health Authy 1986-; MRCP 1969, FRCP 1983; *Recreations* flute playing; *Style—* Dr Martin Farebrother; Cream House, 7 Church St, Burham, Rochester, Kent ME1 3SB (☎ 0634 660550); Acute Unit Headquarters, Medway Hospital, Windmill Rd, Gillingham, Kent ME7 5NY (☎ 0634 830000)

FARRANT, Jeremy Philip; s of Philip Arthur Howard Farrant (d 1958), of Chingford, Essex, and Marie Beryl Louise, *née* Hall; *b* 21 July 1948; *Educ* Christ's Hosp Horsham; *m* 23 Dec 1972, Diana Jane, da of J H Cheesman, of Folkestone; 3 da (Joanna b 1973, Katie b 1975, Melissa b 1981); *Career* exec creative dir Newton and Godin Agency; *Style—* Jeremy Farrant, Esq; Little Trodgers, Lake St, Mark Cross, East Sussex TN6 3NT (☎ 0435 873302); The Newton and Godin Agency, Union House, The Pantiles, Tunbridge Wells, Kent (☎ 0892 510520, fax 0892 510527)

FARRINGTON, David; s of Ellis Farringotn, of Dickley Wood, Ashford Rd, Harrietsham, Kent, and Pauline Eleanor Miles, *née* Toyne; *b* 2 Dec 1948; *Educ* Balshaw's GS Leyland Lancs, UCL (LLB); *Career* called to the Bar Middle Temple 1972,; in practice and tenant Chambers of Louis Blom-cooper, QC Goldsmith Bldgs Temple EC4 1973-76, dep head of chambers Chambers of R Slowe, Esq 4 Kings Bench Walk Temple EC4 1976-85, head of chambers 2 Garden Court Temple EC4 1985; *Books* Know Your Rights (ed, 1976), Law for the Consumer (ed, 1978), A Practical Guide to the Criminal Justice Act 1988 (jtly); *Recreations* theatre, films, ballet, tennis; *Style—* David Farrington, Esq

FARROW, Dr David John Duncan; s of Dr Maurice Duncan Farrow, of Bartons, 36 Bidborough Ridge, Bidborough, Tunbridge Wells, Kent, and Mary Janet, *née* Somerville (d 1986); *b* 29 Nov 1936; *Educ* St Peters, Tonbridge, St Mary's Hosp Med Sch London (MB BS, DObstRCOG, MRCS, LRCP); *m* 9 July 1960, Elizabeth, da of John Frank Notley, of Flat 3, 16 Buckhurst Rd, Bexhill on Sea, Sussex; 3 s (Simon John Duncan b 1964, Paul Matthew b

1966, Andrew David b 1967 d 1978); *Career* family doctor in rural practice 1964-: Hawkhurst and environs, Kent - Sussex borders, Hawkhurst Cottage Hosp; memb: SE London Exec Ctee FPC 1971, Kent FPC 1974-90, Gen Med Servs Ctee 1974-91; pres Hawkhurst Cricket and Squash Clubs 1979-, chm Kent local Med Ctee 1981-85, memb Cncl Cameron Fund 1981-, memb Rural Dispensing Ctee 1988-, chm Gen Med Servs Ctee Rural Practices Sub Ctee 1984-90, memb Prescription Pricing Ctee 1984-90, memb Cncl BMA 1985-92 (fell 1989), pres BMA Tunbridge Wells Div 1987-, memb British Medical Journal Ctee 1987-; Freeman City of Lonodn, Liveryman Worshipful Soc of Apothecaries of London; *Recreations* cricket, country pursuits, francophile, travelling, sports, gardening, living; *Clubs* Farmers, MCC (playing memb); *Style*— Dr David Farrow; Coldharbour Cottage, Merriments Lane, Hurst Green, nr Etchingham, East Sussex TN19 7RG (☎ 0580 860302); North Ridge, Rye Rd, Hawkhurst, Kent TN18 4EX (☎ 0580 753935)

FAULKNER, Sir Eric Odin; MBE (1945), TD; s of Sir Alfred Edward Faulkner, CB, CBE (d 1963), and Edith Florence, *née* Nicoll; *b* 21 April 1914; *Educ* Bradfield, CCC Cambridge (hon fell); *m* 1939, Joan Mary, da of Lt-Col F A M Webster; 1 s, 1 da; *Career* WWII Lt-Col RA; banker; dir: Hudson's Bay Co 1950-70, Vickers plc 1957-79; chm: Union Discount Co 1959-70 (dir 1949-70), Glyn Mills & Co 1963-68, Lloyds Bank Ltd 1968-77; dir and dep chm fin for Indust 1977-80, advsy dir Unilever plc 1979-84; chm Industl Soc 1973-76, pres Br Bankers Assoc 1979-83; warden Bradfield Coll 1965-83; kt 1974; *Recreations* fishing (formerly cricket and associaton football (CUAFC XI 1935)); *Style*— Sir Eric Faulkner, MBE, TD; Farriers Field, Sevenoaks Rd, Ightham, Kent TN15 9AA

FAULKNER, Nicholas Odin; s of Sir Eric Faulkner, MBE, TD, *qv*, of Ightham, Kent, and Lady Joan Mary, *née* Webster; *b* 30 Sept 1948; *Educ* St Ronans Sch Kent, Millfield Somerset; *m* 20 May 1978, Rosalind Beatrice, da of the late Lt-Col A W Noel Cowper; 1 s (Jonathan Frederick Odin b 1980), 1 da (Freya Antonia Noelle b 1984); *Career* Hudson Bay Co Ltd Canada 1967-68, asst to md Firearms Co Ltd Somerset 1968-70; Roneo Vickers Ltd: various sales, sales mgmnt and mktg info posts 1970-75, overseas div exec 1975, gp business devpt exec 1976; head of market res and planning Vickers Dawson Ltd 1977-81, merchanting dir Morris Hanbury Jackson Le May Ltd (Hop Merchants and Factors) 1981-82, history project dir Allied-Lyons plc and Allied Breweries Ltd 1983-88, managing assoc Nicholas Faulkner Assocs 1983-; memb: IOD, Chartered Inst of Mktg, Business Archive Cncl; *Books* Allied Breweries - A Long Life (1988); contrib: Whatman 1740-1990 250 Years of Excellence (1989), Devenish - One Hundred Corporate Years (1990); *Recreations* shooting, sailing, music, fly fishing; *Style*— Nicholas Faulkner, Esq; Gore Cottage, Green Lane, Trottiscliffe, Maidstone, Kent ME19 5DX (☎ 0732 822217)

FAWCETT, Robert; MBE (1945), TD (1946); s of late Percival Charles Fawcett; *b* 16 June 1917; *Educ* Rugby, Trinity Coll Oxford; *m* 1939, Esmé Boileau, da of Lt-Col Nevill George Boileau Henderson, DSO; 1 s, 1 da (and 1 c decd); *Career* Lt-Col RA; served UK and NW Europe; ptnr Messrs Jackson Taylor Abernethy & Co 1948-1976; co dir: Andrew Weir & Co Ltd, Utd Baltic Corporation Ltd, Spink & Son Ltd 1977-84, ret 1984; gen cmmr of Income Taxes 1984-; former chm Investmt Ctee Merchant Navy Offrs Pension Fund; chm: Ensign Trust plc, Merchant Navy Investment Management Ltd; dep chm: CDFC Trust plc, Kent and E Sussex Regnl Ctee Nat Tst; memb cncl Fowney Marsh Historic Churches Tst, churchwarden St Peter and St Paul Appledore; FCA; *Recreations* reading, travelling; *Clubs* MCC; *Style*— Robert Fawcett, Esq, MBE, TD; Vine House, Appledore, Ashford, Kent TN26 2BU (☎ 023 383 260)

FAWSSETT, Robert Seymour; s of Capt Arthur Charles Fawssett, DSO, RN (d 1961), of Lindfield, Sussex, and Sybil Frieda, *née* Salaman (d 1977); *b* 4 May 1931; *Educ* Bradfield, Pembroke Coll Cambridge (BA); *m* 17 May 1958, Philippa Karen, d of George Philip Fox, MBE (d 1970), of Glasshouses, nr Harrogate, Yorks; 1 s (Edward b 1962), 2 da (Nicola b 1961, Katherine b 1965); *Career* Nat Serv 2 Lt RA 1950-51, TA 1951-58, ret Actg Capt RA; admitted slr 1957, sr ptnr Biddle & Co 1976- (ptnr 1958-); memb Lowtonian Soc 1977; *Recreations* gardening, tennis, opera; *Clubs* Naval, City Univ; *Style*— Robert Fawssett, Esq; Biddle & Co, 1 Gresham St, London EC2V 7BU (☎ 071 606 9301, fax 071 606 3305, telex 888197)

FAYERS, Rev Robert Stanley; s of Robert Hitchcock Fayers, of King's Lynn, and Joyce Kathleen, *née* Worth; *b* 7 Feb 1948; *Educ* Alderman Catleugh Sch King's Lynn, St Stephen's House Oxford (Dip in Funeral Directing); *Career* asst curate St Paul with St Mark Deptford 1984-87, vicar St Michael with St Augustine Beckenham 1988-; govr: Churchfields Primary Sch Beckenham, Stewart Fleming Primary Sch Anerley; *Recreations* drama, visual arts, travel, ancient buildings; *Style*— The Rev Robert Fayers

FEARN, Brian Leslie; s of Leslie Fearn, of Stonycroft, Stevenage, and Eileen Lily, *née* Keeley (d 1966); *b* 5 April 1954; *Educ* Hitchin Boys' GS; *m* March 1980, Shree Devi, da of Pradip Patul Rayarappan, of Kuala Lumpur; *Career* info technol strategist; corp structure conslt; ACMA, ACCA, JdipMA; *Recreations* DIY, swimming, piano, golf; *Style*— Brian L Fearn, Esq; Furnace House Farm, Four Elms, Edenbridge, Kent; Midland Bank plc, Poultry, London EC2P 2BX

FEDORCIO, Richard Edward (Dick); s of Jan Adam Fedorcio, of Felsztyn, Poland, and Winifred Elsie, *née* Ambler; *b* 25 March 1953; *Educ* Campion GS Hornchurch Essex, London Coll of Printing; *m* 28 June 1982, Helen Marie, da of William Stokoe (d 1987); 2 s (Alex b 11 June 1987, Leo b 3 May 1990), 1 da (Sarah b 31 July 1984); *Career* PR offr GLC 1974-83, co info offr W Sussex CC 1983-86, head of PR Kent CC 1986-; Inst of PR: chm Local Govt Gp 1985-87, cncl memb on Educn Ctee 1988, chm Professional Practices Ctee 1989-90; MIPR 1984, MAIE 1986; *Recreations* soccer, cricket, sailing, photography; *Style*— Dick Fedorcio, Esq; 19 Clarence Court, Weavering, Maidstone, Kent ME14 5UP (☎ 0622 35049); Kent County Council, County Hall, Maidstone, Kent ME14 1XQ (☎ 0622 671411)

FEHR, Basil Henry Frank; CBE (1979); s of Frank Emil Fehr, CBE (d 1948), and Jane Poulter (d 1961); *b* 11 July 1912; *Educ* Rugby, Ecole de Commerce Neuchatel Switzerland; *m* 1, 1936 (m dis 1951), Jane Marner, *née* Tallent; 2 s (Richard, James), 1 da (Ann); m 2, 1951 (m dis 1974), Greta Constance, *née* Bremner; 1 da (Olinda); m 3, 1974, Anne Norma, *née* Cadman; 1 da (Amanda); *Career* served WWII HAC, later instr Gunnery Sch of Anti-Aircraft RA, ret Maj; joined family firm Frank Fehr & Co 1934, ptnr 1936, governing dir (later chm) Frank Fehr & Co Ltd London 1948, pres (later chm) Fehr Bros (Manufacturers) Inc NY 1949; chm: Cocoa Assoc of London 1952, London Commodity Exchange 1954, London Oil and Tallow Trades Assoc 1955, Copra Assoc London 1957, Inc Oilseed Assoc 1958, United Assocs Ltd 1959, Colyer Fehr Pty Ltd Sydney 1984; elected to Baltic Exchange 1936, dir Baltic Mercantile and Shipping Exchange 1963-69 and 1970- (vice chm 1973-75, chm 1975-77); landowner; jurat of liberty of Romney Marsh 1979; *Recreations* sports, farming; *Clubs* City Livery (Aldgate Ward), MCC, RAC, W Kent CC, Littlestone GC, Little Ship; *Style*— Basil Fehr, Esq, CBE; Slodden Farm, Dymchurch, Romney Marsh, Kent (☎ 0303 872 241); Frank Fehr & Co Ltd, Prince Rupert House, 64 Queen St, London EC4 (☎ 01 248 5066)

FENN, His Excellency Sir Nicholas M; KCMG (1989, CMG 1980); s of Rev Prof J Eric Fenn, of Worcs, and Kathleen M, *née* Harrison; *b* 19 Feb 1936; *Educ* Downs Sch, Kingswood Sch, Peterhouse Cambridge (MA); *m* 1959, Susan Clare, da of Rev Dr G L Russel, of Dorset; 2 s (Robert b 1962, Charles b 1963), 1 da (Julia b 1974); *Career* Flying Offr RAF 1954-56; Burmese studies SOAS 1959-60, vice consul Mandalay Burma 1960-61; third sec Br Embassy Rangoon Burma 1961-63; asst private sec to four successive Secs of State for Foreign and Cwlth Affrs 1963-67; first sec and head of chancery Br Interests Section Swiss Embassy Algiers 1967-69; first sec for public affrs UK Mission to the UN 1969-72; dep head successively of Sci and Technol Dept and Energy Dept FCO 1972-75; counsellor head of chancery and consul-gen Br Embassy Peking 1975-77; RCDS 1978; head of News Dept FCO, spokesman of the FCO and press sec successively to Lord Carrington and Francis Pym 1979-82 (press Sec to Lord Soames, last Governor of S Rhodesia now Zimbabwe 1979-80); HM Ambassador: Rangoon 1982-86, Dublin 1986-; *Recreations* sailing; *Clubs* Utd Oxford and Cambridge Univ, Hibernian Utd Servs Dublin; *Style*— His Excellency Sir Nicholas Fenn, KCMG British Embassy, 33 Merrion Rd, Dublin 4, Republic of Ireland (☎ 0001 695211)

FENNEMORE, Mary Charlotte; da of Percy Alfred Tabb, of North Shields, Tyne and Wear, and Emily Rhoda, *née* Patey; *b* 17 June 1927; *Educ* Plymouth HS for Girls, Totnes Co Sch for Girls; *m* 16 June 1951, Wilfred Bedingfield Fennemore, s of Wilfred Norman Fennemore (ka HMS Kelly 1941); 1 s (Stephen b 1956), 1 da (Sandra b 1959); *Career* Chatham Dockyard 1943-48, Miny of Nat Insur Newcastle upon Tyne 1948-51, Letchworth UDC 1951-56, Bligh Boards Ltd Strood 1976-; memb: Cuxton Women's Inst 1965-, WRVS 1965-76; Rochester upon Medway CC: memb, cncllr for Cuxton and Halling Ward 1976-, dep Mayor 1986-87, Mayor 1987-88; *Style*— Mrs Mary Fennemore; 31 Pilgrims Rd, North Halling, Rochester, Kent ME2 1HN (☎ 0634 240388)

FENNER, Dame Peggy Edith; DBE (1986), MP (Cons Medway 1983-); *b* 12 Nov 1922; *Educ* LCC Sch Brockley, Ide Hill Sevenoaks; *m* 1940, Bernard S Fenner, s of F W Fenner, of Sevenoaks, Kent; 1 da; *Career* chm Sevenoaks UDC 1962 and 1963 (memb 1957-71), vice pres UDCs Assoc 1971, parly candidate (Cons) Newcastle under Lyme 1966, MP (Cons) Rochester and Chatham 1970-74 and 1979-83; parly sec MAAF 1972-74 and 1981-86, govt co chm Womens Nat Cmmn 1983-; memb: Br Delgn to Euro Parl 1974, Cncl of Europe 1987, Western Euro Union (Def) 1987 Select Ctee Membs' Interests; *Style*— Dame Peggy Fenner, DBE, MP; 12 Star Hill, Rochester, Kent (☎ 0634 42124)

FENTON, Ernest John; s of Forbes Duncan Campbell Fenton (d 1970), of Angus, Scotland, and Janet Burnfield, *née* Easson (d 1978); *b* 14 Oct 1938; *Educ* Harris Acad Scot; *m* 2 March 1965, Ann Ishbel, da of Robert Ramsay; 1 s (Forbes b 1965), 2 da (Joanna b 1969, Elizabeth b 1976); *Career* CA, ptnr W Greenwell & Co Stockbrokers 1968-81, dir Greenwell Montagu & Co 1986-87; chief exec: Greenwell Montagu Stockbrokers 1988-, Smith Keen

Cutler Ltd 1988-; ASIA; *Recreations* shooting, curling; *Style*— Ernest Fenton, Esq; Dundale Farm, Tunbridge Wells, Kent (☎ 089 282 2175); 406 Seddon House, The Barbican, London; 114 Old Broad St, London EC2P 2HY (☎ 01 588 8817)

FERGUSON, Barry William Cammack; *b* 18 July 1942; *Educ* Exeter Cathedral Choristers Sch, Clifton, Peterhouse, Cambridge (MA), RCM; *m* 1, 18 Oct 1971, Marjorie Isabelle (d 1987), da of Albert William Kemp (d 1971), of Montgarrie, Aberdeenshire; 1 da (Rachel May b 31 Dec 1972); m 2, 30 Sept 1989, Sandra Monteith, da of Victor Albert Edmund Wibrew, of Chatham, Kent; *Career* asst organist Peterborough Cathedral 1964-71, organist Wimborne Minster 1971-77, organist and master of choristers Rochester Cathedral 1977-, conductor Rochester Choral Soc 1977-85 and 1989-; broadcast and recorded as organist, pianist, singer, conductor, composer; author of many choral and instrumental compositions; directed courses for Royal Sch of Church Music in Croydon, USA, Australia, NZ; co-worker of Mother Teresa Medway Branch, musical advsr Rochester Diocesan Church Music Ctee; FRCO; *Recreations* family, visiting Devon cottage, poetry, seeing the funny side of things; *Style*— Barry Ferguson, Esq; 7 Minor Canon Row, Rochester, Kent ME1 1ST (☎ 0634 400723)

FERRY, Alexander; MBE (1978); s of Alexander Ferry (d 1932), and Susan Cavan Ferry (d 1987); *b* 14 Feb 1931; *Educ* St Patrick's Sr Secdy Sch Dunbartonshire; *m* 15 Feb 1958, Mary, da of late Patrick McAlaney; 2 s (Alexander b 1958 d 1977, Andrew b 1966), 2 da (Carlann b 1960, Mary b 1962); *Career* Nat Serv RAF 1952-54; engr 1951-64; trade union offr AEU 1964-78, gen sec Confedn of Shipbldg and Engrg Unions 1978-; active in Br Lab Pty, bd memb Harland Wolff Belfast 1984-, memb MMC 1986-; *Recreations* golf, reading, crosswords; *Style*— Alexander Ferry, Esq, MBE; 190 Brampton Rd, Bexley Heath, Kent DA7 4YS (☎ 081 303 5338); 140/142 Walworth Rd, London SE17 (☎ 071 703 2215, fax 071 252 7397)

FERRY, David Dawson; s of Brian Ferry, of Blackpool, Lancashire, and Winsome, *née* Dawson (d 1965); *b* 5 Feb 1957; *Educ* Blackpool Coll of Higher and Further Educn, Camberwell Sch of Art and Crafts London (BA), Slade Sch of Fine Art UCL (HDFA); *Career* lectureships incl: full time lectr in fine art Canterbury Coll of Art and Design at Kent Inst of Art 1986-, visiting lectr in postgrad studies in printmaking Camberwell Sch of Art and Crafts 1987-; external assessor in graphic design Croydon Coll of Art and Design; one man exhibitions incl: Paintings, Drawings and Prints (Grundy Art Gallery Blackpool) 1982, graphic work in First Int Contemporary Art Fair (Barbican Centre London) 1984, paintings and prints Second Int Contemporary Art Fair (Olympia London) 1985, The Star Chamber - 1986-87 (Herbert Read Gallery Canterbury Coll of Art) 1987, selected work from Travels & Series 1985-88 (Darwin Coll Univ of Kent) 1988, The Kent Series lithographs and drawings (Drew Gallery Canterbury) 1989, The Star Chamber Series (Museum & Art Gallery Maidstone) 1989; biennales incl: selected Br artist The Int Senefelder Stiftung (Offenbach Am Main Frankfurt W Germany) 1978-88, invited artist Br Section Trace 88 IIIe Biennale D'Estampe Contemporaine FIAP (Paris) 1988; gp exhibitions incl: 53-83 Three Decades of Artists from Inner London Art Schools (Royal Acad of Arts London) 1983, 218 Summer Exhibition (Royal Acad of Arts London) 1986, Five Contemporary Printmakers (Nat Museum of Wales Turner House Penarth, Camarthen Museum) 1987, South East - North West Four Contemporary Artists (Grundy Art Gallery Blackpool) 1987; collections incl: Grundy Art Gallery Blackpool Borough Cncl, Maidstone Museum and Art Gallery, Slade Sch of Fine Art, Special Tstees of St Thomas Hosp London, UCL; various private collections in GB Europe and USA; videos: The Reason For (1989), The Ruin (1989); organiser of exhibitions incl Land, Sea, Air - Ten Contemporary British Artists (3 Canterbury Arts Festival and Herbert Read Gallery); *Books* Shadow on a Rock a Dorset Notebook (1987), Shadow on a Tomb a Rome Notebook (1988), The Kent Series (1989-90); *Style*— David Ferry, Esq; 17 Monastery St, Canterbury, Kent CTI 1NJ

FERRY, Maurice; TD (1969 and bar 1975); s of Eric Walter, of St Leonards, Hastings, E Sussex, and Gladys Florence Wells (d 1980); *b* 11 June 1923; *Educ* Woodford Coll, Coll of Preceptors; *m* 10 June 1948, Elizabeth Willmington, da of Arthur Henry (d 1961), of Victoria, Australia; 3 s (Andrew Michael b 1951, John Patrick b 1958, Mark Richard b 1966); *Career* RAFVR 1940-46, Maj TA 1954-75; Met Police Civil Staff: aliens offr 1950, i/c map room Scotland Yard 1957, press offr 1960, private sec to asst cmmr crime CID 1963, dist liaison offr PR 1965, welfare offr 1972, princ Peel Centre (Hendon Trg Sch) 1976, appts offr 1979; chm: Aylesford Parish Cncl 1972- (memb 1960-), Aylesford Co Primary Sch 1984- (govr 1966-), Aylesford Soc 1985-; vice chm Aylesford HS 1974- (govr 1966-), pres Eccles Branch Royal Br Legion, vice pres Buckhurst Hill Branch Royal Air Forces Assoc; Tonbridge and Malling Borough Cncl (formerly DC): memb 1979-, dep mayor 1984-85, mayor 1985-86; fell Huguenot Soc of GB 1960; *Recreations* genealogy; *Style*— Maurice Ferry, Esq, TD; 1 Brassey Drive, Aylesford, Maidstone, Kent ME20 7QL (☎ 0622 717209)

FFRENCH BLAKE, Maj Martin Arthur O'Brien; DL; s of Lt-Col A O'B ffrench Blake, TD, DL (d 1973), of The Precincts, Canterbury, and Laura Iris (Muff), *née* Walker (d 1976); *b* 10 Jan 1921; *Educ* Eton, RMC, Staff Coll Camberley; *m* 27 July 1946, Betty Rosemarie, da of Brig J F Whitacre Allen, MC, DL (d 1976), of Folkestone; 1 s (Mark b 10 April 1951), 1 da (Carolyn b 27 April 1949); *Career* Reg Offr The Buffs 1940-59; 1 Buffs Western Desert and Italy, GSO3 24 Gds Bde Italy 1945, Staff Capt MS WO 1945-46, Staff Coll 1954, Bde maj 27 Inf Bde Hong Kong 1955-57; memb Stock Exchange 1960-80, ptnr Smith Rice & Hill (later merged with Norris Oakley and Capel-Care Myers); Kent CCC: pres 1982, vice chm 1983-85, chm 1986-88; Freeman City of London, Liveryman Worshipful Co of Mercers (Master 1975 and 1980); *Recreations* shooting, fishing, gardening, cricket; *Clubs* MCC, Band of Brothers; *Style*— Maj Martin ffrench Blake, DL; Stonecroft Hall, Bolderwood Court, Lenham, Maidstone, Kent ME17 2LZ (☎ 0622 858950)

FIELD, John Arthur; s of Lt-Col Arthur William Henry Field, MBE (d 1980), of Bromley, Kent, and Rebecca Annie Rose, *née* Bolt (d 1986); *b* 28 Feb 1932; *Educ* Bromley GS, Keble Coll Oxford (BA,MA), Univ of London (BSc, PGCE, Ac Dip Ed); *m* 11 May 1955, Heather Mavis, da of Eric Douglas Liddiard (d 1986), of Enfield, Middx; 3 s (Andrew b 1962, Richard b 1963, Martin b 1968), 1 da (Alison b 1965); *Career* asst master: City of Norwich Sch 1956-59, Dauntsey's Sch 1959-64; head of sci dept Dover GS 1964-68; headmaster: Springhead Sch Northfleet 1969-81, Wombwell Hall Sch Northfleet 1977-81, Northfleet GS 1981-88; co inspr of secdy educn Kent 1988-; lay reader at Fawkham and Hartley, dir of reader trg Rochester Dio, dep co cmmr Scout Movement Kent, fndr chm Gravesham Town Twinning Assoc 1981-85; memb: SHA, Assoc for Sci Educn, Botanical Soc of Br Isles, Br Biological Soc, Freshwater Biological Assoc; FIBiol 1979; *Recreations* foreign travel, railways, choral music; *Style*— John Field, Esq; Kent County Council, New Rd, Gravesend, Kent DA11 0AT

FIGG, Paul Andrew; s of John Ralph Thomas Figg, of Westbere Court, Canterbury, Kent, and Barbara Diana, *née* Cox; *b* 25 Dec 1958; *Educ* Hele's GS, Avery Hill Coll (BEd); *m* 29 Aug 1981, Penelope Jane, da of Richard Charles Owen, of Haywards Heath, W Sussex; 2 da (Charlotte Grace b 1987, Emma Victoria b 1989); *Career* Stanley Tech HS: teacher 1981-83, head of Physical Educn Dept 1983-84; AE Figg & Son Ltd: contracts mangr 1984-85, projects mangr 1985-86, md 1986-; md Figg (Grounds Maintenance) Ltd 1988-; *Recreations* golf, tennis, travel, good wine; *Style*— Paul Figg, Esq; A E Figg & Son Ltd, Highfield Nursery, Highfield Lane, Mersham, Ashford, Kent TN25 6PG (☎ 0233 629267, fax 0233 620 357)

FINDLAY, Lady Mary Cecilia; *née* Legge; eldest da of 7 Earl of Dartmouth, GCVO (d 1958); *b* 27 Oct 1906; *m* 17 Oct 1929, Cdr Noel Charles Mansfeldt Findlay, RN (d 1976), s of Sir Mansfeldt de Cardonnel Findlay, GBE, KCMG, CB; 2 s (Jonathan b 1933, Martin b 1935), 1 da (Mrs J Debenham b 1930); *Style*— The Lady Mary Findlay; 2 South Close, The Precincts, Canterbury, Kent CT1 2EJ

FINER, Dr Nicholas; s of Sir Morris Finer (d 1974), and Lady Edith, *née* Rubber; *b* 24 Dec 1949; *Educ* The Hall Sch Hampstead, Mill Hill Sch, UCL (BSc, MB BS); *m* 1 May 1974, Susan, da of Prof Charles Dent, CBE (d 1975); 3 da (Emily b 30 Nov 1976, Sarah b 2 Aug 1978, Louise (twin) b 2 Aug (1978); *Career* conslt physician Luton and Dunstable Hosp 1988-, hon lectr United Med and Dental Schs of Guy's and St Thomas' Hosps 1988- (lectr 1981-88); ctee memb Assoc For The Study of Obesity, assoc ed Drugs and Therapeutics Bulletin; MRCP 1977; *Books* contrib: Health Consequences of Obestiy (1988), Progress in Sweeteners (1989); *Style*— Dr Nicholas Finer

FINLEY, Michael John; s of Walter Finley (d 1940), and Grace Marie Butler, *née* Sykes; *b* 22 Sept 1932; *Educ* King Edward VII Sch Sheffield; *m* 19 March 1955, Sheila Elizabeth, da of late Harold Cole, of Osbournby, Lincs; 4 s (Nicholas b 1955, Andrew b 1959, Jonathan b 1967, Robert b 1968); *Career* ed Sheffield Telegraph 1964-69, gen mangr and dir Kent Messenger Gp 1979-82 (editorial dir 1969-79), exec dir Periodical Publishers Assoc 1982-88, dir Fedn Int de la Presse Periodique 1989-; memb Advsy Cncl BBC 1975-80, govr Int Press Fndn 1988-; chm Kent IOD 1980-82, govr Cranbrook Sch 1977-; *Books* Advertising And The Community (contrib, 1969); *Recreations* tennis, golf, snooker, watching rugby, walking; *Style*— Michael Finley, Esq; Sorrento, Staplehurst, Kent; Fipp, Press Foundation House, 5 St Matthew St, London SW1 2JT (☎ 071 873 8158)

FINLINSON, Richard Edward; s of Dennis Whittle Finlinson, of West Malling, Kent (d 1986), and Phylis Maisie, *née* Crowcroft; *b* 16 Dec 1942; *Educ* Blundell's; *m* 5 Sept 1964, Jennifer Mary, da of Bernard John Branson (d 1977), of Moreton Pinkney, Northants; 2 s (Nicholas b 1969, Timothy b 1972), 1 da (Olivia b 1975); *Career* ptnr Finn-Kelcey & Ashendens (estate agents/surveyors) 1970-87, md Ashendens (estate agents/surveyors) 1987 (dir 1987), dir King & Chasemore (estate agents/surveyors) 1988; FRICS 1964; *Recreations* travel, swimming, country pursuits; *Clubs* Maidstone; *Style*— Richard Finlinson, Esq; Forge Hill House, Pluckley, Kent (☎ 023 384 318); King & Chasemore, 36 Earl St, Maidstone, Kent ME14 1PS (☎ 0622 691554, fax 0622 691142, car phone 0860 413149)

FINN, Hugh Roderick; CBE (1974), DL (Kent 1979); s of George William Finn; *b* 12 April 1911; *Educ* Haileybury; *m* 1954, Muriel Enid (Mel), da of Walter Dale; 2 s; *Career* farmer and co dir; chm: Stonegatefarmers Ltd, Kent

Salads Ltd, SSP Ltd; chm: Kent Agric Exec Ctee 1954-68, BBC Agric Advsy Ctee, Gen Advsy Ctee BBC 1966-75, Miny of Agric Regnl Advsy Ctee 1974-80, ARC Hops Tech Ctee 1976-86; memb Lord Chllrs Advsy Ctee (Kent) 1976-86; memb Cncl Protection Rural England 1954-85 (chm Kent Branch 1981-); govr Wye Coll 1948-88 (chm Estates Panel 1954-85); FRZS, FRAgS; *Clubs* Athenaeum; *Style*— Hugh Finn, Esq, CBE, DL; Nackington Farmhouse, Canterbury, Kent CT4 7AD (☎ home: 0227 463 169, office: 0227 763 100)

FINN, John Wilson; s of Edwin Finn (d 1968), and Frances Evelyn, *née* Moody (d 1975); *b* 4 Feb 1916; *Educ* Westminster; *m* 24 Aug 1940, Mildred Mary, da of George Edward Bermingham (d 1966); 1 s (Martin Anthony b 1942), 1 da (Susan Mary b 1944); *Career* joined TA 1939, served WWII Maj RA 1939-45; qualified CA 1938; co sec De la Rue Co Ltd 1974-78 (joined 1958); FCA; *Recreations* construction of miniature antique furniture, beagling, opera; *Style*— John Finn, Esq; Pond Oast, Frittenden, Kent TN17 2BE (☎ 058 080 431); Lloyds Bank, High St, Cranbrook, Kent

FINN, Wilfred John; s of Charles Finn (d 1956), of Chart Sutton, and Lily, *née* Harris (d 1964); *b* 7 Nov 1924; *Educ* Maidstone Tech Sch for Boys; *m* 4 March 1950 June, da of Frederick Gilbert (d 1982), of Maidstone; 1 da (Hilary b 1952); *Career* war serv RCS 1943-47; SE Gas Board (now British Gas Corporation): sr clerk 1950-67, clerk in charge Customer Accounts Dept 1967-70, dep customer accounts offr 1970-72, customer accounts rep 1972-85; clerk Chart Sutton Parish Cncl 1952-60 and 1966-; Ind Order of Odd Fells: sec of Lodge 1956-, tstee Maidstone Dist, prov grand master Maidstone Dist 1987; *Recreations* bowls; *Style*— Wilfred Finn, Esq; 17 Cobfield, Chart Sutton, Maidstone, Kent ME17 3SH (☎ 0622 44885)

FINNIS, John Temple (Jack); s of John Turner Finnis (d 1956), of Marden, and Violet Catherine Temple, *née* Frere (d 1968); *b* 9 Sept 1911; *Educ* Dover Coll; *m* 8 July 1939, Margaret Ismena, da of Arthur John Leech, CIE, MBE (d 1940), of Sevenoaks; 1 s (John b 1954), 1 da (Sarah b 1951); *Career* TA RE 1937-39, WWII cmmnd Royal Norfolk Regt 1940, Staff Capt 4 Inf Bde 1941, DA & QMG 2 Inf Div 1941-43, AAG GHQ India 1943-45, Hon Lt-Col; CA 1936-39; treas Readers' Digest London Paris and Milan 1945-50; practicing CA 1950-74, sr ptnr 1973-74; treas: PCC 1962-, Masonic Lodge 1962-87, Friends of Shoreham Church 1979-; govr: Dover Coll, Royal Sch for Deaf Children; FCA 1956; Cross of Merit (2 class) SMOM 1956; *Recreations* gardening, rugby, football, lawn tennis; *Clubs* Naval and Military; *Style*— Jack Finnis, Esq; 4 Shoreham House, Shoreham, Sevenoaks, Kent (☎ 0959 23333)

FISCHEL, John Roy; s of late Roy Fischel, MC; *b* 2 Sept 1924; *Educ* Cheltenham and RN; *m* 1952, Anita, da of late Capt Maximilian Despard, DSC, RN; 2 s, 3 da; *Career* commodity merchant; L M Fischel & Co Ltd: dir 1960-, chm 1966-, non-exec dir 1984-90; Baltic Mercantile & Shipping Exchange 1975-80; underwriting memb Lloyd's; *Recreations* shooting, sailing (yacht Matawa); *Clubs* Castaways, RCC, RNSA, MCC, Kent CCC; *Style*— John Fischel, Esq; The Mount, Shoreham, nr Sevenoaks, Kent (☎ 095 92 2071)

FISCHER, Dr Peter; s of John Fischer (d 1989), of Torquay, and Elsie, *née* Barns; *b* 17 March 1946; *Educ* Univ of Birmingham (BSc), Univ of Nice, New York Inst of Technol (PhD); *m* 4 Sept 1989, (Rosemary) Anne Catherine, da of John Hampton Francis, of Cranleigh, Surrey; 1 da (Antoinette Jane b 1984); *Career* advsr to HM Cabinet Office on Oil Pollution Control Technol 1963, researcher Rank Organisation 1968, private res Belgium Holland and Germany 1968-71, writer and researcher New York Inst of Technol 1974-80; psychologist: France 1980-87, Ireland and USA 1987-89; chm Alternative Health Europe and UK 1990-; memb Astro-Res Soc 1967- (dir of res 1967-71), fell Acupuncture Res Soc 1980, chm Alternative Med Res Soc 1984-89; *Books* The Welsh Triangle (1979), UFO-UK (1980); *Recreations* horses, sailing, theatre, wine and food, music; *Style*— Dr Peter Fischer; Little Pitchford Manor, Dean St, East Farleigh, Maidstone, Kent (☎ 0622 729011, 0622 720601)

FISHER, Roger Frederick; s of Frederick Barnet Fisher (d 1976), of Sandhurst, Kent, and Dorothy, *née* Harris (d 1987), of Loughton, Essex; *b* 16 April 1935; *Educ* Loughton Secdy Sch, Pitmans Coll London, South Bank Poly (BEd), Royal Coll of Nursing (RGN, RMN, RNT); *Career* Nat Serv RAMC 1953-55; staff nurse London Chest Hosp 1960-62, graduate nurse Univ of Texas USA 1962-63, princ tutor Claybury Hosp 1970-71, regnl nurse SE Thames RHA 1971-; David Salomons House Southborough: princ Regnl Confs and Trg Centre 1985-88, head of Regional Recruitment and Retention Unit; memb Sir David Salomons Soc; memb Royal Coll of Nursing; *publications* Initiatives in Nursing Recruitment (Nursing Times, 1980), Is Anybody There? (Senior Nurse Vol I, 1981), Central Processing of Applications for Nurse Training (Report of Steering Gp, 1981), How The System Would Work (Nursing Times, 1982); *Recreations* music, theatre, Thames sailing barges, heavy horses, exhibitions and galleries; *Style*— Roger Fisher, Esq; 10 Merlin Close, Croydon, Surrey CR0 5UQ (☎ 081 681 3936); SE Thames Regional Health Authority, Thrift House, Collington Ave, Bexhill on Sea, E Sussex TN39 3NO (☎ 0434 730073); David Salomons House, RCTC, Broomhill Rd, Southborough, Kent TN3 0TG (☎ 0892 515152)

FITCH, Brian Hill; s of Stanley Hill Fitch (d 1961), of Hampstead, and Marjorie Winifred, *née* Browne; *b* 19 May 1930; *Educ* Haileybury; *m* 1955, Susan Margaret, da of Cyril Rex Edwards, LDS (d 1935), of Scarborough; 1 s, 1 da; *Career* Lloyd's Insurance broker 1950-65, md The London & Westminster Property Co Ltd 1965- (dir 1956-), chm Caledonian Municipal Investments Ltd 1970-80, chm and md The London & Westminster (Sterling Brokers) Ltd 1972-80, licensed dealer in securities 1974-87, md London Financial Agency Ltd 1980-, underwriting memb Lloyd's 1982-; *Recreations* curio and antique collector, vintage motor cars, shooting, swimming; *Clubs* IOD (fell and life memb), Rolls Royce Enthusiasts, RAS, Br Assoc for Shooting and Conversation; *Style*— Brian Fitch Esq; Grayleigh, St Hubert's Lane, Gerrards Cross, Bucks (☎ 0753 884702, fax 0753 888302); Cheviot Court, Broadstairs, Kent (☎ 0843 63293)

FITZGERALD, Trevor Maurice Patrick; s of John Patrick Fitzgerald, of Bournemouth, and Janet Marjorie, *née* Oclee; *b* 8 March 1959; *Educ* Westbrook House Folkestone, Harvey GS Folkestone, St Peter's RC Sch Bournemouth; *m* 4 June 1988, Alison Michele, da of Keith John Stockwell Bryan, of Dover; 2 s (Maximilian George Patrick b 1988, Archie Valentine b 1990); *Career* retail jeweller Oclee & Son Ltd Folkestone 1977-87, ptnr and mangr Oclee & Son Canterbury 1987-; FGA, memb Nat Arts Collection Fund, friend of V & A; *Recreations* antiques, organic gardening, regional cookery; *Style*— Trevor Fitzgerald, Esq; Oclee & Son, 26 Burgate, Canterbury, Kent CT1 2HA (☎ 0227 767206)

FITZWALTER, 21 Baron (E 1295); (Fitzwalter) Brook Plumptre; JP (Kent 1949); s of George Beresford Plumptre (d 1934), yr bro of 20 Baron (d 1932, but the present Lord FitzWalter was not summoned to Parl until 1953); Lord FitzWalter is eleventh in descent from Frances, w of Sir Thomas Mildmay and half sis of 3 Earl of Sussex (whose 2 w Frances, da of Sir William Sydney, of Penshurst, left £5,000 to establish a Cambridge Coll to be called 'Sydney-Sussex'); Frances was twelfth in descent from Robert FitzWalter, the leading enforcer among the Barons of Magna Carta; by his w (and 1st cousin) Mary Augusta, *née* Plumptre (d 1953); *b* 15 Jan 1914; *Educ* Diocesan Coll Cape Town, Jesus Coll Cambridge; *m* 29 Sept 1951, Margaret Melesina, 3 da of Herbert William Deedes, JP (d 1966), and sis of William Deedes, sometime ed of the Daily Telegraph; 5 s (Julian, Henry, George, William, Francis); *Heir* s, Hon Julian Plumptre; *Career* served WW II Capt; landowner and farmer (2,500 acres); *Recreations* shooting, gardening; *Style*— The Rt Hon the Lord FitzWalter; Goodnestone Park, Canterbury, Kent CT3 1PL (☎ 0304 840218)

FLACK, Cncllr Barry George; s of Jesse Harry Flack (d 1959), of Hoo St Werburgh, and Edith Maud, *née* Rayner (d 1973); *b* 15 Sept 1936; *Educ* Sir Joseph Williamson's Mathematical Sch Rochester, Shoreditch Training Coll; *m* 8 Aug 1959, Marlene Grace, da of George Arthur Cruttenden (d 1977), of Hoo St Werburgh; 3 s (Martin Stuart b 1963, Stuart Roy b 1966, Peter John b 1967), 1 da (Amanda Marlene b 1960); *Career* Nat Serv RAF 1954-56; teacher: Folkestone 1958-61, Aylesford 1961-64, Chatham 1964-70, Snodland 1970-; Mayor of Rochester 1982-83 and 1989-90; memb: Hoo St Werburgh Parish Co 1967-, Rochester City Cncl 1976-; pres Nursing Div Rochester and Strood St John Ambulance; vice pres: Medway Towns Band, Hoo and Dist Gardeners Assoc; memb SE Eng Tourist Bd; *Recreations* reading, DIY, gardening; *Style*— Cncllr Barry Flack; Bramar, 156 Main Rd, Hoo St Werburgh, Rochester, Kent ME3 9HB (☎ 0634 251166)

FLACK, Gillian; da of Derek Flack, of Chatham, and Beryl Irene, *née* Spurway; *b* 5 May 1960; *Educ* Fort Pitt GS For Girls, London Foot Hosp and Sch of Chiropody (Chiropody Dip); *Career* state registered sr II sessional chiropodist Maidstone Health Authy 1981-87, private practitioner 1981-; memb Soc of Chiropodists; *Recreations* hockey, squash, cake decorating; *Style*— Miss Gillian Flack; 561 Maidstone Rd, Bluebell Hill, Chatham, Kent; 205 Robin Hood Lane, Bluebell Hill, Chatham, Kent (☎ 0634 861513)

FLAGG, Rt Rev John William Hawkins (Bill); s of Wilfred John Flagg (d 1974), and Emily, *née* Hawkins (d 1989); *b* 16 April 1929; *Educ* Wolsey Hall, All Nations Missionary Studies; *m* 3 May 1954, Marjorie, da of Norman Lund (d 1968); 2 s (Andrew, Timothy), 4 da (Richenda, Rachel, Rosalind, Patricia); *Career* agric missionary in Southern Chile 1951-58, anglican chaplain and mission supt Paraguay 1959-64, archdeacon Northern Argentina 1965-69; bishop: Paraguay and Northern Argentina 1969-73, Peru and Bolivia 1973-77; asst bishop Liverpool 1978-86, gen sec S American Missionary Soc 1986-, hon asst bishop Rochester 1986-; presiding bishop Anglican Cncl of S America 1973-77; memb: Anglican Consultative Cncl 1973-78, S Atlantic Cncl 1984-, Mission Issues and Strategy Gp (Anglican Cmmn) 1988-; *Recreations* walking, chess; *Style*— The Rt Rev Bill Flagg; 55 Liptraps Lane, Tunbridge Wells, Kent TN2 3BU (☎ 0892 20431); The South American Missionary Society, Allen Gardiner House, Pembury Rd, Tunbridge Wells, Kent TN2 3QU (☎ 0892 38647, 0892 38648, fax 0892 25797)

FLAHERTY, Ronald (Ron); s of John Flaherty Rutherglen (d 1971), of Lanarkshire, Scotland, and Margaret, *née* Dillon (d 1974); *b* 31 May 1944; *Educ* Langside Coll Glasgow, Univ of Strathclyde (BA, post grad dip); *m*

Margaret Grace, da of Lt-Col John Basil Joseph Mulvey (d 1986), of Glasgow; 2 s (Mark Edward Dillon b 24 Feb 1982, Philip Brian Dillon b 25 April 1986), 2 da (Kate Louise b 6 Nov 1980, Fiona Alice b 22 Sept 1989); *Career* admin asst Heriot-Watt Univ Edinburgh 1971, personnel offr City of Edinburgh Educn Dept 1972; Univ of Kent at Canterbury: asst registrar 1973, sr asst registrar 1980; magistrate Co of Kent (Canterbury and St Augustines div) 1977, dir Kent Cncl on Addiction 1981; memb: Community Health Cncl Canterbury and Thanet DHA 1982, Exec Ctee Abbeyfield Soc (Whitstable), Exec Ctee Abbeyfield SE Kent (After Care) Soc 1989; *Recreations* swimming, golf; *Clubs* Rotary (Canterbury), Kent and Canterbury; *Style*— Ron Flaherty, Esq; The University of Kent at Canterbury, Canterbury, Kent (☎ 0227 764000 ext 3253, fax 0227 452196)

FLANAGAN, Prof Terence Patrick (Terry); OBE (1987); s of Thomas Flanagan (d 1933), of Dudley, Worcs, and Harriet Selina, *née* Beard (d 1978); *b* 25 Sept 1924; *Educ* St Josephs Sch Dudley, QMC (BSc, MSc); *m* 1, 9 July 1949 (m dis 1980), Marian Margaret, da of Horace Riddleston (d 1954), of Chesterfield, Derbys; 3 da (Helen (Mrs Russell) b 6 Feb 1955, Jane b 19 Jan 1957, Margaret b 19 Sept 1959); m 2, 31 Jan 1981, Sheila Mary, da of John Wallace McDonald, of Bromley, Kent; *Career* Flt Sgt RAF Aircrew 1943-47; electronics designer Marconi Instruments 1950-57; SIRA Ltd: head of Nucleonics Dept 1957-63, head of Industl Measurement Div 1963-74, exec dir 1974-79, md 1979-87; conslt UKAEA 1964-88, indust conslt 1987-; non-exec dir: Ometron Ltd (chm 1981-87), SIRA Safety Servs Ltd 1987-; ed Measurement and Control series 1987-; visiting prof City Univ London; memb Metrology & Standards Requirements Bd DTI 1980-87, chm Sch of Engrg Advsy Ctee City Univ 1980-, pres Inst of Measurement and Control 1983, govr Ravensbourne Coll of Design & Communication 1984-88; lectr Kent area Understanding Industry Campaign, treas Tenterden Residents Assoc, chm Bromley NSPCC Centenary Ctee 1990-91; Freeman City of London 1982, Liveryman Worshipful Co of Scientific Instrument Makers 1982; Hon DSc City Univ 1990; FIEE, FInstP, FInstMC; *Recreations* cricket, music, DIY, local affairs; *Clubs* 54; *Style*— Prof Terry Flanagan, OBE; 11 Eastgate Rd, Tenterden, Kent (☎ 0580 64070); 19 Foxleas Ct, Spencer Rd, Bromley, Kent (☎ 081 464 4436)

FLANDERS, Dennis; s of Bernard Charles Flanders (d 1964), musician, of Woodford, London, and Jessie Marguerite, *née* Sandell (d 1964), artist; *b* 2 July 1915; *Educ* Merchant Taylors', various art schools; *m* 1952, Dalma Joan Darnley, da of Jack Darnley Taylor (d 1949); 1 s (Julian b 1956), 1 da (Alison b 1953); *Career* Staff Sgt RE 1942-46; artist (drawings of Britain, particularly elaborate architectural compositions - townscapes and landscapes in black and white and water-colour); series of drawings in Yorkshire Post, Birmingham Post, Sunday Times, Illustrated London News; occupied last 50 yrs in proclaiming the superior beauties of the landscapes and townscapes of England, Wales, Scotland and Ireland in more than 3000 drawings and water-colours, 224 of which (half in colour and half in black and white) are reproduced in book (*see below*); RBA 1970, ARWS 1970, RWS 1976; *Books* Dennis Flanders' Britannia (1984); *Recreations* travel; *Clubs* Art Workers' Guild (master 1975); *Style*— Dennis Flanders Esq; 51 Gt Ormond St, London WC1N 3HZ (☎ 071 405 9317); Baker's Cross House, Cranbrook, Kent TN17 3AQ (☎ 0580 712018)

FLEGG, Michael Robert; s of Robert William Flegg (d 1981), and Eileen, *née* Blanshard; *b* 10 March 1938; *Educ* Preston Manor Co GS, Open Univ (BA); *m* 3 Sept 1960, (Ann) Wendy (d 1990), da of Elwyn Pryce Williams, of Richmond, Surrey; *Career* admitted slr 1960; Horwood & James of Aylesbury and Stony Stratford 1960-66, George Wimpey & Co Ltd 1966-73, Faull Best and Knight 1973-77, Port of London Authy 1977-78, Cripps Harries Hall 1979-; memb: 41 Club (former treas 41 Int), Nat Tst; chm of tstees of Kidney Res Aid fund, govr of St James Infants Sch, legal assoc memb RTPI, former memb Round Table; memb Law Soc; *Recreations* photography, cimematography; *Clubs* 41; *Style*— Michael Flegg, Esq; Seymour House, 11 and 13 Mount Ephraim Rd, Tunbridge Wells, Kent TN1 1EN (☎ 0892 515121, fax 0892 544878)

FLEMING, Matthew Valentine; s of Valentine Patrick Fleming, of Stonewall Park, nr Edenbridge, Kent, and Elizabeth Helen, *née* Gibbs ; *b* 12 Dec 1964; *Educ* Eton; *m* 23 Sept 1989, Caroline Mary, da of John Buxton, of Horsey Hall, nr Great Yarmouth, Norfolk; *Career* army offr Royal Greenjackets 1986-89; player for Kent CCC (capped 1990); *Recreations* all sports, fishing and shooting; *Style*— Matthew Fleming, Esq; c/o Kent County Cricket Club, St Lawrence Ground, Canterbury, Kent (☎ 0227 456886)

FLETCHER, Rev Colin William; s of Alan Philip Fletcher, QC, of Royston, Herts, and Annette, *née* Wright; *b* 17 Nov 1950; *Educ* Marlborough, Trinity Coll Oxford (BA, MA); *m* 5 July 1980, Sarah Elizabeth, da of John Webster, of Bradford, W Yorks; 1 s (Jonathan b 1982), 2 da (Pippa b 1984, Kate b 1986); *Career* curate: St Peter Shipley 1975-79, St Andrew Oxford 1979-84; tutor Wycliffe Hall Oxford 1979-84; vicar Holy Trinity Margate 1984-, rural dean Thanet 1988-; vice chm Millmead Neighbourhood Centre, chm Millmead and Dane Valley Community Assoc; *Recreations* walking, cricket, bird watching; *Style*— The Rev Colin Fletcher; 5 Offley Close, Margate, Kent CT9 3PU (☎ 0843 224037); Holy Trinity Church, St Mary's Ave, Margate, Kent CT9 3TN (☎ 0843 294137)

FLETCHER, Daisy; da of Albert Leo Pollard, of Rio De Janeiro, Brazil (d 1951), and Gertrude, *née* Fenton, of Southborough Kent (d 1967); *b* 19 Dec 1925; *Educ* Escola Batista Rio De Janeiro, Faculdade Des Ensinos (Teacher's Certificate), Univ of Michigan (Degree in English Language & History); *m* 14 Nov 1953, Michael James Basil Fletcher, s of John Basil Fletcher, of Burnley, Lancashire (d 1931); 2 s (Basil b 31 Aug 1955, Christopher b 21 Oct 1961); *Career* dep head Br Sch Rio de Janeiro Brazil; princ: Three Departmental American Sch Santos Brasil, Rusthall Boys' Sch Tunbridge Wells; graded post St Paul's C of E Jr Sch Rusthall Tunbridge Wells, dep head St James' Jr Sch Tunbridge Wells, sr lectr Sociedade Brazileira de Cultura Englêsa Brazil, lectr Eversley Coll Folkestone; elected memb Br Community Cncl Santos Brazil, involved with the Leonard Cheshire Homes, treas and memb Townswomens' Guild, fndr chm W Kent Community Active Club (a club for young disabled people); memb: Tunbridge Wells and Dist Cncl For Voluntary Serv, Tunbridge Wells and Dist Sports Advsy Cncl, Pantiles Museum and Art Gallery Working Pty, Area Museums Serv for SE England, Canterbury and Rochester Diocesan Cncl for Social Responsibility; chm Southborough Town Cncl Planning Ctee, rep of Kent Assoc of Dist Cncls on the Kent Ctee for the Employment of Disabled People; cncllr: Tunbridge Wells Borough Cncl, Southborough Town Cncl; govr: Ridgeway Secdy Sch Tunbridge Wells, High Brooms Co Primary Schs Tunbridge Wells; tstee The Holme (Southborough) Fndn; *Recreations* sailing, history; *Clubs* Bewl Valley Sailing, Kent History Teachers Assoc; *Style*— Mrs Daisy Fletcher; 87 Yew Tree Rd, Southborough, Tunbridge Wells, Kent TN4 0BJ (☎ 0892 540618)

FLETCHER, Geoffrey; MBE (1945), TD (1946), JP (1965), DL (1979); s of Brig Harold Fletcher, OBE, TD, JP (d 1964), of Maidstone, and Sylvia Gwendoline, *née* Morling (d 1953); *b* 27 April 1920; *Educ* Repton; *m* 11 Oct 1947, Judy, da of David Howard Lloyd (d 1966), of Newmarket; 2 s (John b 1952, Geoffrey Howard b 1955), 2 da (Lynette b 1948, Rosalind b 1950); *Career* TA: joined 1938, Capt 1940 (despatches), Maj 1941; Surrey Bishop of London (chartered accountants) 1937-39, chm Drake & Fletcher Ltd Agricultural and Motor Engineers 1946-; memb Maidstone Borough Cncl 1950-60, chm Cobtree Charity Tst; FIAgrE; *Recreations* golf, bridge, gardening, reading; *Clubs* Royal St Georges, Farmers; *Style*— Geoffrey Fletcher, Esq, MBE, TD, JP, DL; Drake & Fletcher Ltd, Parkwood, Maidstone, Kent ME15 9NW (☎ 0622 55531)

FLETCHER, Paul Thomas; CBE (1959); s of Stephen Baldwin Fletcher (d 1971), of Maidstone, and Jessie Carrie, *née* Rumsby (d 1963); *b* 30 Sept 1912; *Educ* Nicholson Inst Isle of Lewis, Maidstone GS, Medway Tech Coll (BSc); *m* 12 April 1941, Mary Elizabeth, da of Percy Howard King (d 1936), of Maidstone; 3 s (John b 1947, David b 1949, Peter b 1952); *Career* CEng; chief engr Miny of Works 1951-54 (joined 1939), engrg dir UKAEA Industrial Group 1954-61, dir United Power Co 1961-65; md: GEC Process Engineering Ltd 1965-70, dep chm Atomic Power Construction Ltd 1976-80 (md 1970-75), conslt 1980-; dep pres Br Standards Inst 1981-89 (chm 1979-81), hon fell IMechE 1979 (pres 1975-76); FEng; FICE; FIMechE, FIEE; *Recreations* motoring, photography; *Style*— Paul T Fletcher, Esq, CBE

FLINT, Gillian Margaret (Julie); da of Percy Sydney George (Pip) Flint, of Sevenoaks, and Joyce Marjorie Peggy, *née* Papworth; *b* 1 Jan 1948; *Educ* Talbot Heath Sch Bournemouth, Girton Coll Cambridge (BA); *Career* Rome corr Assoc Press 1974-76, Middle East corr United Press International 1982-84 (Madrid corr 1976-81); radio corr Beirut ABC News 1983-89; corr: Beirut Guardian 1985-89, Beirut Observer 1986-; runner up foreign radio reporter of the year Overseas Press Club of America 1984, foreign reporter of the year What the Papers Say 1988; *Books* Tearing Down the Curtain (1990); *Recreations* swimming, reading, tennis; *Style*— Ms Julie Flint; Observer, Chelsea Bridge House, Queenstown Rd, London SW8 4NN (☎ 071 627 0700, fax 071 627 5570, telex 888963)

FLOOD, David Andrew; s of Frederick Joseph Alfred Flood, of Selsey, W Sussex, and June Kathleen, *née* Alexander; *b* 10 Nov 1955; *Educ* Royal GS Guildford, St John's Coll Oxford (MA), Clare Coll Cambridge (PGCE); *m* 26 June 1976, Alayne Priscilla, da of Maurice Ewart Nicholas, of Farnborough, Hants; 2 s (Christopher Nicholas b 1982, Joshua Samuel b 1986), 2 da (Olivia Kathryn b 1979, Annalisa Harriet b 1989); *Career* asst organist Canterbury Cathedral 1978-86, music master King's Sch Canterbury 1978-86; organist and master of choristers: Lincoln Cathedral 1986-88, Canterbury Cathedral 1988-; organist for enthronement of Archbishop Runcie 1980, organist for visit of Pope John Paul II 1982; asst dir Canterbury Choral Soc 1978-85, fndr and dir Canterbury Cantata Choir 1985-86; musical dir Lincoln Choral Soc 1986-88, Canterbury Music Club 1984-86 and 1988-, hon sr memb Darwin Coll Univ of Kent; FRCO 1976 (chm 1975); *Recreations* travel, motoring, DIY; *Style*— David Flood, Esq; 6 The Precincts, Canterbury, Kent CT1 2EE (☎ 0227 765 219, office 0227 762 862, fax 0227 762 897)

FLOWER, Terence James (Terry); s of Albert George Flower (d 1960), and Joyce Winifred, *née* Hearne (d 1985); *b* 26 July 1953; *Educ* Northfleet Sch For Boys, Goldsmiths Coll Univ of London (BA); *Career* scenery maker 1969-71, theatre and TV propmaker 1971-74, decorative plasterer 1974-82; sculptor; pt/t lecturer: Brighton Poly 1986-, Colchester Inst 1987-; sculpture exhibitions incl: Whitechapel Open (Whitechapel Gallery) 1984, Tout Sculpture Park 1985, Northern Young Contemporaries (Whitworth Gallery) 1985, One Man Show (Red Herring Gallery) 1988, Freedom To Touch (Laing Art Gallery) 1989, One Man Show (Chatham Historic Dockyard) 1989, Morley Gallery 1990; *Recreations* walking, reading, architecture, punting; *Style—* Terry Flower, Esq; The House Carpenters Shop, Chatham Historic Dockyard, Chatham, Kent (☎ 0474 327355)

FLOWERDEW, Anthony David John (Tony); s of Lt-Col George Douglas Hugh Flowerdew, MBE, of 3 Lovelace Rd, Oxford, and Sheila Mary, *née* Bishop; *b* 7 Nov 1935; *Educ* Eton, Univ of Cambridge (MA); *m* 1, 25 July 1959, Elizabeth Marjorie Jennifer (Jenny) (d 1978), da of Prof Norman Bache Lewis (d 1988); 1 s (Dan b 1964), 1 da (Lucy b 1961); m 2, 26 May 1979, Lesley Jean, *née* Murdoch; *Career* Field Investigation Gp NCB 1957-61, Operational Res Dept Richard Thomas & Baldwin Ltd 1961-66, sr planner GLC 1966-68, dep dir of res Cmmn of Third London Airport 1968-70, sr lectr in urban econs LSE 1971-77, prof of mgmnt sci Univ of Kent 1978-89, md Marcial Echenique & Partners 1989- (ptnr 1977-85, chm 1985-89); former: cncl memb ORS, memb Air Transport Users Ctee; *Style—* Tony Flowerdew, Esq

FOLEY, Rev James Patrick; s of James Foley (d 1961) and Frances, *née* O'Brien (d 1975); *b* 2 March 1935; *Educ* Nat Sch; *m* 27 April 1949, Mary, da of John McManus (d 1959); 2 s (James Joseph b 1952, Edmund Paul b 1955); *Career* butler to Hastings William Sackville Russell 12 Duke and Earl of Bedford at Woburn 1948-58; Russell and Bromley Fashion Footwear Retail 1955-90: branch mangr, staff trg offr, mgmnt trg offr (received Distributive Indust Trg Bd Award for Trainer of Instrs 1978); master of ceremonies Passionist Church of Our Lady of the Sacred Heart Herne Bay 1959-80, ordained deacon 1980 (first RC married man to be ordained deacon in Kent since the order of perm deacon was restored by the Fathers of the Second Vatican Cncl "to be confered on married and unmarried men alike" in 1964); involved in extenisve pastoral apostolate and various church orgns in Herne Bay and dist; awarded Cross Pro Ecclesia et Pontifice from Pope Paul VI; *Recreations* walking, cycling, golf (handicap 16, has had hole-in-one three times); *Style—* The Rev Mr James P Foley; 30 Bognor Drive, Herne Bay, Kent CT6 8QP

FORD, Cyril George; s of Albert Edward Ford (d 1976), of Bury St Edmunds, Suffolk, and Alice, *née* Cook (d 1978); *b* 17 Nov 1925; *Educ* West Suffolk Co Sch, Teacher Trg Coll; *m* 28 March 1947, Joan Mary, da of John Samuels (d 1965), of Gravesend; 3 s (David John b 1947, Richard Michael b 1948, Colin Francis b 1951), 1 da (Alison Mary b 1952); *Career* WWII RM 1943-46, demob Lt; acting head St Botolph's C of E Sch Northfleet 1960-66 (formerly dep head); head: Hartlip Endowed Sch 1966-71, Holy Trinity C of E Sch Gravesend 1971-; chm Kent History Teachers' Assoc 1979-88 (fndr memb 1963), chm Gravesham Soc 1983-88 (fndr memb), lectr Local History; ACP 1964, NAHT 1966; *Recreations* collecting slides and illustrations of Gravesend and dist; *Style—* Cyril Ford, Esq; 241 Upper Wrotham Rd, Gravesend, Kent DA11 7LL (☎ 0474 560054); Holy Trinity C of E School, Trinity Rd, Gravesend, Kent DA12 2PG (☎ 0474 534746)

FORD, John Richard; s of Cyril Frank Ford, of Margate, Kent, and Kathleen May, *née* Butler; *b* 14 April 1939; *Educ* Canterbury Tech Sch; *m* 14 March 1964, Joan Maureen, da of Leslie Knight (d 1974); 1 da (Tracy Ann b 29 Jan 1965); *Career* Baldwin Hughes & Drake Ltd: exec dir 1966-71, asst md 1971-76, md 1976-, gp chm 1976-; past pres Rotary Club Ramsgate, past chm Ramsgate Round Table, chm and warden Scout Campsite Ctee; *Recreations* golf, travel, skiing; *Clubs* Ramsgate Rotary, Ramsgate 41, St Augustine's Golf; *Style—* John Ford, Esq; Baldwin Hughes & Drake Ltd, Newington Rd, Ramsgate, Kent (☎ 0843 581351, fax 0843 592619)

FOREMAN, Iain; s of Archie Foreman (d 1973), of Snodland, Kent, and Edith Rose, *née* Fowler (d 1982); *b* 28 July 1941; *Educ* Snodland Secdy Sch, Metropolitan Coll London; *m* 1977, Carol Lyn, da of Leslie Ivor Williams, of Brighton; 1 da (Yvette Marie b 12 Jan 1979); *Career* Road Transport & General Insurance Co Ltd Maidstone 1957-68, photographer Europress Agency London 1968-73, freelance photographer and writer 1973-87, md South East Editorial Ltd 1989-; memb: Ecclesiology Soc London, Royal Photographic Soc, Br Photographers Assoc, The Photographers Guild; holder Freelance Press Servs Dip In Press Photography; Licentiate Mallinson's Sch of Photography, fell Int Soc of Photographers, assoc Inst of Salesmen; *Books* Twigglewood Village (children's book, 1989), On The Banks Of The Medway (1990); *Recreations* photography, reading; *Clubs* Penman (Southend); *Style—* Iain Foreman, Esq; South East Editorial Ltd, 464 Maidstone Rd, Bridgewood, Bluebell Hill, Chatham, Kent ME5 9QJ (☎ 0634 201496, fax 0634 245220)

FORMAN, (Anthony) John; s of Charles Raymond Forman, of Solihull, and Joyce Lily, *née* Legge; *b* 10 Jan 1946; *Educ* Solihull Sch; *m* 11 Aug 1971, Felicty Mary, da of John Francis Ingham, of Birmingham; 3 s (David John b 27 Feb 1976, Christopher James b 21 Aug 1977, Michael Joseph b 18 April 1979), 1 da (Victoria Jane b 12 July 1973); *Career* CA; articled to Spicer & Pegler 1964-70, Peat Marwick Mitchell & Co Birmingham 1971-74; Compair Group: chief accountant Hydrovane Compression Co Ltd 1974-76, fin controller Holman East Africa Ltd 1976-80; fin dir: Fitter & Poulton Ltd 1981-84, Mander Kidd (UK) Ltd 1984-86, EPS Logistics Technology Ltd 1986-87; currently: co sec Chartertrack Holdings Ltd, fin dir The Hanover Group Ltd; committed christian, prev church warden parish treas and served on Solihull Deanery Synod, currently memb St Stephens Church Canterbury; parent govr Simon Langton GS Canterbury; FCA 1970, FBIM 1982; *Recreations* railways, mountain walking, wine making; *Clubs* Nairobi; *Style—* John Forman, Esq; 82 Hackington Rd, Tyler Hill, Canterbury CT2 9NQ (☎ 0227 471 751); Chartertrack Financial Services Ltd, Cornwallis House, Pudding Lane, Maidstone (☎ 0622 686276)

FORRYAN, Jane Hilary; s of John Lambert Forryan, and Barbara Forryan, *née* Edwards; *b* 6 Nov 1958; *Educ* Harrogate HS, Univ of Leeds (BChD); *Career* princ dental surgery 1981-; *Recreations* sailing (dinghy and ocean racing); *Clubs* Royal Cinque Ports Yacht (house ctee); *Style—* Miss Jane Forryan; 81 London Rd, Deal, Kent (☎ 0304 381853); Dental Surgery, 319 London Rd, Dover, Kent (☎ 0304 207416)

FORSTER, Alan Roger; s of Harold Edgar Forster (d 1979), and Annie Dorothy, *née* Wenham; *b* 27 Oct 1933; *Educ* Eastbourne GS; *m* 1, 1956, Diana, da of Herbert Raymond Love; 1 s (Paul b 1957), 1 da (Emma b 1966); m 2, 1979, Valerie, da of James Fisk; *Career* chm: Booker Overseas Trading Ltd, Bookers Sugar Co Ltd, Such & Schooley Ltd; memb Exec Ctee of West India Ctee; *Recreations* horse racing (owner), watching cricket; *Clubs* MCC; *Style—* Alan R Forster, Esq; Little Ridge, Chislehurst Rd, Chislehurst, Kent (☎ 081 467 1094, 081 467 3684); 177/179 Southwark Bridge Rd, London SE1 0EE (telex 8952713, fax 071 403 3631)

FORSYTH, Gordon Scott; s of George Stirling Forsyth (d 1982), of Rutherglen, Scotland, and Betty Agnes, *née* Scott; *b* 20 April 1926; *Educ* Glasgow HS, Univ of Glasgow (MA); *m* 6 March 1954, Nancy Scott, da of John Molesworth Reid (d 1971), of Hale, Cheshire; 1 s (Andrew b 1969), 1 da (Fiona b 1966); *Career* Mil Serv 1945-48, Lt The Highland LI; CA; chief accountant The BP Co plc 1974-81; dir: BP Petroleum Development Ltd 1976-86, BP Oil Development Ltd 1976-86; fin dir BP Exploration Co Ltd 1981-86; hon tres Inst of Petroleum 1985-; *Recreations* golf, walking; *Clubs* Royal Overseas League, Langley Park Golf; *Style—* Gordon Forsyth, Esq; 89 Barnfield Wood Rd, Beckenham, Kent; The Institute of Petroleum, 61 New Cavendish St, London W1M 8AR (☎ 071 636 1004, telex 264380)

FORSYTHE, Dr (John) Malcolm; s of Dr John Walter Joseph Forsythe (d 1988), and Dr Charlotte Constance Forsythe, *née* Beatty (d 1981); *b* 11 July 1936; *Educ* Repton, Guy's Hosp London (BSc, MB BS), LSHTM (MSc), Univ of North Carolina (MRCS, LRCP); *m* 1, 28 Oct 1961, Delia Kathleen, da of late Dr John King Moore; 1 s (Marcus John Malcolm b 30 Sept 1965), 3 da (Suzanne Delia b 9 July 1962, Nicola Kathleen (twin) b 9 July 1962, Sarah Louise b 16 May 1969); m 2, 27 Jan 1984, Patricia Mary, *née* Barnes; *Career* house surgn and house physician Guy's Hosp 1961-62, dep sr admin MO SE Met Royal Hosp Bd 1972-73 (acting sr admin MO 1973-74), area MO Kent Area Health Authy 1974-78; hon conslt Darwin Coll Univ of Kent 1974-; SE Thames RHA: regnl MO 1978-88, dir of planning and serv devpt 1984-, regnl dir of public health 1988-, exec memb 1990-; delegate Kings Coll Hosp Med and Dental Sch 1978-; memb: Public Health Serv Bd 1987-, Bd of Govrs UMDS of Guy's and St Thomas', Med Advsy Bd Nutrisystems Ltd, Health Servs Res Ctee MRC 1987-; dir Inst of Public Health 1990-; Dobst RCOG 1963, MFCM 1972, FFCM 1975, FRCP 1985; *Recreations* squash, sailing; *Clubs* RSA, RSM, Chasers; *Style—* Dr Malcolm Forsythe; Kapalua, 5 Ryders, Langton Green, Tunbridge Wells TN3 0DX; SE Thames Regional Health Authority, Thrift House, Collington AVe, Bexhill, E Sussex; Institute of Public Health, David Solomons House, Broomhill Rd, Southborough, Tunbridge Wells, Kent TN3 0TG

FOSTER, John Stewart; s of Dr Donald Stewart Foster, of Kenilworth, Warwickshire, and Rosemary Margaret Kate, *née* Weber; *b* 16 June 1947; *Educ* The King's Sch Canterbury, Univ of Lancaster (BA); *m* 14 Nov 1969, Alethea Valentine Mary, da of Prof Roberto Weiss (d 1969), of Henley on Thames, Oxfordshire; 2 s (Julien b 1971, William b 1973); *Career* reporter then sr reporter and specialist feature writer Coventry Evening Telegraph 1969-74 (speicial award winner Midlands Journalist of the Year Competition 1974); BBC: regnl journalist TV Birmingham 1974-78, parly journalist Radio News 1978-82, TV reporter and radio and TV presenter of assorted progs on current affrs Scotland 1982-85, home affrs corr TV Scotland 1985, chief parly journalist Corporate News 1985-88, chief parly corr News and Current Affrs 1988-89, chief parly corr and party ed regnl TV News and Current Affrs 1989-; memb House of Commons Press Gallery Ctee 1989; *Recreations* skiing, video-photography, bridge; *Clubs* Belle Toute (Lancaster); *Style—* John Stewart Foster, Esq

FOSTER, Robin Anthony; s of Tom Henry Foster, of Angmering, Sussex, and Gladys Maud, *née* Blyth (d 1988); *b* 4 Nov 1940; *Educ* Eltham Coll; *m* 24 Sept 1966, Georgina Anne, da of George John Cassidy (ka RAF 1943); 2 s (Mark b 1976, Timothy b 1979); *Career* mangr Lloyd Bank Southborough

Branch, chm Southborough Provident Soc; exec memb Southborough Age Concern Ctee, hon treas Sir David Salomons Soc; ACIB 1968; *Recreations* cricket, books; *Clubs* Bidborough cricket (vice pres); *Style*— Robin Foster, Esq; 63 Cranford Rd, Tonbridge, Kent TN10 4HQ (☎ 0732 365119); Lloyds Bank, 151 London Rd, Southborough, Tunbridge Wells, Kent (☎ 0892 32577)

FOSTER, Ronald; s of Joseph Foster, of Chatham (d 1920), and Olive, *née* Beaney; *b* 29 July 1918; *Educ* Chatham Jr Tech Sch, Chatham Dockyard Sch; *m* 21 Sept 1940, Gladys Lilian, da of late Charles Hurley; 2 da (Maureen b 1942, Jacqueline b 1946); *Career* HM dockyard apprentice 1933-38, various dockyard positions 1938-69, dockyard safety offr 1969, ret 1979; former memb: Chatham Borough Cncl, Medway Borough Cncl (now Rochester upon Medway City Cncl); Mayor: of Chatham 1965-66, of Medway 1974-75; Medway Heritage Centre: fndn memb, sec; chm Chatham Veteran's Club, govr 3 local schs, chm organising ctee of River Medway Dutch Week, Kent CC 1980-; Officer of The Order of Oranje Nassau (Holland) 1967; *Recreations* local history, bowls; *Style*— Ronald Foster, Esq; 52 Ingle Rd, Chatham, Kent ME4 5SE (☎ 0634 41540)

FOULSER, Brian George; s of Albert George Foulser (d 1975), of Sydenham, London, and Eva Lilian, *née* Wheeler; *b* 20 Feb 1939; *Educ* Addey and Stanhope GS, Imede Lausanne Switzerland; *m* 20 June 1961, Doreen Ann, *née* Hammett; 1 s (Grahame John b 4 April 1967), 2 da (Juliet Clare b 3 Feb 1963, Joanne Louise b 13 Aug 1964); *Career* area mangr Eskimo Foods 1962-64, northern field sales mangr Fropax-Eskimo Foods 1964-67; Findus: sales planning mangr 1967-70, mktg mangr 1970-73, northern sales mangr 1973-77, nat sales mangr 1977-78; dir and gen mangr Chambourcy Food Co Ltd 1978-84, chm and md BG Foods Ltd 1984-; memb: IOD, Inst of Grocery Distribution; *Recreations* golf, photography, spectator of soccer and cricket; *Clubs* Millwall Executive; *Style*— Brian Foulser, Esq; B G Foods Ltd, Caxton House, 22 St Johns Hill, Sevenoaks, Kent TN13 3NP (☎ 0732 450701, fax 0732 460433)

FOWLER, Ian; s of Norman William Frederick Fowler, OBE, QPM, of Herne Bay, Kent, and late Alice May, *née* Wakelin; *b* 20 Sept 1932; *Educ* The King's Sch Canterbury, St Edmund Hall Oxford (MA); *m* 3 April 1961, Gillian Cecily Fowler, JP, da of late Desmond Allchin; 2 s (Aidan Lewis b 12 May 1966, Edmund Ian Carloss b 18 March 1970), 1 da (Sarah May b 1964); *Career* Nat Serv 2 Lt (Lt TA) 2 Bn The Green Howards 1951-53; called to the Bar Gray's Inn 1957; princ chief clerk and clerk to Ctee of Magistrates Inner London Magistrates' Courts Serv 1979- (joined 1959); cncllr: Herne Bay UDC 1961-74, Canterbury City Cncl 1974-83; Mayor of Canterbury 1976-77; memb Court of Univ of Kent 1976-; *Recreations* reading; *Style*— Ian Fowler, Esq; 6 Dence Park, Herne Bay, Kent (☎ 0227 375530); ILMCS, 3rd Floor, North West Wing, Bush House, Aldwych WC2 (☎ 071 836 9331, fax 071 379 6694)

FOWLER, Ronald Frederick; CBE (1950); s of Charles Frederick Fowler (d 1942), and Amy Beatrice, *née* Hollyoak (d 1976); *b* 21 April 1910; *Educ* Bancroft's Sch, LSE (BCom), Univ of Lille, Univ of Brussels; *m* 17 April 1937, Brenda Kathleen, da of Henry William Smith (d 1970); *Career* asst and lectr in commerce LSE 1932-40, Cabinet Office and Central Statistical Office 1940-50, dir of statistics and under sec Miny of Labour 1950-68, dir statistical res DOE 1968-72; statistic conslt: Statistics Canada Ottawa 1971-72, Prices Cmmn 1973-77; contrib numerous articles in Br and American learned jls; hon treas RSS 1950-60, memb Retail Prices Index Advsy Ctee 1956-86; *Books* The Depreciation of Capital (1934), The Duration of Unemployment (1968), Some Problems of Index Number Construction (1970), Further Problems of Index Number Construction (1973); *Clubs* Reform; *Style*— R F Fowler, Esq, CBE; 10 Silverdale Rd, Petts Wood, Orpington, Kent

FOWLER, Dr Timothy John; s of Eric Fowler (d 1978), of Crowborough, E Sussex, and Agatha Clare, *née* Turner (d 1985); *b* 10 Dec 1937; *Educ* Downside, Oriel Coll Oxford (BA, MA, BM BCh, DM), St Bartholomew's Hosp, MRCP; *m* 6 Sept 1975, Sheila Barbara, da of Harrison Parkin (d 1977); 1 s (Thomas Gregory b 3 July 1979), 2 da (Clare Judith b 10 Nov 1976, Emma Jane b 23 Feb 1978); *Career* house physician St Bartholomew's Hosp, registrar in neurology Queen Elizabeth Hosp Birmingham, registrar and sr registrar in neurology Nat Hosp for Nervous Diseases, sr registrar in neurology St Mary's Hosp London; conslt neurologist 1974-: The Brook Hosp London, West Hill Hosp and Joyce Green Hosps Dartford, Sussex Hosp, Tunbridge Wells Hosp, Pembury Hosp; memb Assoc of Br Neurologists; Kent and MRCP1975, FRCP 1979; *Books* Guide for House Physicians in the Neurological Unit (1982), Neurology (jtly, 1985), Headache (ed, 1987), Clinical Neurology (jtly, 1990); *Style*— Dr Timothy Fowler; The Brook Hospital, Shooters Hill Rd, Woolwich SE18 4LW

FOX, John William Alfred; s of Claude Alfred Fox, of Gravesend, Kent, and Kathleen Elizabeth, *née* Spicer; *b* 30 Dec 1957; *Educ* Gravesend GS for Boys, UEA (BA); *m* 16 Aug 1980, Pamela Barbara, da of Alexander George Sandford (d 1966), of Gravesend, Kent; 1 s (Jonathan Claude b 1984), 1 da (Victoria Elizabeth b 1981); *Career* tax conslt Price Waterhouse London 1983-88, tax adviser Chiltern Fin Services plc 1988-89, sr tax mangr Coopers & Lybrand Deloitte 1989-; memb ctee Gravesend Branch Leukaemia Research Fund, also involved in fund-raising activities with other local charities; memb ICAEW 1984; *Recreations* squash, reading, natural history; *Style*— John Fox, Esq; 39 Singlewell Rd, Gravesend, Kent DA11 7PN (☎ 0474 322530); Coopers & Lybrand Deloitte, P O Box 207, 128 Queen Victoria Street, London EC4P 4JX (☎ 071 454 8380, fax 071 248 3623)

FOX, John William Rawson; s of Sqdn Ldr T R Fox (d 1973), of Ilkley, Yorks and Semer, nr Ipswich, Suffolk, and Jessie (d 1978), of Longton, Staffordshire; *b* 4 July 1930; *Educ* Rugby, Univ Coll Oxford (MA); *m* 11 Dec 1971, Sonia Christine, da of Noman Coe (d 1978), of Salisbury, Wilts; 2 da (Natalie Lorna b 1973, Catherine Louise b 1977); *Career* admin: ICI Ltd 1955-62, Nuffield Fndn 1962-70, asst sec RIBA 1970-74, sr admin Univ of London 1974-84, sr planner NHS 1984-89; hon sec: Univ of Oxford Ski Club 1950-53, Tonbridge and Malling Lib Assoc 1986-89, Kent co cncllr (Social and Liberal Democrats) Malling Rural NE 1989-; *Books* Linking Universities by Technology (1970); *Recreations* gardening, skiing, architectural appreciation; *Clubs* SCGB; *Style*— John Fox, Esq; Merton House, 106 High St, West Malling, Maidstone, Kent ME19 6NE (☎ 0732 840166)

FOX, Kathleen Mary; da of Capt Augustus Nathan Goldman, DCM (d 1985), and Mary Grahamn, *née* Chisnall; *b* 30 June 1948; *Educ* Epworth Public Sch SA, Natal Tech Coll (Dip Fine Art), Univ of Natal, Michael Pettit Sch of Art; *m* 1, 6 Dec 1969 (m dis 1976), John Russell Broom; 2 s (Craig Lynton b 24 March 1971, Nicholas John b 24 April 1972); m 2, 26 July 1977, David Fox, s of Gerald Fox, of Yorkshire and SA; 1 s (Gareth Richard b 2 Oct 1982); *Career* artist; gp exhibitions incl: Cape Town 1981 and 1982, work exhibited at Everard Read Gallery Johannesburg 1986, Peep Show SA Assoc of Arts 1986, Sounds of Cape Town 1987, Exhibition of Portraits Cape Town 1987; solo exhibitions incl: SA Assoc of Arts 1986, Ravensdale Gallery London 1988, Trinity Arts Centre Tunbridge Wells 1990, St Martin in the Fields London 1990; numerous corp collections incl Ernst & Young; memb: SE Arts, Women Artist Slide Library; *Style*— Ms Kathleen Fox; 12 Hopwood Gardens, Tunbridge Wells, Kent TN4 9PU (☎ 0892 543629)

FOX BASSETT, Nigel; s of Thomas Fox Bassett (d 1960), of London, and Catherine Adriana, *née* Wiffen (d 1960); *b* 1 Nov 1929; *Educ* Taunton Sch, Trinity Coll Cambridge (MA); *m* 9 Sept 1961, Patricia Anne, da of Stanley William Lambourne (d 1986), of E Horsley, Surrey; 1 s (Jonathan b 30 July 1966), 1 da (Emma (Mrs Lines) b 19 Jan 1964); *Career* Nat Serv 2 Lt RA 1949-50 (served Canal Zone Egypt with Mauritian Gds), Capt 264 (7 London) Field Regt RA TA 1950-60; admitted slr 1956; sr ptnr Clifford Chance (formerly Coward Chance) 1990- (articled 1953, ptnr 1960); chm Exec Ctee Br Inst of Int and Comparative Law 1986- (cncl memb 1977); cncl memb: Int Assoc for the Protection of Industl Property (Br Gp) Inc 1984-89, Int Law Assoc (Br Branch) 1974-86; ctee chm Int Regulation of Fin Markets 1989-; memb UK Govt Know How Fund Banking and Fin Mission to Poland 1989-; chm Intellectual Property Sub Ctee City of London Slrs Co 1982-87 (sub ctee memb 1969-87), ctee memb Business Section IBA (Anti Tst, Patents and Trademarks, Securities Ctees) 1969-; memb: Law Soc Euro Gp 1969-, American Bar Assoc (Futures Regulation Ctee) 1979-, Assoc Europeenne d'Etudes Juridiques et Fiscales (UK memb) 1969-; cncl memb Taunton Sch; hon legal advsr to Partially Sighted Soc; memb: Glyndebourne Festival Opera Soc and Kent Opera, The Pilgrims of GB 1988-; vice pres Dulwich Hockey Club; chm Old Tautonians Sports Club until 1989; Freeman Worshipful Co of Slrs 1960; memb Law Soc; *Books* English Sections of: Branches and Subsidiaries in the European Common Market (1976), Business Law in Europe (1982 and 1990); *Recreations* shooting, beagling, cricket, art, opera; *Clubs* Garrick, City of London, MCC, Seaview Yacht; *Style*— Nigel Fox Bassett, Esq; Clifford Chance, Blackfriars House, 19 New Bridge St, London EC4V 6BY (☎ 071 353 0211, fax 071 956 0114, telex 887847)

FOXWELL, Rupert Edward Theodore; s of Peter Cottam Foxwell, of Farnham, Surrey, and Marika, *née* Soutzos, of London; *b* 24 Nov 1954; *Educ* Radley, Magdalene Coll Cambridge (MA); *m* 5 May 1979, Penelope, da of Brig Sir Nicholas Somerville, of Greywell, Hants; 3 s (Jonathan b 1980, Mark b 1982, Edward b 1986); *Career* slr Allen & Overy 1979; dir Barclays de Zoete Wedd 1983-86 (md Euro Investmt Banking Div), Prudential-Bache London 1986-88, currently dep md UBS Phillips & Drew; tstee First Challenge Tst; memb Law Soc 1979; *Recreations* shooting, driving; *Style*— Rupert Foxwell, Esq; UBS Phillips & Drew, Broadgate, 100 Liverpool St, London EC2 (☎ 071 901 3333)

FRANCIES, Duncan; s of Joseph Standish Noel Francies (d 1988), and Jeanne Zoe, *née* Dordan-Pyke; *b* 5 June 1945; *Educ* Sutton Valence; *m* 24 June 1983, Patricia Mary, da of Samuel Field, of Brisbane, Aust; 1 s (Edward), 1 da (Olivia); *Career* admitted slr 1968; ptnr Richards Butler; Freeman: Worshipful Co of Slrs 1976, City of London 1978; memb: Law Soc 1963, Slrs Benevolent Assoc 1976; *Recreations* gardening, swimming; *Clubs* Wig and Pen; *Style*— Duncan Francies, Esq; Beaufort House, 15 St Botolph St, London EC3A 7EE (☎ 071 247 6555, telex 9494 94 RBLAW, fax 071 247 5091)

FRANCIS, Ven Edward Reginald; s of Alfred John Francis (d 1978), of 43 Moning Rd, Dover, Kent, and Elsie Hilda, *née* Hiscock; *b* 31 Jan 1929; *Educ*

Monmouth, Dover GS, Rochester Theol Coll; *m* 21 Oct 1950, Joyce Noreen, da of George James Atkins (d 1935); 3 s (Paul, Nigel, Jonathan); *Career* ordained 1961, chaplain Training Ship Arethusa and asst curate All Saints' Frindsbury Rochester 1961-64, vicar St William's Chatham 1964-73, vicar and rural dean Rochester 1973-79, archdeacon of Bromley 1979-; memb Gen Synod 1981-, jt chm Canterbury and Rochester Diocesan Cncl for Social Responsibility 1983-88; ACII 1958; *Recreations* ornithology, walking, rugby football, poetry; *Style*— The Ven the Archdeacon of Bromley

FRANK, Dr Michael Jeffrey; s of Dr C S Grossmark (d 1983); *b* 30 Sept 1941; *Educ* Gillingham GS, Sir Joseph Williamsons Rochester Mathematical Sch, Univ of Manchester (MB ChB, LRCP, MRCS, DRCOG); *m* 19 Jan 1963, Pamela May; 1 s (Stephen Jeffrey b 1964), 1 da (Jacqueline b 1963); *Career* GP; sr govt med offr Turks and Caicos Is WI 1968-70, med offr Chemelil Sugar Estate Kenya 1970-72, GP Rainham and Gillingham; sch govr Dane Court Sch Rainham, conslt Sports Injury Clinic Alexandra Hosp Walderslade Chatham; med offr: Medway Bears Ice Hockey Team, Maidstone United FC (dir); *Style*— Dr Michael Frank; Maryfield, 7 Hoath Lane, Wigmore, Gillingham, Kent; Parkwood Health Centre, Rainham, Kent (☎ 0634 33491)

FRANKLIN, Simon Forbes; s of Alan Forbes Franklin, of Clifffe, Rochester, and Mary Gwenda Franklin, *née* Webster; *b* 7 Jan 1958; *Educ* Sir Joseph Williamson's Mathematical Sch Rochester, Univ Coll Cardiff (LLB), Coll of Law Guildford; *Career* Martin Tolhurst Partnership Slrs Gravesend: articled clerk 1980-82, asst slr 1982-85, ptnr 1985, responsible for Strood Office 1985-; memb: Gravesend and Dist Law Soc, Kent Law Soc, Rochester Chatham and Gillingham Law Soc, The Law Soc; *Recreations* squash, roadrunning, horseriding, rugby, soccer, cricket; *Clubs* High Halston Cricket (former sec), Gravesend Rugby Football, Old Williamsonian; *Style*— Simon Franklin, Esq; 122B High St, Strood, Rochester, Kent ME2 4TR (☎ 0634 290080, fax 0634 290862)

FRANKLIN, Rt Rev William Alfred; OBE (1965); s of George Amos Franklin (d 1956), and Mary Ann Catherine, *née* Scott (d 1980); *b* 16 July 1916; *Educ* Church Sch in London, Kelham Theol Coll Nottingham; *m* 1945, Winifred Agnes, *née* Jarvis; 1 s, 1 da; *Career* ordained: deacon 1940, priest 1941; curate: St John Bethnal Green 1940-43, St John's Palmers Green 1943-45; asst chaplain St Saviour's Anglican Church Buenos Aires 1945-48, rector Holy Trinity Lomas De Zamora Buenos Aires 1948-58, rector canon and sub dean St Andrew's Santiago Chile 1958-65, rector St Alban's Anglican Church Bogota and archdeacon of Colombia (Episcopal church of USA) 1965-71, consecrated lord bishop of Colombia 1972, resigned 1978; full-time asst bishop Diocese Peterborough and hon canon Peterborough Cathedral 1978-86; hon canon emeritus of Peterborough Cathedral 1987, hon asst bishop of Canterbury 1985-; *Recreations* fishing, writing, study of Church growth; *Clubs* Royal Cwlth Soc; *Style*— The Rt Rev William Franklin, OBE; Flat 26c, The Beach, Walmer, nr Deal, Kent CT14 7HJ

FRANKLIN WHITE, Gertrude May; da of Edward Tresoldi Granger (d 1957), of Penarth, South Glamorgan, and Gertrude, *née* Hurcomb (d 1968); *b* 16 April 1920; *Educ* Penarth Co Sch for Girls, The Slade Sch of Fine Art, UCL; *m* 1, 8 Jan 1964, Charles Franklin White, s of Charles White (d 1899), of Reedbeds, Adelaide, S Aust; m 2, 24 Sept 1982, Edmund Hugh Moroney (d 1983), s of Edward Fitzgerald Moroney, of Penarth, S Glamorgan; *Career* princ Samuel Palmer Sch of Art 1976; *Recreations* country life, music; *Style*— Mrs Gertrude Franklin White; Samuel Palmer School of Art, Reedbeds, Shoreham, Sevenoaks, Kent TN14 7SW (☎ 09592 2035)

FRANKS, Anthony Kenric Stapleton; s of Maurice Kenric Franks (d 1955); *b* 13 June 1928; *Educ* Nautical Coll Pangbourne; *m* 1960, Sarah Georgina Cochrane, *née* Watson; 3 s; *Career* md Phicom plc (previously Plantation Holdings Ltd) 1971-84 (chm and chief exec 1984-86), chm Beck Electronics Ltd 1986-; chm Royal Hosp and Home Putney 1988-, dep treas RNLI 1989-; *Recreations* shooting, sailing; *Clubs* Boodle's, Royal Yacht Sqdn, City of London; *Style*— Anthony Franks, Esq; Becketts Grove, Matfield, Tonbridge, Kent TN12 7LH (☎ 089 272 2175)

FRASER, Sir Basil Malcolm; 2 Bt (UK 1921); s of Sir (John) Malcolm Fraser, 1 Bt, GBE (d 1949), and Irene, *née* Brightman; *b* 2 Jan 1920; *Educ* Eton, Queens' Coll Cambridge; *Heir* none; *Career* Capt RE WW II, Madras Sappers and Miners (despatches); *Style*— Sir Basil Fraser, Bt; 175 Beach St, Deal, Kent

FRASER, Shena Eleanor; da of Robert Dick Fraser (d 1936), of 4 Snowdon Place, Stirling, Scotland, and Eleanor Sarah, *née* Hanson (d 1952); *b* 26 May 1910; *Educ* Queen Margaret's Sch Scarborough, RCM (ARCM piano and violin); *m* 19 Jan 1935, Laurence Beale Neame (d 1970), s of Harry Sidney Neame, of Alfred House, Faversham, Kent; 3 s (Colin b 1936, Stuart b 1945, Roderick b 1946), 1 da (Tessa b 1940); *Career* composer; works incl Carillon, To Him Give Praise, Child of Bliss, Full Fathom Five, Sonatina for Flute/Piano, also many part songs and instrumental pieces; pres Faversham Music Club, hon memb Talbot-Lampson Sch for Conductors; memb: Performing Rights Soc, Br Fedn of Music Festivals, Inc Soc of Musicians, Composers' Guild of GB; *Books* Sing at Sight (1986), More Singing at Sight (1989), Listen! (1989); *Recreations* walking, reading; *Clubs* University Women's; *Style*— Miss Shena Fraser

FREEDMAN, Cyril Winston; s of Sydney Freedman (d 1951), and Irene Rosalind, *née* Anekstein; *b* 31 Aug 1945; *Educ* Brighton Coll, Brighton Coll of Art and Design (Dip Graphic Art and Design); *m* 25 March 1970, Christine Mary, da of Cecil Shipman, of Swanwick, Derbys; 1 s (Mark b 1973) 1 da (Anna b 1977); *Career* chm: CWF Advertising Ltd 1971-74, Halls Homes and Gardens 1978-80 (md 1977-78, dir 1974-81); dir Pentos plc and subsidiaries 1979-81, chm Serco Ryan Ltd 1982-87, chief exec WBH Group Ltd (subsidiary of Lopex plc) 1985-88, dir Armour Automotive Products Group 1985-; chm: Deeko plc 1988-90 (dir 1986-90), Hennell Holdings Ltd 1988-; dir Alan Patricof Assocs Ltd 1988-; MCIM; *Recreations* painting, collecting fine art; *Style*— Cyril Freedman, Esq; Alan Patricof Associates Ltd, 24 Upper Brook St, London W1 (☎ 071 872 6300)

FREETHY, Norman Derek; s of Arthur Thomas Freethy (d 1961), and Helen Maud, *née* Cook (d 1977); *b* 23 Feb 1923; *Educ* Pinner Co Sch; *m* 1, 1958; 2 s (Simon Julian b 1964, Conrad Stephen Mark b 1971), 1 da (Nicola b 1962); m 2, 1985, Alison Lesley Vaughan, da of William Arthur Sparke (d 1978); 1 da (Sophie Dawn Vaughan b 1987); *Career* qualified actuary 1957; sr ptnr Hymans Robertson & Co Consulting Actuaries; frequent writer and speaker on pensions and investmt matters; dir: City of London Computer Services Ltd, Coulter Pension Tstees; Liveryman Worshipful Co of Actuaries; FIA; *Recreations* music, gardening, golf; *Clubs* RAC, City Livery, Addington Golf; *Style*— Norman Freethy, Esq; Overcombe, 87 Harvestbank Rd, West Wickham, Kent; Hymans Robertson & Co Consulting Actuaries, 190 Fleet St, London EC4A 2AH (☎ 071 831 9561, fax 071 831 6800, telex 881 3786)

FRIDAY, Malcolm Roland; s of David Friday (d 1980), of Little Coursehorn Farm, Cranbrook, and Helen, *née* Mulligan; *b* 17 July 1951; *Educ* Cranbrook Sch, Univ of Nottingham (BSc); *m* 8 April 1978, Maureen Susan, da of Ernest John Monk, of Southend on Sea, Essex; 3 s (James b 1980, David b 1982, Adam b 1984); *Career* Fridays (Cranbrook) Ltd: dir 1970-, chm 1980-; dir Bumbles Farm Ltd 1984-; offr Br Egg Assoc; *Recreations* tennis, squash, fly fishing; *Clubs* East India; *Style*— Malcolm Friday, Esq; Fridays (Cranbrook) Ltd, Chequer Tree Farm, Cranbrook, Kent TN17 3PN (☎ 0580 714014, fax 0580 713512)

FROST, Robert Frederick; JP; s of Reginald William Frost, and Dorothy May, *née* Porter (d 1983); *b* 27 Nov 1949; *Educ* Sheerness Central Secdy Modern Sch; *m* 3 June 1971, Maureen, da of Reginald Ewen (d 1979); 1 s (Adam Robert b 1980), 2 da (Tracy Louise b 1972, Claire Lisa b 1974); *Career* RCS; United Glass 1972-; branch pres GMBATU; *Recreations* angling, cycling; *Style*— Robert Frost, Esq, JP; 10 Baldwin Rd, Minster, Isle of Sheppey, Kent (☎ 0795 874237); United Glass Ltd, Rushenden Rd, Queenborough, Kent (☎ 0795 580205)

FROY, Robert Anthony Douglas; s of Heinz Louis Froy (d 1981), and Giezela Anna, *née* Salomon; *b* 23 Aug 1936; *Educ* Clarks Coll; *m* 8 July 1960, (Diana) Wendy, da of Maj Clifford Anderson Likeman (d 1980); 2 s (Stephen b 4 April 1963, Nicholas b 21 Feb 1965); *Career* md: Montagu Loebl Stanley 1969-87, Lloyds Bank Stockbrokers 1987-; dir Lloyds Merchant Bank Ltd; non-exec dir: The Otford Group, Hanover Property Unit Trust; dep chm Chambers & Remington Ltd Stockbrokers, chm Sennocke Services Ltd; memb Int Stock Exchange, chm Govrs Sevenoaks Sch; Freeman City of London, Liveryman Worshipful Co of Pattenmakers; AMSIA; *Recreations* sport, walking, gardening; *Clubs* City of London; *Style*— Robert Froy, Esq; 171 Defoe House, Barbican, London EC2Y 8DN (☎ 071 628 0083); Lloyds Bank Stockbrokers Ltd, 48 Chiswell St, London EC1Y 4XX (☎ 071 522 5000, fax 071 522 5563, telex 888301)

FRY, Elaine Caroline Louise; da of Wong Kin Hong, of Kuala Lumpur, Malaysia, and Eileen, *née* Lee (d 1988); *Educ* Godolphin Sch Wiltshire, Queen's Secdy Coll London, Univ of Buckingham (LLB), Inn's of Court Sch of Law; *m* 27 June 1986, (Anthony Joseph) Gordon Fry, s of Gordon Ernest Curtis Fry, of Burton Bradstock, Dorset; *Career* called to the Bar Middle Temple 1987; proprietor: Elaine Fry Fashions 1987, Joyce Heath China and Glass 1990; memb Deal and Walmer C of Trade; *Clubs* Royal Selangor Golf (Kuala Lumpar), Thanet Pistol and Sporting Gun, Ferrari Owners'; *Style*— Mrs Elaine Fry; 123 High St, Deal, Kent CT14 6BB (☎ 0304 365559)

FRY, Rev Canon James Reinhold; s of George Frederick Fry, of Waterloo, Liverpool (d 1979), and Margaret Isobella, *née* Cromie (d 1977); *b* 2 Aug 1930; *Educ* Waterloo Boys' GS, Oak Hill Theol Coll, St Cuthbert's Soc Univ of Durham (BSc, MA); *m* 7 Sept 1957, Wendy Gladys, da of William James Jesse Lacey, of Birchington, Kent; 2 da (Sharon Wendy b 28 June 1958, Susan Margaret b 27 March 1962); *Career* Cadet Pilot RAFVR 1951-53, Lt RA 1953-55; curate St John The Evangelist Bromley 1957-60; vicar: St Luke Deptford 1960-66, Chalk 1966-; rural dean of Gravesend 1981-; canon Rochester Cathedral 1987; chaplain RA Assoc, Mayor of Gravesend 1970; memb: Northfleet and Dist Probus Club, Gravesend Crusade Choir; *Books* Tomorrow's Parents (1977); *Recreations* swimming, tennis, computers, bagpipe playing; *Clubs* Frederick's; *Style*— The Rev Canon James R Fry; The Vicarage, 2a Vicarage Lane, Chalk, Kent DA12 4TF (☎ 0474 567906)

FRY, Dr John; CBE (1988, OBE 1978); s of Dr Ansel Fry (d 1972), and

Barbara, *née* Minton (d 1979); *b* 16 June 1922; *Educ* Whitgift Middle Sch, Univ of London, Guy's Hosp Med Sch (MD); *m* 1, 2 April 1944, Joan Lilian (d 1989), da of James Sabel (d 1941); 1 s (James b 26 Feb 1946), 1 da (Dimity Jane (Mrs Dawson) b 28 May 1947) m 2, 10 Sept 1989, Gertrude Albertine, da of Emil Schwer (d 1954); *Career* GP 1947-; memb cncl RCGP 1957-88, governing tstee Nuffield Provincial Hosp Tst 1957-88, memb GMC Cncl 1970-88, Jephcott prof Univ of Oxford 1981-82; conslt and advsr WHO 1962-90, conslt ed Update 1968-88, civilian conslt in Gen Practice to the Br Army 1967-87; Queen Elizabeth the Queen Mother fell and lectr 1988; FRCS, FRCGP, Hon FRSM 1989; memb: BMA 1944, RSM 1946, RCGP 1952; *Books* Medicine in Three Societies (1969), Common Dilemmas in Family Medicine (1983), Common Diseases (4 edn 1984), Disease Data Book (1986), Primary Health Care: 2000 (1986), General Practice and Primary Health Care 1940s-1980s (1988); *Recreations* reading, writing, running; *Style*— Dr John Fry, CBE; 3 Kings Court, Kelsey Park Avenue, Beckenham, Kent BR3 2TT (☎ 081 650 5414); 138 Croydon Rd, Beckenham, Kent BR3 4DG (☎ 081 650 0568)

FULLER, Michael Frederick; s of Frederick Fuller (d 1984), of Lewes, E Sussex, and Mildred Ruth, *née* Towner; *b* 30 Oct 1945; *Educ* Lewes GS for Boys, St John's Coll Cambridge (MA); *m* 9 Aug 1969, Ursula Dorothy, da of Ronald Grubb Stansfield, of Bishops Stortford, Herts; 1 s (Martin Nicholas b 1974), 1 da (Imogen Sarah b 1976); *Career* faculty asst in res Faculty of Economics and Politics Univ of Cambridge 1968-69, sr lectr in mgmnt sci econometrics and social statistics Univ of Kent 1980- (lectr in quantitative social sci 1969-80); cncllr Canterbury City Cncl 1970-76 (dep cncl ldr 1972-74), Sheriff of Canterbury 1973-74, chm of Govrs Geoffrey Chaucer Sch Canterbury, vice chm Nat Assoc of Govrs and Mangrs Kent 1988-; MIS 1972-, fell RSS 1972-; *Books* Statistics Workbook for Social Science Students (with D A Lury, 1977); *Style*— Michael Fuller, Esq; 75 Beaconsfield Rd, Canterbury, Kent CT2 7LG (☎ 0227 760283); Canterbury Business School, University of Kent, Canterbury, Kent CT2 7PD (☎ 0227 764000, fax 0227 761187)

FULLER, Peter Frederic; s of Frederic Fuller, and Elsie Violet Bertha, *née* Iddenden; *b* 10 April 1929; *Educ* Maidstone Coll of Art; *m* 16 Aug 1975, Rosemary, da of George Edward Blaker (d 1990), of Maidstone; 1 da (Merrie Fleur Blaker b 31 July 1981); *Career* painter in water colours; work exhibited at galleries incl: The Royal Academy of Arts, The Royal Soc of Painters in Water Colours, The Royal Soc of Br Artists, The Royal Inst of Painters in Water Colours, The Royal Soc of Portrait Painters, The New English Art Club; work published in The Artist magazine; memb: Maidstone Art Soc, The Royal Archaeological Inst, Maidstone Archaeological Gp; *Recreations* archaeology, music, reading, all the creative arts; *Style*— Peter Fuller, Esq; 31 Sandling Lane, Penenden Heath, Maidstone, Kent ME14 2HS (☎ 0622 754232)

FULLMAN, Peter Michael; s of John Ernest Fullman (d 1956), of Hockley, Essex, and Hazel Tonkin, *née* Williams (d 1988), of Hockley, Essex; *b* 19 May 1934; *Educ* The London Hosp Med Sch, The Middlesex Hosp London (MB BS); *m* 4 May 1963, Valerie Isobel, da of George Tramschek (d 1974), of Rochford, Essex; 1 s (Adrian b 1970), 1 da (Caroline b 1972); *Career* conslt obstetric and gynaecological surgn Canterbury and Thanet Health Authy 1973; FRCS (Ed), FRCOG; *Recreations* music, gardening; *Style*— Peter Fullman, Esq; 47 London Rd, Canterbury, Kent CT2 8LF (☎ 0227 456352); The Kent & Canterbury Hospital, Canterbury, Kent; The Chaucer Hospital, Canterbury, Kent; Thanet District General Hospital, Margate, Kent

FURNISS, Air Vice-Marshal Peter; DFC (1944), TD (1964); s of John Furniss (d 1930), and Mary Furniss; *b* 16 July 1919; *Educ* Sedbergh; *m* 1954, Denise Andrée Gisèle, da of Charles Cotet, of S France; 1 s, 2 da; *Career* cmmnd Liverpool Scottish TA, Queens Own Cameron Highlanders 1939, seconded to RAF 1942, served in Med theatre of ops, cmd 73 Fighter Sqdn, demob 1946; admitted slr 1948, cmmnd in Legal Branch RAF 1950, dir Legal Servs HQ Air Forces M East, Aden 1961-63, HQ Far E AF Singapore 1969-71, HQ RAF Germany 1973-74, dir Legal Servs RAF 1978-82 (dep 1975-78); pres: Maidstone Branch RAFA, 40 (F) Maidstone Sqdn ATC; *Recreations* country pursuits; *Clubs* RAF; *Style*— Air Vice-Marshal Peter Furniss, DFC, TD; 18 Sevington Park, Loose, Maidstone, Kent (☎ 0622 744620)

G

GALE, Roger James; MP (C) North Thanet 1983-; s of Richard Byrne Gale, and Phyllis Mary, *née* Rowell (d 1948); *b* 20 Aug 1943; *Educ* Hardye's Sch Dorchester, Guildhall Sch of Music and Drama; *m* 1, 1964 (m dis 1967), Wendy Dawn Bowman; m 2, 1971 (m dis), Susan Sampson; 1 da (Misty); m 3, 1980, Suzy Gabrielle, da of Thomas Leopold Marks (d 1972); 2 s (Jasper, Thomas); *Career* formerly: reporter BBC Radio, prodr BBC Radio 4 Today Show, dir BBC Children's TV, prodr and dir Thames Children's TV, editor teenage unit Thames; contested (C) Birmingham Northfield (by-election) 1982; *Recreations* swimming, sailing; *Clubs* Garrick; *Style*— Roger Gale, Esq, MP; House of Commons, London SW1A 0AA (☎ 071 219 4021)

GALL, Henderson Alexander (Sandy); CBE (1988); s of Henderson Gall (d 1963), of Banchory, Scotland, and Jean, *née* Begg (d 1970); *b* 1 Oct 1927; *Educ* Glenalmond Perthshire, Univ of Aberdeen (MA); *m* 11 Aug 1958, Eleanor Mary Patricia Anne, da of Michael Joseph Smyth (d 1964), of London; 1 s (Alexander Patrick Henderson b 17 June 1960), 3 da (Fiona Deirdre b 7 May 1959, Carlotta Maire Jean b 2 Nov 1961, Michaela Monica b 27 March 1965); *Career* Corpl RAF 1945-48; foreign corr Reuters 1953-63: Berlin, Nairobi, Suez, Geneva, Budapest, Johannesburg, Congo; ITN 1963-: roving reporter, newscaster; maker of seven TV documentaries; rector Univ of Aberdeen 1978-81, Sitara-i-Pakistan 1985, Lawrence of Arabia Medal RSAA 1987; Hon LLD Univ of Aberdeen 1981; *Books* Gold Scoop (1977), Chasing the Dragon (1981), Don't Worry About the Money Now (1983), Behind Russian Lines, an Afghan Journal (1983), Afghanistan: Agony of a Nation (1986), Salang (1989); *Recreations* golf, Cresta Run; *Clubs* Turf, Special Forces, Rye Golf, Royal St Georges Golf; *Style*— Sandy Gall, Esq, CBE; Doubleton Oast Hse, Penshurst, Kent TN11 8JA; ITN, 48 Wells St, London W1 (☎ 071 637 2424, fax 0892 870 871)

GALL, Maurice Henry Willis; s of Douglas Crisp Gall (d 1984), of Nutley, Sussex, and Grace Florence, *née* Willis (d 1972); *b* 15 June 1926; *Educ* Kings Canterbury, Cheltenham, Cambridge Univ (MA); *m* 1, 1954 (m dis 1966), Ghyslaine Monique Danielle; 3 da (Chantal b 25 May 1955, Odile b 1 Oct 1958, Alice b 1 Aug 1963); m 2, 16 Aug 1967, Pamela Margaret Alice, da of Sir Guthrie Thomas Russell, KCSI, KCIE (d 1966), of Glasgow; *Career* RNVR 1944-47, Sub Lt 1945, minesweeping Far East and Home Waters; dir H Tinsley & Co Ltd 1959-67, md Precision Varionics Ltd 1968-; Freeman Worshipful Co of Girdlers 1956 (Master 1986), Master Worshipful Co of Scientific Instrument Makers 1984; FIEE FInstP; *Recreations* ocean racing, sailing; *Clubs* RNSA, RNVR Offrs Assoc, IOD; *Style*— Maurice Gall, Esq

GALLOWAY, David Richard; s of John Campbell Galloway (d 1963), of Kent, and Kathleen Adelaide, *née* Herbert; *b* 5 Nov 1931; *Educ* Blackrock Coll Dublin, Lincoln Coll Oxford (MA); *m* 18 May 1963, Ann Penelope Clare, da of William John Clare Gaskell (d 1965), of Kent; 1 s (James b 1969), 2 da (Lucinda b 1964, Natasha b 1967); *Career* writer and fin conslt; dep city ed Sunday Telegraph 1964-67, res ptnr Spencer Thornton (stockbroker) 1967-77, money columnist ('David Hume') Harpers & Queen 1970-, consIt GT Management (fund mangrs) 1977-, chm Imagine (computer graphics) 1985-; memb ctees E Ashford Rural Tst; *Books* The Public Prodigals (1976), Outbid (as 'David Hume', 1984); *Recreations* theatre, opera, concert going, gardening, swimming, skiing, croquet; *Clubs* Garrick, Groucho; *Style*— David R Galloway, Esq; Boughton Court, Ashford, Kent TN25 4EU (☎ 0233 812413)

GAMMON, Supt Peter Alan; s of Cecil William Alan Gammon, of Sweechgate, Broad Oak, Canterbury, Kent, and Dorothy Elizabeth, *née* Harwood; *b* 29 April 1951; *Educ* Simon Langton GS for Boys Canterbury; *m* 5 Aug 1972, Myra Anne, da of Glyndwr John Lane (d 1976), of Canterbury, Kent; 2 da (Julie b 1974, Claire b 1977); *Career* Kent Co Police Constabulary: constable 1970, sgt 1976 (attended special course Police Staff Coll Bramshill Hants), uniformed patrol sgt Sittingbourne 1977, inspr Rochester and other locations 1978, chief inspr 1983, Margate 1983-85, offr i/c Uniform Support Gp 1985, supt and offr i/c res and planning police HQ Maidstone 1987, sub divnl cdr Chatham 1988; sub divnl cdr Canterbury 1989-; memb Canterbury Crime Prevention Panel, vice chm govrs Herne Bay HS, memb PCC St Bartholomews Herne Bay; *Recreations* golf, writing poetry, walking, swimming, photography; *Style*— Supt Peter Gammon; Kent County Constabulary, Police Station, Old Dover Rd, Canterbury, Kent (☎ 0227 762055)

GAMON, Hugh Wynell; CBE (1979), MC (1944); s of His Hon Judge Hugh Reece Percival Gamon (d 1953), of The Lodge, Acomb, York, and Eleanor Margaret Gamon, *née* Lloyd, of Hartford House, Hartley Wintney, Hants; *b* 31 March 1921; *Educ* St Edwards Sch Oxford, Exeter Coll Oxford (MA); *m* 17 Dec 1949, June Elizabeth, da of William Temple (d 1986), of Underriver, Sevenoaks, Kent; 1 s (Charles b 1956), 3 da (Mary-Anne b 1952, Sarah b 1954, Jane b 1959); *Career* WWII 1940-46, Maj 1 Div Signals; served: N Africa, Italy, Palestine; slr and parly agent; sr ptnr Sherwood & Co 1972; HM Govt Agent 1970; *Recreations* gardening, motoring; *Clubs* St Stephens and Constitutional, Westminster; *Style*— Hugh W Gamon, CBE, MC; Black Charles, Underriver, Sevenoaks, Kent TN15 0RY (☎ 0732 833036); Messrs Sherwood & Co, Queen Annes Chambers, 3 Dean Farrar St, Westminster SW1H 9LG (☎ 071 222 0441)

GARDINER, Dr Alan Seath; s of Seath Gardiner (d 1968), and Nora Charlotte, *née* Cooke; *b* 15 Nov 1927; *Educ* Raynes Park Co Sch, Univ of Oxford (MA, BM BCh), RCS (DA); *m* Beryl Rosemary, da of Oliver Wright (d 1968), of Thame; 1 s (Harald b 1962), 1 da (Leila b 1963); *Career* MO Malayan Med Serv 1953, consIt anaesthetist Univ Coll Hosp of the WI 1961, consIt anaesthetist SE Kent Health Authy 1963-; FFARCS, FRSM 1965; *Clubs* Br Med Pilots Assoc, Folkestone Yacht and Motor Boat; *Style*— Dr Alan Gardiner; 9 Earls Ave, Folkestone, Kent

GARDINER, (Charles) Douglas; JP (1974); s of Douglas Gardiner (d 1981), of Dunfermline, and Kate Constable, *née* Spittal; *b* 1 Dec 1925; *Educ* Dunfermline HS, Univ of Edinburgh (BSc), Univ of London (LLB); *m* 24 Oct 1970, Rosemary Gillian Wynne, da of William Stanley Jones Williams, DL (d 1954), of Newport, Gwent; 2 s (Bruce b 1972, Gordon b 1974); *Career* Lt Corps of RE 1946-48; called to the Bar Gray's Inn 1955; SE Electricity Bd: dist mangr Maidstone 1968-70, dist commercial mangr Medway 1970-85, divnl mktg mangr Kent 1985-88; chm Kent branch BIM 1970-72, memb Rotary Club of Chatham 1983-, dep chm Medway bench 1985-89, chm Kentish Players Amateur Operatic and Dramatic Soc 1986-88, pres Medway and Gillingham C of C 1988-90; vice chm Medway Branch Kent Magistrates Courts Ctee 1989- (memb 1986-), govr Mid Kent Coll of Higher and Further Educn 1990-; MIEE 1957, FBIM 1972; *Recreations* theatre, music, golf; *Clubs* Castle (Rochester), Royal St George's Golf (Sandwich), Bearsted Golf (Maidstone); *Style*— Douglas Gardiner, Esq, JP; Dane Close, Hartlip, Sittingbourne, Kent ME9 7TN (☎ 0795 842470); Medway & Gillingham, Chamber of Commerce, 149 New Rd, Chatham, Kent

GARDNER, (Christopher) Mark; s of Lt Col Leslie Browning Gardner (d 1966), and Marjorie Emily, *née* Richards (d 1966); *b* 30 Jan 1939; *Educ* St Boniface's Coll Plymouth; *m* 13 March 1965, Ann, da of Clarence Victor Jeffrey (d 1973); *Career* sports ed Dudley Herald 1959-60, asst municipal corr Birmingham Evening Despatch 1960-63, theatre critic Birmingham Sunday Mercury 1964-68, info offr Swale DC 1974, dist ed Faversham News 1979-89 (asst ed 1968-71); dist ed Faversham Times: 1972-74, 1975-79, 1989-; record reviewer Jazz Journal International 1962-, author of over 700 sleeve notes for jazz record cos worldwide, contrib to nat and int jazz pubns 1960-, compiler of jazz reissues released in Europe USA and Japan; PRO Faversham RNLI Branch Ctee 1982-, life memb The Faversham Soc; *Books* Jam Session (1985), The New Grove Dictionary of Jazz (1988); *Recreations* collecting jazz records, films of the 40's, detective fiction, cycling; *Style*— Mark Gardner, Esq; Faversham Times, 7 West St, Faversham, Kent ME13 7JE (☎ 0795 536555, fax 0795 422389)

GARNER, Anthony James; s of Lt Cdr Frederick Ernest Garner, DSC, RN (d 1976), of Carysfort, Malford Grove, Snaresbrook, Essex, and Sunshine, The Parade, Birchington-on-Sea, Kent, and Gertrude Eleanor, *née* Penwarden (d 1988); *b* 2 May 1925; *Educ* Uppingham, Hertford Coll Oxford (MA); *m* 16 April 1955, Catherine, da of William Talbot (d 1926), of Ramsgate; 2 s (Anthony Frederick John b 1956, William Talbot b 1970), 3 da (Elizabeth Catherine b 1957, Julia Nonie (Mrs Bouverat) b 1962, Mary Ann Frances (Mrs Richardson) b 1966); *Career* WWII volunteered RNVR 1943; Ordinary Seaman: HMS Ganges 1943, HMS Dauntless 1944, HMS King Alfred 1944;

Midshipman 1944, Temp Actg Sub Lt 1944, HMS Woolston 1945; articled clerk Reid Sharman & Co 1947-51, admitted slr 1951, Freshfields 1951-53, Wray Smith Paterson & Co 1954, legal asst to Official Slr the Church Cmmrs 1954, conveyancing slr ICI plc 1957-81; dir: Levancroft Ltd 1978-, Iverna Covat Freehold Co Ltd 1989-; underwriting memb Lloyds 1964-; hon slr 625 Sqdn RAF Assoc; memb numerous orgns and socs incl: Uppingham Assoc and School Soc, Chelsea Cons Assoc, Huguenot Soc, CLA, Friends of Bodleian; Freeman City of London, Memb Worshipful Co of Loriners; friend soc of St John The Evangelist; memb Law Soc 1951; *Recreations* bibliophile, gardening, swimming, music; *Clubs* Boodle's, Hurlingham, St Stephen's Constitutional, Royal Temple YC, City Livery, Canning (Oxford); *Style—* Anthony Garner, Esq; 7 Iverna Ct, Kensington, London W8 6TY (☎ 071 937 1313), The Manor House, Great Mongeham, Deal, Kent CT14 9LR

GARTHWAITE, Sir William Francis Cuthbert; 2 Bt (UK 1919), DSC (1941 and Bar 1942); s of Sir William Garthwaite, 1 Bt (d 1956), and his 1 w, Francesca Margherita, *née* Parfett; *b* 3 Jan 1906; *Educ* Bradfield, Hertford Coll Oxford; *m* 1, 23 July 1931 (m dis 1937), Hon Dorothy, o da of 1 Baron Duveen; m 2, 27 June 1945 (m dis 1952), Patricia Beatrice Eden, er da of late Cdr Charles Eden Neate, RN; 1 s; m 3, 4 April 1957 (m dis), Patricia Merriel, o da of Sir Philip d'Ambrumenil; 3 s (inc twins), 1 da (decd); *Heir* s, William Mark Charles Garthwaite; *Career* Lt Cdr (A) RNR, RN Pilot and with RAF WWII (despatches thrice); underwriter and broker at Lloyds 1927-; Parly candidate (Cons): Hemsworth 1931, Isle of Ely 1935, Wolverhampton 1945; *Recreations* flying, golf, skiing; *Clubs* Portland, Naval, Royal Thames Yacht, Jockey (Paris), Royal Navy Sailing Assoc; *Style—* Sir William Garthwaite, Bt, DSC; Matfield House, Matfield, Kent TN12 7JT (☎ 089 272 2454)

GASKIN, James Joseph; s of James Joseph Gaskin (d 1979), of Berks, and Caroline, *née* Myers (d 1988); *b* 23 April 1945; *Educ* Wembley Co GS; *m* 26 Oct 1968, Linda, da of Thomas William Arundel, of Middx; 1 s (Matthew b 1972), 1 da (Sarah b 1974); *Career* dir 1976-84: Hull Blyth & Co Ltd, Oakwool Group Ltd, Seatronics (UK) Ltd, Wm Jacks (UK) Ltd, Suttons Group Ltd; fin dir: Ocean Cory Investment 1979-80, Ocean Cory Energy 1980-82; md Repcon (UK and Ireland) Ltd 1982-84; dir of external servs FIMBRA; memb Securities Indust Exec Liaison Ctee; FCA; *Recreations* riding, classical music; *Style—* James Gaskin, Esq; 21 Sandiland Crescent, Hayes, Bromley, Kent BR2 7DP (☎ 081 462 4156); FIMBRA, Hertsmere House, Marsh Wall, London E14 9RW (☎ 071 538 8860)

GATER, Paul Raymond; *b* 5 June 1957; *Educ* Portsmouth Poly (BSc), Univ of London (MPhil); *m* 9 April 1988, Caroline Susan, *née* James; *Career* memb: Lab Pty, Canterbury City Co 1987-, Dist of Canterbury Sports Advsy Cncl 1987-, Friends of the Earth; *Recreations* going to meetings; *Style—* Paul Gater, Esq; The Mount Bolts Hill, Chartham, Canterbury, Kent CT4 7JX (☎ 0227 738331)

GATES, Stephen John; s of Joseph Frederick Gates, of 87 Newquay Rd, Catford, London, and Phyllis Kathleen, *née* Owens; *b* 4 Nov 1950; *Educ* Brockley Co GS, Univ of Reading (BA), Univ of Southampton (MSc); *m* 4 Oct 1986, Josephine Mary, da of Norman Belson; *Career* audit sr H Graham King and Co London Bridge 1973-88, audit mangr Brewers London 1988-; memb: Nat Tst, RSPB, Woodland Tst, WWF, Kent Tst for Nature Conservation; FCA; *Recreations* amateur oboe player, photography, natural history; *Style—* Stephen Gates, Esq; 28 Pinchbeck Rd, Green St Green, Orpington, Kent BR6 6DR

GEERING, Kenneth Redman; s of Walter Redman Geering (d 1937), and Edith Amelia (d 1960); *b* 26 Jan 1910; *Educ* Bedford Sch; *m* 6 June 1934, (Mary) Pauline, da of William Davis (d 1937); 1 s (Christopher b 1939 d 1976); *Career* chm: Geerings of Ashford Ltd 1937-64, Office Machinery Ltd 1964-70, Business Machines (SE) Ltd 1974-79; commandant Ashford AFS 1942 (memb 1938-42), col offr E Kent NFS 1943 (memb 1942-46); chm: Ashford UDC 1947 (cncllr 1939-49), Ashford Chamber of Trade 1952-53, Assoc of Imp Typewriter Agents 1963-64; co fndr Ashford Childrens Day 1949; pres: Ashford Rotary Club 1946 (Paul Harris fell 1985), Town Div St John Ambulance Brigade 1947-59, Typewriter Trades Fedn of GB and I 1955-56, Ashford CC 1973-76, Ashford Golf Club 1973-89, AShford Cattle Show 1974, Wengen Curling Club 1986-87; *Recreations* curling, golf, cricket; *Clubs* MCC, Paternosters; *Style—* Kenneth Geering, Esq; Wootton Manor, Charing, Kent TN27 0DU (☎ 0233 712310); Cobbs Wood House, Chart Rd, Ashford, Kent TN23 1EP (☎ 0233 633366, fax 0233 646994)

GEORGE, (William Norman) Bruce; s of Norman Macdonald George (d 1922), and Isobella Elizabeth Dunn (d 1964); *b* 3 Dec 1915; *Educ* Liverpool Univ Sch of Architecture (B Arch), Sch of Planning and Res for Regnl Devpt; *Career* WWII Lt RA 1940-46 (POW Malaya); architect; formerly sr ptnr George/Trew/Dunn/Beckles Willson/Bowes, ret 1984; served: practice ctee and panel of arbitrators: RIBA, CNAA; princ buildings: The Guards' Chapel 1963, Wellington Barracks London 1984, Huddersfield Royal Infirmary 1966, Aberdeen Royal Infirmary 1967 and 1976; other works at: King's Coll Hosp London, King's Coll Hosp Med Sch, Halifax Gen Hosp, New Cross Hosp, Wolverhampton; ARIBA, AMTPI; *Books* The Architect in Practice; *Recreations* sculpture, portrait painting, music, cricket; *Style—* Bruce George, Esq; 1 Copley Dene, Wilderness Rd, Chislehurst, Kent (☎ 081 467 5809)

GEORGE, Glenda Ann; da of Frederick William George, of Maidstone, Kent, and Jean Olive, *née* Weeks; *b* 27 Nov 1951; *Educ* Maidstone Girls GS; *m* 3 Nov 1984, Robert Charles Douglas Ince, s of James Edward Ince, of Oxhey, Herts; 1 s (Daniel George Buck b 4 Nov 1970); *Career* author and poet; public appearances incl: Cambridge Poetry Festival 1979, cross-cultural confs in England and France, performance at the Pompidou Centre Paris; sessional lectr Kent Inst of Art & Design, numerous appearances in literary magazines in Europe USA and Australia; received Yorkshire Arts Assoc New Writers Award for Slit Here; *Books* Slit Here (1976), Dissecting the Corpus (1979), In'hui No 9 (1979), Language; Sex; and... (1980), The Corpse of Elmer Mccurdy (1981), Voix Off/Angleterre (1984), The New British Poetry (1988); *Recreations* back country skiing, hill walking, karate, reading, music, art, gardening; *Style—* Ms Glenda George; 18 Halstead Walk, Allington, Maidstone, Kent ME16 0PN

GIBBONS, David Edward; s of Albert Edward Gibbons (d 1971), of London, and Vera Minnie, *née* Lawrence (d 1974); *b* 12 Oct 1938; *Educ* Christ's Hosp, Guy's Hosp Dental Sch (LDS, BDS, DDPH), Chelsea Coll, Univ of London (MSc), Univ of Kent at Canterbury (MA); *m* 1, 27 April 1963 (m dis 1984), Mary, da of Vernon de Warrenne (d 1981), of London; 2 s (Simon b 5 Nov 1966, Richard b 13 May 1969); m 2, 19 April 1986, Janice Siobhan; *Career* gen dental practitioner Tiverton Devon 1963-65, area dental offr: Worthing Sussex 1965-74, Kent AHA Maidstone 1974-82; hon sr lectr: Kings Coll Hosp Dental Sch 1983-, UMDS Guy's Hosp 1990 (hon clinical tutor 1983-); W Kent Health Authys: dist dental offr 1982-85, specialist in community dental health 1985-, conslt in dental public health 1990-; Medway Health Authy: gen mangr Community Unit and Priority Care Unit 1986-90, dir Primary Care 1990-; memb: Br Assoc for the study of Community Dentistry 1974-, Panel of Examiners Examining Bd for Dental Surgery Assts 1976-, N Kent Bd Young Enterprise; vice pres Br Assoc of Dental Therapists 1979-82, examiner Royal Soc of Health for Dip in Dental Health Educn 1980-; BIM: chm Kent Branch 1988- (vice chm 1986-88), SE Regnl Cncl 1990-; vice chm Govrs and chm Finance Sub-Committee Walderslade HS for Girls; memb BDA 1963-, MRCS, FBIM 1980; *Recreations* squash, walking; *Clubs* Old Blues; *Style—* David Gibbons, Esq; Maidstone Health Authority, Preston Hall, Maidstone, Kent (☎ 0622 710161)

GIBBONS, Rev Paul James; JP (Maidstone, 1983); s of Albert Edward Gibbons (d 1971), of London, and Vera Minnie, *née* Lawrence (d 1974); *b* 28 March 1937; *Educ* Ardingly, Collegii Theologici Cicestrensis; *Career* Nat Serv RAF Cyprus 1955-57; asst priest St Michael and All Angels Croydon 1965-72, parish priest St Michael and All Angels Maidstone 1972-; chm: Howard de Walden Inst Maidstone, St Michael's Primary Sch Govrs Maidstone; *Recreations* donkeys, music; *Style—* The Rev Paul Gibbons, JP; St Michael's Vicarage, 109 Tonbridge Rd, Maidstone, Kent ME16 8JS (☎ 0622 752710)

GIBBS, Jeremy Herbert; s of Rt Hon Sir Humphrey Gibbs, GCVO, KCMG, OBE (3 s of 1 Baron Hunsdon of Hunsdon), and Dame Molly Gibbs, DBE; *b* 26 May 1935; *Educ* Bishops Sch Cape Town, Christ Church Oxford (MA); *m* 8 April 1958, Alison Douglas, da of Col Douglas McCrone Martin, of Dunchattan, Troon, Ayrshire; 4 da; *Career* insur broker; govr: St Mary's Sch Wantage, London House for Overseas Students; *Recreations* fishing; *Clubs* Bulawayo (Zimbabwe); *Style—* Jeremy Gibbs, Esq; Upper Kennards, Leigh, Kent TN11 8RE (☎ 0732 832160; office: 0732 771818)

GIBSON, Elizabeth Scott; da of James Cyril Glen (d 1985), and Joyce Beatrice, *née* Tolhurst; *b* 11 Sept 1949; *Educ* Christ's Hosp Girls' Sch, New Univ of Ulster (BA), Univ of Pa (MA); *m* 19 May 1973, James Melvin Gibson, s of Melvin Morse Gibson, of Rapid City, Dakota, USA; 1 s (Nicholas James St John b 1977), 1 da (Rosemary Katherine Elizabeth b 1980); *Career* teacher St Peter's Sch Pa USA 1973-75, lectr Houghton Coll NY 1976-82; managing ed: MARC Europe Bromley Kent (former ed) 1985-87, Kingsway Publications Eastbourne 1987-, Monarch Publications Eastbourne 1988-; novelist; memb Soc of Writers and Women Journalists; *Books* The Water is Wide (1985), Sons & Brothers (1988), Old Photographs (1990); *Recreations* jogging, swimming; *Style—* Mrs Elizabeth Gibson; Kingsway Publications/Monarch Publications Ltd, 1 St Anne's Rd, Eastbourne, East Sussex BN21 3UN (☎ 0323 410930, fax 0323 411970)

GIBSON, James Melvin; s of Melvin M Gibson, of 1001 Allen Ave, Rapid City, South Dakota, USA, and Kathryn, *née* Fessenden; *b* 25 Jan 1948; *Educ* Houghton Coll NY (BA), Univ of Pennsylvania (MA, PhD); *m* 19 May 1973, Elizabeth Scott, da of James Cyril Glen (d 1985); 1 s (Nicholas James St John b 1977), 1 da (Rosemary Katherine Elizabeth b 1980); *Career* assoc prof of English Houghton Coll NY 1980-85 (asst prof of English 1975-80), bridge clerk elect Rochester Bridge Trust 1990 - (archivist 1987-); pt/t cataloguer Kent Archives Office 1988-, currently editing E Kent volume in Records of Early English Drama for Univ of Toronto Press; memb: Kent Archaeological Soc, Medieval English Theatre Soc; layreader with numerous published sermons at Holy Cross Bearsted 1986; *Books* The Philadelphia Shakespeare Story: Horace Howard Furness and The New Variorum Shakespeare (1990);

Recreations reading, violin playing; *Style—* James Gibson, Esq; 27 Pine Grove, Maidstone, Kent ME14 2AJ (☎ 0622 673050)

GIBSON, Prof Robert Donald Davidson; s of Nicol Aitken Gibson (d 1976), of Leyton, London, and Ann, *née* Campbell (d 1977); *b* 21 Aug 1927; *Educ* Leyton Co HS, King's Coll London, Magdalene Coll Cambridge, Ecole Normale Supéreure Paris; *m* 21 Dec 1953, Sheila Elaine, da of Bertie Goldsworthy (d 1983), of Exeter; 3 s (Ian Campbell b 1955, Graham Campbell b 1958, Robin Campbell b 1962); *Career* Nat Serv Flying Offr RAF Educn Branch 1948-50; asst lectr Univ of St Andrews 1954-55, lectr and head of dept Univ of Dundee 1955-58, lectr Univ of Aberdeen 1958-61, prof of French Queen's Univ Belfast 1961-65, prof of French Univ of Kent at Canterbury 1965-; Rutherford Coll: acting master 1966-67, dep master 1967-71, master 1985-90, public orator Univ of Kent at Canterbury 1971 1976-82 and 1987; author of reviews in: French Studies, Modern Language Review, Times Literary Supplement, Times Higher Education Supplement; author of articles in: Colliers Encyclopaedia, Encyclopaedia Britannica, Penguin Companion to European Literature; memb Soc for French Studies; govr: Eversley Coll 1966-74, Nonington Coll 1966-86, Sittingbourne Coll 1967-76; *Books* The Quest of Alain-Fournier (1953), Modern French Poets on Poetry (1961, new edn 1979), Roger Martin du Gard (1961), La Mésentente Cordiale (1963), Alain-Fournier, Le Grand Meaulnes (1968 edn), The Land Without a Name (1975), Annals of Ashdon (1988), Studies in French Fiction (ed, 1988); *Recreations* walking, talking, writing; *Style—* Prof Robert Gibson; 7 Sunnymead, Tyler Hill, Canterbury, Kent CT2 9NW (☎ 0227 472372); Rutherford College, The University, Canterbury, Kent CT2 7NX (☎ 0227 764000 ext 3470)

GIFFIN, Michael; s of John Metcalfe Giffin (d 1984); *b* 2 May 1935; *Educ* Sevenoaks Sch; *m* 1963, Jane Agnes, da of Col Howard Watson Wright (d 1974); 2 s, 1 da; *Career* md St Olaf Bonding Co Ltd 1974-81, Hays Commercial Services Ltd 1985-89; chm: Hays Business Services Ltd 1981-89, Britdoc Ltd 1981-89; FCA; *Recreations* sailing; *Clubs* RAC, Medway Yacht; *Style—* Michael Giffin, Esq; Tussocks, 19 Burntwood Rd, Sevenoaks, Kent TN13 1PS (☎ 0732 451536)

GILBERT, Michael Francis; CBE (1980), TD (1950); s of Bernard Samuel Gilbert (d 1927), and Berwyn Minna, *née* Cuthbert (d 1966); *b* 17 July 1912; *Educ* Blundell's, Univ of London (LLB); *m* 26 July 1947, Roberta Mary, da of late Col R M W Marsden; 2 s (Richard b 1956, Gerard b 1960), 5 da (Harriett b 1948, Victoria b 1950, Olivia b 1952, Kate b 1954, Laura b 1958); *Career* WWII HAC (Maj) served N Africa, Italy 1939-45 (despatches 1943); ptnr Trower, Still & Keeling 1952-83 (slr 1947), legal advsr to Ruler of Bahrain 1960; memb: Royal Literary Fund Ctee 1964, cncl Soc of Authors 1975; pres Luddesdown Cricket Club 1965; *Books* author of: 24 novels of detection and suspense, over 200 short stories, 4 stage plays, various critical articles; ed of 2 anthologies; *Recreations* walking; *Clubs* Garrick; *Style—* Michael Gilbert, Esq, CBE, TD; The Old Rectory, Luddesdown, Gravesend, Kent DA13 0XE (☎ 0474 814272)

GILBERT, Stuart William; CB (1983); s of Rodney Stuart Gilbert (d 1978), and Ella Edith, *née* Esgate; *b* 2 Aug 1926; *Educ* Maidstone GS, Emmanuel Coll Cambridge (MA); *m* 1955, Marjorie Laws, da of Stanley Aloysius Vallance (d 1975); 1 s, 1 da; *Career* served WW II Sgt RAF, India, Burma; civil servant; dep sec and dir Dept for Nat Savings 1981-86; tstee Bldg Conservation Tst 1987-, treas Bromley Branch Univ of the Third Age 1989-; *Recreations* sailing, music, electronics, painting, woodwork; *Clubs* Oxford and Cambridge, Bewl Valley Sailing; *Style—* Stuart Gilbert, Esq, CB; 3 Westmoat Close, Beckenham, Kent BR3 2BX (☎ 081 650 7213)

GILL, Ian George; LVO; s of George William Gill (d 1975), of Prestwick, Ayrshire, and Lily Francis, *née* Welland (d 1964); *b* 20 Feb 1938; *Educ* Carlisle GS, Univ of Durham (LLB); *m* 25 Aug 1960, Gloria, da of George Maughan (d 1984), of Tynemouth; 1 s (Kevin Ian b 1964), 2 da (Susan b 1962, Tracy b 1969); *Career* admitted slr 1962; legal clerk and asst slr Peterborough Borough Cncl 1959-63, asst and sr asst slr Lincoln CBC 1963-67, dep town clerk Dover Borough Cncl 1967-68, town clerk and HM coroner Dover 1968-74, chief exec Thanet DC 1974-; registrar to Lord Warden of Cinque Ports, jt slr to Confedn of Cinque Ports, hon sec Br Resorts Assoc, exec sec Cncl For Travel and Tourism, dir E Kent Enterprise Agency, govr St Lawrence Coll; *Recreations* walking, reading, travel; *Style—* Ian Gill, Esq, LVO; Thanet Council Offices, PO Box 9, Margate, Kent CT9 1XZ (☎ 0843 225511, fax 0843 290906)

GIRLING, (John) Anthony; s of James William Girling, OBE, of 3 Anna Park, Cliff Rd, Birchington, Kent, and Annie Doris, *née* Reeves; *b* 21 Aug 1943; *Educ* Tonbridge, Guildford Coll of Law; *m* 26 March 1965, Lynne Margaret, da of Raymond Hubert Roland Davis (d 1980); 1 s (Richard b 1971), 1 da (Samantha b 1968); *Career* admitted slr 1966; NP 1968; chm Girlings Solicitors of E Kent 1981- (ptnr 1966-), fndr memb Invicta Radio plc; hon sec Herne Bay Rotary Club 1969-72, chm Herne Bay Round Table 1978, hon sr memb Darwin Coll Univ of Kent, pres Kent Law Soc 1980-81 (hon sec 1974-80), memb Cncl Law Soc for Kent Constituency 1988-, pres Isle of Thanet Law Soc 1983-84; *Recreations* skiing, golf, music, theatre; *Style—* Anthony Girling, Esq; Maypole House, Hoath, Canterbury, Kent CT3 4LN (☎ 0227 86332); Girlings Solicitors, 158 High St, Herne Bay, Kent (☎ 0227 373874, fax 0227 365897)

GLADSTONE, John Neville; s of Stephen Deiniol Gladstone, MC (d 1965), and Mary St Claire, *née* Davidson (d 1976); *b* 12 July 1932; *Educ* Eton; *m* 12 Sept 1959, Jane Gordon, *née* Stephen, da of Maj-Gen Robert Alexander Stephen, CB, CBE, RAMC; 2 s (David b 5 Oct 1960, Peter b 26 June 1963), 1 da (Claire b 8 March 1962); *Career* Nat Serv Queen's Own Royal West Kent Regt in Malaya 1950-52, TA 1952-53; memb Lloyds of London; chm Limpsfield Parish Cncl 1984-86 (memb 1978-); *Recreations* golf; *Style—* John Gladstone, Esq; Old Buckhurst, Mark Beech, nr Edenbridge, Kent (☎ 034 2850 825); Lloyds, London (☎ 071 481 1212)

GLAISHER, Dr Brian Douglas; s of Eric Edward Glaisher (d 1973), of Madrid, Spain, and Libya Emma, *née* Gepp (d 1959); *b* 14 Jan 1923; *Educ* Felsted, Univ of London (MRCS, LRCP); *m* 2 April 1949, (Catherine) Joy Edna, da of Arnold Stämffli (d 1964), of Hildenborough, Kent; 2 s (Charles Frederick b 1957, James Arnold b 1965), 2 da (Judith Caroline b 1950, Julie Valentine b 1954); *Career* Lt RA 1943, transfd to E Surrey Regt and seconded to KAR 1944; qualified in med 1956, princ in gen practice 1958-; *Recreations* walking, swimming, singing, travelling; *Style—* Dr Brian Glaisher; 79 Tonbridge Rd, Hildenborough, Kent TN11 9BH (☎ 0732 838777)

GLASSPOOL, Michael Gillo; s of Frederick Frank Glasspool (d 1972), and Molly Kathleen Glasspool; *b* 8 Aug 1938; *Educ* Clifton, Univ of Cambridge (BA, MB BChir); *m* 9 May 1964, Anna Margaret, da of Percy Kenneth Stiles Wilkinson, of Edenbridge, Kent; 1 s (Jonathan Michael Rennie b 18 March 1965), 2 da (Katherine Louise b 22 Oct 1966, Rachel Naomi b 2 Feb 1969); *Career* res Moorfields Eye Hosp 1968-71, sr registrar Westminster Hosp 1971-73, conslt ophthalmic surgn Queen Mary's Hosp Orpington and Sidcup 1973-; pres Orpington Blind Club, hon conslt ophthalmologist Royal London Soc for the Blind at Dorton House Sch for the Blind Sevenoaks; FRCS, fell Coll of Ophthalmologists; *Books* Problems in Ophthalmology (1982), Atlas of Ophthalmology (1982), Eyes - their problems and treatment (1984), Your Eyes (1990); *Recreations* landscape gardening, painting; *Style—* Michael Glasspool, Esq; Rookery Cottage, Chevening Lane, Knockholt, Sevenoaks, Kent TN14 7LB (☎ 0959 33265); Queen Mary's Hosp, Frognal Ave, Sidcup, Kent DA14 6LT (☎ 081 302 2678)

GLEADALL, Rev John Frederick; s of Frederick James Gledall (d 1963), of Birmingham, and Ivy, *née* Beech (d 1945); *b* 5 Jan 1939; *Educ* Matthew Boulton Tech Coll, Ripon Hall Oxford , Salisbury Theol Coll; *m* 16 Sept 1967, Janet Constance, da of Frank Ernest Hickman (d 1984), of Winchelsea, Sussex; 1 s (Paul James b 27 May 1969), 1 da (Sarah Katherine b 25 July 1972); *Career* engr and tech asst; curate Christ Church; priest in charge: St Francis Ashford, St Margarets Hothfield, St Margarets Hothfield with St Mary, Westwell with Eastwell and Boughton Aluph; vicar and rector of The United Benefice of Hothfield with Westwell and Eastwell with Boughton Aluph; *Recreations* gentle sport; *Style—* Rev John Gleadall; The Vicarage, Eastwell Lane, Westwell, Ashford, Kent TN25 4LQ (☎ 0233 712576)

GLEDHILL, Anthony John; GC (1967); s of Harold Victor Gledhill, of 60 Meon Rd, Milton, Portsmouth, Hants, and Marjorie Edith, *née* Prout; *b* 10 March 1938; *Educ* Doncaster Tech HS; *m* 3 Sept 1958, Marie Lilian, da of William Hughes, of 43 Eastry Ave, Hayes, Bromley, Kent; 1 s (Stewart b 1 Sept 1961), 1 da (Rachel b 13 Sept 1963); *Career* accounts clerk offr's mess RAF Bruggen Germany 1953-56; Met Police: cadet 1956-57, police constable 1957-75, detective sgt 1976-87; PO Investigation Dept 1987, md FCA Ltd 1988-, co exec Landhurst Leasing; memb Royal Br Legion Kent; *Recreations* football, carpentry; *Style—* Anthony Gledhill, Esq, GC; 98 Pickhurst Lane, Hayes, Bromley, Kent, BR2 7JD (☎ 081 462 4033); Landhurst Leasing, 6/7 Queen Street, London EC4N 1SP (☎ 071 236 8702)

GLEDHILL, The Rev Jonathan; *b* 15 Feb 1949; *m* Dr Jane Gledhill; *Career* vicar St Mary Bredin Church 1983-, rural dean of Canterbury 1988-; *Style—* The Rev J M Gledhill; St Mary Bredin Vicarage, Nunnery Fields, Canterbury, Kent CT1 3JN (☎ 0227 462479)

GLENNY, (Alexander) Keith; s of Lt-Col Clifford Roy Glenny, TD, of 28 Crosby Rd, Westcliff On Sea, Essex, and Eileen Winifred, *née* Smith (d 1974); *b* 19 July 1946; *Educ* Charterhouse, Gonville and Caius Coll Cambridge (MA, LLM); *m* 19 April 1975, Rachel Elizabeth, da of Rev A C Fryer, of Byfield House, Byfield, Northants; 2 s (Christopher b 5 Jan 1977, Matthew b 31 Oct 1986), 1 da (Anna b 24 May 1979); *Career* slr British Oxygen Co Ltd 1970-72; Hatten Asplin Channer and Glenny Barking Essex: slr 1972-74, ptnr 1974-88, sr ptnr 1988-; clerk Barking and Ilford United Charities and Barking Gen Charities, govr Barking Abbey Sch; Freeman Worshipful Co of Poulters 1978; memb Law Soc; *Clubs* Wig and Pen, City Livery; *Style—* Keith Glenny, Esq; Netherfield, Powdermill Lane, Leigh, Tonbridge, Kent TN11 8PY (☎ 0732 833 320); 4 Town Quay Wharf, Abbey Rd, Barking IG11 7BZ (☎ 081 591 4131, fax 081 591 1912)

GLOIN, David Barclay; s of Barclay Arthur Gloin (d 1981), of Dulwich, and Dilys Margaret, *née* Williams; *b* 28 Feb 1946; *Educ* Alleyn's Sch Dulwich; *m* 25 July 1970, Elizabeth Mary, da of Leslie George Francis, MBE (d 1975), of

Herne Hill, S London; 1 s (Peter b 1976), 1 da (Janet b 1980); *Career* slr; articled then ptnr Gaunt Foster and Hill 1964-70, legal asst then head of branch Post Office slrs office conveyancing dept 1970-82; British Telecom: div slr slrs office commercial dept 1982-87, dir property law dept 1987-89, dir litigation and advsy dept 1989-; memb: Law Soc, Int Bar Assoc; Freeman City of London Slrs Co 1989, Freeman City of London 1990; *Recreations* singing, reading, walking; *Style*— David B Gloin, Esq; The Solicitor's Office, British Telecommunications plc, British Telecom Centre, 81 Newgate St, London EC1A 7AJ (☎ 071 356 4820, fax 071 356 5894, telex 268413, 071 356 6317, TELECOM GOLD 73:TSY004)

GLOVER, Eric; s of William Arthur Glover (d 1965), of Liverpool, and Margaret, *née* Walker; *b* 28 June 1935; *Educ* Liverpool Inst HS, Oriel Coll Oxford (MA); *m* 1960, Adele Diane, da of Col Cecil Geoffrey Hilliard, of Harrogate; 3 s (Ian, Paul, Jason); *Career* sec-gen Chartered Inst of Bankers 1982-90 (dir of studies 1968-82); *Recreations* golf, squash, tennis; *Clubs* Overseas Bankers; *Style*— Eric Glover, Esq; 12 Manor Park, Tunbridge Wells TN4 8XP (☎ 0892 31221); The Chartered Inst of Bankers, 10 Lombard St, London EC3V 9AS

GLOVER, Myles Howard; y s of Cedric Howard Glover (d 1970), of Regent's Park, London, and Holmbury St Mary, Surrey, and Winifred Mary, *née* Crewdson (d 1978); *b* 18 Dec 1928; *Educ* Rugby, Balliol Coll Oxford (MA); *m* 12 April 1969, Wendy Gillian, da of Cecil Maltby Coleman (d 1985), of Bishop's Stortford, Herts; 1 s (Damian Patrick b 21 July 1970), 2 da (Sophie Louise b 6 Nov 1972, Lucinda Clare b 28 Sept 1974); *Career* called to the Bar Lincoln's Inn 1954; The Skinners' Co: legal asst 1957-58, asst clerk 1958-59, clerk 1959-90; clerk to: Govrs of Tonbridge Sch, Governing Body of Judd Sch Tonbridge, The Skinners' Co's Sch for Boys Tunbridge Wells, The Skinners' Co's Sch for Girls Stamford Hill, Tstees of the Residuary Income of Sir Thomas Smythe's Charity; memb: Ctee of The City & Guilds of London Art Sch 1960-71, Advsy Ctee of Gresham Coll 1985-86, Governing Cncl of St Paul's Cathedral Choir Sch 1986-90, Governing Body of St Leonard's Mayfield Sch 1988-; hon sec Governing Bodies Assoc (Ind Schs) 1967-91, chm Ctee of Clerks to the Twelve Chief Livery Cos of the City of London 1975-81; hon memb The Old Tonbridgian Soc 1986; *Clubs* Savile

GLYNN, Stanley Frederick Henry; *b* 5 Aug 1918; *Educ* Mercers'; *m* 1943, Mary Keith, *née* Dewdney; 2 da; *Career* served with army in N Africa, Egypt, Italy, Greece; Maj; auctioneer and estate agent; Knight Frank and Rutley 1935-79, vice chm Regency Building Soc 1970-; govr BUPA 1970; chm: BUPA Med Fndn 1979, Chislehurst & Sidcup Housing Assoc; memb Lloyd's; Freeman City of London, Liveryman Worshipful Co Tallow Chandlers and Glass-Sellers; *Recreations* tennis, walking, gardening, cricket; *Clubs* Carlton, MCC, Farmers', IOD; *Style*— Stanley Glynn, Esq; Rosemount, Cricket Ground Rd, Chistlehurst, Kent (☎ 081 467 5197)

GOACHER, Deborah Jane; da of Derek Raymond Light, of East Farleigh, Maidstone Kent and Margaret Doris, *née* Campbell; *b* 2 March 1956; *Educ* Maidstone Girls GS; *m* 6 Sept 1975, Philip Goacher, *qv*, s of Howard Leslie Goacher, of Donisthorpe, Ashby De La Zouch, Leicestershire; 1 s (William b 1980), 1 da (Sophia b 1978); *Career* non-residential social worker Kent CC 1974-78, ptnr and brewery owner 1983-; memb Tovil Parish Cncl, sch govr; *Recreations* bellringing, music, cycling, hiking; *Style*— Mrs Philip Goacher; 5 Hayle Mill Cottages, Bockingford, Maidstone, Kent; The Bockingford Brewery, Hayle Mill, Maidstone, Kent (☎ 0622 682112)

GOACHER, Philip; s of Howard Leslie Goacher, of Donisthorpe, Leics, and Florence Emma Pratt (d 1987); *b* 12 March 1944; *Educ* Ashby Boys' GS, Leicester Sch of Architecture, Loughborough Coll of Art (BA); *m* 6 Sept 1975, Deborah Jane, *qv*, da of Dereck Raymond Light, of East Farleigh, Kent; 1 s (William b 1980), 1 da (Sophia b 1978); *Career* design and devpt engr KEF Electronics 1970-73, tech advsr and publicity & advertising mangr Shure Electronics 1973-83, ptnr and brewery owner 1983-; *Recreations* beer, bicycles, bell ringing; *Style*— Philip Goacher, Esq; 5 Hayle Mill Cottages, Bockingford, Maidstone, Kent ME15 6DT; The Bockingford Brewery, Hayle Mill, Maidstone, Kent (☎ 0622 682112)

GODMAN, Arthur; s of Arthur Andrew Godman (d 1958), of London, and Mary Adeline Newman (d 1946); *b* 10 Oct 1916; *Educ* Univ Coll London (BSc), Inst of Educn (Dip Ed); *m* 24 June 1950, Jean Barr, da of James Morton, OBE (d 1973), of Scotland; 2 s (Ian b 1951, Brian b 1953), 1 da (Diana b 1953); *Career* WWII Capt RA 1939: served France, India, Malaya (POW Far E 1946); colonial civil serv educn dept Malaya, Hong Kong, princ asst sec Miny of Educn Malaysia 1946-63; author 1963-; educn conslt Longman Gp 1966-77; hon fell Eliot Coll Univ of Kent 1978-, res fell dept of SE Asian studies Univ of Kent, memb Canterbury Rotary Club 1980-; CChem, MRSC, FRAS; *Books* Dictionary of Scientific Usage (with E M F Payne, 1979), Illustrated Science Dictionary (1981), Illustrated Dictionary of Chemistry (1981), Cambridge Illustrated Thesaurus of Computer Science (1984), Health Science for the Tropics (1962), Chemistry: A New Certificate Approach (with S T Bajah, 1969), Human and Social Biology (1973), Energy Supply (1990); *Recreations* bridge, reading, oriental languages; *Clubs* Royal Overseas League; *Style*— Arthur Godman, Esq; Sondes House, Patrixbourne, Canterbury, Kent CT4 5DD (☎ 0227 830 322); Room L47, Gliot College, Univ of Kent, Canterbury, Kent

GOFF, Nicholette Linda; da of Fred Wood, of Gillingham, Kent, and Jean Patricia, *née* Mulley; *b* 29 March 1949; *Educ* Maidstone Coll of Art (BA), Birkbeck Coll London (Dip A&CE); *m* 1 s (Andrew Spencer b 1975), 1 da (Alison b 1971); *Career* artist; co-ordinator Medway Galleries Group 1986-87, Maidstone Library Gallery 1987-88; Gillingham Adult Educn Centre: tutor, arts and crafts co-ordinator Space Frame Gallery and Arts Educn Prog 1988-, exhibiting artist and artist in residence; exhibition organiser: Women Sculptors (Maidstone) 1989, Women's Creative Roles (Gillingham) 1990; memb: NATFHE, Nat Artists Assoc, Women Artists' Slide Library, West End Studios Group Chatham, SE Arts' Register of Artists; *Style*— Ms Nicholette Goff; 58 Mill Rd, Gillingham, Kent ME7 1HW (☎ 0634 576260); Gillingham Adult Education Centre, Green St, Gillingham, Kent ME7 1XA (☎ 0634 50235)

GOGGIN, Dr Michael James; s of Dr Lawrence James Goggin (d 1953), of Doncaster, and Jean MacLeod, BEM, *née* Hogg (d 1987); *b* 9 April 1934; *Educ* Mount St Marys Coll, St Mary's Hosp Univ of London (MB BS, LRCP, MRCS, MRCP); *m* 10 Sept 1960 (m dis 1977), Jean Anne, da of Stanley Gordon Nash, of Workingham, Berkshire; 2 s (Anthony James b 1963, Paul Lawrence b 1965), 1 da (Julia Elizabeth (Mrs Kennett) b 1961); *Career* conslt physician and dir of renal dept Kent and Canterbury Hosp 1971-; FRCP 1983; *Recreations* photography, tennis, travel; *Style*— Dr Michael Goggin; 32 Dover St, Canterbury, Kent CT1 3HQ (☎ 0227 454335); Kent and Canterbury Hospital, Canterbury, Kent CT1 3NG (☎ 0227 766877 ext 4102)

GOLDMAN, Dr Kenneth Peter; s of Frank Goldman (d 1985), and Lily, *née* Cope; *b* 18 Jan 1928; *Educ* St Paul's, Peterhouse Cambridge (MB, BChir, MD); *m* 8 April 1960, Lorna Vera, da of Henry Stone (d 1983); 2 s (Richard James b 29 Nov 1963, Robert Alexander b 29 Nov 1968), 1 da (Helen Georgina b 15 Oct 1965); *Career* conslt physician Dartford and Gravesham Health Authy 1969-, ed jl Tubercle 1978-90, author numerous articles on tuberculosis; memb: Int Union Against Tuberculosis and Lung Disease, Br Thoracic Soc, BMA; FRCP; *Books* The Chest in Health and Disease (1970); *Recreations* gardening, snooker, walking the dog; *Style*— Dr Kenneth Goldman; 8 Coates Hill Rd, Bickley, Kent BR1 2BJ (☎ 081 467 0257); Chest Clinic, West Hill Hospital, Dartford, Kent DA1 2HF (☎ 0322 223223)

GOLLINGS, Raymond Dennis; s of George Robert Gollings (d 1985), and Renee Mary, *née* Greaves; *b* 5 June 1943; *Educ* Bexleyheath Sch for Boys; *m* 4 Oct 1975, Anne Elizabeth, da of Raymond Lavallan Nugent, JP, of Knockbarragh Park, Rostrevor, Co Down, NI; *Career* dir Hill Samuel Securities Ltd 1983-85, Hill Samuel Bank Ltd 1985-, Hill Samuel International Banking Corporation NY 1986-; Freeman City of London; *Recreations* golf, photography, music; *Clubs* North Down Golf; *Style*— Raymond Gollings, Esq; 36 Pickhurst Park, Bromley, Kent (☎ 081 460 8753); Hill Samuel Bank Ltd, 100 Wood St, London (☎ 071 606 1422, fax 071 606 8175, telex 888471)

GOLLOP, Ralph Ian Hamilton; s of Capt Ralph Cecil Tilly Gollop (d 1948), of St Dogmaels, and Victoria Mary Gollop; *b* 9 Nov 1935; *Educ* Llandovery Coll, St Peter's Oxford (MA, DipEd); *Career* asst schoolmaster: Angusfield House Edinburgh 1958-59, Bradford GS 1959-66; housemaster King's Canterbury 1974-80 (asst schoolmaster 1966-80), headmaster St Lawrence Coll Jr Sch 1980-; active memb Canterbury Cancer Res Ctee and other charities, hon lay reader St Thomas Church St Dogmaels Cardigan; *Recreations* sport, rugby, football, walking, sea fishing, Greece, skiing; *Clubs* Cardigan RFC, Bradford GS RFC, King's Canterbury RFC, St Lawrence Coll RFC; *Style*— R I Gollop, Esq; The Junior School, St Lawrence College, Ramsgate, Kent CT11 7AF (☎ 0843 583570); Sherwood House, St Dogmaels, Cardigan, Dyfed SA43 3LF (☎ 0239 612576)

GOMM, Douglas Rubert; s of Horace Gomm (d 1962), of Canterbury, and Gladys Carden Elizabeth, *née* Weeks; *b* 12 Jan 1937; *Educ* Simon Langton GS For Boys; *m* 22 Dec 1973, Sheila, da of Victor George Arthur Coombes; 2 s (Dominic b 1975, Russell b 1980); *Career* Nat Serv 1955-57, RAPC attached to 1 Bn KOSB; sr accountant McCabe Ford & Williams; cnclr Canterbury City Cncl 1983-, Sheriff of Canterbury 1987-88, govr Briary Co Primary Sch Herne Bay, tstee Herne Parochial Charities, hon life memb and vice pres Canterbury and Dist Table Tennis Assoc (past chm); FFA 1975; *Style*— Douglas Gomm, Esq; Hawthorns, 89A Greenhill Rd, Herne Bay, Kent CT6 7QW (☎ 0227 372 091); McCabe Ford & Williams, 41/43 William St, Herne Bay, Kent (☎ 0227 373 271)

GOODHART, Margaret, Lady; (Margaret Mary) Eileen; da of late Morgan Morgan, of Cray, Powys; *m* 19 Feb 1944, Sir John Gordon Goodhart, 3 Bt (d 1979); 1 s (Sir Robert), 1 da (Mrs John Soul b 1945); *Style*— Eileen, Lady Goodhart; Holtye, 17 Mavelstone Close, Bromley

GOODLIFFE, Brian Wilfred; s of (Wilfred) George Goodliffe (d 1984), of Streatham; *b* 3 Aug 1933; *Educ* Charterhouse; *m* 22 July 1961, Cynthia Katharine, da of Hwfa Hunnard (d 1963), of Dulwich; 2 s (Nicholas George Hunnard b 1964, Robert Brian George b 1969), 1 da (Laura Jayne Hart b 1962); *Career* chm: Smarts Laundries Group 1963, Xylon Ltd 1987; dir: OCS Group Ltd 1971, John Churchills (Valuers) Ltd 1986; pres Textile Services

Assoc 1989-90, memb Glebe Housing Assoc Ctee West Wickham, Master Worshipful Co of Launderers 1978-79; *Recreations* music, history, golf; *Clubs* Livery; *Style*— Brian Goodliffe, Esq; 14 Malmains Way, Beckenham, Kent BR3 2SA (☎ 081 650 9659); OCS Group Ltd, 79 Limpsfield Rd, Sanderstead, Surrey CR2 9LB (☎ 081 651 3211, fax 081 651 4832)

GOODMAN, Richard Antony; s of Antony Marlow Goodman, of Totternhoe, Beds, and Florence, *née* Sowry; *b* 17 June 1952; *Educ* Dunstable GS, Selwyn Coll Cambridge (MA); *m* 14 April 1979, Julie, da of John Edwin Williams, of Chilham, Kent; 2 s (Thomas b 1982, William b 1986), 1 da (Charlotte b 1989); *Career* admitted slr 1976; ptnr Cameron Markby 1981-; memb Law Soc; *Recreations* music, garden, photography; *Style*— Richard Goodman, Esq

GOODSELL, Rev Patrick; s of Joseph Henry Goodsell (d 1988), and Ivy Goodwin, *née* Simmonds (d 1990); *b* 17 March 1932; *Educ* Lewes Co GS for Boys, RN Artificer Apprentices Trg Estabs, Lincoln Theol Coll, Open Univ (BA); *m* 8 Oct 1966, Dorothy, da of Alfred George Cozens, of Wye, Kent; 1 s (Christopher b 1967), 2 da (Ruth b 1969, Elizabeth b 1971); *Career* RN: electrical artificer 1952-60, chief electrical artificer 1960-62; curate: St Jude Thornton Health 1964-65, St John Croydon (i/c St George Waddon) 1965-70; vicar St Michael & All Angels Tenterden 1970-78; priest i/c: Sellindge with Monks' Horton and Stowting 1978-84, Lympne with West Hythe 1982-84; incumbent of United Benefice of Sellindge with Monks' Horton and Stowting and Lympne with West Hythe 1984-; memb Canterbury Diocesan Synod 1970-; govr: Sellindge Co Primary Sch, Stowting C of E (controlled) Primary Sch; area rep Church Computer Users Gp; *Recreations* study, computing, music; *Style*— The Rev Patrick Goodsell; The Vicarage, Harringe Lane, Sellindge, Ashford, Kent TN25 6HP (☎ 0303 813168)

GOODWIN, Graham Cyril; s of Cyril Harry John Goodwin (d 1965), of Lenham, Kent, and Caroline Annie, *née* Thacker; *b* 5 July 1950; *Educ* Norton Knatchbull Sch, Univ of Birmingham (BCom); *m* 24 Jan 1976, Janet, da of Herbert Charles Howes, of Rugby, Warwickshire; 2 s (Timothy Richard b 1982, Samuel John b 1985); *Career* mgmnt accountant Joy Manufacturing Corporation 1973-75, fin accountant Leo Burnet 1975-76, gp chief accountant Firmin Group 1976-86, fin dir and co sec Fullsize Group 1986-; ACIS, ACEA; *Recreations* gardening, food and wine, renovating old buildings; *Clubs* East India; *Style*— Graham Goodwin, Esq; The Old Barn, Rocks Hill, Frittenden, Cranbrook, Kent TN17 2BL; Fullsize Group, Quarry Wood Industrial Estate, Aylesford, Kent ME20 7NF (☎ 0622 717376, fax 0622 882027)

GORDON BOYD, Sally Elizabeth; da of late Stanley Horton, and late Dorothy, *née* Blake; *b* 16 Oct 1933; *Educ* Wycombe Abbey, Univ of London (Dip); *m* 27 Feb 1954, Douglas Gordon Boyd, s of Edwyn Gordon Boyd (d 1959); 3 s (Christopher b 1954, Malcolm b 1956, Graham b 1958); *Career* psychiatric social worker Dept Child Psychiatry Farnborough Hosp Kent 1965-75, sr social worker Queen Mary's Hosp Sidcup 1975-77; involved with Polio Rehabilitation Centre Jamaica 1955-56; memb: Catholic Marriage Advsy Cncl 1965-72, SE Kent CHC 1979-81, SE Kent DHA 1981-89; mangr St Augustine's Hosp 1983-, chm Info Conciliation Ctee Kent FPC (memb 1987-); FRSM; *Books* Report of Seminar on FPC Complaints Procedures (ed, 1989); *Recreations* tennis, classical music; *Style*— Mrs Sally Gordon Boyd; Sackville House, 53 New St, Sandwich, Kent CT13 9BB (☎ 0304 617272)

GOUGH, (Charles) Brandon; s of Charles Richard Gough (d 1957), and Mary Evaline, *née* Goff; *b* 8 Oct 1937; *Educ* Douai Sch, Jesus Coll Cambridge (MA); *m* 24 June 1961, Sarah, da of Maurice Evans Smith (d 1987); 1 s (Richard b 1962) 2 da (Lucy b 1964, Katherine b 1967); *Career* Nat Serv Army 1956-58; Coopers & Lybrand Deloitte (formerly Coopers & Lybrand, previously Cooper Bros and Co): joined 1964, ptnr 1968-83, sr ptnr 1983-90, chm and jt sr ptnr 1990-; memb Exec Ctee Coopers and Lybrand International 1982- (chm 1983), chm Coopers and Lybrand Europe 1989-; govt dir British Aerospace plc 1987-88; chm Auditing Practices Ctee CCAB 1981-84 (memb 1976-84); memb: Accounting Standards Review (Dearing) Ctee 1987-88, Fin Reporting Cncl 1990-; memb: Cambridge Univ Careers Serv Syndicate 1983-86, Cncl for Indust and Higher Educn 1985-; City Univ Business Sch: memb City Advsy Panel 1980- (chm 1986-), cncl memb 1986-, chm Fin Ctee 1988-; memb: Cncl of Lloyd's 1983-86 (Lloyd's Silver Medal 1986), Governing Cncl Business in the Community 1984-88, Mgmnt Cncl GB-Sasakawa Fndn 1985-, Cncl Business in the Community 1988- (memb nat enterprise team 1989-), CBI task force Vocational Educn and Trg 1989, CBI Educn aand Trg Affrs Ctee, UK Nat Ctee Japan-Euro Community Assoc 1989-, Cncl Fndn for Educn Business Ptnrships 1990-; tstee: Guildhall Sch Music and Drama Fndn, Common Purpose within our Cities 1989-; Freeman: City of London 1983, Worshipful Co of CAs 1983; FCA 1974 (memb Cncl 1981-84); *Recreations* music, gardening; *Style*— Brandon Gough, Esq; Long Barn, Weald, Sevenoaks, Kent TN14 6NH (☎ 0732 463714); Coopers and Lybrand, Plumtree Court, London EC4A 4HT (☎ 071 583 5000, fax 071 822 4652, telex 887470 answerback: 887470 COLYLN G)

GOUGH, Robert William (Bob); s of William Gough (d 1955), of Silecroft, Millom, Cumbria, and Gertrude, *née* Hilton (d 1970), of Lytham St Annes, Lancs; *b* 7 July 1935; *Educ* Kirkham GS, Blackpool Tech Coll (Banking Dip), Exec Mgmnt S Africa (Dip Business Mgmnt); *m* 19 Jan 1963, Jean Frances, da of Sir Stanley Matthews, CBE, of Stoke-on-Trent; 1 s (Matthew Robert b 1965), 2 da (Samantha Jean b 1966, Amanda Hilton b 1972); *Career* National Provincial Bank 1956-65 (incl lectr in banking law Blackpool Tech Coll); sales exec: National Cash Register Co 1965-70, ICL (S Africa) 1970-76; exec Hill Samuel Investment Services 1984-89, fin ptnr Jean Frances Bodycare 1987-; vice chm Whitstable Branch Cons Pty, memb Kent CC Whitstable E, pres Dial Kent (disabled information and advice line), govr St Alphege Sch; *Recreations* philately, tennis, walking, interest in all sport; *Clubs* LTA, Wanderers (Johannesburg SA); *Style*— Bob Gough, Esq; Bryanston, 7 Marine Parade, Tankerton, Whitstable, Kent CT5 2BQ (☎ 0227 277315)

GOULDING, Lesley Anne; da of John Derek Sheasby, and Kathleen Maud, *née* Dawts; *b* 17 Jan 1940; *Educ* Devizes GS, Whitley Bay GS, Eastbourne HS, Rosebery GS, Univ of Nottingham, Univ of London (BSc, MSc, PGCE); *m* 21 July 1962, Graham Goulding, s of Samuel Goulding, of Ipswich (d 1953); *Career* physics teacher; former head of physics, Dukinfield Astley GS, head of sci and dep headmistress Cobham Hall Kent 1968-74, headmistress Chatham GS for Girls 1975-; *Recreations* sailing; *Clubs* Medway Yacht, Upnor Sailing; *Style*— Mrs Lesley Goulding; Chatham Grammar School For Girls, Rainham Rd, Chatham, Kent ME5 7EH (☎ 0634 51262)

GOURLEY, Alan Stenhouse; s of Archibald Gourley, and Elizabeth Paterson, *née* Ednie; *b* 13 April 1909; *Educ* Glasgow Acad, DA Edinburgh; *Career* artist: head of design Johnnesburg Tech Coll, designed and executed stained glass windows at Johannesburg and Pretoria Cathedral, elected memb RIOP 1965 (pres 1978-82), has works in Port Elizabeth, Luxemburg and RA galleries; John Laing painting prize 1985; *Style*— Alan Stenhouse Gourley

GOWER-SMITH, (Nicholas) Mark; s of Charles Samuel Smith (d 1983), of Tunbridge Wells, and Margaret Brenda, *née* Isaac; *b* 20 March 1955; *Educ* The Skinners' Sch Tunbridge Wells; *m* 25 July 1987, Christine Lorraine, da of Leslie Frank George Allan, (d 1981); 1 s (Charles b 1989); *Career* CA; sr ptnr Norman Cox & Ashby 1984-, proprietor Gower-Smith & Co 1984-; ACA 1981; *Recreations* music, photography, philately; *Clubs* Royal Cwlth Soc; *Style*— Mark Gower-Smith, Esq; Grosvenor Lodge, 72 Grosvenor Rd, Tunbridge Wells, Kent TN1 2AZ (☎ 0892 22551)

GRACE, Oliver Jeff; MBE (1946), TD (1946), DL (1976); s of Hugh Douglas Charles Grace (d 1952), and Frederica Mary, *née* Jelf (d 1958); *b* 20 May 1909; *Educ* Marlborough, Clare Coll Cambridge; *m* 1 May 1937, Marjorie Foster, *née* Bowman; 1 s (John Grace b 1948), 2 da (Alethea Grint b 1940, Caroline Seear b 1946); *Career* gazetted into TA 91 Field Regt RA (5 Inf Div); served: Dunkirk 1940, Home Forces 1941-43, India, Persia, Palestine 1942-43, invasion of Sicily and Italy 1943-44, Staff Coll Haifa 1944; rejoined 5 Div DAQMC Belgium and Germany 1945; memb Stock Exchange 1933-39 and 1942-74; ptnr Robinson & Glyn (latterly Raphael Robinson & Glyn); dir La Providence French Protestant Hosp Rochester 1957-, tstee Huggins Coll Northfleet 1960- (chm tstees 1964-69), chm Dioscesan Bd of Fin Rochester Diocese 1969-81, memb Chief Band of Brothers CC 1974-82, pres Kent CCC 1976 (hon treas 1970-76); *Clubs* MCC, Hawks (Cambridge); *Style*— Oliver Grace, Esq, MBE, TD, DL; Pilgrims Way, Hollingbourne, Maidstone, Kent ME17 1UT (☎ 0622 880242)

GRACEY, Richard Malcolm Kirkwood; s of Lt Col HMK Gracey (d 1967), of Hilden Grange, Tonbridge, and Margaret Elizabeth, *née* Allen (d 1953); *b* 6 Nov 1936; *m* 31 Aug 1961, Sarah Gray da of John Desmond Cullen (d 1976), of Hildenborough, Kent; 1 s (Patrick Richard Kirkwood b 1963), 1 da (Katharine Jane Gray b 1965); *Career* headmaster Hilden Grange Prep Sch 1961-; amateur rackets doubles champion 1964-65 and 1973-75, Noel-Bruce champion 1957-60 and 1970-76, Masters Champion 1985, Pres Yellowhammers CC 1985-, memb Cricketer Cup winning team on five occasions with Old Tonbridgeians; memb IAPS; *Recreations* cricket, rackets; *Clubs* MCC, FF, Yellowhammers; *Style*— Richard Gracey, Esq; Clock House, Hamptons, Nr Tonbridge, Kent TN11 9SR (☎ 0732 810768); Hilden Grange School, Tonbridge, Kent TN10 3BX (☎ 0732 352706)

GRAHAM, Stuart Twentyman; CBE (1981), DFC (1943); s of Twentyman Graham (d 1923); *b* 26 Aug 1921; *Educ* Kilburn GS; *m* 1948, Betty June, *née* Cox; 1 s (Neil); *Career* Sqdn Ldr RAF 1940-46; Midland Bank Ltd 1938-1982: joined 1938, jt gen mangr 1966-70, asst chief gen mangr 1970-74, chief gen mangr 1974-81, dir 1974-85, gp chief exec 1981-82; dir: Allied-Lyons plc 1981, Sheffield Forgemasters Holdings plc 1983-85, Efamol Holdings plc 1985-; chm: Northern Bank Ltd (head office Belfast) 1982-85, International Commodities Clearing House Ltd 1982-86; *Recreations* music, reading, photography; *Clubs* St James's, RAF; *Style*— Stuart Graham, Esq, CBE, DFC

GRAINGER, (Leonard) Cherry; s of George Grainger (d 1936), and Lucy, *née* Cherry (d 1974); *b* 12 March 1919; *Educ* Westminster Catering Coll (Dip), Ecole Des Hoteliers Zurich; *m* 17 June 1944, (Yvonne) Claudia Marshall, da of Victor Stanley Chambers, OBE (d 1954); 1 s (Lt Cdr Robert Marshall b 1955), 2 da (Lynne b 1945, Jacki b 1947); *Career* RN: Fleet Air Arm 1940-42, Paymaster 1942-46; fndr and chm Graison (Caterers) Ltd 1946-; Chevalier Du Tastevin 1964; chm: London Ctee Catering Trades Benevolent Assoc, tstees Reunion Des Gastronomes (former pres); memb: Ctee Br Hotels and Restaurants Assoc, Mgmnt Ctee City & Guilds; govr

Westminster Coll 1981-; Freeman City of London 1964, Liveryman Worshipful Co of Distillers 1964-, Master Worshipful Co of Cooks 1988-89; FCA, FHCIMA, FRSH; *Recreations* swimming, travel; *Clubs* City Livery, RAC; *Style*— Cherry Grainger, Esq; 102 Hayes Way, Beckenham, Kent BR3 2RS (☎ 081 650 4727, 081 650 4727); Casa 22, Puebla Blanca, Torreblanca, Malaga, Spain

GRAINGER, Frederick George Edward (Stewart); s of Frederick Thomas Grainger (d 1978), of Ashcott, Somerset, and Alice Mary, *née* Syrett; *b* 23 June 1936; *Educ* Dr Mogan's Sch Bridgwater, RMA Sandhurst, Medway Coll of Technol (Dip Civil Engrg), Open Univ (BA), RMCS Shrivenham, RAF Staff Coll, NDC; *m* 31 Oct 1959, Shirley Dorothy, da of Harold Pole (d 1965), of Bridgwater, Somerset; 2 s (Ian Anthony b 10 April 1968, Peter Edward b 8 Feb 1971), 1 da (Karen Shirley b 1 Aug 1965); *Career* paratrooper 1959-62, army pilot 1965-68, jr exec estab Directorate of Army Air Corps 1970-72, offr i/c 60 Field Sqdn 1972-73, CO 72 Engr Regt (Vol) 1976-78, mil advsr to Chief Scientist of the Army 1979-80, sr mil advsr to dir RAE Farnborough 1983, CRE 1 Armd Div 1983-86, Col Doctrine and Weapons RE 1986-89; barrier systems mangr Royal Ordnance plc; chm Army Canoe Union 1975-83 (sec 1970-72); FBIM 1980, AMRAeS 1983; *Recreations* canoeing, skiing; *Clubs* Civil Service, Royal Aeronautical Soc; *Style*— Stewart Grainger, Esq; 24 Studley Crescent, New Barn, Longfield, Kent DA3 7JL; Royal Ordnance plc, Blackburn, Lancashire BB1 2LE (☎ 0254 55131 ext 4996)

GRANT, John Douglas; *b* 16 Oct 1932; *Educ* Stationers' Company's Sch Hornsey; *m* 1955, Patricia Julia Ann; 2 s, 1 da; *Career* journalist, author, conslt; reporter Daily Express 1955-70 (chief industl corr 1967-70); parly candidate (L) Beckenham 1966, MP (L) Islington East 1970-74 (Islington Central 1974-83, (L) to Nov 1981, SDP to 1983); chm Lab and Industl Correspondents' Gp 1967, oppn front bench spokesman Bdcasting and Press Policy 1974, parly sec CSD 1974; parly under-sec state: Overseas Devpt Miny 1974-76, DOE 1976-79; oppn (L) front bench spokesman employment 1979-81, SDP employment and indust spokesman 1982-83, parly advsr to First Div Assoc (a sr civil servants' trade union) 1982-83; head of Communication Electrical Electronic Telecommunication Union 1984-89; memb Radio Authy 1990-; tstee Fedn for Industl Understanding, dir Social Market Fndn; *Style*— John Grant, Esq; Branscombe, Upper St, Kingsdown, nr Deal, Kent CT14 8BJ (☎ 0304 363991)

GRANTLEY-SMITH, (Arthur) Brian; s of Dr Grantley-Smith, of Weston Super Mare, and Millicent Lillian, *née* Pounsford; *b* 19 Oct 1924; *Educ* Watford GS, St Dunstans Coll, Guy's Hosp (LDS); *m* 6 March 1954, Gyllian Ester, da of George Harold Marks (d 1979), of Hythe, Kent; 1 s (Martin), 1 da (Lynn); *Career* RA 1943, surveyer 4 Survey Regt RA 1944; dental surgn; assoc 1953-59, princ 1959-65, sr ptnr 1965-86, assoc 1986-; memb: Local Dental Ctee for Kent (former chm), Kent Dental Advsy Ctee; former chm Planning Sub Ctee Kennington Community Cncl; RCS; *Recreations* boating, travel; *Clubs* Highland Fieldcraft Trg Centre Assoc; *Style*— Brian Grantley-Smith, Esq; 18 Church St, Wye, Kent TN25 5BS (☎ 0233 812717); Leafield, Church Rd, Ashford (☎ 0233 620565)

GRAVELL, David William; s of Canon William James Gravell (d 1968); *b* 9 June 1925; *Educ* Marlborough, Trinity Coll Cambridge; *m* 1955, Cecil Katharine, *née* Eastwood; 3 s, 1 da; *Career* shipbroker; chm: Exec Ctee Br Philippine Soc 1966-67, Killick Martin & Co (dir 1954-89) 1975-89, St Olave's Hart St Patronage Tst 1980-89, London C of C SE Asia Ctee 1982-85; pres Malaysia Singapore and Brunei Assoc 1987-89; memb Br Waterways Bd 1980-83; *Recreations* watching cricket, listening to music, seeing the world; *Clubs* MCC, IOD; *Style*— David Gravell, Esq; Great Barnetts, Leigh, Kent

GRAY, Harold James; CMG (1956); s of John William Gray (d 1930), and Amelia Francis, *née* Miller (d 1961); *b* 17 Oct 1907; *Educ* Dover Co Sch, Univ of London (BSc, MSc, LLB), Gray's Inn, Harvard Univ USA (MPA); *m* 1928, Katherine, da of Sydney George Starling (d 1956); 1 da (Ann); *Career* civil servant 1927-61, examiner Patent Office 1935-39, asst sec Miny of Supply 1939, Cwlth Fund Fellowship 1949-50; under sec BOT 1954, UK sr trade cmmr; econ advsr to: UK High Cmmr Aust 1954-58, S Africa 1958-60; dir: Nat Union of Mfrs 1961-65, CBI 1965-72, chm Numas Management Services Ltd 1970-74 (dir 1961-70); author of various booklets on small firms in UK 1965-72; CPhys, MInstP, FRSA; *Books* Electricity in Service of Man (1949), Economic Survey of Australia (1955), Dictionary of Physics (1956), New Dictionary of Physics (1975); *Recreations* horse riding, swimming, golf; *Style*— Harold Gray, Esq, CMG; Copper Beeches, 58 Tudor Ave, Maidstone, Kent ME14 5HJ (☎ 0672 685978)

GRAY, John Montgomery; s of Dr John Montgomery Gray (d 1984), and Margaret Elizabeth, *née* Welsh (d 1986); *b* 17 Oct 1938; *Educ* Tonbridge, BNC Oxford (BA juris); *m* 2 Sept 1972, Susan Caroline, da of Maj Humphrey Pares, TD; 1 s (Jonathon b 13 March 1974), 2 da (Theresa b 20 May 1976, Anna b 11 May 1978); *Career* called to the Bar Inner Temple 1962, Inner Temple Major Scholar 1962-65, rec 1986; *Recreations* gardening, cabinet making; *Style*— John Gray, Esq; 1 Crown Office Row, Temple, London EC4Y 7HH (☎ 071 583 9292)

GRAYSON, Sir Rupert Stanley Harrington; 4 Bt (UK 1922); s of late Sir Henry Grayson, 1 Bt, KBE (d 1951); suc n Sir Ronald Henry Rudyard Grayson, 3 Bt (d 1987); unc of Lord Rawlinson of Ewell, QC and the Earl of Munster; *b* 22 July 1897; *Educ* Harrow; *m* 1, 1919, Ruby Victoria, da of Walter Henry Banks; m 2, 1950, Vari Colette, da of Maj Henry O' Shea, Royal Dublin Fus, of Cork; *Heir* n, Jeremy Brian Vincent Grayson b 1933; *Career* Ensign in Irish Gds (twice wounded) 1914-18, King's Foreign Serv Messenger 1939-45; novelist, constant traveller; kt of Order of Holy Sepulchre; *Books autobiographies* Voyage Not Completed, Stand Fast The Holy Ghost, *fiction* 26 Gun Cotton, Secret Service Adventures; *Style*— Sir Rupert Grayson, Bt; c/o Midland Bank, Hythe, Kent

GREEN, Dr Donald James (Don); s of Dr Peter Ford Green, of Samburu Cottage, Russell's Green, nr Ninfield, E Sussex, and Hope Mary, *née* Green; *b* 21 Nov 1953; *Educ* Prince of Wales Sch Nairobi Kenya, King Edwards Sch Witley Surrey, Charing Cross Hosp Med Sch (MB BS); *m* 20 May 1978, (Elizabeth) Frances, da of Micheal Handley Grace, of Fairlight, Colt Hill, Odiham, Hants; 1 s (Timothy b 6 Nov 1981), 1 da (Rachael b 21 March 1979); *Career* jr hosp and GP trg Isle of Wight Hosps and Brading Health Centre 1979-83, princ and ptnr in gen practice Tunbridge Wells 1983-; treas and deacon Calvary Free Church Tunbridge Wells; memb BMA 1979-; *Recreations* sailing, photography, motorcaravanning; *Clubs* Bewl Valley Sailing, Caravan; *Style*— Dr Don Green; Bethu-El, 32B Queen's Rd, Tunbridge Wells, Kent (☎ 0892 29481); Grosvenor Lodge Surgery, 72 Grosvenor Rd, Tunbridge Wells (☎ 0892 541634)

GREEN, Dr Frank Alan; s of Frank Green (d 1943), and Winifred Hilda, *née* Payne; *b* 29 Oct 1931; *Educ* Mercers Sch, Univ of London (BSc, PhD); *m* 30 March 1957, Pauline Eleanor, da of George Edward Tayler (d 1980); 1 s (Paul b 19 July 1963), 2 da (Gail b 17 April 1958, Sally b 18 Sept 1960); *Career* md AE Group subsid 1962-66, tech advsr Consormex SA Mexico City 1966-68, mfrg dir Stewart Warner Corp 1968-72, dir market devpt Calor Group 1972-74, md British Twin Disc Ltd (dir Twin Disc International SA) 1974-80, industl advsr (under sec) DTI 1981-84; currently: md Charing Green Ltd, sr conslt Centre for Consultancy Ltd, dir General Technology Systems (Scandinavia), dir Gen Technol Systems (Portugal); advsr to Mexican Govt on mfrg 1966-68, dep chm Newcastle Technol Centre 1983; memb: Kent CBI Ctee and CBI SE Regnl Ctee 1974-80, Professional Bd Inst of Metals 1986- (chm Gen Educn Ctee 1986-88, chm Initial Formation Ctee 1988-, memb Cncl 1990-); currently involved in Understanding Indust Initiative; Freeman City of London 1953; CEng, FIM, FBIM; *Recreations* wine, photography, hill walking, military and local history; *Clubs* Old Mercers; *Style*— Dr Frank Green; Courtwood House, Burleigh Rd, Charing, Kent TN27 0JB (☎ 023 371 3152); Centre for Consultancy Ltd, Boxley Rd, Maidstone, Kent ME14 3DN (☎ 0622 692919, fax 0622 692920)

GREEN, Helen Janet; da of William Ernest Green, and Edna Winifred, *née* Thompson; *b* 24 Feb 1942; *Educ* Haberdashers' Aske's, Architectural Assoc, Univ of London (Dip Arch, Dip Restoration and Conservation of Historic Bldgs); *Career* Hist Bldgs Div GLC 1968-70, project architect Kent CC 1970-73, princ architect PPI Consultant 1973-76, Property Servs Agency Dept of the Environment 1977-; memb: Mid-Kent Branch RIBA, Tunbridge Wells Branch RIBA (Planning Ctee 1973-74); memb: Architectural Assoc 1960-, RIBA 1968-, ARCUK (registered architect) 1968-, SPAB 1969-, ASCHB 1970-; fell ASI 1979-, RIBA SE Regnl Rep Woman of Kent 1980 and 1986; *Recreations* country pursuits, photography, reading, driving, Kentish buildings research; *Style*— Miss H J Green

GREEN, Rev John Herbert Gardner-Waterman; s of George Herbert Green, of Lympne, nr Hythe, Kent (d 1938), and Hilda Benedicta, *née* Gardner-Waterman (d 1954); *b* 17 Oct 1921; *Educ* St Lawrence Coll Ramsgate, Trinity Hall Cambridge (MA); *m* 31 Aug 1955, Angela, da of John Stewart Caulton, of Lincoln (d 1976); 1 s (Simon b 12 Oct 1959), 1 da (Penelope b 17 June 1961); *Career* Intelligence Corps 1941-46, cmmnd Lt 21 Army Gp HQ Brussels 1944, Capt Int Staff 1 Br Corps 1945-46; asst master St Lawrence Coll 1950-58, parish priest (ordained 1959), asst curate New Romney with Ivychurch and Old Romney 1959-63, vicar of Hartlip 1963-68, rector of Sandhurst with Newenden 1968-1990, rural dean of West Charing 1974-81; vice chm Romney Marsh Historic Churches Tst, memb Univ of Cambridge Hockey Club 1947-49 (capt 1948-49); *Books* A Book Of Hockey For Schools (jt ed, 1955), From A Country Rectory Window (1990); *Recreations* hockey, cricket, music, the countryside; *Style*— The Rev John Green; Littlefield House, Rolvenden Layne, Cranbrook, Kent TN17 4NS (☎ 0580 241579)

GREEN, Cncllr Michael Douglas; TD (1955); s of Douglas Harold Green (d 1963), and Maud, *née* Feely (d 1927); *b* 3 Jan 1920; *Educ* Bishops Stortford Coll, Imperial Coll London; *m* 8 Sept 1950, Christelle, da of Leonard Forcey; 2 s (Jonathan Michael b 1951, Andrew David b 1954); *Career* WWII, 1 TBRE 1940-41, cmmnd 2 Lt RE OCTU 1941, Lt RE 1942, Adjt RE 1 Airborne Div 1943; served: N Africa, Sicily, Italy, Norway, Arnhem; 131 Airborne Engr Regt TA, Co Cdr 302 Airborne Park Sqdn RE 1946-55; American Bronze Star 1944; site engr Concrete Structures Ltd; Holland Harman Cubille Ltd: site engr, project mangr, southern area mangr; system design engr Marley Tile

Co; Medway Buildings Ltd: construction mangr, construction dir, tech dir; TRIAD Architects and Planners: res engr (Saudi Arabia), middle east mangr; dir and ptnr Saudi Engineering Group; pres Shoreham Kent Branch Royal British Legion 1979-, memb Sevenoaks Dist Cncl 1987-, chm Shoreham Cons Assoc; MICE, FFB; *Recreations* golf, sailing, gardening; *Clubs* Rock Sailing; *Style*— Cncllr Michael Green, TD; Eyot House, Shoreham, Kent TN14 7RY (☎ 09592 2801)

GREEN, Sam; CBE (1960); s of Fred Green (d 1951), and Alice Ann, *née* Wrigley (d 1950); *b* 6 Feb 1907; *Educ* Oldham Tech Coll (HNC), Manchester Coll of Technol; *m* 18 July 1942, Dr Lilly, da of Lugwig Pollak (d 1942); 1 da (Alison Anne b 18 March 1951); *Career* apprentice Platt Bros (electrical and mechanical engrs), British Northrop Automatic Loom Co 1934-39 (invented Box Motion Automatic Loom), chief engr Betts & Co London 1939-42, works mangr Morphy-Richards 1942-44, gen works mangr Horoplast Ltd 1944-47, indust advsr Industrial & Commercial Finance Corporation 1948-52, md Remploy Ltd 1952-65, chm and md Ralli Bros Industries Ltd 1965-70, chm (govt appt) Dula UK Ltd 1969-, chm and chief exec Spears Bros Ltd 1970-; non exec dir: Grampion Lighting Co Ltd 1966-69, J E Lesser Co Ltd 1969-74, New Day Holdings Ltd 1966-69; lectr Workingmens Coll Crowndale Rd Kings Cross 1949-51, chm and vice pres Inst of Patentees and Inventors 1952-, vice pres Int Fedn of Inventors Assocs 1968-, memb Industl Advsrs to the Blind 1965-72; Royal Br Legion 1965-: memb Benevolent Ctee, dir and vice chm Poppy Factory; dir of industs Maidstone Kent; CEng, FIEE, FIProdE, Fell IOD; 1984 Gold Medal for Services to Invention by WIPO UN; *Recreations* reading, gardening, walking, cycling; *Clubs* Reform, Pickwick Bicycle; *Style*— Sam Green, Esq, CBE; Holly Lodge, 39 Westmoreland Rd, Bromley, Kent BR2 0TF (☎ 01 460 3306); Spear Bros Ltd, 1 Southlands Rd, Bromley, Kent BR2 2QR (☎ 01 460 0039)

GREENAWAY, Sir Derek Burdick; 2 Bt (UK 1933), of Coombe, Surrey; CBE (1974), TD, JP (Kent 1962), DL (1973); s of Sir Percy Walter Greenaway, 1 Bt (d 1956); *b* 27 May 1910; *Educ* Marlborough; *m* 28 April 1937, Sheila Beatrice, o da of Richard Cyril Lockett (d 1950); 1 s, 1 da; *Heir* s, John Michael Burdick Greenaway, Lois Weedon House, Weedon Lois, Towcester, Northants; *Career* Hon Col 44 (HC) Signal Regt (Cinque Ports) (TA) 1966-67, Hon Col 36 (Eastern) Signal Regt (V) 1967-74; High Sheriff Kent 1971-72; life pres Daniel Greenaway & Son Ltd printers; jt Master Old Surrey and Burstow Fox Hounds 1958-66, pres Sevenoaks Div Cons Assoc 1963-66 (formerly chm), chm SE Area Nat Union of Cons Assocs 1975-79 (hon treas 1969-75); Liveryman Worshipful Co of Stationers and Newspaper Makers (Master 1974-75, Silver Medal 1984); *Recreations* hunting, shooting, fishing; *Clubs* Carlton, City of London, MCC; *Style*— Sir Derek Greenaway, Bt, CBE, TD, JP, DL; Dunmore, Four Elms, Edenbridge, Kent TN8 6NE (☎ 073 270 275)

GREENFIELD, Brian William; s of William Forrest Greenfield, of Bromley, and Lilian Violet, *née* Symmons; *b* 3 Aug 1938; *Educ* Wilsons GS London, Inns of Court Sch of Law; *m* 22 June 1962, Ann Madeline, da of Edmund Leon Watt (d 1980); 1 s (Paul Brian Justin b 1966), 1 da (Nichola Carolyne Ann b 1967); *Career* called to the Bar 1970; National Provident Institution: tech advsy servs mangr 1975-79, agency and advsy servs mangr 1979-86, internal legal advsr 1986-; pt/t teacher W Kent Coll 1977-; pres: Tunbridge Wells Insur Inst 1980-81 (educn sec 1972-80), Southborough Lions Club 1987-88, Lions Int Dist 105 SE Zone chm 1988-90 (dep dist govr 1990-); memb Advsy Cncl Nuffield Hosp Tunbridge Wells; ACII 1962; *Recreations* Lions' activities, teaching, occasional golf, garden, DIY; *Clubs* Southborough Lions; *Style*— Brian Greenfield, Esq; Brookbank, Valley Forge Close, Tonbridge, Kent TN10 4EU (☎ 0732 351536); National Provident Institution, Tunbridge Wells, Kent (☎ 0892 515151)

GREENWOOD, Ernest; s of Owen Charles Greenwood (d 1915), of Welling, Kent, and Annie Henrietta Greenwood (d 1965); *b* 12 Feb 1913; *Educ* Gravesend Sch of Art, RCA, Br Sch in Rome; *m* 30 Sept 1939, Eileen Constance, da of Harold Ernest Massenger (d 1961), of Worthing; 1 da (Dorelia Elaine Burrell b 1943); *Career* Nat Serv: RA NI 1940, Ripon 1941, FAEC served France, Belgium, Holland and Germany 1944, lectr Berlin 1944-46; head art and craft Bromley GS for Boys 1938, fndr and teacher Art Dept Chislehurst and Sidcup Tech High for Girls 1946-56; inspr art educn: ILEA County Hall Westminster 1956-71, Kent Educn Ctee Springfield 1971-76; artist; one man exhibitions incl: Kensington Art Gallery 1951-53, Royal Academy 1970, Turkey Court Maidstone 1978, Arizona USA 1987; pres RWS 1976-84 (assoc 1974), ARCA; *Books* The Kent Circulating Art Collection A Guide to its use in Education (in assoc with Kent Educn Ctee); *Style*— Ernest Greenwood, Esq; Brushings Farm House, Broad St, nr Hollingbourne, Kent

GREGOR, Prof Ian Copeland Smith; s of Teresa Copeland; *b* 20 Jan 1926; *Educ* Univ of Durham (BA, PhD) Wadham Coll Oxford; *Career* asst lectr Kings Coll London 1956-58, lectr Univ of Edinburgh 1958-65, sr lectr Univ of Kent 1965-69; memb Assoc of Univ Teachers; *Books* The Moral and Story (with Brian Nicholan, 1962), William Golding: a Critical Study (with Mark Kinkead-Weekes, 1967), Matthew Arnold Culture and Anarchy, The Great Web: the Form of Hardy's Major Fiction (1974), Reading the Victorian Novel: Detail into Form (1980); *Recreations* golf; *Style*— Prof Ian Gregor; 143 Old Dover Rd, Canterbury, Kent (☎ 0227 761098); Rutherford College, University of Kent, Canterbury, Kent (☎ 0227 764000)

GREGORY, Ronald I; s of Thomas Gregory (d 1984), of Port Talbot, S Wales, and Catherine Elizabeth, *née* Evans; *b* 7 Sept 1944; *Educ* Neath GS; *m* 25 April 1970, Christine, da of Stanley Lewis, of Port Talbot, S Wales; 1s (Jason b 1973), 1da (Sharon b 1971); *Career* commenced career in local govt 1964; posts in: Port Talbot, Southend on Sea, Wigan, Met Borough of Calderdale, City of Rochester upon Medway; chief exec City Cncl of Rochester upon Medway 1987- (city housing and environment mangr 1985); memb Soc of Local Authy Chief Execs; *Recreations* travel, good food and wine, swimming, sailing, Grand Prix racing, sport in general; *Style*— Ronald Gregory, Esq; 46 Mayford Rd, Lordswood, Chatham, Kent; City Council of Rochester upon Medway, Civic Centre, Strood, Rochester, Kent ME2 4AW

GRENIER, John Allan; s of Rev George Arthur Grenier; *b* 2 April 1933; *Educ* St John's Sch Leatherhead Surrey; *m* 1980, Valerie, da of James William Cocksey; 2 c; *Career* chm The HLT Group Ltd (Queen's Award for Export 1982); elected chm of British Mgmnt Trg Export Cncl 1985; FCA; *Recreations* off-shore cruising, water skiing; *Clubs* RAC, IOD; *Style*— John Grenier, Esq; The HLT Group Ltd, 200 Greyhound Road, London W14 9RY (☎ 071 385 3377, telex 266386 fax 071 381 3377); Plovers, Horsmonden, Kent

GRIBBON, Angus John St George; s of Maj-Gen Nigel St George Gribbon, OBE, of 99 Pump St, Orford, nr Woodbrige, Suffolk, and Rowan Mary, *née* McLeish; *b* 25 Dec 1951; *Educ* Rugby, New Coll Oxford (MA); *m* 15 May 1965, Mary-Anne, da of Hugh Wynwel Gamon, CBE, MC, of Black Charles Underriver, nr Sevenoaks, Kent; 1 s (Edward b 1981), 2 da (Mary-Clare b 1983, Caroline b 1985); *Career* Clifford-Turner Slrs 1974-79, slr Allied-Lyons plc 1979-89, legal advsr Securicor Group 1989-; *Recreations* sailing, skiing; *Style*— Angus Gribbon, Esq; Pedlam Brook, West Peckham, Maidstone, Kent ME18 5JS (☎ 0732 851732); Securicor Group plc, Sutton Park House, 15 Carshalton Rd, Sutton, Surrey SM1 4LE (☎ 081 770 7000, fax 081 643 1059, telex 8814827)

GRIFFITHS, His Hon Judge David John; s of John Griffiths (d 1936), and Anne Virgo, formerly Griffiths, *née* Jones (d 1967); *b* 18 Feb 1931; *Educ* St Dunstan's Coll Catford; *m* 1, 1959, da of Charles Gosling (d 1963); 3 s (John Richard b 26 June 1961, Huw David b 12 Nov 1963, Bryn Lloyd b 20 July 1965), 1 da (Jane Alison b 23 March 1960); m 2, July 1972, Anita, da of William John Williams (d 1967), of Trimsaram; *Career* RTR 5 Bn BAOR 1949-51, TA City of London Yeo 1951-56; admitted slr 1957; own practice Bromley Kent 1961, NP 1969, acquired Harveys of Lewisham practice 1970, rec 1980, circuit bench 1984; hon slr Bromley Marriage Guidance Cncl 1969-83; pres: Gwalia Male Choir 1962-, Bromley Law Soc 1971-72, Bromley Rotary Club 1978-79, Kent Law Soc 1981-82, Old Duntonian Assoc 1988; memb ed ctee The Law Guardian 1978-71; chm: Nat Jusce Local Tbnls 1977, Bromley and Chislehurst Ctee Cancer Res Campaign 1979-85, Bromley Cncl of Voluntary Servs 1980-87; vice chm: Law Soc Legal Aid (area) Ctee 1983- (memb 1976-84), London Legal Aid Area Ctee 1983-84 (memb 1967); Freeman City of London 1982, Liveryman Worshipful Co of Scriveners; *Recreations* riding, music (male voice); *Style*— His Hon Judge David Griffiths; Crosswell, Fosten Green, Biddenden, Kent TN27 8ER (☎ 0580 291414); The Law Courts, Maidstone, Kent

GRIFFITHS, John Francis Philpin; s of James Maldwyn Griffiths, of Hayes, Bromley, Kent, and Joan, *née* Philpin; *b* 16 Sept 1948; *Educ* St Dunstan's Coll London, Clare Coll Cambridge (MA, DipArch); *m* 16 Sept 1972, Fiona Barbara, da of Lt-Cdr Hugh Desmond Campbell Gibson, of Kilmelford, Argyll, Scotland; 1 s (Leo b 27 July 1980), 1 da (Anna b 16 Jan 1977); *Career* architect; Scarlett Burkett Assoc (Scarlett Burkett Griffiths 1986-): joined 1972, assoc 1975, ptnr 1978; chm: London Reg of Assoc of Conslt Architects 1988-90, AA Part III Examination Bd 1989-; Freeman City of London 1987, Liveryman Worshipful Co of Arbitrators 1987; RIBA 1974, FCIArb 1986, ACA 1985, memb AA 1987; *Recreations* reading, railway memorabilia, woodworking; *Style*— John Griffiths, Esq; Lyndhurst, 98 Hayes Rd, Bromley, Kent BR2 9AB (☎ 081 460 6246); Scarlett Burkett Griffiths, 14 Clerkenwell Close, London EC1R 0PQ (☎ 071 490 5002, fax 071 490 2160)

GROOM, Prof Arthur John Richard; s of Richard George Pearmain Groom (d 1968), of Lincoln, and Edna, *née* Wheatley (d 1978); *b* 5 July 1938; *Educ* City Sch Lincoln, UCL (BSc), Lehigh (MA), Geneva (Dr és sc pol); *m* 17 April 1971, Antoinette Rosemarie, da of Max Robert Corti, of Winterthur, Switzerland; 2 da (Anna b 1976, Helen b 1980); *Career* lectr UCL 1965-77, prof of int rels Univ of Kent at Canterbury 1985- (reader 1978-85), dir Centre for the Analysis of Conflict 1970-; vice chm Br Int Studies Assoc 1987-; memb: Conflict Res Soc, Int Studies Assoc, Anglo-Hellenic League, Int Inst for Strategic Studies; *Books* The Management of Britain's External Relations (ed with R Boardman, 1973), Peacekeeping (1973), British Thinking About Nuclear Weapons (1974), The Study of World Society: A London Perspective (with J W Burton, A V S de Reuck and C R Mitchell, 1974), Functionalism: Theory and Practice in International Relations (ed with Paul Taylor, 1975), International Organisation: A Conceptual Approach (ed with Paul Taylor,

1978), International Relations Theory: A Critical Bibliography (ed with C R Mitchell, 1978), The Commonwealth in the 1980's (ed with Paul Taylor, 1984), Britain Between East and West: A Concerned Independence (with J W Burton, Margot Light, C R Mitchell and D J D Sandole, 1984), International Relations: A Handbook of Current Theory (ed with Margot Light, 1985), International Institutions at Work (ed with Paul Taylor, 1988), Global Issues and the United Nations (ed with Paul Taylor, 1989), Frameworks for International Co-operation (ed with Paul Taylor, 1990); *Recreations* opera, music, travel, wine and food; *Clubs* Royal Cwlth Soc; *Style*— Prof A J R Groom; 8 Cherry Ave, Canterbury, Kent CT2 8EN (☎ 0227 760609); Rutherford College, University of Kent, Canterbury, Kent CT2 7NX (☎ 0227 764000, fax 0227 459025)

GROUT, Noel Alfred Brian; s of Lt Noel Kenneth Grout (d 1964), and Violet Mary, *née* Jolleff; *b* 8 Aug 1927; *Educ* Culford Sch Bury St Edmunds; *m* 12 April 1958, Cynthia Audrey (Thea), da of Leonard Marks (d 1975); 1 s (Simon Kenneth b 1964); *Career* Nat Serv S Lancs Regt and RAOC, later HAC; press offr Western Union International, dir E K Monks Ltd 1963-72, chief exec Royal Masonic Benevolent Institute 1979- (asst sec 1972-78); Freeman: City of London 1979, Worshipful Co of Gold and Silver Wyre Drawers 1979; FBIM 1980; *Recreations* angling, bird watching, church architecture, walking; *Clubs* Royal Naval, Wig and Pen; *Style*— Noel A Grout, Esq; 61 Baston Rd, Hayes, Bromley, Kent BR2 7BS (☎ 081 462 3855); 20 Great Queen St, London WC2B 5BG (☎ 081 405 8341)

GROVES, Rev James Alan; s of William Groves, of Mitcham, Surrey, and Doris Charlotte, *née* Froud; *b* 25 Dec 1932; *Educ* Westminster, Corpus Christi Coll Cambridge, Wells Theol Coll (MA); *m* 28 Dec 1959, Rachel Loveday, da of George Henry Ivan (Jack) Bickford (d 1967), of Looe, Cornwall; 3 s (Peter b 1960, John b 1962, Andrew b 1967), 1 da (Catherine b 1965); *Career* vicar St Andrew Orpington 1966-, select preacher City of London Solicitors Co 1975, acting speakers chaplain 1988; memb Advsy Ctee for the Care of Churches Rochester Diocese 1976-, chaplain to St Mary Cray Sea Cadets, chm Gp Scouts Ctee, vice chm Bromley Econ Teenage Housing Project, memb Mgmnt Ctee Bromley Victim Support, jt chm Canterbury and Rochester Books and Documents Ctee; *Recreations* reading history, playing with toy soldiers; *Style*— The Rev James Groves; St Andrews Vicarage, Anglesea Rd, Orpington, Kent BR5 4AN (☎ 0689 23775)

GROVES, Rev Robert John; s of Ronald John Groves (d 1944), and Rosalind, *née* Knott; *b* 6 Oct 1942; *Educ* Dover GS for Boys, Trinity Coll Bristol (BCTS); *m* 13 March 1965, Mary Kathleen, da of Arthur Percy Manwaring (d 1984); 2 da (Joanna Mary b 10 March 1968, Nicola Jane b 30 September 1971); *Career* tax offr Inland Revenue Dover 1958-62, Northern Assurance Co Ltd 1962-68, supervisor Abbey Life Insurance Co Ltd 1968-71, mangr William Brandts (life and Pensions) Ltd 1971-74; anglican minister: St Luke West Norwood, All Saints Clapham Park, Christ Church Anerley; *Recreations* walking, reading, chess, visiting art galleries, museums and stately homes; *Style*— The Rev Robert Groves; The Vicarage, 234 Anerley Rd, Anerley, London SE20 8TJ (☎ 0817784800)

GRUGEON, Sir John Drury; (DL Kent 1986); s of Drury Grugeon (d 1969), of Westfield Lodge, Broadstairs; *b* 20 Sept 1928; *Educ* Epsom GS, RMA Sandhurst; *m* 1, 1955 (m dis 1986), Mary Patricia, da of Walter James Rickards (d 1957), of Hoath Farm, Canterbury; 1 s, 1 da; m 2, 28 July 1989, Lois, widow of Dr Roland Phillips; *Career* served The Buffs 1948-60, Capt, Regimental Adj (later Adj 5 Bn); served: Europe, ME, Far East; chm Kent CC 1989 (elected 1967, ldr 1973-81, vice chm 1987-89) chm Policy Ctee Assoc CCs 1978-80, vice chm Assoc of CCs 1980-82; memb: Medway Ports Authy 1977-, Consultative Cncl Local Govt Fin; exec mangr Save & Prosper Group Ltd (joined 1960); dir of Liverpool Int Garden Festival 1982-83, chm Tunbridge Wells Health Authy 1984-; kt 1980; *Recreations* shooting, cricket; *Clubs* Carlton, MCC, Kent CCC; *Style*— Sir John Grugeon, DL; 2 Shrublands Court, Sandrock Rd, Tunbridge Wells, Kent TW2 3PS (☎ 0892 31936)

GUILFORD, 9 Earl of (GB 1752); Edward Francis North; DL (Kent 1976); also Baron Guilford (E 1683); patron of three livings; s of Major Lord North (k in accident 1940, himself er s of 8 Earl of Guilford), and Joan, da of Sir Merrik Burrell, 7 Bt, CBE; suc gf, 8 Earl; *b* 22 Sept 1933; *Educ* Eton; *m* 1956, Osyth Vere Napier, da of Cyril Leeston Smith; 1 s; *Heir* s, Lord North; *Style*— The Rt Hon the Earl of Guilford, DL; Waldershare Park, Dover, Kent (☎ 0304 820244)

GULL, Prof Keith; s of David Gull, of Eston, Middlesbrough, and Doris Gull (d 1967); *b* 29 May 1948; *Educ* Eston GS, Univ of London (BSc, PhD); *m* 12 Aug 1972, Dianne Hilary Leonora, da of Frank Edward Elgar, of Manchester; 1 s (David b 22 April 1977), 1 da (Ruth b 27 March 1980); *Career* Univ of Kent: lectr 1972-82, sr lectr 1982-84, reader in cell biology 1984-86, prof 1986-; visiting sr scientist Sandoz Inst Vienna, visiting prof McArdle Laboratory for Cancer Res Univ of Wisconsin Madison USA, Darwin lectureship Br Assoc for the Advancement of Sci 1983; *Recreations* fly-fishing, painting, conversation; *Style*— Prof Keith Gull; 12 Manwood Ave, Canterbury, Kent CT2 7AF (☎ 0227 454224); Biologial Laboratory, University of Kent, Canterbury, Kent CT2 7NJ (☎ 0227 764000, fax 0227 459025)

GUNDRY, Michael Francis; s of Francis Gundry (d 1984), of Chichester, and Mary, *née* Hankins (d 1987); *b* 29 Nov 1939; *Educ* Douai Sch Woolhampton Berks, St Mary's Hosp Med Sch London (MB BS, DO, LRCP, MRCS); *m* 18 April 1968 (m dis 1990), Roxana Margaret, da of Donald Cook, JP (d 1989), of Dorking, Surrey; 2 s (Crispin b 1971, Toby b 1973), 1 da (Imogen b 1979); *Career* house surgn to Lord Porrit St Mary's Hosp 1964-65, sr house offr to Sir George Pinker, KCVO, St Mary's Hosp 1965-66, med offr Union Castle Shipping Line 1966-67, sr house offr in ophthalmology St Mary's Hosp 1967-68, registrar and sr registrar Moorfields Eye Hosp 1968-71, conslt ophthalmic surgn Maidstone Eye Hosp and Gravesend and North Kent Hospital 1971-; sec Rotary Club of Weald of Kent 1982-87; FRCS, Fell Coll Ophthalmology; *Recreations* golf, walking; *Clubs* Cranbrook Golf; *Style*— Michael Gundry, Esq; Kent County Ophthalmic Hospital, Church St, Maidstone, Kent ME14 1DT (☎ 0622 673444)

GUNN, Prof John Charles; s of Albert Charles Gunn, of Charlwood, Surrey, and Lily Hilda Gunn; *b* 6 June 1937; *Educ* Brighton, Hove and Sussex GS, Reigate GS, Univ of Birmingham (MB ChB, MD), Univ of London (DPM); *m* 1, 9 Sept 1959 (m dis 1987), Celia Ann Frances (d 1989), da of Harry Richard Willis, of Charlwood, Surrey; 1 s (Richard Charles b 10 March 1962), 1 da (Frances Margaret b 28 Sept 1964); m 2, 11 Nov 1989, Pamela Jane, da of Rev P Geoffrey Taylor, of Liverpool; *Career* house offr Queen Elizabeth Hosp Birmingham 1961-63, registrar Maudsley Hosp London 1963-67; Inst of Psychiatry: res worker and lectr 1967-71, sr lectr 1971-75, prof of forensic psychiatry 1978-; dir Special Hosps Res Unit 1975-78; memb Home Sec's Advsy Bd on Restricted Patients, advsr House of Commons Social Servs Ctee 1985-86 (Ctee on Violence in Marriages 1975); MRCPsych 1971, FRCPsych 1980; *Books* Violence in Human Society (1973), Epileptics in Prison (1977), Psychiatric Aspects of Imprisonment (1978); *Recreations* walking, photography, theatre, opera, cinema; *Clubs* RSM; *Style*— Prof John Gunn; Institute of Psychiatry, De Crespigny Park, Camberwell, London SE5 8AF (☎ 071 703 5411, 071 701 7063)

GUNNING, James John; s of Cedric Neville Harry Gunning (d 1981), of Dulwich Village, London, and Catherine, *née* Currie Forest (d 1970); *b* 7 June 1931; *Educ* Irvine Royal Acad, Westminster City, Lincoln Coll Oxford (MA); *m* 10 Dec 1966, Sheila, da of Sidney Harold Price (d 1978), of Chislehurst, Kent; 1 s (Christopher Joseph b 1971), 1 da (Catherine Elizabeth b 1968); *Career* Nat Serv RAF 1950-52; asst mangr Lazard Brothers 1966-67 (joined 1956); UK Provident Inst 1967-86: investmt mangr 1975, dir 1980, gen mangr investmts 1984, ret 1986; fin and legal dir nat headquarters The Br Red Cross Soc 1986-; *Recreations* reading history, golf, watching cricket; *Clubs* United Oxford and Cambridge Univ, MCC; *Style*— James Gunning, Esq; Mulberry End, Oldfield Rd, Bickley, Kent BR1 2LF (☎ 081 467 0946); The British Red Cross Society, 9 Grosvenor Crescent, London SW1X 7EJ (☎ 071 235 5454)

GURNEY, David William; s of Rev Horace William Gurney, HCF (d 1983), of Cranbrook, Kent, and Winifred Ruth, *née* Draper (d 1990); *b* 1 Sept 1935; *Educ* Maidstone GS, Chatham House GS Ramsgate, Univ of London (BD, BA, MA); *m* 6 Aug 1960, Sheila May, da of Cncllr Harold Ernest Seccombe, JP (d 1974), of Broadstairs, Kent; 3 s (Andrew b 1962, Richard b 1964, Nigel b 1966); *Career* teacher: St George's Boys' Sch Ramsgate 1961-65, Dane Court Boys' Sch Broadstairs 1965-67, Oldborough Manor HS Maidstone 1972-74, Huntleys Boys' Sch Tunbridge Wells 1974-86; sr asst sec SE Regional Examinations Bd for the CSE 1967-72, chief exec offr Inst of Financial Accountants 1987-; Capt 2 Tunbridge Wells Boys' Brigade Co 1970-83, treas Iden Green Congregational Church 1983-, chm Tunbridge Wells Action Gp of the Bible Soc, vice pres Royal Tunbridge Wells Mixed Voice Choir 1988- (conductor and musical dir 1978-80); FCP 1987; *Recreations* music (church organist and choirmaster), reading (history); *Clubs* IOD; *Style*— David Gurney, Esq; 18 Old Gardens Close, Royal Tunbridge Wells, Kent TN2 5ND (☎ 0892 22841); The Institute of Financial Accountants, Burford House, 44 London Rd, Sevenoaks, Kent TN13 1AS (☎ 0732 458080, fax 0732 455848)

H

HACKING, Susan; da of Arthur Walter David Francis, of Fetcham, Surrey, and Helen, *née* Waggott; *b* 7 Sept 1948; *Educ* Rosebery GS Epsom Surrey, Girton Coll Cambridge (MA); *m* (m dis 1986), Nicholas Ian, s of Burton Ian Hacking, of Mayfield, E Sussex; 1 s (Maximillian b 12 Dec 1973); *Career* fashion model 1971-73, slr Max Barford & Co Tunbridge Wells 1981-86, asst land registrar HM Land Registry Tunbridge Wells 1987-; fndr Kent and Sussex Girtonians Assoc 1989; *Recreations* furniture restoration; *Style—* Ms Susan Hacking; 21 Mountfield Gardens, Tunbridge Wells, Kent TN1 1SJ (☎ 0892 30501); Tunbridge Wells Distist Land Registry, Tunbridge Wells, Kent (☎ 0892 510015)

HACKNEY, Alfred; s of John Thomas Hackney (d 1978), of Staffs, and Anne Mary, *née* Morris (d 1981); *b* 18 May 1926; *Educ* Burslem Coll of Art Staffs, RCA, Edinburgh Coll of Art (DA), France, Italy; *m* 4 Oct 1958, Sheila Anne Macfarlan, *qv*, da of William Ramsay Findlay (d 1976), of Auchlishie, Kirriemuir, Scotland; 2 da (Fiona Anne Seaton b 23 Nov 1959, Isla Katrina b 6 June 1962); *Career* served RE 1944-48, surveyor and draughtsman RE NW frontier India 1945-48; trg at coll of art Stoke on trent and as designer-engraver at Wedgewood Group, visiting lectr London Art Colls; painter based in Chelsea and exhibiting in main London galleries; illustrator of books for London publishing houses incl: Macmillan, Faber & Faber, Harrap, Collins, Penguin Books; head of graphic design Gravesend Sch of Art Kent 1967 and Medway Coll of Art Rochester Kent; works purchased by Royal Acad and also City Art Galleries of: Sheffield (Graves Art Gallery), Stoke on Trent, Nottingham, Carlisle, Bolton, Leeds, and by numerous private collections in GB and abroad; currently working from own studio in Kent and exhibiting in London galleries; RE 1951, RWS 1963; *Recreations* golf; *Clubs* Chelsea Arts, Rochester and Cobham Park Golf; *Style—* Alfred Hackney, Esq; Barnside, Lodge Lane, Cobham, Kent DA12 3BS (☎ 0474 814676)

HACKNEY, Sheila Anne Macfarlane; da of William Ramsay Findlay (d 1976), of Auchlishie, Kirriemuir, Angus, Scotland, and Mary, *née* Seaton; *b* 28 April 1928; *Educ* Webster's Seminary Kirriemuir Scotland, Edinburgh Coll of Art (DA), France, Italy; *m* 4 Oct 1958, Alfred Hackney, *qv*, s of John Thomas Hackney (d 1978), of Staffs; 2 da (Fiona Anne Seaton b 23 Nov 1959, Isla Katrina b 6 June 1962); *Career* working in Chelsea studio as freelance artist, designer and illustrator 1952-; illustrations for numerous London Publishing houses incl: Faber & Faber, Hodder & Stoughton, Macmillan, BBC Pubns, Penguin Books; exhibitions in main London galleries incl: Young Contemporaries, The London Gp, Royal Acad, Royal Scot Acad, Fedn of Br Artists, Br in Watercolours, Royal Soc of Painters - in - Watercolours; works purchased by DOE and Dept of Educn, numerous private collections in GB and USA, currently working from own studio in Kent and Edinburgh; memb cncl Royal Soc of Painters - in - Watercolours; RWS 1968; *Recreations* gardening, golf; *Clubs* Rochester and Cobham Park Golf; *Style—* Ms Sheila Hackney; Barnside, Lodge Lane, Cobham, Kent DA12 3BS (☎ 0474 814676); 5 Randolph Crescent, Edinburgh EH3 7TH (☎ 031 225 6596)

HADMAN, Jillian Murdoch; da of David Hamilton Gardiner, JP, of Kingsdown, Deal, Kent, and Vera Lovis Mary, *née* Horsley (d 1979); *b* 16 May 1936; *Educ* The Friary Sch Lichfield, Univ of London (BA, PGCE); *m* 27 July 1959 (m dis 1988), Derek Seaton Hadman, s of Frederick Hadman, of Ashton, Oundle, Northants; 3 s (Kristjan b 1963, Piers b 1964, Giles b 1966); *Career* acting headmistress Folkestone GS for Girls 1982-83 (dep headmistress 1978-82), first dep head teacher Folkestone Sch for Girls 1983-86, head teacher Dartford GS for Girls 1986-; govr NW Kent Coll of Technol 1987-89, friend of Cncl of Kentish Archaeology; *Recreations* reading, music, walking, archaeology; *Style—* Mrs Jillian Hadman; Radlyn, Kingsdown Hill, Kingsdown, Deal, Kent CT14 8EA (☎ 0304 367267); 56 Chastilian Rd, Dartford, Kent DA1 3JJ (☎ 0322 70555); Dartford Grammer School for Girls, Shepherds Lane, Dartford, Kent DA1 2NT (☎ 0322 223123)

HAGGER, Jonathan Osborne; s of Cyril Francis Osborne Hagger (d 1957), of Loughton, Essex, and Norah Harrison, *née* Broadley (d 1981); *b* 3 Feb 1949; *Educ* Chigwell Sch; *m* 27 April 1974, (Carol) Anne, da of Alan David Luton, of Loughton, Essex; 2 s (William b 1981, James b 1984); *Career* CA; Edward Moore & Sons (CAs) 1968-72, BUPA 1972-75, Willis Faber 1976-85; fin dir: Bain Clarkson 1985-89, FKB Group Plc 1990-, Brook Street Bureau 1990-; Church Organist (deputize at King Charles the Martyr Tunbridge Wells); chm King Charles Music Soc; memb: The Nevill Tennis Club (Tunbridge Wells), Tunbridge Wells Civic Soc; ARCM 1968, FCA 1972; *Recreations* music, tennis; *Style—* Jonathan Hagger, Esq; 104 Warwick Park, Tunbridge Wells, Kent TN2 5EN (☎ 0892 29161)

HAGREEN, Rev John; s of Philip Hagreen (d 1988), and Eileen Mary, *née* Clegg; *b* 24 May 1919; *Educ* Ampleforth; *Career* WWII serv Queen's Own Royal West Kent Regt 1939-46; curate: Forest Hill London 1952-55, St Peter's Hove 1955-60, Northfleet Kent 1960-68; parish priest: Kidbrooke London 1968-75, Stockwell London 1975-84, Tenterden Kent 1984-; guide to Lourdes 1984 and 89; *Style—* The Rev John Hagreen; 47 Ashford Rd, Tenterden, Kent (☎ 05806 2785)

HAINES, Joseph Thomas William (Joe); s of Joseph Haines, and Elizabeth Haines; *b* 29 Jan 1928; *m* 1955, Irene Lambert; *Career* political corr: The Bulletin (Glasgow) 1958-60 (parly corr 1954-58), Scottish Daily Mail 1960-64, The Sun 1964-68; chief leader writer Daily Mirror 1978-90 (feature writer 1977-78), asst ed The Mirror 1985-90; dir: Scottish Daily Record and Sunday Mail Ltd, Mirror Group Newspapers 1986 (gp political ed 1984-90); columnist Daily Mirror, chief press sec to Harold Wilson as PM 1969-70 and 1974-76 and as Leader Oppn 1970-74 (dep press sec 1969); former chm Tonbridge and Malling Lab Pty (resigned), former memb Tonbridge UDC and Royal Cmmn on Legal Servs; *Books* The Politics of Power (1977), Malice in Wonderland (ed, 1986), Maxwell (1986); *Style—* Joe Haines, Esq; 1 South Frith, London Rd, Southborough, Tunbridge Wells, Kent (☎ 0732 365919)

HALL, Alfred Charles; CBE (1977, OBE 1966); s of Alfred Hall (d 1951); *b* 2 Aug 1917; *Educ* Oratory Sch, Open Univ (BA); *m* 1946, Clara Georgievna, *née* Strunina, of Moscow; 5 s, 1 da; *Career* served WWII Intelligence Corps; HM Dip Serv; attached to embassies in: Cairo, Tehran, Moscow; first sec: India, Pakistan, Canada; cncllr: (info) Nigeria, Canberra; attached to Dept of Trade 1969-71, cncllr (econ and devpt) Nigeria 1972-75, dep high cmmr in S India 1975-77; grants offr Save the Children Fund 1979-82; *Recreations* gardening, journalism; *Clubs* Royal Cwlth; *Style—* Alfred Hall, Esq, CBE; White Cliff, St Margarets Bay, Kent (☎ 0304 852230)

HALL, Christopher Sandford; TD (1968), DL (E Sussex 1987); s of Brig Geoffrey Sandford Hall (d 1975), of Ivy Cottage, Eridge, Tunbridge Wells, Kent, and Christine, *née* March; *b* 9 March 1936; *Educ* Rugby, Trinity Coll Cambridge (MA); *m* 8 July 1967, Susanna Marion, da of Richard Harry Bott (d 1976), of Benington Lordship, Stevenage, Herts; 3 s (David Sandford b 1968, Colin James b 1970, Philip Geoffrey b 1973); *Career* Nat Serv 5 Royal Inniskilling Dragoon Gds 1954-56, then as a Territorial Offr; ptnr Cripps Harries Hall 1964-; chm: British Equestrian Promotions Ltd London, A Burslem & Son (Monumental Masons) Tunbridge Wells; dir: Mid-Sussex Water Company, West Kent Water Company; chm S of England Agric Soc 1984-90, pres (Tunbridge Wells) Tunbridge and Dist Law Soc 1987, nat hunt steward Ascot Folkestone and Plumpton, cncl memb Br Horse Soc; Freeman City of London, Master Worshipful Co of Broderers 1980; memb Law Soc; *Recreations* farming, hunting, racing; *Clubs* Cavalry and Guards; *Style—* Christopher Hall, Esq, TD, DL; Great Danegate, Eridge Green, Tunbridge Wells, Kent (☎ 089275 385); Cripps Harries Hall, 84 Calverley Rd, Tunbridge Wells, Kent (☎ 0892 515121, fax 0892 515444)

HALL, Colin James; s of Sqdn Ldr Dr James Stirling Hall, RAF (ret), of Vale Croft, Chesham, Bucks, and Mary Munro, *née* Macphail (d 1982); *b* 13 June 1943; *Educ* City Sch Lincoln, Trinity Hall Cambridge (MA); *m* 21 Nov 1974, Naomi, da of George Alexander Saldanha (d 1974), of Bombay; 2 s (Alastair Colin b 1982, Matthew George Stirling b 1985); *Career* res exec Ogilvy & Mather 1964-66; mktg mangr: Beecham Drinks 1967-69, Benson & Hedges 1969-70; fndr Promotional Campaigns Ltd 1971-; chm: Awards Ctee Inst of Sales Promotion 1979-80, Code of Practice Ctee 1980-82, UK J/24 Assoc 1982-84; memb: ASA/CAP Promotion Ctee 1980-82, Hazlewood Sch Parents Assoc 1990-; hon treas Br Soling Assoc 1978-80, vice chm Int J/24 Assoc 1983-84; fell Inst of Sales Promotion 1987-; *Books* contrib: Managing Sales Promotion (1983), The O & M Business Book (1987); *Recreations* music, yachting; *Clubs* IOD, Royal Southern Yacht, Royal Ocean Racing; *Style—* Colin Hall, Esq; Acremead, Froghole, Crockham Hill, Edenbridge, Kent TN8

6TD (☎ 0732 866286); Promotional Campaigns Ltd, Forest Lodge, Westerham Rd, Keston, Kent BR2 6HE (☎ 0689 53344, fax 0689 62517)

HALL, Edwin Thomas; s of Alexander Edwin Hall (d 1962), of Lyminge, Folkestone, and May, *née* Laker; *b* 10 Feb 1935; *m* 26 Oct 1962, Ruby Yvonne, da of Percy William Clayson (d 1967); 1 da (Jacqueline Anne b 1964); *Career* auctioneer: H F Finn Kelcey, W & B Hobbs, Ashendens (formerly H F Finn Kelcey), G W Finn & Sons, Fordwich; fndr Valley Auctions Lyminge 1979-; *Recreations* photography; *Style—* Edwin Hall, Esq; Claygate, Brady Rd, Lyminge, Folkestone, Kent (☎ 0303 862134)

HALL, Dr Vernon Frederick; CVO (1960); s of Cecil Septimus Hall, and Maud Mary, *née* Fuller; *b* 25 Aug 1904; *Educ* Haberdashers' Aske's, King's Coll London, King's Coll Hosp Med Sch (MRCS, LRCP); *m* 19 Jan 1935, Constance Marcia, da of Rev H T Cavell, rector of Woodford Green, London; 1 s (Desmond Lawrence b 1937), 2 da (Judith Margaret b 1939, Janet Elizabeth b 1943); *Career* WWII RAMC advsr in anaesthetics to SE Asia Cmd, late dir of anaesthetics Indian and Burma Cmd, Brig; fell King's Coll London, fndr memb Faculty of Anaesthetists RCS, pres Assoc of Anaesthetics of GB and Ireland; anaesthetist to HM The Queen for births of her four children, also HRH The Princess Margaret and HRH Duchess of Kent; vice pres The Exmoor Soc; Univ of London: memb Senate, chm Bd of Advanced Med Studies; FFARCS; *Books* History of King's College Hospital Dental School, Scrapbook of Snowdonia; *Recreations* rugby, squash, tennis, riding; *Clubs* RAC; *Style—* Dr Vernon F Hall, CVO; 83A Foxgrove Rd, Beckenham, Kent BR3 2DA (☎ 081 650 2212)

HALL-THOMPSON, Rear Adm Derrick Henry; JP (1957), DL (1976); s of Adm Percival Hall-Thompson, CB, CMG (d 1950), of Tynwald, Hythe, and Helen, *née* Deacon (d 1964); *b* 2 Feb 1902; *Educ* Osborne Naval Coll, Dartmouth Naval Coll; *m* 23 July 1938, Ursula Wakefield, da of Col Harold Street, DSO (d 1959); 2 s (Michael b 1944, Charles b 1951); *Career* Cadet RN 1915 rising to Rear Adm 1955; Mayor of Hythe 1960-62 (memb of town cncl for many years), vice chm Kent CC 1974 (cncllr for 17 years), sch govr; memb: Kent BRCS, local lifeboat orgn; awarded Dannebrog by King of Denmark 1957; *Clubs* Army and Navy; *Style—* Rear Adm Derrick Hall-Thompson, JP, DL

HAMER, Dr Michelle Suzanne Fernande; da of Max Louis Leon Heraud, of Nîmes, France, and Simone Hortense, *née* Janvier; *b* 10 Aug 1952; *Educ* Lycee Montaury Nîmes France, Faculty of Med Montpellier France (MD); *m* 6 Aug 1977, Colin John Hamer, s of Eric John Hamer, of Ashford, Kent; 1 da (Jessica Maîte Michelle b 1981); *Career* sr house ofr St Bart's Hosp London 1979-81, registrar Westminster Hosp 1982-84, sr registrar Royal Free Hosp 1984-88, conslt i/c Intensive Therapy Unit Joyce Green Hsop 1988-; memb: Assoc of Anaesthetists, Intensive Care Soc; memb BMA, FFARCS 1983; *Recreations* outdoor activities, travel, entertaining; *Style—* Dr Michelle Hamer; Joyce Green Hospital, Intensive Therapy Unit, Joyce Green Lane, Dartford, Kent DA1 5PL (☎ 0322 227242, fax 0322 91829)

HAMILL, (William) John; s of Thomas Strahan Hamill (d 1984), of Ballymena, NI, and Mary Elizabeth, *née* Gaston; *b* 11 July 1944; *Educ* Ballymena Acad, Trinity Coll Dublin (BDS, MA); *m* 27 April 1971, Carmel Ann, da of Thomas Mangan (d 1975), of Dangean, Eire; 2 s (Gavin Thomas b 5 Jan 1972, Luke John b 16 Jan 1978), 1 da (Cara Ann b 19 Dec 1973); *Career* dental surgn; memb: Thanet Rotary Club, Ramsgate 41 Club; *Recreations* walking, poetry, photography; *Style—* John Hamill, Esq; Whiteness Cottage, 12 Kingsgate Ave, Broadstairs, Kent CT10 3QP (☎ 0843 62332); 73 Hereson Rd, Ramsgate, Kent CT11 7DS (☎ 0843 581666)

HAMMERTON, Ian Charles; s of Charles Frederick Hammerton (d 1972), of Dartford, and Italia Margherita, *née* Caracó (d 1982); *b* 5 Dec 1921; *Educ* Dartford GS, Coll of St Mark and St John Chelsea; *m* 25 Aug 1952, Barbara Joan, da of Rowland Ernest Broome; 2 s (Michael John b 1954, Colin Marc b 1959), 1 da (Susan Frances b 1956); *Career* 42 bn RTR TA 1939, 43 bn RTR, 101 OCTU RMC 1941, 61 Trg Regt RAC 1941-43, Capt 22 Dragoons RAC 1943-45 (NW Europe D Day - 1945), Staff Capt 43 Wessex Div BAOR 1945-46 (courts martial, war crimes trials), TEM; Hurstmere (Blackfen) Boys' Sch: asst teacher 1949, head of music 1956-, head of year 1973-, sr teacher (actg dep headmaster) 1980-83; lectr: Womens Insts, TGs, retirement clubs, social clubs; memb (former chm) Dartford Symphony Orchestra 1947-87, sec and chm Chislehurst Sidcup and Orpington Music Ctee 1950-65, pt/t memb Kent (Rural) Music Sch Staff and conductor Dartford Youth Orchestra 1957-76, conductor various music festivals 1962-80; Bexley Advsy Cncl: memb Music Panel 1965-82, memb Jt Consultative Ctee; staff rep Hurstmere Parent Teacher Assoc 1968-74, chm and ctee memb Bexley Schs Music Assoc 1968-82, memb Bexley Pastoral Care Ctee 1973-83, sec Bexley NAS/UWT (pres twice), hon life memb NAS/UWT; chm: Save Joyden's Wood Ctee 1986-, Dartford Environment Week Ctee 1987- (memb 1985-), Dartford Arts Cncl 1989- (memb 1983-); voluntary warden (Joyden's Wood) The Woodland Tst 1987-, memb and gp speaker Bexley Branch Ctee RSPB 1988-; memb: Kent Tst for Nature Conservation, Nat Tst, Normandy Veterans Assoc, Royal Br Legion; sec 22 Dragoons Old Comrades Assoc 1979-, UK liason offr (to French) Remember Le Havre 1944 Assoc 1989; Croix de Guerre with silver star; *Recreations* music, walking, bird watching, nature conservation, photography; *Style—* Ian Hammerton, Esq; Tanglewood, 65 Norfield Rd, Wilmington, Dartford, Kent DA2 7NY (☎ 0322 522492)

HAMMOND, Eric Albert Barratt; OBE (1977); s of Arthur Edgar Hammond (d 1963), and Gertrude May, *née* Barratt (d 1983); *b* 17 July 1929; *Educ* Corner Brook Sch Newfoundland; *m* 26 Sept 1953, Brenda Mary, da of George Edgeler; 2 s (Ivan b 1958, Shaun b 1961); *Career* Nat Serv REME 1950-52; EETPU: electrician 1952-64, exec cncllr 1964-84, gen sec 1984-; chm 5 N Fleet Scout Gp 1979-84; cncllr: Gravesend Borough DC 1957-60, Northfleet UDC 1960-63; *Recreations* gardening, photography, watching rugby, reading; *Clubs* Gravesend Rugby; *Style—* Eric Hammond, Esq, OBE; EETPU, Hayes Court, West Common Rd, Hayes Bromley, Kent (☎ 081 462 7755)

HAMMOND, Rev Peter Clark; s of Harry Francis (d 1943), of Singapore, and Joyce Marion, *née* Clark (d 1980); *b* 7 Nov 1927; *Educ* The King's Sch Canterbury, Univ of Oxford (MA), Wells Theological Coll; *m* 17 Sept 1955, Constance Anne, da of Sidney Riches (d 1959), of The Falkland Islands and Ashford, Kent; 1 s (Christopher b 1956), 1 da (Jane b 1959); *Career* rector of Barham Canterbury 1960-66; vicar of: Walmer Kent 1966-85, Rolvenden 1985-; *Books* The Parson and The Victorian Parish (1977), Dean Stanley of Westminster (biog 1987); *Recreations* architecture and reading; *Style—* The Rev Peter Hammond; The Vicarage, Rolvenden, Cranbrook, Kent (☎ 0580 241235)

HANCOCK, Michael Anthony; s of Anthony Ilbert Hancock (d 1954), of Bickley, Kent, and Eileen Mary, *née* King; *b* 11 Sept 1943; *Educ* Tonbridge; *m* 11 July 1967 (m dis 1975), Diana Margaret, da of Albert Edward Peter; 1 s (Froude), 2 da (Claire, Emma); *Career* Bank of England 1961-63, ptnr WN Middleton & Co and Stock Exchange memb 1969-75, chm and chief exec Chart Estates Ltd 1985-; *Recreations* vintage cars, fine wines, antique furniture; *Clubs* Wig and Pen, Kent Woolgrowers; *Style—* Michael Hancock, Esq; Crabbe Farm, Lenham, Heath, Kent (☎ 0622 858 320); Bourg de Borreze, Dordogne, France

HANDLEY JONES, Susan Kathleen (Sue); da of Patrick John Dickinson (d 1984), of Surrey, and Christine Margaret Wells, *née* Weston; *b* 13 July 1955; *Educ* Malvern Girls Coll, Univ of Warwick (BA); *m* 10 Sept 1983, Nicholas, s of Anthony Handley Jones, of Bucks; *Career* recruitment specialist Badenach and Clark, PR consultancy work for Honewell Philips Telephone Rentals 1981-83, recruitment and personnel work 1977-81; *Clubs* Oriental; *Style—* Mrs Susan Handley Jones; Westwood House, Westwood, Southfleet, Kent (☎ 047 483 2156); Badenoch and Clark, 16 New Bridge St, London EC4V 6AU (☎ 01 583 0073, fax 01 353 3908)

HANES, David John; s of Brian Edgar Hanes, of Storrington, Sussex, and Margaret Edith Hanes; *b* 10 Oct 1944; *Educ* Haberdashers' Aske's; *m* 6 Sept 1969, Rosemary Pauline, da of Thomas Brocklehurst Morris; 3s (Nicholas Simon b 1972, Christopher Andrew b 1975, Jonathan David b 1983); *Career* CA 1969; ptnr Foot Davson & Co 1981, dir Foot Davson Investment Consultants Ltd 1984; Pembury Free Church: organist 1970-88, church sec 1979-86, current memb; tstee Buckingham Tst, treas Bennet Meml Diocesan Sch for Girls Govrs Fund; FCA 1969; *Books* My Path of Prayer (ed 1981); *Recreations* music, organist, photography, sailing; *Style—* David Hanes, Esq; Foot Davson & Co, 15 Church Road, Tunbridge Wells, Kent (☎ 0892 38088)

HANKEY, Hon Christopher Alers; OBE (1958); s of 1 Baron Hankey, GCB, GCMG, GCVO, PC, FRS (d 1963); *b* 1911; *Educ* Rugby, Univ of Oxford (MA), Univ of London (BSc); *m* 1, 31 Oct 1945 (m dis 1957), Prudence May, da of Keith Brodribb; 1 da; m 2, 5 Sept 1958, Helen Christine, da of late Alexander John Cassavetti; 1 s; *Career* serv WWII, Maj RM; princ Miny of Overseas Devpt 1964-72, ret; exec Cncl for Tech Educn and Trg in Overseas Countries 1972-78; churchwarden St Mary's Church Westerham 1967-71, hon sec Parochial Church Cncl 1971-; *Recreations* amateur artist; *Style—* The Hon Christopher Hankey, OBE; New Cottage, French St, nr Westerham, Kent

HANKEY, Hon Henry Arthur Alers; CMG (1959), CVO (1960); yst s of 1 Baron Hankey, GCB, GCMG, GCVO, PC, FRS (d 1963); *b* 1 Sept 1914; *Educ* Rugby, New Coll Oxford; *m* 1 Jan 1941, Vronwy, o da of late Rev Thomas Frederic Fisher, Rector of Stilton, Peterborough; 3 s (Christopher, Maurice, Peter), 1 da (Veronica); *Career* ambass to Panama 1966-69, under-sec FCO 1969-74; dir: Lloyds Bank International 1975-80, Autofagasta (Chile) & Bolivia Railway Co 1975-82; sec Br N American Ctee 1981-85; *Clubs* Ski Club of GB, United Univ; *Style—* The Hon Henry Hankey, CMG, CVO; Hosey Croft, Westerham, Kent

HANKEY, 2 Baron (UK 1939); Robert Maurice Alers Hankey; KCMG (1955, CMG 1947), KCVO (1956); s of 1 Baron Hankey, GCB, GCMG, GCVO, PC, FRS, Sec of Cabinet 1915-38, Chllr Duchy of Lancaster 1940 and Paymaster-Gen 1941-42 (d 1963); *b* 4 July 1905; *Educ* Rugby, New Coll Oxford, Univ of Bonn, Sorbonne Paris; *m* 1, 27 Sept 1930, Frances Bevyl (d 1957), da of Walter Stuart-Menteth (4 s of Sir James Stuart-Menteth, 4 Bt); 2 s, 2 da; m 2, 2 Oct 1962, Joanna, da of Rev James Johnston Wright, late chaplain to Edinburgh Castle and asst St Giles Cathedral; *Heir* s, Hon Donald Hankey; *Career* sits as Ind Peer in House of Lords; FO 1927-65; served:

Berlin, Paris, London, Warsaw, Bucharest, Cairo, Teheran, Madrid, Budapest; ambass Stockholm 1954-60, perm UK del OEEC and OECD and chm Econ Policy Ctee 1960-65; dir Alliance Building Soc to 1983; vice pres Euro Inst of Business Admin Fontainebleau (INSEAD) 1966-80, pres Anglo Swedish Soc 1970-78; *Recreations* reading, skiing, tennis, golf; *Clubs* Royal Cwlth Soc; *Style*— The Rt Hon the Lord Hankey, KCMG, KCVO; Hethe House, Cowden, Edenbridge, Kent (☎ 034 286 538)

HANKEY, Dr (Ann) Teresa; da of (Cyril) Patrick Hankey (d 1973), dean of Ely Cathedral 1951-79, and Frances Mary, *née* Harris (d 1966); *b* 11 Feb 1929; *Educ* St Margaret's Sch Bushey, Bedford HS, Bedford Coll Univ of London; *Career* Univ of London: jr res fell The Warburg Inst 1952-54, travelling fell Italy 1954-55, asst lectr then lectr Bedford Coll 1955-67, sr res fell The Warburg Inst 1966-67; Univ of Sussex 1967-88: lectr, reader in classical and medieval studies 1973-88; reader in classical and medieval studies Univ of Kent 1988-; govr Oxted Co Sch 1984-88; *Books* Ricobaldi Ferrariensis Compendium Historiae Romanae (2 volumes, 1 edn, 1984); *Recreations* travel, walking; *Style*— Dr Teresa Hankey; 50 Rough Common Rd, Canterbury, Kent CT2 9DJ (☎ 0227 765770); University of Kent, Canterbury, Kent (☎ 0227 764000)

HANSON, Brian John Taylor; s of Benjamin John Hanson (d 1978), of Norwood Green, Middx, and Gwendoline Ada, *née* Taylor; *b* 23 Jan 1939; *Educ* Hounslow Coll, Law Soc's Coll of Law; *m* 10 June 1972, Deborah Mary Hazel, da of Lt-Col Richard Stewart Palliser Dawson, OBE, of Stowting, Kent; 2 s (James b 1973, Crispin b 1982), 3 da (Sarah b 1975, Rebecca b 1979, Alice b 1986); *Career* admitted slr 1963; ecclesiastical notary, private practice 1963-65, slr Church Cmmn for England 1965-70, asst legal advsr Gen Synod of C of E 1970-74, legal advsr Gen Synod and House of Bishops 1974-; registrar: Gen Synod 1980-, Convocation of Canterbury and Province and Archbishop of Canterbury 1984-, Province of York 1984-; memb Legal Advsy Cmmn of the Gen Synod 1980- (sec 1970-86), guardian of the Shrine of Our Lady of Walsingham 1984-; cncl memb: St Luke's Hosp for the Clergy 1985-, Ecclesiastical Law Soc 1987-; fell of Woodard Corpn 1987-, govr St Michael's Sch Burton Park Sussex 1987-, memb Chichester Diocesan Synod 1987-; *Books* A History of Norwood Parish Church (1970), The Opinions of the Legal Advisory Commission (ed, 6 edn 1985), The Canons of the Church of England (ed, 2 edn 1975, 4 edn 1986); *Recreations* family, gardening, genealogy; *Clubs* Royal Cwlth Soc; *Style*— Brian Hanson, Esq; Daltons Farm, Bolney, W Sussex RH17 5PG (☎ 0444 881890); Church House, Deans Yard, Westminster SW1P 3NZ (☎ 071 222 9011)

HANSON, Christopher John; s of Laurence William Hanson (d 1966), of Oxford, and Carola Mary, *née* Hawes (d 1985); *b* 20 April 1940; *Educ* The King's Sch Canterbury, Univ of Oxford (MA); *m* 26 May 1975, Jayne Gwenllian, da of Evan Morgan Lewis, of Maidstone; 1 s (David William b 1976), 1 da (Elizabeth Jane b 1979); *Career* slr; ptnr Lovell White Durrant; memb insolvency jt working pty Bar and Law Soc 1977-, vice chm Insolvency Sub Ctee City of London Slrs Co; *Style*— Christopher Hanson, Esq; The Shaw, Brasted Chart, nr Westerham, Kent (☎ 0959 63 763); Lovell White Durrant, 21 Holborn Viaduct, London EC1A 2DY (☎ 071 236 0066, fax 071 248 4212, telex 887122 LWD G)

HARDCASTLE, Michael William; s of William Hardcastle (d 1984), of Marden, Kent, and Catherine, *née* Slade; *b* 4 May 1938; *Educ* Haileybury; *m* 16 March 1968, Ruth Margaret, da of Jack Ronald Vernede, of Marden, Kent; 1 s (David Charles b 26 June 1971), 1 da (Claire Elizabeth b 16 June 1969); *Career* admitted slr 1961; ptnr Whitehead Monckton Maidstone 1965-; dep coroner Maidstone, clerk to commissioners of taxes Maidstone divs; Under Sheriff of Kent 1989-; *Recreations* fly fishing; *Style*— Michael Hardcastle, Esq; Fairfield, Sissinghurst, Cranbrook, Kent TN17 2AR (☎ 0580 712817); Whitehead Monckton, 72 King St, Maidstone, Kent ME14 1BL (☎ 0622 690077, fax 0622 690050)

HARDING, Dr Geoffrey Wright; s of Jack Harding, of Gravesend, Kent, and Ethel Florence, *née* Wilkinson; *Educ* King's Coll London (LLB, AKC), Northwestern Univ Sch of Law Chicago (LLM), QMC London (PhD); *m* 7 Oct 1972, Margaret June, da of Eric Oscar Danger; 1 s (Peter James John b 1980), 1 da (Kate Joanna b 1978); *Career* Nat Serv RAF 1951-53; called to the Bar Gray's Inn 1957; asst sec FCEC 1958-60, legal advsr Br Insur (Atomic Energy) Ctee 1960-63, exchange lawyer under Harvard Law Sch Prog Isham Lincoln and Beale Attorneys Chicago 1963-64, asst slr Joynson Hicks 1965-67, ptnr Wilde Sapte 1967- (specialising in banking, competition and computer law); memb Bar and Law Soc Jt Working Pty on Banking Law; business advsr The Prince's Youth Business Tst; memb: Nat Autistic Soc, Kent Autistic Community Tst; Gen Electric Fndn fell Northwestern Univ Sch of Law Chicago; Freeman City of London 1986, memb Guild of Freemen of City of London; memb Law Soc; *Books* Banking Act 1987-Current Law Annotated (1987), Encyclopaedia of Competition Law (jt consltg ed, 1987); *Recreations* piano playing, mountain biking, avoiding domestic DIY; *Style*— Dr Geoffrey Harding; Wilde Sapte, Queensbridge House, 60 Upper Thames St, London EC4V 3BD (☎ 071 236 3050, fax 071 236 9624, telex 887793)

HARDING, Dr Wilfrid Gerald; CBE (1978); s of late Dr Ludwig Ernst Emil Hoffmann, and Marie Minna Eugenie, *née* Weisbach; *b* 17 March 1915; *Educ* Französisches Gymnasium Berlin, Süddeutsches Landerzichungsheim Schondorf Bavaria, Woodbrooke Coll Selly Oak Birmingham, UCL, Univ Coll Hosp Med Sch (MRCS, MRCP, LRCP); *m* 1, 1938 (m dis 1970), Britta Charlotta Haraldsdotter Malmberg; 3 s; m 2, 1973, Hilary Maxwell; *Career* served RAMC 1943-47, Field Units in NW Europe, 1 Corps Staff and Mil Govt, Lt-Col (hygiene specialist); house physician and house surgn UCH 1941-42, asst MOH City of Oxford 1942-43, i/c health servs Ruhr Dist CCG 1947-48, LSHTM 1948-49, career posts in London pub health serv 1949-64, MOH London Borough of Camden and princ sch MO ILEA 1965-74, hon lectr Dept of Sociology Bedford Coll London 1969-77, hon conslt in community med UCH 1971-79, civil conslt in community med to RAF 1974-78, area MO Camden and Islington AHA 1974-79; broadcasts on pub health and community med; author of numerous papers on pub health and community med in med books and jls; Parkes Centenary Meml Lecture (Community Health and Service) 1976; memb: Bd of Studies in Preventative Med and Pub Health Univ of London 1963-79, Cncl for Educn and Trg of Health Visitors 1965-77, Cncl UCH Med Sch 1965-78, Standing Mental Health Advsy Ctee 1966-71, Central Health Servs Cncl and Standing Med Advsy Ctee 1966-71 and 1975-78, Bd of Mgmnt LSHTM 1968-82, Cncl of Action on Smoking and Health 1970-73 and 1978-82, Pub Health Laboratory Serv Bd 1972-83, Armed Servs Med Advsy Bd 1975-78, GMC 1979-84; pres: Cncl Soc of MOH 1971-72 (chm 1966-71), Provisional Bd Faculty of Community Med RCP 1975-78 (chm 1971-72, vice pres 1972-75); hon advsr Office of Health Econs 1977-, chm DHSS Working Gp on Primary Health Team 1978-80 (reported 1981), vice chm Dartford and Gravesham Community Health Cncl 1984-89; cncllr Sevenoaks DC 1979-, chm Farningham Parish Cncl 1983-89; FFCM 1972 (Hon FFCM 1986), FRCP 1972; *Recreations* watching river birds, music, wine; *Clubs* Athenaeum; *Style*— Dr Wilfrid G Harding, CBE; Bridge Cottage, High St, Farningham, Dartford Kent DA4 0DW (☎ 0322 862733)

HARDWICK, Donald Hugh; s of Capt Donald Frederick Hardwick, MC (d 1967), of Purlands, Charing, Kent, and Adeline Marion, *née* Sulston (d 1966); *b* 28 Oct 1936; *Educ* St Edmund's Canterbury, Canterbury Coll of Art (Nat Dip Design); *m* 29 Feb 1964, Kathleen, da of Alfred George Englefield (d 1959); 2 s (Leigh Hardwick b 22 Nov 1967, Giles Hardwick b 27 Oct 1968); *Career* Nat Serv REME attached to 4 Gds Bde BAOR 1956-58; appts in advertising indust 1958-; dir: Appropriate Technology Ltd 1979-, Butler Borg Ltd 1986-; md Jogdean Ltd 1979-; *Style*— Donald Hardwick, Esq; St Margarets, Rochester, Kent (☎ 0634 402632); 4 Gee's Court, Oxford St, London W1M 5HQ (☎ 071 408 2301, fax 071 408 0382, telex 267529)

HARDWICK, Mary Atkinson (Mollie); *née* Greenhalgh; da of Joseph Greenhalgh (d 1940), of Cheadle Hulme, Cheshire, and Anne Frances, *née* Atkinson (d 1959); *Educ* Manchester HS for Girls; *m* 1961, Michael Hardwick, *qv*, s of George Drinkrow Hardwick, of Leeds, W Yorks; 1 s (Julian); *Career* announcer BBC North Region 1940-45, BBC (Radio) Drama Dept 1945-62; freelance author 1962-; FRSA; *Books* Stories from Dickens (1968), Emma, Lady Hamilton (1969), Mrs Dizzy (1972), Upstairs Downstairs: Sarah's Story (1973), The Years of Change (1974), The War to end Wars (1975), Mrs Bridges' Story (1975), The World of Upstairs Downstairs (1976), Alice in Wonderland (play, 1975), Beauty's Daughter (1976, Elizabeth Goudge Award for best historical romantic novel of year), The Duchess of Duke Street: The Way Up (1976), The Golden Years (1976), The World Keeps Turning (1977), Charlie is My Darling (1977), The Atkinson Heritage (1978), Thomas and Sarah (1978), Thomas and Sarah: Two for a Spin (1979), Lovers Meeting (1979), Sisters in Love (1979), Dove's Nest (1980), Willowwood (1980), Juliet Bravo 1 (1980), Juliet Bravo 2 (1980), Monday's Child (1981), Calling Juliet Bravo: New Arrivals (1981), I Remember Love (1982), The Shakespeare Girl (1983), By the Sword Divided (1983), The Merrymaid (1984), Girl with a Crystal Dove (1985), Malice Domestic (1986), Parson's Pleasure (1987), Uneaseful Death (1988) Blood Royal (1988), The Bandersnatch (1989), Perish in July (1989), The Dreaming Damozel (1990); with Michael Hardwick: The Jolly Toper (1961), The Sherlock Holmes Companion (1962), Sherlock Holmes Investigates (1963), The Man Who Was Sherlock Holmes (1964), Four Sherlock Holmes plays (1964), The Charles Dickens Companion (1965), The World's Greatest Sea Mysteries (1967), Writers' Houses: a literary journey in England (1968), Alfred Deller: A Singularity of Voice (1968), Charles Dickens As They Saw Him (1969), The Game's Afoot (Sherlock Holmes Plays, 1969), Plays from Dickens (1970), Dickens' England (1970), The Private Life of Sherlock Holmes (1970), Four More Sherlock Holmes Plays (1973), The Charles Dickens Encyclopedia (1973), The Bernard Shaw Companion (1973), The Charles Dickens Quiz Book (1974), The Upstairs Downstairs Omnibus (1975), The Gaslight Boy (1976), The Hound of the Baskervilles and Other Sherlock Holmes Plays (1982); numerous plays and scripts for radio and television; contributions to women's magazines; *Recreations* reading detective novels; *Style*— Mollie Hardwick; 2 Church St, Wye, Kent TN25 5BJ (☎ 0233 813051)

HARDWICK, Michael John Drinkrow; s of George Drinkrow Hardwick (d

1964), and Katharine Augusta, *née* Townend (d 1964); *b* 10 Sept 1924; *Educ* Leeds GS; *m* 1961, Mollie, *qv*, da of Joseph Greenhalgh (d 1940), of Cheadle Hulme, Cheshire; 1 s (Julian); *Career* Indian Army 1943-47, Capt served in India and Japan; author and dramatist, reporter Morley Observer 1942-43; dir: NZ Nat Film Unit 1948-53, Freedom Newspaper NZ 1953-54, BBC Radio Drama Dept 1958-63; freelance author 1963-; FRSA; *Books* The Royal Visit to New Zealand (1954), Emigrant in Motley: letters of Charles Kean and Ellen Tree (1954), Seeing New Zealand (1955), Opportunity in New Zealand (ed with Baron Birkett, 1955), The Verdict of the Court (1960), Doctors on Trial (1961), The Plague and Fire of London (1966), The Worlds Greatest Air Mysteries (1970), The Discovery of Japan (1970), The Osprey Guide to Gilbert and Sullivan (1972), The Osprey Guide to Jane Austen (1973), A Literary Atlas and Gazetter of the British Isles (1973), The Osprey Guide to Oscar Wilde (1973), Upstairs Downstairs: Mr Hudson's Diaries (1973), Mr Bellamy's Story (1974), On with the Dance (1975), Endings and Beginnings (1975), The Osprey Guide to Anthony Trollope (1974), The Inheritors (1974), The Pallisers (abridger 1974), The Four Musketeers (abridger 1975), The Man Who Would be King (abridger 1976), The Cedar Tree (1976), The Cedar Tree: Autumn of an Age (1977), A Bough Breaks (1978), Regency Royal (1978), Prisoner of the Devil (1979), Regency Rake (1979), Regency Revenge (1980), Bergerac (1981), The Chinese Detective (1981), Regency Revels (1982), The Barchester Chronicles (1982), The Private Life of Dr Watson (1983), Sherlock Holmes: my life and crimes (1984), Last Tenko (1984), Complete Guide to Sherlock Holmes (1986), The Revenge of the Hound (1987), Nightbone (1989); as John Drinkrow: The Vintage Operetta Book (1972), The Vintage Musical Comedy Book (1973); with Mollie Hardwick: The Jolly Toper (1961), The Sherlock Holmes Companion (1962), Sherlock Holmes Investigates (1963), The Man Who Was Sherlock Holmes (1964), Four Sherlock Holmes Plays (1964), The Charles Dickens Companion (1965), The World's Greatest Sea Mysteries (1967), Writers' Houses: a literary journey in England (1968), Alfred Deller: A Singularity of Voice (1968), Charles Dickens As They Saw Him (1969), Dicken's England (1970), The Private Life of Sherlock Holmes (1970), The Bernard Shaw Companion (1973), The Charles Dickens Encyclopaedia (1973), The Charles Dickens Quiz Book (1974), The Upstairs Downstairs Omnibus (1975), The Gaslight Boy (1976); plays: A Christmas Card (1975), Four Sherlock Holmes Plays (jtly, 1964), The Game's Afoot (jtly, 1969), Four More Sherlock Holmes Plays (jtly, 1973), The Hound of the Baskervilles and other Sherlock Holmes Plays (1982); author of many plays and scripts for tv and radio; *Recreations* listening to music, watching old films on television; *Style*— Michael Hardwick, Esq; 2 Church St, Wye, Kent TN25 5BJ (☎ 0233 813 051)

HARDY, Graham John; s of Donald Hardy, of Steeple, Essex, and Gladys Hardy; *b* 15 Nov 1952; *Educ* Goldsmiths Coll London (CertEd), North East London (BEd), Cambridge Inst of Educn (advanced dip); *m* 27 July1975, Kathryn Ann Margaret, da of Derek Francis; 3 s (Luke Daniel b 8 Dec 1981, Martin Adam 10 Dec 1984, Nathan Francis 7 Oct 1987), 2 da (Dominique Mark b 26 Jan 1978, Simon Louise 9 Nov 1979); *Career* special sch teacher; Langdon Comp Sch Newham 1974-77, Bentry Special Sch Barking 1977-78, Wedgwood Special Sch London 1978-80, Corbets Tey Special Sch Havering 1980-83, Kingsley Sch for Physically Handicapped 1983-87, headteacher Bower Grove Special Sch 1987-; NAHT; *Style*— Graham Hardy, Esq; Meadowside, Grafton Underwood, Kettering, Northants NN14 3AA; Bower Grove School, Fant lane, Maidstone, Kent (☎ 0622 26773)

HARDY, Maj-Gen John Campbell; CB (1985), LVO (1978); s of Gen Sir Campbell Hardy, KCB, CBE, DSO (d 1984); *b* 13 Oct 1933; *Educ* Sherborne; *m* 1961, Jennifer Mary Kempton; 1 s, 1 da; *Career* joined RM 1952, 45 Commando 1954, HMS Superb 1956, instr NCOs' Sch at Plymouth 1957, 42 Commando 1959, 43 Commando 1962, Adj Jt Serv Amphibious Warfare Centre 1964, Co Cdr 45 Commando 1965, student RAF Staff Coll Bracknell 1966, instr RNC Greenwich 1967, extra equerry to HRH Prince Philip 1968-69, SO in Dept of Cmdt Gen RM 1969, Rifle Co Cdr 41 Commando 1971, student NDC Latimer 1972, staff of CDS 1973, SO HQ Commando Forces 1975, CO RM Poole 1977, Col 1978, COS and asst def attaché Br Def Staff Washington 1979, ADC to HM The Queen 1981-82, Maj-Gen 1982, COS to Cmdt Gen RM 1982-84, dep COS HQ AFNORTH 1984-87; dir Br Digestive Fndn 1987; *Recreations* current affairs, sailing; *Clubs* Army and Navy; *Style*— Maj-Gen John Hardy, CB, LVO; c/o National Westminster Bank, 51 The Strand, Walmer, Deal, Kent

HARE, John Neville; s of late Capt Lancelot Geldart Hare, MC (d 1957), and Esther Maria, *née* Whales (d 1969); *b* 11 Dec 1934; *Educ* St Edward's Oxford; *m* 17 Sept 1966, Pippa, da of Harding McGregor Dunnett, of Eliot Vale, Blackheath, London; 3 da (Charlotte b 1968, Henrietta b 1970, Emily b 1974); *Career* Lt Oxfordshire and Buckinghamshire LI Royal W Africa Frontier Force 1954-55; sr dist offr Colonial Serv Northern Nigeria 1957-64; dir Macmillan Education Publishers 1966-74, author and conslt Hodder and Stoughton Publishers 1980-89; UN Environment Prog 1989-; *Books* (under pseudonym of Dan Fulani); Hijack (1979), No Condition is Permanent (1979), Primary Hausa Course (1979), Sauna and the Bank Robbers (1980), Sauna, Secret Agent; Sauna to the Rescue (1981), Medicinal Pots of the Cham and Mwana Tribes (1985), No Telephone to Heaven (1985), God's Case No Appeal (1985), The Fight For Life (1986), The Power of Corruption (1986), Flight 800 (1986), The Price of Liberty (1987), Sauna and the Drug Pedlars (1988), Rhino's Horn (1988), Leopard's Coat (1989), Elephant's Tusk (1990); *Recreations* hunting, amateur dramatics, travel, writing; *Clubs* East India; *Style*— John Hare, Esq; School Farm, Benenden, Kent (☎ 0580 240 755)

HARE-SCOTT, Peter Henry Duncan; s of Maj Henry Barton Hare-Scott of St Anthony-in-Roseland, nr Truro, Cornwall, and Ann Gwavas Sophia, *née* Grant-Dalton; *b* 2 March 1948; *Educ* Kelly Coll Tavistock Devon; *m* 26 Apr 1980, Jane Mary, da of Christopher Francis Robert Barclay, of Painswick, Glos; 1 s (Henry William Troutbeck b 1987), 2 da (Rebecca Katherine May b 1981, Natalie Emma Jane b 1983); *Career* Watney Mann 1971-74, Chef and Brewer 1974-84, retail dir Shepherd Neame Ltd 1985- (joined 1984); borough cncllr Ashford (Cons) 1987-; *Recreations* walking, sailing, tennis; *Style*— Peter Hare-Scott, Esq; Shottenden, Westwell, nr Ashford, Kent TN25 4JR (☎ 0233 631548); Shepherd Neame Ltd, 17 Court St, Faversham, Kent ME13 7AX (☎ 0795 532206)

HARMAN, Albert George (Bert); s of Arthur James Harman (d 1965), of Rainham, Kent, and Rose Lilian Harman, *née* Surtees; *b* 7 Nov 1943; *Educ* Chatham Tech HS, Medway Coll of Technol; *m* 22 May 1985, Jacqueline Yvonne (Jacqui), da of Ronald James Healey, of Acton Trussel, Staffs; 1 step s (Simon Terence Hoskins b 1973), 1 step da (Kim Caroline Hoskins b 1971); *Career* Bowater Packaging: prodn controller 1972-75, prodn mangr 1975-78, commercial mangr 1978-85; commercial dir Crest Packaging 1985-; *Recreations* golf, cricket; *Clubs* Faversham Golf, Clarenden Cricket; *Style*— Albert Harman, Esq; Crest Packaging Ltd, Courteney Rd, Gillingham, Kent ME8 0RX (☎ 0634 34444, fax 0634 362473)

HARMER, Sir (John) Dudley; OBE (1963), JP (Kent 1962); s of Ernest Harmer; *b* 27 July 1913; *Educ* Merchant Taylors', Wye Coll London; *m* 1947, Erika Minder-Lanz, of Switzerland; 2 s; *Career* farmer; dep chm Kent Agric Exec Ctee 1964-72, tstee Kent Incorp Soc for Promoting Experiments in Horticulture 1979-; chm SE Area Cons Prov Cncl 1966-71, pres E Kent Euro Cons Cncl 1982- (chm 1979-82); kt 1972; *Style*— Sir Dudley Harmer, OBE, JP; Stone Hill, Egerton, Ashford, Kent (☎ 023 376 241)

HARPER, Brig (Charles) Anthony des Noëttes; CBE (1969, OBE 1964); s of Dr Charles Harold Lefebvre Harper (d 1936), of Finchley; *b* 17 July 1916; *Educ* St Edward's Oxford; *m* 1947, Francesca Marie, da of Col Frank John Beecham (d 1945), of Cape Town; 1 da; *Career* WWII served NW Europe, India, Malaya, Singapore, Germany; mil attaché Moscow 1966-68, Cdr Br Forces Antwerp 1969-71, security advsr HQ CENTO (Turkey) 1971-74, MOD HQ Intelligence Centre 1974-82; diplomat 1971-74, civil servant MOD 1974-82; ldr Ashford Borough Cncl 1985- (memb 1983-); *Clubs* Army and Navy; *Style*— Brig Anthony Harper, CBE; Venus House, The St, Appledore, Ashford, Kent TN26 2BU (☎ 023 383 375)

HARPER, Martin John; s of Frank Harper, of Welford-on-Avon; *b* 26 March 1925; *Educ* King Edward's GS Birmingham, LSE; *m* 1949, Stella, da of Francis Beavis, of Birkdale, Southport; 1 s, 2 da; *Career* merchant banker and conslt; dir: Keyser Ullmann 1971, London Interstate Bank 1980, Charterhouse Japhet 1980 (md 1984-86); chm: Charterhouse Japhet Credit 1983, Johnson Matthey Bankers 1984, Royal Scotland Finance Group 1986-, Minories Finance 1986-; *Recreations* reading, music, walking; *Clubs* Carlton, Overseas Bankers; *Style*— Martin Harper, Esq; 123 Minories, London EC3 (☎ 071 488 2671); Martin Harper & Co, 46a Priestlands Park Rd, Sidcup, Kent DA15 7HJ (☎ 081 300 1264)

HARPHAM, Barry Edward; s of Walter Edward Harpham (d 1960), of Yorks, and Sylvia May, *née* Groves; *b* 5 May 1952; *Educ* Beckenham and Pence GS for Boys, Univ of Kent; *m* 1 July 1986, Lynetta Jane, da of David Street, of Sussex; 1 da (Victoria b 1986); *Career* audit jr, then audit mangr Thomson McLintock & Co (CAs) 1973-82; fin controller: Racal Defence Group 1982-85, ERC Group 1985-87; gp accountant JP Knight Lt 1988-; FCA 1978; *Recreations* model making; *Style*— Barry Harpham, Esq; 40 Meadowdown Close, Hempstead Valley, Gillingham, Kent ME7 3SH (☎ 0634 365687): 348 High Street, Rochester, Kent (☎ 0634 826633, fax 0634 829093)

HARRIES, Hon Mrs (Anne Marjorie); *née* Sidney; da (by 1 m) of 1 Visc De L'Isle, VC, KG, GCMG, GCVO, PC; descent King William IVs natural da Lady Sophia FitzClarence (d 1837) w 1 Baron De L'Isle and Dudley (d 1851); *b* 1947; *m* 1967, David Alexander Harries, *qv*, s of Rear Adm David Hugh Harries, CB, CBE; 2 s (David b 1970, James b 1972), 1 da (Alexandra b 1968); *Style*— The Hon Mrs Harries; Hayselden Manor, Sissinghurst, Kent

HARRIES, David Alexander; s of Rear Adm David Hugh Harries, CB, CBE (d 1980), of Sydney, Aust, and Margaret Emily, *née* Street (d 1982); *b* 14 April 1938; *Educ* Geelong GS Corio Aust, Royal Aust Naval Coll, RNC Dartmouth; *m* 3 June 1967, The Hon Anne Marjorie, *qv*, da of The Rt Hon Viscount De L'Isle, VC, KG, GCMG, GCVO, PC, of Penshurst Place, Kent; 2 s (Henry b 4 May 1970, James b 28 June 1972), 1 da (Alexander b 13 July 1968); *Career* Royal Aust Navy 1955-72, ADC to Govr-Gen of Aust 1962-64, active serv Vietnam 1970; admitted slr 1979; ptnr Thomson Snell & Passmore

1982-; Liveryman Worshipful Co of Broderers; *Recreations* tennis, swimming, walking and family pursuits; *Clubs* Boodle's, Union and Royal Sydney Golf (Sydney); *Style*— David Harries, Esq; Hayselden Manor, Sissinghurst, Cranbrook, Kent TN17 2AE (☎ 0580 714228); Thomson Snell & Passmore, New Rents, Ashford, Kent TN23 1LB (☎ 0233 37303, fax 0233 45222, telex 95194 TS&P G)

HARRIS, Adam Ralph; s of Philip Harris (d 1962), of Glasgow, and René Eva, *née* Cohen; *b* 26 May 1953; *Educ* Woodfarm HS Glasgow, Stevenson Coll Edinburgh (HND); *m* 25 May 1979, Carolyn, da of Harry Davis, of Glasgow; 2 da (Michelle Claire b 25 Nov 1974, Katy Nicole b 25 Oct 1980); *Career* engr IBM 1977-80, euro mktg mangr NEC (UK) 1980-87, md ICS (UK) Ltd 1987-, purchasing and tech dir Opus Computers 1988-; vice chm E Grinstead Jewish Community, memb Radar charity for Disabled; *Style*— Adam P Harris, Esq; Components House, Medway Wharf Rd, Tonbridge, Kent TN2 1RE (☎ 0732 353532, fax 0732 362749)

HARRIS, 6 Baron Harris (UK 1815); George Robert John Harris; s of 5 Baron Harris, CBE, MC (d 1984), and Dorothy Mary (d 1981), da of Rev John Crookes; *b* 17 April 1920; *Educ* Eton, ChCh Oxford; *Career* Capt RA; *Style*— The Rt Hon the Lord Harris; Huntingfield, Faversham, Kent (☎ 0795 282)

HARRIS, Hugh Christopher Emlyn; s of T E Harris, CB, CBE, (d 1955), and M A Harris (d 1980); *b* 25 March 1936; *Educ* The Leys Sch, Trinity Coll Cambridge (MA); *m* 7 Sept 1968, Pamela Susan, da of R A Woollard (d 1980); 1 s (William b 1972), 1 da (Kate b 1970); *Career* Nat Serv Lt RA 1954-56; dir: BE Services Ltd 1979-, Houblon Nominees 1988-, The Securities Mgmnt Tst Ltd 1988-; assoc dir Bank of Eng 1988- (joined 1959, chief of corp servs 1984-88); dir Solefield Sch Educnl Tst Ltd, church warden St Margaret's Lothbury, hon treas Royal Br Legion Kemering branch, memb cncl Business in the Community; ACIB, FIPM, FRSA; *Recreations* rugby, tennis; *Style*— Hugh Harris, Esq; Bank of England, London EC2R 8AH (☎ 071 601 3131)

HARRIS, Sir Philip Charles; s of Charles William Harris, and Ruth Ellen, *née* Ward; *b* 15 Sept 1942; *Educ* Streatham GS; *m* 1960, Pauline Norma, da of Bertie William Chumley (d 1968); 3 s, 1 da; *Career* chm: Harris Queensway plc 1964-88 (chief exec 1987), Harris Ventures Ltd 1988, Carpetright of London 1988, CW Harris Properties 1988, Furniture City 1988; dir Harveys Hldgs plc 1986; non exec dir: Great Universal Stores 1986, Fisons plc 1986; memb: Br Showjumping Assoc, cncl of govrs Utd Med and Dental Schs of Guys and St Thomas's Hosps 1984, Ct of Patrons RGOG 1984; govr Nat Hosp for Nervous Diseases 1985; Hambro Business Man of the Year 1983; Hon Fell Oriel Coll Oxford 1989; kt 1985; *Recreations* showjumping, cricket; *Style*— Sir Philip Harris; Harris Ventures Ltd, Central Court, Knoll Rise, Orpington, Kent BR6 0JA (☎ 0689 75135)

HARRISON, Dr David Lakin; s of Dr James Maurice Harrison, DSC, Surgn Lt RN (d 1971), and Rita Graham, *née* Sorley (d 1970); *b* 1 Oct 1926; *Educ* Malvern Coll, Clare Coll Cambridge (MA, MB BDh, PhD), St Thomas's Hosp; *Career* Flt Lt (med) RAF 1953-55; med practitioner; dir Harrison Zoological Museum Sevenoaks, former conslt in mammalogy Govt of the Sultanate of Oman; author of contribs to numerous scientific jls; former memb Survival Cmmn IUCN (Caprinae Gp), former nat judge Country Life Farm Conservation Competition; *Books* Footsteps in the Sand (1959), The Mammals of Arabia (3 vols 1964-72), Rodents in Desert Enviroments (1975), Mammals of the Arabian Gulf (1981); *Recreations* fishing, squash; *Style*— Dr David Harrison; Bowerwood House, St Botolph's Rd, Sevenoaks, Kent TN13 3AQ (☎ 0732 453114)

HARRISON, Julian Pitman Hyde; s of Lt-Col Jim Willoughby Hyde Harrison, MC (d 1958), and Sylvia Hayward, *née* Pitman (d 1956); *b* 21 Aug 1929; *Educ* Bryanston, Magdalen Coll Oxford (MA); *m* 23 Jan 1965, June Selby, da of Herbert Saysell Colwill (d 1959); 1 s (James b 10 July 1967), 1 da (Sarah b 23 Aug 1965); *Career* memb Lloyd's 1957-, underwriter T R Mountain and others 1970-, chm A R Mountain & Son Ltd 1988-; cnclr (Cons) Camden Borough 1968-71 and 1978-86; contested (C) Stoke-on-Trent (Central) 1959 and 1964; Liveryman Worshipful Co of Merchant Taylors 1956; *Recreations* chess, reading, maintaining a country house; *Clubs* Carlton, City of London; *Style*— Julian Harrison, Esq; Danemore Park, Speldhurst, Kent TN3 OJP (☎ 0892 862 829); 37 Gayton Rd, London NW3 1UB; A R Mountain & Son Ltd, Lloyds, London EC3M 7HL (☎ 071 623 7100 ext 3153)

HARROP, Stuart Reginald; s of Reginald Harrop, of E Yorkshire, and Valerie Mary, *née* Hotham; *b* 11 Jan 1956; *Educ* Beverley GS, Univ of Leeds (LLB); *m* 30 April 1983, Tracy Ann, da of Dennis Roy Green; 2 s (Lee Stuart b 11 May 1986, Joel William b 3 Feb 1990); *Career* admitted slr 1980; slr Costain Gp plc 1982-84, co slr Albright & Wilson Ltd 1984-86, ICI plc 1986-88, dir legal servs Stock Exchange 1988-; memb: Law Soc, Assoc des Juristes Franco-Britanniques; *Recreations* freelance photography, natural history and business; *Style*— Stuart Harrop, Esq; The Stock Exchange, Old Broad St, London EC2N 1HP (☎ 071 588 2355, fax 071 588 3886)

HART, Cncllr Peter John; *Educ* Coll St Pierre; *m* Sylvia Kath Leen Frances; 2 s (John, Ian); *Career* estate agent and valuer; Kent co cncllr 1977-81; chm: Gravesend Cons Assoc 1980-83, Medway Cons Assoc 1983-85, Gravesend borough cncllr 1983-, Mayor of Gravesend 1988-89 (dep Mayor 1987-88); FNAEA; *Style*— Cncllr Peter Hart; 21 Clinton Ave, Strood, Rochester, Kent ME2 3TN (☎ 0634 723097); Peter Hart Estate Agents and Valuers, 183 Parrock St, Gravesend, Kent DA12 1EN (☎ 0474 358282)

HASBURY, Dr Christopher Raymond; s of Raymond John Hasbury, of Sidmouth, and Edith Irene, *née* Archer; *b* 29 March 1951; *Educ* Aston GS Birmingham, Univ of Birmingham Med Sch (BCh); *m* 1 (m dis 1989), Mary Bridget, *née* Bannon; 2 da (Rachel b 1979, Elizabeth b 1981); *Career* conslt anaesthetist Medway AHA; memb: BMA, Coll of Anaesthetists; *Recreations* sailing, skiing; *Clubs* Hollowshore; *Style*— Dr Christopher Hasbury; Medway District Hosp, Windmill Rd, Gillingham, Kent (☎ 0634 830000)

HASWELL, Maj Chetwynd John Drake (Jock); s of Brig Chetwynd Henry Haswell, CIE (d 1956), and Dorothy Edith, *née* Berry (d 1973); *b* 18 July 1919; *Educ* Winchester, RMC Sandhurst; *m* 25 Oct 1947, (Charlotte) Annette, da of Richard Cecil Petter (d 1971); 2 s (Richard b 1948, Charles b 1956), 1 da (Frances b 1950); *Career* cmmnd The Queen's Royal (W Surrey) Regt 1939-60, ret Offr grade II (author) Intelligence Centre 1966-84; tech writer and PR offr Messrs Spembly Ltd 1960-64, md Southern Sales Promotion Ltd 1964-66; memb: Nat Tst, English Heritage, CPRE; chm Regimental Museum Managing Tstees, historian for The Queen's Regt; *Books* under pen name George Foster: Indian File (1960), Soldier on Loan (1961); under own name (Jock Haswell): The Queen's Royal Regiment (1967), The First Respectable Spy (1969), James II, Soldier and Sailor (1972), British Military Intelligence (1973), Citizen Armies (1973), The British Army (1975), The Battle for Empire (1976), The Ardent Queen-Margaret of Anjou (1976), Spies and Spymasters (1977), The Intelligence and Deception of the D Day Landings (1979), The Tangled Web-Tactical and Strategic Deception (1985), The Queen's Regiment (1985), Spies and Spying (1986); *Recreations* gardening, carpentry, building; *Style*— Maj Jock Haswell; The Grey House, Lyminge, Folkestone, Kent CT18 8ED (☎ 0303 862232)

HATTERSLEY, Cncllr Carol Ann; da of Harry Albert Richard Watts, of Gillingham, Kent, and Maisie Dorothy, *née* West; *b* 30 April 1946; *Educ* Woodlands Sch Gillingham; *m* 1, 1965 (m dis 1982), Michael John Stokes; 1 s (Robert Neil b 1971), 3 da (Corrina Jane b 1966, Sharon Lynda b 1968, Sandra Elaine b 1974); m 2, 10 Sept 1983, Clifton Thomas, s of Sydney George Hattersley, of Ash Vale, nr Aldershot; *Career* borough cncllr (C) Riverside Ward Gillingham 1982-; vice chm: Leisure Servs Mgmnt Sub Ctee, Cons Women's Constituency Ctee; chm Riverside branch Gillingham Cons Assoc, vice chm of govrs Arden and Richmond Co Primary Sch, govr Hempstead Co Primary Sch; *Style*— Cncllr Carol Hattersley; 49 Tyler Drive, Rainham, Gillingham, Kent ME8 9LU (☎ 0634 370717)

HATTERSLEY, Cncllr Clifton Thomas; s of Sydney George Hattersley, of 5 Waverley Gardens, Ash Vale, Aldershot, Hants, and Ada Rosalie, *née* Davies; *b* 5 May 1945; *Educ* Dartford GS, Kings Coll London (BSc); *m* 10 Sept 1983, Carol Ann, da of Harry Albert Richard Watts, of 35 Layfield Rd, Gillingham; 1 step s (Robert Neil Stokes b 1971), 3 step da (Corrina Jane Stokes b 1966, Sharon Lynda Stokes (Mrs Couch) b 1968, Sandra Elaine Stokes b 1974); *Career* sr systems analyst UK Paper Co Ltd (formerly Bowaters); memb Gillingham Borough Cncl 1979- (currently chm Housing Mgmnt and Info Technal Panel); tstee Parkwood Community Assoc; former chm: Nat Branches of Disablement Income Gp, Govening Body Forge Len Infant Sch Gillingham, Gillingham Cons Assc 1988; *Recreations* classical guitar, photography, astronomy; *Style*— Cncllr Clifton Hattersley; 49 Tyler Drive, Rainham, Gillingham, Kent ME8 9LU (☎ 0634 370717); UK Paper Co Ltd, Kemsley Mill, Sittingbourne, Kent ME10 2SG (☎ 0795 424488)

HATTERSLEY-SMITH, Dr Geoffrey Francis; s of Maj Wilfred Percy Ashby Hattersley-Smith, DSO (d 1968), of The Crossways, Cranbrook, Kent, and Ethel Mary, *née* Willcocks (d 1937); *b* 22 April 1923; *Educ* Winchester New Coll Oxford (MA, DPhil); *m* 12 May 1955, Maria, da of Dionysius Kefallinos (d 1968), of Zakynthos, Greece; 2 da (Kara Mary, Fiona Anastasia); *Career* Sub-Lt RNVR 1942-46, Normandy Indian Ocean N Atlantic and Arctic; base ldr and glaciologist King George Island Falkland Islands Dependencies Survey 1948-50, scientific staff offr Def Res Bd Ottawa Canada 1951-73, chm Ctee on Glaciers Canadian Nat Res Cncl 1960-66, princ scientific offr Br Antarctic Survey and sec Antarctic Place-names Ctee FCO 1973-90 (Antarctic tour 1988); author of numerous scientific papers; fell: Arctic Inst of N America (formerly govr), RGS (fndr's Gold Medal 1966), Royal Soc of Canada; pres: Arctic Circle Club Canada 1964-67, Arctic Club UK 1976; *Books* North of Latitude Eight (1974), Present Arctic Ice Cover (1974), History of Place-names in the Falkland Islands Dependencies (1980), History of Place-names in the British Antarctic Territory (1991), The Norwegian with Scott (ed, 1984); *Recreations* polar, naval and mountaineering history, gardening; *Clubs* Arctic Circle (Canada), Arctic (UK), Antarctic, Geographical; *Style*— Dr Geoffrey Hattersley-Smith; The Crossways, Cranbrook, Kent TN17 2AG (☎ 0580 712865)

HAWARDEN, 8 Viscount (I 1793); Sir Robert Leslie Eustace Maude; 10 Bt (I 1705); also Baron de Montalt (I 1785); s of 7 Viscount (d 1958), by his w Marion (da of Albert Wright, whose w Margaretta was sis of 20 Baron

FitzWalter); *b* 26 March 1926; *Educ* Winchester, ChCh Oxford; *m* 1957, Susannah, da of Maj Charles Gardner (gggs of 1 Baron Gardner); 2 s, 1 da; *Heir* s, Hon Connan Maude; *Career* served Coldstream Gds 1944-45; landowner and farmer; *Style*— The Rt Hon the Viscount Hawarden; Wingham Court, Canterbury, Kent CT3 1BB (☎ 0227 720222)

HAWES RICHARDS, Derek; s of Arthur Hawes Richards (d 1971), and Eva Evelyn, *née* Small (d 1987); *b* 2 Feb 1933; *Educ* South Devon Technical Coll Torquay; *m* 29 Aug 1959, Hazel Anne, da of Victor Maddison, of Kent; 2 da (Lisa b 1966, Sophie b 1973); *Career* CA; cncllr Kent County Cncl 1985-, pres C of C 1988-FRIBA; *Recreations* cricket, snooker, music, reading; *Style*— Derek Hawes Richards, Esq; Hop Press Oast, Mascalls Court Rd, Paddock Wood, Kent TN12 6NB; 4 St Johns Rd, Tunbridge Wells, Kent (☎ 0892 38777, fax 0892 49849)

HAWKINS, Kerry James; s of Clifford Hawkins, of Hornsey, London, and Joyce, *née* Thresher; *b* 29 April 1946; *Educ* Stationers' Co Sch, Trinity Coll Cambridge (MA); *m* 26 July 1975, (Lilian) Vanessa Rowan, da of Frederick Gardener Rowan Henderson (d 1969), of Gairloch, Wester Ross; 3 s (Andrew b 25 April 1977, Nicholas b 23 Aug 1979, Christopher b 6 Nov 1982); *Career* CA; Coopers & Lybrand: joined 1967, qualified 1970, sr mangr; currently gp fin controller Lloyds Bank (joined 1975); tstee and treas Cornwallis Tst, govr Sissinghurst Sch 1986-88; Master Lodge of Trinity 1986; FCA 1979; *Recreations* golf, tennis, swimming; *Style*— Kerry Hawkins, Esq; White Cottage, Flishinghurst, Cranbrook, Kent (☎ 0580 712358); Lloyds Bank plc, 71 Lombard St, London EC3P 3BS (☎ 071 356 1363, fax 071 283 4819)

HAWKINS, Peter; s of Ernest Hawkins (d 1959), of Bexhill on Sea, and Elsie Mabel Hawkins (d 1954); *b* 30 Jan 1926; *Educ* private; *m* 3 previous m, all dis; 1 s (Stephen John b 1948), 3 da (Jacqueline Mary b 1950, Deborah Shione b 1955, Kay Iona b 1975); *Career* journalist; various positions held on local newspapers 1943-49, news ed Sunday Pictorial 1956-59 (reporter and feature writer 1949-56), foreign corr Daily Mirror newspapers 1959-63, asst news ed Daily Express 1975-79; author and novelist 1963-; screenwriter 1979-; currently working on various screen writing projects incl an original comedy-drama serial for a jt Cinema Verity and BBC TV prodn; chm The Jeanie Campbell Breast Cancer Radiotherapy Appeal 1981- (fndr tstee 1979); memb Writers' Guild of GB 1969-; *Books* novels from 1963: The Daffodil Girls, The Sun Lovers, The Neon Gods, The Naked Spy, The Spying Machine, The Man with Mad Eyes; Prince Rainier of Monaco (authorised biography, 1966); charity pubns: Trying to Put Your Mind at Rest About Breast Cancer 1985, Fighting Breast Cancer Without Losing Your Breast 1988; *Recreations* meeting people, jazz and classical music, travel; *Clubs* Wig and Pen; *Style*— Peter Hawkins, Esq; 29 St Luke's Ave, Ramsgate, Kent CT11 7JZ (☎ 0843 593193)

HAY, Jocelyn Elizabeth Joyce; da of William George Board (d 1951), and Olive Price, *née* Jones (d 1962); *b* 30 July 1927; *Educ* Open Univ (BA); *m* 26 Aug 1950, William Andrew Hunter Hay, TD, s of Sheriff J C E Hay, CBE, MC, TD, DL (d 1975); 2 da (Penelope Jill b 1960, Rosemary Anne b 1961); *Career* freelance journalist and broadcaster 1954-83, Forces Broadcasting Serv Woman's Hour BBC Radio 2 and 4; head of press and PR dept Girl Guide Cwlth Headquaters London 1973-78, princ London Media Workshops 1978- (fndr), examiner CAM Diploma in non-commercial PR 1987-88; fndr chm Voice of the Listener 1983-, dist cmmnr and brownie guider Girl Guides Assoc Gravesend dist; memb Soc of Authors, MIPR; *Recreations* gardening, bee-keeping; *Style*— Mrs Jocelyn Hay; 101 King's Drive, Gravesend, Kent DA12 5BQ (☎ 0474 564676)

HAYES, Sir Claude James; KCMG (1974, CMG 1969); s of James Benjamin Fidge Hayes (d 1951); *b* 23 March 1912; *Educ* Ardingly, St Edmund Hall Oxford (MA, MLitt), Sorbonne Univ Paris, New Coll Oxford; *m* 1940, Joan, da of Edward McCarthy Fitt (d 1984); 2 s (Peter, Robert), 1 da (Rosemary); *Career* Lt-Col BEF 1939, N Africa, Sicily, Italy, Combined Ops NW Europe; cmmr 1949, Civil Serv, HM Treasy 1957-64, princ fin offr Miny of Overseas Devpt 1965-68, chm Crown Agents for Overseas Govts and Admins 1968-74; vice chm E D Sassoon Banking Co Ltd 1968-72; interim cmmr for W Indies 1968-85; *Recreations* garden maintenance and betterment, old oak furniture, Georgian domestic chattels, Wealden timber houses; *Style*— Sir Claude Hayes, KCMG; Prinkham, Chiddingstone Hoath, Kent (☎ 0342 850 335)

HAYES, Jeremy (Jerry); s of John Hayes, of Snodland, Kent, and Agnes Margaret, *née* Pemble; *b* 16 March 1952; *Educ* Holmesdale Co Secdy Sch Snodland, Medway & Maidstone Coll of Technol Maidstone; *m* 1 Dec 1984, Ann Brenda, da of Donald Thomas Worsley, of Snodland, Kent; 1 s (John b 27 Jan 1987); *Career* trainee accountant Reed Int 1970-76; mgmnt accountant: Key Terrain Aylesford 1976-81, Aylesford Paper Mills West Mill 1987-83, Aylesford Paper Mills East Mill 1983-; Lab cncllr: Snodland Town Cncl 1981- (chm Fin Ctee 1982-85 and 1988-, chm Planning and Enviroment Ctee 1985-86 and 1987-88), Tonbridge and Malling Borough Cncl (representing Snodland) 1986-; active memb Lab Pty; ACMA 1978; *Recreations* cycling, walking, reading; *Clubs* Snodland Working Men's, Ham Hill Workman's; *Style*— Jerry Hayes, Esq; 2 Dowling close, Snodland, Kent ME6 5PF (☎ 0634 242720); Reed Paper & Board (UK) Ltd, Aylesford Paper Mills, Aylesford, Maidstone, Kent (☎ 0622 70123 x 3039, fax 0622 79488, telex 965131)

HAYES, Dr (John) Paul Leslie Adolph; s of Leslie Hayes (d 1967), of 30 City Way, Rochester, Kent, and Jeanne Paule Adolphine, *née* Monot (d 1986); *b* 28 Dec 1937; *Educ* Kings Sch Rochester, Mathematical Sch Rochester, St Thomas's Hosp Univ of London (BSc, MB BS); *Career* house surgn in urology St Mary's Hosp Portsmouth 1963, house physician St Paul's Hosp Hemel Hempstead 1963, sr house offr in pathology St George's Hosp London 1965-67; Westminster Hosp London: sr registrar in haematology 1967-70, lectr in haematology 1970-77; memb Kent Archaeological Soc; life memb: Bluebell Railway, City of Rochester Soc; fndr memb N Downs Steam Railway, life fell RSPB; fell RSM, memb BMA, memb Br Soc for Maemoatology; *Recreations* archaeology, railway preservation; *Style*— Dr Paul Hayes; District Laboratory, All Saints Hospital, Chatham, Kent ME4 5NG (☎ 0634 407311, fax 0634 5234)

HAYLEY, Dr Thomas Theodore Steiger; s of Otto Johannes Steiger (d 1945), and Constance Mary, *née* Hayley (d 1971); *b* 4 Oct 1913; *Educ* Clifton, Univ of Cambridge (MA), Univ of Oxford (MA), Univ of London (PhD); *m* 7 Sept 1946, Audrey, da of Sir Keith Cantlie, CIE (d 1977); 3 s (Keith b 1952, Clive b 1957, Robin b 1962), 2 da (Ann b 1954, Emma b 1973); *Career* Indian Civil Serv: dep cmmr sec and dir to the Govt of Assam in depts under PM 1938-50; asst dir Br Branch Int C of C; memb Br Psycho-Analytical Soc and Inst of Psycho-Analysis (chm and vice pres 1969-72); ed: International Journal of Psycho-Analysis 1978-, International Review of Psycho-Analysis 1978-; FRAI; *Books* The Anatomy of Largo Religion and Groups; *Style*— Dr Thomas Hayley; Old East Haxted, Edenbridge, Kent TN8 6PT (☎ 0732 862276); 5 Upper Wimpole St, London W1M 7TD (☎ 071 935 9305)

HAYNES, Edwin William George; CB (1971); s of Frederick William George Haynes (d 1934), and Lilian May, *née* Armstrong (d 1950); *b* 10 Dec 1911; *Educ* Univ of London (BA, LLM); *m* 1942, Dorothy Kathleen; 1 s (Andrew), 1 da (Kathleen); *Career* called to the barr Lincoln's Inn; civil servant, under sec DTI; ret; *Recreations* books, gardens; *Clubs* Civil Service; *Style*— Edwin Haynes, Esq, CB; 92 Malmains Way, Beckenham, Kent (☎ 081 650 0224)

HAYNES, Rev Peter Nigel Stafford; s of (Wilfred) Reginald Haynes, of 11 The Chilterns, Bromley, and Violet Eileen, *née* Gray (d 1984); *b* 22 Jan 1939; *Educ* Kent Coll Canterbury, Sorbonne, Hertford Coll Oxford (MA); *m* 1, 3 June 1964 (m dis 1984), Susan Jane; 2 s (William David Stafford b 5 Dec 1965, Richard Thomas Benjamin b 6 Sept 1967); m 2, 25 May 1984, Annette Justine Susan, da of Rev Richard John Connell, OBE; 2 step s (David De Lisle Murray-Smith b 6 Feb 1964, Anthony Michael Murray-Smith b 20 July 1966); *Career* curate: All Saints' Parish Upper Norwood 1964-68, St Mark's Parish Portsea 1968-72; asst chaplain Holy Trinity Protestant Cathedral Brussels 1972-76, memb General Synod Staff Church House Westminster 1980-85, priest in charge Holy Trinity Parish with Nettlestead 1985-; sec Cncl for Christian Approaches to Def and Disarmament; memb: Div of Int Affrs Br Cncl of Churches, Christians For Europe, Rochester Diocese Cricket XI; *Books* The Brandt Report (1982); *Recreations* cricket; *Style*— The Rev Peter Haynes; The Vicarage, Bush Rd, East Peckham, Tonbridge TN12 5LL (☎ 0622 871278)

HAYWARD, Sir Anthony William Byrd; s of Eric Hayward (d 1964), of Dane St House, Chilham, nr Canterbury, and Barbara Olive, *née* Bird (d 1976); *b* 29 June 1927; *Educ* Stowe, Ch Ch Oxford; *m* 1955, Jenifer Susan, da of Dr Francis Howard McCay (d 1985); 2 s, (Simon, Charles), 2 da (Charlotte, Emma); *Career* temp Sub-Lt RNVR 1945-48, served in Scotland, SE Asia, Persian Gulf; family business in India 1948-57, dir Shaw Wallace and Co India 1957-78 (chm and md 1970-78), pres Associated Chambers of Commerce and Indust of India 1977-78, md Guthrie Berhad Singapore 1978-81, pres and chief exec offr Private Investmt Co for Asia (PICA) SA 1982-84, dir of various cos; FRSA; kt 1978; *Recreations* shooting, fishing, golf, photography; *Clubs* Boodles, Oriental, Rye Golf; *Style*— Sir Anthony Hayward; Dane St House, Chilham, near Canterbury, Kent (☎ 0227 730221)

HAYWARD, Sir Richard Arthur; CBE (1966); s of late Richard Bolton Hayward, and Jessie Emmeline Elisabeth Hayward; *b* 14 March 1910; *Educ* Catford Central Sch; *m* 1936, Ethel Wheatcroft; 1 s, 1 da; *Career* dep gen sec Union of PO Workers 1951 (asst sec 1947), sec gen Civil Serv Nat Whitley Cncl 1956-66; chm: Supplementary Benefits Cmmn 1966-69, NHS Staff Cmmn 1972-75, New Towns Staff Cmmn 1976-77; memb: Civil Serv Security Appeals Panel 1967-82, PO Bd 1969-71, Home Office Advsy Panel on Security (Immigration Act 1972) 1972-81, Parole Bd for England and Wales 1975-79, Slrs Disciplinary Tbnl 1975-82; life vice pres: Civil Serv Sports Cncl 1973- (chm 1968-73), Assoc of Kent Cricket Clubs 1984- (pres 1970-84); tstee Kent County Playing Fields Assoc 1975-89, chm Southborough Soc 1983-87; pres Civil Serv: Cricket Assoc, FA; hon life memb: Nat Assoc of Young Cricketers; Freeman City of London 1980; kt 1969; *Recreations* sport, history of Southwark; *Style*— Sir Richard Hayward, CBE; Lower Cowley, Parracombe, Barnstaple, N Devon EX31 4PQ (☎ 059 83 373)

HAYWARD, Richard Wellesley; s of Harold Joseph Hayward, MC, and

Olive Mary, *née* Stanley (d 1988); *b* 4 Aug 1928; *Educ* Colston's Sch Bristol, Brixton Sch of Bldg (now S Bank Poly); *m* 14 June 1952, Jill Patricia, da of Wing Cdr Arthur Leslie Grice (ka), of Hatch End, Middlesex; 1 da (Jenny (Mrs Spivey) b 29 July 1958); *Career* sr ptnr Burrell Hayward and Budd 1974-80; memb gen cncl RICS 1971-79, chm RICS (Central London Branch) 1979-80, dir and sec School Mistresses and Governesses Benevolent Inst 1980-; memb The Clapham Soc; Freeman: City of London 1977, Worshipful Co of Tallow Chandlers 1978, Worshipful Co of Chartered Surveyors 1977-87; ARICS 1954, FRICS 1965; *Recreations* reading, walking the dog, Georgian and Victorian glass; *Style*— Richard Hayward, Esq; Flat 3, 23 West Side, Clapham Common, London SW4 9AN (☎ 071 228 5232); SGBI Office, Queen Mary House, Manor Park Rd, Chislehurst, Kent BR7 5PY (☎ 081 468 7997)

HAYWARD, Maj-Gen (George) Victor; s of George Harold Hayward (d 1971), of Stratford-on-Avon, and Daisy, *née* Ball (d 1975); *b* 21 June 1918; *Educ* Blundell's, Univ of Birmingham (BSc); *m* 18 July 1953, Gay Benson, da of Hamilton Barrett Goulding (d 1947), of Dublin; 1 s (Stephen George Hamilton b 1954), 1 da (Victoria Clare b 1956); *Career* served WWII 1939-45, cmmnd 1940, transf to REME 1942, GSO1 REME Training Centre 1958, cdr REME 2nd Div 1960, asst mil sec WO 1962, Col RARDE, Fort Halstead 1963, CO 38 Central Workshop 1965, Dep Cmdt Technical Gp REME 1966, Cmdt REME Trg Centre 1969, Cmdt Technical Gp REME 1971-73, Col Cmdt REME 1973-78; planning inspr DOE 1973-88; CEng, FICE, FIMechE, FBIM; *Recreations* sailing, skiing, shooting; *Clubs* Army and Navy; *Style*— Maj-Gen Victor Hayward; Chart Cottage, Chartwell, Westerham, Kent TN16 1PT (☎ 0732 866253)

HAYWOOD, Bernard Arthur Charles; s of Arthur Haywood, of Burnham on Sea, Somerset, and (Mildred) Mary, *née* Jenden; *b* 3 Sept 1945; *Educ* St Richards Secdy Sch Bexhill on Sea, Hastings Coll of FE; *m* 26 Sept 1964, Margaret, da of Frederick James Bond (d 1975); 1 s (Anthony b 1965), 2 da (Natalie b 1967, Louise b 1969); *Career* Br Fire Bde (14 yrs), asst dist fire prevention offr Merton and Sutton Health Authy (6 yrs), currently dist fire prevention offr S E Kent Health Authy; MIFPO 1983, MNAHFO, memb GIFireE; *Recreations* hospital radio, sea fishing, caravanning, armchair gardening; *Style*— Bernard Haywood, Esq; Hunros, 40 Essella Rd, Ashford, Kent TN24 8AN (☎ 0233 645353); St Mary's Hospital, Fire Training Centre, Etchinghill, Kent

HAYWOOD, Ian Robert; s of Walter Robert Haywood (d 1974), of Finchley, and Eileen Mary, *née* Warren (d 1987); *b* 13 Oct 1941; *Educ* Bedford Sch, St Thomas' Hosp Med Sch Univ of London; *m* 28 March 1970, Margaret Comrie, da of John Hannah, MBE (d 1984), of Annan, Dumfries and Galloway; 2 da (Jennifer b 1971, Susan b 1973); *Career* cmmnd Beds Regt TA 1959, reg cmmn RAMC 1965-; house appts: St Thomas' Hosp, Addenbrookes Hosp Cambridge; regtl med offr RWF, jr staff appts in surgery RAMC 1968-78, lectr in surgery Westminster Hosp Med Sch 1975, lectr Bart's Hosp Med Sch 1977-78, conslt surgn RAMC 1978, jt prof of mil surgery RCS and Royal Army Med Coll 1985, Ben Eiseman Visiting Prof Uniformed Univ Health Scis Bethesda Maryland 1987, examiner RCSE; author of numerous papers in learned jls; memb Exec Cncl Br Assoc for Immediate Care (chm Inter-Serv Liason and Disaster Planning Ctee); FRSM, FRCS 1970, FRCSE 1989; OStJ; *Books* Medicine for Disasters (contrib, 1988), Problems in General Surgery (contrib, 1989); *Recreations* history and photography; *Style*— Ian Haywood, Esq

HAYWOOD, Michael Robert; s of Robert Oliver Haywood (d 1962), of Edinburgh, and Helen Agnes, *née* O'Halloran (d 1986); *b* 9 Oct 1941; *Educ* Edinburgh Acad, Univ of Edinburgh, Trinity Hall Cambridge; *m* 2 August 1966, Stella Margaret, da of Angus McPherson Lyle (d 1971), of 10 Silverknowes Terrace, Edinburgh; 2 s (Nicholas Angus b 12 May 1970, Oliver Gabriel b 31 May 1975), 2 da (Sarah Helen b 21 Sept 1967, Rebecca Emily b 20 Jan 1969); *Career* offr cadet Edinburgh Univ OTC 1959-63, Lt TAVR 1964-70; asst history master Dulwich Coll 1964-70; head of History Dept and housemaster Dollar Acad 1970-80 (dep rector 1975-80), headmaster Sutton Valence 1980-; chm St James' Vestry Dollar; memb: Community Cncl Dollar, Maidstone Rotary Club 1981-83; govr: Rosehill Prep Sch Tunbridge Wells, Underhill Prep Sch Chart Sutton; memb: HMC, SHA 1980; *Recreations* reading, music, hill walking, sailing; *Clubs* East India, Devonshire, Public Schools; *Style*— Michael Haywood, Esq; The Headmaster's House, Sutton Valence School, Sutton Valence, Maidstone, Kent ME17 3HL (☎ 0622 842381)

HEAD, (Edwin) Leonard; AFC; s of John William Head, of Mortlake, Surrey, and Maud, *née* Richards; *b* 4 Jan 1910; *Educ* Mortlake Elementary Sch; *m* 18 Sept 1937, Kathleen Marjorie, da of John Lynch, of Waldemar Ave, Fulham; 1 s (Michael John b 19 March 1943), 1 da (Susan Patricia b 31 Aug 1939); *Career* pilot RAF 1939-46; municipal offr 1924-39, chm E L Head Ltd 1946-89; privately studied biological use of oxygen 1946-89; privately sponsored res Univ of Cardiff into biological functions of electrons and oxygen 1970-80; discovered: chronic bronchitis linked to peak high barometric pressure (Hg 30.7 ins) 1946, poliomyelitis epidemics linked to peak low barometric pressure (Hg 29.5 ins) 1952, possible use of oxygen to prevent devpt of common cold and influenza 1960, atmospheric electrons linked to biological functions 1965, application of high voltage electrons to biological tissue to relieve arthritic pain and promote healing of burns 1978, that biological oxygen remains inert in body until activated by uptake of biological electrons at cellular level 1982; ind evaluation undertaken by Prof David Denison prof of clinical physiology Nat Heart and Lung Inst (results not yet published); *Books* Electron Therapy (1989); *Recreations* golf, bridge; *Style*— Leonard Head, Esq, AFC; E L Head Ltd, Eddington Works, Herne Bay, Kent CT6 5TR (☎ 0227 372217, fax 0227 367124)

HEAP, Sir Desmond; s of William Heap, of Burnley, Lancs, and Minnie Heap; *b* 17 Sept 1907; *Educ* The GS Burnley, Univ of Manchester (LLB, LLM); *m* 6 Oct 1945, Adelene Mai, da of Frederick Lacey, of Harrogate; 1 s (John Nicholas Desmond b 5 July 1951), 2 da (Sally Elizabeth Adelene b 10 Aug 1946, Joanna Mary Alison b 29 April 1948); *Career* admitted slr 1933; chief asst slr City of Leeds 1938-40 (prosecuting slr 1935-38), dep town clerk Leeds 1940-47, comptroller and city slr to Corporation of London 1947-73; lectr Leeds Sch of Architecture 1935-47; RTPI: legal memb 1935-, cncl memb 1947-77, pres 1955-56; assoc memb RICS 1953- (cncl memb 1957-84); memb: Colonial Office Housing and Town Planning Advsy Panel 1953-65, Editorial Bd of Planning and Environment Law 1948-, Cncl on Tribunals 1971-77; vice pres Statute Law Soc 1982-, dep pres City of London branch BRCS 1956-76, chm of govrs Hurstpierpoint Coll 1975-82; hon assoc Worshipful Co of Solicitors of City of London 1987, Liveryman Worshipful Co of Carpenters, hon memb Court of Worshipful Co of Chartered Surveyors; Law Soc: cncl memb 1954-78, chm Law Reform Ctee 1955-60, chm Town Planning Ctee 1964-70, pres 1972-73; Hon LLD Univ of Manchester; FRSA (cncl memb 1974-78); kt 1970; *Books* Planning Law for Town and Country (1938), Planning and the Law of Interim Development (1944), An Outline of Planning Law (1949, 10 edn 1990), Encyclopaedia of Planning Law and Practice (1960), Encyclopaedia of Betterment Levy (1967), How to Control Land Development (1974, 2 edn 1981); *Recreations* swimming, pedal biking, stage and theatre; *Clubs* Athenaeum, City Livery, Guildhall; *Style*— Sir Desmond Heap; Hammond Suddards, 10 Piccadilly, Bradford BD1 3LR (☎ 0274 734700); Sugden and Spencer, Arndale House, Charles St, Bradford BD1 1ER (☎ 0274 732271)

HEATH, Rt Hon Edward Richard George; MBE (1946), PC (1955), MP (C) Bexley Sidcup 1974-; s of late William George Heath and his 1 w Edith Annie, *née* Pantony; the family has been traced back in a continuous male line to one William Heath, of Cliston in Blackawton, Devon (d 1546); Mr Heath's f was a builder, his gf a railwayman, his ggf a merchant seaman, his gggf a coastguard, his ggggf a mariner; *b* 9 July 1916; *Educ* Chatham House Sch Ramsgate, Balliol Coll Oxford ; *Career* served WWII RA (Maj 1945, despatches); Lt-Col cmdg 2 Regt HAC (TA) 1947-51; Master Gunner within the Tower of London, 1951-54; admin Civil Service 1946-47, worked in journalism and merchant banking 1947-50; MP (C) Bexley 1950-74, oppn leader 1965-70 and 1974-75, PM 1970-74; asst oppn whip 1951, lord cmmr Treasury 1951, jt dep chief whip 1952, dep chief whip 1953-55, parly sec Treasy and govt chief whip 1955-59, Min Labour 1959-60, Lord Privy Seal with FO responsibilities (negotiating UK entry EEC) 1960-63, sec state Indust, Trade, Regnl Devpt and pres BOT 1963-64; memb of Ind Cmmn on Int Devpt Issues (the Brandt Cmmn 1977-80 Advisory Ctee), chm IRIS 1981-83; chm LSO Tst 1963-70 (memb 1974-), vice-pres Bach Choir 1970-, pres EEC Youth Orch 1977-, hon memb LSO 1974-; lectures: Godkin at Harvard 1968, Cyril Foster Meml Oxford 1965, Montagu Burton Leeds 1976, Edge Princeton 1976, Romanes Oxford 1976, Ishizaka Japan 1979, Felix Neubergh Gothenburg 1979, 10 STC Communication London 1980, Noel Buxton Univ of Essex 1980, Alastair Buchan Meml London 1980; Hoover Univ of Strathclyde 1980; Stanton Griffs Disting, Cornell Univ 1981; Edwin Stevens, RSM, 1981; William Temple, York 1981; City of London, Chartered Insce Inst 1982; John Findley Green, Westminster Coll, Missouri 1982; Mizuno, Tokyo, 1982; ITT European, Brussels, 1982; Bruce Meml, Keele Univ 1982; Gaitskell, Univ of Nottingham 1983; Trinity Univ, San Antonio 1983; lect to mark opening Michael Fowler Centre, Wellington, NZ 1983; Bridge Meml, Guildhall 1984; David R Calhoun Jr Meml Washington Univ, St Louis 1984; Corbishley Meml RSA 1984; John Rogers Meml Llandudno 1985; George Woodcock, Univ of Leicester 1985; Royal Inst of Int Affairs, Chatham House 1985; Int Peace Lecture, Univ of Manchester 1985; London Business Sch Lecture, Regent's Park 150 Anniversary of the Tamworth Manifesto 1985; 4 Annual John F Kennedy Mem Lectr, Oxford 1986; Employment Inst, Josiah Mason Lectr, Birmingham 1986; The Netherlands Inst for Int Relations 1986; Address to both Houses of the Swiss Parliament, Zurich 1986; Lothian Fndn Lectr 1987, Maitland, Edward Boyle Meml Lectr, Sir John Keswick Meml Lectr Southern Methodist Univ Texas 1988, Edward Boyle Memorial Lecture Leeds Univ 1988; visiting Chubb Fell Yale 1975, Montgomery Fell Dartmouth Coll 1980; Hon DCL Oxford, DTech Bradford, DCL Kent; Hon Doctorate Sorbonne; hon fell Balliol Coll Oxford; Nuffield Coll Oxford, Inst of Devpt Studies at Univ of Sussex; hon FRCM, FRCO and Fell Royal Canadian

Coll of Organists, Hon DL Westminster Coll Fulton Missouri; Liveryman Worshipful Co of Goldsmiths, Hon Freeman Musicians' Co; *Books* One Nation: A Tory Approach to Social Problems (co-author 1950), Old World, New Horizons (1970), Sailing-A Course of My Life (1975), Music-A Joy for Life (1976), Travels-People and Places in My Life (1977), Carols-The Joy of Christmas (1977); music: chm London Symphony Orch Tst 1963-70, 1971 conducted Orch in Elgar's 'Cockaigne' Overture at its gala concert in the Royal Festival Hall London, has since conducted orchestras in London Cologne and Bonn, also conducted Royal Philharmonia Orchestra, Philharmonia, London Sinfonia, Liverpool Philharmonic Orch, Bournemouth Symphony Orch, Bournemouth Sinfonia, the English Chamber Orch, the Thames Chamber Orch and the Sarum Chamber Orch, Berlin Philharmonic Orch, Chicago Symphony Orch, Philadelphia Symphony Orch, Cleveland Symphony Orch, the Minneapolis Symphony Orch, the Grand Teton Festival, the Jerusalem Symphony Orch, The Shanghai Philharmonic Orch, the Beijing Central Symphony Orch, the Swiss-Italian Radio Television Symphony Orch and the Zurich Chamber Orch, Singapore Symphony Orchestra; was instrumental in founding the European Community Youth Orch of which he is pres, and conducted it on its 1978 Easter tour and 1978, 1979 and 1980 Summer tours of Europe, he has also conducted at the World Festival of Youth Orchs in Aberdeen in 1977 and 1978; Freiherr Von Stein Fndn Prize, Charlemagne Prize 1963, Estes J Kefauver Prize 1971, Stresseman Gold Medal 1971, Gold Medal of City of Paris 1978, World Humanity Award 1980, Gold Medal European Parl; sailing (bought ocean racer 'Morning Cloud' 1969, won Sydney to Hobart race 1969, Capt British team Admiral's Cup 1971 and 1979, Capt British team Sardinia Cup 1980); *Recreations* music, sailing; *Clubs* Royal Yacht Sqdn, Buck's, Carlton, St Stephen's; *Style—* The Rt Hon Edward Heath, MBE, MP; House of Commons, London SW1A 0AA

HEATH, Raymond Bartlett; s of Frederick William Heath (d 1930), and Elizabeth Augusta Heath (d 1958); *b* 14 March 1928; *Educ* Royal Masonic Sch, Univ of Sheffield (MB ChB, MD); *m* 1952, Edith, da of Edwin Swift (d 1966); 1 s (David b 1953, d 1978), 1 da (Katherin b 1955); *Career* RAF 1946-48; prof of virology Bart's Hosp 1975-90 (sr lectr 1960-74); memb Soc Gen Microbiology; memb RSM, MRCPath; *Books* Modern Trends in virology (co-ed, vol 1 1967, vol 2 1970), Virus Diseases (ed, 1979), Virus Diseases and the Skin (1983); *Recreations* golf, gardening, birdwatching; *Clubs* Athenaeum; *Style—* Prof Raymond Heath; The Cottage, Leybourne Rd, Broadstairs, Kent (☎ 0843 61618); Dept of Virology, St Bartholomew's Hospital, London EC1A 7BE (☎ 071 601 7351)

HEATHER, Colin Michael; s of Harold James Alfred Heather (d 1980), of Gillingham, Kent, and Ellen Elizabeth, *née* Tidey; *b* 7 Jan 1940; *Educ* Sir Joseph Williamsons Mathematical Sch Rochester, HM Dockyard Upper Sch Chatham; *m* 11 Sept 1963, Pamela Elizabeth, da of Charles Ernest Stevens (d 1952); 2 da (Lynette Elizabeth b 1964, Tracey Marie b 1966); *Career* planning technician 1972-74, planning offr 1974-89, town clerk Paddock Wood Town Cncl 1978-; *Recreations* philately, music, travel; *Style—* Colin Heather, Esq; Yew Tree Cottage, Tong Rd, Brenchley, Tonbridge, Kent TN12 7AN (☎ 0892 723527)

HEDDLE, Robert Miller; s of Robert Shearer Heddle, of Ringwood, Hampshire, and Edith, *née* Miller (d 1948); *b* 22 April 1942; *Educ* Trinity Sch Wood Green London, King's Coll London, Westminster Med Sch (MB BS); *m* 28 Feb 1970, Valerie Anne, da of Thomas Donnelly; 2 s (Robert Sinclair b 1975, William Flett b 1982), 1 da (Anabel b 1972); *Career* sr registrar Westminster Hosp 1975-80, conslt surgn Canterbury 1981-; Harvard fell Boston Mass USA 1973-74; FRCS, FRCSEd; memb: Assoc Surgns GB and I, Vascular Surgical Soc GB and I; *Books* Treatment of Cancer (contrib, 1990); *Recreations* angling; *Clubs* Kent and Canterbury; *Style—* Robert Heddle, Esq; 5 Dover St, Canterbury, Kent

HEFFORD, Patricia (Pat); da of Sidney Thomas Hinkley (d 1977), of Derby, and Frances Elizabeth, *née* Wells (d 1979); *b* 7 Nov 1936; *Educ* Parkfields Cedars GS Derby; *m* Paul Brian Hefford; 2 da (Sarah Eve b 2 Nov 1968, Rachel Paula b 27 Nov 1971); *Career* chm Rede Action Gp (green belt conservation) 1982-88, memb Tradescant Tst; *Style—* Mrs Pat Hefford

HEMMING, Alexander Cameron; s of Alexander Henry Hemming (d 1972), of London, and Catherine Margaret, *née* Dickinson (d 1975); *b* 8 Dec 1925; *Educ* Dulwich; *m* 5 Sept 1953, Joan Mary, da of Gilbert Frederick William Goodliffe (d 1965), of Worthing, Sussex; 1 s (Ian Alexander b 1963), 1 da (Sarah Joan b 1958); *Career* dir: Office Cleaning Services Ltd 1971-86, Cannon Hygiene Ltd 1977-86; capt Old Alleynian FC 1950-53, memb RFU 1970-83; pres: Kent Co RFU 1976-79 (capt 1951-53), Alleyn Club 1988-89; RFU liaison offr for int tours from NZ Aust Tonga and USA; *Recreations* rugby (played in England rugby trial 1950), cricket, golf, travel; *Clubs* MCC, British Sportsmans, Alleyn; *Style—* Alexander Hemming, Esq; Twaskent, 44 Baston Rd, Hayes, Bromley, Kent BR2 7BE (☎ 081 462 1844)

HEMMING-CLARK, Rev Stanley Charles; s of Charles George Clark (d 1937), of Aldershot, and Alice, *née* Netley (d 1962); *b* 1 March 1929; *Educ* Collyer's Sch, Peterhouse Cambridge (BA), Ridley Coll Cambridge (MA); *m* 13 Aug 1955, Stella Audrey, da of Arthur James Hemming (d 1976), of Guildford; 1 s (John b 1960), 1 da (Margaret b 1957); *Career* Nat Serv RAF 1947-49; C of E deacon 1954, priest 1955; asst curate: Holy Trinity Redhill 1954-56, St John Woking 1956-59; vicar Crockenhill 1959-, chaplain Parkwood Convalescent Home Swanley 1959-65, pt/t teacher 1965-88; clerk Crockenhill Almshouses; memb: Rochester Diocesan Synod, Rochester Diocesan Bd of Educn; *Recreations* gardening, walking, lit; *Style—* The Rev Stanley Hemming-Clark; The Vicarage, Eynsford Rd, Crockenhill, Swanley, Kent BR8 8JS; 84/86 High Path Rd, Merrow, Guildford, Surrey GU1 2QL (☎ 0322 62157)

HEMPSTOCK, (Nigel) Duncan; s of Christopher Mathew Hempstock (d 1954), of Solihull, and Sarah Helen, *née* Hopkinson (d 1952); *b* 7 Jan 1940; *Educ* Kings Sch Macclesfield, Warwick Sch; *m* 30 April 1962, Jenifor Mary, da of Frank Walker (d 1981), of Solihull; 1 s (Christopher Duncan b 1974), 2 da (Sarah Elizabeth b 1963, Ruth b 1965); *Career* cadet offr and 3 offr P&O St NAV Co Ltd 1955-60; trainee mangr MCD 1960-64, mangr Capol Transport 1964-68, commercial mangr Crescent Shipping 1968-75, export sales and distribution mangr Sheerness Steel 1975-83, md Crescent Shipping Ltd 1983-, md Crescent Wharves Ltd 1983-, dir Hays Marine Servs 1983-, dir Br Motor Ship Owners Assoc 1983-; fell Inst of Transport; *Recreations* sailing, fishing, walking; *Style—* Duncan Hempstock, Esq; 11-13 Canal Rd, Rochester, Kent ME2 4DS (☎ 079589 431, office 0634 290092, fax 0634 290111, telex 96276)

HENDERSON, George Poland; s of George James Henderson (d 1963), and Emma Rouse Wilson (d 1949); *b* 24 April 1920; *Educ* Westminster City, University of London; *m* 27 April 1953, (Shirley) Prudence Ann Cotton, da of Kenneth W Cotton, Librarian, Bank of England (d 1942); 2 s (Crispin Alastair Poland b 1955, Antony James Willis b 1957); *Career* Capt RA 1940-46; commercial reference librarian Guildhall Library London 1946-63, dir Kellys Directories Ltd 1963-66; pres: Assoc of Br Directory Publishers 1974-75, Euro Assoc Directory Publishers 1976-78; Freeman City of London 1961; FInstD 1970; *Books* Current British Directories 6 edns (1953-71), European Companies A Guide to Sources of Information 3 edns (1961-72), Directory of British Associations 10 edns (jtly, 1965-90); *Recreations* travel, gardening, postal history; *Style—* George Henderson, Esq; CBD Research Ltd, 15 Wickham Rd, Beckenham, Kent BR3 2JS (☎ 081 650 7745, fax 081 650 0768)

HENDERSON, Giles Ian; s of Charles David Henderson (d 1980), of Henfield, Sussex, and Joan, *née* Firmin; *b* 20 April 1942; *Educ* Michaelhouse Natal SA, Witwatersrand Univ SA (BA), Magdalen Coll Oxford (MA, BCL); *m* 21 Aug 1971, Lynne, da of Charles William Fyfield, OBE, of Alnmouth, Northumberland; 2 s (Mark b 1974, Simon b 1975), 1 da (Clare b 1978); *Career* admitted slr 1970, ptnr Slaughter and May 1975-; *Recreations* sport, music; *Style—* Giles Henderson, Esq; Slaughter and May, 35 Basinghall St, London EC2V 5DB (☎ 071 600 1200, fax 071 726 0038, 071 600 0289, telex 883486)

HENDERSON, Gordon Leonard; s of William John Butler-Henderson, JP, and Pauline, *née* Pullen (d 1954); *b* 27 Jan 1948; *Educ* Fort Luton Boys Sch, Rochester Mathematical Sch, Medway Coll of Technol; *m* 1 (m dis 1978), Marilyn Louise, *née* Rawlings; 1 da (Tamara Louise b 17 July 1972); m 2, 1979, Benita Kathleen, *née* Jemmett; *Career* mangr FW Woolworth 1964-79, restauranteur 1979-83, political agent Cons Pty 1983-85, sr contracts offr GEC Avionics 1985-; elected Kent CC 1989; chm: Sheppey Conservatives, Kent Assoc of Boys Clubs Media & PR Ctee 1990; vice chm Faversham Constituency Cons Assoc, dir SWIM; govr: Lady Anne Cheyne Sch, Sir Thomas Cheyne Sch, Eastchurch Primary Sch; tstee Leysdown Charity; *Recreations* writing, politics and sports; *Style—* Gordon Henderson, Esq; 6 The Crescent, Halfway, Minster, Sheppey ME12 3BQ (☎ 0795 667113)

HENLEY, Capt John Arthur Cameron; DSC (1952); s of Vice Adm Joseph Charles Walrond Henley, CB, DL (d 1968), of The Down House, Lamberhurst, Kent, and Esmé Gordon, *née* Cameron (d 1968); *b* 18 Feb 1913; *Educ* West Downs, RNC Dartmouth; *m* 27 Oct 1942, Frances Mary, da of Lt-Gen Francis Home Griffiths, OBE, DL (d 1962); 3 s (David Edward b 23 Jan 1944, Richard John b 22 May 1946 d 1989, Christopher Francis b 27 April 1957); *Career* HMS Queen Elizabeth 1930-33, Staff of C-in-C Home Fleet 1941-42 (present at sinking of Bismarck), HMS Mauritius for D Day Landings 1944, in cmd HMS Charity in Korean War 1950-52; Capt: HMS Diamond 1957-58, HM Signal Sch 1959-61, HMS Centaur 1961-62; Naval ADC to HM The Queen 1962-63, ret 1963; attached to MOD 1963-73; pres Lamberhurst Branch Royal Br Legion 1963-, fndr Kent and Sussex Border Control Soc 1973, chm Lamberhurst Branch Cons and Unionist Assoc 1982-88; *Recreations* shooting, fishing, natural history; *Clubs* Army and Navy, Band of Brothers; *Style—* Capt John Henley, DSC, RN; The Old Stables, Scotney Castle, Lamberhurst, Tumbridge Wells, Kent TN3 8JD (☎ 0892 890322)

HERBERT, Rev David Alexander Sellars; s of Arthur Thomas Alexander Herbert (d 1982), of Hastings, and Edith Florence, *née* Harrison (d 1955); *b* 30 April 1939; *Educ* William Morris Sch Walthamstow, Univ of Bristol (BA), St Stephen's House Oxford (Theol Studies); *Career* teacher 1960-67, asst priest Christ Church St Leonards-on-Sea 1967-81, vicar St George's Bickley

Kent 1981-; sec gen Fedn of Catholic Priests 1973-82; chm: Hastings Cncl of Churches 1975-78, Hastings Cncl Vol Serv 1978-81, Rochester Fedn of Catholic Priests 1985-; memb Gen Synod C of E 1985-; *Recreations* cooking, travel, reading, drama; *Style—* The Rev David Herbert; St George's Vicarage, Bickley Park Rd, Bromley, Kent BR1 2BE (☎ 081 467 3809)

HERBERT, William Henry; s of Gerald Herbert (d 1977), of Kuling, Kiangsi, China, and Margrethe, *née* Clemmensen (d 1977); *b* 13 June 1936; *Educ* St Edward's Oxford, Bristol GS, Univ of Bristol (BA, MA); *m* 30 July 1964, Jennifer Mary, da of Joseph John Powell (d 1968), of Weston Super Mare; 2 s (Richard b 1973, John b 1975); *Career* head master: The British Sch Helsinki 1964-66, Lochinver House Sch Potters Bar 1966-71, Knights Templar Sch Baldock Herts 1971-76, Fulston Manor Sch Sittingbourne 1977-; memb Classical Assoc, past pres Kent Branch NAHT; FRGS, FCP; *Books* Excavations at Weston in Gordano (1961); *Recreations* music, walking; *Style—* William Herbert, Esq; 8 St Thomas Hill, Canterbury, Kent CT2 8EH; Fulston Manor Sch, Brenchley Rd, Sittingbourne, Kent ME10 4EG (☎ 0795 475228, fax 0795 428144)

HEROYS, Nicholas; s of Vladimir Héroys (d 1977), and Sheila Mary, *née* Walton; *b* 1 April 1937; *Educ* Tonbridge Sch, Sidney Sussex Coll Cambridge (MA); *m* 12 June 1965, Susan Evelyne, da of Allan Edward Moxham Janes, OBE (d 1987); 2 s (Michael b 13 June 1966, Alexander b 6 April 1968); *Career* Nat Serv 1955-57, cmmnd 2 Lt Royal Leics Regt (Cyprus); head of gp planning and fin Lamson Industries Ltd 1965-77; fin dir: McCorquodale plc 1977-87, Slaughter and May slrs 1987-; played cricket and racquets for Univ of Cambridge, Captained MCC against Univ of Cambridge 1974; Kent CCC: vice chm 1986-, tstee 1989-; hon sec Band of Brothers 1975-, tstee Tonbridge Sch XXth Century Fund 1984-; govr: Claremont Prep Sch St Leonards on Sea 1983-, Cobham Hall Girls Sch 1986-87; ctee memb: Old Tonbridgian CC 1969-, Yellowhammers CC 1972-, Bluemantles CC 1962-76; FCA; *Recreations* cricket, sport generally, gardening, reading; *Clubs* Hawks (Cambridge), MCC, XL; *Style—* Nicholas Héroys, Esq; St Catherines, 10 London Rd, Southborough, Tunbridge Wells, Kent TN4 0RR (☎ 0892 39971); Slaughter and May, 35 Basinghall St, London EC2V 5DB (☎ 071 600 1200, fax 071 600 0289)

HERRIN, John Edward; CBE (1985); s of Harold John Herrin (d 1974), of Humecourt, Hythe, Kent, and Gertrude Mary, *née* MacDermot (d 1989); *b* 15 Sept 1930; *Educ* Bancrofts Sch, Rugby Coll of Technol; *m* 4 April 1959, Heather Yeoman, da of Leslie Kirkpatrick Reid, JP (d 1980), of Mill House, Hale, Cheshire; 1 s (Jeremy b 1970), 2 da (Johanna b 1961, Caroline b 1962); *Career* Lt Cdr RNR 1953-55; chm Welwyn Electronics Ltd 1972; md: Royal Worcester plc 1975-83, Crystalate Hldgs plc 1983-88; dep chm Crystalate 1988-89; dir: Oxley Devpts Co Ltd 1989-, Queensgate Instruments Ltd 1989-; chm Yeoman Technol 1989-; pres Euro Electronics Component Mfrs Assoc 1986-88; memb: cncl of Electronic Component Indust Fedn (chm 1981-82), Nedo Electronics SG; chm N Regnl Cncl for Sport and Recreation 1982-84; Freeman City of London, Liveryman Worshipful Co of Scientific Instrument Makers (Sr Warden 1989-90); CEng, FIEE; *Recreations* sailing, shooting, fishing; *Style—* John Herrin, Esq, CBE; Petteridge Oast, Matfield, Kent TN12 7LX; Crystalate Holdings plc, Wharf House, Medway Wharf Rd, Tonbridge, Kent TN9 1RE (☎ 0732 361414)

HERRINGTON, Timothy John; s of John Herrington, of 16 Scotney Rd, Basingstoke, Hants, and Barbara Jean Margaret, *née* Toon; *b* 22 April 1954; *Educ* Queen Mary's GS Basingstoke Hants, Univ of Bristol (LLB); *m* 20 Feb 1982, Kathleen Mary, da of Peter Loy Chetwynd Pigott, of Botswana; 1 s (James b 1987); *Career* admitted slr 1978; ptnr: Coward Chance 1985 (joined 1978), Clifford Chance 1987-; memb Law Soc Standing Ctee on Co Law 1988- (chm Fin Servs Gp); Freeman: City of London 1977, The Worshipful Co of Slrs 1985; memb Law Soc; *Books* Life After Big Bang (contrib, 1987); *Recreations* cricket, travel, walking, gardening; *Clubs* Hampshire CCC; *Style—* Timothy Herrington, Esq; Clifford Chance, Royex House, Aldermanbury Sq, London EC2V 7LD (☎ 071 600 0808, fax 071 726 8561)

HEWSON, Michael John; s of George Alfred Hewson (d 1959), of Portsmouth, and Marjorie Phyllis, *née* Hall; *b* 17 March 1944; *Educ* Southern GS Portsmouth; *m* 21 July 1970, Sharland Elisabeth, da of Frank Templeman, of Grimsby; 1 s (Martin Philip b 1970); *Career* Nationwide Anglia Bldg Soc: branch mangr Oxford 1982-85 (Northampton 1976-81, Boston Lincs 1973-75), regnl mangr S E London 1988- (Surrey 1987, S E 1986); FCBSI 1973, MBIM 1973; *Recreations* mountaineering, rock climbing; *Style—* Michael Hewson, Esq; 9 Widmore Rd, Bromley, Kent BR1 1RP (☎ 081 464 0929)

HEYES, Dr Martyn Peter; s of John Harold Heyes (d 1988), of Liverpool, and Joyce Marion, *née* Willder; *b* 14 June 1943; *Educ* Alsop HS Liverpool, King's Coll London (BSc, MEng, PhD); *m* 24 Dec 1966, Hazel Norma, da of Alfred Concar, of Southport; 2 da (Tracy Ann b 17 April 1971, Wendy Jane b 21 Dec 1973); *Career* tport engrg consultancy 1966-74, chief asst engr Devon CC 1975-80, head of transportation planning Surrey CC 1980-83, dep co engr Gtr Manchester CC 1983-86, princ asst co surveyor Kent CC 1987-; memb: Co Surveyors Soc, Nat Tst; vice chm Co Rd Safety Offrs Assoc; CEng, MICE, MCIT, MBIM; *Recreations* travel, gardening; *Style—* Dr Martyn Heyes; Exeleigh Lodge, New Rd, Cranbrook, Kent TN17 3LE (☎ 0580 714737); Kent County Council, Highways & Transportation Dept, Sandling Block, Springfield, Maidstone, Kent ME14 2LQ (☎ 0622 671411, ext 6816, fax 0622 691028)

HEYWOOD, Francis Melville; s of Rt Rev Bernard Oliver Francis Heywood (d 1960), Bishop of Southwell, Hull and Ely, and Maude Marion, *née* Lempriere (d 1957); *b* 1 Oct 1908; *Educ* Haileybury, Gonville and Caius Coll Cambridge (BA, MA); *m* 28 Dec 1937, Dorothea Kathleen (d 1983), da of Sir Basil Edgar Mayhew, KBE (d 1966), of Felthorpe Hall, Norwich; 1 s (Simon b 1945 d 1985), 2 da (Susan, Janion), 1 adopted s (Michael b 1940); *Career* asst master Haileybury 1931-35, fell asst tutor and praelector Trinity Hall Cambridge 1935-39, Master of Marlborough 1939-52, Warden of Lord Mayor Treloar Coll 1952-69; *Books* A Load of New Rubbish (1985); *Recreations* formerly: cricket, rugby, squash, gardening; now walking; *Style—* F M Heywood, Esq; 30 The Bayle, Folkestone, Kent (☎ 0303 52366)

HICKS, Dr Brendan Hamilton; s of Bryan Hamilton Hicks (d 1968), of London, and Winefrede, *née* O'Leary; *b* 22 Feb 1942; *Educ* St Brendan's Coll Bristol, Univ of London (BSc, MB BS, MD); *m* 8 Oct 1966, Jacqueline Ann Hamilton, da of William R Box, of Reading; 1 s (Benjamin John Hamilton b 18 June 1974), 1 da (Amelia Clare Hamilton b 10 Oct 1970); *Career* lectr in med Guys Hosp Med Sch 1969-72, NIH int fell of the US Public Health Serv 1972-73, postgrad dean to United Med and Dental Schs of Guy's and St Thomas' Hosps Univ of London 1985- (sr lectr in med and conslt physician and endocrinologist 1974-84); chm educn section and cncl memb Br Diabetic Soc; Freeman City of London, Freeman Worshipful Soc of Apothecaries 1985 (memb ct of examiners); FRCP 1982; *Books* contrib A New short Textbook of Medicine (1988); *Recreations* good books, theatre & films, cocker spaniels, sailing and walking; *Style—* Dr Brendan Hicks; Pembury House, 3 Brewery Rd, Bromley Common, Kent BR2 8LG (☎ 081 462 3244); Guy's Hospital, Department of Endocrinology, London SE1 9RT (☎ 071 955 5000)

HIGGINS, Harold Robert (Harry); s of Perceval Edward Higgins (d 1979), and Lilian Blanche, *née* Hogg; *b* 25 June 1931; *Educ* Birkenhead Inst Eaton Hall Offr Cadet Sch, Royal Mil Coll of Sci, UMIST; *m* 24 Nov 1956, Gwenyth Joan, da of Ernest Smith (d 1972); 1 s (Guy Simon Stuart b 1961), 1 da (Sarah Jane b 1959); *Career* enlisted RAOC 1950, cmmnd 1951, serv Korea, Egypt, Cyprus, Borneo; exchange cmd appointment NZ Army 1975-78, Dep Garrison Cdr CoD Bicester 1978-81, Cmdt CAD Kineton 1981-83, Garrison Cdr Donnington 1983-85 (ret); dist gen mangr Medway Health Authy 1985-; pres Civil Serv Retirement Fellowship 1983-85, memb Shropshire Enterprise Tst 1984-85; FBIM 1979 (pres Shropshire Branch 1983-85); *Recreations* off shore sailing; *Clubs* RAOC Officers; *Style—* Harry Higgins, Esq; Medway Health Authority, Medway Hospital, Windmill Rd, Gillingham, Kent (☎ 0634 830000)

HIGGINS, Prof Peter Matthew; OBE (1987); s of Peter Joseph Higgins (d 1952), of 120 Powys Lane, Palmers Green, London, and Margaret Higgins (d 1982); *b* 18 June 1923; *Educ* St Ignatius Coll London, UCL, UCH London (MB BS); *m* 27 Sept 1952, Jean Margaret Lindsay, da of John Currie, DSO (d 1932), of Darlington, Co Durham; 3 s (Nicholas b 1954, Anthony b 1956, David b 1958), 1 da (Jane b 1959); *Career* Lt RAMC 1948, serv Libya, Capt 1949; UCH: house physician 1947 and 1950, res med offr 1951-52, asst med registrar 1953; princ in gen practice: Rugeley Staffs 1954-66, Castle Vale Birmingham 1966-68; sr lectr in gen med and head Gen Practice Res Unit Guy's Hosp Med Sch 1968-73, princ in gen practice Thamesmead 1968-73, regnl advsr in gen practice 1970-88, prof of gen practice Guy's Hosp Med Sch 1974-88; vice chm SE Thames RHA 1976- (memb 1974-), chm Kent Family Health Servs Authy 1990-; memb: Chislehurst Soc, Court Univ of Kent, W Kent Med Soc, Nat Cncl Family Serv Units; chm Thamesmead Family Serv Unit Mgmnt Ctee; tstee Thamesmead Community Assoc Tst; former memb: Attendance Allowance Bd, Editorial Bd Health Trends, Standing Med Advsy Ctee DHSS; former govr Linacre Centre for Study of Med Ethics; FRSA, FRSM 1950, FRCP, FRCGP; *Recreations* squash, tennis, swimming, music; *Style—* Prof Peter Higgins, OBE; Wallings, Heathfield Lane, Chislehurst, Kent BR7 6AH (☎ 081 467 2756)

HIGGS, Dr Frederick David; s of Charlie Higgs, BEM, JP (d 1981), of Home Farm, Isle of Grain, and Joyce Alice, *née* White; *b* 13 Feb 1939; *Educ* Bethany Sch Goudhurst, Mill Hill Sch, St John's Coll Oxford (MA), Guy's Hosp (BM BCh); *m* 28 Feb 1970, Josephine, da of Dr Arthur Hartland Wright (d 1987), of Zaire and Umberleigh, N Devon; 2 s (James b 1974, John b 1977), 2 da (Sarah b 1971, Mary b 1980); *Career* house physician Guy's Hosp 1964, med offr Save The Children Fund Algeria 1966, SHO Hammersmith Hosp 1967, paediatric registrar Southmead Hosp Bristol 1969, physician specialist Solomon Islands W Pacific 1970-77, ptnr in gen practice Sevenoaks Kent 1979-; MRCP; *Style—* Dr Frederick Higgs; Meadow Gate, Chart Lane, Brasted, Westerham, Kent TN16 1LN (☎ 0959 62507); Amherst Medical Centre, London Rd, Sevenoaks, Kent TN13 2JD (☎ 0732 459255)

HIGH, Katherine; da of Douglas Arthur Brown, of Exeter, and Gwyneth, *née* Jones; *b* 20 March 1957; *Educ* Manchester HS for Girls, Somerville Coll Oxford (BA, MA); *m* 25 Sept 1982, Desmond Charles Fitzpatrick High, s of

Geoffrey Charles High, of Tunbridge Wells; *Career* trainee accountant Ernst & Whinney London 1978-82 (qualified 1981), audit supervisor (then insolvency specialist) Coopers & Lybrand Sydney Aust 1982-85, mangr corporate recovery Peat Marwick McLintock Maidstone 1986-88, fin controller and co sec Sports & Leisure Devpt plc Gillingham Kent 1988-; ctee memb Maidstone Choral Union, memb Methodist Church; ACA 1982; *Style—* Mrs Katherine High; 29 Paynes Lane, Loose, Maidstone, Kent; Sports & Leisure Developments plc, The Ice Bowl, Gillingham Business Park, Gillingham, Kent (☎ 0634 376800, fax 0634 374065)

HIGHE, Jackie; da of John Barraclough (d 1988), and Lily, *née* Senior (d 1989); *b* 17 Sept 1947; *Educ* Univ of Leeds; *m* 5 April 1968, Brian Highe, s of Philip Highe, of Yorkshire; 1 s (Philip b 1971), 1 da (Jane b 1969); *Career* assoc ed Living Magazine 1984-86, ed Parents Magazine 1986-88; ed in chief: Bella Magazine 1988-90, First For Women 1990-; memb: UK Women's Forum, Br Soc of Magazine Eds; *Recreations* music, walking, reading; *Style—* Mrs Jackie Highe; First For Women, 270 Sylvan Ave, Englewood Cliffs NJ 07632 USA

HIGHFIELD, Jane Elizabeth; da of Peter Frederick Highfield, of Ponsanooth, Cornwall, and Iris Joyce, *née* Heath (d 1970); *b* 24 Aug 1956; *Educ* Bruton Sch for Girls Sunnyhill, Malmesbury GS, Claremont Sch Esher, RAM (LRAM, GRSM), Guildhall Sch of Music; *m* 23 Aug 1980, John Graham Lacy, s of William Lacy; *Career* prof Blackheath Conservatoire of Music 1980-83, prof of singing Jr Acad RAM 1987- (teacher 1976-), lectr local adult educn authys and ILEA, vocal coach Nat Youth Choir of GB, freelance singer in recitals concerts and opera (debut Wigmore Hall), soloist major venues GB and abroad (incl Purcell room, Queen Elizabeth Hall and St John Smith Square), broadcast for BBC, sang for Bayreuth Opera Festival 1989 and 1990; memb: Trio d'Amici, Rondel Ensemble, Quintette, Cncl for Music in Hosps, Equity, Int Fund for Animal Welfare, Nat Tst, First Church of Christ Scientist Bromley, The Mother Church Boston Massachusetts; *Recreations* tennis, walking, travel; *Clubs* RAM; *Style—* Miss Jane Highfield; 1 Ullswater Close, Bromley, Kent BR1 4JF (☎ 081 460 3503); Simply Singers, 339 Portobello Rd, London W10 5SA (☎ 071 960 1594); Helen Sykes Artists' Management, 11 Elm Rd, East Sheen, London SW14 7JL (☎ 071 224 3881)

HIGTON, (Desmond) Ian Ralph; s of John William Higton (d 1966), of Haslemere, and Olive Gwendoline, *née* Smith (d 1979); *b* 9 Dec 1934; *Educ* Farnham GS Surrey, King's Coll London, King's Coll Hosp Med Sch (MB BS, AKC, MRCS, LRCP); *m* 20 June 1959, Margaret Jean, da of Sir Wilfred John Neden, CB, CBE (d 1978); 1 s (John Robert b 8 Oct 1964), 1 da (Elisabeth Mary Jean b 11 July 1960); *Career* conslt surgn Bromley Health Authy attending Beckenham, Bromley, Farnborough, Sloane and Chelsfield Park Hosps 1970-, recognised teacher of Univ of London 1983; memb: Bromley Health Authy, BMA; FRSM, FRCS; *Books* Colour Atlas of Minor Surgery in General Practice (with John Fry and John Stephenson, 1990); *Clubs* Chelwood; *Style—* Ian Higton, Esq; Courtneys, 36 Forest Drive, Keston, Kent BR2 6EF (☎ 0689 51936); Farnborough Hospital, Farnborough Common, Orpington, Kent (☎ 0689 53333)

HILL, David Beatty; s of Frederick Charles Hill (d 1964), and Jane Elizabeth, *née* Garlick (d 1934); *b* 5 Nov 1918; *m* 29 March 1952, Patricia, da of Thomas Walsh (d 1982), of Cornell House, Manor Park, Chislehurst, Kent; 2 da (Stevanne, Nikki); *Career* WWII RN 1939-40, special ops 1940-44, Fleet Air Arm 1944-45; asst ed Kentish Times 1946; ed: Ford Times 1946, European Esquire 1951; asst ed Daily Sketch 1953, ed Weekend 1956; ed-in-chief and md: Harmsworth Publications 1958, Weekend Publications 1958, Harmsworth Press 1977; dir Associated Newspapers 1979; hon citizen New Orleans USA 1969; Freeman City of London 1967, Liveryman Worshipful Co Stationers and Newspaper Makers; *Books* The Cat Race (1952); *Recreations* golf, indolence as a fine art; *Clubs* Special Forces; *Style—* D Beatty Hill, Esq; Hill Court, Manor Park, Chislehurst, Kent

HILL, Maj John Arnold; TD (1943), DL (1973); s of (John) Arnold Hill (d 1961), of Penco, St Mary's Rd, Long Ditton, Surrey, and Lucie Ann, *née* Bucknell (d 1963); *b* 17 March 1903; *Educ* Westminster; *m* 1 Feb 1941, Esmé Evelyn, da of (Alfred) Ernest Yarrow (d 1943), of How Green, Hever, Kent; 2 s ((John) Antony Yarrow b 30 June 1943, Roderic Gordon b 27 July 1944), 2 da (Diana Esmé b and d 1942, Angela Rosemary (Mrs Fossick) b 26 July 1947); *Career* joined HAC 1921, Maj 1935, cmd B Batty; CA 1926; Price Waterhouse 1926-28, dir Argentine Land Investment Co 1958 (sec 1928), ptnr Bird Potter CAs 1935-58; dir: Securicor 1948-, Essex Water Co 1958-85; church warden St Peter's Church Hever 1946-49, joined Kent CC 1961 (chm 1969-72); memb: senate Univ of Kent at Canterbury, SOS Soc, govr Sevenoaks Sch 1969-82; memb: Worshipful Co of Broderers 1935 (Master 1966), Fitzroy Lodge 1932 (Centenary Master 1949); memb Inst of CAs 1926; *Recreations* golf, tennis, gardening, riding, walking; *Clubs* The Bath, Argentine, City Carlton, St Stevens; *Style—* Maj John Hill, TD, DL; Mountfield, Bayleys Hill, Sevenoaks Weald, Kent TN14 6LY (☎ 0732 463257)

HILL, Pauline (Mrs Briggs); da of Antony George Dyce (d 1986), of Rochester, and Doris Olive, *née* Tweed; *b* 21 Oct 1934; *Educ* St Angela's Ursuline Convent London, Bognor Regis Trg Coll (Cert Ed); *m* 1, 1954, Stanley Hill (d 1975); 2 s (David Roger b 1961, Martin Alistair b 1963); m 2, 26 March 1983, Anthony Arthur Briggs, s of late Martin Briggs, of London; *Career* freelance writer; writes workshops for academic instns and professional gps; involved in SE Arts; *Books* Noisiest Class in the School (1981), Noisiest Class at the Beach (1983); *Recreations* travel, entertainment; *Clubs* Soc of Authors, Pen International Soc of Women Writers; *Style—* Ms Pauline Hill

HILLEN, John Malcolm; s of Clarence Albert Hillen, of Great Barr, Birmingham, and Winifred Mary Hillen, *née* Bristow; *b* 13 May 1952; *Educ* King Edward VI GS Aston, Lincoln Coll Oxford (BA, MA); *m* 5 Oct 1985, Monica Lillian Marie, da of Harry Frewin Curtice, of Aldwick, West Sussex; 1 s (Guy Albert Curtice b 23 March 1989), 1 da (Florence Elizabeth b 11 Dec 1987); *Career* called to the Bar Middle Temple 1976; memb: South Eastern Circuit, Central Criminal Ct Bar Mess, Kent Bar Mess, Criminal Bar Assoc; *Recreations* theatre, cinema; *Style—* John Hillen, Esq; 3 New Square, Lincolns Inn, London WC2 3RS (☎ 071 242 2523, fax 071 831 6968); 62 London Rd, Maidstone, Kent ME16 8QL (☎ 0622 685049, fax 0622 691178)

HILLIER, David Philip Ian; s of David William John Hillier, of Parsonage Farm, Church Rd, Eastchurch, Sheerness, Kent, and Yvonne Judy, *née* Fairservice; *b* 28 April 1963; *Educ* St Andrews Rochester Kent, Reaseheath Cheshire Agric Coll, Hadlow Agric Coll; *Career* dir Bourne & Hilliers Creameries Ltd 1987-; chm N Kent Nat Dairymans Assoc 1988 (vice chm SE region 1990), memb: Nat Dairymans Benevolent Inst, RAS, NFU; *Recreations* cricket, hockey, country pursuits; *Clubs* Gore Court Cricket, Cantagrians Assoc, Castle (Rochester); *Style—* David Hillier, Esq; Little Oakhurst, Ashford Rd, Bethersden, nr Ashford, Kent TN26 3BQ (☎ 023 382865); Bourne & Hilliers Creameries Ltd, 7 Revenge Rd, Lordswood, Chatham, Kent ME5 8TP (☎ 0634 864477, fax 0634 201800)

HILLIER, Jennifer Mary; da of Mark George Templeman, of Farnborough, Kent and Marjorie Alice, *née* Brugh; *b* 12 Nov 1937; *Educ* Beckenham Convent, Chelsea School of Pharmacy (MRPharmS); *m* 9 Oct 1965, Christopher Hillier, s of Alfred George Lesley Hillier, of Beckenham, Kent; 1 s (Christopher George b 30 May 1969), 1 da (Elizabeth Marjorie Katherine b 17 Oct 1972); *Career* pharmacist Bromley Health Authy; borough cncllr, Farnborough Ward Bromley 1974-, chm various ctees and sub-ctees (mostly Educn and Servs), sch govr; memb: Bromley Health Authy, St Olavs Fndn; treas local Cons Assoc, mayor Bromley 1990-91; *Recreations* botany, english history, music, architecture; *Style—* Mrs Jennifer Hillier; Willow Tree Cottages, 327 Crofton Rd, Locks Bottom, Farnborough, Kent BR6 8NR (☎ 0689 51773)

HILLS, Maurice John; s of Herbert Percy Redvers Hills (d 1988), of Tunbridge Wells, and Kathleen Marion, *née* Geer; *b* 27 March 1941; *Educ* Sutton Valence Sch, Br Sch of Osteopathy (Dip); *m* 17 Sept 1966, Margaret, da of Arthur Stanley Phillips, of Tunbridge Wells; 2 s (Matthew b 1970, Jolyon b 1973), 1 da (Catherine b 1968); *Career* private osteopath 1963-; cncl memb and Registrar Gen Cncl and Register of Osteopaths, MRO; *Recreations* art and antiques, fly fishing, wine; *Style—* Maurice Hills, Esq; Tarquin, Roedean Rd, Tunbridge Wells, Kent TN2 5JX (☎ 0892 29730)

HILLYER, John Selby; OBE (1975); s of Stanley Gordon Hillyer, OBE (d 1965), of Sussex, and late Margaret, *née* Selby; *b* 14 Feb 1925; *Educ* Stowe, Trinity Coll Oxford (MA); *m* 2 June 1951, Elizabeth Ann, da of Sinclair Jeavons Thyne, CBE, of Tasmania; 1 s (James b 1952), 2 da (Sarah b 1955, Caroline b 1958); *Career* Lt Coldstream Gds; called to the Bar Inner Temple 1949; ptnr Hill Vellacott, CA 1954-88, sr ptnr Chantrey Vellacott 1988-89; dir: T H White Ltd 1954-, Capel-Cure Myers Unit Trust Management Ltd; chm cncl Barnardo's 1970 (memb 1962-); Master Worshipful Co of Fanmakers 1969; *Recreations* gardening, keeping ornamental ducks; *Clubs* Royal Automobile, City Livery; *Style—* John S Hillyer, Esq, OBE; Copden House, Biddenden, Kent

HILTON, Geoffrey Charles; s of Harry Roscoe Hilton, of Rayleigh, Essex, and Lilian, *née* Dyas; *b* 16 March 1949; *Educ* Southend on Sea GS, Hatfield Poly (BA), Kingston Poly (Dip Mktg); *m* 6 July 1974, Susan Mary, da of Edward Butcher; 1 s (Simon Geoffrey b 1981), 1 da (Emma Jane b 1978); *Career* overseas mktg exec Bowater Scott Corporation 1971-76, product mangr and market mangr Kimberley Clark Ltd 1976-79; md BFN Storefitters Ltd (mktg mangr and mktg dir 1979); MInstM; *Recreations* squash, dingy sailing, windsurfing; *Clubs* Biddenden Squash, Bewl Valley Sailing; *Style—* Geoffrey Hilton, Esq; Palmerston, High Halden, Ashford, Kent TN26 3LY (☎ 023385 496); BFN Storefitters Ltd, Lower Rd, Gravesend, Kent DA11 9BE (☎ 0474 560671, fax 0474 334282)

HIND, John Wheelton; s of Dr Alan Wheelton Hind, of Thimbles, Piddinghoe, nr Newhaven, Sussex, and Margaret, *née* Fearnehough; *b* 2 Aug 1950; *Educ* Reed's Sch Cobham Surrey, Univ of Wales (BEcon); *m* 2 Aug 1975, Susan Helen; 1 s (James Wheelton b 1981), 1 da (Emma b 1979); *Career* admin Bromley Hosps 1974-79, actg asst dist admin Bromley Health Authy 1982-83 (sr princ admin 1979-82); SE Kent Health Authy: admin Ashford Hosps 1983-86, gen mangr community health servs 1983-; assoc memb IHSM 1983;

Recreations family life, rugby, reading, Tolkein; *Style—* John Hind, Esq; Rustlings, Woolpack Hill, Smeeth, nr Ashford, Kent TN25 6RT (☎ 030381 3195); 1 Radnor Park Rd, Folkestone, Kent (☎ 0303 850202)

HINKS, Frank Peter; s of Henry John Hinks, of Stamford, Lincs, and Patricia May, *née* Adams; *b* 8 July 1950; *Educ* Bromley GS, St Catherine's Coll Oxford (BA, BCL, MA); *m* 31 July 1982, Susan Mary, da of Col John Arthur Haire, of Bickley, Kent; 3 s (Julius b 1984, Alexander b 1985, Benjamin b 1987); *Career* called to the Bar Lincoln's Inn 1973, Chancery Bar 1974-; memb Shoreham PCC; Freeman Worshipful Co of Innholders 1988; *Recreations* poetry, gardening, collecting jugs; *Style—* Frank Hinks, Esq; The Old Vicarage, Shoreham, Sevenoaks, Kent (☎ 095 92 4480); 13 Old Sq, Lincoln's Inn, London WC2 (☎ 071 242 6105, fax 071 405 4004)

HINKS, Simon Graham; s of Graham Thomas Hinks, of Gravesend, and Mary Winifred, *née* Welch; *b* 12 Oct 1960; *Educ* St Georges Gravesend; *Career* Kent CCC: joined 1980, debut against Hants 1982, first full season scored 1500 runs; Kent cap 1985, captained Kent against WI 1988; highest score 234 v Middx 1990; *Recreations* most sports, gardening, sports cars, wine and food; *Clubs* Gravesend Cricket; *Style—* Simon Hinks, Esq; Kent County Cricket Club, St Lawrence Ground, Old Dover Rd, Canterbury, Kent (☎ 0227 456886)

HINWOOD-ZEIDLER, Kathleen Mary (Kay); da of Lt Robert Wylie, MC (d 1941), of 43 Rodway Rd, Bromley, Kent, and Maimie Emilie, *née* Malling (d 1981); *b* 26 Nov 1920; *Educ* Stratford House Sch Bickley Kent; *m* 1, 26 July 1941 (m dis), George Yorke Hinwood (d 1960), s of late Frederick Hinwood, of Malmesbury, Wilts; 1 s (Peter Wylie b 17 May 1946), 1 da (Georgina Mary (Mrs Fowkes) b 18 April 1942); m 2, 17 Feb 1966, Lt Cdr Douglas Louis Zeidler (d 1967); *Career* ambulance driver CD 1939-41; studied art: studio of Edouard MacAvoy Paris 1937, privately in London with Sonia Mervyn, final studies with Kratochwil Kathleen Brown Studios Chelsea; exhibitions: RP, RBA, ROI, NEAC, SWA, Pastel Soc, UA; paintings in private collections in: Eng, France, Spain, Canada, USA, Aust; winner of Award for Pastel 1986 from Mall Galleries (UA exhibition 1984); memb: Pastel Soc, United Soc of Artists, Fedn Br Artists; signs work K Hinwood; *Recreations* reading, writing, photography; *Clubs* Chelsea Arts; *Style—* Mrs Kay Hinwood-Zeidler

HISCOCK, Robert Heath; s of Frederick Heath Hiscock (d 1963), of Highfields, 257 Singlewell Rd, Gravesend, Kent, and Edith Rose, *née* Turnbull; *b* 18 Aug 1920; *Educ* Kings Sch Rochester, Univ of London (LLB); *m* 2 July 1947, (Kathleen) Patricia, da of Herbert Septimus Humphreys (d 1952), of Powers Court, 25 The Ave, Gravesend, Kent; 1 s (Robert Grigor Heath b 1948), 1 da (Catherine Patricia (Mrs Leadbetter) b 1952), 1 step s (Michael Ronald Tong b 1943); *Career* Sgt Home Guard; admitted slr 1944; articled clerk Thomas Anthony Tolhurst 1938; ptnr Tolhurst & Hiscock 1948-70, pt/t Martin Tolhurst Partnership (formerly Martin Tolhurst Allen & Hiscock) 1986- (ptnr 1970-); NP 1953; author of various local histories, church guides and articles in Archaeoligia Cantiana; fell Soc of Antiquaries of London 1970; memb cncl Kent Archaeological Soc, vice chm Kent Historic Bldgs Ctee, chm Gravesend Hist Soc; memb: Law Soc, Soc of Provincial Notaries; FSA; *Recreations* gardening, walking; *Style—* Robert Hiscock, Esq, FSA; 10 Old Rd East, Gravesend, Kent DA12 1NQ (☎ 0474 567378); 7 Wrotham Rd, Gravesend, Kent DA11 0PD (☎ 0474 325531, fax 0474 560771)

HITMAN, Dr Graham Alec; s of Maxwell Hitman (d 1987), and Annette Hitman (d 1976); *b* 19 Jan 1953; *Educ* Bromley GS, Univ Coll Hosp Med Sch (MB BS); *m* Avril Fiona, da of Ivor Sevitt, of 63 Court Rd, Eltham; 1 s (Oliver b 1980), 1 da (Nadia b 1978); *Career* sr house offr and registrar Kings Coll Hosp London, RD Lawrence res fell Bart's Hosp; The Royal London Hosp: lectr Med Unit, asst dir, sr lectr, hon conslt; memb: Br Diabetic Assoc, Med Res Soc; FRCP 1990 (MRCP); *publications* incl: Polymorphisms in the 5'flaking region of the insulin gene and non-insulin dependent diabetes (jtly, 1984), Type 1 diabetes and a highly variable locus close to the insulin gene on chromosome 11 (jtly, 1985), New HLA DNA polymorphism associated with auto-immune diseases (jtly, 1986), Genes and diabetes mellitus (with M J Niven, 1986), The genetic predisposition to fibrocalculous pancreatic diabetes (jtly, 1989), 2'-5 oligoadenylate Synthetase and its relationship to HLA and genetic markers of insulin dependent diabetes mellitus (jtly, 1989); *Recreations* windsurfing, reading, tennis; *Style—* Dr Graham Hitman; 17 Toynbec Close, Chislehurst, Kent BR6 7TH (☎ 081 467 3331); Medical Unit, The Royal London Hospital, Whitechapel, London E1 1BB (☎ 071 377 7111, fax 071 377 7677)

HOARE, Lady Christina Alice; *née* McDonnell; only da of 8 Earl of Antrim, KBE, JP, DL (d 1977), and Angela Christina, *née* Sykes (d 1984); *b* 18 Sept 1938; *Educ* Les Oiseaux Convent, Slade Sch of Art (Dip of Fine Arts); *m* 23 Jan 1963, Joseph Andrew Christopher Hoare, *qv*, s of Sir Reginald Hoare, KCMG (d 1954); 1 s (Charles William Reginald b 1966), 2 da (Jane Alice Patience b 1963, Lucy Mary Christina b 1968); *Career* artist; fndr Christian Art Centre 1988; memb Lloyd's 1979-; *Recreations* painting, gardening, meeting friends; *Clubs* Arts; *Style—* The Lady Christina Hoare; Hartridge Manor Farm, Cranbrook, Kent TN17 2NA; Christian Art Centre, 342C South Lambeth Rd, London SW8 1UQ

HOARE, Joseph Andrew Christopher; o s of Sir Reginald Hervey Hoare, KCMG (d 1954), and Lucy Joan (d 1971), da of William George Frederick Cavendish-Bentinck, JP, and sis of 8 and 9 Dukes of Portland; *b* 23 March 1925; *Educ* Eton, Balliol Coll Oxford (MA); *m* 23 Jan 1963, Lady Christina Alice McDonnell, da of 13 Earl of Antrim, KBE, DL (d 1977); 1 s, 2 da; *Career* Flt Offr: RAF Regt 1946-47, 604 Sqdn R AUX AF 1951-57; dir Canadian Overseas Packaging Industries 1962-; memb Stock Exchange 1957-77, underwriting memb Lloyd's 1985; chm Assoc of Chartered and Tech Analysts 1970-73; farmer 1972-; *Recreations* devising and maintaining models for forecasting 11 leading world economics; *Clubs* Brooks's; *Style—* Joseph Hoare, Esq; Hartridge Manor Farm, Cranbrook, Kent TN17 2NA

HOARE, Quintin Vincent; OBE (1944); s of Maj Vincent Robertson Hoare (ka 1915), and Elspeth Florence, *née* Hogg (d 1965); *b* 21 June 1907; *Educ* Eton, Oriel Coll Oxford; *m* 1, 2 May 1936 (m dis 1948), Lucy Florence, da of Very Rev Gordon Selwyn, Dean of Winchester; 3 s ((Benjamin) Quintin b 1938, Gavin Quintin b 1940 d 1986, Richard Quintin (Tigger) b 1943); m 2, Rosemary, da of Lt-Col Charles Hezlet, DSO (d 1965); 2 s (David Quintin b 1954 d 1981, Nicholas Quintin b 1956), 1 da (Belinda Rosemary Cash b 1958); *Career* 2 Rangers TA 1933-36, 8 KRRC 1939-45, AA and QMG (formerly SO) 6 Armed Div 1940-45; sr ptnr C Hoare & Co (joined 1928, managing ptnr 1935); *Recreations* golf, bridge; *Clubs* White's, Portland, Royal St George's Golf, Royal Cinque Ports Golf, Rye Golf; *Style—* Quintin Hoare, Esq, OBE; Stuart House, Delf St, Sandwich, Kent (☎ 0304 612 133); 37 Fleet St, London EC4 (☎ 071 353 4522)

HOBDAY, Dr Paul Jeremy; s of Arthur Samuel Hobday, of Birchington, Kent, and Elsie Mabel, *née* Baigent; *b* 22 July 1956; *Educ* Purley GS Surrey, Univ of London and Guy's Hosp Med Sch (MB BS, MRCGP, DRCOG, FPA Cert); *m* 20 Oct 1979, Marion Pamela, da of Joseph Gooch, of Hailsham, Sussex; 3 da (Louisa Jessica b 1984, Natasha Nicole b 1986, Leila Daisy b 1989); *Career* house physician and house surgn Lewisham Gen Hosp 1979-80, hosp Dr West Kent Hosp Maidstone 1980-82, GP Sutton Valence Kent 1983-, prison med offr East Sutton Park 1985-; memb: BMA, LMC; *Style—* Dr Paul Hobday; 374 Loose Rd, Maidstone, Kent ME15 9TT (☎ 0622 695240); Surgery, South Lane, Sutton Valence, Kent ME17 3BD (☎ 0622 842212)

HODDER-WILLIAMS, Mark; s of Lt-Col Paul Hodder-Williams, OBE, TD, of Court House, Exford, Somerset, and Felicity, *née* Blagden (d 1986); *b* 31 March 1939; *Educ* Rugby, CCC Oxford (MA); *m* 10 Oct 1961, Janette Elspeth (Jinty), da of Harry Archibald Cochran, OBE (d 1973), of Shoreham, Kent; 3 s (Andrew b 1963, James b 1964, Peter b 1968), 1 da (Susanna b 1969); *Career* Hodder and Stoughton Holdings Ltd: dir 1971-73, dep chm 1989-; dir The Lancet Ltd 1973-88; Publishers' Assoc Distribution Ctee: memb 1970-87, chm 1978-80; memb: Publishers' Assoc Tech Devpt Gp 1984-86, Teleordering Users' Cncl (chm 1983), Book Trade Electronic Communications Ctee 1987-; FRSA 1990-; *Recreations* golf, skiing, gardening, music; *Clubs* Vincents (Oxford), Wildernesse (Sevenoaks); *Style—* Mark Hodder-Williams, Esq; Little Birches, 38 Greenhill Rd, Otford, Kent TN14 5RS (☎ 0959 22180); Hodder & Stoughton Ltd, Mill Rd, Dunton Green, Sevenoaks, Kent TN13 2YA (☎ 0732 450111, fax 0732 460134)

HODGES, David Reginald Eyles; s of Edward Reginald George Hodges, of Dolphin Square, London, and Irene Muriel, *née* Turner; *b* 26 Aug 1942; *Educ* Micklebурgh; *m* 1, 19 Dec 1969, Yolande Wadih (d 1988), da of Joseph Yuja (d 1975), of San Pedro Sula, Honduras; 1 s (Crispin James David b 1973), 1 da (Patricia Irene b 1964); m 2, 22 July 1989, Patricia Emma, da of Cesar Augusto Pancorvo Noriega Del Valle (d 1983), of Lima, Peru; *Career* dir Cayzer Steel Bowater International Ltd 1975-86, dir and chm Ridgelawn Associates Ltd 1986-, conslt J H Davies (Underwriting Agency) Ltd 1986-; memb Lloyds; *Recreations* sailing, travel, skiing; *Clubs* Turf; *Style—* David Hodges, Esq; c/o Messrs C Hoare and Co, 37 Fleet St, London EC4 (☎ 071 481 4455 or 071 821 0179 or 0227 721224)

HODGES, Joseph Thomas Charles; s of Joseph Henry Hodges (d 1977), of Welling, Kent, and Hilda Ellen Susan, *née* Hermitage; *b* 25 July 1932; *Educ* East Ham GS for Boys; *m* 15 Sept 1962, Joan, da of James Bremner Swan (d 1983), of Welling, Kent; 2 s (Kevin b 1966, David b 1968), 1 da (Julia b 1969); *Career* Nat Serv RAF 1949-51; Lloyd's: mangr Audit Dept 1966-73, head of advsy and legislation 1973-80, sec gen 1980-84; dir: Mark Loveday Underwriting Agencies Ltd 1984-, Cater Allen Members Agency Ltd 1987-; Freeman: City of London 1982, Worshipful Co of Insurers 1982; FCA 1965, FCIS 1980; *Recreations* caravanning; *Style—* Joseph Hodges, Esq; 246 Halfway St, Sidcup, Kent; Lloyd's, Lime St, London EC3

HODGSON, Roy William; s of William French Hodgson (d 1930), of Chatham, Kent, and Ivy Matilda Dale, *née* Barnard; *b* 2 Jan 1928; *Educ* Holcombe Jr Tech Sch Chatham; *m* 23 Sept 1957, Isabel Victoria; *Career* Clerical and Admin Branch RAF 1945-48, cmmnd Trg Branch RAFVR 1970-76; theatre and cinema mgmnt 1948-52; chiropodist 1952-89, ret; audio theatre writer and prodr responsible for numerous audio plays and an audio documentary on WWII The Glorious Years 1986-; chm Sandwich Video Prodn;

memb Inst of Chiropodists 1967-; *Recreations* playright, videography; *Clubs* RAF; *Style*— Roy Hodgson, Esq; The Barbican, 2 High St, Sandwich, Kent CT13 9EA (☎ 0304 617332)

HOFFMAN, Thomas; s of Dirk Hoffman (d 1986), of Cambridge, and Marie-Luise, *née* Leyser; *b* 9 Aug 1945; *Educ* The Leys Sch Cambridge, Univ of Exeter (LLB); *m* June 1971, Verena, *née* Fairs; 1 s (Alexander b 29 Dec 1975); *Career* CA; Spicer & Oppenheim CAs Cambridge 1963-70, Arthur Anderson & Co CAs London 1970-71; int banker: Williams & Glyns Bank Ltd 1971-76, Hill Samuel & Co Ltd 1976-78; dir Capital Mkts Lloyds Bank International Ltd 1978-84, dep md Fuji International Finance Ltd 1984-89, head of corporate banking in the UK Algemene Bank Nederland 1989-; memb: Royal Soc for Asian Affrs, Anglo Netherlands Soc; hon treas Cordwainer Ward Club City of London; Freeman City of London (memb Guild), Liveryman Worshipful Co of Tylers and Bricklayers; FRSA, FCA 1971; *Recreations* travel, gardening, opera, ballet; *Clubs* Royal Cwlth, City Livery; *Style*— Thomas Hoffman, Esq; Old Curteis, Biddenden, Ashford, Kent; 72 Gainsford St, Tower Bridge Square, London SE1; 61 Threadneedle St, London EC2 (☎ 071 628 4272)

HOGG, John Goldsborough; s of F G Hogg (d 1969); *b* 21 Jan 1925; *Educ* Harrow, Trinity Coll Cambridge; *m* 1955, Hon Sarah Edith, yst da of 1 Baron Noel-Buxton, PC (d 1948); 2 da; *Career* insur broker Lloyd's 1947-85, dep chm Hogg Robinson Group 1979-85; *Recreations* golf, shooting, fishing, skiing, flying; *Clubs* Boodle's; *Style*— John Hogg, Esq; Old Broad Oak, Brenchley, Kent (☎ 089 272 2318); Hogg Group plc, Lloyds Chambers, 1 Portsoken St, London E1 8DF (☎ 071 480 4000; telex 884633)

HOGWOOD, Paul Arthur; s of Robert Thomas Hogwood, of Forest Hill, London, and Hilda Jesse, *née* Marshall; *b* 18 July 1949; *Educ* Haberdashers' Aske's, Univ of Hull (BSc); *m* 30 Oct 1971, Sylvia Ann, da of Gordon John McCulloch (d 1971); 2 s (James b 26 Aug 1978, Christopher b 28 June 1980); *Career* mangr Coopers & Lybrand CAs 1970-77, project fin asst dir Morgan Grenfell & Co Ltd Merchant Bankers 1982-86 (chief internal auditor 1977-82); co sec: Morgan Grenfell Securities Holdings Ltd 1986-89, Morgan Grenfell Asset Management Ltd 1989-, Anglo & Overseas Investment Trust plc 1989-, Overseas Investment Trust plc 1989-; FCA 1974; *Style*— Paul Hogwood, Esq; 10 Ravenshill, Chislehurst, Kent BR7 5PD (☎ 081 467 1918); Morgan Grenfell Asset Management, 20 Finsbury Circus, London EC2M 7AS (☎ 081 826 0036)

HOHLER, Frederick Christopher Gerald; s of Edward Christopher Hohler, of Lydersagensgate 23, Oslo, Norway, and Mary Alice Olga Sophia Jane Scrivener, *née* Lane; *b* 30 Aug 1943; *Educ* Eton, Oriel Coll and St Antony's Coll Oxford (MA, DPhil); *m* 7 Sept 1968, Sarah Virginia, *qv*, da of Ian Herbert Gillet Gilbert, of Trotton, W Sussex; 4 da (Alice b 1970, Emily b 1971, Isobel b 1979, Ophelia b 1982); *Career* ed Hong Kong Section Far Eastern Economic Review 1964-65, lectr Univ of Ghana 1967-68, HM Dip Serv 1969-85, asst dir de Zoete & Bevan/BZW 1985-88, chief exec The Whitney Group (Europe) Ltd 1988-; chm Writers in Business 1989-; *Books* Sino-Ghanaian Relations, 1956-1966 (1970); *Clubs* Boodles, Beefsteak, Academy; *Style*— Frederick Hohler, Esq; The Court Lodge, Stansted, Sevenoaks, Kent TN15 7PG (☎ 0732 823347)

HOHLER, Sarah Virginia; da of Ian Herbert Gillett Gilbert, of Rectory Cottage, Trotton, Rogate, W Sussex, and Violet Edith Heelas (d 1984); *b* 20 May 1945; *Educ* Prior's Field Sch Godalming Surrey, St Hugh's Coll Oxford (MA); *m* 7 Sept 1968, Frederick Christopher Gerald Hohler, *qv*, s of Christopher Hohler, formerly of Long Crendon Manor, Aylesbury, Bucks; 4 da (Alice b 1970, Emily b 1971, Isobel b 1979, Ophelia b 1982); *Career* asst Euro sales mangr Pergamon Press; ed: Oxford Univ Press Hong Kong, Macmillan Education Basingstoke; librarian Spence Sch New York, Eng lang asst Br Cncl Brussels; Kent CC: elected memb for Malling Rural North 1989, vice chm Highways Sub Ctee; govr: Stansted C of E Sch, St George's C of E Sch, Holmesdale Sch; *Style*— Mrs Frederick Hohler; The Court Lodge, Stansted, Sevenoaks, Kent TN15 7PG

HOILE, Ronald William; *b* 23 Nov 1944; *Educ* Charing Cross Hosp Med Sch Univ of London (MB BS, MS); *m* 1, 1967 (m dis 1971); m 2, 1972 (m dis 1977); 2 s (Christopher Malcolm b 26 Dec 1973, Adrian Robert 29 Sept 1976); m 3, 12 Jan 1980, Patricia Helen Murray; 1 s (Nicholas William b 22 Jan 1985), 1 da (Alexandra Claire b 1 Aug 1982); *Career* conslt surgn Medway Health Dist 1983, private surgical practice BUPA Alexandra Hosp Chatham; asst clinical co-ordinator Nat Confidential Enquiry into Perioperative Deaths, examiner in anatomy RCS, recognised teacher in surgery Univ of London, referee for British Medical Journal and British Journal of Surgery; FRCS; *Books* Your Below Knee Amputation (1989); *Recreations* computor science; *Clubs* RSM; *Style*— Ronald Hoile, Esq; 6 Water Meadow Close, Hempstead, Gillingham, Kent ME7 3QF (☎ 0634 377070); Medway Hospital, Windmill Rd, Gillingham, Kent ME7 5NY (☎ 0634 830000, fax 0634 829470); BUPA Alexandra Hospital, Impton Lane, Walderslade, Chatham, Kent ME5 9PG (☎ 0634 400677)

HOLDEN, Alan Keith; s of George Dovestone Holden, of Manea, Cambs, and Hilda Lillian, *née* Whibley (d 1981); *b* 14 Dec 1947; *Educ* Western Secdy Boys' Sch Grimsby South Humberside; *m* 1, 1972 (m dis 1976) Eileen Lynch; 1 s (Stuart John b 1969), 1 da (Paula Louise b 1970); m 2, 3 June 1978, Monica Christine, da of Denis John Waters, of Coxheath, Kent; *Career* VSO Vanuatu SW Pacific 1971-72, social worker Kent CC 1974-; borough cncllr (Democrat) Bridge Ward Maidstone; memb: W Area Planning Ctee, Housing Ctee, Gen Purposes Ctee; vice chm Maidstone Health Authy 1988-; posts incl: mangr Maidstone Hosp Psychiatric Wing, Mental Health Care Gp, Kent Ambulance Ctee, Maidstone Ambulance Ctee, Maidstone Health Promotion Panel; memb: Maidstone Community Health Cncl 1982-88, Maidstone Age Concern Ctee; youth ldr 1970-, govr St Michael's C of E Sch Maidstone, memb 6024 Preservation Soc; Freemason Fleur-de-Lis Lodge Maidstone; MRSH 1988; *Recreations* photography, astronomy, aquaria, railways; *Style*— Alan Holden, Esq; 41 Hastings Rd, Maidstone, Kent ME15 7SH (☎ 0622 62770); Kent County Council, Social Services Dept, Bishops Terrace, Maidstone, Kent (☎ 0622 54933)

HOLLAMBY, Edward Ernest; OBE (1970); s of Edward Thomas Hollamby (d 1979), of Kent, and Ethel May Kingdom; *b* 8 Jan 1921; *Educ* Sch of Arts and Crafts Hammersmith, Univ of London (DipTP and DipCD); *m* 1941, Doris Isabel, da of William John Parker, of London; 1 s (Andrew b 1953), 2 da (Marsha b 1946, Jillian b 1948); *Career* Royal Marine Engrs Far East 1941-46; architect, designer, town planner; sr architect London CC 1949-62, dir of architecture and town planning London Borough of Lambeth 1969-81 (borough architect 1962-69), conslt London Docklands Development Corporation 1985-88 (chief architect and planner 1981-85); town planning projects incl: Erith Township Kent (Thamesmead prototype), Brixton town centre, relocation Covent Garden Market, Isle of Dogs, London Dockland, Wapping and Limehouse, Royal Docks, Becton; works incl conservation of historic bldgs: Brandon Est, Kennington, Offices and Rec Centre Brixton, Lambeth housing, Christopher Wren and Burlington Schs Hammersmith, special schs handicapped children Brixton and Kennington, holiday home for disabled Netley, public library and civic hall W Norwood; numerous design awards including 2 DOE bronze medals; RIBA: cncl memb 1961-72, hon treas 1967-70, memb NW Kent Branch SE Region; memb: Historic Bldgs Cncl for Eng 1971-83, London Advsy Ctee Eng Heritage 1986-, London Borough Bexley Cons Area Advsy Panel; fndr memb: William Morris Soc, Bexley Civic Soc; FRTPI, FRSA; hon assoc Landscape Inst; *Books* Docklands Heritage - A Study in Conservation and Regeneration in London Docklands (1987); *Recreations* travel, music, theatre, opera, gardening; *Clubs* Arts; *Style*— Edward Hollamby, Esq, OBE; Red House, Red House Lane, Upton, Bexleyheath, Kent (☎ 081 303 8808)

HOLLAND, (Robert) Einion; s of Robert Ellis Holland, and Bene, *née* Williams; *b* 23 April 1927; *Educ* Univ Coll N Wales Bangor (BSc); *m* 1955, Eryl Haf (d 1988); 1 s (Gareth), 2 da (Sian, Eluned); *Career* Pearl Assurance plc: joined 1953, chief mangr 1977-83, dir and chm 1983-89; dir: Aviation and General Insurance Co Ltd 1973-89, Pearl Assurance (Unit Funds) Ltd 1975-89, Crawley Warren Group plc, New London Properties Ltd 1984-89, Queens Ice Skating Ltd 1984-89, Pearl Group plc 1986-90 (chm 1986-89), BR Property Board 1987-; FIA; *Recreations* golf, Welsh lit; *Style*— Einion Holland, Esq; 55 Corkscrew Hill, West Wickham, Kent BR4 9BA (☎ 081 777 1861)

HOLLAND, Maj Stanley; TD (1950); s of Albert John Holland (ka 1915), and Amy Alice Smith (d 1972); *b* 4 Aug 1912; *Educ* Lancashire Hill Sch, Stockport Coll; *m* 26 Feb 1946, Marjorie Edwina, da of John Edwin Haslam (d 1938), of Prestatyn, N Wales; *Career* TA RA Field Regt 1938, Staff Capt and instr Sch of Mil Engrg, Staff Maj G2 supreme HQ Mil Mission to Denmark, ret Army Res 1962; incorporated commercial conslt; JP 1964-; memb Lloyds 1970-; hon memb Anglo-Danish Soc, hon sr memb Univ of Kent at Canterbury 1989; memb: Devpt Bd Univ of Kent 1990, Court of Univ of Kent 1990, Nat Tst; tstee Stockport Sunday Sch; vice pres Edenbridge and Oxted Agric Show; Freeman City of London 1970, Liveryman Worshipful Co of Wheelwrights 1970 (memb court 1980); FBSC 1946 (sr vice pres); Knight (1 class) Order of Dannebrog Denmark 1946, Decoration of Hon (Denmark 1990); *Recreations* world travel, viewing wildlife; *Style*— Maj Stanley Holland, TD

HOLLENDEN, 3 Baron (UK 1912); Gordon Hope Hope-Morley; o s of Hon Claude Hope-Morley (d 1968, yr s of 1 Baron), and Lady Dorothy Edith Isabel Hobart-Hampden-Mercer-Henderson (d 1972), da of 7 Earl of Buckinghamshire; suc unc 1977; *b* 8 Jan 1914; *Educ* Eton; *m* 27 Oct 1945, Sonja, da of late Thorolf Sundt, of Bergen, Norway; 3 s; *Heir* s, Hon Ian Hampden Hope-Morley; *Career* served Black Watch 1939-45, Maj; alderman City of London 1954-58, former chm I and R Morley Ltd, ret; *Clubs* Brooks's, Beefsteak; *Style*— The Rt Hon the Lord Hollenden; Hall Place, Leigh, Tonbridge, Kent (☎ 0732 832255)

HOLLIS, Arthur Norman; OBE (1985), DFC (1943); s of Egerton Clark Hollis (d 1967), of Eastbourne, Sussex, and Vera Lina, *née* Leigh (d 1944); *b* 11 Aug 1922; *Educ* Dulwich; *m* 2 Dec 1944, Elizabeth, da of Reginald Chase Edmunds (d 1986), of Westwell, nr Ashford, Kent; 1 s (Richard b 1953), 2 da (Jennifer b 1945, Sylvia b 1949); *Career* RAFVR 1941-46, Sqdn Ldr 1945-46; memb HAC 1978; CA; ptnr: Limebeer & Co 1953-75, Russell Limebeer

1975-88; sr ptnr based in City of London specialising in countries of W Europe; dir various cos; memb Mgmnt Ctee Yehudi Menuhin Sch 1964-88 (vice pres 1989), govr Live Music Now 1977-90, offr of various Cons assocs; chm: Ashford constituency 1980-83, Kent E Euro constituency 1985-88 (vice pres 1988), Westwell Parish Cncl 1976-79; Master Worshipful Co of Woolmen 1982-83; FCA 1958, FRSA 1983; *Recreations* travel, shooting, country pursuits; *Clubs* Travellers, City of London, United and Cecil; *Style*— Arthur Hollis, Esq, OBE, DFC; Court Lodge, Westwell, nr Ashford, Kent TN25 4JX (☎ 023 371 2555)

HOLLOWAY, Frank; s of late Frank Holloway; *b* 20 Oct 1924; *Educ* Burnage HS Manchester; *m* 1949, Elizabeth, *née* Beattie; 3 da; *Career* various sr fin appts in The United Steel Companies and later British Steel Corpn 1949-72; md: supplies and prodn control British Steel Corpn 1973-76, fin and supplies 1976-80, supplies and tport and bd memb 1978-; chm British Steel Corpn (Chemicals) Ltd; FCA, FBIM; *Recreations* cricket, collecting books; *Style*— Frank Holloway, Esq; 11 Copperfield Way, Chislehurst, Kent (☎ 081 467 9559); BSC, Supplies and Transport Div, 9 Albert Embankment, London SE1 7SN (☎ 071 735 7654; telex 916061)

HOLMAN, David McArthur; s of Alexander McArthur Holman (d 1979), of Springland, Millbrook, Jersey, CI, and Hon Margery Amy, *née* Boot (d 1987); *b* 11 Dec 1928; *Educ* Rugby; *m* 1, 1952 (m dis 1965), Felicity Frances, da of Capt Rickard Donovan, CBE, RN (d 1956); 1 s (Mark Rickard b 1957 d 1987); m 2, 1966, Valerie Brythonig, *née* Pryor; 2 s (Michael Jesse b 1967, Andrew McArthur b 1968); *Career* Lt RHG 1946-49; chm and md: John Holman & Sons Ltd 1953-, David Holman & Co Ltd 1971-; chm Phyllis Holman Richards Adoption Soc 1970-; memb Lloyds 1954; *Recreations* field sports; *Clubs* Cavalry and Guards', City of London; *Style*— David Holman, Esq; Crundale House, Crundale, Canterbury, Kent CT4 7EH (☎ 0227 731020)

HOLT, Clifford Gordon; s of Gordon Robarts Holt (d 1963), of Stanford, Ashford, Kent, and Florence May, *née* Taylor (d 1977); *b* 6 Aug 1928; *Educ* Ashford GS; *m* 20 June 1953, Evelyn Joan, da of Hans Jorgen Hansen (d 1958), of Hawkinge, Folkestone, Kent; 1 s (Alastair David b 1958), 2 da (Fiona Nova b 1955, Katrina Clare b 1965); *Career* arable and sheep farmer; Kent and E Sussex NFU: chm Potatoes and Vegetables Ctee, memb Exec Ctee, memb Fin and Gen Purposes Ctee, memb PR Ctee; memb and chm Swingfield and Elham Branch NFU, vice chm Canterbury Farmers' Club 1989; memb: CLA and NFU Kent Channel Link Gp, Stanford Parish Hall Ctee; chm Stanford Parish Cncl; vice chm and treas Southern Shepherds ATB Gp, chm and dir Woodchurch Farmer's & Growers; memb: RASE, NSA; supporter of Young Farmers' Club; *Recreations* fly-fishing, travel; *Clubs* Canterbury Farmers'; *Style*— Clifford Holt, Esq; Hayton Manor Farm, Stanford, Ashford, Kent TN25 6DQ (☎ 0303 812282)

HOLT, Dr Phyllis Marie; da of Alan Holt, of Welwyn, and Phyllis Mary, *née* McCann; *b* 29 Oct 1951; *Educ* Univ of Manchester Med Sch (MB ChB, MD, MRCP); *m* 26 May 1990, Franz Von Dickmann, s of Col Caspar Von Dickmann (d 1946); *Career* sr registrar in cardiology: Nat Heart Hosp London 1983, Guy's Hosp 1984-87; conslt physician and cardiologist 1987-: Maidstone Hosp, Guy's Hosp; lectr in arrhythmias in England N America and Europe; memb: Br Cardiac Soc, Br Pacing and Electrophysiological Gp, American Coll of Cardiology, N American Soc of Pacing and Electrophysiology, NY Acad of Sci, Br Heart Fndn; involved in local fund raising for equipment for cardiac unit at Maidstone Hosp; *Books* Electrical Therapy for Cardiac Arrthymias (contrib, 1990), Current States of Clinical Cardiology; Cardiac Arrthymias (1989); *Recreations* flying light aircraft, skiing; *Style*— Dr Phyllis Holt; Maidstone Hospital, Hermitage Lane, Barming, Maidstone, Kent ME16 9QQ (☎ 0622 729000 ext 455)

HONNYWILL, Godfrey Coleridge; s of John Christopher Honnywill (d 1984), of Tunbridge Wells, and Mary Rosalind, *née* Gair; ggggs of Samuel Taylor Coleridge; *b* 14 March 1934; *Educ* Sherborne; *m* 18 June 1962, Helen Newbery, da of Dudley Searle Freeman (d 1978), of Chiddingstone, Kent; 3 s (Charles Gair b 1963, Thomas Dudley b 1965, David Weston b 1967), 1 da (Alice Mary (twin) b 1967); *Career* slr 1957; dir Crown Chemical Co (Hldgs) Ltd 1972-86; pres: Kent Law Soc 1974, Tunbridge Wells Law Soc 1980; memb Law Soc; *Recreations* travel, gardening; *Clubs* Tonbridge Rugby Football; *Style*— Godfrey Honnywill, Esq; The Timberyard, Lamberhurst, Kent TN3 8DT (☎ 0892 890417); The Priory, Tunbridge Wells, Kent (☎ 0892 510222, fax 0892 510333)

HONYWOOD, Sir Filmer Courtenay William; 11 Bt (E 1660), of Evington, Kent; s of Col Sir William Wynne Honywood, 10 Bt, MC (d 1982), and Maud, yr da of William Hodgson-Wilson, of Hexgrave Park, Southwell, Notts; *b* 20 May 1930; *Educ* Downside, RMA Sandhurst, RAC Cirencester (MRAC Dip); *m* 1956, Elizabeth Margaret Mary Cynthia, 2 da of late Sir Alastair George Lionel Joseph Miller, 6 Bt; 2 s (Rupert Anthony b 1957, Simon Joseph b 1958), 2 da (Mary Caroline b 1961, Judith Mary Frances b 1964); *Heir* s, Rupert Honywood; *Career* 3 Carabiniers (Prince of Wales's Dragoon Gds); asst surveyor MAFF Maidstone 1966-73, surveyor Cockermouth Cumbria 1973-74, sr lands offr SE Regn CEGB 1974-78 (regnl surveyor and valuer 1978-88); FRICS; *Style*— Sir Filmer Honywood, Bt; Greenway Forstal Farmhouse, Hollingbourne, Maidstone, Kent ME17 1QA (☎ 0622 880418)

HOOK, Rt Rev Dr Ross Sydney; MC (1946); s of Sydney Frank Hook (d 1959), of Woodchurch, and Laura Harriet, *née* Dale (d 1973); *b* 19 Feb 1917; *Educ* Christ's Hosp, Peterhouse Cambridge (BA, MA), Ridley Hall Cambridge; *m* 26 Aug 1948, Ruth Leslie, da of Rev Herman Masterman Biddell (d 1946), of Sandown, IOW; 1 s ((Ross) Philip b 1950), 1 da ((Ruth) Deborah b 1956); *Career* chaplain RNVR RM Commandos 1943-46; chaplain Ridley Hall Cambridge 1946-48, select preacher Univ of Cambridge 1948, rector Chorlton Cum Hardy Manchester 1948-52, rector and rural dean Chelsea 1952-61, residentiary canon Rochester 1961-65, bishop Grantham 1965-72, dean Stamford 1971-72, bishop Bradford 1972-80, COS to Archibishop of Canterbury 1980-84, asst bishop Canterbury 1980-; Freeman City of London 1981; Hon DLitt Univ of Bradford 1981; *Recreations* watching cricket; *Clubs* Army and Navy; *Style*— The Rt Rev Dr Ross Hook, MC; Mill Rock, Newchurch, Romney Marsh, Kent TN29 0DN (☎ 0303 873115)

HOPE-MORLEY, Hon Andrew James Sundt; s of 3 Baron Hollenden; *b* 16 Sept 1952; *Educ* Eton; *Style*— The Hon Andrew Hope-Morley

HORD, Brian Howard; CBE (1989); s of Edwin Charles Hord, of Hampstead, London (d 1938), and Winifred Hannah, *née* Harris; *b* 20 June 1934; *Educ* Reedham Sch, Purley Co GS, Sch of Architecture and Surveying Regent St Poly London; *m* 11 June 1960, Christine Marian, da of Reginald Marcel Lucas, of Bexhill-on-Sea; 2 s (Colin James b 1962, Ian Edward b 1964); *Career* RAF Air Traffic Control 1957-59; Co Planning Dept Middx CC 1950-51, GL Hearn & Ptnrs Surveyors London 1951-57, asst estates mangr United Drapery Stores London 1959-61, mangr Pearsons Chartered Surveyors Beckenham 1961-62, chief surveyor Town & Commercial Properties Ltd London 1962-65, devpt surveyor Maybrook Properties Ltd London 1965-67, sr devpt controller Costain Property Investments 1967-70; dir: CAPCO (UK) Ltd 1970-75, Capital & Counties plc London 1970-75; sr ptnr: Howard Hord & Palmer Chartered Surveyors London 1975-84, Brian Hord & Ptnrs 1984-86; parly candidate (Cons) for Darlington 1973-74, memb Euro Parl for London West 1979-84 (memb: Budgets Ctee, Agric Ctee, Econ and Monetary Ctee, ACP/EEC Ctee), cncl memb London World Trade Centre 1982-, fell Indust and Parl Tst 1984-, chm Bexley Health Authy 1986-; FRICS 1970 (ARICS 1957); *Recreations* swimming, bee-keeping, gardening, music; *Clubs* Carlton, United and Cecil, Cricketers; *Style*— Brian Hord, Esq, CBE; Whitesides, Pilgrims Way East, Otford, Sevenoaks, Kent TN14 5QN (☎ 081 301 2333); 221 Erith Rd, Bexleyheath, Kent DA7 6HZ

HORNAK, Lady Patricia Sybil; *née* Douglas; da of 11 Marquess of Queensberry (d 1954); *b* 1918; *m* 1, 1938 (m dis 1950), Capt Count John Gerard de Bendern; 1 s, 2 da; m 2, 1954 (m dis 1960), Herman Hornak; 2 s; *Style*— Lady Patricia Hornak; 36 St James's Rd, Tunbridge Wells, Kent

HORNE, Christopher Malcolm; s of Gerald Fitzlait Horne (d 1970), and Dora, *née* Hartley; *b* 14 June 1941; *Educ* King Edward VI Chelmsford; *m* 12 Sept 1964, Christine Ann, da of Reginald Arthur Fradley (d 1985); 2 s (Darren James b 7 Feb 1968, Alec Gerald b 20 Jan 1970); *Career* Coutts & Co 1958-: head of personnel 1980-88, assoc dir 1980-89, sec of Bank 1988-, sr assoc dir 1989-; memb Vines Rochester URC; MInstD; *Recreations* golf, gardening, interest in most sports; *Clubs* Rochester and Cobham Park Golf; *Style*— Christopher Horne, Esq; Silver Birches, 151 Maidstone Rd, Chatham, Kent ME4 6JE (☎ 0634 847594); Coutts & Co, 440 The Strand, London WC2R 0QS (☎ 071 379 6262)

HORNE, Frederick Samuel Elbourne; s of William Smart Horne (d 1957), of Nash Court, Westwell, Ashford, Kent, and Anne Elisabeth, *née* Elbourne (d 1937); *b* 13 Nov 1901; *Educ* Ashford GS; *m* 22 Oct 1935, Georgiana Carter, da of John William White (d 1945), of Bedford; 1 s (George Frederick Elbourne b 28 Nov 1939), 1 da (Rosamund Georgiana b 18 April 1938 d 1979); *Career* landowner, breeder of thoroughbred horses; memb local hunts; *Recreations* hunting, racing; *Style*— Frederick Horne, Esq; Nash Court, Westwell, Ashford, Kent (☎ 0233 620567)

HORNE, Godfrey Allan; s of Alfred Henry Horne, of 19 Sherwood Way, West Wickham, Bromley, Kent, and Mildred Filicitus Thamur, *née* Farmer; *b* 5 July 1943; *Educ* Clapham Coll, St Mary's Coll Strawberry Hill; *m* 8 April 1972, Linda Christine, da of Arthur Henry Golding, of 52 Sussex Rd, Tonbridge, Kent; 1 s (Godric Peter b 1980), 1 da (Felicity Ann b 1977); *Career* teacher; Surrey 1964-65, London Borough of Merton 1965-72, head Dept of Geography Sevenoaks Sch for Girls 1972-; memb: S E Regnl Examinations Bd 1976-87, Working Pty for Geography Southern Exams Bd on GCSE; Tonbridge and Malling Borough Cncl 1976-: chm Devpt Servs Ctee 1984-87, memb Kent Economic Devpt Ctee 1987, chm Traffic Mgmnt Ctee 1987, dep Mayor 1987-88, Mayor 1988-89, chm Health and Leisure Servs 1990-; vice chm: St Margaret Clitheroe Primary Sch (govr 1977-), Hillview Secdy Sch (govr 1977); *Recreations* reading, bridge; *Style*— Godfrey Horne, Esq; 44 Royal Ave, Tonbridge, Kent TN9 2DB (☎ 0732 357233); Tonbridge and Malling Borough Council, Air Station, West Malling, Kent (☎ 0732 844522)

HORNE, Dr Nigel William; s of Eric Charles Henry Horne (d 1963), and late Edith Margaret, *née* Boyd; *b* 13 Sept 1940; *Educ* Lower Sch of John Lyon Harrow, Univ of Bristol (BSc), Univ of Cambridge (PhD); *m* 30 Oct 1965, Jennifer Ann, da of William Henry Holton (d 1988); 1 s (Peter b 1970), 2 da (Catherine b 1967, Joanna b 1973); *Career* dir and gen mangr GEC Telecommunications Ltd 1976-81, md GEC Information Systems Ltd 1981-83; dir: Tech and Corp Devpt STC plc 1983-90, Abingworth plc 1985-; chm Info Technol Advsy Bd DTI 1988-; memb: Advsy Cncl on Sci and Technol, Cabinet Office, Espirt Advsy Bd Euro Cmmn; Freeman City of London; memb Guild of Info Technologists, FIIM 1979, FENG 1982, FRSA 1983, FIEE 1984; *Recreations* piano, music, gardening; *Clubs* United Oxford and Cambridge; *Style—* Dr Nigel Horne; IT Partner, KPMG Peat Marwick McLintock, 8 Salisbury Square, London EC4Y 8BB (☎ 071 236 8000)

HORSFALL TURNER, Jonathan; s of Harold Horsfall Turner, CBE (d 1981), and Eileen Mary, *née* Jenkins; *b* 27 Nov 1945; *Educ* The King's Sch Canterbury, Gonville and Caius Coll Cambridge (MA); *m* 25 Aug 1973, Yvonne Roberts, da of Angus Monroe Thomson (d 1972); 1 da (Olivia Jane b 1980); *Career* admitted slr 1970; ptnr Allen and Overy 1973-; carried out res on Eng Mediaeval Graffiti of Canterbury Cathedral 1963-67 (manuscripts in cathedral library and results published by Canterbury Cathedral Chronicles); Freeman Worshipful Co of Slrs 1973; memb Law Soc 1970; *Recreations* architecture, antiques, opera, canals; *Clubs* Garrick; *Style—* Jonathan Horsfall Turner, Esq; Greenwich, London; Palace St, Canterbury, Kent

HORTON, Clive Fielding; s of Frank Fielding Horton (d 1970), and Hilda Elizabeth, *née* Powell (d 1983); *b* 3 July 1931; *Educ* Dover Coll; *m* 4 April 1959, Wendy Bradley, da of Henry Jordan (d 1983), of Maidstone; 3 da (Jane b 1963, Susan b 1963, Katie b 1966); *Career* cmmnd RA 1954, served Malaya 1955-56; qualified CA 1954; sr ptnr Day Smith and Hunter 1979- (ptnr 1958); pres SE Soc of CAs 1972-73, memb Cncl ICAEW 1973-77; hon treas Kent Assoc for the Blind, cncl memb Maidstone Hospice Appeal; *Recreations* golf; *Clubs* Royal St George's Golf, Bearsted Golf (capt 1974); *Style—* Clive Horton, Esq; 14 Conway Rd, Maidstone, Kent ME16 0HD (☎ 0622 753695); Day Smith and Hunter, Star House, Maidstone, Kent ME14 1LT (☎ 0622 690666)

HORTON, Kenneth Edward; s of Edward Thomas Samuel Horton, of Rochester (d 1949), and Hilda Eleanor, *née* Smith (d 1978); *b* 24 March 1921; *Educ* Medway Tech Coll; *m* 1, 12 July 1947 (m dis 1972), Nora Winifried, da of Ernest Levi Cumberland, of Rochester (d 1979); 2 s (Peter Richard b 28 Aug 1949, Nigel Edward b 26 Feb 1952); m 2, 29 Sept 1979, José Helena, *née* Hood; *Career* Capt Kent Home Guard 1940-45 and 1956-60, trained in signals; engrg design conslt engaged on: BP refinery Isle of Grain Rochester, SEGB power station Isle of Grain Rochester; elected memb: Rochester upon Medway City Cncl 1979-87, Kent CC 1985 (former sec of a tenants assoc and youth club worker); memb: Kent and Essex Sea Fisheries Ctee 1985-, Southern Water Land Drainage Ctee 1985-; Lab Pty: joined 1937, contested various seats in local elections 1947-, former holder of several offices; FInstPet 1966; *Recreations* wine making, photography, travelling abroad; *Style—* Kenneth Horton, Esq; Danelea, 41 Barleymow Close, Chatham, Kent (☎ 0634 861805)

HORTON, Malcolm Charles; s of Charles Harry Horton (d 1990), of Bexleyheath, and Irene Alice, *née* Povey (d 1989); *b* 29 Aug 1940; *Educ* Erith Tech Sch; *m* 1, 13 Aug 1966 (m dis 1983), Leila Mary, da of Julius Ungerson (d 1988), of Truro; 2 s (Jeremy b 1967, Frazer b 1969), 1 da (Rachel b 1972); m 2, 8 Oct 1983, Valerie May, da of Harry Stow (d 1944), of London; *Career* articled clerk Davies Bros and Co Chartered Accountants 1959-67, qualified City London 1966, chief accountant Beck and Pollitzer Ltd 1967-70, fin and admin mangr BOC International 1970-73; md: Williams Lea and Co Ltd 1973-78, Westerham Press Ltd 1979-82, Malcolm Horton Assoc Ltd 1982-87, Contemporary Watercolours Ltd 1987-; sole practitioner Malcolm Horton and Co 1985-; borough cncllr London Borough of Bexley 1971-74; treas: Bexley Community Rels Cncl 1973-76, Gravesend Chamber of Trade 1987-89; SDP parly candidate for Gravesend 1983; memb Concert Artists Assoc London; *Recreations* squash, walking, travel; *Style—* Malcolm Horton, Esq; Swale Cottage, Uplees, nr Faversham, Kent ME13 0QU (☎ 0795 531954); Malcolm Horton & Co, 165 Parrock St, Gravesend, Kent DA12 1ER (☎ 0474 328882)

HOSKIN, Ernest Jabez; s of Jabez Edmund Hoskin (d 1957), of Elmside House, Elmside, Exeter, and Eva Maud, *née* Anstey; *b* 15 Sept 1920; *Educ* Heles Sch Exeter; *m* 14 Nov 1946, (Hilda) Joyce, da of William Arthur Mawhinney (d 1966), of Torquay and Belfast; 1 s (Peter b 17 Sept 1948); *Career* Gunner 163-55 LAA Regt TA 1939, served France, Norway, Ceylon, cmmnd 1 Punjab Regt IA 1943, Lt 1944, Capt (Adj) 1944, Actg Maj 1945, served India and Burma, demob 1946; City Treasurer's Office Exeter 1938-49, sr inspr HM Customs and Excise 1949-79 (represented UK at Customs and Indirect Taxation Ctees of EEC 1974-79), led EEC delgn (indirect taxation) to Andean GP to promote a common market between Peru Bolivia Ecuador Colombia and Venezuela 1979-80, registrar VAT Tbnls for the UK 1980-83, VAT conslt Coopers & Lybrand Deloitte 1983-; managing conslt ed VAT Intelligence 1985-89; memb Kent Dahlia Soc; Freeman: City of London 1980, Worshipful Co of Blacksmiths 1980; FTII 1986; *Books* Community Law and UK VAT (1988), Appealing to a VAT Tribunal (1989), VAT and Community Law (1989), Community Law Cases (1990); *Recreations* genealogy, golf, gardening; *Clubs* Chislehurst Golf; *Style—* Ernest Hoskin, Esq; Woodhayes, 76A The Ave, Beckenham, Kent BR3 2ES

HOSKING, John Everard; CBE, JP; s of J Everard Hosking, OBE (d 1978), and Eveline Margaret, *née* Shaxson; *b* 23 Oct 1929; *Educ* Marlborough, Wye Coll London (BSc); *m* 16 Sept 1953, Joan Cecily, da of John Wilfrid Whitaker, OBE (d 1980); 2 s (Julian Bernard b 1957, Bruce Adrian b 1960); *Career* farmer and landowner in Kent 1953-69; md Eastes and Loud Ltd 1965-69; dir: Ashford Corn Exchange Co 1965-69, Newgrain-Kent 1969-74, Agroup Ltd 1987-, Bureau Europeen de Recherches SA 1987-, European Intelligence Ltd 1987-; chm Agra Europe (London) Ltd 1989 (chief exec 1974-89); chm: Ashford Magistrates' Court 1975-85, Centre for Euro Agric Studies Assoc 1977-83, Kent Magistrates' Courts Ctee 1984-88; vice pres Magistrates' Assoc (chm of Cncl 1987-90); memb Royal Agric Soc 1960; *Books* Rural Response to the Resource Crisis in Europe (ed, 1981); *Recreations* the arts, the countryside; *Clubs* Farmers', Royal Overseas; *Style—* John Hosking, Esq, CBE, JP; Agra Europe (London) Ltd, 25 Frant Rd, Tunbridge Wells, Kent TN2 5JT (☎ 0892 33813, fax 0892 24593, telex 95114 AGRATW G)

HOSKINS, Arthur Henry James; CBE; s of Alfred George Hoskins; *b* 14 Jan 1923; *m* 1949, Margaret Lilian Rose, da of Albert Davis (d 1959); 1 child; *Career* certified accountant, chartered sec; md and dep chm Matthew Hall plc 1939-86; *Recreations* reading, walking; *Style—* Arthur Hoskins, Esq, CBE; 2 Acorn Close, Chislehurst, Kent BR7 6LD (☎ 081 467 0755)

HOSKINS, (Herbert) Turnley; s of Capt Cecil John Hoskins (d 1936), and Ivy Doris, *née* Cuff (d 1976); *b* 16 Aug 1930; *Educ* Shoreham GS, Worthing HS, Brighton Tech Coll (PhC), Univ of Kent at Canterbury (MSc); *m* 31 Oct 1953, Audrey Elsie, da of Christopher Weldrick Martin (d 1985); 1 s (Malcolm John b 10 Oct 1962), 1 da (Elizabeth Mary b 4 April 1961); *Career* Sgt RAMC; dir Weald Pharmacies Kent 1962, dist pharmaceutical offr Canterbury and Thanet Health Authy; Br Standards 1976-; chm: Nat JAC Pharmacy Computer System, E Kent Branch Pharmaceutical Soc; MRPhS, MCPP, MIPhM; *Recreations* golf, sailing, photography, squash; *Clubs* Kent and Canterbury, Broome Park Golf and Country; *Style—* Turnley Hoskins, Esq; Kent and Canterbury Hospital, Ethelbert Rd, Canterbury, Kent CT1 3NG (☎ 0227 766877 ext 4303)

HOUGHAM, John William; s of William George Hougham, of Ash, Canterbury, Kent, and Emily Jane, *née* Smith; *b* 18 Jan 1937; *Educ* Sir Roger Manwood's Sch Sandwich Kent, Univ of Leeds (BA); *m* 26 Aug 1961, Peggy Edith, da of Ernest Grove (d 1972), of Hales Owen, Worcs; 1 s (Simon b 1967), 1 da (Elizabeth b 1965); *Career* Royal Regt of Artillery 1955-57 (2 Lt 1956), TA 1957-60 (Lt 1959); dir industl rels Ford Espana SA Valencia Spain 1976-80, dir industl rels mfrg Ford of Europe Inc 1982-86, exec dir for personnel Ford Motor Co Ltd 1986-; memb: Cncl CRAC, Bd Personnel Mgmnt Servs Ltd, CBI Employment Policy Ctee, Engrg Indust Trg Bd, Cncl Engrg Trg Authy Ltd, IPM Ctee on Equal Opportunities, Trg and Employment Advsy Bd NI; FIPM 1980, CBIM 1986; *Recreations* walking, collecting books on Kent, fishing; *Style—* John Hougham, Esq; Ford Motor Co Ltd, Warley, Brentwood, Essex CM13 3BW (☎ 0277 253 000, fax 0277 262 066)

HOUGHTON, David John; s of Walter John Houghton, of St Neots, Cambs; *Educ* Hitchin Boys' GS, St Thomas's Hosp Med Sch Univ of London (MB BS, MRCOG); *m* 19 June 1976, Theresa Ann, da of Reginald James Wherrell; 2 s (Giles Phillip b 1980, Guy Marcus b 1985), 1 da (Charlotte Emily b and d 1983); *Career* St Thomas's Hosp: house surgn 1971, obstetric and gynaecological res 1972-73; house physician Professorial Unit Southampton 1972, jr lectr anatomy Nottingham Med Sch 1974-75, sr house offr in surgery Poole 1975-76, registrar in surgery Dorchester 1976-77, jr researcher Queen Charlotte's Hosp 1978, registrar and sr registrar in gynaecology St Bartholemew's Hosp 1978-83, conslt gynaecologist Chatham 1983-; author of: various pubns on placental proteins 1982, articles on female genital cancer; memb: Hosp Conslts' and Specialists' Assoc, Br Fertility Soc; memb BMA, FRCS 1976; *Recreations* swimming and keep fit, wine appreciation, photography; *Clubs* Queen Charlotte's Hosp Dining, Maidstone and Sevenoaks Post House Health and Fitness; *Style—* David Houghton, Esq; All Saints' Hospital, Chatham, Kent (☎ 0634 407311); Bupa Alexandra Hospital, Impton Lane, Walderslade, Chatham, Kent (☎ 0634 687166)

HOUSE, Hon Mrs (Susan Anne); *née* Irving; o da of Baron Irving of Dartford, PC, DL (Life Peer, d 1989); *b* 1946; *m* 1966, John House; *Style—* The Hon Mrs House; c/o The Lady Irving of Dartford, 10 Tynedale Close, Dartford, Kent

HOUSTON, Dr James Caldwell; CBE (1982); s of David Houston (d 1955), and Minnie Walker Caldwell (d 1973); *b* 18 Feb 1917; *Educ* Mill Hill, Guy's Hosp Med Sch (MD); *m* 1946, Dr Thelma Cromarty, da of Prof John Cruickshank, CBE (d 1966), of Aberdeen; 4 s (Kenneth, Brian, Alan, Andrew); *Career* dean: Guy's Hosp Med and Dental Schs 1965-82, United Med and Dental Schs of Guy's and St Thomas's Hosps 1982-84; emeritus conslt physician Guy's Hosp, dir Clerical Med and Gen Life Assur Soc 1964-87, vice pres Med Def Union 1970-; FRCP; *Recreations* golf, gardening; *Clubs* Addington Golf; *Style*— Dr J Caldwell Houston, CBE; Discovery Cottage, St Katharine-by-the-Tower, London E1 9UG (☎ 071 481 8912); Cockhill Farm, Detling, Maidstone, Kent (☎ 0634 31395); Keats House, Guy's Hospital, London SE1 9RT (☎ 071 955 5000)

HOWARD, Rt Hon Michael; PC (1990), QC (1982), MP (C) Folkestone and Hythe 1983-; s of late Bernard Howard, and Hilda Howard; *b* 7 July 1941; *Educ* Llanelli GS, Peterhouse Cambridge; *m* 1975, Sandra Clare, da of Wing Cdr Saville Paul; 1 s, 1 da, 1 step-s; *Career* pres Cambridge Union 1962; called to the Bar Inner Temple 1964; chm Bow Gp 1970; contested (C) Liverpool Edge Hill 1966 and 1970, chm Coningsby Club 1972-73; memb: Cons Gp for Europe, Euro Movement Exec Ctee 1970-73; PPS to SG 1984-85, parly under sec of state for consumer and corporate affrs 1985-87, min for local govt 1987-88; min for water and planning 1988-90; sec of state for employment 1990-; *Recreations* watching sport, reading; *Clubs* Carlton; *Style*— The Rt Hon Michael Howard, QC, MP; House of Commons, London SW1

HOWARD, Ronald Walter; s of John Howard (d 1952), of Adelaide, S Aust, and Selma Hertha, *née* Heine (d 1975); *b* 13 June 1929; *Educ* Adelaide HS, Univ of Adelaide (BEng); *m* 30 July 1955, Enid Gretta, da of Herbert William Harrington (d 1946), of Adelaide; 2 da (Julie Rosanna b 11 Jan 1961, Jane Clare b 29 Nov 1962); *Career* electronics engr; specialised in systems for missiles and aircraft especially automatic flight controls for combat and tport aircraft; scientific offr Dept of Supply Aust 1951-54; Elliott Bros (London) Ltd: joined 1954, dir and gen mangr 1965; dir and gen mangr Marconi-Elliot 1965; GEC Avionics Ltd: md 1987, chm 1989; chm Aviation Div Electronic Engrg Assoc 1973-75; memb: Plenary Bd Royal Aircraft Estab 1986-, Airworthiness Requirements Bd CAA 1987-, Aeronautical Res Cncl 1977-79, Offshore Energy Technol Bd Dept of Energy 1979-, Aviation Ctee DTI 1982-; cncl memb CBI; SBAC: chm Tech Bd 1978-80, pres 1989-90; author of numerous technical papers on aeronautical automatic controls; memb: parish cncl, village ctees; FRAeS 1974 (Simms Prize 1974 and 1981, Bronze Medal 1976, Br Gold Medal 1986), FRSA (1988); *Recreations* private flying and gliding, listed buildings and antique furniture restoration, local history, genealogy; *Style*— Ronald Howard, Esq; Yew Trees House, Boxley, Maidstone, Kent ME14 3DR (☎ 0622 752929); GEC Avionics Ltd, Airport Works, Rochester, Kent ME1 2XX (☎ 0634 744400, fax 0634 832664, telex 96333)

HOWLETT, Gen Sir Geoffrey Hugh Whitby; KBE (1984, OBE 1972), MC (1952); s of Brig Bernard Howlett, DSO (ka 1943), and Joan, *née* Whitby; *b* 5 Feb 1930; *Educ* Wellington, RMA Sandhurst; *m* 1955, Elizabeth Anne, da of Sqdn Ldr Leonard Aspinal, of Speldhurst; 1 s, 2 da; *Career* cmmnd Queen's Own Royal West Kent Regt 1950, transfd Parachute Regt 1959, Mil Asst to C-in-C North (Oslo) 1969-71, cmd 2 Para 1971-73, RCDS 1973-75, cmd 16 Para Bde 1975-77, dir Army Recruiting 1977-79, GOC 1 Armoured Div (Lower Saxony, W Germany) 1979-82, Cmdt RMA Sandhurst 1982-83, GOC SE Dist 1983-85; C-in-C Allied Forces Northern Europe (Oslo) 1986-89; Col Cmdt: Army Catering Corps 1981-89, The Parachute Regt 1983-90; chm Serv Sound and Vision Corp 1990- (vice chm 1989); chm Leonard Cheshire Fndn 1990- (tstee 1988-); pres: CCF 1989-, Stragglers of Asia CC 1989-; cmmr Royal Hosp Chelsea 1989-, chm Reg Forces Employment Assoc 1990- (vice chm 1989); *Recreations* cricket, shooting; *Clubs* Naval and Military, MCC; *Style*— Gen Sir Geoffrey Howlett, KBE, MC; c/o Lloyds Bank, Tonbridge, Kent

HUBBARD, Dr Dudley Charles; s of Cyril Charles Hubbard, of Perry Barr, Birmingham, and Gwendoline May, *née* Baldock; *b* 7 Sept 1943; *Educ* King Edward VI GS Aston Birmingham, Univ of Birmingham Med Sch (MB ChB); *m* 1, 8 May 1965 (m dis 1979), Elizabeth Frances, da of Albert Edward Taylor, of Great Barr, Birmingham; 3 s (Mark Charles Edward b 1966, Jonathan Robert b 1968, Andrew William b 1971), 1 da (Diane Gail Jean b 1970); m 2, 14 Feb 1987, Christine Joyce, da of (Albert) Cyril Phillips, of Oakwood Park, Derby; *Career* house offr: Queen Elizabeth Hosp Birmingham 1966-67 and 1968, Wordsley Hosp 1967-68; GP Rochester 1968-, clinical asst diabetes St Bartholomews Hosp Rochester 1972-, co med advsr AKZO Chemicals Ltd 1984-90; cncllr Rochester upon Medway CC 1987-, staff offr St John Ambulance Bde 1969-, vice chm Mgmnt Ctee Fiveways Leisure Centre; chm: Parsonage Farm Open Space Gp, Bd Govrs Thomas Aveling Sch Rochester; SBStJ; *Style*— Dr Dudley Hubbard; The Pines, 7 Shaws Way, Rochester, Kent ME1 3DY; 67 City Way, Rochester, Kent ME1 2AY (☎ 0634 843351)

HUBBARD, Jack; s of Arthur Fredrick Hubbard (d 1984), and Alice Mary, *née* Fairman (d 1985); *b* 11 Oct 1932; *Educ* Rochester Tech Sch, Univ of Cardiff (BSc); *m* 11 Sept 1960, Christine Lilian, da of Francis Held (d 1985); 2 s (Andrew b 14 June 1961, Peter b 30 Oct 1964); *Career* Nat Serv RAF 1953-55; Reed Int: central engrg 1956-57, head engrg res 1967-69, PA to dep chm 1969-71, md Timperley Engrg 1971-73, divnl chief exec 1973-87; chief exec Medway Packaging Ncb Sweden 1987-, ret 1990; involved in church activities; Liveryman Worshipful Co of Horners; MIEE, MIMechE; *Recreations* rambling; *Style*— Jack Hubbard, Esq; Medway Packaging, New Hythe Lane, Larkfield, Maidstone, Kent ME2 6SH (☎ 0622 717 179, fax 0622 76360, car tel 0836 231 274, telex 965131)

HUBERT, John (Jack) Francis Drake; s of John McFarlane Hubert (d 1980), of Sydney, Aust, and Grace Francis, *née* Drake (d 1951); *b* 29 June 1934; *m* 21 Sept 1957, Joan Dorothy Emma, da of Alfred William Henry McIntyre (d 1985); 1 da (Katharine Emma (Kate) b 1967); *Career* Nat Serv RAF instrument fitter Germany 1952-54; asst mangr Frys Motor Works Lewisham (formerly estimator) 1956-61, dir and ptnr Lennox C Holman Ltd consltg engrs and assessors 1985- (engr and assessor 1961-85); vice chm Wilmington Meml Ctee; memb: Dartford CAB Ctee, Wilmington Parish Cncl, Dartford Borough Cncl; MIMI; *Recreations* walking, gardening; *Style*— John Hubert, Esq; 23 Walnut Tree Ave, Wilmington, Dartford, Kent DA1 1LT (☎ 0322 26654); Lennox C Holman Ltd, 29 Abbeville Rd, London SW4 9LA (☎ 081 675 5315, fax 081 673 4446)

HUDSON, (Norman) Barrie; s of William Hudson, of Coventry, and Lottie Mary, *née* Taylor; *b* 21 June 1937; *Educ* King Henry VIII Sch Coventry, Univ of Sheffield (BA), UCL (MSc); *m* 5 Oct 1963, Hazel, da of Capt Frederick Cotterill (d 1965); 2 s (Richard b 12 March 1965, Mark b 22 Jan 1974), 1 da (Jane b 13 Nov 1966); *Career* economist: Tube Investments Ltd 1960, Economist Intelligence Unit 1962, nat accounts advsr Govt of Jordan 1963, econ advsr Br Devpt Div Beirut 1967, sr econ advsr ODA 1973, head of Br Devpt Divn Bangkok 1974, under sec (principal estabs offr) ODA 1981, under sec ODA (Africa) 1986; *Recreations* theatre, music, reading, watching football and cricket; *Style*— Barrie Hudson, Esq; The Galleons, Sallows Shaw, Sole St, Cobham, Kent DA13 9BP (☎ 0474 814419); Overseas Development Administration, Eland House, Stag Place, London SW1 (☎ 071 273 0549)

HUDSON, Prof Robert Francis; s of John Frederick Hudson (d 1966), of Bottesford, Nottingham, and Ethel Lizzie, *née* Oldfield (d 1968); *b* 15 Dec 1922; *Educ* Brigg GS Lincs, Imperial Coll London (BSc, DIC, PhD); *m* 3 Aug 1945, Monica, da of Charles Ashton Stray (d 1939), of Lowestoft; 1 s (John Martin Edward b 1949), 2 da (Sarah Elizabeth b 1952, Mary Alexandra b 1952); *Career* asst lectr Imperial Coll London 1945-47, lectr QMC London 1947-59, gp dir CERT Geneva 1960-66; visiting prof: Rochester USA 1970, Bergen Norway 1971, Paris 1973, Mainz Germany 1979, Queens Univ Ontario Canada 1983; Frontiers lectr Case-Western Reserve Univ Cleveland USA 1970, Nuffield lectr Canada 1975, Quest lectr Queens Univ Kingston Ontario Canada 1983, industl conslt 1983-, emeritus prof of organic chemistry Univ of Kent 1985- (prof 1967-85); memb: Cncl of Chem Soc 1967-70, Dalton Cncl RSC 1973-76, Perkin Cncl RSC; vice pres Inst of Sci and Technol 1970-76, fndn chm Reaction Mechanisms Gp RSC 1973-75; FRS, FRSC; *Books* Wool-Its Physics and Chemistry (1954), Structure and Mechanism in Organophosphorus Chemistry; *Recreations* music, cricket; *Clubs* Athenaeum; *Style*— Prof Robert Hudson, FRS; 37 Puckle Lane, Canterbury, Kent CT1 3LA (☎ 0227 761340); University of Kent, Chemical Lab, Canterbury, Kent CT2 7NZ (☎ 0227 764000)

HUGHES, Dr David Treharne Dillon; s of Maj-Gen W D Hughes, CB, CBE, of Vine House, Summer Court, Tilford Rd, Farnham, and Kathleen Linda Elizabeth, *née* Thomas (d 1976); *b* 31 Oct 1931; *Educ* Cheltenham, Trinity Coll Oxford (BSc, MA), London Hosp Med Coll (BM BCh); *m* 11 Nov 1959, Gloria Anna; 1 s (David Edward Treharne b 29 April 1974), 2 da (Carly Anna b 22 Sept 1960, Mandy Lou b 19 Oct 1962); *Career* Capt RAMC served 1959-61 (jr med specialist BMH Hong Kong); jr res fell MRC Univ of Oxford 1953-54, res fell Univ of California 1963-64, conslt physician London Hosp 1970- (jr appts 1957-68), head Dept Clinical Investigation Wellcome Res Laboratories 1978-; memb: Hunterian Soc (former pres), Int Soc of Internal Med (former pres); Freeman City of London, Jr Warden Worshipful Soc of Apothecaries (memb Court 1981); memb RSM, FRCP; *Books* Tropical Health Science (1967), Human Biology and Hygiene (1969), Lung Function for the Clinical (1981); *Recreations* cricket, horseracing; *Clubs* Savage; *Style*— Dr David Hughes; The London Hospital, London E1 1BB (☎ 071 377 7417)

HUGHES, Rev Dr Edward Marshall; s of Edward William Hughes (d 1940), of Kent, and Mabel Frances, *née* Faggetter (d 1947); *b* 11 Nov 1913; *Educ* City of London Sch, King's Coll London (AKC), Cuddesdon Coll Oxford (MTh, PhD); *Career* warden St Peter's Coll Jamaica 1952-61, fell St Augustine's Coll Canterbury 1961-65; vicar of Dover 1971-84, chaplain to HM The Queen 1973-83, hon chaplain of the co assoc Men of Kent and Kentish Men 1979- (of which his father was a fndr memb 1897); *Recreations* gardening, exercising the dogs, computing; *Style*— The Rev Dr Edward Hughes; Woodlands, Sandwich Rd, Woodnesborough, Sandwich, Kent CT13 0LZ (☎ 0304 617098)

HUGHES, Dr Graham Robert Vivian; s of Robert Arthur Hughes, and Emily Elizabeth Hughes (d 1989); *b* 26 Nov 1940; *Educ* Cardiff HS For Boys, London Hosp Med Coll (MD); *m* 2 March 1966, Monica Ann; 1 s (Richard John Vivian b 7 July 1971), 1 da (Sarah Imogen b 19 Oct 1967); *Career* reader in med and head Dept of Rheumatology Royal Postgrad Med Sch London, conslt rheumatologist and head of Lupus Arthritis Res Unit St Thomas' Hosp

London, conslt rheumatologist RAF 1987; 500 pubns on arthritis res; chm Nat Lupus Gp, tstee Br SLE (Lupus) Aid Soc; hon memb: Aust Rheumatology Soc, Scandinavian Rheumatology Soc, Hong Kong Rheumatology Soc Portugese Rheumatology Soc; memb: American Lupus Hall of Fame, Assoc of Physicians of GB and I; FRCP; *Books* Modern Topics in Rheumatology (1978), Systemic Lupus Erythematosus (1982), Connective Tissue Diseases (3 edn 1987), Lecture Notes in Rhematology (1987), Problems in The Rheumatic Diseases (1988), SLE: A Guide for Patients (1988); *Recreations* tennis, piano; *Style—* Dr Graham Hughes; Lupus Arthritis Research Unit, Rayne Institute, St Thomas' Hospital, London SE1 (☎ 071 928 9292 ext 2888)

HUGHES, Howard; s of Charles William Hughes (d 1969), of W Kirby, Ches, and Ethel May, *née* Howard; *b* 4 March 1938; *Educ* Rydal Sch; *m* 1, 20 June 1964, Joy Margaret (d 1984), da of Charles Francis Pilmore-Bedford (d 1966), of Keston, Kent; 2 s (Quentin b 1969, Edward b 1971), 1 da (Charlotte b 1974); m 2, 2 April 1988, Christine Margaret, da of Walter George Miles, of Tunbridge Wells, Kent; *Career* articled Bryce Hammer & Co Liverpool 1955-60; Price Waterhouse London: joined 1960, ptnr 1970-, memb Policy Ctee 1979-, dir London Office 1982-85, managing ptnr (UK) 1985, md Europe 1988-, memb World Bd 1988-; memb: Cncl Royal London Soc for Blind, Agric Wages Bd; FCA 1960; *Recreations* golf, music; *Clubs* Carlton, Wildernesse GC; *Style—* Howard Hughes, Esq; Witham, Woodland Rise, Seal, nr Sevenoaks, Kent TN15 0HZ (☎ 0732 61161), Price Waterhouse, Southwark Towers, 32 London Bridge St, London SE1 9SY (☎ 071 407 8989, fax 071 378 0647, telex 884657/8)

HUGHES, Melvyn; s of Evan Llewellyn Hughes, of Newcastle upon Tyne, and Irene Kathleen, *née* Spires; *b* 18 Nov 1950; *Educ* Royal GS Newcastle upon Tyne, St Catherine's Coll Oxford (MA); *m* 6 July 1974, Diane, da of Percival Moffett (d 1987); 2 s (Richard b 2 Nov 1983, David b 9 March 1990), 1 da (Alexandra b 28 Oct 1980); *Career* personnel ptnr Slaughter and May 1989- (asst slr 1976-83, articled clerk 1974-76, ptnr 1983-); Freeman City of London; memb: City of London Slrs, Law Soc; *Recreations* reading, cars, sport; *Style—* Melvyn Hughes, Esq; Little Steading, Godden Green, Sevenoaks, Kent TN15 0JS (☎ 0732 61 610); Slaughter and May, 35 Basinghall St, London EC2V 5DB (☎ 071 600 1200, fax 071 726 0038/071 600 0289)

HUGHES-MORGAN, His Hon Judge; Sir David John; 3 Bt (UK 1925), of Penally, Pembroke; CB (Mil 1983), CBE (Mil 1973, MBE Mil 1959); s of Sir John Vernon Hughes-Morgan, 2 Bt (d 1969); *b* 11 Oct 1925; *Educ* RNC Dartmouth; *m* 1959, Isabel Jean Blacklock Gellatly Milne, da of John Milne Lindsay (d 1969), of Annan, Dumfriesshire; 3 s; *Heir* s, Parry Hughes-Morgan, *qv*; *Career* Sub Lt RN, ret 1946; admitted slr 1950; cmmnd Army Legal Servs 1955, Brig Legal HQ UKLF 1976-78, dir Army Legal Servs BAOR 1978-80, dir Army Legal Servs (Maj Gen) MOD 1980-84; rec SE Circuit 1983-86, circuit judge 1986-; *Style—* His Hon Judge Sir David Hughes-Morgan, Bt, CB, CBE; c/o National Westminster Bank Ltd, 1 High St, Bromley, Kent BR1 1LL

HUGHES-MORGAN, (Ian) Parry David; s and h of Sir David John Hughes-Morgan, 3 Bt, CB, CBE, *qv*; *b* 22 Feb 1960; *Style—* Parry Hughes-Morgan, Esq

HULL, Vernon Allan; s of Percy Hull, and Rita, *née* Shotbolt; *b* 22 Oct 1947; *Educ* Univ of Keele (BA), Univ of Lancaster (MA); *m* 1, 27 July 1971 (m dis 1979), Gillian Frances; m 2, 26 Oct 1981, Catherine Jane, da of William Berry; 1 s (Thomas Edward Percy b 20 April 1982); *Career* lectr Lowestoft Coll Further Educn 1972-75, head of Adult Educn S Bedford 1975-78, dist sec S E Dist Workers Educnl Assoc 1978-; city cncllr Rochester Upon Medway 1983-; Lab parly candidate: Mid Kent constituency 1983, Medway Constituency 1987; memb TGWU; *Recreations* walking, reading, cricket, visual arts and music; *Style—* Vernon Hull, Esq; 9 King Edward Rd, Rochester, Kent ME1 1UB (☎ 0634 408573); 4 Castle Hill, Rochester, Kent ME1 1QQ (☎ 0634 842140)

HULSE, Dr (John) Anthony; s of Eric Cecil Hulse, of Ditchling, Sussex, and Joan Mary Hulse; *b* 12 May 1948; *Educ* Woking Co GS, Trinity Coll Cambridge (MD), St Thomas' Hosp Med Sch (MB BChir, MA, MRLP); *m* 6 July 1974, Doriel Maura, da of Theodore Beggs; 1 da (Charlotte Olivia Aurelie b 24 March 1988); *Career* res registrar Hosp for Sick Children Gt Ormond St 1978-80, sr registrar in paediatrics St Thomas' Hosp London 1980-88, res fell Univ of California San Francisco 1984, conslt paediatrician Maidstone Hosp; currently hon conslt paediatrician: Hosp for Sick Children Gt Ormond St, St Thomas' Hosp; Author: 22 papers on growth and endocrine disorders in childhood, books for students on gen paediatrics; memb: BMA, BPA, various paediatric working ptys and ctees; sec Hadlow Gardeners' Soc, clinical dir child health Maidstone Health Dist; FRSM; *Books* Treatment and Prognosis in Paediatrics (1989); *Recreations* gardening, travel, theatre, restoring old houses; *Clubs* RSM; *Style—* Dr Anthony Hulse; Costens, Carpenters Lane, Hadlow, Tonbridge, Kent TN11 0EY (☎ 0732 851404); Maidstone Hospital, Hermitage Lane, Barming, Maidstone, Kent ME16 9QQ (☎ 0622 729000)

HUMPHERY-SMITH, Cecil Raymond Julian; s of Frederick Humphery-Smith, MBE (d 1979), and Violet Agnes Humphery-Smith (d 1990); *b* 29 Oct 1928; *Educ* St John's Hurstpierpoint, Univ of London Sch of Hygiene and Tropical Med, Parma, Univ of Kent; *m* 1951, Alice Elizabeth Gwendoline, da of late Charles Thomas Cogle; 1 s, 5 da; *Career* mangr Consumer Servs Dept H J Heinz Co 1955-60, conslt De Rica SpA 1961-72, md Achievements Ltd 1961-81 (chm 1981); fndr princ and tstee Inst of Heraldic and Genealogical Studies, ed Family History 1961-; co-fndr Kent Family History Soc; lectr in extra mural studies: Univ of London 1951-, Univ of Kent 1964-; visiting prof Univ of Minho 1970-72; cncl memb: Heraldry Soc 1953-, Manorial Soc of GB 1979-, Sub-Priory B Adrian Fortescue 1981-87; memb Domesday Nat Ctee 1984-85; Freeman and Liveryman Worshipful Cos of Broderers and Scriveners (hon historian); fell Heraldry Soc; FSA, FSG; Academician l'Académie Internationale d'Héraldique 1967 (memb Cncl); memb: Confédération Internationale des Sciences Généalogique et Héraldique (vice pres 1980-86, pres 1986-90), UNESCO, ISSC; Knight of Obedience SMOM; *Publications* books incl: The Colour of Heraldry (jtly), General Armory Two, Heraldry in Canterbury Cathedral, Chronicles of Thomas Chough, Anglo-Norman Armory (2 volumes), An Atlas and Index of Parish Registers, A Genealogist's Bibliography, Our Family History, Introducing Family History, Sonnets of Life, Hugh Revel; numerous articles and lectures on Canterbury Cathedral Heraldry; *Recreations* writing sonnets, walking, listening to good music; *Clubs* Challoner, Royal British (Lisbon); *Style—* Cecil Humphery-Smith, Esq, FSA; Alcroft Grange, Hackington, Canterbury, Kent CT2 9NN (☎ 0227 462308); Fazarga, Moita-Fatima, 2495 Portugal

HUNT, David Roderic Notley; QC (1987); s of Dr Geoffrey Notley Hunt (d 1982), of Pembury, Kent, and Deborah Katharine Rosamund, *née* Clapham; *b* 22 June 1947; *Educ* Charterhouse, Trinity Coll Cambridge (MA); *m* 27 April 1974, Alison Connell, da of Lt-Col Arthur George Jelf (d 1958); 2 s (Thomas b 8 Feb 1976, Robert b 20 Feb 1979); *Career* called to the Bar Gray's Inn 1969, asst rec; *Recreations* sailing, golf, skiing; *Clubs* Bewl Valley Sailing, Nevill Golf; *Style—* David Hunt, Esq, QC; Queen Elizabeth Building, Temple, London EC4 (☎ 071 936 3131, fax 071 353 1937, telex 8951414)

HUNTER, Dennis James; s of late Ernest James Hunter, and late Florence, *née* Ofield; *b* 10 June 1923; *m* (Margaret) Elizabeth Hunter; 3 s (Antony Paul b 20 May 1950, Philip b 29 Aug 1953, Dominic b 5 March 1965), 2 da (Jacqueline Avril b 27 April 1947, Rosemary b 9 Feb 1963); *Career* co cncllr, tstee Whitstable Improvement Tst, govr Sir William Nottidge Sch, former pres Fedn of Assocs of Materials Handling; *Recreations* yachting; *Clubs* RYA, Royal Temple Yacht, Cruising Assoc; *Style—* Dennis Hunter, Esq; Highfield House, 96 Joy Lane, Whitstable, Kent CT5 4DF (☎ 0227 272318)

HUNTRODS, (Vernon) Guy; CBE (1985); s of Joseph Guy Huntrods (d 1945), and Ethel Fanny, *née* Clapperton (d 1982); *b* 18 May 1923; *Educ* Felsted, Kings Sch Rochester; *m* 9 Nov 1945, Betty Margaret, da of Arthur Sanders Gough (d 1974); 3 s (Richard Guy Gough b 9 Aug 1947, Crispin Joseph Agar b 19 May 1953, Guy Justin Rupert b 4 May 1958); *Career* RN 1941-46, LT RNVR 1944; Bank of England: joined 1946, advsr Central Bank of Brasil Rio De Janeiro 1965-66, asst chief Overseas Devpt 1966-67, alternate exec dir for UK Int Monetary Fund Washington 1967-70, advsr 1971-73, resigned 1973; conslt Commercial Bank of Australia 1973, advsr Euro Latin American Bank 1974, chief of mission to Banco de la Republica Bogota Colombia 1974, exec dir Latin America Div Lloyds Bank International 1975-85; dir: Bank of London and South America, Bank of London and Montreal, LBI (Bahamas), Banco Anglo Colombiano Bogota; memb and fin advsr of UK Delgn at UN Econ Cmmn for Latin America Conf in: Panama 1959, Santiago 1961; chm Latin American Trade Advsy Gp 1977-79, memb BOTB 1978-80, Br banks rep Int Banks Advsy Ctee on Argentina 1982-85, Br banks rep and dep chm Int Banks Advsy Ctee on Brasil 1982-85; Cdr Ordem Nacional Do Cruzeiro Do Sul Brasil 1985; *Recreations* golf, tennis; *Clubs* Overseas Bankers, Canning; *Style—* Guy Huntrods, Esq, CBE; Collingwood House, London Rd, Tunbridge Wells, Kent TN1 1DX (☎ 0892 26785)

HURST, Peter Thomas; s of Thomas Lyon Hurst (d 1981), of Cheshire, and Norah Mary, *née* Delaney (d 1977); *b* 27 Oct 1942; *Educ* Stoneyhurst, Univ of London (LLB); *m* 1968, Diane, da of Ian George Irvine, of Cheshire; 1 s (Charles b 1975), 2 da (Elizabeth b 1970, Catherine b 1972); *Career* slr Supreme Court 1967; ptnr: Hurst and Walker slrs Liverpool 1967-77, Gair Roberts Hurst and Walker slrs Liverpool 1977-81; Master Supreme Court 1981-; chm: Liverpool Young Slrs Gp 1979, NW Young Slrs Conf 1980; *Books* Butterworths Costs Service (1986), Costs in Criminal Cases, Solicitors' Remuneration, Cordery on Solicitors (contrib 8 edn, 1988); *Style—* Peter Hurst, Esq; Supreme Court Taxing Office, Royal Courts of Justice, The Strand, London WC2

HUSSAIN, Dr (Mian) Farrukh; s of Mian Maqbool Hussain, of Pakistan, and Sarfraz Hussain; *b* 26 Dec 1940; *Educ* St Anthony's HS Lahore, Karachi (MB BS, RCPSI DPM), London (DPM); *m* 29 July 1973, Dr Shahnaz Akthar, da of C H Abdul Majeed; 3 s (Omar b 1976, Mustafa b 1978, Usman b 1980); *Career* conslt psychiatrist and specialist in mental illness: St Augustines Chartham Kent, Chaucer Hosp Canterbury, St Martin's Hosp Canterbury,

Kent and Canterbury Hosp Canterbury; memb: BMA Canterbury, Southern Div Royal Coll Psychiatrists, Simon Langton PTA; registrar Rotary Club Canterbury, treas Kent Fedn PTA; MRCPsych; *Recreations* chess, badminton; *Style*— Dr Farrukh Hussain; 6 Cadnam Close, Canterbury, Kent CT2 7SQ (☎ 0227 762267); Chaucer Hospital, Hackington Rd, Canterbury (☎ 0227 455466)

HUTCHINSON, Cncllr Jill; da of John Maldwyn Pughe (d 1967), of Orpington, Kent, and Gladys, *née* Pearey; *b* 25 July 1934; *Educ* Holy Trinity Convent Sch Bromley Kent, Westminster Hotel and Catering Coll London; *m* 19 Sept 1959, Alan James, s of Harry Hutchinson (d 1983), of Bromley, Kent; 3 s (James Alexander (Jamie) b 1962, Matthew Harry b 1964, Toby Maldwyn b 1968); *Career* mangr of employment agency London 1962-76; cncllr Tonbridge and Malling Borough Cncl 1976- (former Mayor), non exec memb Tunbridge Wells Health Authy; chm: CRUSE (bereavement care) W Kent, St Stephens Co Primary Sch, Thomas Delarue Sch; vice chm Hardwick Sch, govr Fosse Bank Sch, memb SE Arts Cncl; *Recreations* golf; *Style*— Cncllr Jill Hutchinson; Tonbridge and Malling Borough Council, The Air Station, West Malling, nr Maidstone, Kent (☎ 0732 844 522)

I

IGGLESDEN, Alan Paul; s of Alan Trevor Igglesden, of Westerham, and Gillian Catherine, *née* Relf; *b* 8 Oct 1964; *Educ* Churchill Sch Westerham; *m* 20 Jan 1990, Hilary Moira, da of William Henry Middleton, of Cape Town, SA; *Career* winter cricket coach Townships of Cape Town SA (incl Athlone and Langa) 1985-89, represented Western Province and played for Avendale CC (a multi-racial club) Cape Town, SA; Kent CCC: first class debut 1986, capped player 1989, leading wicket taker 1989; represented England in 1989 Ashes Series against Aust, toured with England A to Kenya and Zimbabwe 1990; *Recreations* golf, spending time with my wife, music, good movies; *Clubs* Crystal Palace Football; *Style—* Alan Igglesden, Esq; Kent County Cricket Club, St Lawrence Ground, Old Dover Rd, Canterbury, Kent CT1 3N2 (☎ 0227 456886, fax 0227 76168)

ILCHESTER, 9 Earl of (GB 1756) Maurice Vivian de Touffreville Fox-Strangways; Lord Ilchester of Ilchester, Somerset, and Baron Strangways of Woodford Strangways, Dorset (GB 1741), and Lord Ilchester and Stavordale, Baron of Redlynch, Somerset (GB 1747); s of 8 Earl of Ilchester (d 1970), and Laure Georgine Emilie, *née* Mazaraki; the 1 Earl was unc of Charles James Fox and brother of 1 Lord Holland; from 1889 Holland House reverted to the Earls of Ilchester before being bombed in WWII; it is now a youth hostel; *b* 1 April 1920; *Educ* Kingsbridge Sch; *m* 29 Nov 1941, Diana Mary Elizabeth, da of George Frederick Simpson, of Carrington, Oxford; *Heir* bro, Hon Raymond Fox-Strangways, *qv*; *Career* RAF 1936-76 (ret Gp Capt); vice chm Nottingham Building Society 1985-87 (dir 1982-90); md: Biggin Hill News Ltd, Bromley Borough News Ltd, County Border News Ltd 1983-; pres: Soc of Engrs 1974-75, Edenbridge Town Band 1976-, Biggin Hill Branch RAFA 1976-, 2427 (Biggin Hill) Sqdn ATC 1977-, SE Area RAFA 1978-, Inst Nuclear Engrs 1983-85; vice chm Biggin Hill Airport Consultative Ctee 1976-86 and 1989-, chm of govrs Cannock Sch 1978-, memb House of Lords Select Ctee on Sci and Technol 1984-89; Freeman City of London, Liveryman Guild of Air Pilots and Air Navigators; CEng, MRAeS, FINucE, Hon FSE, FBIM, FInstD, FRSA; *Recreations* outdoor activities, passive enjoyment of the arts; *Clubs* RAF; *Style—* The Rt Hon the Earl of Ilchester; Farley Mill, Westerham, Kent TN16 1UB (☎ 0959 62314); Biggin Hill News Ltd, Winterton House, Westerham, Kent TN16 1AJ (☎ 0959 64766)

IMAM, Dr Nilufar (Mrs Karim); da of Ali Imam (d 1943), and Mrs A Imam; *b* 5 May 1940; *Educ* Univ of Dhaka (MB BS); *m* 6 Aug 1962, Dr Mahbub Karim, s of Dr A Karim (d 1979); 1 s (Mahzuz b 1969), 1 da (Naila (Dr Karim) b 1963); *Career* various trg posts in hosps in Dhaka Oxford Banbury and Winchester 1962-72, sr trg dr in family planning Medway Health Authy 1972-77, sr ptnr all female gen practice 1977-; memb: Cervical Cytology Working Pty Medway, Medway Post Grad Soc; memb Bd of Govrs: Byron Rd Primary Sch Gillingham, Chatham GS for Girls; Dhaka Gold Medallist 1962; memb BMA, MRCOG, FRCSEd 1971, FRCOG 1989; *Recreations* gardening, travelling, music, walking, welfare of neighbourhood and environment; *Style—* Dr Nilufar Imam; Byron House Surgery, 30 Byron Rd, Gillingham, Kent ME7 5QH (☎ 0634 576347)

IND, Jack Kenneth; s of Rev William Price Ind (d 1956), of Harlington, Beds, and Doris Maud, *née* Cavell; *b* 20 Jan 1935; *Educ* Lichfield Cathedral Choir Sch, Marlborough, St John's Coll Oxford (MA), Univ of London (PGCE); *m* 2 Sept 1964, Elizabeth Olive, da of Gordon Edgar Toombs (d 1956), of Wokingham, Berks; 2 s (Mark Alexander b 1967, Hugh Timothy b 1969), 2 da (Rebecca Jane b 1965, Katharine Elizabeth b 1972); *Career* Nat Serv 2 Lt RA 1953-55; asst master Wellingborough Sch 1960-63, housemaster Tonbridge Sch 1970-81 (asst master 1963-81), headmaster Dover Coll 1981-; memb: HMC, Governing Body Gt Walstead Sch W Sussex, Jt Assoc of Classics Teachers 1960; reader C of E 1963-; vice pres: Dover Opera and Dramatic Soc, Dover Soc; *Recreations* music, reading; *Clubs* Public Schools'; *Style—* Jack K Ind, Esq; Headmaster's House, Dover College, Dover, Kent CT17 9RH (☎ 0304 205 905/969, fax 0304 242 208)

INGLEFIELD-WATSON, Lady; Therese; da of late Prof Charles Bodon, of Budapest; *m* 1946 (as his 2 w), Sir Derrick Inglefield-Watson, 4 Bt (d 1987); *Style—* Lady Inglefield-Watson; Ringshill House, Wouldham, nr Rochester, Kent ME1 3RB (☎ 0634 61514)

INGLETON, Kenneth John (Ken); s of Harold Ingleton (d 1982), of Minster, and Gwendaline Joyce, *née* Stables; *b* 21 April 1944; *Educ* Sheerness Tech Sch, Mid Kent Tech Coll (BSc); *m* 20 May 1967, Moira Catherine, *née* Bolter; 1 da (Charlotte Anne b 1968); *Career* civil engr; dir D Ingleton Ltd 1964-76, princ K Ingleton 1976-; chm: Swale Housing Assoc, Minster Co Primary Sch Govrs; Mayor of Swale 1986-87 (cncl memb 1979-90), hon alderman Borough of Swale; Isle of Sheppey Round Table: memb 1970-85, chm 1975-76, Kent area chm 1980-81; *Recreations* local history, photography; *Clubs* Past Tablers; *Style—* Ken Ingleton, Esq; Prospect Villa, 418 Minster Rd, Minster on Sea, Sheerness, Kent ME12 3NZ (☎ 0795 873709); 495 Minster Rd, Minster on Sea, Sheerness, Kent ME12 3NZ (☎ 0795 873709)

INGRAM, Dr David John Edward; s of John Evans Ingram (d 1967), of Ships Lantern, Bexhill on Sea, and Marie Florence, *née* Wéller (d 1965); *b* 6 April 1927; *Educ* King's Coll Sch Wimbledon, New Coll Oxford, Clarendon Laboratory Oxford (MA, DPhil, DSc); *m* 4 July 1952, (Ruth) Geraldine Grace, da of Donald McNair (d 1975), of The Old Grammar School, Cirencester, Glos; 3 s (Jonathan b 1953, Bruce b 1960, Marion b 1956); *Career* lectr and reader Dept of Electronics Univ of Southampton 1952-59, dep vice chllr Univ of Keele 1964 and 1968-71 (prof and head of physics 1959-73), princ Chelsea Coll Univ of London 1973-80, vice chllr Univ of Kent 1980-; memb: Enterprise Agency of E Kent, Kent CC Educn Ctee; vice chm Canterbury-Reims Twinning Assoc, pres Kent Fedn of Amenity Socs 1986-87; chm: Chaucer Hosp Community Advsy Bd, Kent Co Consultative Ctee for Industry Year 1986, Nat Unit on Staff Devpt for Univs 1988, Br Cncl Ctee on Europe 1989; tstee Canterbury Cathedral Appeal Tst; memb Bd Govrs: King's Sch Canterbury, Cobhall Hall Sch, West Heath Sch; Fell Roehampton Inst 1988; Hon DSc: Univ of Clermont-Ferrand 1960, Univ of Keele 1983; fell King's Coll London; FInstP; *Books* Spectroscopy at Radio and Microwave Frequencies (1955, 2 ed 1967), Free Radicals as Studied by Electron Spin Resonance (1958), Biological and Biochemical Applications of Electron Spin Resonance (1969), Radiation and Quantum Physics (1973), Radio and Microwave Spectroscopy (1976); *Recreations* sailing, DIY; *Clubs* Athenaeum; *Style—* Dr David J E Ingram; 22 Ethelbert Rd, Canterbury, Kent CT1 3NE (☎ 0227 65855); The Registry, The University, Canterbury, Kent CT2 7NZ (☎ 0227 764 000, fax 0227 451 684, telex 965449)

INMAN, Stephen Eric; s of John Eric Inman (d 1978), and Vera Alice, *née* Willis (d 1985); *b* 14 Oct 1935; *Educ* All Saints Sch Bloxham, St Thomas's Hosp Med Sch Univ of London (MB BS); *m* 1 July 1961, Ione Elizabeth Jill, da of Maurice Scott Murdoch (d 1963); 2 s (Paul b 1966, Dominic b 1973), 1 da (Nicola b 1962); *Career* resident med offr: Queen Charlotte's Hosp 1965-66, Chelsea Hosp for Women 1966-67; lectr St Thomas's Hosp 1968-70, sr registrar St Thomas's Hosp 1970-74, conslt obstetrician and gynaecologist W Surrey/NE Hants Health Dist 1974; chm Div of Obstetrics Gynaecology and Paedriatrics Frimley Park Hosp; memb Hosp Conslts and Specialists Assoc 1974; FRCOG 1981; *Recreations* sailing, swimming, squash, tennis; *Clubs* Royal Aldershot Officers'; *Style—* Stephen E Inman, Esq; Folly Hill House, Farnham, Surrey (☎ 0252 713389)

INNES, David Archibald; s of Lt-Col J A Innes, DSO, (d 1948), of Horringer Manor, Bury St Edmunds, Suffolk, and Evelyn Adelaide, *née* Dawnay (d 1985); *b* 1 May 1931; *Educ* Eton, Magdalene Coll Cambridge (MA); *m* 10 June 1955, Philippa, da of Maj Sir Alastair Penrose Gordon Cumming, MC (d 1939); 2 s (Guy b 1956, John b 1959), 1 da (Davina b 1957); *Career* ptnr Rowe and Pitman 1958-84, memb Stock Exchange Cncl 1979-83; farmer 1976- (breeder of Limpsfield Herd of Pedigree Friesians); memb: Bd of Tstees Chevening Estate 1983-, Kent Ctee CLA 1989-, Kent and E Sussex Ctee Nat Tst 1989-; tstee Kent Gdns Tst 1987-; *Recreations* shooting, golf, gardening; *Clubs* Boodles, Cavalry and Guards, Rye Golf; *Style—* David Innes, Esq; Hensill House, Hawkhurst, Kent TN18 4QH (☎ 0580 752162)

INSTANCE, David John; s of Horace Arthur Instance, and Ellen Rosina, *née* Perkins; *b* 15 Dec 1938; *Educ* Woolwich Poly (HNC Engrg); LSPGA (Dip Printing Mgmnt); *m* 19 Oct 1963, Lydia Fiamma, da of Carlo Lago (d 1984); 2 s (Simon David, Andrew Edward); *Career* Nat Serv Lt RE, served Malaya; chm and md Instance Group of Companies; holder of many patents covering engrg/printing application; dir of numerous subsid cos incl: Ditchling Press Ltd, Inprint Systems Italy, Inprint Systems France, Inprint Systems USA,

Cybertest USA; *Recreations* reading, opera, skiing, walking; *Style—* David Instance, Esq; Guinea Hall, Sellindge, nr Ashford, Kent TN25 6EG (☎ 030 381 3115); David J Instance Ltd, T/A Inprint Systems, Maidstone Rd, Paddock Wood, Tonbridge, Kent TN12 6DF

IRELAND, Richard Henry; s of George Thomas Ireland (d 1970), of Fulham, and Irene Edith, *née* Lunt; *b* 30 April 1946; *Educ* London Tech Sch; *m* 30 Sept 1967, Joan Florence, da of William Thomas Smith (d 1958), of Lewisham; 1 s (Robert b 1972), 1 da (Suzanne b 1975); *Career* admitted slr 1978; Slaughter and May 1978; ptnr: Eaton & Burley 1982, Rowe & Maw 1984; memb Law Soc 1978; *Recreations* fly fishing, walking, reading; *Style—* Richard Ireland, Esq; Verdon, Old Perry St, Chislehurst, Kent BR7 6PP (☎ 071 248 4282); Rowe & Maw, 20 Black Friars Lane, London EC4V 6HD (☎ 071 248 4282, fax 071 248 2009, telex 262787)

IRVING, Rear Adm Sir Edmund George; KBE (1966, OBE 1944), CB (1962); s of George Clerk Irving (d 1956), and Ethel Mary Frances, *née* Poole (d 1964); *b* 5 April 1910; *Educ* St Anthony's Eastbourne, RNC Dartmouth; *m* 1, 1936, Margaret Scudamore (d 1974), da of Richard Edwards, MBE; 1 s, 1 da; m 2, 1979, Esther Rebecca Ellison; *Career* joined RN 1924, served WWII, Capt 1951, Rear Adm 1960, ADC to HM The Queen 1960, Hydrographer of the Navy 1960-66, ret; memb NERC 1967-74; pres: RIN 1967-69, RGS 1970-72; tstee Nat Maritime Museum 1972-81; acting conservator of the River Mersey 1975-85; FRGS, FRICS, FRIN, FRSA; *Recreations* horticulture; *Clubs* Army and Navy; *Style—* Rear Adm Sir Edmund Irving, KBE, CB; Camer Green, Meopham, Kent DA13 0XR (☎ 0474 813 253)

IRVING, Hon Stephen John; s of Baron Irving of Dartford, PC, DL (Life Peer, d 1989); *b* 1959; *m* 1984, Lesley Anne, yr da of R Neil Herbert, of Wilmington, Kent; *Style—* The Hon Stephen Irving; 25 Princes Ave, Dartford, Kent DA2 6NF

IRVING OF DARTFORD, Baroness; Mildred; *née* Weedy; da of Charlton Weedy, of Morpeth; *m* 1942, Baron Irving of Dartford, PC, DL (Life Peer, d 1989); 1 s (Hon Stephen John, *qv*), 1 da (Hon Susan Anne (Hon Mrs House), *qv*, (and 1 s decd); *Style—* The Rt Hon the Lady Irving of Dartford; 10 Tynedale Close, Dartford, Kent (☎ 0322 225105)

ISAACSON, James William (Peter); s of Capt James Melville Isaacson (d 1962), of Sutton, Surrey, and Margaret Anne, *née* Yoole (d 1969); *b* 20 Dec 1920; *Educ* King Edward VI School Norwich; *m* 1, 1943 (m dis 1958), Jane Mary Lyell, da of Robert Lyell Williamson (d 1926), of Rangoon; 1 s (Charles b 1949), 2 da (Prudence b 1945, Rosemary b 1952); m 2, 1964, Jean Margaret Clements, da of Malcolm Terence Prichard Rule (d 1969), of Deal; *Career* RN Paymaster Cadet 1938, staff of Flag Offr Dover 1942-43; Nato Int Staff 1962-65, ret 1965; P & O SN Co 1966-78, Townsend Car Ferries Dover 1980-86; Dover DC Lower Walmer Ward 1983-, Mayor of Deal 1985-86 (dep Mayor 1984-85); vice chm Health & Housing Ctee 1986- (chm 1989), chm Lower Walmer Cons Assoc 1986-89, memb Canterbury & Thanet Community Health Cncl 1987-, pres Assoc of Port Health Authys 1990, vice chm Deal CAB 1990; *Recreations* walking, reading, bridge; *Style—* Lt Cdr Peter Isaacson; 4 Beachlands Court, The Strand, Walmer, Deal, Kent CT14 7DL (☎ 0304 361522)

ISITT, Kenneth Frederick; s of Frederick William Isitt (d 1964), of Ruislip, and Florence Agnes Adelaide, *née* Hockleyford; *b* 10 Feb 1930; *Educ* Erith Tech Coll, Brixton Tech Coll, Westminster Tech Coll; *m* 16 Sept 1950, Winifred Patricia, da of Augustus Charles Clark (d 1977), of Chartham; 3 s (David Frederick b 1951, Guy Francis b 1954, Ralph Charles b 1959), 2 da (Karen Lisa b 1961, Yvonne Terese b 1964); *Career* active serv in Bde of Gds (Grenadiers) 1948-50; architectural technician Port of London Authy 1950-54, Buenfeld Isitt Partnership 1954-59, sr asst Sir T P Bennett & Son Architects 1960-62, chief asst to Sir George Langley-Taylor chm of The CPRE and New Forest Verderers 1962-63, assoc ptnr and office mangr Bernard Engle Partnership Architects 1963-76, assoc and conslt to Ketley Goold & Clark Architects 1976-84, tech dir Keith Day Partnership 1984-; dir: BIAT Services Co Ltd, Atrium Building Magazine; memb: Construction Indust Cncl, Royal Soc of Health; Br Inst of Architectural Technicians: former pres, nat cncllr for Kent Sussex and Surrey, dir; assoc memb Inst of Architects and Surveyors (Bldg Surveying Div), fell Faculty of Bldg; *Recreations* walking, gardening, photography; *Clubs* Charing Sports (vice pres); *Style—* Kenneth Isitt, Esq; Copperfields, Pett Lane, Charing, Kent TN27 0DL (☎ 023371 2951); Keith Day Partnership Ltd, Chartered Architects, 6 Ambley Green, Gillingham Business Park, Gillingham, Kent ME8 0NJ (☎ 0634 379982, fax 0634 379983)

IVES, David Gell; s of John Henry Gell Ives (d 1980), of IOW, and Blanche Emilie Hayter, *née* Jones; *b* 12 March 1936; *Educ* Monkton Combe Sch, Worcester Coll Oxford (MA); *m* 9 April 1960, Rachel Diana Luxmoore, da of Paul Luxmoore May, of Dunsford, nr Godalming; 2 s (Martin b 1961, Duncan b 1968), 1 da (Susan b 1962); *Career* head of French Monkton Combe Jr Sch 1959-67; headmaster: Smallwood Manor, Denstone Coll Prep Sch 1968-80, Holmewood House Tunbridge Wells 1980-; chm IAPS 1988-89 (former cncl memb), tstee Jt Educnl Tst; *Recreations* rugby, fine wines, travel; *Clubs* Vincents (Oxford); *Style—* David Ives, Esq; Mulberry Cottage, Barrow Lane, Langton Green, Tunbridge Wells, Kent TN3 0EA (☎ 0892 862546)

J

JACKSON, Christopher Murray; MEP (C) Kent East 1979-; s of Rev Howard Murray Jackson (d 1955), of York, and Doris Bessie, *née* Grainger; *b* 24 May 1935; *Educ* Kingswood Sch Bath, Magdalen Coll Oxford (BA, MA), LSE, Univ of Frankfurt; *m* 11 June 1971, Carlie Elizabeth, da of Bernard Sidney Keeling, of Oxted, Surrey; 1 s (David Bernard Murray b 1972), 1 da (Catherine Anna Helen b 1974); *Career* Nat Serv PO RAF 1954-56; sr mangr Unilever 1967, gen mktg mangr Save & Prosper Group 1969-71; dir: S and P Services 1970, MacPherson Group 1971-74, dir of corp devpt Spillers Ltd 1974-80; underwriting memb Lloyds 1985-88; dir Westminster Communications Group Ltd 1988-; Cons Pty spokesman on: rels with developing countries 1981-87, agric 1987-89; rapporteur gen ACP EEC Jt Assembly 1986, dep chm Cons MEPs and EDG 1989-; pres Kent Hotels and Restaurants Assoc; vice pres: Assoc of Dist Cncls, Assoc of Local Cncls, Assoc of Port Health Authys, Canterbury Reims Twinning Assoc; *Recreations* gardening, sailing, skiing, music, tennis; *Style—* Christopher Jackson, Esq, MEP; Kent Office: 8 Wellmeade Drive, Sevenoaks, Kent TN13 1QA; European Democratic Group, 2 Queen Anne's Gate, London SW1; European Parliament, Rue Belliard, Brussels, Belgium (☎ 0732 456688, fax 0732 740007)

JACKSON, Colin Thornton Sanford; s of William Athel Jackson (d 1969), of Under River, Sevenoaks, Kent, and Susan Elizabeth Nina, *née* Pipon; *b* 10 March 1936; *Educ* Stancliff Hall Derbyshire, Uppingham; *m* 1, 1 July 1961 (m dis 1972), Hilary Vaughan, da of Erik Chitty (d 1976), of Harrow, Middx; 1 s (Timothy b 1965), 2 da (Clare b 1963, Erica b 1967); m 2, 23 May 1980, Ann Rosalind, da of Roger Henry Charles Human (d 1942); *Career* mgmnt trainee Jenson and Nicholson 1956-63, industl sales mangr BJN Paints (Scotland) Ltd 1963-66, commercial mangr and regnl sales mangr Crown Paints (Industl Paints Div) 1966-72; Key Terrain (subsid Reed International plc): product mangr, market devpt mangr, business devpt mangr, building prods; gen mangr Startrit Ltd, business devpt dir and md Fieldhurst Southern, mktg mangr Caradon Terrain Ltd, sr conslt Centre for Consultancy (Kent) Ltd, dir Key Corporation Ltd; chm: Hucking Parish Meeting (Cncl), Parkinson's Disease Soc Maidstone; memb: Hucking Parochial Church Cncl, N Downs Soc Ctee, N Downs Rail Concern; memb: BIM, Charterd Inst of Mktg; *Recreations* squash, cricket, bee keeping; *Clubs* Reed Squash, Under River CC; *Style—* Colin Jackson, Esq; Little Scragged Oak Cottage, Hucking, Hollingbourne, Maidstone, Kent ME17 1QU (☎ 0622 880275); Centre for Consultancy (Kent) Ltd, 3 Harbourland Court, Boxley, Maidstone, Kent ME14 3DM (☎ 0622 692919, fax 0622 692920)

JACKSON, Enid, Lady; Enid; da of Stanley Hugh Groome (d 1965), of Kingston-upon-Thames; *m* 1, 1937 (m dis 1950), as his 2 w, (Alfred) Chester Beatty (d 1983); m 2, 1953, Sir John Montrésor Jackson, 6 Bt (d 1980); *Style—* Enid, Lady Jackson; Rose Cottage, Charing, Kent TN27 0EN

JACKSON, Dr Peter Douglas; s of Percy Jackson (d 1964), of Scarborough, and Ethel, *née* Harding (d 1980); *b* 9 May 1930; *Educ* Kingswood Sch Bath, Jesus Coll Cambridge (BA, MB BChir), UCH London (DLO); *m* 1 Aug 1955, Janet Mary; 2 s (Simon d 1957, Nicholas), 3 da (Jane, Elizabeth, Ann); *Career* sr house offr and registrar in pediatric surgery Liverpool 1957-59, RSO W Bromwich 1960-62; RN Med Serv 1962-78 incl: MDIC RN Hosp Mauritius, head of ENT Dept RN Hosp Plymouth 1971-76; sr lectr Inst of Laryngology 1978-81, conslt ENT surgn SE Thames Health Authy 1981-89; Methodist local preacher (on trial 1990), sec BMA Regnl Cncl SE Thames, rep Lewisham Div BMA 1985-89; FRCSEd, FRCS; *Books* ENT Nursing (jtly, 1986); *Recreations* singer (baritone); *Style—* Dr Peter Jackson; 70 Loampit Hill, Lewisham, London SE13 7SX (☎ 081 692 5615)

JACKSON, Dr Peter John Edward; s of David Charles Jackson (d 1977), of Kent, and Sarah Ann, *née* Manester; *b* 14 May 1944; *Educ* Brockley County GS, Sprachen und Dolmetscher Inst Hamburg, Univ of London (LLB), Univ of Tübingen W Germany (Dr Jur); *m* 23 Sept 1967, Ursula Henny, da of Paul Schubert (d 1945), of Hamburg; 2 da (Philippa b 1972, Pia b 1984); *Career* called to the Bar Middle Temple and N Ireland; dep circuit judge 1979-81, asst rec 1982-83, rec of Crown Court 1983-; *Recreations* horse riding, German language, German law; *Style—* Dr Peter Jackson; 2 Pump Court, Temple, London EC4Y 7AH (☎ 071 583 9389 and 353 5579, fax 071 583 5122); D 7000 Stuttgart 50, Seelbergstrasse 8 (☎ 0711 561465, fax 0711 552407); Vienna and Olton, Switzerland

JACKSON, William Unsworth (Bill); CBE (1985); s of William Jackson (d 1959), and Margaret Esplen, *née* Sunderland (d 1984); *b* 9 Feb 1926; *Educ* Alsop HS Liverpool; *m* 27 Sept 1952, Valerie Annette, da of Robert Henry Llewellyn (d 1966); 1 s (Philip Robert b 1957), 1 da (Deborah Ann b 1954); *Career* slr; dep co clerk Kent CC 1970-73, chief exec Kent CC 1973-86; dir Kent Econ Devpt Bd 1982-86; pres Soc of Local Authy Chief Execs 1985-86, memb Tunbridge Wells DHA 1986-, tstee Charity Aid Fndn 1986-, chm UK Steering Ctee on Community Tsts 1988-, adjudicator on political restrictions in local govt Engand Wales 1989-; *Recreations* gardening; *Clubs* Royal Over-Seas; *Style—* Bill Jackson, Esq, CBE; 34 Yardley Park Rd, Tonbridge, Kent TN9 1NF (☎ 0732 351078)

JACOB, Charles William; MBE; s of Louis Edward Jacob (d 1926), of Forest Hill, London, and Amelia Adelaide, *née* Gams (d 1985); *b* 24 Jan 1921; *Educ* Catford Commercial Sch; *m* 23 Sept 1950, Margaret Aylmer, da of Louis William (d 1947), of Forest Hill, London; 3 da (Pamela b 9 Oct 1951, Jacqueline b 9 Sept 1954, Barbara b 7 July 1959); *Career* ptnr: Nathan & Rosselli 1961-64, James Capel and Co 1965-69; fin advsr Newsvendors Benevolent Inst 1961-85, investmt mangr Central Fin Bd Methodist Church 1972-87, md Linvest Securities Ltd 1979-87; dir: First Investors and Savers 1973-74, Methodist Insurance Co plc 1978-90, London United Investments plc 1987-; originator Stewardship Unit Tst (first UK ethical unit tst); pres Bromley Relate; memb: Ctee of Reference Friends Provident - Stewardship Unit Tst, Cncl and Bd Central Fin Bd Methodist Church, Soc of Investmt Analysts; lay preacher; *Recreations* church and charity work, drama, general sports; *Clubs* IOD; *Style—* Charles Jacob, Esq, MBE; 23 Prince Consort Drive, Chislehurst, Kent BR7 5SB (☎ 081 467 4629)

JACOBS, Prof Arthur David; s of Alexander Susman Jacobs (d 1972), and Estelle, *née* Isaacs (d 1981); *b* 14 June 1922; *Educ* Manchester GS, Univ of Oxford (MA); *m* 4 Nov 1953, Betty Upton Hughes; 2 s (Julian b 1957, Michael b 1960); *Career* served WWII 1942-46; music critic Daily Express 1947-52, freelance writer on music 1953-, prof RAM 1964-79, head Music Dept Huddersfield Poly 1979-84, fndr ed British Music Yearbook 1972, memb Bd Eds Opera magazine 1962-; *Books* incl: Music Lover's Anthology (1948), Gilbert and Sullivan (1951), Choral Music (1963), Libretto of Opera One Man Show by Nicholas Maw (1964), Pan Book of Opera (with Stanley Sadie, expanded edn 1984), A Short History of Western Music (1972), The New Penguin Dictionary of Music (new edn 1978), Arthur Sullivan: a Victorian musician (1984), Pan Book of Orchestral Music (1988), The Penguin Dictionary of Musical Performers (1990); many opera translations incl Berg's Lulu; *Style—* Prof Arthur Jacobs; 10 Oldbury Close, Sevenoaks, Kent TN15 9DJ (☎ 0732 884006)

JAKEMAN, (David) Christopher; s of George Jakeman, of Tadcaster, Yorks, and Cecilia Catherine Monica, *née* Devine; *b* 4 Oct 1952; *Educ* Tadcaster GS; *m* 11 June 1977, Wendy Ann, da of Frederick William Studd, of Sittingbourne, Kent; 2 da (Deborah b 1981, Rebecca b 1983); *Career* joined Royal Insurance 1970, reinsurance mangr Hughes Gibb & Co Ltd 1979-81, reinsurance dir Hodgson McCreery & Co Ltd 1981-83, md Unity Insurance Services Ltd 1985-, ptnr Fairview Leisure; memb St Vincent de Paul Soc; ACII 1977, memb IBRC 1985, FInstIC 1986, MBIM 1987; *Recreations* cricket, opera, BBC World Service, real ale, greyhound racing; *Style—* Christopher Jakeman, Esq; Lyn-Mor, Chestnut Wood Lane, Borden, Kent; Unity Insurance Services Ltd, 53 West St, Sittingbourne, Kent (☎ 0795 423424)

JAMES, Alan Murray; s of Harold Birkett James (d 1961), of Sutton, Surrey, and Nellie Beatrice, *née* Covington (d 1981); *b* 24 Feb 1925; *Educ* Sutton Valence, Univ of Birmingham (RE Army Course), Clare Coll Cambridge (MA); *m* 7 June 1952, Janette Mary, da of Harold Pridmore Lack (d 1974); 3 da (Linda b 1954, Susan b 1956, Mandy b 1961); *Career* WWII RE 1943-47, cmmnd 1945, KGVO Bengal Sappers and Miners 1945-47, Capt 1947, served Indonesia and Malaysia; md and chm Tate and Lyle Technical Services 1961-75, dir Sugar Industry Technologists Inc 1965-78, md Tate and Lyle Enterprises 1969-75, chm Sugar Knowledge International 1981-; Lloyds underwriting memb 1982-; pres Sugar Processing Res 1972-74; Freeman:

City of London 1948, Worshipful Co of Loriners; *Recreations* tennis, squash, travel; *Clubs* RAC, Bromley Cricket, Middleton, Richmond Football, Cambridge Rugby Union Football; *Style*— Alan James, Esq; 12 Shornefield Close, Bickley, Kent BR1 2HX (☎ 081 467 4579, telex 934968); 16 Crossbush Rd, Felpham, W Sussex PO22 7LS

JAMES, Hon Charles Walter Henry; eldest s & h of 5 Baron Northbourne, qv; *b* 14 June 1960; *Educ* Eton, Magdalen Coll Oxford; *m* 3 Oct 1987, Catherine Lucy, o da of W Ralph Burrows, of Prescot, Lancs; 1 s (Henry Christopher William b 3 Dec 1988); *Career* dir: Rede Investments Ltd, Redesdale Investments Ltd, Betteshanger Farms Ltd, Kent Salads Holdings Ltd; *Style*— The Hon Charles James; Northbourne Court, Northbourne, Deal, Kent (☎ 0304 374617); Betteshanger Farms Ltd, Home Farm, Betteshanger, Deal, Kent (☎ 0304 611281, telex 0304 965837)

JAMES, Mark Stephen; s of Clive John James, of Bearsted, Maidstone, Kent, and Maureen Ann, *née* Farrow; *b* 10 July 1963; *Educ* Bexleyheath Sch Kent, UCL (BSc); *Career* clerical offr GLC 1984-85, mgmnt servs asst Kent CC 1985-88, corp planner Thurrock Borough Cncl 1988-90, corp planning mangr Nat Assoc of CABs 1990-; sec Mid-Kent Constituency Lab Pty 1984-86; Kent CC: contested Maidstone Rural North Div 1985, Lab memb Gravesend North Div 1989-; memb Bearsted Parish Cncl 1987-, prospective Lab party canidate S Thanet 1990; *Recreations* transport, photography; *Style*— Mark James, Esq; 60 Peverel Drive, Bearsted, Maidstone, Kent ME14 4PS (☎ 0622 36759); National Association of Citizens Advice Bureaux, Myddleton House, 115-123 Pentoville Rd, London N1 91Z (☎ 071 833 2181 ext 306)

JAMES, Paul (Paul William John Webzell); s of William Thomas Webzell (d 1972), of Gravesend, and Violet May, *née* Butcher; *b* 19 July 1947; *Educ* Southfields Secdy Sch, Gravesend Art Sch; *m* 1, (m dis 1982), Vivian Jane, *née* Stanbridge; m 2, 10 Oct 1986, Gisella Maria, da of Giuseppe Bianchet, of Varese, Italy; 1 da (Emily Charlotte b 20 Dec 1987); *Career* worked for Brian Epstein and The Beatles, wrote produced and starred in three Christmas shows for Gravesend Woodville Theatre, presenter BBC Radio Kent Sunday Request Show, one of Kent's leading comedians; fndr The Don and Paul Fun Club (for the BBC to help Kent charities with fund-raising events), memb Concert Artiste Assoc; *Style*— Paul James, Esq; BBC Radio Kent, Sun Pier, Chatham, Kent ME4 4EZ (☎ 0634 811111)

JAMES, (William) Paul; s of Sir Frederick Seton James, KCMG, KBE (d 1934), and Lady Doris Francis James (d 1956); *b* 22 Aug 1921; *Educ* Haileybury, PCL (Dip Arch); *m* 4 Jan 1947, (Florence) Peggy, da of Josephy Harvey; 1 s (Julian Paul b 1958), 3 da (Jennifer b 1948, Fenella b 1952, Caroline b 1954); *Career* WWII RAF 1940-45; architect on staff of Lord Holford 1950-60, princ in private practice 1960-67, seconded planning conslt DHSS 1967-68, fndr ptnr and chm Hosp Design Partnership (London, Leeds and Birmingham) 1968-79, int conslt in hosp planning 1979-; author of numerous articles in professional jls 1970-85; chm Royal Tunbridge Wells Civic Soc; FRIBA 1970 (ARIBA 1950); *Books* Hospitals - Designs and Development (1986); *Recreations* lawn tennis, walking, reading, travel, writing; *Clubs* Sloane; *Style*— Paul James, Esq; Lawnside, 3 Hungershall Park, Tunbridge Wells, Kent (☎ 0892 25726)

JAMES, Paula (Mrs Howitt); da of Reginald Alan James (d 1980), and Arabella, *née* Seppings (d 1980); *b* 12 June 1934; *Educ* St Albans HS; *m* 1, 1954 (m dis 1968), John Charles William Woodeson; 1 s (Nicholas Martin b 1956), 2 da (Elizabeth Jane (twin) b 1956, Tamsin Sarah Ivy b 1968); m 2, 1974, Frank Howitt; *Career* Daily Mirror 1958-78: reporter, feature writer Royal corr; freelance columnist Aust America and Japan 1978-87, news ed S Kent Newspapers 1987-; life memb Newspaper Press Fund; memb: NUJ 1958-84; *Books* Princess Anne at 18 (1968), Diana - Royal Bride (1981); *Recreations* travel, cooking, swimming, enjoying good food and good friends, hang-gliding, climbing; *Style*— Miss Paula James; South Kent Newspapers, Westcliffe House, Westcliffe Gardens, Folkestone, Kent CT20 1SZ (☎ 0303 850999, fax 0303 850618)

JAMES, Sarah Alison Livingston; da of Alistair Livingston Gunn (d 1970), of Chislehurst and Harley St, London, and Sibyl Marian, *née* Thomas (d 1986); *b* 4 Aug 1938; *Educ* St Leonard's Sch, St Andrews, Fife; *m* 15 July 1961, Hywel Morgan Cledwyn James, s of David Gwilym James Univ (d 1969); 3 s (Edward b 1963, William b 1965, Wattie b 1970), 1 da (Charlotte b 1966); *Career* Spicer & Pegler CAs 1957-; memb: Gen Synod of C of E, Bishop's Cncl of Rochester Diocese; lay chm Bromley Deanery Synod, reader St Nicholas Church Chislehurst, central vice pres Mother's Union; FCA 1973 (ACA 1963); *Recreations* calligraphy, tapestry; *Style*— Mrs Hywel James; Eldridge, Southill Rd, Chislehurst, Kent (☎ 081 467 1075)

JARRETT, Alan George; s of George James Jarrett, of Bexley Heath, and Mabel Constance, *née* Hipkin; *b* 2 April 1943; *Educ* Erith GS, Univ of Wales at Aberystwyth (BSc, DipEd); *m* 27 July 1968, Margaret, da of Lt Brian Walker (d 1981), of 10 Whitmarsh, Mere, Wiltshire; 2 s (Nicholas Stephen b 23 Aug 1971, Jonathan Christopher b 31 July 1978), 1 da (Samantha Jane b 11 April 1970); *Career* teacher; head Sci Dept Seychelles Coll 1968-77, lectr sci educn Seychelles Trg Coll 1972-75, head of sixth form and second i/c Sci Dept Sandown Court Sch Kent 1978-80, first dep headmaster Hewett Sch Norwich 1984-87 (head of sixth form and dep head upper sch 1981-84), headmaster The Howard Grammer/High Sch 1988-; memb: Young Enterprize Area Mgmnt Ctee (N Kent), Secdy Heads Assoc; *Books* The Cowries of the Seychelles (1970), The Cone Shells of Seychelles (1970); *Recreations* tennis, bowls, malacology, gardening, philately; *Style*— Alan Jarrett, Esq; The Howard Grammer/High Sch, Derwent Way, Rainham, Gillingham, Kent ME8 0BX (☎ 0634 35466)

JEFFRIES, Peter Jocelyn; s of Colin Jocelyn Jeffries, MBE, of Plowmans, Yeoman's Meadow, Kippington, Sevenoaks, Kent, and Veronica Constance Jeffries (d 1985); *b* 17 Feb 1940; *Educ* Canford; *m* 5 Sept 1970, Lavinia Keppel, da of George Montagu North (d 1953), of Lodge, Udimore, Rye, E Sussex; 1 s (Charles Jocelyn b 12 July 1973), 1 da (Alexandra Keppel b 13 Aug 1971); *Career* ptnr West Wake Price & Co CAS 1968-82, chm Gt Knights Wines 1983, md City Fine Wines 1985; treas: Ide Hill Cons Assoc, Ide Hill Village Hall; auditor Ide Hill Soc; Freeman City of London, Liveryman Worshipful Co of Masons; FCA 1973; *Recreations* sailing; *Style*— Peter Jeffries, Esq; Brownings House, Ide Hill, Sevenoaks, Kent (☎ 073 275 480); 4 London Rd, Sevenoaks, Kent (☎ 0732 457873, fax 0732 455905, telex 95130)

JEMPSON, Cncllr William John (Bill); s of Charles Jempson (d 1953), and Rosa Jane, *née* Good (d 1963); *b* 23 June 1909; *m* 6 Aug 1934, (Margaret) Eileen, da of Alfred Sydney Offer (d 1976); 3 s (Peter b 1935, David b 1938, John b 1942), 1 da (Joy b 1940); *Career* Civil Def 1941-45; poultry farm worker 1923-27, poultry farmer 1927-33, gentleman's hairdresser 1933-47, market gardener with poultry 1947-51, sales rep 1951-55, co sec and mangr 1955-59, estate agents negotiator 1959-66, mangr 1966-74; fndr memb Cranbrook and Dist Ratepayer's Assoc, memb Baptist Church, pastor Mount Hermon Baptist Church Warbleton (formerly lay preacher); memb Cranbrook Parish Cncl 1944-51 and 1954-, chm Cranbrook RDC 1948-62 (memb 1946-74); Ind memb: Tunbridge Wells Borough Cncl 1973- (Mayor 1978-79), Kent CC 1970-77 and 1981-85; Hon Freeman of the Borough of Tunbridge Wells 1986; *Recreations* gardening; *Style*— Cncllr Bill Jempson; Heatherlea, New Rd, Cranbrook, Kent TN17 3LE (☎ 0580 712126)

JENKINS, Nicholas Stephen; s of Walter Walker Jenkins (d 1982), of Tanglewood, Pyrford, Surrey, and Teresa Davis, *née* Callens; *b* 8 Feb 1954; *Educ* Salesian Coll Chertsey, Harlow Coll; *m* 25 Oct 1974, Marion Joanne, da of Henry Alex Findlay (d 1966), of Chatham, Kent; 2 s (Joel, Jordan); *Career* PR conslt; formed Jenkins Group 1975-; MIPR; *Recreations* tennis, helicopters; *Clubs* Castle (Rochester), Roffen; *Style*— Nicholas Jenkins, Esq; Castle Chambers, Castle Hill, Rochester, Kent; Berkeley House, 186 High St, Rochester, Kent ME1 1EY (☎ 0634 408 325, fax 0634 830 930, car tel 0860 414285, telex 94015848 JORG G)

JENKINSON, Valerie Robertson; da of late William Mar Erskine, and Flora Ernestine, *née* Robertson; *b* 16 March 1934; *Educ* St Paul's Girls Sch Hammersmith; *m* 1 March 1962, Eric Reginald Jenkinson, s of Percy Jenkinson; *Career* qualified SRN 1960; various posts Medway Health Authy 1960-79, registered clinical nurse tutor 1973, commissioning nurse New Maidstone Dist Gen Hosp Maidstone Health Authy 1973-83, dir nursing servs Canterbury Gen Unit Canterbury and Thanet Health Authy 1983-89; *Recreations* cooking, gardening, music; *Style*— Mrs Eric Jenkinson; Invermar, 26 Richdore Rd, Waltham, nr Canterbury, Kent CT4 5SJ (☎ 0227 70 477)

JENNISON, Prof Roger Clifton; s of George Robert Jennison (d 1948), and Elsie Grace, *née* Clifton (d 1959); *b* 18 Dec 1922; *Educ* Clee GS Grimsby, Hull Tech Coll, Univ of Manchester; *m* 7 Nov 1952, Jean Gordon, da of Douglas George Gordon Gray (d 1967), of Stonehaven; 2 s (Michael Alexander Clifton b 22 Oct 1956, Timothy Martin Clifton b 10 Nov 1963), 2 da (Heather Clifton b 11 Oct 1960, Jacqueline Clifton b 8 Sept 1962 d 1962); *Career* RAF aircrew 1943-47; Mackinnon student of the Royal Soc 1951-53; Univ of Manchester: lectr in radio astronomy 1953-60 (sr lectr 1960-64), sr lectr in physics 1965; Univ of Kent: fndn prof in physical electronics 1965, dir of laboratories 1965-81, additional personal chair in radio astronomy 1982; past pres Inst of Electronics, memb Int Astronomical Union, past chm Ctee of Cospar (UK nat del 1983-90), pres Canterbury Soc of Art, exec memb Canterbury Arts Cncl, past govr Medway and Maidstone Coll of Technol, past memb Electronics Research Cncl, dep master Eliot Coll 1966-75, memb Court of City Univ; author of numerous articles in learned jls; CEng, CPhys, FIEE, FInstP, FRAS, FRSA; *Books* Fourier Transforms and Convolutions for the Experimentalist (1960), Introduction to Radio Astronomy (1966); *Recreations* painting, sculpture, amateur radio, DIY, tennis, sailing, being with my wife; *Style*— Prof Roger Jennison; Wildwood, Nackington, Canterbury, Kent CT4 7AY (☎ 0227 761530); Electronic Engineering Laboratories, The University, Canterbury, Kent (☎ 0227 764000)

JEQUIER, Dr Peter Winton; s of Lt Philip Winton Jequier, DSC, of 19 Wilsford Green, Oak Hill, Edgbaston, Birmingham, and Mary Steward, *née* Tardrew, RRC (d 1975); *b* 25 May 1949; *Educ* Caterham Sch Caterham Surrey, UCL (BSc), UCH London (MB BS); *m* 4 Oct 1975, Sarah Frances, da of Oliver Keeble (d 1988); 1 s (Andrew David b 1982), 1 da (Nicola Judith b 1977); *Career* hosp med registrar 1975-80; GP: Tunbridge Wells 1980-84,

Folkestone 1984-; sec Folkestone Med Soc 1989-; memb BMA; *Recreations* golf, squash, windsurfing, sailing; *Style*— Dr Peter Jequier; 64 Radnor Park Rd, Folkestone, Kent CT19 5AY (☎ 0303 221167, 0303 221220)

JERROM, Michael George Lindsay; s of Maj Michael Francis Jerrom, and Irene Edith, *née* Fry; *b* 14 April 1942; *Educ* Sherborne, Univ of Oxford (MA); *m* 1, 1 June 1968 (m dis), Rosalind Mary, da of Dr Bernard James Sanger, of Fairhaven, Leveretts Lane, Walberswick, Suffolk; 1 s (Charles Lindsay b 11 May 1973, 1 da (Amanda Suzanne b 25 Aug 1970); m 2, 8 Sept 1979, Dorothy Fay Allgood; *Career* audit mangr Thornton Baker & Co London 1968-70 (accountancy articles 1964-67), section leader Overseas Containers Ltd 1971-72, co sec International Caledonian Assets Ltd and Argyle Services Ltd 1972-73; dir: Jardine Properties Ltd 1973-75, Norwest Holst International Ltd 1975-77, CCL Fin Servs Ltd 1977-, Axis Property Mgmnt Ltd; md: Selective Construction Projects plc 1984, CCL Devpts plc 1986; chm The Vector Collection plc 1988, dir Look at Languages Communications Experts Ltd 1989; memb Pubns Review Panel ICAEW, ctee memb (former capt): Old Shirburnian Golfing Soc, Wrotham Health Golf Club; memb Oxford and Cambridge Golfing Soc; FCA 1968; *Recreations* golf, local affairs, ex chairman conservative branch; *Clubs* East India, Thorpe Hall, Wrotham Heath, Royal Cinque Ports, Oxford Soc; *Style*— Michael Jerrom, Esq; 107 Jermyn St, London SW1Y 6EE (☎ 071 930 8367, fax 071 839 4598)

JESSEL, Betty, Lady; (Joan) Betty; *née* Ewart; da of late Dr David Ewart, OBE, of Chichester; *m* 1, 1933 (m dis 1946), 2 Baron Russell of Liverpool, CBE, MC (d 1981); 1 da; m 2, 1948, as his 2 w, Sir George Jessel, MC, 2 Bt (d 1977); *Recreations* gardening; *Clubs* Army and Navy; *Style*— Betty, Lady Jessel; Ladham House, Ladham Lane, Goudhurst, Kent TN17 1DB (☎ 0580 211203)

JESSEL, Sir Charles John; 3 Bt (UK 1883), of Ladham House, Goudhurst, Kent; s of Sir George Jessel, MC, 2 Bt (d 1977); *b* 29 Dec 1924; *Educ* Eton, Balliol Coll Oxford, Inst of Optimum Nutrition (Dip); *m* 1, 1956, Shirley Cornelia (d 1977), da of John Waters, of Northampton; 2 s, 1 da; m 2, 1979 (m dis 1983), Gwendolyn Mary, da of late Laurance Devereux, OBE, and widow of Charles Langer; *Heir* s, George Jessel, *qv*; *Career* Lt 15/19 Hussars (despatches) WWII; Northampton Inst of Agric 1951-52, farmer 1953-85, in ptnrship with son 1985-, nutrition conslt 1987-; JP Kent 1960-78; chm: Ashford NFU 1963-64, Canterbury Farmers Club 1972; pres: Kent Branch Men of the Trees 1979-83, Br Soc of Dowsers 1987-; hon fell Psionic Med Soc 1977; memb Inst of Allergy Therapists 1990; *Recreations* gardening, planting trees; *Clubs* Cavalry and Guards; *Style*— Sir Charles Jessel, Bt; South Hill Farm, Hastingleigh, nr Ashford, Kent (☎ 023 375 325)

JESSEL, George Elphinstone; s and h of Sir Charles Jessel, 3 Bt, *qv*, and Shirley Cornelia, *née* Waters (d 1977), of South Hill Farm, Hastingleigh, Ashford, Kent; *b* 15 Dec 1957; *Educ* Milton Abbey, RAC Cirencester; *m* 10 Dec 1988, Rose Amila Coutts-Smith; *Career* cmmnd Lt 15/19 Royal Hussars, Germany, Canada and Cyprus 1978-82; farmer, ptnr with father 1985-; *Recreations* skiing, travelling; *Clubs* Cavalry and Guards, Farmers; *Style*— George Jessel, Esq; Stoakes Cottage, Hastingleigh, Ashford, Kent TN25 5HG (☎ 023 375 216); South Hill Farm, Hastingleigh, Ashford, Kent TN25 5HL (☎ 023 375 325)

JESSEL, Oliver Richard; s of Cdr Richard Frederick Jessel, DSO, OBE, DSC (d 1988), of Marden, Kent; er bro of Toby Jessel, MP; *b* 24 Aug 1929; *Educ* Rugby; *m* 1950, Gloria Rosalie Teresa, *née* Holden; 1 s, 5 da; *Career* chm: many cos in Jessel Gp 1954-89, Charles Clifford Industs (non-ferrous metals gp) 1978-81; former chm London Australian & Gen Exploration Co; fndr: New Issue Unit Tst, Castle Communications plc; *Clubs* Garrick; *Style*— Oliver Jessel, Esq; Merrington Place, Rolvenden, Cranbrook, Kent TN17 4PJ (☎ 0580 241428)

JESSUP, Graham Marcus; s of Basil Graham Jessup (d 1979), of Ash Platt, Kent, and Jessie Laura, *née* Chappell (d 1979); *b* 14 Feb 1947; *Educ* Sevenoaks Sch, Univ of Bristol (BSc); *m* 17 Aug 1967, Susan Janet Melland, da of Peter William Gilpin, of Culvers Close, Oxon; 2 s (Simon b 1972, Richard b 1974); *Career* client servs dir Newton & Godin Ltd; dir: Newton & Godin Ltd 1982-, Promotional Campaigns Ltd 1982-, Dowton Advertising Ltd 1980-82; *Recreations* golf, sailing; *Clubs* Knole Park Golf; *Style*— Graham M Jessup, Esq; Parksland Cottage, 7 Weald Rd, Sevenoaks, Kent; Newton & Godin Ltd, Union House, The Pantiles, Tunbridge Wells, Kent (☎ 0892 510520, car ☎ 0860 325 374)

JISKOOT, Barbara Dorothy; da of Harold Reginald Wilkins (d 1933), and Ruth Wilkins (d 1962); *b* 13 Feb 1923; *Educ* Various Convents, St Michaels Sch, Leigh on Sea, Clarks Coll; *m* 21 Jan 1948, Joost Jacob Jiskoot, *qv*, s of Joost Jacob Jiskoot, of Netherlands (d 1985); 3 s (Robert b 3 Jan 1951, Patrick b 12 Oct 1952, Mark, *qv*, b 16 Feb 1959), 1 da (Johanna b 15 July 1956); *Career* WRNS 1941-45, PO WREN; dir Boddington Milnard & Co 1949-50; fin dir: Jiskoot Autocontrol Ltd 1961-87, Jiskoot Holdings 1985-; fell Inst Fin Accountants 1981-; *Recreations* golf, swimming, walking, history; *Clubs* Limpsfield Golf; *Style*— Mrs Barbara Jiskoot; Jiskoot Autocontrol Ltd, 85 Goods Station Rd, Tunbridge Wells, Kent (☎ 0892 22291, fax 0892 23694)

JISKOOT, Joost Jacob; s of Joost Jacob Jiskoot (d 1986), of Netherlands, and Johanna Maria, *née* Soepnel (d 1981); *b* 1 Nov 1923; *Educ* Tech MHS Rotterdam; *m* 21 Jan 1947, Barbara Dorothy, *qv*, da of Harold Reginald Wilkins (d 1933), of Chingford, Essex; 3 s (Robert Jerome Julian b 3 Jan 1951, Patrick Andre b 12 Oct 1952, Mark Anthony, *qv*, b 16 Feb 1959), 1 da (Johanna Christina Dorothy b 15 July 1956); *Career* Lt REME Royal Dutch Army served Indonesia 1948-50; Bristowes Machinery Ltd Enfield 1950-55, design engr Constructors John Brown Ltd London 1955-61, md Jiskoot Autocontrol Ltd Tunbridge Wells 1961-89, chm and chief exec offr Jiskoot Holdings Ltd; active memb Int Standards Orgn and Inst of Petroleum Ctees; author of numerous papers; originator of several patents in field of: digital closed loop control, flow measurement control, and other related technol; memb Lloyd's; MIED, FInstPet; *Recreations* sailing, swimming, golf; *Clubs* Royal Fowey Yacht, RYA, Lloyd's YC, Edenbridge Golf; *Style*— Joost J Jiskoot, Esq; Pittfield, Swan Lane, Edenbridge, Kent TN8 6AJ (☎ 0732 863115); Jiskoot Holdings Ltd, Tunbridge Wells, Kent TN1 2DJ (☎ 0892 22291, fax 0892 23694)

JISKOOT, Mark Anthony; s of Joost Jacob Jiskoot, of Edenbridge, Kent, and Barbara Dorothy, *née* Wilkins; *b* 16 Feb 1959; *Educ* Hazelwood Sch Limpsfield Surrey, Tunbridge Sch Tunbridge, Imperial Coll London (BSc); *m* 10 Jan 1987, Jody Lynn, da of Leslie Dibert, of Bowling Green, Ohio, USA; *Career* pres Jiskoot Inc Houston Texas 1983- (VP engr and start up operation 1982-83), sales and mktg dir Jiskoot Autocontrol 1987 (R&D engr 1980-82, relocated UK 1987); written and presented tech papers: microprocessors Golf Coast Short Course 1984, jet mixing AICHE Protetech 1986, flowmeters IBC Industl Flow 1987; ACGI; *Recreations* squash, skiing, scuba diving; *Style*— Mark Jiskoot, Esq; 33 Elmhurst Gardens, Tonbridge, Kent TN10 3QT (☎ 0732 356531); Jiskoot Autocontrol Ltd, 85 Goods Station Rd, Tunbridge Wells, Kent (☎ 0892 22291, fax 0892 23694)

JOHN, Dr George; s of Philipose John, and Saramma, *née* George; *b* 14 Aug 1947; *Educ* Christian Coll Sch Madras, Univ of Mysore (MB BS), Univ of Nottingham (rotational psychiatric trg scheme), RCPsych (MRCPsych), St Thomas's Hosp London, Inst of Psychiatry (external student); *m* 31 May 1973, Anna, da of V I Varkey; 2 s (Kieran George b 1974, Philip George b 1985); *Career* registrar: Professorial Unit Nottingham 1975-76, Regnl Addiction Unit Nottingham 1976-77; sr registrar St Thomas' Hosp 1977-80, conslt in psychological med Dartford and Gravesham Health Authy 1980-, clinical tutor Hayes Grove Priory Hosp 1987-89, med dir Godden Green Clinic 1989-; memb Regnl Psychiatric Specialty Sub Ctee SE Thames RHA 1974-90, chm Psychiatric Div Dartford and Gravesham Health Authy 1984-90; memb Dartford Rotary Club 1983-88; *Books* Phenothiazines: Clinical Aspects and Pharmacokinetics (1982); *Recreations* golf; *Style*— Dr George John; Mangalam, St George's Rd, Bickley, Kent BR1 2LD (☎ 081 467 8625); Godden Green Clinic, Godden Green, Sevenoaks, Kent TN15 0JR (☎ 0732 63491, fax 0732 63160)

JOHNS, Andrew Norman; s of Norman William Johns, of Frinton, Essex, and Violet Mary, *née* Littlemore; *b* 9 Jan 1948; *Educ* Brentwood Sch, St John's Coll Cambridge (MA, MB BChir), Guy's Hosp Med Sch; *Career* conslt ENT surgn Maidstone and Medway Health Authys 1982-, lectr City Univ London; chm BMA Div 1986-88, chm Conslts' Cncl and Dist Med Ctee Maidstone, memb Dist Mgmnt Bd Maidstone Authy 1985-; memb RSM, FRCS; *Books* Voice Disorders and their Management (contrib, 1986); *Recreations* badminton, crosswords; *Style*— Andrew Johns, Esq; Glengyle, 16 Bower Mount Rd, Maidstone, Kent (☎ 0622 692154)

JOHNSON, Charles Richard Alexander; s of Richard Matthew Adam Johnson (d 1975), of Romney Marsh, and Victoria, *née* Roberts; *b* 23 Oct 1936; *Educ* Sutton Vallence, Univ of Kent at Canterbury (BA), Kings Coll London (MA); *m* 18 March 1966, Helen Penelope, da of Martin Franklin; 1 s (Stephen b 1972), 1 da (Elizabeth b 1969); *Career* Nat Serv 1954-56; National Westminster Bank PLC: joined 1957, clerk 1957-64, asst mangr 1964-70; farmer and landowner 1970-; involved with fund raising for local charities, memb local Cons Assoc; *Recreations* collecting porcelain, fishing, golf, painting; *Style*— Charles Johnson, Esq; c/o West Cottage, Rocky Lane, Ryash, nr West Malling, Kent

JOHNSON, Rev Christopher Frederick; s of Frederick Christopher Johnson (d 1984), of West Malling, Kent, and Kate, *née* Goodwin; *b* 13 Nov 1943; *Educ* S Bromley Coll, Brixton Sch of Bldg, Ripon Hall Oxford; *m* 25 March 1967, Kathleen Marie, da of Frederick Jones; 1 s (Timothy b 1970), 1 da (Catherine b 1973); *Career* quantity surveyor 1959-71; min of religion 1974-; vicar: Slade Green 1978-85, Wilmington 1985-; chaplain: Ellenor Hospice Home Care Team, Wilmington Old Peoples' Homes; ARICS 1967; *Recreations* music (especially jazz), walking; *Style*— The Rev Christopher Johnson; The Vicarage, Church Hill, Wilmington, Dartford, Kent DA2 7EH (☎ 0322 220561)

JOHNSON, Donal Keith; s of Edmund Donald Johnson (d 1971), and Jean Marion, *née* Chapter (d 1970); *b* 11 June 1928; *Educ* Magdalen Coll Sch Oxford; *m* 8 Aug 1955, Hilary Anita, da of Capt Frank Smith (d 1938), of Stanhope Farm, Stanwell, Middx; 1 s (Neil b 1960), 1 da (Sarah b 1958); *Career* CA; sr ptnr Bryden Johnson and Co 1970- (ptnr 1958); Liveryman

Worshipful Co of Needlemakers 1969, Freeman City of London 1968; FCA 1953; *Recreations* golf; *Clubs* RAC; *Style*— Donal Johnson, Esq; The Downe House, Ricketts Hill, Tatsfield, Westerham, Kent (tel: 0959 77318); Bryden Johnson and Co, Kings Parade, Lower Coombe Street, Croydon, Surrey CRO 1AA (☎ 081 686 0255, fax 081 688 5620, telex 928110 BJCO G)

JOHNSON, Joan; *b* 8 Oct 1938; *Career* asst teacher Whitby Rd Jr Sch Sheffield 1959-67; dep headteacher: Jr Dept Royal Alexandra and Albert Sch Reigate 1968-69, Woodlea Co Primary Sch Woldingham Surrey 1969-72; headteacher: Crockham Hill C of E Primary Sch 1972-82, Crockham Hill C of E First Sch 1982-; memb: NAHT, Cncl Edenbridge Headteachers, Crockham Hill Bonfire Assoc, Edenbridge Three Tier Assoc; *Recreations* music, photography, reading, travel, badminton; *Style*— Miss Joan Johnson; 45 Spencer Way, Redhill, Surrey RH1 5LF (☎ 0737 771482); Crockham Hill C of E First School, Crockham Hill, Edenbridge, Kent TN8 6RP (☎ 0734 866 374)

JOHNSON, Peter; s of Arthur Henry Johnson (d 1959), of Arundel, Sussex, and Marjory Sybil, *née* Meeking (d 1973); *b* 2 May 1922; *Educ* Highgate Sch, Regent St Poly; *m* 31 May 1947, Pauline, da of Cyril Holland Child, MBE (d 1965), of East Cliff, Dover; 1 s (James Matthew b 1959), 1 da (Catherine Louise b 1961); *Career* chartered quantity surveyor; Bristow Johnson and Partners: joined 1949, ptnr 1953, opened Dover office 1953, sr ptnr 1975, ret 1988; co-author as memb Aqua Gp of various books on Practice and Procedure in Construction Contracts; chm: Kent Branch RICS 1972-73, SE Branch CIArb 1986-87; rep for RICS on Jt Contracts Tbnl for Standard Form of Bldg Contract, served on various local and nat RICS ctees; JP 1965-90, dep chm Dover and E Kent Magistrates Court 1973-90, chm Juvenile Court 1975-87; served on: Kent Magistrates Court Ctee, Kent Police Authy; memb and later chm Bd of Visitors Dover Borstal; pres Dover Community Assoc, vice pres The Dover Soc, govr Dover Coll (chm 1974-82); FRICS 1958 (RICS 1946), FCIArb 1959; *Recreations* walking, gardening, cinematography; *Clubs* East India, Kent CCC; *Style*— Peter Johnson, Esq; Dover

JOHNSON, Brig Peter Dunbar; s of Dr P Dunbar Johnson (d 1984), of Tapshaw, Male Hill, St Leonards-on-Sea, Sussex, and Barbara Leigh, *née* Hutton; *b* 15 April 1931; *Educ* Sherborne, RMA Sandhurst, Staff Coll (psc), Jt Servs Staff Coll (jssc), Royal Coll of Defence (RCDS); *m* 1961, Marthe Marie Eugenie, da of Marquis Yvés de Simon de Palmas (d 1975), of La Raterie, Corbery, Loches, France; 3 s (Mark, Stephen, Paul); *Career* cmmnd Royal Sussex Regt 1951, CO 5 Queens 1971-73; dep dir Manning 1981-84; ADC to HM The Queen 1983-; gen sec Offr Assoc 1984-; *Recreations* golf, skiing, gardening; *Clubs* Army and Navy, Royal St George's (Sandwich); *Style*— Brig P D Johnson; Homestall, Doddington, Kent ME9 0HF (☎ 079 586 212); Officers Association, 48 Pall Mall, London SW1

JOHNSON, Rex Sutherland; s of Adam Sutherland Johnson (d 1950), and Grace Elizabeth, *née* Bedwell (d 1988); *b* 24 Aug 1928; *Educ* Royal HS Edinburgh, George Heriots Sch Edinburgh, Northern Poly Sch of Architecture (Dip Arch); *m* 24 Aug 1957, Betty Elsie, da of Herbert Charles Manning (d 1974), of Witham, Essex; 2 s (Mark Sutherland b 1958, Michael Charles b 1960); *Career* RN 1947-48; sr architect TP Bennett & Son London 1946-61, jr ptnr Oliver Law & Partners London 1961-63, ptnr Ronald Ward & Partners London 1963-89; dir: Ronald Ward International Ltd 1980-89, QE Design Ltd 1989-; ptnr RWP 1989-; cncl memb London C of C and Indust 1976-, former chm Platt Cons Soc Kent 1976-79, pres United Ward Club of the City of London 1989, former pres and rotarian Westminster and Pimlico Rotary Club, memb Br Acad of Experts 1989; Freeman City of London 1969, Sr Warden Guild of Freeman City of London 1990; Liveryman: Worshipful Co of Carmen, Worshipful Co of Woolmen (memb Court); FRIBA 1968, FCIArb 1971; *Recreations* golf, photography, architecture, travel; *Clubs* City Livery, Caledonian; *Style*— Rex Johnson, Esq; Whitepines, Longmill Lane, Crouch, nr Sevenoaks, Kent TN15 8QB; RWP, The Pump House, Jacob's Well Mews, George St, London W1H 5PD (☎ 071 224 4788)

JOINER, Dr Charles Louis; s of Maj C A Joiner (d 1952), of Whyteleafe, Surrey, and Kathleen, *née* O'Malley (d 1978); *b* 21 Jan 1923; *Educ* Tonbridge, Guy's Hosp Med Sch (MB BS, MD); *m* 9 Dec 1947, Helen Mary, da of Basil Reginald Lovell, MBE (d 1984), of Littleton, Hants; 1 s (David b 1961), 1 da (Sarah b 1958); *Career* RAMC 1946-48; physician to Guy's Hosp, Bromley Gp of Hosps 1959-88, hon physician to the Army 1974-88, chief conslt physician Sun Alliance Insurance Co; FRCP, FRSM; *Books* Short Text Book of Medicine (1969); *Recreations* shooting, English lit and history, antique porcelain; *Clubs* Athenaeum; *Style*— Dr Charles Joiner; Ashton, Mead Rd, Chislehurst, Kent (☎ 081 467 4060); Suite 302, Emblem House, 27 Tooley St, London SE1 (☎ 071 407 0292)

JONES, Brian William; s of William Robert Jones, and Ada Edna, *née* Smith; *b* 10 Dec 1938; *Educ* Ealing GS, Univ of Cambridge (MA); 1 s (Stephen Patrick b 1962), 1 da (Catherine Rachel b 1965); *Career* poet; work featured on BBC Omnibus and other TV progs; past reviewer of poetry biography and fiction for The London Magazine and Tribune; awards: Eric Gregory Award for Poetry, Cholmondeley Award; area vice princ NW Kent Adult Educn Serv, memb Amnesty Int; *Books* Poems (1966), A Family Album (1968), Interior (1969), For Mad Mary (1974), The Spitfire on the Northern Line (1976), The Island Normal (1980), The Children of Separation (1986), Freeborn John (1990); *Recreations* music, cricket; *Style*— Brian Jones, Esq; 39 Punch Croft, New Ash Green, Longfield, Kent (☎ 0474 873627)

JONES, David Evan; s of Evan Jones, of Caernarvon, Gwynedd, and Mary, *née* Davies; *b* 16 May 1945; *Educ* Sir Hugh Owen GS Caernarvon, Univ of Liverpool (BDS), Univ of London (DDPH); *m* 6 Dec 1970, Pamela Anne, da of Maj Robert John Flanders (d 1983), of Bebington, Wirral; 2 s (Peter b 1971, Mark b 1973), 1 da (Claire b 1974); *Career* gen dental practitioner 1969-70, dental offr Cheshire CC and Cheshire AHA 1970-76, sr dental offr Clwyd Health Authy 1976-78, asst area dental offr Kent AHA 1978-83, dists dental offr Canterbury and Thanet and SE Kent Health Authys 1983-; former chm Maidstone Round Table, memb Maidstone 41 Club; MBIM 1981; *Recreations* music, badminton, walking, photography; *Style*— David Jones, Esq; 2 Stable Mews, Ridghill Farm, Etchinghill, nr Folkestone, Kent CT18 9DE; Community and Mental Handicap Unit, 41 Old Dover Rd, Canterbury, Kent CT1 3HJ (☎ 0227 459371 ext 2040)

JONES, David Thomas Lloyd; s of John Thomas Jones (d 1954), and Elizabeth Jane, *née* Lloyd (d 1987); *b* 31 July 1931; *Educ* Plaistow Co GS, Univ of Exeter (BSc); *m* 1 Aug 1959, Lilian May Beryl, da of Frederick Henry Chilvers (d 1970), of Kings Lynn, Norfolk; 3 s (Philip Lloyd b 1963, Nicholas John b 1967, Richard David b 1970); *Career* Lt RN 1953-56; res physicist: Duplate Canada Ltd Canada 1956-58, Beckman Instruments California 1959-62, Cementation Ltd 1962-64; lectr and head of dept: Harrow Middx Poly, NW Kent Colls 1964-72; princ: Redhill Tech Coll Surrey 1972-79, NW Kent Coll of Technol 1980-; visiting lectr: Further Educn Staff Coll, Industl Soc; md NW Kent Business Services Ltd; various consultancies, holder of three industl patents, author of numerous industl and educnl published papers; magistrate Godstone Div Surrey; memb: Assoc of Colls of Further Educn and Higher, Assoc of Princs of Colls, Assoc of Coll Mgmnt, Magistrates Assoc; *Books* The Education of Scientists For Industry (1969), Accountability and Budgets in Colleges (1986); *Recreations* music, theatre, travel, education; *Style*— David Jones, Esq; North West Kent College of Technology, Miskin Rd, Dartford, Kent DA1 2LU (☎ 0322 225471)

JONES, Gareth; s of Henry Rees Jones (d 1985), of Nantymoel, Wales, and Elisabeth Irene Brown (d 1987); *b* 6 Nov 1935; *Educ* Ogmore GS, Caerleon Teachers' Coll (CertEd Univ of Wales); *m* 8 Aug 1959, Pamela Margaret, da of Ernest Percy Green (1988), of Bridgend, Wales; 2 s (Gordon Wyn b 8 Oct 1965, David Gareth b 15 Dec 1976), 1 da (Beverley Ann b 11 Jan 1963); *Career* teacher Middlesex and Kent 1958-67, dep headteacher Lordswood Jr Sch 1967-71; headteacher: Winston Jr Sch 1971-86, Tunbury Co Primary Sch 1986-; pres Medway NAHT 1983; orch memb: Nat Youth Schoolboy, Kent Sinfonia, Maidstone Symphony, Rochester Arts; *Recreations* violinist in local and Kent symphony orchestras, travel, caravanning; *Clubs* Saracens Rugby, RA Rugby, Medway Lions; *Style*— Gareth Jones, Esq; Ty Newydd, 108 Princes Ave, Walderslade, Chatham, Kent ME5 8AH; Tunbury Country Primary School, Tunbury Ave, Walderslade, Chatham, Kent ME5 9HY (☎ 0634 863085)

JONES, Sir Glyn Smallwood; GCMG (1964, KCMG 1960, CMG 1957), MBE (1944); s of Gwilym Ioan Jones (d 1942); *b* 9 Jan 1908; *Educ* King's Sch Chester, St Catherine's Coll Oxford (MA); *m* 1942, Nancy Madoc Featherstone; 1 da (and 1 s decd); *Career* entered Colonial Serv (N Rhodesia) 1931, min for native affrs and chief cmmr N Rhodesia 1959, chief sec Nyasaland 1960-61, govr Nyasaland 1961-64, govr gen and C in C Malawi 1964-66; advsr on govt admin to PM of Lesotho 1969-71; Br Govt observer Zimbabwe elections 1980; dep chm Lord Pearce Cmmn for test of Rhodesian opinion 1971-72; hon fell St Catherine's Coll Oxford; KStJ; *Recreations* fishing, golf; *Clubs* MCC, Athenaeum, Royal Commonwealth Soc; *Style*— Sir Glyn Jones, GCMG, MBE; Little Brandfold Cottage, Goudhurst, Kent TN17 1JJ (☎ 0580 211386)

JONES, Ivor Walter Morris; s of David Jones (d 1969), of Crynant, and Margaret Ellen, *née* Williams (d 1981); *b* 21 Aug 1930; *Educ* Neath GS, Univ of Wales (BSc, DipEd); *m* 9 Aug 1958, Mavis, da of Redvers Paddison (d 1961), of Ystrad Mynach; 2 s (Gareth b 1962, Alun b 1966), 1 da (Siân b 1964); *Career* short serv cmmn RAF, Flying Offr 1953-56; industl consultancy and lecturing appts 1956-68, head Dept Mgmnt and Business Studies Twickenham Coll of Technol 1968-74, princ Bromley Coll of Technol 1975- (vice princ 1974-75); nat cncl memb Assoc of Princs of Colls 1983-86; memb: Bromley Health Authy 1977-, NW Surrey Youth Employment Ctee 1969-74; chm W London Productivity Assoc 1964-67; memb Rotary Int 1969-, pres Rotary Club of Bromley 1979-80; Inst of Admin Mgmnt: memb 1962-, fell 1990-, memb Educn Ctee 1989; *Recreations* rugby union football, photography; *Style*— Ivor Jones, Esq; 79 The Ridge, Orpington, Kent BR6 8AG; Rookery Lane, Bromley, Kent BR2 8HE (☎ 081 462 6331, fax 081 462 7780)

JONES, Jack Anthony; s of Jack Jones (d 1973), and Patricia, *née* Hackett (d 1989); *b* 12 Oct 1957; *Educ* Chatham House GS Ramsgate, Univ of Nottingham (BSc), Imperial Coll of Sci and Technol (MSc); *m* 30 May 1981,

Bridget Jane, da of Peter Linington, of Somali Farm, Birchington, Kent; 1 s (Christopher Peter b 24 Sept 1987), 1 da (Katherine Patricia b 20 Sept 89); *Career* mining engr: Gold Fields of SA 1979-80, Shell (SA) 1980-82, Shell (Botswana) 1982-83; stockbroker UBS Phillips & Drew 1984-; MIMM 1985, CEng 1986; *Style—* Jack Jones, Esq; Ashleigh, 11A Johns Rd, Meopham, Kent DA13 0LP (☎ 0474 814 720); UBA Phillips & Drew, 100 Liverpool St, London EC2M 2RH (☎ 071 901 1319)

JONES, Michael Frederick; s of Glyn Frederick Jones, of Glos, and Elizabeth, *née* Coopey; *b* 3 July 1937; *Educ* Crypt Sch Glos; *m* 28 Feb 1959, Sheila Joan, da of Charles Dawes, of Chaldon, Surrey; 3 s (Edward b 1966, John b 1968, Richard b 1970); *Career* reporter; Maidenhead Advertiser 1956-59, Northern Echo 1959-61, Manchester Evening News 1961-64; lab reporter: Financial Times 1964-65, The Daily Telegraph 1965-67; news ed asst ed The Times Business News 1967-70, managing ed The Asian Hong Kong 1971; The Sunday Times: assoc news ed 1972-75, political corr 1975-84, political ed 1984-; chm parly press gallery 1989; memb Inst of Journalists 1987; *Recreations* recovering; *Style—* Michael Jones, Esq; The Sunday Times, 1 Pennington St, Wapping, London E1 (☎ 0481 4100, fax 071 782 5658, telex 262 139 TIMES G)

JONES, Peter Alan; s of Alan Barnard Jones (d 1985), of Lymington, Hants, and Isobel Caroline, *née* Banham; *Educ* Purley Co GS, King's Coll London, Westminster Med Sch (MB BS, MS); *m* 1 (m dis), Elizabeth Anslie Friend, *née* Spiller; 3 da (Samantha b 17 Jan 1975, Victoria (twin) b 17 Jan 1975, Katie b 23 March 1977); m 2, 22 May 1980, Dr Susan Elizabeth, da of R C Basson, of Iden Court Mews, Staplehurst, Kent; 1 s (Frederick b 9 April 1987), 2 da (Charlotte b 9 March 1983, Sophie b 1 Oct 1985); *Career* lectr in gen surgery St George's Hosp London 1977-79, sr registrar in gen surgery Westminster Hosp 1979-83, conslt gen surgn The Maidstone Hosp 1983-; pres Maidstone Div BMA, former ctee memb Pancreatic Soc of GB and I, fell Assoc of Surgns; memb: Br Soc of Gastroenterology, Br Assoc of Urological Surgns; FRCS, FRSM; *Recreations* tennis, swimming; *Clubs* 69; *Style—* Peter Jones, Esq; Old Timbers, Reed Place, Dairy Lane, Chainhurst, Marden, Kent TN12 9ST (☎ 062 72 840); Maidstone Hospital, Hermitage Lane, Barming, Maidstone, Kent ME16 9QQ (☎ 0622 729000, fax 0622 674706)

JONES, Peter Eldon; s of Wilfrid Eldon Jones (d 1985), of Kingston upon Thames, and Jessie Meikle, *née* Buchanan (d 1970); *b* 11 Oct 1927; *Educ* Surbiton GS, Kingston Poly, UCL (DipTP); *m* 1, 1954 (m dis 1984), Gisela Marie, da of Maj Landforstmeister Karl Heinrich von Arnswaldt (d 1985) of Celle, Germany; 2 s (Christopher b 1955, Andrew b 1958), 1 da (Hella b 1962); m 2, 1985, Claudia Ann Mary Milner-Brown, da of John Alan Laurence, of Gt Waltham, Essex; *Career* sr asst architect Powell and Moya 1950-54, joined LCC Arch Dept 1954, dep sch architecture LCC 1960-65, town devpt architect/planner GLC 1965-71, tech policy architect GLC 1971-74, acting dir of architecture ILEA 1980-82 (educn architect 1974-82), dir architecture and superintending architect Met Bldgs GLC/ILEA 1982-86, dir Watkins Gray Peter Jones Ltd 1986-; conslt: Watkins Gray Int, DES; chm: Abbeyfield, Pirbright Bldg Ctee; pres Soc Chief Architects of Local Authys 1983-84, memb EEC Advsy Ctee on Educn and Trg of Architects 1986-; Freeman: City of London 1968, Worshipful Co of CAs 1988; vice pres RIBA 1985-86, FRIBA, FRTPI, FRSA, FCSD; *Books* Good House Design (1956); *Recreations* photography, travel, bridge, golf; *Clubs* Woking Golf; *Style—* Peter Jones, Esq; Watkins Gray Peter Jones Ltd, Alexander House, 1a Spur Rd, Orpington, Kent (☎ 0689 36141, fax 0689 35152)

JONES, (Eric) Reginald Lloyd; s of Eric Lloyd Jones, of 30 Osborne Rd, Litherland, Liverpool, and Royal Audrey Joan, *née* Johnstone-Brown; *b* 5 Oct 1939; *Educ* Waterloo GS Liverpool, King's Coll Univ of London, King's Coll Hosp Med Sch (MB BS, LRCP); *m* 28 March 1964, Shelagh Ann (Candy), da of Henry John Hayward (d 1960), of Horton Heath, Dorset; 2 s (Peter b 11 Feb 1966, Alex b 17 April 1970), 2 da (Sarah b 1 Jan 1965, Debbie b 4 March 1969); *Career* med house offr Freedom Fields Hosp Plymouth 1962, accident house offr Luton and Dunstable Hosp 1964, surgical house offr Devonport Hosp Plymouth 1965; Frenchay Hosp Bristol: SHO in neurosurgery and plastics surgery 1966, surgicical registrar 1967; orthopaedic registrar Kings Coll Hosp London 1968 (house offr 1963), sr registrar on King's rotation 1970, conslt orthopaedic and accident surgn to SE Kent and Canterbury and Thanet DHAs 1972; hon med offr: Kent CCC, Folkestone Boxing Club; hon orthopaedic surgn Folkestone and Shepway FC; memb: Folkestone Med Soc, Bird Stamp Soc, MCSA; memb: RSM, BMA; fell Br Orthopaedic Assoc, FRCS 1967; *Publications* Radial Neck Fractures and of Sacral Cysts (published in Journal of Bone and Joint Surgery 1972), Lettsom and The Royal Sea Bathing Hospital proceedings of the RSM (1978); *Recreations* wildlife filming and photography, bird stamps; *Style—* Reginald Jones, Esq; Broadmead, 1 Cherry Garden Ave, Folkestone, Kent CT19 5LB (☎ 0303 75907)

JORDAN, Francis Leo (Frank); CBE (1989), QPM (1982); s of Leo Thomas Jordan (d 1967), of Stone, Staffs, and Mary, *née* Moloney (d 1982); *b* 15 June 1930; *Educ* St Joseph's Coll; *m* 1951, Ruth, da of James Ashmore (d 1970), of Cheshire; 1 s (Francis b 1958), 2 da (Karen b 1957, Diane b 1962); *Career* joined Staffs Police 1950 attaining rank of Chief Supt, seconded to Cyprus Police during EOKA emergency 1956-58, staff offr to HO Police Inspectorate 1975, Asst Chief Constable W Midlands 1976, Dep Chief Constable of Kent 1979, Chief Constable of Kent 1982-89; chm Kent Children's House Soc 1979-81 (hon patron), vice pres Assoc of Kent CCs 1982-89; memb: Kent Co Ctee SSAFA 1986-89, Kent Agric Soc, Assoc Men of Kent and Kentish Men, Band of Brothers; appointed to Parole Bd 1990; CBIM 1985, FRSA 1990; OStJ 1988; *Recreations* shooting, walking, old buildings, travel; *Clubs* Royal Over-Seas League, Hopper's Tie; *Style—* Frank Jordan, Esq, CBE, QPM; c/o Police Headquarters, Sutton Rd, Maidstone, Kent ME15 9BZ (☎ 0622 690690, telex 96132)

JOSE, (Thomas) Leonard; JP; s of William José (d 1967), of Penzance, and Jessie, *née* Brown Wark (d 1974); *b* 11 May 1926; *Educ* schs in Cornwall Scotland and England; *m* 29 March 1952, Gwendoline Joyce, da of Archibald Butler (d 1945), of Hounslow; 1 s (Alan), 2 da (Karen, Miranda); *Career* London Scottish (Gordon Highlanders) TA 1948-52, Lance-Corpl 1949, Corpl 1950, Sgt 1951; pt/t Kenya Police Res Inspr 1953-55, Lloyd's 1944-87 (memb 1977), HP Motor Policies 1944-48, Hogg Robinson & Capel Cure Ltd 1948-49, Arbon Langrish & Co Ltd 1949-55, Ernest A Notcutt & Co Ltd 1955-87 (later Eastern Produce Holdings, Clarkson Puckle, now Bain Clarkson), dir Telecommunications Network Ltd 1990-; registered insur broker; Magistrate Bromley Bench 1979, ed Bromley Business, PR exec Bromley Borough C of C; govr: Valley Primary Sch Shortlands, Princess Plain Primary Bromley, The Emily Dowling Fndn; sidesman and chm Rooms Ctee Bromley Parish Church; life memb: Nat Tst for Scotland, Cornwall Naturalists Tst; memb: Guild of Freeman, The Hon Soc of Knights of the Round Table, London Cornish Assoc, Royal Cornwall Agric Assoc, Kent Co Agric Soc, Bd Kent Business Fedn, Chartered Insur Inst; vice chm W Kent Cornish Assoc; Freeman City of London 1959, Liveryman Worshipful Co of Carmen 1982; *Books* Road Transport Safety and Security Handbook (contrib, 1982); *Recreations* cooking, golf, reading, walking; *Clubs* Bromley Conservative, City Livery, Chelwood, Shortland Golf; *Style—* Leonard José, Esq, JP; 14 The Glen, Shortlands, Bromley, Kent BR2 0JB (☎ 081 464 3548)

JOYCE, Roger Allen; s of Ronald George Joyce, and Ernestine Francesca, *née* Ungaro (d 1990); *b* 31 July 1945; *Educ* Sir Joseph Williamson's Mathematical Sch Rochester, Canterbury Sch of Architecture (Dip Arch), AA (Dip Bldg Conservation); *m* 1, 8 July 1967 (m dis 1980), Gloria June, da of Colin Lewis, of Bridge; 1 da (Nicola Louise b 9 July 1977); m 2, 3 April 1982, Kathryn Jane (Kate), da of Frank Richmond (d 1963), of Folkestone; 1 da (Hannah Amy b 1 April 1984); *Career* architect; Co Architects Office 1970-72, assoc Cheney & Thorpe 1972-78, conslt to Anthony Swaine 1977-80, Roger A Joyce Chartered Architect 1977-; ARIBA; *Recreations* theatre, travel, food and wine; *Clubs* OW, FHODS; *Style—* Roger Joyce, Esq; Stowting Court Barn, Stowting, Ashford, Kent TN25 6BB (☎ 0303 863288)

JOYNES, Roger Arthur; JP (Folkestone and Hythe 1988); s of Eric Arthur Joynes (d 1983), of Barking, Essex, and Olive Christina Burge; *b* 12 Nov 1941; *Educ* Eastbury Secdy Modern Sch, E Ham Tech Coll (HNC), Havering Tech Coll (CDip Eng Man), Barking Coll of Technol (CDip Acc); *m* 25 Feb 1967, Jane Elizabeth, da of Thomas James Winter, of Caister-on-Sea, Norfolk; 2 s (Richard b 1971, Simon b 1977), 1 da (Helen b 1974); *Career* apprentice marine engr 1958-63, marine engr offr 1964-65; project engr CEGB 1980- (mechanical maintenance engr 1966-80); memb Rotary Club Romney Marsh; MBIM 1980, MINucE 1983; *Recreations* sailing; *Clubs* Royal Cinque Ports Yacht; *Style—* Roger Joynes, Esq, JP; Malindi, Blenheim Rd, Littlestone, New Romney, Kent TN28 8RD (☎ 0679 66367); Nuclear Electric plc, Project Management Branch, South East Sites Office, Dungeness, Romney Marsh, Kent TN29 9PL (☎ 0679 20531, fax 0679 20594, telex 96218)

JUDD, Clifford Harold Alfred; CB (1987); s of Alfred Ernest Judd (d 1966), and Florence Louisa, *née* Peacock; *b* 27 June 1927; *Educ* Christs Hosp, Keble Coll Oxford; *m* 9 Aug 1951, (Elizabeth) Margaret, da of late Albert William Holmes; 2 da (Caroline b 1969, Rosemary b 1970); *Career* Nat Serv 2 Lt RA 1947-48 (invalided out); HM Treasy: exec offr 1948, through ranks princ 1964, sr princ 1969, asst sec 1973, under sec Treasy Offr of Accounts 1981-87; memb Royal Patriotic Fund Corp 1987-; *Recreations* cricket, golf, DIY; *Clubs* Sevenoaks Vine Cricket, Knole Park Golf; *Style—* Clifford Judd, Esq, CB; 4 Colets Orchard, Otford, Sevenoaks, Kent TN14 5RA (☎ 09592 2398)

JUKES, Rt Rev John Peter Ignatius; s of Francis Jukes, and Florence Maud, *née* Stampton; *b* 7 Aug 1923; *Educ* St Joseph's Acad Blackheath, Rome (degree and licence in theology); *Career* appointed Bishop of Strathearn by Pope John Paul II and consecrated 1980, auxiliary bishop RC Archdiocese of Southwark, RC area bishop Kent; chm World of Work Ctee of the Bishop's Conference of Eng and Wales, memb and Res Ctee memb Canon Law Soc of GB and I, memb Order of Friars Minor Conventual 1949-, provincial Eng Province of Greyfriars 1979; contrib to: Canon Law Soc of GB and I Newsletter, Studia Canonica, New Life; *Recreations* mountain climbing and walking; *Style—* The Rt Rev John Jukes; The Hermitage, More Park, West Malling, Kent ME19 6HN (☎ 0732 845486, fax 0732 847888)

JURY, Cncllr Kenneth Ernest Thomas (Ken); s of Arthur William Jury (d

1976), of Cheltenham, and Gwendoline Gladys, *née* Edwards (d 1942), of Chatham; *b* 19 Dec 1926; *Educ* Rochester Cathedral Choir Sch, The Kings Sch Rochester; *m* 16 Sept 1950, Joan Barbara, da of Cdr Edward Clement Newport, RNVR (d 1980), of Gillingham; *Career* Parachute Regt 1944-47; sales and distribution exec: J Lyons & Co Ltd 1948-52, Quaker Oats Ltd 1952-54; regnl mangr Holdfast Footwear Ltd Bristol 1954-62, dir Newport & Jury Ltd Sevenoaks 1962-69; admin offr Gillingham Borough Cncl 1969-74, sr admin offr Sevenoaks DC 1974-83; Gillingham Borough Cncl: elected Cons memb Parkwood Ward May 1979, chm Health and Housing Ctee, chm Housing Mgmnt Sub Ctee, chm Gen Purposes Ctee, Mayor elect 1990-91; tstee Parkwood Community Assoc, govr of several schools, memb Inst Advanced Motorists; *Recreations* motoring, gardening, travel; *Style*— Cncllr Ken Jury; The Mayor's Parlour, Gillingham Borough Council, Municipal Buildings, Gillingham ME7 5LA (☎ 0634 282038, fax 0634 282040)

K

KAMDAR, Batookrai Anopchand; s of Anopchand Keshavlal Kamdar, and Lilavati, *née* Shah; *b* 29 Oct 1939; *Educ* Gujarat Univ (MB BS), MRCS (tutor); *m* 27 May 1964, Dr Beni Kamdar, da of Dr Chandulal Chhotalal Shah, of Baroda, India; 1 s (Neel b 1965), 1 da (Sujata b 1967); *Career* orthopaedic registrar: Hammersmith Hosp 1970-71, Heatherwood Hosp Ascot Berks 1971-72; sr orthopaedic registrar Royal Free Hosp London 1973-75, conslt orthopeadic surgn Dartford and Gravesham Health Dist 1975-; memb: RSM, BMA, Br Orthopaedic Assoc; FRCSEd; *Pubns:* Complications Following Total Knee Replacement (1974), Soft Tissue Calcification Following Total Hip Replacement (1976), Early Soft Tissue Release in CTEV (1977); *Recreations* reading, music, philately, cricket; *Clubs* MCC; *Style—* Batookrai Kamdar, Esq; 7 Liskeard Close, Chislehurst, Kent BR7 6RT (☎ 081 467 9851); West Hill Hospital, Dartford, Kent; Blackheath Hospital, Blackheath, London; Fawkham Manor Hospital, Fawkham, Kent (☎ 0322 23223)

KAY, Thelma (Thelma Kay Green); da of William Ernest Green, and Edna Winifred, *née* Thompson; *b* 30 Oct 1943; *Educ* Haberdashers' Aske's, Ravensbourne Coll of Art, Maidstone Coll of Art, Chelsea Studios; *Career* specialist in animal portraiture and action painting; princ works incl: Interior State Mews Buckingham Palace, November Morning (sold for HM The Queen's Jubilee Fund), Pippin and Friends at Handen Farm, West Kent Payment (Champion Foxhound), Capt D C McIntosh - The Scinde Horse, Exercising The Limekilns, Full of Hope (The Willows), Tack On (Style Place Farm); exhibitions incl: ROI Summer Salon, Art International; former hon sec BHS Co Branch; *Recreations* equestrian pursuits especially eventing and point-to-pointing, breeding donkeys; *Style—* Miss Thelma Kay; Spinnakers, Nettlestead Green, nr Wateringbury, Kent ME18 5HN

KEE, His Hon William; s of Robert Kee (d 1958), and Dorothy Frances, *née* Monkman (d 1964); *b* 15 Oct 1921; *Educ* Stowe; *m* 1953, Helga Wessel, da of Erling Christian Haneborg Eckhoff (d 1980); 1 s (Peter William b 1960), 3 da (Christine Frances b 1954, Susanna Helga b 1957, Karen Mary b 1964); *Career* Army 1941-46, Orkneys and India, attached 9 Gurkha Rifles, Staff Capt; Inner Temple 1948; jt chm Ind Sch Tbnl 1971-72; circuit judge 1972-90, princ judge for Co Courts in Kent 1985-90; *Books* Divorce Case Book (1950), Encyclopaedia of Court Forms and Halsbury's Laws of England (contrib); *Recreations* walking, listening to music; *Style—* His Hon William Kee

KEEN, Brian James; s of Percy Archibald Keen, of Hoath, nr Canterbury, and Cicely Bertha, *née* Keen (d 1979); *b* 1 Jan 1949; *Educ* Simon Langton GS for Boys Canterbury, Univ of Reading (BSc); *m* 10 Sept 1979, Ceinwen Vivienne, da of Percy Vivian Hopkins (d 1947), of Leeds, Yorks; *Career* asst city estates offr Canterbury City Cncl 1980-84, ptnr James B Terson & Son Dover 1984-86, md Swan Property Services Canterbury 1986-, dir Davis Zuber Associates Lanzarote Canary Is 1986-; co sec: Swan Country Inns 1987-, Rice Mans Insurance Brokers 1989-; life memb Old Langtonians Assoc; memb: Nat Tst, WWF, Woodland Trust, RHS; tstee Canterbury Investmt Club; FRICS 1985, fell RSPB 1988; *Clubs* Chisley & Dist CC (chm), Arbrix; *Style—* Brian Keen, Esq; 19 Sunnymead, Tyler Hill, Canterbury, Kent (☎ 0227 472395); 75 St Dunstans St, Canterbury, Kent CT2 8BN (☎ 0227 463709, fax 0227 454826)

KEEN, Linda Anne; da of Alfred Boutle, of Southend on Sea, Essex, and Doris, *née* Redman (d 1984); *b* 10 Sept 1947; *Educ* Southend on Sea GS, Univ of Kent (BA, MA) Christchurch Coll (PGCE), Mid-Kent Coll (DMS), RAM; *Career* previous posts incl: tutor Open Univ, social worker, journalist, music teacher; sr lecturer Pub Sector Mgmnt Mid Kent Coll; cncllr Canterbury Dist 1983-, prospective parly candidate (L) Canterbury 1987, ctee memb Three Towns Assoc twinning Canterbury with Vladimir USSR and USA town; memb NATHE; *Recreations* chess, music; *Clubs* Whitstable Labour; *Style—* Ms Linda Keen; 19 Ersham Rd, Canterbury, Kent (☎ 0227 66314); Mid-Kent College, Horsted, Chatham, Kent

KEIR, Dr Michael Ian Stenhouse; s of Sir David Lindsay Keir (d 1973), of Hillsborough, Lincombe Lane, Boars Hill, Oxford, and Anna Clunie, *née* Dale; *b* 16 May 1934; *Educ* Charterhouse, New Coll Oxford (MA, BM BCh); *m* 14 Jan 1961 (m dis 1986), Maria Grazia, da of Gen Joseph Piana (d 1969), of Rome; 2 s (Mark Robert b 1961, Thomas Joseph b 1968); *Career* conslt dermatologist: Kent and Canterbury Hosp 1969-77, Whipps Cross Hosp London 1980-; hon lectr Bart's Med Coll 1987-; memb: Dermatological Section RSM, BMA, Br Assoc of Dermatologists, Huntarian Soc; memb fell Royal Soc of Tropical Med and Hygiene; FRCPE 1977; *Recreations* swimming, travelling; *Style—* Dr Michael Keir

KEITH-LUCAS, Prof Bryan; CBE (1983); s of Dr Keith Lucas, FRS (ka 1916), and Alys, *née* Hubbard 1955); *b* 1 Aug 1912; *Educ* Gresham's, Pembroke Coll Cambridge (MA), Univ of Kent at Canterbury (DLitt); *m* 24 Oct 1946, Mary Ross, MBE (Sheriff of Canterbury 1971), da of Dr J Hardwicke (d 1940), of Woolpit, Suffolk; 1 s (Peter b 1950), 2 da (Jane (Mrs Bird) b 1948, Polly (Mrs Dangerfield) b 1950); *Career* enlisted Buffs 1939; Sherwood Foresters: cmmnd 1940, Adj 2/5 Bn 1941, serv N Africa and Italy 1942-44, (despatches 1943), Maj DAAG Cyprus 1945-46; admitted slr 1937; asst slr: Royal Borough of Kensington 1937-46, Nottingham 1946-48; sr lectr Univ of Oxford 1948-65, bursar Nuffield Coll 1957-65 (fell 1950-65), prof of govt Univ of Kent at Canterbury 1965-77, Master Darwin Coll 1970-74; parish cncllr Cumnor 1950-56, city cncllr Oxford 1950-65; chm: Cmmn on Elections Sierra Leone 1954 (Mauritius 1955-56), Nat Assoc of Parish Cncls 1964-70, Canterbury Soc 1972-75; memb: Roberts Ctee on Public Libraries 1957-59, Mallaby Ctee on Staffing in Local Govt 1964-67, Local Govt Cmmn for England 1965-66, Royal Cmmn on Elections in Fiji 1975; pres: Kent Assoc of Parish Cncls 1976-81, Kent Fedn of Amenity Socs 1976-81, Stour Valley Soc 1982-, Kent Soc 1985-88; hon fell Inst of Local Govt Studies Birmingham Univ 1973; *Publications*: The English Local Government Franchise (1952), English Local Government in the 19th and 20th Centuries (1977), History of Local Government in the 20th Century (with P G Richards, (1978), The Unreformed Local Government System (1979), Parish Affairs (the Government of Kent under George III) (1986); *Recreations* walking; *Clubs* Nat Lib; *Style—* Prof Bryan Keith-Lucas, CBE; 7 Church St, Wye, Ashford, Kent TN25 5BN (☎ 0233 812 621)

KELLY, Brian Owen; s of George Alfred Kelly (d 1984), and Delia, *née* Cafferkey (d 1984); *b* 9 Jan 1943; *Educ* Presentation Coll Reading, Farnborough Coll of Technol; *m* 17 Oct 1970, (Anne) Christine, da of Fred Payne (d 1985); *Career* scientific asst Servs Electronics Res Laboratory 1959-64, experimental offr Admty Compass Observatory 1964-70, sr engr Bendix Aerospace Michigan USA 1970-73, vice pres United Detector Technology LA 1973-78, gen mangr Centronic Optical Systems Ltd Croydon 1978-85, md Centronic Ltd 1985-; chm: Dosimeter Corporation of America USA, Mini Instruments Ltd Essex, Centronic Inc USA; memb Cncl Def Mfrs Assoc; govr: Rowdown HS Croydon, Addington HS Croydon; MIERE 1975, MInstP 1979, FBIM 1980, CPhys; *Recreations* golf, bridge, chess; *Style—* Brian Kelly, Esq; Green Roofs, Dower House Crescent, Tunbridge Wells, Kent TN4 0TT; Centronic House, King Henry's Drive, Croydon CR9 0BG (☎ 0689 42 121, fax 0489 43 053, telex 876 474 CENTRO G)

KELLY, Shaun Andrew; s of Robert Christopher Kelly (d 1989), of 109 Spot Lane, Bearsted, Kent, and Elsie May, *née* Tyler; *b* 11 Nov 1960; *Educ* Maidstone GS; *m* 14 Oct 1989, Susan Jane Elizabeth, da of John West, of Crosby House, Sandy Lane, West Malling; *Career* National Westminster Bank plc: joined Maidstone 1979, PA to sr mangr Sittingbourne 1985, Kent Area Office Advances 1987, SE Regnl Office Advances 1988, managerial appt Tonbridge 1989; memb: Tonbridge Business Luncheon Club, Chartered Inst of Bankers; fndr David Coleman Appreciation Soc, active involvement in fund raising for Maidstone Hosp CORDA (Coronary Artery Disease Res Assoc); *Recreations* golf, squash, climbing, watercolours, motor racing; *Clubs* Whitehouse Squash, British Racing and Sportscar; *Style—* Shaun Kelly, Esq; 164 Southwood Rd, Rusthall, Tunbridge Wells, Kent (☎ 0892 511605); National Westminster Bank plc, 130 High St, Tonbridge, Kent TN9 1DE (☎ 0732 357766, fax 0732 770754)

KEMP, David Stephen; s of Stephen Nicholas Kemp (d 1967), of Bromley, Kent, and Mary Grace, *née* Gibbs (d 1976); *b* 14 Dec 1928; *Educ* Tonbridge, Brasenose Coll Oxford (MA); *m* 16 April 1966, Marion Elizabeth, da of late Dr Maurice Sibley Blower, of Rake, Hants; 3 s (Anthony David b 1967, William James Stephen b 1971, Peter John b 1973); *Career* 2 Lt Duke of Wellington's Regt 1948; articled clerk E F Turner & Sons 1952, admitted slr 1955; Tonbridge Sch: asst master 1956, housemaster 1969, second master

1971, actg headmaster 1990; played hockey for Kent; Mental Health Act mangr Leybourne Grange Hosp, chm Govrs Marlborough House Sch, govr Claremont Sch, ctee memb Kent CCC; Liveryman Worshipful Co of Skinners 1954; *Recreations* cricket, golf, reading; *Clubs* Vincents, MCC, Bude & N Cornwall Golf; *Style—* David Kemp, Esq; Summerlands, Portman Park, Tonbridge, Kent TN9 1LW (☎ 0732 350 023)

KEMP, Michael Alfred Lawrence; s of Alfred Lawrence Kemp (d 1968), and Margaret, *née* Smith; *b* 19 March 1941; *Educ* Greenwich Central Sch; *m* 1, 1965, Janet Anne, da of Charles Blogg, OBE; 1 s (Lawrence Michael b 1968); m 2, Patricia Deborah, da of Jack Kitching (d 1986); 1 s (Paul Lawrence Michael b 1971), 1 da (Lindsey b 1974); *Career* md: G & L Ralli Investment & Trustee Co Ltd 1977 (dir 1973-), G & L Ralli Finance Co Ltd 1977- (dir 1972-), Ralli Investment Co Ltd 1979-; dir Frowds Ltd 1983-, chm Ralli Bondite Ltd 1989- (dir 1981-); AMSIA; *Recreations* gardening, rugby union supporter, horseracing; *Clubs* City of London; *Style—* Michael A L Kemp, Esq; 5 Westott Close, Bickley, Kent BR1 2TU (☎ 081 468 7347)

KEMP, Robert Thayer; s of Robert Kemp (d 1968), and Ada, *née* Thayer; *b* 18 June 1928; *Educ* Bromley GS, Univ of London (BA); *m* 1951, Gwendolyn Mabel, da of Rev Charles Stanley Minty (d 1930); *Career* former dir Int Gp Export Credits Guarantee Dept 1985-88 (asst 1970-75, under sec 1975-85), export credit conslt and non-exec dir Sedgwick James Credit Ltd 1989-; *Publications* Review of Future Status Operations for ECGD (1989); *Recreations* gardening, theatre, music; *Clubs* Overseas Bankers; *Style—* Robert Kemp, Esq; 294 Tubbenden Lane South, Farnborough, Orpington, Kent BR6 7DN (☎ 0689 53924)

KENNEDY, George MacDonald; s of George W MacDonald Kennedy (d 1988), of Leith, Scotland; and Marion D C, *née* Grainger; *b* 4 Aug 1940; *Educ* Leith Acad Scotland, IMEDE Lausanne Switzerland; *m* 28 May 1976, Christine E, da of David Balcomb, of Lydd, Kent; 2 s (George D MacDonald b 19 May 1978, Paul D MacDonald b 18 Feb 1981); *Career* md Portby Ltd Hythe Kent 1973; chm SI Medical Systems Gp, exec dir Smiths Industs plc, non exec dir Arthur Lee & Son plc; chm: Br Healthcare Trade and Indust Cncl, SE Kent Productivity Assoc 1977; memb Manpower Services Corporation 1977; memb RSM 1986; *Style—* George Kennedy, Esq; Deepwell House, Chilham Castle Estate, Chilham, Canterbury, Kent CT4 8DB (☎ 0227 730363); 765 Finchley Rd, Childs Hill, London NW11 8DS (☎ 081 458 3232, fax 0227 730175)

KENT, Joan (Mrs Alan Whibley); da of Henry William Coultrip (d 1952), of Canterbury and Faversham, and Eliza Ann, *née* Kemp (d 1968); *b* 19 April 1922; *Educ* Blean and Eastling Village Sch; *m* 30 Aug 1941, Alan Whibley, s of Herbert Whibley (d 1962); 1 s (Christopher Martin b 1953), 3 da (Linda Ann b 1942, Marianne Joan b 1948, Jillian b 1963); *Career* farming 1935-46, author of weekly Country Girl column in South Wales Echo 1965-, country based articles printed in various magazines, regular speaker for various orgns for handicapped disabled and elderly people; *Books* Binder Twine And Rabbit Stew (1975), Woodsmoke And Pigeon Pie (1977), Hay Wains And Cherry Ale (1980); *Recreations* gardening, reading, winemaking, local rural history; *Style—* Mrs Joan Kent; Beam Ends, 57 Wynn Rd, Tankerton, Whitstable, Kent CT5 2JN (☎ 0227 263998)

KERBY, John Vyvyan; s of Dr Theo Rosser Fred Kerby (d 1947), and Constance Mary, *née* Newell (d 1954); *b* 14 Dec 1942; *Educ* Eton, ChCh Oxford (MA); *m* 23 June 1978, Shirley Elizabeth, da of Sydney John Pope (d 1970); 1 step s, 1 step da; *Career* temp asst princ Colonial Office 1965-67, asst princ Miny of Overseas Devpt 1967-70, private sec to Parly Under Sec FCO 1970-71, memb Civil Serv Selection Bd 1974-75, head Br Devpt Div in SA 1983-86, under sec and princ estabs offr ODA 1986- (princ 1971-74 and 1975-77, asst sec 1977-83); *Recreations* gardening, entomology, cricket; *Style—* John Kerby, Esq; Overseas Development Administration, Eland House, Stag Place, London, SW1 (☎ 01 273 0380)

KERSHAW, David Robert; s of Noel Ernest Kershaw, TD, and Dorothy Anne, *née* Cheyne; *Educ* Urmston GS, Trinity Coll Cambridge (MA); *m* 1978, Christine Anne, da of late John Spear Sexton; 3 s (Oliver James b 1979, Toby Thomas b 1984, Charles Henry Alexander b 1986), 1 da (Isabelle Alice Katharine b 1989); *Career* admitted slr 1978; specialist in corporate fin, mergers and acquisitions and banking; ptnr Ashurst Morris Crisp 1986-; *Recreations* classical guitar, windsurfing, tennis, literature; *Style—* David Kershaw, Esq; Ashurst Morris Crisp, Broadwalk House, 5 Appold St, London EC2A 2HA (☎ 01 638 1111, fax 01 972 7990)

KETT, George Anthony; s of George Robert Kett, and Lilian Hester, *née* Groves (d 1987); *b* 15 Feb 1943; *Educ* Christ's Coll Blackheath; *m* 23 May 1970, Margaret Anne; 1 s (Nicholas George b 1 June 1973), 1 da (Georgina Anne b 14 Sept 1978); *Career* subst underwriter Red Star Policies Lloyd's 1960-65, underwriter Corinthian Motor Policies Lloyd's 1977 (dep underwriter 1965-77), chm Rose Thomson Young Ltd 1990- (dir 1982-90); govr Christs Coll Blackheath; *Recreations* golf, gardening, reading; *Style—* George Kett, Esq

KEYES, Hon Adrian Christopher Noel; s of 2 Baron Keyes *qv*; *b* 1962; *Educ* Lancing; *Style—* The Hon Adrian Keyes

KEYES, Hon Charles William Packe; s and h of 2 Baron Keyes *qv*; *b* 8 Dec 1951; *m* 1, 1978 (m dis), Sadiye Yasmin, da of Mahir Coskun, of Istanbul; m 2, 1984, Sally da of Thomas Jackson, 1 da (Anne Merula b 1985); *Style—* The Hon Charles Keyes

KEYES, 2 Baron (UK 1943); Sir Roger George Bowlby Keyes; 2 Bt (UK 1919); s of Adm of the Fleet 1 Baron Keyes, GCB, KCVO, CMG, DSO (d 1945), and Eva Mary Salvin, *née* Bowlby (d 1973); *b* 14 March 1919; *Educ* King's Mead Sch Seaford, RNC Dartmouth; *m* 6 Dec 1947, Grizelda Mary, da of late Lt-Col William Packe, DSO; 3 s (Hon Charles *qv*, Hon John *qv*, Hon Adrian), 2 da (Hon Mrs Crompton b 1950, Hon Mrs Young b 1958); *Heir* s, Hon Charles Keyes; *Career* WWII serv RN N Sea and Med 1939-45, ret 1949; co dir, conslt; author; *Books* Outrageous Fortune (1984),Un Règne Brisé (1985), Echec au Roi (1986), Een Beproeft Koning (1986), Complot Tegen de Koning (1988); *Clubs* Anglo-Belgian, Institute of Directors; *Style—* The Rt Hon the Lord Keyes; Elmscroft, Charlton Lane, West Farleigh, nr Maidstone, Kent ME15 0NY (☎ 0622 812477)

KHAMBATA, Ardeshir Shiavax; s of Shiavay Sorabjee Khambata (d 19690), of Bombay, India, and Coomi, *née* Lam; *b* 13 Oct 1935; *Educ* Cathedral Sch Bombay India, Grant Med Coll Bombay India (MBBS); *Career* conslt ENT surgn Dartford and Gravesham Health Dist and Queen Mary's Hosp Sidcup 1973-; FRCS; *Publications* Music and the Brain (contrib, 1977), Scott Brown's Diseases of ENT (contrib), Voice (contrib), Yehudi Menuhin's Music Guides (for Young Musicians) (1983); *Recreations* classical music, singing, opera, travel; *Style—* Ardeshir Khambata, Esq; 152 Harley St, London W1M 1HH (☎ 071 9358868); Fawkham Manor Hosp, Fawkham, Kent DA3 8ND (☎ 0474 879900)

KHAN, Daniel; s of Fizizool Khan, of Trinidad, W Indies, and Azina, *née* Khan; *b* 6 Aug 1951; *Educ* Naparima Coll, SW London Coll (ACCA), City of London Poly (MA), New Testament Bible Inst (Dip Theol); *m* 3 June 1976, Marion Jane, da of Arthur Leslie James Lawrence, of Rainham, Kent; 1 s (Matthew b 23 May 1985), 1 da (Rebecca b 12 Feb 1983); *Career* auditor Pannell Kerr Forster 1970-73; accountant Amber Seafords Ltd 1973-74, chief accountant Dansteel Ltd 1976-77, accountant Univ of the WI 1977-80, mgmnt accountant Allied Lyons plc 1980-81, accountant Univ of London 1981-84, princ Daniel Khan and Co Certified Accountants 1984-; Gillingham Borough Cncl: chm Fin Ctee, chm Health and Housing Ctee, chm New Age Leisure; ordinary memb and auditor: Rainham and Wigmore Community Assoc, Medway and Gillingham Racial Equality Cncl; vice chm of govrs Fairview CP Sch; govr: Mierscourt CP Sch (chm Fin Ctee), Rainham Mark GS; memb King's Church Chatham; *Recreations* table tennis, football, swimming; *Clubs* Brasenose; *Style—* Daniel Khan, Esq; 9 The Rise, Hempstead, Gillingham, Kent ME7 3SS (☎ 0634 31992); Ibis House, 14 Canterbury St, Gillingham, Kent ME7 5TX (☎ 0634 574639)

KHAN, Dr Tariq Ali; s of Hashmat Ali Khan, of Lucknow, India, and Qudsia Begum, da of Khan Sahib Faiyaz Ali Khan (title of Khan Sahib was awarded by Br Empire in India); *b* 10 Aug 1940; *Educ* Christian Coll Lucknow India, Lucknow Univ India (BSc, Dip Public Admin), King Georges Med Coll Lucknow (MB BS), FPA (UK); *m* 6 Nov 1980, Christine Reid Robertson (Yasmin), da of Edward Thompson (d 1971); 1 s (Hasan Ali b 19 Dec 1982), 1 da (Shaheen b 9 Nov 1981); *Career* house surgn and sr houseman Buckland Hosp Dover Kent 1971-73, sr house offr Mothers Hosp London 1973-74, clinical asst Margate Dist Hosp Kent 1974-80, ptnr in gp gen practice Dover 1976-, pt/t clinical asst in trauma and orthapaedics 1981-, sr ptnr in practice 1983, trainer in gen practice 1983, pt/t MO to HM Youth Custody Centre Dover 1983; MO East Kent Car Co Automobile Assoc; memb: Cons Pty, Local Med Ctee Kent 1984-88, Kent Family Practise Ctee 1985-90, Dover Dist Cncl 1987; govr Whitfield Primary Sch 1988; memb BMA; *Recreations* cricket, gardening, music; *Clubs* Moat House, Dover; *Style—* Dr Tariq Khan; North-End, Beechwood Close, Whitfield, Dover, Kent CT16 3JZ (☎ 0304 820158); The Surgery, 27 Park Ave, Dover, Kent CT16 1ES; The Surgery, 43 Sandwich Rd, Whitfield, Dover, Kent (☎ 0304 206463, 0304 820756)

KIDD, John Edward Aitken; s of Maj Edward Daltrey Kidd (d 1979), and The Hon Janet Gladys, *née* Aitken (d 1988); *b* 12 Dec 1944; *Educ* Harrow; *m* 2 April 1973, Wendy Madeleine, da of Sir John Rowland Hodge, MBE; 1 s (Jack Edward b 1973), 2 da (Jemma Madeleine b 1974, Jodie Elizabeth b 1978); *Career* showjumper; Jr Individual Showjumping Euro Champion, represented GB 1964-72; polo: represented England II v The Cwlth Int Day at Windsor; dir: London Utd Investments plc 1977-81, Aitkens Hume plc 1982-86, Care Plus (USA) plc 1987-, All England Jumping Course Hickstead 1989-; chm Columbia Labs Inc (USA) plc 1987-; *Books* Reins Our Hands (1966), Take Off (1974), Biographies on Showjumping Career; *Recreations* polo; *Clubs* Bucks; *Style—* John Kidd, Esq; Hilliers, Petworth, W Sussex; Holders House, St James, Barbados; 745 Fifth Ave, Suite 1809, NYC, NY USA

KIDD, Martin Norman; s of Norman Stanley Kidd, of Belfast, N Ireland, and Evelyn Adair, *née* Mills; *b* 21 Nov 1952; *Educ* Royal Belfast Academical Instn, Queens Univ Belfast (MB BCh, BAO); *Career* trg in ophthalmic surgery Royal Victoria Hosp Belfast 1979-86, visiting prof Univ of California San Francisco

1986-87, conslt ophthalmic surgn Kent Co Ophthalmic & Aural Hosp Maidstone 1988-; memb: BMA, Glaucoma Gp of the UK, Shaffer Soc of Glaucoma Fells; fell Coll of Ophthalmologists, FRCSEd; *Recreations* skiing; *Clubs* Westborough Sports Centre; *Style*— Martin Kidd, Esq; Kent County Ophthalmic & Aural Hospital, Church St, Maidstone, Kent (☎ 0622 673444)

KIDDY, Dennis; s of Thomas William Kiddy (d 1987), and Violet, *née* Snead; *b* 6 Dec 1951; *Educ* Blackpool GS, Worcester Coll Oxford (MA); *Career* musician, organ scholar Worcester Coll Oxford Univ 1970-73, dir of music: Beaudesert Park 1974-75, Repton Prep Sch 1975-83, Wymondham Coll 1983-84; devpt offr St Edmund's Sch Canterbury 1984-; hon sr memb Darwin Coll Univ of Kent 1986, dir of music Lambeth Conf 1988; *Recreations* cooking; *Style*— Dennis Kiddy, Esq; St Edmund's School, Canterbury, Kent CT2 8HU (☎ 0227 454 575)

KILLBERY, Ian Douglas; s of Douglas Charles Killbery, of Ryde, IOW, and Elizabeth, *née* Bryson; *b* 1 Feb 1947; *Educ* Wadham Coll Oxford (MA); *m* 1964, Vivienne; 2 s (Martin James b 1965, Stephen Paul b 1968), 1 da (Emma b 1971); *Career* head of economics and enviromental studies Dover GS for Boys, dir Kent Educnl TV Centre 1981-; author of Computer Software for Schools published by Computer in the Curriculum Project Kings Coll Univ of London 1978-85; cncllr Dover Dist Cncl 1973- (prev Deal Borough Cncl and Micklefield Yorks Parish Cncl), various offices Dover and Deal Constituency Lab Party, parly candidate (Lab) Thanet E 1979, fndr tstee of Crabble Com Mill Tst; *Books* Network for a Nation (1990); *Recreations* walking, reading; *Style*— Ian Kilbery, Esq; 74 Middle Deal Rd, Deal, Kent CT14 9RH (☎ 0304 362569); KETV, Barton Rd, Dover, Kent CT16 2ND (☎ 0304 202827)

KILLICK, Sir John Edward; GCMG (1979, KCMG 1971, CMG 1966); s of Edward William James Killick (d 1972); *b* 18 Nov 1919; *Educ* Latymer Upper Sch, UCL (fell), Univ of Bonn; *m* 1, 1949, Lynette du Preez, da of William Oxenham Leach (d 1984); m 2, 1985, Irene Monica Harries Killick, OBE, da of Malcolm Henry Easton; *Career* WWII Capt (Army) W Africa and W Europe; dip serv 1946-; asst under sec of state 1968-71, ambass USSR 1971-73, dep under sec of state 1973-75, ambass and perm UK rep to NATO 1975-79, ret; dir Dunlop SA 1980-85; pres Br Atlantic Ctee; chm Southborough Soc; *Recreations* golf; *Clubs* Brooks's, Garrick, East India Devonshire, Sports and Public Schs; *Style*— Sir John Killick, GCMG; Challoner's Cottage, 2 Birchwood Ave, Southborough, Kent TN4 0UE

KINCH, (Alec) Anthony; CBE (1987); s of Edward Alec Kinch, OBE (d 1986), and Catherine Teresa, *née* Cassidy (d 1955); *b* 13 Dec 1926; *Educ* Ampleforth, ChCh Oxford (MA); *m* 26 July 1952, Barbara Patricia, da of Brig E J Paton Walsh (d 1985), of Wimbledon; 4 s (Christopher b 1953, Peter b 1956, David b 1960, Stephen b 1967), 2 da (Katherine b 1957, Mary b 1964); *Career* RAF 1944-48, RAFVR 1948-54; called to the Bar Middle Temple 1951; govt contracts mangr The Plessey Co Ltd 1957-60, legal advsr and insurance conslt R & H Green and Silley Weir Ltd 1960-66, dir Federation of Bakers 1966-73; Commission of the European Communities: head Div for Processed Food Products and the Food Indust 1973-82, memb Team 92 Speakers Panel London Office, memb Panel European Movement, Chef de Division Honoraire 1987; head Div Operations of Euro Regnl Fund 1982-86, conslt Euro Affairs; JP Bromley Bench 1970-73, fndr chm Brussels SDP Area Pty 1981-85, memb SDP Cncl Social Democracy 1981-90, Alliance candidate Kent East constituency Euro Elections 1984, SDP candidate London SE constituency Euro Elections 1989; active in ecumenical movement; Knight Cdr with star Order of The Holy Sepulchre; *Recreations* living; *Style*— Anthony Kinch, Esq, CBE; 36 Greenways, Beckenham, Kent BR3 3NG (☎ 081 658 2298)

KINDERSLEY, Hon Anna Lucy; da of 3 Baron Kindersley, *qv*; *b* 1965; *Style*— The Hon Anna Kindersley

KINDERSLEY, Hon Dickon Michael; s of 3 Baron Kindersley, *qv*; *b* 1962; *Style*— The Hon Dickon Kindersley

KINDERSLEY, The Rt Hon the Lord Robert Hugh Molesworth Kindersley; s of 2 Baron Kindersley, CBE, MC (d 1976), and Nancy Farnsworth (d 1977); *b* 18 Aug 1929; *Educ* Eton, Trinity Coll Oxford, Harvard Business Sch; *m* 1, 4 Sept 1954 (m dis 1989), Venice Marigold (Rosie), da of late Capt Lord (Arthur) Francis Henry Hill, (yr s of 6 Marquess of Downside); 3 s (Rupert John Molesworth b 11 March 1955, Hugh F b 22 June 1956, Dickon Michael b 9 Feb 1962), 1 da (Anna Lucy b 19 June 1965); m 2, 1989, Patricia Margaret (Tita), o da of late Brig Hugh Ronald Norman, DSO, MC, of St Clere, Kemsing, Kent, and formerly w of Henry Colum Crickton-Stuart; *Career* Lt Scots Guards served Malaya 1949; dir: London Assurance 1957-, Witan Investment Co Ltd 1958-85, Steel Co of Wales 1959-67, Lazard Bros and Co Ltd 1960-, Marconi Co Ltd 1963-68, Sun Alliance & London Insurance Group 1965-, English Electric Co Ltd 1966-68, GEC Ltd 1968-70, British Match Corporation Ltd 1969-73, Swedish Match Co 1973-85, Maersk Co Ltd 1986-; chm Commonwealth Development Corporation 1980-89, Siam Selective Growth Trust 1990-; dep chm ECGD Advsy Cncl 1975-80; fin advsr to Export Gp for the Constructional Industs 1961-85; chm BBA 1976-78, pres Anglo-Taiwan Trade Ctee 1976-86; memb Inst Int d'Etudes Bancaires 1971-85; memb Court Worshipful Co of Fishmongers 1973-, Prime Warden 1989-90; *Recreations* all sports, deer, gardening; *Clubs* All England Lawn Tennis and Croquet (memb Ctee), Queen's, MCC, Pratt's; *Style*— The Rt Hon The Lord Kindersley; West Green Farm, Shipbourne, Kent TN11 9PU (☎ 0732 810293); 25 Grafton Square, London SW4 0DB (☎ 071 622 1198); 21 Moorfields, London EC2P 2HT (☎ 071 588 2721, fax 071 628 2485)

KING, Alexander John (Alex); s of Alexander King (d 1977), of Banstead, Surrey, and Ivy Ellen King (d 1989); *b* 9 Nov 1947; *Educ* Reigate GS, Sch of Business Ealing Tech Coll (BA); *m* 28 April 1979, Susan Frances, da of Kenneth Plumbe, of Grange Over Sands, Cumbria; 2 s (Adrian Mark b 1980, Laurence Charles b 1981), 1 da (Gemma Ann Louise b 1984); *Career* gp personnel mangr Bristol Myers Co 1972-78, gp personnel and admin mangr Crystalate Holdings plc 1978-86; dir: Crystalate Services Ltd 1982-86, Royal Worcester Spode Ltd 1984-86; personnel mangr Rotaprint plc 1986-88, chm The King Partnership Ltd 1987-; memb: Fin and Gen Purposes Ctee Tunbridge Wells Cons Assoc 1987-, Kent CC 1989-, CC Devpt Planning and Transportation Ctee 1989-, CC Policy and Resources Ctee 1990-; chm CC Econ Devpt and Tourism Sub Ctee 1990-; FIPM, FBIM, MInstD, assoc Inst of Mgmnt Conslts; *Recreations* DIY, Travel, Politics; *Style*— Alex King, Esq; Whispering Firs, Maidstone Rd, Horsmonden, Kent TN12 8NE (☎ 089 272 2292, fax 089 272 3828)

KING, Brian Maurice; s of Maurice James King, and late Grace Mary, *née* Escott; *b* 8 Aug 1933; *Educ* Westcliff HS, Southend Sch of Architecture; *m* 23 Aug 1958, Joan, da of Arthur Rouse; 2 s (Andrew James b 1961, Daniel John b 1963); *Career* architect and landscape architect; formed own practice 1982; chm Wells Housing Assoc, served in Friends Ambulance Unit Int Serv 1956-58; ARIBA; *Recreations* dinghy sailing, painting, drawing, walking; *Clubs* Wilsonian; *Style*— Brian King, Esq; 67 Kingswood Rd, Bromley, Kent BR2 0NL (☎ 081 460 7658); 34 Hill Rise, Richmond, Surrey TW10 6UA (☎ 081 948 8191)

KING, John Beverley; s of Prof Ronald King, and Margaret Anne, *née* Williams; *b* 8 June 1944; *Educ* Hampton Sch, London Hosp Med Coll (MB BS); *m* 1 Aug 1967, Deirdre Joanne, da of Dennis Henry George Walker (d 1979); 1 s (Toby St John b 8 July 1969), 1 da (Polly Megan b 11 Sept 1971); *Career* sr lectr in orthopaedic and trauma surgery and dir Dept of Sports Med London Hosp Med Coll, hon conslt The Royal London Hosp; author of 50 papers on orthopaedics trauma and sports med; memb: Med Bd The Nat Sports Centre at Crystal Palace, Bd London Sports Med Inst; sometime cncl memb: Br Assoc Sport and Med, Br Assoc for Surgery of the Knee, Int Knee Soc, Br Orthopaedic Assoc, RSM, BMA, Biological Engrg Soc, Bioelectricial Repair and Growth Soc, Acad of Surgical Res; FRCS 1974; *Books* Sports Injuries (co-ed, 1986); *Recreations* windsurfing; *Clubs* Athenaeum; *Style*— John King, Esq; The Royal London Hospital, London E1 1BB (☎ 071 377 7000)

KING, Vice Adm Sir Norman Ross Dutton; KBE (1989); s of Sir Norman King, KCMG (d 1963), and Mona, *née* Dutton (d 1982); family name which was adopted from town of Dutton in Cheshire can be traced back to Sir Thomas Dutton of Dutton, Sheriff of Cheshire in 1226; *b* 19 March 1933; *Educ* Fonthill Sch, RNC Dartmouth; *m* 1967, Patricia Rosemary, da of Dr Lionel Brian Furber (d 1981); 2 da (Annabelle b 1970, Melissa b 1978); *Career* CO HMS Leopard 1967-68, XO HMS Intrepid 1972-73, NA to Second Sea Lord 1975-77, RCDS 1978, CO HMS Newcastle 1979-80, Dir of Naval Offr Appts (Seamen Offrs) 1983-84, Cmdr Br Navy Staff Washington, Br Naval Attaché Washington, UKNLR to SACLANT 1985-86, Naval Sec 1987, COS to Cdr Allied Naval Forces S Europe 1988-; *Recreations* tennis, music, chess; *Clubs* Royal Navy of 1765 and 1785; *Style*— Vice Adm Sir Norman King, KBE; c/o Lloyds Bank, Faversham, Kent

KING, Dr Ronald Charles; s of William Charles King (d 1979), and Edith Jane, *née* Lockyer (d 1978); *b* 8 July 1924; *Educ* Peter Symonds' Sch Winchester, St Bartholomew's Hosp Med Coll Univ of London (MB BS, MD, MRCP); *m* 9 April 1949, Patricia, da of Harold Frederick Jackson (d 1952); 2 s (Christopher b 22 Sept 1950, David b 13 Aug 1952), 2 da (Susan b 8 Feb 1956, Rosemary b 19 June 1960); *Career* Lt-Col RAMC (AER) ret 1960; instr and res assoc Univ of Michigan USA 1956-57, casualty physician St Bartholomew's Hosp London 1958-60, conslt physician Tunbridge Wells DHA 1960-84, clinical tutor Tunbridge Wells Health Dist 1966-74, reg advsr RCP 1974-80, dean of Postgrad Med Educn SE Thames RHA 1984-90, asst dir Br Postgrad Med Fedn 1984-90, chief exec Jt Centre for Educnl Res and Devpt in Med 1990-, princ med offr Nat Provident Inst; fndr tstee Tunbridge Wells Postgrad Centre Tst, chm Advsy Ctee of Deans of Eng and Wales; memb: SE Thames RHA, NHS Trg Authy, BMA; FRCP, FRSA, FRSM; *Books* Practical Therapeutics (jtly, 1962); *Recreations* skiing, canal cruising, hill walking, jogging, victorian oils and watercolours, victorian books; *Style*— Dr Ronald King; Broadlands, Camden Park, Tunbridge Wells, Kent TN2 4TW (☎ 0892 25586); Joint Centre for Educational Research and Development in Medicine, 33 Millman St, London WC1N 3EJ (☎ 071 831 6222, fax 071 831 7599)

KING, Sir Wayne Alexander; 8 Bt (UK 1815), of Charlestown, Roscommon;

s of Sir Peter Alexander King, 7 Bt (d 1973); *b* 2 Feb 1962; *Style*— Sir Wayne King, Bt; 146 High St, Almonte, Ontario, Canada KOA 1AO

KINKEAD-WEEKES, Prof Mark; s of Lt-Col Alfred Bernard (Bill) Kinkead-Weekes, MC (d 1960), and Vida May, *née* Kinkead (d 1946); *b* 26 April 1931; *Educ* Potchefstroom Boys HS, Univ of Cape Town, Brasenose Coll Oxford; *m* March 1959, (Margaret) Joan, da of Benjamin Irvine (d 1966); 2 s (Paul b 1962, Timothy Guy b 1963); *Career* lectr Univ of Edinburgh 1958-65 (asst lectr 1956-58); Univ of Kent at Canterbury: lectr 1965-66, sr lectr 1966-74, prof of English and American lit 1974-84, pro vice chllr 1974-77, emeritus prof 1984-; govr: ChCh Coll Canterbury, Kings Sch Rochester, London Contemporary Dance Tst; *Books* William Golding: A Critical Study (with I Gregor, 1967, 2 edn 1984), Samuel Richardson: Dramatic Novelist (1973), D H Lawrence: The Rainbow (ed, 1989); *Recreations* golf; *Style*— Prof Mark Kinkead-Weekes; 5 Albion Place, Ramsgate, Kent CT11 8HQ (☎ 0843 593168); Rutherford College, The University, Canterbury CT2 7NX (☎ 0227 764000 ext 3437)

KIRKE, Rear Adm David Walter; CB (1967), CBE (1962, OBE 1945); s of Percy St George Kirke (d 1966), and Alice Gertrude (d 1959), da of Sir James Gibson-Craig, 3 Bt; *b* 13 March 1915; *Educ* RNC Dartmouth; *m* 1, 1936 (m dis 1950), Tessa, da of Capt Patrick O'Connor; 1 s; m 2, 1956, Marion Margaret, da of late Dr James Gibb; 1 s, 1 da; *Career* chief of Naval Aviation Indian Navy New Delhi 1959-62, Flag Offr Naval Flying Trg 1965-68; *Recreations* golf; *Clubs* Army and Navy; *Style*— Rear Adm David Kirke, CB, CBE; Lismore House, Pluckley, Kent (☎ 023 384 439)

KIRKNESS, (Rosemary) Jane; da of Dr Cedric Angus Selway, of Harlow, Essex, and Josephine, *née* Geeson; *b* 17 Feb 1960; *Educ* Loughton Co HS Loughton Essex, Middlesex Hosp London (SRN), London Sch of Fashion (Higher Dip); *m* 6 July 1985, Julian Patrick, s of Lt-Col Desmond Kirkness (d 1980), of Chilham, Kent; *Career* staff nurse: Middlesex Hosp 1982-83 (nurse 1979-82), London Clinic 1983-84; product specialist in diabetes coronary heart disease and lipids Farmitalia Carlo Erba St Albans 1987-88, branch mangr Mann & Co Estate Agents Canterbury 1988-; *Recreations* dress designing, reading, squash, tennis; *Style*— Mrs Jane Kirkness; 47A Court St, Faversham, Kent (☎ 0795 532 485); 26 Watling St, Canterbury, Kent (☎ 0227 454 125)

KIRKWOOD, Hon James Stuart; s of 2 Baron Kirkwood (d 1970), and hp of bro, 3 Baron; *b* 19 June 1937; *Educ* Rugby, Trinity Hall Cambridge; FRICS; *m* 1965, Alexander Mary, da of late Alec Dyson, of Holt, Norfolk; 2 da; *Style*— The Hon James Kirkwood; The Cearne, Kent Hatch, Crockham Hill, Edenbridge, Kent

KIRWAN, Helen Ann Hermione; da of John Gilbert Roberts (d 1985), of Ludlow, and Irene Marguerite Hermione, *née* Graham; *b* 4 June 1949; *Educ* The Ladies' Coll Cheltenham Glos, Trinity Coll Dublin, The New Univ of Ulster Coleraine NI; *m* 3 July 1976, Reginald William Kirwan, s of Maj Lionel E Kirwan (d 1923), of Coonor, India; *Career* social worker London Borough of Ealing 1972-74, sr social worker Royal Borough of Richmond upon Thames; called to the Irish Bar 1980; practised 1980-85; called to the Bar Middle Temple 1983; principal legal offr Revenue Slr's Office Somerset House 1985-89, practised at English Bar 1989-; memb Royal Cwlth Soc; *Recreations* gardening, art, listening to music; *Style*— Mrs Helen Kirwan; Heron Manor, Chilham, Kent CT4 8DG (☎ 0227 730256); Stour Chambers, Barton Mill House, Barton Mill Rd, Canterbury, Kent CT1 1BP (☎ 0227 764899, fax 0227 764941)

KITTEL, Gerald Anthony; s of Francis William Berthold Kittel, of Faraway, South View Rd, Pinner Hill, Middx, and Eileen Winifred, *née* Maybanks (d 1973); *b* 24 Feb 1947; *Educ* Merchant Taylors', Univ of Poitiers (History Dip), Ealing Poly; *m* 26 April 1975, Jean Samantha, *née* Beveridge; 2 s (Christian b 1969, Ashley b 1976), 1 da (Natalie b 1979); *Career* md Northey Bunting Kittel Advertising & Marketing and Paulsgrove Ltd; memb Int Advertising Assoc; MIPA, MInstM; *Recreations* riding, squash, tennis; *Clubs* St James, Park Place, Old Merchant Taylors' Soc; *Style*— Gerald Kittel, Esq; Valence End, Hosey Hill, French St, Westerham, Kent TN16 1PN; 20 Lime Court, Gipsy Lane, Putney, London SW15 5RJ

KNIGHT, Capt Christopher Moreton; s of Moreton Thorpe Knight, JP (d 1982), and Laura, *née* Noble (d 1964); *b* 31 May 1934; *Educ* Felsted, Sir John Cass Coll London (Master Mariner); *m* 26 Nov 1987, Janet Vivien, da of Alfred Arthur Aston (d 1984); 1 s (Peter b 14 Feb 1989); *Career* dir JP Knight Ltd 1964; chm: Shaftesbury Homes and Arethusa 1973-, Br Tugowners Assoc 1974-76, Victoria League for Cwlth Friendship 1990-; memb: Nautical Inst 1975, Chm's Advsy Panel BSI 1981, Bd of Cwlth Tst 1989; Liveryman Hon Co of Master Mariners 1973; Freeman: City of London 1973, Worshipful Co of Watermen and Lightermen 1985; *Recreations* wood carving, bee keeping; *Clubs* Naval and Military, Cwlth Tst; *Style*— Capt Christopher Knight; Cooling Castle, Cliffe-at-Hoo, Kent ME3 8DT; J P Knight Ltd, 348 High St, Rochester, Kent ME1 1DH (☎ 0634 826633, fax 0634 829093)

KNIGHT, Peter John Talbot; s of John Knight, and Gillian Ann, *née* Leather; *b* 12 Oct 1961; *Educ* Malvern; *m* 21 May 1988, Deborah Ann, da of Ronald Frederick Hunter, of Reading; *Career* former gp md: Jackson Property Services, Halifax Property Services; md: Phoenix New Homes, P & I Properties, La Manga Property Services; *Recreations* golf; *Clubs* Sundridge Park Golf; *Style*— Peter Knight, Esq; 2 East St, Bromley, Kent BR1 1QX (☎ 081 313 3132, fax 081 290 4562)

KNIGHT, Stephen Charles; s of Reginald Frank Knight, of 32 Grangemill Road, London, and Sheila Ethel Clarice, *née* Jones; *b* 25 Nov 1954; *Educ* Colfe's Sch, Bromley Coll; *m* 30 July 1977, Lesley Joan, da of Harold Leonard Davison, of 4 Donaldson Rd, London; 1 s (Timothy David Stephen b 1988); *Career* gen mangr mktg and devpt Newcross Building Soc 1983-84, vice pres Citibank 1984-87, chm Private Label Mortgage Services Ltd 1987-; FCBSI 1977, MBIM 1978, MInstM 1979; *Recreations* squash, cricket, freelance writing; *Clubs* IOD; *Style*— Stephen Knight, Esq; Little Grange, Orpington Rd, Chislehurst, Kent BR7 6RA (☎ 0689 33667); Brettenham House, 14-15 Lancaster Place, London WC2E 7EB (☎ 071 379 5232, fax 071 379 4078, car tel 0836 773240 and 0836 243659)

KNOTT, Air Vice-Marshal Ronald George; CB (1967), DSO (1945), DFC (1944), AFC (1956); s of Capt George Knott (d 1952), and Edith Rose, *née* Anderson (d 1981); *b* 19 Dec 1917; *Educ* Borden GS; *m* 1941, Hermione Violet, da of Col Robert Bernard Phayre (d 1964); 3 s (Terence, Nicholas (decd), Andrew), 1 da (Alexandra); *Career* RAF Dir of Op Requirements MOD 1963-67, Sr Air Staff Offr ME Air Force 1967-70, Air Offr Admin Air Support Cmd 1970-72, ret; chm Weald of Kent Preservation Soc; *Recreations* wine growing, property restoration; *Style*— Air Vice Marshal Ronald Knott, CB, DSO, DFC, AFC; Pilgrims Cottage, Charing, Ashford, Kent TN27 0DR

KNOWLES, Prof Christopher John; s of Frank Knowles, of Knott End, Lancashire, and Alice Clayton, *née* Sims; *b* 2 March 1943; *Educ* Univ of Leicester (BSc, PhD); *m* 14 July 1968, Denise Henriette, da of Paul Georges Fouquet (d 1976); 1 s (Peter b 1969); *Career* post-doctoral fell: Dartmouth Coll USA 1967-69, Univ of Warwick 1969-70; Univ of Kent at Canterbury: lectr 1970-77, sr lectr 1977-80, reader 1980-84, prof microbial biochemistry 1984-; sec Euro Environmental Res Orgn; CChem, FRSC 1986, FRSA 1987; *Recreations* walking, skiing, cooking; *Style*— Prof Christopher Knowles; Biological Laboratory, University of Kent, Canterbury, Kent (☎ 0227 764000)

KOFLER, Rev Leonhard; s of Johan Kofler, and Maria, *née* Ausserlechner; *b* 12 April 1935; *Educ* secdy sch Hall Tyrol Austria, Brixen, N Italy, Diocesan Seminary, Mill Hill, Wellington Univ NZ, Trent Univ Italy (DSoc), Salzburg Univ (PhD); *Career* teacher of Greek and Latin Ireland 1959-60, mission propaganda Tyrol Austria 1960-62, work among the Maoris NZ 1962-67, i/c Boys' Hostel 1968-73, lectr in pastoral psychology, counselling and Biblical Greek Missionary Inst London 1978-80, vice rector Mill Hill Coll 1979-80, extra mural lectr in pastoral psychology Univ of London 1979-85, pres and lectr Missionary Inst 1980-85, fndr dir Inst of St Anselm Damascus House London 1985- (Inst moved to Cliftonville Kent 1986); *Style*— The Rev Leonhard Kofler; Institute of St Anselm, Edgar Rd, Cliftonville, Kent CT9 2EU (☎ 0843 221865)

KOOWAREE, Serge Joseph Georgie (George); s of Raymond Joseph André Koowaree, and Eva Marie, *née* Achille; *b* 9 July 1934; *Educ* Windsor Coll, Kilburn Poly; *m* 15 Dec 1962, Joy Muriel; 3 da (Linda Marie b 21 April 1963, Carole b 19 Oct 1967, Eva b 30 Jan 1972); *Career* Nat Serv RAF 1959-61; registered mental nurse 1979, charge nurse 1981-85; memb Advsy Ctees: St Mary's Youth Club, Ashford Parochial Charities, Ashford Twinning Assoc, SE Kent Community Health Cncl; borough cncllr 1987-; memb Royal Coll of Nursing 1979-, hon memb Psychiatric Nurses Assoc 1979-; *Recreations* driving, photography, reading; *Style*— George Koowaree, Esq; 56 Birling Rd, Ashford, Kent TN24 8BB (☎ 0233 34760)

KRUDY von WALDENUZZI, Elemer Arpad; s of Dr Elemer Stephen Krudy, of 9 Thorsden Way, London, and Dr Aranka Elisabeth Krudy, *née* Gallai; *b* 6 June 1945; *Educ* Kolcsey Ferenc Gimnazium Budapest, Croydon Tech Coll, Univ of Aston (BSc); *m* 19 Aug 1972, Carol Anne, da of Collet Herbert Samuel James Penny (d 1974); 2 s (Christopher b 19 Sept 1974, Edward b 15 Aug 1976); *Career* sr internal auditor The Hertz Corporation 1979-80, accounting mangr Hertz Europe Ltd 1980-82, asst controller Hertz France 1982-83, controller Hertz Belux 1983-86, asst euro controller Hertz Europe Ltd 1986, fin controller Harting Elektronik 1987-, fin dir Harting Elektronic (UK) Ltd and int controller Harting Elektronic GMBH 1990-; ACA; *Style*— Elemer Krudy von Waldenuzzi, Esq; 21 Clockhouse Rd, Beckenham, Kent (☎ 081 658 9221); Harting Elektronik Ltd, Airport Estate, Biggin Hill, Kent TN16 3BW (☎ 0959 71411)

KUMAR, Prof (Jagdish) Krishan; *b* 11 Aug 1942; *Educ* William Ellis Sch London, St John's Coll Cambridge (BA, MA), LSE (MSc); *Career* prodr Talks Dept BBC 1972-74, prof of social thought Univ of Kent 1987- (lectr in sociology 1967-77, reader in sociology 1977-87); tstee Action Soc Tst; *Books* Prophecy and Progress (1978), Utopia and Anti-Utopia in Modern Times (1987), Rise of Modern Society (1988); *Style*— Prof Krishan Kumar; Keynes College, University of Kent, Canterbury CT2 7NP (☎ 0227 764000)

KVERNDAL, Ole Sigvard; s of Thor Bjorn Kverndal (d 1953), of Duchess of Bedford Walk, Campden Hill, London, and Agnes Tschudi, *née* Madsen (d

1982); *b* 3 Nov 1926; *Educ* The Abbey Sch Beckenham, Haileybury and Herts, Univ of Glasgow; *m* 22 March 1952, Brenda Olive, da of A C Skinner, of Bickley, Kent; 1 s (Simon Richard b 1958), 2 da (Deborah Jane b 1955, Vanessa Helen b 1965); *Career* W K Webster and Co: joined 1948, ptnr 1953, sr ptnr 1961; dir: Pandl Claims Ltd, Ship Surveys Ltd, SE Region Lloyds Bank (non-exec); former Kent co rep and memb Exec Ctee RFU, hon sec and later pres Kent Co RFU, hon treas and later pres London RFU, chm Kent Co Playing Fields Assoc, hon treas and chm Scandinavian Benevolent Soc, life govr and memb Cncl and Fin and Gen Purposes Ctee Haileybury and ISC; pres: Norwegian-Br C of C, Haileybury Soc; memb Court of Assts Worshipful Co of Shipwrights of London; Chev First Class of Order of the Dannebrog (Denmark), Chev First Class of the Royal Order of St Olave (Norway); *Recreations* tennis, squash, swimming, windsurfing, travel; *Clubs* Naval, Den Norske Klub; *Style*— O S Kverndal, Esq; Colgates, Shoreham Lane, Halstead, Sevenoaks, Kent TN14 7BY (☎ 0959 34267); W K Webster and Co, 6 Lloyds Ave, London EC3N 3AX (☎ 081 300 7744, fax 081 309 1266)

L

L'ESTRANGE, Rev Canon Guy James Albert; s of Rev Canon Frederick H P L'Estrange (d 1963), of Dublin, and Kathleen, *née* Hurford (d 1947); *b* 13 March 1924; *Educ* Ellesmere Coll Shropshire, St Columba's Coll Dublin, Royal Acad Inst Belfast, Univ of Dublin (BA, MA); *m* 29 Sept 1965, Helen Margaret, da of Harry Ashton (d 1967), of Batley, Yorkshire; 1 s (Timothy John Nicholas b 23 Dec 1967); *Career* asst priest St Martin Belfast 1947-51, dean's vicar minor canon and chapter clerk St Patrick's Cathedral Dublin 1951-63, press offr Church of Ireland 1960-63, precentor of Canterbury Cathedral 1963-68, headmaster Canterbury Cathedral Choir Sch 1963-64, rector of Saltwood 1968-89, rural dean of Elham 1974-80, canon of Canterbury Cathedral 1981-89, archbishop's sec for Bd of Miny 1985-88, canon emeritus of Canterbury Cathedral 1989-; nat trg offr for Ireland Boys' Bde 1954-63, chm sch govrs; *Style—* The Rev Canon L'Estrange; 36 St Stephen's Hill, Canterbury, Kent CT2 7AX (☎ 0227 763226)

LACAMP, Philippe Frederick; s of Philippe Albert Lacamp (d 1982), of Milton Regis, Kent, and Dorothea Jeanette, *née* Barker; *b* 12 March 1940; *Educ* City of London Sch; *m* 31 July 1965, Marie-Louise, da of Capt Peter Stephens Impey, of High Barn, Finstall, Worcs; 1 s (Philippe Paul b 5 Feb 1969), 2 da (Melissa b 26 April 1971, Camilla b 18 Dec 1972); *Career* dir Allders Ltd 1973-82, independent conslt 1982-; mangr C of E Primary Sch, tstee Contacts Charity for Handicapped Children, chm St Mary's Norton Restoration Ctee; Freeman: City of London 1961, Worshipful Co of Blacksmiths 1966; MBCS 1963; *Books* Microcomputers in Retail (1984); *Recreations* singing, piano, tennis, golf; *Clubs* Kent and Canterbury; *Style—* Philippe Lacamp, Esq; Prospect House, High St, Westerham, Kent TN16 1RG (☎ 0959 644 22, fax 0959 644 22)

LACY, John Trend; CBE (1982); s of Rev Hubert Lacy (d 1982), and Gertrude Markham (d 1983); *b* 15 March 1928; *Educ* Kings Sch Ely Cambs; *m* 16 June 1956, Pamela, da of Jack Guerin; 1 s (Nicholas b 23 Dec 1957); *Career* RN 1945-48; Cons Pty agent London and Bucks 1950-60, CCO agent W Mids N and SE 1960-85, gen dir Cons Pty Campaigning 1989- (dir 1985-89); memb Nat Soc Cons and Unionist Agents; *Recreations* politics, family; *Clubs* St Stephens, Carlton; *Style—* John Lacy, Esq, CBE; Conservative Central Office, 32 Smith Square, London SW1P 3HH (☎ 071 222 9000, fax 071 222 1135)

LADER, Prof Malcolm Harold; s of Abe Lader (d 1979), of Liverpool, and Minnie, *née* Sholl; *b* 27 Feb 1936; *Educ* Liverpool Inst HS, Univ of Liverpool (BSc, MB ChB, MD), Univ of London (PhD, DPM, DSc); *m* 16 April 1961, Susan Ruth, da of Louis Packer (d 1990), of Hendon, Middx; 3 da (Deborah b 1966, Vicki b 1969, Charlotte b 1972); *Career* memb external scientific staff MRC 1966-, conslt Bethlem Royal and Maudsley Hosp 1970-, prof clinical psychopharmacology Univ of London 1978-; tstee Mental Health Fndn; memb Advsy Cncl Misuse of Drugs; FRCPsych 1971; *Books* Psychiatry on Trial (1977), Dependence on Tranquillizers (1984), Guide to the use of Psychotropic Drugs (1986); *Recreations* antiques, English watercolours; *Clubs* RSM; *Style—* Prof Malcolm Lader; 11 Kelsey Way, Beckenham, Kent BR3 3LP (☎ 081 650 0366); 10 Dedham Mill, Dedham, Essex CO7 6DH; Inst of Psychiatry, Decrespigny Park, London SE5 8AF (☎ 071 703 0770, fax 071 703 5796)

LAINTON, Keith Frederick; s of Frederick Lainton (d 1990), of Sheffield, and Eva, *née* Corker; *b* 4 Jan 1940; *Educ* Manchester GS, Univ of Manchester (BA), Open Univ (BA); *m* 2 March 1968, Edith Mary, da of Walter Shaw (d 1967), of Altrincham; 2 da (Julia Alexandra Helen b 1969, Ruth Elizabeth b 1974); *Career* res planner Proctor and Gamble 1961-64, commercial offr Reckitt and Coleman 1964-65, head of market res and statistics ICI 1965-69, mktg res mangr Abbott Laboratories 1969-72, dir MI (PA) Ltd 1972-73, md Survey Force Ltd 1973-; former nat chm Br Pharmaceutical Market Res Gp; former memb: Canterbury Diocesan Synod, Canterbury Diocesan Bd of Fin; church warden St Peter and St Paul Borden, former chm Parent Teachers Assoc Westlands, govr Borden Primary Sch; *Books* Advertising Research (1965), Techniques in Copy Testing (1968), Rôle of Marketing Research (1986), Directing Sales Force (1987); *Style—* Keith Lainton, Esq; Survey Force Ltd, 18 High St, Maidstone, Kent ME9 8HW (☎ 0795 423778)

LAIRD, Gavin Harry; CBE (1988); s of James Laird, and Frances Luxton Laird; *b* 14 March 1933; *Educ* Clydebank HS; *m* 4 Oct 1956, Catherine Gillies (Reena), *née* Campbell; 1 da (Fiona Campbell b 14 April 1961); *Career* AEU: elected regnl offr Scotland 1972, exec cncl memb 1975-82, gen sec 1982-; non-exec dir: Highlands and Islands Development Board 1973-75, Scottish TV 1986-, Court of The Bank of England 1986-, FS Assurance 1988- (became Britannia Life 1990); pt/t memb: British National Oil Corporation 1976-86, Scottish Development Agency 1986-; memb: Gen Cncl of Scottish TUC 1972-75, Arts Cncl of GB 1983-86, Ed Bd European Business Journal; govr: London Business Sch 1988-, Atlantic Coll 1988-; Napier Technical Coll 1989-; hon fell Paisley Tech Coll; *Recreations* hill walking, music, reading, avoiding work; *Clubs* Royal Scottish Automobile, North Kent Ramblers Assoc; *Style—* Gavin Laird, Esq, CBE; 35 Southlands Grove, Bromley, Kent BR1 2DA; Amalgamated Engineering Union, 110 Peckham Road, London SE15 5EL (☎ 071 703 4231, fax 071 701 7862)

LAIRD, Robert Edward; s of Robert Laird (d 1975), of Seaford, Sussex, and Esther Margaret, *née* Stoney (d 1976); *b* 25 Dec 1940; *Educ* Aldenham, Harvard Univ; *m* 8 Aug 1964, Mary Theresa, da of Martin Cooke (d 1969), of Galway, Ireland; 2 s (Robert Richard Martin b 1964, Julian Alexander b 1968) 1 da (Caroline b 1971); *Career* various appts Unilever Ltd 1959-76, dir Carnation Foods 1977-80, md Vandemoortele 1980-86, chm Polar Entertainment Group 1986-88, dir Keith Butters Ltd 1988-89, head of mktg Tate & Lyle Sugars 1989; cncl memb Coronary Prevention Gp; Freeman: City of London 1984, Worshipful Co of Upholders 1984; MInsTM 1978, FBIM 1980, MIOD 1982; *Recreations* golf, squash, jogging, reading, genealogy; *Clubs* Old Aldenhamians, Harvard Business Sch Club of London, The Sportsman; *Style—* R E Laird, Esq; 42 Elsham Rd, Kensington, London W14 8HB (☎ 071 602 2843); Tate & Lyle Sugars, Enterprise House, 45 Homesdale Rd, Bromley, Kent BR2 9TE (☎ 081 464 6556, fax 081 290 0721, telex 917184)

LAKE, Terence Edward; s of Walter Joseph Lake (d 1978), and Maud, *née* Ford (d 1951); *b* 26 July 1933; *Educ* East Ham GS for Boys, Univ of Leicester (BSc); *m* 11 June 1955, Margaret, da of Gerald Steechman: 2 da (Hazel (Mrs Anwell) b 2 June 1957, Helen (Mrs Kitchingham) b 24 Jan 1959); *Career* Nat Serv 1954-56, Sch of Ammunition Bromley (Sgt ammunition examiner); gp fin controller Elliott Automation 1960-68, commercial dir and md Instrument Maintenance and Erection Co 1968-75, dir Roxby Engineering Ltd 1981-; Liveryman Worshipful Co of Scientific Instrument Makers; *Recreations* reading, gardening, travel, wine; *Style—* Terence Lake, Esq; 7 Lawpings, New Barn, Longfield, Kent DA3 7NH (☎ 04 747 4190); Roxby House, Station Rd, Sidcup DA15 7EJ (☎ 081 300 3393, fax 081 300 4400, telex 896172 ROXBY G)

LAKEY, Prof John Richard Angwin; s of late William Richard Lakey, and late Edith, *née* Hartley; *b* 28 June 1929; *Educ* Morley GS, Univ of Sheffield (BSc, PhD); *m* 22 Dec 1955, Dr Pamela Janet Lakey, JP, da of late Eric Clifford Lancey; 3 da (Joanna Margaret, Philippa Mary (Mrs Lewry), Nicola Janet (Dr King)); *Career* res posts Simon Carves Ltd, secondment to AERE Harwell and GEC 1953-60; RNC Greenwich: asst prof 1960-80, prof 1980-89, dean 1984-86 and 1988-89; reactor shielding conslt DG Ships 1967-89, radiation conslt WHO 1973-74, visiting prof Univ of Surrey 1988, fndr John Lakes Assocs 1989, memb CNAA Physics Bd 1973-82, pubns dir Int Radiation Protection Assoc 1979-88, external examiner Univ of Surrey 1980-86, visiting lectr Harvard Univ 1984-, memb Ed Bd Physics in Med and Biology 1980-83, news ed Health Physics 1980-88; regnl scientific advsr No5 Region 1984-, chm UK Liaison Ctee for Scis Allied to Med and Biology 1984-87, pres Inst Nuclear Engrs 1988-90 (vice pres 1983-87), vice pres London Int Youth Sci Fortnight 1988-, pres Int Radiation Protection Assoc 1988-; vice pres Euro Nuclear Soc 1989-, memb Medway Health Authy 1987-90; Freeman City of London 1988, Liveryman Worshipful Co of Engineers 1988; Eur Ing, CEng, FINucE, FInstE, CPhys; memb: Soc for Radiological Protection, American Nuclear Soc; *Books* Protection Against Radiation (1961), Radiation Protection Measurement: philosophy and implementation (1975), ALARA principles and practices (1987), Non Ionising Radiation Guidelines (1990), papers on nuclear safety, radiological protection and management of emergencies; *Recreations* yachting, photography, conversation; *Clubs* Athenaeum, Medway Yacht, RNSA; *Style—* Prof John Lakey; John Lakey Associates, 5 Pine Rise, Meopham, Gravesend, Kent (☎ 0474 812551)

LAMBERT, Chief Supt David Philip; s of William John Lambert, of Royal Hosp, Chelsea, and Norma Ella, *née* Roberts (d 1982); *b* 20 Nov 1947; *Educ* LSE (BSc); *m* 6 May 1967, Sheila Patricia, da of Staff Sgt Robert Neudegg; 1 s (Mark Paul b 1967), 2 da (Jane Marie b 1969, Sophie Louisa b 1980); *Career* Beds Police 1967-87 (Chief Inspr 1986), Chief Supt (ops) Kent Co Constabulary 1990- (Supt i/c computing 1987-90); *Recreations* badminton, caravanning, gardening; *Style—* Chief Supt David Lambert; Police Headquarters, Sutton Rd, Maidstone, Kent ME15 9BZ (☎ 0622 690690)

LAMBERT, Harry Paul; s of James Lambert (d 1979), of Kent, and Irene, *née* Kennedy; *b* 20 Feb 1944; *Educ* Chorlton Tech High, Stockport Coll; *m* 1974, Shan Elizabeth Rose, da of Trevor Watkins, of Kent; 1 s (Mark James Trevor b 1981), 1 da (Katie Elizabeth b 1982); *Career* chm and chief exec The Adscene Group plc (dir 1974-); dir Assoc of Free Newspapers 1983-; *Style—* Harry Lambert, Esq; Newspaper House, Wincheap, Canterbury, Kent CT1 3YR

LAMPARD, Peter; s of Desmonde Robert Lampard (d 1987), of Maidstone, Kent, and Nora Edith, *née* Startup (d 1983); *b* 16 March 1945; *Educ* Maidstone GS, Univ of Reading (BSc); *m* 6 Dec 1980, Penelope, da of Wilfred Mordue, of Perth, WA; 1 da (Holly b 1981); *Career* farmer 1970-; memb: Longley Parish Cncl 1986-, Linton Angling Soc 1985-, Game Conservancy 1986-; ctee memb: Maidstone Branch NFU 1980-, Kent NFU Potato and Vegetable Ctee; *Recreations* shooting, fishing, cricket; *Clubs* E Sutton Cricket; *Style—* Peter Lampard, Esq; The Rectory Farm, Langley, Maidstone, Kent (☎ 0622 861377)

LANCASTER, John Meredith; s of Dr Zikmund F Foltin, and Alica Foltinova, *née* Polakova; *b* 23 Aug 1919; *Educ* Komenius Univ Bratislava, Coll of Aeronautical Engrg London, LSE; *m* 12 June 1943, Jean Gertrude, da of Lt-Col George William Thomas Coles, TD; 2 s (Michael John b 1944, David John b 1967), 3 da (Jane Deirdre (Mrs Brentnall) b 1949, Sally Jean (Mrs de Elye Cole) b 1951, Judith Elisabeth b 1953); *Career* RAOC Workshop Unit 6 AA Div 1940-42, cmmnd E Surrey Regt 1942, Intelligence Corps, Interservice Topographical Dept 1943-46, Maj GSO2; head of mkt res Rio Tinto Co Ltd 1947-51, mktg exec Metallo-Chemical Refining Co 1952; The British Sulphur Corporation Ltd: joined 1953, md 1954-85, chm 1970-89, non-exec dir 1989-; dir CRU Holdings Co Ltd 1986-; chm and md: L & B Consultants Ltd 1985-, Seven Rocks Mining Ltd 1989-; chm: Orlestone Parish Cncl 1961-, Hamstreet Victory Hall 1966-, Hamstreet and Warchorme Branch Ashford Cons Assoc 1963- (memb Exec Ctee); memb: CPRE, Romney Marsh Level, Fertiliser Soc; Francis New Meml Medal; Lord of the Manor of Orlestone 1969-; Freeman City of London 1978, Liveryman Worshipful Co of Stationers and Newspaper Makers 1978; *Books* World Survey of Sulphur Resources (1966); *Recreations* swimming, skiing, gardening; *Clubs* Carlton; *Style—* John Lancaster, Esq; Court Lodge, Orlestone, Ashford, Kent (☎ 0233 732 339); 4 Eccleston Square, London SW1; 31 Mount Pleasant, London WC1X 0AD (☎ 071 837 5600, fax 071 837 0292, telex 918918 LONDON SULFEX G)

LANCASTER SMITH, Dr Michael John; s of Ronald George Lancaster Smith, of Hastings, E Sussex, and Marie Elizabeth, *née* Wright; *b* 4 Sept 1941; *Educ* Hastings GS, London Hosp Med Coll, Univ of London (BSc, MD); *m* 11 April 1964, Susan Frances Bayes, da of Arthur Bannister (d 1946); 1 s (Daniel James b 1969), 2 da (Catherine Claire b 1966, Naomi Louise b 1971); *Career* London Hosp: house offr and sr house offr 1966-68, registrar and sr registrar 1969-73; sr lectr Bart's 1973-74, conslt physician Queen Mary's Hosp 1974-, past clinical tutor (Univ of London) Queen Mary's Hosp Sidcup; numerous pubns in med jls and presentations to learned soc; past vice chm Bexley Health Authy; formerly represented Sussex at soccer and athletics; memb BMA, MBSG, FRCP; *Books* Ulcer and Non Ulcer Dyspepsia (1987), Problems in Practice - Gastroenterology (1982), Problems in Management - Gastroenterology (1985); *Recreations* cricket, theatre; *Style—* Dr Michael Lancaster Smith; Stableside House, 36 Southborough Rd, Bickley, Bromley, Kent BR1 2EB (☎ 081 467 4184); Queen Mary's Hospital, Frognal Lane, Sidcup, Kent DA14 6LT (☎ 081 302 2678)

LANDERS, Brian Whitfield; s of William Reginald Harry Whitfield Landers (d 1964), of Beckenham, and Gladys Winifred, *née* Widgery (d 1979); *b* 22 March 1921; *Educ* City of London Sch; *m* 7 Sept 1943, Elizabeth Joan Marguerite, da of John Pearce, of Wooburn Green, Bucks (d 1950); 2 da (Valerie Elizabeth b 1947, Rosalind Mary b 1954); *Career* Pilot RAF 1941-46, Flt Lt, Flying Boat Capt with coastal cmd; slr; sr ptnr Waterhouse and Co London 1982-86; chm Castle Baynard Ward Club 1973-74; pres: City of Westminster Law Soc 1977-78, John Carpenter Club 1981-82; Liveryman Worshipful Co of Basketmakers 1956-; *Recreations* photography, cricket; *Clubs* MCC, Forty, City Livery, John Carpenter (Old Citizens' Assoc); *Style—* Brian W Landers, Esq; Cobbleston, The Glen, Farnborough Park, Kent BR6 8LR (☎ 0689 856209)

LANE, Rev Canon Gerald; s of Gerald Lane (d 1964), of Gillingham, Kent, and Susanna Elizabeth Eleanor, *née* Leeder (d 1989); *b* 10 Aug 1929; *Educ* Gillingham Co GS, Univ of Durham (BA), Sarum Theol Coll; *m* 31 July 1971, Linda Mary Sibun, da of Laurence Sibun Hastings (d 1976); 1 da (Jennifer Mary b 1973); *Career* vicar: St Philip and St Mark Old Kent Rd 1959-67, St Nicholas Plumstead 1967-73, St Augustine Gillingham 1973-78, Hadlow 1978-; chaplain St Nicholas Hosp Plumstead 1967-73, hon chaplain to Hadlow Coll of Agric and Horticulture 1978-, hon canon Rochester 1987-; ctee memb: Hadlow Parish Cncl, Gillingham Careers Advice, Plumstead Hosp; memb and home ctee memb Rochester Diocesan Synod, sch govr; *Books* Realizing God (1975); *Recreations* music, piano and violin, reading, time with family and dog; *Style—* The Rev Canon Gerald Lane; The Vicarage, Maidstone Rd, Hadlow, Tonbridge, Kent TN11 0DJ (☎ 0732 850238)

LANE, John; CB (1981); s of Roger James Iddison Lane (d 1972), and Mary Elizabeth Lily, *née* Roberts (d 1982); *b* 23 Oct 1924; *Educ* John Lyon Sch, Harrow, Univ Coll Hull, LSE (BSc); *m* 1954, Ruth Ann, da of Thomas Victor Crocker (d 1941); 1 s (Robert); *Career* civil servant; under sec Depts of the Environment and Tport 1972-78, dep dir Central Statistical Office 1978-81, dep sec, ret; *Recreations* theatre, music, golf; *Clubs* Civil Service; *Style—* John Lane, Esq, CB; Fern Hill, 67 Mount Ephraim, Tunbridge Wells, Kent

LANE, Richard Ernest; s of Stanley William Lane, of 4 The Glebe, Penshurst, Tonbridge, Kent, and Nora, *née* Cheason; *b* 26 Sept 1943; *Educ* Cranbrook Sch Kent; *m* 19 April 1980, Paula Francesca Mary, da of George Slack Paul Hadley, of 5 Valley View Grove, Bradford, W Yorks; 1 s (Simon Paul William b 22 Sept 1981), 1 da (Rachel Mary b 13 Nov 1984); *Career* qualified CA with Deloittes 1968; ptnr Crane & Partners 1971- (joined 1970-); fndr and first chm Bromley Enterprise Agency Tst 1983-87; chm: Young Enterprise Bromley 1986-89, S E London Area Soc of CAs 1989-90, Croydon Family Health Serv Authy 1989-, Govrs Bromley Coll of Technol 1990- (govr 1987-); govr St Olave's Sch 1988-, memb S W Thames RHA 1990-; FCA 1976; *Recreations* skiing, golf, hockey umpire; *Clubs* Bromley Cricket, Bromley Hockey; *Style—* Richard Lane, Esq; 13 St Michaels Close, Bickley, Bromley, Kent BR1 2DX (☎ 081 464 4517); Crane & Partners, Rutland House, 44 Masons Hill, Bromley, Kent BR2 9EQ (☎ 081 464 0131, fax 081 464 6018)

LANGDON, Capt Jonathan Bertram Robert Louis; s of Capt John Edward Langdon, RN, of Hayling Is, and Nancy Langdon; *b* 1 Nov 1939; *Educ* Hurstpierpoint Coll, RNC Dartmouth; *m* 31 March 1962, Hilary Jean, da of John William Fox Taylor, OBE (d 1988), of Spain; 2 s (Andrew William b 1964, Stephen John (twin) b 1964), 1 da (Claire Fiona b 1967); *Career* RN RNC Dartmouth 1958, HM Ships Bermuda, Lincoln, Daring 1960-68; called to the Bar Gray's Inn 1970; Far East legal advsr Hong Kong 1973-75, RN Supply Sch 1975-77, Cdr 1977, HMS Norfolk 1977-79, MOD 1979-81, staff of C in C Naval Home Cmd 1981-83, asst rec SE Circuit 1983, sec to Naval Sec MOD 1983-86, Capt 1986, postgrad trg int law 1987-88, Chief Naval Judge Advocate 1988-90, rec SE Circuit 1989, sec to C in C Naval Home Cmd 1990-; *Recreations* sailing, gardening, history; *Style—* Capt Jonathan Langdon, RN; c/o Lloyds Bank, High Street, Sittingbourne, Kent

LANGFORD, Philip Baber; s of Percy Norman Langford (d 1968), and Elizabeth Ellen, *née* Jones (d 1987); *b* 23 March 1934; *Educ* Bromsgrove, BNC Oxford (MA), Univ of London (LLB); *m* 10 March 1987, Catherine Judith, da of William Arthur Gibbon, of 132 The Close, Salisbury, Wiltshire; 2 step s (Edward b 1977, Richard b 1979); *Career* Nat Serv 2 Lt RAEC attached to 2 bn Coldstream Gds 1959-61; admitted slr 1959; asst slr Kent CC 1961-63, ptnr Thomson Snell & Passmore 1965- (joined 1963); former chm SE Area Legal Aid Ctee, former pres Tunbridge Wells Tonbridge and Dist Law Soc; memb Law Soc; *Recreations* tennis, reading, travel; *Style—* Philip Langford, Esq; Baber House, Ticehurst, Wadhurst, East Sussex TN5 7HT (☎ 0580 200978); Thomson Snell & Passmore, 3 Lonsdale Gardens, Tunbridge Wells, Kent TN1 1NX (☎ 0892 510000, telex 95194 TSANDP G, fax 0892 549884)

LANGLEY, Kenneth William; s of William Thomas Charles Langley (d 1984), of Osmont House, Grove Park, Wanstead, London, and Ada Winifred, *née* Looke (d 1979); *b* 13 Jan 1932; *Educ* East Ham Tech HS, East Ham Tech Coll; *m* 16 March 1957, Daisy Rosina, da of Frederick Charles Parsons (d 1956), of 14 Durell Rd, Dagenham, Essex; 3 da (Gillian b 1959, Susan b 1961, Elizabeth b 1964); *Career* Nat Serv Sgt RE Egypt and Jordan; memb: Greenwich Chamber of Trade, Kent Branch Jt Consultative Ctee for Bldg Indust, CBI, Divnl Cncl RICS, Rotary Club Gravesend; Freeman City of London 1972, Liveryman Worshipful Co of Basketmakers 1977; FCIOB 1957, FRICS 1960, ACIArb 1966; *Recreations* music, reading, golf; *Clubs* City Livery; *Style—* Kenneth Langley, Esq; Wm Bryen Langley & Co, 58 Footscray Rd, London SE9 2SU (☎ 081 850 7775, fax 081 850 6772)

LANGTON, John Leslie; s of Arthur Laurence Langton (d 1976), and Sarah Jane, *née* Baker; *b* 23 Nov 1948; *Educ* Roan GS Greenwich; *m* 10 Aug 1979, Raymonde, da of Raymond Glinne, of Gembloux, Belgium 5030; 1 da (Jennifer Marie-Anne b 8 Dec 1983); *Career* Strauss Turnbull & Co 1965-69, Scandinavian Bank Ltd 1969-73, Williams & Glyns Bank 1973-74, Bondtrade in Brussels 1974-77, Morgan Stanley International 1977-78, dir Amex Bank Ltd 1979-80, sr exec dir Orion Royal Bank Ltd 1980-85, exec dir Security

Pacific Hoare Govett Ltd 1986-87, md Gintel & Co Ltd 1987-89, bd memb AIBD Zurich 1981-, chm AIBD (Systems & Info) Ltd 1990-; chief exec and sec gen The Assoc of Int Bond Dealers; *Recreations* wine, food, books, backgammon, travel; *Style*— John L Langton, Esq; 8 Beckenham Rd, West Wickham, Kent BR4 0GT (☎ 081 777 1202); Schwanengasse 2, 8001 Zurich, Switzerland; The Association of International Bond Dealers, Rigistrasse 60, CH-8033, Zurich, Switzerland (☎ 010 411 363 4222, fax 010 411 363 7772, telex 815812); AIBD (Systems & Info) Ltd, 7 Limeharbour, Docklands, London E14 9NQ (☎ 071 538 5656, fax 071 538 4902, telex 8813069)

LANKESTER, Richard Shermer; s of Richard Ward Lankester (d 1969), and Elsie Marion, *née* Shermer; *b* 8 Feb 1922; *Educ* Haberdashers' Aske's, Jesus Coll Oxford (MA); *m* 30 May 1950, Dorothy, da of Raymond Jackson (d 1966), of Worsley, Lancs; 3 s (Simon b 1951 d 1989, Toby b 1960, Thomas b 1964), 1 da (Ruth b 1955); *Career* serv Hants RHA Regt Italy 1943-45, RA 1942-45, Lt; Clerks Dept House of Commons 1947, co ed The Table 1962-67, clerk of Standing Ctees 1973-75, clerk to Expenditure Ctee 1975-79, registrar of Members' Interests 1976-87, clerk of Select Ctees House of Commons 1979-87; *Style*— Richard Lankester, Esq; The Old Farmhouse, The Green, Boughton Monchelsea, Kent (☎ 0622 43749)

LARCOMBE, Jennifer Rees; s of Tom Rees (d 1971), of Hildenborough Hall, Sevenoaks, Kent, and Jean, *née* Sinclair (d 1981); *b* 19 Oct 1942; *Educ* Fossbank Sch Tonbridge, Nursery Nursing Trg Colchester, Constant Spry Finishing Sch Berkshire; *m* 6 Aug 1966, Antony John Larcombe, s of Sydney Larcombe (d 1985); 3 s (Justyn b 1969, Duncan b 1975, Richard b 1977), 2 da (Sarah b 1968, Naomi b 1972), 1 god da and ward (Jane b 1970); *Career* author of children's novels and adult non-fiction; sch teacher 1960-68, antique dealer 1966-76, disabled by viral encephalitis 1982-90, author and lectr on subject of coping with disablement; regular contrib to magazines incl: Link, Renewal, Christian Woman, Family, Evangelism Today; columnist for local newspaper; memb: Disabled Christians Fellowship, Christian Viewpoint, Pembury Free Church, Women's Inst; *Books* incl: Curse of Craigyburn (1965), Firebrand (1981), Broken Stone (1984), Beyond Healing (1968), Gods Gloves (1987), Where Have You Gone God? (1988), Keeping A Spiritual Journal (1989); *Recreations* reading, walking, golf, music, singing; *Style*— Mrs Jennifer Larcombe; 17 Sutherland Rd, Tunbridge Wells, Kent TN1 1SE (☎ 0892 548171)

LATHAM, Peter John; s of Rev Frederick Latham (d 1985), of Hythe, Kent, and Dorothy Shirley, *née* Currah (d 1985); *b* 8 June 1937; *Educ* Kent Coll Canterbury, Canterbury Coll of Art (NDD), Brighton Coll of Art (ATC); *m* 28 April 1962, Prudence Helen Clare, da of Harry Knowles; 1 s (Alexis John b 22 Feb 1965), 1 da (Anna Clara Gail b 8 Sept 1962); *Career* Nat Serv 2 Lt Royal Regt Malaya 1957-59; sculptor and printmaker; lectr in sculpture and fndn studies Newport Coll of Art 1964-70, design conslt Technacryl Ltd 1966-, private client work and industl cmmns 1966-; visiting lectr: Christchurch Coll Canterbury 1973-76, Dept of Plastics Sheffield Poly 1975, maj study ldr visual studies Medway Coll of Design 1982- (lectr in 3D fndn studies 1970-82), furniture sold in maj London stores and exported to Europe ME W Africa Scandinavia and USA also used by DOE in embassies and embassy residences abroad, worked at Cité International des Arts Paris 1985-86, conducted seminar on applications of drawing at Ecole Nationale Superieure de Creation Industrielle Paris 1986, worked in Afghan refugee camps in Pakistan preparing paintings and drawings for later exhibition 1989; exhibitions incl: Wales Tomorrow 1969, Bio 5 1973, New Members Exhibition (E Kent Art Soc) 1979, Medway Artists '84 1984, one man show Canterbury Gallery 1986, Royal Acad Summer Exhibition 1987, Afghans (one man show at 3 venues in Kent) 1990; *Recreations* swimming, foreign travel, drawing; *Style*— Peter Latham, Esq; Tenterden House, 209 The Street, Boughton, Near Faversham, Kent ME13 9BL (☎ 0227 751593)

LAUGHLAND, Iain Hugh Page; s of Hugh Norman Wilson Laughland (d 1984), and Morag Laughland; *b* 29 Oct 1935; *Educ* Merchiston Castle Sch; *m* 1972, Ann Stewart, da of Andrew Blackwood Stewart Young, of Belhaven, Troon, Ayrshire, Scot; 1 s (Andrew Iain Stewart b 1965), 1 da (Rosemary Ann b 1963); *Career* 2 Lt 1 Bn Seaforth Highlanders, serv Egypt, Aden, Gibraltar 1955-56; dir press: Coomberlands 1964-68, Benn Publications Ltd 1977-87, Farm Holiday Guides Ltd 1981-84; 31 Caps Scotland Rugby XV 1959-66, capt 1965, record 5 wins Middx Sevens; *Recreations* golf; *Clubs* Rye, Caledonian, London Scottish Football; *Style*— Iain Laughland, Esq; School House Farm, School House Lane, Horsmonden, Tonbridge, Kent TN12 8BN

LAW, Gordon Malcolm; s of Robert Law (d 1989), of Sheffield, and Elizabeth Black, *née* Cassells; *b* 7 Nov 1932; *Educ* King Edward VII GS Sheffield, Univ of Sheffield (BA); *m* 31 Aug 1957, Elaine, da of Thomas Whittingham (d 1942); 3 da (Helen b 15 Nov 1959, Mary b 4 Feb 1961, Charlotte b 12 Oct 1965); *Career* Nat Serv 12th Royal Lancers (POW) 1955-57; staff offr Jessop-Saville Ltd Sheffield 1960-62 (graduate trainee 1957-60), gp estab offr Shepherd Building Group Ltd York 1965-70 (personnel offr 1962-65); Woolwich Building Society: personnel mangr 1970-72, asst gen mangr personnel 1972-76, gen mangr personnel and trg 1976-90, ret 1990; cncl memb: Nat Interactive Video Centre, Nat Cncl for Educnl Technol, Chartered Bldg Socs Inst (CBSI); memb: York Tourist Advsy Bd 1968-70, York Crime Prevention Ctee 1967-70; govr Thames Poly (chm Court of Govrs 1985-88), past pres York Jr C of C; Freeman City of London, Liveryman Worshipful Co of Distillers; hon FCBSI 1977, hon FBIM 1975, FIPM 1960; *Books* Personnel Policy and Line Management (1974, revised 1983); *Recreations* golf, philately; *Clubs* City Livery, W Kent Golf; *Style*— Gordon Law, Esq; 6 Hawthorne Close, Bickley, Bromley, Kent BR1 2HJ

LAW, Ronald James John; s of Arthur Sydney Law (d 1970), of Ash, nr Canterbury, and Emily Adams (d 1981); *b* 13 Feb 1924; *Educ* Westmarsh C of E Sch Ash; *Career* RN Sick Berth Branch 1942-49, served on HMS Beguam HMS Sussex and HMS Belfast; SRN 1951, matron Linton Hosp Maidstone 1964, princ nursing offr Maidstone Gen Hosps 1975, dir of nursing servs Greenwich Health Dist 1976, chief nursing offr and dir of quality assur and trg Dartford and Gravesham Health Authy 1979, ret 1988; memb Canterbury and Thanet Health Authy 1986-, regnl trg offr in SE for Assoc of Cricket Umpires; sec Maidstone Cricket Umpires Assoc, pres Leeds and Bromfields Cricket Club, vice chm Maidstone Dist Assoc of Kent Clubs; *Recreations* cricket, classical music, theatre; *Style*— Ronald Law, Esq; 16 Cremer Place, Wildish Rd, Faversham, Kent (☎ 0795 539863)

LAWRENCE, Agnes May; da of William Frederick Milbourne (d 1973), and Agnes May, *née* Weadon (d 1967); *b* 26 Sept 1913; *Educ* St Andrews Church Sch Bournemouth; *m* 25 Dec 1937, Jack Lawrence, s of Herbert Lawrence, (d 1971); 1 s (Michael John b 1947), 1 da (Janet Avril b 1944); *Career* lay supt Luton and Dunstable Hosp First Aid Post 1939-44; St John Ambulance Bde: co staff offr for cadets Bedford, formed first Ladies Div at Electrolux Works Luton, co supt Cheshire, hon sec and memb cncl for Cheshire, co supt Kent (ret), memb cncl for Kent, served 4 years on Community Health Cncl; hon sec: Standing Ctee of Voluntary Youth Orgns, Cripples Help Soc, Capel Women's Inst (for 6 years); Long Service Medal and bars St John Ambulance Bde, Defence Medal; DStJ 1979; *Recreations* music, various voluntary work; *Clubs* Royal Cinque Ports Yacht; *Style*— Mrs Agnes Lawrence; 177 The Gateway, Marine Parade, Dover, Kent, CT16 1LL (☎ 0304 205544)

LAWRENCE, Clive Wyndham; s of Lt-Col Sir (Percy) Roland Bradford Lawrence, MC and hp to Btcy of bro, Sir David (Roland Walter) Lawrence; *b* 6 Oct 1939; *Educ* Gordonstoun; *m* 1966, Sophia Annabel Stuart, da of Ian Hervey Stuart Black; 3 s; *Career* late Lt Coldstream Gds; *Style*— Clive Lawrence, Esq; Woodside, Frant, nr Tunbridge Wells, Kent TN3 9HW

LAWRENCE, Geoffrey; s of Capt Leslie Arthur Lawrence (d 1980), and Nancy, *née* Wilkinson; *b* 14 Sept 1943; *Educ* Gravesend GS, Dartford GS, Canterbury Sch of Architecture (Dip Arch); *m* 29 Oct 1966, Bonita, da of Sidney James Adams, of Ladywood Rd, Lanes End, Dartford, Kent; 2 da (Catherine b 21 Sep 1967, Sarah b 8 Aug 1973); *Career* architect; Gas Energy Mgmnt Award 1979; design architect: Raysut Cement Complex Oman 1981-82, Khaldyia Cement Complex Jordan 1982; memb Dartford C of C; memb: Arcuk 1980, RIBA 1981, IAAS 1980; ACA 1988; *Recreations* reading; *Style*— Geoffrey Lawrence, Esq; 16 Tower Rd, Dartford, Kent DA1 2HA (☎ 0322 223720, telex MBX 32291021)

LAWRENCE, Sandra; da of Alexander Edward Vail, of London, and Violet Alice, *née* Bennett; *b* 13 Jan 1948; *Educ* Thomlas Bennet Sch Crawley Sussex; *m* 1, 2 Aug 1969 (m dis 1982), John Glyn James; 2 s (Simon John, Paul Alexander); m 2, 2 Nov 1984, John Lindsay Lawrence, s of Edwin Harvey Lawrence, of Somerset; *Career* sec to sales mangr Wards Construction (Medway) Ltd 1980, asst to chm and md Ward Holdings plc 1983-, dir Troy Developments (subsid of Ward Holdings) 1987; *Recreations* travel, skiing, good food and wine; *Style*— Mrs Sandra Lawrence; Troy Developments, 2 Ashtree Lane, Chatham, Kent (☎ 0634 55111, fax 0634 577172)

LAWREY, Keith; JP (Inner London); s of Capt George William Bishop Lawrey, of Bognor Regis, W Sussex, and Edna Muriel, *née* Gass; *b* 21 Aug 1940; *Educ* Colfe's Sch, Birkbeck Coll London (LLB, MScEcon); *m* 20 Dec 1969, (Helen) Jane, da of James Edward Marriott, MBE, and Betty Evelyn, *née* Church; 2 s (David Keith b 1972, Andrew Charles b 1976), 2 da (Sarah Jane b 1970, Katherine Jane b 1979); *Career* called to the Bar Grays Inn 1972; educn offr Plastics and Rubber Inst 1960-68, lectr and sr lectr Bucks Coll of Higher Educn 1968-74, head Dept Business Studies Mid-Kent Coll of Higher and Further Educn 1974-78, sec gen The Library Assoc 1978-84, dean of Faculty of Business and Mgmnt Harrow Coll of Higher Educn 1984-, sec and ragistrar RCVS 1990-; hon treas Coll of Preceptors 1987- (also examiner), lay preacher Methodist church; Freeman City of London, Liveryman Worshipful Co of Chartered Secretaries and Administrators; FCIS 1967, FCollP 1980; *Recreations* preaching, sailing, swimming, theatre, gardening; *Clubs* Dell Quay Sailing, Old Colfeians' Assoc; *Style*— Keith Lawrey, Esq, JP; Royal College of Vetinary Surgeons, 32 Belgrave Square, London SW1X 8QP (☎ 071 235 4971)

LAWSON, Jeremy Thomas; s of Walter Harold Lawson (d 1967), and Marion Greta, *née* Broom (d 1944); *b* 16 Jan 1929; *Educ* Merchant Taylor's; *m* 10 July 1954, Gillian Eveline Mary (Jill), da of Eric James Harrison (d 1978); 2 s

(Matthew Jeremy b 11 May 1961, Nicholas James b 9 Feb 1965), 2 da (Rachel Marion (Dr Penney) b 4 Nov 1959, Deborah Jane (Mrs Philip Betts) b 20 Oct 1962); *Career* dir London Fancy Box Co 1952-; ldr and assoc Crusader Bible Class; past pres Box and Packaging Manufacturers Assoc, past Master Worshipful Co Joiners and Ceilers; *Recreations* cabinet making, wood turning; *Style*— Jeremy Lawson, Esq; London Fancy Box Co, Poulton Close, Dover, Kent CT17 0BX (☎ 0304 201598)

LE FORT, Norman Harry Frank; s of Harry Charles Le Fort (d 1951), of Chiswick, and Edith, *née* Steel (d 1964); *m* 3 Aug 1963, Gerbera Elizabeth, da of late Leo Dominic McHugh (Lt in Aust Navy); 1 s (Douglas b 1966), 2 da (Hilary b 1967, Jennifer b 1969); *Career* admitted slr 1963; Trower Still & Keeling Lincoln's Inn 1963-68, sr ptnr Braund & Fredrick 1978- (ptnr 1968-78); non-exec dir Bexley Health Authy 1990-; memb: Sidcup Literary and Scientific Soc (pres 1987-88), Parochial Church Cncl of St John The Evangelist Sidcup (vice chm 1988), Kent Law Soc, Sidcup Cncl of Churches, Bexley and Dartford Law Soc (pres 1990-91); fndr memb: Chislehurst and Sidcup Housing Assoc (vice chm 1988-), Sidcup Chamber of Trade and Indust (former sec); chm Govrs Harenc Sch Tst Footscray 1988- (fndr govr), govr Longlands Co Primary Sch Sidcup 1988-, vice pres Chislehurst and W Kent CC, patron Sidcup Symphony Orchestra, tstee Bexley United Charities; memb Law Soc 1963, IOD (assoc memb) 1988; *Recreations* music, people, travel; *Style*— Norman Le Fort, Esq; 12 Victoria Rd, Sidcup DA15 7HD (☎ 081 300 3849); 10 Hatherley Rd, Sidcup, Kent (☎ 081 300 6515, fax 081 300 7710)

LEA, Rev Canon Richard John Rutland; s of Douglas Rutland Lea (d 1942), of Brighton, and Sonia Constance, *née* Glaum (d 1983); *b* 2 Oct 1940; *Educ* Haileybury, Trinity Hall Cambridge (BA, MA); *m* 26 June 1965, Rosemary Helen, da of Maurice Ivan Douse, of Hove; 2 s (Nicholas John b 28 Aug 1966, Simon David b 10 Dec 1973), 1 da (Josephine Anna b 19 March 1968); *Career* curate: Edenbridge Kent 1965-68, Hayes Bromley 1968-71; vicar of Larkfield and Leybourne 1971-85, rural dean of Malling 1979-84, vicar of St Stephen's Chatham 1986-88, residentiary canon and precentor Rochester Cathedral 1988-; chm: Rochester Choral Soc, Rochester Diocesan Church Music Ctee; *Recreations* music, literature, walking; *Style*— The Rev Canon Richard Lea; 2, King's Orchard, Rochester, Kent ME1 1TG (☎ 0634 41491)

LEADBEATER, Kenneth Frank Martin; s of Ralph Sydney Kenneth (d 1980), and Rosa Elizabeth (Betty), *née* Skousbo (d 1988); *b* 31 Jan 1956; *Educ* King's Sch Rochester, Queens' Coll Cambridge (BA), Jordanhill Coll of Educn Glasgow (cert Ed), Univ of Glasgow (Dip Ed); *Career* teacher in Aberdeen 1978-80, Stock Exchange 1980-81, Touche Ross & Co 1981-, qualified CA 1984; memb Dartford Borough Cncl 1983- (dep ldr Bd of Mgmnt 1990-), memb Kent CC 1985-89, chm Govrs Kent Coll for Careers Serv; govr: Dartford GS, Leigh City Technol Coll Dartford, Joydens Wood Primary Sch; memb ICAEW 1984, GTC 1978; *Recreations* opera, fell-walking, psephology; *Style*— Kenneth Leadbeater, Esq; 46 Water Mill Way, South Darenth, Dartford, Kent DA4 9BE (☎ 0322 866375); Hill House, 1 Little New St, London EC4A 3TR (☎ 071 936 3000 ext 3133)

LEAH, Nancy Marguerite Jane; s of Capt Howard James Adair Swann (d 1982), of Timberdown, Heathfield, Sussex, and Beatrix Anne, *née* Walton; *b* 24 April 1954; *Educ* Timberdown Home Sch Heathfield Sussex, RADA; *m* 1 Oct 1983, Barry David Leah, s of Cyril Leah, of 10 The Buildings, Manswood, Dorset; *Career* reviewer of children's lit and freelance journalist; buyer for Hatchards Bookshop 1985-, innovator of a series of talks for children on new children's lit 1986, major contrib to Christmas reading lists for Kent Reading and Language Devpt Centre 1987 and 1988, author of children's book reviews in Kent Companion 1988; memb: Lit Panel SE Arts 1987-, Fedn of Children's Book Gps; *Recreations* yoga, theatre, music; *Style*— Mrs Nancy Leah; Hatchards Bookshop, The Great Hall, Mount Pleasant Rd, Tunbridge Wells, Kent TN1 1QQ (☎ 0892 35318/9)

LEAKEY, Dr David Martin; s of Reginald Edward Leakey (d 1969), of Redhill, Surrey, and Edith Doris, *née* Gaze (d 1974); *b* 23 July 1932; *Educ* Imperial Coll London (BSc, PhD, DIC); *m* 31 Aug 1957, Shirely May, da of George Clifford Webster (d 1968), of Bridlington, Yorks; 1 s (Graham Peter b 1967), 1 da (Pamela Susan b 1961); *Career* tech dir GEC Telecoms Ltd 1969-84; dir: Fulcrum Telecommunications Ltd 1985-, Mitel Inc Canada 1986-; chief scientist BT 1986- (dep engr-in-chief 1984-86); Liveryman Worshipful Co of Engrs, Freeman City of London; FEng, FIEE, FCGI; *Recreations* horticulture; *Style*— Dr David Leakey; British Telecom Centre, 81 Newgate St, London EC1A 7AJ (☎ 071 356 5315, telex 883051)

LEARY, Brian; QC; s of late A T Leary, and late M C Leary, *née* Bond; *b* 1 Jan 1929; *Educ* Kings Sch Canterbury, Wadham Coll Oxford (MA); *m* 14 April 1965, Myriam Ann, da of late Kenneth Bannister, CBE, of Mexico City; *Career* called to the Bar Middle Temple 1953; sr prosecuting counsel to Crown 1971-78 (jr 1964-71), master of the bench 1986; chm Br Mexican Soc; *Recreations* travel, sailing, growing herbs; *Style*— Brian Leary, Esq, QC; East Farleigh House, East Farleigh, Kent (☎ 0622 726295); 5 Paper Buildings, Temple EC4 (☎ 071 583 6117)

LEATES, Margaret; da of Henry Arthur Sargent Rayner, and Alice, *née* Baker; *b* 30 March 1951; *Educ* Lilley and Stone Girls' HS Newark, King's Coll London (LLB, LLM, AKC); *m* 26 May 1973, Timothy Philip Leates; 1 s (Benjamin b 15 April 1982), 1 da (Lydia b 14 July 1983); *Career* admitted slr; dep parly counsel 1986-; memb Law Soc; *Recreations* junk, gardening; *Clubs* Whitstable Yacht; *Style*— Mrs Margaret Leates; The Office of the Parliamentary Counsel, 36 Whitehall, London SW1 (☎ 071 210 3000)

LEATHERS, Hon Jeremy Baxter; s of 2 Viscount Leathers; *b* 11 April 1946; *Educ* Rugby, Trinity Coll Dublin; *m* 1969, Fiona Lesley, eldest da of late George Stanhope Pitt, of Rowbarns Manor, Horsley, Surrey; 2 da (Tara Charlotte b 1972, Fern Griselda b 1979), 1 s (Luke Alexander b 1974); *Style*— The Hon Jeremy Leathers

LEAVER, Hon Mrs (Margaret); *née* Cavendish; da of 6 Baron Waterpark (d 1949); *b* 1907; *m* 1934, Wallace Thomas Leaver (d 1972); 2 da (Mrs Peter Wiggins b 1938, Elizabeth b 1942); *Style*— The Hon Mrs Leaver; St Benets, Beech Hill, Bridge, Canterbury, Kent

LEBOR, Jill Ann; da of Sub Lt Ernest William David Rodwell (d 1981), of Ipswich, Suffolk, and Violet Ann May, *née* Snelgar; *b* 17 Sept 1947; *Educ* Sch of the Holy Child Lahleham Abbey, Sch of Art Carmarthen (NDD), Leicester Coll of Art (BA, Dip AD); *m* 8 June 1974, Stanley Harvey Lebor, s of Lois Isaac Lebor (d 1976), of London; 3 s (David Alexander Meyer b 1976, Thomas Arthur William b 1977, Michael Ernest Lois b 1979); *Career* PR offr Rank Advertising 1971-73 (EMI 1969-71), freelance advertising mangr 1973-76, designer and prodr of jewellery 1980-84; involved in starting new branch of Nat Childbirth Tst Canterbury; chm: Planning Ctee of Swale, Parent Teachers Assoc at local sch (rep of Nat Assoc); borough cncllr Boughton Ward; memb: Boughton-under-Blean Parish Cncl, borough cncl, local Lib Democrats; *Recreations* reading, gardening, family, walking; *Style*— Mrs Jill Lebor; 160 The Street, Boughton-under-Blean, Faversham, Kent ME13 9AL (☎ 0227 750294); Swale House, East St, Sittingbourne, Kent ME10 3HT (☎ 0795 24341, fax 0795 28773)

LEDWARD, Avril Monica; da of Arthur Eastwood Crabtree (d 1943), of North Yorkshire, and Margaret Evelyn, *née* Marshall; *b* 17 April 1925; *Educ* Heathfield Sch Berks, Elmwood Ottawa Canada; *m* 10 June 1949, Denis Richard Ledward (d 1983), s of Jocelyn Charles Ledward (d 1966), of Rye, E Sussex; 3 s (Simon b 1950, Colin b 1952, William b 1958); *Career* 3 Offr WRNS 1943-46; memb: Cons Assoc, Arthritis and Rheumatism Cncl; elected Kent CC 1977; *Recreations* music, theatre, sport; *Style*— Mrs Avril Ledward; Grantley Court, Tunbridge Wells, Kent (☎ 0892 26036); County Hall, Maidstone, Kent (☎ 0622 671411, fax 0622 59905)

LEDWARD, Rodney Spencer; s of Arthur Ledward (d 1984), of Stone, Staffs, and Beatrice Maud, *née* Pritchard (d 1986); *b* 30 June 1938; *Educ* Alleynes GS, Univ of Manchester (BSc, MPS), Univ of Liverpool (MB ChB), Univ of Virginia Charlottesville, Brown Univ RI, Univ of Nottingham (DM); *m* 26 Aug 1983, Lady Jane Annabelle Howard; 1 s (Bertie Arthur Ruthven b 7 Nov 1985); *Career* conslt in obstetrics and gynaecology SE Kent Health Dist 1980-; private gynaecological practice: St Saviour's Hosp Hythe Kent, Chaucer Hosp Canterbury, London Med Centre, London Bridge Hosp; md Tutorial Systems International; hon sr teaching fell Dept Obstetrics and Gynaecology The Royal London Hosp, dean Ross Univ Med Sch Ross Univ NY; FRCS 1974, FRSM 1974, FRCOG 1986; *Books* Drug Treatment in Obstetrics (1982, 2 edn 1990), Drug Treatment in Gynaecology (1984), Handbook of Obstetrics and Gynaecology (1986); *Recreations* swimming, riding; *Clubs* RSM; *Style*— Rodney Ledward, Esq; Beaulieu, The Riviera, Sandgate CT20 3AB (☎ 0303 40104); Consulting Rooms, St Saviours Hospital, Hythe (☎ 0303 265 581); Chaucer Hospital, Canterbury (☎ 0227 455 466); 144 Harley St, London (☎ 071 935 0023); London Bridge Hospital (☎ 071 403 488)

LEE, Prof David John; CBE (1989); s of Douglas Lee (d 1987), and Mildred Amy, *née* Checkley (d 1955); *b* 28 Aug 1930; *Educ* Chislehurst & Sidcup Co GS, Univ of Manchester (BSc), Imperial Coll London (DIC); *m* 6 Dec 1957, Helga; 1 s (Graham b 1961), 1 da (Caroline b 1960); *Career* Nat Serv RE 1950-52, Col Engr and Tport Staff Corps RE (TA) 1990 (Maj 1978, Lt-Col 1982); chm G Maunsell & Partners 1984- (joined 1955, ptnr 1966, managing ptnr 1978-84), dir Maunsell International Group; visiting prof: Imperial Coll London, Univ of Newcastle upon Tyne; author of many papers published in learned jnls; Freeman City of London, Liveryman Worshipful Co of Engrs; FICE 1966, FIStructE 1968 (pres 1985-86), FEng 1980; *Books* Theory and Practice of Bearings and Expansion Joints for Bridges (1971), Civil Engineering Reference Book (contrib); *Clubs* East India; *Style*— Prof David Lee, CBE; G Maunsell & Partners, Yeoman House, 63 Croydon Rd, Penge, London SE2O 7TP (☎ 081 778 6060, fax 081 659 5568, telex 946171)

LEE, James Giles; s of John Lee, CBE, and Muriel, *née* Giles; *b* 23 Dec 1942; *Educ* Trinity Coll Glenalmond, Univ of Glasgow, Harvard Univ; *m* 1966, Linn, *née* MacDonald; 1 s, 2 da; *Career* conslt McKinsey & Co 1969-80, dep chm and chief exec Pearson Longman 1980-83; chm: Penguin Publishing Co 1980-84, Longman Gp 1980-84; dir S Pearson & Son 1981-84, dep chm Yorkshire TV 1982-88, chief exec Goldcrest Films and TV 1983-85 (chm 1981-85), chm Direct Bdcasting by Satellite Consortium 1986-87, dir Boston Consulting Gp Ltd 1987-; *Books* Planning for the Social Services

(1978), The Investment Challenge (1979); *Recreations* photography, travelling, sailing; *Clubs* Reform, Harvard (NY); *Style*— J G Lee, Esq; Meadow Wood, Penshurst, Kent (☎ 0892 870309); Devonshire House, Mayfair Place, London W1X 5FH (☎ 01 493 3222, telex 28975, fax 01 499 3660)

LEE, Peter John; s of Capt Reginald George Lee (d 1960), of London, and Christina Eliza, *née* Foulser; *b* 6 Aug 1938; *Educ* George Heriots Sch Edinburgh; *m* 23 Aug 1966, Maureen Ann, da of Victor John Braybrook, of London; 2 da (Jennifer b 1967, Catherine b 1970); *Career* CA in pub practice; ptnr Morison Stoneham & Co London 1972-77, proprietor Peter Lee & Co 1978-82, sr ptnr Dendy Neville Gradons 1987- (ptnr 1982-); involved in: Hollingbourne Soc, Maidstone C of C and Indust, local charitable work, preservation of the environment; FCA 1962; *Recreations* treasure hunting, writing, country walking, music; *Clubs* Maidstone; *Style*— Peter Lee, Esq; Autumn Cottage, Musket Lane, Hollingbourne, Kent (☎ 0622 880 580); 1 Bower Mount Rd, Maidstone, Kent (☎ 0622 686441, fax 0622 690221, telex 966297 DENLEE G)

LEES, Susan; da of Capt Jack Maylam (d 1988), of Ashford, Kent, and Ivy Patricia, Maylam, *née* Higson (later Mrs McKinlay); *b* 28 Aug 1940; *Educ* Northern GS Portsmouth, Univ of London (extra mural); *m* 28 Sept 1963, Robert Frederick, s of Robert Lees; 2 s (Stephen b 1965, Jamie b 1967); *Career* exec offr Miny of Tport 1960-65; clerk Alkham Parish Cncl, ctee memb Alkham Valley Preservation Soc, memb Kent Family History Soc; *Books* Pictorial Study of Alkham Parish (1985), History of Alkham Church (1988); *Recreations* local history, genealogy, bird keeping, handicrafts; *Style*— Mrs Susan Lees; Forstal Cottage, Alkham, Dover, Kent CT1S 7DE (☎ 0304 822661)

LEESE, Arthur; s of Henry Leese (d 1969), and Edith Mabel, *née* Baker (d 1952); *b* 4 May 1931; *Educ* Battersea GS; *m* 18 July 1959, Marian, da of Walter Thomas Bryant (d 1989); 1 s (Simon b 1967), 1 da (Sarah b 1971); *Career* dir: Columbia Pictures Corporation Ltd 1980-, Columbia Pictures Video Ltd 1982-, Colgems Productions Ltd 1983-, Columbia Video Europe Ltd 1990, Seven Seas Films Ltd 1990-, Darby Films Ltd 1990-; *Recreations* reading, walking, fishing; *Style*— Arthur Leese, Esq; 53 Chieveley Drive, Tunbridge Wells, Kent TN2 5HQ (☎ 0892 30706); 19/23 Wells St, London W1P 3FP (☎ 071 580 2090, telex 263392, fax 071 528 8980)

LEGG, Dr Owen Campbell; s of Frank George Colby Legg, and Amy, *née* Quarendon; *b* 1 Aug 1935; *Educ* Alleyn's Coll, Guy's Hosp Med Sch (MB BS, DRCOG, LRCP, MRCS); *m* 10 June 1961, Helen Christina, da of Leslie Harvey; 1 s (Ian Campbell b 30 March 1962), 1 da (Sarra Caroline b 1 July 1967); *Career* med practitioner in Hadlow gen practice 1969-; printer of private press books incl: Armourers Play (York Cycle), Cut in the Chalk, Rubayyat of Omar Khayaam, The Garden by Vita Sackville West; *Recreations* reading, Welsh; *Style*— Dr Owen Legg; 152 Hadlow Rd, Tonbridge, Kent; The Surgery, Hadlow, Kent (☎ 0732 850248)

LEHMANN, Dr Geoffrey Donald; MBE (1974); s of Paul Samuel Lehmann (d 1950), of Woodland House, Woodford Wells, Essex, and Lilian Ruth, *née* Harris (d 1954); *b* 5 Jan 1904; *Educ* Highgate Sch, Queen Mary's Coll London, Univ Coll Oxford (BSc, DPhil), UCH London (MRCS, LRCP), Univ of Liverpool (DTM, DOMS); *m* 16 Sept 1933, Monica Elizabeth, da of Henry Deacon Allen (d 1919), of The Retreat, Cawnpur, India; 1 s (Donald John b 21 May 1940), 3 da (Prilla (Mrs Coole) b 25 Jan 1935, Petronella (Mrs Young) b 25 March 1938, Su (Mrs East) b 15 Dec 1946); *Career* Vol IMS India 1942-46, Staff Maj DADP, Central Cmd Meerat India; specialist in eye surgery, pioneered certain new surgery techniques India, jt fndr with Mrs Monica Lehmann Herbertpur Christian Hosp Himalayan Doon Valley 1936 (sole permanent dir until 1973), chm Wyberg Allen Sch Mussouria India 1973-84; engr; dir: Lehmann Archer (later International Tools), Dunsterville Allen plc (Property Co); fndr dir International Films Ltd; chm: Sunda Ltd, Calamus Ltd; Name at Lloyds 1954; fndr of Charitable Tst; fndr: Herbertpur Tst UK 1935, NEED Non-profit Corp USA 1956, Herbertpur Tst Assoc India 1976; fell Soc of Tropical Medicine and Hygiene; *Books* incl: Lyrics (1980), On the Trial of a Spy (1981), The Red Gang (with B Norman, 1983), Danger on The Sonita (1985), Saved by Fire (1990); *Recreations* tennis, golf; *Style*— Dr Geoffrey Lehmann, MBE

LEIGH, David Irvine; s of Frederick Leigh (d 1980), of Glasgow, Scotland, and Mary, *née* David; *b* 16 April 1944; *Educ* Glasgow Sch of Art, Edinburgh Coll of Art, Heriot-Watt Univ (DA); *m* 30 Aug 1975, Lynda, da of Frank Thomas Taylor (d 1970), of Hawkhurst, Kent; 1 s (Elliot b 1983), 1 da (Claire Francesca b 1971); *Career* architect; ptnr R J Wood Chapman and Hanson 1974, chm and md Chapman and Hanson 1989- (dir 1981); designed HQ bldgs: Charrington & Co London 1978, R S Components Corby 1984, Electrocomponents Knightsbridge 1987, W M Lighting Northampton 1989; chm Fairlight Tennis Club; MRIBA 1969; *Recreations* tennis, swimming, cycling, computing; *Clubs* St Stephens, Inigo Jones; *Style*— David Leigh, Esq; Chapman & Hanson, Chartered Architects and Interior Designers, 29 Widmore Rd, Bromley, Kent BR1 1RT (☎ 081 460 8834, fax 081 460 8838)

LEIGH, (William) Rowland Llewellyn; o s of Capt Rowland Llewellyn Leigh (d 1942), of Yalding, Kent, and Evelyn Mary Adeline, *née* Carey-Wilkins (d 1989); *b* 27 June 1942; *Educ* Tonbridge; *m* 18 April 1970, Lindsay Elizabeth, o da of Gp Capt Peter James Simpson, DSO, DFC (d 1987), of Tunbridge Wells, Kent; 1 s (Peter Rowland Llewellyn b 1975); *Career* fin dir and co sec: SEET plc 1974-88, The Savoy Hotel plc 1988-; Freeman City of London, memb ICAEW; *Recreations* music, photography; *Style*— Rowland Leigh, Esq; Chancel House, Church St, Hadlow, Tonbridge, Kent TN11 0DB (☎ 0732 851329); The Savoy Hotel Hotel plc, 1 Savoy Hill, London WC2R 0BP (☎ 071 836 1533, fax 071 379 5421)

LEIGH PEMBERTON, Jeremy; s of late Robert Douglas Leigh Pemberton, MBE, MC, JP, and late Helen Isabel, *née* Payne-Gallwey; bro of Rt Hon Robin Leigh-Pemberton, *qv*; *b* 25 Nov 1933; *Educ* Eton, Magdalen Coll Oxford (MA), INSEAD Fontainebleau (MBA); *m* 1, 30 May 1968 (m dis 1980), Mary, da of John Ames, of Boston, Mass; 1 s (Richard b 13 Dec 1971); m 2, 3 June 1982, Virginia Marion, da of Sir John Curle, KCVO, CMG, qv; *Career* Nat Serv Grenadier Gds 1952-54, cmmnd 2 Lt 1953; Brooke Bond Liebig 1957-69 (rising to gp mktg controller), md W & R Balston Gp 1973-74 (gp mktg controller and corporate planner 1970-73), dep chm Whatman plc (formerly Whatman Reeve Angel plc) 1990- (md 1974-89); chm: Mid Kent Hldgs plc, Kent Co Crematorium plc; dir: London & Manchester Group plc, Fleming Fledgeling Investment Trust plc, Kent Economic Development Bd, Bailey Products Ltd, Kent TEC (Dev) Ltd, Genzyme (UK) Ltd, Southern Advsy Bd National Westminster Bank plc; CBI: memb Nat Cncl, memb Econ and Fin Policy Ctee, memb Fin and Gen Purposes Ctee, fndr chm Kent Area Ctee (later chm SE Regnl Cncl); visiting prof in mktg at INSEAD 1965-70; pres: INSEAD Int Alumni Assoc 1962-66, Kent branch Chartered Inst of Mktg 1988-89; chm Fin Ctee Kent Branch Red Cross, SE memb Nat Employers' Liaison Ctee, memb Rates Consultative Ctee Kent CC; tstee: Understanding Indust Tst (chm Mgmnt Bd), Lord Cornwallis Meml Fund; FCIM, FInstD; *Recreations* opera, fishing; *Style*— Jeremy Leigh Pemberton, Esq; Hill House, Wormshill, Sittingbourne, Kent ME9 OTS; Whatman plc, Springfield Mill, Maidstone, Kent ME14 2LE (☎ 0622 692 022, fax 0622 691 425)

LEIGH PEMBERTON, John David; s of Rt Hon R Leigh-Pemberton, PC, *qv*, of Torry Hill, Sittingbourne, Kent, and Rosemary Davina, *née* Forbes; *b* 16 March 1955; *Educ* Eton, Magdalen Coll Oxford; *m* 1, 1980 (m dis 1983), Rosamund, *née* Jessel; m 2, 6 Sept 1986, Kathryn Felice, da of Martin Robert Lampard, of Theberton House, Theberton, nr Leiston, Suffolk; 1 s (Arthur Evelyn b 1989); *Career* with Smith New Court plc London; memb Kent Branch Ctees: CLA, The Game Conservancy Cncl; *Recreations* botany, pomology, architecture, motorcycling; *Style*— John Leigh Pemberton, Esq; Yokes Court, Frinsted, nr Sittingbourne, Kent ME9 OST; Smith New Court plc, 30 St Swithins Lane, London EC4

LEIGH-PEMBERTON, Rt Hon Robin (Robert); PC (1987); s of Capt Robert Leigh-Pemberton, MBE, MC (d 1964), of Torry Hill, Sittingbourne, Kent, and Helen Isabel, *née* Payne-Gallwey (d 1985); *b* 5 Jan 1927; *Educ* Eton, Trinity Coll Oxford; *m* 8 July 1953, Rosemary Davina, da of Lt-Col David Walter Arthur William Forbes, MC (ka 1943), of Callander, Falkirk, and Diana (d 1982; who m 2, 1946, 6 Marquess of Exeter who d 1981), gda of 1 Baron Faringdon; 5 s (John b 16 March 1955, *qv*, James b 10 Dec 1956, Edward b 10 Jan 1959, Thomas b 22 Sept 1961, William b 20 march 1964); *Career* Lt Grenadier Gds, served Palestine 1946-48; Hon Col: Kent and Sharpshooters Yeo Sqdn, 265 (KCLY) Signal Sqdn (V), 5 (Vol) Bn The Queen's Regt; pres: SE TA & VR Assoc, Kent SSAFA; hon pres: Kent Wing Air Trg Corps; called to the Bar Inner Temple 1954, practised London and SE Circuit 1954-60, hon bencher 1983; dir: Birmid Qualcast 1966-83 (dep chm 1970, chm 1975-77), University Life Assurance Society 1967-78, Redland Ltd 1972-83, Equitable Life Assurance Society 1979-83 (vice pres 1982-83); chm: National Westminster Bank 1977-83 (dir 1972-83, dep chm 1974), Ctee of London Clearing Bankers 1982-83; govr Bank of England 1983-; Lord-Lieut of Kent 1982- (DL 1970, vice Lord-Lieut 1972-82), JP 1961-75, Kent Co Cncllr 1961-77 (chm cncl 1972-75); memb NEDC 1982-; tstee: Royal Acad of Arts Tst 1982-87 (now tstee emeritus), Kent CCC, Kent Co Playing Fields Assoc, Kent Co Agric Soc, Rochester Cathedral Tst, The Kent Fndn; chm Canterbury Cathedral Appeal Tst Fund; pres: Kent Co Agric Soc 1984-85, Kent Rural Community Cncl, Kent Assoc of Youth Clubs, St John Cncl for Kent; hon fell Trinity Coll Oxford 1984, pro chllr Univ of Kent 1977-83, seneschal of Canterbury Cathedral 1983-; Hon DCL Univ of Kent 1983; memb RSA, FCIB, KStJ 1983; *Recreations* country pursuits, the arts; *Clubs* Brooks's, Cavalry & Guards, Kent CCC; *Style*— The Rt Hon Robin Leigh-Pemberton; Torry Hill, Sittingbourne, Kent ME9 0SP; Bank of England, Threadneedle St, London EC2R 8AH (☎ 071 601 4444)

LEITH, Pauline Thelma; da of Stacey Smart (d 1966) of Norwich, and Kathleen Lilian, *née* Egglestone (d 1981); *b* 23 April 1927; *Educ* Crome Girls Sch; *m* 26 July 1947, Frank David Leith, s of Hugh Clarke Leith; 3 s (Andrew, Trevor, Simon); *Career* cncllr: Sandwich Borough Cncl 1964-73, Sandwich Town Cncl 1973-, Kent County Cncl 1973-; chm SEECC, vice chm Canterbury and Thanet Community Health Cncl, Mayor of Sandwich 1987-; Twinning assocs with Sandwich / Ronse - Sonsbeck / Honfleur; assoc memb:

Br Legion, Deal and Dist CAB, historical link Flanders - Kent; vice pres Thanet Mencap; *Recreations* music, reading; *Style—* Mrs Pauline Leith; 83 St Barts Rd, Sandwich, Kent CT13 0AS (☎ 0304 613246)

LEMON, Sir (Richard) Dawnay; CBE (1958), QPM; s of Lt-Col Frederick Joseph Lemon, CBE, DSO (d 1952); *b* 1912; *Educ* Uppingham, RMC; *m* 1939, Sylvia Marie, da of Lt-Col L W Kentish, of Burnham, Bucks; 1 s, 2 da (1 decd); *Career* joined W Yorks Regt 1932; Met Police 1934-37, Leics Constabulary 1937-39; chief constable: E Riding Yorks 1939-42, Hampshire and IOW 1942-62, Kent 1962-74; cncl memb Friends of Canterbury Cathedral; kt 1970; *Recreations* golf; *Clubs* Band of Brothers Cricket, Free Foresters Cricket, Naval and Military, Royal St George's Golf; *Style—* Sir Dawnay Lemon, CBE, QPM; Rosecroft, Ringwould, nr Deal, Kent (☎ 030 45 67 554)

LENOX-CONYNGHAM, Charles Denis; s of Capt Alwyn Douglas Lenox-Conyngham, RN, of Benenden, Kent, and Margaret Cecilia, *née* Clear; *b* 24 Jan 1935; *Educ* Winchester, Magdalen Coll Oxford (MA), Wharton Sch of Business Admin, Univ of Pennsylvania; *m* 15 April 1972, Helga Gerrit, da of Lt-Gen Hans von Liebach (d 1966), of Berlin; 1 s (Patrick b 1972), 1 da (Laura b 1974); *Career* cmmnd 2 Lt Royal Hussars, served Germany 1954-56; md: Blue Funnel Line 1970, Price and Pierce 1985; exec dir: Ocean Transport & Trading 1972-85, chm and chief exec Sealink (UK) Ltd 1985-; *Recreations* gardening, tennis, squash, skiing; *Clubs* RAC; *Style—* Charles Lenox-Conyngham, Esq; Yew Tree House, Benenden, Kent TN17 3EJ (☎ 0580 240 630); Sealink UK Ltd, 20 Upper Ground, London SE1 9PF (☎ 071 928 6969, telex 914028, fax 071 928 1469)

LEONARD, (James) Nigel Robert; s of Norman Arthur Leonard, of Limpsfield Chart, Surrey, and Patricia Jessie, *née* Barrett; *b* 23 March 1952; *Educ* Forest Sch, RCM; *Career* operatic bass; work at ENO incl: Aida and Damnation of Faust 1980, Fidelio and Tosca 1981, The Flying Dutchman and Boris Godunov 1982, Don Carlos and The Magic Flute 1983, Rigoletto and Mazeppa 1984, Faust and the Mastersingers 1985, Don Giovanni and Parsifal 1986, Akhnaten and Queen of Spades 1987, La Bohème and King Lear 1988-89; Simone Boccanegra Royal Opera House 1980; notable roles incl: Sarastro in The Magic Flute, Zaccariah in Nabucco, King Philip in Don Carlos, Fiesco in Simone Boccanegra; TV appearances incl: Rigoletto, Lady Macbeth, Akhnaten, Mary Stuart; ARCM; *Recreations* sailing, collecting fountain pens, bridge; *Clubs* Players Theatre; *Style—* Nigel Leonard, Esq; 2 Lower Chart Cottages, Chart Lane, Brasted Chart, nr Westerham, Kent TN16 1LN (☎ 0959 62847); c/o English Nat Opera, St Martins Lane, London WC2; FLat 2, 24 Sutherland St, London SW1

LESTER, Jeremy Michael; s of Michael Edwin Lester, of Stanton, Worcs, and Denise Wadsworth, *née* Dowling (d 1975); *b* 2 May 1945; *Educ* St Edward's Oxford, Univ of Bristol (LLB); *m* 15 Aug 1970, Elizabeth Maria, da of Lt Col Lechna Stanislaw (d 1981); 2 s (Marek b 1979, Martin b 1984), 2 da (Wiktoria b 1973, Frances b 1975); *Career* admitted slr 1969; Lester Dixon and Jeffcote Nuneaton 1969-70, ptnr Daynes Chittock and Back Norwich 1972-81 (joined 1970), Chanter Burrington and Foster Barnstaple 1981-86, ptnr The Buss Murton Partnership Tunbridge Wells 1987- (joined 1986); treas Norwich Cncl of Churches 1979-81, memb Law Soc, cncl memb Tunbridge Wells Tonbridge and Dist Law Soc; *Recreations* swimming, sailing, family; *Style—* Jeremy Lester, Esq; Marlinspike, 79 Culverden Park, Tunbridge Wells, Kent TN4 9QS (☎ 0892 33193); The Buss Murton Partnership, The Priory, Tunbridge Wells, Kent TN4 9QS (☎ 0892 510222, fax 0892 515457)

LETTS, John Robert; s of Capt Robert Frederick Letts, of Mulberry Down, Vicarage Lane, Blean, Kent, and Helen Ann Cecille, *née* Sturgis; *b* 22 Dec 1950; *Educ* King's Sch Canterbury; *m* 21 June 1975, Alison Margaret Muir, *née* Rogers; 2 s (Richard, Christopher), 1 da (Katherine); *Career* admitted slr 1975; princ Letts & Co (family firm); memb: Law Soc, Kent Law Soc, Slrs Benevolent Assoc; *Recreations* hockey, golf, old cars, France; *Clubs* Herne Bay Hockey and Tennis; *Style—* John Letts, Esq; Yew Tree Farm, 33 Blean Common, Blean, Canterbury, Kent (☎ 0227 471572); Bartletts, Tyler Hill Rd, Blean, Canterbury, Kent (☎ 0227 471555, fax 0227 471556)

LEVETT, John Lionel; s of Theodore Angelo Roderick Levett, CBE, of Oxted, Surrey, and Muriel Greta, *née* Lockwood (d 1957); *b* 2 May 1928; *Educ* Haileybury, Queens' Coll Cambridge (BA, LLB, MA); *m* 17 July 1954, (Mary) Lorna, da of Dr William Glasse Watson (d 1947), of Cambridge; 2 s (Richard John b 1957, Stephen Paul Martin b 1960); *Career* 2 Lt RA 1947; admitted slr 1954; Levett Son and Baldwin: articled clerk 1951-54, ptnr 1954-68, sr ptnr 1968-88; conslt Hill Bailey 1988-; pres Bromley Chamber of Commerce 1966-67 (1960-61), vice pres Glebe Housing Assoc 1984; *Recreations* classical music, walking, vintage railways; *Style—* John Levett, Esq; Hill Bailey Solicitors, Wells House, 15/17 Elmfield Rd, Bromley, Kent BR1 1QP (☎ 081 2901177, fax 081 4643328)

LEWIS, Dr (Edward) Brian; s of Rev George Owen Lewis (d 1967), of Hereford, and Ethel Mary, *née* Hay (d 1977); *b* 8 July 1930; *Educ* Hereford Cathedral Sch, St John's Coll Cambridge (MA, MBBChir), West London Hospital Med Sch (DA); *m* 28 Sept 1963, (Yolande) Aurea Ruston, da of Peter Dunstan Bennett (d 1969), of Rugby, Warwickshire; 1 s (Edward b 1965), 1 da (Sophie b 1967); *Career* conslt anaesthetist SE Kent DHA 1967-, memb cncl BMA 1970- (chm rep body 1978-81, fell 1981), dir BUPA 1980-, pres Nat Assoc of Theatre Nurses 1982-85, vice pres Assoc of Anaesthetists of GB and Ireland 1986-88, pres Folkestone Med Soc 1988-89; St John Ambulance Bde: Kent County Cmmr 1983-86, Kent County Cdr 1986-90, vice chm cncl Order of St John in Kent 1986-90, surgn in chief 1988-, CStJ 1988-; author numerous med articles; Liveryman Worshipful Soc of Apothecaries 1964, Freeman City of London 1966; memb GMC 1979, fell BMA 1981, FRSM 1986, LMSSA, FFARCS; *Recreations* aeromedical repatriation, photography; *Clubs* Savage, RSM; *Style—* Dr Brian Lewis; High Hopes, 5 North Rd West, Hythe, Kent CT21 4BD (☎ 0303 266569); William Harvey Hospital, Ashford, Kent TN24 0LZ (☎ 0233 633331)

LEWIS, Brian Geoffrey Marshall; s of Col Geoffrey Archibald Ernest Lewis (d 1977), of Tunbridge Wells, and Joan Isabel, *née* Stratford; *b* 1 Dec 1943; *Educ* Bethany Sch Goudhurst; *m* 29 June 1974, Elizabeth Jane, da of John Alexander Miller, of Heathfield, Sussex; 3 da (Sarah Isabel b 2 Aug 1976, Anna Charlotte b 10 April 1979, Claire Victoria (twin) b 10 April 1979); *Career* exec positions H J Heinz Ltd and Canada Dry (UK) Ltd; md Heron Cruisers Ltd Kent, dir Stanton Asset Management Kent; *Recreations* motor sports, point-to-point, eventing; *Style—* Brian Lewis, Esq; Stanton Asset Management Ltd, Stanton House, Romford Rd, Pembury, Kent TN2 4AY (☎ 089 282 5454, fax 089 282 2482, telex 94013002 LEAS G)

LEWIS, Brian Russell; s of Iorwerth Lewis (d 1986), and Ethel Eliza Gertrude Lewis; *b* 15 Nov 1944; *Educ* St Augustine's Coll Westgate; *m* 10 Oct 1967, Gloria, da of Lawrence Birch, of Ashford, Kent; 3 da (Joanna Michelle b 29 July 1968, Janiva Elizabeth b 24 Oct 1969, Julia Trudie b 25 Sept 1971); *Career* dep ed Kent Messenger 1983-86; ed: Kentish Express Ashford Extra, Folkestone Extra, Dover Extra, Hythe Extra, Deal Extra, Tenterden Extra; memb: Ashford C of C and Indust, Ashford Carnival Assoc; memb Guild of Br Newspaper Eds; *Recreations* fishing, skiing, walking, gardening, reading, travel; *Clubs* Elwick (Ashford); *Style—* Brian Lewis, Esq; Kentish Express, Pearl House, Station Rd, Ashford, Kent TN23 1PT (☎ 0233 623232, fax 0233 626545)

LEWIS, Ian Talbot; s of Cyril Frederick Lewis, CBE, and Marjorie, *née* Talbot; *b* 7 July 1929; *Educ* Marlborough; *m* 1, 1962, Patricia Anne, da of Rev William Dalrymple Hardy (d 1982); 2 s (James b 1964, Charles b 1966); m 2, 1986, Susan Lydia, da of Henry Alfred Sargant, of Putney, London; *Career* Nat Serv KOH and QOH followed by AER Serv (Capt) 1952-61; under sec (legal) Treasy Slrs Office 1982-90, memb Law Cmmn Working Gp on Commonhold 1986-87; pres Fordcombe Village Hall 1989-, chm Fordcombe Soc 1990-, govr Fordcombe C of E (Aided) Primary Sch 1990-; ctee memb Marlburian Club 1984-87, pres Blackheath FC (RU) 1985-88, hon vice pres Blackheath CC; Liveryman Worshipful Co of Merchant Taylors; *Recreations* sport, countryside, theatre, reading, films; *Clubs* Cavalry and Guards, MCC, Blackheath FC (RU), Piltdown Golf; *Style—* Ian Lewis, Esq; South Cottage, Fordcombe, Tunbridge Wells, Kent TN3 0RY (☎ 0892 740413)

LEWIS, James Laurence; s of Arthur Wells, of Laguna Niguel, California, and Evelyn, *née* Eisner; *b* 6 June 1949; *Educ* St Paul's, Guy's Hosp Med Sch Univ of London (MB BS, MS, MRCP); *m* 2 da (Carrie Laura b 1981, Megan Rachel b 1985); *Career* res fell Harvard Med Sch Boston Massachusetts 1979-80, sr registrar Guy's Hosp London 1981-87 (surgical registrar 1975-79), conslt gen surgn and urologist Tunbridge Wells Health Authy 1987-; memb: BMA, Hosp Conslts and Specialists Assoc, Br Tennis Umpires Assoc, Br Sub Aqua Club; assoc memb Br Assoc of Urological Surgns; memb BMA, FRCS; *Recreations* theatre, writing, diving, travel; *Style—* James Lewis, Esq; 5 Harescroft, St Marks Rd, Tunbridge Wells, Kent TN2 5XE (☎ 0892 549124); Pembury Hosp, Dept of Surgery, Tunbridge Wells, Kent TN2 4QJ (☎ 0892 823535, ext 3177)

LEWIS, Michael; s of Stanley Herbert Lewis, Oldroyd House, 55 London Rd, Canterbury, Kent, and Renée Hilda, *née* Enticknap; *b* 7 April 1933; *Educ* Truro Sch, Law Soc Coll; *m* 11 Oct 1961, Margaret Alison, da of Dr Frederick Walter Pringle (d 1967); 1 s (Douglas Keith Toten b 7 June 1965), 2 da (Patricia Alison Hilda b 13 Jan 1963, Sarah-Anne Douglas b 12 June 1964); *Career* Nat Serv Pilot Offr RAF 1957-59; slr 1957-; leader Gillingham Borough Cncl 1974-89 (memb 1960-); memb: Rochester Bridge Tst, Medway Ports Authy, Medway (Chatham) Dock Co Ltd, Rotary, 41 Club; Freemason; memb Law Soc; *Recreations* music, watching Gillingham FC; *Clubs* Wig and Pen, Crew's Quaters (Chatham); *Style—* Michael Lewis, Esq; Ewhurst, 5 Park Ave, Gillingham; Kingsley Smith & Co, 48 Canterbury St, Gillingham (☎ 0634 577261, fax 577270, telex 965112)

LEWIS, William Edward (Bill); s of Edward Francis Lewis (d 1969), and Helen, *née* Brown (d 1990); *b* 2 Aug 1953; *Educ* Westborough Secdy Modern, Medway Coll of Art and Design; *m* 17 Oct 1981, Ann Frances, da of Alan Frank Morris, JP, of Ditton, nr Maidstone; *Career* poet; fndr memb The Medway Poets Gp 1977, work has been translated into Spanish by Latin American poets Claribel Alegria and Clara Allen; readings incl: The Kent Lit Festival 1980 and 1982-84, The Cambridge Int Festival 1981, The Brighton Festival 1985 and 1987, The Angels of Fire Festival of Radical Poetry

(London) 1985, The Elephant Fayre (Cornwall) 1986, The Gillingham Arts Festival 1987 and 1988, The Casa Benjamin Linder (Nicaragua), ICA, The Drill Wall, The Hazlit Theatre (Maidstone), The Orchard Theatre (Dartford), The Zap Club (Brighton); subject of TVS documentary film 1982, writer in residence Brighton Festival 1985, has made various TV and Radio appearances in GB USA and Aust, sections of Rage Without Anger read out by membs of FMLN Guerillas on Radio Farbundo Marti in El Salvador 1989; lyricist and performer; former teacher of poetry at Maidstone Prison, has read at E Sutton Park Borstal for Girls; took part in: Life Prisoners Summer Sch, Prisoner 92 Project; memb: Amnesty International, Chile Ctee for Human Rights, Christian Socialist Movement, Shelter; involved in: Medway Poets tour for Amnesty International 1987, readings and fund raising for Oxfam and Christian Aid; *Books* Poems 1975-83 (1983), Night Clinic (1984), Communion (1986), Rage Without Anger (1987); *Recreations* films, readings, travel, study of Latin American Literature; *Style*— Bill Lewis, Esq; 66 Glencoe Rd, Chatham, Kent ME4 5QE (☎ 0634 827308)

LILLICRAP, Dr David A; s of Albert E Lillicrap (d 1984), of St Leonards-on-Sea, Sussex, and Margaret E, *née* Baldwin; *b* 26 Oct 1930; *Educ* St Edwards Sch Oxford, St Edmund Hall Coll Oxford (MA, BM, BCR), Guy's Hosp; *m* 15 June 1957, Gwyneth Elizabeth, da of Philip Roberts (d 1987), of Cliftonville; 3 s (Stephen b 17 March 1958, Richard b 20 May 1964, Peter b 22 June 1965), 1 da (Susan b 24 Feb 1960); *Career* sr registrar Guy's Hosp 1962-66, res fell John Hopkin's Hosp Balitmore 1965, conslt physician Thanet Dist Gen Hosp 1966-, conslt endocrinologist Kent and Canterbury Hosp 1966-; memb: Margate Rotary Club, Canterbury and Thanet Health Authy, Holy Trinity Church CLiftonville; *Recreations* squash, sailing; *Clubs* Thanet Squash, Margate Sailing; *Style*— Dr David Lillicrap; 29 Princes Gardens, CLiftonville, Margate, Kent CT9 3AR (☎ 0843 292335); Thanet District General Hosp, St Peters Rd, Margate, Kent CT9 4AN (☎ 0843 225544)

LILLICRAP, Dr David Anthony; s of Albert Ernest Lillicrap (d 1984), and Margaret, *née* Baldwin (d 1958); *b* 26 Oct 1930; *Educ* St Edwards Sch Oxford, St Edmund Hall Oxford, Guy's Hosp London (BM, BCh, MA); *m* 15 June 1957, Gwyneth Frances, da of Philip Lister Roberts (d 1987); 3 s (Stephen b 1958, Richard b 1964, Peter b 1965), 1 da (Susan b 1960); *Career* sr registrar in med Guy's Hosp 1962-66, res fell John Hopkins Hosp Baltimore 1964-65, conslt physician Thanet Dist Hosp 1966-, conslt endocrinolist Canterbury Hosp Kent 1966-; memb: Margate Rotary Club, Dist Health Authy Canterbury Thanet; FRCP 1974; *Recreations* squash, dinghy sailing, bridge; *Style*— Dr David Lillicrap; 29 Princes Gdns, Cliftonville, Margate, Kent CT9 3AR (☎ 0843 292 335); Thanet Dist Gen Hosp, Margate, Kent (☎ 0843 225 544)

LILLY, Prof Malcolm Douglas; s of Charles Victor Lilly (d 1977), and Amy, *née* Gardner; *b* 9 Aug 1936; *Educ* St Olave's GS, UCL (BSc, PhD), Univ of London (DSc); *m* 19 Sept 1959, Sheila Elizabeth, da of George Frederick Andrew Stuart (d 1973); 2 s (Andrew Stuart b 14 Nov 1966, Duncan Stuart b 12 May 1968); *Career* RNVR 1953-54, Nat Serv RN 1954-56; prof biochem engrg UCL 1979- (lectr 1963-72, reader 1972-79), dir Whatman Biochemicals 1968-71, visiting prof Univ of Pennsylvania USA 1969, chm Int Orgn for Biotechnol and Bioengrg 1972-80, cncl memb Soc of Gen Microbiology 1979-83, memb Br Gas Res Ctee 1982-, dir Inst Biotechnol Studies 1983-89, visiting res fell Merck Sharp and Dohme USA 1987, bd memb Public Health Lab Serv 1988-, fell UCL 1988-, dir Int Inst of Biotechnol 1989-; vice chm Govrs St Olaves GS Orpington, observer SE Gp Inst of Advanced Motorists; FIChemE 1980, FEng 1982; *Books* Fermentation and Enzyme Technology (jtly, 1979); *Recreations* advanced motoring, sailing, swimming; *Style*— Prof Malcolm Lilly; Collingwood, 8 Tower Rd, Orpington, Kent BR6 0SQ (☎ 0689 21762); Dept of Chemical and Biochemical Engineering, University College London, Torrington Place, London WC1E 7JE (☎ 071 380 7368, fax 071 388 0808)

LIMENTANI, Alexander Esmond; s of Uberto Limentani, and Barbara Cicely, *née* Hoban (d 1984); *b* 21 Sept 1949; *Educ* Perse Sch Cambridge, Guys Hosp Med Sch Univ of London (MBBS); *m* 12 June 1975, Jeanette, da of Arthur Edward Lawrence, of Bromley; 1 s (Christopher b 1981), 1 da (Elizabeth b 1977); *Career* specialist in community med 1981-82, dist MO Canterbury and Thanet Health Authy 1982-; memb Rutherford Coll Univ of Kent, conslt Health Servs Res Unit; LRCP 1973, MRCS 1973, MFCM 1981, FFCM 1988, memb Soc for Social Med; *Recreations* watercolours, beekeeping, walking, swimming; *Style*— Alexander Limentani, Esq; Regency Buildings, 3 Royal Crescent, Ramsgate, Kent (☎ 0843 594592)

LINDLEY, (Raymond) Peter; s of Frederick George Lindley, and Edith Elizabeth, *née* Evans (d 1979); *b* 26 May 1929; *m* 1953, Lilian May, *née* Scales; 1 da; *Career* insur broker, ret; former dir: Reed Stenhouse UK Ltd 1969-85, Reed Stenhouse Ltd 1979-85; conslt to various cos and slrs; FCII; *Recreations* flyfishing, genealogy, music, collecting porcelain; *Style*— Peter Lindley, Esq; Springrove House, Redwings Lane, Pembury, Tunbridge Wells, Kent (☎ 089 282 2172)

LINDSAY, Robert Keith; s of Robert Lindsay (d 1978); *b* 15 Nov 1936; *Educ* Lancing, Magdalene Coll Cambridge; *m* 1961, Elisabeth, *née* Smith; 2 s, 1 da; *Career* dir Tennant Trading Ltd 1974-79, md New Metals and Chemicals Hldgs Ltd 1979-; CEng, FICemE; *Recreations* squash, gardening; *Clubs* IOD, Wilderness Squash; *Style*— Robert Lindsay, Esq; Russell House, Station Rd, Otford, Sevenoaks, Kent (☎ 09592 2352); Abbey Chambers, Highbridge St, Waltham Abbey, Essex (☎ 0992 711111)

LINFOOT, (Arthur) Denis; s of Arthur Lindsay Linfoot (d 1977), of Sunderland, Co Durham, and Jessie Fenwick, *née* Thatcher (d 1985); *b* 9 April 1931; *Educ* Bede Sch Sunderland, Univ of Durham (BA), Trinity Coll Cambridge (Major Open Scholar, MA); *m* 7 Aug 1958, Edith Osborne, da of Charles John Osborne, of Sunderland; 3 s (Charles Robert Fenwick b 1961, Matthew James Arthur b 1964, Edmund William Francis b 1966); *Career* Nat Serv 1952-54, Sgt Intelligence Corps Malaya 1953-54 (despatches); lectr comparative linguistics SOAS Univ of London 1956-57; Univ of Birmingham: various admin posts 1957-61, dep registrar 1961-1963; registrar Univ of Warwick 1963-69; University of Kent at Canterbury: fin offr 1969-84, registrar 1981-; chm: Br Univs Fin Offrs' Conf 1979, Conf of Registrars and Secs 1990; *Recreations* reading, walking, gardening, music; *Style*— Denis Linfoot, Esq; The University, Canterbury, Kent CT2 7NZ (☎ 0227 762349)

LING, Maj-Gen Fergus Alan Humphrey; CB (1958), CBE (1964), DSO (1944), DL (1969); s of John Richardson Ling (d 1938), of Bath, and Mabel, *née* Pratchitt (d 1948); *b* 5 Aug 1914; *Educ* Stowe, RMC Sandhurst; *m* 20 March 1940, Sheelah Phyllis, da of William Godfrey Molyneux Sarel (d 1950), of Berks; 2 s (Anthony b 1941, Philip b 1946), 3 da (Virginia b 1948, Elizabeth and Diana b 1950); *Career* cmd 2/5 Bn Queen's Royal Regt Italy 1944, DS Staff Coll Camberley 1951-53, cmd 5 Bn Queen's Royal Regt 1954-57, asst mil sec WO 1957-58, Cdr 148 Inf Bde (TA) 1958-61, Dep Adj-Gen Rhine Army 1961-65, Gen Offr cmd 54 E Anglian Div (TA) and Cdr E Anglian 1965-67, GOC Eastern Dist 1967-69, ret; dir: Caffin Holdings Ltd 1969-72, Lundi Appeal 1969; fndr admin dir Inst for the Study of Conflict 1970-72, def conslt ISC 1972-82; chm Surrey TAVR Assoc 1973-78, Col The Queen's Regt 1973-77 (Col 1969-73); vice Lord-Lieut Surrey 1973-82; chm SE TAVR Assoc 1978-79 (vice chm 1973-78); *Recreations* grandchildren, gardening; *Clubs* Royal Cwlth Soc; *Style*— Maj-Gen Fergus A H Ling, CB, CBE, DSO, DL; Mystole Coach House, nr Canterbury, Kent CT4 7DB (☎ 0227 738496); Shepherd House, Netherwasdale, nr Seascale, Cumbria (☎ 0940 6312)

LINNITT, (Frederick) Basil Wellesley; s of Lt Col Charles Linnitt, JP (d 1968), of Weymouth, Dorset, and Winifred May Linnitt (d 1970); *b* 15 June 1917; *Educ* Weymouth GS, Univ of Southampton; *m* 29 Aug 1942, Brenda, da of Alfred Eason; 1 da (Jane Brenda b 9 July 1958); *Career* WWII RAOC, latterly Staff Capt legal aid section West Cmd; slr; local govt offr (40 yrs) appointments incl: dep town clerk Royal Borough of Windsor, chief exec Malling Rural DC (ret); memb KCC for Malling Rural North Div (12yrs), former fndr pres Malling Rotary Club, pres West Malling Branch Royal Br Legion; *Recreations* football, cricket, tennis; *Clubs* MCC, Surrey CC, Kent CC; *Style*— Basil Linnitt, Esq; 6 Friars Court, Queen Anne Rd, Maidstone, Kent ME14 1ER (☎ 0622 672923)

LINTON, (George) David Hough; TD (1962); s of George Blyth Linton (d 1943), of Croydon, and Annie Maude, *née* Hough (d 1958); *b* 20 Sept 1916; *Educ* Tonbridge; *m* 7 June 1947, (Ellen) Pamela, da of Stanley Flood (d 1940), of Herne Bay; 2 s (Jeremy b 1948, Peter b 1952), 1 da (Anne b 1956); *Career* HAC 1940, cmmnd RA 1940, served in India and Burma as GSO3 air liaison offr 1946, cmmnd Intelligence Corps TA 1950, ret 1962; press offr Miny of Civil Aviation Heathrow Airport 1947-49, Shell Petroleum Co Ltd London and Borneo 1949-58, dep head Greenlys PR Ltd 1960-64, involved with editorial work and overseas exhibitions London C of C 1966-70, dir pub affrs Inst of Work Study Practitioners 1970-71; ed: House Information Services Ltd 1973-74, Benn's Press Directory Tonbridge 1976-81; mangr Hollis Directories Ltd 1974-76, archivist History of Advertising Tst 1986-87; currently: press historian and bibliographer, book reviewer on media and military subjects, indexer; hon PRO and cncl memb Friends of the Imperial War Museum 1987-89 (memb Editorial Ctee 1987-), museum tstee Intelligence Corps Ashford, ctee memb and publicity offr Royal Br Legion Shoreham, dir and ctee memb and hon librarian London Press Club; memb: Soc of Indexers, Friends of Inst of Hist Res, HAC, Air PR Assoc, Old Tonbridgian Soc, Shoreham Soc; vice pres Warlingham RFC; FIPR 1978 (MIPR 1950); *Books* The Newspaper Press in Britain: An Annotated Bibliography (co-ed, 1987); *Recreations* tennis; *Style*— David Linton, Esq, TD; Vine Cottage, 1 High St, Shoreham, Sevenoaks, Kent TN14 7TB (☎ 095 92 4507)

LISHMAN, Prof (William) Alwyn; s of George Hackworth Lishman (d 1984), of Whitburn, Tyne and Wear, and Madge Scott, *née* Young (d 1980); *b* 16 May 1931; *Educ* Houghton-Le-Spring GS, Univ of Birmingham Med Sch (BSc, MB ChB, DPM, MD, DSc); *m* 4 June 1966, Marjorie, da of Cecil Victor Loud (d 1987), of Portsmouth, Hants; 1 s (James William Michael b 11 June 1973), 1 da (Victoria Alison b 12 Oct 1971); *Career* conslt in psychological med: Nat Hosp Queen Square 1966-67, RPMS 1967-69, Bethlem and Maudsley Hosps 1967-; prof of Neuropsychiatry Univ of London 1979-, civilian conslt to RAF 1987-; examiner: Univ of Oxford 1975-79, Univ of Birmingham 1984-87, Nat Univ of Malaysia 1989; memb: Neurosciences Bd MRC 1976-78, Experimental Psychology Soc 1978-, Assoc of Br Neurologists 1979-; scientific advsr DHSS 1979-82, chm Br Neuropsychiatry Assoc 1987-; MRCP 1958, FRCP 1972, FRCPsych 1972; *Books* Organic Psychiatry: The Psychological Consequences of Cerebral Disorder (1978, 2 edn 1987); *Recreations* organ, piano, harpsichord, travel; *Style*— Prof Alwyn Lishman; Institute of Psychiatry, De Crespigny Park, London SE5 8AF (☎ 071 703 5411)

LISTER, Anthony Charles Bramham; s of David Bramham Lister (d 1980), and Monica Joan, *née* Russell; *b* 31 Aug 1939; *Educ* Sutton Valence, Coll of Estate Mgmnt St Albans Grove London; *m* 1 June 1963, Susan Kitty, da of (Harold) Norman Funnell, of Great Paddock Farm, Challock, Ashford; 3 s (Giles Anthony Bramham b 12 Jan 1966, Timothy Norman Bramham (twin) b 12 Jan 1966, Guy Bramham b 16 Oct 1968); *Career* equity ptnr Geering and Colyer Chartered Surveyors 1972-82, Black Horse Agencies 1982-90 (memb Bd Mgmnt 1982, head Residential Agency 1988), Keswick Holdings Ltd 1990; RICS: chm Kent Jr Orgn 1972-72, memb Ctee Kent Branch 1973-74; chm: Ashford Chamber of Trade 1974, Challock and Molash Branch Cons Assoc 1975-80, Maidstone and Dist Estate Agents Assoc 1981; Freeman City of London 1961, Liveryman Worshipful Co of Leathersellers 1964 (Freeman 1961, 3 Warden 1988-89); AMBIM 1968, FRICS 1970; *Recreations* sheep farming, golf, sailing; *Clubs* Rye Golf, Whitstable Sailing; *Style*— Anthony Lister, Esq; Dean Court, Westwell, Ashford, Kent TN25 4NH (☎ 0233 712924); Keswick Holdings Ltd, Kent House, Station Rd, Ashford, Kent TN23 1PP (☎ 0233 640220)

LITTLE, Cncllr James Frederick; s of John Little (d 1976), of Belfast, and Rozeina, *née* Lennox (d 1980); *b* 2 Oct 1927; *Educ* St Mary's Christian Brothers Sch Belfast, City of London Coll, Regent St Poly, Catford Coll of Commerce, Woolwich Poly; *m* 26 March 1955, June, da of Joseph Benstead, of London; 4 s (John Stephen b 15 May 1956 d 22 May 1972, David James b 23 March 1959, Simon Joseph b 8 Aug 1962, Hugh Brendan b 21 Nov 1963), 1 da (Ruth Patricia b 11 March 1958); *Career* BR employee for 30 years incl: traffic costing accountant, organiser of traffic surveys and nat market res prog, headquarters passenger offr and mktg offr; Lab Pty: joined 1946, former chm sec and treas Gravesend, former memb Nat Local Govt Advsy Ctee, chm Southern Regnl Cncl 1988-, chm Regnl Local Govt and Policy Ctee; former memb: Bermondsey Met Borough Cncl, Swanscombe Urban Dist Cncl 1961-62, Northfleet Urban Dist Cncl 1962-65, Gravesend Borough Cncl 1966-69 and 1971-74, Gravesham Dist Cncl 1973-74; memb: Gravesham Borough Cncl 1974-76 and 1983-, Kent CC 1965-67 and 1974- (oppn ldr); contested parly elections as: Lab and Co-op candidate Lewes Feb and Oct 1974, Lab candidate Thanet West 1979, Lab candidate Bexleyheath 1987; memb Political Ctee and Kent Branch Ctee Co-op Wholesale Society Ltd SE Retail Gp, sec Gravesend and Dist Co-op Pty; former chm: Educn Ctee Gravesend Co-op Society Ltd, Dartford and Gravesham Community Health Cncl; former memb: Tport Salaried Staffs Assoc (chm four branches), Mgmnt Staffs Jt Ctee BR Headquarters; memb: Dartford and Gravesham Health Authy, Kent Ambulance Ctee 1983-88, Fabian Soc, Meopham Fabian Soc, Gravesend Community Rels Cncl, NHS Unlimited; chm and mental health mangr Mabledon Unit House Ctee for Polish and East Euro Patients, has given evidence to Select Ctees of the House of Commons and prepared briefs for Lab spokesmen in both Houses of Parl; Gold Cross of Merit Repub of Poland in Exile, Gold Medal Tport Salaried Staffs' Assoc, TUC Silver Medal for Trades Cncl Offrs; memb: Inst of Tport Admin, Inst of Materials Management, MRS; MCIT; *Recreations* gardening, wine making; *Clubs* Irish, Invicta (Gravesend), Gravesend Trades Hall; *Style*— Cncllr James Little; 17 Singlewell Rd, Gravesend, Kent DA11 7PN (☎ 0474 566912); Kent County Council, County Hall, Maidstone, Kent ME14 1XQ (☎ 0622 671411, fax 0622 681097)

LITTLE, Dr Margaret Isabel; da of John Terry Little (d 1945), of Bedford, and Lilian Helen, *née* Dixson (d 1954); *b* 21 May 1901; *Educ* Bedford HS for Girls, Bedford Coll for Women, St Mary's Hosp Med Sch Univ of London; *m* Aug 1966, Reginald Sizen, MC; *Career* GP; clinical asst Elizabeth Garrett Anderson Hosp 1930-36, dist med offr Burnt Oak Edgeware 1930-39; memb professional staff: Tavistock Clinic 1938-42, London Clinic of Psychoanalysis 1945-62; asst med offr Brook House London 1939-40, trg analyst Inst of Pschoanalysis 1950-71, lecture tours in USA 1958 and 1964, ret 1976; co-fndr Hendon Branch Family Welfare Assoc (now CAB), memb Dunton Green Gardening Soc; memb: Br Psychoanalyical Soc, Int Psychoanalytical Assoc; founding memb MRCPsych 1971, MRCS, LRCP 1927; *Books* Transference Neurosis and Transference Psychosis - Toward Basis Unity (1980), Psychotic Anxieties and Containment (1990); *Recreations* painting in oil and gouache, mosaic, gardening; *Clubs* Free Painters and Sculptures, Knockholt Art; *Style*— Dr Margaret Little; 1 Mayfield, 72 London Rd, Dunton Green, Sevenoaks, Kent TN13 2UG (☎ 0732 462421)

LIVESEY, Dr Carole Andrea; da of Arnold Livesey, and Pauline Livesey; *b* 2 Oct 1947; *Educ* Whyteleaf Co GS, Middx Hosp Sch of Nursing (SRN), Middx Hosp Med Sch Univ of London (MB BS); *m* 23 Sept 1972, David Robert Clarke; 1 s (Hugo David Lee b 27 Nov 1980), 1 da (Poppy Anna Lee b 7 April 1979); *Career* staff nurse Middx Hosp 1970-72, house surgn and physician Medway Hosp 1977-78, clinical asst in nephrology Kent and Canterbury 1979-; currently: community and family planning Dr Maidstone and Medway Area Health Authy, sessional Dr dealing with women's problems in gen practice at Med Centre Sittingbourne; *Recreations* gardening, reading; *Style*— Dr Carole Livesey; Hartlip House, Hartlip, Sittingbourne, Kent ME9 7TL (☎ 0795 842569); 32 London Rd, Sittingbourne, Kent ME10 1ND (☎ 0795 472109)

LIVESEY, Dr Peter Gerard; s of Edmund Livesey (d 1978), of Chorley, Lancs, and Sarah, *née* Baxendale; *b* 23 April 1944; *Educ* The Catholic Coll Preston, Univ of Leeds Med Sch (MD, MB, ChB, DObstRCOG); *m* 22 July 1972, Tessa Mary, da of Capt (David) Rodney Burles, RE, of Thorpe Bay Essex; 2 s (Paul Nicholas b 1973, Christopher Michael b 1980); *Career* Royal Infirmary Leeds: house offr 1968-69, registrar in med and nuclear med 1969-72; Anglo-German Wellcome Fellowship Award Univ of Munich 1972-73, trainee GP with Dr R Jeremy Barnes Gloucester 1974-75, princ GP (ptnr) Cossington House Surgery 1975-90, hon clinical asst in nuclear med Kent and Canterbury Hosp 1977-90, trainer in gen practice at Canterbury 1983-90, med offr Kent Coll Canterbury 1985-90, peripatetic lectr on gen practice 1987-, assoc advsr in gen practice SE Thames Region 1990-; Mustard Seed Registered Charity Day Centre for Mentally Ill Canterbury: memb 1980-90, chm and dir 1987-89; govr Blean Co Primary Sch 1985-90, memb local med ctee 1989-90; *Books* Study of Some Thyroid Function Tests (MD Thesis, 1976), Partners in Care: The Consultation in General Practice (1986), articles and poems on general practice; *Recreations* tennis, art, architecture, wine; *Clubs* Chestfield CC; *Style*— Dr Peter Livesey; Kiln House, Tile Kiln Hill, Blean, Canterbury CT2 9EE (☎ 0227 471433); Cossington House, Cossington Rd, Canterbury CT1 3HX (☎ 0227 763377)

LIVESEY, Robert; s of Stanley Livesey (d 1960), and Mable, *née* Heigh; *b* 23 Aug 1938; *Educ* Grace Ramsden GS, Huddersfield Coll of Technol; *m* 28 Oct 1961, Joan, da of Clifford Ledgard; 4 s (Stephen Alan b 1962, David Andrew b 1964, Graham Michael b 1967, Jonathan Robert b 1973); *Career* chartered measurement and control technologist; chm and fndr Chemitrol Process Equipment Ltd 1977-; Fisher Process Equipment Ltd 1972-77; MIMC; *Recreations* restoration of medieval buildings; *Style*— Robert Livesey, Esq; Chainhurst Farm, Hunton Rd, Marden, Kent; Cook Lubbock House, St Faith's St, Maidstone, Kent

LIVINGSTONE, Linda; da of Richard George Thomas Morrison, of Dover, Kent, and Mary Jean Morrison, *née* Abbott; *b* 11 March 1948; *Educ* Dover GS for Girls; *m* 23 Sept 1972, Roger David Walter Livingstone, s of Cecil Walter Livingstone (d 1986); 2 s (Robert David b 23 April 1981, Iain Richard b 30 June 1984); *Career* prodn dept asst Reader's Digest Assoc 1969-72, PA City Engr Canterbury City Cncl 1972-81, parish clerk Chestfield Parish Cncl 1988-; RNLI (Whitstable): fndr branch sec 1973-86, chm 1986-88 (received award for services to Life-Boat); *Recreations* piano, family history; *Clubs* Whitstable Book, Dover Soc; *Style*— Mrs Linda Livingstone

LIYANAGE, Dayantha Porambe (Dai); s of Wilmot Porambe Liyanage (d 1971), of Colombo, Sri Lanka, and Valerie Porambe, *née* Rupasinghe, of Finchley, London N3; *b* 18 May 1944; *Educ* Royal Coll Colombo Sri Lanka, Paddington Tech Coll London, Brunel Univ Uxbridge; *m* 27 May 1972, Mary Assumpta, da of Michael Quirke, of Limerick, Eire; 2 da (Aoife Sunitha b 11 Jan 1981, Claire Ruwani b 16 Nov 1983); *Career* work study offr: GLC 1970-71, London Borough of Barnet 1971-73; mgmnt servs offr London Borough of Ealing 1973-74, sr O & M analyst British Shoe Corporation 1974-75, head of work study and O & M Zambia Consolidated Copper Mines 1976-80, princ mgmnt servs offr City of Westminster 1980-86, project mangr for mgmnt consltg gp performance review and policy studies mangr London Borough of Tower Hamlets 1986-; chm Gillingham Lib Assoc 1985, memb Mgmnt Ctee Woodlands Youth Centre Gillingham, cncllr for Gillingham NW 1985-, memb Kent Police Authy 1985-89, vice chm Home Cos Libs 1986, chm Kent Lib Fedn (currently Kent SLD) 1986-, vice chm SE (Regnl) Lib Democrats 1988, memb Kent Educn Ctee, chm Vocational Servs Ctee Medway Rotary Club 1990, govr of three local schs; FMS, MBIM; *Recreations* family, travel; *Clubs* Medway Rotary; *Style*— Dai Liyanagé, Esq; 28 Woodpecker Glade, Wigmore, Gillingham, Kent ME8 0JR (☎ 0634 388979); London Borough of Tower Hamlets, Town Hall, Patriot Square, London E2 9LN (☎ 081 980 4831 ext 5035, fax 081 980 5949)

LLEWELLYN, Anthony David; s of William Henry Llewellyn (d 1977), of Rickmansworth, Herts, and Ida Elsie, *née* Davies (d 1980); *b* 23 March 1940; *Educ* Watford GS; *m* 23 May 1967, Jacqueline Hilary, da of William Frederick Curtis, of Croydon, Surrey; 2 da (Felicity b 1973, Lucinda b 1975); *Career* tax ptnr Touche Ross & Co CAs 1972-; memb Bd of Mgmnt and Fin and Gen Purposes Ctee LSHTM 1988-; ACIB 1963, FTII 1969, FCA 1977 (ACA 1970); *Recreations* tennis, skiing, bridge; *Style*— Anthony Llewellyn, Esq; Kingswood, Parkfield, Sevenoaks, Kent TN15 OHX; Touche Ross & Co, Friary Court, 65 Crutched Friars, London EC3N 2NP (☎ 071 936 3000, fax 071 480 6958)

LLOYD, Sir Richard Ernest Butler; 2 Bt (UK 1960), of Rhu, Co Dunbarton; o s of Maj Sir (Ernest) Guy Richard Lloyd, 1 Bt, DSO, DL (d 1987), and Helen Kynaston, *née* Greg (d 1984); *b* 6 Dec 1928; *Educ* Wellington, Hertford Coll Oxford (MA); *m* 6 June 1955, Jennifer Susan Margaret, er da of Brig Ereld Boteler Wingfield Cardiff, CB, CBE (d 1988), of Easton Court, nr Ludlow, Shropshire; 3 s (Timothy, Simon b 26 July 1958, Henry b 22 Feb 1965); *Heir* s, (Richard) Timothy Butler Lloyd b 12 April 1956; *Career* former Capt Black Watch, Mil Serv Malaya 1947-49; banker; exec then dir Glyn Mills & Co 1952-70, chief exec Williams & Glyn's Bank 1970-78, chm Hill Samuel Bank Ltd 1987- (dep chm 1978-80, dep chm and chief exec 1980-87, jt chm 1987-88); Freeman City of London 1964, Liveryman Worshipful Co of Mercers 1965, memb Guild of Freemen of Shrewsbury 1978; CBIM, FCIB; *Recreations* fishing, gardening, walking; *Clubs* Boodle's; *Style*— Sir Richard Lloyd, Bt; Sundridge Place, Sundridge, Sevenoaks, Kent TN14 6DD (☎ 0959 63599); Hill Samuel Bank Ltd, 100 Wood St, London EC2P 2AJ (☎ 071 628 8011, fax 071 726 2818, telex 888822 HSAMUK)

LLOYD-DAVIS, Glynne Christian; s of Col G St G Lloyd-Davis (d 1956), and Daphne Mary, *née* Barnes; *b* 9 March 1941; *Educ* St Paul's, Ealing Tech Coll, Royal Sch of Mines (Univ of London); *m* 20 April 1963, Dorothy Helen, da of Michael O'Shea, of Aust; 1 s (Simon b 1966), 1 da (Sarah b 1964); *Career* chartered sec; asst sec The RTZ Corporation plc 1976, dir subsid cos; FCIS; *Recreations* reading, walking, sketching; *Clubs* Royal Overseas League; *Style*— Glynne Lloyd-Davis, Esq; Forge Cottage, Whitehill, Ospringe, Faversham, Kent; 6 St James's Square, London SW1Y 4LD (☎ 071 930 2399, telex 24639)

LLOYD-ROBERTS, Dr Robert Edmund; TD (1972); o s of Richard Lloyd Roberts (d 1939), of Pinner, Middx, and Margaret Sarah Lloyd-Roberts, *née* Evans (d 1987); representative of a cadet branch of the ancient house of Nannau, N Wales, derived from the Princes of Powys; *b* 22 July 1925; *Educ* Merchant Taylors', St Thomas's Hosp (MB BS, LRCP); *m* 2 July 1955, Elizabeth, yr da of Dr Mandale Byers (d 1923), of Mowhan House, Co Armagh, and St Anne's-on-Sea, Lancs (the Byers of Mowhan descend from the Byres of Coates, Scotland); 2 s (Richard b 1956, Meyrick b and d 1958), 2 da (Arabella b 1959, Sophia b 1963); *Career* Lt-Col RAMC RARO formerly TA, DADMS 44 (Home Counties) Divn TA 1962-67, CO 144 Field Ambulance RAMC(V) and SMO 44 Parachute Bde (V) 1969-73; hon treas Airborne Med Soc 1973-83; princ in gen med practice 1957-90; visiting med offr: Nunnery Fields Hosp 1957-90, Mount Hosp Canterbury 1985-89; med offr: Christ Church Coll 1962-90, St Edmund's Sch Canterbury 1986-90; chm War Pensions and Industl Injuries Med Bds DHSS, local med advsr Med Advsy Serv, Civil Serv Dept, med examiner Insur Cos, Br Red Cross Soc; in attendance on HH Pope John Paul II at his visit to Canterbury Cathedral 29 May 1982; memb: Br Geriatric Soc, Canterbury Police Advsy Ctee; former memb Dist Gen Practitioners Ctee; fndr: The Welsh Registry 1990, The Royal Third Dining Club 1990; FRSM, MRCSEng; OStJ 1967; *Recreations* history, heraldry, genealogy, membership of various socs; *Clubs* Army and Navy, Kent and Canterbury (Canterbury); *Style*— Dr R E Lloyd-Roberts, TD; Plas Glanafon, Talybont, Merioneth, Gwynedd; Longport House, 8 Longport, Canterbury, Kent CT1 1PE

LOBLEY, (Charles Frederick) Martyn; s of Fredrick Lomas Lobley, of 89 Long Lane, Chadderton, and Ada Oates (d 1980); *b* 18 Nov 1957; *Educ* The Hulme GS Oldham, St George's Hosp Med Sch Univ of London (MB BS); *Career* house surgn Royal Cornwall Hosp 1981, house physician St James' Hosp London 1982; sr house offr Newham Hosp: accident and emergency 1983, paediatrics 1983, obstetrics and gynaecology 1984; sr house offr psychiatry Goodmayes Hosp Essex 1984, lectr in gen practice Guy's Hosp Med Sch 1985-, GP Thamesmead Med Assocs 1985-, freelance med journalist; memb GP Writers Assoc; MRCGP 1985, DRCOG 1985; *Recreations* writing, cooking, motor racing; *Style*— Dr Martyn Lobley; Gallions Reach Health Centre, Bentham Rd, Thamesmead, London SE28 8BE (☎ 081 3111010)

LOBO, Anthony Finton; s of John Vincent Gaspar Lobo (d 1942), of Jabalpur, India, and Maria Isabel, *née* Rebello (d 1939); *b* 17 Feb 1923; *Educ* St Aloysius HS Jabalpur India, Univ of Nagpur (BA), Univ of Saugor (LLB), Univ of London (Dip); *m* 5 Aug 1961, Margaret, da of Reginald Morgan Herbert; *Career* called to the Bar Lincoln's Inn 1958; Office of Fair Trading: legal asst 1961-73, sr legal asst 1973-83; sec Indian Catholic Assoc, fndr memb Indian Christian Assoc; chm: Catholic Congress Continuation Gp 1981-84, Catholic Assoc for Racial Justice 1984-, Br Cncl of Churches Econ Empowerment of the Black Community Sub Ctee 1989-90, Bexley Dental Servs Sub Ctee 1987-; memb: Congress of Black Catholics Steering Ctee, Greenwich and Bexley FPC 1985; organising sec Marlborough and Shenstone Summer Schs for Handicapped Children 1981-87; Papal Award Pro Ecclesia et Pontifice 1984; *Recreations* golf, squash, hockey; *Style*— Anthony Lobo, Esq; 8 Jaquets Court, North Cray Rd, Bexley, Kent DA5 3NF (☎ 0322 524436)

LOCK, Rev Canon Peter Harcourt D'Arcy; s of Edward Herbert William Lock (d 1977), and Ruth D'Arcy, *née* Jones (d 1958); *b* 2 Aug 1944; *Educ* Kingston GS, Univ of London (AKC), St Boniface Warminster Wilts; *m* 6 July 1968, Susan Russ, da of Maj Frederick John Reed, of Angmerring, Sussex; 1 s (Adam Russ D'Arcy b 7 Feb 1973), 1 da (Rebecca Russ D'Arcy b 4 May 1970); *Career* ordained: deacon 1968, priest 1969; curate parish of Meopham 1968-72; sr curate: parish of Wigmore 1972-73, parish of S Gillingham 1973-77; rector: Hartley 1977-83, parish of Fawkham and Hartley 1983-84; vicar of Dartford (Holy Trinity) 1984-, hon canon Rochester Cathedral 1990-; memb Gen Synod of C of E 1980-, vice chm Govrs of Dartford GS; chm: Dartford Almshouse Charity, Rochester Diocesan Liturgical Ctee, Govrs Holy Trinity C of E Primary Sch Dartford; *Recreations* playing and watching cricket, singing, music, calligraphy; *Clubs* Rotary Dartford 1985-; *Style*— The Rev Canon Peter Lock; The Vicarage, High St, Dartford, Kent DA1 1RX (☎ 0322 222782)

LOCKHART-MURE, Thomas Ochterlon (Tom); s of Dr Thomas Valiant Lockhart-Mure (d 1925), and Isabella Dodds McGown (d 1941); *b* 25 Aug 1904; *Educ* Edinburgh Acad; *m* 18 July 1936, Sheila, da of John MacKinnon (d 1938); 3 s (Peter Thomas b 1941, John Kevin b 1945, James Edward b 1937, d 1965); *Career* Maj KAR serv Abyssinian Campaign (despatches); Cmd HQ Inspectorate of Mechanical Tport; ptnr Manchester Airways (A Barnstorming Co) 1923; dir: Kenyan Co rep General Motors prods 1924-, Airspray Kenya; former pres: AA of E Africa, Areo Club of E Africa; conslt Caspair Air Charter; *Recreations* rugby, hockey, cricket; *Clubs* Mt Kenya Safari, Mombasa, Nairobi, Aero (E Africa); *Style*— Tom Lockhart-Mure, Esq; Mawingo, Benenden, Cranbrook, Kent (☎ 0580 241722)

LODER-SYMONDS, Roderick Francis (Roddy); s of Brig Robert Guy Loder-Symonds, DSO, MC (ka 1945), of Three Chimneys, Heytesbury, Warminster, Wilts, and Mrs Merlin Audrey Houghton Brown, *née* Allen (d 1988); *b* 16 Nov 1938; *Educ* Radley, RAC Cirencester; *m* 20 July 1987, Caroline Anne, da of Cdr M F L Beebee (d 1988), of Womaston House, Presteigne, Radnorshire; 2 s (Robert b 31 Aug 1971, James b 28 May 1974), 1 da (Sacha b 19 Nov 1968); *Career* farmer Wellshead Farm Exford Somerset 1960-67, asst surveyor Knight Frank and Rutley 1962-72, ptnr Strutt & Parker 1976- (joined 1973); church warden Womenswold Church 1970-82; chm: Farmers Club 1976, Parish Cncl 1978-86, Canterbury Farmers Club 1982, Kent Branch CLA 1986-87; bd memb Enterprise Agency E Kent 1985-, jt chm NFU/CLA Channel Tunnel Working Pty 1986-87; FRICS 1976; *Recreations* shooting and hunting; *Clubs* Farmers, Army and Navy; *Style*— Roddy Loder-Symonds, Esq; Denne Hill Farm, Womenswold, Canterbury, Kent CT4 6HD (☎ 0227 831203); Strutt & Parker, 2 St Margaret's St, Canterbury, Kent CT1 2TG (☎ 0227 451123, fax 0227 762509); 13 Hill St, London W14 8DL (☎ 071 627 7282)

LOMAS, John Raymond; s of Raymond Lomas (d 1988), of Halifax, Yorkshire, and Edith, *née* Blagg; *b* 16 May 1949; *Educ* Crossley and Porter Sch Halifax, Manchester Poly, Sheffield City Coll of Educn (Dip Special Educn); *m* 7 Feb 1976, Lynn Margaret, da of Eric Bateson, of Bishopthorpe, York; 2 da (Hannah Louise Mary b 25 March 1982, Noami Jane Ruth b 29 Oct 1983); *Career* teacher of children with special needs; dep headteacher: Taxal Lodge Sch Whaley Bridge 1978-81, Woodlands Sch Scarborough 1981-84; headteacher Broomhill Bank Sch Tunbridge Wells 1984-; *Recreations* sailing, climbing, hill walking, cycling; *Clubs* Bewl Valley Sailing, Medway Yacht, Filey Sailing, Tunbridge Wells Mountaineering; *Style*— John Lomas, Esq; Headteacher's Flat, Broomhill Bank School, Rusthall, Tunbridge Wells Kent TN3 OTB (☎ 0892 22666)

LONDON, John Frederick; s of Eric Horton London, MBE, of Bexhill-on-Sea, and Doris Emma, *née* Browning; *b* 17 Nov 1934; *Educ* Tonbridge; *m* 6 Oct 1962, Merrill Anne, da of Alfred Edward James Prior (d 1969), of Sevenoaks; 1 s (James Frederick Justin b 8 Nov 1964), 2 da (Anne-Louise Merrill b 27 Oct 1967, Sally Anne Claire b 3 Aug 1969); *Career* dir Gerald Quin Cope and Co Ltd 1974-85 (asst dir 1972-74), md Quin Cope Ltd 1985-89; chm: Sevenoaks Mental Health Assoc 1962-70, Sevenoaks UDC 1970-71 (memb 1959-62 and 1963-74), Sevenoaks Scout Cncl 1971-88; Sevenoaks Town Cncl: memb 1973-, Mayor 1973-74 and 1988-89; vice chm Sevenoaks Constituency Cons Pty 1989-; *Recreations* sailing, gardening, motoring, reading; *Clubs* Overseas Bankers, Chipstead Sailing; *Style*— John London, Esq; 18 Knole Way, Sevenoaks, Kent TN13 3RS (☎ 0732 456327)

LONG, Martin William; s of Sidney William Long, and Vera Nellie, *née* Pope; *b* 25 March 1958; *Educ* Bromley GS for Boys, Ravensbourne Sch for Boys, Univ of Southampton; *Career* CA; audit mangr Touche Ross & Co Papua New Guinea 1984-86 (Dartford 1979-84), internal audit Marley plc Sevenoaks 1986-88, fin accountant Marley Foam Ltd 1988-; memb ICAEW 1982; *Recreations* squash, nature; *Clubs* Walnuts; *Style*— Martin Long, Esq; Marley Foam Ltd, Lenham, Kent ME17 2DE (☎ 0622 859491)

LONG, Timothy John; s of Dr Aiden G G Long, of Bridge Cottage, Church Rd, Brasted, Kent, and Helen C, *née* Ulasto; *b* 25 Dec 1957; *Educ* St Edmunds Sch Canterbury, London College of Furniture; *Career* fndr Timothy Long Restoration 1978, specialist in restoration of seventeenth to nineteenth century furniture; memb Br Antique Furniture Restorers Assoc 1984-; *Recreations* sailing; *Style*— Timothy Long, Esq; 26A High St, Seal,

Sevenoaks, Kent (☎ 0732 62606); 26 High St, Seal, Sevenoaks, Kent (☎ 0732 62606)

LORD, Alan; CB (1972); s of Frederick Lord; *b* 12 April 1929; *Educ* Rochdale, St John's Coll Cambridge; *m* Joan; 2 da; *Career* former cmmr Inland Revenue and second perm sec Treasy; dir Allied Breweries, md Dunlop Holdings 1980- (md Dunlop Int 1978-), dir Bank of England 1983-; *Style—* Alan Lord, Esq, CB; Mardens, Hildenborough, Tonbridge, Kent (☎ Hildenborough 832268)

LORD, John William; s of William James Lord (d 1970), of 54 St Albans Close, Gravesend, Kent, and Bessie Maria, *née* Watkins; *b* 28 May 1931; *Educ* Gravesend GS for Boys; *m* 28 April 1956, Patricia Jane, da of Maj Frank Palmer (d 1979); 3 s (David b 1964, Richard b 1966, Peter b 1971); *Career* Nat Serv RAF 1953-55; articled clerk MacIntyre Hudson and Co 1948-53, qualified CA, audit mangr Evnas Fripp Deed and Co 1955-57, tax mangr Midgley Snelling and Co 1957-60, sr ptnr Carley and Co 1983- (mangr 1961, ptnr 1962-); dir and sec Gravesend Masonic Hall Co Ltd, memb Assoc of Ex Round Tablers; FCA 1953, ATII 1962; *Recreations* golf, tennis, gardening; *Clubs* Mid Kent Golf; *Style—* John Lord, Esq; Lark Rise, Pondfield Lane, Shorne, nr Gravesend, Kent DA12 3LD; 8 Overcliffe, Gravesend, Kent DA11 OHJ (☎ 0474 569032, fax 0474 320410)

LOTEN, Alexander William; CB (1984); s of late Alec Oliver Loten, and late Alice Maud Loten; *b* 11 Dec 1925; *Educ* Churcher's Coll Petersfield, Corpus Christi Coll Cambridge (BA); *m* 1954, Mary Diana Flint; 1 s, 1 da; *Career* served WWII, RNVR 1943-46; engr: Rolls-Royce Ltd Derby 1950-54, Benham & Sons Ltd London 1954-58; Air Miny Work Directorate 1958-64; MPBW: sr engr 1964-70, superintending engr (mechanical design) 1970-75; pres CIBS 1976-77, under sec DOE 1981-85, dir Mechanical and Electrical Engrg Servs PSA 1981-85 (dir of works Civil Accommodation 1975-81); *Style—* Alexander Loten, Esq, CB; Mansers Farm, Nizels Lane, Hildenborough, Tonbridge, Kent TN11 8NX (☎ 0732 833204)

LOUDON, James Rushworth Hope; s of Francis William Hope Loudon (d 1985), and Lady Prudence Katharine Patton, *née* Jellicoe; *b* 19 March 1943; *Educ* Eton, Magdalene Coll Cambridge (BA); *m* 17 May 1975, Jane Gavina, *née* Fryett; 2 s (Hugo John Hope b 1978, Alexander Guy Rushworth b 1980), 1 da (Antonia Louise Cameron b 1977); *Career* fin dir Blue Circle Industries plc 1987-; *Recreations* tennis, cricket, opera; *Clubs* MCC; *Style—* James Loudon, Esq; Olantigh, Wye, Ashford, Kent TN25 5EW (☎ 0233 812294); Blue Circle Industries plc, 84 Eccleston Square, London SW1 (☎ 071 828 3456)

LOUDON, Lady Prudence Katharine Patton; 5 da of Adm of the Fleet 1 Earl Jellicoe (d 1935), and Florence Gwendoline, *née* Cayzer (d 1964); *b* 30 Aug 1913; *Educ* N Foreland Lodge Broadstairs; *m* 22 Dec 1936, Francis William Hope Loudon (d 1985), s of James Hope Loudon (d 1952), of Olantigh, Kent; 1 s (James Rushworth Hope b 1943), 2 da (Katharine (Lady Wilkinson) b 1937, Annabella (Mrs I J Scott) b 1939); *Career* JP Kent 1963-76; former memb Cncl Univ of Kent, former govr Christ Church Coll Canterbury, past pres Kent Fedn Amenities Socs, chm Ashford Sch 1961-79, pres St Augustine's Hosp 1972-, acting chm Bd Tstees Burrswood Kent 1981-82 (memb 1970-84); *Recreations* sketching; *Style—* The Lady Prudence Loudon, JP; Little Olantigh, Wye, nr Ashford, Kent (☎ 0233 812916)

LOUGHLIN, (James) John; JP (1981); s of Michael Loughlin (d 1986), of Wicklow, and Catherine, *née* English (d 1983); *b* 15 Feb 1939; *Educ* Stratford Sch Co Wicklow; *m* 23 July 1966, Bridget, da of Michael Nyland (d 1983), of Co Mayo; 2 s (Graham John b 12 July 1969, Alan Michael b 6 Dec 1970), 1 da (Anne Marie b 13 May 1962); *Career* tport mangr 1985-88, commercial admin offr 1988-; borough cncllr Gravesham 1979- (dep ldr oppn 1983-86); memb: IBA for Local Radio 1985-86, Gravesend and Dist Mencap; dep chm Gravesham Bench 1989-, fndr govr St John's RC Sch Gravesend; memb Inst of Tport Admin; *Recreations* charity work, town twinning activities and visits; *Style—* John Loughlin, Esq, JP; 170 Old Road West, Gravesend, Kent DA11 0LZ (☎ 0474 568186); Kentish Bus & Coach Co Ltd, Apex House, London Rd, Northfleet, Kent DA11 0PD (☎ 0474 325533, fax 0474 325073)

LOVATT, Dr George Earle; s of Edward Ernest Lovatt (d 1970), of Paignton, Devon, and Alice Mary, *née* Earle (d 1965); *b* 23 June 1922; *Educ* King Edward VI GS Totnes, Univ of London (BSc, MB BS), Royal Coll of Physicians and Surgns Canada; *m* 14 May 1956, Patricia Moira (Paddy), da of Edwin Albert Kirby (d 1974), of Aldeburgh, Suffolk; 2 da (Sarah Madeleine b 1965, Jessica Anne b 1970); *Career* conslt physician London Ontario Canada 1964-71, dir med educn Univ of W Ontario 1965-71, clin res physician Wellcome Foundation Ltd 1971-87; hon consltg physician: Hammersmith Hosp London 1971-76, Hackney Hosp London 1976-87; memb: Canadian Diabetic Assoc 1964-71, American Diabetic Assoc 1964-71, Br Diabetic Assoc 1971-87, Age Concern 1987-; FRCP Canada; *Recreations* sitting, sometimes thinking; *Style—* Dr George Lovatt; Cornwood, Combe Bank Drive, Sundridge, Kent TN14 6AD (☎ 0959 62509)

LOVE, Heather Beryl; da of the late John Sydney Love, and Joyce Margaret, *née* Cracknell; *b* 17 Nov 1953; *Educ* Mayfield Sch Putney; 1 s (Matthew Paul Hodges b 1982); *Career* IPC Magazines: publicity mangr 1980, gp publicity mangr 1981, assoc publisher 1985, publisher 1988, publishing dir (Women's Journal, Marie Claire, Country Homes and Interiors) 1988-; memb Nat Small Bore Rifle Assoc; *Recreations* pistol shooting, interior design, workaholic; *Style—* Miss Heather Love; 2 Hatfields, London SE1 (☎ 071 261 5508, fax 071 261 4277)

LOWE, Peter Arthur Geary; s of Capt Kenneth Rylands Lowe (d 1967), of The Pinfold, Bleasby, Notts, and Corinne Barbara, *née* Geary; *b* 1 Sept 1951; *Educ* Canford, Univ of Bristol (BA); *m* 11 Sept 1982, Penelope Jean, da of Dr Robert William Cope (d 1976); 2 s (Christopher, Timothy); *Career* admitted slr 1978; fndr Peter Lowe & Co Slrs 1982; asst dir: Int Maritime Bureau 1984, Counterfeit Intelligence Bureau; dir: Medical Express (UK) Ltd, Heslow Enterprises Ltd; treas St Marys Church Laddingford; memb Law Soc 1978, FRGS 1980; *Recreations* skiing, tennis, squash, badminton; *Clubs* Lansdowne; *Style—* Peter Lowe, Esq; Uptons Farmhouse, Yalding, Kent (☎ 0622 872499); Peter Lowe & Co Slrs, Uptons House, Laddingford, Yalding, Kent; Maritime House, Linton Rd, Barking, Essex (☎ 081 591 3000, fax 081 594 2833, telex 8956492)

LOWNIE, His Hon Judge Ralph Hamilton; s of James Hood Wilson Lownie (d 1961), of Edinburgh, and Jessie, *née* Aitken (d 1952); *b* 27 Sept 1924; *Educ* George Watson's Coll Edinburgh, Univ of Edinburgh (MA, LLB), Univ of Kent (PhD); *m* 12 Nov 1960, Claudine Theresa, da of Pierre Claude Lecrocq (d 1976), of Reims, France; 1 s (Andrew James Hamilton b 1961), 1 da (Solange Helen Hamilton b 1963); *Career* WWII RE 1943-47, served NW Europe; called to the Bar Inner Temple 1962; practised privately as WS 1952-54, in Judicial and Legal Depts of Kenya Govt 1954-65, in Judicial Dept Bermuda Govt 1965-72, met stipendiary magistrate 1974-86, circuit judge 1986-; memb Faculty of Advocates 1959; *Style—* His Hon Judge Lownie

LOWRIE, Anthony Carmel (Tony); s of Vincent Lowrie, of Rhodesia and SA (d 1988), and Gwendoline, *née* Stephens; *b* 24 March 1942; *Educ* Llewellyn HS N Rhodesia, RMA Sandhurst; *m* 3 Nov 1969, Liv Torill, da of Torbjon Ronningen; 1 s (Alexander Christian b 27 Jan 1975), 1 da (Louise Therese (twin) b 27 Jan 1975); *Career* Cadet Rhodesian Army 1960-62, 2 Lt Platoon Cdr Middx Regt, Lt Support Platoon Queen's Regt, Capt 10 PMO Gurkha Rifles cmdg support co, Maj 1/2 Gurkha Rifles cmdg C company; bd dir Hoare Govett stockbrokers 1986- (trainee 1973, Devpt Asian Equity Sales, ptnr 1978-, dir Hoare Govett Asia, head of SE Asia Devpt Singapore), chm Hoare Govett International Securities 1988-, bd dir Security Pacific Hoare Govett; dir: The SESDAQ Fund, The Scottish Asian Fund, The Thai Euro Fund, The Malaysian Emerging Companies Fund; non-exec dir: J D Weatherspoon, City Wine Bars; non-exec chm Superchalet Ltd; memb London Stock Exchange 1984; *Recreations* rugby, golf, tennis, skiing; *Clubs* Blackheath, Walton Health Golf, Addington; *Style—* Tony Lowrie, Esq; 7 Orchard Drive, Blackheath, London SE3 (☎ 081 852 0652); Glassenbury Cottage, Cranbrook, Kent (☎ 0580 713148); Hoare Govett Ltd, Security Pacific House, 4 Broadgate, London EC2M 7LE (☎ 071 374 1256/071 601 0101, fax 071 256 9961, telex 297801)

LOWTHORPE, Michael; s of Leonard George Lowthorpe (d 1986), and Doreen, *née* Sparke; *b* 27 Oct 1946; *Educ* Maidstone GS, Medway and Maidstone Coll of Technol; *Career* Larking & Larking: articled clerk 1964-69, sr asst 1970-78, qualified CA 1974; tax sr Finnie & Co 1978-82, taxation accountant Reed International plc Publishing and Info 1982-90, gp tax mangr Reed Business Publishing Ltd 1990-; memb local accountants soc, sidesman and bible reader St Faith's Church Maidstone; FCA; *Recreations* electric organ, music, photography, travel, languages, swimming, walking; *Clubs* Lansdowne; *Style—* Michael Lowthorpe, Esq; 24 Shernolds, Maidstone, Kent ME15 9QH

LUBBOCK, Hon Lyulph Ambrose Jonathan Mark; s and h of 4 Baron Avebury, and his 1 w, Kina Maria, *née* O'Kelly de Gallagh; *b* 15 June 1954; *Educ* St Olaves GS, Univ of Birmingham (BSc); *m* 1977, Susan Carol, da of Kenneth Henry MacDonald, of Cliffsea Cottage, 10 Sunridge Close, Swanage, Dorset; 1 s (Alexander Lyulph Robert b 17 Jan 1985), 1 da (Vanessa Adelaide Felicity b 1983); *Career* local govt offr Computer Dept; *Recreations* golf, astronomy; *Style—* The Hon Lyulph Lubbock; 53 Worlds End Lane, Orpington, Kent

LUCAS, Prof Ian Albert McKenzie; CBE (1977); s of Percy John Lucas (d 1970), and Janie Inglis Hamilton (d 1984); *b* 1 July 1926; *Educ* Clayesmore Sch, Univ of Reading (BSc), McGill Univ (MSc); *m* 20 Dec 1950, Helen Louise, da of Ernest Struban Langerman (d 1930), of SA; 1 s (Michael Ian b 27 Feb 1952), 2 da (Karen Elizabeth b 25 March 1953, Catherine Helen b 17 July 1967); *Career* lectr Harper Adams Agric Coll 1949-50, princ sci offr (formerly sci offr, sr offr) Rowett Res Inst Aberdeen 1950-61, DSIR res fell Ruakura Res Station NZ 1957-58, prof of agric Univ Coll N Wales 1961-77, princ Wye Coll London 1977-88; memb: Br Soc Animal Prodn, Agric Educn Assoc, RASE, Royal Welsh Agric Soc; hon memb Br Cncl 1987; FRAgS 1972, FIBiol 1978; *Recreations* sailing; *Clubs* Farmers; *Style—* Prof Ian Lucas, CBE; Valley Downs, Brady Rd, Lyminge, Folkestone, Kent CT18 8DU (☎ 0303 863 053)

LUCAS, Dr Jeremy Simon; s of Diana Vaughan Lucas; *b* 2 Nov 1953; *Educ*

Highgate Sch London, King's Coll London (BSc, PhD); *m* 24 July 1982, Katharine Anne, da of Paul Denis Donovan, of Tunbridge Wells, Kent; 1 s (Peter Simon b 17 Aug 1989), 2 da (Hannah Victoria b 8 March 1984, Eleanor Katharine b 8 March 1986); *Career* freelance writer and journalist; staff writer at FT Magazines; current memb Eng fly-fishing team, winner of numerous nat and int fly-fishing awards, Euro fly-fishing Champion 1987 (runner-up 1989 and 1990), Benson & Hedges Nat Champion 1987, Benson & Hedges Int Silver Medallist 1987, Gold Medallist 1990; *Books* Whale, The Longest Flight, Fur, The Faroes Venture, The Last Salmon, Fly-Fisher; *Recreations* fly-fishing; *Style*— Dr Jeremy Lucas; FT Magazines (Resident Abroad Magazine), 102-108 Clerkenwell Rd, London EC1M 5SA (☎ 071 251 9321, fax 071 251 4686)

LUCAS, Nigel David; s of Joseph Lucas (d 1986), of Purley, Surrey, and Dorothy Mary, *née* Collier; *b* 14 May 1941; *Educ* Whitgift Sch, Westminster Hotel Sch; *m* 1, 19 Sept 1970, Linda Elisabeth (d 1979), da of Sidney Alfred Stanton (d 1972); 2 da (Sarah b 1973, Catherine b 1974); m 2, 5 May 1982, Janette Muriel, da of Harold Stanley Vian-Smith; 2 s (Matthew Peter b 12 Nov 1988, Andrew James (twin) b 12 Nov 1988); *Career* restaurateur and wine wholesaler; dir Castle Inn Ltd 1964-; memb: Hotel Catering and Institutional Mgmnt Assoc, Cooking and Food Assoc; Freeman City of London 1983; *Recreations* family and home; *Style*— Nigel D Lucas, Esq; Withers, Chiddingstone, Edenbridge, Kent TN8 7AE (☎ 0892 870694); Castle Inn, Chiddingstone, Edenbridge, Kent TN8 7AH (☎ 0892 870247)

LUCKHAM-DOWN, Melvyn Raymond; s of Sydney Claude Luckham-Down (d 1958), of The Glen, Plympton, Devon, and Florence Gard, *née* Oatey (d 1957); *b* 20 Aug 1926; *Educ* Plymouth Coll, Univ of London, Royal Dental Hosp (LDS, RCS); *m* 3 April 1954, Margaret Gwendoline, da of John Rees Davies (d 1950), of The Tonn, Llandovery, Wales; 2 s (John b 1956, Edwin b 1965), 1 da (Sarah b 1959); *Career* cmmnd Devonshire Regt 1944, Capt GSO3 Greece 1948, Maj RADC 1955-59; dental surgn and co dir; memb: Marine Biological Assoc, Fedn Dentaire Internationale; Freeman City of London 1977, Liveryman Worshipful Co of Wheelwrights; memb American Dental Assoc; *Recreations* fly fishing, golf, shooting, orchid growing; *Style*— Melvyn Luckham-Down, Esq

LUCY, (Judith) Elizabeth; da of Edmund Morton Butterworth, of Bedford, and Brenda, *née* Fitton; *b* 22 April 1947; *Educ* Ware GS; *m* m dis; 1 da (Gayle b 8 Feb 1982); *Career* sr housing offr Sevenoaks DC 1985-; *Recreations* sailing, gliding; *Style*— Mrs Elizabeth Lucy; Sevenoaks District Council, Council Offices, Argyle Road, Sevenoaks, Kent (☎ 0322 865040)

LUCZYC-WYHOWSKA, Hon Mrs (Oriel Annabelle Diana Skeffington); da of 13 Visc Massereene and Ferrard; *b* 6 Feb 1950; *Educ* Downham, Tunbridge Wells Tutors, La Sorbonne; *m* 1971, Dominik Albin Thomas Luczyc-Wyhowska, s of Stanislaus Luczyc-Wyhowska, of Dalcove, Roxburgh; 2 da (Sofia b 1973, Kassia b 1980); *Style*— The Hon Mrs Luczyc-Wyhowska; Chilham Castle, Chilham, nr Canterbury, Kent (☎ 0227 730319)

LUMLEY, John Adrian; s of Thomas Lumley (d 1983), and Patience, *née* Henn Collins (d 1987); *b* 29 May 1942; *Educ* Eton, Magdalene Coll Cambridge (MA); *m* 14 June 1969, Catita, da of Hans Lieb (d 1959), of Algeciras, Spain; 1 s (Joshua b 1970), 2 da (Eliza b 1973, Olivia b 1981); *Career* dir Christie's (Christie, Manson & Woods Ltd) 1969 (joined 1964); memb Kent and E Sussex Regnl Ctee Nat Tst 1981-87; Liveryman Worshipful Co of Goldsmiths 1984; *Clubs* Brooks's; *Style*— John Lumley, Esq; Court Lodge, Egerton, Ashford, Kent (☎ 023 376 249); Christie's, 8 King St, London SW1 (☎ 071 839 9060)

LUNNON, Rev Robert Reginald; s of Reginald Percy Lunnon, of 53 Kynaston Rd, Orpington, and Dorothy May, *née* Pinker (d 1986); *b* 22 June 1931; *Educ* Gravesend GS for Boys, King's Coll London (BD); *m* 6 Sept 1958, Pamela, da of Cyril John Homes (d 1980); 2 s (Jeremy Mark, Michael Simon John), 2 da (Juliet Katharine, Joanna Clare Sarah); *Career* Nat Serv Sgt RAEC 1950-52; curate: St Michael and All Angels Maidstone 1956-58, Deal Parish Church 1958-62; vicar of: Sturry 1963-68, St Stephen Norbury 1968-77, Orpington 1977-; rural dean of Orpington 1979-; AKC 1955; chaplain: Orpington branch Br Legion, Orpington branch Men of Kent and Kentish Men; govr Blenheim Primary Sch, fndn govr St Olave's and St Saviour's Schs; *Recreations* transport, current affairs, travel; *Style*— The Rev Robert Lunnon; The Vicarage, 1A Keswick Road, Orpington, Kent BR6 0EU (☎ 0689 24624)

LYLE, Dr Eric Herbert; s of Dr Herbert Willoughby Lyle (d 1956), of Portishead, Bristol, and Ada, *née* Selfe (d 1906; *b* 10 Jan 1906; *Educ* Dulwich, Clare Coll Cambridge (MA), Kings Coll Hosp (MD, BCh, LMSSA); *m* 21 July 1934, Elizabeth Ellen, da of Frederick Renatus Hughes (d 1923), of Hale, Cheshire; 1 s (Timothy John b 1937), 1 da (Sally Elizabeth b 1940); *Career* Maj: RAMC 1939-45, Reg Army Reserve of Offrs 1945-61; ophthalmic surgn to: Bromley Educn Ctee 1935-81, Bromley Hosp 1936-72, Beckenham Hosp 1952-71; *Recreations* rugby football, walking, gardening; *Style*— Dr Eric Lyle; Farley Cottage, Farley Lane, Westerham, Kent TN16 1UD (☎ 0959 64600)

LYONS, Peter William; s of William Thomas Lyons (d 1983), of Chestfield, Kent, and Benedicta Louise, *née* Bridgeland; *b* 28 Aug 1940; *Educ* Kent Coll Canterbury; *m* 7 Aug 1971, Marion Rose, da of Frederick George Vare Oxley (d 1972), of Enfield; 1 s (Geoffrey b 18 June 1974), 1 da (Julie Rose b 4 Aug 1977); *Career* accountant; articles with Larking and Larking Canterbury 1958-64, qualified sr Spicer and Pegler London 1964-66, analyst Vivian Gray and Co Stockbrokers London 1966-68, invesmt analyst Hoare Govett stockbrokers London 1968-70, sr investmt analyst McAnally Montgomery and Co stockbrokers London 1970-75, area mangr (SE) Manchester Exchange Bank Ltd 1975-77, asst mangr Corp Fin Dept London branch Deutsche Bank AG 1977-84, mangr London branch Commerzbank AG 1984-86, in practice as CA acting as fin corp and investmt conslt 1986-, former mangr Corp Banking Dept Singer & Friedlander Ltd merchant bankers London, assoc C W Lyons & Sons (Canterbury) Ltd, sr mangr funding CSL Group Limited 1989-; FCA 1964, AMSIA 1968, FBIM 1988; *Books* The Big Four Clearing Banks; *Recreations* golf; *Clubs* Canterbury Golf (former capt and hon treas), Royal Overseas League, Canterbury Cons; *Style*— Peter Lyons, Esq; 1 Westfield, Blean, Kent CT2 9ER (☎ 0227 471320); CSL Group Ltd, Consilium House, City Forum, City Rd, London EC1V 2NY (☎ 071 982 0071, fax 071 490 4474)

LYONS, Russell John Stewart; s of John Gerald Lyons, and Jean Hutcheon Horne, *née* Smith; *b* 11 May 1950; *Educ* Forest Sch, City Univ Graduate Sch (MBA); *m* 1, May 1970 (m dis 1986), Yvonne Noelly; 1 da (Caroline Jane b 26 Oct 1982); m 2, 1 June 1987, Margaret Roberta, da of Col George Lennie, MBE; *Career* dep md Nippon International 1977, md Icon International 1980, dir sales and mktg Torch Computers plc 1981 (fndr shareholder), chm Mgmnt Innovation Gp 1983-, md XAT software 1985; FCA 1973 and 1978, memb CMI 1975; *Recreations* sailing, waterskiing, riding, playing several musical instruments; *Clubs* Public Schs, East India; *Style*— Russell Lyons, Esq; Century House, Pluckley Rd, Charing, Kent (☎ 023371 3512; 9 New Rd, Rochester Kent (☎ 0634 814931, fax 0634 815878)

LYONS, Terence Patrick; s of Maurice Peter Lyons (d 1978), of Pevensey Bay, Sussex, and Maude Mary Elizabeth, *née* O'Farrell (d 1958); *b* 2 Sept 1919; *Educ* Wimbledon Coll, King's Coll London, LSE; *m* 11 June 1945, Winifred Mary, da of James Basil Ward Normile (d 1965), of Sutton, Surrey; 2 da (Moira Teresa b 16 Nov 1947, Celia Mary b 19 May 1952); *Career* Gunner RA and Offr Cadet IA 1940-41, 2 Lt Indian Armed Corps (attached RIASC) 1941-46, Capt 1942; head Staff Dept Unilever Ltd 1948-54, chief personnel offr Philips Industries (Croydon) 1954-60, gp personnel mangr Ilford Ltd 1960-66, dir of personnel Staveley Industries Ltd 1966-69, exec dir (personnel) Williams & Glyn's Bank 1969-82, dir Industl Trg Serv 1983-, conslt 1983-; pres IPM 1981-83; memb: CBI Educn Fndn Cncl 1974-86, MMC 1975-81, Open Univ Cncl 1980-90, MSC 1981-82; chm: CBI Manpower Servs Advsy Panel 1975-82, Fedn of London Clearing Bank Employers 1976-78, CBI Educn and Trg Ctee 1976-77; CIPM, FCIB; *Books* The Personnel Function in a Changing Environment (second edn 1985); *Recreations* golf, sailing, bridge, music; *Clubs* Army and Navy, Wildernesse Golf, Royal Eastbourne Golf, Chipstead Sailing, Riverhead Bridge; *Style*— Terence Lyons, Esq; Winter Ride, 2 Rosefield, Kippington Rd, Sevenoaks, Kent

M

McALISTER, Maj-Gen Ronald William Lorne; CB (1977), OBE (1968, MBE 1958); s of Col Ronald James Frier McAlister, OBE (d 1963), of Edinburgh, and Mrs Nora Ford Collins, *née* Prosser; *b* 26 May 1923; *Educ* Sedbergh; *m* 25 Jan 1964, Sally Ewart, da of Dr Gordon King Marshall (d 1974), of Broadstairs, Kent; 2 da (Angela Frances b 15 May 1965, Caroline Jane b 14 Sept 1966); *Career* cmmnd 3 QAO Gurkha Rifles 1942, Adj 1/3 Gurkha Rifles Burma 1945 (despatches), 10 Gurkha Rifles 1948, Adj 2/10 Gurkha Rifles Malaya 1949-52 (despatches), instr Sch of Infantry Warminster 1952-55, Staff Coll 1956, Bde Maj Malaya 1957-58, Jt Serv Staff Coll 1961, asst sec Chiefs of Staff Ctee MOD 1962-65, CO 1/10 Gurkha Rifles Borneo 1966 (despatches), Hong Kong 1967, instr Jt Servs Staff Coll 1968, CO Berlin Infantry Bde 1968-71, Canadian Nat Def Coll 1971-72, exercise controller to UK Cs-in-C 1972-74, Maj Gen Bde of Gurkhas and Dep Cdr Hong Kong Land Forces 1975-77, ret 1977; bursar Wellesley House Prep Sch Broadstairs 1977-88; chm: Gurkha Brigade Assoc 1980-, Buckmaster Memorial Home for Ladies Broadstairs 1983-; Capt Royal St Georges GC Sandwich 1989; *Books* Bugle and Kukri Vol 2(1986); *Recreations* golf, gardening; *Clubs* Army and Navy, Senior Golfers Soc; *Style—* Maj-Gen Ronald McAlister, CB, OBE; The Chalet, 41 Callis Court Rd, Broadstairs, Kent

McALPINE, Kenneth; DL (Kent 1975); s of Sir Malcolm McAlpine, KBE (d 1968), of Fairmile Court, Cobham, Surrey, and Maud Dees (d 1969); *b* 21 Sept 1920; *Educ* Charterhouse; *m* 24 Nov 1955, Patricia Mary, da of Capt Francis William Hugh Jeans, CVO, RN (d 1968), of Summerfold, Rudgwick, Sussex; 2 s (Richard Hugh b 24 April 1958, James Thomas Hemery b 29 Sept 1960); *Career* flying offr RAFVR 1942-46; dir Newarthill plc 1972-, proprietor Lamberhurst Vineyards 1972-; High Sheriff Kent 1973; memb: cncl Fedn Civil Engrg Contractors 1967-80, Construction Indust Trg Bd 1967-73, Shrievalty Assoc Cncl 1976-81, Cncl Business Aircraft Users Assoc 1961-88 (chm 1968-72), Int Business Aviation Cncl Ltd 1981-88, Cncl Br Helicopter Advsy Bd 1968- (chm 1976-85), Cncl Euro Helicopter Assoc 1981-85 (chm 1981-83); Bart's: govr 1972-74, special tstee 1982-; govr and dep chm Eastbourne Coll 1968-84, tstee Inst of Econ Affrs 1968-89; FRAeS; *Recreations* sailing, shooting, gardening; *Clubs* Royal Yacht Sqdn, Air Sqdn, Br Racing Drivers, Royal Hort Soc; *Style—* Kenneth McAlpine, Esq, DL; The Priory, Lamberhurst, Kent TN3 8DS (☎ 0892 890205); Lamberhurst Vineyards, The Ridge, Lamberhurst Down, Kent TN3 8ER (☎ 0892 890734, fax 0892 890106)

MCCALLUM, Ian Stewart; s of John Blair McCallum (d 1972), and Margaret Stewart, *née* Hannah (d 1989); *b* 24 Sept 1936; *Educ* Kingston GS; *m* 1, 26 Oct 1957 (m dis 1984), Pamela Mary, da of James Herbert Shave; 1 s (Andrew Stewart b 12 Sept 1958), 2 da (Sheila Anne (Mrs Curling) b 8 July 1960, Heather Jean (Mrs Drury) b 26 June 1963); m 2, 15 Sept 1984, Jean, da of Patrick Wittingstall Lynch, of 95 Oakwood Rd, Bricket Wood, Herts; 2 step da (Michelle b 6 Feb 1971, Donna b 8 May 1974); *Career* Highland LI 1954-56; Eagle Star Insurance Co Ltd 1953-54 and 1956-58, FE Wright & Co 1958-63, M Clarkson Home Ltd 1963-68, currently exec sales mangr Save & Prosper Group Ltd (joined 1968); Mayor Woking Borough Cncl 1976-77 (ldr 1972-76 and 1978-81, dep ldr 1981-84); hon vice pres Woking Cons Assoc 1976-, chm Assoc of DCs 1979-84 (ldr 1976-79); pres Woking Swimming Club 1977-84; vice chm: UK Steering Ctee on Local Authy Superannuation 1974-84, Standing Ctee Local Authys & the Theatre 1977-81, The Sports Cncl 1980-86; memb: Consultative Cncl on Local Govt Fin 1975-84, Local Authys Conditions of Serv Advsy Bd 1978-84, Cncl for Business & the Community 1981-84, Audit Cmmn 1983-86, Health Promotion Res Tst 1983-; LIA; *Recreations* swimming, jogging, walking, reading; *Style—* Ian McCallum, Esq; 5 Minters Orchard, Maidstone Rd, St Marys Platt, nr Sevenoaks, Kent TN15 8QJ (☎ 0732 883653); Save & Prosper Group Ltd, 1 Finsbury Ave, London EC2M 2QY (☎ 071 588 1717)

McCALLUM, John (Ian); s of Hugh McCallum (d 1978), of Old Kilpatrick, Dunbartonshire, and Agnes Falconer Wood, *née* Walker (d 1983); *b* 13 Oct 1920; *Educ* Allan Glen's Sch Glasgow, Univ of Glasgow (BSc); *m* 19 June 1948, Christine Peggy (d 1989), da of Thomas Edwin Sowden (d 1973), of Paignton, Devon; 2 s (Hugh b 1951, Angus b 1953); *Career* asst lectr in naval architecture and marine engrg Univ of Glasgow 1943-44; Lloyd's Register of Shipping: ship surveyor Newcastle-upon-Tyne 1944-49, ship surveyor Glasgow 1949-53, sr ship surveyor with roving troubleshooting cmmn (London HQ) 1953-60; recalled to John Brown & Co Clydebank (his apprenticeship co) as chief naval architect and tech dir 1960-70; chief designer of QE2, Kungsholm (now Royal Princess) and other large ships; recalled to Lloyd's Register of Shipping London as chief ship surveyor 1970-81 (supervising design approval, construction, maintenance, repair, research and development of 11,700 ships in all maritime nations); conslt naval architect 1981-; author of over 40 technical papers in learned jnls; Freeman City of London 1975, Liveryman Worshipful Co of Shipwrights 1975 (memb Educn Ctee 1976-); FEng 1977, FRINA (past chm, now vice-pres), FICE (life fell 1978), 1 cncl memb Smeatonian Soc of Civil Engrs 1979, life fell SNAME (NY) 1981, medallist of ATMA Paris 1978, MIES 1962; over 40 technical papers in learned journals; *Recreations* golf, piano, crayon painting; *Style—* Ian McCallum, Esq; Dala, Garvock Drive, Kippington, Sevenoaks, Kent TN13 2LT (☎ 0732 455462)

MCCOY, Rev Father Alban Peter Edmund; s of John Patrick McCoy, of Manchester, and Sheila, *née* Kyte; *b* 1 Aug 1951; *Educ* St Bede's Coll Manchester, Univ of Kent (BA), St Benet's Hall Oxford (M Litt); *Career* entered Franciscan order (OFM Conv) 1968, final profession 1972, ordained priest 1975, curate Catholic church Sleaford Lincs 1976-79, chaplain RAF Digby Lincs 1976-79, asst prov 1980-82 and 1985-88, guardian St Anthony's Friary Canterbury 1982-88, lectr in philosophy Franciscan Study Centre 1982-; pt/t lectr: in medieval theology Univ of Kent 1984-, in philosophy Allen Hall Chelsea 1990-; memb standing advsy ctee for religious educn Kent Co Educn Ctee 1989-, nat spiritual asst secular Franciscan order of GB 1988-; *Recreations* cycling, swimming, music, history; *Style—* The Rev Father Alban McCoy; Franciscan Study Centre, Giles Lane, Canterbury, Kent CT2 7NA (☎ 0227 454647/ 452802/ 769439)

MACDONALD, Kenneth Carmichael; KCB (1990, CB 1983); s of William Thomas MacDonald, and Janet Millar Macdonald; *b* 25 July 1930; *Educ* Hutcheson's GS, Univ of Glasgow (MA); *m* 1960, Ann Elizabeth Pauer; 1 s, 2 da; *Career* MOD: second perm sec 1988-90 (procurement exec 1980-84, dep under sec of state Resources and Progs 1985-88); *Recreations* golf; *Style—* Sir Kenneth Macdonald, KCB; c/o Barclays Bank, 357-366 The Strand, London WC2R 0NX

MACDONALD, Michael Stanley; s of Stanley Roche Macdonald (d 1958), and Elsie Roche, *née* Nichols; *b* 12 Sept 1923; *Educ* Churchers Coll Petersfield, Cranleigh; *m* 27 Sept 1947, Cynthia Mary, da of Horace Winstone Harrison (d 1959); 1 s (Martin Stanley Harrison b 1951), 2 da (Michele Annette Cynthia (Mrs Foot) b 1949, Penelope Mary (Mrs Hughes) b 1952); *Career* WWII RAF 1941-46, AC2 wireless operator, cmmnd PO (Intelligence), served in India and Burma 1942-45, Flt Lt ADC to AOC Malaya 1945-46; md: Taylors Eagle Brewery and Austine Cravers 1946-51, Carlsberg Sales Ltd 1951-74, Carlsberg Distributors Ltd 1974-81; Carlsberg Brewery Ltd: sales dir 1981-85, md 1985-88, non-exec dir 1988-; church warden St Winifreds Harrogate 1964-74; JP: City of Manchester 1965-71, Harrogate 1971-74; chm Canterbury Diocesan Bd of Fin 1990, memb Archbishop's Cncl 1990; Freeman City of London, Liveryman Worshipful Co of Distillers; Knight of the Danebrau (Denmark); *Recreations* golf, tennis, swimming, gardening; *Clubs* RAF; *Style—* Michael Macdonald, Esq; Carlsberg Brewery Ltd, Bridge St, Northampton NN1 1PD (☎ 0604 234333)

MacDONALD, Lt-Col (Ewen) William; OBE (1965); s of Ewen Henry MacDonald (1951), of Cranbrook, Kent, and Eva Emma, *née* Nicholls (d 1971); *b* 6 Aug 1922; *Educ* Cranbrook Sch; *m* 1, 16 Dec 1949, Patricia Grace (d 1978), da of Geoffrey Walter (d 1973), of Bradford, Yorkshire; 1 da (Eva Patricia Anne b 1951); m2, Jennifer Ann Pilcher, *née* Cattell; *Career* cmmnd 1 KGVO Gurkha Rifles 1942, French Indo-China (despatches 1946), regt cmmn The Buffs 1948, cmd The Queen's Own Buffs 1964, served in every continent during 36 years serv; memb Kent War Pensioners Ctee, various offices in Rolvenden Br Legion; Cdr Order of The Dannebrog 1965; *Recreations* supporting Kent cricket (played for Army in Far East), gardening, reading; *Style—* Lt-Col William MacDonald, OBE; Horseshoes, Frensham Rd, Rolvenden Layne, Cranbrook, Kent TN17 4NJ (☎ 0580 241 250)

McDONNELL, Prof James Anthony Michael (Tony); s of Michael Francis McDonnell, of Madeley, nr Crewe, Cheshire, and Very Phyllis, *née* Redding (d 1987); *b* 26 Sept 1938; *Educ* St Joseph's Coll, Stoke on Trent, Univ of Manchester (BSc, PhD); *m* 22 July 1961, Jean Mary, da of George Gordon (d 1976); 2 s ((Benedict) Michael b 27 Feb 1965; Roger (James) b 1 June 1971), Louise (Anne) b 21 Aug 1962); *Career* res asst Nuffield Radio Astronomy Laboratories 1964-65, post-doctoral res assoc NASA Goddard Spaceflight Centre USA 1965-67; Univ of Kent: lectr physical electronics 1967-72, sr lectr electronics 1972-77, reader space sciences 1977-85, prof space physics head of space sci 1985; contrib to Planetary Science in Europe JAM McDonnell (Planetary and Interstellar Dust) 1980; various chapters of Advanced Space Res incl: Progress in Planetary Exploration 1981, Recent Researches into Solid Bodies and Magnetic Fields in the Solar System 1982, Cosmic Dust and Space Debris 1986, organiser and orator of welcome address Comet Nucleus Sample Return ESA Cornerstone Workshop Canterbury 1986; ctee memb Space Astronomy and Radio Div SERC 1979-81; memb: UK Halley Watch Steering Ctee (later CHUKCC) 1983-87, space sci prog Br Nat Space Centre 1988-; COSPAR: memb and sec Panel 3 C 1973-79, memb sub-cmmn B1 ISC B 1982-86 exec memb ISC B 1984-88, chm ISC B 1988-, memb Organising Ctee IAU Cmmn 22 1979; memb: Meteoroid Shield Design Workshop ESA Comet Halley Mission 1981, ESA Lunar Polar Workshop 1981; govr Workshop on Planetology European Sci Fndn 1981, chm Organisation Ctee Symposium 6 COSPAR/IAU/IUTAM 1982, discipline specialist Int Halley Watch 1983, memb ESA/NASA Primitive Bodies Study Team 1984; conslt: space station design USRA 1985, Comet nucleus sample return CNSR 1985-87, CAESAR assessment study 1986, UESTA phase A 1987; memb: Solar System Working Gp 1988-90, Rosetta Mission Definition Team ESA 1988; FRAS, FBIS 1987; *Books* Cosmic Dust (ed and co-author with John Wiley, 1978); *Recreations* tennis, woodwork; *Style—* Prof Tony McDonnell; Unit for Space Sciences, Physics Laboratory, University of Kent, Canterbury, Kent CT2 7NR (☎ 0227 459616, fax 0227 762616, telex 965449)

MACEY, Rear Adm David Edward; CB (1984); s of Frederick William Charles Macey (d 1978), of Strood, Kent, and Florence May, *née* Macey (d 1986); *b* 15 June 1929; *Educ* Sir Joseph Williamson's Mathematical Sch Rochester, Britannia RNC Dartmouth; *m* 1, 1958, Lorna Therese (d 1976), er da of His Hon Judge Oliver William Verner (d 1957); 1 s (Hugo), 1 da (Anna); m 2, 1982, Fiona Beloe, o da of Vice Adm Sir William Beloe, KBE, CB, DSC (d 1966); 3 step s; *Career* RNC Dartmouth, Midshipman 1948, cruisers carriers and destroyers 1950-63, Cdr 1963, American Staff Coll 1964, Cdr RNC Dartmouth 1970, Capt 1972, Directorate Naval Plans 1972-74, RCDS 1975; dir: RN Staff Coll 1976-78, Naval Manpower 1979-81; ADC to HM the Queen 1981, Rear Adm 1981, Dep Asst Chief of Staff (Ops) Staff of the Supreme Allied Cdr 1981-84, ret; receiver gen Canterbury Cathedral 1984-, gentleman usher of the Scarlet Rod 1985; *Recreations* walking, cricket, cooking; *Clubs* MCC; *Style—* Rear Adm David Macey, CB; Petham Oast, Garlinge Green, Canterbury, Kent CT4 5RT (☎ 0227 70291); The Receiver General, Cathedral House, The Precincts, Canterbury, Kent CT1 2EG (☎ 0227 762862)

MCGETTRICK, Rev Monsignor James Francis; s of John McGettrick (d 1943), of Dublin, and Ellen, *née* Brown (d 1983); *b* 18 April 1939; *Educ* St Joseph's Acad Blackheath London, St John's Seminary Wonersh Guildford; *Career* curate Sacred Heart Camberwell 1964-68, chllr sec diocese of Southwark 1970-79 (asst diocesan dec 1968-70), parish priest: Crayford 1979-87, Maidstone 1988-; judge Diocesan Appeal Tbnl 1981-87, chm Catholic Schs Cmmn 1985-, memb Kent Ecumenical Cncl; *Recreations* archaeology, golf; *Style—* The Rev Monsignor James McGettrick; 126 Week St, Maidstone, Kent ME14 1RH (☎ 0622 756217)

McGONIGAL, Christopher Ian; s of Maj H A K McGonigal, MC (d 1963), of Beverley, E Yorks, and Cora, *née* Bentley (d 1946); *b* 10 Nov 1937; *Educ* Ampleforth, CCC Oxford (MA); *m* 28 Sept 1961, (Sara) Sally Ann, da of Louis David Mesnard Fearnley Sander (d 1975); 3 s (Dominic b 1962, Gregory b 1967, Fergus b 1969), 1 da (Alice b 1964); *Career* slr 1965; Coward Chance: asst slr 1965-68, ptnr 1969-87, sr litigation ptnr 1972-79, sr resident ptnr ME 1979-83, sr litigation ptnr 1983-87; slr Hong Kong 1981, jt sr litigation ptnr Clifford Chance 1987-; asst rec 1989-; memb Lamberhurst Local History Soc; Freeman Worshipful Co of Slrs 1972; *Recreations* local history, gardening, walking; *Style—* Christopher McGonigal, Esq; Sandhurst Farm, Clayhill Rd, Lamberhurst, Kent TN3 8AX (☎ 0892 890595); Clifford Chance, Blackfriars House, 19 New Bridge Street, London (☎ 071 353 0211, fax 071 489 0046, telex 887847)

MCGREGOR, Maj (James) Alastair; DSO, MC; s of James McGregor (d 1928), of Reigate and Grantown-on-Spey, and Gladys Victoria, *née* Pollard (d 1962); *b* 15 Sept 1918; *Educ* Epsom Coll, RMC Sandhurst; *m* 10 June 1942, Magdolna Maria Julia Judith, da of Bela Féher (d 1960), of Budapest and London; 1 s, 1 da; *Career* cmmnd The Royal Scots 1938, served France and Belgium 1938-42, 5 Parachute Bn 1942, 2 SAS N Africa and Italy (despatches) 1943, served France and Germany (despatches, Croix De Guerre) 1944-45; attached to: Foreign Legion Greek Commando Bde in Civil War (Greek War Cross) 1947-50; formed 22 SAS Malaya 1951-54; Euro mktg dir Rank Hotels 1970, London International Futures Exchange 1980, md Lossie Travel 1982-; memb Broadstairs and St Peters Town Cncl 1988-; *Recreations* gardening, travel, pink gins; *Clubs* Naval & Military, Special Forces; *Style—* Maj Alastair McGregor, DSO, MC; Swinburne Lodge, Swinburne Ave, Broadstairs, Kent CT10 2DP (☎ 0843 602449)

McGUIRE, Air Cdre Edward John; s of Charles Aloysius McGuire, and Eileen Maude, *née* Bisgood; *b* 7 Dec 1924; *Educ* Epsom Coll, Guy's Hosp Univ of London (MB BS); *m* 21 May 1949, Rowena, da of Sidney Charles Sanders; 1 s (Simon John b 5 Dec 1952), 2 da (Gabrielle b 9 Feb 1951, Colina b 4 March 1956); *Career* RAF med branch 1950-81: OC RAF Aviation Medicine Training Centre 1963-69, on staff to Air Attaché Washington 1969-72, dep dir Aviation Medicine MOD Air 1972-75, OC RAF Hosp Wroughton 1975-78, dep PMO HQ Strike Command 1978, dir health and res MOD Air 1978-81; late Hon Physician to HM The Queen; dist community physician Mid Downs Health Authy 1981-83, dep dist gen mangr and dir of public health Tunbridge Wells Health Authy 1983-; memb: RAF Assoc, Royal Br Legion; Freeman City of London, Liveryman Worshipful Soc of Apothecaries; MFOM, FFCM, FRSM; *Recreations* photography, music, amateur theatre; *Clubs* Royal Airforce; *Style—* Air Cdre Edward McGuire; The Bricklayers, Clay Hill, Goudhurst, Kent TN17 1AB (☎ 0580 211 277); Tunbridge Wells Health Authority, Sherwood Park, Pembury Rd, Tunbridge Wells, Kent (☎ 0892 511577)

MACILDOWIE, Douglas Malcolm; s of John MacIldowie, FRGS, of Tunbridge Wells, and Betty MacIldowie (d 1983); *b* 1 Oct 1942; *Educ* Vernon Holme, Kent Coll Canterbury, The Skinners' Sch Tunbridge Wells, Univ of Leeds (BA, PGCE); *m* 10 Aug 1966, Elizabeth Gardner, da of Dr Edward Race (1972), of Blackburn, Lancs; *Career* second eng master Pudsey GS Yorks 1965-69, head of Eng Sharston HS Manchester 1969-73, sr teacher Bredbury Comp Sch Cheshire 1973-76, dep head Hazel Grove HS Stockport 1976-83, headmaster Swanley Sch Kent 1983-; fndr memb Swanley Town Twinning Ctee with Verriéres le Buisson France; memb: cncl Amherst Rotary Club 1986-88, Nat Union of Head Teachers, Mensa, Otford Players; *Recreations* walking, quizzing, bat and trap, model making; *Style—* Douglas MacIldowie, Esq; 20 Chesterfield Drive, Riverhead, nr Sevenoaks, Kent TN13 2EG (☎ 0732 450964); Swanley School, St Mary's Rd, Swanley, Kent BR8 7TE (☎ 0322 65231)

McILWRAITH, Dr George Robert; s of Alexander Herd McIlwraith (d 1971), of Ruislip, Middx, and Kathleen Joan, *née* Heaton; *b* 15 July 1941; *Educ* Merchant Taylors', Univ of St Andrews (MB ChB); *m* 24 July 1982, Isabel Margaret, da of Harry Jack Manwaring (d 1988), of Collier St, Marden, Kent; 1 s (Harry Alexander b 1987); *Career* various jr appts in UK hosps; asst prof of internal med Pulmonary Div Univ of Michigan Med Sch USA 1979-80, conslt physician Maidstone Dist Hosps 1981-; author of pubns chapters papers and articles on cardiological and respiratory med matters; memb: Br Thoracic Soc, Br Geriatric Soc; FRCP 1988; *Style—* Dr George McIlwraith; Noah's Ark Farmhouse, East Sutton Rd, Headcorn, Ashford, Kent TN27 9PS (☎ 0622 891278); The Maidstone Hospital, Hermitage Lane Barming, Maidstone, Kent (☎ 0622 29000)

McINTOSH, Kinn Hamilton; MBE (1988); da of Robert Aeneas Cameron McIntosh (d 1978), and Violet Jessie, *née* Kinnis (d 1988); *b* 20 June 1930; *Educ* Waverley Sch Huddersfield Yorkshire, Greenhead HS; *Career* detective novelist as Catherine Aird; asst treas World Assoc of Girl Guides and Girl Scouts 1978-84, chm UK Fin Ctee Girl Guides Assoc 1983-87, vice chm Crime Writers Assoc 1989-; Hon MA Univ of Kent at Canterbury 1985; *Books* The Religious Body (1966), A Most Contagious Game (1967), The Complete Steel (1969), Henrietta Who? (1968), A Late Phoenix (1971), His Burial Too (1973), Slight Mourning (1975), Parting Breath (1978), Some Died Eloquent (1979), Passing Strange (1981), Last Respects (1982), Harms's Way (1984), A Dead Liberty (1986), The Body Politic (1990); *Recreations* bridge; *Clubs* The English-Speaking Union; *Style—* Miss Kinn McIntosh, MBE

MCINTYRE, Donald Conroy; CBE (1985, OBE 1975); s of George McIntyre, and Hermyn, *née* Conroy; *b* 22 Oct 1934; *Educ* Mount Albert GS New Zealand, Auckland Teachers Trg Coll, Guildhall Sch of Music London; *m* 29 July 1961, Jill Redington, da of Norton Mitchell, DFC (d 1989), of Barnstaple, Devon; 3 da (Ruth Frances b 1965, Lynn Hazel b 1967, Jenny Jane b 1971); *Career* princ bass: Sadler's Wells Opera 1960-67, Royal Opera House Covent Garden 1967-, annual appearances at Bayreuth Festival 1967-81; roles incl: Wotan and Wanderer (Der Ring), Dutchman (Der Fliegende Hollander), Telramund (Logengrin), Barak (Die Frau ohne Schatten), Pizzaro (Fidelio), Golaud (Pelleas et Melisande), Kurwenal (Tristan and Isolde), Gurnemanz, Klingsor and Amfortas (Parsifal), Heyst (Victory), Jochanaan (Salome), Macbeth, Scarpia (Tosca), The Count (Marriage of Figaro), Nick Shadow (The Rake's Progress), Hans Sachs (Die Meistersinger), Doctor (Wozzeck), Cardillac (Cardillac Hindemith); recordings incl: Pelleas et Melisande, Oedipus Rex, Il Trovatore, Ring, Parsifal, Damnation de Faust, Messiah; Fidelio Medal Oct 1989; *Recreations* swimming, tennis, farming, walking; *Style—* Donald McIntyre, Esq, CBE

MacINTYRE, Robert Hamilton (Sandy); s of Robert Hamilton MacIntyre (d 1964), of 4 Bede House, Manor Fields, London, and Doris, *née* Bateman (d 1978); *b* 2 March 1932; *Educ* St Pauls; *m* 3 March 1956, Jean-Anne, da of James Pizzey (d 1975); 2 s (Robert b 1965, Richard b 1967), 2 da (Lisbeth-Anne b 1959, Amanda b 1961); *Career* mil serv Sgt RAPC; ptnr MacIntyre Hudson (CAs), dir Surrey Building Society; former chm W Wickham Round Table; FCA; *Recreations* motoring, motor sport, swimming; *Clubs* Leander Rowing, Thames Rowing; *Style*— Sandy MacIntyre, Esq; 87 Copse Ave, West Wickham, Kent BR4 9NW; 26/28 Ely Place, London EC1N 6RL (fax 071 405 4786)

MACKAY, Iain Andrew; s of John Andrew Mackay (d 1979), of Sydenham, London, and Eileen Beatrice, *née* Wade; *b* 19 March 1943; *Educ* Wilson GS, Sir John Cass Coll; *m* 15 June 1968, Teresa Margaret, da of George Leslie Barrett, of Blackheath, London; 3 da (Elinore b 1971, Rowena b 1974, Imogene b 1982); *Career* tech offr British Non-Ferrous Metals Research Association 1960-68, tech author The British Aluminium Co 1968-73, regnl sales Alcan Extrusions 1973-78, sales mangr Cego Extrusions 1978-82, dir sales and mktg Adams Rite Europe Ltd 1987- (gen sales mangr 1982-87); sch govr, vice pres Aluminium Window Assoc; memb: IOD, Chartered Inst of Marketing; fell Br Inst Management; *Recreations* swimming, squash; *Style*— Iain Mackay, Esq; Adams Rite Europe Ltd, Unit 6, Moreton Industrial Estate, London Rd, Swanley, Kent BR8 8TZ (☎ 0322 69211, fax 0322 613230)

MACKAY, Michael Alexander; s of Dr Ian Bannerman Mackay, of Mickleton, Gloucs, and Helen, *née* Walker (d 1974); *b* 16 Dec 1946; *Educ* Repton, Coll of Law Lancaster Gate; *m* 31 May 1974, Mary Jacintha, da of William Canning (d 1979); 2 s (Ian Michael b 1978, William James b 1980); *Career* slr; articled Amery-Parkes and Co London 1966-71; admitted slr 1971; ptnr Sole Sawbridge and Co Grays Inn 1971-79, fndr Mackay and Co Faversham 1979; hon slr Faversham C of C; *Recreations* tennis, Times crossword; *Clubs* Broome Park, Law Soc; *Style*— Michael Mackay, Esq; 6a East St, Faversham, Kent ME13 8AD (☎ 0795 536061, fax 0795 538813)

MacKENZIE, Rt Hon (James) Gregor; PC (1977); s of James MacKenzie (d 1984), and Mary, *née* Wood (d 1972); *b* 15 Nov 1927; *Educ* Queens Park Sch, Royal Tech Coll, Univ of Glasgow Sch of Social Studies; *m* 1958, Joan Swan, da of John Campbell Provan; 1 s, 1 da; *Career* joined Lab Pty 1944; contested (Lab): Aberdeenshire E 1950, Kinross and Perth 1959; MP Rutherglen 1964-87, PPS to Rt Hon James Callaghan 1965-70, shadow oppn spokesman Posts and Telecommunications 1970-74, min of state for Indust 1975-76 (parly under sec 1974-75), min of state Scottish Office 1976-79; JP Glasgow 1962; *Style*— The Rt Hon Gregor MacKenzie; 8 Buchanan Drive, Newton Mearns G77 6HT

MACKENZIE, Michael Philip Uvedale Rapinet; s of Brig MR Mackenzie, DSO (d 1985), of Mayfield, Sussex, and Vivienne, *née* Price; *b* 1937; *Educ* Downside, Lincoln Coll Oxford; *m* 1966, Jill, da of Charles Foweraker Beckley, of Chislehurst, Kent; 1 s (William b 1966), 1 da (Elizabeth b 1970); *Career* United Biscuits plc 1966-86: prodn dir of various businesses 1974-83, md DS Crawford Bakeries 1983-86; DG Food and Drink Fedn; FRSA 1988; *Clubs* Travellers; *Style*— Michael Mackenzie, Esq; Ebony Cottage, Ebony, nr Tenterden, Kent TN30 7HT; Food & Drink Federation, Catherine St, London WC2B 5JJ

MACKILLIGIN, Robert Guy Walter; MC (1944, and bar 1945); s of late Hector Rennie Mackilligin; *b* 11 Oct 1918; *Educ* Charterhouse, Camborne Sch of Mines; *m* 1949, Daphne Gwendoline, *née* Cooper; 3 da; *Career* serv WWII 51 Highland Div RA 1939-46; petroleum engr Shell International Petroleum Co Ltd 1946-53, mangr Shell International Co Ltd 1954-73, exec dir Bisichi Mining plc 1974-, chm Dragon Markets Ltd 1984-; *Recreations* genealogy, gardening, ornithology; *Style*— Robert Mackilligin, Esq, MC; Walnut Tree Cottage, Woodlands, Pembury Rd, Tunbridge Wells (☎ 0892 30392, 071 236 3539)

MACKINNON, Hon Mrs (Patricia Ann); *née* Souter; da and co heiress of 25 Baron Audley; *b* 10 Aug 1946; *m* 1969, Carey Leigh Mackinnon; 1 s, 1 da; *Style*— The Hon Mrs Mackinnon; Holts Crest, Fordcombe, Tunbridge Wells, Kent

MACKLEN, Victor Harry Burton; CB; s of Harry Macklen (d 1965), of Brighton, Sussex, and Annie Clara, *née* Hayward (d 1972); *b* 13 July 1919; *Educ* Varndean Secdy Sch Brighton, King's Coll London (BSc); *m* 22 Sept 1950, Scylla Ursula Irene, da of Henry Hope Fellows (d 1924); *Career* Capt Army Operational Res Gp 1943, Capt GHQ Cairo 1943-44, special Operational Res Gp WO and Air Miny 1944, Maj sci advsr staff WO 1944-45, Lt Col GSO1 Sci 2 WO 1945-49; princ sci offr: sci 2 WO 1949, operational res section HQ BAOR 1950-54; dep chief sci offr Chief Sr Advsr's Staff MOD 1958-60 (sr princ sci offr 1954-58), head of Tech Secretariat Rector Gp UKAEA 1960-64, dep dir Tech Ops Reactor Gp UDAEA 1964-67, asst chief sci advsr (Nuclear) MOD 1967-69, dep sec and dep chief advsr Projects and Nuclear MOD 1969-79, special advsr to chm Dynamics Gp BAe 1980-81, personal advsr to chm Br Telecom 1981-87; chm Hartlip Parish Cncl 1983-, pres Sittingbourne and Milton Regis Branch Royal Br Legion; FRSA; *Clubs* Army & Navy; *Style*— Victor Macklen, Esq, CB; Stepp House, The Street, Hartlip, Sittingbourne, Kent ME9 7TH (☎ 0795 842 591)

McLACHLAN, John James; s of William McLachlan (d 1980), of Birkenhead, and Helen, *née* Duffy; *b* 28 Aug 1942; *Educ* Rock Ferry High GS Cheshire; *m* 24 Sept 1966, Heather Joan, da of George Smith (d 1975), of Heswall; 1 s (Alexander b 4 Jan 1975), 1 da (Deborah b 19 Feb 1972); *Career* mgmnt accountant Norwest Construction 1966-67, investmt analyst Martins Bank Trust Co 1967-69, investmt res mangr Barclays Bank Trust Co 1969-71, dep investmt mangr 1971-74, investmt mangr BR Pension Fund 1974-83, dir pensions investmt 1983-84, investmt mangr Reed International plc 1984-88, investmt mangr and dir United Friendly Insurance plc 1988-; former chm Investmt Ctee Nat Assoc of Pension Funds; former memb: Panel on Take Overs and Mergers, Institutional Shareholders Ctee; non-exec dir: Iceland Frozen Foods Holdings, Investment Management Regulatory Organisation; FCA, AMSIA, FRSA; *Recreations* squash, watching cricket and soccer, collecting Wisdens; *Style*— John McLachlan, Esq; United Friendly Insurance plc, 42 Southwark Bridge Rd, London SE1 9HE (☎ 071 928 5644, fax 071 261 9077, telex 8813953)

MacLACHLAN, Simon; MBE (1983); s of Geoffrey Cheasty MacLachlan (d 1965), of Ipswich, and Violet Edith Gasgoigne, *née* Hicks; *b* 17 Dec 1934; *Educ* Downside Sch; *m* 11 May 1963, Julie, da of John Mannering (d 1985), of River House, River, Kent; 2 s (Justin b 1964, Luke b 1965), 2 da (Martha b 1968, Hannah b 1972); *Career* 2 Lt Queens Own Royal West Kent Regt 1953-55, seconded 5 Bn Kings African Rifles 1953-54 (served in Kenya and mentioned in Despatches), Lt 4/5 BN Queens Own Royal West Kent Regt (TA) 1955-62; slr 1959, ptnr Clifford-Turner 1964, Assigning Ptnr Co Dept 1980-87, ptnr clifford Chance 1987-, vice chm Ctee on Securities Int Bar Assoc 1986-; chm New Islington and Hackney Housing Assoc 1983; tstee: Circle 33 Housing Tst 1978-, George V Playing Fields Sissinghurst; Law Soc 1959-, Int Bar Assoc 1979-; *Books* Life After Big Bang (1987); *Recreations* gardening, tennis; *Clubs* RAC; *Style*— Simon MacLachlan, Esq, MBE; Sissinghurst Place, Sissinghurst, Cranbrook, Kent TN17 2JP; Royex House, Aldermanbury Sq, London EC2 (☎ 071 600 0808, fax 071 600 1064, telex 887847)

MacLAREN, Alexander Geoffrey (Alex); s of Geoffrey Cecil MacLaren, of White Croft, Sussex Gardens, East Dean, Eastbourne, East Sussex, and Joy, *née* Parks; *b* 13 April 1944; *Educ* Harrow; *m* 8 July 1968, Carole Beatrice, da of Capt Dilwyn Vaughan Davies, of Hill Crest, Southborough, Tunbridge Wells, Kent; 2 da (Rosemary b 26 April 1974, Miranda b 19 Feb 1982); *Career* Deliotte Plender Griffiths & Co: articled clerk, audit sr 1962-69; asst fund mangr Hill Samuel & Co 1969-71, rep Daniel Greenaway & Sons 1971-72, London rep Northwest Ban Corp 1972-74, vice pres Irving Trust Company 1974-, md Historic Design 1988-; *Recreations* music, theatre, architecture; *Style*— Alex MacLaren, Esq; Frogs Hill House, Newenden, Cranbrook, Kent TN18 5PX (☎ 07974 3268); Irving Trust Co, 46 Berkeley St, London (☎ 071 322 6324)

MACLEAN, Dr Isabel Forrester; da of John Henderson, DL, JP, MP (d 1973), of Glasgow, and Agnes, *née* Brander; *b* 2 April 1928; *Educ* Queen's Park Glasgow, Univ of Glasgow (MB, ChB); *m* 2 July 1954, Donald Buchanan Maclean, s of Donald Maclean, MBE (d 1950), of Glasgow; *Career* Glasgow Royal Infirmary 1951-54: SHO, house surgn, house physician; London Borough of Bromley: clinical med offr 1955-78, sr clinical med offr 1978-88; *Recreations* painting, travel, golf; *Clubs* Sundridge Park Golf (Lady Capt 1987); *Style*— Dr Isabel Maclean

MCLELLAN, Prof David Thorburn; s of Robert Douglas McLellan (d 1973), and Olive May, *née* Bush; *b* 10 Feb 1940; *Educ* Merchant Taylor's, St John's Coll Oxford (BA, MA, DPhil); *m* 1 July 1967, Annie, da of André Brassart; 2 da (Gabrielle b 8 Nov 1968, Stephanie b 8 May 1970); *Career* Univ of Kent: lectr 1966-70, sr lectr in politics 1970-75, prof of political theory 1975; visiting prof State Univ of NY 1969, visiting fell Indian Inst of Advanced Study Simla 1970; *Books* The Young Hegelians and Karl Marx (1969), Marx before Marxism (1970), Karl Marx: The Early Texts (1971), Marx's Grundrisse (1971), The Thought of Karl Marx (1971), Marx (1971), Karl Marx: His Life and Thought (1973), Engels (1977), Karl Marx: Selected Writings (1977), Marxism after Marx (1980), Karl Marx: Interviews and Recollections (1983), Marx: The First Hundred Years (ed, 1983), Karl Marx: The Legacy (1983), Ideology (1985), Marxism: Selected Texts (ed, 1987), Marxism and Religion (1987), Simone Weil: Utopian Pessimist (1990); *Style*— Prof David McLellan; 13 Ivy Lane, Canterbury, Kent CT1 1TV (☎ 0227 463579); Eliot College, University of Kent, Canterbury, Kent CT2 7NS (☎ 0227 764000)

MCLELLAN, Philip Stuart; s of William Lester McLellan (d 1980), and Vera Gladys, *née* Willetts; *b* 6 Oct 1948; *Educ* Sir Roger Manwoods GS Sandwich, Loughborough Library Sch, Open Univ (BA); *m* 2 March 1974, Doreen Elizabeth, da of Cyril Stanley Hills, of Rochester; 1 s (John David b 1982), 1 da (Claire Elizabeth b 1984); *Career* professional librarian and info offr Kent CC and CEGB 1969-82, admin offr Nuclear Electric plc; chm Mid Kent SLD, sec Chatham SLD, jt local organiser Action Aid; *Recreations* cricket, golf, kids; *Style*— Philip McLellan, Esq; Nuclear Electric plc, Canal Road, Gravesend, Kent DA12 2RS (☎ 0474 351122)

MacLEOD, Rev Murdo Allan; s of John MacLeod (d 1971), of Inverness, and Christina MacLeod (d 1972); *b* 5 Sept 1926; *Educ* Inverness Royal Acad, Univ of Edinburgh (MA), Free Church of Scotland Coll Edinburgh; *m* 11 Sept 1954, Nancie Margaret, da of Frank Johnstone (d 1981), of Westcliff-on-Sea, Essex; 2 s (John b 1955, Donald b 1959), 2 da (Ruth b 1957, Catherine b 1963); *Career* ordained min Free Church of Scotland 1955, dir and gen sec Christian Witness to Israel 1970-, int pres Lausanne Consultation on Jewish Evangelism 1983-, moderator Free Church of Scotland Gen Assembly 1984; *Books* contrib to: Hold Fast Your Confession (1962), International Bible Encyclopedia (4 volumes, 1979), Illustrated Bible Dictionary (3 volumes 1980), Witness of the Jews to God (1982); *Recreations* antique furniture, photography, walking; *Style*— The Rev Murdo MacLeod; 11 St Martins Drive, Eynsford, Dartford DA4 0EY (☎ 0322 863277); 44 Lubbock Rd, Chislehurst, Kent BR7 5JX (☎ 081 467 2296, fax 081 295 1586)

MacLEOD-SMITH, Alastair MacLeod; CMG (1956); s of Robert Arthur Smith (d 1950), and Catherine Ethel Welsh, *née* Kellner (d 1977); *b* 30 June 1916; *Educ* Wells House Malvern Wells, Ellesmere Coll Salop, Queen's Coll Oxford (BA); *m* 18 Aug 1945, Ann, da of George Francis Langdale Circuitt (d 1966); 1 s (Geoffrey Langdale b 1953), 1 da (Catherine Amanda b 1955); *Career* Colonial Admin Serv; Nigeria 1939-49, econ and fin advsr Windward Islands 1949-52, fin sec Western Pacific High Cmmn 1952-57, fin sec Sierra Leone 1957-61; jt dir Selection Trust 1975-80 (joined 1961), ret; conslt National Westminster Bank 1980-82; *Recreations* golf; *Clubs* United Oxford and Cambridge Univs, Knole Park Golf (Sevenoaks); *Style*— Alastair MacLeod-Smith, Esq, CMG; Roughetts Lodge, Coldharbour Lane, Hildenborough, Kent TN11 9JX (☎ 0732 833239)

MCMURRAY, Rev Brian Harold; s of Harold Stephen McMurray, of Downpatrick, I, and Ester Elizabeth, *née* Erwin; *b* 9 Jan 1944; *Educ* The Royal Sch Armagh, Trinity Coll Dublin, Church of Ireland Theol Coll; *Career* asst curate in Eng and I 1967-75; chaplain: York Gen Hosp 1975-81, Holy Trinity Sliema Malta 1982-84, Bede House Staplehurst 1984-85; parish priest St Giles Skelton York 1975-81, precentor Gibraltar Cathedral and officiating chaplain RN Gibraltar 1981-82, vicar SS Peter and Paul Borden 1985-; chm Borden C of E Primary Sch Bd of Govrs, tstee Barrow Charity; memb: Soc of the Holy Cross, Br Inst of Organ Studies; *Recreations* swimming, music, opera, organ design; *Clubs* Yorkshire; *Style*— The Rev Brian McMurray; Borden Vicarage, Sittingbourne, Kent ME9 8JS (☎ 0795 72986)

MACNAB, Brig Sir Geoffrey Alex Colin; KCMG (1962, CMG 1955), CB (1951); s of late Brig-Gen Colin Macnab, CMG, and Beatrice Bliss; *b* 23 Dec 1899; *Educ* Wellington, RMC Sandhurst; *m* 1930, Norah Cramer-Roberts (d 1981); *Career* first cmmn Royal Sussex Regt, instr Small Arms Sch Hythe 1925-28, Staff Coll Camberley 1930-31, Capt Argyll and Sutherland Highlanders 1931, GSO 3 WO 1933-35, BM 10 Inf Bde 1935-38, mil attaché Prague and Bucharest 1938-40, served WWII (despatches 1940), campaigns Western Desert, Greece, Crete, Brig 1944, mil mission Hungary 1945, DMI ME 1945-47, mil attaché Rome 1947-49, Paris 1949-54, Gold SO at coronation of HM Queen Elizabeth 1952, ret; sec Govt Hospitality Fund 1957-68, local pres Royal Br Legion; *Clubs* MCC, Army and Navy; *Style*— Brig Sir Geoffrey Macnab, KCMG, CB; Stanford House, Stanford, Ashford, Kent (☎ 030 381 2118)

MCQUEEN, John; s of R. Leonard George McQueen, and Mira Milstead, *née* Birch; *b* 20 May 1942; *Educ* Rugby, Trinity Coll Cambridge, St Thomas's Hosp Med Sch (MA, MBBChir); *m* Dorothy, da of Gilbert Dyke; 5 da (Katy b 1968, Deborah b 1971, Philippa b 1977, Sarah b 1984, Laura b 1987); *Career* sr registrar Queen Charlottes Hosp and Chelsea Hosp, currently conslt obstetrician gynaecologist Bromley Health Authy; author of various papers on obstetrics, gynaecology and the menopause; memb Int Menopause Soc; FRCS 1972, FRCOG 1985 (memb 1973); *Recreations* travel, golf; *Clubs* London Obstetric, Gynaecological Society; *Style*— John McQueen, Esq; Downs View, Heritage Hill, Keston, Kent BR2 6AU (☎ 0689 59058); Beckenham Hospital, Croydon Rd, Beckenham, Kent BR3 3QL (☎ 01 650 0125)

MCQUIGGAN, John; MBE (1955); s of John McQuiggan (d 1937), of Liverpool, and Sarah Elizabeth, *née* Sim (d 1960); *b* 24 Nov 1922; *Educ* St Edward's Coll Liverpool; *m* 17 June 1950, (Doris) Elsie, da of Gilbert Henry Hadler (d 1973), of Bromley; 3 s (Anthony b 8 March 1956, Simon b 21 July 1959, David b 29 April 1963), 1 da (Sarah b 13 Sept 1961); *Career* served RAF 1942-47; Dominions Office 1940-42, CRO 1947-50, admin offr Canberra 1950-54, 2 sec and consul Lahore and Dacca 1954-57, 1 sec (inf) Lahore and Peshawar 1957-58, dep dir UK Info Serv 1958-61; dir Br Info Servs: E Nigeria 1961-64, Uganda 1964-69 (1 sec Kigali Rwanda); FCO London 1969-73, HM Consul Chad (London based) 1970-73, dep high cmmr and Commercial Cnsllr Lusaka Zambia 1973-76; ret (own request) HM Dip Serv 1976; princ John McQuiggan Assoc 1976-78 and 1987-, exec dir UK S Africa Trade Assoc 1978-86, DG Br Indust Ctee on S Africa 1986; numerous contribs to trade and econ jls; FIOD, MIPR; pubns: num contribs to Trade & Economic Jls; *Recreations* tennis, carpentry, craftwork (wood); *Clubs* Royal Overseas League London, Bickley Park Cricket; *Style*— John McQuiggan, Esq, MBE; 7 Meadowcroft, Bickley, Kent BR1 2JD (☎ 071 467 0075)

MACRAE, Barry John; s of Hugh Fleming Muncie Macrae (d 1983), of Ramsgate, and Eileen Joyce, *née* Chapman; *b* 10 March 1947; *Educ* Chatham House GS Ramsgate; *m* 1, 1971 (m dis 1973), Wilma Ann, *née* Wright; m 2, 5 Jan 1974, Lillian, da of Lawrence Sparkes, of Milton Keynes; 1 da (Heather Louise b Nov 1981); *Career* Ramsgate Borough Cncl 1963-65, Deal Borough Cncl 1967-68, first PR offr Strood RDC (Medway) 1971-73 (joined cncl 1969); Thanet DC: tourism offr 1974-77, econ devpt offr 1978-79, head of corp affrs 1980; mktg offr Peterborough New Town 1981-83, head of tourism, publicity and econ devpt Canterbury City Cncl 1983-, conslt in mktg Berks CC 1973-74; chm East Kent Resorts Assoc 1985-; memb RTPI: Andover 1967-69, Rochester 1970-73, Reading 1973, Bristol 1974, Margate 1974-80, Peterborough 1981-83; AIPR 1973-75, AInstM 1974-76; *Recreations* caravanning, reading, swimming; *Style*— Barry Macrae, Esq; 65 Broad Oak Rd, Canterbury, Kent CT2 7PN (☎ 0227 450681); Canterbury City Council, Military Rd, Canterbury, Kent CT1 1YW (☎ 0227 763763, fax 0227 763727)

MacTAGGART, Lady; Irene; da of late Ferdinand Richard Holmes Meyrick; *m* 1, 1939 (m dis 1954), 6 Earl of Craven (d 1965); m 2, 1961, Sir Andrew MacTaggart (d 1978); *Style*— Lady Irene MacTaggart; Clatfields, Marsh Green, Edenbridge, Kent (☎ 0732 2819)

MADDOCKS, Rt Rev Morris Henry St John; s of Rev Canon Morris Arthur Maddocks (d 1953), and Gladys Mabel, *née* Sharpe; *b* 28 April 1928; *Educ* St John's Sch Leatherhead, Trinity Coll Cambridge, Chichester Theol Coll; *m* 1955, Anne, da of late William Oliver Miles; *Career* Nat Serv 2 Lt RASC; curate: St Peter's Ealing 1954-55, St Andrew's Uxbridge 1955-58; vicar: Weaverthorpe Helperthorpe and Luttons Ambo 1958-61, St Martin-on-the-Hill Scarborough 1961-71; suffragan bishop of Selby 1972-83; hon asst bishop: Diocese of Bath and Wells 1983-87, Diocese of Chichester 1987-; chm of Churches Cncl for Health and Healing 1982-85 (co-chm 1975-82), advsr to the Archbishops of Canterbury and York for the Miny of Health and Healing 1983-; co-fndr (with wife) of Acorn Christian Healing Tst; FRSM 1988; *Books* The Christian Healing Ministry (1981), The Christian Adventure (1983), Journey to Wholeness (1986), A Healing House of Prayer (1987), Twenty Questions About Healing (1988); *Recreations* walking, gardening, music; *Clubs* Army and Navy; *Style*— The Rt Rev Morris Maddocks; St Mary's, Burrswood, Groombridge, nr Tunbridge Wells, Kent TN3 9PY (☎ 0892 863637 ext 221); Acorn Christian Healing Trust, Whitehall Chase, Bordon, Hampshire GU35 OAP (☎ 0420 478121/2)

MADGWICK, Ernest James; s of Henry James Madgwick (served WWI, d 1948), and Harriet Alice, *née* Nicholls (d 1966); *b* 26 March 1920; *Educ* Teynhan C of E Sch; *m* 1, 1 July 1946 (m dis 1951), Patricia Mary; m 2, 30 March 1957, Louisa May, da of late G Peacock, of 6 Rose Gardens, Ealing; 3 step s (William, David, Roger), 3 step da (Sheila, Jennifer, Brenda); *Career* WWII served: RASC 1940, 8 Light Ambulance Corps Eng and N Africa (Alamein), Libya (allied mil govt occupied territory) 1943, joined American Voluntary Ambulance Corps (Br attached in Italian Campaign) 1943, Vienna Garrison 1945, demobbed Lance Sgt 1986; Kent Co Cncllr; Swale Borough Cncl (formerly Sittingbourne Urban Dist): cncllr, vice chm of Devpt Control, sr cncllr of borough; memb: Kent Co Cncl Adoption Custodianship Agency (foster parent to 40 children), Kent Co Cncl Social Servs Ctees; fndr memb: Sittingbourne Milton Regis Carnival Assoc, Sittingbourne Community Soc (now Sittingbourne Soc), American Field Serv Student Exchange; pres Faversham Constituency Lib Democrats; *Recreations* motoring; *Style*— Ernest Madgwick, Esq; The Milestone, 201 Canterbury Rd, Sittingbourne, Kent ME10 4UL (☎ 0795 79308)

MAGAN, George Morgan; s of Brig William Morgan Tilson Magan, CBE, and Maxine, *née* Mitchell; *b* 14 Nov 1945; *Educ* Winchester; *m* 1972, Wendy Anne, da of Maj Patrick Chilton, MC; 2 s (Edward b 1975, Patrick b 1984), 1 da (Henrietta b 1977); *Career* merchant banker; dir: J O Hambro Magan & Co Ltd, Asprey plc, WCRS Gp plc, CCA Pubns plc; govr Hawtrey's Sch; FCA; *Clubs* Royal Yacht Squadron, Turf, Boodle's; *Style*— George Magan, Esq; J O Hambro Magan & Co Ltd, 30 Queen Anne's Gate, London SW1 (☎ 071 222 2020); St Michael's House, nr Tonbridge, Kent

MAGAN, Brig William Morgan Tilson; CBE (1957, OBE 1946); s of Lt-Col Arthur Tilson Shaen Magan, CMG (d 1965), of Killyon Manor, Hill of Down, Co Meath, and Kathleen Jane, *née* Biddulph (d 1969); *b* 13 June 1908; *Educ* Rossall Sch, Sandhurst; *m* 30 Nov 1940, Maxine, da of Sir Kenneth Grant Mitchell, KCIE (d 1966), of Black Horse Farm, Wickhambrook, Suffolk; 4 s (Thomas b 1941 d 1943, George b 1945, Hugh b 1946 d 1983, James b 1957); *Career* cmmnd 1928, IA Sam Browne's Cavalry (12 Frontier Force) 1929-37, Hodson's Horse 1937, various appts up to GSOI during WWII, GSOI Palestine 1946, Brig Gen Staff GHQ Egypt 1947-48, resigned cmmn 1948; estab civil WO (later MOD) 1948, under sec 1953-68, ret 1968; dir Cuckoobird Productions Ltd 1968-90; *Books* Umma-More, The Story of An Irish Family; *Recreations* painting, writing; *Clubs* Cavalry and Guards; *Style*— Brig William Magan, CBE; St Michael's House, Peckham Bush, Tonbridge, Kent TN12 5NH (☎ 0622 812368)

MAHMOOD, Dr Shahid; s of Sheikh Mohammad Amin (d 1987), of Lahore, and Hameeda Amin (d 1983); *b* 11 April 1939; *Educ* Govt Boys Sch, Govt

Coll Lahore, King Edward Med Coll Lahore (BSc), Univ of Punjab (MB BS); *m* 25 Nov 1972, Susan Elizabeth, da of Thomas Owen Cole, of Sandacre, W Hythe; *Career* Capt GDMO Armed Forces of Pakistan 1965-66, awarded war medal Indo-Pakistan War 1965-66; various hosp appts in Pakistan 1963-73, med offr to Pakistan International Airway 1964-65, trainee GP Liverpool 1974-75, jr ptnr Northwich Cheshire April-Oct 1975; single-handed GP: Chatham 1977-80, Dymchurch 1980-; FRCS (Glasgow) 1971; *Recreations* tennis, badminton, hang-gliding; *Clubs* Romney Marsh Rotary; *Style—* Dr Shahid Mahmood; The Surgery, 9 Orgarswick Ave, Dymchurch, Kent (☎ 0303 873156)

MAIDSTONE, Archdeacon of; *see*: Evans, Ven Patrick Alexander Sidney

MAIDSTONE, Bishop of 1987-; Rt Rev David James Smith; s of Stanley James Smith (d 1965), and Gwendolen Emie, *née* Nunn (d 1960); *b* 14 July 1935; *Educ* Hertford GS, King's Coll London AKC; *m* 2 Dec 1961, Mary Hunter, da of Eric John Moult (d 1970); 1 s (Christopher b 1966), 1 da (Rebecca b 1965); *Career* asst curate: All Saints Gosforth 1959-62, St Francis High Heaton 1962-64, Longbenton 1964-68; vicar: Longhirst with Hebron 1968-75, St Mary Monkseaton 1975-81, Felton 1982-83; archdeacon of Lindisfarne 1981-87, bishop to HM Forces 1990-; *Style—* The Rt Rev the Bishop of Maidstone; Bishop's House, Pett Lane, Charing, Ashford, Kent TN27 0DL (☎ 023 3712950)

MAIS, Baron (Life Peer UK 1967), of Walbrook, City of London; (Alan) Raymond Mais; GBE (1973, OBE 1944), ERD (1958), TD (1944), JP (City of London 1962), DL (Kent 1976, Co of London subsequently Gtr London 1951-76); s of late Capt Ernest Mais, of Mornington Court, Kensington; *b* 7 July 1911; *Educ* Banister Court Hants, Coll of Estate Mgmnt Univ of London; *m* 1936, Lorna Aline, da of Stanley Aspinall Boardman, of Addiscombe, Surrey; 2 s (Hon Richard Jeremy Ian, *qv*, b 1945, Hon Jonathan Robert Neal b 1954), 1 da (Hon Angela Clare (Hon Mrs Beckman) b 1946); *Career* 2 Lt Royal West Kent Regt 1929, RE 1931-70; dir Royal Bank of Scotland 1969-81, chm Peachey Property Corp 1977-81; formerly: with Richard Costain, chm Trollope & Colls; alderman Walbrook Ward 1962-81, Lt City of London 1963 (Sheriff 1969-70), Lord Mayor of London 1972-73 (first Lab Lord Mayor), Cmmr of Income Tax 1972-81, Sitting as Lib peer in House of Lords 1981- (formerly Lab); memb: Court of City Univ 1973, Cwlth Scholars Cmmn 1978, Govt Ctees for Works and Bldgs Emergency Orgn; pres London C of C & Indust 1975-78, past pres London Master Builders' Assoc, vice pres Inst of Structural Engrs; Freeman: Worshipful Co of Marketors 1977 (Master 1983-84), Worshipful Co of Cutlers (Master 1966-67), Worshipful Co of Pavior's (Master 1974-75); Hon DSc: Univ of Ulster, City Univ; FICE, FIStructE, FRICS, KStJ; *Style—* The Rt Hon Lord Mais, GBE, ERD, TD, JP, DL; Griffins, Sundridge Ave, Bromley, Kent (☎ 081 460 9896)

MAIS, Hon Richard Jeremy Ian; s of Baron Mais, OBE (Life Peer), *qv*; *b* 2 Nov 1945; *Educ* Cumnor House Sch, Stowe, Ewell Tech Coll; *m* 17 June 1972, Janice, da of Ralph Dean, of Hurley, Berks; 1 s (Alexander b 1975), 2 da (Vanessa b 1977, Lydia b 1981); *Career* property developer; with Higgs & Hill Ltd 1963-69, J M Jones & Sons Ltd 1969-71, Lyon Group Ltd 1971-75; md Clarke Nickolls & Coombs plc 1975-; chm: Becontree Estates Ltd; Altbarn Properties Ltd, CNC Properties Ltd, CNC Developments Ltd, CNC Benfleet Ltd, Philpot Managment Ltd, Beacontree Plaza Ltd, CNC Delaware Inc, CNC California Investments Inc; vice chm St Pancras Housing Assoc; Freeman of the City of London 1968, Liveryman Worshipful Co of Cutlers 1968; MCIOB 1980, FIOD 1984; *Recreations* motor racing, sailing, skiing, badminton; *Clubs* Br Automobile Racing; *Style—* The Hon Richard Mais; 79 Seal Hollow Rd, Sevenoaks, Kent TN13 3RY (☎ 0732 454886); Clarke, Nickolls & Coombs plc, 33 High St, Sunninghill, Ascot, Berks SL5 9NR (☎ 0344 28721, fax 0344 28711, car tel 0836 230248)

MAITLAND, Colin Neil; s of Col Otis Edward Maitland, MBE (d 1977), of Surrey, and Margaret Joan, *née* Haslehurst (d 1955); *b* 7 July 1940; *Educ* Old Buckenham Hall Norfolk, Embley Park Romsey Hants, Univ of Southampton; *m* 30 Sept 1967, Judy, da of Col Howard Watson Wright; 2 s (Mark Otis b 1976, Sam Ragen b 1980), 1 da (Kate Margaret b 1978); *Career* offr RM 1958-69 (45 Commando 1959-61, Cdr Trg Sch 1962-63, ADC 1965-69); NOP 1969-70, Louis Harris 1970-71, res dir Leo Burnett LPE 1971-73; md: Eyes Can 1973-83, ISIS Research 1984-; chm Embley Park Sch 1969; *Books* New Product Launch Planner (1988); *Style—* Colin Maitland, Esq

MALLET, Philip Louis Victor; CMG (1980); s of Sir Victor Alexander Louis Mallet GCMG, CVO (d 1969), and Christiana Jean, *née* Andreae (d 1984); descended from Jacques Mallet du Pan, chronicler of the French Revolution; *b* 3 Feb 1926; *Educ* Winchester, Balliol Coll Oxford (BA); *m* 1953, Mary Moyle Grenfell, da of Rev Granville William Borlase (d 1953); 3 s (James, Stephen, Victor); *Career* HM Dip Serv (ret); high cmmr Guyana, non-res ambass Suriname 1978-82; *Clubs* Brooks's; *Style—* Philip Mallet, Esq, CMG; Wittersham House, Wittersham, Kent TN30 7ED (☎ 0797 270238)

MALONE, Andrew David; s of Richard Michael Delve Malone, of Dorking, Surrey, and Christine Frances, *née* Rayner; *b* 26 March 1965; *Educ* Hertfordshire Coll of Art, Canterbury Coll of Art (BA), St Martins Sch of Art; *Career* exhibitions 1987-90: St Augustines Gardens Canterbury, Wendens Ambo Essex, Canterbury Fringe Festival, Royal Nat Rose Soc Gardens St Albans, Scottish Sculpture Workshop, Univ of Kent, Herbert Read Gallery Canterbury; *Recreations* ornithology, cycling; *Style—* Andrew Malone, Esq; Derringstone Hill House, Derringstone Hill, Barham, nr Canterbury, Kent CT4 6QD (☎ 0227 831304); Ground Floor Studio, The Granary, Railway Hill, Barham, nr Canterbury, Kent

MANATON, John Westacott; s of William Alfred Westacott Manaton, and Linda Maud, *née* Townsend; *b* 10 Jan 1926; *Educ* Dulwich, Downing Coll Cambridge; *m* 23 June 1951, Mavis June, da of Frederick George Langton (d 1959), of Dartford, Kent; 1 da (Gillian Clare b 15 May 1964); *Career* Fleet Air Arm RN 1945-47; Lt Inns of Court Regt and 3/4 Co of London Yeo (Sharpshooters) TA; Royal Exchange Assurance 1947-51, Legal & General Assurance Society Ltd 1951-56, Canada Life Assurance Co Ltd 1956-59, Scottish Provident Institution 1959-63, pensions mangr National Mutual Life Association of Australasia Ltd 1964-67, gen mangr (UK) Swiss Life Insurance and Pension Co 1967-89, chm Westacott & Manton Ltd 1977-90; Freeman City of London 1980, Liveryman Worshipful Co of Actuaries 1980; AIA 1968, FPMI 1976; *Recreations* sailing (yachtmaster); *Clubs* United Oxford and Cambridge Univ, Little Ship, RNSA, Alleynian SS; *Style—* John Manaton, Esq; 2 Blair Drive, Sevenoaks, Kent TN13 3JR (☎ 0732 458528); Westacott & Manaton Ltd, 6 Stoneydeep, Twickenham Rd, Teddington, Middx TW11 8BL (☎ 081 943 1653)

MANNERING, Clive Trevor; TD; s of Frederick Mannering, of Springview, 6-10 Crescent Rd, Enfield, Middlesex, and Ella Norah, *née* Mace (d 1982); *b* 10 Sept 1938; *Educ* Highgate Sch; *m* 8 Sept 1962, Prudence Mary, da of Ivan Whitfeld (d 1984), of Oxford; 2 s (Michael Paul b 1965, Richard John b 1968); *Career* CA; articled clerk Pridie Brewster 1954-59; fin dir: Whitworths Food Gp plc 1975-86, Jamaica Producers Mktg Co Ltd (UK ops), JP Fruit Distributors Ltd 1987-; treas Nat Inst of Fresh Produce 1989-; assoc memb ICAEW 1960, FCA 1971, ATII 1962; *Recreations* farming; *Style—* Clive Mannering, Esq, TD; JP Group, 120 Main Rd, Sidcup, Kent DA14 6NH (☎ 081 309 0056, fax 081 309 0396)

MANSOUR, Dr Nagy Youssef; s of Mansour Hanna (d 1974), of Egypt, and Linda Yanni, *née* Mikhale; *b* 5 Dec 1938; *Educ* Cairo (MB BCh, DA), RCS London 1974 (LRCP, MRCS); *m* 8 Feb 1962 (m dis 1984); 1 s (Samer b 4 Dec 1965), 1 da (Sahar b 8 Jan 1964); *Career* conslt anaesthetist and i/c Intensive Care Unit Medway Health Dist 1975-78, estab Pain Relief Centre at Medway Hosp 1979-; FFARCS 1971; *Recreations* travel, garden design, classical music, organising conferences on regional blockade and pain relief; *Style—* Dr Nagy Mansour; 3A Vicary Way, Queens Ave, Maidstone, Kent ME16 0EJ (☎ 0622 756407); Alexandra Hospital, Impton Lane, Walderslade, Chatham, Kent ME5 9PG (☎ 0634 687166, fax 0634 686162)

MAR, Lady Janet Helen of; da of 30 Earl of Mar; *b* 31 Jan 1946; *Educ* Univ of St Andrews; *m* 1969, Lt Cdr Laurence of Mar (formerly Laurence Duncan McDiarmid Anderson, of Winton Castle, E Lothian) recognized in surname of Mar by warrant of Lord Lyon 1969; 2 da (Elizabeth b 1970, Catherine b 1971); *Style—* The Lady Janet of Mar; c/o Midland Bank, 26 Biggin St, Dover, Kent CT16 1BJ; Princes Ct, Brompton Rd, London SW3

MARCHAND, Rev (Rex) Anthony Victor; s of Maj Rex Marten Victor Marchand, TD, of Hurstpierpoint, W Sussex, and Rose Evelyn, *née* Rose-Innes; *b* 12 Jan 1947; *Educ* Eastbourne Coll, King's Coll London (BD, AKC); *m* 19 July 1969, Madelaine Margaret, da of Sqdn Ldr Anthony Neville Rowland, DSO, DFC (d 1980), of Weston Super Mare, Avon; 3 s (Jonathan b 1971, Timothy b 1975, Christopher b 1979), 1 da (Rachel b 1973); *Career* curate St Francis Leigh Park Hants 1970-73, dist vicar St John's Hatfield Herts 1973-80, rector of Deal 1980-; chaplain: Victoria Hosp Deal, Downs Branch Royal Br Legion Deal; *Recreations* tennis, cycling, caravanning, family; *Style—* The Rev Anthony Marchand; St Leonard's Rectory, Addelam Rd, Deal, Kent CT14 9BZ (☎ 0304 374076)

MARDON, Roger Clifford; s of Clifford Henry Mardon, of Chatham, Kent and Lilian, *née* Snowdon (d 1980); *b* 29 Feb 1944; *Educ* King's Sch Rochester; *m* 28 Sept 1968, Margaret Ann, da of Edward William Stanley Carter (d 1980), of Gillingham, Kent; 2 s (Anthony Clifford b 28 Sept 1972, Clive Edward b 11 Nov 1976); *Career* slr; articled clerk Stigant Son & Taylor 1961-66, admitted slr 1966, sr asst slr Bromley London Borough Cncl 1967-73 (asst slr 1966-67), asst slr Wallis & Co 1973-74, sec and slr Gravesham Borough Cncl 1988- (asst borough sec 1974-88); memb: Law Soc, Assoc of Dist Secs, Gravesend and Dist Law Soc (pres 1985-86); *Recreations* photography, music; *Style—* Roger C Mardon, Esq; Gravesend Borough Council, Civic Centre, Gravesham, Kent DA12 1AU (☎ 0474 337258, fax 0474 337453)

MARGARY, Harry Herbert; s of Thomas Alfred George Margary (d 1947), of Bournemouth, and Mabel Elizabeth, *née* Bilham (d 1978); *b* 16 July 1913; *Educ* Wolverhampton Sch, Univ of Cambridge (MA), Univ of Manchester (BA); *m* 29 July 1940, Deirdre, da of Samuel Johnston Moore, MD (d 1926), of Glasgow; 2 s (Aubyn Moore b 1941, Giles Donald Moore b 1951); *Career* RN Scientific Serv 1939-71, publisher of reproductions of historic maps especially of London 1971-; memb Cons Pty 1939-, chm Lympne Parish Cncl 1967-74, cncllr Shepway Dist 1973-; Freeman City of London, Liveryman

Worshipful Co of Salters 1934-; CEng, memb Civil Mechanical and Electrical Engrs, FSA; *Recreations* fly fishing; *Style*— Harry Margary, Esq; Lympne Castle, nr Hythe, Kent CT21 4HQ

MARGO, David Philip; s of Gerald Margo, of 4 The Grove, Bexleyheath, Kent, and Rene, *née* Goldstein; *b* 14 May 1951; *Educ* Chislehurst and Sidcup GS for Boys; *m* 14 Nov 1976, Lezley Susan, da of Maurice Kaye, of 43 Bath Hill Court, Bournemouth, Dorset; 1 s (Alexi Nicholas b 1981), 2 da (Jodi Rochelle b 1980, Kerri Mirian b 1984); *Career* admitted slr 1975; ptnr Saunders Sobell Leigh & Dobin; memb Law Soc; *Recreations* bridge, swimming; *Style*— David Margo, Esq

MARKENDALE, Nicholas John; s of Maj Joseph Leo Markendale, of 22 Greenleas Rd, Wallasey, Merseyside, and Mary *née* Dixon; *b* 3 March 1953; *Educ* Wallasey GS, Exeter Coll Oxford (BA); ptnr, Rosslyn Ann Macdonald; 1 s (Joseph Penrice b 10 May 1984); *Career* admitted slr 1980; ptnr Playford & Pope Sittingbourne 1986-; advsr to Swale Relate 1983-, legal advsr on Radio Invicta's Openline 1987-; memb Law Soc; *Style*— Nicholas Markendale, Esq; 9 London Rd, Sittingbourne, Kent ME10 4NQ (☎ 0795 76321, fax 0795 78414)

MARKS, (Frances) Leslie; da of Frank West (d 1970), and Ida Edith Mary, *née* Coombs; *b* 2 Aug 1930; *Educ* Milton Mount Coll Sussex, Birkbeck Coll London (BA), LSE (dip social policy and admin, dip social work studies); *m* 21 June 1958, Alan Frederick Marks, s of Frederick Marks; 2 s (Jonathan b 1961, Toby b 1964), 1 da (Nicola b 1962); *Career* gen sec Croydon Guild of Voluntary Orgns 1974-82, dep dir London Voluntary Serv Cncl 1982-85, chief exec and co sec Greater London Assoc for Disabled People 1985-88, dir Nat Assoc for the Welfare of Children in Hosp 1990-; Health Authy memb: Leybourne Grange HMC 1970-72, T Wells Leybourne 1972-74, Kent AHA 1974-81, Dartford and Gravesend 1981-88, Bromley 1988-90; advsr Nat Devpt Team for Mentally Handicapped People 1976-, memb Central Appeals Advsy Ctee (BBC/IBA) 1984-88, chm Informal Caring Advsy Forum (Kings fund) 1985-88, tstee Thames/LWT Telethon Tst 1987-, memb Charities Aid Fndn Grants Cncl 1988-, chm Jt Planning Working Gp Nat Cncl for Voluntary Orgns 1984-89; memb: Exec Ctee Bromley Cncl for Voluntary Serv, Bromley Soc for Mentally Handicapped Children, Bromcare Homes; *Clubs* Reform, LSE; *Style*— Mrs Leslie Marks

MARRIOTT, Alan Ogilvie; s of Spencer George Marriott, and Catherine Mary, *née* Burdett; *b* 3 July 1940; *Educ* Cranbrook Sch; *m* 11 Dec 1971, Joan Elizabeth, da of William George Jacobs; *Career* called to the Bar Inner Temple 1971; princ asst Worthing Magistrates Ct 1964-72, clerk the Canterbury & St Augustine Justices 1972-, clerk to the Faversham & Sittinghbourne Justices 1987-; pres Kent branch of Justices' Soc 1985-, hon sec Kent branch of Magistrates Assoc 1983-; memb Justices' Clerks Soc; *Recreations* sport, music, travel; *Clubs* Kent County Cricket, Chestfield Cricket, Kent & Canterbury; *Style*— Alan Marriott, Esq; The Magistrates' Courts, Broad St, Canterbury, Kent CT1 2UE (☎ 0227 454731)

MARRIOTT, Rev Canon David John; s of Alfred James Marriott (d 1961), of Northampton, and Emily, *née* Whyman; *b* 17 March 1929; *Educ* Campbell Square Sch Northampton, St Chad's Coll Durham (BA, Dip); *m* 1 April 1967, (Frances) Elizabeth, da of Brig A C C Willway, CB, CBE (d 1980), of Wye; *Career* curate St James Manston Leeds 1956-59, chaplain Cranleigh Sch Surrey 1959-63, headmaster Cathedral Choir Sch Canterbury 1963-67, vicar Wye 1967-, chaplain Wye Coll; promotions sec Friends of Vellore (India), chm Wye and Brook India Tst, govr Ashford Sch; mangr: Lady Joanna Thornhill Sch Wye; *Recreations* walking, swimming, gardening; *Style*— The Rev Canon David Marriott; The Vicarage, Wye, Ashford, Kent TN25 5AS (☎ 0233 812450)

MARSH, Hon Christopher; yr s of Baron Marsh by his 1 w; *b* 1960; *Style*— The Hon Christopher Marsh; Blackfen, Sidcup, Kent

MARSH, Francis Patrick (Frank); s of Horatio Septimus Marsh, of Leeds, Yorks, and Violet Mabel Constance, *née* Murphy; *b* 15 April 1936; *Educ* Gonville and Caius Coll Cambridge (BA, MB BChir, MA), London Hosp Med Coll Univ of London (MRCP); *m* 31 Aug 1963, Pamela Anne Campbell, da of Richard Campbell Bradbury (d 1963), of London; 1 s (Nicholas b 1966), 2 da (Penelope b 1964, Alexandra b 1971); *Career* The London Hosp: house offr 1960-61, registrar in med 1963-65, res fell Med Unit Med Coll 1965-67, lectr Med Coll 1967-70, sr lectr in med 1970-, conslt physician 1971-, dean of med studies Med Coll 1990-; SHO Kent and Canterbury Hosp 1961-62, registrar in med Royal Free Hosp 1962-63; chm NE Thames Regnl Med Advsy Ctee; memb: Jt Formulary Ctee Br Nat Formulary, Special Advsy Ctee on Renal Disease RCP, Jt Ctee on Higher Med Trg RCP, Euro Renal Assoc, BR Transplant Soc; memb RSM, FRCP 1976; *Books* incl: Urology (contrib, 1976), Price's Textbook of Medicine (contrib, 1978), Oxford Textbook of Medicine (contrib, 1982, 1987), Postgraduate Nephrology (ed, 1985), Hutchisons Clinical Methods (contrib, 1989), Drugs and the Kidney (contrib, 1990); *Recreations* music, sailing, skiing; *Clubs* Blizard; *Style*— Dr Frank Marsh

MARSH, Peter Dudley; s of Dudley Graham Marsh (d 1969), of Canterbury, and Norah Marion *née* Wacher (d 1974); *b* 16 Feb 1926; *Educ* Dulwich, St Johns Coll Hurstpierpoint, Univ of Edinburgh, Sch of Architecture Canterbury Coll of Art; *m* 1, 18 Aug 1949, June, *née* Saxby (d 1969); 2 s (Richard b 1957, Jonathan b 1961), 1 da (Anne Crouch b 1953); m 2, 23 May 1970, Valerie, da of Charles Alfred Williams (d 1983); 1 s (Henry b 1977); *Career* architect in private practice 1952-, Surveyor to the Fabric Canterbury Cathedral 1969-; chm: Canterbury Branch RIBA 1969, Cathedral Architects Assoc 1984-87; pres Rotary Club of Dover 1970; memb: Tech Sub Ctee Euro Cathedrals Assoc 1986-, Fabric Advsy Ctee Rochester Cathedral, Canterbury Conservation Advsy Ctee; govr Kent Inst of Art and Design; Freeman City of London, Liveryman Worshipful Co of Masons 1978; memb EASA, ARIBA 1953, FSA 1982; *Recreations* bee keeping; *Style*— Peter Marsh, Esq, FSA; Little Watersend, Temple Ewell, Dover, Kent CT15 7EP (☎ 0304 822022)

MARSH, Steven Andrew; s of Melvyn Graham Marsh, of Walderslade, Chatham, Kent, and Valerie Ann, *née* Box; *b* 27 Jan 1961; *Educ* Walderslade Secdy Sch for Boys, Mid-Kent Coll of Higher and Further Educn (OND); *m* 27 Sept 1986, Julie Ann, da of Robert Colin Wilson, of The Martins, Frinsted, Sittingbourne, Kent; 1 da (Hayley Ann b 1987); *Career* co cricketer; Kent CCC: debut 1986, wicket keeper and right handed batsman, highest score 120 versus Essex 1988, record holder for most dismissals in a Refuge Assurance League season 1989; *Recreations* golf, horse racing, football; *Clubs* Kent Hoppers Tie; *Style*— Steven Marsh, Esq; Kent County Cricket Club, St Lawrence Ground, Old Dover Rd, Canterbury, Kent

MARSHALL, Michael Leicester John; s of Sir James Marshall, JP, DL (d 1977), and Rebecca Mary, *née* Gotley (d 1966); *b* 26 May 1924; *Educ* Eastbourne Coll, Coll of Estate Mgmnt; *m* 6 June 1959, Tessa Rosemary, da of Charles Miles Skerrett-Rogers (d 1972); 2 s (Julian b 24 April 1960, Thomas b 1 July 1964), 1 da (Antonia b 6 June 1961); *Career* Maj 5 Royal Gurkha Rifles (FF); active serv: Arakan 1943-44 (wounded), Kohima 1944, Burma 1944-45; Capt 4 Bn Queens Regt TA 1947-50, ret; chartered surveyor; sr ptnr Chestertons, receiver Church Cmmrs for England, surveyor Royal Masonic Sch for Boys, hon surveyor Charterhouse Sch; memb Court of Assts Corp of Sons of the Clergy (former sr treas); memb Court Worshipful Co of Tylers and Bricklayers (Master 1986-87); Lambeth Degree MA Oxon 1989; FRICS 1952; *Recreations* gardening, walking; *Clubs* Army and Navy, MCC; *Style*— Michael Marshall, Esq; East Brabourne House, Brabourne, Ashford, Kent TN25 5LR (☎ 030 381 2112)

MARSHALL, Stuart Walter; s of Walter Clement Marshall, and Elsie Vera, *née* Hawkins; *b* 9 Sept 1935; *Educ* Beckenham and Penge GS; *m* 5 Aug 1961, Patricia Ann, da of Hugh Lawrence Bentley; 1 s (Adrian b 1967), 1 da (Anne b 1970); *Career* Coutts & Co: joined 1952, dep head branch 1981-86, head Mgmnt Serv Div 1986-90, dir 1989, head Commercial Banking 1990-; cncl memb and hon treas Invalid Childrens Aid Nationwide, tstee WALK Fund, govr Colfe's Sch; FCIB; *Recreations* fishing, shooting, skiing, opera, gardening; *Style*— Stuart Marshall, Esq; Chelsfield, Kent; Coutts & Co, 440 Strand, London WC2R 0QS (☎ 071 379 6262); Coutts & Co, 27 Bush Lane, Cannon Street, London EC4R 0AA (☎ 071 623 3434)

MARTEL, Keith Alistair; s of Basil Walter Martel, and Lilias Patricia Martel (d 1988); *b* 24 Sept 1949; *Educ* Guernsey GS for Boys, Ealing Tech Coll; *m* 1, 10 July 1981 (m dis 1988), Susan Elizabeth; 1 s (James Martel b 8 Jan 1978), 1 da (Caroline Patricia Martel b 27 March 1976); m 2, 10 April 1988, Dorothy, da of John Conlin; *Career* trainee mangr Royal Garden Hotel London 1971-72, asst and dep mangr Wiltshire Hotel Swindon 1972-75, dep gen mangr Great Danes Hotel Kent 1975-78, asst project mangr Rank Hotels Ltd London (gp of 17 hotels) 1978-80, project and gen mangr St Pierre Park Hotel Guernsey CI 1980-87, project and gen mangr Effingham Park Hotel West Sussex 1987-; MBIM 1984, MHCIMA 1985, FInstSMM 1986; *Recreations* golf, swimming, wind surfing; *Style*— Keith Martel, Esq; Effingham Park Hotel, Copthorne, West Sussex RH10 3EU (☎ 0342 714994, fax 0342 716039)

MARTIN, Anthony Loft (Tony); s of Leslie Commerford Martin (d 1968), of Shorne, and Ella Gertrude, *née* Loft (d 1959); *b* 15 May 1925; *Educ* Kings Sch Rochester, Gravesend GS for Boys; *m* 4 April 1951, Valerie Murray, da of Herbert James Mitchell (d 1980), of 60 Portland Ave, Gravesend; 1 s (David Commerford Martin b 15 June 1953), 1 da (Hilary Murray Green (*née* Martin) b 22 Feb 1955); *Career* LAC RAF 1943-47; admitted slr 1950; presently sr ptnr family firm of slrs Martin Tolhurst Partnership (joined 1947, ptnr 1956); pres: Gravesend & Dist Law Soc 1980, Kent Law Soc 1984-85; chm Gravesend Round Table 1964-65, pres Rotary Club Gravesend 1980-81; memb Law Soc; *Recreations* gardening and walking; *Style*— Tony Martin, Esq; The Tanyard, Tanyard Hill, Shorne, Gravesend, Kent (☎ 0474 822145); 7 Wrotham Rd, Gravesend, Kent (☎ 0474 325531, fax 0474 560771)

MARTIN, Dr Neil David Tait; s of Dr J W Martin, and M Martin, *née* Nicholls; *b* 10 Aug 1952; *Educ* Watson's Coll Edinburgh, Univ of Edinburgh (BSc), Univ of London (MB BS, MD); *m* 9 May 1981, Gillian Ann Philipa, da of Mr J W Dobson; 2 s (Jack Lewis b 21 July 1983, Frederick James b 20 May 1986), 1 da (Lily Rose b 17 Oct 1988); *Career* paediatrician and neonatologist Kent and Canterbury Hosp 1987-; memb: BPA, Williams Syndrome and Infantile Hypercalcaemia Fndn; *Recreations* squash, gardening; *Style*— Dr Neil

Martin; The Kent and Canterbury Hospital, Ethelbert Rd, Canterbury, Kent CT3 3RG (☎ 0227 766877)

MARTIN-QUIRK, Howard Richard Newell; s of George Donald Martin, of Milton on Stour, Dorset, and Nellie Katie, *née* Newell; *b* 8 Aug 1937; *Educ* Lancing, Christ's Coll Cambridge (BA,MA), UCL (BSc, MLitt); *m* 1, Sally Anne (d 1976), da of Ernest Davies, MP, of London; m 2, 1 Oct 1976, Mary Teresa (Mitzi), da of Dudley C Quirk, JP; 1 s (Inigo b 3 Dec 1989); *Career* architect; sr tutor Sch of Architecture Kingston Poly 1970-, ptnr Martin Quirk Associates 1983-; chief oenologist Chiddingstone Vineyards Ltd 1985-; *Books* incl: Meaning and Metaphor in Architecture (1983), The Crime of the Century (1989); *Recreations* chess, squash rackets, gardening, cricket, wine, music; *Clubs* Soc of Architectural Historians, Victorian Soc, Architectural Assoc, Wagner Soc, EVA; *Style—* Howard Martin, Esq; Chiddingstone Vineyards Ltd, Vexour Farm, Chiddingstone, Kent TN8 7BB (☎ 0892 870277); Kingston Polytechnic, Kingston upon Thames KT1 2QJ (☎ 081 549 6151); Martin Quirk Associates, Sorrel, Vexour Farm, Chiddingstone, Kent TN8 7BB (☎ 0892 870439)

MARWOOD, David Christopher Laborde; er s of Hubert George Marwood (d 1962), of Tonbridge, Kent, and Gertrude Sendall, *née* Laborde; *b* 12 Feb 1923; *Educ* St Catharine's Coll Cambridge (MA); *m* 15 Sept 1951, Jean Margaret Burrington, da of George Frederick Sharp (d 1966); 2 s (Philip b 4 April 1954, Dr Richard Marwood b 21 Oct 1956); *Career* enlisted Royal Scots Regt 1941, Offrs Trg Sch Bangalore India 1942, cmmnd 2 Lt IA 1942, served India, Assam, Burma RIASC 1942-46, demob Capt 1946; city merchant bank 1949-51, MI 1951-53, New Town Corporation 1953-54; International Computers Ltd 1954-84: co sec 1961, gp sec 1968, admin dir 1976, ret 1984; chm ICL Pension Trust Ltd 1980-89, dir STC Pension Tst Ltd 1989-; pres Chartered Secs and Admins 1975 (memb Cncl 1964-87); memb London Regnl Cncl CBI 1980-84, govr Birkbeck Coll London 1983-86, tstee High Hilden Old People's Home; memb: Kent CC 1985-, Tonbridge Volunteer Bureau Mgmnt Ctee, Tonbridge Investmt Club, Tonbridge NADFAS, Tonbridge Historical Soc, Kent Branch Cambridge Soc, Assoc of Men of Kent and Kentish Men, Kent Co Playing Fields Assoc; vice chm Tonbridge & Malling Cons Assoc 1984-87 (currently chm Patrons Club); Master Worshipful Co of Chartered Secretaries and Administrators 1982 (fndr memb 1977); FCIS 1958 (assoc 1954), FBIM, FRSA; *Recreations* sailing, walking, antiques, reading; *Clubs* United Oxford & Cambridge Univ; *Style—* David Marwood, Esq; 36 The Ridgeway, Tonbridge, Kent TN10 4NJ (☎ 0732 354303)

MASON, (Michael) Andrew; s of Lt-Col Geoffrey Mason, MBE (ret), of Otley, Suffolk, and Daphne Mason; *b* 27 April 1948; *Educ* Steyning GS, Royal Free Hosp Sch of Med Univ of London (MB BS, LRCP); *m* 10 June 1978, Eleanor Mason; 1 s (Timothy b 9 Aug 1980), 1 da (Jennifer b 14 Sept 1983); *Career* dir Accident and Emergency Servs Medway Health Authy, conslt and specialist in Accident and Emergency Med Medway Hosp 1985-, ed British Journal of Accident and Emergency Medicine; memb: Br Assoc for Accident & Emergency Med, RSM, Br Assoc of Immediate Care Schemes; memb BMA, FRCS; *Recreations* gardening, bringing up children, food and wine; *Style—* Andrew Mason, Esq; The Accident Centre, Medway Hospital, Windmill Rd, Gillingham, Kent ME7 5NY (☎ 0634 830000 ext 3334, fax 0634 829470)

MASON, Ven Richard John; s of Vice Adm Frank Trowbridge Mason, KCB (d 1988), of 114 High St, Hurstpierpoint, W Sussex, and Dora Margaret, *née* Brand; *b* 26 April 1929; *Educ* Shrewsbury, Lincoln Theol Coll; *Career* Nat Serv RA 1947-49; newspaper journalist 1949-55; asst curate Bishop's Hatfield 1958-64, domestic chaplain to Bishop of London 1964-69; vicar of: Riverhead 1969-73, Edenbridge 1973-83; priest i/c: Dunton Green 1963-73, Crockham Hill 1981-83; leader Chiddingstone Gp of Parishes 1974-77, archdeacon of Tonbridge 1977-, min St Luke Sevenoaks 1983-; memb Edenbridge Rotary Club 1973-83, pres East Grinstead & Dist Guild of Church Bell Ringers 1976-; Freeman Worshipful Co of Shipwrights; *Recreations* watching cricket; *Style—* The Ven the Archdeacon of Tonbridge; St Luke's House, 30 Eardley Rd, Sevenoaks, Kent TN13 1XT (☎ 0732 452462)

MASSEREENE AND FERRARD, 13 & 6 Viscount (I 1660 & 1797); John Clotworthy Talbot Foster Whyte-Melville Skeffington; DL (Co Antrim 1957); also Baron of Loughneagh (I 1660), Baron Oriel of Collon (I 1790), and Baron Oriel of Ferrard (UK 1821, which sits as); patron of one living; s of 12 (& 5) Viscount, DSO, JP, DL (d 1956, himself ggs of Harriet, w of 2 Viscount Ferrard, and Viscountess Massereene in her own right; Harriet's f was the 4 & last Earl of Massereene; the Viscountcy of Massereene (but not that of Ferrard) is the only Irish Peeerage heritable by a female), and Jean Barbara Ainsworth, JP (d 1937), da of Sir John Stirling Ainsworth, MP ; *b* 23 Oct 1914; *Educ* Eton; *m* 15 March 1939, Annabelle Kathleen, er da of late Henry David Lewis, of Combwell Priory, Hawkhurst; 1 s, 1 da; *Heir* s, Hon John David Clotworthy Whyte-Melville Skeffington; *Career* Lt Black Watch SR 1933-36 and 1939-49 WWII invalided, served invasion, small vessels pool RN 1944; sits as Cons in House of Lords; driver leading Br Car Le Mans Grand Prix 1937, gold staff offr Coronation of HM The Queen 1953, Peers memb Inter-Parly Union Delgn to Spain 1960, jt chm Cons Peers Ctee (IUP) House of Lords 1965-70, (Cons whip 1958-65); promoted and ran 1st scheduled air serv Glasgow, Oban, Isle of Mull; memb parly delegation to Malawi 1976, an original pioneer in commercial development of Cape Canaveral USA, presented operetta Countess Maritza at Palace Theatre London; former dir Aviation & Shipping Ltd, chm Sunset & Vine plc (TV), former chm Ferrard Holdings Ltd; former chm: London Scottish Clas Assoc, Victoria League for Kent; former pres Kent Hotels & Restaurants Assoc and other socs, MFH Ashford Valley Foxhounds 1953-54, vice pres Animal Welfare Year 1976-77, memb Deer Ctee Br Field Sports Soc, pres Monday Club 1981-; Freeman City of London, memb Worshipful Co of Shipwrights; Cross Cdr Order of Merit SMOM; *Books* The Lords (1973); *Recreations* sailing - (yacht 'Benmore Lady'); *Clubs* Royal Yacht Sqdn, Turf, Carlton, Pratt's, House of Lords YC (former cdre); *Style—* The Rt Hon the Viscount Massereene and Ferrard, DL; Chilham Castle, Canterbury, Kent (☎ 0227 730319); Knock, Isle of Mull, Argyll (☎ 06803 356)

MASTERS, Sheila Valerie (Mrs Barry Noakes); da of Albert Frederick Masters, of Eltham, London, and Iris Sheila, *née* Ratcliffe; *b* 23 June 1949; *Educ* Eltham Hill GS, Univ of Bristol (LLB); *m* 3 Aug 1985, (Colin) Barry Noakes, s of Stuart Noakes, of Brenchley; *Career* Peat Marwick McLintock: joined 1970, ptnr 1983-, ptnr in charge Pub Sector Practice 1986-; seconded to: HM Treasy as accounting/ commercial advsr 1979-81, Dept of Health as fin dir on NHS Mgmnt Exec 1988; elected to: London Soc of CAs 1984, Cncl ICAEW 1987; appointed to Ctee of Enquiry MAFF 1988; FCA, ATII; *Books* Tolley's Stamp Duties (1980); *Recreations* skiing, horse-racing, opera, early classical music; *Style—* Ms Sheila Masters; Spyways, High St, Goudhurst, Kent TN17 1AL (☎ 0580 211 427, fax 0580 212244); Peat Marwick McLintock, Blackfriars, London EC4V 3PD (☎ 071 236 8000, fax 071 248 6552)

MATHIESON, Jeffery George; OBE (1988); s of Walter Douglas Mathieson, OBE, MC (d 1983), of Middleton Thatch, Freshwater, IOW, and Florence Winifred, *née* Burley (d 1988); *b* 17 Feb 1925; *Educ* Whitgift Sch Croydon; *m* 16 Sept 1961, Patricia (d 1988), da of Fredrick Murton Faers (d 1975); 2 da (Jacqueline b 31 May 1963, Ann b 12 Sept 1966); *Career* RAF 1943-47, Navigator/Wireless Operator (Air Crew); asst valuer Corp of Birmingham 1952-54, asst estates offr Basildon Devpt Corp 1954-59; Corp of London: asst estates offr 1959-63, princ asst estates offr 1963-79, dep city surveyor 1979-90; Freeman City of London 1970, Liveryman Worshipful Co of Chartered Surveyors 1982; FRICS 1976; *Recreations* golf, gardening, cooking; *Style—* Jeffery Mathieson, Esq, OBE; 2 Sandown Close, Tunbridge Wells, Kent TN2 4RL (☎ 089282 2839)

MATTHEWS, Jeffery Edward; s of Henry Edward Matthews (d 1960), and Sybil Frances, *née* Cooke (d 1951); *b* 3 April 1928; *Educ* Alleyn's, Brixton Sch of Building (NDD); *m* 12 Sept 1953, (Sylvia Lilian) Christine, da of Cecil Herbert William Hoar (d 1974), 1 s (Rory b 1956), 1 da (Sarah Jane b 1958); *Career* graphic designer J Edward Sander 1949-52, pt/t tutor 1952-55, lettering and calligraphy assesor SIAD 1970-; designs for the PO: decimal 'To Pay' labels 1971, font of numerals for definitive stamps 1981, new range of colours for stamps 1987; stamps: United Nations 1965; British Bridges 1968, definitives for Scotland Wales NI and IOM 1971, Royal Silver Wedding 1972, 25th Anniversary of the Coronation 1978, London 1980, 80th Birthday of the Queen Mother 1980, Christmas 1980, Wedding of Prince Charles and Lady Diana Spencer 1981, Quincentenary of the College of Arms 1984, 60th Birthday of the Queen 1986, Wedding of Prince Andrew and Sarah Ferguson 1986, Order of the Thistle Tercentenary of Revival 1987, 150 Anniversary The Penny Black 1990; also: first day covers, postmarks, presentation packs, souvenir books and posters; designer film Picture to Post 1969, other work includes: title banner lettering and coat of arms Sunday Times 1968, cover design and lettering for official programme Royal Wedding 1981, The Royal Mint commemorative medal Order of the Thistle 1987, official heraldry and symbols HMSO, hand-drawn lettering COI, calligraphy, packaging, promotion and book binding designs, logotypes, brand images and hand-drawn lettering; for various firms incl: Unicover Corp USA, Harrison & Sons Ltd, Metal Box Co, DRG, Reader's Digest Association Ltd, Encyclopaedia Britannica International Ltd, ICI, H R Higgins (Coffee-Man) Ltd; work exhibited in A History of Bookplates in Britain and at V & A Museum 1979; Citizen & Goldsmith of London (Freedom by Patrimony) 1949; FCSD 1978, FRSA 1987, AIBD 1951; *Books* Designers In Britain (contrib 1964, 2 edn 1971), 45 Wood-Engravers (contrib, 1982), Royal Mail Year Book (contrib, 1984, 1986, 1987); *Recreations* furniture restoration, playing the guitar, gardening, DIY; *Style—* Jeffery Matthews, Esq

MATTHIAE, Rev David; *b* 29 July 1940; *Educ* Trinity Sch of John Whitgift Croydon, Fitzwilliam House Cambridge (MA), Lincoln Theol Coll; *Career* curate Charlton Dover 1970-75 (St Edward New Addington 1965-70); incumbent: Canterbury All Saints 1975-84, Tunstall with Rodmersham 1987- (priest in charge 1984-87), Rural Dean of Sittingbourne 1988-; memb Rotary Club of Sittingbourne and Milton Regis, chm Seaside Camps for London Boys and Girls Inc (Hawkshill) Walmer Deal Kent 1978-; *Style—* The Rev David Matthiae; The Rectory, Tunstall, Sittingbourne, Kent ME9 8DU (☎ 0795

23907)

MATTOCK, John Clive; s of Raymond Jack Mattock, of 10 Brownlands Rd, Sidmouth, E Devon, and Eva Winifred Zoë, *née* Ward; *b* 21 Jan 1944; *Educ* Dartford GS; *m* 1985, Susan, da of Richard Clulow, of 97 Upper Mealines, Harlow, Essex; 2 s (Anthony b 1986, Christopher b 1988); *Career* stockbroker, md UTC Securities plc; dep chm: UTC Gp plc 1985, Peak Tst Ltd 1988, Southwest Resources plc 1989; dir: Stalwart Assur Gp plc 1986, Takare plc 1986; FCA 1967; *Recreations* tennis, country pursuits; *Clubs* Bexley Lawn Tennis (vice pres), Cannons; *Style*— J C Mattock, Esq; Chippens Bank House, Hever, Kent; UTC Securities plc, 23 Finsbury Circus, London EC2 (☎ 071 628 7090)

MAUDE, Hon (Robert) Connan Wyndham Leslie; s and h of 8 Viscount Hawarden; *b* 23 May 1961; *Educ* St Edmund's Sch Canterbury, RAC Cirencester; *Career* farming, including vineyards; *Recreations* shooting, motorcycling, indoor cricket, skiing; *Style*— The Hon Connan Maude; 2 Dene Cotts, Adisham Rd, Wingham, Canterbury, Kent CT3 1NU

MAUDE, Hon Henry Cornwallis; yr s of 7 Viscount Hawarden (d 1958), and Marion, *née* Wright (d 1974); *b* 3 March 1928; *Educ* Marlborough, Worcester Coll Oxford (MA); *m* 8 Aug 1964, Elizabeth Georgina, o da of David McNaught Lockie, of Grasse, France; 2 s, 2 da; *Career* schoolmaster, farmer; High Sheriff of Kent 1989-90; *Recreations* swimming, reading, gardening; *Style*— The Hon Henry Maude; Wingham Well House, Wingham, Canterbury, Kent

MAUDE, Hon Thomas Patrick Cornwallis; s of 8 Viscount Hawarden; *b* 1 Oct 1964; *Career* farmer; *Recreations* hockey, shooting, skiing, tennis; *Clubs* Polo Farm Sports (Canterbury), Kent and Canterbury; *Style*— The Hon Thomas Maude

MAURICE, Brian Armstead; s of Norman Brocklehurst Maurice, OBE (d 1975), and Dorothy, *née* Armstead (d 1966); *b* 27 July 1928; *Educ* Oundle, Trinity Hall Cambridge (BA, MA, MChir); *m* 13 Sept 1958, Marjorie Anne, da of Ernest Frederick Sammons (d 1985); 2 s (Adrian b 1959, Christopher b 1965), 1 da (Laura b 1961); *Career* Nat Serv Flying Offr MO 2FTS Hullavington 1954, Flt Lt surgn RAF Hosp St Athan 1955; former surgical registrar Warwick Hosp; former sr surgical registrar: St Thomas' Hosp (house surgn, lectr in anatomy, registrar), KCH; conslt surgn Kent and Sussex Hosp Tunbridge Wells; now ret; surgical tutor RCS; memb: Cncl of Hosp Conslts and Specialists Assoc, Registered Homes Tbnl; Freeman: City of London 1955, Worshipful Co of Barbers 1987; Master Worshipful Co of Playing Card Makers 1970 (Freeman 1956); FRCS 1958; *Books* Surgery for General Practioners (1988); *Recreations* golf, bridge, koi keeper; *Clubs* Livery, Santa Cristina Golf; *Style*— Brian Maurice, Esq

MAW, Dr (Dane Stephen) Jonathan; s of Daniel Scarrat Maw (d 1989), and Gulielma, *née* Colbert; *b* 8 Sept 1937; *Educ* Kingswood Sch, Univ of London St Mary's Hosp (MB BS); *m* 18 Dec 1965, Barbara Vokins, da of Arthur Edward Priest (d 1989); 1 s (David Nicholas b 1967), 1 da (Elizabeth Tacye b 1970); *Career* professional posts in London until 1972; conslt physician: Tunbridge Wells Health Authy, Pembury Hosp Pembury, Kent & Sussex Hosp Tunbridge Wells 1972-; visiting physician Sir Archibald McIndoe Burns Unit Queen Victoria Hosp E Grinstead, conslt memb Med Appeals Tbnl 1988-, princ med offr Nat Provident Inst Tunbridge Wells 1990-; memb Mgmnt Ctee The Horder Centre for Arthritics Crowborough, pres Tonbridge Wells Branch Br Diabetic Assoc; FRCP FRSA; *Recreations* the arts, good wine, travel, walking; *Style*— Dr Jonathan Maw; Chasedale, 53 Madeira Park, Tunbridge Wells, Kent TN2 5SY (☎ 0892 34815); Pembury Hospital, Pembury, Kent TN2 4QJ (☎ 089 2823535)

MAXTED, Cncllr Robert Frederick; s of Thomas Maxted (d 1952), of London, and Ada Maxted (d 1956); *Educ* Randall Place Sch, Elfrida Sch Bellingham Kent; *m* 24 March 1945, Mary Margaret, da of Frederick John Gibb (d 1956), of Southend, Essex; *Career* RAFVR 1937, RN 1939, RM 1944-46, served Pacific Area Aust; Prescott & Co London 1935-39, Silver and Edgington Civil and Military Outfitters 1948-75, estate offr London Borough Greenwich; semi pro pianist and singer; former dep Mayor and Mayor 1943-45, cncllr 1960-, dep ldr Cons Gp Dartford Cncl 1965-68, former chm Housing and Environmental Health Ctees, memb Dartford and Gravesham Community Health Ctee; chm of Govrs Wentworth Infant and Jr Sch; former mangr: St Albans Sch, The Downs Sch; chm Dartford Sea Cadet Corps, dep chm Thameside Jt Ctee on Pollution, dir N Kent Enterprise Agency; *Recreations* walking, dancing, music; *Style*— Cncllr Robert Maxted; 55 Fleet Rd, Dartford, Kent DA2 6JE (☎ 0322 222562)

MAXTED, Rev Robin Leslie; s of Leslie Joseph Maxted (d 1988), of Holy Innocents, Orpington, and Eileen Rose, *née* Hackney (d 1973); *b* 8 Feb 1950; *Educ* St Stephen's Secdy Sch Welling, Jr Seminary St Joseph's Mark Cross, Sr Seminary St Johns Wonersh; *Career* ordained priest St Georges Cathedral 1975; asst priest Parish of: Strood Kent 1975-79, Purley Surrey 1979-83, Ashford Kent 1983-87, Orpington Kent 1987-; memb: Amnesty Int, UNA, Aids Support Gp Orpington; *Recreations* squash, wind-surfing, golf, skiing; *Style*— Rev Robin Maxted; Holy Innocents Presbytery, Strickland Way, Orpington BR6 9UE (☎ 0689 32995)

MAXTED, Stephen Paul; s of Ernest John Maxted, of Deal, Kent, and Evelyn Grace, *née* Cook; *b* 17 May 1956; *Educ* Walmer Secdy Sch, Canterbury Coll of Technol, Maidstone Coll of Printing; *m* 11 Sept 1977 (m dis 1990), Janet Patricia, da of Frederick John Ballard, of Broadstairs, Kent; 3 da (Tracy b 1981, Katy b 1983, Nicola b 1985); *Career* compositor East Kent Mercury 1973, computer typesetter System Graphics Folkestone; elected to Dover Dist Cncl serving on Fin and Tourism Ctee, Deal Charter Tstee 1985-89; memb: Bd of Govrs Downs Primary Sch 1985-88, Exec Ctee Dover and Deal CLP 1983-86; *Recreations* natural history, family; *Style*— Stephen Maxted, Esq; 79 Station Rd, Walmer, Deal, Kent CT14 7RE (☎ 0304 368309)

MAXTONE GRAHAM, Robert Mungo; s of Anthony James Oliphant Maxtone Graham (d 1971), of Cultoquhey, Crieff, Perthshire, and Joyce Anstruther (d 1953, 'Jan Struther' author of 'Mrs Miniver'); the Maxtone of Cultoquhey line is traced back to 1410 (see Burke's LG, 18 edn, Vol III, 1972); *b* 6 May 1931; *Educ* USA, Stowe, Trinity Coll Cambridge (MA), Univ of Edinburgh; *m* 1962, Claudia Eva Elizabeth Page-Phillips, da of Frederick Tannert (d 1980), of 238a Southlands Rd, Bickley, Kent; 1 da (Ysenda b 1962), and 1 stepda (Livia b 1958); *Career* Nat Serv cmmnd Scots Gds 1949-51 serv Malaya; advocate of the Scots Bar 1957, legal assoc Royal Town Planning Inst, town planning conslt, fndr and proprietor Malthouse Arcade Hythe Kent; *Recreations* genealogy, book-collecting, photography; *Style*— Robert Maxtone Graham, Esq; 6 Moat Sole, Sandwich, Kent (☎ 0304 613270); 8 Atholl Crescent Lane, Edinburgh 3 (☎ 031 228 3338); 55 rue des Teinturiers, Avignon, France (☎ 90865292)

MAY, Kenneth Walter; JP (Kent, 1962); *b* 24 July 1919; *Educ* Queen's Coll Oxford (MA); *m* 21 April 1947, Helena Frances, *née* Pettitt; 2 s (Richard b 1954, Stephen b 1958), 1 da (Jacquetta b 1960); *Career* war serv RA RAEC 1940-46, demob Capt; teacher Tonbridge Sch 1948-81, pt/t tutor WEA 1956-, pt/t tutor and cnsllr Open Univ 1976-, pt/t lectr Kent Coll for Careers Serv 1972-82, pt/t tutor Univ of Sussex 1987-; chm: Tonbridge UDC 1958-59 (memb 1952-74), Kent and Sussex Accident Prevention Fedn 1970-74, Tonbridge CAB 1970-85, West Kent Div Educn Exec 1972-74; parly candidate 1959-70; memb: Bd of Visitors Blantyre House HM Prison 1974-89, WEA Nat Exec Ctee 1978- (chm SE Dist 1975-87); currently vice chm Tonbridge and Malling Twinning Ctee (chm 1966-85); hon Alderman Tonbridge and Malling 1974-; *Style*— Kenneth May, Esq, JP; 1 Mayor House, Blackham, Tunbridge Wells, Kent TN3 9UE

MAY, Dr Roger William; JP 1988; s of Thomas George May (d 1963), of Surbiton, Surrey, and Grace Alice Cole; *b* 28 Aug 1936; *Educ* Surbiton Co GS, Guy's Hosp Med Sch (MB BS, LRCP, MRCS, DRCOG); *m* 18th May 1959, Diana Elizabeth, da of Percy Grant Robertson (d 1989), of Hook, Surrey; 3 s (Timothy John b 1960, Robert Alexander Grant b 1963, Jonathan Roger b 1967), 2 da (Stephanie Diana b 1962, Philippa Susan b 1965); *Career* ptnr in gen practice 1963, assoc advsr in gen practice SE Thames 1988 (asst advsr 1987-88); memb: Kent Local Med Ctee 1967-74, Bromley AHA and FPC 1974-77, Bromley Local Med Ctee 1974-87; examiner RCGP 1982-89; hon memb Chislehurst Rotary Club (past pres 1980-81), chm Nat Leader Trainee Advsy Bd The Scout Assoc, former HQ cmmr for the handicapped 1983-88 (prev asst co cmmr and dist cmmr); tstee and hon sec Health Projects Abroad, memb Mgmnt Ctee Bromley Y Project; Churchill fell USA 1986, Mayor of Bromley's Award for Voluntary Servs 1987; MITD, FRCGP 1988 (MRCGP 1972); *Books* Neurology (1985), Let's Integrate (1987); *Recreations* opera, theatre, mountain walking, jogging (very slowly); *Style*— Dr Roger May, JP; 5 Little Thrift, Petts Wood, Orpington, Kent BR5 1NQ; The Surgery, 42 High St, Chislehurst, Kent BR7 5AX (☎ 081 467 5551)

MAYHEW, Sir Patrick Barnabas Burke; PC (1986), QC (1972), MP (C) Tunbridge Wells 1974-; s of (Alfred) Geoffrey Horace Mayhew, MC (d 1985), of Sevenoaks Weald, Kent, and Sheila Margaret Burke, *née* Roche; *b* 11 Sept 1929; *Educ* Tonbridge, Balliol Coll Oxford (MA); *m* 15 April 1963, Jean Elizabeth, 2 da of John Gurney, of Walsingham Abbey, Norfolk; 4 s (James b 1964, Henry b 1966, Tristram b 1968, Jerome b 1970); *Career* served 4/7 Royal Dragoon Gds, Capt (Nat Serv and AER); bencher Middle Temple 1982 (barr 1956); contested (C) Camberwell and Dulwich 1970, vice chm Cons Home Affrs Ctee and memb Exec Ctee 1976-79, parly under sec Employment 1979-81, min of state Home Office 1981-83, SG 1983-87, AG 1987-; pres: Tonbridge and Tunbridge Wells Dist MENCAP, Tunbridge Wells Constitutional Club, Kilndown CC; vice pres: Tunbridge Wells RFC, Goudhurst CC; kt 1983; *Recreations* sailing, country pursuits; *Clubs* Pratt's, Beefsteak, Garrick; *Style*— The Rt Hon Sir Patrick Mayhew, PC, QC, MP; House of Commons, London SW1A 0AA

MAYLAM, Richard Thomas; s of Maj Thomas John Maylam (d 1990), of Tonbridge, Kent, and Evelyn Mary, *née* Epps; *b* 5 May 1942; *Educ* Tonbridge Sch; *m* 14 May 1988, Sophie Jane, da of Maj Robin Dacres Dixon, of Wadhurst, Sussex; *Career* chartered surveyor; ptnr Fox & Manwaring 1974-; vice chm Tonbridge Branch of The Assoc Men of Kent and Kentish Men; played Hockey for Kent Co, 12 man for Kent CCC, hunted with Ashford Valley Foxhounds; AMRSH 1971, FRICS 1973; *Recreations* horses, hockey, cricket, dieting, work, riding in Arab races; *Style*— Richard Maylam, Esq; Peacock Farm, Emmet Lane, Yalding, Maidstone, Kent ME18 6BG; Fox & Manwaring, 4 London Rd, Tonbridge, Kent TN10 3AE (☎ 0732 771212)

MAYNARD, Edwin Francis George (Frank); s of Edwin Maynard, and Nancy Frances, *née* Tully; *b* 23 Feb 1921; *Educ* Westminster, ME Staff Coll; *m* 1, May 1945 (m dis 1962), Patricia Baker; 1 s (John Edwin b 1947), 1 da (Ann b 1948); m 2, Feb 1963, Anna Maria McGettrick; 2 s (Gareth b 1964, James b 1966); *Career* Royal Fusiliers 1939-40, cmmnd 4/8 Prince of Wales Own Punjab Regt, Capt 1941 ME & Burma HQ 17 Indian Div 1943-45, Maj GSO II (I) 1945, instr Intelligence Sch India 1946; BBC French Serv 1948; FO 1949, consular & oriental sec Jedda 1950, 1 sec Benghazi 1952, FO 1954, commercial sec and supt Consul Bogota 1956, 1 sec Info Khartoum 1959, FO 1960, Baghdad 1962, fndr dir Dip Serv Language Centre 1966, cnsllr Aden 1967, commercial cnsllr New Delhi 1968-72, commercial min Buenos Aires 1972-76, Chargé d'Affaires 1974-75, dep high cmmr Calcutta 1976-80; business conslt and dir; memb local Cons Soc; *Recreations* shooting, fishing, languages, gardening; *Clubs* Brooks's, Circulo de Armas Buenos Aires, Bengal; *Style*— Frank Maynard, Esq; Littlebourne Court, Littlebourne, Canterbury, Kent

MAYNARD, (Arthur) John Everard; s of Arthur John Maynard (d 1931), of Shawford, Winchester, and Edith Dorothy, *née* Jackson (d 1986); *b* 16 April 1931; *Educ* Charterhouse; *m* 1, 9 April 1955, Daphne Langdon (d 1978), da of Capt E T Cooper, CBE, DSO, RN (d 1979), of Broughton, Hants; 2 s (Charles Edward b 1958, Timothy John b 1960), 2 da (Catherine Mary b 1956, Jill Daphne b 1963); m 2, 25 Aug 1984, Marguerite Rosalie, da of Rodney Edwin Rogers; *Career* Nat Serv Flying Offr RAF 1953-55, Sword of Honour OCTU 1953; de Havilland Aircraft: prof engrg trg 1949-53, engr and dep personnel mangr and co personnel mangr 1955-64; sr industl rels advsr Engineering Employers Federation 1964-73; Reed Paper and Board: personnel dir and md Mill Group 1973-87; dir Oxford Univ Business Summer Sch on Sabbatical 1983; author of numerous articles on aviation; treas Royal Aeronautical Soc Medway Branch; *Recreations* aviation, gardening, worldwide travel; *Clubs* RAF; *Style*— John Maynard, Esq; Pheasant Cottage, Stangate Rd, Birling, W Malling, Kent ME19 5JJ (☎ 0634 240181); Empire Paper Mill Ltd, Greenhithe, Kent DA9 9EH (☎ 0322 843322, fax 0322 846685)

MAYNARD, Sheila Pauline Margaret; da of Harry McQuitters (d 1957), and Peggy Cogger *née* Prise; *b* 1 Nov 1952; *Educ* Rochester GS, Nonington Coll of Physical Educn; *m* 4 Aug 1973, Peter Albert Maynard, s of Albert Henry Robert Maynard; 1 s (Benjamin David b 17 July 1978), 1 da (Katy-Jane b 30 March 1981); *Career* teacher: Rainham Girls Sch 1974-80, Fulmar Sch Strood 1983-85; head of Specific Learning Difficulties Unit Upbury Manor Gillingham 1985-; sec Kent Branch Nat Cncl for Special Educn, ctee memb Upbury Manor Dyslexia Gp, involved in res project for American Res on Scotopic Sensitivity Syndrome; *Recreations* squash, swimming, petanque, amateur dramatics; *Style*— Mrs Sheila Maynard; 6 Fowler Close, Wigmore, Gillingham, Kent ME8 0LX (☎ 0634 379246); Upbury Manor, Marlborough Rd, Gillingham, Kent (☎ 0634 52341)

MEAD, Rev (Thomas) Eric Arthur; s of James Charles Eric Mead (ka 1943), and Margaret, *née* Sheehan (d 1960); *b* 24 March 1941; *Educ* Clapham Coll, Open Univ (BA); *Career* asst priest Orpington 1965-74, priest i/c S Bermindsey 1974-75, chaplain King's Coll Hosp 1975-76; asst priest: Bromley 1976-79, Orpington 1979-83; parish priest Northfleet 1984-; diocesan chaplain Catholic Nurses' Guild, memb Diocesan Kent Ecumenical Cmmn; FSA(Scot); *Style*— Rev Eric Mead; Stella Maris, 3 The Hill, Northfleet, Kent DA11 9ES (☎ 0474 533689)

MEAD, Richard Barwick; s of Thomas Gifford Mead, MBE, of 4 Wyndham Lea, W Chiltington, W Sussex, and Joyce Mary, *née* Barwick; *b* 18 Aug 1947; *Educ* Marlborough, Pembroke Coll Cambridge (MA); *m* 25 June 1971, Sheelagh Margaret, da of James Leslie Thom, of Holly Cottage, Stoke St Milborough, Ludlow, Shropshire; 2 s (Timothy b 1973, Rupert b 1977), 1 da (Nicola b 1975 d 1976); *Career* audit supervisor Arthur Young 1969-73, corporate fin exec Brandts Ltd 1973-75, dir and head Corporate Fin Dept Antony Gibbs and Sons 1975-83, dir corporate fin Credit Suisse First Boston Ltd 1983-85, ptnr and nat dir corporate fin Ernst & Young 1985-; FCA 1972; *Recreations* gardening, history, music, family; *Style*— Richard Mead, Esq; Shambles, Watts Cross, Hildenborough, Tonbridge, Kent TN11 9NB (☎ 0732 832 858); Ernst & Young, Rolls House, 7 Rolls Buildings, Fetter Lane, London EC4A 1NH (☎ 071 928 2000, fax 071 405 2147, telex 888604)

MEANS, Hon Mrs (Juliet Evelyn Mary); *née* Deedes; eldest da of Baron Deedes (Life Peer), *qv*; *b* 1948; *m* 7 April 1990, Robert Dale Means, eldest s of Robert Means, of Blythe, California, USA, and Mrs Clyda Holbrook, of Hemet, California, USA; *Style*— The Hon Mrs Means; 1707 E St, Eureica, CA 95501, USA

MELLING, Elizabeth; da of William Alexander Melling (d 1962), of Wigan, Lancs, and Jessie Helena Alice Melling, JP, *née* Stone (d 1980); *b* 4 Sept 1926; *Educ* Abbey Sch Malvern Wells, Worcs, Univ of Durham (BA), Univ of Liverpool (DAA); *Career* asst archivist Kent CC and asst co archivist 1950-80; memb: Exec Ctee Kent Fedn of Amenity Socs 1967-75 and 1982- (sec to membs 1982-), Ctee Mid Kent Nat Tst Centre 1984-85, Exec Ctee Kent Branch CPRE 1985-, Ctee Mid Kent Decorative and Fine Arts Soc (and visits sec) 1990-; vice chm Soc of Archivists 1976-78, vice pres Kent Archaelogical Soc 1984- (memb Cncl 1975-); *Books* Kentish Sources (volumes 1-6, 1959-69), History of the Kent County Council (1975), Sir Garrard Tyrwhitt-Drake and the Cobtree Estate, Maidstone (1988); *Recreations* reading, listening to music, visiting art galleries, gardening; *Style*— Miss Elizabeth Melling; 81A Bower Mount Rd, Maidstone, Kent ME16 8AS (☎ 0622 754217)

MELLOR, Robin Frederick; s of Philip James Mellor, of Swansea, and Marguerita, *née* Sutton (d 1976); *b* 16 Nov 1944; *Educ* Dynevor GS, Swansea Coll of Educn (teaching certificate), Univ of London (BEd); *m* 1, 31 Aug 1967 (m dis 1988), Carolyn, *née* Lewis; 2 s (David James b 1975, Paul Kenneth b 1981); m 2, 13 June 1988, (Frances) Anne, da of Kenneth Brignall Harris, of Braunton, Devon; 1 step s (Hayden Peter b 1975), 1 step da (Katherine Ruth b 1977); *Career* poet; work published in magazines incl: Poetry Wales, Junior Education, Infant Projects; involved in Poetry Soc's Poets in Schools Scheme; *Books* Tree Roots And Evening Ice (poems for children, 1986), Wild Monkey (poems for children, 1987); *Recreations* walking, photography; *Style*— Robin Mellor, Esq; 51 Bush Rd, Cuxton, Rochester, Kent ME2 1LS (☎ 0634 719668)

MENZIES, Ian William; s of Adam Menzies (d 1946), of Muirhead, Glasgow, and Margaret McDermid Stewart, *née* Colvin (d 1961); *b* 30 Dec 1927; *Educ* Coatbridge Sch Strathclyde, Royal Tech Coll Glasgow (BSc), Univ of London (LLB); *m* 1, 3 May 1952, June Alice (d 1978), da of Joseph Mullard (d 1951), of Liverpool; 3 da (Margaret b 1952, Sheena b 1955, Alison b 1957); m 2, 8 Oct 1983, Dr Monica Patricia Hunter, da of Thomas Burrows, of Swansea; 3 step-da (Nicola b 1963, Francesca b 1965, Lizette b 1972); *Career* Nat Serv 2 Lt RAEC 1947-49, 2 Lt RE RARO 1949-82; res engr Kuwait 1954-56, ptnr Menzies & Durkin Zambia 1956-59, res engr Ghana 1960-62, ptnr Charles Weiss & Ptnrs 1975-87, dir Charles Weiss Partnership Ltd 1987-; memb: cncl CIArb (vice-pres), Tonbridge Civic Soc; govr W Kent Coll; Freeman of City of London, Liveryman of Worshipful Co of Arbitrators; FICE, MIStructE, FCIArb, FRSA; *Recreations* armory, genealogy, cosmology; *Style*— Ian Menzies, Esq; Charles Weiss Partnership Ltd, 139/151 Sydenham Rd, London SE26 5HJ (☎ 01 778 6099, fax 01 659 5595, telex 8951165 CTBXXXG)

MERCER, Rev Timothy James; s of Clement Mercer, of Hadlow, Kent, and (Grace) Miriam, *née* Dawson; *b* 11 Aug 1954; *Educ* Ashford GS, Cranbrook Sch, Fitzwilliam Coll Cambridge (MA); *m* 12 Aug 1978, Pamela, da of Ronald Wynne, of Grove Park, London; 2 da (Joanna b 1 Sept 1981, Francesca b 4 April 1989); *Career* deacon 1981, priest Rochester 1982, curate Bromley Parish Church 1981-85, rector of Swanscombe 1985-; memb: West Kent Assoc for Pastoral Care and Counselling, Clergy Against Nuclear Arms; govr: St Botolph's C of E Primary Sch, Swanscombe HS; tstee: The Consolidated Almshouse Charity of Swanscombe, Dr Plume's Tst; memb Rochester Diocean Synod, The Mayor's chaplain Swanscombe and Greenhithe Town Cncl 1988; *Recreations* gardening, walking, reading, cycling; *Clubs* Sion College; *Style*— The Rev Timothy Mercer; The Rectory, Swanscombe St, Swanscombe, Kent DA10 0JZ (☎ 0322 843160)

MICHAEL, Dr William Francis; s of Dr Stephen Ernest Michael (d 1971), of Croydon, and Dr Janet Michael, *née* Young; *b* 22 June 1936; *Educ* Winchester, New Coll Oxford (MA, DM); *m* 27 May 1972, Mary Ann, da of Bernard Sadler (d 1982), of Reading; 2 da (Victoria b 1974, Juliet b 1977) ; *Career* Nat Serv, 2 Lt RA 1955-56; jr med appts: St Thomas's Hosp, National Hosp 1967-70, Bart's 1970-74; conslt neurologist SE Thames Regnl Neurological Unit 1974-; memb: assoc Br neurologists 1974, RSM; FRCP 1981 ; *Recreations* music, books gardening, skiing; *Style*— Dr William Michael

MICHAELS, Prof Leslie; s of Henry Michaels (d 1979), of Nottingham, and Minnie Michaels (d 1982); *b* 24 July 1925; *Educ* Parmiter's Sch London, Westminster Hosp Med Sch Univ of London (MB BS, MD); *m* 21 Sept 1951, Edith, da of Friedrich Waldstein (d 1943); 2 da (Ruth b 1953); *Career* house appts Westminster Hosp 1949-50, trg in pathology Univ of Bristol and Univ of Manchester 1953-57, lectr in pathology St Marys Hosp Med Sch London 1957-59, asst prof Albert Einstein Coll of Med 1959-61, prov pathologist Northern Ontario Canada 1961-69, prof of pathology Inst of Laryngol 1973- (sr lectr in pathology 1970-73); FRCPath 1973; *Books* Pathology of the Larynx (1984), Ear, Nose and Throat Histopathology (1987), Atlas of Ear, Nose and Throat Pathology (1990); *Recreations* music, walking; *Style*— Prof Leslie Michaels

MILES, Adrian Spencer; s of Herbert Beale Miles (d 1952), of London, and Marjorie Phyllis, *née* Harris; *b* 16 Nov 1947; *Educ* Rutlish Sch, QMC London (LLB); *m* 28 June 1975, Hilary, da of William Nelson (d 1980); 1 s (Jonathan Francis b 20 May 1968), 2 da (Julie Clare b 11 Oct 1978, Anna Kirsty b 7 July 1980); *Career* admitted slr 1972, Boodle Hatfield 1972-74, Norton Rose 1974-76, ptnr Wilde Sapte 1976-; memb Law Soc; *Recreations* chess, tennis, music; *Style*— Adrian Miles, Esq; Queensbridge House, 60 Upper Thames St, London EC4V 3BD (☎ 071 236 3050, fax 071 236 9624, telex 887793)

MILLER, (Edwin) John Royston; s of Edwin Claud Miller, of Bexhill-on-Sea, and Lilian Henrietta, *née* Whiting (d 1979); *b* 7 April 1935; *Educ* Ealing Coll W

London, Pembury Hosp (RGN), Bethlem Royal & Maudsley Hosp London (RMN); *Career* chief nursing offr Medway Health Authy 1986-88 (dep chief 1984-86), dir quality assur and trg and chief nursing offr Dartford and Gravesham Health Authy 1988-89, asst regnl dir of nursing SE Thames RHA 1989-; chm Tenterden Railway Co Ltd 1983-85 (hon archivist 1978-, dir 1979-85); memb Tenterden and Dist Museum Ctee (railway nominated) 1977-; memb Royal Coll of Nursing; *Books* Opening a Hospital is Easy - Isn't It? (1983); *Recreations* industrial archaeology, light railway history; *Style—* John Miller, Esq; 121 High St, Tenterden, Kent (☎ 05806 5350); SE Thanet Regional Health Authority, Thrift House, Collington Ave, Bexhill on Sea (☎ 0424 730073)

MILLER, Kenneth Harry; s of late Harry Miller, DSM, and late Alice Emily, *née* Cook; *b* 11 April 1936; *m* 2 June 1956, Margaret Mason, da of late George Carson Graham; 1 s (Neil Quenton b 1964), 1 da (Gillian Shelley (Mrs Bateman) b 1962); *Career* admitted slr 1966; slr of Supreme Court, ptnr Markbys (now Cameron Markby Hewitt) 1966, cmmr for oaths 1970; sec Int Carnation Propagators Assoc; memb: Law Soc, The City of London Slr's Co; *Recreations* arts, painting, theatre, walking; *Style—* Kenneth Miller, Esq

MILLER, Ronald Kinsman; CB (1989); s of William Miller (d 1986), of Kelvedon, Essex, and Elsie May, *née* Kinsman (d 1956); *b* 12 Nov 1929; *Educ* Colchester Royal GS; *m* 1952, Doris Alice, da of Patrick Dew (d 1984), of Greenwich; 1 s (Timothy John b 1960); 1 da (Felicity Jane b 1958); *Career* Nat Serv RN 1948-50; called to the Bar Gray's Inn 1953; Inland Revenue: slr's off 1965, law officers' dept 1977-79, slr 1986 (princ asst slr 1981); *Recreations* music, reading, gardening; *Clubs* Athenaeum; *Style—* Ronald Miller, Esq, CB; 4 Liskeard Close, Chislehurst, Kent BR7 6RT; Somerset House, Strand, London WC2R 1LB (☎ 071 438 6645)

MILLS, William; s of William Frederick Mills (d 1963), of Blackheath, London, and Ada Maud, *née* East (d 1984); *b* 7 July 1938; *Educ* Sutton Valence; *m* 27 Feb 1965, Pamela Anne, da of Stanley Gilbert Dean; 1 s (James William b 11 July 1974), 2 da (Melissa Jane b 17 May 1970, Kate Emma b 24 Jan 1972); *Career* RE 1957-59; Prudential Assurance: taxation mangr 1977-80, controller 1980-84, chief accountant 1984-85; Prudential Corporation Group 1985-89, md Prudential Mortgage Co 1989-; Freeman: City of London, Worshipful Co of Painters and Stainers; FCCA 1973; *Recreations* opera, gardening; *Style—* William Mills, Esq; Sunbury, Foxhole Lane, Matfield, Tonbridge, Kent (☎ 089 272 3464); Prudential Mortgage Co, Chichester House, 278-282 High Holborn, London WC1V (☎ 071 962 4550)

MILLWARD, Edwina Carole; da of Eric Millward (Capt RADC), of Bridlington, N Humberside, and Frances Morris, *née* Norton; *b* 20 Sept 1943; *Educ* Maltby GS Yorks, Thornes House Sch Wakefield Yorks, Ilkley Coll of Housecraft Yorks, Univ of London (LLB); *m* 11 Nov 1972, David Charles Bicker, s of Arthur Charles Bicker, of Maidstone, Kent; *Career* teacher of housecraft 1964-67, slr's articled clerk 1967-72, slr and ptnr Gill Turner & Tucker 1972-; dep Co Court and Dist High Court registrar 1988; nat pres UK Fedn of Business and Professional Women 1985-87, memb exec ctee Womens' Nat Cmmn 1986-87, appeal patron Lucy Cavendish Coll Cambridge 1986, chm Constitution Advsy Ctee and tstee Int Fedn of Business and Professional Women 1988-, co sec Maidstone Hospice Appeal, former pres Maidstone Business and Professional Womens' Club, dinner sec and chm Lectures Sub Ctee, memb SE Region Electricity Consumers Ctee; memb: Kent Law Soc 1980-, Law Soc 1972; *Recreations* swimming, reading, needlework; *Style—* Miss Edwina Millward; Loan Head, Simmonds Lane, Otham, Nr Maidstone, Kent ME15 8RH; Gill Turner & Tucker, Colman House, King St, Maidstone, Kent ME14 1JE (☎ 0622 59051, fax 0622 62192, telex 965343)

MILLWATER, Dennis Curtis; s of William Milson Millwater (d 1974), of Rogerstone, Gwent, and Kathleen Irene Millwater (d 1969); *b* 31 March 1934; *Educ* Bassaleg GS Gwent, Univ of Bristol; *m* 5 Aug 1957, Marlene Beatrice, da of Kenneth Collins, of Cliffs End, Ramsgate; 3 s (Christopher b 26 April 1961, Grahame b 28 April 1963, Jonathan b 23 Aug 1967 d 1989), 1 da (Sara b 20 July 1977); *Career* pensions supt Northern Assurance Co Ltd 1957-68, pensions controller Commercial Union Group 1968-69, dir De Falbe Halsey Ltd 1969-71; gp dir: H Clarkson (Insurance Holdings) Ltd 1971-81, Clarkson Puckle Group Ltd 1981-87, Bain Clarkson Ltd 1987; chief exec Bain Clarkson (Fin Services) Ltd; gen cmmr of taxes; FPMI, ACII; *Recreations* golf, music, cycling; *Clubs* Royal St Georges Golf (Sandwich); *Style—* Dennis Millwater, Esq; The Shieling, 32 Harkness Drive, Canterbury, Kent CT2 7RW (☎ 0227 463026); Bain Dawes House, 15 Minories, London EC3 (☎ 071 481 3232, fax 071 481 2324)

MILMAN, David Patrick; er s and h of Lt-Col Sir Derek Milman, 9 Bt, MC; *b* 1945; *m* 1969, Christina, da of John William Hunt; 1 s (Thomas Hart b 1976), 1 da (Katharine Jane b 1975); *Style—* David Milman, Esq; 71 Camden Rd, Sevenoaks, Kent

MING, Sexton Divadip; s of Ronald Waghorne, and Doris, *née* Deakin; *b* 17 Sept 1961; *Educ* Southfields Comp Gravesend; *Career* one of the six original Medway poets; participated in: Cambridge Poetry Festival 1981, Cambridge Fringe Poetry Festival 1982, Swindon Poetry Festival 1983, Travers All Day Poetry Festival Belgium 1983; appearances on TV incl: Nationwide North 1981, Getting it On 1982; LP records incl: Old Horse of the Nation 1987, The Mindreaders, Ban the Mind Reader 1987, Six More Miles to the Graveyard 1988, The Medway Poets 1988, Wild Billy Childish and the Natural Born Lovers 1989; films incl: The Cheated 1988, Dr X vs Billy Childish 1988; writer of short stories for Deadline magazine; *Books* incl: Which Dead Donkey Daddy? (1978), Position X (1980), The Old Onion of the Mountain (1980), Muscle Horse in Holland (1981), Virginia Woolf vs Lady Ottolin Morrel (1981), Fan Club Book (1982), The Cheesy Bug Gazzett (1986), The Man Who Created Himself (1987), Fish Glue in Eskimo Land (1988), Sermons (1989); included in following anthologies: Rivers of Life (1980), The Medway Poets (1980), Ving (1980), The Cheap Review (1981), Fracture Clinic (1981); *Recreations* music, gardening, painting; *Style—* Sexton Ming, Esq; Le Tronchai, 53700 St Aubin Du Desert, Villaines La Juhel, France

MINGAY, Prof Gordon Edmund; s of Lt Cdr William Edmund Mingay, RN (d 1979), of Southsea, and Florence Mabel, *née* Tuckwood, (d 1962); *b* 20 June 1923; *Educ* Sir Joseph Williamson's Mathematical Sch Rochester Kent, Univ of Nottingham (BA, PhD); *m* 5 Jan 1945, Mavis, da of Albert Edwin Tippen, (d 1984), of Hythe; *Career* lectr LSE 1957-65; Univ of Kent: reader in economics and social history 1965-68, prof of agrarian history 1968-86, emeritus prof 1986-; ed The Agricultural History Review 1973-83; pres Br Agric History Soc 1987-89; FRHistS; *Books* English Landed Society in the Eighteenth Century (1963), The Agricultural Revolution (with J D Chambers, 1966), The Victorian Countryside (ed, 1981), The Transformation of Britain 1830-1939 (1986), A Social History of the English Countryside (1990); *Recreations* swimming, walking, travelling, music; *Style—* Prof Gordon Mingay; Rutherford College, University of Kent, Canterbury, Kent CT2 7NX

MITCHELL, Malcolm; s of Frank Mitchell (d 1985), of Dover, and Nellie Florence, *née* Watts (d 1988); *b* 7 Feb 1933; *Educ* Sir Walter St John's GS Battersea, Ashford (Kent) GS; *m* 1, 16 Sept 1961 (m dis 1979), Alison, da of late John Macmillan, of Chartham, Kent; m 2, (Elizabeth Anne) Judith, da of Col Geoffrey Elliott, DSO, OBE (d 1981); 1 s (David) Justin b 14 March 1966), 1 da (Harriet Mary Rachel (twin) b 14 March 1966); *Career* ed Mid Kent News 1955-57, dep ed Kentish Gazette 1975-82; ed: Thanet Extra 1982-83, E Kent Mercury 1983-; previously: presenter and interviewer Southern TV, broadcaster BBC radio; former memb: Canterbury Round Table, Canterbury Rotary Club; hon memb Sr Common Room Darwin Coll Univ of Kent at Canterbury; *Recreations* listening to jazz, botany, angling, bird watching; *Style—* Malcolm Mitchell, Esq; The Old Cottage, The Street, Bishopsbourne, nr Canterbury CT4 5HT (☎ 0227 830645); East Kent Mercury, 9 St George's Place, Canterbury (☎ 0227 768181)

MITCHELL, William Vernon; s of Peter Mitchell (d 1976), and Ann Mitchell (d 1986); *b* 1 May 1923; *Educ* Dollar Acad, Liverpool Tech Coll; *m* 1944, Muriel Olive, *née* Cooke; 2 c; *Career* tech dir Lever Brothers Ltd to 1983; tech advsr Br Exec Serv Overseas; MRIC; *Recreations* golf, microscopy, philately; *Style—* William Mitchell, Esq; 15 Uplands Way, Sevenoaks, Kent (☎ 0732 456887)

MITCHELL LAMBERT, Ian William; s of Ernest Joseph Lambert (d 1976), of Coventry, and Ivy Muriel, *née* Mitchell; *b* 3 March 1942; *Educ* Slough GS, King Henry VIII Sch Coventry, Univ of Wales (UC Swansea), Univ of Kent; *m* 21 Oct 1978, Mavis Crazencea, da of Agrippa Amado Rogers (d 1980), of SA; 1 s (Derek b 1969); *Career* theologian, author, industl relations conslt; lay pastor Weald Methodist Church; chm and md: Job Generation (Hldgs) Ltd, Job Generation Ltd; chm Job Generation Trg Tst; dir: IPSET, Centre for the Study of Early Christianity (UK off); chm Emeritus Professional Assoc of Teachers; memb: Industrial Tribunals; fell Coll of Preceptors; FBIM; *Clubs* Royal Cwlth; *Style—* Ian Mitchell Lambert, Esq; Tangnefedd, Windmill Rd, Weald, Sevenoaks, Kent TN14 6PJ (☎ 0732 463460)

MITCHENSON, Francis Joseph Blackett (Joe); s of Francis Mitchenson, and Sarah, *née* Roddam; *Educ* privately, Fay Compton Studio of Dramatic Art; *Career* WWII, RHA 1941-43; actor and theatrical historian; first stage appearance Libel! 1934, rep at Cheltenham 1936, joined as stage mangr Portfolio Playhouse 1937 (appearances incl Fenton in Merry Wives of Windsor 1939), season at Gateway Notting Hill Gate 1944, mangr Grand Croydon 1945, dir and actor in Charley's Aunt and The Ghost Train, toured Euro in ENSA 1945-46, Freddy in Pygmalion with ENSA (Germany); other plays incl: Quiet Wedding, George and Margaret; many TV and radio appearances; fndr (with late Raymond Mander) and full time dir Theatre Collection 1939; author, conslt; *Books* Hamlet Through the Ages (1952), Theatrical Companions to: Shaw (1954), Maugham (1955), Coward (1957), A Picture History of British Theatre (1957), The Theatres of London (1961), Musical Comedy (1969), Revue (1971), Pantomime (1973), Victorian and Edwardian Entertainment from Old Photographs (1978), Guide to Somerset Maugham Theatrical Paintings at the National Theatre (1980); *Recreations* collecting anything and everything theatrical, sunbathing; *Style—* Joe Mitchenson, Esq; The Mansion, Beckenham Place Park, Beckenham, Kent BR3 2BP (☎ 071 658 7725)

MITSON, (Sydney) Allen; s of Sydney Mitson, of Snaresbrook and St Margaret's Bay, Kent, and Catherine, *née* Gooding; *b* 24 May 1933; *Educ*

Exeter Sch, Forest Sch (BA); *m* 1, 1959 (m dis 1971), Elizabeth Angela, da of R Garner (d 1966), of Buckhurst Hill, Essex; 2 s (Andrew b 1963, Michael b 1966); m 2, 1973, Valerie Angela, da of J Sherratt (d 1988), of Waltham Abbey, Essex; 1 step s (John b 1967); *Career* Nat Serv Royal Signals; sales promotion mangr Rotaflex 1960-65, formed Emess Lighting 1966 (became public co 1980), md Emess Lighting (UK) Ltd 1980-89, chief exec and dep chm Inlite Group 1989-; underwriting memb Lloyds 1977-; Freeman City of London 1983, Liveryman Worshipful Co of Gold and Silver Wyre Drawers 1983; *Recreations* walking, swimming; *Style—* Allen Mitson, Esq; Inlite Group Ltd, 9/10 Grafton St, London W1 (☎ 071 493 0702, fax 071 493 0832)

MOATE, Roger Denis; MP (C) Faversham 1970-; s of late Harold Stanley Moate, of Chiswick, and Elizabeth Freestone; *b* 12 May 1938; *Educ* Latymer Upper Sch; *m* 1 (m dis), Hazel Joy, da of late F J Skinner, of Somerset; 1 s, 1 da; m 2, Auriol, da of late W B G Cran, of Huddersfield; 1 da; *Career* registered insur broker; underwriting memb Lloyds, past chm Lloyds Brokers Frank Bradford & Co Ltd, past chm Theatre Prodns plc; dir: Hunter Murray and Co Ltd, Robinco UK Ltd, Euro Mktg Info Ltd; hon sec Br American Parly gp 1974-81, chm Br Norwegian Parly Gp 1988-, memb Ct of Referees; *Recreations* skiing, tennis; *Style—* Roger Moate Esq, MP; The Old Vicarage, Knatchbull Rd, London SE5

MOGFORD, Stephen George; *b* 20 June 1914; *Educ* Exeter, Univ of London (BA, BSc); *m* 1946; 1 s (Stephen); *Career* int banker; formerly: dep chm Italian International Bank Leadenhall St vice chm Barclays Bank International, dir Barclays Bank plc; *Recreations* gardening, music; *Clubs* Reform, Overseas Bankers; *Style—* Stephen Mogford, Esq; Warrington Place Farmhouse, Paddock Wood, Kent TN12 6HE

MOIR, John Pirie; TD (1978); s of Prof J Chassar Moir, CBE (d 1977), of Oxford, and Grace Hilda, *née* Bailey; *b* 26 Sept 1946; *Educ* Dragon Sch Oxford, Tonbridge Sch Kent, Oriel Coll Oxford (MA); *m* 1972, Michelle, da of late Emile Tastevin, of Digne, France; 1 s, 1 da; *Career* 5 Royal Inniskilling Dragoon Gds 1968-79, Capt TAVR 1974; marine reinsurance broker LLoyds London 1969-70, mktg exec BTA London, Paris, Toronto 1971-78, dep dir of devpt Highland Regnl Cncl Inverness 1978-84, chief exec Dover DC 1984-; dir: The Enterprise Agency of E Kent Ltd, Dover Trade and Export Centre Ltd; Univ of Oxford half-blues for mod pentathlon 1966 and polo 1968, hon sec Bullingdon Club point to point steeplechases 1967; memb ctee: Nat Conf on Local Govt and Tourism, Oriel Soc, E Kent branch Oxford Soc; vice pres: Sandwich branch Royal Br Legion, Dover Operatic and Dramatic Soc; memb exec ctee and del for social affrs Conf of Peripheral Maritime Regions of the European Community 1980-84, memb The Tourism Soc 1983, hon sec Kent Assoc of DCs 1984-86, chm The Channel Ferry Disaster Fund 1987-, tstee The Nat Battle of Br Meml Fund; Soc of Local Authy Chief Execs (SOLACE): memb exec cncl, memb civil def panel, hon sec int panel, bicentennial exchange ptnr Aust 1988; FBIM 1983, FRSA 1990; *Recreations* skiing, sailing, fishing, gardening; *Clubs* Royal Cinque Ports Yacht, Royal Overseas League; *Style—* John Moir, Esq, TD; Dover District Council, Honeywood Rd, Whitfield, Dover, Kent CT16 3PJ (☎ 0304 821199, fax 0304 824917)

MOLOCK, Derrick Arthur; s of Arthur Molock (d 1955), of Ramsgate, and Eileen Lily Molock (d 1961); *b* 1 Sept 1921; *Educ* St George's Sch Ramsgate, Chatham House GS Ramsgate; *m* 18 Oct 1962, (Margaret) Joyce, da of Harold Pardoe (d 1955), of Green Roofs, Crow Hill, Broadstairs; *Career* writer and ed East Kent Critic 1947-49 and 1963-85, freelance journalist; memb: Ramsgate Borough Cncl 1968-74, Kent CC 1973-77 and 1981-, Thanet Dist Cncl 1974-83, Fabian Soc, Lab Pty, League Against Cruel Sports, Ramsgate Soc; sch govr, pres Cliffsend Residents' Assoc; *Books* Life and Times of the East Kent Critic (1986); *Recreations* cricket (no longer a player, alas), music, writing; *Clubs* Kent CCC; *Style—* Derrick Molock, Esq; Starlings, 44 Foad's Hill, Cliffsend, Ramsgate, Kent CT12 5EN (☎ 0843 591833)

MONCADA, Dr Salvador Enrique; Salvador Moncada, Tegucigalpa, Honduras, and Jenny Seidner (d 1985); *b* 3 Dec 1944; *Educ* Univ of El Salvador (MD), Univ of London (PhD); *m* 1 April 1966, Dorys, *née* Lemus; 1 s (Salvador Ernesto b 6 May 1972 d 19 May 1982), 1 da (Claudia Regina b 15 Nov 1966); *Career* Gp Social Serv of El Salvador 1969, instr of preventative med Univ of El Salvador 1969-70; The Wellcome Res Laboratories England: dept of pharmacology RCS 1971-73, section leader and sr scientist Prostaglandin res gp 1975-77, head of dept of Prostaglandin res 1977-85, dir of theraputic res div 1984-86, dir of res 1986-; assoc prof of pharmacology and physiology dept of physiological sciences 1974-75 (instr of physiology and pharmacology 1970-71); editorial work: gen pharmacology section ed jl Prostaglandins 1975-80, conslt ed Prostaglandins 1980; memb editorial bd: Br Jl of Pharmacology 1980-85, Atherosclerosis 1980, European Jl of Clinical Investigation 1986, Thrombosis Res 1989, Clinica e Investigacion en Arteriosclerosis 1989; memb editorial ctee of Archives Venezolanos de Farmacologia y Terapeutica 1980, scientific ed The British Medical Bulletin no 39 Part 3; recipient of numerous int med awards; inventor of various patented pharmaceutical compositions; memb Br Pharmacological Soc 1974, hon memb Colombian Soc of Int Med 1982, hon memb Peruvian Pharmacological Soc 1983; FRS 1988; *Books* Prostacyclin in Pregnancy (ed jtly, 1983); *Recreations* music, theatre, literature; *Style—* Dr Salvador Moncada; 25 Hitherwood Drive, London SE19 1XA (☎ 081 670 0298); The Wellcome Research Laboratories, Langley Court, Beckenham, Kent BR3 3BS (☎ 081 658 2211, fax 081 658 2278, car 0836 243472)

MONCKTON, Hon Anthony Leopold Colyer; yst s of 2 Viscount Monkton of Brenchley, CB, OBE, MC, DL; *b* 25 Sept 1960; *Educ* Harrow, Magdalene Coll Camb; *m* 1985, Philippa Susan, yr da of late Gervase Christopher Brinsmade Wingfield; 1 s (Edward Gervase Colyer b 1988), 1 da (Camilla Mary b 1989); *Career* cmmnd 9/12 Royal Lancers 1982, Capt 1984; *Clubs* MCC, Cavalry and Guards'; *Style—* Capt The Hon Anthony Monckton; BFPO 33, W Germany

MONCKTON, Hon Christopher Walter; s and h of 2 Viscount Monckton of Brenchley, CB, OBE, MC, by his w Marianna Laetitia, da of Cdr Robert Tatton Bower, RN; *b* 14 Feb 1952; *Educ* Harrow, Churchill Coll Cambridge (MA), Univ Coll Cardiff (Dip Journalism); *m* 19 May 1990, Juliet Mary Abbe, yst da of Jørgen Malherbe Jensen, of Doughty Street, London WC1; *Career* reporter Yorks Post 1974-75 (ldr writer 1975-77), press offr Cons Central Off 1977-78, ed the Universe 1979-81, managing ed Telegraph Sunday Magazine 1981-82, ldr writer The Standard 1982, asst ed Today 1986-; special advsr to PM's Policy Unit (Home Affrs) 1982-; memb: Int MENSA Ltd 1975-, St John Ambulance Bd (Wetherby Div) 1976-77, Hon Soc of the Middle Temple 1979-; sec: Health Study Gp 1981-, Employment Study Gp 1982-; kt SMO Malta 1973, OStJ 1973; *Books* The Laker Story (co-author with Ivan Fallon, 1982); *Recreations* clocks and sundials, computers, cycling, fell-walking, inventions, motor-cycling, number theory, politics, public speaking, punting, recreational mathematics, sci fiction, Yorks; *Clubs* Beefsteak, Brooks's, Pratt's; *Style—* The Hon Christopher Monckton; 71 Albert Rd, Richmond, Surrey (☎ 081 940 6528); Runhams Farm, Harrietsham, Maidstone, Kent (☎ 0622 85 313)

MONCKTON, Hon Jonathan Riversdale St Quintin; s (twin) of 2 Viscount Monckton of Brenchley, CB, OBE, MC; *b* 15 Aug 1955; *Educ* Ladycross, Worth; *Career* monk of the Order of St Benedict Worth Abbey; *Style—* The Hon Jonathan Monckton

MONCKTON OF BRENCHLEY, 2 Viscount (UK 1957); Maj-Gen Gilbert Walter Riversdale Monckton; CB (1966), OBE (1956), MC (1940), DL (Kent 1970); s of 1 Viscount Monckton of Brenchley, GCVO, KCMG, PC, MC, QC (d 1965), by his w Mary, da of Sir Thomas Colyer-Fergusson, 3rd Bt; *b* 3 Nov 1915; *Educ* Harrow, Trinity Coll Cambridge (MA); *m* 1950, Marianna Laetitia, OStJ, Dame of Honour & Devotion (Sovereign Mil Order Malta), Pres St John's Ambulance Kent 1972-80, and High Sheriff Kent 1981-82, 3 da of Cdr Robert Tatton Bower, of Gatto-Murina Palace, Mdina, Malta, by his w Hon Henrietta, *née* Strickland, 4 da of 1 and last Baron Strickland; 4 s, 1 da; *Heir* s, Hon Christopher Walter Monckton, *qv*; *Career* serv WWII; dep dir Personnel Admin 1962, DPR War Office (Maj-Gen) 1963-65, CoS HQ BAOR 1965-67; Liveryman Worshipful Co of Broderers 1962 (Master 1978); pres: Kent Assoc of Boys' Clubs 1965-78, Inst of Heraldic and Genealogical Studies 1965, Kent Archaeological Assoc 1968-75, Medway Productivity Assoc 1968-74, Maidstone and Dist Football League 1968, Br Archaeological Awards; vice chm Scout Assoc Kent 1968-74; pres Anglo-Belgian Union 1974-80; chm Cncl of the OStJ for Kent 1969-74; Grand Offr Order of Leopold II (Belgium 1978), Cmdr Order of the Crown (Belgium) KStJ; Bailiff Grand Cross Obedience Sov Mil Order Malta, Grand Cross Merit 1980; FSA; *Clubs* Brooks's, MCC, Casino Maltese; *Style—* The Rt Hon the Viscount Monckton of Brenchley, CB, OBE, MC, DL; Runhams Farm, Runham Lane, Harrietsham, Maidstone, Kent (☎ 0627 850 313)

MONSON, Hon Anthony John; s of 10 Baron Monson (d 1958); *b* 1944; *Educ* Malvern; *Style—* The Hon Anthony Monson; 35 Lynwood Grove, Orpington, Kent

MONTAGUE, Robert Joel; s of Robert L Montague, of Seveoaks, Kent, and Freda, *née* Lance; *b* 22 June 1948; *Educ* Bedstone Sch Shropshire, Caius Sch Brighton; *m* 12 Feb 1972 (m dis), Susan Jane; 2 s (Robert Kenneth b 9 June 1975, Benjamin James b 4 Feb 1980), 1 da (Victoria Louise b 11 May 1973); m 2, 23 Sept Sept 1988 (m dis), Jane Laura; *Career* sales and mktg Esso Petroleum Co Ltd 1964-69, dep md Cables Montague Ltd 1971-80 (joined 1969), fndr Tiphook plc 1978-; memb: cncl Asthma Res Cncl, Cons Pty; Freeman: City of London, Worshipful Co of Carmen; FCIT; *Recreations* shooting, fishing, squash, running; *Style—* Robert Montague, Esq; Tiphook plc, Lancaster House, 7 Elmfield Rd, Bromley, Kent BR1 1LT (☎ 081 460 6060, telex 8952546, fax 081 466 1505)

MOOLAN-FEROZE, Sir Rustam; s of Dr Jehangir Moolan-Feroze (d 1962), and Diana Lester; *b* 4 Aug 1920; *Educ* Sutton Valence, Univ of London (MB BS, MD); *m* 1947, Margaret, da of Harry Dowsett (d 1975); 3 s, 1 da; *Career* Surgn Lt RNVR Atlantic and Far E 1943-46; conslt obstetrician Queen Charlotte's Hosp London 1952-73, conslt gynaecologist Chelsea Hosp for Women 1952-73, conslt obstetrician and gynaecologist KCH London 1952-85, dean Inst of Obstetrics and Gynaecology Univ of London 1954-67; now ret;

contrib med books 1981-84; pres RCOG 1981-84, currently hon pres Euro Assoc of Gynaecologists and Obstetricians (first pres 1985-88); FRCS, FRCOG; kt 1983; *Recreations* swimming, gardening; *Clubs* RAC; *Style*— Sir Rustam Moolan-Feroze; 21 Kenwood Drive, Beckenham, Kent BR3 2QX (☎ 081 650 2972)

MOORE, Brian Baden; s of Baden Kimberley Moore (d 1969), of Benenden, Kent, and Elsie Norah, *née* Sharpe (d 1987); *b* 28 Feb 1932; *Educ* Cranbrook Sch Kent; *m* 19 March 1955, Eileen Betty, da of William Cole (d 1973), of Bromley, Kent; 2 s (Christopher b 1958, Simon b 1961); *Career* Nat Serv PO RAF 1950-52; sports reporter and sub ed: World Sports 1955, Exchange Telegraph 1957, The Times 1958; football commentator and presenter BBC Radio 1960-67, football commentator and sports presenter ITV 1967-, presenter of documentary series Brian Moore Meets...; dir Gillingham FC 1978-85; *Style*— Brian Moore, Esq; London Weekend Television, London SE1 (☎ 071 261 3264)

MOORE, Edward; OBE (1954), DL (Kent, 1979); s of Edward Moore (d 1931), of Brentfield, Dartford, and Jessie Rosaline, *née* Thompson (d 1957); *b* 24 April 1914; *Educ* Holy Trinity Gravesend; *m* 2 Sept 1939, Sylvia Mary, da of Robert Grange (d 1964) of Beltinge, Herne Bay; 1 s (Edward Fabian b 24 Aug 1941) 1 da (Rosemary Ann b 4 March 1940); *Career* ptnr Moore Bros soft drinks mfrs 1931-38; Moore Bros (Swanscombe) Ltd: dir 1938-40, md 1940-59, chm and md 1959-68; Edward Moore Ltd: dir 1938-40, md 1940-58, chm and md 1958-69; pres SE Soft Drinks Assoc 1956-66, dir and exec ctee memb Nat Assoc Soft Drinks Mfrs Ltd 1954-68; Kent CC: memb for 39 years, alderman 1961-74, chm 1981-82; memb: Swanscombe UDC 1941-46, Dartford Hosp Mgmnt Ctee 1952-62, Dartford RDC 1961-63; vice chm: Dartford and Stone Hosp Mgmnt Ctee 1962-74, Kent Area AHA 1977-80 (memb 1974-82), Dartford and Gravesham Health Authy 1982-90; pres: Chislehurst Div Cons Assoc 1970-74 (chm 1950-70), New Cobham Coll 1988-89, Joyce Green Hosp League of Friends, Darenth Sr Citizens Club; past pres Rotary Club of Dartford, fndr chm Dartford Round Table, sr warden Rochester Bridge Tst 1988-89 (asst 1981-), fin and property advsr Rochester Cathedral (steward), past churchwarden St Albans Church Dartford, tstee Age Concern Kent (memb Exec Ctee); sch govr: Darenth Sch, Joyce Green Hosp Sch; *Recreations* watching sports, reading, writing, travel, TV; *Style*— Edward Moore, Esq, OBE, DL; Vicarage Place, 29 The Street, Shorne, Gravesend, Kent DA12 3EA (☎ 047 482 26180); County Hall, Maidstone, Kent ME14 1XQ (☎ 0622 671411 ext 4256)

MOORE, Hubert Rogers; s of Will Grayburn Moore (d 1978), and Elizabeth Ursula Joy Moore (d 1976); *b* 8 Feb 1934; *Educ* Kingswood Sch Bath, Univ of Oxford (BA, MA); *m* 5 April 1961, Diana Jean, da of Laurence Murray Kelly, MBE, of Betchworth, Surrey; 1 s (Andrew Lawrence b 23 Oct 1966), 3 da (Alison Jean (Mrs Bovey) b 15 Feb 1962, Hilary Joy (Mrs Thompson) b 24 July 1964, Elinor Mary b 14 March 1971); *Career* asst teacher: Rose Lane Secdy Biggleswade 1957, Kingswood Coll Grahamstown S Africa 1958, Sherborne Sch Dorset 1958-68; head of Dept of English Cranbrook Sch Kent 1968-; rugby footballer: Oxford Blue 1956, Blackheath, Southern Cos, Rhodes Univ; *Books* Down By A Bicycle (1978), Namesakes (1988); *Style*— Hubert Moore, Esq; The Moat, Carriers Rd, Cranbrook, Kent TN17 3JY (☎ 0580 712151)

MOORE, Sir John Michael; KCVO (1983), CB (1974), DSC (1944); s of Algernon William Moore (d 1970), and Amy Elizabeth, *née* Jeffreys (d 1940); *b* 2 April 1921; *Educ* Whitgift Middle Sch Croydon, Selwyn Coll Cambridge; *m* 1, 1947 (m dis 1963), Kathleen, da of Capt C C Pawley (d 1982); 1 s, 1 da; m 2, 1963 (m dis 1985), Margaret, da of J Ward (d 1935); *Career* Lt RNVR 1940-46, with Miny of Transport and DOE 1946-72, dep sec (personnel mgmnt) CSD 1972-78, second Crown Estate cmmr 1978-83; Humane Soc Bronze Medal 1942; *Recreations* sailing, mountain walking; *Style*— Sir John Moore, KCVO, CB, DSC; High Spinney, Old Coach Rd, Wrotham, Kent TN15 7NR (☎ 0732 822340)

MOORE, Nigel Sandford Johnson; s of Raymond Johnson Moore (d 1977), and Lucy Mary, *née* Kirby; *b* 12 April 1944; *Educ* Radley; *m* 16 Aug 1969, Elizabeth Ann, da of Joseph Henry Bowker (d 1986); 1 s (Peter b 9 Jan 1983), 2 da (Louise b 20 Feb 1974, Rachel b 1 Mar 1977); *Career* Buckley Hall Devin & Co 1962-68; CA Ernst and Young: Sydney Aust 1969-71, ptnr (UK) 1973-, human resources 1973-81, Practice Devpt Dept 1983-86, managing ptnr London Office 1986-88, euro liaison and devpt 1988-89, dir client servs Europe 1989-90, regnl managing ptnr Eastern Europe 1990-; FCA 1977; *Recreations* theatre, golf, tennis; *Clubs* City of London, IOD, The Pilgrims, Wildernesse; *Style*— Nigel Moore, Esq; Vinesgate, Chart Lane, Brasted Chart, Westerham, Kent TN16 1LR (☎ 0959 64510); Becket House, 1 Lambeth Palace Rd, London SE1 7EU (☎ 071 931 3444, fax 071 928 1345, telex 885234)

MOORE, Prof Peter Gerald; TD (1963); s of Leonard Jiggens Moore, of Wimbledon, and Ruby Silvester, *née* Wilburn (d 1978); *b* 5 April 1928; *Educ* Kings Coll Sch Wimbledon, UCL (BSc, PhD), Princeton Univ USA; *m* 27 Sept 1958, Sonja Enevoldson, da of William Ivor Thomas, of Cooden (d 1973); 2 s (Charles b 1967, Richard b 1973), 1 da (Penelope (Mrs Lawrenson) b 1960); *Career* 2 Lt 3 Regt RHA 1949-51, 2 Lt (later Lt then Capt) 290 Field Regt (City of London) RA TA 1951-61, Capt (later Maj) 254 Field Regt RA TA 1961-65; lectr UCL 1951-56, asst econ advsr NCB 1956-59, head statistical servs Reed Paper Group 1959-65; London Business Sch: prof of statistics 1965-, dep princ 1972-84, princ 1984-89; pt/t ptnr Duncan C Fraser 1974-77; pt/t dir: Copeman Paterson Ltd 1984-, Elf Aquitaine UK plc 1989-; fell UCL 1988; memb: Drs and Dentists Renumeration Body 1971-89, Ctee on 1971 Census Security 1971-73, UGC 1978-84 (vice chm 1980-83); conslt Wilson Ctee on Fin Insts 1977-80; cncl memb: Univ of Sci and Technol Hong Kong 1986-, UCL 1989; Liveryman Tallow Chandlers Co (memb Ct 1987-); Hon DSc Heriot Watt Univ 1985; pres: RCS 1989- (fell 1952), Inst of Actuaries 1984-86 (fell 1956); CBIM 1985; *Books* Anatomy of Decisions (1976), Reason By Numbers (1980), The Business of Risk (1983); *Recreations* golf, walking, travelling; *Clubs* Athenaeum, Knole Park Golf; *Style*— Prof Peter Moore, TD; 3 Chartway, The Vine, Sevenoaks, Kent TN13 3RU (☎ 0732 451 936); London Business School, Sussex Place, Regent's Park, London NW1 4SA (☎ 071 262 5050, fax 071 724 7875)

MOORE, Steven Ronald; MBE (1989); s of Douglas Michael Moore (d 1990), of 25 Gainsborough Drive, Beltinge, Kent, and Anson Margaret Christabel, *née* Meade; *b* 3 March 1963; *m* 4 Oct 1986, Hilary Anne, da of Clifford Charles Eaton, of 2 Rutland Gardens, Cliftonville, Kent; *Career* waterskier; Br team memb 1981-90, Euro champion 1985-88, Br champion 1985-89, World Cup champion 1986, World champion 1988-89, Euro Cup champion 1989; *Recreations* water skiing, football, squash, most fast sports; *Clubs* Whitstable Water Ski; *Style*— Steven Moore, Esq, MBE; 2 Dane Park Villas, Park Lane, Cliftonville, Kent CT9 1RH (☎ 0843 298205)

MOORMAN, Bernard George; JP (1967); s of George Moorman (d 1967), of Ashford, and Margaret Ethel, *née* Horton (d 1978); *b* 24 Oct 1932; *Educ* Ashford South Co Middle Sch; *m* 1, 11 April 1955 (m dis 1978), Christine Rita, da of Charles Birch Cooper (d 1972), of Hythe, Kent; m 2, 1 Jan 1983, Sylvia Joan Marsden, da of Walter Herbert Sinden (d 1965), of Deal Kent; *Career* office mangr and funeral dir Frank Knock & Co Ashford 1956-71, chm East Kent Assoc of Funeral Dirs 1968-70, office mangr R J Barwick (Ashford) Ltd 1971-; Ashford Young Conservatives: sec 1952-54, chm 1954-56, treas 1956-62; chm: Ashford Cons Local Govt Ctee 1984-87, N Ashford Conservatives 1981-; Ashford Urban Dist Cncl: memb 1955-74, Cons leader 1963-74, chm 1967-69; tstee Ashford Parochial Charities 1969-; Ashford Borough Cncl: memb 1973-76 and 1977-, leader 1973-75; Mayor of Ashford 1990-; *Recreations* gardening, boating, philately, model railways; *Clubs* Elwick (Ashford); *Style*— Bernard Moorman, Esq, JP; 10 Wall Rd, Ashford, Kent TN24 8NZ (☎ 0233 620299); R J Barwick (Ashford) Ltd, Tennyson Rd, Ashford, Kent TN23 2LR (☎ 0233 627963)

MORGAN, Kenneth S; s of Edward Henry Morgan, and Florence May, *née* Wheeler; *b* 6 Aug 1925; *Educ* Battersea, Dartford GS; *m* 1 Nov 1952, Patricia Eva, da of Joseph Hunt, of Kingsway, Derby; 1 s (Richard b 1962), 1 da (Lindsay b 1956); *Career* ed Official Report (Hansard) House of Commons 1979-89; pres Cwlth Hansard Eds Assoc; *Books* The Falklands Campaign (digest of parly debates); *Recreations* military history; *Style*— Kenneth S Morgan, Esq; 3 Highfield Rd, Bexleyheath, Kent (☎ 0322 525333); House of Commons (☎ 071 219 3388)

MORGAN, Peter Bainbridge; s of Raymond Bainbridge Morgan (d 1980), and Ena Mence, *née* Hartwright (d 1980); *b* 2 Nov 1942; *Educ* Tonbridge, Trinity Coll Oxford (MA); *m* 4 Sept 1971, Mary Louise, da of Arthur Eric Perkins, of Dulverton, Somerset; 2 da (Charlotte Alicia b 1975, Madeleine Elinor b 1980); *Career* admitted slr 1967, ptnr Girlings 1972-; memb Kent Law Soc Ctee, chm Social Security appeals Trib; memb Law Soc 1967-; *Recreations* tennis, music (fndr memb The Dark Blues), after dinner speaking; *Clubs* Hoppers' Tie, Oxford Soc, Kent CCC (life memb); *Style*— Peter Morgan, Esq; 3-6 Dane John, Canterbury, Kent (☎ 0227 768374, fax 0227 450498)

MORGAN, Cncllr Peter James; s of Joshua Morgan (d 1970), of Penarth, South Wales, and Nesta Mabel, *née* James; *b* 16 May 1926; *Educ* Monmouth, Lewis Sch Pengam, St Paul's Teacher Trg Coll Cheltenham; *m* 29 March 1951, June, da of Lesley S Colthup (d 1987); 3 da (Jane Elizabeth (Mrs Cheetham) b 5 Sept 1953, Anne Louise (Mrs Goldsmith) b 24 June 1955, Claire Suzanne (Mrs Yeo) b 15 Jan 1958); *Career* serv in RAF Educn Branch SE Asia Cmd 1945-48; asst teacher: Milton The Butts Elementary Boys Sch 1948-52, Westlands HS 1952-87; formerly: pres local branch NUT, chm Kent Lib Fedn, pres Sittingbourne & Sheppey Athletics Assoc, chm Swale & N Downs Soc, chm Sittingbourne Volunteer Bureau, chm Sittingbourne Branch Parkinson's Disease Soc; mayor of Swale 1987-88, Lib parly cand Feb & Oct 1974, pres and sec Free Church Fed Cncl and The Cncl of Churches in Sittingbourne, local organiser Christian Aid; elected memb: Sittingbourne & Dist UDC, Swale Borough Cncl; chm: Sittingbourne CAB, Crossroads Care, Dolphin Barge Museum Tst; vice pres Orpheus Choral Soc Sittingbourne, Lib Democrat cand Kent CC by-election 1990; *Recreations* music, nature study, reading; *Clubs* KTNC, Nat Tst, English Heritage, Friends of Canterbury Cathedral, Friends of The Earth; *Style*— Cncllr Peter Morgan; 65 Park Rd,

Sittingbourne, Kent ME10 1DY (☎ 0795 423215)

MORIARTY, Michael John Patrick; s of Alexander Hugo Moriarty; *b* 22 Nov 1942; *Educ* St Stephen's, Welling, Kent; *m* 1965, Pearl Joy; 1 s, 2 da; *Career* memb Stock Exchange 1977; dir: Shaw & Marvin Ltd 1978-80, Zootopia 1979-83; *Recreations* gardening; *Style*— Michael Moriarty Esq; Woodside, Foxendown Lane, Meopham, Kent (☎ 0474 812232)

MORLAND, Nicholas Vermuyden Courtenay; s of John Courtenay Morland (d 1961), of Londiani, Kenya, and Gwendoline Louise, *née* Bastow; *b* 7 Sept 1935; *Educ* Durban HS SA, Loughborough Coll of Technol (Dip Mechanical Engrg); *m* 27 June 1964, Gwendeline Marie, da of Lt-Col Roland Charles Greenwood; 1 s (Daniel Courtenay b 27 May 1978), 2 da (Clara Frances b 16 March 1966, Heather Louise b 5 Dec 1968); *Career* devpt engr: Hawker Aircraft 1958-64, Hymatic Engineering 1964-67, Boeing Vertol USA 1968-70; design and devpt engr AMF Legg 1971-81; mechanical engrg design conslt 1981-; advsr CAB; MIMechE 1970; *Recreations* gliding, camping, travel, family; *Clubs* Lasham Gliding Soc; *Style*— Nicholas Morland, Esq

MORLEY-CLARKE, Ian Wentworth; s of Maj Francis Edward Morley Clarke (d 1959), of Southampton, and Vera Dagmar, *née* Bates (d 1953); *b* 9 Jan 1927; *Educ* St Piran's Maidenhead Berks, Wellington Crowthorne Berks; *m* 1, 1950 (m dis 1958); 2 s (Richard Stuart b 23 Sept 1951 d 15 Oct 1983, David Charles Edward b 23 March 1953); m 2, 10 May 1958 (m dis 1969); 1 s (John Robert b 26 Aug 1961); m 3, 18 Aug 1969, Kathleen Joyce, da of Arthur Frederick William Wells (d 1970), of Worthing; *Career* enlisted in Army 1943, reg commission in Queen's Royal Regt 1946, seconded to Parachute Regt, resigned commission as Capt 1955; fndr: Buildtay Ltd (publishing) 1958, Planned Action Ltd (Midas Books) 1968, Spellmount Ltd 1983, The Nutshell Publishing Co Ltd 1989; involved with publicity for: Nat Assoc of Youth Clubs, PHAB; played hockey for; Combined Servs, Army, Kent, Berks; *Recreations* rugby, cricket, hockey, athletics; *Clubs* Tramps Hockey, Guildford Hockey, Invalids' CC, Grasshoppers' CC, Berks Gents' CC, Blues CC; *Style*— Ian Morley-Clarke, Esq; 12 Dene Way, Speldhurst, nr Tunbridge Wells, Kent TN3 0NX (☎ 0892 862860, office 0892 863861)

MORRIS, Charles Evan Henry (Harry); CBE (1990); s of Thomas Silvan Morris, MC, JP (d 1981), of Swansea, West Glamorgan, and Mary Isobel, *née* Williamson; *b* 7 May 1926; *Educ* Rugby, Univ of Cambridge (BA); *m* 5 Feb 1955, Mansil, da of Dr I O Martin, of Swansea; 3 s (Martyn b 1956, Stephen b 1959, Thomas b 1962 d 1987); *Career* RN Instr 1947-49; Br Steel Corpn: dir Steel Co of Wales div 1967-70 (dir ops 1966-67), md (tech) 1970-77; pres Ferrco Engrg Ltd (Canada) 1977-83, vice pres Co Steel Inc (Canada) 1983-85, chief exec Sheerness Steel Co 1985-; pres: Inst of Metals 1988-89, Br Ind Steel Prodrs Assoc 1988; chm SE Region CBI 1989-; Liveryman Worshipful Co of Engrs 1990 (memb 1988); FIMechE 1976, FIM 1984, FEng 1988; *Recreations* golf, photography; *Style*— Harry Morris, Esq, CBE; Old Forge House, Boughton Aluph, Ashford, Kent TN25 4JB (☎ 0233 643301); Sheerness Steel Co plc, Sheerness, Kent ME12 1TH (☎ 0795 663333)

MORRIS, Hon Edward Patrick; yr twin s of 2 Baron Morris (d 1975), and Jean Beatrice, *née* Maitland-Makgill-Crichton (d 1989, having m 2, Baron Salmon (Life Peer); gs of 1 Baron Morris (d 1935, last PM of Newfoundland 1909-18 and memb of War Cabinet 1916-18); *b* 9 Dec 1937; *Educ* Downside; *m* 1963, Mary Beryl, da of Lt-Col D H G Thrush, of Canterbury; 1 s (Edward Patrick b 1965), 1 da (Elizabeth Mary b 1968); *Career* co dir (Export) Barrow Hepburn 1973-75, export mangr Portex Ltd Hythe Kent 1976-83, sales dir Concord Laboratories Ltd Folkestone 1983-84; *Recreations* golf, veteran car (1930 Rolls-Royce); *Style*— The Hon Edward Morris; Dormer Cottage, Petham, Canterbury, Kent (☎ 0227 70 329)

MORRIS, Hon Michaela Mary; da of 3 Baron Morris; *b* 1965; *Style*— The Hon Michaela Morris

MORRIS, Paul William; s of William Henry Morris (d 1987), of Bexhill-on-Sea, and late Norah, *née* Abbott; *b* 20 May 1942; *Educ* Downsmeade Sch Eastbourne; *m* 30 Jan 1965, Carole, da of William Joseph Cornelius Owden, of Tunbridge Wells; 2 s (Nicholas b 1967, Dominic b 1972), 2 da (Karen b 1969, Elizabeth b 1979); *Career* articled clerk HS Humphrey and Co Eastbourne 1966, sr tax ptnr BDO Binder Hamlyn 1988- (joined 1972); Freeman City of London, Liveryman Worshipful Co of Painter Stainers; FCA 1966; *Recreations* cricket, tennis, walking, painting, art, theatre; *Style*— Paul Morris, Esq; BDO Binder Hamlyn, 20 Old Bailey, London EC4M 7BH (☎ 071 489 9000, fax 071 489 6060, telex 8812282)

MORRIS, Peter Christopher West; s of Christopher Thomas Richard Morris, of Westbrook, Rottingdean, Sussex, and Lillian Beatrice, *née* Briggs; *b* 24 Dec 1937; *Educ* Seaford Coll, Christ's Cambridge (MA, LLB); *m* 1, 20 June 1959 (m dis), Joy Florence; 2 s (Mark b 1962, James b 1964), 1 da (Amanda b 1960); m 2, 1987, Terese Lindsay; 1 step s (Maxim b 1974), 2 step da (Phillippa b 1972, Victoria b 1976); *Career* Nat Serv 76 Co Lt RASC 1956-58 (cmmnd 2 Lt 1957); admitted slr 1965; ptnr Wild Hewitson and Shaw of Cambridge 1965, called to the Bar Middle temple 1982; recorder of the Crown Court 1980-84, voluntary removal from roll of slrs 1982, resigned recordership 1984; hockey player for Wales 1982-85; co dir 1985-; *Recreations* hockey, tennis, golf; *Clubs* Hawks; *Style*— Peter Morris, Esq

MORRIS, Richard Francis Maxwell; s of Maxwell Morris, of Broomershill House, Pulborough, Sussex, and late Frederica Eugenie, *née* Abelson; *b* 11 Sept 1944; *Educ* Eton, New Coll, Oxford (MA); *m* 1, 15 June 1974 (m dis 1978), Sarah Penelope, da of Jeffrey Quill; m 2, 9 April 1983, Marian Claire, da of late Michael Sperling; 2 da (Harriet 1984, Jessica 1986); *Career* admitted slr 1969; mangr SG Warburg and Co Ltd 1974-79, jt md Hodder and Stoughton Holdings Ltd Kent 1989- (dir 1979-), md Edward Arnold (publishers) Ltd 1987-89, dir: The Lancet Ltd 1985-, Invicta Sound plc, Kent Opera (Regional Opera Trust Ltd); jt fndr Almaviva Opera; *Recreations* music, visual arts, golf, tennis; *Clubs* Athenaeum; *Style*— Richard Morris, Esq; Holdfast House, Edenbridge, Kent TN8 6SJ (☎ 0732 862439); Hodder & Stoughton Ltd, Mill Rd, Dunton Green, Sevenoaks, Kent TN13 2YA (☎ 0732 450111, fax 0732 460134, telex 95122)

MORRISH, Peter Sydney; s of Sydney Victor Morrish (d 1969), of Hove, Sussex, and Elizabeth McLaren, *née* Dewar (d 1969); *b* 30 Dec 1924; *Educ* Sutton Valence, Emmanuel Coll Cambridge (MA); *m* 18 Sept 1954, June Seymour, da of Lancelot Stephen Richard Monckton (d 1979), of Bearsted, Kent; 1 s (Lancelot Peter b 19 Oct 1956), 1 da (Annabel June b 24 Feb 1959); *Career* Sub Lt RNVR 1942-46, Channel, Far East Coastal Forces and attached Fleet Air Arm; land agent and chartered surveyor; ptnr Burrows Clements Winch & Sons 1952-55; chm: Castlemaine Farms Ltd 1955-, Wealden Hops Ltd 1986-; Friends of Kent Churches; Freeman City of London 1964; memb: Worshipful Co of Broderers 1964, Worshipful Co of Fruiterers 1975; ARICS 1946; *Recreations* skiing, golf, environment; *Clubs* Farmers', Royal St George's Golf, Rye Golf; *Style*— Peter S Morrish, Esq; Castlemaine, Horsmonden, Tonbridge, Kent (☎ 089 272 2213); Castlemaine Farms Ltd, Horsmonden, Tonbridge, Kent TN12 8HG; Wealden Hops Ltd, Nettlestead Oast, Paddock Wood, Kent (☎ 089 283 6061)

MORSE, Rodney John; s of James Morse (d 1986), and Elsie, *née* Cripps; *b* 26 Jan 1944; *m* 25 May 1968, (Maureen) Ann, da of John Kenny Woodward, of Leighton Buzzard, Beds; 1 da (Carrie Alisa b 25 Aug 1971); *Career* underwriter Lloyds 1986-, dir Wellington Underwriting Agencies Ltd 1986-; ACII; *Style*— Rodney Morse, Esq; Linwood, Sevenoaks Rd, Ightham, Sevenoaks, Kent (☎ 0732 882537); 120 Fenchurch St, London EC3M 5BA (☎ 071 929 2811, fax 071 220 7234, telex 268892 WELTN G)

MOSCOW, Dr David; s of Emanuel Moscow (d 1981), and Rachel, *née* Davidovitch; *b* 3 May 1937; *Educ* Parmiter's GS London, Univ of London (BSc), Univ of Leicester, Univ of Leeds (PhD); *m* 1, 1960 (m dis 1972), Jennifer Dianne, da of William Thomas Redgate (d 1986); 4 da (Sarah b 1964, Susan b 1967, Emma b 1968, Linda b 1969); m 2, 1975, Patricia Ann, da of Frank Edward Gostling, OBE, of Oxshott, Surrey; *Career* personnel offr BAC 1960-63, lectr Univ of Leeds 1963-67, res assoc Netherlands Inst for Preventive Med 1967-70, jt md Sheppard Moscow and Assoc Ltd 1984-86 (chm 1970-84); conslt to: ICI, Shell, nat orgns NHS, Bank of England; FID 1977; FBIM 1983, FIMC 1986; *Recreations* golf, sculpture; *Style*— Dr David Moscow; Cross Keys House, Cross Keys, Sevenoaks, Kent (☎ 0732 457411)

MOSS, Dr Martin Leslie; s of Leslie Moss, of Bury St Edmunds, Suffolk, and Dorothy Violet, *née* Long; *b* 21 March 1954; *Educ* King Edward VI GS Bury St Edmunds Suffolk, Guy's Hospital Med Sch of London (MB BS, LRCP); *m* 16 Sept 1978, Sylvia Rosemary Diane, da of Capt Harry Albert Saunders, of Cobham, Surrey, 2 s (Christopher Martin James b 1981, Edward Alfred Peter b 1983) 1 da (Katherine Sylvia Marija b 1988); *Career* house surgn Guy's Hosp London 1977, house physican St Nicholas Hosp Plumstead 1978, sr house offr Maidstone Vocational Trg Scheme 1978-81, GP Drs Vaux Bonds Manners Moss and Laurent 1982-, clinical asst in cardiology The Maidstone Hosp 1987-; memb: Maidstone Child Abuse Review Gp 1986-88, Maidstone Div BMA 1978 (pres 1986), Soc of Genealogists, Inst Heraldic and Genealogical Studies, Suffolk Genealogy Soc; Charles Forster Cardiology Prize 1977; CMF 1977; MRCS 1977, FRSM 1987; *Recreations* genealogy, local history, skiing; *Style*— Dr Martin Moss; Old Forge House, Busbridge Rd, Loose, Maidstone, Kent ME15 0ER (☎ 0622 745175); The Surgery, Yeoman Lane, Bearsted, Maidstone, Kent; Mill Cottages, Hollingbourne, Kent (☎ 0622 37326, 0622 38344)

MOSSELMANS, Hon Mrs (Prudence Fiona); da of 1 and last Baron McCorquodale of Newton (d 1971), and Winifred Sophia Doris Clark (d 1960); *b* 27 June 1936; *m* 1962, Carel Maurits Mosselmans, TD; 2 s; *Style*— The Hon Mrs Mosselmans; Seameads, Sandwich Bay, Kent (☎ 030 461 3558); 15 Chelsea Square, London SW3 (☎ 071 352 0621)

MOUBRAY-JANKOWSKI, Anthony; s of Capt Josef Marian Orzel-Jankowski (d 1966), and Barbara, *née* Moubray (d 1964); *b* 2 Oct 1946; *Educ* King's Sch Canterbury, Canterbury Coll of Art Sch of Architecture (Dip Arch); *m* 13 Oct 1969, Danielle Marian, da of H L A Green, of Canterbury; 1 s (Arran Jason b 6 Aug 1970), 2 da (Selena Cassandra b 2 Oct 1972, Barbara Christabel b 20 Feb 1979); *Career* architect; sr ptnr Lee Evans Partnership Canterbury Ashford London and Hereford; conslt architect: Kings Sch Canterbury, Strutt & Parker, Leeds Castle Estate, Knole Estate, Dover Coll; former chm Canterbury Area Branch RIBA, vice pres Canterbury Festival, sponsor Canterbury Urban Studies Centre Summer Sch; memb: St Mary's Church

Chartham PCC, The Chartham Soc; tstee Village Hall Ctees; *Recreations* skiing, travel, gardening, buildings; *Style*— Anthony Moubray-Jankowski, Esq; Kenfield House, Petham, Canterbury, Kent CT4 5RN (☎ 022 770 721); Lee Evans Partnership, Lee Court, Castle St, Canterbury, Kent CT1 2PX (☎ 0227 452127, fax 0227 456345)

MOULAND, Harry Seagrave; s of William Harry Mouland, of Lower Halstow, Sittingbourne, Kent, and Grace Seagrave, *née* Muggeridge (d 1971); *b* 8 May 1936; *Educ* Collyers GS Horsham; *m* 6 June 1959, Valerie, da of Walter Sydney Townsend, of Boxley, Maidstone, Kent; 1 s (Michael Harry b 13 Dec 1960), 2 da (Gillian Valerie b 18 Nov 1961, Alison Julia b 25 June 1963); *Career* farmer; breeder pedigree Charolais and Chianina cattle; chm Br Chianina Cattle Soc 1980-86, pres Int Chianina Assoc 1981-85, cncl memb SE Charolais Cattle Assoc 1978-, nat cncl memb Charolais Cattle Assoc 1990-; *Books* The New Wildfowler in the 1970s (contrib chapter duck rearing, 1969), Duck Rearing (1970); *Recreations* shooting, fishing; *Clubs* Farmers; *Style*— Harry Mouland, Esq; Harval Farm, Lower Halstow, Sittingbourne, Kent ME9 7EB (☎ 0795 842357); Great Barksore Farm, Lower Halstow, Sittingbourne, Kent ME9 7EE (☎ 0795 842272)

MOULTON, Jonathan Paul (Jon); s of Douglas Cecil Moulton, of Stoke-on-Trent, and Elsie Turner Moulton (d 1984); *b* 15 Oct 1950; *Educ* Hanley HS, Univ of Lancaster (BA); *m* 13 Aug 1973, Pauline Marie, da of Stanley Dunn, of Stoke on Trent; 1 s (Spencer Jonathan b 1980), 1 da (Rebecca Clare b 1978); *Career* mangr Coopers & Lybrand 1972-80; Citicorp Venture Capital: dir NY 1980-81, gen mangr London 1981-85, managing ptnr Schroder Ventures 1985-; non-exec dir: Hornby Hobbies plc 1981-, Halls Homes & Gardens plc 1982-, Parker Pen Ltd 1986-, Haden MacLellan Holdings plc 1987-, Interconnection Systems Ltd 1987-, Technology Holdings plc 1989-, Appledore Holdings Ltd 1990-; FCA 1983, FBIM; *Recreations* chess, fishing; *Style*— Jon Moulton, Esq; 57 Kippington Rd, Sevenoaks, Kent TN13 2LL (☎ 0732 450025); Schroder Ventures, 20 Southampton St, London WC2E 7QG (☎ 071 632 1000, fax 071 240 5072)

MOUNTBATTEN OF BURMA, Countess (UK 1947); Patricia Edwina Victoria Knatchbull; CD (1976), JP (Kent 1971), DL (Kent 1973); also Viscountess Mountbatten of Burma (UK 1946), Baroness Romsey (UK 1947); da of Adm of the Fleet 1 Earl Mountbatten of Burma, KG, GCB, OM, GCSI, GCIE, GCVO, DSO, PC, FRS (assas 1979) and Hon Edwina Ashley, CI, GBE, DCVO (d 1960, da of 1 and last Baron Mount Temple, himself gs of 7 Earl of Shaftesbury, the philanthropist); Edwina's mother was Maud, da of Sir Ernest Cassel, the banker and friend of Edward VII; sister of Lady Pamela Hicks; *b* 14 Feb 1924; *Educ* Malta, England, NYC; *m* 26 Oct 1946, 7 Baron Brabourne; 4 s (and 1 s k 1979, with his gf), 2 da; *Heir* s, Lord Romsey; *Career* served 1943-46 WRNS; Col-in-Chief Princess Patricia's Canadian Light Inf 1974; vice Lord Lieut Kent 1984; vice-pres: BRCS, Kent Rural Community cncl, SSAFA, FPA, Nat Childbirth Tst, Royal Life Saving Soc, Shaftesbury Soc, Royal Coll of Nursing, Nat Soc for Cancer Relief, Royal Nat Coll for the Blind; vice patron Burma Star Assoc; patron: Commando Assoc, VAD (RN) Assoc, HMS Kelly Reunion Assoc, East Kent Hospice, Kent Cncl on Drug Addiction, Kent Chest Heart and Stroke Assoc, Mote House, Cheshire House, Kent Handicapped Orphans' Caring Assoc, Kent Childrens' Houses Soc, Chatham Dockyard Hist Soc, Ashford Samaritans, Ashford Umbrella Club, T S Churchill Sea Cadets Ashford; dep vice chm NSPCC, chm Sir Ernest Cassel Educn Tst; pres: SOS Children's Villages, Shaftesbury Homes and Arethusa, Kent Branch Save the Children Fund, Kent Branch Relate, Friends of William Harvey Hosp; govr Ashford Sch, memb Cncl Caldecott Community Kent, tstee The Kent Community Housing Tst; DStJ 1981; *Style*— The Rt Hon the Countess Mountbatten of Burma, CD, JP, DL; Newhouse, Mersham, Ashford, Kent TN25 6NQ (☎ 0233 623466); 39 Montpelier Walk, London SW7 1JH (☎ 071 589 8829)

MOWLL, Rev (John) William Rutley; s of Wilfred Rutley Mowll (d 1979), and Mary Gifford, *née* Holden; *b* 24 March 1942; *Educ* Canterbury Cathedral Choir Sch, King's Sch Canterbury, Sarum Theol Coll; *m* 16 April 1966, Susan Frances Lisle, da of William Alexander Bullen; 2 s (Benjamin b 1967, Joshua b 1970); *Career* deacon Sheffield Cathedral 1966, priested 1967; curacies: diocese of Sheffield 1966-69, diocese of Birmingham 1969-72; first living: parish of Upper Arley diocese of Worcester and Industl chaplain Kidderminster 1973-78; second living: vicar of Upton Snodsbury with Broughton Hackett, Grafton Flyford, Flyford Flavell and North Piddle (diocese of Worcester) 1978-83; third living: Boughton Under Blean with Dunkirk 1983- and Hernhill 1989-; hon memb Guild of Master Craftsmen 1984 (memb 1979); reg contrib to Argus Specialist Publications on subject of Victorian Shipping, advsr to Ship's Plan's Serv (HMS Warrior, 1860), memb Soc for Nautical Res South, Gold medal winner Wembley Model Engrg Exhibiton 1982, author and playwright, community magazine ed; *Books* The SS Great Britain - The Model Ship (1982); *Recreations* music, engineering, shipping, miniature craft work; *Style*— The Rev William Mowll; The Vicarage, 101 The Street, Boughton Under Blean, Faversham, Kent ME13 9BG (☎ 0227 751410)

MUCKLE, Ann; da of Percival Alfred Wyatt (d 1984), of Dartford, Kent, and Frances Mary, *née* Gardiner (d 1985); *b* 12 April 1937; *Educ* Dartford W Secdy Modern Sch For Girls; *m* 2 Aug 1958, John Ivan Muckle, *qv*, s of William John Arthur Muckle (d 1966), of Dartford; 1 s (Tony b 25 Aug 1963), 1 da (Carol (Mrs Miller) b 7 Dec 1959); *Career* sec for firm of CAs 1952-59, asst chief clerk insur co 1969-74, personal asst Trade Union 1974; treas NW Kent Branch RSPCA, memb Mgmnt Ctee local CAB, chm Sch Govrs Temple Hill Schs 1973-84, sch govr Westgate Sch 1973-84; Dartford Constituency Lab Pty: cncl memb, branch sec, membership sec; Dartford borough cncllr (Lab) 1983- (dep Mayoress of Dartford 1972-73, Mayoress of Dartford 1973-74); *Recreations* charity work, swimming, theatre; *Style*— Mrs Ann Muckle; 69 Farnol Rd, Dartford, Kent DA1 5NG (☎ 0322 23295); 94 London Rd, Crayford, Kent DA1 4BT (☎ 0322 57627)

MUCKLE, John Ivan; s of William John Arthur Muckle (d 1966), of Dartford, Kent, and Daisy Muckle, *née* Woods; *b* 22 Feb 1933; *Educ* Banstead Co Sch; *m* 2 Aug 1958, Ann, *qv*, da of Percival Alfred Wyatt (d 1984), of Dartford, Kent; 1 s (Tony b 25 Aug 1963), 1 da (Carol (Mrs Miller) b 7 Dec 1959); *Career* Nat Serv sr Aircraftsman RAF 1954-56; apprentice patternmaker: John Smith Engry Carshalton Surrey 1947-51, A Sprinks & Son Dartford 1951-54; foreman patternmaker Alpha Pattern Co Northfleet, local govt offr and housing mangr London Borough Southwark 1981-; Dartford Borough Cncl: Lab cncllr 1967-, chm Planning Ctee, dep ldr 1974-83 (oppn 1983-); Kent co cncllr 1988-; Mayor of Dartford 1973-74 (dep mayor 1972-73); memb Dartford Dist Twinning Assoc, branch chm Dartford Constituency Lab Pty (memb GC and EC); chm Mgmnt Ctee Temple Hill and Highfield Youth Club, chm of Govrs Down Sch; *Recreations* golf, photography; *Clubs* Dartford Golf, Dartford Photographic; *Style*— John Muckle, Esq; 69 Farnol Rd, Dartford, Kent DA1 5NG (☎ 0322 23295); 47A East Dulwich Rd, East Dulwich, Greater London SE22 (☎ 081 693 3399)

MUIRHEAD, William Mortimer; s of Denis Butler Muirhead; *b* 11 July 1947; *Educ* Armidale Sch NSW, St Dunstans Coll SE6; *m* Jeanne Elizabeth, *née* Meins; 2 s; *Career* dir: Saatchi & Saatchi Garland-Compton, Saatchi & Saatchi Compton 1980-; *Recreations* rugby, tennis, squash, skiing; *Clubs* RAC, Zanzibar, Mortons; *Style*— William Muirhead Esq; 'Ightham', Merlewood Drive, Chislehurst, Kent; 'Tramontana', Encounter Bay, Victor Harbour, S Australia

MULLARKEY, David Charles; s of Daniel Francis Mullarkey, of Finchley, London, and Alice Cecelia, *née* Dillon; *b* 4 Feb 1956; *Educ* Fincley Catholic GS, Univ of Nottingham (LLB); *m* Aug 1984, Beverley Ann, da of Anthony George Carter, of Beckenham, Kent; 1 s (Daniel Nicholas b 14 Aug 1989), 1 da (Lura Ann b 10 June 1987); *Career* admitted slr 1982; Linklaters & Paines: tax dept 1982-84, Hong Kong Off 1984-86, ptnr 1988; memb Tax Ctee Unit Assoc; memb: Law Soc, Int Bar Assoc; *Style*— David Mullarkey, Esq

MULLIGAN, Reginald Graham; s of Frederick George Mulligan, of Marbella, Spain, and Gladys Mulligan; *b* 4 Dec 1944; *Educ* Ottershaw Sch, Coll of Air Trg Hamble; *m* 10 Nov 1974, Linda Mary, da of Lenord Wood; 2 s (Maxwell Thomas b 6 Dec 1976, Daniel Graham b 24 April 1979); *Career* pilot: BEA 1965-66, BOAC 1966-78; chm Fairflight 1978-; *Recreations* golf; *Clubs* Royal MD Surrey GC; *Style*— Reginald Mulligan, Esq; Fairflight Ltd, Biggin Hill Airport, nr Westerham, Kent TN16 3B (☎ 0959 74651, fax 0959 71929)

MULLINS, Col Gerald Oliver; DL (Kent, 1983); s of George Arthur Mullins (d 1966), and Ivy Winifred, *née* Goddard (d 1982); *b* 19 Aug 1928; *Educ* Shrewsbury, RMA Sandhurst; *m* 27 Aug 1960, Caroline Sylvia Mary, da of Brig J M Rymer-Jones, CBE, MC, QPM; 3 s (Toby Jonathan b 1961, Nicholas Gerald b 1963, Andrew Oliver b 1964), 1 da (Sophie Minette b 1970); *Career* cmmnd Buffs 1948, served 1 Bn Buffs 1949-54; served Parachute Regt: 3 Bn and 2 Bn 1954-69, 10 vol Bn 1969-72, regtl Col 1975-78; instr Nat Def Coll 1972-75, chm Jt Cadet Exec MOD 1978-80; psc 1960, NDC 1972; sec SE Territorial Auxiliary and Vol Assoc; Freeman City of London 1979; *Recreations* watching cricket, gardening; *Style*— Col Gerald Mullins, DL; Lion House, High Halden, Ashford, Kent (☎ 0233 850446); South East TAVR Assoc, Sandling Place, Chatham Rd, Maidstone, Kent (☎ 0622 690402, fax 691944)

MULLINS, Nicholas Richard John; s of Colin Mullins, of Leicestershire, and Valerie Margaret, *née* Branson; *b* 31 Jan 1966; *Educ* Stonehill HS, Longslade Coll Leics, Poly of Central London (BA); *m* 21 July 1990, Rachael Elizabeth, da of Christopher McLaren Allen, of Leics; *Career* news reporter: Loughborough Trader 1981-83, Loughborough Echo 1983-85; sports reporter BBC Radio Leicester 1985-87, sports ed BBC Radio Kent 1989- (sports reporter 1987-89); *Recreations* eating out, wines, country walking, reading, photography, music; *Style*— Nicholas Mullins, Esq; Seymour Cottage, 88 High St, Snodland, Kent ME6 5AL (☎ 0634 245165); BBC Radio Kent, Sun Pier, Chatham, Kent ME4 4EZ (☎ 0634 830505, fax 0634 830573)

MUNASINGHE, Dr (Don) Ranjith; s of Don Martin Munasinghe (d 1946), of Sri Lanka, and Dona Margaret, *née* Jayakody; *b* 5 Nov 1935; *Educ* St Lawrence Sch Colombo, St Peter's Coll Colombo, Royal Coll Colombo, Univ of Ceylon Colombo (MB BS, MD); *m* 3 June 1966, (Srimathi) Beatrice, da of Simon Semage Christian Kulatilake (d 1983), of Wanchawela, Sri Lanka; 1 s

(Chanaka Sumith b 1972), 1 da (Kumudini Renuka b 1969); *Career* registrar in med Univ of Ceylon Colombo 1963-66, hon clinical asst Bristol Royal Infirmary and UCH 1966-68, Smith and Nephew res fell Hammersmith Hosp 1971, sr registrar geriatric med Canterbury and Thanet Hosp and St Thomas' Hosp 1975-79; conslt physician: Matale dist Sri Lanka 1969-70, Colombo S Hosp Sri Lanka 1973-75, geriatric med Dartford and Gravesham Health Dist 1979-; memb Br Geriatrics Soc; FRCP, FRCPE; *Recreations* travel, philately; *Style—* Dr Ranjith Munasinghe; Gilda, Gresham Ave, Hartley, nr Longfield, Kent DA3 7BT (☎ 04747 7780); Joyce Green Hospital, Dartford, Kent DA1 5PL (☎ 0322 227242)

MUNDY, Anthony Richard; s of Peter Gordon Mundy, of Bedford Ave, London, and Betty, *née* Hall; *b* 25 April 1948; *Educ* Mill Hill Sch, Univ of London (MB BS, MS); *m* 20 Sept 1975, Marilyn June, da of Edward Ashton, of South Ockendon, Essex; 1 s (Harry b 1986), 1 da (Emily b 1977); *Career* CO and conslt surgn Muscat Oman 1977-78, conslt urological surgn Lewisham Hosp 1981-86, sr lectr in urology UMDS 1981-, conslt urological surgn Guy's Hosp 1981-, sr lectr in urology and conslt urological surgn Inst of Urology 1986-; ctee memb Br Assoc Urological Surgns; MRCP 1974, FRCS 1975; *Books* Urodynamics: Principles Practice and Application (1984), Scientific Basis of Urology (1986), Current Operative Surgery-Urology (1988); *Style—* Anthony Mundy, Esq

MUNRO, Ian Arthur Hoyle; s of Gordon Alexander Munro (d 1984), of Bradford, Yorks, and Muriel Rebecca, *née* Hoyle (d 1938); *b* 5 Nov 1923; *Educ* Huddersfield Coll, Royal Lancaster GS, Paston Sch North Walsham, Royal Liberty Sch Romford, Univ of London Guy's Hosp Med Sch (MB, BS); *m* 4 Aug 1948, Dr Olive Isabel, da of Ernest John Jackson (d 1946); 3 s (Andrew b 1950, Robert b 1960, John b 1965), 2 da (Jane b 1952, Deborah b 1956); *Career* RAMC 1947-50, radiologist Br Mil Hosp Klagenfurt BTA; editorial staff The Lancet 1951- (ed 1976-88); FRCP 1984; *Recreations* cricket, crosswords; *Clubs* Athenaeum, Yorks CCC; *Style—* Ian Munro, Esq; Oakwood, Bayley's Hill, Sevenoaks, Kent TN14 6HS (☎ 0732 454993)

MUNRO, Michael Hector; s of Capt Alan Hector Munro, RA (d 1961), of Amersham, Bucks, and Aileen Stewart, *née* Brown (d 1974); *b* 19 Aug 1927; *Educ* Epsom Coll, Univ of London (MRPharmS); *m* 11 June 1955, Pamela Gwyn, da of Capt Trevor Robinson (d 1968), of Bristol; 2 s (Robin Stewart b 20 Nov 1959, Nicholas Stewart b 21 Dec 1962); *Career* asst mangr A H Hobbs Pharmacy 1954-56, med rep British Drug Houses 1956-60; Crown Chemical Company: asst sales mangr 1960-61, sales mangr 1961-64, sales dir 1964-77, admin dir 1977-85; dir Harkers Veterinary Remedies 1966-83; chief exec: British Distributors of Animal Medicines 1982-85, Animal Health Distributors Assoc (UK) 1985-87; branch chm Pharmaceutical Soc: Bath 1959, Weald of Kent 1972; memb: Tonbridge Round Table 1965-68, Rotary Club (Tunbridge Wells 1976-78, Tonbridge 1978-); fndr chm Tonbridge 41 Club 1968, chm Headway (Tunbridge Wells and Dist) National Head Injuries Assoc Ltd 1988-; former: Memb IOD, MIPharmM, FBIM; *Recreations* golf, fishing; *Style—* Michael Munro, Esq; High Cedar, Nevill Ridge, Nevill Park, Tunbridge Wells, Kent TN4 8NN (☎ 0892 541250)

MURDOCH, Robert Clive; s of Lt-Col Clive Murdoch, DSO (d 1944), and Janet Homewood, *née* Motion (d 1963); *b* 7 March 1922; *Educ* Wellington; *m* 1, 1951 (m dis 1976), Mary Anne, da of late Capt A K MacEwan; 3 da (Miranda Jane b 1954, Serena Janet b 1957, Camilla Anne b 1958); m 2, Susan Mary, da of late Eric Graham Mattingley; *Career* WWII Capt Grenadier Gds, served N Africa, Italy 1942-46; farmer 1947-; dir Hops Mktg Bd 1955-82, Checkers and Checkers Growers Ltd 1957-88; *Recreations* farming, all country pursuits; *Clubs* Farmers; *Style—* Robert C Murdoch, Esq; Wester Hill, Linton, Maidstone, Kent ME17 4BT (☎ 0622 7452277); Murdoch & Allfrey Ltd, Clockhouse, Linton, Maidstone, Kent (☎ 0622 743173)

MURRAY, Hon Catherine Anne; da of Baron Murray of Gravesend (Life Peer) (d 1980); *b* 1964; *Educ* Emmanuel Coll Cambridge; *Style—* The Hon Catherine Murray

MURRAY, Sir Donald Frederick; KCVO (1983), CMG (1973); s of Archibald Thomas Murray (d 1960), and Freda May, *née* Byfield (d 1964); *b* 14 June 1924; *Educ* Colfes GS, Kings Sch Canterbury, Worcester Coll Oxford; *m* 17 Dec 1949, Marjorie, da of Charles Culverwell (d 1977); 3 s (Ian b 1951, Neil b 1958, Alexander b 1960), 1 da (Gillian b 1953); *Career* RM (41 Commando) 1943-46; Foreign Serv: entered FO 1948, third sec Warsaw 1948, FO 1951, second sec Vienna 1953, first sec political office ME Forces 1956, FO 1957, first sec commerce Stockholm 1958, first sec and head of chancery Saigon 1962, FO 1964, cnsllr 1965, head of SE Asia Dept 1966, cnsllr Tehran 1969, RCDS 1973, HM ambass Tripoli 1974, asst undersec of state FCO 1977, HM ambass Stockholm 1980, ret 1984; assessor chm Civil Serv Selection Bd 1984-86, dir Goodlass Wall & Co Ltd 1985-; chm Kent Co SSAFA 1985-90, tstee World Resource Fndn 1986-, complaints cmmr Channel Tunnel 1987-; Grand Cross Order of North Star Sweden 1983; *Style—* Sir Donald Murray, KCVO, CMG; Oxney House, Wittersham, Kent TN30 7ED

MURRAY, Neil Alastair Charles; s of Alastair Richardson Murray, of Hong Kong, and Patricia Stella Ray, *née* Jones; *b* 25 Feb 1954; *Educ* King George V Sch Hong Kong, Univ of Southampton (LLB), City Univ (MA); *m* 1 Sept 1984, Patricia Susan, da of John Herbert Mulholland, of Connecticut, USA; 1 s (James b 4 July 1987), 1 da (Stephanie b 18 June 1989); *Career* admitted slr 1980; Boodle Hatfield & Co London 1978-80, Legal Dept ICI 1980, Norton Rose 1980-85, ptnr Travers Smith Braithwaite 1987- (joined 1985); Freeman Worshipful Co of Slrs; memb Law Soc; *Recreations* music, golf, squash, fitness; *Clubs* Wig and Pen; *Style—* Neil Murray, Esq

MURRAY, Hon Mrs (Sally Ann Hale); *née* Willis; da of Baron Willis (Life Peer); *b* 8 Jan 1951; *Educ* Chislehurst and Sidcup Girls' GS, Crownwoods Sch; *m* 1974, Robin James Murray, s of James Patrick Murray, of Bexley; 1 s (James Edward b 24 Sept 1980), 2 da (Alice Louise b 14 July 1982, Helen Jane (twin) b 14 July 1982); *Career* Civil Serv 1974-77, advice worker CAB 1977-80, legal cashier 1988-; *Recreations* cooking, embroidery, needlework; *Style—* The Hon Mrs Murray; Inglenook Cottage, 12 Pump Close, Leybourne, W Malling, Kent ME19 5HH (☎ 0732 870917)

MURRAY, Hon Timothy John; s of Baron Murray of Gravesend (Life Peer, d 1980); *b* 1966; *Style—* The Hon Timothy Murray

MURRAY OF GRAVESEND, Baroness; Margaret Anne; *née* Wakeford; JP (1971); da of Frederick Charles Wakeford, of Crayford; *b* 6 Dec 1928; *m* 1960, Baron Murray of Gravesend (Life Peer) (d 1980); 1 s (Timothy John, *qv*, b 1966), 1 da (Catherine Anne, *qv*, b 1964); *Career* mangr Gravesend Churches Housing Assoc; memb: Lambeth Cncl 1958-65, Dartford and Gravesend Dist Health Authy 1982-89, Co-Op Pty, Fabian Soc, Soroptimists, Lab Pty; pres: N Kent Sunday Football League 1980-, Gravesend Branch Nat Assoc of Widows 1981-, Gravesend Branch NSPCC 1985-; vice pres Gravesend Cncl for Racial Equality, chm Wrotham Cncl for Gravesend; govr: Holy Trinity C of E Sch, St John's RC Sch; clerk to Knights Almshouse Tst Northfleet; *Style—* The Rt Hon Lady Murray of Gravesend, JP; 13 Parrock Rd, Gravesend, Kent (☎ 0474 365958); Gravesend Churches Housing Association, 28 Harmer St, Gravesend (☎ 0474 357361)

MUSHIN, Alan Spencer; s of Dr Louis Mushin (d 1984); *b* 31 Jan 1938; *Educ* Haberdashers' Aske's, London Hosp Med Coll (MB BS); *m* 27 Feb 1972, Joan Carolyn, da of Dr Simon Behrman, of Harley St, London; 1 s (James b 1976), 1 da (Rosalind b 1974); *Career* conslt: ophthalmic surgn Moorfield Eye Hosp London, London Hosp, Queen Elizabeth Hosp for children; memb: Ophthalmological Soc of the UK, Br Paediatric Assoc; BMA, FRSM, FRCS; *Books* papers on paediatric ophthalmology; *Recreations* photography, philately, gardening; *Clubs* Savage; *Style—* Alan S Mushin, Esq; 935 Finchley Rd, London NW11 7PE (☎ 071 455 7212); 82 Harley St, London W1N 1AE (☎ 071 580 3116); The Dower House, Oxney, St Margarets-at-Cliffe, Kent

N

NAIRN, Andrew; s of Capt Andrew Nairn, MC (d 1971), of Glasgow, and Margaret Cornfoot, *née* Turner (d 1972); *b* 31 July 1944; *Educ* Strathallan Sch; *m* 1, 25 April 1970 (m dis 1983), Susan Anne, da of Richard Alphonse Napier; 1 s (Jonathan Richard b 1981), 1 da (Penelope Margaret b 1976); m 2, 1983, Glynis Vivienne, *née* Sweet; 1 step s (Barnaby Craggs b 1971), 1 step da (Charlotte Craggs b 1974); *Career* trainee CA Thomson Jackson Gourlay and Taylor 1962-67; Kidsons Impey (formerly Hodgson Impey): joined 1967, ptnr 1970-, London region managing ptnr 1990-; dep chm Dulwich Cons Assoc 1978; MICAS; *Recreations* fly fishing, golf; *Clubs* Vagabonds, Saville; *Style*— Andrew Nairn, Esq; 52 Redhill Wood, New Ash Green, Kent DA3 8QP (☎ 0474 873 724); Hodgson Impey, 20-26 Cursitor St, London EC4A 1HY (☎ 071 405 2088, fax 071 831 2206)

NASH, (Denis Frederic) Ellison; OBE (1982), AE (1944); s of late Frederic Arthur Nash; *b* 10 Feb 1913; *Educ* Dulwich, Bart's Hosp Med Coll London; *m* 1938, Joan Mary, *née* Andrew; 2 s, 2 da; *Career* consulting surgn Bart's, formerly dean of Medical Coll Univ of London; interest in special educn with contribs recognised by naming of schs (Nash House at W Wickham and Dulwich Coll Prep Sch); FRCS; *Recreations* gardening, photography, work with disabled; *Clubs* Guild of Freemen, City of London; *Style*— D F Ellison Nash, Esq, OBE, AE; 28 Hawthorne Rd, Bickley, Kent (☎ 081 467 1142)

NASH, Eric Charles; s of Charles Nash (d 1984), and Ellen, *née* Fowkes (d 1981); *b* 6 March 1927; *Educ* Carshalton Sch; *m* 15 March 1952, Jean, da of James Murray Miller (d 1963); 2 s (Ian b 18 March 1953, Andrew b 24 Dec 1955); *Career* Army 1944-48; Distillers Co Ltd 1948-58, non marine mangr W E Found & Co Ltd 1958-76; account exec: Alexander Howden & Co Ltd 1976-87, How F Devitt & Sons Ltd 1987; pres Southern Co Athletic Assoc, vice pres AAA; Freeman: City of London, Worshipful Co of Bakers 1982; MBIM; *Recreations* athletics; *Clubs* City Livery; *Style*— Eric Nash, Esq; 12 Margaret Rd, Bexley, Kent DA5 1DU (☎ 081 303 4573)

NASH, Michael John; adopted s of John William Nash (d 1975), of Minster, and Elizabeth Sarah Nash (d 1938); *b* 24 March 1931; *Educ* Roan Sch for Boys Blackheath London; *m* 10 March 1956, June Veronica, da of Nicholas William Cooper (d 1979), of Blackheath; 2 da (Jacqueline Anne b 1957, Teresa Jane b 1960); *Career* Nat Serv Royal Signals and City of London Yeo 1949-54; md Sandbrook Nash & Co Ltd 1964-88, chm Sandbrook Nash Scannell Ltd 1988-; ctee memb: Kent Assoc Boys Clubs, Kent Co Playing Fields Assoc; publicity offr Maidstone Hospice Appeal; FInstD (ctee memb), MIPA; *Recreations* golf, sailing, travel, music; *Clubs* Lamberhurst Golf, Royal Temple Yacht; *Style*— Michael Nash, Esq; The Oast, Five Wents, Chart Sutton, Kent ME17 3RT; Sandbrook Nash & Co Ltd, 41 Earl St, Maidstone, Kent ME14 1PF (☎ 0622 690069, fax 0622 692314)

NAYLOR, Rev Canon Peter Aubrey; s of Erasmus Aubrey Davenport Naylor (d 1971), and Joyce Evelyn, *née* Leeds (d 1988); *b* 22 Nov 1933; *Educ* KES Stourbridge, Kelham Theological Coll, Ely Theological Coll; *m* 21 Nov 1959, Anna Flora, da of Herbert Moore Phillips, CMG, of Plan De La Tour France (d 1987); 2 s (Andrew Peter b 9 July 1961, Patrick Aubrey b 6 Nov 1963), 1 da (Viginia Martha Kate b 15 Aug 1966); *Career* curate: St Stephen Shepherds Bush 1958-62, St Mark Portsea 1962-66; Vicar: Holy Innocents Kidderminster 1966-74, All Saints Maidstone 1974-; Hon Canon of Canterbury 1979-; chaplain to: Maidstone Borough Cncl, Kent Co Ophthalmic Hosp; *Recreations* golf, travel, shooting; *Style*— The Rev Canon Peter Naylor; The Vicarage, Priory Rd, Maidstone, Kent (☎ 0622 56002)

NEALL, Brian Howard; s of Frank William Neall (d 1973), of Bexleyheath, and Phyllis Agnes, *née* Richards (d 1986), of Hartley; *b* 6 June 1939; *Educ* Dartford GS, Woolwich Poly (HNC); *m* 23 June 1962, Margaret Elizabeth, da of Bernard John Orwin (d 1974), of Hartley; 2 da (Susanne Christine b 1965, Joanne Louise b 1969); *Career* Esso Petroleum: laboratory technician 1955-68, plant supervisor 1968-80, sr supervisor Lubes and Grease Prodn 1980-83, liaison supervisor Modernisation Project Fuels 1983-85 and Lubricants Modernisation 1985-89, ret 1989; asst safety and security mangr Babcock Construction Ltd 1990-; hon mktg mangr North Downs Steam Preservation Soc 1989-, memb Mid Hants Railway Soc, qualified first aider St John Ambulance; FIP (London), assoc memb Inst Occupational Safety and Health (SE); *Recreations* golf, driving, railway preservation; *Style*— Brian Neall, Esq; Landaura, 4 Round Ash Way, Hartley, Longfield, Kent DA3 8BT (☎ 04747 3731)

NEAME, Basil Desmond; CBE (1970); s of Sir Thomas Neame (d 1972), of Preston Lea, Faversham, Kent, and Gwendolyn Mary, *née* Thompson, CBE (d 1972); *b* 14 Oct 1921; *Educ* Cheltenham; *m* 3 April 1948, Stella, da of Lt-Col William Edward Roe (d 1956), of Valence Dene, Godmersham, nr Canterbury, Kent; 2 s (Andrew b 1951, Charles b 1957), 2 da (Patricia (Mrs Cuomo) b 1949, Bridget (Mrs Schillereff) b 1954); *Career* Signalman Royal Signals 1941, cmmnd 2 Lt Cadet RE 1942, Field Co attached Madras Sappers & Miners 1942, Lt 405 Ind Field Co, Capt 1944, Maj 1945, demob 1946, despatches 1946; Kent farmer; chm E Kent Packers Ltd 1973-80 (dir 1970-), local dir Royal Insur Co 1955-87; NFU: chm Kent 1956-58, memb Nat Cncl 1960-66, memb Agric Apprenticeship Ctee Kent (chm 1953-61, chm Nat Cncl 1960-67); chm Agric Trg Bd 1966-70; govr: Wye Coll 1971-87, E Malling Res Station 1960-87 (tstee 1985); memb Pear Res Cncl 1989; *Recreations* bird watching; *Clubs* Farmers; *Style*— Basil Neame, Esq, CBE; Macknade Manor, Faversham, Kent ME13 8XF (☎ 0795 532 070); Macknade, Faversham, Kent ME13 8XF (☎ 0795 532 216)

NEAME, Christopher Desmond; s of Sir Thomas Neame, MBE (d 1973), of Faversham, and Gwendolyn Mary Neame, CBE, *née* Thomson (professional name Astra Desmond, d 1973); *b* 20 July 1927; *Educ* Cheltenham, Gonville and Caius Coll Cambridge (BA); *m* 28 April 1956, Elizabeth Mary Swifte, da of Basil Newton Parsons, of London; 2 s (Geoffrey Michael b 1961, Thomas b 1967), 3 da (Rebecca Christina b 1957, Victoria Mary b 1959, Antonia Jane b 1965); *Career* fruit and vegetable farmer; formerly in family business, independently 1964-; memb various ctees: Kent NFU, CLA; cncl memb RASE 1960-, chm Southern Regnl Flood Def Ctee Nat Rivers Authy; *Recreations* gardening, mineralogy; *Style*— Christopher D Neame, Esq; Colkins, Faversham, Kent ME13 9LU (☎ 0227 752249)

NEAME, Robert Harry Beale; s of Jasper Beale Neame (d 1961), and Violet Evelyn, *née* Cobb (d 1976); The Neame family have been resident in E Kent and can be traced back 500 years; *b* 25 Feb 1934; *Educ* Harrow; *m* 1, 11 March 1961 (m dis), Sally Elizabeth, da of Jack Corben; 1 s (Jonathan b 30 Jan 1964), 2 da (Charlotte b 11 Jan 1962, Sarah b 25 July 1966); m 2, 29 May 1974, Yvonne Mary, da of Alexander McKensie; 1 da (Moray b 7 March 1975); *Career* cmmnd 17/21 Lancers 1953-55 (army racquets champion 1954); chm Shepherd Neame Ltd 1971- (joined 1956, dir 1957, mktg dir 1961), former dir and chm Faversham Laundry Co; chm: Folkestone Racecourse 1988- (dir 1986), SE Eng Tourist Bd 1979-; regnl dir Nat Westminster Bank plc 1982-; dir Kent Econ Devpt Bd 1984-, local dir Royal Insur (UK) Ltd 1971-; memb Faversham CC 1965-, ldr Kent CC 1982-84, chm Int Union of Local Authys 1986-; memb Assoc of Brewing; *Recreations* shooting, riding, cricket, golf, squash, rackets, skiing; *Clubs* MCC, I Zingari, Butterflies, Escorts, Jesters, Band of Brothers, Press, Roy St George's Golf, Free Foresters; *Style*— Robert Neame, Esq; Dane Court Farmhouse, Kits Hill, Selling, Faversham, Kent (☎ 030381 284); c/o Shepherd Neame Ltd, 17 Court St, Faversham, Kent (☎ 079 5822206)

NEAME, Stuart Fraser Beale; *b* 14 Jan 1945; *Educ* Pembroke Coll Cambridge (MA); *Career* vice chm Shepherd Neame Ltd 1985-, dir Quotient plc 1987-; hon lectr in computing Univ of Kent at Canterbury; *Style*— Stuart Neame, Esq; Shepherd Neame Ltd, 17 Court St, Faversham, Kent ME13 7AX

NEARN, Graham Bradshaw; s of Henry John Nearn (d 1986), and Eva Charlotte, *née* Sayers; *b* 29 Sept 1933; *Educ* Purley Co GS, City of London Coll; *m* 5 March 1966, (Margaret) Jane, da of Dr John Stewart Norwell (d 1984); 2 s (Robert Bradshaw b 24 April 1967, Simon John 27 March 1969), 2 da (Eliza Alexandra Jane b 2 Nov 1972, Janina Charlotte b 5 May 1977); *Career* md Caterham Cars Ltd (mfr Caterham super 7 Sports car, formerly Lotus Super 7) 1970- (dir 1959-70), dir District Finance Ltd 1970, chm London Property Conversions Ltd 1972-; chm Specialist Car Mfrs Gp Soc of Motor Mfrs and Traders; *Books* The Caterham & Lotus Sevens (1986); *Recreations* golf, sailing, motor sport; *Clubs* Edenbridge Golf, Whitstable Yacht, Aston Martin Owners, Lotus 7; *Style*— Graham Nearn, Esq; Winburne, Ashurst, Kent TN3 9TB (☎ 0892 740341); 34 Island Wall,

Whitstable, Kent; Caterham Cars Ltd, Seven House, Townend, Caterham, Surrey CR3 5UG (☎ 0883 346666, fax 0883 349086, car tel 0836 340683)

NEESON, David Ivor; s of (Horace) Ivor Charles Neeson, of Belchamp, St Paul, Essex, and Jean Gibson, *née* Wade; *b* 19 Oct 1946; *Educ* Beal GS Ilford Essex; *m* 28 Dec 1972, Christine Pearl, da of Frank Hunt (d 1980), of Romford, Essex; 1 s (Rory), 1 da (Eloisa); *Career* investmt asst Corpn of Lloyds 1965-67, stock (jobber) and ptnr Bisgood Bishop and Co 1967-76, vice pres Merrill Lynch Int 1976-82; Morgan Stanley Int: joined 1982, vice pres 1984, exec dir 1985, md 1986-; memb Int Stock Exchange; *Recreations* golf, tennis, shooting, hiking; *Clubs* Wentworth, Wildernesse Golf (Seal); *Style*— David Neeson, Esq; Morgan Stanley International, Kingsley House, 1A Wimpole St, London W1 (☎ 01 709 3898)

NELSON, Robert Franklyn; QC (1985); s of Clarence William Nelson, of North Rigton, Harrogate, Yorks, and Lucie Margaret, *née* Kirkby; *b* 19 Sept 1942; *Educ* Repton, St Johns Coll Cambridge (BA, MA); *m* 14 Sept 1968, Anne-Marie Sabina, da of Francis William George Hall, of Bellingham House, Hook Green, Wilmington, Kent; 2 s (Joshua b 1970, Bartholomew b 1973); *Career* called to the Bar Middle Temple 1965, rec 1986-; *Recreations* opera, cricket, golf; *Style*— Robert Nelson, Esq, QC; Fairseat Manor, Fairseat, nr Wrotham, Kent; 1 Paper Buildings, Temple, London EC4

NESHAM, Rosaleen Mary Patricia (Paddy); da of Surgn Capt James Percy Shorten, DSC, RN (d 1978), and Eileen Madeleine, *née* O'Keeffe (d 1969); *b* 13 Aug 1920; *Educ* Sacred Heart Sch Tunbridge Wells, Sorbonne; *m* 30 Nov 1939, John Edward Crossley Nesham, MBE, MC, s of Col E W Nesham, MBE, TD, RE (d 1960); 3 s (Robert b 1944, Jeremy b 1947, Patrick b 1955), 1 da (Joanna b 1940); *Career* pres: Kent Assoc For The Blind, Kent Schs Sailing Assoc; vice pres: E Kent Girl Guides, Kent Assoc of Girl Guides, Kent Assoc of Youth Clubs; govr of secdy primary and special schs; memb: Women's Inst, Duke of Edinburgh Award Scheme; parish cncllr 1967-; Kent CC: elected 1970, Social Servs and Educn Ctee, vice chm educn 1981-83, vice chm 1983-85, first female chm 1985-87; Cncl of Univ of Kent at Canterbury; Hon DCL Univ of Kent at Canterbury; *Recreations* sailing, gardening, needlework; *Style*— Mrs Paddy Nesham; Scarbutts Manor, Boughton, Faversham, Kent ME13 9AP (☎ 0227 751401)

NEVILL, Lady Beatrix Mary; da of Lord Lambton; *b* 1949; *m* 1982, Guy Nevill, *qv*; *Style*— The Lady Beatrix Nevill; The Garden House, Eridge Park, Tunbridge Wells, Kent; 25 Musgrave Rd, New King's Rd, London SW6

NEVILL, Guy Rupert Gerard; er s of Lord Rupert Nevill, CVO, JP, DL (d 1982), by his w Lady Anne, *née* Wallop, da of 9 Earl of Portsmouth; hp to unc, 5 Marquess of Abergavenny; *b* 29 March 1945; *Educ* Eton; *m* 1982, Lady Beatrix Lambton, *qv*, da of Lord Lambton; *Career* page of honour to HM 1958-61; *Style*— Guy Nevill, Esq; The Garden House, Eridge Park, Tunbridge Wells, Kent; 10c Bramerton St, London SW3; 25 Musgrave Rd, New King's Rd, London SW6

NEVILL, John Robert Ralph Austin; s of Frederick Reginald Nevill (d 1949), of Rosecroft, Newbury, Berks, and Jeanne, *née* Fageol (d 1975); *b* 15 Feb 1928; *Educ* Ampleforth; *m* 30 July 1955, Ann Margaret Mary, da of Archibald Corble (d 1944), of Cookham, Berks; 4 s (Dominic b 1957, Ralph b 1959, Christopher b 1962, Anthony b 1966), 2 da (Cecilia b 1956, Caroline b 1960); *Career* Lt DCLI 1947-48; dir: Nevill Developments 1956-, The Nevill Gallery; formerly: dir Family Housing Assoc Folkestone Area, chm and vice pres Canterbury and E Kent Branch English Speaking Union, chm and pres SE Region English Speaking Union, ctee memb SE Arts Assoc; ctee memb Canterbury Arts Cncl; Freeman City of London, Liveryman Worshipful Co of Gardeners; memb Hon Soc of Gray's Inn 1951; Knight of Honour and Devotion Br Assoc Sovereign Mil Order of Malta 1975; *Recreations* travelling, fishing, photography, painting; *Clubs* Carlton, English Speaking Union; *Style*— John Nevill, Esq; 5 Tite St, London SW3 4JU; 8 Radnor Cliff, Folkestone, Kent CT20 2JN (☎ 071 352 7368/0303 48403); Nevill Gallery, 43 St Peter's St, Canterbury, Kent CT1 2BG (☎ 0227 65291)

NEWBURY, Hon Mrs (Julia Elizabeth Heather); *née* Hamilton; da of 13 Lord Belhaven and Stenton; *b* 1956; *m* 1, 1975 (m dis) Richard Newbury; m 2, 1979, Stephen Hobbs; *Style*— The Hon Mrs Hobbs

NEWCOMB, Charles Buckle; s of Gerald Buckle Newcomb (d 1928), and Dorothy Lester, *née* Willis, MBE (d 1987); *b* 11 Sept 1926; *Educ* Epsom Coll; *m* 17 Nov 1970, Loretta Anne, da of Frank Porter (d 1988); *Career* CA; RASC 1944-48; ptnr: Jackson Pixley & Co 1960-75, Clark Pixley 1975-78; dir F & H Newcomb Ltd 1960-87, Glaxo Holdings plc 1983-88; former treas Rochester and Chatham Cons Assoc; Freeman City of London 1957, memb Worshipful Co of Coopers 1957; FCA 1951; *Recreations* golf; *Clubs* East India; *Style*— Charles Newcomb, Esq; Woodland House, Hawkhurst, Kent TN18 5EJ (☎ 0580 2189)

NEWEY, His Hon Judge John Henry Richard; QC (1970-); s of Lt-Col Thomas Henry Newey, ED (d 1983), and Irene Kathleen Mary Newey, JP (d 1989); *b* 20 Oct 1923; *Educ* Ellesmere Coll Shropshire, Queens Coll Cambridge (MA, LLM); *m* 31 July 1953, Mollie Patricia, da of Herbert Chalk (d 1982); 3 s (Robert b 1956, Guy b 1959, Michael b 1963), 2 da (Jane b 1962, Annabel b 1966); *Career* served Capt, Central India Horse, Indian Army 1942-47 in India, Middle East, Italy and Greece; called to the Bar Middle Temple 1948; bencher Middle Temple 1977, prosecuting counsel to PO SE circuit 1963-64, standing counsel to PO at Common Law 1964-70, personal injuries jr to Treasy 1968-70, dep chm Kent Quarter Sessions 1970-71, Commissary Gen of City and Diocese of Canterbury 1971-, rec 1972-80, Judge of Official Referees Court in London 1980-, Parly boundary cmmnr for Eng 1980-88; chm: Sevenoaks Soc 1962-65, Sevenoaks Div Cons Assoc 1965-68; alternate chm Burnhar and other Teachers Remuneration Ctees 1969-80, churchwarden St Luke's Sevenoaks 1970-73; FCIArb 1979; US Bronze Star 1944; *Recreations* excursions, history; *Style*— His Hon Judge Newey, QC; St David's, 68 The Drive, Sevenoaks, Kent TN13 3AF (☎ 0732 454597); Offical Referees' Court, St Dunstan's House, 133-137, Fetter Lane, London EC4A 1HD

NEWFIELD, Edward; s of Davis Newfield (d 1949), and Maud Adele Sylvia, *née* Sheppard; *b* 1 Dec 1945; *Educ* Woodhouse Sch London, Univ of Hull (LLB), UCL; *m* 1 June 1973 (m dis 1986), Margaret Mary, da of Capt Horrace Peter Lee-Roberts, of Faversham, Kent; 1 s (Thomas b 15 March 1977), 1 da (Louise b 1 May 1974); m 2, 10 July 1989, June Wendy, da of late Lawrence Green, of Faversham, Kent; 1 da (Natalie b 6 May 1990); *Career* barr 1969-73, princ local govt offr 1973-77, sr ptnr in firm of slrs 1977-; clerk: Preston Charities 1977-88, Queen Elizabeth Sch Govrs 1978-84; govr Bysingwood Primary Sch 1980-, chm Faversham Round Table 1982-83, treas Kentish Sail Assoc; memb Law Soc, FBIM 1983; *Recreations* yachting; *Clubs* RYA, Hollowshore Cruising; *Style*— Edward Newfield, Esq; Abion House, South Rd, Faversham, Kent; 130 Friern Park, London N12; Newfield & Co, 67 High St, Milton Regis, Kent (☎ 0795 427501)

NEWMAN, His Hon Judge Cyril Wilfred Francis; QC (1982); s of Wilfred James Newman (d 1970), and Cecilia Beatrice Lily Newman (d 1977); *b* 2 July 1937; *Educ* Sacred Heart Coll Droitwich, Lewes Co GS, Merton Coll Oxford (MA); *m* 1966, Winifred, da of Theodore de Kok, of Zürich, Switzerland; 2 s, 1 da; *Career* barr 1960; asst cmmr Parly Boundary Cmmn for Eng 1976, rec SE circuit 1982-, memb Criminal Injuries Compensation Bd 1985-86, circuit judge SE circuit 1986-; pres Oxford Univ Law Soc 1959, memb OU Middle Temple Soc 1959; *Recreations* sailing, country sports, skiing, swimming, opera, church music; *Clubs* Bar Yacht (hon treas 1973-88, rear cdre 1985); *Style*— His Hon Judge Cyril Newman, QC; Orlestone Grange, Orlestone, nr Ashford, Kent TN26 2EB (☎ 023 373 2306)

NEWMAN, Cncllr Jean Margaret; da of Sydney Henry Charters, OBE, of Woodlands Ave, Emsworth, Hants, and Maggie Rogan Charters (d 1988); *Educ* Wykeham House Fareham Hants; *m* 23 Oct 1954, Capt Douglas John Newman, OBE (Ben), s of John Gilbert Newman, of St Margarets Bay, Dover, Kent; 2 s (Peter John b 1958, David Alec b 1968), 2 da (Elisabeth Jean b 1961, Kirsty Helen b 1964); *Career* former civil servant Hendon and Chichester; govr Luddenham Sch, chm of Govrs Teynham C of E Sch; memb: Medway Community Health Cncl, Men of Kent and Kentish Men Lynsted, Exec Ctee SE Arts Cncl, Kent Rural Community Cncl, Royal Soc of St George Sittingbourne; dep chm Faversham Constituency Cons Assoc, Swale borough cncllr for the Teynham and Lynsted Ward 1982-, dep Mayor of Swale 1989-90 and 1990-91, chm Ospringe Parish Cncl; *Recreations* managing a small flock of geese, gardening, eating; *Style*— Cncllr Jean Newman; Little Brook Manor, Vicarage Lane, Ospringe, Faversham, Kent ME13 8XT (☎ 0795 532589)

NICE, Geoffrey; s of William Charles Nice, and Mahala Anne, *née* Tarryer (d 1982); *b* 21 Oct 1945; *Educ* St Dunstans Coll Catford, Keble Coll Oxford; *m* 1974, Philippa, da of Kemlo Abbot Cronin Gross, OBE, ERD; 3 da (Amelia b 1975, Taffa b 1976, Mahalah b 1980); *Career* barr, rec Crown Court 1987-, QC 1990; Parly candidate Dover (SDP/Lib Alliance) 1983 and 1987; *Recreations* music, tennis, skiing; *Style*— Geoffrey Nice, Esq; Manor Farm, Adisham, Canterbury (☎ 0304 840156); Farrars Building, Temple, London EC4 (☎ 071 583 9241)

NICHOLAS, Alan Peter; s of Dennis Leonard Albert Nicholas, of Eastbourne, Sussex, and Elsie Queenie, *née* Mason; *b* 1 June 1944; *Educ* Twickenham Tech Coll (HNC); *m* 7 March 1970, Annegret, da of Johannes Engelke (d 1966), of Hildesheim, Germany; 1 s (Martyn b 30 Jan 1978), 1 da (Clare b 20 Oct 1975); *Career* sales mangr Alderman & Ryder Ltd 1976-82, jt md Paterex Ltd 1986- (commercial dir 1982-86); *Recreations* badminton, gardening; *Style*— Alan Nicholas, Esq; Rosegarth, 54 Woodland Way, Bidborough, Tunbridge Wells, Kent TN4 0UY (☎ 0892 28831); Paterex Ltd, Cray Ave, Orpington, Kent BR5 3RR (☎ 0689 31555, fax 0689 27612, car tel 631579, telex 262717)

NICHOLLS, (Frank) Kim Ian; s of Frank Nicholls, DSO, MC (d 1979), of Loughton, Essex, and Nellie Hay, *née* Mills (d 1986); *b* 2 Sept 1923; *Educ* Sherborne, Univ of Glasgow; *m* 9 April 1946, Jean, da of Walter Sedgwick (d 1986), of Middlesbrough; 2 s (Peter Alastair b 1948, Mark Ian b 1959), 1 da (Rosamund Shane b 1951); *Career* navigator RAF 1941-46, sqdn cdr Air Cadets RAFVR 1966-78; Nicholls and Clark Ltd: trainee 1946-50, tport mangr 1950-56; tport mangr: North and West NAAFI 1962-63 (North 1956-59, Middle East 1959-62), various tport functions Ford Motor Co; chm Abbeyfield

Canterbury Soc; tstee: United Municipal Charities, United Parochial Charities; memb Men of Kent and Kentish Men Ctee Canterbury Div; cncllr Canterbury Cncl, Mayor of Canterbury 1987-88; *Recreations* fishing, flying, gardening; *Style—* Kim Nicholls, Esq; 13 Dane John, Canterbury, Kent CT1 2QU (☎ 0227 453958)

NICHOLS, Robin Anthony; s of Thomas George Nichols (d 1981), of Eastcote, Middx, and Irene Joan Buck; gs of Thomas George Nichols, OBE (despatches thrice, 1935); *b* 28 April 1944; *Educ* Pinner Co GS, City of London Coll for Chartered Bldg Soc Exams; *m* 5 March 1967, Paula Theresa, da of Joseph Severin Spiegelhalter (d 1984), of Wembley, Middx; 1 s (Grant Anthony b 1970), 1 da (Sarah Kate b 1973); *Career* md Greenwich Building Society 1981-, dir Building Society Ombudsman Co Ltd 1987; cncl memb Bldg Soc Assoc 1983, Bldg Soc Ombudsman 1987; govr Blackheath HS 1987-; FCBSI; *Recreations* sport, music, theatre, MENSA; *Style—* Robin Nichols, Esq; 15 Highfield Drive, Shortlands, Bromley, Kent BR2 0RX (☎ 081 460 3369); 279 Greenwich High Rd, London SE10 8NL (☎ 081 858 8212)

NICKLESS, Christopher John; yr s of Rev Canon Victor George Nickless, of Ford Place, Ford Lane, Wrotham Heath, and Grace Kathleen, *née* Hepburn-Whyte; *b* 17 Sept 1947; *Educ* King's Sch Rochester, Univ of Birmingham (BA); *m* 11 April 1987, Mairi, da of Lt-Col Robert Andrew Garden, of Naini, 164 St George's Rd, Sandwich; *Career* King's Sch Rochester: asst master 1968-82, dep master Jr Dept 1982-87, dep headmaster Jr Dept 1987-, headmaster Pre-Prep Sch 1988-; steward Cathedral Church of Christ and The Blessed Virgin Mary Rochester, govr RNLI, pres Borstal CC; ind memb Rochester CC St Margaret's Ward 1972; memb: Medway DC 1973, Medway Borough Cncl 1976 and 1979, Rochester upon Medway CC 1983 and 1987; *Recreations* cricket, music, gardening, walking; *Style—* Christopher Nickless, Esq; The Hawthorns, 121 Maidstone Rd, Chatham, Kent ME4 6JA (☎ 0634 841037); Rookwood, King Edward Rd, Rochester, Kent ME1 1UB (☎ 0634 829498)

NICOLSON, Nigel; MBE (1945); s of Hon Sir Harold Nicolson, KCVO, CMG, sometime MP Leics W (d 1968, the biographer, critic and broadcaster, 3 s of 1 Baron Carnock), and Hon 'Vita' (Victoria) Sackville-West, CH, JP (also a writer, author of The Edwardians), only child of 3 Baron Sackville; bro of late Benedict Nicolson, the art historian; hp to 1 cousin, 4 Baron Carnock; *b* 19 Jan 1917; *Educ* Eton, Balliol Coll Oxford; *m* 1953, Philippa, da of Sir Eustace Tennyson d'Eyncourt, 2 Bt; 1 s (Adam b 1957, m 1982 Olivia Fane), 2 da (Juliet, b 9 June 1954 and 1977 James Macmillan Scott (2 da, Clementina b 1981, Flora b 1985); Rebecca b 1963); *Career* dir Weidenfeld and Nicolson 1946-; MP (C) Bournemouth and Christchurch 1952-59; FRSL; author; *Books Incl:* Lord of the Isles (1969), Great Houses of Britain (1965), Harold Nicolson; Diaries and Letters 1930-39 (1966), 1939-45 (1967), 1945-62 (1968; ed 3 vols), Portrait of a Marriage (1973), Alex (Field Marshal Alexander of Tunis) (1973), Letters of Virginia Woolf (ed 6 vols 1975-1980), Mary Curzon (1977, Whitbread Prize); *Recreations* archaeology; *Clubs* Beefsteak; *Style—* Nigel Nicolson, Esq, MBE; Sissinghurst Castle, Cranbrook, Kent (☎ 0580 714239)

NIGHTINGALE, Heather Mary; da of Handley Nightingale (d 1970), and Anne, *née* Whitaker; *b* 11 March 1932; *Educ* Hamilton House Tunbridge Wells, Nightingale Sch St Thomas' Hosp, London Sch of Business; *Career* asst matron Wessex Neurological Centre Southampton 1969-71, sr nursing offr Western Hosp Southampton 1971-75, divnl nursing offr Acute Servs Salisbury 1975-79, area nurse personnel Kent AHA 1979-82; Canterbury and Thanet Health Authy: chief nursing offr 1982-, unit gen mangr for mental health 1986-; pres: Soroptimist Int GB and Ireland Canterbury Club 1986-87, SE England Div Union of Soroptimist of GB and Ireland 1989-90; govr Simon Langton Girls Sch Canterbury; memb Royal Coll of Nursing, IHSM; *Style—* Miss Heather Nightingale; 7 Richmond Gardens, Canterbury, Kent CT2 8ES (☎ 0227 769167); Regency Buildings, 3 Royal Crescent, Ramsgate, Kent CT11 9PF

NIGHTINGALE OF CROMARTY, Michael David; OBE (1960); Baron of Cromarty (feudal); s of Victor Russell John Nightingale (d 1951), of Wormshill, Kent, and Bathsheba, *née* Buhay (d 1942); *b* 6 Dec 1927; *Educ* Winchester, Wye Coll Univ of London (BSc), Magdalen Coll Oxford (B Litt); *m* 28 April 1956, Hilary Marion Olwen, da of John Eric Jones (d 1933), of Swansea; 2 s (John b 1960, Alexander b 1964), 3 da (Emma b 1957, Rebecca b 1958, Rachel b 1966); *Career* asst investmt mangr Anglo-Iranian Oil 1951-53, investmt advsr Univ of London 1954-66, dir Charterhouse Japhet Ltd 1965-70; chm: Anglo-Indonesian Corporation plc 1971-, The Chillington Corporation plc 1986-89, Anglo-Eastern Plantations plc, Thomas Seager Ltd; sec Museums Assoc and ed Museums Journal 1954-60, sec Museum Ctee Carnegie UK Tst 1954-60; memb: Advsy Cncl for Export of Works of Art 1954-60, Br Ctee Int Cncl of Museums 1956-60, Hollingbourn Rural Dist Cncl 1961-74, Canterbury Diocesan Advsy Ctee 1964-79, Kent CC 1973-77, Maidstone Borough Cncl 1973- (chm Planning Ctee 1973-77, ldr 1976-77), Exec Ctee SE Arts Assoc 1974-77, Area Archaeological Advsy Ctee SE England 1974-79; Panel of Chairmen Gen Synod C of E 1984-85 (memb 1979-85); chm: Churches Ctee of Kent Archaeological Soc 1973-, North Downs Soc 1983-; bd memb Cwlth Devpt Corp 1985-; Esquire Bedell Univ of London 1953-, dep Steward Royal Manor of Wye 1954-, Mayor of Maidstone 1984-85, warden Rochester Bridge 1989- (memb 1985-), pres Cobham New Coll 1989-, Lord of the Level of Romney Marsh, Lord of the Manors of Wormshill, Eastbridge and Bobbing; Freeman City of London; FSA (1956); *Recreations* antiquarian, musical; *Clubs* Athenaeum; *Style—* Michael Nightingale of Cromarty, OBE, FSA; Cromarty House, Ross and Cromarty (☎ 038 17 265); Wormshill Ct, Sittingbourne, Kent (☎ 062 784 235)

NIVEN, Sir (Cecil) Rex; CMG (1954), MC (1918); s of late Rev Dr George Cecil Niven, and Jeanne Niven, of Torquay, Devon; *b* 20 Nov 1898; *Educ* Blundell's Sch Tiverton, Balliol Coll Oxford (MA); *m* 1, 1925, Dorothy Marshall (d 1977), da of David Marshall Mason, formerly MP Coventry and E Edinburgh (d 1956); 1 da (and 1 da decd); m 2, 1980, Pamela Mary Catterall, da of George Catterall Leach (d 1937), of Sibton Park Kent; *Career* 2 Lt RFA 1918-19, Corpl Lagos Def Force 1939-42; admin offr and finally sr resident Nigeria 1921-54, speaker N Nigeria Assembly 1953-60, special cmmr N Nigeria 1960-62; dep sec Southwark Diocesan Office 1962-70; memb: cncl RSA, Paddington Hospital's Mgmnt Ctee 1962-72, Cncl Imperial Soc of Knights Bachelor 1966-, Gen Synod of C of E 1975-80; patron Deal Protection Soc, fndr pres NE Kent Br Oxford Soc 1986-; FRGS 1919, life memb BRCS 1983; kt 1960; *Books* author of 13 books on Africa incl A Nigerian Kaleidoscope (1983); *Clubs* Royal Over Seas League; *Style—* Sir Rex Niven, CMG, MC; 12 Archery Sq, Walmer, Kent CT14 7HP (☎ 0304 361863)

NIX, Prof John Sydney; s of John William Nix (d 1968), of SE London, and Eleanor Elizabeth, *née* Stears (d 1978); *b* 27 July 1927; *Educ* Brockley Co Sch, Univ Coll of the South-West (BSc), Univ of Cambridge (MA); *m* 7 Oct 1950, Mavis Marian, da of George Cooper, of Teignmouth; 1 s (Robert David John b 10 Jan 1955), 2 da (Alison Mary b 23 July 1952, Jennifer Ann b 7 May 1959); *Career* Instr Lt RN 1948-51; sr res offr Farm Econs Branch Univ of Cambridge 1957-61 (1951-61); Wye Coll London: farm mgmnt liaison offr and lectr 1961-70, sr tutor 1970-72, sr lectr 1972-75, head Farm Business Unit 1974-89, reader 1975-82, prof of farm business mgmnt (personal chair) 1982-89, emeritus prof 1989-; fndr memb Farm Mgmnt Assoc 1965, prog advsr Southern TV 1966-81; chm: Educn Ctee Farm Management (CMA) 1971-, Bd of Farm Mgmnt (BIM) 1979-81; Nat Award for Outstanding Contrib to Advancement of Mgmnt in Agric Indust BIM 1982, author of numerous articles for jls, memb many nat study gps and advsy ctees; CBIM 1983, FRSA 1984, FRAgS 1985; *Books* Farm Planning and Control (with C S Barnard, 2 edn 1979), Farm Mechanisation For Profit (with W Butterworth, 1983), Land and Estate Management (2 edn 1989), Farm Management Pocketbook (21 edn 1990); *Recreations* theatre, cinema, travel, rugby, cricket; *Clubs* Farmers; *Style—* Prof John Nix; Wye Coll, Wye, Ashford, Kent TN25 5AH (☎ 0233 812 401, fax 0233 813 320, telex 96118)

NOBLE, David Brunel; s and h of Sir Marc Brunel Noble, 5 Bt, *qv*; *b* 25 Dec 1961; *m* 26 Sept 1987, Virginia Ann, yr da of late Roderick Lancaster Wetherall, MBE, of Platt Oast, St Mary's Platt, Kent; 2 s (Roderick Lancaster Brunel b 8 Dec 1988, Alexander David b 28 Feb 1990); *Style—* David Noble, Esq

NOBLE, Sir Marc Brunel; 5 Bt (UK 1902), of Ardmore and Ardardan Noble, Cardross, Co Dumbarton; s of Sir Humphrey Brunel Noble, 4 Bt, MBE, MC (d 1968, whose mother Celia Brunel James, was gda of Isambard Kingdom Brunel, the celebrated Victorian engineer), of Walwick Hall, Hexham, Northumberland, and Celia, *née* Weigall (d 1982); *b* 8 Jan 1927; *Educ* Eton; *m* 27 Jan 1956, Jennifer Lorna, yr da of late John Mein-Austin, of Flint Hill, W Haddon, Rugby, Northants; 2 s, 1 da (and 1 da decd); *Heir* s, David Brunel Noble, *qv*; *Career* Maj (ret) King's Dragoon Gds (cmmnd 1947), transfd 1 Royal Dragoons 1958; Cwlth cmmr Scout Assoc 1972-, chm Ctee of Cncl Scout Assoc 1979-80; co pres Kent Scout Cncl, govr Sibton Park Sch; High Sheriff of Kent 1985-86; *Recreations* shooting, travel; *Clubs* Cavalry and Guards; *Style—* Maj Sir Marc Noble, Bt; Deerleap House, Knockholt, Sevenoaks, Kent TN14 7NP (☎ 0959 33222)

NOLAN, Hon Mr Justice; Hon Sir Michael Patrick Nolan; yr s of James Thomas Nolan and Jane, *née* Walsh; *b* 10 Sept 1928; *Educ* Ampleforth, Wadham Coll Oxford; *m* 1953, Margaret, yr da of Alfred Noyes, CBE, the poet, by his w Mary, da of Capt Jasper Graham Mayne, CBE, of Gidleigh Park, Chagford, Devon, by his w Cecily; 1 s, 4 da; *Career* serv RA 1947-49 and TA 1949-55; High Court Judge (Queen's Bench) 1982-; presiding judge Western Circuit 1985-88; rec Crown Ct 1975-82, QC 1968, QC (NI) 1974, called to the Bar NI 1974, called to the Bar Middle Temple 1953, memb Bar Cncl 1973-74, memb Senate Inns of Ct and Bar 1974-81, treas 1977-79; memb Sandilands Ctee Inflation Accounting 1973-75; memb Governing Body Convent of Sacred Heart Woldingham 1973-82, govr Combe Bank Sch 1974-82; kt 1982; *Style—* The Hon Mr Justice Nolan; Royal Courts of Justice, Strand, London WC2A 2LL

NORFOLK, Cdr Edward Lionel Stanley; JP (Maidstone 1985-); s of Capt Stanley Edward Norfolk, RN (d 1980), of Sevenoaks, and Enid Margaret, *née* Powell (d 1988); *b* 6 Aug 1930; *Educ* Downside, RNC Dartmouth, RNC

Greenwich; *m* 5 Dec 1957, Janet Sykes, da of Henry Leslie Wilson (d 1964), of Pannal, Harrogate; 1 s (Robert Michael Stanley b 13 Oct 1967), 1 da (Charlotte McDowell b 30 July 1964); *Career* Cdr RN ret 1972; chartered sec 1973, CA 1976, ptnr Day Smith & Hunter Maidstone 1979-84, princ Norfolk Chartered Accountant 1984-; memb: Maidstone Health Authy 1984-90, Kent Probation Ctee 1982-85, Detling Parish Cncl 1974-88; chm: Mgmnt Ctee Fleming House Probation Hostel Maidstone 1977-82, Homeless & Offender Projects & Enterprises Ltd 1990-; MBIM; *Clubs* Naval & Military, Maidstone; *Style*— Cdr Edward Norfolk, JP, RN

NORRIS, Dr Alexander Donald Craig; s of Dr Donald Craig Norris (d 1968), of 53 Portland Place, London, and Hélène, *née* Righthouse (d 1957); *b* 2 April 1936; *Educ* Charterhouse, Trinity Coll Cambridge (MA), London Hosp Med Coll (MB BChir); *m* 19 Sept 1964, Beryl, da of Harry Marshall (d 1943), of Rochester; 2 s (Julian Alexander Craig b 1965, Adrian Charles Douglas b 1968); *Career* conslt physician SE Kent Health Dist 1971-, hon conslt Cardiac Dept Guy's 1980-; memb: BMA, Br Cardiac Soc; FRCP; *Recreations* music, skiing, photography; *Style*— Dr Alexander Norris; Stone Stile Oast, Selling, Faversham, Kent ME13 9SD (☎ 0227 730539); BUPA St Saviours Hospital, Seabrook Rd, Hythe, Kent (☎ 0303 265581)

NORTH, Hon Charles Evelyn; s of 8 Earl of Guilford (d 1949); *b* 1918; *Educ* Eton, Univ of London (BSc); *m* 1, 1942 (m dis 1957), Maureen O'Callaghan, da of Maj F C B Baldwin; 1 s, 1 da; m 2, 1959, Joan Aston, da of Maj F B Booker (d 1954), of Edenmore House Raheny, Co Dublin; *Career* PO RAFVR 1940, Flt Lt 1942, on staff Air Miny and MAP; dir J M W North and Co Ltd London, professional engr DOE, ret 1983; memb Inst of Advanced Motorists, MIMechE; *Recreations* rural life, riding, steam engines; *Style*— The Hon Charles E North; Park End House, Eythorne, Dover, Kent (☎ 0304 830368)

NORTH, Michael Alexander; s of Wilfrid Samuel North (d 1967), and Alice Kathleen, *née* Cook; *b* 22 Dec 1945; *Educ* Chigwell Sch Essex, Oriel Coll Oxford (MA); *m* 19 Jan 1974, Susan Elizabeth, da of Oliver Eustace Tidman, MBE, of 9 Field Close, Bromley, Kent; 2 da (Gemma Alexandra b 1976, Laura Elizabeth b 1979); *Career* admitted slr 1972; NP 1987; memb Bromley C of C; *Recreations* squash, tennis; *Clubs* Utd Oxford and Cambridge Univ; *Style*— Michael North, Esq; Clarkson Wright & Jakes, Valiant House, 12 Knoll Rise, Orpington, Kent BR6 0PG (☎ 0689 871621, fax 0689 878537)

NORTH, Lord; Piers Edward Brownlow; s and h of 9 Earl of Guilford, DL; *b* 9 March 1971; *Style*— Lord North; Waldershare Park, Dover, Kent

NORTHBOURNE, 5 Baron (UK 1884); Sir Christopher George Walter James; 6 Bt (GB 1791); only s of 4 Baron Northbourne (d 1982), of Northbourne Court, Kent, and Katharine Louise (d 1980), yr da of late George Nickerson, of Boston, Mass, and his w Ellen (d 1950), who m as her 2 husb Rear Adm Hon Sir Horace Hood, KCB, MVO, DSO (ka Jutland 1916), and was by him mother of 6 and 7 Viscounts Hood; *b* 18 Feb 1926; *Educ* Eton, Magdalen Coll Oxford (MA); *m* 29 July 1959, Marie-Sygne, *qv*, da of Henri Louis Claudel and gda of Paul Claudel, poet and diplomat; 3 s (Hon Charles Walter Henri b 14 June 1960, Hon Anthony Christopher Walter Paul b 14 Jan 1963, Hon Sebastian Richard Edward Cuthbert b 7 March 1966), 1 da (Hon Ophelia Mary Katherine Christine Aliki b 23 Aug 1969); *Heir* eldest s, Hon Charles James b 14 June 1960; *Career* co dir sits as Ind in House of Lords; FRICS; *Clubs* Brooks's, Farmers', Royal Yacht Squadron; *Style*— The Rt Hon the Lord Northbourne; Coldharbour, Northbourne, Kent (☎ 0304 611277); 11 Eaton Place, SW1 (☎ 071 235 6790); Evistones, Otterburn, Northumberland; office: Betteshanger Farms Ltd and Kent Salads Ltd, Betteshanger, Deal, Kent (☎ 0304 611281)

NORTHBOURNE, Baroness; Marie-Sygne; da of Henri Louis Claudel, of France, and Christine, *née* Diplarakos; *b* 13 Feb 1937; *Educ* Lyceé Francais de Bruxelles, Sorbonne; *m* 29 July 1959, 5 Baron Northbourne, *qv*; 3 s, 1 da; *Career* dir Invicta Radio 1984-; chm of govrs Northbourne Park Sch 1979, memb Cncl Univ of Kent at Canterbury 1984, tstee Kent Fndn 1987, chm Kent Community Housing Tst 1990; *Style*— The Rt Hon Lady Northbourne; Coldharbour, Northbourne, Deal, Kent (☎ 0304 611 277); 11 Eaton Place, London SW1 (☎ 071 235 6790); Invicta Radio, Invicta Sound plc, 15 Station Rd East, Canterbury, Kent (☎ 0227 767 661, car tel 0860 464 127)

NOTHARD, Malcolm Albert; s of Albert Edward Nothard, of Bromley, Kent (d 1985), and Rose, *née* Woodruff (d 1949); *b* 24 June 1938; *Educ* Bromley GS, Open Univ (BA); *m* 6 Feb 1965, Carol Hilda, da of Thomas Anthoney (d 1982), of London; 2 da (Tanya b 1968, Sarah b 1971); *Career* Nat Serv RAF Habbaniya Iraq and Nicosia Cyprus 1956-58; dir Shephard & Co Insurance Brokers (ptnr 1981-88); govr Sutton at Hone C of E Primary Sch, tstee Leigh City Technol Coll Dartford, vice chm Kent Assoc of Dist Cncls, vice pres Kent Assoc of Parish Cncls, parish cncllr 1972-, borough cncllr 1976- (leader 1983-), chm Orchard Bd; ACII 1962; *Recreations* travel, photography, reading; *Style*— Malcolm Nothard, Esq; 24 Cedar Drive, Sutton At Hone, Dartford, Kent DA4 9EN (☎ 0322 863470, fax 0322 864886); Shephard & Co Ltd, 29 London Rd, Bromley, Kent BR1 1DH (☎ 081 460 9999, fax 081 464 6665); Dartford Borough Council, Civic Centre, Home Gardens, Dartford DA1 1DR (☎ 0322 343434, fax 0322 343422)

NUTLEY, Ronald Frank; s of Walter Francis Nutley (d 1987), of Tonbridge, Kent, and Lucy, *née* Sabin (d 1962); *b* 17 April 1932; *Educ* Sussex Road Sch Tonbridge, London Coll of Printing; *m* 22 June 1957, Patricia, da of Charles James Percy Waghorn (d 1988), of 2 Priory St, Tonbridge, Kent; 1 da (Jennifer Jane b 1963); *Career* signaller 1 Bn Queen's Own Royal West Kent served Malaya 1950-52; BR engr, works and Personnel dir Brown Knight & Truscott Ltd 1972-80 (gen mgmnt 1955-80), md David Evans & Co, dir Sekers Int plc 1982, chief exec Sekers Silks Ltd 1986, dir Richard Allan Scarves, ret with consultancies for the Food and Agric Orgn UN and the UK Silk Indust; MIOP, FBIM, FInstD; *Recreations* reading, art and design, jogging, swimming, tennis, golf, community service; *Clubs* Tonbridge Lions, IOD, RAC; *Style*— Ronald Nutley, Esq; Aalsmeer, 13 Higham Lane, Tonbridge, Kent TN10 4JB (☎ 0732 351 017)

O

O'BRIEN, Michael Anthony; s of Dr Donal O'Brien, and Patricia Mary, *née* Dowdall; *b* 7 Sept 1950; *Educ* The Oratory Sch Reading, Trinity Coll Dublin (BA, BAI); *m* 7 Sept 1971, Robin Patricia Antonia, da of Roger Greene, (d 1954), of Wellington Quay, Dublin; 4 da (Louise b 1974, Pippa b 1976, Tara b 1977, Alice b 1987); *Career* CA; asst dir C T Bowring & Co (Lloyd's Insurance Brokers) 1975-78, gp fin controller Mining Investmt Corpn Ltd 1978-79, chief exec Anglo Int Mining Corpn Ltd 1979-82; chm and chief exec: Bannertill Ltd, KDM Leasing Ltd, Leisure Projects Int Ltd, Loupiptar plc, Mineral and Energy Resources Corp Ltd, Mineral and Energy (UK) Ltd; FCA; *Recreations* horses, ponies, swimming, tennis; *Clubs* Br Show Pony Soc, S of England Agric Soc; *Style—* Michael O'Brien, Esq; 57 High St, Tunbridge Wells, Kent TN1 1XU (☎ 0892 511866, fax 0892 548440)

O'BRIEN, (Charles) Michael; s of Richard Alfred O'Brien, CBE (d 1970), of Beckenham, Kent, later of Queensland, Aust, and Nora, *née* McKay (1956); *b* 17 Jan 1919; *Educ* Westminster, Ch Ch Oxford (MA); *m* 4 Nov 1950, Joyce, da of Rupert Henry Prebble (d 1956), of Beckenham, Kent; 2 s (Philip b 1952, Christopher b 1954); *Career* WWII, cmmnd 2 Lt RA 1940, Capt RA Burma (despatches), demobbed 1946; actuary; asst actuary Equitable Life Assurance Society 1952, gen mangr and actuary Royal National Pension Fund for Nurses 1955-84, dir M & G Assurance Group Ltd 1984-; govr Westminster Sch 1972-, memb Limpsfield Common Mgmnt Ctee NT, chm Federated Pension Servs 1983-89; FIA 1949 (hon sec 1961-63, pres 1976-78), FPMI; *Recreations* shooting, training and working gundogs; *Style—* Michael O'Brien, Esq; The Boundary, Goodley Stock, Crockham Hill, Edenbridge, Kent TN8 6TA (☎ 0732 866349)

O'CONNOR, Rev Canon (Brian) Michael McDougal; s of Brian McDougal O'Connor (d 1985), of Hove, Sussex, and Beryl Mary, *née* Kinmond; *b* 20 June 1942; *Educ* Lancing, Coll of Law Guildford, St Catherine's Coll Cambridge (BA, MA), Cuddesdon Theol Coll Oxford; *m* 6 Jan 1968, Alison Margaret, da of Harry Gordon Tibbutt (d 1982), FSA, of Kempston, Bedford; 2 s (Andrew b 1972, Simon b 1972); *Career* admitted slr 1964; asst curate St Andrew Headington 1969-72, vicar Merton Coll Oxford 1972-76, sec Oxford Diocesan Pastoral Ctee 1972-79, vicar Rainham Kent 1979-, rural dean Gillingham 1981-88; memb: Gen Synod 1975- (Standing Ctee Gen 1985-), Crown Appts Cmmn 1987-, Anglican Consultative Cncl 1989-; hon canon Rochester Cathedral 1988-; sch govr; *Clubs* National Liberal; *Style—* The Rev Canon Michael O'Connor; The Vicarage, 80 Broadview Ave, Rainham, Gillingham, Kent ME8 9DE (☎ 0634 31538)

O'DONOGHUE, Michael John; s of Desmond O'Donoghue (d 1971), of Leicester, and Sarah Ann, *née* Ward; *b* 30 Nov 1934; *Educ* Wyggeston Sch Leicester, Univ of Cambridge (MA); *m* 1, June 1959 (m dis 1967), Janet Rose, *née* Wheeler; m 2, 26 Feb 1968, (Elizabeth) Anne Hawkins, da of Henry John Hawkins Borley, CBE, of Felpham, Sussex; 1 s (Michael Peter Desmond b 5 Oct 1971), 2 da (Lucy Sarah Anne b 6 Nov 1967, Charlotte Clare Mary b 7 Oct 1969); *Career* curator: Nat Library of Scot 1960-62, Br Museum 1962-82, Br Library Sci Technol and Indust 1982-90; lectr in gemmology City of London Poly 1967-, free lance mineralogist and gemstone consIt 1990-, gemstone consIt UN Indust Devpt Orgn, dir Precious Stone Trg Servs Ltd 1980-; memb Central London Samaritans 1967-, pastoral asst St John's Church Sevenoaks 1989- (ed About St John's monthly community newsheet); ed: Gemmological Newsletter, Synthetic Crystals Newsletter, Geological Information Gp Newsletter; past ed Gems and Mineral Realm; FGA (cncl memb), fell Geological Soc of London, lectr Sotheby's Looking at Jewellery Course, ldr field trips to investigate mineral deposits and lecture on man-made crystals in Pakistan Japan Denmark Finland USSR Sweden Norway Hungary Austria Yugoslavia Poland Turkey Greece USA (o lectr France Italy Germany Hong Kong); memb: Mineralogical Soc of GB, Mineralogical Assoc of America, Deutsche Gemmologische Gesellschaft (past cncl memb), Br Iris Soc, Russell Soc (mineralogical), author of over 100 papers in scientific jls and eleven monographs; *Books* incl Encyclopedia of Minerals and Gemstones (1976), Identifying Man-Made Gemstones (1983), Quartz (1987), Gemstones (1988), Field Guide to Rocks and Minerals (1990), A Dictionary of Anonymous and Pseudonymous Publications in English 1475-1640 (jt author); *Recreations* organ, botany and horticulture; *Style—* Michael O'Donoghue, Esq; 7 Hillingdon Ave, Sevenoaks, Kent TN13 3RB (☎ 0732 453503)

O'DONOVAN, Prof Katherine; da of Prof John O'Donovan, TD (d 1982), of Dublin, Ireland, and Kathleen, *née* Mahon; *b* 7 Feb 1942; *Educ* Nat Univ of Ireland (BCL), Faculté de Droit Univ De Strasbourg, Harvard Law Sch (LLM), Univ of Kent (PhD); *m* 5 June 1971, Julian, s of F Victor Davey; 1 da (Julia Davey b 5 Nov 1979); *Career* lectr in law 1965-87 (Queen's Univ of Belfast, Univ of Sussex, Univ of Kent); prof of law Univ of Kent 1987 (formerly lectr); visiting appts: HSI Univ Ethiopia, Univ of Malaya, Univ of Hong Kong; sch govr Canterbury; memb: Nat Tst, Specialist Panel CNAA, RSPB, Cncl SPTL, Royal Cwlth Soc, Women's Legal Defence Fund; *Books* Sexual Divisions in Law (1985), Equality and Sex Discrimination Law (1988); *Recreations* child rearing, writing, aerobics; *Clubs* Cwlth Tst, Hong Kong; *Style—* Prof Katherine O'Donovan; University of Kent, Rutherford College, Canterbury, Kent CT2 7NX (☎ 0227 764000)

O'REILLY, Elizabeth Janet Eve; da of Lt Cdr Douglas de Valder Duff, DSC (d 1978), and Janet, *née* Wallace (d 1959); *b* 23 Aug 1936; *Educ* King Edward VI Girls' GS Louth, Northern Cos Trg Coll of Domestic Sci Newcastle on Tyne, Leeds Gen Infirmary Dietetic Sch Leeds (Dip in Dietetics); *m* 12 June 1965, Joseph Michael O'Reilly (d 1972), s of James Emmet O'Reilly (d 1932); *Career* chief dietician: W Middx Hosp 1961-64 and 1967-70, Central Middx Hosp 1973-75; dietician: Hong Kong 1964-65, Br Diabetic Assoc 1970-73; dist dietician Canterbury & Thanet Health Authy 1975-; memb Br Dietetic Assoc 1959; *Books* Measure for Measure Diabetic Cookery (1973); *Recreations* reading and burmese cats; *Style—* Mrs Elizabeth O'Reilly; Thanet District General Hospital, St Peters Rd, Margate, Kent (☎ 0843 225544 x 2306)

O'TOOLE, Kenneth; JP; s of Thomas O'Toole, of London, and Nancy Alice, *née* Bright; *b* 23 March 1935; *Educ* St Clement Danes GS London, Chatham House GS Ramsgate; *m* 30 April 1960, Pamela Christina; 2 s (Kevin b 1961, Michael b 1962); *Career* surveyor Ordnance Survey to 1957, cartographical draughtsman France 1957-60, estate agent 1960-90; sch govr; treas of Lest We Forget Margate; *Style—* Kenneth O'Toole, Esq, JP; 62 Royal Esplanade, Westbrook, Margate, Kent CT9 5ET (☎ 0843 34534); Benefield & Cornford, Town Hall Buildings, Westgate-on-Sea, Kent CT8 8RG (☎ 0843 31010)

OCKENDEN, Brig Robert Vaughan (Rob); CBE (1982, OBE 1977); s of William Ockenden (d 1983), of Chigwell, Essex, and Norah Vaughan, *née* Paterson (d 1981); *b* 14 April 1933; *Educ* Chigwell Sch, RMA; *m* 13 April 1963, Patricia Alice Walker Taylor, da of Robert Cauwood (d 1987), of Wheal Vor, Cornwall; 1 s (Paul b 1967), 1 da (Jessica b 1969); *Career* cmmnd 2 RTR 1953, Col Staff Offr to QMG 1979-82, Col Staff Offr to SACEUR 1983-85, dir Def Operational Requirements 1985-88; chief exec NRA 1988-; FBIM 1988; *Recreations* the countryside, bird watching, gardening, motoring; *Clubs* Army and Navy; *Style—* Brig Rob Ockenden, CBE; Glovers Cottage, Faversham Rd, Lenham, Kent; National Rifle Assoc, Bisley Camp, Brookwood, Woking, Surrey (☎ 0483 797777, fax 0483 797 285)

ODGERS, Graeme David William; s of William Arthur Odgers (d 1950), and Elizabeth Minty, *née* Rennie (d 1987); *b* 10 March 1934; *Educ* St John's Coll Johannesburg, Gonville and Caius Coll Cambridge, Harvard Business Sch (MBA); *m* 1957, Diana Patricia, *née* Berge; 1 s (John), 2 da (Mary, Juliet) and 1 da decd; *Career* dir Keith Shipton & Co Ltd 1965-72, chm Odgers & Co (Mgmnt Consits) 1970-74, C T Bowring (Insurance) Holdings Ltd 1972-74, dir Indust Devpt Unit DOI 1974-77, assoc dir (fin) GEC 1977-78, gp md Tarmac plc 1983-86 (gp fin dir 1979-83); BT: pt/t memb bd 1983-86, UK govt dir 1984-86, dep chm and chief fin offr 1986-87, gp md 1987-90; non exec dir: Dalgety 1987-, National and Provincial Building Society; chief exec Alfred McAlpine plc 1990-; *Recreations* golf; *Clubs* City of London, Wildernesse; *Style—* Graeme Odgers, Esq; Brome House, High St, W Malling, Kent ME19 6NE

OGLEY, Robert; s of John Roberts Ogley (d 1974), of Sevenoaks, Kent, and Florence Mary, *née* Reardon (d 1982); *b* 15 July 1939; *Educ* Sevenoaks Sch; *m* 31 Oct 1966 (sep 1981), Rosemary Lucy; 2 da (Caroline Sarah b 12 Nov 1966, Elizabeth Claire b 8 Sept 1969); partner, Fern Flynn; *Career* journalist 1956-89, ed Sevenoaks Chronicle 1969-89, author and publisher 1987- (raising over £60,000 for conservation appeals), Kent Journalist of Year Special Award 1988; memb Rotary Club Sevenoaks 1976-; *Books* In the Wake of The

Hurricane (1987, 1988), Hurricane Gilbert (co-author, 1989), Eye on the Hurricane (1989), Biggin on the Bump - The Most Famous Fighter Station in the World (1990); *Recreations* cricket, cycling, walking, swimming, gardening, travel; *Clubs* Buckhurst CC (fndr 1956); *Style*— Robert Ogley, Esq; (fax 0959 65365)

OLIVEY, Alan Keith; s of Hugh Norman Olivey (d 1980), of Upper Norwood, London, and Kathleen, *née* Mills; *b* 14 Oct 1947; *Educ* Heath Clark GS Croydon; *m* 11 Sept 1971, Janet Mary, da of Raymond Edgar Crewes Hutton, of Beckenham, Kent; 1 s (Richard b 1981), 1 da (Louise b 1977); *Career* CA; Sydenham Snowden Nicholson & Co 1964-71, ptnr Ernst & Young 1980- (joined 1971); FCA 1970, ATII 1970; *Recreations* badminton, gardening, philately, photography; *Style*— Alan Olivey, Esq; 75 Elwill Way, Beckenham, Kent BR3 2RY (☎ 081 658 1519); Becket House, 1 Lambeth Palace Rd, London SE1 7EU (☎ 071 931 3293, fax 071 928 1345, telex 885234 ERNSLO G)

OLSEN, (James) Wilfred; s of August Mauritz Olsen (d 1957), of East Sheen, London, and Ellen, *née* Lyche (d 1959); *b* 6 Feb 1920; *Educ* Kings Coll Sch Wimbledon; *m* 28 Feb 1953, Georgina Frances; 2 s (Roger, Jeremy); *Career* Lt (Special Branch) RNVR 1940-46, Naval Intelligence Div Admty 1940-45, SO (Intelligence) Kristiansand S Norway 1945; sec: D & W Gibbs Ltd (Unilever) 1948-51, Hudson & Knight Ltd (Unilever) 1951-55; former chief accountant Associated Newspapers Ltd; chm PO Advsy Ctee Bromley, former chm Bromley and Dist Consumers Gp, local referee CAs Benevolent Assoc, memb Knights of St George; Liveryman Worshipful Co of CAs 1980; FCA 1947, ACIS 1948; Christian X Freedom Medal (Denmark) 1945; *Recreations* bridge, consumerism, caravanning; *Clubs* Royal Over-Seas League; *Style*— Wilfred Olsen, Esq; Correnden, 4 Waldegrave Rd, Bromley, Kent BR1 2JP (☎ 081 467 5218)

OPPEN, Richard John Stuart; s of Arthur Harrie Oppen (d 1976), and Muriel Evelyn, *née* Dent (d 1984); *b* 29 Jan 1937; *Educ* Dulwich, City of London Sch; *m* 1 June 1963, Wendy, da of Leslie William Day Suffield (d 1979); 1 s (James b 11 July 1969), 1 da (Lucy b 27 Jan 1972); *Career* Nat Serv 3 Carabiniers (3DG) 1955-57; dir Galbraiths Ltd 1984-88, md Berge of CIA (UK) Ltd 1989-; Freeman City of London 1980, Liveryman Worshipful Co of Shipwrights 1982; *Recreations* country pursuits; *Clubs* Naval & Military; *Style*— Richard Oppen, Esq; 1 Clarendon Way, Chislehurst, Kent (☎ 0689 25253); 47 Albermarle St, London W1 (☎ 071 499 3186, fax 071 495 4808, telex 261675)

ORAM, Daphne Blake; da of James Oram, MBE, JP (d 1964), of Devizes, Wiltshire, and Ida Murton Talbot (d 1972); *b* 31 Dec 1925; *Educ* Sherborne; *Career* music balancer BBC 1943-57, co-fndr and dir BBC Radiophonic Workshop 1958; dir: Oramics Studio 1959-, Essconic Ltd 1959-75; visiting lectr: Morley Coll London 1959, Christ Church Coll Canterbury 1982-89; Gulbenkian Fndn Awards 1962 and 1965, Arts Cncl bursary 1986, RVW Tst 3 year grant 1986-89; lectures and concerts: Edinburgh Festival, Mermaid Theatre, Inst of Physics, various univs and schs; inventor oramics (graphic sound); various compositions for film, TV, radio, ballet; memb: Music Ctee Arts Cncl 1968-78, Mgmnt Ctee Performing Right Soc London (Members Fund); *Books* An Individual Note of Music, Sound and Electronics; *Recreations* megalithic archaeology, reading, animals; *Style*— Daphne Oram; Tower Folley, Fairseat, Wrotham, Sevenoaks, Kent TN15 7JR

ORMEROD, Brig Denis Leonard; CBE (1976, MBE 1950); s of Harold Eric Ormerod, CBE (d 1959), and Kathleen Mary, *née* Bourke (d 1957); *b* 17 Feb 1922; *Educ* Downside; *m* 7 Oct 1950, Frances Mary Shewell, da of Brig Charles Edward Francis Turner, CBE, DSO, of Wadhurst, E Sussex; 2 s (Giles b 1957, Jonathan b 1962), 6 da (Jennifer (Mrs P Tolhurst) b 1951, Julia (Mrs A Wells) b 1953, Teresa (Mrs M Bromley Gardner) b 1959, Jessica b 1960, Clare (Mrs A Torrance) b 1964, Katherine b 1968); *Career* cmmnd 1941 2 KEO Gurkhas (IA) served in India, Italy, Greece 1941-47, transferred to RIF 1947, served in Palestine, Egypt 1947-48, Malaya 1948-50 (seconded to 1/2 Gurkhas), (despatches 1949), Regt Serv RIF NI, BAOR, Berlin, Tripoli 1950-60, RN Staff Coll 1960-61, Staff Sch of Inf 1961-63, CO 1 Bn RIF 1965-67 (BAOR, UK, Swaziland, Bechuanaland, Aden), Asst Mil Sec Southern Cmd, Army Strategic Cmd 1967-69, Col GS MOD 1969-71, Cmd Ulster Def Regt (11 Bns) 1971-73 (despatches 1973), Brig Inf 1 (BR) Corps 1973-76, sec NW England and IOM TA and VR Assoc 1976-87; DL Merseyside 1983-87; *Recreations* country pursuits, horses, music, gardening; *Clubs* Rhinefield Polo; *Style*— Brig Denis Ormerod, CBE; Kirkbank House, High Halden, Kent TN26 2JD (☎ 023 3850 249)

ORSON, Rasin Ward; CBE (1985); s of Rasin Nelson Orson, and Blanche, *née* Hyre; *b* 16 April 1927; *Educ* Stratford GS, LSE (BSc); *m* 1, 1950, Marie Goodenough; 2 s; m 2, 1979, Lesley Jean Vallance; *Career* memb The Electricity Cncl 1976-88; dir Chloride Silent Power Ltd 1974-88; COMPIEE; *Style*— Rasin Orson, Esq, CBE; The Old Garden, Dunorlan Park, Tunbridge Wells TN2 3QA (☎ 0892 24027)

OSBORNE, Andrew Harold; s of Rev John Andrew Osborne (d 1972), and Margret Ethel, *née* Hartley Sharpe (d 1988); *b* 10 March 1931; *Educ* Sir Roger Manwoods Sch Sandwich, Canterbury Coll of Art Sch of Architecture; *m* 15 Oct 1955, Ann, da of George William Smith (d 1974); 2 s (Simon Andrew b 25 Feb 1959, David William b 9 Sept 1962, 1 da (Ruth Ann (twin) b 9 Sept 1962); *Career* Nat Serv RE 1955-57; sr architect CWS Ltd 1954-65, princ architect Canterbury City Cncl 1965-71, architect Historic Bldgs Div of Planning Dept Kent CC 1971-74, dep borough planning offr Maidstone Borough Cncl 1974-87 (ret); planning conslt Lambert and Foster 1987-; fndr memb Faversham Soc 1961 (hon architect until 1967); memb: Faversham Borough Cncl 1968-74, Swale Borough Cncl 1974-86, Faversham Town Cncl 1974-88; tstee: Faversham Municipal Charities 1972-, Bensteds Charity 1988-; govr QE Sch Faversham 1978-, chm Faversham Conservation Advsy Ctee 1980-86, Mayor of Faversham 1987-88, hon alderman of Borough of Swale; ARIBA; *Recreations* sailing; *Clubs* Kent Trust for Nature Conservation; *Style*— Andrew H Osborne, Esq; 3 Priory Rd, Davington, Faversham, Kent ME13 7EJ (☎ 0795 533244); Lambert and Foster Ltd, 77 Commercial Rd, Paddock Wood, Kent TN12 6DR (☎ 0892 832325, fax 0892 834700)

OSMOND, Lady; Olivia Sybil; *née* Wells; da of Ernest Edward Wells, JP, (d 1948), of Kegworth, Leics, and Olivia Maud, *née* Orton (d 1956); *Educ* St Elphins Sch Darley Dale, Newnham Coll Cambridge (MA, MSc); *m* 5 Feb 1942, Sir Paul Osmond, CB, *qv*, 2 s (Oliver b 1944, Andrew b 1949); *Career* economist and statistician Nat Inst of Econ and Social Res 1938-39, Miny of Econ Warfare 1939-41, FO 1942-44, Int Fedn of Agric Prodrs 1951-60, econ advsr Miny of Health 1967; memb: Br Section Exec European Union of Women 1961-86, Bd of Govrs Bethlem Royal and Maudsley Hosp 1968-82 (vice-chm 1980-82), Cncl Cambridge Soc 1980- (chm Exec Ctee 1988-), Cncl Independant Schs Careers Orgn 1986-; govr St Elphins Sch 1967-, assoc Newnham Coll 1977-90; *Recreations* gardening, travel, theatre; *Clubs* Utd Oxford and Cambridge Univ; *Style*— Lady Osmond, JP; 20 Beckenham Grove, Shortlands, Bromley, Kent BR2 0JU (☎ 081 460 2026)

OSMOND, Sir (Stanley) Paul; CB (1966); s of late Stanley C Osmond (d 1966), of Bristol; *b* 13 May 1917; *Educ* Bristol GS, Jesus Coll Oxford; *m* 1942, Olivia Sybil, JP, *qv*, da of late Ernest E Wells, JP; 2 s; *Career* The Buffs, WWII Glos Regt and staff 1940-46; Home Civil Serv 1939-75; sec to the Church Cmmrs 1975-80, pres Bromley Marriage Guidance Cncl 1982-90; kt 1980; *Clubs* Athenaeum; *Style*— Sir Paul Osmond, CB; 20 Beckenham Grove, Bromley, Kent BR2 OJU (☎ 081 460 2026)

OSTROM, Neil Ian Eric; s of Erik Hugo Magnus Ostrom (d 1981), and Florence Louise, *née* Mees (d 1971); *b* 26 July 1923; *Educ* Bedford Sch, Univ of Cambridge, Univ of London (BA); *m* 23 May 1953, Fay, da of William Henry Ceney (d 1982); 2 s (Mark, Toby), 1 da (Tessa); *Career* RAFVR 1942-47: trg as Air Observer 1942-43, Bomber Cmd 1944, Pathfinder Force Navigator 1944, (POW 1944-45); dir: E V Hawtin Ltd 1958-68, Glynn Manson Orgn Ltd 1973; chm: Stewart Nairn Gp plc 1974-82, Central London Branch BIM 1989-; FInst D 1984, FBIM 1984; *Recreations* languages, travel, writing, water sports, astronomy, music, investments; *Style*— Neil Ostrom, Esq; Priestfield, Watts Lane, Chislehurst, Kent BR7 5PJ (☎ 01 467 1989)

OTTON, Sir Geoffrey (John); KCB (1980, CB 1978); s of late John Alfred Otton; *b* 10 June 1927; *Educ* Christ's Hosp, St John's Coll, Cambridge (MA); *m* 1952, Hazel Lomas, *née* White; 1 s, 1 da; *Career* second permanent sec DHSS 1979- (under-sec 1971-75, dep sec 1975-79); chief advr to Supplementary Benefits Cmmn 1976-; *Style*— Sir Geoffrey Otton, KCB; 72 Cumberland Rd, Bromley, Kent (☎ 01 460 9610)

OVENDEN, Chief Inspector Ian; s of Harold Arthur Ovenden, of Paddock Wood, Kent, and Joan, *née* Brisley; *b* 12 Jan 1944; *Educ* Harvey GS Folkstone; *m* 7 Oct 1967, Eileen Teresa, da of William Costello (d 1985), of Eire; 2 da (Fiona b 1968, Amanda b 1970); *Career* Kent Police: cadet force 1960-63, Constable 1963, Sgt 1969, Inspr 1978, Chief Inspr 1987, offr in charge Tonbridge Police Station Band: fndr memb, concert mangr; *Recreations* swimming, painting, gardening, music; *Style*— Chief Inspector Ian Ovenden; Tonbridge Police Station, Pembury, Tonbridge Kent TN9 2HS (☎ 0732 771055)

OWEN, John Arthur; s of Herbert Owen (d 1956), of St Leonards-on-Sea, E Sussex, and Amelia Emma, *née* Wellstead (d 1976); *b* 20 Feb 1934; *Educ* Hastings GS, Laton House Sch Hastings; *m* 2 April 1960, Mavis, da of Alfred Thomas Wakeford (d 1958), of Hastings, E Sussex; 2 s (Michael b 1966, James b 1967), 1 da (Anne b 1974); *Career* Nat Serv RAF 1956-58; CA; mangr Price Waterhouse & Co Nassau Bahamas 1961-73, ptnr Day Smith & Hunter Maidstone 1973-, dir Star Secretariat; South Eastern Soc of CAs: ctee memb 1981-, rep on Tech Advsy Ctee of ICAEW 1979-83; treas: Detling Community Assoc, Friends of Rochester Arts Orchestra, St Faiths PCC Maidstone; dir Maidstone & Mid-Kent Motor Club Ltd; FICA 1956; *Recreations* pianoforte (as soloist and choir accompanist), church organist, cycling, motor sport; *Clubs* Maidstone Rotary; *Style*— John Owen, Esq; 19 Hockers Lane, Detling, Maidstone, Kent ME14 3JL (☎ 0622 37940); Star House, Pudding Lane, Maidstone, Kent ME14 1LT (☎ 0622 690666, fax 0622 690955)

OWENS, (John) Robin; s of Col Theobold David Cogswell Owens, MC (d 1984), of Chichester, Hampshire, and Irene Hamilton, *née* Franklyn (d 1949);

b 26 May 1939; *Educ* Wellington, Welbeck Coll, RMA Sandhurst, Emmanuel Coll Cambridge (MA); *m* 21 Dec 1963, Margaret Ann, da of Harry Arthur Overton (d 1979), of Ormesby St Margaret, Norfolk; 1 s (Nicholas b 1966), 1 da (Philippa b 1969); *Career* 2 i/c Hong Kong Fortress Sqdn 1964-67, projects offr 1 Bn RE 1967-68, ret Capt 1968; chm Airlease International Finance 1977-78; dir: Midland Montague Leasing Ltd 1978-80, Forward Tst Gp 1980-84, Gat Lease Finance Ltd 1984-85; md: Park Place Finance Ltd 1985-86, Medens Trust Ltd 1986-89; dir Brown Shipley 1989-; FCA 1972; *Recreations* tennis, sailing; *Clubs* Utd Oxford and Cambridge Univ; *Style*— Robin Owens, Esq; Park Cottage, Teston, Maidstone, Kent (☎ 0622 812208); Founders Court, Lothbury, London EC2R 7HE (☎ 071 726 4058)

OWTRAM, Godfrey Herbert; s of Col Herbert Hawkesworth Owtram, TD, OBE (d 1952), of Newland Hall, nr Lancaster, and Ethel, *née* Fair (d 1921); *b* 13 Feb 1907; *Educ* Shrewsbury, Brasenose Coll Oxford; *m* 1, 3 June 1930, Joan, da of Capt Oswald Gardner (ka 1916); 2 da (Susan Caroline b 1936, Christine Angela b 1938); m 2, 5 Oct 1946, Margaret Elizabeth, da of Ven Archdeacon Hamerton (d 1971); 1 s (Julian Godfrey Hermon b 1948); *Career* served WWII special duties; chm/fin dir many public cos incl: Horrockses Crewdson & Co Ltd 1937-40, Petrochemicals Ltd (now Shell Chemicals) 1952-56, E H Bentall Gp 1957-65, Lewis & Peat Chemicals 1965-77; *Recreations* shooting, fishing, golf, bridge; *Clubs* Boodle's; *Style*— Godfrey H Owtram, Esq; Oak Lodge, Matfield, nr Tonbridge (☎ 089 272 2106); Davers Stretton & Co Ltd, Petteridge (☎ 089 272 2710)

OXLADE, Roy; s of William Oxlade (d 1955), of Bexley Heath, Kent, and Emily, *née* Fenn; *b* 13 Jan 1929; *Educ* Bromley Coll of Art, RCA (PhD); *m* 10 Aug 1957, Rose, da of Alexander Forrest Wylie, OBE (d 1964), of Hythe, Kent; 1 s (Luke-John b 7 Aug 1958), 2 da (Elizabeth b 11 April 1960, Henrietta b 18 July 1966); *Career* painter; gp exhibitions: Young Contempories 1952 1953 and 1954, Borough Bottega 1954 and 1955, Winnipeg Biennale 1960, John Moores 1964, Hayward Annual 1982, Odette Gilbert Gallery 1984 and 1985-90, Royal Acad Summer Exhibition 1984 1985 1989 and 1990, Rocks and Flesh 1985, Olympia Art Fair 1986, Chicago Art Fair 1987, Los Angeles Art Fair 1987, Waddington Schiel Toronto 1987, Jan Turner Los Angeles 1988, Cleveland Int Drawing Biennale 1989; one-man exhibitions: Vancouver Art Gallery 1963, Midland Gp Gallery 1975, New Metropole Gallery Folkestone 1983, Air Gallery 1983, Odette Gilbert Gallery 1985 1987 and 1988, Univ of Kent 1987; *Publications* David Bomberg - RCA Papers III (1981), The Visual Arts in Adult Education and The Arts (contrib, 1981), Modern Painters Magazine (contrib); *Style*— Roy Oxlade, Esq; Odette Gilbert Gallery, 5 Cork St, London W1 (☎ 071 437 3175)

OXLEY, Raymond Leslie; s of Leslie Elgar Oxley (d 1974), of Maidstone, Kent, and Amelia Maud, *née* Pearmain (d 1985); *b* 13 April 1926; *Educ* Maidstone GS; *m* 8 February 1947, Annie Margaret (Ann) (d 1979), da of Percy Cawthorne (d 1972), of Chatham, Kent; 2 da (Janet Ann b 1952, Gillian Margaret b 1956); *Career* RA 1943-47; with various local authys 1943-52; joined E Malling Res Station 1952, sec and treas E Malling Res Assoc 1987-; sec to Pubn Ctee Journal of Horticultural Science 1957-, clerk E Malling Tst for Horticultural Res 1987-; memb Kent Special Constabulary 1955-86 (divnl cmdt 1981-86); memb Rotary Club of Malling 1963- (pres 1970-71), dist govr Kent and E Sussex Rotary 1982-83, chm Malling and Dist Crime Prevention Panel 1988-, pres Malling Dist Youth Brass 1990-; *Recreations* philately, motoring, walking; *Style*— Raymond Oxley, Esq; 1 Bradbourne Oast Cottages, East Malling, Kent ME19 6DZ (☎ 0732 849076; office tel: 0732 843833, fax 0732 847117)

OXTOBY, Kenneth; s of William Heighley Oxtoby (d 1973), of Hallgarth, Eastgate, North Newbald, E Yorks, and Jessie, *née* Mason (d 1981); *b* 5 March 1945; *Educ* Market Weighton Sch E Yorks, Rose Bruford Coll of Speech and Drama Sidcup Kent; *Career* actor; worked extensively in regnl repertory theatre; appeared in: Malta Arts Festival 1975, Edinburgh Festival 1987, There's A Girl In My Soup (Comedy Theatre), The Changing Room (Globe Theatre), The Dresser (Queen's Theatre); numerous TV appearances incl: Coronation St, Crown Court, Return of the Saint, Lady Killers, All Creatures Great and Small, Shine on Harvey Moon, Never the Twain; films incl: Seasong, Spy (Camp 020), O Lucky Man!; *Recreations* Spanish, patio gardening, eating and drinking with friends; *Style*— Kenneth Oxtoby, Esq; c/o The Spotlight, 7 Leicester Place, London WC2H 7BP (☎ 071 4375881)

P

PACKER, Robin John; s of Eswin James Packer, and Alma, *née* Lodge; *b* 6 May 1948; *Educ* Catford Sch; *m* 1 Aug 1970, Diane Irana, da of Kenneth Derek Jones; 2 da (Melanie b 28 Dec 1973, Natalie b 1 Aug 1977); *Career* de Zoete & Gordon 1964-66, Goveti Sons 1966-74, Cazenove 1974-76; Wood MacKenzie & Co: joined 1976, ptnr 1984-87, dir 1986-87: currently dep md UK Equities UBS Phillips & Drew (joined 1987); memb local Cons Assoc; memb Stock Exchange; *Recreations* golf, game fishing; *Style*— Robin Packer, Esq; Southfields, Telegraph Hill, Higham by Rochester, Kent ME3 7NW (☎ 0634 721420); UBS Phillips & Drew, 100 Liverpool St, London EC2 (☎ 071 901 1386)

PAGE, Jeremy Neil; s of Harold Percy Page, of Folkestone, and Doris Irene, *née* Hawker; *b* 23 Feb 1958; *Educ* Harvey Folkestone, Univ of Warwick (BA), Univ of Bristol (MA); *Career* teacher and teacher trainer: International House Hastings 1983, International House London 1984-1990, Accademia Britannica Tuscany 1987-88; actor Eleventh Hour Theatre Co 1978; ed: The Frogmore Papers 1983-; memb: New Folkestone Soc, RSPB, Old Harveians Assoc, BFI; supporter of Greenpeace, signatory to Charter '88; *Books* Bliss (1989), Frogmore Poetry (ed with Antony Powell, 1989); *Recreations* cricket, theatre, cinema; *Style*— Jeremy Page, Esq; International House, 106 Piccadilly, London W1V 9FL (☎ 071 491 2598)

PAGET, Hon Mrs (Enid Louise); da of 1 and last Baron Queenborough (d 1949); *b* 1923; *m* 1947 (m dis) Count (Roland) de la Poype; 1 da; resumed the surname Paget; *Style*— The Hon Mrs Paget

PALLETT, Norman Ivor; s of Walter Albert Stanley Pallett (d 1949), of Hastings, and Helen Rebecca, *née* Shearman (d 1977); *b* 22 April 1929; *Educ* Alleyns Sch Dulwich; *m* 20 Sep 1952, Margaret Evelyn, da of Marcus Edward Turk, of Hastings; 1 s (Robert Nigel b 1954); *Career* CH Dobbie conslt engrs 1951- (ptnr 1970-84, managing ptnr 1984-); work incl: coastal engrg, public health, highways, railways; FICE, MIHT, MConsSE, FBIM; *Recreations* archaeology, railways, the Arab world; *Clubs* St Stephen's Constitutional; *Style*— Norman Pallett, Esq; Dobbie & Partners, Consulting Structural and Civil Engineers, 17 Lansdowne Rd, Croydon CR9 3UN (☎ 081 686 8212, fax 081 681 2499, telex 917220)

PALMBY, (Phillip) Michael; s of Gerald Dorrien Palmby, BEM (d 1987), of Maidstone, and Joan, *née* Rees; *b* 8 Aug 1948; *Educ* St Andrews Coll, Mid Kent Coll of Technol (Dip in Municipal Admin); *m* 6 June 1970, Susan Mary, da of John Hills (d 1970), of Maidstone; 3 da (Catherine, Annemarie, Sophie); *Career* personnel offr: Westminster City Cncl 1972-75, Kent CC 1975-88; force personnel and trg offr Kent Co Constabulary 1988-; Maidstone Borough Cncl: chm Personnel Gp 1984-86, chm Arts and Recreation Ctee 1986-; ACIS 1980; *Recreations* sport, reading, travel, films, dog showing; *Style*— Michael Palmby, Esq; 27 Grace Ave, Maidstone, Kent (☎ 0622 64934)

PALMER, John; JP; s of Herbert Palmer, of Elham, Canterbury, and Blanche Eleanor, *née* Weller (d 1989); *b* 19 Oct 1934; *Educ* Kent Coll Canterbury, QMC London (BSc); *m* 18 April 1961, Eleanor Ann, da of Frank Noble (d 1958), of Altrincham, Cheshire; 3 s (David b 1962, Richard b 1964, Joseph b 1969), 1 da (Elizabeth b 1966); *Career* Nat Serv RAF; area mktg mangr Esso Petroleum Co Ltd 1960-85, farmer, ptnr Parsonage Farm Rural Heritage Centre, dir Elham Valley Railway Co Ltd 1989; Univ of London Purple for Rowing 1959; memb: Shepway Dist Cncl 1974-82 (vice chm 1978), Kent CC (Elham Valley Div) 1981-; chm: Folkestone and Hythe Cons Assoc 1986-89, Swingfield and Elham Br NFU 1974-76; govr: Harvey GS, Sellinge Co Primary Sch, Saltwood C of E primary, Selsted C of E Sch; *Recreations* playing the trombone; *Clubs* Univ of London Boat Club Assoc, Thames Rowing, Exec (Folkestone); *Style*— John Palmer, Esq; North Elham Farm, Elham, Canterbury, Kent CT4 6UY (☎ 0303 84356)

PALMER, Prof John Michael; da of Henry William Palmer (d 1974), and Hilda May, *née* Ball (d 1955); *b* 24 April 1936; *Educ* Yeovil GS, Univ of Reading (BSc), Univ of Oxford (DPhil); *m* 29 July 1959, Irene Alice, da of Sidney Arthur Ricketts, of 16 Cromwell Rd, Yeovil, Somerset; 1 s (Stephen John b 1969), 2 da (Alison Hilary b 1965, Helen Melinda b 1967); *Career* NATO res fell Univ of California 1962-64, lectr in plant physiology KCL 1964-71, prof of plant biochemistry Imp Coll London 1985- (reader in enzymology 1971-85); warden Kent Tst for Nature Conservation; memb: Cncl S London Botanical Inst, Br Mycological Soc, Soc for Experimental Biology, Micrological Soc 1984; *Books* The Physiology and Biochemistry of Plant Respiration (1984); *Recreations* photography, natural history, music; *Clubs* Orpington Field, Kent Field; *Style*— Prof John Palmer

PALMER, (Ronald) Richard; s of Ronald Walter Palmer (d 1973), and Alice Elizabeth, *née* Rablin; *b* 31 Dec 1939; *Educ* Dulwich; *m* Sept 1961, Frances, da of Alfred Henry Smith (d 1979); 1 s (Corin Brian b 11 Aug 1967), 1 da (Anna Veronica b 26 March 1970); *Career* project mangr Bank of England 1959-82; Kent Repertory Co: fndr 1983, dir of over 20 prodns incl 7 Shakespeare plays, responsible for devpt of Hever Castle Lakeside Theatre, rep on the Theatrical Mgmnt Assoc; *Recreations* theatre, music, literature; *Clubs* Alleyn; *Style*— Richard Palmer, Esq; Kent Repertory Company, Hever Castle, Edenbridge, Kent TN8 7NG (☎ 0732 866654)

PALMER, Rozanne; da of Basil Henry Palmer (d 1962), of Ramsgate, and Violet, *née* Pullen (d 1976); *Educ* Convent of The Assumption Ramsgate, Canterbury Coll of Art, Beckenham Sch of Art, RCA (Dip RCA), Acad of Fine Arts Rome; *Career* artist; won Italian govt scholarship sponsored by Br Cncl, prizewinner Ansvar 1976; exhibited: Royal Acad, Beaux Arts Trafford Galleries, New English Art Club RCA, Retrospective London Royal Scot Acad, New Metropole, Ogle Gallery (one man show), Nevill Galleries Canterbury and Bath, Compton Windsor, Ashbarn Petersfield, Guildford House, S Eastern Arts, Positano Art Workshop, Marshall Field Chicago (one man show), Carlisle Museum and Towner Gallery Eastbourne 1987; *Style*— Ms Rozanne Palmer; 112 Middle St, Deal, Kent CT14 6JX (☎ 0304 367241)

PALMER, Victor Douglas; s of Arthur Palmer (d 1963), and Ethel May, *née* Bolton (d 1956); *b* 20 Nov 1918; *Educ* Eltham Secdy Sch; *m* 26 May 1951, Muriel Dorothy, da of Wallace Charles Sweatman, JP (d 1969); 2 s (Michael b 1952, John b 1958); *Career* War Serv code and cypher Sgt RAF 1939-45; co sec and accountant; Walker Brothers (London) Ltd 1958-65, SA Industrial Suppliers Ltd 1965-83, Philip Frame Properties (London) Ltd 1965-83; elder United Reformed Church; FICA 1952; *Recreations* community service, music; *Style*— Victor Palmer, Esq; 52 Derry Downs, St Mary Cray, Orpington, Kent BR5 4DU (☎ 0689 30567)

PANTON, Dr Francis Harry; MBE (1948); s of George Emerson Panton; *b* 25 May 1923; *Educ* City Sch Lincoln, UCL, Univ of Nottingham; *m* 1952, Audrey Mary, *née* Lane (d 1989); 2 s; *Career* MOD: asst chief sci advsr (nuclear) 1969-76, dir Propellants Explosives and Rocket Motors Estab Waltham Abbey and Westcott 1976-80, head of Rocket Motor Exec 1976-80; dir Royal Armament Rand D Estab Fort Halstead 1980-84; conslt: Cabinet Office, BT, MOD 1985-; dir Heritage Projects (Canterbury) Ltd; chm: Mgmnt Ctee Canterbury Archaeological Tst, Canterbury Visitor Info Centre; cncl memb Kent Archaeological Soc; *Recreations* local history, bridge; *Clubs* Reform; *Style*— Dr Francis Panton, MBE; Cantis House, 1 St Peter's Lane, Canterbury, Kent (☎ 0227 452902)

PARGITER, Hon Donald; s of Baron Pargiter, CBE (Life Peer); *b* 1921; *m* 1947; *Style*— The Hon Donald Pargiter; 68 Tonbridge Rd, Maidstone, Kent

PARISH, Christopher Henry Woodbine; s of Patrick Edward Gladstone Woodbine Parish, OBE (d 1979), of Empshott Lodge, Liss, Hampshire, and Marion Aimée Lyon Parish, MBE, *née* Garnett (d 1971); *b* 4 Oct 1937; *Educ* Eton, Trinity Coll Oxford (MA); *m* 1 Aug 1969, Angela Phoebe, da of Peter Gray Benham, of Wrays, Hookwood, Horley, Surrey; 1 s (Matthew b 1971), 4 da (Daisy b 1973, Laura b 1975, Priscilla b 1977, Elisabeth b 1979); *Career* Nat Serv 2 Lt Welsh Gds 1956-58; asst master Cheam Sch 1958; MacFarlanes Slrs: articled clerk 1961, slr 1965, ptnr 1969-; dir Olgivy Gillanders & Co Ltd 1984-89; dir Hedley Fndn 1986-; memb Law Soc 1965; *Recreations* tennis, singing; *Clubs* Garrick, MCC, Wig & Pen; *Style*— Christopher Parish, Esq; Frittenden House, Frittenden, Cranbrook, Kent TN17 2DG (☎ 071 831 9222, fax 071 831 9607)

PARKER, Christopher John McKellen; s of Alfred Derek McKellen Parker, of Beltinge, Herne Bay, Kent, and Muriel Joyce, *née* Hargreaves; *b* 25 July 1945; *Educ* Dulwich, LSE (BSc); *m* 27 Dec 1969, Alison Eyre, da of Robin Gordon Miller, of Shepherdswell, Dover, Kent; 3 s (Thomas b 1972, Jonathan b 1974, Samuel b 1980); *Career* dir: Arbuthnot Latham & Co Ltd 1978-82, Caird Gp plc (formerly A Caird & Sons plc) 1982- (chm 1982-87); ACA 1969,

FCA 1979; *Style—* Christopher Parker, Esq; Dennes House, Waltham, Canterbury, Kent CT4 5SD (☎ 022 770 389); 163 Andrewes House, Barbican, London EC2Y 8BA (☎ 071 638 5009); 33 Sekforde St, London EC1R 0HH (☎ 071 250 3003, fax 071 250 3001, car tel 0836 676622)

PARKER, Prof Edward Andrew; s of Edward Parker (d 1966), of Orpington, Kent, and Mary, *née* Barber; *b* 29 April 1942; *Educ* Bromley GS, St Catharine's Coll Cambridge (MA, PhD); *m* 31 July 1964, Naomi, da of Cyril Richard Wright, of Richmond, London; 2 s (Giles b 1970, Geoffrey b 1971); *Career* Univ of Kent: asst lectr 1967, lectr 1968, reader in radio communications 1977-81, chartered electrical engr 1981-, prof of radio communications 1987-; memb Bd of Dirs Kent Scientific and Industrial Projects Ltd 1988-; author of numerous papers on antennas; memb: IEE, Prof Gp EII of IEE, Ctee E Kent Assoc of Nat Tst; FRAS; *Recreations* local history, antiquarian horology, eating, walking, photography; *Style—* Prof Edward Parker; University of Kent, Electronic Engr Labs, The University, Canterbury, Kent CT2 7NT (☎ 0227 764000)

PARKER, Dr John Richard Robert; s of Richard Robert Parker (d 1987), and Elsie Winifred, *née* Curtis; *b* 5 Nov 1933; *Educ* SE London Tech Coll, Regent St Poly (Dip Arch), UCL (Dip TP), Central London Poly (PhD); *m* 1959, Valerie Barbara Mary, da of Edward James Troupe Duguid (d 1952); 1 s (Jonathan b 1965), 1 da (Joanna b 1968); *Career* Nat Serv 2 Lt RE served Canal Zone, Cyprus 1952-54, TA (Lt) 1954-64; private architects and commercial firms 1954-59, architect LCC 1961-64, urban designer London Borough of Lambeth 1964-70, head Central Area Team GLC 1970-86; fndr and md Gtr London Conslts 1986- (dir Environment Appraisal Unit 1989-), princ John Parker Associates (architectural and planning conslts) 1990-; originator of devpt nr tport interchanges related to pedestrian movement 1967-87, project mangr Piccadilly Circus redevpt 1972-86, planning cnslt for Addis Ababa 1986; Winston Churchill fell 1967; RIBA Pearce Edwards Award 1969, Br Cncl Anglo-Soviet Award 1988; ARIBA, FRTPI, FRSA; *Publications* subjects incl: urban design, environmental planning, pedestrians and security; *Recreations* tennis, golf, drawing; *Clubs* Royal Cwlth, IOD, Shortlands Golf, Catford Wanderers Sports (chm); *Style—* Dr John Parker; 4 The Heights, Foxgrove Rd, Beckenham, Kent BR3 2BY (☎ 081 658 6076); Greater London Consultants, St Brides's House, 32 High St, Beckenham, Kent BR3 1BD (☎ 081 663 6330, fax 081 650 3456, telex 262 433 (ref W6861))

PARKINSON, Prof Cyril Northcote; s of William Edward Parkinson, princ York Sch of Art, and Rose Emily Mary, *née* Curnow; *b* 30 July 1909; *Educ* St Peter's Sch York, Emmanuel Coll Cambridge (BA), King's Coll London (PhD); *m* 1, 1943 (m dis 1950) Ethelwyn Edith, da of Francis Graves, editor Windsor Express; 1 s (Christopher b 1945), 1 da (Alison b 1943); m 2, 1952, (Elizabeth) Ann (d 1983), da of Lt-Col Fry, MC, RA; 2 s (Charles b 1955, Jonathan b 1961), 1 da (Antonia b 1958); m 3, 1 June 1985, Iris Hilda (Ingrid), da of Norman Victor Waters; *Career* 2 Lt TA Reserve 1932, Lt 22 London Regt (The Queen's) 1933, Capt Blundell's Sch Tiverton OTC, Capt 166 OCTU 1940, Maj Gen Staff 1943, demob 1944, Hon Lt-Col Alabama Militia; author, historian and journalist; seigneur of Anneville, Mauxmarquis and Beavoir; sr history master Blundell's Sch Tiverton, master RNC Dartmouth 1938 and 1944-46, lectr Univ of Liverpool 1947-50, Raffles prof of history Univ of Singapore 1950-58, prof emeritus Troy State Univ Alabama USA 1970-; chm Leviathan House (publishers) 1972-; author of numerous books and novels; contribs to: Encyclopaedia Britannica, The Economist, The Guardian, Punch, Saturday Evening Post and other jnls; fell of Emmanuel Coll Cambridge; Hon LLD, DLitt, Hon Dr of Business Orgns; FRHistS; *Recreations* painting, travel; *Clubs* Army and Navy, Royal Channel Islands Yacht; *Style—* Professor C Northcote Parkinson; 36 Harkness Drive, Canterbury, Kent CT2 7RW (☎ 0227 452742)

PARRY-CROOKE, David John; s of Maj Charles Philip Parry-Crooke, JP (d 1978), of Friston, Suffolk, and Winifred Rosa Parry-Crooke, JP, *née* Wales (d 1976); *see* Burke's Landed Gentry 18 Ed Vol III 1972; *b* 3 March 1923; *Educ* Radley, Univ Coll Oxford; *m* 1, 22 Jan 1948, Griselda Mary Powell, da of Rev Canon Norman Powell Williams (d 1942), of Christ Church Oxford; 1 s (John Paul b 1953), 2 da (Charlotte Mary b 1950, Georgiana Mary b 1956); m 2, 1 Nov 1979, Elizabeth Dorothea, da of Dr William Crampton Gore, RHA (d 1945), of Enniskillen Co Fermanagh; *Career* WWII 19 King George V's Own Lancers IA 1942-46; Capt: India, Burma, Malaya; sometime rubber planter Malaya, farmer and travel conslt, landowner; voluntary work: The Samaritans London, Suffolk Cons Pty; involved with church and local cncls; Master Worshipful Co of Tylers and Bricklayers 1976-77; *Recreations* model railways, photography, shooting, travel; *Clubs* MCC, Army and Navy; *Style—* David Parry-Crooke, Esq; 5 Dixwell Rd, Folkestone, Kent (☎ 0303 55 690)

PARSONS, Derek George; s of George Frederick Parsons (d 1959), and Ethel Olive, *née* King (d 1980); *b* 18 Nov 1929; *Educ* Dartford GS; *m* 23 July 1955, Wendy Maud, da of Charles George Heydon (d 1967); 1 s (Jeremy Rawdon b 1963), 1 da (Nicola Lindsey b 1959); *Career* head of Trade Marks Div Shell International Petroleum Co Ltd 1979-89; vice pres Euro Trade Mark Practitioners' Assoc 1986 (cncl memb 1984-89), cncl memb Inst of Trade Mark Agents 1979-89, leader of Dartford Borough Cncl 1969-72 (Cons cncllr 1966-72 and 1976-87), govr Dartford GS; fell Inst of Trade Mark Agents 1987; *Recreations* visiting galleries and theatres; *Clubs* Players; *Style—* Derek Parsons, Esq; 76 Watling St, Dartford, Kent DA2 6AE (☎ 0322 224879)

PARTRIDGE, (Walter Michael) James; s of Maj Michael Harry Partridge, of Betchworth, Surrey, and Diana Marjorie, *née* Chamberlain; *b* 14 March 1958; *Educ* Lancing, Trinity Coll Cambridge (BA); *m* 16 July 1983, Sarah Mercy, da of Wallace Barrie Page, of Killearn, Scotland; 1 s (Harry Michael James b 1989), 1 da (Georgiana Diana Margaret b 1987); *Career* cmmnd RA (Volunteer) 1979, Maj 1990-, 201 (Hertfordshire and Bedfordshire Yeomanry) Field Battery; admitted slr Supreme Court 1983; asst slr Lawrence Graham 1983-86, ptnr Thomson Snell & Passmore 1987-; memb Law Soc; *Recreations* sailing, walking, reading; *Clubs* Cavalry & Guards; *Style—* James Partridge, Esq; Thomson Snell & Passmore, 3 Lonsdale Gardens, Tunbridge Wells, Kent TN1 1NX (☎ 0892 510000, fax 0892 549884)

PARTRIDGE, Simon Harry Wood; OBE (1983); s of Rt Rev Frank Partridge (d 1941), of Bishopswood, Fareham, Hants, and Elizabeth Maud, *née* Barton (d 1965); *b* 17 Aug 1919; *Educ* Uppingham, Trinity Coll Oxford (MA); *m* 26 May 1951, Barbara Dagmar, da of Anton Emil Schou Bech (d 1981), of Copenhagen, Denmark; 2 s (Andrew b 17 March 1954, Jonathan b 8 Jan 1956); *Career* 57 HTR RAC 1939-40; chm and md: Butterworth Law Publishers Ltd 1974-76, Butterworth & Co (UK) Ltd 1976-82; dir Lloyd's of London Press Ltd 1982-; memb Editorial Bd Statutes in Force 1984-; Liveryman Worshipful Co of Merchant Taylors 1952; *Recreations* golf, chess; *Clubs* Garrick; *Style—* Simon Partridge, Esq, OBE; High Rede, Kilndown, Cranbrook, Kent TN17 2RT (☎ 0892 890413)

PASSMORE, John Francis Wolfe; s of Leonard Wolfe Passmore (d 1944), and Winifred, *née* Sladden (d 1981); *b* 9 Oct 1921; *Educ* Cranleigh; *m* 14 May 1949, Pamela Madeline, da of Otto Dunkels (d 1955); 3 s (Nicholas John Wolfe b 1950, Jeremy Cedric b 1952, David William b 1955); *Career* serv RE 1940-46, cmmnd 1941; sr ptnr Thomson Snell and Passmore (Slrs) 1979-86; *Recreations* gardening, photography, bridge; *Clubs* Naval and Military, Piccadilly; *Style—* John Passmore, Esq; Maynards, Groombridge, Tunbridge Wells TN3 9PR (☎ 0892 864335); 3 Lonsdale Gardens, Tunbridge Wells TN1 1NX (☎ 0892 510000, telex 95194, fax 0892 49884)

PASSMORE, Michael Bramwell; s of Brian Alfred Passmore (d 1985), of The Dog and Duck, W Wittering, Sussex, and Eileen Barbara, *née* Church; *b* 18 Sept 1928; *Educ* Bryanston; *m* 14 Sept 1957, Anne Gillian, da of Joseph Hurrell Pillman, CBE (d 1968), of Ballards Corner, Limpsfield, Surrey; 2 s (Christopher b 1959, Stephen b 1960), 1 da (Stella b 1962); *Career* dir Albaster Passmore and Sons Ltd 1955-, chm Passmore International 1981-89; pres Inst of Printing; *Recreations* sailing, walking; *Clubs* Royal Naval Sailing Assoc, Little Ship; *Style—* Michael Passmore, Esq; Scraces, Rectory Lane, Barming, nr Maidstone, Kent ME16 9NE (☎ 0622 726237)

PATEL, Dr Hasmukh Rambhai; s of Rambhai Patel, of London, and Shardaben Patel; *b* 1 Jan 1945; *Educ* King's Coll London, King's Coll Hosp Med Sch (MB BS, MRCS); *m* 16 July 1969, Mrudula Hasmukh, da of Revabhai Patel, of Baroda India; 1 s (Veran b 31 July 1972), 1 da (Nesha b 7 May 1975); *Career* conslt paediatrician Joyce Green Hosp Kent 1976-, clinical tutor Univ of London 1982-, coll tutor RCP 1986-; memb: Royal Med Benevolent Fund, BPA; FRCPE 1985, FRCP 1986; *Recreations* travel, swimming, photography; *Style—* Dr Hasmukh Patel; 9 Irene Rd, Orpington, Kent BR6 0HA; Postgraduate Medical Centre, Joyce Green Hospital, Dartford, Kent (☎ 0322 229414)

PATEMAN, Jack Ernest; CBE (1970); s of William Edward Pateman, and Lucy Varley, *née* Jetten; *b* 29 Nov 1921; *Educ* Gt Yarmouth GS; *m* 1949, Cicely Hope, *née* Turner; 1 s (John b 1954), 1 da (Susan b 1951); *Career* RAF 1940-46; res engr Belling and Lee 1946-48, Elliott Bros (London) Ltd 1948-51 (formed Aviation Div at Borehamwood 1951-62), md Elliott Flight Automation Ltd 1971-86 (dep chm and jt md 1962-71); dir: Canadian Marconi Co 1971-87, GEC Computers Ltd 1971-89, Elliott Bros (London) Ltd 1979-89, Marconi Electronic Devices Ltd 1980-87, GEC Marconi Ltd 1979-89, GEC Marconi (China) Ltd 1979-89, GEC Info Systems Ltd 1982-86, GEC Avionics Projects (UK) Ltd 1984-89, GEC plc 1986-88; dep chm GEC Avionics Ltd 1986-; Br Gold Medal RAeS 1981; chm Kent Co Engrg Soc, dir Kent Trg and Enterprise Cncl; FEng, FRSA; *Recreations* sailing, gardening; *Style—* Jack Pateman, Esq, CBE; Spindles, Ivy Hatch, Sevenoaks, Kent TN15 0PG (☎ 0732 810364); GEC Avionics Ltd, Airport Works, Rochester, Kent ME1 2XX (☎ 0634 816333, fax 0634 832664)

PATERSON, Robert Andrew (Robin); o s of John Leggat Paterson (d 1983), of Beith, Ayrshire, and Winifred Purdon, *née* Ballantyne (d 1983); *b* 27 Oct 1936; *Educ* Strathallan Sch; *m* 27 July 1963, Diane Margaret, o da of Malcolm George Lillingston (ka 1941; *see* Burke's Landed Gentry, 18 edn, vol I, 1965), and Mary Lyons, yst da of Sir William McLintock, 1 Bt, GBE, CVO; 1 s (Jamie John Lillingston-Paterson (assumed additional surname of Lillingston on 18th birthday) b 6 Aug 1967), 1 da (Joanna Mary Lillingston b 16 May 1965); *Career* CA; ptnr Grieveson Grant & Co 1970-86, dir Kleinwort Benson Securities Ltd 1986-88, chm Paterson Printing Ltd 1988-, memb Stock

Exchange; *Recreations* golf, skiing, gardening; *Clubs* New (Edinburgh); *Style*— Robin Paterson, Esq; Lees Court, Matfield, Tonbridge, Kent TN12 7JU (☎ 089 272 2892); Paterson Printing Ltd, 21 Chapman Way, Tunbridge Wells, Kent TN2 3EF (☎ 0892 511212)

PATEY, Mark; MBE; s of David Howard Patey (d 1978), and Gladys Joyce, *née* Summers (d 1981); *b* 17 Feb 1930; *Educ* Bryanston, Trinity Hall Cambridge (MA); *m* 16 Nov 1957, Cecile O'Connell, da of William Leil Cock (d 1966); 3 da (Helen b 1958, Claire b 1960, Mary-Ann b 1966); *Career* Nat Serv RAF 1948-50 (pilot offr 1949-50); judicial cmmr Colonial Serv Swaziland 1967-70 (dist offr 1954, dist cmmr 1957), chief adjudicator Immigration Appeals UK 1984- (adjudicator 1970); *Recreations* gardening; *Style*— Mark Patey, Esq, MBE; Immigration Appeals (UK), Thanet House, 231 The Strand, London WC2

PATTERSON, Maj-Gen Arthur Gordon; CB (1969), DSO (1964), OBE (1961), MC (1945); s of late Arthur Abbey Patterson; *b* 24 July 1917; *Educ* Tonbridge, RMC Sandhurst; *m* 1949, Jean Mary Grant; 2 s, 1 da; *Career* dir of Army Trg 1969-72, ret; *Style*— Maj-Gen Arthur Patterson, CB, DSO, OBE, MC; Burnt House, Benenden, Cranbrook, Kent

PATTERSON, Felicity Barbara Anne; da of Gordon William Raybould, of Sundridge, Kent, and Barbara, *née* Wilkins (d 1986); *b* 21 June 1945; *Educ* Benenden Sch, Whitelands Coll of Educn Univ of London (certEd, AMBDA), Dyslexia Inst (Dip), Open Univ (Dip Reading Devpt); *m* 5 July 1970, (George) Benjamin Patterson, MEP, *qv*, s of Eric James Patterson (d 1972); 1 s (Alexander b 1974), 1 da (Olivia b 1977); *Career* posts in Chm's Office and English Picture Dept Sotheby's 1964-70; ILEA Adult Literacy Scheme 1973-76, Berkshire Co Educn Authy Adult Literacy Scheme 1976-86; Dyslexia Inst: joined 1986, area princ 1989, regnl princ (SE Area) 1990; memb: Br Dyslexia Assoc, The Orton Soc, UK Reading Assoc, Professional Assoc of Teachers, Mid Kent Dyslexia Assoc; *Recreations* oboe, piano, tennis, portrait drawing; *Style*— Mrs Felicity Patterson; The Dyslexia Institute, 32 Avebury Ave, Tonbridge, Kent TN9 1VA (☎ 0732 352762)

PATTERSON, George Benjamin (Ben); MEP (EDG Kent West 1979-); s of Prof Eric James Patterson (d 1972), of Stonehedge, Alphington Cross, Exeter, Devon, and Dr Ethel Patterson, *née* Simkins; *b* 21 April 1939; *Educ* Westminster, Trinity Coll Cambridge (MA), LSE; *m* 6 Dec 1970, Felicity Barbara Anne, *qv*, da of Gordon W Raybould, of Little Combe Bank, Sundridge, Sevenoaks, Kent; 1 s (Alexander b 6 Dec 1974), 1 da (Olivia b 15 April 1977); *Career* tutor Swinton Coll Masham Yorks 1961-65, ed CPC Monthly Report 1965-73, dep head Euro Parly London Office 1973-79, dir Wiltenbridge Ltd 1980-; EDG spokesman on economic monetary and industl policy in the Euro Parly 1984-89, policy co-ordinator EDG 1989-; cncllr London Borough of Hammersmith 1968-71; MInstD; *Books* The Character of Conservatism (1973), Direct Elections to the European Parliament (1974), The Purse-strings of Europe (1979), Vredeling and All That (1984), VAT: The Zero Rate Issue (1988), A Guide to EMU (1990); *Recreations* squash, walking; *Clubs* IOD, Bow Group; *Style*— Ben Patterson, Esq, MEP; Elm Hill House, Hawkhurst, Kent TN18 4XU (☎ 0580 753260); European Parliament, 89-91 Rue Belliard, 1090 Brussels, Belgium (☎ 010 32 2 234 3801, fax 010 32 2 231 11 83)

PAUL, Dr David Manuel; s of Kenneth Paul (d 1960), and Rachel, *née* Favell (d 1965); *b* 8 June 1927; *Educ* Selhurst GS Croydon, St Bartholomew's Hosp Med Coll, London Hosp Med Coll (DRCOG, DA, DMJ, MRCS, LRCP); *m* 14 Feb 1948, (Gladys) Audrey, da of William Garton, of The Wallhatch Hotel, Forest Row, Sussex; 2 da (Judith Audrey (Mrs Stevens) b 25 Nov 1948, Alison Jane (Mrs Putman) b 4 July 1950); *Career* GP Drs Duncan & Ptnrs 1955-67; Purley War Meml Hosp: clinical asst anaesthetist 1956-68, clinical asst obstetrician 1958-68; clinical asst anaesthetist Croydon Gp of Hosps 1956-68, divn surgn Met Police 1956-68; coroner: City of London 1966-, Northern Dist London 1968-; dept of forensic med Guy's Hosp: hon lectr, hon conslt in clinical forensic med and court practice 1966-; hon conslt in clinical forensic med Surrey Constabulary 1967, pres Br Acad of Forensic Sciences 1987-88 (chm med section 1983-87 and exec cncl 1984-87); chm Warlingham and Dist Horse Club 1964-68; Freeman City of London 1966, Liveryman Worshipful Soc of Apothecaries 1966; memb Assoc of Police Surgs 1956, BAFS 1964; memb: Medico Legal Soc 1964, Forensic Sci Soc 1964, RSM; *Books* chapters in Gradwohl's Legal Medicine (3 edn, 1976), Modern Trends in Forensic Medicine (1973), Taylor's Principles and Practice of Medical Jurisprudence (13 edn, 1984); *Recreations* travel, photography, equitation, fishing, work; *Style*— Dr David Paul; Cobhambury Farm, Edenbridge, Kent TN8 5PN (☎ 0732 863280); Coroner's Court, Milton Court, Moor Lane, London EC2 7BL (☎ 071 260 1598); Coroner's Court, Myddelton Rd, Hornsey, London N8 7PY (☎ 081 348 4411); Shirley Oaks Hospital, Poppy Lane, Shirley Oaks, Croydon, Surrey CR9 8AB (☎ 081 655 2255, fax 081 656 2868)

PAUL, Julian Braithwaite; s of Dr Michael Braithwaite Paul, of Orchard House, Newchurch, Burton on Trent, Staffs, and Patricia Elisabeth Ann, *née* Mumm; *b* 18 May 1945; *Educ* Wrekin Coll Wellington Shropshire, St John's Coll Oxford (BA, MA); *m* 3 Nov 1973, Diana, da of Ernest Trevor Davies (d 1981), of Epsom, Surrey; 1 s (Rupert b 1981), 2 da (Arabella b 1975, Henrietta b 1978); *Career* CA; Arthur Anderson & Co 1966-71, Citibank NA 1971-74, dep md Banco Hispano Americano Ltd 1974-87, md Guinness Mahon & Co Ltd Merchant Bankers 1987-; chm Govrs Valence Sch Westerham, vice chm Govrs Sundridge and Brasted C of E Primary Sch; pres: Brasted and Sundridge Horticultural Soc; Cons memb for Sevenoaks W Kent CC 1985-; ACA 1969, FCA 1979; *Recreations* politics, travel; *Clubs* Carlton, Coningsby, Bow Group; *Style*— Julian Paul, Esq; The Mount House, Brasted, Westerham, Kent (☎ 0959 63617); 32 St Mary At Hill, London EC3 (☎ 071 623 9333, fax 071 283 4811, telex 884035)

PAULSON-ELLIS, Jeremy David; s of Christian William Geoffrey Paulson-Ellis (d 1982), and Vivien Joan Paulson-Ellis (d 1966); *b* 21 Sept 1943; *Educ* Sherborne; *m* 27 April 1973, Jennifer Jill, da of Harry Milne (d 1958); 2 s (Nicholas b 1976, Matthew b 1984), 1 da (Vivien b 1974); *Career* Citicorp Scrimgeour Vickers International Ltd (formerly Vickers da Costa & Co): joined 1964, ptnr 1970, dir 1974, chm 1985-88; chm: Genesis Investment Management Ltd, Genesis Emerging Markets Fund Ltd, Genesis Chile Fund Ltd, Genesis Malaysia Maju Fund Ltd; dir Korea Asia Fund Ltd; memb investmt advsy cncl: Korea International Trust 1982-87, Seoul International Trust (chm) 1985-87, Thailand Fund 1986-88; ind memb Heathrow Airport Consultative Ctee 1984-88; memb London Stock Exchange 1970; AMSIA; *Recreations* tennis, travel; *Style*— Jeremy Paulson-Ellis, Esq; Broomlands, Langton Green, Tunbridge Wells, Kent TN3 0RA (☎ 0892 863 555); Genesis Investment Management Ltd, 21 Knightsbridge, London SW1X 7LY (☎ 071 235 5090, fax 071 235 8065, telex 919062 GIML, car tel 0860 534 116)

PAWLEY, Margaret Grozier; da of James John William Herbertson, MVO, OBE (d 1974), of Folkestone, and Lilian Annie Charlotte, *née* Rawlinson Wood (d 1985); *b* 22 March 1922; *Educ* Stratford House Sch Bickley, St Anne's Coll Oxford (MA), St Hugh's Coll Oxford; *m* 11 Jan 1958, Ven Bernard Clinton Pawley (d 1981), formerly Archdeacon of Canterbury, s of Lt Cdr Sylvester George Pawley, RN (d 1975), of Southwold; 1 s (Matthew James b 1962), 1 da (Felicity Ann b 1961); *Career* Lt Special Op Exec FANY Corps 1943-46, ME and Italy; tutor Open Univ 1975-84; *Books* Rome and Canterbury Through Four Centuries (with B C Pawley, 1974), Donald Coggan, Servant of Christ (1987), One Light for One World and The Unity we Seek (The Sermons of Archbishop Runcie, ed, 1988 and 1989), Praying with the English Tradition (1990); *Recreations* reading, foreign travel; *Style*— Mrs Bernard Pawley; 3 North Court Oast, Old Wives' Lees, Canterbury, Kent (☎ 0227 730818)

PAYNE, Harold Lloyd; OBE (1972); s of Horace Frederick Payne (d 1956), of Blackheath, and Dora Kate, *née* Lloyd (d 1972); *b* 16 Oct 1920; *Educ* City of London Sch; *m* 12 June 1942, Mary Mildred, da of William George Hill (d 1951), of Blackheath; 1 da (Lorna b 1949); *Career* TA HAC 1939, II Regt RHA 1939, cmmnd 137 FD Regt RA 1941 (Japanese POW 1942-45); dir Lloyds Insurance Brokers 1937-80, memb Lloyds 1949-88; forest owner 1974-; vice chm: Far East Fund, Cncl Br Serv Ex-Serv Orgns; tstee Queen Mary's Roehampton Hosp Tst, pres Nat Fedn of Far Eastern POW Assocs; memb: Bd Govrs Westminster Hosp Gp 1970-74, Central Advsy Ctee War Pensions, Kent W War Pensions Ctee, Br Membs Cncl World Veterans Fedn, BMC/NUF Med Advsy Ctee; Freeman City of London 1951, Liveryman Worshipful Co of Carmen 1952; *Recreations* rugby, gardening; *Clubs* City Livery, Guild of Freemen; *Style*— Harold L Payne, Esq, OBE; Long View, 18 Whybourne Crest, Tunbridge Wells, Kent TN2 5BS (☎ 0892 27024); Foresters, Girnwood, Hawick, Roxburghshire, Scotland TD9 7PN (☎ 045088 203)

PAYNE, Michael Douglas; s of Ewart Douglas Payne, of Tunbridge Wells, and Anne Elizabeth, Elizabeth, *née* Bailey; *b* 30 June 1959; *Educ* Tonbridge, Univ of London (BSc); *Career* dir Payne and Son (Silversmiths) Ltd 1985- (joined 1981); Retail Jewellers dip 1983, Gemmological Assoc dip 1984, Rayner Prize for Gemmology 1984; memb: Univ of London Convocation, Retail Ctee C of C Tunbridge Wells, Young Exec Section Nat Assoc of Goldsmiths (chm SE Branch 1988-90), Nat Assoc of Goldsmiths; registered valuer; FGA 1984; *Recreations* music, cycling, local history, agriculture and conservation; *Clubs* Agricola; *Style*— Michael Payne, Esq; Clock House, 37 High St, Tunbridge Wells, Kent TN1 1XL (☎ 0892 25874)

PAYNE, Michael William; s of Albert Leonard Payne, MM, RFC (d 1955), of Orpington, Kent, and Grace Maud, *née* Lyon (d 1974); *b* 18 April 1927; *Educ* Dulwich; *m* 2 June 1951, Angela Margaret Westmacott, da of Hugh Sherwood Leary (d 1955); 2 s (Thomas b 1965, William b 1968), 2 da (Susan b 1952, Sally b 1956); *Career* Sgt RAF 1945-48; trainee underwriter 1948-50, dep underwriter 1950-57, gen mangr 1957-68, sr ptnr Michael Payne & Partners 1967-; active underwriter: Sir William Garthwaite & Others 1969-71, Michael Payne & Others 1973-; exec chm: Janson Payne Management Ltd 1986-, Michael Payne Syndicates Pty Ltd 1987-; chm Michael Payne Agencies Ltd 1989-, dir Janson Green Holdings Ltd 1986-; memb Lloyds Law Reform Ctee 1968- (jt chm 1973-84), vice pres Insur Inst of London 1969-; Freeman City of London 1979, memb Worshipful Co of Insurers 1980; *Books* Modern Requirements in Liability Insurance (1968); *Recreations* golf, opera, music;

Clubs City of London; *Style*— Michael Payne, Esq; Wroughton, 47 Sundridge Ave, Bromley, Kent (☎ 081 460 4924); Shene Cottage, Vicarage St, Colyton, Devon (☎ 0297 52621); 85 Gracechurch St, London EC3V OBH (☎ 071 623 6423, fax 071 283 4531, telex 8813816)

PAYNTER, Cecil de Camborne Pendarves; s of late Col E Pendarves Paynter, TD, of Fernchase Manor, Ashurst Park, Fordcombe, Kent, and late Cicely Marion, *née* Hadow; *b* 17 July 1930; *Educ* Summerfields, Wellington, RMA Sandhurst; *m* 29 July 1961, Fiona Marion Naismith; 2 s (Michael John Pendarves b 1963, Andrew Francis de Camborne b 1965); *Career* Capt 3 Kings Own Hussars, Airborne Trg Offr N Somerset Yeo; regnl mangr Rank Hovis McDougal, md Magnet Signs and Joinery, chm LGT Vending, dir The English Wine Consortium; dir: Wine Standard's Bd, Bd of Tstees Wine and Spirits Educn Tst, Court of Vintners' Co; memb cncl England Agric Show and Soc, gp chm Royal Br Legion W Kent; *Recreations* country pursuits, golf, cricket, growing vines; *Clubs* Army and Navy; *Style*— C de C P Paynter, Esq; Rookery Cottage, Hever, nr Edenbridge, Kent (☎ 034 286 350)

PEACEY, Col John Capel (Charles); *b* 11 Dec 1928; *Educ* Marlborough, Bournemouth Municipal Coll (Dip Mech Eng); *m* 17 July 1954, Dr Jean Menzies Peacey, *née* Thirlby; 2 da (Susan (Mrs Graves), Diana (Mrs Taine)); *Career* various appts mainly of professional engrg interest UK Malaya Germany and Singapore 1950-71, SO I Logistics Petroleum AFSOUTH Naples Italy 1971-73, chief instr Electrical and Mechanical Sch RSME Chatham 1973-75, CRE specialist team RE acting as consltg engrs for Govt of Malta 1975-77, cdr RE team Br Mil Mission to Saudi Nat Gd Riyadh Saudi Arabia 1978-80, ret; chief infrastructure progs and SACEURS rep on NATO Infrastructure Ctee 1980-83; dep sec ACE (asst sec from 1984); Freeman City of London, Liveryman Worshipful Co of Engrs 1986; FICE, FIMechE; *Recreations* golf, family bridge, gardening, conservation, local history; *Style*— Col Charles Peacey; 11 Prospect Row, Brompton, Gillingham, Kent ME7 5AL (☎ 0634 843123); 46 Riverside Court, Nine Elms Lane, London SW8 5BY (☎ 071 627 2818); Association of Consulting Engineers, Alliance House, 12 Caxton St, London SW1H 0QL (☎ 071 222 6557, fax 071 222 0750)

PEAD, David William; s of William Henry Pead, and Ellen, *née* Bygrave; *b* 3 Nov 1949; *Educ* Haberdashers' Aske's, Leicester Business Sch (BA); *m* 17 June 1978, Shirley Florence Ann, da of William Alexander Fuller, of London; 1 da (Rachel Sarah b 26 Aug 1981); *Career* CA; asst mangr Price Waterhouse & Co 1976-78, gp taxation and planning mangr and dir Rush & Tompkins Group plc 1981-85; Consolidated Tern Investments plc: fin controller 1985-86, gp fin dir 1986-87; gp fin dir Ward Holdings plc 1987-; FCA 1982; *Recreations* ballet, opera, theatre, antique clocks, porcelain, furniture; *Style*— David W Pead, Esq; Muretto, 36 Mays Hill Rd, Shortlands, Bromley, Kent BR2 0HT (☎ 081 460 1158); Ward Holdings plc, 2 Ash Tree Lane, Chatham, Kent ME5 7BZ (☎ 0634 55111, fax 0634 577172)

PEAL, Rev John Arthur; s of Arthur Sydney William Peal, of Bognor Regis, Sussex, and Elizabeth, *née* Norris; *b* 27 April 1946; *Educ* Chichester HS, Chichester Coll of Further Educn, Kings Coll London (BD), St Augustine's Coll Canterbury; *m* 25 July 1990, Jacqueline, da of Leslie John Wyeth; 1 s (Adam b 1974), 1 da (Joanna b 1979); *Career* National Provincial Bank 1962-66; curate: All Saints Portsmouth and St John Baptist Rudmore 1971-74, Westbury with Westbury Leigh and Dilton 1974-77; vicar: Borstal 1977-82, Christ Church Educn 1982-; chaplain HM Prison Cookham Wood 1978-82, priest i/c St John Baptist Erith 1986-; AKC; *Recreations* mountain walking, bird watching, stamp collecting; *Style*— The Rev John Peal; Christ Church Vicarage, Victoria Rd, Erith, Kent DA8 3AN (☎ 0322 334729)

PEARCE, Brian Harold; s of (John) Harold George Pearce (d 1982), of Sevenoaks, and Dorothy Elsie Pearce; *b* 30 July 1931; *Educ* Tonbridge, UCL (BSc); *m* 1, 3 Sept 1955, Jean Isabel, *née* Richardson (d 1985); 2 s (Nicholas Michael John b 1959, Jonathan Brian Miles b 1966), 1 da (Gillian Sarah (Mrs Mueller-Pearce) b 1961); m 2, 2 Aug 1988, Veronica Mary, *née* Maund, formerly Mrs Magraw; *Career* Nat Serv RE 1953-55 (cmmnd 2 Lt 1954); gp chm Pearce Signs Ltd and subsids 1981- (joined 1955, gp md 1975); vice chm Royal London Soc for the Blind, bd memb Deptford Enterprise Agency; cncl memb: Goldsmith Coll London, Business in the Community; memb Bd London C of C and Indust (and other offices); pres: Br Sign Assoc, Euro Fedn of Illuminated Signs; govr New Beacon Sch Sevenoaks; Freeman: City of London, Worshipful Co of Lightmongers; *Recreations* sailing; *Clubs* RAC, Little Ship, Royal Cornwall Yacht; *Style*— Brian Pearce, Esq; Pearce Signs Ltd, Insignia House, London SE14 6AB

PEARCE, Det Chief Insp John Silby; s of Silby Henry Pearce, of Rainham, Kent, and Edith Doris, *née* Roots (d 1988); *b* 8 April 1947; *Educ* Gillingham Boys' GS; *m* 27 June 1970, Susan Ann, da of Leonard Campbell, of Chatham, Kent; 1 s (Stephen Jonathan b 1975), 1 da (Nicola Jaime b 1973); *Career* joined Kent Co Constabulary 1968; service at: Sittingbourne, Margate, Sevenoaks, Tunbridge Wells, Force Trg Sch and HQ Maidstone; specialist in detective trg forensic sci and criminal intelligence, has served in both CID and uniformed branch; hon sec Kent Police Male Voice Choir; *Recreations* male voice choir, singing, German language and culture; *Style*— Det Chief Inspr John Pearce; Kent County Constabulary, Headquarters, Sutton Rd, Maidstone, Kent ME15 9BZ (☎ 0622 690690 ext 4670, fax 0622 690511)

PEARCE, Marshall Davie; JP (1988); s of Jack Author Pearce, of Ontario, Canada, and Eileen Elizabeth, *née* Davie; *b* 28 Nov 1944; *Educ* T L Kennedy HS, Southlands Coll (Cert Ed), King Alfred's Coll (Dip Ed); *m* 27 Oct 1973; 1 da (Hannah b 9 April 1980); *Career* dep head teacher John Farmer Sch Dorset 1975-80, head teacher St Bartholemew Special Sch 1981; *Recreations* running, sailing, mountaineering; *Clubs* Seasalter Sailing; *Style*— Marshall Pearce, Esq, JP; St Bartholomew School, Attlee Way, North St, Milton Regis, Kent (☎ 0795 477888)

PEARCE, Mike; s of Victor Pearce (d 1982), of Whitstable, Kent, and Hilda Kate Pearce (d 1975); *b* 31 Dec 1943; *Educ* Faversham GS, Redhill GS; *Career* prodn ed Associated Kent Newspapers 1975-86; ed: Isle of Thanet Gazette 1986-, Thanet Times 1986-; former memb Whitstable Urban Cncl; former chm: Whitstable Carnival Ctee, East Kent Carnival Assoc; *Recreations* gardening, village pubs, collecting historic amusement machines; *Style*— Mike Pearce, Esq; Sunnyside, Dargate, Faversham, Kent ME13 9HG (☎ 0227 751356); Isle of Thanet Gazette, Gazette Building, Union Row, Margate, Kent CT9 1BB (☎ 0843 221313, fax 0843 291799)

PEARL, Howard George; s of (George Edward) Roy Pearl, of Boldventure, Chagford, Devon, and Patricia Evelyn, *née* Kirby; *b* 27 Sept 1944; *Educ* Cranbrook; *m* 1, 31 May 1969, Sally-Ann Hunter (d 1988), da of S Hunter (d 1980); 1 s (Robert Howard b 22 July 1970), 1 da (Louise Ann b 9 May 1972); m 2, 3 Jan 1989, Elizabeth, *née* Hodgson formerly Mrs Jaaback; *Career* CA; asst controller American Ultramar Ltd 1973, fin co-ordinator Ultramar plc 1981; chm and fixtures sec Sevenoaks RFC, memb Chevening PCC; FCA 1969; *Recreations* rugby football, cricket; *Clubs* Kent County CC, Sevenoaks Rugby Football; *Style*— Howard Pearl, Esq; 10 Barnfield Rd, Riverhead, Sevenoaks, Kent (☎ 0732 451641); Ultramar plc, 141 Moorgate, London EC2 (☎ 071 256 6080, fax 071 256 8556)

PEARS, Terence Edward; s of Edwin Pears (d 1964), of London, and Doris, *née* Wood (d 1958), of London; *b* 12 May 1930; *Educ* Grocers Sch London, London Poly, Stanford Univ Graduate School of Business USA; *m* Rita, da of Frederick Cottle (d 1955), of London; 1 s (Christopher Terence b 4 April 1965), 1 da (Julia Jane b 12 June 1968); *Career* former pres: Germiston Rotary Club SA, Fedn of Master Builders; former chm Inst of Building S African Branch, memb of Kent CC for Canterbury North 1989-, chm Canterbury Constituency Cons Assoc; Freeman City of London, Liveryman Worshipful Co of Paviours; Fell Chartered Inst of Building, FCIArb, PrEng (Professional Engr SA); *Recreations* philately, golf; *Clubs* City Livery, Canterbury Rotary, Broome Park Golf; *Style*— Terence Pears, Esq; Woodlands, Palmars Cross Hill, Harbledown, Canterbury, Kent CT2 9BL (☎ 0227 462944)

PEARSALL, Phyllis Isobel; MBE (1986); da of late Alexander Grosz, and late Isobel,*née* Crowley; *b* 25 Sept 1906; *Educ* Roedean, Collège e Jeunes Filles Fécamp, Sorbonne; *m* 1926, (m dis 1938), Richard Montague Stack Pearsall; *Career* artist; one-woman exhibitions 1924-89 incl: Brooke St Gallery London 1926, Upper Grosvenor Galleries London 1967-69, Arts Club 1977-79, RGS 50 Anniversary Geographers' A-Z Map Co 1986; work exhibited with: Orléans 1924, Art Inst Chicago 1931, RA 1935-39, Leicester Galleries London 1938, Upper Grosvenor Galleries 1967-72, Brighton Art Gallery 1970-71, Chilham Gallery Kent 1975, Rye Art Gallery Sussex 1976, Nevill Gallery Canterbury 1976-82, V&A Museum and Museum of London; represented in private art collections UK, USA, France, Canada, Aust, Turkey; Geographers' A-Z Map Co Ltd: fndr and dir 1936-, chm and md 1958-; Geographers Map Tst: fndr and dir 1966-, chm 1987; FRGS; *Books* Castillian Ochre (1934), Fleet Street, Tite Street, Queer Street (1983), Only the Unexpected Happens (1985), Women 1939-40 (1985); *Recreations* cooking, opera, theatre; *Clubs* Arts, Univ Women's; *Style*— Mrs Phyllis Pearsall, MBE; Geographers' A to Z Map Co Ltd, Vestry Rd, Sevenoaks, Kent TN14 5EP (☎ 0732 41152)

PEDERSEN, Cecil Ivan; s of Ivan Pedersen (d 1963), of London, and Ethel Mary, *née* McCormick; *b* 31 May 1931; *Educ* Owens Sch London; *m* 4 June 1960, (Anne) Isabel, da of Samuel James Curry, OBE, JP, of Coleraine, Co Londonderry NI; 2 da (Catherine b 1961, Hilary b 1964); *Career* RAF: Nat Serv Cmmn 1949, short serv cmmn, sponsored to study Russian London Univ 1953, instr in Russian Jt Servs Sch for Linguists 1956-58; sr ed asst The Iron and Steel Inst 1959-61; press offr: DSIR 1961-62, PR Prodn Engrg Res Assoc (PERA) 1962-66, Decca Radar Ltd 1966-67; asst sec The Inst of Physics 1967-84 (mannaging ed 1967-70, dir of publishing 1970-84), md Adam Hilger Ltd 1976-84, publishing conslt 1985-, chief exec Br Assoc Industl Eds 1986-; FInst D, FAIE (Fell Br Assoc of Idustl Eds); *Recreations* bridge, outdoor activites, photography; *Clubs* Danish, Royal Cwlth Soc, Remenham (Henley); *Style*— Cecil Pedersen, Esq

PEISLEY, Tracie Ann; da of Frederick William Peisley, of Canterbury, Kent, and Andrea Jackqulene, *née* Clayton; *b* 24 May 1965; *Educ* Bath College of Higher Educn (BA), City of Birmingham Poly (MA); *Career* artist; exhibitions: Young Painters (Metropolitan Arts Centre Folkestone) 1987, Young Painters (Maidstone Library Gallery) 1988 and 1989, Royal Overseas League Artists

89 (London) 1989, MA Fine Art 89 (Ikon Gallery Birmingham) 1989, Peter Kinley Award Exhibition (Victoria Art Gallery Bath) 1990, Portobello Art Fair (The Tabernacle Gallery London) 1990, Free Spirit (Maidstone Library) 1990, New Works (ESC Gallery London) 1990; works in Kent CC collections; painting used for book cover of In The Gold of Flesh; *Style*— Ms Tracie Peisley; Bothey Cottage, Staple St, Hernhill, nr Faversham, Kent ME13 9UB, (☎ 0227 751699)

PELLEREAU, Maj-Gen Peter John Mitchell; s of Col John Cyril Etienne Pellereau (d 1973), of Tebbs Corner, Igtham, Kent, and Aileen Nora Vidal, *née* Betham; family became Br following ceding of Isle de France to Britain becoming Mauritius; *b* 24 April 1921; *Educ* Wellington, Trinity Coll Cambridge (BA, MA); *m* 1949, Rosemary, da of Sydney Robert Garnar (d 1981), of Wrotham, Kent; 2 s (Matthew, David); *Career* cmmnd RE 1942, serv NW Europe, Maj OC 26 Armd Engr Sqdn RE (Hameln) 1946-47, Tech Staff Offr Fighting Vehicles Design Estab Chobham 1948-49, Dep Cdr Engr Base Installations Singapore 1953-55, sec Def Res Policy Ctee MOD 1959-60, Lt-Col Mil Sec's Dept MOD 1960-62, cmdg 131 Parachute Engr Regt RE TA 1963-64, Col Mil Dir of Studies RMCS Shrivenham 1965-67, asst dir RE Equipment Devpt MOD 1967-70, Brig Sr Mil Offr Royal Armament Res and Devpt Estab Fort Halstead Sevenoaks 1970-73, pres Ordnance Bd 1975-76; sec ACE 1976-87; past pres: RE Lawn Tennis Club, Oxted Hockey Club; ctee memb Wolfe Soc, memb Seveoaks Cons Assoc; CEng, FIMechE, FBIM; *Clubs* Knole; *Style*— Maj-Gen Peter Pellereau; Woodmans Folly, Crockham Hill, Edenbridge, Kent (☎ 0732 866309)

PENDER, 3 Baron (UK 1937); John Willoughby Denison-Pender; s of 2 Baron Pender, CBE (d 1965), and Camilla Lethbridge, da of late Willoughby Arthur Pemberton; *b* 6 May 1933; *Educ* Eton; *m* 1962, Julia, *qv*, da of Richard Nevill Cannon, OBE, of Coombe Place, Lewes, Sussex; 1 s, 2 da (Hon Emma Charlotte b 1964, Hon Mary Anne Louise b 1965); *Heir* s, Hon Henry John Richard Denison-Pender b 19 March 1968; *Career* formerly Lt 10 Royal Hussars and Capt City of London Yeo; former dir Globe Trust Ltd, chm J J & D Frost plc; sits as Cons in House of Lords; *Recreations* golf, racing, gardening; *Clubs* White's, Pratt's; *Style*— The Rt Hon The Lord Pender; North Court, Tilmanstone, Kent

PENDER, Baroness; Julia; da of Richard Nevill Cannon, OBE (d 1986), of Coombe Place, Lewes, Sussex, and Lelia, *née* Farmar; *b* 1 March 1943; *m* 19 Nov 1962, 3 Baron Pender, *qv*, s of 2 Baron Pender, CBE (d 1965); 1s (Hon Henry John Richard Denison-Pender b 1968), 2 da (Hon Emma Charlotte Denison-Pender b 1964, Hon Mary Anne Louise Denison-Pender b 1965); *Career* formerly: memb Br Red Cross WRVS, involved with Gtr London Fund for the Blind; memb: Kent CC for Sandwich 1981-, Kent Probation Ctee, Kent Social Servs Ctee, Police Authy; chm: Kent Adoption Panel 1983-, Kent CC Social Servs Adoption Sub Ctee 1983-, Kent CC Community Residential Sub Ctee, Dover Police Advsy Ctee, Board of Govrs Sandwich HS; govr Sir Roger Manwoods GS; *Recreations* gardening, reading, listening; *Style*— Lady Pender; North Court, Tilmanstone, nr Deal, Kent CT14 OJP (☎ 0304 611726)

PENRY, (William) Cedric Rhys; s of Benjamin William Penry (d 1972), and Ethel Evelyn Penry (d 1972); descended from John Penry, Christian martyr (1563-1593); *b* 21 June 1927; *Educ* Gowerton GS, Univ of Wales (BSc), Stanford-Insead Fontainbleau; *m* 1952, Margaret Winifred, da of Charles Starvington Cetta (d 1978); 1 s, 1 da; *Career* RAF 1945-48; works mangr Richard Thomas and Baldwins 1951-63; dir: Halivourgiki Athens 1963-69, British Steel Corporation (International) Ltd 1977-, British Steel Corporation (Overseas Services) 1976-87, Slater Steel Corporation Canada 1977-86; int business conslt 1987-; FIM; *Recreations* golf, gardening; *Clubs* Directors'; *Style*— Cedric Penry, Esq; Swallows Corner, Islet Rd, Maidenhead, Berks SL6 8LG (☎ 0628 72701)

PENTIN, David John; s of Sydney Edward Pentin (d 1971), of Canterbury, and Amelia, *née* Winkel (d 1989); *b* 26 June 1935; *Educ* Kent Coll Canterbury, Univ of London (LLB); *m* 11 June 1960, Alicia Henrietta Althea Pentin, JP, da of Gp Capt Ivor Morgan Rodney, OBE; 3 s (John b 1964, Richard b 1969, Edward b 1971), 1 da (Caroline b 1962); *Career* Nat Serv RAF 1959-61; CA; articles 1953-58, ptnr 1960-86, sr ptnr Pentins CAs 1986-; chm: Canterbury and Dist Round Table 1971-72, Gp Study Exchange Ctee Rotary Dist 1978-80, Canterbury Volunteer Bureau 1980-83; fndr pres Forest of Blean Rotary Club 1977-78; Canterbury City Cncl: memb 1983-, chm of Fin and Gen Purposes Ctee 1985-90, dep ldr of Cncl 1987-90, ldr 1990-; FCA 1959; *Recreations* walking, skiing, cycling, music; *Clubs* Kent and Canterbury; *Style*— David Pentin, Esq; Ashley House, Brewery Lane, Bridge, Canterbury, Kent CT4 5LD (☎ 0227 830278); Pentins, Chartered Accountants, Lullingstone House, Castle St, Canterbury, Kent CT1 2QF (☎ 0227 763400, fax 0227 762416)

PEPPER, Gillian Clare; JP (Tunbridge Wells and Cranbrook); da of Lt-Col William Helier Huelin (d 1968), of Ravenscliff, St Brelade, Jersey, Channel Isles, and Gwyneth Clare Huelin, OBE *née* Locker; *b* 3 Aug 1937; *Educ* Tudor Hall Wykham Park Banbury Oxon; *m* 30 Aug 1958, Gordon Terry Pepper, CBE, *qv*, s of Harold Terry Pepper (d 1972), of Jersey; 3 s (Alasdair b 13 May 1960, Harry b 1 Nov 1967, Mark b 10 June 1969), 1 da (Linda (Ninna) b 8 Dec 1961); *Career* memb: Biddenden and Dist Barnardo's Ctee, Hawkhurst Cottage Hosp League of Friends Exec Ctee; govr Cranbrook Primary Sch; local organiser RNLI; *Recreations* family, tennis, golf, walking, sailing, reading; *Style*— Mrs Gillian Pepper, JP; Staddleden, Sissinghurst, Cranbrook, Kent (☎ 0580 712852)

PEPPER, Gordon Terry; CBE; s of Harold Terry Pepper (d 1973), and Jean Margaret Gordon, *née* Furness (d 1963); *b* 2 June 1934; *Educ* Repton, Trinity Coll Cambridge (MA); *m* 30 Aug 1958, Gillian Clare, *qv*, da of Lt-Col William Helier Huelin (d 1978); 3 s (Alasdair b 1960, Harry b 1967, Mark b 1969), 1 da (Linda (Ninna) b 1961); *Career* Nat Serv cmmnd RCS 1952-54; Equity and Law Life Assurance Soc 1957-60; W Greenwell & Co: joined 1960, ptnr 1962, jt sr ptnr 1980; chm Greenwell Montagu & Co 1986-87, dir and sr advsr Midland Montagu (Holdings) Ltd 1987-90, chm Payton Pepper & Sons Ltd 1987 (dir 1986), hon visiting prof City Univ Business Sch 1987-, dir Centre For Financial Markets 1988-; memb: Ctee on Indust and Fin Nat Econ Devpt Cncl 1988-, Econ and Social Res Cncl 1989-; author of articles in various econ and fin jls; memb Stock Exchange; FIA 1961, fell Soc Investmt Analysts, CBIM; *Recreations* sailing, tennis, skiing, walking, family; *Clubs* Reform, Royal Ocean Racing, Royal Channel Islands Yacht; *Style*— Gordon Pepper, Esq, CBE; Staddleden, Sissinghurst, Cranbrook, Kent TN17 2AN (☎ & fax 0580 714853); City University Business School, Frobisher Crescent, Barbican Centre, London EC2Y 8HB (☎ 071 920 0111, fax 071 588 2756)

PEPPERELL, Peter Frederick; s of Amos Victor Pepperell (d 1947), and Elizabeth Sarah Gower (d 1943); *b* 12 May 1926; *Educ* Newport GS, Leeds Univ; *m* 1 Oct 1955, Joyce Johnston, da of David Henderson Adamson (d 1975); 1 s (David 1958), 1 da (Susan b 1960); *Career* serv Royal Hampshire Regt 1944-48; with Duncan Bros & Co Ltd Calcutta 1950-73, with Walter Duncan Gp UK 1973-; dir: Western Dooars Hldgs plc 1973, Walter Duncan & Goodricke plc 1982, Lawrie Gp plc 1985, Assam-Dooars Hldgs plc 1986; chm Lawrie Plantation Servs Ltd 1979, etc; *Recreations* golf; *Clubs* Oriental, Bengal (Calcutta); *Style*— Peter Pepperell, Esq; Lawrie Plantation Service Ltd, Wortham Place, Wrotham, Sevenoaks, Kent TN15 7AE

PEPPITT, John Raymond; QC (1976); s of Reginald Peppitt, MBE (d 1962), and Phyllis Claire, *née* French (d 1978); *b* 22 Sept 1931; *Educ* St Paul's, Jesus Coll Cambridge (BA); *m* 2 April 1960, Judith Penelope, da of Maj Lionel Frederick Edward James, CBE; 3 s (Matthew b 1962, William b 1964, Edward b 1968); *Career* Nat Serv 2 Lt RA 1950-51; called to the Bar Gray's Inn 1958; rec Crown Court 1976-, bencher 1982; *Recreations* collecting watercolours, rearing sheep; *Style*— John Peppitt, Esq, QC; Chegworth Manor Farm, Chegworth, Harrietsham, Kent ME17 1DD (☎ 0622 859313); Chambers: 3 Gray's Inn Place, London WC1 (☎ 071 831 8441, fax 071 831 8479, telex 295 119 LEXCOL G)

PERCHARD, Colin William; OBE (1985); s of William George Perchard, of La Chasse, St Martin, Jersey, CI, and Winifred Sarah, *née* Horn; *b* 19 Oct 1940; *Educ* Victoria Coll Jersey, Univ of Liverpool (BA), Int Inst for Educn Planning UNESCO Paris (Advanced Dip Educn Planning and Admin); *m* 4 April 1970, Elisabeth Penelope Glynis, da of Sir Glyn Jones, GCMG, MBE, QV, of Brandfold Cottage, Goudhurst, Kent; 3 s (Nicholas b 1972, Jonathan b 1976, Adam b 1985); *Career* Br Cncl: asst rep Blantyre Malawi 1964-68, regnl offr Africa S of Sahara 1968-71, asst rep Calcutta 1971-72, offr i/c Dhaka 1972, rep Seoul 1973-76, dir Tech Coop Trg Dept 1976-79, Int Inst for Educn Planning Paris 1979-80, rep Harare 1980-86, controller Africa Div 1986-90, dir Turkey 1990-; *Recreations* theatre, music, cooking; *Style*— Colin Perchard, Esq, OBE; The British Council, 10 Spring Gardens, London SW1A 2BN (☎ 071 930 8466, fax 071 839 6347, telex 8952201)

PERCIVAL, Arthur John; MBE (1976); s of Eric Harman Percival (d 1960), of Wembley, and Kathleen Langridge, *née* Heath; *b* 10 Sept 1933; *Educ* Mercers' Sch, Wadham Coll Oxford (BA); *m* 21 March 1964, Dorothy, da of William Salthouse (d 1961), of New Eltham; 1 da (Helen Clare b 1967); *Career* curator of Collection of Prints and Drawings and researcher for Blue Plaques County Hall London 1956-65; Civic Trust: librarian 1965-67, liaison offr 1967-87, asst dir Community Enterprise Unit 1987-; author of numerous books; adult educn lectr in Faversham and elsewhere; memb: London and Middlesex Archaeological Soc 1947-, Kent Archaeological Soc 1954-, Noise Advsy Cncl 1970-71, RTPI Working Pty on Pub Participation in Planning 1981-82, NZ Historic Places Tst 1988-, Japan Nat Tst 1989-; helped lead successful campaign to avert demolition of St Mary's Sandwich 1953; chm: Historic Bldgs Preservation Ctee of London and Middlesex Archaological Soc 1960-66, Mgmnt Ctee Darlington Quiet Town Experiment 1976-78; The Faversham Soc: fndr 1962, hon sec 1962-73, vice chm 1973-75, hon dir Fleur de Lis Heritage Centre 1977-; jt fndr: Kent Fedn of Amenity Socs 1964, Tport 2000 1971; hon ed Faversham Papers 1964-, helped draft Civic Amenities Act 1967 in 1966, hon sec The Sheppey Gp 1967-80, assessor for Interpret Britian Awards 1983-; initiated: pilot Environment Week in W Yorks Humbs and Lincs 1984, Lorry Mgmnt Study 1985; conslt for Heritage Centre in Auckland NZ 1987, involved in Br Cncl sponsored lecture tour in Japan 1989; Freeman City of London 1954; FSA 1968; *Books* A Chronicle of the Old

Mercers Club, 1904-1954 (1954), The Dutch Influence on English Vernacular Architecture (1966), The Organisation of a Local Amenity Society (1967), Local Government and Local Amenity Societies (1967), The Faversham Gunpowder Industry and its Development (1967), Heavy Lorries (1970), Final Report on the UK Contribution to European Architectural Heritage Year 1975 (1976), Understanding Our Surroundings (1979), The Great Explosion at Faversham, 2 April 1916 (1986), Old Faversham (1988); *Recreations* enjoying places, wine-making, listening to music of most kinds; *Style—* Arthur Percival, Esq, MBE, FSA; 22 Stone St, Faversham, Kent ME13 8PU (☎ 0795 533261); Civic Trust, 17 Carlton House Terrace, London SW1Y 5AW (☎ 071 9300914, fax 071 3210180)

PERCIVAL, Lady; Audrey Emily; da of Alfred Ernest Smith, and Dorothy Emily, *née* Pack; *b* 27 March 1929; *Educ* Bromley Co GS, Br Sch of Osteopathy; *m* 1990, Sir Anthony Edward Percival, CB; *Career* Br Sch of Osteopathy: qualified with Golf Medal Award 1951, leader of basic sci course 1958-62, PA to princ 1959-62, vice princ and head of faculty 1962-86, dir 1968-86; clinic supt 1951-54, pt/t private osteopathic practice Beckenham 1951-, designer of BSc course in osteopathy for Victoria Aust 1979, conslt to Course Advsy Ctee for BSc osteopathy Philip Inst of Technol Melbourne Aust 1984-; author of 10 papers printed in Br osteopathic jls 1961-83; memb: Gen Cncl and Register of Osteopaths 1951- (cncl memb 1967-69), Osteopathic Assoc of GB 1951-; pres Osteopathic Assoc of GB 1964-65; awarded Little John Award by Osteopathic Assoc of GB for servs to the profession 1980; friend of Abbeyfield Bromley Soc (involved with fund raising); hon life membership of Aust Osteopathic Assoc 1979, hon fellowship Br Sch of Osteopathy 1987; *Recreations* dog walking, classical music, gardening; *Clubs* Soroptimist Int, Beckenham and Dist; *Style—* Lady Percival; 16 Beckenham Rd, Beckenham, Kent BR3 4LS (☎ 081 650 4313)

PERCIVAL, Rt Hon Sir Ian; PC (1983), QC (1963); s of Eldon Percival (d 1947), and Chrystine, *née* Hoyle (d 1979); *b* 11 May 1921; *Educ* Latymer Upper Sch, St Catharine's Coll Cambridge (MA); *m* 1942, Madeline Buckingham, da of Albert Cooke (d 1928); 1 s (Robert), 1 da (Jane); *Career* served WWII Maj The Buffs N Africa and Burma 1940-46; called to the Bar Inner Temple 1948; bencher 1970, rec of Deal, later of the Crown Court 1971-, slr gen 1979-83, master treas Inner Temple 1990; memb Sidley and Austin USA and Int Attorneys 1984-; MP (C) Southport 1959-87; landowner; memb Royal Econ Soc; Liveryman and memb Worshipful Co of Arbitrators; FTII, FCIArb; kt 1979; *Recreations* golf, parachuting, windsurfing, tennis; *Clubs* Carlton, Beefsteak, Royal Birkdale Golf, Rye Golf, City Livery; *Style—* The Rt Hon Sir Ian Percival, QC; Oxenden, Stone-in-Oxney, nr Tenterden, Kent (☎ 023 383 321); 2 Harcourt Buildings, Temple, London EC4 (☎ 071 583 2939); 5 Paper Buildings, Temple, London EC4 (☎ 071 583 4555, telex 8956431 ANTON G, fax 071 583 1926)

PEREIRA, Sir (Herbert) Charles; s of Herbert John Pereira (d 1952); *b* 12 May 1913; *Educ* St Alban's Sch, Univ of London (BSc, PhD, DSc); *m* 1941, Irene Beatrice, da of David James Sloan (d 1916); 3 s, 1 da; *Career* RE 1939-46; Colonial Serv 1946-67, dep dir E Africa Agric and Forestry Res Orgn 1955-61; dir: ARC of Rhodesia and Nyasaland 1961-63, ARC of Central Africa (Rhodesia Zambia and Malawi) 1963-67; chm ARC of Malawi 1967-74, dir E Malling Res Station 1969-72, chief scientist (dep sec) MAFF 1972-77, res conslt in tropical agric to World Bank and other orgns 1978-, memb Bd of Tstees Royal Botanic Gdns Kew 1983-86; Haile Selassie Prize for Res in Africa 1966; FRS 1969; kt 1977; *Books* Land Use and Water Resources (1973), Policy and Practice in the Management of Tropical Watersheds (1989); *Recreations* sailing, swimming, mountain walking; *Clubs* Athenaeum, Harare; *Style—* Sir Charles Pereira, FRS; Peartrees, Nestor Court, Teston, Maidstone, Kent ME18 5AD (☎ 0622 813333)

PERKINS, Prof (Michael) John; s of George Karl Perkins (d 1987), and Eva, *née* Richardson; *b* 29 Sept 1936; *Educ* Warwick Sch, King's Coll Univ of London (BSc, PhD, DSc); *m* 24 March 1962, Pauline Mary, da of Herbert Edwin Attwood (d 1948); 3 da (Inger b 1963, Georgina b 1964, Alexandra b 1971); *Career* lectr Kings Coll London 1960-72; prof: Chelsea Coll London 1972-84, Royal Holloway and Bedford New Coll 1985- (head of dept 1985), author of papers published in various jls incl Journal of the Chemical Soc, sometime co author and co ed Organic Reaction Mechanisms series; Corday-Morgan medallist Chem Soc 1972; FRSC, CChem; *Recreations* hill walking, photography; *Style—* Prof John Perkins; Department of Chemistry, Bourne Laboratory, Royal Holloway and Bedford New College, Egham, Surrey TW20 0EX (☎ 0784 439903, fax 0784 437520, telex 935504)

PERKS, His Hon (John) Clifford; MC (1944), TD; s of late John Hyde Haslewood Perks; *b* 20 March 1915; *Educ* Blundell's, Balliol Coll Oxford; *m* 1940, Ruth Dyke, *née* Appleby; 2 s (1 s and 2 da decd); *Career* called to the Bar Inner Temple 1938; dep chm Devon QS 1965-71, circuit judge 1970-85; *Style—* His Hon Clifford Perks, MC, TD; 32 Melbury Close, Chislehurst, Kent

PERRETT, Anthony James; s of Henry Thomas Perrett, of Loxwood, W Sussex, and Florence Delphie, *née* Conran; *b* 14 Oct 1939; *Educ* Monkton Combe Sch, Open Univ (BA); *m* 4 Oct 1980, Francisca Wolthera Josphine, da of Robert Daniel Crommelin (d 1965); 2 s (Robert Quintin Henry b 1981, Timothy John Alexander b 1986), 2 da (Florence Claudine Sophie b 1982, Elizabeth Anne Louise b 1984); *Career* electrical engr: RA Lister & Co Ltd 1958-63, RA Lister & GA Sacs 1964-65, RA Lister & Ptnrs Ltd 1965-70; called to the Bar Lincolns Inn 1972; barr Govt Legal Serv 1973-: DTI 1973-74, Treasy Slrs' Dept 1974-, seconded to OFT 1958-88, asst registrar of Friendly Socs 1989-, legal advsr to Building Socs Cmmn 1989-; MIEE, CEng; *Recreations* reading, gardening; *Style—* Anthony Perrett, Esq; The Old Vicarage, The Square, Chilham, New Canterbury, Kent CT4 8BY; Registry of Friendly Societies, 15 Great Marlborough Street, London WIV 2AX

PERRY, John Howard; s of late Howard William Maurice Perry, of Cheam, Surrey, and Jane Anne, *née* Wood; *b* 13 May 1932; *Educ* Glynn Sch Epsom; *m* 21 Aug 1965, Doreen Jose, da of Frank Devereux; 2 s (Nicholas John b 16 Dec 1968, Simon Christopher b 29 Nov 1970); *Career* admin and fin ptnr Scrimgeour Kemp-Gee and Co (stockbrokers) 1968-87, admin dir Smith New Court plc 1987-90; farmer 1983-; memb Kent CC 1985-; ACIS 1955, FCCA 1955; *Clubs* Kennel, City of London; *Style—* John Perry, Esq

PERRY, Michael Anthony; s of Anthony Frank Perry, and Barbara Mary Perry; *b* 18 Jan 1957; *Educ* Swanley Sch, South Bank Poly; *m* 10 Nov 1984, Michelle Bhimattie, da of Pulchan Gajadhar; 1 s (Michael Anthony Edmund b 1987), 1 da (Letitia Michelle Cherrill b 1985); *Career* CA; trained and qualified Shipley Blackburn 1976-81, audit mangr John Baker Sons & Bell 1981-83, founded Perry & Co 1983-; ACA 1980; *Style—* Michael Perry, Esq; Perry House, The Square, Wrotham, Sevenoaks, Kent; 19-21 Swan St, West Malling, Maidstone, Kent (☎ 0732 882488)

PETERS, William; CMG (1980), LVO (1961), MBE (1959); s of John William Peters (d 1983), of Morpeth, Northumberland, and Louise, *née* Woodhouse (d 1965); *b* 28 Sept 1923; *Educ* King Edward VI GS Morpeth, Balliol Coll Oxford (MA), LSE, SOAS; *m* 1944, Catherine Bertha, da of Daniel Bailey (d 1928), of Edinburgh and Paisley; *Career* WWII serv Britain and Far East Queen's Royal Rifles, KOSB, 9 Gurkha Rifles, demob as Capt 1946; joined Colonial Serv, asst dist cmmr Gold Coast (now Ghana) 1950, ret as acting sec regnl cmmr (Cabinet rank) Northern Ghana; joined CRO as asst princ 1959, princ CRO 1959; 1 Sec: Dacca 1960-63, Cyprus 1963-67; head Zambia and Malawi Dept CRO 1967-68, head Central African Dept FCO 1968-69, dir Int Affrs Div Cwlth Secretariat 1969-71, cnsllr and head Chancery Canberra 1971-73, dep high cmmr Bombay 1974-77, ambass Uruguay 1977-80, high cmmr Malawi 1980-83; chm: LEPRA, Tibet Soc of UK; pres Royal Br Legion (Downs Branch), hon tres Tibet and China Ctee; memb: Abbeyfield (Walmer) Soc, Educn Bd Royal Soc for Asian Affairs; past pres Deal Rotary Club 1989-90, govnr Walmer Secdy Sch; *Books* Diplomatic Service Formation and Operation (1972); *Recreations* music, walking, archaeology; *Clubs* United Oxford & Cambridge Univ, Royal Commonwealth Soc, Royal Soc for Asian Affrs; *Style—* William Peters, Esq, CMG, LVO, MBE; 12 Crown Court, Middle St, Deal, Kent (☎ 030 4362822);

PETERSEN, Sir Jeffrey Charles; KCMG (1978, CMG 1968); s of Charles Petersen; *b* 20 July 1920; *Educ* Westcliff HS, LSE; *m* 1962, Karin Kristina Hayward; 2 s, 4 da; *Career* RN 1939-46; Dip Serv 1948-80; ambass to: Republic of Korea 1971-74, Romania 1975-77, Sweden 1977-80; chm British Materials Handling Board, North Sea Assets plc, AKC Larson Ltd; pres: Anglo-Korean Soc, Anglo-Swedish Soc; vice pres Swedish C of C for the UK; knight Grand Cross Royal Order of the Polar Star Sweden 1984, Order of Diplomatic Merit South Korea 1984; *Clubs* Travellers, Kent and Canterbury; *Style—* Sir Jeffrey Petersen, KCMG; 32 Longmoore St, London SW1 (☎ 071 834 8262); Crofts Wood, Petham, Kent (☎ 022 770 537)

PETRI, Dr Michael Philip; s of Philip Ludvis Carr Petri (d 1977), and Beryl Katherine, *née* Wood; *b* 17 April 1956; *Educ* Univ of London (MB BS, MRCP); *m* 22 May 1976, Linda Mary, da of Alan Powell; 1 s (Robert b 1988), 2 da (Lydia b 1982, Marissa b 1983); *Career* currently conslt physician Polle; *Style—* Dr Michael Petri; Poole General Hosptial, Poole, Dorset ☎ 0202 675100

PETTIT, Frederick George (Fred); s of George Arthur Pettit (d 1971), of Bexley, Kent, and Winifred, *née* Smith; *Educ* Sandringham Central Sch; *m* 27 May 1950, Iris Joan, da of Edward David Shopland (d 1981), of Southborough, Tunbridge Wells; 1 s (Martin Frederick b 1955 d 1971), 1 da (Janet Iris b 1952); *Career* RN 1942-46; CA; Stafford Rudkin & Co: articled 1946-51, sr asst 1951-56; Creaseys: ptnrs' asst 1956-68, ptnr 1966-88, sr ptnr 1988-; memb: ICAEW (careers advsr), CAs Benevolent Inst, SE Soc of CAs, West Kent Freemasons, Nat Tst; FCA 1962 (ACA 1952); *Recreations* gardening, family, DIY, travel; *Style—* Frederick Pettit, Esq; 25 Brian Crescent, Southborough, Tunbridge Wells, Kent TN4 0AP (☎ 0892 28980); Creaseys, 1 East Street, Tonbridge, Kent TN9 1HP (☎ 0732 770600, fax 0732 771881)

PHEILS, Peter John; s of Prof Murray Theodore Pheils, of Sydney Australia, and Unity Louise, *née* McCaughey; *b* 7 March 1944; *Educ* Leighton Park Sch Reading, St Thomas's Hosp Med Sch Univ of London (MS); *m* 29 May 1971, Sylvia, da of Tom Robinson, of Prestbury, Cheshire; 1 s (Jonathan David b 29 June 1977), 1 da (Laura Catherine b 21 Aug 1974); *Career* surgical registrar: High Wycombe and Amersham Hosps 1973-74, Brighton Hosp 1974-75; St

Thomas's Hosp London: surgical registrar 1975-76, lectr in surgery 1976-78; sr surgical registrar Bart's 1978-83, conslt surgn Canterbury and Thanet Health Authy 1984-, clinical tutor Thanet Dist Gen Hosp 1988-; memb: Br Assoc of Surgical Oncology, Nat Assoc of Clinical Tutors; fell Assoc of Surgns of GB and I; FRCS, FRSM; *Books* Master of Surgery (Thesis, 1982, Univ of London); *Recreations* gardening, cycling, tennis; *Clubs* Chelsea (St Thomas's Hosp London); *Style—* Peter Pheils, Esq; Thanet District General Hospital, St Peter's Rd, Margate, Kent CT9 4AN (☎ 0843 225544)

PHILLIPS, Rev Canon Dr Anthony Charles Julian; s of Arthur Reginald Phillips (d 1965), of Mawnan Smith, Falmouth, Cornwall, and Esmee Mary, *née* Aikman (d 1987); *b* 2 June 1936; *Educ* Kelly Coll Tavistock, King's Coll London (BD, AKC), Gonville and Caius Coll Cambridge (PhD), Coll of the Resurrection Mirfield; *m* 11 April 1970, Victoria Ann, da of Vernon Bruce Stainton, OBE (d 1946), of Rawalpindi, Punjab; 2 s (Christopher Charles Withiel b 6 Aug 1971, James Alexander Withiel b 27 June 1973), 1 da (Lucy Karenza Withiel b 10 Feb 1975); *Career* curate Good Shepherd Cambridge 1966-69, dean chaplain and fell Trinity Hall Cambridge 1969-74; St John's Coll Oxford: chaplain and fell 1975-86, domestic bursar 1982-84; lectr in theol: Jesus Coll Oxford 1975-86, Hertford Coll Oxford 1984-86; SA Cook Bye fell Gonville and Caius Coll Cambridge 1984, hon chaplain to Bishop of Norwich 1970-71; examining chaplain to: Bishop of Oxford 1979-86, Bishop of Manchester 1980-86, Bishop of Wakefield 1984-86; inter faith conslt for Judaism Archbishops of Canterbury and York 1984-86; headmaster The King's Sch Canterbury 1986-, canon theologian dio of Truro 1986-, hon canon Canterbury Cathedral 1987-; author of various articles in learned jls; *Books* Ancient Israel's Criminal Law (1970), Denteronomy (1973), God BC (1977), Israel's Prophetic Tradition (ed, 1982), Lower than the Angels (1983), Preaching from the Psalter (1987); contributor: Words and Meanings (ed P R Ackroyd and B Lindens, 1968), Witness to the Spirit (ed W Harrington, 1979), The Ministry of the World (ed G Cuming, 1979), Heaven and Earth (ed A Linzey and P Wexler, 1986); *Recreations* gardening, beachcombing; *Clubs* Athenaeum; *Style—* The Rev Canon Dr Anthony Phillips; The King's School, Canterbury, Kent CT1 2ES (☎ 0227 475501)

PHILLIPS, Ian; s of Wilfrid Phillips (d 1976), and Dorothy McLellan, *née* Taylor (d 1963); *b* 16 July 1938; *Educ* Whitgift Sch Croydon; *m* 21 Oct 1961, Fay Rosemary, da of George Sharpe Stoner (d 1986); 2 s (Jonathan Peter b 13 April 1964, Simon James b 3 Sept 1966); *Career* bd memb (fin) London Tport Exec 1980-84, dir fin and planning BR Bd 1985-88, dir fin BBC 1988-; FCA; *Recreations* golf; *Style—* Ian Phillips, Esq; 113 Lower Camden, Chislehurst, Kent BR7 5JD (☎ 081 467 0529); Bakers Cottage, Church Rd, Quenington, Cirencester, Glos; BBC, Broadcasting House, London W1A 1AA (☎ 071 927 4312, fax 071 323 6820, telex 265781, car tel 0860 748109)

PHILLIPS, Prof Neville Crompton; CMG (1973); 2 s of Samuel Phillips, of Christchurch, NZ, and Clara Phillips ; *b* 7 March 1916; *Educ* Dannevirke HS, Palmerston North Boys' HS, Canterbury Univ Coll NZ, Merton Coll Oxford; *m* 1940, Pauline Beatrice, 3 da of Selby Palmer, of Havelock North, NZ; 1 s, 2 da; *Career* serv RA 1939-45, Maj, N Africa, Italy (despatches); emeritus prof Univ of Canterbury Christchurch NZ 1966 (prof of history 1949-66, vice chllr and rector 1966-77), ret; chm: Mgmnt Ctee Canterbury Archaeological Tst 1980-83, Paths Gp Canterbury Dist Cncl 1981-85; Hon LittD Univ of Canterbury NZ 1977; presented with Festschrift 1984; *Books* Italy, vol I (Sangro to Cassino), NZ Official War Histories (1957), History of University of Canterbury (ed and contrib, 1973), Yorkshire and English National Politics 1783-84 (1961); *Recreations* walking, cricket, wine, things italian; *Style—* Professor Neville Phillips, CMG; Tyle House, Hackington Rd, Tyler Hill, Canterbury, Kent CT2 9NF (☎ 0227 471708)

PHYSICK, Dr John Frederick; CBE (1984); s of Nino William Physick (d 1946), of London, and Gladys, *née* Elliott (d 1978); *b* 31 Dec 1923; *Educ* Battersea GS, (DrRCA); *m* 28 May 1954, Eileen Mary, da of Cyril Walter Walsh (d 1970), of London; 2 s (Alastair b 2 Dec 1955, Nigel b 9 June 1958), 1 da (Helen b 6 Jan 1960); *Career* WWII RN 1942-46, AFHQ Algiers/Caserta 1942-45, RNVR until 1956; V & A Museum: joined 1948, sec to Advsy Cncl 1973-83, asst to dir 1974-83, keeper of museum servs 1975-83, dep dir 1983; memb: Drawings Ctee RIBA 1975, Cathedrals Advsy Ctee 1977-81; pres Church Monuments Soc 1984-86, chm Monuments Sub Ctee Cncl for the Care of Churches 1984- (memb 1978-); memb: Westminster Abbey Architectural Advsy Panel 1985-, Rochester Cathedral Fabric Ctee 1987-, Canterbury and Rochester Jt Diocesan Books and Documents Ctee, Canterbury and Rochester Jt Diocesan Archaeological Sub Ctee; vice chm: Rochester Diocesan Advsy Ctee for the Care of the Churches 1987- (memb 1965-), Friends of Kent Churches (chm Grants Ctee); FSA, FRSA; *Books* Catalogue of the Engravings of Eric Gill (1965), Designs for English Sculpture 1680-1860 (1969), The Wellington Monument (1970), Marble Halls (1975), The Victoria and Albert Museum, the History of its Building (1982), Sculpture in Britain 1530-1830 (ed, 2 edn 1988), The Royal College of Art (contrib, 1987); *Style—* Dr John Physick, CBE, FSA; 49 New Rd, Meopham, Kent DA13 0LS; 14 Park St, Deal, Kent CT14 6AG

PICHOWSKI, Nigel James; s of Henry Theodore James, of 31 Foxglove Green, Willesborough, and Irene Iris, *née* Hayes; *b* 27 Aug 1945; *Educ* Dartford GS, Beckenham and Penge GS, Shenstone Coll (Cert Ed), Christ Church Coll (Advanced Academic Dip Ed), Univ of Sussex (MA), Open Univ (Advanced Academic Dip Ed); *m* 1 Jan, 1972, Kathleen Margaret, da of Leonard Creasor (d 1986); 1 s (Timothy b 4 March 1976), 1 da (Lyra b 15 Sept 1973); *Career* teacher: Anerley Jr Sch 1968-70, Ramsden Jr Sch 1970-73, Mottingham Jr Sch 1973-76; dep head Lydd Jr Sch 1976-83, KCC Mobile Pool appt 1983, lectr in educn Christ Church Coll of Higher Educn 1985; headteacher: Hillyfields Jr Sch 1987-89, Napier Primary Sch 1989-; tutor S Lambeth Evening Inst 1975-86; memb Nat Assoc of Headteachers, Fell Coll Preceptors (assoc 1988); *Recreations* cricket, golf; *Clubs* Ashford Cricket, Hythe Imperial Golf; *Style—* Nigel Pichowski, Esq; 29 Sandilands, Willesborough, Ashford, Kent TN24 ORD (☎ 0233 627136); Napier Primary School, Napier Rd, Gillingham, Kent (☎ 0634 574920)

PICKERING, Dr David George Lowthian; s of Dr Ian George Walker Pickering, VRD (d 1984), of E Horsley, Surrey, and Jean Winifred, *née* Lowthian (d 1975); *b* 19 Aug 1949; *Educ* Epsom Coll, Westminster Hosp Univ of London (MB BS, MRCP); *m* 24 May 1975, Nita, da of Brahm Prakash Mankanday, of Croydon; 2 s (Shalin Ian b 1985, Vyan Niel George b 1987); *Career* RN Med Serv 1974-79; registrar radiotherapy and oncology Westminster Hosp 1979-81, sr registrar radiotherapy and oncology RPMS and Hammersmith Hosp 1981-87, conslt clinical oncologist Pembury Hosp 1987-; author of various papers in professional jls; memb: Standing Ctee on Med Oncology RCP, Project Team Mid Kent Radiotherapy Centre Maidstone; FRCR; *Recreations* sailing, sub aqua diving; *Style—* Dr David Pickering; Bishop's Lodge, 129 Forest Rd, Tunbridge Wells, Kent TN2 5EY (☎ 0892 29278); Pembury Hosp, Tunbridge Wells, Kent TN2 4QT (☎ 0892 823535)

PICKFORD, David Michael; s of Aston Charles Corpe Pickford (d 1945); *b* 25 Aug 1926; *Educ* Emanuel Sch London, Coll of Estate Mgmnt; *m* 1956, Elizabeth Gwendoline, da of John Hooson, of Segrwyd Hall, Denbigh (d 1972); 1 s (Charles b 1960), 2 da (Penelope b 1952, Elizabeth b 1958); *Career* chartered surveyor; chm: Haslemere Estates plc 1983-86 (md to 1983), Lilliput Property Unit Trust, Exeter Park Estates plc, Compco Holdings plc, Gulliver Developments Property Unit Trust; dir Youth with a Mission, vice pres Drug and Alcohol Fndn; chm: Prison Fellowship, Mission to London; pres Christians In Property, organizer of Residential Christian Conference Centre for 15-25 year-olds (2000 visitors each year); *Recreations* sheep farming, youth work; *Style—* David Pickford, Esq; Elm Tree Farm, Mersham, nr Ashford, Kent TN25 7HS (☎ 023 3720 200); 33 Grosvenor Sq, London W1X 9LL (☎ 071 493 1156)

PILE, Sir William Dennis; GCB (1978, KCB 1971, CB 1968), MBE (1944); s of James Edward Pile; *b* 1 Dec 1919; *Educ* Royal Masonic Sch, St Catharine's Coll Cambridge; *m* 1, 1939 (m dis 1947) Brenda Skinner; m 2, 1948, Joan Marguerite Crafter; 1 s, 2 da; *Career* chm Bd of Inland Revenue 1976-79, dir Nationwide Building Soc 1980-, Distillers' Co Ltd 1980-; *Clubs* United Oxford and Cambridge Univ, Hawks (Cambridge); *Style—* Sir William Pile, GCB, MBE; The Manor House, Riverhead, nr Sevenoaks, Kent (☎ 0732 54498)

PINCHIN, Rev Antony Pinchin; s of Frank James Pinchin, of Epsom, Surrey, and Barbara Ann, *née* Cornforth; *b* 27 Sept 1957; *Educ* Whitgift Sch Croydon, St John's Coll Cambridge (BA, MA), Coll of The Resurection Mirfield (theol trg); *Career* ordained: deacon 1981, priest 1982; curate Holy Trinity Hawley 1981-1984, asst administrator Shrine of Our Lady of Walsingham 1984-1987, vicar of Higham with Merston Rochester 1987-; ed Living Stones (theol jl) 1986-; govr Higham Co Primary Sch, chm Observer Mace Schs Debating Assoc, memb Dickens Country Protection Soc ; *Recreations* squash, travel, music; *Style—* The Rev Antony Pinchin; The Vicarage, Hermitage Rd, Higham, Rochester, Kent ME3 7NE (☎ 0634 717360)

PINCHIN, David Robert George; s of George Robert Pinchin (d 1962), of Harford Drive, Watford, Herts, and Audrey Edwina Kathleen, *née* Hancox; *b* 31 Jan 1945; *Educ* Watford GS; *m* 17 Dec 1977, Roberta Mary E (Bobby), da of late Gordon Thomas Howell Jones, of Llanelli, Dyfed; 2 s (Mark Edward David b 1980, Stuart William Robert b 1981); *Career* asst sec to Bd of Govrs Bethlem Royal and Maudsley Hosps 1970-72, dep gp sec Barnet Hosp Mgmnt Ctee 1972-74, acting dist admin Barnet AHA 1974-82; Bexley Health Authy: dist admin 1982-86, dist gen mangr 1987-; memb Inst of Health Serv Mgmnt SE Thames Regnl Cncl 1984- (chm 1984-86); life memb Watford Operatic Soc (memb and musical dir 1963-82), musical dir Abbots Langley Gilbert and Sullivan Soc 1967-77, memb Barnet and E Barnet Rotary club 1972-82; memb Inst of Health Serv Mgmnt 1969; *Recreations* singing, acting, conducting, piano, violin, theatre, football, tennis, badminton, snooker; *Clubs* Chelsfield Park Cricket (memb and social sec); *Style—* David Pinchin, Esq; Paynesfield House, Tatsfield, Westerham, Kent (☎ 0959 77267); Bexley Health Authority, 221 Erith Road, Bexleyheath, Kent (☎ 081 301 2333)

PINKER, Maj Richard Walrond; s of Henry George Pinker (d 1961), and May Simcoe (d 1963), da of Rev Walrond Clarke (*see* Burke's Landed Gentry, 1871 edn, Clarke of Tremlett); *b* 19 July 1913; *Educ* Wrekin Coll Sherborne;

m 16 Sept 1940, Caroline Mary, da of Charles Gordon Darroch Farquhar (d 1946) (*see* Burke's Landed Gentry, 18 edn, Vol I, 1965, Farquhar of Acheron); 1 s (Charles), 1 da (Anne (wid of Lt-Col David Blair, Queens Own Highlanders, ka 1979 NI)); *Career* cmmnd Devonshire Regt 1932, served India, Malta, UK (acting Lt-Col), ret from Army 1947; in wine trade with Mentzendorff & Co, dir (late md) Simon Bros & Co Ltd, wine buyer NAAFI, ret 1973; *Recreations* shooting, golf, gardening; *Clubs* Army and Navy; *Style*— Maj Richard W Pinker; Pilgroves, Brasted Chart, Westerham, Kent TN16 1LY (☎ 0959 62579)

PITT, Rev Trevor; s of Arthur Edwin Pitt (d 1990), of Luton, Beds, and Bessie May, *née* Taylor; *b* 10 Jan 1945; *Educ* Dunstable GS, Univ of Hull (BA, MA)), Union Theol Seminary New York City (STM); *m* 1, 19 Aug 1967, Elizabeth (d 1979), da of Albert Turner (d 1986), of Folkestone, Kent; 2 da (Emma Elizabeth Jane b 20 Dec 1970, Charlotte Georgina b 10 July 1974); m 2, 29 July 1981, Linda Joyce, da of Richard Birch (d 1969), of Folkestone; *Career* asst curate St George Sheffield 1970-74; Gleadless Valley Sheffield: team vicar 1974-77, team rector 1977-79; priest i/c Elham Canterbury 1979-81, vicar of Elham Denton and Wootton Canterbury 1981-, vice princ Canterbury Sch of Ministry 1981-, six preacher Canterbury Cathedral 1985-; asst prodr religions progs Radio Hallam Sheffield 1974-79, govr various schs sheffield 1974-79, chm Elham Sch Govrs 1979-; *Recreations* photography, cricket; *Style*— The Rev Trevor Pitt; The Vicarage, Elham, Canterbury, Kent CT4 6TT (☎ 0303 840219); 1 Lady Wootton's Green, Canterbury, Kent CT1 1TL (☎ 0227 459401)

PITT, William; *b* 17 July 1977; *Educ* London Nautical Sch, South Bank Poly London (BA); *m* 1967, Janet, *née* Wearn; 1 da; *Career* housing offr Lambeth Borough Cncl 1975-81; joined Lib Party 1959; contested Croydon NW 1974 and 1979, MP (SDP-Liberal Alliance) Croydon North-West 1981-83; *Style*— William Pitt Esq; 9 Queens Rd, Broadstairs, Kent

PLAISTOWE, Alan David; s of David Plaistowe, of Connemara, Co Galway, and Rhona Elizabeth, *née* French; *b* 18 June 1932; *Educ* Marlborough, Ramsey Laboratories UCL (BSc); *m* 14 June 1957, Jane, da of Donovan Candler, of London; 1 da (Victoria b 1966); *Career* Lt RE Libya 1950-52; with Design Engrs (gas processing, oil refining) 1955-58; Stone and Webster Engineering 1958-65; fndr and md Chemical Systems International 1965, pres Chemical Systems Group 1986-; FIChemEng, FIPet; *Recreations* flying, golf, gardening, jazz; *Clubs* RAC; *Style*— Alan Plaistowe, Esq; Wanden, Egerton, Kent; Chemical Systems Ltd

PLANT, Baroness; Gladys; *née* Mayers; da of Sampson Mayers; *m* 1931, Baron Plant, CBE (Life Peer UK (1978), d 1986); 2 s, 1 da; *Style*— The Rt Hon Lady Plant; 8 Apple Tree Close, North St, Barming, Maidstone, Kent ME16 9HQ

PLATT, Norman; OBE (1985); s of Edward Turner Platt (d 1956), and Emily Jane Platt (d 1972); *b* 29 Aug 1920; *Educ* Bury GS, King's Coll Cambridge (BA); *m* 1, 1942, Diana Franklin, da of Sir Charles Travis Clay, CB (d 1975); 1 s (Tristan), 1 da (Marianna); m 2, 1963, Johanna Sigrid, da of Jesse Stewart Bishop; 1 s (Benjamin b 1965), 2 da (Rebecca b 1966, Lucinda b 1969); *Career* singer, actor, writer, translator, opera prodr, teacher; princ Sadler's Wells Opera 1946-48, Eng Opera Gp 1948; memb Deller Consort, fndr and artistic dir Kent Opera 1969-89; co-fndr (with Robin Jessel) The Canterbury Theatre and Festival Tst, chm Canterbury Festival Planning Ctee 1984-86; dir of first Acting in Opera course 1989; Hon DCL Kent; *Recreations* listening to music, being read to by my wife; *Style*— Norman Platt, Esq, OBE; Pembles Cross, Egerton, Ashford, Kent TN27 9EN (☎ 023 376 237)

PLAYFORD, Geoffrey John; s of Frank Reginald John Playford, of 43a Upper Queens Rd, Ashford, Kent, and Kathleen Agnes Mary, *née* Pentecost; *b* 1 June 1945; *Educ* Ashford GS, Coll of Law Lancaster Gate; *m* 15 April 1983, Lorraine, da of Robert Bevington, of Brockton Manor, Charing Heath, nr Ashford, Kent; 1 s (Robert Glynne b 5 Sept 1978), 1 da (Alexandra Helen Frances b 5 Sept 1988); *Career* admitted slr 1967; NP 1972; parly liason offr (Swale Dist) for Kent Law Soc; govr: Norton Knatchbull Sch Ashford 1970, Friars Sch Gt Chart Ashford 1984; chm: Ashford Hockey Club 1982, Ball Lane Pavilion Club 1988; memb: Law Soc 1967, Kent Law Soc 1967, Provincial Notaries Soc 1972, FIMBRA 1988; *Recreations* hockey; *Clubs* Ashford Hockey, Ball Lane Pavilion; *Style*— Geoffrey Playford, Esq; 40 Court St, Faversham, Kent (☎ 0795 536535, fax 0795 539088, home 0233 647112)

PLEASANCE, Roy Thomas; s of James Harold Pleasance (d 1981), and Mary Catherine, *née* Harris (d 1982); *b* 11 Feb 1926; *Educ* Rutlish Sch Merton; *m* 1, 12 June 1948, Gwendoline May; m 2, 3 Oct 1964, Anne; m 3, 29 June 1984, Norman Mary Germaine, da of Sir Norman King (d 1963); *Career* CA taxation specialist; head of taxation dept BP Co Ltd 1958-73, chm UK Oil Ind Taxation Ctee 1964-74; *Books* UK Taxation of Offshire Oil and Gas (with R Hayllar, 1977); *Recreations* opera, architecture, history; *Style*— Roy Pleasance, Esq; Arden's House, Abbey St, Faversham, Kent ME13 7BH (☎ 0795 534 124); 80 Preston St, Faversham, Kent (☎ 0795 535 249)

PLUMPTRE, Hon Francis Charles; yst s of 21 Baron FitzWalter, and Margaret Melisina, *née* Deedes; *b* 30 May 1963; *Educ* St Edmund's Sch Canterbury Kent; *Style*— The Hon Francis Plumptre; Goodnestone Park, Canterbury, Kent

PLUMPTRE, Hon (Wyndham) George; s of 21 Baron FitzWalter, *qv*, and Margaret Melesina, *née* Deedes; *b* 24 April 1956; *Educ* Radley, Jesus Coll Cambridge; *m* 1984, Alexandra Elizabeth, da of Prince Michael Cantacuzene, Count Speransky and Mrs James Edwards; 2 s (Wyndham James Alexander b 1986, Piers Harry Constantine b 1987); *Career* Sotheby's rep in Kent 1991-; author; *Books* Royal Gardens (1981), Collins Book of British Gardens (1985), The Fast Set (1985), Homes of Cricket (1988), The Latest Country Gardens (1988), Cricket Caricatures and Cartoons (1989), Garden Ornament (1989), The Golden Age of Cricket (1990), Barclays World of Cricket (ed, 1986), Back Page Cricket (ed, 1987), Back Page Racing (ed, 1989); *Clubs* Beefsteak; *Style*— The Hon George Plumptre; Rowling House, Goodnestone, Canterbury, Kent CT3 1QB (☎ 0304 813287)

PLUMPTRE, Hon Julian Brook; s and h of 21 Baron FitzWalter, and Margaret Melesina, *née* Deedes; *b* 18 Oct 1952; *Educ* Radley, Wye Coll London (BSc); *m* March 1988, Alison Sally, *née* Quiney; 1 s (Edward Brook b 26 April 1989); *Career* land agency; *Style*— The Hon Julian Plumptre; Goodnestone Park, Canterbury, Kent

PLUNKET, Hon Mrs (Denis) Kiwa; Pamela Mary; da of late James Watherston, of Christchurch, NZ; *m* 1962, the Hon (Denis) Kiwa Plunket (d 1970), s of 5 Baron Plunket, GCMG, KCVO, KBE (d 1920); *Style*— The Hon Mrs Kiwa Plunket; 16 Town Hill, W Malling, Kent ME19 6QN (☎ (0732) 1197)

PLURENDEN, Baroness; Dorothee Monica; da of Maj Robert Bateman Prust, OBE, of Vancouver, BC, Canada; *m* 1951, 1 and last Baron Plurenden (d 1978); 2 da (Rosanne, Francesca); *Style*— The Rt Hon the Lady Plurenden; Plurenden Manor, High Halden, Ashford, Kent; Lidostrasse 63, 6314 Unterägeri, Switzerland

POCOCK, Air Vice-Marshal Donald Arthur; CBE (1975, OBE 1957); s of Arthur Pocock (d 1970), of Hampstead, and E Pocock, *née* Broad; *b* 5 July 1920; *Educ* Crouch End; *m* 1947, Dorothy Monica, da of D Griffiths; 2 s, 3 da; *Career* cmmnd RAF 1941; cmd RAF Regt Wing 1957-58, MOD 1958-59, HQ AAFCE 1959-62, sr ground def SO NEAF 1962-63, MOD 1963-66, sr ground def SO FEAF 1966-68, ADC to HM The Queen 1967, Cmdt-Gen RAF Regt 1973-75; gen mangr (Iran) British Aerospace Dynamics Group 1976-79; dir Br Metallurgical Plant Constructors' Assoc 1980-85; *Style*— Air Vice-Marshal Donald Pocock, CBE; 16 Dence Park, Herne Bay, Kent CT6 6BQ (☎ 0227 374773)

POCOCK, Robert William Richard; s of Geoffrey Robert Pocock (d 1939), of Blandford, Dorset, and Sybil Frances Hall, *née* Richards; *b* 2 Aug 1937; *Educ* Blundells Sch Tiverton Devon; *m* 5 March 1960, Deanna Anne, da of Howard Leslie Chant (d 1975), of Montacute, Somerset; 2 s (Stephen b 1961, John b 1968), 1 da (Jane b 1965); *Career* Nat Serv 1959-61, cmmnd Duke of Edinburgh's Royal Regt 1960; ptnr Messrs Hobbs Parker Chartered Surveyors Kent 1971-88, regnl dir Abbey National Estate Agents Cornerstone 1988-90; memb: Ashford Round Table 1961-72, local businessmen's clubs, local sports clubs; FRICS 1970, former assoc memb Chartered Auctioneers and Estate Agents Inst 1959; *Recreations* sport, foreign travel; *Clubs* Farmers, Elwick (Ashford), Folkestone RFC; *Style*— Robert Pocock, Esq; Ridge Cottage, Etchinghill, Folkestone, Kent CT18 8DE (☎ 0303 862183, fax 0303 862627)

POLLOCK, Peter Glen; s of Jack Campbell Pollock (d 1953), and Rebecca Shields Marshall, *née* Clarke (d 1985); *b* 6 Sept 1946; *Educ* Nautical Coll Pangbourne; Univ of St Andrews (MA); *m* 3 Sept 1977, Nicola Sara, da of Derek William Bernard Clements, of Cirencester, Glos; 2 s (Jonathan William Campbell b 1982, Matthew Charles Simon b 1984); *Career* fin dir: Hawker Siddeley Power Transformations Ltd 1978-83, Fisher Controls Ltd 1983-85; gp chief exec ML Holdings plc 1985; ctee memb RUKBA 1985-, memb Cncl SBAC 1989-; FICA; *Recreations* golf, shooting, fishing, skiing, sailing; *Clubs* Knole Park Golf; *Style*— Peter Pollock, Esq; Hamilton House, Temple Ave, London EC4Y DHA (☎ 071 353 4212)

POLLOCK, Hon Mrs (Rosemary Tyrwhitt); da and co-heiress of Baroness Berners; *b* 20 July 1931; *Educ* Stonar Sch Cottles Park nr Melksham Wilts, Dorset House Sch of Occupational Therapy Oxford; *m* 1959, Kelvin Alexander Pollock, s of Kelvin Clayton Pollock; 2 s; *Career* practising occupational therapist 1952-59; *Recreations* outdoor pursuits; *Style*— The Hon Mrs Pollock; Malt House, Hollingbourne, Kent

POOLE, (Francis) Henry (Michael); s of Charles Frederick John Kaitting Poole (d 1976), of Mixtow House, Lanteglos-by-Fowey, Cornwall, and Stella Mary Grant, *née* Morris; *b* 23 Sept 1949; *Educ* Eton, Trinity Hall Cambridge; *m* 20 Sept 1975, Diana Mary Olga, da of Eric Arthur Parker (d 1983), of Summerhill Farm House, Headcorn, Kent; 1 s (Frederick Henry Eric b 1983), 2 da (Angelica Lucy Daphne, Stella Antonia Felicity); *Career* dir Laing and Cruikshank Institutional Equities 1985- (joined 1971, ptnr 1979), non-exec dir Rockware Gp 1986-87; memb: Kensington Cons Assoc, London Stock Exchange 1979-; *Books* European Paper Directory (1988); *Recreations* bridge, riding, mountain walking; *Style*— Henry Poole, Esq; 74 Hornton St, London W8 4NU; Gibbet Oast, Leigh Green, Tenterden, Kent TN30 7DH; Laing &

Cruickshank, Broadwalk House, 5 Appold St, London EC2A 2DA (☎ 071 588 4000, telex 888397/8, fax 071 588 0290)

POOLE, Monica Mary; da of Charles Reginald Poole (d 1961), of Tonbridge, and Gladys Aline, *née* Haskell (d 1962); *b* 20 May 1921; *Educ* Abbotsford Sch Broadstairs, Central Sch of Arts and Crafts (Dip); *m* 28 May 1952, Alastair George Murison Small, s of Alexander Small, of Melrose; *Career* wood engraver; exhibitions incl: Royal Acad, Int Exhibitions of Botanical Art Pittsburgh USA 1972 and 1979, Int Soc of Wood Engravers Exhibitions 1979 and 1983; perm collections containing work incl: V&A London, Ashmolean Museum Oxford, Fitzwilliam Museum Cambridge, Hunterian Museum Glasgow, Boston Public Library USA, Södentale Art Gallery Sweden, Museum Boymans Van Beunengen Rotterdam, Kent CC Collection; fell Royal Soc of Painter-Etchers and Engravers 1967; *Books* The Wood Engravings of John Farleigh (1985); *Style—* Miss Monica Poole; 67 Hadlow Rd, Tonbridge, Kent TN9 1QB (☎ 0732 353806)

PORTER, Arthur Gordon; TD; s of John Alfred Graham Porter (d 1978), and Mary Elizabeth, *née* Whitling; *b* 11 Sept 1913; *Educ* King's Sch Canterbury; *m* 20 Dec 1947, Annette Mary, da of John Edmund Fryer (d 1989), of Fort William, Canada; 2 s (John Graham b 1951, David Arthur b 1959), 2 da (Jane Mary b 1954, Judith Edna b 1958); *Career* Reckitt and Colman (overseas) Ltd in Mexico, Cuba, Peru 1946-65; Cncllr Whitstable UDC 1970-74; Canterbury City Cncl: leader 1974-82, Mayor 1982-83, Lord Mayor 1989-90; memb Assoc of Dist Cncls; *Recreations* gardening, theatre, travel; *Clubs* Special Forces; *Style—* Arthur Porter, Esq, TD; South Tythe Barn, The Drive, Chestfield, Whitstable CT5 3NS (☎ 0227 792700)

PORTER, John Andrew; TD, DL (Kent); s of Horace Augustus Porter, DFC, MP (d 1948), of Southfleet, and Vera Marion, *née* Andrew (d 1967); *b* 18 May 1916; *Educ* Radley, Sidney Sussex Coll Cambridge (MA); *m* 23 Aug 1941, Margaret Isobel, da of Samuel Wisnom (d 1944), of Stanmore; 2 da (Jocelyn Virginia b 1942, Angela Ruth b 1945); *Career* RA 1937-46 Lt Col; chartered surveyor; Porter Putt & Fletcher: ptnr 1938, sr ptnr 1948-81 (later Porter & Co BB); Kent County Building Society: dir 1947, chm 1965-68; Hastings & Thanet Building Society: dir 1968, chm 1972-78; Anglia Building Society: chm 1978-81, dir 1978-87; Gravesend & Dartford Reporter: dir 1946, chm 1969-74; dir Gravesend & District Real Estate Company 1947-; JP 1952-85 (chm Gravesham Bench 1976-83), gen commr of taxes 1970-; pres: Gravesend Cons Assoc 1965-77, Kent CCC 1985-86; chm govrs Cobham Hall Sch 1988-, played hockey for Kent 1946-47; FRICS (twice chm Kent Branch); *Recreations* cricket, reading, gardening; *Clubs* MCC, RAC, Hawks (Cambridge); *Style—* John Porter, Esq, TD, DL; Leaders, Hodsoll St, nr Wrotham, Kent TN15 7LH (☎ 0732 822260)

PORTER OF LUDDENHAM, Baron (Life Peer 1990), of Luddenham in the Co of Kent; Sir George; OM (1989); s of late John Smith Porter, and Alice Ann, *née* Roebuck; *b* 6 Dec 1920; *Educ* Thorne GS, Univ of Leeds (BSc), Emmanuel Coll Cambridge (MA, PhD, ScD); *m* 12 Aug 1949, Stella Jean, da of Col George Brooke (d 1973), of Caring, Leeds, nr Maidstone, Kent; 2 s (John Brooke b 22 Sept 1952, Andrew Christopher George b 17 Aug 1955); *Career* Radar Offr RNVR Western Approaches and Med 1941-45; demonstrator physical chemistry Univ of Cambridge 1949-52, asst dir of res physical chemistry and fell Emmanuel Coll Cambridge 1952-54, asst dir Br Rayon Res Assoc 1954-55, Firth prof of chemistry and head Dept Chemistry Univ of Sheffield 1963-66 (prof of physical chemistry 1955-63); The Royal Instn of GB: dir 1966-85, dir The Davy Faraday Res Laboratory 1966-85, Fullerian prof of chemistry 1966-87; chllr Univ of Leicester 1986-, res prof and fell Imperial Coll London 1987-, Gresham prof of astronomy and physical sciences 1990-; visiting prof: Pennsylvania State Univ 1961, UCL 1967-86, Caltech 1974, Univ of California at Berkeley 1978, Imperial Coll London 1978-; hon fell: Emmanuel Coll Cambridge 1967, Royal Scot Soc of Arts 1975, Royal Med Soc Edinburgh 1987, Imperial Coll London 1987; foreign fell Indian Nat Acad of Sciences 1990; fell: Royal Soc of Edinburgh 1983, Queen Mary and Westfield Coll London 1986; awarded: Corday-Morgan Medal of Chem Soc 1955, Nobel Prize for Chemistry 1967, Silvanus Thompson Medal of Br Inst of Radiology 1968, Davy Medal of Royal Soc 1971, 1976 Kalinga Prize (UNESCO) for Popularisation of Sci 1977, Robertson Prize of Nat Acad Sci 1978, Rumford Medal of Royal Soc 1978, Communications Award of Euro Physical Soc 1978, Faraday Medal of Chem Soc 1980, Longstaff Medal of RSC 1981, Melchett Medal of Inst of Energy 1987, Porter Medal 1988; author of over 300 scientific papers, many lectures given on scientific subjects, numerous TV and radio appearances, producer of scientific films and videos; pres: Comité International de Photobiologie 1968-72, Chem Soc 1970-72 (Faraday Div 1973-74), Nat Assoc for Gifted Children 1975-80, Res and Devpt Soc 1977-82, Assoc for Sci Educn 1985, Br Assoc for Advancement of Sci 1985-86, Royal Soc 1985-90, London Int Youth Sci Fortnight 1987-89; vice pres UK Soc for Promotion of Sci and Technol in Pakistan 1989-; hon memberships incl: NY Acad of Sciences 1968, Chem Soc of Japan 1982, Royal Inst GB 1988; memberships incl: Res Grants Ctee DSIR 1963-65, Aeronautical Res Cncl 1964-66, BBC Sci Consultative Gp 1967-75, Open Univ Cncl 1969-75, Advsy Cncl Sci Museum 1970-73, Pontifical Acad of Sciences 1974, Euro Acad of Arts Sciences and Humanities 1980, Cncl RSA 1978-80; foreign memberships incl: Soviet Acad of Sciences, Japan Acad, Academia Lincei, La Real Academia de Ciencias Madrid 1978, Indian Nat Acad of Sciences 1986; foreign assoc Nat Acad of Sciences Washington 1974; tstee: Br Museum 1972-74, The Bristol Exploratory 1986-; Hon Liveryman Worshipful Co of Salters 1981, Freeman City of London 1981; Hon Doctorate of 30 Univs, Hon Professorship of 2 Univs and 2 Insts; FRS 1960, PRS 1985; kt 1972; *Books* Chemistry for the Modern World (1962); *Recreations* sailing; *Clubs* Athenaeum; *Style—* The Rt Hon Lord Porter of Luddenham, OM, PRS; The Old Rectory, Luddenham, nr Faversham, Kent ME13 0TE; Chairman of the Centre for Photochemistry and Photosynthesis, Dept of Biology, Imperial College of Science and Technology, South Kensington, London SW7 2AZ (☎ 071 589 5111, fax 071 584 7596)

POSNETTE, Dr Adrian Frank (Peter); CBE (1976); s of Frank William Posnette (d 1956), of Cheltenham, Glos, and Edith Mary, *née* Webber (d 1969); *b* 11 Jan 1914; *Educ* Cheltenham GS, Christ's Coll Cambridge (BA, MA, ScD), Imp Coll of Tropical Agric (AICTA), Univ of London (PhD); *m* 15 July 1937, Isabelle, da of Dr Montgomery De Forest La Roche (d 1958), of New York City; 1 s (John b 1950), 2 da (Jane b 1939, Suzanne b 1942); *Career* Colonial Agric Serv Gold Coast 1937-55: appointed botanist 1937-44, head of botany and plant pathology W African Cocoa Res Inst 1944-49, seconded to E Malling Res Station Maidstone Kent 1949, appointed princ scientific offr 1955; dir E Malling Res Station 1972-79 (head Plant Pathology Section 1957-69, dep dir 1969-72), prof of plant sciences Wye Coll London 1971-78; author of: series of eight res pubns on virus diseases of cocoa trees 1947-55, numerous pubns on virus diseases of fruit trees and strawberries 1953-80; govr Redhill Sch E Sutton; awarded Ridley Medal of the Worshipful Co of Fruiterers 1978 (Hon Freeman 1982); FIBiol 1963, FRS 1971, VMH 1982; *Recreations* ornithology; *Clubs* Farmers, Hawks's (Camb); *Style—* Prof Adrian Posnette, CBE, FRS; Walnut Tree, East Sutton, Maidstone, Kent ME17 3DR (☎ 0622 843282)

POSWILLO, Prof David Ernest; CBE (1989); s of Ernest Joseph Poswillo, JP (d 1979), of Gisborne, NZ, and Amelia Mary, *née* McCormick; *b* 1 Jan 1927; *Educ* Gisborne Boys' HS, Univ of Otago NZ (BDS, DDS, DSc), Westminster Med Sch Univ of London (MRCPath), Univ of Zurich (MDhc); *m* 27 June 1956, Elizabeth Alison, da of John Whitworth Russell (d 1982), of Nelson, NZ; 2 s (Stephen b 22 Nov 1962, Mark b 10 Dec 1964), 2 da (Jane (Mrs Caton) b 13 Oct 1958, Jill (Mrs Battye) b 8 Jan 1960); *Career* OC Southern Dists Hosp RNZDC 1948-50, 30 Field Ambulance RAMC BAOR 1951; dir oral surgery N Canterbury Hosp Bd NZ 1953-68, prof of teratology RCS 1969-77, conslt oral surgn Queen Victoria Hosp E Grinstead 1969-77, prof of oral pathology and oral surgery Univ of Adelaide South Aust 1977-79, sr oral and maxillofacial surgn Royal Adelaide and Childrens Hosp South Aust 1977-79; prof: of oral Surgery Royal Dental Hosp London 1977-83, of oral and maxillofacial surgery Guy's Hosp London 1983-; memb: Human Task Force WHO 1976-78, Cncl Royal Dental Hosp London 1977-83; conslt advsr to chief MO DHSS 1979-86, tstee Tobacco Prods Res Tst 1980-, memb Bd of Faculty of Dental Surgery RCS 1981-89; vice pres and cncl memb Med Def Union 1983- (chm Dental Ctee), sec gen Int Assoc of Oral and Maxillofacial Surgeons 1983-90, memb Govrs Cncl UMDS of Guys and St Thomas' Hosps 1983-89; pres: Odontology Section Royal Soc of Med 1989-90, Br Assoc Oral and Maxillofacial Surgns 1990-91; Hunterian Prof RCS 1968 and 1976, Regent's Prof Univ of California 1987; lectures: Arnott Demonstrator 1972, Erasmus Wilson 1973, Darwin-Lincoln and Johns Hopkins 1975, Waldron (Harvard) 1976, Richardson (Harvard) 1981, Tomes RCS 1982, President's BAOMS 1985, Sarnat (UCLA) 1989, William Guy RCS of Educn 1990; RNZADC prize 1948, Tomes prize 1966, Down medal 1973, Kay-Kilner prize 1975, ASOMS res award 1976, Hunter medal and Triennial prize 1976, Orthog Surgery award Univ of Texas 1982, Edison award Univ of Michigan 1987; memb: German Acad of Natural Scis (Leopoldina) 1988, Inst of Med Nat Acad of Sci Washington USA 1989; hon FFDRCSI 1974; FDSRCS 1952, FRACDS 1966, FIBiol, CBiol, FRCPath 1981; *Recreations* gardening, DIY, skiing, sailing; *Style—* Prof David Poswillo, CBE; Ferndale, Oldfield Rd, Bickley, Kent BR1 2LE (☎ 081 467 1578); Floor 24 Guy's Hosp Tower, London SE1 9RT (☎ 071 955 4338)

POTTER, Hon Mrs (Vanessa Jane); *née* Robson; da of Sir Lawrence William Robson (d.1982), and Baroness Robson of Kiddington, J P; *b* 2 Sept 1949; *Educ* Wycombe Abbey, St Thomas's Medical Sch; *m* 1973, Jonathan Martin Potter; 1 s, 2 da; *Career* medical practitioner; *Style—* The Hon Mrs Potter; Tyler Hall, Tyler Hill, Canterbury, Kent

POULSEN, Christian Graeme; s of Otto Marius Poulsen (d 1966), of Folkestone, and Eileen Theresa, *née* Puxley; *b* 25 Aug 1953; *Educ* Harvey GS Folkestone; *m* 16 Oct 1982, Susan Jane, da of Frederick Robert Henry Luckhurst, of Folkestone; *Career* insur underwriter; Commercial Union Group 1971-74; Burlington Insurance Services Ltd: commercial insur account exec 1974-, ptnr 1982-, main bd dir 1985-; memb Insur Inst of Folkestone and S Kent 1975- (pres 1981-82); ACII 1978; *Recreations* tennis, photography, bridge, wine and good food; *Clubs* The Danish; *Style—* Christian Poulsen,

Esq; Bilton House, 13 Godwyn Rd, Folkestone, Kent CT20 2LA (☎ 0303 42313); Burlington Insurance Services Ltd, Westbourne House, Coolinge Lane, Folkestone, Kent CT20 3RH (☎ 0303 850555, fax 0303 44914)

POULTON, Christopher Geoffrey; s of Sqdn Ldr Geoffrey Poulton, DFC, and Margery, *née* Hillman; *b* 4 June 1943; *Educ* Dulwich Coll, Churchill Coll Cambridge (MA); *m* 2 Sept 1967, Judith, *née* Barton; 3 da (Annabel, Rebecca, Victoria); *Career* Baring Bros & Co 1972-75, asst dir Charterhouse Japhet 1975-84, dir Cadogan Oakley 1984-86, divnl md CL-Alexanders Laing & Cruickshank 1986-; *Recreations* fishing, music, sailing; *Style—* Christopher Poulton, Esq; The Manor House, Sundridge, Kent; Piercy Hse, Copthall Ave, London, EC2R 7BE

POULTON, Doris Olive Elizabeth; da of Thomas Poulton (d 1947), of Banbury, and Martha Jane, *née* Thomas; *b* 22 Dec 1913; *Educ* Banbury GS, Brighton Diocesan Coll (Dip), Gullan Speech Coll (Dip); *Career* staff memb: St Bartholomew's Sch Dover 1935-37, Hythe Girls' Sch 1937-39, Black Fen Sch Sidcup 1939-59; headmistress Longlands Sch Sidcup 1959-77; memb: NUT (local pres 1947), Bexley Advsy Ctee of Teachers (chm 1970-77), Bexley Educn Ctee 1970-77, Ctee Barnado's 1977-, Bexley Cancer Res Gp, Nat Tst, RSPB, Dorothy L Sayers Soc; awarded Queen's Jubilee Medal 1977 (for servs to educn); *Recreations* reading, theatre, gardening, flower arranging; *Style—* Miss Doris Poulton; 154 Sidcup Hill, Sidcup, Kent DA14 6JW

POULTON, William Dacres Campbell; s of Maj Arthur Stanley Poulton (d 1931), of Battle, Sussex, and Winifred Evelyn, *née* Montgomery Campbell; *b* 15 Dec 1937; *Educ* Dover Coll, New Coll Oxford (BA, MA); *m* 3 Jan 1970, Carolyn Frances, da of Flt Lt Francis Macken (d 1961); 2 s (Charles b 1970, Andrew b 1976), 1 da (Elinor b 1972); *Career* Nat Serv 1956-58, 2 Lt Royal Sussex Regt 1957, Somaliland Scout 1957 -58; lectr in law New Coll Oxford 1963-68; called to the Bar Middle Temple 1965, S E circuit, asst rec 1987; memb Sevenoaks Deanery Synod; *Recreations* gardening, walking, skiing; *Style—* William Poulton, Esq; Quarry Chase, Seal Hollow Rd, Sevenoaks, Kent (☎ 0732 451 389); 12 New Square, Lincolns Inn, London WC2 (☎ 071 405 3808, fax 071 831 7376)

POWELL, Albert Edward; JP (1961); s of Albert Edward Powell (d 1938), of Morden Surrey, and Mrs Mary Daisy Fewtrell; *b* 20 May 1927; *Educ* Holy Family RC Sch Morden Surrey; *m* 1947, Margaret da of Thomas Neville (d 1942); 1 s (Michael), 2 da (Susan, Deirdre); *Career* London organiser Nat Union Printing, Bookbinding and Paperworkers 1957, organising sec SOGAT 1967 (gen pres 1973-83); dep chm Bexley Magistrates and Bexley Juvenile Bench of Magistrates; memb: Indust Trg Bd 1968 (chm 1974), Central Arbitration Ctee 1978, Industl Tribunal 1984, Parole Bd 1986, Social Security Appeal Tribunal 1985; MTM Assoc of UK; former govr London Coll of Printing, tstee: Bookbinders Charitable Assoc, Mgmnt Ctee of Printers Charitable Assoc; former memb: London Electricity Consultative Ctee, NEDO Printing Industs Ctee; FIMS, HM The Queens Silver Jubilee Medal; *Recreations* golf, chess, gardening, music (classic); *Style—* Albert Powell Esq, JP; 31 Red House Lane, Bexley Heath, Kent DN6 8JF (☎ 081 304 7480)

POWELL, John Lawrence; s of John Edmund Powell (d 1974), and Hilda, *née* Lawrence (d 1973); *b* 19 Oct 1934; *Educ* St Philips GS Edgbaston Birmingham; *m* 20 Oct 1962, Ann, da of Herbert Felton (d 1984); 1 s (David b 1963); *Career* RAF 1954-56; CA; City of Birmingham 1950-53, Agar Bates Neal & Co Birmingham 1956-63; sr accounting and secretarial appts: Mann Egerton Norwich 1963-66, Marley Sevenoaks 1968-73, Radford Group Tunbridge Wells 1973-77; gp chief accountant John E Wiltshier Group plc 1977-88; fin dir Wiltshier South East Ltd 1988-; memb Wingham Br E Kent Pilgrims Hospice Ctee, chm Wingham Lawn Tennis Club; FCA 1963; *Recreations* music, tennis; *Clubs* Kent CC, Wingham Lawn Tennis; *Style—* John Powell, Esq; 9 St Mary's Meadow, Wingham, Canterbury, Kent CT3 1DF (☎ 0227 720348); Wiltshier South East Ltd, Stour St, Canterbury, Kent (☎ 0227 768421)

POWELL-COTTON, Christopher; CMG (1961), MBE (1951), MC (1945), JP; s of Maj P H G Powell-Cotton; *b* 23 Feb 1918; *Educ* Harrow, Trinity Coll Cambridge; *Career* Uganda Admin: dist cmmr 1950, prov cmmr 1955, min of security and external rels 1961, ret 1962; dir Powell-Cotton Museum of Natural History and Ethnography; landowner; *Clubs* MCC; *Style—* Christopher Powell-Cotton, Esq, CMG, MBE, MC, JP; Quex Park, Birchington, East Kent CT7 0BH (☎ 0843 41836)

POWELL-JACKSON, Dr Paul Richard; s of Donald Powell-Jackson (d 1949), and Joan, *née* Henry; *b* 17 March 1947; *Educ* Haywards Heath GS, Gonville and Caius Coll Cambridge (BA, MA), Guys Hosp Med Sch (MB BChir, MRCP, MD); *m* 22 Dec 1980, Valerie, da of Walter Alfred Binsted, of Westham, Sussex; 1 s (Edward b 1982), 2 da (Eleanor b 1984, Rebecca b 1985); *Career* lectr in med Kings Coll Sch of Med and Dentistry 1977-87, conslt physician Maidstone Health Authy 1988-, author of numerous papers on liver disease and drug metabolism; memb RSPB, Nat Tst; memb: Br Soc of Gastroenterology, Br Assoc for Study of the Liver; *Recreations* golf, birdwatching, travel; *Clubs* Royal Ashdown Forest Golf; *Style—* Dr Paul Powell-Jackson; Maidstone Hospital, Hermitage Lane, Maidstone, Kent ME16 9QQ (☎ 0622 729000)

POWLING, Wing Cdr Ronald Henry Charles; DL; s of George William Powling (d 1987), of Tankerton, Kent, and Amelia Powling (d 1968); *b* 2 Nov 1920; *Educ* Simon Langton Sch Canterbury; *m* 15 Nov 1941, Silvia, da of Harold Marshall (d 1973), of Southport; 3 s (Neil Patrick, Nicholas Michael, Mark Adrian Rufus), 1 da (Katrina Beverley); *Career* WWII Fighter Pilot RAFVR 1939-46, Flying and Admin Cmd RAF 1946-73; chm: Kent CC, SE Provincial Cncl of Local Authorities; memb Jt Cncl Local Authorities; pres Tankerton Cons Assoc; *Recreations* golf, gardening, swimming, walking; *Style—* Wing Cdr Ronald Powling, DL; Browndown, 73 Bennells Ave, Tankerton, Whitstable, Kent CT5 2HP (☎ 0227 274 893)

PRAGNELL, Anthony William; CBE (1982, OBE 1960), DFC (1944); s of late William Hendley Pragnell, and late Silvia Mary Pragnell; *b* 15 Feb 1921; *Educ* Cardinal Vaughan Sch London, Univ of London (LLB Ext); *m* 1955, Teresa Mary (d 1988), da of late Leo Francis Monaghan, of Maidstone; 1 s, 1 da; *Career* served RAF 1942-46, Flt Lt Bomber Cmd; civil servant; asst examiner Inland Revenue 1939-50, GPO 1950-54; dep dir gen Independant TV Authority (became Independant Broadcasting Authority 1972) 1961-83 (joined 1954, sec 1955-61), dir Channel 4 TV 1983-88; fell: Royal TV Soc 1980, Euro Inst for the Media, Univ of Manchester 1983-; Emile Noël Euro Prize 1987; memb BBC Radio Kent Religious Advsy Gp 1988-, chm Sevenoaks and Dist Cncl for Churches 1990-; *Recreations* reading, listening to music, watching TV; *Clubs* RAF, Kent CCC; *Style—* Anthony Pragnell, Esq, CBE, DFC; Ashley, Grassy Lane, Sevenoaks, Kent TN13 1PL (☎ 0732 451463)

PRATT, Lord Michael John Henry; s of 5 Marquess Camden (d 1983), and 2 w, Averil (d 1977), da of late Col Henry Sidney John Streatfield, DSO (through whom she was ggda of 2 Earl of Lichfield); *b* 15 Aug 1946; *Educ* Eton, Balliol Coll Oxford; *Career* author and researcher; *Clubs* White's, Pratt's, MCC, Beefsteak; *Style—* The Lord Michael Pratt; 16 Coulson St, London SW3 (☎ 071 581 2200); Bayham Manor, Lamberhurst, Kent (☎ 0892 890500)

PRESTON, Simon Douglas Nelson; s of Jocelyn Panizzi Preston (d 1970), of Romsey, and Emily Geraldine Morval Kirby, *née* Nelson; *b* 5 Aug 1933; *Educ* Sherborne, Trinity Coll Cambridge (MA); *m* 30 June 1962, Celia Mary, da of Frank Bodenham Thornely, MC (d 1958), of Tunbridge Wells; 4 s (Rupert b 1963, Adam b 1966, John b 1975, Charles b 1975), 1 da (Emma b 1965); *Career* Nat Serv Lt RM Commandos Austria special duties 1952-54; PR offr Stock Exchange 1959-64, info offr Lazard Bros & Co Ltd 1964-66; dir: Fin PR Ltd 1966-68, Charles Barker City Ltd 1968-71, Mixed Media Ltd 1982-87; fin dir Leo Burnett Ltd 1971-74, md and dir Dewe Rogerson Ltd 1974-81, dep chm St James PR Ltd 1987-90; chm: City Liason Gp 1973-74 and 1979-83, Br Enterprise Award Ctee 1981-84; memb Cncl Assoc Ind Business 1978-79, dir Think Br Campaign 1982-; memb Inst PR (hon tres 1981-82); *Recreations* farming, sailing, entomology; *Clubs* Travellers; *Style—* Simon Preston, Esq; Badsell Park Farm, Matfield, Tonbridge, Kent (☎ 0892 832 549); Finaancial Public Relations Ltd, 76 Shoe Lane, London EC4 (☎ 071 353 8907, fax 071 353 7550)

PRESTON, Terry; s of Kenneth Preston, of 42 Central Ave, Syston, Leicestershire and Constance Mary, *née* Toon; *b* 2 Oct 1938; *Educ* Roundhill HS, Thurmaston, Leicestershire; *m* 17 May 1962, Ena, da of John Edward George Newman, of 63 Hythe Rd, Dymchurch, Romney Marsh, Kent; 1 s (Andrew b 5 Feb 1971), 1 da (Rachel b 13 Oct 1967); *Career* Nat Serv Corpl RHMC 1957-59; ptnr (with w and parents-in-law) Sutton Farm Christian Guest House 1959-69, proprietor The Hythe Aquarium 1969-76, security offr Portex Ltd 1976-; lay preacher Methodist Church, memb Synod and Policy Ctee London SE Dist of Methodist Churches; chm Mgmnt Ctee Dymchurch Village Hall, vice chm Governing Body Dymchurch Primary Sch; memb: Romney Marsh RDC 1968-74, Shepway DC 1973-, Dymchurch Parish Cncl 1973-; Ldr Lib Gp Shepway DC 1973-83 (chm Personnel Ctee 1989-), memb Assoc of SLD Cnllrs, elected as jurat of Corp of Romney Marsh 1987; *Recreations* walking, cycling, aquatist, reading; *Style—* Terry Preston, Esq; Egerton, 63 Hythe Rd, Dymchurch, Romney Marsh, Kent TN29 OLL (☎ 0303 873647)

PRESTON, Thomas Davis; s of Thomas William Samuel Lane Preston (d 1952), of Eastbourne, Sussex, and Madeleine Irene, *née* Davis (d 1966); *b* 1 Dec 1932; *Educ* Gillingham Sch; *m* 23 March 1963, Jennifer Katherine, da of Dr James Anderson, OBE; 2 da (Carolyn b 1969, Lesley b 1971); *Career* Colonial Serv Kenya: dist offr 1954-62, dist cmmr 1962-63, ret 1963; Phillips Harrisons & Crosfield Kenya: mktg mangr 1963-69, mktg dir 1970-73, chm and md 1974-79, chm 1979-88; dir Harrisons & Crosfield plc London 1981-, chm and chief exec Harrisons & Crosfield Aust 1982-; chm: Harcros Chemicals Aust 1982-, Harcros Timber Aust 1982-, Harrisons & Crosfield Papua New Guinea 1982-, New Britain Palm Oil Development Papua New Guinea 1982-, Linatex Aust 1984-, Kapiura Plantations Papua New Guinea 1986-; *Recreations* golf; *Style—* Thomas Preston, Esq; High St, Sevenoaks, Kent; Melbourne Mansions, Queens Club Gardens, London; Elemang Ave, Kirribilli, Sydney, Australia; 20 St Dunstans Hill, London EC3R 5AB (☎ 071 626 4333, fax 929 3785, telex 885 636)

PRESTON-DUNLOP, Dr Valerie Morthland; *née* Preston; da of Arthur Llewellyn Preston (d 1936), Bishop of Woolwich, and Nancy Robina, *née* Napier (d 1977); *b* 14 March 1930; *Educ* Downe House Newbury, Art of Movement Studio (Dip), London Univ (Dip Ed), London Univ (MA), Laban Centre (PhD); *m* 16 Sept 1961, John Henderson Dunlop, s of Sir John Kinninmont Dunlop, KBE, CMG, MC (d 1976), of Ridge Lea, Sevenoaks; 1 s (Roger Napier b 1965), 1 da (Emma Preston b 1971); *Career* sr lectr Dartford Coll of PE 1954-63, dir Beechmont Movement Study Centre 1965-73, sr post grad tutor Laban Centre for Movement and Dance 1978-, int lectr and writer on dance (princ areas of res Rudolf Laban and Choreology), pioneer of dance scholarship, fndr Beechmount Action Centre Tst for the Disadvantaged, govr Walthamstow Hall Sch; FICKL 1961, fndr memb Dance Res Soc 1982; *Books* Practical Kinetography (1969), Dancing and Dance Theory (1979), Dance in Education (1980), Point of Departure (1984); *Recreations* gardening, music; *Clubs* Royal Society of Arts; *Style—* Dr Valerie Preston-Dunlop; Corners, The Street, Ightham, Kent (☎ 0732 884882); Laban Centre, Newcross, London SE14 (☎ 081 692 4070)

PREVETTE, Kenneth George Charles; OBE (1983); s of George William Prevette (d 1966), of Dartford, Kent, and Rosina Hannah, *née* Gray-Wright (d 1966); *b* 17 May 1917; *m* 29 Aug 1946, Sheila, da of Herbert Henry Spencer, of Blackpool, Lancs; 1 s (Martin Kenneth William Spencer b 20 July 1948), 1 da (Linda Ann b 21 Feb 1951); *Career* cremator 1935-82; dir: The London Cremation Co plc 1971-, Kent Co Crematorium plc 1973-, Norwich Crematorium plc 1978-83; gen sec The Cremation Soc of GB 1964-82, sec-gen Int Cremation Fedn 1979-81, tstee Golders Green Fndn 1982-; *Style—* Kenneth Prevette, Esq, OBE; 80 Ware St, Bearsted, Maidstone, Kent ME14 4PG (☎ 0622 38261)

PRICE, Jonathan Meredith; s of William Gerald Maxence Price, and Eleanor Joan, *née* Edmunds; *b* 4 July 1938; *Educ* Tonbridge, Pembroke Coll Cambridge (MA); *m* 28 Dec 1968, Ingrid Friederike Maria Price-Gschlössl, da of Josef Seidl (d 1984); 1 s (Alexander b 8 Feb 1979), 1 da (Kathrin b 23 Jan 1976); *Career* Nat Serv 2Lt RA Cyprus; articled clerk Jackson Pixley & Co 1962-66, auditor Arthur Anderson & Co 1966-67, accountant Morgan Crucible Gp 1967-68, fin planning and asst gp chief accountant Rio Tinto-Zinc Corp 1968-72, gp fin dir Christies Int plc; ARCM 1961, FCA 1967, FRSA 1987; *Recreations* golf, music; *Clubs* Brooks's, Royal & Ancient; *Style—* Jonathan Price, Esq; Christies International plc, 8 King St, London SW1Y 6QT (☎ 071 8399060, fax 071 8391611)

PRICE, (John) Maurice; QC (1976); s of Edward Samuel Price; *b* 4 May 1922; *Educ* Grove Park Sch Wrexham, Trinity Coll Cambridge; *m* 1945, Mary, da of Dr Horace Gibson, DSO; 2 s; *Career* RN 1941-46, Lt RNVR, called to the barr Gray's Inn 1949, memb Senate of Inns of Ct and the Bar 1975-78; *Clubs* Flyfishers'; *Style—* Maurice Price, Esq, QC; Bowzell Place, Weald, Sevenoaks, Kent TN14 6NF; 2 New Sq, Lincoln's Inn, WC2A 3RU (☎ 071 242 6201)

PRICE, Peter Nicholas; MEP (EDG) Lancs W 1979-84, London SE 1984-; s of Rev Dewi Emlyn Price, of Worcester; *b* 19 Feb 1942; *Educ* Worcester Royal GS, Aberdare Boys' GS, Univ of Southampton; *Career* slr; sr ptnr Peter Price & Ptnrs 1969-80; chm Budgetary Control Ctee Euro Parl 1989- (vice chm 1979-84); EDG spokesman: on Legal Affrs Ctee 1984-87, on Budgets Ctee 1986-89; rapporteur for several budgetary and legal reports; former nat vice chm: Young Cons, Cons Political Centre; former sec Foreign Affrs Forum; former memb Cons Nat Exec Ctee; memb: EDG, ACP-EEC Jt Assembly, RIIA; *Recreations* theatre, music, photography; *Style—* Peter Price, Esq, MEP; 60 Marlings Park Ave, Chislehurst, Kent BR7 6RD (☎ 0689 20681, fax 0689 890622); European Parliament, 97-113 Rue Belliard, 1040 Bruxelles, Belgium (☎ 010 32 2 234 3610)

PRICE, Vivian William Cecil; QC (1972); s of late Evan Price; *b* 14 April 1926; *Educ* Judd Sch Tonbridge, Trinity Coll Cambridge, Balliol Coll Oxford; *m* 1961, Elizabeth Anne, da of late Arthur Rawlins; 3 s, 2 da; *Career* RN 1946-49; barr Mid Temple 1954, Hong Kong 1975, Singapore 1979, bencher Mid Temple 1979, dep high ct judge (Chancery Div) 1975-; *Clubs* Travellers'; *Style—* Vivian Price, Esq, QC; Redwall Farmhouse, Linton, Kent (☎ Maidstone 43682); New Court, Temple, London EC4 (☎ 01 353 1769)

PRICHARD, (Elizabeth) Anne; da of Donald Geere Blaskett, of New Milton, Hampshire, and Phoebe Edith, *née* Harding (d 1976); *b* 16 June 1936; *Educ* The Abbey Sch, Reading, Berks; *m* 6 June 1959, Brian Henry Prichard, s of William Henry Prichard (d 1975); 1 da (Victoria b 1970); *Career* med scientist; jt owner (with husband) Wootton Park Vineyard; parish clerk: Swingfield Shepway Dist 1979-, Guston Dover Dist 1987-; former parish cncllr and clerk of Denton with Wootton, govr Dover GS For Girls 1982-88, hon treas and membership sec Kent Youth Music Assoc 1988-; memb: Soc of Local Cncl Clerks, The Eng Vineyards Assoc, The S of Eng Airedale Club, The Wild Flower Soc, Kent Guild of Spinners Dyers and Weavers; *Recreations* breeder of Tymewell Airedale terriers, crafts incl spinning and weaving, gardening, fuchsias, botany; *Style—* Mrs Anne Prichard; The Gables, Wootton, Canterbury, Kent CT4 6RT

PRIME, Brian Salisbury; s of George Henry Luke Prime (d 1975), of Northwood, Middx, and Dilys Salisbury, *née* Jones (d 1978); *b* 14 Aug 1932; *Educ* Harrow GS, LSE (BSc); *m* 10 March 1962, Susan Mary Eveline, da of Thomas Holdstock (d 1983), of Redhill; 2 s (Jonathan b 1965, Richard b 1967), 1 da (Sally-Ann b 1963); *Career* Lt RA 1954-56; trained as CA and mgmnt accountant; md Kingsway Gp plc (dir 1967-), Celcon Blocks Ltd 1975-, Ryarsh Brick Ltd 1980-, Compton Aggregates Ltd 1978-, Eurospace Furniture Packs Ltd 1983-, New Horizon Furniture Ltd 1985-, Nymoelle Stenindustri Ltd 1986-, Busboard Parker Ltd 1986-, Contrology Products Ltd 1987-, Brantham Engrg Ltd 1987-, Elremco Products Ltd 1987-, Hormigones Celulares SA 1989-, Essex Electronics Ltd 1989-, Earthspan plc 1990-; memb: cncl Chartered Inst of Mgmnt Accountants, Lloyds 1982; CBIM, FCA, FCMA; *Recreations* skiing, gardening; *Clubs* Directors, Danish; *Style—* Brian S Prime, Esq; White Gables, 18 Bromley Common, Bromley, Kent (☎ 081 460 9245); Kingsway Gp plc, Celcon House, 289-293 High Holborn, London WC1V 7HU

PRINCE, Dr Arthur Wilfred; s of Wilfred Charles Prince, DCM (d 1979), of Borth-y-West Porthmadog, Gwynedd, N Wales and Cossette Lydia, *née* Haddad; *b* 23 Oct 1944; *Educ* Yscol Eifionydd Secdy Sch Porthmadog Gwynedd, Univ of Newcastle Upper Tyne Med Sch (MB BS); *m* 21 Sept 1968, Carina Hilda Dawe, da of Josiah Dawe Parsons, CBE (d 1975), of Leylands, Hunton, Maidstone, Kent; 1 s (Nicholas b 1974), 2 da (Hilary b 1976, Caitlin b 1979); *Career* house physician and surgn Nottingham Gen Hosp 1969-70, trainee GP Newcastle upon Tyne Vocational Trg Scheme 1970-73; GP: Ashington Northumberland 1973-77, Herne Bay Kent 1977-; postgrad teacher in gen practice 1975-, med offr in family planning Broadstairs and Margate 1977-86, clinical asst in gen med Herne Bay Hosp 1986-; former chm Herne Bay Branch Cons Assoc 1979-82; DRCOG 1971, MRCGP 1973, honours and winner of Frazer Rose Gold Medal RCGP, FPCert RCOG/RCGP 1976, memb BMA; *Recreations* golf; *Style—* Dr Arthur Prince; Golfmount, 38 Pigeon Lane, Herne Bay, Kent CT6 7ES (☎ 0227 361424); St Annes Surgery, 161 Station Rd, Herne Bay, Kent (☎ 0227 366945)

PRIOR-WILLEARD, Christopher Howard; s of Peter Arnold Prior-Willeard, of Kent, and Anne Jocelyn, *née* Prior; *b* 7 March 1956; *Educ* Gresham's; *m* 18 Oct 1980, Penelope Jane, da of David John Steen, of Sevenoaks, Kent; 1 s (Mark b 1982), 1 da (Annabel b 1984); *Career* MN 1974-80; fndr London Meat Futures Exchange, sr conslt International Equities Stock Exchange, sr mangr UK Equities Stock Exchange, European Divisional Executive Corporate Trust, Chase Manhattan Bank; *Books* Farming Futures; *Recreations* farming, shooting; *Clubs* Farmers', City Univ; *Style—* Christopher H Prior-Willeard, Esq; Crookfoot, Rye Lane, Otford, Kent TN14 5JF

PROCTER, John Howard Adlington; *b* 11 June 1950; 25 Great Footway, Langton Green, Tunbridge Wells, Kent TW3 ODT (☎ 0892 86 3355); C E Heath Insurance Broking Ltd, 150 Minories, London EC3N 1NR (☎ 071 488 2488, fax 071 481 4561, telex 8813001)

PRODGER, Angela Jane; da of George Walter Avery, and Vera Bertha, *née* Meadows (d 1982); *b* 21 Aug 1944; *Educ* Bexhill Girls GS; *m* 1, 26 Sept 1964 (m dis), David Graham Walters; 1 s (Andrew b 1968); m 2, 18 Dec 1973, Brian Edward Prodger; 1 s (Nathaniel b 1982), 1 foster s (Nbe b 1973); *Career* sec: Mid Kent Cons Assoc, Andrew Rowe MP; chm of govrs Walderslade Boys HS; memb: Nat Tst, Eng Heritage; *Recreations* embroidery, gardening; *Style—* Mrs Angela Prodger

PROUDFOOT, (John Hugh) Christopher; s of (William) Frank Proudfoot, of Limpsfield, Surrey. and Beryl, *née* Nops (d 1986); *b* 31 Dec 1946; *Educ* Westminster, Trinity Coll Cambridge (BA); *m* 29 June 1974, Karin Elizabeth, da of Rodney Fleetwood Tatchell, LVO, of Bury St Edmunds, Suffolk; 1 s (William b 1981), 1 da (Helen b 1985); *Career* Christie Manson and Woods Ltd 1970-74, dir Christie's S Kensington 1983- (joined 1975), Kent rep for Christie's 1985-; ctee memb: Kent Building Preservation Tst, Musical Box Soc of GB; *Books* Collecting Phonographs and Gramophones (1980), Woodworking Tools (1984); *Recreations* collecting mechanical and architectural junk; *Style—* Christopher Proudfoot, Esq; The Old Rectory, Fawkham, Longfield, Kent DA3 8LX (☎ 04747 7513); Christie's South Kensington, 85 Old Brompton Rd, London SW7 3LD (☎ 071 581 7611, fax 071 584 0421)

PRYNNE, Andrew Geoffrey Lockyer; s of Maj-Gen Michael Whitworth Prynne, CB, CBE (d 1977), and Jean Violet, *née* Stewart (d 1977); *b* 28 May 1953; *Educ* Marlborough, Univ of Southampton (LLB); *m* 30 July 1977, Catriena Mary, da of Maj Henry Gordon Brougham (d 1958); 2 da (Jessica Jean, Miranda Wendy); *Career* called to the Bar Middle Temple 1975; memb Gen Cncl of Bar; *Recreations* sailing, fishing, shooting, theatre, music; *Clubs* Royal Solent Yacht, Island Sailing; *Style—* Andrew Prynne, Esq, Mount Le Hoe, Benenden, Kent (☎ 0580 241583); 107 Elm Park Mansions, Park Walk, London SW10

PULESTON JONES, Haydn; s of Iago Oliver Puleston Jones (d 1971), and Elizabeth Ann, *née* Morris; *b* 16 Sept 1948; *Educ* Welshpool HS, King's Coll London (LLB, AKC); *m* 9 June 1973, Susan Elizabeth, da of Lt Cdr George Karn (d 1970); 2 s (Simon b 1975, Nicholas b 1978); *Career* ptnr Linklaters & Paines 1979- (joined 1971); memb: Banking Law Sub Ctee City of London Law Soc 1980-, Montgomery Soc (ctee memb) 1974-; tstee Montgomeryshire

Charitable Tsts 1983-; memb: Law Soc 1973, The City of London Slrs' Co 1980-; *Recreations* gardening, classical music, genealogy; *Style*— Haydn Puleston Jones, Esq; Ducks Farm, Dux Lane, Plaxtol, nr Sevenoaks, Kent TN15 ORB; Linklaters & Paines, Barrington House, 59/67 Gresham St, London EC2V 7JA (☎ 071 606 7080, fax 071 606 5113, telex 884349)

PULLEN, Doris Evelyn; da of George Ernest Lord (d 1949), and Ellen Harriett, *née* Holley (d 1967); *b* 4 Oct 1920; *Educ* South Hill Coll Sydenham, Rachel McMillan's Coll of Educn Deptford, Open Univ, Inst Heraldry and Genealogical Studies; *m* 1, 29 July 1939 (m dis 1952), Ronald Ernest Rushbrook; 1 s (Anthony John b 20 May 1947), 2 da (Rosalyn Anne b 9 Feb 1942, Ellena Jane b 27 Jan 1944); m 2, 17 May 1952, George Victor Raymond Pullen, s of late George Henry Pullen, of Penge; 1 da (Diana Mary Evelyn (Mrs Pigot) b 21 May 1954), 2 step s (Dennis Raymond b 14 May 1942, Terence Antony b 8 Feb 1949); *Career* sec for Monumental Inscriptions Soc of Genealogists 1975-, record agent private cmmns, genealogy tutor at evening insts 1980-85; memb: Red Cross VAD 1938-42, PCC Holy Trinity Church 1960-71, Soc of Genealogists 1968-, Nat Tst 1970-, Hist Assoc 1970-, Lewisham Local Hist Soc 1973-90, Sydenham Soc 1975-90, BACSA 1980-, Inst of Heraldic and Genealogical Soc 1980-90, Bd of Govrs Alexandra Jr and Infant Schs 1989-90; ctee memb: Cons Assoc Beckenham 1972-90, Bromley Local History Soc 1975-90; fndr memb: NW Kent Family History Soc, Crystal Palace Fndn; parents ctee memb Guides 1960-63, ctee memb and press offr Townswomen's Guild 1972-75, cncl memb AGRA 1983-90 (memb 1975-); FIBA 1986-87; *Books* Sydenham (1974), Penge (1978), Forest Hill (1980), Dulwich (1984), Beckenham (1985), Wartime Memories (1986); *Recreations* writing, gardening, music; *Style*— Mrs Doris Pullen; 155 Venner Rd, Sydenham, London SE26 5HX (☎ 081 7787189)

PULLEN, Trevor Keith; s of Ronald Pullen, of Bexley, Kent, and Pamela Ann *née* Berry; *b* 22 Nov 1948; *Educ* Roan GS Greenwich, Lanchester Poly Coventry (BA); *m* 1, 13 Sept 1969 (m dis 1980), Glenise May; 1 s (Andrew b 1973), 1 da (Samantha b 1971); m 2, 31 March 1988, Pauline; *Career* Prudential Portfolio Managers: UK equity dir 1982, global securities dir 1988; investmt dir Prudential Holborn 1987, chm Barnard Enterprises 1987; *Recreations* golf, squash, skiing ; *Clubs* Addington Golf; *Style*— Trevor Pullen, Esq; 9 Prince Consort Drive, Chislehurst, Kent (☎ 081 467 9522); 142 Holborn Bars, London EC1N 2NH (☎ 071 548 3145, telex 265082, car tel 0860 527092)

PURCHESE, John; s of Horace Robert Leopald Purchese (d 1935), of Muswell Hill, London, and Hannah Harriet, *née* Kennedy (d 1981); *b* 21 Feb 1925; *Educ* Steyning GS Sussex, Ardingly Coll; *m* 27 Nov 1947, Mollie Joan (Anne), *née* Harvey, da of Charles Harvey, of Worthing, Sussex; 2 s (Anthony Charles Nesfield b 6 April 1949, Timothy John Kennedy b 6 Oct 1961), 3 da (Helen Francesca b 13 Sept 1950, Catherine Lindsay b 7 Feb 1953, Hilary Caroline b 26 March 1958); *Career* RAF WWII, demob 1947; worked in film indust 1947-70: two years as a documentary dir, twenty one years as a sound recordist incl news coverage of the Abervan tragedy; set up own printing co 1970; former chm ACTT Sound Section, candidate in all gen elections 1979-, memb for Canterbury Central Div Kent CC 1984-, pres Canterbury Lib Democrats, churchwarden St Peter's Bekesbourne, hon sec East Bridge Deanery Synod, govr Canterbury HS; *Recreations* writing, recording and directing Son-Et-Lumiere in churches; *Style*— John Purchese, Esq; Mill Cottage, Bekesbourne, Canterbury, Kent CT4 5HD (☎ 0227 830937); A & J Purchese Ltd, Cow Lane, Wincheap Industrial Estate, Canterbury, Kent CT1 3RW (☎ 0227 761508, 0227 470282, fax 0227 472915)

PURNELL, Roger Glanvill (Peter); DFC (1945), DFM (1942); s of Christopher James Purnell, CBE (d 1959), of London, and Letitia Lucy, *née* Glanvill (d 1969); *b* 7 Sept 1914; *Educ* Dulwich, LSE (BCom); *m* 27 May 1944, Doris (Vicky), da of Arthur Price (d 1934), of Banbury; 1 s (Christopher b 1949), 1 da (Clare b 1952); *Career* trainee pilot RAF 1939-40; bomber pilot: Sgt 106 Sqdn 1941, Sqdn Ldr 619 Sqdn 1944-45; cmmnd pilot instr 1942-43; accountant; articled to Ogden Hibberd Bull & Langton 1934; Delta Metal Co: asst sec 1946-52, sec 1952-56, dir 1956-75, ret 1975; hon treas London Homes for the Elderly 1973-88, ambulance driver 1976-88, chm Age Concern Orpington 1985-87 (hon treas 1977-85); FCA 1960 (ACA 1937), FIIS 1979; *Recreations* amateur dramatics, swimming; *Clubs* RAF; *Style*— Peter Purnell, Esq, DFC, DFM; New Orchard House, Sevenoaks Rd, Pratts Bottom, Orpington, Kent BR6 7SE (☎ 0689 54463)

PURSEGLOVE, Prof John William; CMG (1973); s of late Robert Purseglove; *b* 11 Aug 1912; *Educ* Lady Manners Sch Bakewell, Univ of Manchester, Gonville and Caius Coll Cambridge, Imp Coll of Tropical Agric Trinidad; *m* 1947, Phyllis Agnes Adèle, da of late George Turner, of Falkland Islands; 1 s, 1 da decd; *Career* tropical crops specialist ODA E Malling Res Station Kent 1967-75; memb Green Alliance, friend of Kew Gardens; FLS 1944, FIBiol 1970; *Books* Tobacco in Uganda (1951), Tropical Crops Dicotyledons (2 vols, 1968), Monocotyledon (2 vols, 1972), Spices (1981, Japanese edn 1986); *Recreations* natural history; *Style*— Prof John Purseglove, CMG; Walnut Trees, Sissinghurst, Cranbrook, Kent TN17 2JL (☎ 0580 712836)

Q

QUEALY, Richard Anthony; s of Thomas Quealy (d 1941), of Dungarvan, Co Waterford, Eire, and Mary, *née* Power (d 1988); *b* 10 June 1939; *Educ* Cistercian Coll Roscrea Co Tipperary Eire, Univ Coll Galway and Dublin (BDS), RCS (DOrth), RCPS (FDS); *m* 20 June 1964, Joan GLynn, da of James GLynn (d 1961), of Dunmore, Co Galway, Eire; 3 s (Diarmuid b 1 May 1965, Conor b 16 Aug 1966, Emmet b 19 Jan 1972); *Career* gen dental practice Sheerness and Sittingbourne 1963-72, post grad study Eastman Dental Hosp London, registrar and sr registrar orthodontics Guy's Hosp London 1973-78, conslt orthodontist Maidstone and Medway Health Authys 1978-; chm: Kent Branch Cleft Lip and Palate Assoc, Bd of Govrs Nativity Sch Sittingbourne; past chm: Assoc of Medway Dentists, Med Staff Ctee KCOA Hosp Maidstone; *Recreations* golf; *Clubs* Princes Golf, Rodmersham Squash, Sandwich; *Style—* Richard Quealy, Esq; Sunnested, Ave of Remembrance, Sittingbourne, Kent ME10 4DE (☎ 0795 424532); 86 Rock Ave, Gillingham, Kent ME7 5PS (☎ 0634 53935)

QUINN, Cncllr (Frank Ernest) Geoffrey; s of Ernest Quinn (d 1970), of Syston, Leicester, and Dorothy Mathilda, *née* North (d 1976); *b* 2 Sept 1924; *Educ* Wyggeston GS Leicester, Air Serv Trg Coll Hamble, Regis Coll Johannesburg; *m* 2 Oct 1954, Diana Olivia, da of Allen Borman (d 1964); 3 s (Christopher Ernest b 30 July 1958, Mark Lockhart-Muir b 31 May 1960, Michael Geoffrey b 6 April 1965 d 3 Aug 1965), 1 da (Sara Dorothy Olivia b 2 Nov 1967); *Career* Engrg Branch Fleet Air Arm RN 1943-46; apprentice I L Berridge & Co Ltd 1941-43, engr Experimental Dept Auster Aircraft Co Ltd 1946-47, tech rep De Havilland Engine Co UK M E Norway Congo S Africa 1949-57, Mobil Oil Corporation 1957-87 (chm and md Mobil Aviation and Marine Sales Ltd); cncllr Sevenoaks DC, chm Bd of Dirs Sevenoaks Direct Contracts, parish cncllr Kemsing, exec ctee memb Age Concern Sevenoaks and Dist, govr Kemsing Primary Sch, sidesman St Marys Kemsing, treas Kemsing Allotment Assoc; ACIS; *Recreations* gardening, looking after elderly people; *Clubs* Probus (Sevenoaks); *Style—* Cncllr Geoffrey Quinn; 7 Beechy Lees Rd, Otford, Nr Sevenoaks, Kent TN14 5QJ (☎ 09592 2831)

QUIRK, Dudley Cecil; s of George Henry Quirk (d 1932), and Ethel Jane, *née* Sargent (d 1959); *b* 12 May 1920; *Educ* Whitgift Sch, RNC; *m* 5 July 1941, Joan Mary, da of Sidney Herbert Salmon (d 1972); 2 s (Jonathan) Piers b 27 Dec 1943, Matthew b 25 May 1954), 1 da (Mary-Teresa (Mrs Martin-Quirk) b 9 May 1947); *Career* served RNVR 1939-46: coastal forces 1940-43, passed RN Staff Course Greenwich 1943, staff offr ops Taranto Italy 1944-46; chartered surveyor, farmer and landowner, vineyard proprietor; JP Kent 1963; Freeman City of London, Liveryman Worshipful Co of Chartered Surveyors; FRICS 1948, FRS 1959; *Recreations* sailing, skiing, reading; *Clubs* Travellers; *Style—* Dudley Quirk, Esq, FRS; Vexour, Chiddingstone, Kent (☎ 0892 870277, 0892 870198)

QUIRK, (Jonathan) Piers; s of Dudley Cecil Quirk, JP, of Chiddingstone, Kent, and Joan Mary, *née* Salmon; *b* 27 Dec 1943; *Educ* Winchester, Coll of Estate Mgmnt Univ of London (BSc); *m* 3 Sept 1983, Sally, da of (Arthur) Richard Kemp, of Chiddingstone, Kent; 1 s (Frederick b 1986), 1 da (Zoe b 1988); *Career* ptnr Messrs Parris & Quirk Chartered Surveyors of Tunbridge Wells and London 1971-87; pres Royal Tunbridge Wells C of C 1986; Freeman City of London 1984, Liveryman Worshipful Co of Chartered Surveyors 1984; FRICS 1974; *Recreations* photography, woodwork, paintings, rugs; *Style—* Piers Quirk, Esq; The Oasts, Chiddingstone, Kent TN8 7AQ (☎ 0892 870 701); Fox & Sons, 27 Mount Pleasant, Tunbridge Wells, Kent TN1 1PP (☎ 0892 515 252, fax 0892 515 868)

R

RACE, Russell John; s of Russell Edgar Race (d 1982), and Winifred Olive, *née* Clissold; *b* 28 May 1946; *Educ* Sir Joseph Williamson's Mathematical Sch Rochester, Univ of Liverpool (BA); *Career* economist White Fish Authy 1967-70, dir Hoare Govett 1985- (investmt analyst 1970-76, corp fin 1976-); memb: Soc of Business Economists, Soc of Investmt Analysts; *Recreations* hockey, cricket, music; *Style—* Russell Race, Esq; 86 Ingle Rd, Chatham, Kent ME4 5SE (☎ 0634 406 347); Hoare Govett Corporate Finance Ltd, 4 Broadgate, London EC2M 7LE (☎ 071 374 1861, fax 071 374 4494)

RADNOR, 8 Earl of (GB 1765); Sir Jacob Pleydell-Bouverie; 11 Bt (GB 1714); also Viscount Folkestone, Baron Longford (both GB 1747), and Baron Pleydell-Bouverie (GB 1765); patron of two livings; s of 7 Earl of Radnor, KG, KCVO (d 1968), and his 1 w, Helena (who m 2, 1943, Brig Montacute William Worrell Selby-Lowndes, and d 1985), da of late Charles Adeane, CB (whose w Madeline, CBE, JP, was gda of 1 Baron Leconfield); *b* 10 Nov 1927; *Educ* Harrow, Trinity Coll Cambridge; *m* 1, 1953 (m dis 1962), Anne, da of Donald Seth-Smith, MC; 2 s; m 2, 1963 (m dis 1985), Margaret, da of Robin Fleming, of Catter House, Drymen; 4 da; m 3, 1986, Mrs A C Pettit; *Heir* s, Viscount Folkestone; *Career* landowner and farmer; chm Br Dyslexia Assoc 1971-76, pres Dyslexia Fndn 1975-, memb Home of Lords Select Ctee (agriculture, food and consumer affrs) 1985-; *Recreations* field sports; *Clubs* White's, Farmers; *Style—* The Rt Hon the Earl of Radnor; Longford Castle, Salisbury, Wilts SP5 4EF (☎ 0722 29732)

RAE, Nicola Elizabeth Auriel; da of Stephen Douglas Rae, of 8 Beech Dell, Keston Park, Kent, and Elizabeth Jane, *née* Tawse; *b* 14 Jan 1961; *Educ* St Michael's Sch Petworth, Kingston Poly, Canterbury Coll of Art (BA); *Career* artist; 8 solo exhibitions incl: The Showrooms Wolverhampton 1985, The Canal Brasserie Canalot Studios 1989, Hotel de Ville Dieppe 1989, The Drew Gallery Canterbury 1988 and 1990; 20 gp exhibitions incl: Galeri Carwyn Rogers LLandysul 1985, Towner Gallery Eastbourne 1989, Young Artists SE 1987 1988 and 1989, Britain's Painters Mall Galleries 1988 1989 and 1990, Portobello Open Print Exhibition 1990; involved in various SE Arts projects; *Style—* Miss Nicola Rae; Ground Floor Flat, 119 Victoria Way, Charlton SE7 7NX (☎ 081 853 5200)

RAE, Nola Margaret; da of John Irvine Rae, and Margaret Kathleen, *née* Simms; *b* 12 June 1949; *Educ* Manley Girl's HS Sydney Aust, Nesta Brooking Sch of Ballet and Educn London, Royal Ballet Upper Sch London, Ecole Int de Mime Marcel Marceau Paris; *Career* dancer Malmo Stadsteaker 1967-69, soloist Tivoli Pantomime Theatre Copenhagen 1969; fndr memb: La Troupe Kiss Internationale France 1970-71, Friends Roadshow England 1972-74; actress Bristol Old Vic 1974-75, co fndr London Mime Theatre 1975, solo mime artist 1976-; has cr 10 shows incl: Mime and Clown 1976, Some Great Fools From History 1977, Upper Cuts 1983, Elizabeth's Last Stand 1990; has toured in over fifty countries in N America, S America, Europe, Africa, The Middle East, Asia and Australasia; TV appearances incl: Tonight, Arena, Play School, The Neil Innes Show, The Denis Waterman Show; co-organiser of first Br Mime Gala for Charity in aid of Dr Barnado's 1987; former memb GLA Dance and Mime panel, memb Action Gp; *Recreations* playing the piano, reading, watching television, strolling; *Style—* Miss Nola Rae; 22a Farnaby Rd, Bromley, Kent BR1 4BJ (☎ 081 4609885)

RAE SMITH, David Douglas; CBE (1976), MC (1945); s of Sir Alan Rae Smith, KBE (d 1961), of Copynsfield, Westerham, Kent, and Mabel Grace *née* Eales (d 1963); *b* 15 Nov 1919; *Educ* Radley, ChCh Oxford (MA); *m* 12 April 1947, Margaret Alison, da of James Watson (d 1968), of Holyrood House, Hedon, E Yorks; 3 s (James b 1949, John b 1952, Alan b 1960), 1 da (Katherine b 1957); *Career* Capt RA 1939-46 (despatches), ME, Italy, France and Germany; CA; sr ptnr Deloitte Haskins & Sells 1973-82 (ptnr 1954-82), Thomas Tilling plc 1982-83, Sandoz Products Ltd 1983-, Bankers Trustee Co Ltd 1984-; hon treas RIIA 1961-81, memb Licensed Dealers Tbnl 1974-88, chm Radley Coll 1976- (memb Cncl 1966-); *Recreations* horseracing, golf; *Clubs* Gresham; *Style—* David Rae Smith, Esq, CBE, MC; Oakdale, Crockham Hill, Edenbridge, Kent (☎ 0732 866220)

RAEBURN, (Sir) Michael Edward Norman; (4 Bt, UK 1923, but does not use his title); s of Sir Edward Alfred Raeburn, 3 Bt (d 1977), and Joan, da of Frederick Hill, of Boston, USA; *b* 12 Nov 1954; *m* 1979, Penelope Henrietta Theodora, da of Alfred Louis Penn (d 1963), of London; 2 s, 2 da; *Heir* s, Christopher Edward Alfred Raeburn, b 4 Dec 1981; *Career* civil servant; *Style—* Michael Raeburn, Esq; Little Spring Cottage, Fletching Street, Mayfield, East Sussex TN20 6TN; HM Land Registry, Curtis House, Forest Rd, Hawkenbury, Tunbridge Wells, Kent

RAINE, (Charles) Peter Everton; s of David Edward Raine (d 1979), of Birmingham, and Margaret Clare, *née* Everton; *b* 13 April 1951; *Educ* Uppingham, Univ of Aberdeen (MA), UCL (MSc); *Career* accountant: Touche Ross & Co Birmingham 1972-77, Friends of the Earth Birmingham 1977-79; dir: Centre for Alternative Technol Wales 1979-86, Kent Tst for Nature Conservation 1989- (joined 1987); memb: Cncl Montgomery Wildlife Tst 1981-86, Ctee for Wales RSPB 1982-86; *Books* The Rough Guide to Mediterranean Wildlife (1990); *Recreations* watching wildlife, travel, amateur dramatics; *Style—* Peter Raine, Esq; Kent Trust for Nature Conservation, 1A Bower Mount Rd, Maidstone, Kent ME16 8AX (☎ 0622 753017)

RALLI, Sir Godfrey Victor; 3 Bt (UK 1912), TD; s of Sir Strati Ralli, 2 Bt, MC (d 1964); *b* 9 Sept 1915; *Educ* Eton; *m* 1, 24 June 1937 (m dis 1947), Nora Margaret, o da of late Charles Forman, of Lodden Court, Spencers Wood, nr Reading; 1 s, 2 da; m 2, 24 March 1949, Jean, da of late Keith Barlow; *Heir* s, David Charles Ralli; *Career* Ralli Brothers Ltd 1936-62 (apart from army service 1939-45); chm: G & L Ralli Investment & Tstee Co Ltd 1962-75, Greater London Fund for the Blind 1962-82; *Recreations* golf, fishing, gardening; *Clubs* White's, Naval and Military; *Style—* Sir Godfrey Ralli, Bt, TD; Great Walton, Eastry, Sandwich, Kent CT13 0DN

RAMPTON, Sir Jack Leslie; KCB (1973, CB 1969); s of Leonard Wilfrid Rampton, and Sylvia, *née* Davies; *b* 10 July 1920; *Educ* Tonbridge, Trinity Coll Oxford (MA); *m* 1950, Eileen Joan, *née* Hart; 1 s, 1 da; *Career* joined Treasy 1941, asst private sec to Chllrs of the Exchequer 1942-43, private sec to Fin Sec 1945-46, econ and fin advsr to Cmmr Gen SE Asia and Br High Cmmr Malaya 1959-61, under sec 1964-68; dep sec: Mintech 1968-70, DTI 1970-72, second perm sec DTI 1972-74, perm under sec Dept of Energy 1974-80; dir: London Atlantic Investment Trust 1981-, Sheerness Steel Co 1982-87 (dep chm 1985-87), ENO 1982-88, Carnarvon Mining 1984, Flextech 1985-; pt/t conslt Sun Oil 1982-87; memb: Cook Soc 1977 (chm 1987-88), Honeywell Advsy Cncl 1981-, Cncl Victoria League (dep chm 1985-), Cncl Br-Aust Soc 1986- (dep chm 1989-); govr: Cwlth Tst 1988- (dep chm 1989-); London House for Overseas Students 1990-; Hon DSc Univ of Aston; CBIM, FInstPet, FInst GasE; *Recreations* gardening, travel, photography; *Style—* Sir Jack Rampton, KCB; 17 The Ridgeway, Tonbridge, Kent (☎ 0732 352117); c/o Britain Australia Society, Borax House, Carlisle Place, London (☎ 071 976 5611)

RAMRAYKA, Peter; JP (Inner London 1981); s of Samaroo Ramrayka (d 1979), of Br Guiana, and Rosalind, *née* Singh (d 1948); *b* 10 Oct 1943; *Educ* St George's Anglican Georgetown Br Guiana, Univ of London, Poly of Central London (MBA); *m* 2 da (Nadia Sunita Devi b 21 Sept 1975, Tara Laxmi Devi b 18 Feb 1977); *Career* RAF Med Branch 1961-70; staff offr and dep hosp admin UCH London 1970-73, dep and hosp admin Newham Health Dist 1973-75, sector admin NE Sector Greenwich Health Dist 1975-77, asst and dep dist admin Lewisham Health Dist 1977-82; Dartford and Gravesend Health Authy: dep dist admin 1982-85, dist admin 1985-86, dir of admin personnel and estate mgmnt and sec to the Authy 1986-; govr Churchdown Adult Educn Inst 1979-82, memb SE Thames Regnl Cncl of the Inst of Health Serv Mgmnt, sec and tstee Indo Caribbean Cultural Assoc UK; FHSM, FBIM, FRSH; *Recreations* public affrs, cricket, travelling; *Style—* Peter Ramrayka, Esq, JP; 43 Fairby Rd, Lee, London SE12 8JP (☎ 081 852 7812)

RAMSAY, Col George Patrick Maule; s of Capt Archibald Henry Maule Ramsay (d 1955), and Ismay Lucretia Mary, *née* Hon Ismay Preston (d 1975); *b* 15 Nov 1922; *Educ* Eton, RMA Sandhurst; *m* 1, 1947; 2 s (Alexander, Patrick), 3 da (Catherine, Diana, Fiona); m 2, 1980, Bridget, da of Ronald Hornby (d 1984); *Career* WWII serv Scots Gds: Italy (wounded), Malaya, Egypt, Kenya, Germany; Col cmdg Scots Gds 1964-67; dir: Hill Samuel 1968-79, Kornferry International 1979-82, Goddard Kay Rogers 1982-87; memb Royal Co of Archers Queens Body Guard for Scotland; *Recreations* shooting, fishing, gardening; *Clubs* Boodle's, Army and Navy, Pratt's,

Beefsteak; *Style*— Col George Ramsay; The Old School House, The Square, Elham, Canterbury, Kent CT4 6TJ

RAMSEY, Vivian Arthur; s of Ian Thomas Ramsey (d 1972 former Bishop of Durham), and Margretta, *née* McKay; *b* 24 May 1950; *Educ* Abingdon Sch, Harley Sch Rochester NY USA, Oriel Coll Oxford (MA), City Univ (Dip Law); *m* 14 Aug 1974, Barbara, da of Lt-Col Gerard Majella Walker, of Farnborough, Hants; 2 s (Nicholas b 1981, James b 1986), 2 da (Helen b 1980, Katharine b 1984); *Career* graduate engr Ove Arup & Ptnrs 1972-77, called to the Bar Middle Temple 1979; practising barr 1981-, ctee official referee Bar Assoc 1986-, arbitrator (incl ICC arbitration) 1988-; ed Construction Law Jl 1984-; treas: St Swithuns Hither Green 1977-84, Swanley Village Sports and Social Club 1986-; MICE 1977; *Recreations* pantomime, building renovation; *Style*— Vivian Ramsey, Esq; 10 Essex St, Outer Temple, London WC2R 3AA (☎ 01 240 6981, fax 01 240 7722, telex 8955650)

RANDALL, (Charles) Peter; s of Charles Gregory Randall (d 1983), of Sittingbourne, Kent, and (Myra) Winifred, *née* Coates (d 1972); *b* 8 April 1931; *Educ* Borden GS Sittingbourne, LSE (BSc), UCL (MPhil), Barnett Coll London (Cert Ed, BEd); *m* 23 July 1955, Valerie Anne, da of Flt Lt Frank Barker, of Maidstone, Kent; 1 s (Justin b 1972), 1 da (Anne-Marie (Mrs Bray) b 1962); *Career* Nat Serv, Sgt instr RAEC 1950-51, TA RA; tax offr Chief Inspr's Div Bd of Inland Revenue 1949-61; res offr: Jt Intelligence Bureau and Defence Intelligence Staff 1961-66, Miny of Housing and Local Govt and DOE 1966-72; HM planning inspr DOE 1972-75, gp ldr Planning Dept East Sussex CC 1975-81, planning conslt 1981-, lectr in economics Dept of Business and Mgmnt Mid Kent Coll of Higher and Further Educn 1981-; cncllr for Leeds Maidstone Borough Cncl 1986-; memb: Old Bordenians Assoc, SE Branch RTPI; *Style*— Peter Randall, Esq; Linton Cottage, Linton Hall, Linton, Kent (☎ 0622 743879); Mid Kent College of Higher and Furthur Education, Oakwood Park, Tonbridge Rd, Maidstone, Kent ME16 8AQ (☎ 0622 691555)

RANDALL, Rona (Mrs F W Shambrook); da of late Leonard Standage Green, of London, and late Jessie Sophia, *née* Randall; *Educ* Claughton Higher Grade Sch Cheshire, Pitman's Coll London; *m* Frederick Walter Shambrook; 1s (Paul Standage William); *Career* drama student then actress with Frank Forbes-Robertson's Co and Nancy Price's Co; acted in: The Rose Without a Thorn (Duke of York's Theatre), Alice in Wonderland (Duke of York's Theatre), Josephine (Her Majesty's Theatre); formerly: ed asst Women's Journal, journalist, short story and serial writer; currently: novelist (books translated into 12 languages), non-fiction author, lectr on writing career, author of articles on aspects of authorship for various writing jls, occasional bdcaster for progs dealing with craft of writing; winner of: RNA jt maj award, Exclusive Selections award, Literary Guild and Doubleday Book Clubs award; memb: SE Arts Assoc, Ctee Soc of Sussex Authors, Soc of Women Writers and Journalists, Kent Potters' Assoc; fndr and chm Tunbridge Wells Writers' Weekends, former vice chm Women's Press Club of London, fell Int PEN; *Books* 57 titles incl: Dragonmede, Watchman's Stone, The Mating Dance, The Eagle At The Gate, Ladies Of Hanover Square, Curtain Call, Glenrannoch, Knight's Keep, 3 volumes of The Drayton Trilogy, Jordan & The Holy Land (non-ficton, foreword by HM King Hussein of Jordan), The Model Wife - 19th Century Style (non-fiction); *Recreations* ceramic modelling, travel, theatre, reading; *Style*— Ms Rona Randall; Conifers, Pembury Rd, Tunbridge Wells, Kent TN2 4ND; c/o Curtis Brown Ltd, Literary Agents, 162-168 Regent St, London W1R 5TB (☎ 071 872 0331, fax 071 437 9700)

RANDELL, Elaine (Mrs Rose); da of Henry William Randell (d 1979), and Daphne Pauline, *née* Standing; *b* 21 Sept 1951; *Educ* Kings Warren GS Plumstead, Goldsmiths' Coll London, Mid Kent Coll, Tavistock Clinic London; *m* 1, 1972 (m dis 1981), Barry MacSweeney; m 2, 14 Feb 1982, Ian Christopher Rose, s of Kenneth Percy Rose, MBE, of Bucks; 3 da (Phoebe Helena b 21 Sept 1983, Beatrice Isabella b 31 Oct 1985, Naomi Florence b 9 Aug 1987); *Career* social worker in mental health and child care for over 15 years; sr practitioner: Kent CC, Children Need Families Project C of E Children's Soc Tunbridge Wells; author of numerous social work papers, published poet and prose writer; *Books* incl: Collected poems Beyond All Other (1988), Gut Reaction (1989); included in following anthologies: New British Poetry (1989), Affirming Flame (1989), In the Gold of Flesh (1990); *Style*— Ms Elaine Randell; The Stable, Snoadhill, Bethersden, Ashford, Kent TN26 3DY (☎ 0233 82735)

RAO, Dr (Chitaldroog) Ramachandra; s of Santebennur Ranga Rao, and Rukmini Bai, *née* Padaki; *b* 4 March 1931; *Educ* Mysore Med Coll Karnataka (MB BS), MRCP Edinburgh, Univ of Liverpool (DTM & H); *m* 16 Jan 1960, Beryl, da of Islwyn James; 1 s (Kiran b 1963), 2 da (Anita b 1960, Brinda b 1962); *Career* univ teaching appts and conslt physician Karnataka Med Colls 1961-67, fell in cardiology Canada 1968-69; Bangalore Med Coll 1969-77: prof of med and cardiology, conslt physician, conslt cardiologist; hon physician govr of Karnataka Med Colls 1969-77, conslt physician Welsh Regnl Hosp Bd 1977-79, conslt physician and geriatrician SE Thames RHA 1979-; author of numerous jl articles on heart disease and the role of indigenous herbs in modern med; organiser: Bangalore Mahaloodhi Sce Hypertension Clinic For The Poor 1963-67, Bangalore Lyons Club Heart Disease Detection and Advice Campus For The Poor 1976-77; chm and examiner undergraduate and postgrad med examinations Univ of Bangalore and Mysore 1966-75, memb Editorial Bd Indian Heart Journal 1974-77, Lyons Int Citizen of the Year Bangalore 1977; former fell: USA Coll of Chest Physicians, American Coll of Cardiology; fell Royal Coll of Tropical Med and Health; memb: Br Geriatric Soc, BMA; life memb: Assoc of Physicians of India, Cardiological Soc of India, Indian Assoc For The Advancement of Med Educn; FRCPE 1974 ; *Recreations* travel, golf; *Clubs* Rotary (Bangalore and UK), Bangalore Masonic Lodge, North Foreland Golf (Kent), Bangalore (India); *Style*— Dr C R Rao

RASHID, Dr Abutaleb Muhammed Fazlur (Faz); s of Dr A M M A Rouf (d 1972), of Barisal, Bangladesh, and Shamse Ara, *née* Ahmed; *b* 29 Dec 1937; *Educ* Univ of Dhaka Bangladesh (MB BS, MSc), RCPath London; *m* 9 June 1968, Faozia Sultana, da of M Habibullah (d 1987), of Chandpur, Bangladesh; 2 da (Tina Farzana b 1971, Samantha Fahima b 1972); *Career* various trg posts in pathology Dhaka Med Coll and Hosp Bangladesh 1962-70, asst prof of pathology Inst of Post Grad Med and Res Dhaka Bangladesh 1970-74, asst in pathology Inst of Pathology Free Univ of Berlin W Ger 1974-75, registrar in pathology Royal Sussex Co Hosp 1975-78, sr registrar in pathology Southampton Gen Hosp and Poole Gen Hosp 1978-80, conslt pathologist Joyce Green Hosp 1980-; coll tutor RCPath; past pres Dartford Bengali Assoc, past treas London and SE Branch Bangladesh Med Assoc in UK; memb: Central Exec Ctee Bangladesh Med Assoc in UK, Regnl Exec Ctee BMA Dartford and Medway, ACP, BSCC, ODA; FRCPath; *Recreations* swimming, jogging, snooker, gardening, DIY, computers; *Style*— Dr Faz Rashid; Joyce Green Hospital, Dartford, Kent DA1 5PL (☎ 0322 227242 ext 325)

RAWLINGS, Keith John; s of Jack Frederick Rawlings (d 1985), and Eva, *née* Mullis; *b* 24 April 1940; *Educ* Kent Coll Canterbury; *m* 21 Dec 1965, Susan Mary, da of Thomas Johnson (d 1967); 1 s (Jonathan James Ashley b 27 March 1965), 1 da (Sarah Louise (Mrs Watson) b 15 Feb 1967); *Career* insur broker and ind fin advsr, chm Burlington Insurance Group 1969-; dir: London & Edinburgh Trust plc 1986-87, Rutland Trust plc 1987-, Whitehouse Moorman & Partners Ltd 1988-, Greville Baylis & Parry Ltd 1988-, Norminster Associates Ltd 1988-, Atticus Financial Services Ltd 1988-; *Recreations* golf, tennis, skiing, sailing, bridge, travel; *Clubs* St James's; *Style*— Keith Rawlings, Esq; Summerhayes, Cliff Rd, Hythe, Kent CT21 5XQ (☎ 0303 267014); Burlington Insurance Services Ltd, Westbourne House, Coolinge Lane, Folkestone, Kent CT20 3RH (☎ 0303 850555, fax 0303 44914, telex 96240, car 0836 274010)

RAWLINS, Gordon John; OBE (1986); s of Arthur James Rawlins, of New Milton, Hants, and Joyce Rosemary, *née* Smith; *b* 22 April 1944; *Educ* Welbeck Coll, RMA Sandhurst, RMCS (BSc); *m* 1, 28 Aug 1965, Ann Rose (d 1986), da of Alfred George Beard (d 1981); 1 s (Richard James b 1968); m 2, 25 Oct 1986, Margaret Anne (Meg), da of James Martin Edward Ravenscroft; 1 step s (Hamish Richmond Haddow b 1970), 1 step da (Islay Elizabeth Haddow b 1972); *Career* cmmnd REME 1964; recent career: Staff Coll (Maj) 1977-78, Maj GSO2 ASD 1 MOD 1978-80, Maj 21C 5 ARMD WKSP 1981-82, Lt-Col CO 7 ARMD WKSP 1982-84, Lt-Col Mil Asst to MGO MOD 1984-86, Col PB21 MOD 1986, Col Sec to COS Ctee MOD 1987, Brig Comd Maint 1 (BR) Corps 1988, serv Aden, Oman, Jordan, UK, Hong Kong and BAOR, ret 1989 as Brig; Sec IProdE and chief exec Inst of Indust Mangrs 1988-; MRAeS, CEng 1982, FIProdE, FIIM 1989; *Recreations* rugby, cricket, music; *Clubs* Army and Navy; *Style*— Gordon Rawlins, Esq, OBE; Institute of Production Engineers and Industrial Managers, Rochester House, 66 Little Ealing Lane, London W5 4XX (☎ 081 579 9411, fax 081 579 2244)

RAY, Mary Eva Pedder; da of William John Ray (d 1959), of Birmingham, and Dora Florence, *née* Moule (d 1985); *b* 14 March 1932; *Educ* Rugby HS, Coll of the Ascension Selly Oak (Dip Social Science), Univ of Kent at Canterbury; *Career* civil servant ECGD 1962-78, author of children's hist fiction; lay reader The Church of England; *Books* The Voice Of Apollo (1964), The Eastern Beacon (1965), Standing Lions (1968), Spring Tide (1969), Living in Earliest Greece (1969), Shout Against The Wind (1970), A Tent For The Sun (1971), The Ides of April (1974), Sword Sleep (1975), Beyond The Desert Gate (1977), Song of Thunder (1978), Rain From The West (1980), The Windows of Elissa (1982), The Golden Bees (1984); *Recreations* choral singing, gardening, travel; *Style*— Miss Mary Ray; 2 Harcourt Drive, Canterbury, Kent CT2 8DP (☎ 0227 455035)

RAYER, John Bernard; s of John William Rayer, and Kathleen Patricia, *née* Heath; *b* 29 Oct 1947; *Educ* St Joseph's R C Primary Sch Bermondsey, Clapham Coll; *m* 12 Dec 1940, Anne Elizabeth, da of late John Leahy; 1 s (Stephen John b 20 March 1974), 1 da (Jane Elizabeth b 11 Feb 1976); *Career* CA; articled clerk Allan Charlesworth & Co 1967, CA 1972, Coopers and Lybrand 1973; Robson Rhodes: joined 1974, ptnr 1978, estab Personal Fin Planning Gp and Lloyd's Underwriter's Specialist Gp 1980, currently lead ptnr in Kent and responsible for personal taxation in SE Eng; frequent lectr on Lloyd's; pres Swanley Catenian Assoc 1988-89; FCA, ATII; *Recreations* photograghy, wine; *Style*— John Rayer, Esq; Robson Rhodes, 52 St Margaret's St, Rochester, Kent ME1 1TY (☎ 0634 829300, fax 0834 829082)

RAYNES, Lady (Frederica) Rozelle Ridgway; *née* Pierrepont; da of 6 Earl Manvers (d 1955); *b* 1925; *Educ* Queen Elizabeth's GS Mansfield Notts; *m* 1, 1953 (m dis 1961), Maj Alexander Montgomerie Greaves Beattie; m 2, 1965, Richard Hollins Raynes; *Career* served 1939-45 war as Leading Wren Stoker WRNS; writer, school care worker (ILEA), asst purser Merchant Navy; *Books* North in a Nutshell, Maid Matelot, The Sea Bird, The Tuesday Boys; *Recreations* sailing; *Clubs* Royal Cruising, Royal Naval Sailing Assoc, Royal Cinque Ports Yacht; *Style—* The Lady Rozelle Raynes; Dolphin's Leap, St Margaret's Bay, Kent; 88 Narrow St, London E14 8BP

REA, Hon Mrs Findlay; Helen Margaret; *née* Richardson; da of Bernhard Hermann Richardson (decd), of Edinburgh; *m* 1, 1936, Donald Crawford Reid; m 2, 1959, as his 3 w, Hon Findlay Russell Rea (d 1984), 3 and yst s of 1 Baron Rea; *Style—* The Hon Mrs Findlay Rea; Weald Cottage, Weald, Sevenoaks, Kent

RECORD, Rev John; s of Frederick Thomas Record, of Bridport, Dorset, and Ivy May, *née* Crespin; *b* 6 Nov 1947; *Educ* Colfox Sch, Univ of Durham (BA), Westcott House Cambridge; *m* 5 Aug 1972, Felicity Joan Slade, da of Lt Cdr Anthony Claud Higgens, DSC, RN, of West House, Old Harlow, Essex; 2 s (Thomas Adam Crespin b 1980, Nicholas John Crespin b 1983), 1 da (Anna Katherine Crespin b 1977); *Career* curate: St John the Evangelist Hyde Park Crescent London 1973, Witney 1975; vicar: Little Compton with Chastleton Cornwell Salford and Little Rollright 1978, Hawkhurst 1983-; rural dean West Charing 1989-; memb Tunbridge Wells Health Authy, ind mangr Ticehurst House, vocations advsr Archdeaconry of Maidstone, chm govrs Hawkhurst Primary Sch; chaplain: Hawkhurst Cottage Hosp, Bowles Lodge, Br Legion, Weald of Kent Scouts; *Recreations* family, performing arts, country matters; *Style—* The Rev John Record; The Vicarage, Hawkhurst, Kent TN18 4BQ (☎ 0580 753397)

REDMAN, Mark; s of Frederick George Redman (d 1976), of Swiss Cottage, West Wickham, Dulwich and Cliftonville, and (Unity Anne) Veronica, *née* Bland; *b* 5 June 1948; *Educ* Dulwich, The Coll of Law Lancaster Gate; *m* 28 July 1979, Lorna Alexia, da of Robert Young, of Deal; 3 da (Polly Alexia b 2 June 1981, Hannah Victoria b 26 Oct 1983, Camilla Beth b 18 June 1990); *Career* slr; articles with Nicholson Graham & Jones 1967-72, equity ptnr Girlings 1975 (ptnr 1974), nursing homes proprietor and sr ptnr The St Anselm's Nursing Home Group, dir Lerril Ltd; tstee Matthew Young Appeal Fund, former pres Brotherhood of Cheerful Sparrows, master Foreland Masonic Lodge 1987-88; memb: sundry local ctees, Law Soc, Kent Law Soc, Isle of Thanet Law Soc (hon sec 1981-88); *Recreations* parenthood, current affrs, property devpt; *Clubs* Wig and Pen; *Style—* Mark Redman, Esq; Ripple House, Ripple, Deal, Kent; Girlings, Crown Chambers, Margate, Kent (☎ 0843 220274, fax 0843 297828)

REED, Frederick William (Freddie); MBE; s of Thomas George Reed, and Julia, *née* Pond; *b* 21 July 1914; *m* 12 Aug 1939, Kathleen, da of Ernest Ridley, of Newcastle on Tyne; 2 s (Michael Ridley Graham b 25 Nov 1944, David Brian b 27 Feb 1948); *Career* art ed Daily Mirror 1943 (staff photographer 1930), chief photographer Picture News 1946-79 (ed 1944); int freelance 1979-, Royal Photographer of Year twice, former Sports Photographer of Year six times runner up Photographer of Year; chm: Visual Journalism Paanel for Qualifications of RPS; FRPS, FBIPP; *Books* Queen Mother and Her Family (1979), A Friend in Need (1985), Freddie Reed's Royal Tours (1989); *Recreations* golf; *Clubs* Wildernesse (Kent); *Style—* Freddie Reed, Esq, MBE; 8 Turners Gardens, Sevenoaks, Kent TN13 1QE

REES, Prof Lovat Victor Charles; s of Sqdn Ldr Daniel George Rees (d 1960), of Nairnm Scotland, and Margaret Jane, *née* Urquhart Stephen (d 1967); *b* 7 Nov 1927; *Educ* Robert Gordon's Coll Aberdeen, Univ of Aberdeen (BSc, PhD, DSc); *m* 12 Aug 1953, Elizabeth Margaret, da of Joseph Main (d 1989), of Stonehaven, Scotland; 1 s (Lovat Michael Graham b 1959), 3 da (Lesley Elizabeth b 1957, Shauna b 1961, Gillian Main b 1963); *Career* asst lectr Univ of Aberdeen 1952-53, sr scientific offr Awre Aldermaston 1953-57, prof Imperial Coll Univ of London 1958-; FRSC, CChem 1984; *Recreations* rifle shooting, golf; *Clubs* St Nicholas Rifle & Pistol, Chislehurst Brechin GC; *Style—* Prof Lovat Rees; Pantiles, Yester Park, Chislehurst, Kent BR7 5DQ (☎ 081 467 2928); Imperial College of Science Technology and Medicine, Chemistry Department, S Kensington, London SW7 2AY (☎ 071 589 5111 ext 4606, fax 071 584 7596, telex 261503)

REES, Rev (Richard) Michael; s of Rev Richard Rees (d 1975), of Bedford, and Margaret Patricia, *née* Head; *b* 31 July 1935; *Educ* Brighton Coll, St Peter's Coll Oxford (MA), Tyndale Hall Bristol; *m* 6 Sept 1958, Yoma Patricia, da of Maj the Rev Cyril Herbert Hampton, of Branksome Park; 2 s (Timothy b 1960, Killadeas b 1961); *Career* ed Missionary Mandate 1956-69; curate: All Saints Crowborough Sussex 1959-62, Christ Church with Emmanuel Clifton Bristol 1962-64; chaplain Bristol ATC 1963-64, vicar Christ Church Clevedon Avon 1964-72, chaplain Clevedon Maternity Hosp, vicar Holy Trinity Church Cambridge 1972-84, chm Cambridge Cncl of Churches, chief sec Church Army 1984-; tstee: Disabled Christians Fellowship 1962- (chm 1962-72), Cambridge Work Relations Gp 1984-, Simeon's Tstees 1969-; govr St Brandon's Sch Clevedon 1969-87; *Recreations* photography, tropical fish, classical music; *Style—* The Rev Michael Rees; 6 Pickwick Way, Chislehurst, Kent BR7 6RZ (☎ 081 467 9167); The Chief Secretary, Church Army, Independents Rd, Blackheath, London SE3 9LG (☎ 081 318 1226, fax 081 318 5258)

REES-DAVIES, William Rupert (Billy); QC (1973); s of Sir William Rees-Davies, KC, JP, DL (sometime Lib MP for Pembroke and chief justice Hong Kong, d 1939); *b* 19 Nov 1916; *Educ* Eton, Trinity Coll Cambridge; *m* 1, 1959, Jane Lesa, *née* Mander; 2 da; m 2, 1982, Sharlie Kingsley; *Career* served WWII Welsh Gds; called to the Bar Inner Temple 1939; MP (C): Isle of Thanet 1953-74, Thanet W 1974-83; chm: All Party Ctee for Tourism 1965-68, Cons Ctee for Tourism; Cons ldr Select Ctee Health and Social Servs 1980-83; *Clubs* MCC, Hawks, Turf; *Style—* William Rees-Davies Esq, QC; 1 Crown Office Row, Temple, London EC4 (☎ 071 583 3724); 5 Lord North St, London SW1; Gore Street Manor, Monkton, Thanet, Kent

REEVE, Nigel John; s of George Edward Reeve, of Ipswich, Suffolk, and Edna May, *née* Chenery; *b* 19 Aug 1952; *Educ* Everton House Ipswich Suffolk; *m* 1, 13 Aug 1982 (m dis 1988), Marytyje Geertruida, *née* Lamberts; m 2, 7 Oct 1988, (Marion) Lindsay, da of Capt Trevor Maldwyn Jones; *Career* admin Eastern Counties Newspapers 1969-76, sales exec Radio Orwell Ipswich 1976-81, sales mangr Two Counties Radio Bournemouth 1982-83, sales dir County Sound Guildford 1983-85; Invicta Sound: sales dir 1985-87, dep md 1987-88, md 1988-; dir: Mellow 1557 Ltd Colchester Essex, Invicta Continental SARL France; dir and tstee Invicta Charity for the Disabled of Kent; memb: SE Eng Publicity Club (former sec), Cons Pty, IOD, Mktg Ctee and Radio Award Ctee Assoc of Ind Radio Contractors; *Recreations* golf, soccer; *Clubs* Broom Park Golf; *Style—* Nigel Reeve, Esq; Invicta Sound plc, 15 Station Rd East, Canterbury, Kent CT1 2RB (☎ 0227 767661, fax 0227 451312)

REEVES, (Charles) Christopher Seward; s of late Maj Charles Westcott Reeves, OBE, of Enfield, Middx, and Winifred Mary Reeves; *b* 6 Oct 1917; *Educ* Aldenham; *m* 1, 3 April 1948, Betty Rosanne Roberts (d 1987); 1 s (Robert Christopher b 1952), 1 da (Bettina b 1949); m 2, 10 Dec 1988, Elizabeth Mary (Bunty), da of late Arthur Brown; *Career* WWII Home Guard 1941-45; selling and admin Fitch and Son Ltd (now Fitch Lovell Group) 1939-53, selling EM Denny Ltd 1953-55, selling Danish Bacon Co Ltd 1955-63, sales mangr Mathews and Skailes Ltd London 1963-73, mangr Atalanta (UK) Ltd London (subsid of Atlanta Corpn NY USA), now ret; fndr chm Enfield Young Cons 1946, memb local Cons Pty 1946-, pres Chislehurst Cons Commons Branch, chm Bromley Youth Tst, govr four local schs, chm of govrs Kemnal Manor Sch 1982-88; cncllr London Borough of Bromley 1967-, Mayor of Bromley 1986-87, memb Bromley Family Practitioners Ctee, chm Nat Benevolent Inst; Liveryman Worshipful Co of Skinners; *Recreations* bridge, sailing, petanque; *Style—* Christopher Reeves, Esq; 6 Manor Place, Chislehurst, Kent BR7 5QH (☎ 071 467 5247); 114 Bay View, Hermanus Cape, RSA

REICH, David Keith; s of Cecil Dominic Reich (d 1967), of Tunbridge Wells, and Megan Eluned, *née* Jones; *b* 5 July 1943; *Educ* Tonbridge, Imperial Coll London (BSc); *m* 7 Aug 1974, (Anne) Jennifer, da of John Oswald Anthony Gardner, of Ventnor, Isle of Wight; 3 s (Christopher b 1978, Anthony b 1980, Michael b 1981); *Career* L Reich and Sons Ltd: joined 1967, dir 1969, chm and md 1973; memb Cncl of the Nat Assoc of Goldsmiths of GB and Ireland 1973-; pres Royal Tunbridge Wells Chamber of Trade 1978, chm Tonbridge and Dist Branch of the Nat Assoc of Goldsmiths 1978; memb Tunbridge Wells Borough Cncl 1968-71 and 1972-74; *Recreations* golf, bridge, oenology, skiing; *Clubs* Nevill Golf, West Kent; *Style—* David Reich, Esq; L Reich & Sons Ltd, 48-50 Monson Rd, Royal Tunbridge Wells, Kent TN1 1LP (☎ 0892 26552)

REID, Sir Norman Robert; s of Edward Daniel Reid (d 1956); *b* 27 Dec 1915; *Educ* Wilson's GS Camberwell, Edinburgh Coll of Art, Univ of Edinburgh (DA); *m* 1941, Jean Lindsay, da of Alexander Taylor Bertram, of Brechin; 1 s, 1 da; *Career* WWII served A & SH, Maj 1946; Tate Gallery: joined 1946, dep dir 1954, keeper 1959, dir 1964-79; memb: Cncl Friends of the Tate Gallery 1958-79, Arts Cncl Panel 1964-74, Advsy Panel ICA 1965-, Advsy Ctee Paintings in Hosps 1965-69, Br Cncl Fine Arts Ctee 1965-77 (chm 1968-75), Cultural Advsy Ctee UK Nat Cmmn for UNESCO 1966-70, Studies in History of Art Bd London Univ 1968, The Rome Centre 1969-77 (pres 1975-77), Burlington Magazine Bd 1971-75, Advsy Cncl Paul Mellon Centre 1971-78, Cncl of Mgmnt Inst of Contemporary Prints 1972-78, Contemporary Arts Soc Ctee 1973-77 (and 1965-72), Cncl RCA 1974-77; pres Penworth Soc of Arts, tstee Graham and Kathleen Sutherland Fndn 1980-86; Hon LittD UEA; FMA, FIIC; Offr of the Mexican Order of the Aztec Eagle; kt 1970; *Clubs* Arts; *Style—* Sir Norman Reid; 50 Brabourne Rise, Park Langley, Beckenham, Kent

REMINGTON-HOBBS, Col Edward; DSO (1945), OBE (1947); s of A Remington-Hobbs, MD (d 1928), and gs of Sir Joseph Wilkinson (d 1902); *b* 7 Feb 1916; *Educ* Westminster, RMC Sandhurst; *m* 1, 1950, Angela Susan (k in air crash 1953), only da of Capt Marshall Owen Roberts (d 1931), of 15 Grosvenor Sq, London W1; 1 da (Julie Marguerite b 1951); m 2, 1957 (m dis

1967), Ann; m 3, 1972, Susan Mary Sheila; *Career* WWII serv Argyll and Sutherland Highlanders: UK, BNAF, NW Europe (wounded), SEAC; instr Staff Coll Camberley 1944, ret 1950; gold staff offr Coronation of HM The Queen 1953, usher (silver stick) Silver Jubilee Thanksgiving Serv 1977; underwriting memb of Lloyd's 1959-; chm and md: Polyseal Ltd 1960-75, Bellfax Int Ltd 1975-84; chm Snuffers Ltd 1984-; memb OStJ Cncl for Sussex 1965-69 (Order Cross Bearer 1966-); memb Chapter Gen 1972-; Freeman City of London 1960, memb Guild of Freemen 1987, Liveryman Worshipful Co of Gunmakers 1988-; The Pilgrims 1971-; KStJ 1976; *Recreations* cricket, shooting, golf; *Clubs* Boodle's, Pratt's, MCC, I Zingari, Free Forresters, Butterflies, Swinley Forest; *Style*— Col Edward Remington-Hobbs, DSO, OBE; The Maidens' Tower, Leeds Castle, Maidstone, Kent ME17 1PL (☎ 0622 880272); 3 Lyall Mews, London SW1X 8DJ (☎ 071 235 0930); 123-124 Newgate St, London EC1A 7AA (☎ 071 600 8387)

REMINGTON-HOBBS, Mrs Edward; Susan Mary Sheila; *née* Winn; da of Hon Charles Winn (2 s of 2 Baron St Oswald, JP, DL), by his 1 w Hon Olive, da of 1 and last Baron Queenborough, GBE, JP (gs of 1 Marquess of Anglesey); *b* 27 April 1923; *Educ* Owleston Croft, Cambridge, French Sch Paris; *m* 1, 20 July 1946, Hon Geoffrey Denis Erskine Russell (now Baron Ampthill); 3 s (David Whitney Erskine b 1947, James Nicholas Geoffrey b 1948 d 1969, Anthony John Mark b 1952), 1 da (Vanessa Mary Linda b 1960); m 2, 19 Dec 1972, Col Edward Remington-Hobbs, DSO, OBE, *qv*; *Career* joined Red Cross 1939, serv VAD 1941-45; *Recreations* reading, walking, photography; *Style*— Mrs Edward Remington-Hobbs; The Maidens' Tower, Leeds Castle, Maidstone, Kent ME17 1PL (☎ 0622 880272); 3 Lyall Mews, London SW1X 8DJ (☎ 071 235 0930)

RHODES, Barry; s of James Henry Rhodes, of Crawley, West Sussex, and Victoria Alice, *née* Harris; *b* 10 Sept 1947; *Educ* Thomas Bennett Comprehensive Sch Crawley, Coll of Law Lancaster Gate London; *m* 3 June 1972, Margaret Elizabeth, da of Douglas Percy Wright, of Crawley, West Sussex; 2 s (Paul Edward b 24 Feb 1978, Stephen Antony b 29 May 1980); *Career* articled clerk Arbeid and Co Hove (now Helman and Co) 1966-71, unadmitted conveyancing asst Stuart Hunt and Co 1972; asst slr: Gillingham Borough Cncl 1972-73, Watson Flint and Gunter 1973-; memb: Nat Trust, English Heritage, Benevolent Asssoc 1980; chm exec Ctee 22 Gillingham Scout Gp, life govr Imperial Cancer Research Fund; memb: Law Soc, Br Legal Assoc; vice pres Kent Law Soc; *Recreations* badminton, history especially the Napolionic period; *Style*— Barry Rhodes, Esq; Longwood, The Platters, Rainham, Kent (☎ 0634 362000); Watson Flint and Gunter, 35 Railway St, Chatham, Kent (☎ 0634 844618, 844619, fax 0634 842557)

RIBBANDS, Mark Jonathan; s of Henry Stephen Ribbands, of Hornchurch, and Christina Ivy, *née* Saggers (d 1984); *b* 6 Jan 1959; *Educ* Forest Sch Snaresbrook, N E London Poly (BSc); *m* 30 May 1987, Maya, da of Flt Offr Wassoudeve Goriah, DFC (d 1969); *Career* md Ribbands Explosives Ltd 1982-; involved with: explosives disposals demoliton, purchase and supply of arms and ammunition specialising in antiarmour weaponry, supply of explosive ordnance disposal personnel worldwide; memb cncl Inst of Explosives Engrs 1988; FGS 1983, FRGS 1983, MIExpE 1985; *Recreations* scuba diving, flying (helicopters), shooting; *Style*— Mark Ribbands, Esq; 18 Kingsgate Castle, Broadstairs, Kent CT10 3PH

RICHARDSON, James; s of Kenneth Eason Richardson (d 1982), of Coventry, W Midlands, and Margaret Joan, *née* Simpson, of Chichester, W Sussex; *b* 8 April 1952; *Educ* King Henry VIII Sch Coventry, Univ of Manchester (LLB); *m* 9 Nov 1985, Christine Margaret, da of Robert Raymond Pittam, of Croydon, Surrey; *Career* asst town clerk Gillingham Borough Cncl 1982-87; Kent CC: slr 1987-88, sr slr 1988-89, first sr slr (Land and Planning) 1989-; parish church sidesman; memb Law Soc 1982-; *Recreations* theatre, music, walking, reading, National Trust; *Style*— James Richardson, Esq; 13 Allsworth Close, Newington, Sittingbourne, Kent ME9 7NW (☎ 0795 843989); Kent County Council, County Hall, Maidstone, Kent ME14 1XQ (☎ 0622 671411 ext 4481, fax 0622 694402)

RICHARDSON, Michael John; s of George Frederick Richardson (d 1979), and Mabel Alice, *née* Cox; *b* 28 March 1935; *Educ* Epsom Coll; *m* 22 Aug 1959, Helen Patricia, da of Percival Bluett Bray (d 1942); 1 s (David b 16 Jan 1962), 1 da (Susan b 2 Jan 1965); *Career* CA; FW Smith Riches 1952-60, Price Waterhouse 1960-63, dir 3i Group (3i Corporate Finance Ltd) 1963-80, fin dir Shandwick Group 1980-81, dir Chartered West LB Ltd (formerly Standard Chartered Merchant Bank Ltd) 1986- (joined 1981); circuit steward Sevenoaks Methodist Church; Freeman City of London, Liveryman Worshipful Co of CAs; FCA; *Books* Going Public (1973); *Recreations* singing, swimming, gardening; *Style*— Michael Richardson, Esq; 19 Mount Harry Rd, Sevenoaks, Kent TN13 3JJ (☎ 0732 453839); Chartered West LB Ltd, 33-36 Gracechurch St, London EC3V 0AX (☎ 071 623 8711, fax 071 626 1610, telex 884689)

RICHARDSON, Air Marshal Sir (David) William; KBE (1986); *b* 10 Feb 1932; *Educ* Univ of Birmingham, Cranfield Inst of Technol (MSc); *m* 1954, Mary Winifred, *née* Parker; 2 s (b 1956 and 1958), 1 da (b 1960); *Career* RAF 1953, AOC Maintenance Gp HQ RAF Support Cmd 1981-83, Air Offr Engrg RAF Strike Cmd 1983-86, RAF Chief Eng 1986, ret 1988; dir Aero & Industrial Technology Ltd; tstee MONITOR (charity investigating motor neurone disease); CEng, FIMechE, FRAeS; *Clubs* RAF; *Style*— Air Marshal Sir William Richardson, KBE; c/o Lloyds Bank, Southborough

RICHMAN, Richard Andrew; s of Derek Rudolph Valentino Richman, of 11 Donet Close, Rainham, Gillingham, Kent, and Jill, *née* Ambrose; *b* 12 Jan 1962; *Educ* Howard Sch for Boys, Mid Kent Coll Rochester and Chatham; *Career* TA REME 1982-85; mechanical engr: trg Blaw Knox Rochester 1978-82, Engis Ltd 1982-86; ptnr Design Tooling 1986- (SE winners of Best Business Award 1988); designed a track product for BR 1987-89; memb: Gillingham Lions Club (IO5E Dist) Kent 1988-, Br Motorcycle Two Stroke Club 1990-; sponsored by Kent Jet Ski Centre for their racing team 1990; *Recreations* TA, keep fit, vintage motorcycles; *Style*— Richard Richman, Esq; 54 Old Castle Walk, Rainham, Gillingham, Kent ME8 9TZ (☎ 0634 374565); R W Regrind, Unit D, 256 Lower Twydall Lane, Gillingham, Kent ME8 6QP (☎ 0634 376150, fax 0634 35124)

RICHMOND-WATSON, Colin Irving; s of Richmond Watson (d 1944), of Chalfont Grove, Chalfont St Giles, Bucks, and Gwendolen Llewethlyn Avis, *née* Davis (d 1971); *b* 24 Oct 1925; *Educ* Winchester New Coll Oxford; *m* 5 June 1954 (m dis 1973), Anne Isabel, da of Francis Luther Fane (d 1954), of Wormsley, Watlington, Oxon; 2 s (Harry b 1956, Angus b 1958 d 1984), 2 da (Elizabeth b 1960, Sarah b 1962); *Career* now ret; chm Kent Gardens Tst, pres Charing and Westwell Soc; *Recreations* gardening; *Style*— Colin Richmond-Watson, Esq; Pett Place, Charing, Kent TN27 0D5 (☎ 023 371 2850, fax 023 371 3220)

RICKAYZEN, Prof Gerald; s of Solomon Rickayzen (d 1969), and Jane, *née* Culank (d 1975); *b* 16 Oct 1929; *Educ* Teignmouth GS, Central Fndn Boys' Sch, QMC London (BSc), Christ's Coll Cambridge (PhD); *m* 20 Dec 1953, Gillian Thelma, da of Maurice Lewin (d 1971); 3 s (Alan Michael b 15 Jan 1957, Martin Asher b 28 Dec 1960, Benjamin David b 1 June 1963), 1 da (Sonia Ruth b 29 Nov 1958); *Career* res fell Admiralty 1954-57, res assoc Univ of Illinois 1957-59, lectr Univ of Liverpool 1959-65; Univ of Kent: reader in theoretical physics 1966-, dean Faculty of Natural Scis 1977-81, pro vice chllr 1981-90, dep vice chllr 1984-90; chm of govrs Simon Langton Girls' Sch; govr: Simon Langton Boys' Sch, Christ Church Coll Canterbury; fell Inst of Physics; *Books* Theory of Superconductivity (1965), Green's Functions and Condensed Matter (1980); *Recreations* playing the cello, tennis; *Style*— Prof Gerald Rickayzen; The Physics Laboratory, The University, Canterbury, Kent CT2 7NR (☎ 0227 764000, fax 0227 762616)

RICKAYZEN, Gillian Thelma; da of Maurice Lewin (d 1971), of Dunstable, and Ethel, *née* Michaelis (d 1986); *b* 4 Dec 1929; *Educ* Luton HS for Girls, Univ of Glasgow (MA), Oxford Delegacy for Social Studies (Dip Pub and Social Admin); *m* 20 Dec 1953, Gerald Rickayzen, *qv*, s of Solomon Rickayzen (d 1969), of London; 3 s (Alan Michael b 15 Jan 1957, Martin Asher b 28 Dec 1960, Benjamin David b 1 June 1963), 1 da (Sonia Ruth b 29 Nov 1958); *Career* social worker London CC 1952-53, remedial teacher Baldock Primary Sch 1953-56, fndr and hon sec Monday Music 1974-; fndr and ctee memb Canterbury Assoc for Advancement of State Educn 1965-, exec Nat Confedn for Advancement of State Educn 1971-75 (prodn ed of Nat CASE newsletter), govr Kent Music Sch 1971-74, memb of exec Canterbury Arts Cncl, fndr memb and first sec Univ of Kent Women's Club (chm 1986-89); life memb: Nat Tst, Henry Doubleday Res Assoc; *Recreations* organising music, collecting chamber music, playing viola, sheep-rearing, esperanto; *Style*— Mrs Gillian Rickayzen; 27 Ross Gardens, Rough Common, Canterbury, Kent CT2 9BZ (☎ 0227 464996)

RIDDLE, Howard Charles Frazer; s of Cecil Riddle (d 1987), of Sevenoaks, Kent, and Eithne, *née* McKenna; *b* 13 Aug 1947; *Educ* Judd Sch Tonbridge, LSE (LLB); *m* 31 Aug 1974, (Susan) Hilary, da of Dr André Hurst, of Ottawa, Canada; 2 da (Stephanie b 1979, Poppy b 1984); *Career* SSRC Canada 1971-76, sr ptnr Edward Fail Bradshaw & Waterson 1985-; memb Law Soc 1978 (London Area Ctee 1986); *Recreations* rugby football; *Style*— Howard Riddle, Esq; Norton Cottage, Bethersden, Kent; Edward Fail Bradshaw & Waterson, 402 Commercial Rd, Stepney, London E1 0LG (☎ 071 790 4032, fax 071 790 2739)

RIDLEY, Jasper Godwin; s of Geoffrey William Ridley (d 1957), of 24 Victoria Park, Dover, and Ursula Mary, *née* King (d 1974); *b* 25 May 1920; *Educ* Felcourt Sch, The Sorbonne, Magdalen Coll Oxford; *m* 1 Oct 1949, Vera, da of Emil Pollak (d 1974), of Prague, Czechoslovakia; 2 s (Benjamin Nicholas b 1952, John Simon b 1956), 1 da (Barbara Susan b 1950); *Career* called to the Bar Inner Temple 1945; practicing barr 1946-52; author; vice pres Eng section Int PEN, vice chm Tunbridge Wells and Dist Writers' Circle (chm 1987-90); chm Tunbridge Wells Gp Rambler's Assoc, memb Soc of Sussex Authors; memb Court of Assts Worshipful Co of Carpenters (Master 1988-89 and 1990-91); FRSL; *Books* Nicholas Ridley (1957), The Law of Carriage of Goods (1957), Thomas Cranmer (1962), John Knox (1968), Lord Palmerston (1970), Mary Tudor (1973), Garibaldi (1974), The Roundheads (1976), Napoleon III and Eugénie (1979), The History of England (1981), The Statesman and the Fanatic (1982), Henry VIII (1984), Elizabeth I (1987), The

Tudor Age (1988), The Love Letters of Henry VIII (1989); *Recreations* chess, walking; *Style*— Jasper Ridley, Esq; 6 Oakdale Rd, Tunbridge Wells, Kent TN4 8DS (☎ 0892 22460)

RIDOUT, Dr Alan John; s of George Alfred Ridout (d 1958), and Dorothy Evelyn, *née* Gardner (d 1985); *b* 9 Dec 1934; *Educ* Haberdashers' Aske's, Guildhall Sch of Music, RCM; *Career* composer; works incl: operas, ballets, orchestral works, choral works, chamber music, instrumental music, liturgical music; teacher: Univ of Birmingham, Univ of London, Univ of Cambridge, Univ of Oxford: prof RCM 1962-82; John Collard fell Worshipful Co of Musicians 1968-71; DMus Central Sch of Religion 1980; FRCM 1981; *Books* Background to Music (1982), Background to Musical Form (1964), The Music of Howard Ferguson (1989); *Style*— Dr Alan Ridout

RIDOUT, John Edward; s of W D Edward Albert Ridout, RM (ka June 1942 Malta Convoy), and Margaret Mary, *née* Sloan; *b* 24 May 1936; *Educ* Castle HS Deal, Dover Poly Coll (HNC Engrg); *m* 25 March 1967, Barbara Mary, da of Stanley Hodgson, MBE, of 2 Willow Court, Embrook Rd, Sandgate, Folkstone; 1 s (Matthew John b 4 Jan 1983); *Career* apprentice engrg draughtsman 1951-56; Petbow Ltd: mechanical electrical draughtsman 1956-58, control systems designer 1958-60, estimator power plant 1960-63, asst sales mangr 1963-68, sales mangr 1968-70, sales and publicity mangr 1970-80, euro sales mangr 1981-82, mktg mangr 1982-86; gp mktg mangr: Petbow Holdings plc 1986-88, Anglo Nordia Power Generation Ltd 1988; former ctee memb Inst of Mktg Kent Branch; memb Nat Assoc of Res (Mktg), Chartered Inst of Mktg; author of technical articles and papers relating to power generation, world markets and statistical analysis in mktg studies; *Books* 50 Years In Power (ed, 1982); *Recreations* photography, gardening, writing, swimming, family, travel; *Style*— John Ridout, Esq; Sea Lodge, Kingsdown Rd, Walmer, Deal, Kent CT14 8AR (☎ 0304 361019); Anglo Nordic Power Generation Ltd, Sandwich, Kent CT13 9NE (☎ 0304 613311, fax 0304 613358)

RIMER, Colin Percy Farquharson; QC (1988); s of Kenneth Rowland Rimer, of Beckenham, Kent, and Maria Eugenia, *née* Farquharson; *b* 30 Jan 1944; *Educ* Dulwich, Trinity Hall Cambridge (MA, LLB); *m* 3 Jan 1970, Penelope Ann, da of Alfred William Gibbs, of Beckenham, Kent; 2 s (David b 1972, Michael b 1974), 1 da (Catherine b 1971); *Career* res asst Inst of Comparative Law Paris 1967-68; called to the Bar Lincoln's Inn 1968; practising since 1969; *Recreations* music, photography, novels, walking; *Style*— Colin Rimer, Esq, QC; 13 Old Square, Lincoln's Inn, London WC2A 3UA (☎ 071 404 4800)

RING, Sir Lindsay Roberts; GBE (1975), JP (Inner London 1964); s of George Arthur Ring; *b* 1 May 1914; *Educ* Dulwich Coll, Mecklenburg Germany; *m* 1940, Hazel Doris, da of A Trevor Nichols, CBE; 2 s, 1 da; *Career* serv WWII Maj RASC; memb Court of Common Cncl (Bishopsgate Ward) City of London 1964-68, alderman (Ward of Vintry) 1968, sheriff City of London 1967-68, Lord Mayor of London 1975-76; FCIS 1976; chm Ring & Brymer (Birchs) Ltd (caterers); memb Gaming Bd for GB 1977-; Hon DSc (City U) 1976, Freeman City of London 1935; Hon DLitt (Ulster) 1976; KStJ 1976; *Style*— Sir Lindsay Ring, GBE, JP; Chalvedune, Wilderness Rd, Chislehurst, Kent BR7 5EY (☎ 01 467 3199); Ring & Brymer Ltd, 30 Sun St, London EC2 (☎ 01 377 2552)

RIX, Dr (Edward) Martyn; s of Edward Lionel Reussner Rix, of Kent, and Elizabeth Joyce, *née* Martyn-Linnington (d 1978); *b* 15 Aug 1943; *Educ* Sherborne, Trinity Coll Dublin (MA), Corpus Christi Coll Cambridge (PhD), Univ of Zurich; *m* 10 Sept 1983, Alison Jane, da of Geoffrey Herbert Goatcher, of Washington, Sussex; 1 da (Emma May b 19 June 1987); *Career* botanist RHS Gardens Wisley Surrey 1975-78; *Books* The Art of the Botanist (1981), Growing Bulbs (1983); with Roger Phillips: The Bulb Book (1981), Freshwater Fish (1985), Roses (1988), Shrubs (1989); Garden Open Today (ed with Alison Rix, 1987); *Recreations* fishing; *Style*— Dr Martyn Rix; Grove House, Sellinge, nr Ashford, Kent

RIX, Richard Harry; s of Maj Edward Lionel Reussner Rix, of Grove House, Sellindge, nr Ashford, and Elizabeth Joyce, *née* Martyn-Linnington (d 1978); *b* 22 Aug 1950; *Educ* Sherborne, Wye Coll London (BSc); *m* 20 April 1974, Sarah Elizabeth, da of Lt Cdr Charles Cecil Gardner (d 1976), of Symnel Cottage, Aldington; 1 s (Charles b 1984), 1 da (Lizzie b 1981); *Career* admitted slr 1979, slr of Supreme Court 1979; fin ptnr Hallett & Co 1982- (ptnr 1980-); churchwarden Sellindge Parish Church, vice chm of govrs Aldington Primary Sch; memb Law Soc, licentiate Royal Photographic Soc; *Recreations* gardening, fishing, photography; *Style*— Richard Rix, Esq; Messrs Hallett & Co Solicitors, 11 Bank St, Ashford, Kent TN23 1DA (☎ 0233 625711, fax 0233 643841)

RIZZA, George Joseph; s of James Rizza (d 1974), and Emily Neri (d 1943); *b* 5 Nov 1925; *Educ* Gordons Sch Huntly, Royal Scottish Acad of Music; *m* 25 March 1969, Margaret, da of Harvey Gibson (d 1947); 1 da (Jane Diane b 1971); *Career* Novello & Co Ltd 1973, Laurel Music 1970, Cinderella 1978, Lorna Music 1978, Woodside Music 1978-82, Mayheu Music 1978-82, Fairfield 1975, Goodwin & Tabb 1975, Elkin 1975, Mercury Music 1973, Paxton 1976, Performing Rights Society 1973, Jazz Journal 1973-83, Austria Travel 1986, Park Lane Gp 1964-80, J W Chester Ltd 1962-72; ARCM; *Style*— George Rizza, Esq; 14 Vine Avenue, Sevenoaks, Kent (☎ 0732 452429); Novello & Co Ltd, Fairfield Road, Borough Green, Kent TN15 8DT (☎ 0732 883261, telex 95583)

ROBBINS, Stephen Dennis; s of Lt-Col J Dennis Robbins, OBE, TD (d 1986), of Inworth Hall, Essex, and Joan, *née* Mason; *b* 11 Jan 1948; *Educ* Marlborough, Coll of Europe Bruges; *m* 28 Sept 1974, Amanda Robbins, JP, da of J Michael Smith, of Foden Bank Farm, Macclesfield, Ches; 3 da (Harriet b 1976, Victoria b 1979, Camilla (twin) b 1979); *Career* barr 1969; practice S Eastern circuit 1972-, recorder Crown Courts 1987-; London Common Law Bar Assoc and Senate Overseas Rels, chm Disciplinary Ctee Potato Mktg Bd 1988-; *Recreations* Scottish hill walking, fishing, swimming, shooting, cross country skiing, music, collecting ephemera; *Style*— Stephen Robbins, Esq; Hillcrest Farm, Sevington, nr Ashford, Kent (☎ 0233 629732); The Studios, Edge St, London W8 (☎ 071 727 7216); 1 Harcourt Buildings, Temple, London EC4 (☎ 071 353 9421)

ROBERTS, John Leonard; s of Maj Robert Edward Roberts, and Dorothea, *née* Goodchild; *b* 19 Jan 1939; *m* 22 Oct 1963, Gillian Lesley, da of Leslie Low; 1 s (Alexander b 12 Dec 1972); *Career* reporter; sub ed and dir City Press 1957-63, fin ed Thomson Newspapers 1963-67, exec Minster Trust 1967-68, asst ed Investors Chronicle 1968-73, city ed Daily Express 1974-76, freelance business journalist and broadcaster BBC Radio 4 and World Serv 1976-; award for business journalism for Men in the Middle 1977; *Books* Megalomania, Managers and Mergers (1987); *Recreations* beekeeping, gardening, standing on rainswept pitch watching son play rugby ; *Style*— John Roberts, Esq

ROBERTS, (Roberta) Julie; da of Robert Harry Green (d 1981), of Hawkinge, nr Folkestone, Kent, and Pearl Green, *née* Andrews; *b* 3 July 1952; *Educ* Folkestone GS For Girls, QMC (LLB); *m* 11 April 1984, Christopher John Roberts; *Career* admitted slr 1976; slr: Keene Marsland and Co 1976-79, Hamlin Grammer and Hamlin 1979-81, Thomson Snell and Passmore 1981-; *Style*— Mrs Julie Roberts; 30 Minter Ave, Densole, Folkestone, Kent (☎ 0303 89 2097); New Rents, Ashford, Kent TN23 1LB (☎ 0233 37303, fax 0233 45222)

ROBERTS, Malcolm John Binyon; s of Sqdn Ldr Kenneth Arthur Norman Roberts (d 1973), and Greta Kathleen, *née* Cooper; *b* 3 July 1951; *Educ* St Edmund's Sch Canterbury; *m* 28 April 1984, Caroline Mary, da of John Harry Scrutton; 1 s (Frederick), 1 da (Iona); *Career* ptnr Montagu Loebl Stanley 1979-86, dir Fleming Private Asset Management 1986-; memb Stock Exchange 1978; govr Granville Sch Sevenoaks; Freeman Worshipful Co of Barbers

ROBERTS, Peter David Thatcher; s of Leonard Charles Roberts (d 1978); *b* 1 March 1934; *Educ* Alleyns Sch Dulwich, Sir John Cass Coll Univ of London; *m* 1959, Elizabeth June Dodds; 1 s, 2 da; *Career* MN 1951-59, Lt RNR; Leinster/Hispania Maritime Ltd: Joined 1980, dir 1963, md 1965; dir Hays plc 1983- (joined 1969), chm: Hays Marine Services Ltd, Hays Commercial Services Ltd, Hays Personnel Services Ltd; dir: Shipowners P & I Association Ltd, Minories Holdings Ltd; memb Gen Ctee Lloyds Register of Shipping; Jr Warden The Co of Watermen and Lightermen of River Thames, Liveryman Worshipful Co of Shipwrights; MICS 1962, FBIM 1981; *Recreations* offshore sailing, golf; *Clubs* Royal Ocean Racing, RAC, Wildernesse Golf; *Style*— Peter Roberts, Esq; Callenders Cottage, Bidborough, nr Tunbridge Wells, Kent (☎ 0892 29053, office 0483 302203)

ROBERTSON, Douglas Laurence; s of Ronald John Robertson, of Milton Keynes, and Agnes McKay (Nanette), *née* Reid; *b* 12 June 1952; *Educ* Dalkeith HS, Langley Park Sch for Boys, St Edmund Hall Oxford (MA); *m* 1 Nov 1975, Susan Winifred, da of John Clair (d 1989), of Marden, Herefordshire; 1 s (Iain b 1979), 1 da (Carolyn b 1982); *Career* admitted slr 1977; ptnr Kenneth Brown Baker Baker 1981, Turner Kenneth Brown 1983; life memb Friends of Kent Churches; Freeman: City of London 1986, Worshipful Co of Slrs 1986; memb Law Soc 1977; *Recreations* rugby and football (spectating only), reading; *Clubs* Vincents, Utd Oxford and Cambridge Univ, Blackheath Football; *Style*— Douglas Robertson, Esq; Farleigh Cottage, Ricketts Hill Rd, Tatsfield, Westerham, Kent TN16 2NA (☎ 0959 77283); Turner Kenneth Brown, 100 Fetter Lane, London EC4A 1DD (☎ 071 242 6006, fax 071 242 3003)

ROBINSON, (George) Adrian; s of Thomas Gerard Robinson, BEM, of Preston, Lancs, and Elizabeth, *née* Gillow; *b* 3 Nov 1949; *Educ* Preston Catholic Coll, Pembroke Coll Oxford (MA); *m* 6 April 1974, Susan Margaret, da of James Hopwood Edmondson, of Accrington, Lancs; 2 s (Philip Adrian b 9 Sept 1984, Andrew James b 3 May 1987); *Career* various appts Midland Bank Ltd 1971-80; Airbus Industries: sales fin mangr 1980-82, dep sales fin dir 1982-84, sales fin dir 1984; corporate fin dir Midland Bank plc 1985; md special fin gp Chemical Bank 1987-89 (dir Aerospace 1986-87), dep gen mangr The Nippon Credit Bank 1990; ACIB 1973; *Recreations* golf, tennis, shooting; *Style*— Adrian Robinson, Esq; City Tower (10th Floor), 40 Basinghall St, London EC2V 5DE (☎ 071 638 6411, fax 071 920 0901, telex 893 273)

ROBINSON, Alexander Paul; s of Albert Edward Robinson (d 1975), and

Mabel Elizabeth Robinson (d 1987); *b* 30 March 1923; *Educ* Woolwich Poly, South West Essex Tech Coll (Nat Cert); *m* 3 May 1947, Edna Anne, da of William Hodges, of Camberwell; 2 s (Paul David b 7 March 1948, Michael John b 13 Nov 1961), 3 da (Pamela Jean b 4 Feb 1950, Jennifer Mary b 28 Oct 1952, Carol Elizabeth b 17 Nov 1964); *Career* RAF Bomber Cmd 1941-46; electrical engr; Jones and Jennings Electrical and Mechanical Engineers 1940-41 and 1947-50, AEI Group 1950-53, CEGB 1953-56, Kent CC Property Servs Dept 1956-84, ret 1984; memb: SE Thames RHA (chm Air Ambulance Helicopter Public Appeal Ctee), Ex-POW Assoc, Welfare Ctee Kent Co Nat Assoc of Local Govt Offrs; asst sec Tonbridge and Malling Trades Cncl, former pres Kent Branch NALGO; *Recreations* gardening; *Clubs* 158 Squadron Bomber Command Assoc; *Style*— Alexander Robinson, Esq; Santa Fe, Rectory Drive, Bidborough, Tunbridge Wells, Kent TN3 0UN (☎ 0892 29102)

ROBINSON, Arthur Geoffrey; CBE (1978); s of Arthur Robinson (d 1987), and Frances May Mason (d 1970); *b* 22 Aug 1917; *Educ* Lincoln Sch, Jesus Coll Cambridge (MA), SOAS Univ of London; *m* 1, 1943, Patricia (d 1971), da of William MacAllister (d 1922), of Wetherby; 3 s (Matthew b 1944, Thomas b 1950, George b 1961), 1 da (Sophy b 1955); m 2, 1973, Gai Rencie, wid of Martin Treves and da of Baron Salmon of Sandwich; *Career* served RA Staff Capt 1939-46; admitted slr 1948; Treasy Slrs Dept 1954-62, PLA 1962-66, md Tees and Hartlepool Port Authy 1966-77; chm: English Industl Estates Corp 1974-84, Medway Ports 1978-87; memb Nat Ports Cncl 1980-81, chm Br Ports Assoc 1983-85; *Books* Hedingham Harvest (1977); *Recreations* music; *Clubs* United Oxford and Cambridge Univ; *Style*— A G Robinson, Esq, CBE; Salts End, Gosshall Lane, Ash, Canterbury CT3 2AN (☎ 0304 812366); La Baume, Uzes 30700, Gard, France (☎ 010 33 66 22 55 44)

ROBINSON, Hon Mrs (Gai Rencie); da (by 1 m) of Baron Salmon (Life Peer); *b* 1933; *m* 1, 1955, Martin Treves (d 1970); 3 s, 1 da; m 2, 1973, Geoffrey Robinson, CBE, *qv*; *Style*— The Hon Mrs Robinson; 19 Millers Court, Chiswick Mall, London W4 (☎ 081 748 2997); Salts End, Ash, nr Canterbury, Kent (☎ 0304 812366)

ROBINSON, Rosina Elizabeth Violet May; da of Frederick Thomas Moon (d 1988), and Violet Maud, *née* Hughes; *b* 24 Aug 1950; *Educ* Bennett Memorial C of E Sch for Girls Tunbridge Wells; *m* 9 June 1973, Graham Anthony Robinson, s of Capt Ernest Leonard Alfred Robinson; *Career* student med laboratory technician 1967-68, Sec of State's Private Office NI Office 1972-87; Home Office: UN and Cncl of Europe Dept 1968-72, Health and Safety 1987-88, user assurance coordinator Prison Serv Info Technol Gp 1988-; area coordinator Br Diabetic Assoc Kent and E Sussex; involved with: The Paula Carr Trust Ashford, Br Diabetic Assoc Tunbridge Wells (Medway Day Centre), Cap du Nord Dunkerque France, French Diabetic Assoc, The Mission to Lepers, work of the church, animal charities; memb Double Reed Soc; memb Inst of Professional Civil Servants; *Recreations* playing piano violin and oboe, listening to classical music and opera, ancient history, religion, swimming, tennis, crochet; *Style*— Mrs Rosina Robinson; 38 Chenies Close, Tunbridge Wells, Kent TN2 5LL (☎ 0892 35380); Prison Information Technology Gp, Home Office, HM Prison Service Headquarters, Room 140, Cleland House, Page St, London SW1P 4LN (☎ 071 2176688, fax 071 6305082)

ROBSON, Col Felix Guy; s of Guy Coburn Robson (d 1945), and Beryl Sinclair, *née* Nicholson; *b* 20 July 1921; *Educ* Merchant Taylors'; *m* 10 Aug 1954, Elizabeth Winifred, da of Cdr William Trinick, OBE, RD RNR, (d 1957); 2 s (Rupert b 1959, Angus b 1961); *Career* 2 Lt RA Field Branch 1941, Capt and Air Observer Pilot Italy 1944-46, 3 RHA 1947, Staff Coll Camberley PSC 1951, Mil Asst on Montgomery's Personal Staff Paris 1956, GSO2 Allied Forces Fontainebleau 1957-59, War Office 1961-62, Lt-Col Mil Attaché Br Embassy Cambodia 1964-66; Col Gen Staff: HQ BAOR 1970-73, HQ Allied Forces Central Euro 1973-76; ret 1976; corps secretary HQ Intelligence Corps 1976-86; village & church affrs, tstee of two local museums; memb RUSI 1962, MBIM 1973; *Books* Short History & Guide To Church Of St Mary Westwell (1988); *Recreations* country pursuits, military and local history; *Clubs* Naval; *Style*— Col Felix Robson; Dunn St Cottage, Pilgrims Way, Westwell, Ashford, Kent TN25 4NJ (☎ 023371 2521)

ROBSON, Raymond; s of Ronald Herbert Robson (d 1980), and Gertrude Francis, *née* Gallaghan; *b* 17 Dec 1951; *Educ* St Joseph's Acad GS, Univ of Aston Birmingham (BSc); *m* 9 Sept 1978, Yvonne, da of Gordon Hobday-Pepper (d 1971); 1 s (David b 20 Nov 1981); *Career* surveyor Gardiner & Theobald 1969-77, contract surveyor Mansells 1978, sr surveyor Spicer Partnership 1979-82, started own surveying practice Bromley 1982 (additional offices Acton, Maidstone, Cambridge); organiser: Lewisham Businessmens Club London, Acton & Ealing Businessmens Club London; FRICS 1988, (ARICS 1975); *Recreations* flying (own aeroplane), squash, travelling; *Clubs* Civil Air Flying, Bromley Town Squash; *Style*— Raymond Robson, Esq; Cobden Court, Unit 3, Wimpole Close, Stanley Rd, Bromley, Kent BR2 9JF (☎ 081 466 6742, fax 081 466 6860)

ROCHESTER, 105 Bishop of 1988-; Rt Rev Anthony Michael Arnold Turnbull; patron of seventy-six livings, of the Archdeaconries of Rochester, Tonbridge and Bromley, two Residentiary Canonries, and of all the Honorary Canonries; s of George Ernest Turnbull (d 1954), and Adeline Turnbull; *b* 27 Dec 1935; *Educ* Ilkley GS, Keble Coll Oxford (MA), St John's Coll Durham (DipTheol); *m* 25 May 1963, Brenda Turnbull, JP, da of Leslie James Merchant; 1 s (Mark b 1966), 2 da (Rachel b 1964, Rebecca b 1970); *Career* curate Middleton and Luton 1960-65; chaplain: Archbishop of York 1965-69, Univ of York; rector of Heslington 1969-76, chief sec Church Army 1976-84, archdeacon of Rochester and canon residentiary Rochester Cathedral 1984-88; memb Bd of Govrs Church Cmmrs, vice chm Central Bd of Finance C of E, chm Bible Reading Fellowship, religious advsr to TVS; patron: Dartford Almshouses Centenary Appeal, Medway Towns Spastic Soc, Kenward Tst, Lions Hospice Gravesend, Kent Assoc of Victim Support Schemes, Medway and Gillingham Community Relations Cncl, The Friends of Kent Churches; vice pres Royal London Soc for the Blind, pres Medway Towns Parkinsons Disease Soc; *Books* Gods Front Line (1978), Parish Evangelism (1980); *Recreations* cricket, books, walking; *Clubs* Athenaeum, MCC; *Style*— The Rt Rev the Bishop of Rochester; Bishopscourt, Rochester, Kent ME1 1TS (☎ 0634 842721)

ROCHESTER, Archdeacon of; *see*: Warren, Ven Norman Leonard

RODGER, George William Adam; s of George F Eck Rodger (d 1956), and Hilda Seebohm Rodger (d 1961); *b* 19 March 1908; *Educ* privately, St Bees Coll; *m* 1, 1942, Cicely Joane Hussey-Freke (decd); m 2, 1953, Lois Witherspoon; 2 s (Jonathan George b 1962, Peter Anthony b 1965), 1 da (Jennifer b 1959); *Career* war corr Life magazine 1940-45; service incl: W Africa (Free French), Eritrea (Foreign Legion), Ethiopia (Indian Army), (American Army); photographer BBC 1936-39, staff photographer Life 1945, fndr memb Magnum Photos Inc 1947; in 1948 started 2 yr Cape-Cairo expedition resulting in the famous pictures of Kordofan; 1 man exhibitions incl: Photographers Gallery London 1974 1979 and 1987, S Africa 1978, Grenoble 1982, Marseilles 1984, Gerona 1986, Cyprus 1987, Founders Exhibition In Centre of Photography NY 1989, Musée d'Elysées Lausanne 1990, Musée de la Photographie Charle Roi Belgium 1990, Le Blitz Paris 1990, The Blitz 1940 1990 (London in July, Washington in Sept, Bradford Oct-Dec); won first prize Peace to the World exhibition Moscow 1985; *Books* Red Moon Rising (1943), Desert Journey (1943), Far on the Ringing Plains (1943), Les Villages des Noubas (1955), World of the Horse (1977), George Rodger en Afrique by Carole Naggar (1984), George Rodger - Magnum Opus by Dirk Nishen (1987), The Blitz: Photographs by George Rodger (1990); *Style*— George Rodger, Esq; Waterside House, Smarden, Kent (☎ 023 377 322)

RODGERS, Ian Louis; s of Charles Augustus Rodgers (d 1942), and Doris, *née* Hanneman; *b* 12 Jan 1943; *Educ* Christ's Hospital; *m* 3 June 1967, Susanna, da of Rev Stanley James Pert (d 1974); 2 s (Mark b 1969, Paul b 1971); *Career* with Laurence Kenn & Gardner 1959-71, ptnr Laurence Prust 1977-86 (joined 1971); dir: Framlington Investment Management Ltd 1986-89, Framlington Investment Trust Services 1986-89; appeal dir Christ's Hosp 1989-; dir and memb Gen Cncl S American Missionary Soc, memb Investmt Ctee Girls Bde, donation govr Christ's Hosp; Freeman City of London 1978, Liveryman Worshipful Co Poulters 1979l; memb: Stock Exchange 1973-86, IOD 1989, ICFM 1989; *Recreations* fly fishing, music, theatre, photography; *Clubs* City Livery; *Style*— Ian Rodgers, Esq

RODGERS, Sir John Charles; DL (Kent 1973); 1 Bt (UK 1964), of Groombridge, Kent; s of late Charles Rodgers, of York, and late Maud Mary, *née* Hodgson; *b* 5 Oct 1906; *Educ* St Peter's Sch York, Ecole des Roches France, Keble Coll Oxford (MA); *m* 23 Dec 1930, Betsy Rodgers, JP, da of Francis Aikin-Sneath, JP (d 1939), of Burleigh Court, Glos; 2 s (Tobias, Piers b 1944); *Heir* s, Tobias Rodgers b 2 July 1940; *Career* FO WWII; J Walter Thompson Co: joined 1931, dir 1936-60, dep chm 1960-70; MP (C) Sevenoaks 1950-79, PPS to Rt Hon Viscount Eccles at Minys of Works Educn and BOT 1951-57, parly sec BOT and min Regnl Devpt and Employment 1958-60, memb Cncl of Europe and Western European Union; chm Radio Luxenbourg (London) 1979-84, vice chm Cocoa Merchants Ltd 1980; memb: BBC Gen Advsy Cncl 1946-52, Exec Cncl Fndn for Mgmnt Educn 1959-, Cncl Nat Tst 1978-; govr BFI 1958, fndr govr Admin Staff Coll; chm: Br Market Res Bureau, New Eng Library; Freeman City of London 1947, Master Worshipful Co of Masons 1968-69, memb Merchant Adventurers of York; CBIM, FSS, FIS, FRSA; awarded high hons: Spain, Portugal, Belgium, Taiwan, Sweden, Finland, Luxembourg, Liechtenstein; Cncl of Europe Medal of Merit; *Books* The Old Public Schools of England (1938), The English Woodland (1941), English Rivers (1948), One Nation (jtly, 1950), York (1951), Thomas Gray (ed, 1953); *Recreations* travel, theatre; *Clubs* Brooks's, Pratt's, Royal Thames Yacht; *Style*— Sir John Rodgers, Bt, DL; The Dower House, Groombridge, Kent (☎ 089 276 213)

ROE, James Kenneth; s of Kenneth Alfred Roe (d 1988), of Spain, and Zirphie Norah, *née* Luke (d 1940); *b* 28 Feb 1935; *Educ* King's Sch Bruton; *m* 15 March 1958, Marion Audrey (MP for Broxbourne and parly under sec of state for DOE 1987-88), da of William Keyte (d 1977), of Chagford, Devon; 1 s (William b 1969), 2 da (Philippa b 1962, Jane b 1965); *Career* Nat Serv cmmnd RN; banker; chm: Equity Consort Investment Trust plc 1973- (dir

1967-), N M Rothschild & Sons (Channel Islands) Ltd 1981-; dir: N M Rothschild & Sons Ltd 1970-, Rothschild Trust Corporation 1970-, Kleeneze Holdings plc 1985-; Jupiter European Investment Trust plc 1990-; AMSIA, FRSA; *Clubs* Carlton; *Style*— James Roe Esq; Petleys, Downe, Kent BR6 7JS (☎ 0689 54901); New Court, St Swithin's Lane, London EC4P 4DU (☎ 071 280 5000)

ROGERS, Evelyn Uarda; da of Brig F W Bewsher, CBE, DSO, MC (d 1950); *b* 1 Dec 1923; *Educ* Queen Anne's Sch Caversham; *m* 1 Dec 1943, Maj David Morrison Rogers (d 1987); 3 s; *Career* regnl chm Historic Houses Assoc of SE Eng 1984-88; memb: Exec Cncl Historic Houses Assoc, Ctee Kent Gardens Tst; patron Holy Trinity Church Cookham-on-Thames; *Recreations* heritage, gardening, editing family papers; *Style*— Mrs David Rogers; Riverhill House, Sevenoaks, Kent (☎ 0732 452557)

ROGERSON, Philip Graham; s of Henry Rogerson, and Florence, *née* Dalton; *b* 1 Jan 1945; *Educ* William Hulmes GS Manchester; *m* 21 Dec 1968, Susan Janet, da of Jack Kershaw, of 12 Brampton Ave, Cleveleys, nr Blackpool, Lancs; 1 s (Simon Andrew b 19 July 1974); 2 da (Penelope Rose b 2 Dec 1971, Hannah Rosemary b 7 April 1988); *Career* various appts with the ICI Group 1978-, gen fin mangr ICI plc 1989-; FCA, MCT; *Recreations* golf, tennis, theatre; *Style*— Philip Rogerson, Esq; Baywood, 4 New Beacon Bungalows, Brittains Lane, Sevenoaks, Kent TN13 2ND (☎ 0732 461 402); Imperial Chemical Industries plc, 9 Millbank, London SW1P 3JF (☎ 071 834 4444, fax 071 834 2042, telex 21324)

ROOKE, His Hon Judge Giles Hugh; TD (1963); s of Lt-Col Charles Eustace Rooke, CMG (d 1947), and Irene Phyllis, *née* Paterson (d 1969); *b* 28 Oct 1930; *Educ* Stowe, Exeter Coll Oxford (MA); *m* 30 Nov 1968, Anne Bernadette Seymour, da of His Hon Judge Perrett, of Lichfield; 4 s (Alexander b 1969, Nicholas b 1970, George b 1979, Charles b 1989), 1 da (Elizabeth b 1972); *Career* Nat Serv RA 2 Lt 1949-51, TA Kent Yeo 1951-61, Kent and Co of London Yeo 1961-65; called to the Bar Lincoln's Inn 1957, practised SE Circuit 1957-81, QC 1979, hon rec Margate 1980-, circuit judge 1981; hon sec Margate 1980-, circuit judge 1981; SE Circuit Bar Mess: jr 1959-60, treas 1961-65; chm Kent Bar Mess 1975-79; *Recreations* cultivant son jardin; *Style*— His Hon Judge Rooke, QC, TD; c/o The Sessions House, Longport, Canterbury, Kent

ROOME, Capt David Gordon; LVO (1962); s of Maj-Gen Sir Horace Eckford Roome, KCIE, CB, CBE, MC, DL, late RE (d 1964), late of IOW, and Helen Isabel Roome, *née* Walford (d 1970); *b* 8 Feb 1923; *Educ* Wellington; *m* 25 Jan 1949, Anne Patricia, da of Rear Adm Humfrey John Bradley Moore, CBE (d 1985), of Kent; 2 s (Geoffrey b 1951, Rowland b 1956), 1 da (Julia b 1950); *Career* RN 1940-72; WWII served: N Atlantic, Med, Far East; Royal Yacht 1960-62, IDC 1963, sr Naval Offr W Indies 1970-72 (as Cdre), ret as Capt RN; ADC to HM The Queen 1971; Civil Serv 1972-87; *Recreations* sailing, cider making, walking; *Clubs* Civil Serv; *Style*— Capt David Roome, LVO, RN; East Hall, Boughton Monchelsea, Maidstone, Kent ME17 4JX (☎ 0622 743410)

ROSE, Eliot Joseph Benn (Jim); CBE (1979); s of Col Ernest Albert Rose, CBE (d 1976), of Old Kiln, Churt, Surrey, and Julia, *née* Levy (d 1969); *b* 7 June 1909; *Educ* Rugby, New Coll Oxford; *m* 1, 1940 (m dis 1945), Mollie Lipscombe; m 2, 14 Feb 1946, Susan Pamela, da of Thornely Carbutt Gibson; 1 s (Alan b 1949), 1 da (Harriet b 1950); *Career* WWII 1939-45: RAF 1939-41, Govt CCs Bletchley, Wing-Cdr Dep Dir Intelligence Air Miny 1945; sec Lord Baldwin's Fund for German Refugees 1938-39, literary ed The Observer 1948-51, first dir Int Press Inst 1951-62, dir Nuffield Survey of Race Relations in Br 1963-69, ed dir Westminster Press 1970-73, chm and chief exec Penguin Books 1974-80; fndr 33 club for German Jewish Refugees 1933-39, co-fndr and chm The Runnymede Tst, chm Inter-Action Tst 1968-84, memb Rampton Ctee of Enquiry into Educn of Ethnic Minority Children 1979-81; tstee Writers and Scholars Educnl Tst, memb Bd UNICEF UK; US Legion of Merit 1945; *Books* Colour and Citzenship (1969); *Recreations* music and walking; *Clubs* Garrick; *Style*— E J B Rose, Esq, CBE; 37 Pembroke Square, London W8 (☎ 071 937 3772); Rocks Farm, Groombridge, Kent (☎ 0892 864 223)

ROSS, Harry Edward Thomas; TD (1945); s of Harry Ross (d 1958), and Rhoda, *née* Smith (d 1941), of Beckenham, Kent; *b* 3 June 1903; *Educ* St Dunstans Coll; *m* 16 Sept 1937, Vera Elizabeth, da of James Robert Davis, of Lahloo Hayes, Kent; 2 s (Robert b 1941, Timothy b 1948), 1 da (Elizabeth b 1953); *Career* ret md Port Line (Cunard); former dir: Montreal Australian New Zealand Line, London Steam-ship Owners Mutual Insurance Association Ltd, Port of London Authy, Cunard House Ltd; shipowners rep Pilotage Ctee of Trinity Ho, chm London Gen Shipowners Soc 1964-65; memb: London Shipowners Dock Labour Ctee, Lloyds Register of Shipping Gen Ctee, Chamber of Shipping; *Recreations* gardening, philately, rugby football; *Style*— Harry Ross, Esq, TD; 12 Kirk Court, Sevenoaks TN13 3JW (☎ 0732 454 724)

ROSS MARTYN, John Greaves; s of Dr William Ross Martyn, of Wilmslow, Cheshire, and Ida Mary Martyn, *née* Greaves; *b* 23 Jan 1944; *Educ* Repton, Univ of Cambridge (BA, LLM); *m* 4 Aug 1973, Pauline, da of Ronald Jennings (d 1979), of Morley, Yorks; 1 s (Philip b 1978), 1 da (Elizabeth b 1975); *Career* asst lectr Birmingham Coll of Commerce 1966-68, called to the Bar Middle Temple 1969, in practice at Chancery Bar 1970-, asst rec 1988, SE circuit; memb Chancery Bar Assoc; *Books* Williams, Mortimer and Sunnucks on Executors, Administrators and Probate (jt ed, 1982), Family Provision: Law and Practice (1985); *Recreations* gardening, skiing; *Style*— John Ross Martyn, Esq; 5 New Square, Lincoln's Inn, London WC2A 3RJ (☎ 071 404 0404, fax 071 831 6016)

ROTHNIE, Sir Alan Keir; KCVO (1980), CMG (1967); s of John Rothnie (d 1962), of Aberdeen, and Dora Rothnie; *b* 2 May 1920; *Educ* Montrose Acad, St Andrews Univ; *m* 1953, Anne Cadogan, da of late Euan Cadogan Harris, 2 s, 1 da; *Career* WWII serv RN Atlantic and N Russia; joined FO 1945, 1 sec 1952, cnsllr Baghdad 1963-64, Moscow 1965-68, consul-gen Chicago 1969-72; ambass to: Saudi Arabia 1972-76, Switzerland 1976-80; Hon LLD St Andrews 1981; *Clubs* White's, MCC, Royal and Ancient (St Andrews); *Style*— Sir Alan Rothnie, KCVO, CMG; Little Job's Cross, Rolvenden Layne, Kent TN17 4PP

ROWE, Prof Adrian Harold Redfern (Jack); s of Harold Ridges Rowe (d 1945) of Lymington, Hants and Emma Eliza, *née* Matthews (d 1979); *b* 30 Dec 1925; *Educ* King Edward VI GS Southampton, Guys Hosp Dental Sch (BDS, MDS, MCCD, RCS); *m* 30 March 1951, Patricia Mary, da of Henry Roland Peter, *née* Flett (d 1969), of Forest Hill, London; 3 s (Paul Harold b 1952, Timothy David b 1954, Simon John b 1961); *Career* RADC Lt 1949, Capt 1950-51; head of Dept of Conservative Dental Surgery Guys Hosp Dental Sch 1967- (sen lectr 1963-67), dean of Dental Sch UMDS 1985- (reader in conservative dental surgery 1967-71, prof 1971-); chief ed Companion to Dental Studies; memb: UGC Dental Sub Ctee 1974-83, Cncl Med Def Union 1977-, Bd of Faculty of Dental Surgery RCS 1980-; dir Med Sickness Soc 1987-; BDA, FDI, BSRD, FICD 1969, FDS; *Recreations* golf, DIY, gardening; *Style*— Prof A H R Rowe

ROWE, Andrew John Bernard; MP (C) Mid Kent 1983-; s of John Douglas Rowe (d 1976), of Andover, and Mary Katherine, *née* Storr; *b* 11 Sept 1935; *Educ* Eton, Merton Coll Oxford (MA); *m* 1, (m dis); 1 s (Nicholas James Sebastian b 20 Nov 1966); m 2, 5 Nov 1983, Sheila Leslie, *née* Finkle (formerly Dr Wirz); 2 step da (Kathryn Leslie b 26 Sept 1968, (Helen) Louise b 15 Feb 1971); *Career* sub Lt RNVR 1954-56; asst master Eton 1959-62, princ Scot Home and Health Dept 1962-67, lectr Univ of Edinburgh 1967-74, dir Community Affrs Cons Central Office 1975-79, self employed conslt 1979-83; chm: Parly Panel for the Personal Social Servs, Cons Backbench Ctee on Employment; memb Speaker's Cmmn on Citizenship, tstee CSV, fndr Kent Co Engrg Soc; *Books* Democracy Renewed; *Recreations* photography, gardening; *Clubs* Carlton, Maidstone; *Style*— Andrew Rowe, Esq, MP; House of Commons, London SW1A 0AA (☎ 071 219 6358)

ROWLAND PAYNE, Dr Christopher Melville Edwin; s of Maj Edwin Rowland Payne, and Rosemary Ann, *née* Bird; *b* 19 May 1955; *Educ* Clifton, Univ of London, St Bartholomew's Hosp (MB BS, MRCP); *Career* conslt dermatologist and landowner; house surgn Bart's Hosp London 1978; house physician: Med Prof Unit Royal Infirmary Edinburgh 1978, Roy Marsden Hosp 1979; dermatological registrar St Thomas's Hosp London 1980-83, dermatological sr registrar Westminster Hosp 1983-89; professeur universitaire Faculté de Medicine de Paris 1985-86; conslt dermatologist: Kent and Canterbury Hosp, William Harvey Hosp Kent, Thanet Hosp Kent, Chaucer Hosp Kent, St Saviours Hosp Kent, Lister Hosp London 1990-; clinical prof of dermatology Ross Univ NY 1990-; HAC 1975-76; memb: Societé Francaise de Dermatologie, Br Assoc Dermatologists; Liveryman Worshipful Soc of Apothecaries, Freeman City of London; Roxburgh Prize 1977; Br Assoc Dermatologists Awards: 1984, 1985, 1986, 1989; Dowling Club Prizes: 1985, 1986, 1987, 1988; *Books* contrib: British Medical Journal, Journal Royal Soc Med and others; *Recreations* shooting, cycling, military history; *Style*— Dr Christopher Rowland Payne; High St, Elham, Kent (☎ 0303 840569); 29 Hans Place, London SW1 (☎ 071 584 7435)

ROWLEY, Christopher Owen Bergin; s of Owen Rowley (d 1987), and Sylvia Rowley; *b* 12 Aug 1938; *Educ* Rugby, Clare Coll Cambridge (MA); *m* 6 Aug 1964, Ann Mary, da of Roy Clarkson (d 1975), of Oxted, Surrey; 2 da (Katya b 1967, Juliet b 1969); *Career* drama coordinating offr ITV 1964-65, KYW-TV Philadelphia and Westinghouse Broadcasting USA 1965-66, prog planning exec Rediffusion TV 1966-67 (studio scheduling offr 1962-64); Thames TV: exec prodr In Sickness and In Health 1971 and Third World War 1972, prodr BAFTA award winning The Sun Is God, dep controller Factual Progs to 1973; IBA TV scheduling offr 1974-84, head of planning TV 1984-90, md Five TV Network Ltd 1990-; fndr tstee One World Bdcasting Tst; memb: RTS, cncl Media Soc, BAFTA, Soc Int Devpt; *Style*— Christopher Rowley, Esq

ROYCE, Norman Alexander; s of Joseph Samuel Royce (d 1960), of London, and Margaret, *née* Fraser (d 1954); *b* 4 Feb 1915; *Educ* Abbey Sch Beckenham, Bromley Coll of Art, Architectural Assoc (DipArch); *m* 10 Sept 1948, Molly Walden, da of late Alfred William Clarke, OBE; 3 s (Christopher b 1950, Darryl b 1952, Dominic b 1964), 1 da (Lesley b 1954); *Career* RAF 1940-46: Pilot Staff Offr 1945, Sqdn Ldr, served Europe and ME; sr ptnr

Royce Hurley & Stewart Architects 1938-, pres CIArb 1942, vice pres RIBA 1968 (assoc 1940, fell 1960), pres Concrete Soc 1977; chm: Joint Contracts Tbnl 1978-83, London Ct Int Arbitration 1980; chm: 444 (Shoreditch) Sqdn ATC, Biggins Hill Airport Consultative Ctee; memb: Ctee Royal London Soc for the Blind, Ctee Old peoples Home and Sheltered Housing Bencurtis House Beckenham; vice chm Biggin Hill RAF Assoc; Freeman City of London 1952; Master: Worshipful Co of Gardeners 1973, Worshipful Co of Fanmakers 1979, Worshipful Guild of Air Pilots and Air Navigators 1981, Worshipful Co of Arbitrators 1983, Worshipful Co of Chartered Architects; CIArb 1957 (former pres); *Recreations* flying, gardening, cricket; *Clubs* Carlton, RAF, City Livery, MCC; *Style—* Norman Royce, Esq; 4 Waldon Gdns, Shortlands, Bromley, Kent BR2 0JR (☎ 081 464 3256); 3 Field Ct, Grays Inn, London WC1R 5EF (☎ 071 242 5957, fax 071 405 5724)

ROZE, Rev Fr Ignatius Claude-Paul-Marie; OSB; s of Eugene Roze (d 1985) and Geneviève, *née* Cauchis (d 1984); *b* 19 June 1940; *Educ* classical baccalauréat, Le Bec-Hellouin Abbaye France; *Career* professed Benedictine Monk, ordained priest; Bec Abbey: monk, priest, glazier in ceramics, asst guestmaster; St Augustine's Abbey: educnl parochial and chaplaincy work; missionary Diocese of Pietersburg homeland of Lebowa (Sotho tribe) 1984, expelled from SA due to anti- apartheid views and sympathies; marathon and long distance runner in support of charities incl: Cafod, Across, Help the Aged, UNICEF, Multiple Sclerosis, Herne Handicapped Children, Mother Theresa Co-Workers, RSPCC; former memb Thanet Road Runners Club; *Style—* The Rev Fr Dom Ignatius Roze, OSB; St Augustine's Abbey, St Augustine's Rd, Ramsgate CT11 9PA, (☎ 0843 593045), St Augustine's College, 125 Canterbury Rd, Westgate-on-Sea, Kent CT8 8NL, (☎ 0843 32441)

RUCINSKI, Dr Jacek; s of Teodor Rucinski (d 1961), of Poland, and Lucja Rucinska; *b* 15 May 1946; *Educ* Music Sch, Kosciuszko Lyceum Poland, N Copernicus Univ, Med Acad Gdansk (DM), RCP and RCS (DPM, MRCPsych); *m* 23 Oct 1975, Dr Ewa Cybulska, da of Henryk Cybulski; 1 s (Kajetan Olaf b Jan 1980), 1 da (Tatiana Joanna b 20 Feb 1977); *Career* internship and jr clinical asst in psychiatry Fromb Hosp 1973-75, sr house offr Bexley Hosp 1975-77, registrar in psychiatry Guy's and St Olave's Hosps and Bexley Hosp 1977-78, sr registrar in psychiatry Tooting Bec Hosp and St Thomas Hosp London 1978-81; Medway Health Authy: appointed conslt in psychiatry with special interest in community psychiatry and rehabilitation 1981, assumed responsibility for old age psychiatry 1986, currently responsible for Old Age Psychiatry Serv for the Medway towns; author of various articles in med press on numerous psychiatric and med subjects; memb BMA; *Recreations* classical music, folk and jazz, literature, theatre, painting, photography, supervision of my children's musical education (flute, cello, piano and music theory), travelling, swimming, mountaineering; *Style—* Dr Jacek Rucinski; A Block, Department of Psychiatry, Medway Hospital, Gillingham, Kent ME7 5NY (☎ 0634 830000)

RUDD, (Antony) Harvey Richard; s of Guy Grainger Rudd, of Bridlington, E Yorks, and Enid Mary, *née* Milner; *b* 24 Feb 1960; *Educ* Headlands Sch Bridlington, Leeds Poly (BA); *m* 16 April 1988, Janine, da of John D'Aguanno, of Bridlington; *Career* admitted slr 1985; articled clerk Leeds City Cncl 1982-85; Dover Dist Cncl: asst slr 1985-89, sr asst slr 1989-; pres Folkestone Rotaract Club 1988-89 (memb 1986); *Style—* Harvey Rudd, Esq; Dover District Council, Council Offices, Honeywood Rd, Whitfield, Dover, Kent CT16 3PE (☎ 0304 821199, fax 0304 824917)

RUDDLE, Rev Canon Donald Arthur (Don); s of Herbert Ruddle (d 1977), of Barnet, Herts, and May Violet, *née* Stroud; *b* 12 April 1931; *Educ* Friern Barnet GS, Soc of the Sacred Mission Kelham, Lincoln Theol Coll; *m* 5 May 1956, Penelope Ann, da of Wilfred Owen Penderel Hodder, OBE, of E Malling; 1 s (Stephen b 1957), 2 da (Sarah b 1959, Emma b 1967); *Career* regtl educn instr Sherwood Foresters 1949-51; served Colonial Police Nyasaland (Malawi) 1954-64, curate SS Peter and Paul Kettering 1966-70; vicar: St Anne's Church Earlham Norwich 1970-79, St James The Great East Malling Rochester Diocese 1979-; rural dean Malling Deanery 1984-, hon canon Rochester Cathedral 1988-; chm: Elizabeth Smith Almshouses E Malling, Twisden and Lane Charity; tstee Kent Nursing Inst; memb Holme Fndn, Maidstone Malling Police Advsy Ctee; sec Rochester Diocesan Cncl for Mission and Unity; *Recreations* travel, walking, sport; *Style—* The Rev Canon Donald Ruddle; The Vicarage, East Malling, Kent ME19 6AJ (☎ 0732 843282)

RUMINS, John Sandford; *b* 16 Dec 1934; *Educ* Univ of Bristol (BA); *m* 13 Sept 1960, (Margaret) Ruth; 1 s (Christopher John b 9 Sept 1965), 2 da (Philippa Ann b 31 Dec 1961, Tanya Helen b 5 July 1969); *Career* RAF 1959-62, PO 1959-61, flying offr 1961-62; CA; qualified with Tansley Witt 1959, Cooper Brothers & Co (later Coopers & Lybrand) 1962-72, currently head of Fin and Resource Planning Div Bank of England (joined 1972); FCA 1959; *Recreations* tennis; *Style—* John Rumins, Esq

RUNCIE, Most Rev and Rt Hon Robert Alexander Kennedy; *see*: CANTERBURY, Archbishop

RUSHTON, Dr David Nigel; s of Dr Roland Rushton, of Bromley, and Pamela Anne, *née* Galzini; *b* 21 Dec 1944; *Educ* Kings Sch Canterbury, Trinity Coll Cambridge (BA), King's Coll Hosp Med Sch (MB BChir), Univ of Cambridge (MD); *m* 30 March 1968, Anne, da of Leo Gallagher (d 1967), of Liverpool; 1 s (Samuel b 1982), 2 da (Nicola b 1970, Susannah b 1976); *Career* clinical scientific staff MRC Neurological Prostheses Unit 1971-, reader Dept of Neurology Inst of Psychiatry 1990; hon conslt Maudsley Hosp 1979-, hon conslt neurologist King's Coll Hosp 1984-; contrib scientific articles on neurology and neurological prostheses; memb: Assoc of Br Neurologists, Physiological Soc; Freeman Worshipful Co of Spectacle Makers 1979; FRCP 1989; *Books* Treatment in Clinical Medicine - Neurological Disorders; *Recreations* medieval house reconstruction, steam road vehicles; *Style—* Dr David Rushton

RUSS, Colin Albert Harry; s of Albert Henry Webb Russ (d 1986), of Sutton, Surrey, and Delcie Ada, *née* Dye (d 1975); *b* 19 March 1930; *Educ* Sutton Co GS, Univ of London (BA, MA); *m* Zsuzsanna, da of Jenö Kelemen (d 1957), of Budapest; *Career* asst and lectr in German Univ of Glasgow 1955-66, lectr and sr lectr in German Univ of Kent at Canterbury 1966-; visiting prof: Columbia Univ, Univ of California, Univ of Utah, Univ of Jyväskylä; ed of various German lit texts; past pres Br Chess Problem Soc, UK del World Chess Fedn, Perm Cmmn for Compositions, memb Br Chess Fedn Cncl; *Books* Der Schriftsteller Siegfried Lenz (ed, 1973), Miniature Chess Problems from Many Countries (1981); *Recreations* chess; *Style—* Colin Russ, Esq; Darwin College, University of Kent at Canterbury, Canterbury, Kent CT2 7NY (☎ 0227 764000)

RUSSELL, Sir Charles Ian; 3 Bt (UK 1916), of Littleworth Corner, Burnham, Bucks; s of Capt Sir Alec Charles Russell, MC, 2 Bt (d 1938); *b* 13 March 1918; *Educ* Beaumont Coll, Univ Coll Oxford; *m* 18 Jan 1947, Rosemary, da of late Maj Sir John Theodore Prestige, of The Court House, Bishopsbourne, Canterbury; 1 s, 1 da ; *Heir* s, Charles Dominic Russell; *Career* serv WWII Capt RHA (despatches); slr 1947, former sr partner Charles Russell & Co, of Hale Court, Lincoln's Inn, WC2, currently conslt; *Clubs* Garrick, Army and Navy, Royal St George; *Style—* Sir Charles Russell, Bt; Hidden House, Strand St, Sandwich, Kent

RUSSELL, Derek Charles; s of Raymond Charles Russell, and Alice Elizabeth, *née* Jones; *b* 21 July 1944; *Educ* South Bank Poly (Graduate Dip Arch), Thames Poly (Dip Arch); *m* 27 Aug 1966, (Margaret) Ann, da of Tom Joseph Boulton (d 1985), of Barking, Essex; 2 da (Nicola b 1969, Stephanie b 1973); *Career* architect; BBC 1964-66, Westminster City Cncl 1966-67, Plymouth City Cncl 1967-69, John Lewis Partnership 1969-85, Grainger & Day & Partners 1985-88, Russell Dadds Page Partnership 1988-; memb RIBA; *Recreations* golf, sailing; *Clubs* Tudor Park Country; *Style—* Derek Russell, Esq; Heathfield Lodge, Penenden Heath Rd, Maidstone, Kent (☎ 0622 673218); Russell Dadds Page Partnership, Sutton House, 76 College Rd, Maidstone ME15 6SJ (☎ 0622 692243, fax 0622 688014)

RUSSELL, George; CBE (1985); s of William Henry Russell (d 1972), of Gateshead, Co Durham, and Frances Annie, *née* Atkinson (d 1973); *b* 25 Oct 1935; *Educ* Gateshead GS, Univ of Durham (BA); *m* 19 Dec 1959, Dorothy, da of Ernest Victor Brown (d 1969), of Gateshead, Co Durham; 3 da (Erica Frances b 1963, Livia Jane b 1966, Alison Victoria b 1969); *Career* vice pres and gen mangr: Welland Chemical Co of Canada 1968, St Clair Chemical Co Ltd 1968; chm Luxfer Hldgs Ltd 1976, Alcan UK Ltd 1978, Basys International Ltd 1987-88, IBA 1989-; md: Alcan Aluminium (UK) 1977-81, Alcan UK Ltd 1981-82 (asst md 1977-81); md and chief exec Br Alcan Aluminium 1982-86; dir: Alcan Aluminiumwerke GMBH Frankfurt 1982-86, Northern Rock Building Soc 1985-, Alcan Aluminium Ltd 1987-, chm and chief exec Marley plc 1986-, dep chm 4 TV Co Ltd 1987-88; visiting prof Univ of Newcastle-upon-Tyne 1978; memb: Bd Northern Sinfonia Orchestra 1977-80, Northern Industl Bd 1977-80, Washington Corp 1978-80, IBA 1979-86, Bd Civil Serv Pay Res Unit 1980-81, Megaw Inquiry into Civil Serv Pay 1981-82, Widdicombe Ctee of Inquiry into Conduct of Local Authy Business 1985-86; tstee: Beamish Devpt Tst 1985-89, Thomas Bewick Birthplace Tst 1986-89; Hon DEng Newcastle-upon-Tyne 1985; *Recreations* tennis, badminton, bird watching; *Style—* George Russell, Esq, CBE; 46 Downshire Hill, Hampstead, London NW3 1NX; Marley plc, London Rd, Riverhead, Sevenoaks, Kent TN13 2DS (☎ 0732 455255, fax 0732 740694, telex 95231)

RUSSELL, Ingeborg Elisabeth Anna Else; da of Maj Horst Ferdinand Quade (d 1954), of Bonn, Germany, and Elisabeth Charlotte, *née* Wilke; *b* 26 Oct 1926; *Educ* Goethe Sch Leipzig, Bach Sch Leipzig (Interpreter Dip); *m* 2 May 1952, Maj Raymond Wycliffe Russell, s of Canon A F Russell, of Dalethorpe, Dedham, Essex; 1 da (Victoria b 12 Oct 1956); *Career* ct interpreter BAOR 1947-50, Miny of Justice Bonn Germany 1950-52, pt/t teacher Benenden Sch 1970-86; chm: Benenden Cons Orgn, Benenden Collectors Club; pres Benenden Womens Club; borough cncllr Tunbridge Wells 1980-90; memb Benenden Parish Cncl; govr Benenden Primary Sch; *Clubs* Naval and Mil; *Style—* Mrs Ingeborg Russell; Millers Meadow, Benenden, Cranbrook, Kent (☎ 0580 240579)

RUSSELL, Dr James Rowland; s of Adm The Hon Sir Guy Russell GBE, KCB, DSO (d 1977), of Wisborough Green, West Sussex, and The Hon Lady

Russell, *née* Blades, of Onslow Sq, London SW7; *b* 28 March 1940; *Educ* Radley, Clare Coll Cambridge (MA, MB BCh), Middx Hosp Med Sch (DObstRCOG); *m* 2 Sept 1965, Glenys Pearl, da of George Lofing, of Nairobi, Kenya; 1 s (Lt Robert Russell, RAMC b 23 Aug 1966), 3 da (Katharine b 11 Dec 1968, Elizabeth b 27 July 1970, Mary b 8 Aug 1973); *Career* Surgn Lt RN 1965-68, sr med offr Beira Patrol 1966-67, res obstetrician RN Hosp Malta 1967-68; house surgn to Sir Thomas Holmes Sellors Middx Hosp 1964, house physician to Lord Waverley Royal Berkshire Hosp 1965; princ in gen practice: Betchworth Surrey 1969-80, Sittingbourne Kent 1980-; hon med advsr Swale Marriage Guidance Bureau 1981; chm Stockbury Parish Cncl 1988; *Recreations* cricket, golf; *Clubs* RAC, Band of Brothers, Stockbury CC (hon treas) 1988, Free Foresters, Royal St George's Golf; *Style*— Dr James Russell; Sheepcote Harrow Court, Stockbury, Sittingbourne, Kent ME9 7UQ (☎ 0795 844005); Dr Kerr and Partners, 32 London Rd, Sittingbourne, Kent ME10 1ND (☎ 0795 72109 or 72100)

RUSSELL, Lady; (Aliki) Olga; *née* Diplarakos; da of George Diplarakos, of Athens; *Educ* Lycee Victor-Duruy Paris, Piano Conservatoire; *m* 1, Cmdt Paul-Louis Weiller; 1 s (Paul-Annik b 1933, m 1965, Donna Olimpia Torlonia, gda of King Alfonso XIII of Spain and gggda of Queen Victoria); m 2, 1945, Sir John Wriothesley Russell, GCVO, CMG (d 1984); 1 s (Alexander b 1950, m 1986, Elizabeth Diana Manners), 1 da (Georgiana b 1947, m 1976, Brooke Boothby; *Career* Order of Isabel la Catolica (Spain); *Recreations* sculpting, music; *Style*— Lady Russell; Flat 1, 48 Queen's Gate Gardens, London SW7 5ND; The Vine Farm, Northbourne, Deal, Kent (☎ 0304 374 794)

RUSSELL, Simon John; s of William John Hugo Russell, of Chippenham, Wiltshire, and Angela Frances, *née* Morland; *b* 3 June 1951; *Educ* Chippenham GS, Univ of Leicester (BSc); *m* 21 April 1973, Anne Denise, da of Dennis Charles Sumner, of Oxford; 2 s (Matthew John b 24 Feb 1977, Gavin Francis b 12 Mar 1989), 2 da (Sally Victoria b 6 Feb 1983, Gemma Louise b 8 June 1984); *Career* mining engr NCB 1974-79; ARC Ltd: geologist 1972-74, quarry mangr 1979-82, area ops mangr 1982-88; area dir Home Counties ARC Aggregates 1988-90; md Greenways Landfill Ltd 1990-; neighbourhood engr Cranbrook Sch sponsored by Engrg Cncl; CEng 1978, MIMM 1978, Fell Inst of Quarrying 1984; *Recreations* salmon fishing, collecting fine art prints, hill walking, family; *Style*— Simon Russell, Esq; Hillcroft, Hartley Rd, Cranbrook, Kent TN17 3QP; Greenways Landfill Ltd, The Ridge, Chipping Sodbury, Bristol BS17 6AY (☎ 0454 327999, fax 0454 317030)

RUSSELL VICK, His Hon Judge Arnold Oughtred; QC (1980); s of His Hon Judge Sir Godfrey Russell Vick, QC (d 1958), and Marjorie Hester Russell Vick, JP (d 1985), yst da of John A Compston, KC; *b* 14 Sept 1933; *Educ* The Leys Sch, Jesus Coll Cambridge (MA); *m* 5 Sept 1959, Zinnia Mary, da of Thomas Brown Yates (d 1968), of Godalming, Surrey; 2 s (Philip b 1960, Mark b 1964), 1 da (Tessa b 1963); *Career* serv RAF 1952-54, qualified pilot (Flying Off); called to the Bar Inner Temple 1958; memb Bar Cncl 1964-68, dep rec Rochester City QS 1971, memb Lord Chllr's Co Court Rules Ctee 1972-80, rec of Crown Court 1972-82, circuit judge 1982-; princ co court judge Kent 1990-; govr New Beacon Sch Sevenoaks 1982-; Master Worshipful Co of Curriers' 1976-77; *Books* A Hundred Years of Golf at Wildernesse (1990); *Recreations* golf, cricket, gardening, bridge; *Clubs* MCC, Hawks (Cambridge), Wildernesse Golf (capt 1978); *Style*— His Hon Judge Russell Vick, QC; Law Courts, Barker Rd, Maidstone, Kent (☎ 0622 54966)

RUSSELL VICK, Mary; OBE (1980); da of Pierre de Putron, OBE (d 1950), of La Bertozerie, Guernsey, CI, and Christobel, *née* Whitehead (d 1982); *b* 16 July 1922; *Educ* Beehive Sch Bexhill on Sea, Somerville Coll Oxford (MA); *m* 2 Dec 1944, Clive Compston Russell Vick (d 1990), s of His Hon Judge Sir Godfrey Russell Vick, QC (d 1958); 3 da (Rosemary (Mrs Scott) b 21 Sep 1945, Susan (Mrs Clear) b 28 Feb 1950, Christabel b 1 Sep 1956); *Career* 3 Offr WRNS 1943-45; played hockey for Sussex and England 1947-49 and 1951-53, pres All England Women's Hockey Assoc 1976-86, chm GB Women's Hockey 1981-, chm GB Hockey Bd 1989; vice pres: Sevenoaks Hockey Assoc, Sussex Ladies Hockey Assoc, Southern Counties Women's Hockey Assoc; *Recreations* sport, gardening; *Style*— Mrs Clive Russell Vick, OBE; Ameroak, Seal, Sevenoaks, Kent TN15 0AG (☎ 0732 61 154)

RUTMAN, Laurence David; s of Sidney Rutman, and Anne, *née* Smith; *b* 8 Oct 1937; *Educ* Hendon Co Sch, UCL (LLB), Yale Univ (LLM); *m* 26 July 1964, Sandra Christine, da of Philip Colvin; 2 s (Simon b 1966, Paul b 1970), 1 da (Laura b 1968); *Career* ptnr: Paisner & Co 1960-74, Ashurst Morris Crisp 1974-; *Recreations* farming, opera, books; *Style*— Laurence Rutman, Esq; Broadwalk House, 5 Appold St, London EC2A 2HA (☎ 071 638 1111, fax 071 972 7990, telex 887067)

RYAN, Richard Kevin de Burgo; s of Richard Jarlath de Burgo Ryan, and Ursula Clare, *née* Bradshaw; *b* 19 Oct 1957; *Educ* Bedford Sch, Univ of Leeds (BA), RMA Sandhurst; *Career* cmmnd 1 Bn Royal Green Jackets 1979-82, serv London and NI, Capt 1982, 4 Bn Royal Green Jackets (TA) 1983-, Maj; insurance broker with Willis Faber & Dumas 1982-87; stockbroker with Capel- Cure Myers 1987-, Sheppards 1989-; *Recreations* shooting, fishing, music; *Clubs* Royal Green Jackets, Cavalry and Guards'; *Style*— Richard K de B Ryan, Esq; 87 Strathville Road, Earlsfield, London SW18 4QR (☎ 071 870 7754); Brookside, Cranbrook, Kent; 65 Holborn Viaduct, London EC1A 2EU (☎ 071 236 5101, telex 885556, fax 071 236 4558); 1 London Bridge, London SE1 9QU (☎ 071 378 700, fax 071 378 7585, telex 888282)

RYLE, Alun; s of George Bodley Ryle, CBE (d 1978), and Margaret, *née* Bevan; *b* 10 June 1937; *Educ* Reigate GS, Britannia RNC Dartmouth, Emmanuel Coll Cambridge (BA, MA); *m* 23 Dec 1961, Carole Ann, da of Wing Cdr MF Clyne (d 1946); 1 s (James Bodley b 1969), 1 da (Susannah Caroline b 1964); *Career* weapon and electrical engr various ships and land estabs 1959-81 incl: HMS Mounts Bay, HMS Cavendish, HMS Hermes, HMS Mohawk, HMS Danae; Lt Cdr 1968, Cdr 1974, Capt 1981, dir NATO Maritime Electronic Warfare Support Group 1981-84, head Tech Naval Intelligence MOD 1984-87, Capt HMS Cochrane 1987-88, Royal Coll of Defence Studies 1989; dir Assoc of Old Crows 1981-87, chm RN & RM Amateur Rowing Assoc 1983-86; FIEE 1986; *Recreations* running, squash; *Style*— Capt Alun Ryle

RYLE, Lt-Col (Ian) Nigel; OBE (1960), MC (1945), DL (Kent 1976); s of Arthur John Ryle (d 1921), and Mary Gertrude, *née* Edwards (d 1970); *b* 7 April 1914; *Educ* Epsom Coll; *m* 1, 27 July 1958 (m dis 1965), Jytte Lilian, *née* Scouby-Christensen; 1 da (Jacqueline Lilian b 28 Aug 1959); m 2, 1969, Joanna Browne (d 1970), da of Mathew Hawksworth (d 1958), of London; *Career* cmmnd Royal E Kent Regt (The Buffs) 1940, served N E Europe 1944-45, slightly wounded 1945, transferred RTR 1946, attended Staff Coll 1947; served: Egypt 1948-51, NATO Oslo Norway 1956-58, Cyprus 1958-61, ret 1964; sec: Worcestershire T & AFA 1965-68, SE TA & VRA 1968-79; awarded American Bronze Star 1944; Freeman City of London 1984; *Recreations* hunting, shooting, fishing; *Clubs* Army and Navy; *Style*— Lt-Col Nigel Ryle, OBE, MC, DL; 6 Ashlawn, The Green, Benenden, Cranbrook, Kent TN17 4DN (☎ 0580 240857)

S

SABIN, Paul Robert; s of Robert Reginald Sabin (d 1988), and Dorothy Maude, *née* Aston; *b* 29 March 1943; *Educ* Oldbury GS, Univ of Aston (DMS); *m* 19 June 1965, Vivien, da of Harry Furnival; 1 s (Martin Lawrence b 1969), 2 da (Ann Hazel b 1973, Caroline Jane b 1978); *Career* West Bromwich CBC 1961-69, chief fin offr Redditch Devpt Corp 1975-81 (joined 1969); City of Birmingham: joined 1981, city treas 1982-86, dep chief exec 1984-86; chief exec Kent CC 1986-; memb DTI/SERC Information Technology Advsy Bd (ITAB), dir Kent Economic Devpt Bd; bd memb: Kent Trg and Enterprise Cncl, Kent Trg Centres Ltd; Hon Citizen of the City of Baltimore USA 1985; DMS, IPFA 1966, FBIM, FRSA; *Recreations* antique maps and books, music; *Style—* Paul Sabin, Esq; Kent County Council, Chief Executive's Office, County Hall, Maidstone, Kent ME14 1XQ (☎ 0622 694001, fax 0622 681097)

SACKS, Roger Ian; s of Joseph Sacks (d 1989), of Ramsgate, and Jessie Marie, *née* White; *b* 29 Feb 1948; *Educ* Hereson Secdy TS Arethusa, St George's CE HS Ramsgate, Open Univ; *m* 1, 1 May 1971 (m dis 1973), Gillian Dawn, *née* Clarke; m 2, 23 April 1977, Sheila Eleanor Jane, da of Charles Herbert Temple (d 1980); 2 s (Christian Paul b 1977, Andrew Charles b 1980), 1 da (Samantha Joanne b 1984); *Career* author and illustrator of childrens' books: Cervia the Steam Tug (1986), The Rock Garden; playwright: numerous incl Out of the Dog House, It Takes All Salts (runner up in BBC Radio Kent and Channel Theatre Ten Minute Radio Play Competition), Confessions of a Telephone Answering Machine Salesman; hist novelist The Gentlemen Go By, author of numerous songs short stories and poems; memb: E Kent Maritime Tst Ramsgate, Spinal Injuries Assoc London, St Laurence Church Ramsgate, Parent Teacher Assoc St George's CE HS 1990; vice chm Parent Teacher Assoc CP Sch Ramsgate 1985-; involved with Guide Dogs for the Blind; *Recreations* amateur dramatics, art, patronising charitable functions and fund raising, music especially guitar and keyboards, photography, socialising, studying history, reading; *Clubs* Thanet Amateur Dramatics Soc, Everyman Arts Gp; *Style—* Roger Sacks, Esq; 1 Convent Walk, Goodwin Park, Pegwell, Ramsgate, Kent CT11 0JR (☎ 0843 583338); Cervia the Steam Tug Publications and Club, The Clockhouse, Pier Yard, Royal Harbour, Ramsgate, Kent CT11 8LS (☎ 0843 587765)

SACKVILLE, 6 Baron (UK 1876); Lionel Bertrand Sackville-West; proprietor of Knole, one of the most spacious homes in private hands in the country, started, around 1456, by Thomas Bourchier, then Archbishop of Canterbury, and expanded in the early seventeenth century by Thomas Sackville, to whom it was made over by Elizabeth I; patron of eleven livings; s of late Hon Bertrand George Sackville-West (bro of 4 Baron and unc of Vita (Victoria) Sackville-West, w of Hon Sir Harold Nicolson, KCVO, CMG) and Eva, da of late Maj-Gen Inigo Richmond Jones, CB, CVO; suc cous 1965; *b* 30 May 1913; *Educ* Winchester, Magdalen Coll Oxford; *m* 1, 1953, Jacobine Napier (d 1971), da of J R Menzies-Wilson and widow of Capt John Hitchens, RA; 5 da; m 2, 1974 (m dis 1983), Arlie Roebuck, da of Charles Woodhead, of Romany Rye Brisbane Aust, widow of Maj Hugh Dalzell Stewart and formerly w of Maj-Gen Sir Francis Wilfred de Guingand, KBE, CB, DSO; m 3, Jean, JP, da of Arthur Stanley Garton (d 1963), and widow of Sir Edward Imbert-Terry, 3 Bt, MC (d 1978); *Heir* bro, Hugh Inigo Sackville-West; *Career* late Coldstream Gds, served WW II (POW); Lloyd's underwriter, ret; *Style—* The Rt Hon the Lord Sackville; Knole, Sevenoaks, Kent (☎ 0732 455694)

SACKVILLE-WEST, Hugh Rosslyn Inigo; MC; s of late Hon Bertrand Sackville-West (bro of 4 Baron Sackville) and Eva, da of Maj-Gen Inigo Richmond Jones, CB, CVO; hp of bro, 6 Baron; *b* 1 Feb 1919; *Educ* Winchester, Magdalen Coll Oxford; *m* 1957, Bridget Eleanor, da of Capt Robert Lionel Brooke Cunliffe, CBE, RN (ggs of 3 Bt); 2 s, 3 da; *Career* Capt RTR, serv WWII (Croix de Guerre); admin offr N Nigeria 1946-59; ARICS; *Style—* Hugh Sackville-West, Esq; Knole, Sevenoaks, Kent

ST CLAIR, Joy; da of Jesse Pearce (d 1984), of Chesham and Margate, and Ada, *née* Burgin (d 1975); *b* 10 Jan 1930; *Educ* Pitman's Coll London; *m* 10 April 1950, Frank Edward Sinclair, s of Edward Sinclair (d 1974), of Ramsgate; 1 s (Michael b 1952), 1 da (Shelley (Mrs Lycett) b 1956); *Career* romantic novelist; work published in 20 countries and 5 languages, author of 10 novels, over 100 short stories and articles, award winning poet; sec Margate C of C 1975-88, former sec and chm Margate Trefoil Guild; memb Broadstairs Writers Circle, Parkinsons Disease Soc, Soc of Women Writers and Journalists, Romantic Novelists Assoc; fndr Baldrick Appreciation Turnip Soc to raise money for Nat Children's Home; *Books incl* Run Barbie Run (winner SWWJ Clemence Dane Cup 1980), Love's Tangled Web (1989); *Recreations* travel, modern sequence dancing, cryptic crosswords, playing piano; *Style—* Mrs Joy St Clair; 6 Thanet Rd, Margate, Kent; 108 Model Village, Creswell, Derbys

SALAMA, Nabil Youssef; s of Dr Youssef Salama (d 1985), and Malak Zaklama; *b* 5 Dec 1949; *Educ* Med Sch Univ of Cairo Egypt (MB BCh); *m* 30 Aug 1980, Susan Frances, da of James Willson Beale; 1 s (Adam b 5 Sept 1983), 2 da (Georgina b 8 March 1985, Helen Louise b 5 Sept 1990); *Career* conslt oto-laryngologist Lewisham and N Southwark and Greenwich Health Dists 1983-, private conslt Blackheath Hosp 1984-, surgical tutor Lewisham Hosp; author articles in various med jls; memb: BMA, RSM; BAOL, FRCS; *Style—* Nabil Salama, Esq; 7 Elm Rd, Beckenham, Kent BR3 4JB (☎ 081 658 3751); The Blackheath Hospital, 40-42 Lee Terrace, Blackheath, London SE3 9UD (☎ 081 318 7722, 081 852 8468, 267335 AMILDN G, 081 318 2542)

SALMON, John Dyster; s of The Rev Harold Dyster Salmon (d 1962), of Woodbridge, The Ridge, Woldingham, Surrey, and Margaret Elizabeth, *née* Underwood (d 1963); *b* 22 Dec 1928; *Educ* Haileybury, Queens' Coll Cambridge (MA), Bart's Hosp (MB BChir); *m* 17 June 1980, Georgina Mary, da of John Austwick Payne, of Biggin Hill; 3 s (Paul Harold b 4 Oct 1982, Andrew Dyster b 13 April 1985, Robert John b 23 March 1987), 2 da (Abigail Mary b 3 July 1981, Rachel Margaret b 30 Aug 1989); *Career* Nat Serv RAMC E Africa 1955-57; house surgn Bart's 1958, registrar Moorfields Eye Hosp 1960-63; sr registrar: Bart's 1963-65, St John's Hosp Jerusalem 1967; conslt surgn Kent and Sussex Hosp Tunbridge Wells 1970-; fndr and hon treas Sight by Wing 1971, pres Southern Ophthalmological Soc of UK 1990-, Christian Medical Fellowship, Stag Owners Club; FRCS, FOphth; *Recreations* DIY, sailing; *Style—* John Salmon, Esq; 2 Chilston Rd, Tunbridge Wells, Kent TN4 9LR (☎ 0892 26686); Kent and Sussex Hosp, Mount Ephrain, Tunbridge Wells, Kent TN4 8AT (☎ 0892 26111)

SALMON, Peter James; s of Arthur Alfred Salmon, JP (d 1973), of Faversham, and Winifred Charlotte, *née* Pepper (d 1981); *b* 16 May 1935; *Educ* City of Canterbury Coll of Art; *m* 27 Aug 1960, Maureen Jessie, da of George Henry Hammond (d 1941), of Cheshunt; 2 da (Anne Lucy b 1962, Carole Felicity b 1970); *Career* Nat Serv RAF Biggin Hill; silver engraver; engravings incl: works for Royal Family, many major trophies; Swale Borough Cncl: dep Mayor Faversham, Mayor Faversham 1989-90 and 1990-91; fndr memb Faversham Soc 1962, organiser Faversham in Bloom Competition in Britain in Bloom entry; *Recreations* mug collecting, philately, photography, gardening; *Style—* Peter Salmon, Esq; 121 St John's Rd, Faversham, Kent (☎ 071 405 5187); R H Wilkins, 31-35 Kirby St, Hatton Garden, London EC1N 8TC

SALMON, Col William Alexander; OBE (1956); s of Lt-Col William Harry Broome Salmon, Indian Army (d 1962), and Lillian Mabel (d 1963); *b* 16 Nov 1910; *Educ* Haileybury, RMC Sandhurst; *m* 1939, Jean Barbara (d 1982), da of late Rt Rev John Macmillan, OBE, DD (Bishop of Guildford 1935-49); 1 s, 2 da; *Career* cmmnd 2 Lt HLI 1930, ADC to govr of Sind 1936-38; serv WWII: France 1939, Middle E, Italy, Greece, Bde Maj 1942, GSO2 HQ Aegean Force 1943, CO 2 Beds and Herts Regt 1945-46, CO 2 Royal Irish Fus 1946-47, GSO1 (Trg) HQ Scottish Cmd 1947-49, COS to Lt Gen Glubb Pasha HQ Arab Legion 1950-53, CO 1 Bn HLI 1953-55, Col General Staff (O & T Div) SHAPE 1957-59, AQMG (QAE2) W O 1959-62, AAG (AG14) W O 1962-63, ret 1963; asst ecclesiastical sec to Lord Chllr and PM 1965-77; *Books* Churches and Royal Patronage (1983); *Recreations* shooting, fishing, writing; *Clubs* Army and Navy; *Style—* Col W A Salmon, OBE; Apartment 1, Great Maytham Hall, Rolvenden, Kent TN17 4NE (☎ 0580 241239)

SALTER, John Rotherham; s of Herbert Salter (d 1978), of Cooden, Bexhill, and Nora, *née* Waters (d 1978); *b* 2 May 1932; *Educ* Queen Elizabeth's Sch, Ashridge Coll, Lincoln Coll Oxford (MA), King's Coll London; *m* 3 June 1961, Cynthia Rotherham, da of Frederick Brewer (d 1982), of Sevenoaks; 1 s

(Jeremy b 1964), 2 da (Rachel b 1962, Christy b 1970); *Career* Nat Serv 2 Lt RA 65 Regt 1952, Lt RA 1953; slr; ptnr Denton Hall Burgin & Warrens 1961-; conslt UNIDO 1983-84; vice chm: Int Bar Assoc Ctee of Energy and Nat Resources Law 1976-79, Int Bar Assoc Ctee on Int Environmental Law 1979-82, ABA Ctee on Comparative Govt Law 1988-90; chm: Section on Business Law Int Bar Assoc 1986-88, SBL Ctee on Construction in the Oil Indust 1989-90; tstee: Petroleum Law Educn Tst 1980-, Int Bar Assoc Educn Tst 1983-; treas Anglo-American Real Property Inst 1985-86; cncl memb: IBA 1982-, SBL 1982-, Town and Country Planning Assoc 1984-88; govr: Lady Boswell's Sch 1980-, Copthorne Sch 1982-; memb: Lantle Middlesex Archaeological Soc, Soc for Promotion of Knowledge about Roman Britain, W Kent Branch Oxford Soc; Freeman: City of London 1984, City of Glasgow 1986; Liveryman: Incorporation of Hammermen 1988, Worshipful Co of Slrs 1989, Worshipful Co of Fanmakers 1990-; memb Law Soc 1959, FBIM 1984, FRSA 1984, FRGS 1987, ACIArb 1987; hon memb Bar of Madrid 1987; *Books* Planning Law for Industry (jt ed, 1981), UK Onshore Oil and Gas Law (1986), Oil and Gas Law (contrib 1984), Halsbury's Laws of England (contrib, 1986), Law of the European Communities (contrib, 1986), numerous articles for Int Bar Assoc; *Recreations* the arts, archaeology, sailing; *Clubs* Oxford and Cambridge; *Style*— John Salter, Esq; Five Chancery Lane, Clifford's Inn, London EC4 1BU (☎ 071 242 1212)

SALUSBURY-TRELAWNY, Sir John Barry; 13 Bt (E 1628), of Trelawny, Cornwall; s of Sir John William Robin Maurice Salusbury-Trelawny, 12 Bt (d 1956), by his 1 w, Glenys Mary, da of John Cameron Kynoch; *b* 4 Sept 1934; *Educ* HMS Worcester; *m* 1958, Carol Knox, yr da of C F K Watson, of The Field, Saltwood, Kent; 1 s, 3 da; *Heir* s, John Salusbury-Trelawny *qv*; *Career* Nat Serv RNVR; dir: Martin Walter Group Ltd 1971-74, Korn/Ferry International 1977-83, Goddard Kay Rogers & Associates 1984- (mgmnt conslts); JP Kent 1973-78; FInstM; *Clubs* Army and Navy, Buck's; *Style*— Sir John Salusbury-Trelawny, Bt; Beavers Hill, Saltwood, Hythe, Kent (☎ 0303 66476); 32 St James's Sq, London SW1 (☎ 071 930 5100)

SALUSBURY-TRELAWNY, John William Richard; s and h of Sir John Salusbury-Trelawny, 13 Bt *qv*; *b* 30 March 1960; *m* 16 Aug 1980, Anita, yr da of Kenneth Snelgrove and Mrs L E Thorpe, of Iver Heath, Bucks; 1 s (Harry John b 10 Dec 1982), 1 da (Victoria Hayley b 1981); *Style*— John Salusbury-Trelawny Esq; 45 St Leonard's Rd, Hythe, Kent (☎ 0303 65571)

SANDEFORD, John Herbert; s of Maj Charles Herbert Sandeford, MC (d 1970), of Chiswick, and Millicent Elizabeth Ann, *née* Taylor (d 1973); *b* 4 April 1929; *Educ* Latymer Sch Hammersmith; *m* 31 July 1954, (Joan) Heather, da of Arthur William Tee (d 1963); 5 s (Christopher) Paul b 29 Sept 1956, John Michael b 7 Jan 1959, Mark Charles b 21 July 1962, Richard James b 25 Dec 1972, William Aubrey b 3 June 1974); *Career* bank mangr Sittingbourne 1974-80, sr bank mangr Dartford 1980-90, lawyer's admin 1990-; chm: Sittingbourne C of C, Dartford C of C, Ctee Against Closure of Sittingbourne Meml Hosp; memb Police Advsy Ctee, sch govr, past pres Rotary Club; *Recreations* sailing, golf, history WWII; *Clubs* Purchasers, Sittingbourne Rugby Football (pres); *Style*— John Sandeford, Esq; Wenlock Edge, Gorse Wood Rd, Hartley, Kent DA3 7DF (☎ 047 47 4515); Essex House, Essex Rd, Dartford, Kent (☎ 0322 79211)

SANDERS, Peter Eric; s of John Sanders, and Margaret Jean, *née* Bass; *b* 3 June 1960; *Educ* Ardingly, Br Sch of Osteopathy; *Career* registered osteopath 1983-; memb: Bromley Baptist Church, Bromley Boys Bde; church music, railway memorabilia; *Style*— Peter Sanders, Esq; 258 Chislehurst Rd, Petts Wood, Orpington, Kent BR5 1NT (☎ 0689 76582)

SANDERSON, Roy; OBE (1983); s of George Sanderson (d 1938), and Lillian, *née* Charlesworth (d 1939); *b* 15 Feb 1931; *Educ* Leicester, Kings Richards Royal GS; *m* 25 Aug 1951, Jean Lillian, s of James Booth; 3 s (Roy James, Alan (d 1973), Kevin); *Career* Nat Serv Lance-Corpl REME 1949-51; convenor of shop stewards Lucas Aerospace Hemel Hempstead 1952-67, nat sec EETPU 1987- (asst educn offr 1967-69, nat offr 1969-87); non-exec dir UKAEA 1987-; memb: Exec Ctee Industrial Soc, Armed Forces Pay Review Body, Exec Cncl Confedn of Shipbuilding and Engrg Unions, Econ and Social Ctee of Euro Communities; *Recreations* golf, snooker, supporter of Watford FC; *Clubs* Shendish (Hemel Hempstead); *Style*— Roy Sanderson, Esq, OBE; 162 Belswains Lane, Hemel Hempstead, Hertfordshire (☎ 0442 42033); Hayes Court, West Common Rd, Hayes, Bromley, Kent (☎ 081 462 7755)

SANSON, (Lionel) Alec; CBE (1984, OBE 1971); s of Theodore Alfred Sanson (d 1968), of Bromley, Kent, and Elvira Elizabeth, *née* Smyrloglou (d 1979); *b* 11 March 1923; *Educ* Dulwich, Univ of London; *m* 28 May 1949, Gwenda Dorothy, da of William Barrit; 1 s (Andrew Theodore b 1958), 2 da (Patricia Elvira b 1950, Anthea Elizabeth b 1953); *Career* Euro diesel sales mangr Napier 1954-57 (res engr 1943-54), exec vice pres Napier Canada 1957-62, mangr Napier Commercia 1962-63, guided weapons sales and serv mangr British Aircraft Corporation 1963-68, mktg dir British Aerospace Dynamics 1977-83, corp mktg dir British Aerospace plc 1983-87, ret 1987; former chm Sales and Export Ctee SBAC; FRSA 1989; *Recreations* model engineering, gardening; *Clubs* IOD; *Style*— Alec Sanson, Esq, CBE; Forest Springs, The Nightingales, Sissinghurst Rd, Biddenden, Kent TN27 8HN (☎ 0580 714770)

SANSUM, Cncllr Anthony John David; s of David Charles Michael Sansum (d 1985), and Margaret Mary, *née* Kearney; *b* 26 July 1952; *Educ* St Edmunds RC Secdy Sch Dover, Canterbury Coll of Technol (MQB Electricians Cert of Competence Class I, II); *m* 1, 4 Aug 1979 (m dis); m 2, 21 Dec 1989, Sharon Jane; *Career* electrician Tilmanstone Colliery 1967-84; serv engr: Indesit 1975-88, ADS 1988-89, self employed 1989-; cncllr Eythorne Ward Dover DC, chm Eythorne Parish Cncl, memb Governing Body St Edmund RC Comprehensive (formerly Secdy) Sch Dover; dep ldr Dover DC Lab Gp; *Recreations* local govt; *Style*— Cncllr Anthony Sansum; 19 Stonehall, Lydden, Dover, Kent CT15 7JT (☎ home: 0304 823080; business: 0304 211440)

SAPHIR, Nicholas Peter George; s of Emanuel Saphir, MBE, and Anne Saphir; *b* 30 Nov 1944; *Educ* City of London, Manchester Univ (LLB); *m* 1971, Ena, da of Raphael Bodin; 1 s; *Career* barr; chm Hunter Saphir plc; former chm Food From Britain; memb Food & Drinks EDC; *Recreations* horses, modern art; *Clubs* Farmers'; *Style*— Nicholas Saphir, Esq; Hunter Saphir plc, Whitstable Rd, Faversham, Kent ME13 8BQ

SARGENT, David George; s of Albert George Sargent, of Hastings, Sussex, and Dorothy Victoria Lilian, *née* Bowden; *b* 17 April 1947; *Educ* Hastings GS; *m* 16 March 1974, Susan Margaret, da of David Paton Fauvelle (d 1983), of St Leonards on Sea, Sussex; *Career* CA; articles Mannington Bishop & Bryant Hastings 1964-69, Layton-Bennett Billingham & Co London 1969-73; chief accountant: J and F Stone Ltd 1973-75, Hunterprint Ltd 1976-77; fin dir BEW (Auto Products) Ltd 1980- (joined 1978); FCA 1969; *Recreations* theatre, music, sport; *Style*— David Sargent, Esq; BEW (Auto Products) Ltd, Seaplane House, Sir Thomas Longley Rd, Frindsbury, Rochester, Kent ME2 4HX (☎ 0634 290884, fax 0634 290895)

SAUNDERS, John Albert; s of John Albert Saunders, and Annie Maria, *née* Brown; *b* 9 May 1917; *Educ* Wilsons GS; *m* 22 Aug 1941, Doris Emilia, da of George Charles Elliott; 1 s (John Charles b 1945), 1 da (Ann Veronica (Mrs Doré) b 1946); *Career* War Serv involved with the Dunkirk Evacuation; memb E Peckham Parish Cncl 1970-85, chm Tonbridge and Malling DC 1980-81 (memb 1974-85); hon alderman Tonbridge and Malling Borough Cncl 1986; *Style*— John Saunders, Esq; Wood View, Wells Cottages, Maidstone Rd, Nettlestead Green, Maidstone, Kent ME18 5HH (☎ 0622 813174)

SAUNDERS, Stephen Frederick; s of Stanley Charles, of Southsea, Hampshire, and Joan Marianne Barnet, *née* Clarke; *b* 26 July 1942; *Educ* Sherborne; *m* 15 Oct 1966, (Jean) Lindsay, da of Stanley MacEwan (d 1975), of Southampton; 1 s (Craig Philip b 1973), 1 da (Nicola Gail b 1970); *Career* co sec and fin controller Liberty plc 1977-81; fin dir and co sec: Liberty Retail Ltd 1981, Liberty of London Prints Ltd 1981; dir Hampshire Building Soc 1981-88; Waddington Galleries Ltd: co sec and fin controller 1982-85, fin dir and co sec 1985-; Friend of Kent Opera, Friend of Royal Acad, NACF, FCA 1966; *Recreations* tennis, cricket, opera; *Clubs* Hampshire CCC; *Style*— Stephen Saunders, Esq; Bybrook House, Canterbury Rd, Kennington, Ashford, Kent (☎ 0233 33916); Waddington Galleries Ltd, 11 Cork St, London W1 (☎ 071 437 8611, fax 071 734 4146, telex 266772)

SAVAGE, Peter Edmund Annesley; s of Gordon Annesley Savage (d 1988), and Margaret Emma, *née* Hyson; *b* 25 Nov 1935; *Educ* Welwyn Garden City GS, St Mary's Hosp Med Sch (MB BS); *m* 1, (m dis 1973) Margaret Ann, *née* Sweetman; 1 s (Michael b 1964), 1 da (Elizabeth b 1965); m 2, Anne Lowden, *née* Robertson (d 1989); 2 s (James b 1975, Robert b 1976); *Career* conslt surgn Queen Mary's Hosp Sidcup 1974-; *Books* Disasters - Hospital Planning (1979), Vascular Surgery (1985); *Recreations* hill walking; *Clubs* RSM; *Style*— Peter Savage, Esq; 52 Grosvener Rd, Petts Wood, Orpington, Kent BR5 1QU (☎ 0689 825053); Queen Mary's Hospital, Sidcup, Kent DA14 6LT (☎ 081 3022678)

SAVIDGE, Dr Geoffrey Francis; *b* 16 Dec 1940; *Educ* Univ of Cambridge (MB BChir, MA), Karolinska Inst Stockholm Sweden (MD); *m* 24 July 1964, Paula Margaretha; 2 s (Tor b 1964, Kevin b 1975), 1 da (Kim b 1966); *Career* lectr: Dept of Neurology Karolinska Hosp Stockholm 1969-71, Dept of Pathology and Clinical Chemistry St Gorans Hosp Stockholm 1974-77 (Dept of Med 1971-74); res assoc Inst Coagulation Res Karolinska Inst Stockholm 1976-79, physician Dept of Coagulation Disorders Karolinska Hosp Stockholm 1977-79; St Thomas' Hosp London: dir Haemaphilia Reference Centre 1979-, sr lectr and hon conslt 1979, dir coagulation res Rayne Inst 1988-; memb: Br Soc of Thrombosis and Haemostasis 1983, American Soc of Haematology 1988, Am Heart Assoc 1989; memb: NY Acad of Sci 1986; *Books* Factor VIII-von Willebrand Factor vol 1 (1989), Factor VII-von Willebrand Factor vol 2 (1989); *Recreations* music, reading, sport; *Clubs* United Oxford & Cambridge Univs; *Style*— Dr Geoffrey Savidge; Haemophilia Centre, St Thomas' Hospital, Lambeth Palace Rd, London SE1 7EH (☎ 071 620 0378, fax 071 401 3125)

SAX, Richard Noel; s of Lt-Col George Hans Sax, of Leeford Oaks, Whatlington, nr Battle, E Sussex, and Yvonne Anna Marcelle Sax; *b* 26 Dec 1938; *Educ* Tonbridge, St John's Coll Oxford (MA); *m* 8 April 1967, Margaret, da of Ronald Frank Penny (d 1988); 3 da (Catherine b 1968,

Josephine b 1971, Charlotte b 1974); *Career* Nat Serv cmmnd 2 Lt RASC 1957, attatched 1 Gds Bde Irish Gds Cyprus (GSM Cyprus Clasp), Lt 1959; admitted slr 1967; managing ptnr Rubinstein Callingham 1984- (equity ptnr 1968-84); memb Law Cmmn's Working Pty on Family Property 1974, former chm Slrs Family Law Assoc 1987-, memb Law Soc's Family Law Ctee 1990-, dep registrar Princ Registry Family Div; Liveryman Worshipful Co of Skinners; memb Law Soc 1967; *Recreations* current affairs, gardening, history and archaeology, travel, art; *Clubs* MCC; *Style—* Richard Sax, Esq; 29 Kelsey Way, Beckenham, Kent BR3 3LP; 2 Raymond Buildings, Grays Inn, London WC1R 5BZ (☎ 081 650 8272, fax 071 831 7413, telex 894 100 RUBCAL G)

SAXTON, Patrick Vincent; s of Patrick Cyril Saxton (d 1979), and Zara Pearl, *née* Moore; *b* 6 Sept 1929; *Educ* High Oakham Sch Mansfield; *m* 19 July 1980, Vera (Vee) Margaret, da of Alexander John Temple (d 1958), of Sanderstead, Surrey; *Career* Nat Serv RA; Willis Faber and Dumas 1950-53, clerk to agency supt Caledonian Insur Co 1953-63; Chartered Insur Inst: Careers Advsy Office 1964-, asst sec 1965-, admin sec 1979-, sec gen 1983-; lay asst St Georges Church Beckenham; sec Insur Indust Trg Cncl 1972-80; chm: Br Insur Law Assoc 1981-83, Insur Trg Ctee of Comité Européen des Assurances, All Saints Educational Tst, Inst Trg and Devpt 1984-86; memb London Univ Careers Advsy Bd; Freedom City of London 1973; Liveryman: Worshipful Co of Gold and Silver Wyre Drawers 1973, Worshipful Co of Insurers 1984; assoc memb Inst of Insur Sci for services to Anglo-German insur educn; Hon FICO 1977; FCII 1956, FITD 1978, FBIM 1982; *Books* Allured to Adventure (1974); *Recreations* chess, music, photography, watching sport; *Clubs* MCC, Cripplegate Ward; *Style—* Patrick Saxton, Esq; 24 Lakeside, Wickham Road, Beckenham, Kent (☎ 081 658 6298); Chartered Insurance Institute, 20 Aldermanbury, London EC2V 7HY (☎ 071 606 3835, fax (group 2 + 3) 071 726 0131, telex 957017)

SAY, Rt Rev Dr (Richard) David; KCVO (1988); s of Cdr Richard Say, OBE, RNVR (d 1958), of London, and Kathleen Mary, *née* Wildy; *b* 4 Oct 1914; *Educ* Univ Coll Sch, Christ's Coll Cambridge (BA, MA), Ridley Hall Cambridge; *m* 16 Oct 1943, Irene Frances Say, OBE, JP, da of Seaburne Rayner (d 1952), of Exeter; 2 s (Richard William Gurney b and d 1950, William David b 1952), 2 da (Mary Penelope (Mrs Thompson) b 1945, Anne Caroline (Mrs Langley) b 1948); *Career* ordained: deacon 1939, priest 1940, bishop Canterbury Cathedral 1961; curate: Croydon Parish Church 1939-43, St Martin-in-the-Fields 1943-50; gen sec: C of E Youth Cncl 1944-47, Br Cncl of Churches 1947-55; rector of Hatfield Herts and chaplain to the 5 Marquess of Salisbury 1955-61, hon canon St Albans 1957-61, 104th Bishop of Rochester 1961-88, chaplain to Pilgrims of GB 1968-, Lord High Almoner to HM The Queen 1970-88, asst Bishop of Canterbury 1988-; C of E del to World Cncl of Churches 1948 1954 and 1961; select preacher: Univ of Cambridge 1954, Univ of Oxford 1963; chaplain and sub-prelate OStJ 1961, memb House of Lords 1969-88, chm Ctee on State Aid for Churches in Use 1971-90, pro-chllr Univ of Kent 1983- (dep pro-chllr 1977-83), memb Court of Ecclesiastical Causes Reserved 1984-; vice-pres: UN Assoc of GB 1986, Age Concern England 1990- (chm 1986-89); pres Friends of Kent Churches 1988-; hon memb Inst of RE 1987; Freeman City of London 1953; Hon Freeman: Borough of Tonbridge and Malling 1987, City of Rochester upon Medway 1988; DD Lambeth 1961; Hon DCL Univ of Kent at Canterbury 1987; *Recreations* walking, travel; *Clubs* United Oxford and Cambridge Univ; *Style—* The Rt Rev Dr David Say, KCVO; 23 Chequers Park, Wye, Ashford, Kent TN25 5BB (☎ 0233 812720)

SAYER, Arthur Frederick; s of Frederick Charles Sayer (d 1973), of Bexhill, Sussex, and Wynsome Brooke, *née* Taylor; *b* 10 June 1924; *Educ* Archbishop Tenisons GS; *m* 13 March 1944, Doreen (d 1988), da of Reginald Squire Park (d 1966), of Leeds; 2 s (Graham Paul b 1946, Philip John b 1948); *Career* Sgt RM 1942-46; insur broker; clerk GP Turner & Co 1939-48, asst marine mangr P Wigham-Richardson & Co Ltd 1948-53, res inspr for Gold Coast British Commonwealth Insurance Co 1953-55, Allied Insurance Brokers Ltd 1955-83 (mangr, assoc dir, dir), dir Sasserath Alfred Ltd 1983-; underwriter dir: Allied Underwriting Agencies 1983-, Cedar Insurance Co Ltd 1988-; cncllr Tunbridge Wells Borough Cncl 1978- (dep Mayor 1987-88, Mayor 1988-); Culverden Ward: chm Recreation and Leisure Ctee 1984-88, chm Tourism 1984-88, chm Devpt Ctee 1990-; chm Tunbridge Wells/Wiesbaden Assoc; memb: Friends of Pembury Hosp, League of Friends Kent and Sussex Hosp; vice pres RN Assoc, cncl rep RTW Indoor Bowls Club and St George's Children Community Project, pres Sherwood Ward Conservatives; City of Wiesbaden Medal 1984; *Recreations* art, sports and meeting people; *Clubs* RTW Constitutional (vice pres), RTW Cons; *Style—* Arthur Sayer, Esq; 6 Brooklands, Brook Rd, Tunbridge Wells, Kent TN2 (☎ 0892 31481)

SAYERS, Maurice George; s of George William Walter Sayers (d 1981), and Elsie Victoria Sayers (d 1978); *b* 4 Sept 1928; *Educ* Dover GS; *m* 27 March 1954, Pamela Ellen, da of Leonard George Dennis Hopkins, of 87 Lower Rd, River, Dover; 1 s (John Maurice b 10 Aug 1966), 2 da (Jennifer Kate b 9 Feb 1962, Patricia Ellen b 17 March 1964); *Career* Nat Serv 1946-49; Stilwell and Harby Solicitors: office jr 1942, articled clerk, admitted slr 1961, ptnr 1963, sr ptnr 1971-; pres: Dover Inc C of C 1969, Dover Round Table 1976 (chm 1966), Kent Law Soc 1978, Dover Deal and Sandwich Law Soc 1987-88, Dover RFC (capt 1958-59), Alkham Valley Soc, Dover Ex Tablers Club; capt Dover Swimming Club 1954-60; memb: Law Soc, Kent Law Soc, Dover Deal and Sandwich Law Soc; *Recreations* swimming, rugby, ornithology; *Clubs* Royal Cinque Ports Yacht, Dover RFC; *Style—* Maurice G Sayers, Esq; Malmains Manor, Alkham, Dover, Kent (☎ 0304 822397); Stilwell and Harby Solicitors, 110 Maison Dieu Rd, Dover, Kent CT16 1RT (☎ 0304 206850, fax 0304 206950, telex 96174)

SAYNOR, Joy Margaret; da of Alfred Thomas D'Eye, of Friars, Shoreham, Sevenoaks, Kent, and Margaret Edith, *née* Francis (d 1980); *b* 26 March 1926; *Educ* Bromley GS, Barmouth GS Gwynedd, Lady Margaret Hall Oxford (MA), Univ of London (dip); *m* 4 Feb 1949, Peter James Saynor, s of Elias James Saynor (d 1980), of Springthorpe, Lincolnshire; 2 s (John Stephen b 1953, James Oliver b 1958); *Career* lectr in Kentish history 1960-: Sch of Continuing Educn Univ of Kent at Canterbury, Extra-Mural Dept Univ of London, SE Dist WEA; Kent History Fedn: memb Lectrs Panel, memb Exec Ctee and Ctee; memb: CPRE, Cncl Kent Archaeological Soc, Soc of Friends of Shoreham Church, Snowdonia Nat Park Soc, Shoreham Women's Inst (former vice pres); sec Shoreham Village Hall Mgmnt Ctee; *Publications* Gravesend in 1851- A Census Study (1971), The Parish Administration of Shoreham 1782-84 (in Archaeologia Cantiana LXXXVII 1972), Bexley Mosaic (1977), Shoreham Remembers 1939-45 (1985), Shoreham - A Village in Kent (with M White, 1989); *Recreations* dirt archaeology, reading, restoring family cottage, speaking to Kentish history socs, researching family history; *Style—* Mrs Joy Saynor

SCAMELL, Ernest Harold; s of Capt Ernest Harold Scamell (d 1981), and Lilian Kate, *née* Hall; *b* 9 March 1928; *Educ* Frays Coll Uxbridge, King's Coll London (LLB, LLM, AKC); *m* 1, 22 Aug 1952 (m dis), Patricia Annie, da of Percy Bullock (d 1979); 2 s (Grant b 11 Nov 1956, Adrian b 9 July 1958), 2 da (Joanna b 9 May 1960, Amanda b 19 Oct 1963); m 2, 11 Sept 1977, Ragnhild Bennedsen, da of Viggo Holdt, of Nyborg, Denmark; 1 step child (Cleere b 16 Nov 1967); *Career* called to the Bar Lincoln's Inn 1949; prof English law Univ of London 1966-90 (reader 1960-66), head of chambers Lincoln's Inn 1971-, vice provost UCL 1978-84; memb Bar Cncl; *Books* Precedents for the Conveyancer (1970-77), Lindley on Partnership (co ed, 1984), Butterworths Property Law Handbook (2 edn, 1989); *Recreations* flying, model building; *Clubs* Holy Trinity Meccano, Air Touring Flying; *Style—* Ernest Scamell, Esq; Oak Farm, Kennington, Ashford, Kent TN24 9BH (☎ 0233 628453); 5 New Sq, Lincoln's Inn, London WC2A 3RJ (☎ 071 405 6171/4797)

SCANLON, Baron (Life Peer UK 1979), of Davyhulme, Greater Manchester; Hugh Parr Scanlon; s of Hugh Scanlon; *b* 26 Oct 1913, in Australia; *Educ* Stretford Elementary Sch, Nat Council of Labour Colls; *m* 1943, Nora, da of James Markey; 2 da; *Career* apprentice instrument maker; chm Engrg Industry Training Bd to 1982; memb British Gas Corp 1976-, pres AEUW 1968-78 (formerly div organiser and memb London Exec Cncl); Hon DCL Kent 1988; *Style—* The Rt Hon the Lord Scanlon; 23 Seven Stones Drive, Broadstairs, Kent

SCARLETT, His Hon James Harvey Anglin; s of Lt-Col James Alexander Scarlett, DSO, RA (d 1925), and Muriel, *née* Blease (1945); *b* 27 Jan 1924; *Educ* Aysgarth Sch, Shrewsbury, Christ Church Oxford (MA); *Career* Lt RA 1944-47 (attached to Indian Mountain Artillery 1945); called to the Bar Inner Temple 1950; barr Malayan Civil Serv 1955-58, rec 1972-74, circuit judge 1974-89; pres Kent Family Conciliation Serv; *Recreations* gardening, fell walking; *Clubs* Athenaeum; *Style—* His Hon James Scarlett; Little Netters, Chilmington Green, Great Chart, nr Ashford, Kent TN23 3DP; The Law Courts, Barker Rd, Maidstone, Kent ME16 8EW (☎ 0622 54966)

SCARMAN, Baron (Life Peer UK 1977), of Quatt, Co Shropshire; Leslie George Scarman; OBE (1944), PC (1972); s of late George Charles Scarman; *b* 29 July 1911; *Educ* Radley, BNC Oxford (MA); *m* 1947, Ruth Clement, da of late Clement Wright; 1 adopted s (John Clement b 1946); *Career* sits as Ind peer in House of Lords; called to the bar 1936; QC 1957, judge of the High Court 1961-72, Lord Justice of Appeal 1972-77, Lord of Appeal in Ordinary 1977-86; chm: Law Cmmn 1965-72, Tbnl and Inquiry NI 1969-72; author of report into Brixton riots 1981; chllr Univ of Warwick 1977-89, visitor St Hilda's Coll Oxford, pres RIPA 1981-87, former memb Arts Cncl; pres Thanet Archaeological Soc; hon memb American Philosophical Soc, hon fell BNC Oxford; Hon DCL Univ of Oxford 1982; Hon MD: Univ of Glasgow, Univ of Kent, Univ of Dundee, Univ of London, Univ of Warwick, Univ of Wales, Univ of Freiburg, Univ of Keele, Univ of Exeter; kt 1961; *Style—* The Rt Hon the Lord Scarman, OBE, PC; House of Lords, London SW1

SCHOLES, James Edward; s of Vernon Dean Scholes (d 1942), of Oldham, Lancs, and Ruth (now Mrs Ryan), *née* Ashworth; *b* 25 Dec 1942; *Educ* High Storrs GS, Univ Of Leicester (BSc); *m* 10 May 1969, (Rowena) Jane, da of Roy Canon Bishop, of Leicester; 1 s (Paul James b 17 August 1972), 1 da (Marion Louise b 12 May 1970); *Career* mathematician English Electric

Whetstone Leics 1964, programmer Laycock Engineering Sheffield 1965-67, computer conslt Computer Automation Systems London 1967-70; Grieveson Grant (Stockbrokers) London: project leader 1970-77, data processing mangr 1977-84, capital ptnr 1984-86; asst dir Kleinwort Benson London 1986-89, project mangr Barclays Commercial Services Hastings 1989-; author of various articles in Chess magazine 1964-65; Tunbridge Wells Borough Cncl: borough cncllr, past chm Enviromental Ctee, past vice chm Fin Ctee, memb Central Area Planning Ctee, memb Computer Ctee, bd memb TWB Servs; dep Mayor Tunbridge Wells 1990-91; sch govr: Ramslye Jr and Broadwater Infant Schs 1976-87, Broomhill Bank Sch for ESN 1976-82, Broadwater Down Co Primary Sch 1987-88, Claremont Co Primary Sch 1988; membership sec St Marks Cons Branch, sidesman King Charles the Martyr C of E, table tennis Champion div 3 & 4 Tunbridge Wells 1978-79; chm Tunbridge Wells Chess Club 1986-89; memb: Univ Olympic Chess Team 1964, Kent 1st chess team; chess champion: Eng Jr Int 1961, Br Univs champ 1962-64, UK Bank 1988, Tunbridge Wells 1989; MBCS, AFIMA; memb: Inst of Computer Sci, Stock Exchange; *Recreations* chess, table tennis, politics, walking, bridge; *Style*— James Scholes, Esq; Barclays Commercial Services, Aquila House, Breeds Place, Hastings, Kent TN34 3D9 (☎ 0424 430824, ext 378)

SCHUEPPERT, (Charles) Clancy; s of Charles William Schueppert, of Menasha, Wisconsin, USA, and Margaret Mary, *née* Clancy (d 1990); *b* 12 April 1936; *Educ* Marquette Univ (BS), Harvard Univ (MBA); *m* 27 Dec 1961, Deidre Virginia, da of Michael Joseph O'Brien (d 1980), of Vancouver, BC, Canada; 2 s (Mark Christopher b 1963, Michael Tehan b 1966), 2 da (Margaret Madigan b 1964, Kathleen Clancy b 1970); *Career* chm and chief exec: Sheerness Steel Co 1971-85, Hilger Analytical Ltd 1986-; *Recreations* tennis, skiing; *Clubs* Wildernesse; *Style*— Clancy Schueppert, Esq; Wildwood, Seal, Kent TN15 0EH (☎ 0732 61119); Hilger Analytical Ltd, Westwood, Margate, Kent CT9 4JL (☎ 0843 225131, fax 0843 224402)

SCHWABE, Prof Walter Wolfgang; s of Dr Walter Schwabe (d 1962), of Wimbledon, and Anne, *née* Lagershausen (d 1954); *b* 1 June 1920; *Educ* Regent St Poly, Imperial Coll London (BSc, ARCS, PhD, DIC, DSc, DAghc); *m* 15 Nov 1958 (m dis); 1 s (John b 1965), 2 da (Fiona b 1960, Ruth b 1962); *Career* princ scientific offr ARC 1958-65, plant physiologist and prof of horticulture Univ of London and Wye Coll 1965-85; former memb Governing Body (Exec Ctee) E Malling Res Station; memb: Nat Vegetable Res Station, Glasshouse Crops Res Station; ed in chief Jl of Experimental Botany; currently assoc ed: Jl Hort Sci Physiologia Plantarum (Scandinavia), Elais (Malaysia); *Recreations* hill walking, skiing; *Style*— Prof Walter W Schwabe; Audlea, Bilting, nr Ashford, Kent (☎ 0233 812 482); Department of Horticulture, Wye College, University of London, Wye, nr Ashford, Kent (☎ 0233 812 401)

SCHWARZ, Lewis Patrick (Lew); s of Anthony Augustine Schwarz (d 1948), of Glasgow, and Alice, *née* Henry (d 1973); *b* 16 April 1925; *Educ* St Aloysius Coll Glasgow, Holyrood Sr Secdy Glasgow, Univ of Glasgow, Köln Univ; *m* 3 April 1956, Margaret Sarah, da of Francis Glen (d 1968); 3 s (Conrad Anthony b 1957, Timothy John b 1959, Mark Andrew b 1962), 2 da (Michele Margaret b 1958, Alexandra Jane b 1963); *Career* professional scriptwriter for TV and Film 1954-; over 600 TV credits incl: The Army Game 1959-61, Bootsie & Snudge 1962, The Charlie Drake Show 1963, The Worker 1965-66 and 1969-70, The Liver Birds 1969, Nearest & Dearest 1971-73, Touch of Wisdom 1975; films: HMS Petticoat 1962, The Cracksman 1963, Cuckoo Patrol 1964, Laughter In Paradise 1969; *Books* The Craft of Writing TV Comedy (1989); *Recreations* fishing; *Clubs* Aircrew Assoc; *Style*— Lew Schwarz, Esq; 138 Gladstone Rd, Deal, Kent CT14 7EP (☎ 0304 365804)

SCOBLE-HODGINS, (Charles Wilfrid) Julius; s of Maj Richard Douglas Scoble-Hodgins, RA (d 1973), of Kynance, Pheasant Lane, Loose, nr Maidstone, Kent, and Gladys, *née* Chambers (d 1983); *b* 8 June 1930; *Educ* Sutton Valence, Law Society's Coll of Law Lancaster Gate; *m* 1, 25 Aug 1956 (m dis 1980), Belinda Jane Hackett (now Walker), da of Arthur Wallis Kendall, VRD (d 1973), of Wimbledon; 1 s (Nicholas Mark b 4 July 1958), 1 da (Sara Ann b 11 June 1961); m 2, 16 Jan 1988, Elizabeth Mary (wid of Francis John Dare), da of Lawrence Victor Walker, of 8 Morkyns Walk, Alleyn Park, Dulwich, London; *Career* Nat Serv: cmmnd RA, courts martial prosecuting offr Directorate Army Legal Servs; served Kent Yeomanry Tunbridge Wells Battery; admitted slr 1954; dep chief slr Assoc Electrical Industries plc 1957-60; sec: AEI Charitable Tst 1957-60, AEI Estates Ltd 1957-60; ptnr: Haslewoods 1960-65, Keene Marsland 1965-; clerk to Cinque Cottages and Cuthbert Gift Charities Wimbledon 1970-, tstee Soc of Big Brothers, memb Tunbridge Wells Branch Assoc Men of Kent and Kentish Men, fndr memb Tower Ward Club of the City of London; Freeman Worshipful Co of Slrs 1965; memb: Law Soc, Kent Law Soc, Slrs Benevolent Assoc; *Recreations* sailing, motoring, cycling; *Clubs* Little Ship, Salcombe Yacht, Hoo Ness, MG Car; *Style*— Julius Scoble-Hodgins, Esq; Fairmead, Goudhurst, Kent (☎ 0580 211437); 6 Clanricarde Gardens, Tunbridge Wells, Kent TN1 1PH (☎ 0892 26442, fax 0892 510486)

SCOTT, Jeremy Robert Andrew Berresford; s of Anthony Christopher Multon Battiscombe Scott, of Green Mile, Babworth, Nottingham, and Mary, *née* Beresford; *b* 19 June 1946; *Educ* Harrow, Trinity Coll Dublin (BA); *m* 11 Oct 1969, (Rosemary) Jane, da of Dr G B Locke, of Leigh Lodge, Knutsford, Cheshire; 2 s (Jake b 1972, Cassian b 1975), 1 da (Flora b 1977); *Career* merchant banker 1970-73, farmer 1973-; parish cncllr, chm Sevenoaks NFU 1985-87; ctee memb: W Kent Hunt, Bolebroke Beagles, SE Br Field Sports Soc; *Recreations* hunting, opera, travel; *Style*— Jeremy Scott, Esq; Ash Manor, Ash Green, Sevenoaks, Kent (☎ 0474 872238)

SCOTT, Dr John Graham; s of Walter Francis Scott (d 1985), of Beckenham, Kent, and Sybil, *née* Doré (d 1975); *b* 14 Feb 1938; *Educ* St Pauls, St Mary's Hosp Univ of London (MBBS); *m* 9 July 1970, Christina Sui-Lin, da of FS Lian (d 1987), of Kuala Lumpur, Malaysia; 1 s (William Francis b 10 Aug 1973); *Career* sr house offr in anaesthetics Edgeware 1963; registrar in anaesthetics: Portsmouth 1964, Royal Free Hosp 1965; sr registrar in anaesthetics E Grinstead 1966, visiting fell in anaestheology N Western Univ of Chicago 1968; conslt anaesthetist: Nigerian Armed Forces Med Serv 1969, Bromley Health Dist 1970-; memb: Assoc of Anaesthetists, BMA; FFARCS 1966; *Recreations* skiing, golf; *Clubs* Old Pauline; *Style*— DR John Scott; 8 Regents Drive, Keston, Kent BR2 6BU (☎ 0689 51542); Dept of Anaesthesia, Bromley Hospital, Cromwell Rd, Bromley, Kent (☎ 081 460 9933)

SCOTT, Dr Kenneth; s of Sidney Scott (d 1965), of London, and Rachel, *née* Silverman (d 1976); *b* 4 April 1925; *Educ* City of London Coll, Guy's Hosp Univ of London (MB BS); *m* 22 Feb 1951, Anita Cecily, da of Barnet Levin (d 1957); *Career* served RAF 1945-48; princ in gen practice 1956-; London Borough of Bromley: co-opted memb Health and Welfare Ctee 1965-74, Social Servs Ctee 1978-; Bromley DHA: gen mangr Community and Mental Handicap Unit 1986-, memb Mgmnt Bd 1986-; memb: Mgmnt Ctee Cane Hill Hosp 1958-74, Bromley Family Practitioner Ctee 1974- Exec Ctee Bromley Div BMA 1981-; chm: Bromley Area Med Ctee 1979-82, Bromley Local Med Ctee 1986- (memb 1974-86); vice chm Bromley Dist Mgmnt Team 1983-86 (gp rep 1977-86); fell Med Soc of London, FRCGP, DRCOG; *Style*— Dr Kenneth Scott; Silverley, 16 Court Downs Rd, Beckenham, Kent BR3 2LS (☎ 081 650 4244); Elm House Surgery, 29 Beckenham Rd, Beckenham, Kent BR3 4PR (☎ 081 650 0173, fax 081 6633911)

SCOTT-ORDISH, Lesley; da of Kenneth Scott Adie (d 1968), of One Oak, Dovehouse Lane, Solihull, W Midlands, and Enid, *née* Reffitt (d 1978); *b* 25 March 1932; *Educ* The Laurels Sch, Wroxall Abbey; *m* 4 Sept 1953, Peter Guy Ordish, s of Thomas Guy Ordish (d 1970), of Brueton Ave, Solihull, W Midlands; 2 s (Nicholas Guy b 25 Nov 1956, Jonathan Scott b 5 Jan 1959); *Career* freelance journalist; fndr and dir PRO-Dogs (nat charity providing free community servs for children and elderly or incapacitated) 1976-, ed ARGOS (pubn for membs of PRO-Dogs); co fndr and dir Hearing Dogs for the Deaf (scheme to train dogs to assist people with hearing difficulties), devised Pets As Therapy (nat dog visiting scheme to hosps and homes for elderly) 1983- (became separate nat charity 1990), joined Bd of Assistance Dogs for Disabled People; inaugurated Malling Airfield Action Gp 1972, served on Ditton Parish Cncl, govr Leybourne Grange Special Sch; *Books* Are Dogs a Health Risk? (1978), Planned Puppies Only (1980), Dogs in Town (1980), Your Dog - Without You (1989), Heroic Dogs (1990); *Recreations* studying people with animals, walking the dogs; *Style*— Mrs Lesley Scott-Ordish; Arden House, Holt Wood, Aylesford, Kent ME20 7QH (☎ 0622 717301); Rocky Bank, New Rd, Ditton, Kent ME20 6AD (☎ 0732 848499)

SCRUTON, Robert; s of George Henry Kirman Scruton (d 1981), and Kitty, *née* Van Der Vord; *b* 6 April 1952; *Educ* Havelock Sch Grimsby, Univ of Kent at Canterbury (BSc), Open Univ (MSc); partner, since 1981, Barbara Brown, da of John Albert Cox, of Canterbury; 2 c (Martin Brown b 1973, Jenni Brown b 1975); *Career* CA; currently fin ptnr and ptnr responsible for computer servs Reeves & Neylan (joined 1973, ptnr 1980-); Kent Assoc of Parish Cncls: memb of exec 1985-, chm Canterbury area 1987-; memb of court Univ of Kent 1986-, tstee Canterbury Hosp Bdcasting Network 1987-, memb of exec Temporary Accommodation for Rootless and Homeless Young Adults 1988-, parish cncllr Womenswold 1983-; memb London Mathematical Soc 1973; FCA 1982 (ACA 1977); *Recreations* badminton; *Style*— Robert Scruton, Esq; Nethersole House, Womenswold, Canterbury, Kent (☎ 0227 831248); 37 St Margarets St, Canterbury, Kent (☎ 0227 768231, fax 0227 458383)

SEABROOK, Roger Albert; *b* 15 May 1941; *Educ* Sexeys GS, Univ of Reading; *m* 26 Sept 1964, Jennifer Leonie; 2 s (Clive b 2 May 1967, Gareth b 1 March 1969), 3 da (Melanie b 20 June 1970, Hannah b 1 Jan 1973, Lindsey b 19 Nov 1978); *Career* graduate trainee Dexion plc 1961-62, mangr Vickers plc 1962-65, formed own printing co 1965-68, formed Marketing Aids Group 1968-; involved with various childrens charities; *Recreations* most sports apart from golf, current affairs, travel, stimulating conversation (mainly listening); *Style*— Roger Seabrook, Esq; The Thatched House, St Mary's Platt, Kent TN15 8NR (☎ 0732 882421); Marketing Aids Group, Nix's Hill, Alfreton, Derbyshire DE5 7FQ (☎ 0773 520800, fax 0773 831199)

SEAGER, Eric Victor John; s of Victor Ernest Buckledee Seager (d 1977), and Hester Kate, *née* Hendry (d 1969); *b* 21 Sept 1941; *Educ* Sudbury GS,

IPFA; *m* 16 March 1968, Margaret Lysbeth, da of William Harold Allen, of Eastbourne, Sussex; 2 s (Clive Paul b 1970, Jonathan Mark b 1974), 2 da (Julie Ruth b 1971, Claire Elizabeth b 1976); *Career* dep treas Gillingham Borough Cncl 1969-73, chief exec Gravesham Borough Cncl 1988- (borough treas 1973-88); memb Fin Panel Soc of Local Authy Chief Execs (SOLACE), elder Gillingham Baptist Church; *Recreations* walking, swimming, reading; *Style—* Eric Seager, Esq; Civic Centre, Gravesend, Kent DA12 1AU (☎ 0474 337300, fax 0474 337453)

SEAGER, Maisie Elizabeth; da of Albert Edward Taylor (d 1968), of Kensington, London, and Emma Ann Elizabeth, *née* Fisher (d 1972); *b* 7 Sept 1928; *Educ* St Georges Sch Camden Hill, St Mary Abbotts Sch Kensington; *m* 21 Sept 1960, John Edward Seager; 1 s (John Francis b 1963); *Career* ptnr Electrical Contractors; sec Herne Bay and Dist C of C, trophy sec Nat Roller Hockey Assoc of Eng, sec and treas Kent Co Roller Hockey Assoc, treas Herne Bay and Whitstable Crime Prevention Panel; *Style—* Mrs Maisie E Seager; Copperfields, 47 Bank St, Herne Bay, Kent CT6 5AW (☎ 0227 362175)

SEARLE, Dr John Baynes; s of Alfred Broadhead Searle (d 1967), of Sheffield, and Mary Elizabeth, *née* Moulds (d 1967); *b* 27 April 1915; *Educ* Bootham Sch York, Univ of Oxford (BA BM, BCh); *m* 10 June 1949, Margaret Beryl (Berry), da of Alfred James Mansfield (d 1966), of Bristol; 2 s (Robert James Baynes, Charles Jonathan Baynes); *Career* Surgn Lt RNVR served on destroyers 1942-46; house surgn: UCH London 1941, Bradford Royal Infirmary 1941; clinical asst Nuffield Dept of Anaesthetics Radcliffe Infirmary Oxford 1946-50, Dip Anaesthetics RCS 1948, conslt anaesthetist SE Kent Royal Hosp Bd; former pres Folkestone Med Soc; memb: Oxford Graduates Med Soc, Oxford Soc; former memb SE Kent Hosp Mgmnt Ctee; FFARCS 1951, fell Coll of Anaesthetists RCS 1988; *Recreations* golf, sailing; *Clubs* Royal Naval Medical; *Style—* Dr John Searle; 1 Bodenham Rd, Folkestone, Kent (☎ 0303 54245)

SEARLE, Muriel Vivienne; da of (Alfred Charles) Noel Searle (d 1983), of Bromley, and Ellen Rose (Nellie), *née* Jessop (d 1978); *Educ* Bromley Co GS for Girls; *Career* author; awarded Booksellers' Assoc Dip 1964, contrib to 2 local newspapers, lectures on local and railway history for many local orgns; involved in: HA Bromley and Beckenham, Bromley Borough Local History Soc, ENBRO (Environment Bromley); *Books* incl: Spas and Watering Places (1977), Bathing Machines and Bloomers (1977), John Ireland, The Man and His Music (1979), Lost Lines (1982), Down the Line To Dover (1983), Bromley Yesterdays (1983), Down the Line to Southend (1984), Bromley in Old Picture Postcards (1985), Down the Line to Brighton (1986), Down the Line to Bristol (1986), Bromley's Hurricane (1988), Old Bromley (1989), Bickley and Widmore in Old Picture Postcards (1990); *Recreations* travel, countryside, preserved railways, pets (cats); *Style—* Miss Muriel V Searle; 164 Queen Anne Ave, Bromley, Kent BR2 OSF (☎ 081 466 5133)

SEAWARD, Colin Hugh; CBE (1987); s of Sydney Widmer Seaward (d 1967), and Molly Wendela, *née* Darwen (d 1985); *b* 16 Sept 1926; *Educ* RNC Dartmouth, Univ of Cambridge; *m* 1, Jean, *née* Bugler (d 1971); 3 s (Jonathan Louis b 1952, Nicholas William b 1956, Thomas Edward b 1967), 1 da (Petronella Jane (Mrs Seccombe) b 1950); m 2, Judith Margaret, da of Canon W T Hinkley, of Alnwick, Northumberland; 2 da (Candida Harriet b 1974, Jessica Lucy b 1976); *Career* War Serv HMS Ajax 1944-45, served Far East 1946-48, Med 1951-52, Admty 1953-55, cmd HMS Aberford 1956-58, Asst Naval Attaché Moscow and Naval Attaché Warsaw 1958-60, HMS Centaur 1960-62, MOD 1962-64, ret; joined HM Dip Serv 1965, dep high cmmr The Gambia 1966-68, FCO 1968-71, Rio de Janeiro 1971, Prague 1972-73, FCO 1973-76; Sr Offrs War Course RNC Greenwich 1976, cnsllr (econ and commercial) Islamabad 1977-80, HM consul-gen Rio de Janeiro 1980-86, ret 1986, re-employed Protocol Dept FCO 1987-; hon sec Anglo-Brazilian Soc 1986; Freeman City of London 1987; Hon Citizen State of Rio de Janeiro 1985; *Recreations* country life; *Style—* Colin Seaward, Esq; Brasted House, Brasted, Westerham, Kent, TN16 1JA

SEDDON, (Edward) Jeremy; s of Col Roland Nelson Seddon, OBE, of Stourton Caundle, Dorset, and Dorothy Ida Kathleen, *née* Canning (d 1982); *b* 14 April 1941; *Educ* Kings Sch Bruton, Univ of Southampton (BSc); *m* 20 Sept 1975, Prudence Mary, da of Arthur William George Clarke (d 1955); 1 s (Thomas b 1985), 2 da (Serena b 1979, Alexandra b 1980); *Career* Associated Electrical Industries Ltd 1958-68, Dalgety Ltd 1968-73, md Barclays de Zoete Wedd Ltd 1978- (head of public sector unit), non exec dir Victaulic plc 1983-; Freeman City of London 1976; *Recreations* sailing, music, gardening; *Clubs* Royal Thames Yacht, Special Forces; *Style—* Jeremy Seddon, Esq; Jesters, Oak Lane, Sevenoaks, Kent TN13 1UF (☎ 0732 461 180); Barclays de Zoete Wedd Ltd, Ebbgate House, 2 Swan Lane, London EC4R 3TS (☎ 071 623 2323)

SEDGWICK, Robert Mannering; s of Patrick Cardinall Mason Sedgwick, CMG (d 1982), and Beth Mannering, *née* Thompson; *b* 17 Oct 1948; *Educ* St Lawrence Coll Ramsgate, UCL (LLB), Coll of Law; *m* 14 June 1974 (m dis 1988), Patricia Anne, da of Lt Col Harry Orson Oakes (d 1970); 3 s (Simon b 1975, Timothy b 1977 d 1990, Nicholas b 1981); m 2, 18 Aug 1989, Sally Jean, da of Noel Dowson; *Career* slr; Buss Stone & Co: articled clerk 1971-73, asst slr 1973-74, ptnr 1974-85; ptnr Buss Murton Partnership 1985-; memb: Royal Tunbridge Wells Round Table 1976-89, Rotary Club of the Pantiles 1987-90; conservator Tunbridge Wells Commons 1980-88; memb Law Soc 1973; *Style—* Robert Sedgwick, Esq; 7 Grecian Rd, Tunbridge Wells, Kent TN1 1TG (☎ 0892 25691); The Buss Murton Partnership, The Priory, Tunbridge Wells, Kent TN1 1JJ (☎ 0892 510222, fax 0892 510333, telex 95195)

SEEX, David Stewart; s of William Ernest Seex (d 1985), of Eastbourne, Sussex, and Joan Marie; *b* 29 Sept 1946; *Educ* Gregg GS, Ealing London; *m* 20 March 1970, Wendy Ann; 2 s (Daren Mark b 1972, Daniel Lee Samuel b 1974); *Career* md Comma Oil and Chemicals Ltd 1975-; dir: Sonic Transport Services Ltd 1977-89, Lassi Aviation Ltd 1983-, Br Lubricants Fedn Ltd 1984-, Bookash Ltd 1989-; vice pres Br Lubricants Fedn, chm London Amateur Aviation Soc Int; *Recreations* flying (private pilot); *Style—* David Seex, Esq; Wayside, Wrotham Hill Farm, Wrotham, Sevenoaks, Kent TN15 1JG (☎ 0732 822028); Comma Oil and Chemicals Ltd, Comma Works, Gravesend, Kent DA12 2QX (☎ 0474 864311, fax 0474 333000)

SENIOR, Sir Edward Walters; CMG (1955); s of late Albert Senior, CBE, of Sheffield; *b* 29 March 1902; *Educ* Repton, Univ of Sheffield; *m* 1928, Stephanie Vera (d 1990), da of Basil M Heald, of Torquay; 1 s (John), 1 da (Jennifer); *Career* RA (TA) 1920-52, Maj 1938; JP Sheffield 1937-50; memb Iron and Steel Control 1940-44, controller Ball and Roller Bearings 1944-45, DG British Iron and Steel Fedn 1962-66 (dir 1949-62); chm George Senior & Sons Ltd; kt 1970; *Clubs* Naval and Military; *Style—* Sir Edward Senior, CMG; Hollies, Church Close, Brenchley, Tonbridge, Kent (☎ 089 272 2359)

SEWELL, Rev (Michael) Brocard; s of Cecil Arthur Seymour Sewell (d 1953), and Ethel Dorothy, *née* Grylls (d 1912); *b* 30 June 1912; *Educ* Weymouth Coll Dorset, St Edmunds Coll Ware, Collegio Sant' Alberto Rome; *Career* editorial asst GK's Weekly 1928-31, Saint Dominic's Press Ditchling 1932-37, entered Carmelite Order 1952, ordained priest 1954, ed The Aylesford Review 1955-68, dir St Albert's Press 1955-58, lectr in 1980's studies Dept of Eng St Francis Xavier Univ of Antigonish NS; *Books* Olive Custance: Her Life and Works (1975), Cecil Chesterton (1975), The Private Presses (1979), Cardinal of Norfolk, Philip Thomas Howard (1980), Like Black Swans: some People and Themes (1982), In the Dorian Mode: A Life of John Gray 1866-1934 (1983); *Recreations* RSA; *Style—* The Rev Brocard Sewell; Whitefriars, Tanners St, Faversham, Kent ME13 7JW (☎ 0795 532449)

SEWELL, David John; s of Geoffrey George Sewell, of Bromley, Kent, and Hilda Elizabeth, *née* Williams; *b* 11 July 1960; *Educ* Eltham Coll London, Lady Margaret Hall Oxford (BA), Trent Poly Nottingham, Manchester Poly; *Career* admitted slr 1986; Whitehead Monckton Maidstone: articled clerk 1984-86, asst slr 1986-88, ptnr 1988-; pt/t lectr in law Mid Kent Coll of Higher and Further Educn Maidstone 1985-; NP 1990; Methodist local preacher Orpington Headcorn 1988-, candidate reader Canterbury Dio C of E 1989-; memb: Law Soc, Kent Law Soc, Marden Soc; assoc memb The Notaries' Soc; *Recreations* reading, walking; *Style—* David Sewell, Esq; 22 Ballard Close, Marden, Tonbridge, Kent TN12 9HW; Whitehead Monckton, 72 King St, Maidstone, Kent ME14 1BL (☎ 0622 690077, fax 0622 690050)

SHABBIR-AHMAD, Dr Shabbir; s of Aziz Ahmad (d 1974), of Kenya, and Meirage Begum (d 1930); *b* 10 May 1927; *Educ* Duke of Gloucester Sch Nairobi, Panjab Univ Lahore (MB BS, DLO); *m* Zarina Begum, da of Faqir Ahmad (d 1950), of Lahore; 4 s (Shakil b 1953, Aquil b 1956, Zamir b 1959, Tanvir b 1961), 1 da (Farah Azma b 1963); *Career* area surgn St Johns Ambulance W Kenya 1955-80, med dir and cmo Kisumu Nursing and Maternity 1965-80, conslt primary care physician KFAF Hosp Jeddah 1984-89, hon conslt Dept Islamic Med King Fahd Med Res Univ of Jeddah 1986-, owner St Leonards Care Home for Elderly West Malling; vice pres and chm Kenya Family Planning Assoc, fndr pres Nyanza Family Planning Assoc Kenya, memb World Population Cncl; fndr and chm: Rotary Club of Kisumu Kenya, Nyanza Hockey Assoc Kenya, Nyanza Lawn Tennis Assoc Kenya; pres Nyanza Muslim League Kenya, vice chm Hockey Assoc of Kenya (formerly a national selector), former table tennis champion of Pakistan; OStJ, MRCGP; *Books* Prophet's Health Guidance, HOPE (vols I, II and III); *Style—* Dr Shabbir Shabbir-Ahmad; St Leonard's Care Home for the Elderly, Malling Place, West Malling, Kent ME19 6PD (☎ home 0732 843102, business 0732 847979)

SHAKESPEARE, Elizabeth, Lady; Elizabeth; da of Brig-Gen Robert Hare, CMG, DSO, DL (d 1953; great n of 2 Earl of Listowel), and Helen Mary, *née* Atkinson (d 1972); *b* 4 May 1914; *m* 29 Feb 1952, as his 2 w, Rt Hon Sir Geoffrey Shakespeare, 1 Bt, PC (d 1980); *Career* served WWII Section Offr WAAF (despatches); Bronze Star (USA); Freeman City of London 1974; *Recreations* gardening, travel; *Style—* Elizabeth, Lady Shakespeare; Flat 6, Great Ash, Lubbock Rd, Chislehurst, Kent BR7 5JZ

SHANNON, Susan, Countess of; Susan Margaret Boyle; da of the late J P R Hogg, and E S Haywood, *née* Kidd; *b* 24 Aug 1930; *Educ* Battle Abbey Sch, Central Sch of Arts and Crafts; *m* 28 May 1958 (m dis 1979), 9 Earl of

Shannon, s of 8 Earl (d 1963); 1 s (Viscount Boyle b 19 Jan 1960), 2 da (Lady Georgina Shannon b 7 Feb 1961, Lady Caroline Waters b 12 Oct 1965); *Career* artist; furniture decorator; memb Weald of Kent Preservation Soc; *Style*— The Countess of Shannon; Brandfold Barn Cottage, Goudhurst, Cranbrook, Kent TN17 1JJ (☎ 0580 211942)

SHARMA, Dr Bharat Kumar; s of Shri Kapildeo Kumar (d 1981), of India, and Shrimat Sundarpati, *née* Devi, of Bihar State, India; *b* 20 Oct 1935; *Educ* Krist Raja Bettiah India, Univ of Patna (MB BS); *m* 30 April 1955, Saroj, da of Shri Jwala Prasad Singh, of Bihar State India; 2 s (Praveen b 1960, Ashutosh b 1968), 2 da (Alka (Mrs Sharma) b 1962, Anjali b 1967); *Career* MO IAF 1961-67; med registrar Durham Health Dist 1972-74, sr registrar Middlesborough Gen Hosp 1974-78, conslt rheumatologist Medway Hosp 1978-; memb: BMA, IMA, BSR; chm: Medway Gravesham Div BMA, Medway ODA, Fundraising Appeal Ctee for a hydrotherapy pool at the Medway Hosp; MRCP; *Recreations* Indian music, tabla playing; *Style*— Dr Bharat Kumar; 123 Robinhood Lane, Walderslade, Chatham, Kent ME5 9NL; Medway Hosp, Windmill Rd, Gillingham, Kent ME7 5NY (☎ 0634 830000 x 3427)

SHARP, Dr David Henry; OBE (1982); s of Rev Douglas Simmonds Sharp (d 1938), and late Gwendoline Helen, *née* Roberts; *b* 24 Feb 1917; *Educ* Tynemouth HS, Queen Elixabeth's GS Blackburn, Univ Coll Southampton, Univ of London (BSc, PhD); *m* 18 July 1942, Enid Catherine, da of Rev Emlyn Maurice Williams (d 1953), of Caernarvon; 2 s (Roger b 28 Jan 1946, Richard b 24 Aug 1952), 1 da (Lalage b 11 Nov 1956); *Career* sci offr Chemical Def Res Dept 1937-44, head of res Sutcliffe Speakman & Co Ltd 1944-48, section head Br Ceramic Res Assoc 1948-51, works mangr asst to md Fisons Ltd 1951-61; tech dir FBI and CBI 1961-67; gen sec: Inst Chemical Engrs, Soc of Chemical Indust 1967-82; assoc ed Ellis Horwood Ltd Chichester 1982-, served on various govt ctees including Key Ctee on Disposal of Solid Toxic Waste; active memb and office holder Methodist Church; FRSC 1943, FIChemE 1968, FRSH 1972; Das Grosse Verdienstkreuz, Federal Republic of Germany 1981; *Books* The Chemical Industry (jt ed 1981), Bioprotein Manufacture (1989); *Recreations* swimming, colour photography, model railways; *Clubs* Anglo-Belgian, Probus (Sevenoaks); *Style*— Dr David Sharp, OBE; Greenhill House, Shoreham Rd, Otford, Sevenoaks, Kent TN14 5RN (☎ 095 92 3332)

SHARPE, Dannatt Robert; s of Lt Robert Sharpe, RN (d 1977), and Winifred Dorothy, *née* Norton; *b* 6 April 1943; *Educ* St John's Coll Southsea Hants, Univ of Leicester (BSc), Univ of Southampton (DipEd), Lady Spencer Churchill Coll Oxford (Cert Ed for the deaf), Univ of Bath (cert in use of radioactive isotopes); *m* 28 Dec 1978, Jennifer Ursula, da of Alexander Grant, of St Ives, Cornwall; 1 s (Christopher), 1 da (Nadine); *Career* RN Aux Serv 1965-68; teacher St John's Coll Southsea 1965-68, head of Sci ODM Alliance HS Kikuyu Kenya 1968-75, head Unit for Hearing Impaired Children Hugh Christie Sch Tonbridge 1975-; contrib to various jls; memb: ROC 1 Gp, ROC Assoc 1 Gp (long serv medal 1988), RN Amateur Radio Soc, Radio Soc of GB; awarded Meritorious Service Certificate by the Lord Lieutenant of East Sussex 1989; MIBiol 1968, CBiol 1968, FZS 1965, AMMA 1966; *Books* Univ of Southampton Biological Bulletin 1964-65, The School Science Review; *Recreations* amateur radio, gardening; *Style*— Dannatt Sharpe, Esq; The Hugh Christie Sch, Unit for Hearing Impaired Children, Norwich Ave, Tonbridge, Kent (☎ 0732 358288/353544)

SHAW, David Lawrence; MP (C) Dover 1987-; *b* 14 Nov 1950; *Educ* King's Sch Wimbledon, City of London Poly; *m* 1986, Dr Lesley Christine Shaw, *née* Brown; 1 s (James b 1989); *Career* qualified CA 1974; Coopers & Lybrand 1971-79, County Bank 1979-83, fndr and md Sabrelance Ltd 1983-; dir: Invicta Sound plc, The Adscene Group plc, Hoskins Brewery plc, Palladian Estates plc; joined Cons Pty 1970, cncllr Royal Borough of Kingston upon Thames 1974-78, contested Leigh 1979, vice chm Kingston and Malden Cons Assoc 1979-86, chm Bow Gp 1983-84; sec Cons Pty: Smaller Business Ctee, Social Security Ctee; co-chm All-Pty Dolphin Protection Gp; fndr Bow Gp/Ripon Soc Transatlantic Confs; VFCA 1974; *Style*— David Shaw, Esq, MP; House of Commons, London SW1A OAA

SHAW, Frederick Henry; s of Alfred John Shaw (d 1979), of London, and Florence Maud, *née* Dallimore (d 1977); *b* 20 Jan 1940; *Educ* Wilsons GS London, City of London Coll; *m* 15 Nov 1958 (m dis 1990), Astrid; 2 s (Steven Frederick Timothy b 1960, Christopher Jeffrey Andrew b 1968), 3 da (Angela Astrid Inga b 1959, Jacqueline Gillian b 1965, Pamela Sandra b 1966); *Career* accountant: Stephenson Clarke Ltd 1957-63, Vickers Ltd 1964-72, Aveley Laboratories Ltd 1973-78, APV Kestner Ltd 1978-83, Kestner Engineering Co Ltd 1983-; chm: NW Kent Enterprise Agency, Kent Enterprise Agencies Consortium; ctee memb Dartford and Crayford Sea Cadet Corps; FCCA; *Recreations* travel, antiques; *Style*— Frederick Shaw, Esq; Kestner Engineering Co Ltd, Station Rd, Greenhithe, Kent DA9 9NG (☎ 0322 843281, fax 0322 846684)

SHAW, Laurence Marcus Alan; s of Lionel Shaw (d 1986), and Winifred Mary Hilda, *née* Lilley; *b* 17 Sept 1952; *Educ* Quainton Hall Sch Harrow, Merchant Taylor's, Bart's Univ of London (MB BS); *m* 27 July 1985, Keren Ann, da of Dr Fritz Starer, of Watford, Herts; 1 s (Sebastian Leon Jonathan b 11 Oct 1986), 1 da (Zoë Antonia b 2 Sept 1989); *Career* jr Dr: Bart's, Westminster and Hammersmith Hosps; conslt in obstetrics and gynaecology Canterbury and Thanet Health Authy 1988-; Liveryman Worshipful Co of Apothecaries 1989- (yeoman 1985-89); MRCOG; *Recreations* sport, music; *Clubs* Kent and Canterbury; *Style*— Laurence Shaw, Esq; Kent and Canterbury Hospital, Ethelbert Rd, Canterbury, Kent CT1 3NG (☎ 0227 766877)

SHAW, Michael Gordon (Mike); s of Leslie Shaw, of Buckhurst Hill, and Pauline, *née* Gordon (d 1971); *b* 8 July 1931; *Educ* Epsom Co GS; *m* 1, 23 Nov 1957 (m dis 1981), Ann, da of Henry Newbury; 3 s (Kevin b 1958, Simon b 1959, Adam b 1962), 2 da (Zoe b 1963, Melanie b 1969); m 2, 30 March 1989, Ann Hatton-James; *Career* Nat Serv RAF 1949-51; advertising copywriter and creative dir; Cunningham Hurst 1979, Progress Advertising 1981; author of three computer books; memb Mensa 1975; *Recreations* writing, computing, photography (video); *Style*— Mike Shaw, Esq; 45 Beechfield Rd, Bromley, Kent BR1 3BT (☎ 01 464 0853); No 2 Parkwest Place, Kendal Street, London W2 2QZ (☎ 071 402 9361)

SHAW, Prof Robert Alfred; s of Walter Schlesinger (d 1964), and Lily Karoline, *née* Plahner (d 1954); *b* 2 Nov 1924; *Educ* Univ of London (BSc, PhD, DSc); *m* 23 Aug 1980, Dr Leylâ Süheylâ Shaw, da of Yusuf Gözen, of Tarsus, Turkey; 1 s (Robert b 28 March 1984), 1 da (Lily b 30 May 1989); *Career* WWII Royal Fusiliers and Queen's Royal Regt UK, India, SE Asia command 1944-47; Birkbeck Coll Univ of London: asst lectr 1953-56, lectr 1956-65, prof of chemistry 1965-90, prof emeritus 1990-; author of numerous articles dealing with chemistry educn and third world countries; memb Academic Policy Ctee Inter Univ Cncl for Higher Educn Overseas 1976-81, UNESCO conslt to Turkish Govt 1977, main speaker and memb of Organising Ctee of Conference sponsored by Institut Mondial du Phosphate Rabat Morocco 1977, main speaker on Lifelong Educn in Koblenz W Germany 1978, fndr and steering ctee memb Univ of the Third Age London; Dr hc Univ Paul Sabatier Toulouse 1978; memb Soc of Chemical Indust; C Chem, FRSC; *Recreations* reading, music, gardening, travelling, skiing, fencing; *Style*— Prof Robert A Shaw; Brettargh Holt, Camden Way, Chislehurst, Kent BR7 5HT (☎ 081 467 5656); Department of Chemistry, Birkbeck College, University of London, Gordon House, 29 Gordon Square, London WC1H 0PP (☎ 071 380 7475, fax 071 380 7464)

SHEA, Christopher William; s of Frederick William Shea, of Otley, W Yorks, and Elaine Mary, *née* Keane (d 1971); *b* 25 June 1954; *Educ* St Thomas Aquinas GS Leeds, Christs Coll Cambridge (MA); *m* 27 June 1981, Susan, da of Gordon Shepherd, of Liskeard, Cornwall; 3 s (Marc b 1984, Stephen b 1986, Justin b 1989); *Career* CA; articles Thomson McLintock & Co 1976-81; accountant: BP Oil International 1981-83, Gill and Duffus Ltd 1983; dir: Gill and Duffus Ltd 1987, Gill and Duffus London Ltd 1988, London Fox (non-exec) 1987; ACA 1979; *Style*— Christopher Shea, Esq; 145 St Johns Rd, Tunbridge Wells, Kent TN4 9UP (☎ 0892 24271); Gill and Duffus Ltd, Sugar Quay, Lower Thames St, London EC3R 6DV (☎ 071 623 1800, telex 887162)

SHELLEY, Brian Stanley; s of Stanley Arnold Shelley (d 1983), of Nottingham, and Ivy May, *née* Allen; *b* 22 March 1948; *Educ* Univ of Surrey (BSc), Univ Coll Cardiff (post grad Cert Educn), Univ of Nottingham (MEd); *m* 25 March 1968, Jane Margaret, da of Laurence Edward King; 2 s (Daniel b 16 Dec 1973, Adam b 7 Sept 1975); *Career* teacher: Dale Sch Derby 1971-73, Parkside Sch Eastwood Notts 1973-79; dep head teacher Bennerley Fields Sch Ilkeston Derbys 1979-83, head teacher Orchard Sch Canterbury 1984-; memb NAHT, local cncllr Erewash (Derbys) 1979-83, sec Wincheap Centre Canterbury 1986-; *Style*— Brian Shelley, Esq; Centrio, The Street, Bossingham, Canterbury CT4 6DX (☎ 0227 87424); Orchard School, Cambridge Rd, Canterbury (☎ 0227 69220)

SHEPHARD, Air Cdre Harold Montague; CBE (1974, OBE 1959); s of Rev Leonard Benjamin Shephard (d 1961), of Wareham, Dorset, and Lilian Shephard (d 1982); *b* 15 Aug 1918; *Educ* St John's Leatherhead; *m* 20 May 1939, Margaret Isobel, da of Frederick Girdlestone, of Ewell; 1 s (David Harold Andrew), 1 da (Angela Margaret (Mrs Colgate)); *Career* RAF 1941-74, Air Cdre, provost marshal and dir RAF Security 1971-74; Met Police (CID) 1937-41; MBIM 1970-74; *Recreations* sport, reading; *Clubs* RAF, Tenterden Golf, Tenterden Cricket (vice pres); *Style*— Air Cdre Harold Shephard, CBE; 6 Bennetts Mews, West Cross, Tenterden, Kent TN30 6JN (☎ 05806 4945)

SHEPHERD, Lord Malcolm Newton Shepherd; PC (1965); 2 Baron (UK 1946); s of 1 Baron Shepherd, PC, sometime Chief Labour Whip Lords, Capt Yeomen of the Gd and Hon Corps Gentlemen at Arms, also Nat Agent Lab Pty (d 1954), and Ada, *née* Newton; *b* 27 Sept 1918; *Educ* Friends' Sch Saffron Walden; *m* 15 Nov 1941, Allison, The Lady Shepherd, JP, da of Patrick Redmond (d 1980); 2 s (Graeme George b 1951, Douglas Newton b 1954); *Heir* s, Hon Graeme Shepherd; *Career* chm: Mitchell Cotts & Co (FE) Ltd 1950-56, Fielding Brown & Finch (FE) Ltd 1951-62, National Bus Company 1980-85, Cheque Point International 1988-; dir: Sterling Group of Cos 1976-82, Sum Hung Kai Ltd 1980-85; chief whip House of Lords 1964-67 (oppn chief whip 1960-64), min of state FO 1967-70, lord privy seal and leader House of Lords 1974-76; chm: MRC 1976-80, Civil Serv Pay Res Unit Bd 1976-81, Packaging Cncl; pres Inst Road Tport Engrs 1987-; *Recreations* golf; *Clubs* Tenterden Golf; *Style*— The Rt Hon the Lord Shepherd, PC; 29 Kennington Palace Court, Sancroft St, London SE11 (☎ 071 582 6772); Cheque Point International, Berkeley St, London W1 (☎ 071 409 0868)

SHERRED, Peter William; s of Capt William Percival Charles Sherred (d 1955), and Elizabeth Ann, *née* McKeen (d 1987); *b* 21 Dec 1947; *Educ* Bearwood Coll Wokingham Berks, Eliot Coll Univ of Kent at Canterbury (BA); *m* 1 Aug 1987, Mary Elizabeth, da of John William Todd, formerly of 334 Southborough Lane, Bromley, Kent; 2 s (James Andrew Jolyon b 30 Nov 1988, Charles William Alexander b 19 Jan 1990); *Career* asst slr London Borough of Camden 1973, dep dir legal servs Dover DC 1976-81 (asst slr 1974-76), ptnr Stilwell & Harby 1981-; pres: Dover C of C 1988-89, pres Rotary Club of Dover 1990-; treas Kent Soc Univ of Kent, sch govr St Mary's C of E Primary Sch Dover, lay reader St Peter and St Paul Church Charlton-in-Dover; life memb: Kent CCC, Assoc of Men of Kent and Kentish Men; memb: Court Univ of Kent, Kent Law Soc, Law Soc Slrs Benevolent Assoc; *Recreations* antiquarian books, philately, model railways, travel; *Clubs* Royal Cinque Ports Yacht (Dover); *Style*— Peter Sherred, Esq; Copthorne, 73 Castle Ave, Dover, Kent CT16 1EZ; Stilwell & Harby, 110 Maison Dieu Rd, Dover, Kent CT16 1RT (☎ 0304 206850, fax 0304 206950, telex 96174)

SHIELDS, Rev Michael Penton; s of Albert James Shields (d 1949), of Newport, IOW, and Violet Marguerite, *née* Capon; *b* 6 Aug 1930; *Educ* King James's GS IOW, Kelham Theol Coll, Bishops' Coll Cheshunt; *Career* Nat Serv RAF 1949-50, RAFVR 1951-61; corp sec Thomas Cook & Son Ltd 1954-62; ordained deacon 1964, priest Diocese of London 1965; curate: St Andrew Kingsbury 1964-67, All Saints Friern Barnet 1967-69; vicar St Matthias Colindale 1969-76; chaplain: Colindale Hosp 1969-74, West Hendon Hosp 1975-76; vicar St John the Baptist Sevenoaks 1976-, chaplain Sevenoaks Hosp 1978-, rural dean Sevenoaks 1984-; memb Co of Mission Priests; *Recreations* reading, driving, television; *Style*— The Rev Michael Shields; St John's Clergy House, 62 Quakers Hall Lane, Sevenoaks, Kent TN13 3TX (☎ 0732 451710)

SHILLING, Wilfrid Joseph; s of William Henry Shilling (d 1964), of Sittingbourne, Kent, and Lilian Bertha, *née* Burton (d 1980); *b* 21 May 1913; *Educ* Elementary Sch; *m* 24 May 1952, Kathleen Eileen, da of James Boucher (d 1970), of Cookham, Berks; 2 s (Michael James Anthony b 22 April 1956, David George Martin b 18 July 1958), 1 da (Angela Christine (Mrs Taylor) b 9 Nov 1953); *Career* Lt RNVR 1943-47; CA; cost accountant: De Havilland Aircraft Co Ltd Stag Lane and Hatfield 1935-43, Telephone Manufacturing Co Ltd 1947-51; co sec and chief accountant Daniel Greenaway & Sons Ltd 1952-80 (dir 1976); Kent CC: cnclr for Maidstone Rural West 1989-, fin spokesman Lib Democrats; govr Barming Primary Sch, sec Clare Park Maidstone Bowls Club; memb: London Philharmonic Choir 1947-52, Mote Park Maidstone Indoor Bowls Club; treas: Maidstone Lib Democrats, Tonbridge Rd Maidstone Methodist Church; FCCA, FCMA; *Recreations* music, bowls, bridge, travel; *Style*— Wilfrid Shilling, Esq

SHORT, Michael Edward; s of Thomas Edward Short, of Blackheath, and Anne Elizabeth, *née* Roffe; *b* 16 Sept 1941; *Educ* Greenwich Boys Tech Coll; *m* 12 May 1962, Maureen, da of Christoher Thorington (d 1984); 1 s (Ian Michael Edward b 1973), 1 da (Joanne Maureen (twin) b 1973); *Career* gp md Pearce Group Holdings Ltd; chm: Pearce Maintenance Ltd, Pearce Southern Ltd, Pearce Northern Ltd, Pearce Gowshall Ltd, Davand Plastics Ltd; md Haaxman Lichtreclame BV; FIOD 1974; *Recreations* golf, badminton, music; *Clubs* RAC, Pall Mall; *Style*— Michael Short, Esq; Rowans, High Halstow, Kent ME3 8SF; Pearce Group Holdings, Insignia House, New Cross, London SE14 6AB (☎ 081 692 6611, fax 081 692 1753/081 694 8015, car 0863 360309)

SHOTTER, Very Rev Edward Frank; s of Frank Edward Shotter (d 1970), of Grimsby, and Minnetta, *née* Gaskill (d 1976); *b* 29 June 1933; *Educ* Humberstone Fndn Sch Ctee, St David's Coll Lampeter, Univ of Wales (BA), St Stephen's House Oxford; *m* 9 Dec 1978, Dr Jane Shotter, da of Dr John Oliver Pearce Edgcumbe; 2 s (James b 1982, Piers b 1984), 1 da (Emma b 1987); *Career* ordained: deacon 1960, priest 1961; asst curate St Peter's Plymouth 1960-62, intercollegiate sec Student Christian Movement London 1962-66; dir: London Medical Gp 1963-89, Inst of Medical Ethics 1974-89; chaplain Univ of London 1969-89, prebendary St Paul's Cathedral London 1977-89, dean of Rochester 1990-; memb: Editorial Bd Journal of Medical Ethics, working party on ethics of med involvement in torture, Inst of Med Ethics; FRSM; Patriarchal Cross Romanian Orthodox Church 1975; *Books* Matters of Life and Death (ed, 1970), Life Before Birth (jt author, 1986); *Recreations* Romania, restoring country houses, hill walking; *Clubs* Reform, Castle (Rochester); *Style*— The Very Rev the Dean of Rochester; The Deanery, Rochester, Kent ME1 1TG (☎ 0634 844023); Northseat of Auchedly, Tarves, Aberdeen

SHOVELTON, Walter Patrick; CB (1976), CMG (1972); s of Sydney Taverner Shovelton, CBE (d 1968), and May Catherine Kelly (d 1958); *b* 18 Aug 1919; *Educ* Charterhouse, Keble Coll Oxford (MA); *m* 1968, Helena, da of Denis George Richards, OBE; *Career* WWII 1940-46, Maj; civil servant; dep sec 1946-78, dir gen GCBS 1978-85; dir: Br Airports Authy 1982-85, The Maersk Co Ltd 1985-87 (vice chm 1987-); chm Birmingham Euro Airways 1988-; advsr: House of Lords Ctee on Euro Communities 1985-86, House of Commons Select Ctee on Tport 1986; chm Maritime Ctee William & Mary Tercentenary Tst 1985-; *Recreations* golf; *Clubs* Brooks's, Royal Ashdown Forest Golf, Rye Golf, Hampstead Golf, Seniors Golf; *Style*— W P Shovelton, Esq, CB, CMG; 63 London Rd, Tunbridge Wells, Kent TN1 1DT (☎ 0892 27885)

SIDEBOTHAM, Rev Canon Stephen Francis; s of Rev Edward Maurice Sidebotham (d 1967), and Evelyn Rose, *née* Budd (d 1981); *b* 31 May 1935; *Educ* Marlborough, Queens' Coll Cambridge (BA, MA), Lincoln Theol Coll; *m* 31 Jan 1961, Margaret Joy (Peggy), da of Leonard Douglas Palmer (d 1978); 1 s (Peter b 1963), 2 da (Heather b 1962, Mei Ling b 1964); *Career* Nat Serv Gunner RA 1953-54, 2 Lt RPC 1954-55; St John's Cathedral Hong Kong: chaplain 1964-66, precentor 1966-70, dean 1976-82; vicar Christ Church Kowloon Tong Hong Kong 1970-76, rector St George's Church Gravesend 1983-; memb Rochester Diocesan Synod, chaplain Gravesend and North Kent Hosp, chm govrs Holy Trinity Church of Eng Primary Sch, hon chaplain Probus Club of Gravesend; *Recreations* carpentry, walking, reading, classical music; *Style*— The Rev Canon Stephen Sidebotham; St George's Rectory, Gravesend, Kent DA11 0DJ (☎ 0474 534965)

SIDNEY, Maj Hon Philip John Algernon; MBE (1977); s and h of 1 Viscount De L'Isle, VC, KG, GCMG, GCVO, PC, *qv*, and his 1 w, Hon Jacqueline Corinne Yvonne, *née* Vereker (d 1962); *b* 21 April 1945; *Educ* Tabley House Cheshire; *m* 15 Nov 1980, Isobel Tresyllian, da of Sir Edmund Gerald Compton, GCB, KBE; 1 s (Philip William Edmund b 2 April 1985), 1 da (Sophia Jacqueline Mary b 25 March 1983); *Career* cmmnd Grenadier Gds 1966, served BAOR, NI, Belize, GSO3 Ops/SD HQ 3 Inf Bde NI 1974-76, ret 1979; farmer and landowner; dir and chm Wood Products of Westerham 1984-; memb: Ctee CLA Kent (chm 1983-85), Kent Archives Office Advsy Ctee; Freeman City of London, Liveryman Worshipful Co of Goldsmiths; *Clubs* White's, Pratt's, The Brook (NY); *Style*— Maj The Hon Philip Sidney, MBE; Estate Office, Penshurst Place, Penshurst, Tonbridge, Kent TN11 8DG (☎ 0892 870304)

SILCOCK, Rev Donald John; s of William George Silcock (d 1984), of Woldingham, Surrey, and Alice Sophia, *née* Shelley (d 1988); *b* 26 Oct 1930; *Educ* Oxted Co GS, Kings Coll London (AKC); *m* 30 Aug 1958, Dorothy Hilda, da of Frederick William Terry (d 1965), of Bellingham, Catford; 1 s (Timothy b 1965), 2 da (Katharine b 1960, Judith b 1962); *Career* curate St John at Hackney London 1960-63, minister in charge William Temple Church Abbey Wood 1963-69, curate and priest in charge St Nicholas Middleton on Sea and St Mary Felpham 1967-74; rector: St Peter Ightham 1974-84, St Helen Cliffe with Cooling 1984-, rural dean of Strood 1985-; *Recreations* classical music, sailing, photography; *Style*— The Rev Donald Silcock; St Helen's Rectory, Church St, Cliffe, Rochester, Kent ME3 7PY (☎ 0634 220220)

SIMMONS, Rev Brian Dudley; s of Frederick Roberts Simmons (d 1981), of Watlington, Oxford, and Ellen Dorothy, *née* Carr (d 1987); *b* 31 Aug 1935; *Educ* Salesian Coll Oxford, King Edward VII Coll London, Univ of Southampton Sch of Navigation (Master Mariner), St Stephen's House Oxford; *m* 31 July 1959, Mary Linda, da of Sir Percival Liesching, GCMG, KCB, KCVO (d 1973), of Tunbridge Wells; 3 s (Mark b 1961, David b 1963, John b 1965), 1 da (Sarah b 1967); *Career* master mariner Furness Withy and Co 1952-63, ordained priest 1965 (deacon 1964), asst curate St Peters Bournemouth 1964-67; The Missions to Seamen: sr chaplain Nat Sea Trg Sch Gravesend 1967-71, Chaplain Trg Ship Worcester 1967-71; vicar Holy Trinity Lamorbey Sidcup 1971-1990, rector of Hever with Mark Beech and Four Elms 1990-; former memb London Borough Bexley Educn Ctee; memb Rochester Diocesan Bd of Educn and Bd of Fin, chm of govrs Hever Sch; memb and diocesan advsr Hon Co of Master Mariners 1974; *Recreations* industrial archaeology, walking, reading; *Style*— The Rev Brian Simmons; Hever Rectory, Kent TN8 7LH (☎ 0732 862249)

SIMPSON, Very Rev John Arthur; s of Arthur Simpson (d 1958), and Mary Esther, *née* Price (d 1982); *b* 7 June 1933; *Educ* Cathays HS Cardiff, Keble Coll Oxford (BA, MA), Clifton Theol Coll; *m* 15 Aug 1968, Ruth Marian, da of Leo Dibbens (d 1966); 1 s (Damian b 1972), 2 da (Rebecca b 1970, Helen b 1974); *Career* curate: Leyton 1958-59, Christ Church Orpington 1959-62; tutor Oak Hill Coll London 1962-72, vicar Ridge Herts 1972-79, dir Ordinands and Post-Ordination Trg Diocese of St Albans 1975-81, hon canon St Albans Cathedral 1977-79, residentiary canon St Albans and priest i/c of Ridge 1979-81, archdeacon of Canterbury and residentiary canon of Canterbury Cathedral 1981-86, dean of Canterbury 1986-; dir Ecclesiastical Insurance Group 1983-; chm: (Canterbury) Cathedral Gifts Ltd 1986-, The Canterbury Cathedral Co Ltd; chm Govrs Kings Sch Canterbury 1986-; *Recreations* travel, theatre, opera; *Clubs* Athenaeum; *Style*— The Very Rev the Dean of Canterbury; The Deanery, Canterbury, Kent CT1 2EP (☎ 0227 765983); Cathedral House, 11

The Precincts, Canterbury CT1 2EH (☎ 0227 762862)

SIMPSON, Lady Juliet; da of late 4 Earl of Cranbrook by 2 w, Fidelity (*see Dowager Countess of Cranbrook*); *b* 1934; *m* 1958 (m dis 1970), Charles Colin Simpson, TD; 2 s (Charles b 1962, Edward b 1965), 2 da (Fidelity b 1960, Amanda b 1964); *Style—* The Lady Juliet Simpson; The White House, Rooks Hill, Underriver, Sevenoaks, Kent

SIMPSON, Rosemary Irene; da of Capt William Watson (d 1990), and Doris, of Broadstairs and St Peters; *b* 3 Aug 1947; *Educ* The Charles Dickens Sch Broadstairs, Dane Court Sch Broadstairs, Gipsy Hill Coll of Educn (Cert Ed), Thanet Tech Coll, Canterbury Tech Coll (BTech); *m* 21 Jan 1975, Graham Cooper Simpson, s of late (Kenneth) Roy Simpson, of Margate; 1 s (Benjamin Christopher b 14 Dec 1975), 1 da (Jessica Ellen b 3 July 1977); *Career* teacher The Charles Dickens Sch Broadstairs 1968-71 (pt/t 1982-83), VSO The Govt Girls' Sch Yola NE State Nigeria 1971-73; professional housewife and mother; Broadstairs and St Peter: town cncllr 1987-, dep Mayor 1988-89, Mayor 1989-90; memb: VSO, NSPCC, Br Women's Pilots' Assoc, Kent Microlight Assoc; *Recreations* hockey, reading, flying, fencing; *Clubs* Thanet Flying, Thanet Nomads Hockey; *Style—* Ms Rosemary Simpson; Broadstairs, Kent CT10 1BQ

SIMPSON, William John; s of John Alexander Simpson (d 1978), of Petham, and Joan Emma, *née* Vanderplank; *b* 21 March 1936; *Educ* Pretoria Boys HS SA, Univ of Natal, Univ of Exeter; *m* 9 July 1959, June Irene, da of Cecil David Gold (d 1974), of Kokstad, E Griqualand; 1 s (Harold Alexander b 27 Aug 1964), 2 da (Lucy Emma b 12 May 1966, Victoria Beatrice b 8 Nov 1967); *Career* asst librarian Univ of Exeter 1964-70, librarian Wolverhampton Poly 1970-73, dep librarian Univ of Kent 1973-77, librarian Univ of Kent 1977-; FRSA; *Style—* William Simpson, Esq; 58 High St, Bridge, Canterbury, Kent CT4 5LA (☎ 0227 830722); Univ of Kent, Canterbury, Kent CT2 7NU (☎ 0227 764000, fax 0227 459025)

SIMS, Roger Edward; MP (C) Chislehurst 1974-; s of Herbert William Sims (d 1981), of Chislehurst, and Annie Amy, *née* Savidge (d 1987); *b* 27 Jan 1930; *Educ* City Boys' GS Leicester, St Olave's GS Tower Bridge London; *m* 15 June 1957, Angela, da of John Robert Mathews (d 1951), of Chislehurst; 2 s (Matthew Robert b 31 March 1962, Toby Edward b 27 July 1966), 1 da (Virginia Claire b 29 May 1959); *Career* Campbell Booker Carter Ltd 1953-62, advsr Dodwell & Co Ltd 1974-90 (dept mangr 1962-74), dir Inchcape International Ltd 1981-90; memb Chislehurst and Sidcup UDC 1956-62, JP Bromley 1960-72, chm Juvenile Court 1970-72, PPS to Home Sec 1979-83, vice chm Cons Health Ctee; chm 1912 Club; memb: Central Exec Ctee NSPCC 1980- (pres Bromley and Dist Branch), Gen Med Cncl 1989-; *Recreations* swimming, singing (Royal Choral Soc); *Clubs* Bromley Cons; *Style—* Roger Sims, Esq, MP; House of Commons, London SW1A 0AA (☎ 071 219 5000/4404)

SINCLAIR, David Anthony; s of (Francis) Kenneth Sinclair (d 1979), of 57 New England Rd, Pietermaritzburgh, Natal, SA, and Pamela Margaret, *née* Chaldecott; *b* 29 July 1936; *Educ* Aldenham, Merton Coll Oxford (MA); *m* 1 April 1961 (m dis 1978), Angela Nellie, da of George Peacock, of Tillington, nr Petworth, W Sussex; 3 s (Alistair b 18 April 1963, Julian b 13 July 1968, Benjamin b 18 March 1972), 1 da (Catherine b 12 Oct 1964); *Career* Nat Serv cmmnd 2 Lt RAOC 1954-56; administrator Kings Coll Hosp; mktg sales exec: Fibreglass Ltd, Pilkington plc; jt chm Galleon Group; jt chm Galleon Group; memb: Tunbridge Wells Community Health Cncl 1981-82, PO Users Complaints Cncl and Telephone Advsy Cncl 1985-87; first SDP memb: Tunbridge Wells Borough Cncl 1983-87, W Kent memb Cncl for Social Democracy 1984-86, Kent CC 1985-; exec memb: Kent Assoc for the Blind 1985-, Southern Regnl Assoc for the Blind 1985-; SDP/Lib Alliance candidate for Wealden E Sussex Gen Election 1987, vice chm Tunbridge Wells SDP 1987-88; govr: St Peters Primary Sch Tunbridge Wells 1988, St James Infant Sch Tunbridge Wells 1989-; *Recreations* cooking, reading, the arts; *Style—* David A Sinclair, Esq; The Coach House, 6 Ferndale, Royal Tunbridge Wells, Kent (☎ 0892 545387)

SINGER, Hugh Roland; s of Cyril Roland Singer (d 1990), of Island Wall, Whitstable, Kent, and Dorothy, *née* Roberts (d 1975); *b* 14 Nov 1930; *Educ* Faversham GS, Woolwich Poly, Guy's (LDS), Univ of London (BDS); *m* 20 March 1956, Marion Hilda, da of Charles Lamin Boyd; 1 s (Guy b 1966), 1 da (Monique b 1960); *Career* 1 Bn Buffs ACF 1945-49, 10 Bn Parachute Regt TA 1949-52, RADC 1956-58; gen dental practitioner 1956-, md Whitstable Diving Co 1961-; memb: BSAC, Pudding Pan Res Gp, Radio Soc of GB; *Recreations* sub aqua, amateur radio, boating; *Style—* Hugh Singer, Esq; 1 Neptune Gap, Whitstable, Kent (☎ 0227 272449)

SINGER, Dr Norbert; CBE (1990); s of Salomon Singer (d 1970), and Mina, *née* Korn (d 1976); *b* 3 May 1931; *Educ* Highbury Co Sch, QMC London (BSc, PhD); *m* 23 May 1980, Dr Brenda Margaret Singer, da of Richard Walter, of Tunbridge Wells; *Career* project ldr Morgan Crucible Co Ltd 1954-58; N London Poly 1958-70 (lectr, sr lectr, princ lectr, dep head of Dept of Chemistry), prof and head of Life Sci Dept Poly of Central London 1971-74, asst dir (later dept dir) Poly of N London 1974-78, dir Thames Poly 1978-; cncl memb CNAA 1982-88; CChem, FRSC 1954; *Recreations* reading, walking; *Style—* Dr Norbert Singer, CBE; Croft Lodge, Bayhall Road, Tunbridge Wells, Kent TN2 4TD (☎ 0892 23821); Thames Polytechnic, Wellington St, Woolwich, London SE18 6PF (☎ 081 316 8000)

SINGH, Makhan; s of Daulat Singh, of Punjab, India, and Tej Kaur, *née* Nijjor; *b* 1 Aug 1941; *Educ* Inst of Higher Educn Doncaster (HNC), South Bank Poly (BSc); *m* 25 Dec 1962, (Surinder) Kaur, da of Daya Singh Heire, of Kent; 2 s (Manjit b 1964, Ranjit b 1965), 1 da (Harinder b 1966); *Career* apprentice electrician, electrician, electrical engr, lectr, lectr and head of electrical section Kilburn Poly, currently lectr and course tutor electrical installation Woolwich Coll; organised and lectured on 15 edn of IEE regulations; gen sec and treas Sikh Temple Gravesend 1976-78 (pres 1971-73), Gravesham borough cncllr 1983-, chm Gravesend Community Rels Cncl 1987-90 (memb and exec ctee memb 1987-90); memb: Kent FPC, Kent Police Advisory Consultative Ctee; involved with orgn of sports festival in Asian Games Gravesend; *Clubs* Guru Nanak Kabaddi; *Style—* Makhan Singh, Esq; 29 Milton Hall Rd, Gravesend, Kent DA12 1QN (☎ 0474 357500); Woolwich College, Villas Rd, Plumstead, London SE18 (☎ 081 855 1216)

SINKER, Patrick Andrew Charles Chisholm; s of Capt Leonard Chisholm Sinker, RN (d 1970), and Nancy, *née* Johnston; *b* 14 Jan 1939; *Educ* Pangbourne Nautical Coll; *m* 3 April 1964, Letitia Ann, da of Robert King Anderson, of Whitstable, Kent; 2 da (Kate Letitia b 1967, Polly Anna b 1969); *Career* co dir; FCA; *Recreations* sailing, golf; *Clubs* Chestfield Golf; *Style—* Patrick Sinker, Esq; The Orchard, Alexandra Rd, Whitstable, Kent; Brent's Boatyard, Brents, Faversham, Kent (☎ 0795 537 809)

SISSONS, Peter George; s of George Robert Percival Sissons (d 1964), and Elsie Emma, *née* Evans; *b* 17 July 1942; *Educ* Liverpool Inst HS for Boys, Univ Coll Oxford (MA); *m* Sylvia; 2 s, 1 da; *Career* tv journalist and presenter; ITN 1964-78: gen trainee then scrip writer, gen reporter, foreign correspondent, news ed, indust correspondent, indust ed; presenter News at One 1978-82, presenter Channel Four News 1982-89, chm Question Time and presenter 6 O'Clock News BBC 1989-; Broadcasting Press Guild's Best Front of Camera Performer 1984, Royal TV Soc's Judges Award 1989; *Recreations* relaxing; *Style—* Peter Sissons, ESq; c/o BBC TV Centre, Wood Lane, London W12 7RJ (☎ 081 576 7776)

SKINGSLEY, Air Chief Marshal Sir Anthony Gerald; KCB (1986, CB 1983); *b* 19 Oct 1933; *Educ* Univ of Cambridge (MA); *m* 1957 Lilwen Dixon; 2 s, 1 da; *Career* joined RAF 1955, HQ 2 ATAF (ACOS Offensive Ops) 1977-78, Hon ADC to HM The Queen 1976-77, RCDS course 1978, dir Air Plans MOD 1979-80, ACOS Plans and Policy SHAPE 1980-83, Cmdt RAF Staff Coll Bracknell 1983-84, Asst Chief of Air Staff 1985-86, air memb for Personnel 1986-87, C-in-C RAF Germany, Cdr 2 Allied Tactical AF 1987-89, Dep C-in-C AFCENT 1989-; *Recreations* off-shore sailing, golf, travel; *Clubs* RAF; *Style—* Air Chief Marshal Sir Anthony Skingsley, KCB; c/o National Westminster Bank plc, 43 Swan St, West Malling, Kent ME19 6LE

SKINNER, Dr Richard Osmond; s of Osmond Skinner, MBE (d 1980), of Whiteways, Sissinghurst, Kent, and Hazel Agnes, *née* Goodbun (d 1987); *b* 5 April 1935; *Educ* Tonbridge, London Hosp Med Coll (MB BS, DObstRCOG); *m* 8 Aug 1959, Shirley Ann, da of Horace Matthews (d 1983); 3 s (Timothy b 1963, Stephen b 1966, William b 1969), 1 da (Caroline (Mrs Letchford) b 1960); *Career* capt RAMC 1960-63; house physician Royal Victoria Hosp Folkestone 1958, house surgn Ashford Hosp 1959, house surgn in obstetrics Willisbrough Hosp Ashford 1959-60, princ in gen practice Staplehurst 1963-; memb: Gen Cncl of Leprosy Mission England and Wales, Canterbury Diocesan Stewardship Ctee 1966-69, Staplehurst PCC, Staplehurst Parish Cncl 1970-87 (chm 1979-87); tstee Staplehurst Village Hall Tst 1970-88; memb BMA 1958-88; *Style—* Dr Richard Skinner; Minton House, Staplehurst, Kent (☎ 0580 891395)

SLEIGHT, (George) Robin; s of George Ernest Sleight, of 1 Portmark Ave, Alloway, Ayr, Scotland, and Mary Thomspon, *née* McIntyre (d 1979); *b* 11 Nov 1937; *Educ* Ayr Acad, Univ of Glasgow (BSc); *m* 28 April 1962, Eilen Isobel, da of Eugene Owens, of 51 Adamton Rd, Prestwick, Ayrshire, Scotland; 1 s (David Eugene b 30 Nov 1966), 1 da (Fiona Caroline b 25 Dec 1968); *Career* aerodynamicist Vickers Aircraft Weybridge 1959-61; Elliott Automation (merged into GEC Avionics): systems engr Mil Autopilots 1961-64, project mangr Displays 1964-69, mangr Dallas Fort Worth office 1969-71, project mangr Navigation Systems 1971-75, tech mangr Airborne Display Div 1975-85, divnl mangr Airborne Display Div 1985-88, gen mangr 1988-89, asst md 1989-; CEng, MRAes; *Style—* Robin Sleight, Esq; GEC Avionics Ltd, Airport Works, Rochester, Kent ME1 2XX (☎ 0634 816259)

SMALLMAN, Barry Granger; CMG (1976), CVO (1972); s of Charles Stanley Smallman, CBE (d 1981), of Worthing, Sussex, and Ruby Marian, *née* Granger (d 1949); *b* 22 Feb 1924; *Educ* St Paul's, Trinity Coll Cambridge (MA); *m* 6 Sept 1952, Sheila Maxine, da of William Henry Knight, of Sissinghurst, Kent; 2 s (Mark b 1955, Robin b 1957), 1 da (Joy b 1953); *Career* served 1939-45, Lt Intelligence Corps; Br dep high cmmr: Sierra Leone 1963-64, NZ 1964-67, IDC 1968; consul gen Br Embassy Thailand 1971-74, Br high cmmr Bangladesh 1975-78, res chm Dip Serv, Civil Serv Selection Bd 1978-81, Br high cmmr Jamaica and ambass Haiti 1982-84; fndr and dir Granger Consultancies 1984-; memb: Cncl St Lawrence Coll Ramsgate 1984-, The Leprosy Mission 1984-, The Soc for Promoting Christian Knowledge 1984-; chm Cncl Beneden Sch 1986-; *Recreations* reading, writing, short stories and verse, singing, piano, bird watching, tennis, golf; *Clubs* Royal Cwlth Soc; *Style—* Barry Smallman, Esq, CMG, CVO; Beacon Shaw, Benenden, Kent TN17 4BU (☎ 0580 240 625)

SMEATON, Wilson; s of John James Smeaton (d 1988), of Northumberland, and Catherine, *née* Wilson (d 1989), of Northumberland; *b* 27 Feb 1942; *Educ* Blyth GS Northumberland, Queen Elizabeth Coll Univ of London (sister-tutor dip), Sunderland Poly (BEd); *m* 1, 7 March 1964 (m dis 1983), Diane, da of Robert Moore, of Northumberland; 1 s (Philip Andrew b 1966), 1 da (Annette Nicola b 1964); m 2, 8 Oct 1983, Josephine Lesley, da of Timothy Francis Edward King, MBE, of Leatherhead, Surrey; 1 step s (Ian Henry Brodie b 1966), 1 step da (Karen Emma Brodie b 1968); *Career* sr tutor: general and mental nursing Gateshead Health Authy 1975-82, staff devpt Airedale Health Authy W Yorks 1982-84; dir of nurse educn SE Kent Health Authy, currently seconded to Christ Church Coll of Higher Educn, author of articles in nursing jls; chm Folkestone and Dist Sporting Gun Club, memb Br Assoc for Shooting and Conservation; RGN, RMN, RNT; *Recreations* shooting, skiing; *Style—* Wilson Smeaton, Esq; 2 The Corner, Aldington, Ashford, Kent TN25 7EE (☎ 0233 720321); Christ Church College, North Holmes, Canterbury, Kent CT1 1QU (☎ 0227 762444)

SMITH, Allen Donald Warren; OBE (1984); s of Donald Charles Wesley Smith (d 1983), and Olive Kathleen Smith (d 1979); *b* 20 Oct 1922; *Educ* Ipswich Sch, Univ of London (BSc); *m* 12 Aug 1949, June Mary, da of Kenneth Pearce (d 1946); 3 s (Andrew b 1951, Christopher b 1953, Nicholas b 1958); *Career* RAF Airfield Construction Serv 1944-47, Flt Lt, serv France, Belgium, Holland, Germany and Singapore; various engrg appts 1948-62: E Suffolk CC, Surrey CC, W Riding of Yorks CC, Somerset CC, Sir Alexander Gibbs Partners (Conslt Engrs); dep county surveyor; E Sussex CC 1962-68, Kent CC 1968-71; county surveyor Kent 1972-84, conslt transportation planning and highways; pres County Surveyor's Soc 1978-79, parish cncllr Frittenden Kent, chm Engrg Cncl Regnl Orgn Kent and Sussex; Freeman City of London 1984, Liveryman Worshipful Co of Engrs 1984; FEng, FICE, FIHT, MIWM, FRSA; *Books* A History of the County Surveyors' Society 1885-1985 (1985); *Recreations* music, gardening, reading; *Clubs* RAC; *Style—* Allen Smith, Esq, OBE; Kippens, Frittenden, Cranbrook, Kent TN17 2DD (☎ 058 080 358)

SMITH, Cncllr Anthony John (Tony); s of Henry John Smith (d 1981), of Bexleyheath, and Annie Nelda, *née* Miller; *b* 15 Feb 1941; *Educ* St Mary's Coll Sidcup; *m* 1 Oct 1969, Wendy Marion, da of Robert Sidney Brind (d 1965), of Basildon, Essex; 2 s (Adam John b 31 Jan 1970, Robert Anthony b 18 March 1972); *Career* Prudential Assurance Company: agent 1962-75, fire and accident inspr 1975-83, gen branch conslt 1983-; Dartford Borough Cncl: cons cncllr 1973-83, re-elected 1986-, chm Highways and Transportation 1989-; Mayor of Dartford 1988-89 (dep Mayor 1987-88); pres: Borough 19 Motor Club, Borough United FC, Dartford div St John Ambulance Cadets; memb London Regnl Passengers Ctee, vice chm Orchard Theatre Bd, chm govrs Dartford West HS for Boys, memb Section Exec Ctee Nat Union of Insur Workers; *Recreations* motor sport, swimming; *Style—* Cncllr Tony Smith; 16 Maida Vale Rd, Dartford, Kent DA1 3BT (☎ 0322 70130); 110-112 The Broadway, Bexleyheath, Kent DA6 7EF (☎ 081 303 1087)

SMITH, Dr Colin Haigh; s of Sydney Herbert Smith (d 1983), and Constance Maude, *née* Sidney; *b* 5 March 1933; *Educ* Charterhouse, Trinity Coll Oxford (MA, BM BCh, MSc, DCH), (MRCGP); *m* 10 Dec 1960, Celia Jane, da of Ralph Douglas Perkins (d 1961); 1 s (Peter Ralph Haigh b 1961), 3 da (Clare Caroline b 1963, Philippa Mary b 1967, Diana Lucy b 1969); *Career* govt med offr Basutoland 1960-63, princ in gen practice 1965-; course organiser for vocational trg in gen practice Medway Dist, SE Thames faculty rep Cncl RCGP; chm Dickens' Country Protection Soc 1972-, actively involved in protection of countryside and environment both locally and nationally; FRCGP 1988; *Recreations* singing, ecology; *Style—* Dr Colin Smith; Findhorn, Gads Hill, Higham, Rochester, Kent ME3 7PE (☎ 047482 2009)

SMITH, Lady Corisande; *née* Bennet; da of 8 Earl of Tankerville (d 1971), and his 2 w, Violet; *b* 1938; *m* 1963, Lt Cdr Timothy Bain Smith, RN; 2 s; *Style—* The Lady Corisande Smith; Wickens Manor, Charing, Kent

SMITH, Rt Rev David James; *see*: Maidstone, Bishop of

SMITH, Prof (Norman John) David; s of Norman Samson Smith, (d 1962), of Kensington, London, and Eileen Tatton, *née* Oakley (d 1971); *b* 2 Feb 1931; *Educ* King's Coll Sch, King's Coll Hosp Med Sch Univ of London (BDS, MPhil), Univ of London (KCHMS BDS), Royal Free Hosp Sch of Med (MSc); *m* 1, 2 Oct 1954 (m dis), Regina Eileen, da of Reginald Lugg (d 1961), of Highgate, London; 1 s (Malcolm David Oakley b 1964); m 2, 21 Sept 1983, Mary Christine, da of Alfred Thomas Pocock (d 1977); 1 da (Clare Zillah Mary b 1983); *Career* serv MN, apprentice Pacific Steam Navigation Co 1948-52, offr serv Royal Mail Lines 1953-58, gen dental practice jr hosp experience 1964-73, head Dept Dental Radiology King's Coll Sch of Med 1973-; memb: Southwark Cncl 1974-78, GLC 1977-86, Thames Water Authy 1977-83, South East Thames RHA 1978-86, Hon Co of Master Msariners; *Books* Simple Navigation by the Sun (1974), Dental Radiography (1980), Dental Radiography (2nd ed, 1988); *Recreations* nature, photography, walking; *Style—* Prof David Smith; Department of Dental Radiology, King's College School of Medicine and Dentistry, Caldecot Rd, London SE5 9RW (☎ 071 274 6222 ext 2503)

SMITH, Edward Richard; s of Albert Edward Smith (d 1961), of Finchley, London, and Elsie Florence, *née* Turner; *b* 19 March 1936; *Educ* Highgate Sch; *m* 10 Sept 1960, Pamela Margaret, da of Alfred Montague Mundy (d 1977), of Gidea Park and Tunbridge Wells; 2 s (Donald Edward Philip b 1966, Philip Richard Jeremy b 1969); *Career* Nat Serv RAOC 1954-56; Martins Bank Ltd 1954-68; dir: Hill Samuel Bank Ltd 1974-, Gross Hill Properties Ltd 1983-, Sydney and London Properties Ltd 1986-, Consolidated Land Properties Ltd, Control Securities plc 1988-, European Equity Corporation Ltd 1988-; Freeman City of London, Liveryman Worshipful Co of Pattenmakers; FCIB 1982; *Recreations* antiquarian books, gardening; *Clubs* East India, RAC, MCC; *Style—* Edward R Smith, Esq; Phildon Lodge, Seal Hollow Rd, Sevenoaks, Kent TN13 3SL (☎ 0732 456928); Hill Samuel Bank Ltd, 100 Wood St, London EC2P 2AJ (☎ 071 628 8011, fax 071 606 5073)

SMITH, (James Ellis) Felix; s of John Ellis Smith, of Bagham Lodge, Chilham, Canterbury, Kent, and Constance May, *née* Bloxham; *b* 2 June 1935; *Educ* Kent Coll Canterbury; *m* 19 Sept 1960; 1 s (Richard Ellis b 1964), 1 da (Helen (Mrs Jarrett) b 1962); *Career* RAVC 1955-57; dairy farmer; chm NFU Canterbury 1978-80, borough cncllr Ashford 1970-, Mayor of Ashford 1981-82; *Recreations* gardening, shooting; *Style—* Felix Smith, Esq; Stile Farm, Chilham, Canterbury, Kent CT4 7DE (☎ 0227 730441)

SMITH, Horace Anthony; s of Osbourne Smith (d 1975), and Gertrude Mabel, *née* Reason; *b* 17 Jan 1941; *Educ* De Aston Sch Market Rasen; *m* 1, 4 June 1959 (m dis 1981), Catherine Mary, da of Flt Lt J A Tindall, DFC, of E Yorks; 2 s (David b 1960, Richard b 1962); m 2, 30 Aug 1984, Imelda, da of Jesus Paez, of Manila; 2 da (Annalisa b 1985, Emma Jade b 1987); *Career* sr exec offr Dept of Employment 1965-73, overseas dir Professional and Exec Recruitment 1973-85, md Int Trg and Recruitment Link 1985-, md Coppas International Group Ltd 1989-; chm Wychling CC; MRGS 1974; *Books* Guide to Working Abroad (1983, 1985, 1986, 1987, 1988); *Recreations* cricket, horseracing, bridge, oriental studies; *Clubs* Lions Int; *Style—* Horace Smith, Esq; 21 Tilton Rd, Borough Green, Kent TN15 8RS; ITRL, 51A Bryanston St, London W1H 7DN (☎ 071 706 3646, fax 071 724 3948, telex 928079 TRL G)

SMITH, John Geoffrey; s of Geoffrey Smith, of Meppershall, Beds, and Lillian Smith, *née* Simnor (d 1983); *b* 6 March 1956; *Educ* Ellesmere Port GS, Univ of Bath; *m* 25 Aug 1979, Daphne Ann, da of Ronald Howard, of Chester; 2 s (Mark b 1987, Peter b 1988); *Career* mktg planning mangr SKF (UK) Ltd 1980-82 (product mangr 1978-80), commercial exec Pillar Engineering Ltd 1982-85, commercial mangr AEM (Stansted) Ltd 1985-86, md Aviation Engineering and Maintenace Ltd 1989-; *Recreations* rock climbing, mountaineering, skiing; *Style—* John Smith, Esq; Aviation Engineering & Maintenace Ltd, Wilton Rd, Ramsgate, Kent CT12 5HE (☎ 0843 591381)

SMITH, Rev Joseph Anthony; s of William James (d 1988), and Margaret Campbell (d 1987); *b* 20 April 1940; *Educ* St Columb's Coll Derry, St Patrick's Coll, Carlow Ireland; *Career* ordained Catholic priest 1966 then served at: West Norwood, Our Lady of The Rosary, St Josephs Roehampton; as first parish priest at the Church of St Vincents built new church house and complex; memb local church cncl, chm of govrs St Anselm Sch, chm Handicapped Childrens Tst; *Style—* The Rev Joseph Smith; St Vincents, Temple Hill, Dartford, Kent DA1 5HU (☎ 0322 79955)

SMITH, Keir; s of Walter Henry William Smith, of Northfleet, and Joan Irene, *née* Mitten; *b* 1 Feb 1950; *Educ* Univ of Newcastle upon Tyne, Chelsea Sch of Art; *Career* pt/t lectr: Sheffield Coll of Art 1976-79, Stourbridge Coll of Art; head of Sculpture Birmingham Poly Sch of Fine Art (formerly sr lectr in sculpture); exhibitions of sited sculpture incl: Realm of Taurus (Grizedale Forest Cumbria) 1979-80, Toward The Open Sea (South Hill Park Bracknell) 1983, A Small Dream of Freedom (Rufford Country Park) 1984, Fires That Burn Unseen (Ramsgate Library and Art Gallery) 1984, From My Window: The Vespers (Univ of Bath) 1985, Topsail (Baltic Wharf Bristol) 1986, The Dreaming Track (BR Peterborough) 1988, The Way of Clouds (Usher Gallery Temple Gdns Lincoln) 1990; one man exhibitions incl: Flint Axe (Hays Gallery Sheffield) 1977, Like Nimrod's Tower (Acme Gallery London) 1980, Ceres (Spectro Gallery Newcastle upon Tyne) 1981, Sailing Ancient Seas (Ceolfrith Gallery Sunderland and Ikon Gallery Birmingham) 1982, The Coniston Variations (Richard Demarco Edinburgh) 1983, Navigator (Rochdale Art Gallery, Aspex Gallery Portsmouth, Ramsgate Art Gallery, Chapter Arts Centre Cardiff) 1984-85, Towards The Iron Road (Bluecoat Gallery Liverpool) 1985, The Dust of Learning (Art Site Gallery Bath) 1986, Project Drawings 1983-87 (Posterngate Gallery Hull) 1987, The Dreaming Track (Laing Art Gallery Newcastle upon Tyne) 1989; contributed to various mixed exhibitions incl: Here and Now (from the collection of SE Arts) 1982, Sculptors and Modellers (Tate Gallery London) 1983, Feeling Through Form (Barbican Art Gallery Sculpture Court) 1986, Wonders Wild and New (Walton Hall Cheshire)

1986, Artists in National Parks (V & A Museum and Tour) 1988, Sculpture in the Close (Jesus Coll Cambridge) 1988, The Cutting Edge (Manchester City Art Gallery) 1989, Poets and Painters in Print (Arts Council and Tour) 1990; author of various articles and contrib to various jls 1974-89; *Style—* Keir Smith, Esq; 39 Lewis Rd, Istead Rise, Northfleet, Kent DA13 9JQ (☎ 0474 83321); 19 Florence Rd, New Cross, London SE14 6TW (☎ 081 692 6420)

SMITH, Kenneth David; s of Percival Smith (d 1985), and Doris Lillian, *née* Townsend; *b* 27 Feb 1944; *Educ* Beckenham Tech Sch, Beckenham Art Sch, S E London Tech Coll; *m* 28 Aug 1964, Pamela Jean Smith; 1 s (Ivan David b 26 Feb 1969), 2 da (Julia Hazel b 4 Dec 1966, Michelle Christine b 18 Aug 1970); *Career* designer; Elsom PackRoberts (chartered architects, and town planners) 1978-86, ptnr EPR Design Partnership 1985-89, md EPR Design Ltd 1988, Freeman: City of London 1981, Worshipful Co of Paviors (ctee memb 1988-); FCSD; *Recreations* art, theatre, music; *Clubs* Travellers'; *Style—* Kenneth Smith, Esq; Hartfield Cottage, 91 Harvest Bank Rd, West Wickham, Kent (☎ 081 462 1797); 90 Meddon St, Bideford, North Devon; EPR Design Ltd, 56-62 Wilton Rd, London SW1V 1DE (☎ 071 834 2299, fax 071 834 7524, telex 917940 PRLON G)

SMITH, Rev Lawrence Paul; s of Bernard Martin Smith, of Gravesend, and Audrey Doreen, *née* Smith; *Educ* St George's CE Sch Gravesend, Univ of London, Christ Church Coll Canterbury (CertED), Chichester Theol Coll (Certificate), Univ of Southampton (B Theol); *Career* head of religious studies Chartham Secdy Sch 1972-76, asst curate and deanery youth chaplain St John the Baptist Margate 1979-84, pastoral responsibility for Barfreston 1985, priest in charge Shepherdswell and Coldred 1985; rector: Eythorne and Waldershare 1984, Eythorne and Elvington with Waldershare and Barfreston with Shepherdswell and Coldred 1987-; memb: E Kent Counselling Assoc, community of L'Arche; parish cncllr Eythorne, chaplain to Little Ewell and Cana; *Recreations* travel, music, local history; *Style—* The Rev Lawrence Smith; St Peter and St Paul's Rectory, Barfreston Rd, Eythorne, Dover, Kent CT15 4AH (☎ 0304 830241)

SMITH, Martin Phillip; s of Eric Philip Stratton Smith, of Polperro, Cornwall, and Jean Catherine, *née* Martin; *b* 1 Jan 1951; *Educ* Chapel End Secdy Modern Sch, Coll of Law Chancery Lane; *m* 1 Sept 1973 (m dis); 1 s Benjamin Phillip b 8 June 1978), 1 da (Amy Deborah b 20 Sept 1980); *Career* legal exec: Birbeck Montague & Co 1967-72, Hart-Leverton and Roscoe-Phillips 1972-76, Hepburns 1976-80; admitted slr 1984; ptnr Messrs Bassets 1985- (joined 1980), NP 1988; memb: Law Soc Chancery Lane, Law Soc Rochester Chatham and Gillingham, Rochester Round Table, Mgmnt Ctee London Legal League, Notaries Soc; FInstLEx 1976; *Recreations* sport, reading, music, philately; *Clubs* The Roffen; *Style—* Martin Smith, Esq; The Mole Hole, 49 Heritage Drive, Gillingham, Kent ME7 3EQ (☎ 0634 574226); Bassets, 33/5 Balmoral Rd, Gillingham, Kent ME7 4QB (☎ 0634 575464, fax 0634 576516); Bassets, 156 High St, Rochester, Kent ME1 1ET (☎ 0634 400161, fax 0634 408251)

SMITH, (Gilbert Kenneth) Michael; s of Edward James Marston Alban Smith (d 1961), of Cambridge, and Ada Elsie Mary, *née* Pleasance; *b* 1 Jan 1922; *Educ* St Johns Coll Choir Sch Cambridge, Chesterton Sr Sch Cambridge; *m* 1 (m dis 1972), Mary Forbes, *née* Gibb (d 1989); 1 s (Robin Michael b 1967), 3 da (Linda b 1949, Alison Jane b 1966, Clare Louise b 1968); m 2, June 1975, Sylvia (formerly Ms Williams), da of Richard Martin (d 1969), of Bexleyheath; *Career* record librarian and broadcaster Br Forces Broadcasting Serv 1962-66; music prodr and freelance presenter: BBC Radio Medway 1971-, BBC Radio Kent 1971-; fndr and chm Cambridge Music Circle 1949-61, chm Gillingham Recorded Music Soc 1975-, vice chm Fedn of Recorded Music Socs 1987-; *Discographies:* D and E series (78 RPM gramophone recordings) HMV, L and LX series recordings (with Ian Coseus) Columbia, C Plum Label Series (with Frank Andrews) HMV; *Recreations* reading, concerts, writing; *Style—* Michael Smith, Esq; BBC Radio Kent, Sun Pier, Chatham, Kent ME4 4EZ (☎ 0634 830505)

SMITH, Michael Jeffrey Wellard; TD; s of Herbert Allnutt Smith, JP (d 1979), of Monkton, and Marjorie Kathleen Sara, *née* Hoey (d 1974); *b* 29 Aug 1918; *Educ* St Lawrence Coll Ramsgate; *m* 10 June 1947, Jean Elizabeth, da of Philip Tom Stanbury Brook (d 1982), of Sturry, nr Canterbury; 2 s (Julian Brook b 1 Nov 1949, Philip Michael Brook b 12 Oct 1951), 1 da (Joanna Catherine Rosso b 6 March 1960); *Career* War Serv 1939-46: France, Malta (Capt ADC to Maj-Gen Sir John Scobell, KBE, CMG, DSO and Maj-Gen Beak, VC, DSO, MC), Middle East, Aegean Islands (despatches 1943), Brunswick Oflag VIII F (POW); farmer 1934-85: breeder and exporter of first all white pedigree turkey flock in world; former JP; former chm: Kent Branch Br Turkey Fedn, SE Counties Dairy Shortham Soc, Thanet Ploughing Match Assoc, Canterbury Farmers' Lecture Club, Monkton Branch Conservatives; former vice chm Sandwich and Dist Growers Farmers Co-op; former memb: Br Turkey Fedn Mgmnt Ctee, Breeders Res Sub Ctee, NFU Poultry Ctee Kent, NFU Publicity Ctee Kent, Kent Co Agric Advsy Poultry Ctee, Eastry Rural DC; memb: MAFF Adhac Ctee, Monkton Parish Cncl; rep Thanet CPRE; pres: Monkton Conservatives, Minster Br Legion, Minster Playhouse; vice pres Monkton Sports Club, sch govr Monkton; *Recreations* golf, tennis, travel; *Clubs* Army and Navy; *Style—* Michael Smith, Esq, TD; Monkton Court Farms, Monkton, nr Ramsgate, Thanet, Kent CT12 4JR (☎ 0843 821227, fax 0843 47172)

SMITH, Muriel Winifred Goldwin; MBE (1977); da of Edgar Thomas Goldwin Smith (d 1941), and Mabel Mary, *née* Verinder (d 1962); *b* 28 Oct 1915; *Educ* James Allen's Girls' Sch Dulwich, Regent St Poly London; *Career* sec Whitelands Trg Coll 1939-44, worked in office of RHS at Wisley 1947-54, transfd to Miny of Agric Nat Fruit Trials at Wisley (moved to Brodgale Farm, responsible for compiling Nat Apple Register of the UK Faversham 1960), ret 1978; memb: ctee of local charity concerned with relieving the needy 1962- (sec and treas 1962-88), Tstees of Faversham Municipal Charities 1978-; asst sec Sheppey Gp; *Recreations* going to concerts, attending classes of further edcuation; *Style—* Miss Muriel Smith, MBE

SMITH, Norman Jack; s of Maurice Leslie Smith (d 1967), of Newton Abbot, Devon, and Ellen Dorothy, *née* Solly; *b* 14 April 1936; *Educ* Henley GS, Oriel Coll Oxford (MA), City Univ (MPhil); *m* 4 March 1967, Valerie Ann, da of Capt Arthur Ernest Frost (d 1978), of Ramsgate, Kent; 1 s (Malcolm b 1970); 1 da (Gail b 1974); *Career* market analyst Dexion Ltd 1957-60, comm evaluation mangr Vickers Ltd 1960-69, business devpt mangr Baring Bros and Co Ltd 1969-80; dir: Burnstisland Engineers and Fabricators Ltd 1974-76, Zenith Reed Ltd 1975-76, International Economic Services Ltd 1975-76, SAI Tubular Services Ltd 1983-88, Atkins Oil and Gas Engineering Ltd 1984-86, Smith Rea Energy Analysts Ltd 1985-, Gas Transmission Ltd 1989-, Smith Rea Energy Aberdeen Ltd 1990-; dir gen Offshire Supplies Office 1978-80; chm: British Underwater Engineering Ltd 1981-83, Mentor Engineering Consultants Ltd 1988-; md Smith Rea Energy Assocs Ltd 1983-; *Recreations* archaeology, walking, swimming, gardening; *Clubs* United Oxford and Cambridge Univ; *Style—* Norman Jack Smith, Esq; Smith Rea Energy Associates Ltd, Hunstead House, Nickle, Chartham, Canterbury, Kent CT4 7PL (☎ 0227 738822)

SMITH, Canon (Anthony Michael) Percival; s of Canon Kenneth Percival Smith (d 1951), and Audrey Mary, *née* Clarke (d 1972); *b* 5 Sept 1924; *Educ* Shrewsbury, Gonville and Caius Coll Cambridge (MA), Westcott House Cambridge; *m* 16 July 1950, Mildred Elizabeth, da of William Brown, OBE (d 1978), of Covington, Huntingdon, Cambridgeshire; 2 da (Susan Percival b 1951, Claire Percival b 1954); *Career* Lt Rifle Bde 1943-46 N Euro; domestic chaplain to Archbishop of Canterbury 1953-58; vicar: All Saints' Upper Norwood S London 1958-66, Yeovil 1966-72; rural dean of Murston 1968-72, prebendary of Wells Cathedral 1970-72, vicar St Mildred's Addiscombe Croydon 1972-80, archdeacon of Maidstone 1980-90; diocesan dir Ordinands 1980-, hon canon Canterbury Cathedral 1980; *Recreations* reading; *Style—* Canon A M P Smith

SMITH, Peter; s of Ernest Sidney Smith (d 1950), of Yotes Cottage, St Mary's Platt, Sevenoaks, Kent, and Ellen Smith (d 1967); *Educ* Sevenoaks Sch; *m* 1 (m dis), Christina De Vries; m 2, 17 Oct 1953, Pamela Mary, da of Cyril Leigh Francis, MM (d 1972), of 33 Goldington Ave, Bedford; 1 s (Richard Peter b 26 May 1954), 3 da (Jane Alexander b 28 July 1945, Susan Christina b 27 Oct 1947, Sally Ann b 1 May 1956); *Career* 2 Lt Royal W Kent Regt 1955; chm Borough Green Sawmills Ltd 1967-90 (md 1962); pres Full Gospel Business Mens Fellowship Maidstone Chapter 1989; memb: Boughton Monchelsea Parish Cncl 1972-90, Boughton Monchelsea PCC 1973-90, Rochester Deanery Synod 1982-87; church warden St Peter's Boughton Monchelsea; *Recreations* walking, racing; *Clubs* Lingfield Park, Folkestone Racing; *Style—* Peter Smith, Esq; The White House, Boughton Monchelsea, Maidstone, Kent (☎ 0622 743555); Borough Green Sawmills Ltd, Borough Green, Kent (☎ 0732 882012)

SMITH, Rev (Thomas) Roger; s of Thomas George Smith (d 1964), of Truro, Cornwall, and Constance Hannah, *née* Kelly; *b* 26 Feb 1948; *Educ* Truro Cathedral Sch, Univ of London, Christ Church Coll Canterbury, Canterbury Sch of Ministry; *Career* Hillside Sch Folkestone: sch master Eng and music 1969, head of year 1971; Wyndgate Sch Folkestone: dir of music 1972, head of fifth year 1977; curate of Lyminge Peddlesworth Stanford and Postling until 1985, rector of Biddendefn and Smorden 1985-; Dio of Canterbury: sec Bd of Ministry, bishop's offr for non-stipendiary ministry; conductor Tenterden Choral Soc, chm of govrs John Moyne Sch Biddenden; *Recreations* music, reading, antiques; *Style—* The Rev Roger Smith; The Rectory, Biddenden, Ashford, Kent TN27 8AH

SMITH, Dr (Carlyle) Wilhelm Ernst; JP (Margate); s of William August Carlyle Smith (d 1943), of Ceylon, and Maureen Victoria, *née* Ernst; *b* 14 July 1934; *Educ* St Thomas' Coll Mount Lavinia Colombo Ceylon, Univ of Colombo (MB BS); *m* 11 April 1959, Sheila June, da of Walwin Harold de Kretser (d 1975), of Melbourne, Australia; 3 da (Karel Jeanne b 26 June 1960, Beverley Anne b 7 Oct 1962, Sandra Michelle b 17 Sept 1966); *Career* hosp med appts Ceylon 1958-64, hosp NHS appts GB 1964-69, conslt chest physician Canterbury Kent 1969-70, conslt physician geriatric med Canterbury and Thanet Health Authy 1970-, assoc prof clinical gerontology servs Univ of Saskatoon Saskatchewan Canada 1987; memb: Rotary Club Ramsgate, BMA, Multiple Sclerosis Soc; FCRP; *Recreations* travel, wild life, flying (private pilot); *Style—* Dr Wilhelm Smith, JP; Ramsgate Hospital, West Cliff Rd, Ramsgate, Kent CT11 9NR (☎ 0843 581441)

SMITHERS, Prof Sir David Waldron; s of Sir Waldron Smithers, JP, MP (d 1954); *b* 17 Jan 1908; *Educ* Charterhouse, Clare Coll Cambridge; *m* 1933, Gwladys Margaret, *née* Angel; 1 s, 1 da; *Career* prof radiotherapy Inst of Cancer Res and Royal Marsden Hosp 1943-72; hon conslt radiotherapist; Brompton Hosp Diseases of the Chest, RN; kt Cdr SMOM 1972, KStJ; kt 1969; *Books* Jane Austen in Kent (1982), Therefore Imagine - The Works of Clemence Dane (1988), Not a Moment to Lose Some Reminiscences (1989), This Idle Trade: on doctors who were writers (1989); *Recreations* book collecting, growing roses, arts; *Style—* Prof Sir David Smithers; Ringfield, Knockholt, Kent (☎ 0959 32122)

SMYTH, David Michael; s of (Robert Samuel) Walter Smyth (d 1985), of 14 Cranmore Gardens, Belfast, NI, and (Beatrice) Aileen Barett, *née* Gould; *b* 11 Jan 1938; *Educ* Royal Belfast Academical Instn, Queen's Univ Belfast; *m* 21 Dec 1963 (Helen) Vanessa, da of Edward Winterbon (d 1953), of Pinner, Middx; 1 s (Fergus Carmichael b 1984), 2 da (Nicola Abigail b 1975, Gemma Siobhan b 1977); *Career* md Teleconnect Holdings Ltd 1980-86 (Teleplan Ltd 1979), chm and md HUS Publications Ltd 1988-; chm Malling and Dist C of C 1988-, pres Kent Business Fedn 1989-; *Recreations* travel, boating, reading; *Style—* David Smyth, Esq; 233 London Rd, W Malling, Kent ME19 5AD (☎ 0732 842613); Teleconnect Ltd, 2 High St, Aylesford, Kent; HUS Publications Ltd, Swan Mill, Mill Yard, W Malling, Kent ME19 6LP (☎ 0732 871000, fax 0732 844580)

SMYTH, (John) Rodney; s of John Clifford Smyth, of Heswall, Merseyside, and Norah Myfannwy, *née* Powell; *b* 23 Aug 1953; *Educ* Shrewsbury, Magdalene Coll Cambridge (MA); *Career* barr 1975-79; admitted slr 1980; asst slr: Holman Fenwick & Willan 1980-82, Lovell White Durrant (formerly Durrant Piesse) 1982-85 (ptnr 1985-); memb Law Soc; *Recreations* birdwatching, paintings; *Style—* Rodney Smyth, Esq; Brickhouse Farm, Main Rd, St Mary Hoo, Rochester, Kent ME3 8RP (☎ 0634 270 326); Lovell White Durrant, 65 Holborn Viaduct, London EC1A 2DY (☎ 071 236 0066, fax 071 248 4212, telex 887122 LWD G)

SNAITH, Peter Stuart; s of Gordon Stuart Snaith, of Laughton-En-Le-Morthen, S Yorks, and Eileen Joan, *née* Myers; *b* 1 April 1955; *Educ* Dinnington Camp Sch, Univ of Manchester (LLB); *m* 4 Oct 1980, Ruth Lorna, da of John Guy, of Gravesend, Kent; *Career* admitted slr 1979; ptnr Farmar & Moody 1980, co sec Aegis Development plc 1988-; ctee memb Otford and Dist Hist Soc, hon sec Kent Branch IOD; memb: Law Soc 1979, IOD 1984; *Recreations* sailing, squash; *Style—* Peter Snaith, Esq; Estate House, 2 Pembroke Rd, Sevenoaks, Kent TN13 1XR (☎ 0732 455012, fax 0732 460038)

SNELL, John Bernard; s of Harold Emley Snell (d 1966), of Suva, Fiji, and Edna Muriel, *née* Mackenzie (d 1943); *b* 28 March 1932; *Educ* St Peters Sch Cambridge NZ, Bryanston, Balliol Coll Oxford; *Career* various positions: London Transport Central Buses 1957-64, Br Railways Eastern Regn HQ 1964-67; md Romney Hythe & Dymchurch Railway plc 1972-; called to the Bar Lincoln's Inn 1972; *Books* Early Railways (1960), Britain's Railways Under Steam (1965), Railways: Mechanical Engineering (1970), One Man's Railway (1984); *Recreations* travel, photography; *Style—* John Snell, Esq; 15 Tudor Ave, Dymchurch, Kent; Romney Hythe & Dymchurch Railway plc, New Romney, Kent (☎ 0679 62353)

SNELLING, Michael Victor; s of Victor Frederick Snelling (d 1986), of Gloucester, and Vera Gwendoline Iris, *née* Bunyard; *b* 17 Dec 1945; *Educ* Ilford GS for Boys; *m* 7 June 1969, Heather June, da of Arthur Leonard Brown (d 1979), of Dagenham; 2 da (Abigail Louise b 27 May 1972, Kirsten Rachel b 21 Feb 1975); *Career* National Westminster Bank: employee since 1962, admin mangr Gravesend 1984, lending mangr Bromley 1987, corporate account exec Dartford 1989; borough cncllr (Meopham Ward) Gravesham, dep Mayor Gravesham 1990-91; govr Gravesend GS for Girls (treas Parents Assoc), exec memb Gravesend Cons Assoc; memb: Meopham Cons, Fin Ctee St John's Church Meopham; *Recreations* politics and squash (memb local squash league); *Style—* Michael Snelling, Esq; 5 Dormers Drive, Meopham, Kent DA13 0ES (☎ 0474 812404); National Westminster Bank plc, 12 High St, Dartford, Kent DA1 1DD (☎ 0322 76831, fax 0322 93226)

SOLOMON, John William; s of George William Solomon (d 1957), of Roehampton, London, and Ivy Louie (Pat), *née* Castle; *b* 22 Nov 1931; *Educ* Charterhouse; *m* 1, 25 July 1953 (m dis 1972), Anne, da of (David) Robert Thomas Lewis (d 1976), of Carshalton, Surrey; 3 s (Andrew b 1954, John b 1956, Gregory b 1964); m 2, 5 Dec 1972, Barbara Arthur; *Career* md William P Solomon Ltd 1957-83 (joined 1951), md John Solomon Inc Ltd 1983-; Tobacco Trade Benevolent Assoc: hon treas 1970-76, vice chm 1976-82, chm 1982-86, vice pres 1980-; chm Imported Tobacco Prods Advsy Ctee 1984-86 (1976-80 and 1990-); The Croquet Assoc: chm 1962-64, vice pres 1975-83, pres 1983-; nat titles in assoc croquet: ten GB open championship, ten GB mens championship, ten GB open doubles championship, one GB mixed doubles championship, nine times holder presidents cup, twice winner NZ open championship, twice winner NZ open doubles championship, four times winner championship of champions; Worshipful Co of Tobacco Pipe Makers and Tobacco Blenders: Freeman 1960, Liveryman 1962, memb Court 1974, Master 1989-90; *Books* Croquet (1966); *Recreations* music, golf, acting, croquet; *Clubs* Hurlingham; *Style—* John Solomon, Esq; Pipersfield, Rusper Rd, Newdigate, Dorking, Surrey RG5 5BX (☎ 0293 871320); John Solomon Inc Ltd, 6 Edenbridge Trade Centre, Hever Rd, Edenbridge, Kent TN8 5EA (☎ 0732 864222, fax 0732 866727)

SONDES, 5 Earl (UK 1880); Henry George Herbert Milles-Lade; also Baron Sondes (GB 1760) and Viscount Throwley (UK 1880); s of 4 Earl Sondes (d 1970, descended from 1 Baron Monson through the latter's 2 s, who was cr Baron Sondes) and Pamela, da of Lt-Col Herbert McDougall, of Cawston Manor, Norfolk; *b* 1 May 1940; *Educ* Eton; *m* 1, 1968 (m dis 1969), Primrose Anne, da of late Lawrence Stopford Llewellyn Cotter (s of 5 Bt); m 2 1976 (m dis 1981), Altgräfin Sissy, da of Altgraf Niklas zu Salm-Reifferscheidt-Raitz; *Style—* The Rt Hon The Earl Sondes; Stringman's Farm, Faversham, Kent

SOUTER, Hon Amanda Elizabeth; da and co-heiress presumptive of 25 Baron Audley; *b* 5 May 1958; *Style—* The Hon Amanda Souter; c/o Friendly Green, Cowden, nr Edenbridge, Kent TN8 7DU

SOUTHBY, Iris, Lady; Iris Mackay; *née* Heriot; da of late Lt-Col Granville Mackay Heriot, DSO, RM, and Marta Luisa, da of William Paynter; *m* 1, Brig Ian Charles Alexander Robertson; m 2, 1979, as his 4 w, Lt-Col Sir (Archibald) Richard Charles Southby, 2 Bt, OBE (d 1988); *Style—* Lady Southby; Greystone House, Stone, Tenterden, Kent; No 7 Bolur Ave, Kenilworth 7700, Cape, S Africa

SPANTON, (Harry) Merrik; OBE (1975); s of Henry Broadley Spanton (d 1947), of Canterbury, and Edith Jane, *née* Castle; *b* 27 Nov 1924; *Educ* Eastbourne Coll, Royal Sch of Mines London (BSc); *m* 3 Feb 1945, Mary Margaret, da of George Westcombe Hawkins (d 1958), of Bournemouth; 1 s (Graham Leslie b 1949); *Career* colliery mangr 1950, agent 1954, gp mangr 1956, dep area prodn mangr 1958, dep prodn dir Yorkshire 1960, asst area gen mangr 1962, gen mangr Kent 1964, area dir N Notts 1967-80, memb NCB 1980-85; dir: J H Sankey & Son (chm 1982-83), Br Mining Conslts 1980-87 (chm 1981-83), Compower 1981-85 (chm 1984-85), NCB (Coal Products) Ltd 1981-83, Br Fuel Co Ltd 1983-87; chm Br Coal Enterprise Ltd 1984-; memb: W Euro Coal Prodrs Assoc 1980-85, CBI Overseas Ctee 1981-85; jt sec Coal Indust Social Welfare Orgn 1983-85, vice pres Coal Trade Benevolent Assoc 1979- (chm 1978); Hon FIMinE 1986; ARSM 1945, CEng, CBIM 1979; *Recreations* travel, shooting; *Style—* Merrik Spanton, Esq, OBE; 4 Roselands Gardens, Canterbury, Kent CT2 7LP (☎ 0227 769356); Hobart House, Grosvenor Place, London SW1X 7AE (☎ 071 630 5304)

SPARKS, (John Robert) Godfrey; s of John Leo Sparks, of Cheltenham, and Winifred Mary, *née* Atkinson; *b* 21 April 1936; *Educ* Salesian Coll Oxford, Univ of Durham; *m* Valerie Christine, da of John Frederick Ody, of Margate, Kent; 2 s (Ian b 1965, Paul b 1966), 1 da (Emma b 1966); *Career* Cmmnd RAF Legal Branch 1959-61; articled clerk to His Hon Judge Harold Hewitt 1955-59, admitted slr 1959; sr ptnr Bassets Solicitors 1984- (ptnr 1984); lectr in law RN Supply Sch 1965-83; legal advsr Rochester CAB 1965-90; memb: Rochester Chatham and Gillingham Law Soc (pres 1983), Gillingham Rotary Club; Lord of the Manor of Bearsted; *Recreations* vintage motoring and engineering, antiques particularly porcelain; *Clubs* Aston Martin Owners, Jaguar Drivers, Manorial Society, RAF; *Style—* Godfrey Sparks, Esq; Mote Hall, Bearsted, Kent ME14 4EE (☎ 0622 30248); Bassets Solicitors, 156 High St, Rochester, Kent ME1 1ET (☎ 0634 400161, fax 0634 408251)

SPARKS, Hon Mrs (Juliet Jane Margaretta); *née* Moynihan; da of 2 Baron Moynihan, OBE, TD (d 1965); *b* 1934; *m* 1, 1958, Thomas Edwin Bidwell Abraham (d 1976); 2 s; m 2, 1978, Harry Hougham Sparks; *Style—* The Hon Mrs Sparks; Uplands, Bonnington, W Ashford, Kent

SPEAKMAN, Kenneth Floyd; s of Thomas Alcock Speakman (d 1939), of Barlaston, Staffs, and Ellen, *née* Floyd (d 1969); *b* 25 July 1912; *Educ* Orme Sch Newcastle-under-Lyme; *m* 7 March 1942, Joanna Marg, da of Alfred Edward Caswell (d 1923), of Sedgeley, Staffs; 1 da (Penny b 18 Sept 1944); *Career* served with The Buffs 1942, Inspecting Ordnance Offr RAOC 1943, Capt attached to MI 10 WO and Gen Staff Intelligence (specialising in enemy ammunition and explosives) India; slr; Borough of Wednesbury Staffs: articled to town clerk 1929-34, asst slr 1934-36; Borough of Ramsgate: asst slr 1936-48, town clerk 1948-74; hon sec: Ramsgate Station RNLI 1952-74, E Kent Deer Control Soc; memb: Assoc of Men of Kent and Kentishmen, Buffs Past and Present Assoc, Royal Br Legion, Thanet Pistol and Sporting Gun Club, Nat Rifle Assoc of America; *Recreations* shooting, deer stalking, study of firearms ammunition and ballistics; *Clubs* St Hubert of GB, Rotary (Ramsgate); *Style—* Kenneth Speakman, Esq; 15 Park Rd, Ramsgate, Kent CT11 7QN (☎ 0843 593571)

SPEAR, (Christopher) Eric; s of Thomas Christopher Spear, of Alsager, Cheshire, and Mary Spear (d 1979); *b* 23 Aug 1940; *Educ* Helsby GS, Bilston GS, Alsager Coll (Teacher's Cert), Crewe and Alsager Coll (BEd), Goldsmith's Coll London (MA); *m* 13 Aug 1966, Barbara Alice, da of Albert

John Hawke (d 1944), of Walthamstow; 2 da (Kathryn b 1969, Victoria b 1972); *Career* headmaster: Sidney Williams Sch Manzini Swaziland 1972-74, Istead Rise Jr Sch 1977-82, Staplehurst Co Primary Sch 1982-; pres Gravesham Headteachers' Assoc 1980; Kent Branch Nat Assoc of Headteachers: pres 1985-86, primary ctee chm; vice chm and primary rep Mid-Kent Cncl of Headteachers; *Books* Primary Sch Management in Action (contrib, 1987), Managing the Primary Classroom (contrib, 1988), Primary Headship in the 1990s (contrib, 1989), A Guide to School Management (contrib, 1990), From Forster to 44 The Story of Staplehurst School 1871-1944 (1990); *Recreations* gardening, walking, photography; *Style*— Eric Spear, Esq; Cobwebs, Mill Lane, Smardon, Ashford, Kent (☎ 0233 77350); Staplehurst CP School, Gybbon Rise, Staplehurst, Tonbridge, Kent (☎ 0580 891765 ext 891)

SPECTOR, Prof Roy Geoffrey; s of Paul Spector, and Esther, *née* Cohen; *b* 27 Aug 1931; *Educ* Univ of Leeds (MB ChB, MD), Univ of London (PhD, Dip Biochemistry); *m* 1960 (m dis 1979), Eva Freeman; 2 s (David Marshall b 1960, Colin Richard b 1964), 1 da (Gillian Sarah b 1962); *Career* sr lectr Paediatric Res Unit Guys Hosp 1961-66 (former lectr), prof applied pharmacology United Medical Schools of Guys and St Thomas' Hosps 1967-89 (former reader, sub dean for admissions 1975-89), visiting prof clinical pharmacology West China Med Univ Sichuan 1986-87, emeritus prof Univ of London 1989-; vice chm Br Univs Film and Video Cncl 1976-87, memb Dartford and Gravesham Health Authy 1988-89; memb RSM; FRCP, FRCPath; *Books* Psychiatry-Common Drug Treatments (1984), The Nerve Cell (1986), Textbook of Clinical Pharmacology (1986), Aids to Clinical Pharmacology (1989), Drugs People Use (1989), Therapeutics In Dentistry (1989); *Recreations* music, walking; *Style*— Prof Roy Spector; 60 Crescent Drive, Petts Wood, Orpington, Kent BR5 1BD (☎ 0689 875885); Drug Research Unit, Guy's Hospital, Newcomen St, London SE1 1YR (☎ 071 378 1772, fax 071 403 4409)

SPEED, (Herbert) Keith; RD (1967), MP (C) Ashford 1974-; s of Herbert Victor Speed (d 1971), of Bletchley, Bucks, and Alice Dorothy Barbara, *née* Mumford; *b* 11 March 1934; *Educ* Bedford Mod, RNC Dartmouth, RNC Greenwich; *m* 14 Oct 1961, Peggy Voss, da of Cedric Cyril Clarke (d 1983); 3 s (Herbert Mark Jeffrey b 1963, Crispin Nicholas b 1965 d 1967, Nicholas William b 1968), 1 da (Emma Jane b 1970); *Career* offr RN (incl Korean War) 1947-57, Lt Cdr RNR; sales mangr Amos (Electronics) 1957-60, mktg mangr Plysu Products 1960-65, CRD 1965-68; MP (C) Meriden 1968-74, asst govt whip 1970-71, Lord Cmmr Treasy 1971-72; parly under sec: Environment 1972-74, Def (RN) 1979-81; MP (C) Ashford 1974-; oppn spokesman: Environment 1975-77, Home Affrs 1977-79; parly conslt to Professional Assoc Teachers 1982-, memb Parly Assembly Cncl of Euro and Western Euro Union 1987-; chm: Westminster Communications Gp 1983-, Machine Tool Trades Assoc 1984-; dir Folkestone Water Co 1986-; patron: E Ashford Rural Tst, Ashford Branch BDA; memb Governing Cncl and Exec Ctee SPCK; *Books* Blueprint for Britain (1964), Sea Change (1982); *Recreations* classical music, opera, reading; *Clubs* Garrick; *Style*— Keith Speed, Esq, RD, MP; House of Commons, London SW1 1AA (☎ 071 219 4516)

SPENCE, Donald Ian Fleming; s of Brig I F M Spence, OBE, MC, TD (d 1966), of London, and Ruth May Bakewell, *née* Peacock (d 1960); *b* 18 Dec 1935; *Educ* Marlborough, Univ of Grenoble; *m* 8 May 1965, Bridget Mary, da of Maj-Gen M W Prynne, CB, CBE; 1 s (Robert b 14 June 1969), 1 da (Arabella b 16 Dec 1967); *Career* Nat Serv 3 Kings Own Hussars 1954-56; A Baumann & Co Kenya and Uganda 1960-65, dep head of res E D & F Man Ltd London 1983- (joined 1979); cncllr Sevenoaks Dist 1987-, Cons rep Penshurst and Fordcombe; *Recreations* cricket, bridge; *Clubs* MCC; *Style*— Donald Spence, Esq; South Lodge, Redleaf, Penhurst, Kent TN11 8HY (☎ 0892 870388); E D & F Man Ltd, Sugar Quay, Lower Thames St, London EC3R 6DU (☎ 071 626 8788)

SPENS, Dowager Baroness; Kathleen Annie Fedden; da of Roger Dodds, of Bath and Northumberland; *m* 1963, as his 2 w, 1 Baron Spens, KBE, PC (d 1973); *Style*— The Rt Hon the Dowager Lady Spens; Gould, Frittenden, Kent

SPENS, Hon Mallowry Ann; da of 2 Baron Spens; *b* 30 Sept 1949; *Career* int show jumper 1968-72, runs Equestrian Livery and Trg Yard; *Recreations* hunting; *Style*— The Hon Mallowry Spens; Missingham Farm, East Brabourne, Ashford, Kent (☎ 023 375 444)

SPENS, 3 Baron (UK 1959); Patrick Michael Rex; s of 2 Baron Spens (d 1984), and Joan Elizabeth, da of late Reginald Goodall; *b* 22 July 1942; *Educ* Rugby, Corpus Christi Coll Cambridge (MA); *m* 1966, Barbara, da of Rear Adm Ralph Fisher, CB, DSO, OBE, DSC; 1 s, 1 da (Hon Sarah b 1970); *Heir* s, Hon Patrick Nathaniel George Spens b 1968; *Career* md Henry Ansbacher & Co 1982-; FCA; *Style*— The Rt Hon Patrick Spens; Gould, Frittenden, Kent

SPERRING, Donald James; s of John Roland Sperring, of Sussex, and Edna Joan, *née* Ashton; *b* 5 March 1951; *Educ* Ravensbourne Kent; *m* 18 April 1981, Laura Jane, da of Desmond Champ; 3 s (Ben b 1983, Sam b 1985, Thomas b 1987); 1 da (Alice b 1990); *Career* dir Grandfield Rork Collins (advertising agency) 1981-86, md Young & Rubicam (advertising agency) 1986-; *Recreations* golf, squash; *Clubs* RAC; *Style*— Donald Sperring, Esq; 3 Maywood Close, Beckenham Place Park, Beckenham, Kent (☎ 081 650 9807); Les Fraisiers Sauvages, Avenue D'Auteuil, Le Touquet, France; Young & Rubicam, Greater London House, Hampstead Rd, London NW1

SPINKS, John Charles; s of Arthur Edward Charles Spinks (d 1977), of Dartford, Kent, and Lilian May, *née* Lovegrove; *b* 29 Aug 1943; *Educ* Dartford GS, Univ of London (BSc); *m* 31 Aug 1968, Sylvia Mary, da of Herbert William Bennett (d 1951), of Eynsford, Kent; 2 da (Katherine Mary b 1972, Rachel Lucy b 1973); *Career* CEng; Elliott Brothers (London) Ltd: mathematician and engr 1964, tech mangr Instrument and Controls Divs 1978, mangr Displays Div 1983, gen mangr 1985; asst md GEC Avionics Ltd 1987-; dir: Lear Astronics Corp Ca (USA), Developmental Sciences Corp Ca (USA); memb Royal Aeronautical Soc; *Recreations* golf, shooting, photography, travel; *Style*— John Spinks, Esq; Watermill House, Salts Lane, Loose, Maidstone ME15 0BD (☎ 0622 743108); GEC Avionics Ltd, Airport Works, Rochester, Kent ME1 2XX (☎ 0634 816940, fax 0634 832664)

SPINKS, Mary; da of William White (d 1952), and Mary White (d 1987); *b* 21 Feb 1947; *m* 1968, Henry Spinks; 1 s (Michael b 1975), 1 da (Susanna 1972); *Career* memb Gen Cncl Nat Asthma Campaign, memb Asthma Res Cncl, sponsor King's Med Res Tst, fndr and hon organiser of The Starlight Ball 1985-90 (in aid of the Asthma Res Cncl); *Recreations* family life, voluntary fund raising, armchair politics; *Style*— Mrs Mary Spinks; Tantons, Leesons Hill, Chislehurst, Kent BR7 6QH (☎ 0689 38388)

SPON-SMITH, Robin Witterick; s of Maj Alan Witterick Spon-Smith, and Joyce Margaret, *née* Bache (d 1988) ; *b* 11 Oct 1942; *Educ* Eltham Coll London; *m* 11 June 1966, Jennifer Dorothy, da of William Frederic Delabere Walker; 2 s (Jolyon b 1973, Phillip b 1975); *Career* 1 Bn London Scottish (TA) 1960-65; slr Supreme Court 1965; called to the Bar Inner Temple 1976; rec 1987; cncllr London Borough Bromley 1968-71, govr Eltham Coll Tst 1974-; Freeman City of London 1980; *Style*— Robin Spon-Smith, Esq; 1 Mitre Court Buildings, Temple, London EC4Y 7BS (☎ 071 353 0434, fax 071 353 3988)

SPOONER, Prof Frank Clyffurde; s of Harry Gordon Morrison Spooner (d 1967), and Ethel Beatrice, *née* Walden (d 1985); *b* 5 March 1924; *Educ* Christ's Coll Cambridge (BA, MA, PhD, LittD); *Career* WWII RNVR 1942-46, Sub Lt (S); served: HMS Shippigan, HMS Swiftsure, HMS Newfoundland, HMS Roame Head; Chargé de Recherches Centre Nat de la Recherche Sciëntifique Paris 1949-50, Allen scholar Univ of Cambridge 1951, fell Christ's Coll 1951-57; Cwlth Fund fell: Univ of Chicago 1955-56, Univs of NY Columbia and Harvard 1956-57, Ecole Pratique des Hautes Etudes Paris 1957-63; lectr: Ctee for Advanced Studies Univ of Oxford 1958-59, econs Harvard Univ 1961-62; Irving Fisher res prof of econs Yale Univ 1962-63; Univ of Durham: lectr 1963, reader 1964, prof 1966, emeritus prof of econ history 1985, Leverhulme fell 1977-79 and 1985-86; Prix Limantour, Lauréat de l'Académie des Sciences Morales et Politiques (1957); FRHistS 1970, FSA 1983; *Books* L'économie mondiale et les frappes monétaires en France, 1493-1680 (1956), The International Economy and Monetary Movements in France, 1493-1725 (1972), Risks at sea: Amsterdam insurance and maritime Europe, 1766-1780 (1983); *Recreations* music, walking, photography; *Clubs* United Oxford and Cambridge Univ; *Style*— Prof Frank Spooner, FSA; 31 Chatsworth Ave, Bromley, Kent BR1 5DP (☎ 081 857 7040); Dept of Economics, University of Durham, 23 Old Elvet, Durham DH1 3HY (☎ 091 374 2272)

SPRINGALL, Diana; da of William Gordon Alexander, CBE (d 1971), of Beckenham, Kent, and Stella Alice, *née* Fuller; *b* 16 Sept 1938; *Educ* Lillesden Sch Hawkhurst, Goldsmiths' Coll Sch of Art, Univ of London; *m* 9 July 1960 (m dis 1979), Ernest Thomas Springall; 2 s (Richard Gordon b 29 Nov 1965, Lawrence Thomas b 5 Nov 1969); *Career* teacher of art craft and needlecraft West Heath Sch for Girls Sevenoaks 1961-63, lectr in embroidery Maidstone Coll of Art 1963-68, princ lectr in art Stockwell Coll of Educn Bromley 1963-80, visiting lectr Manchester Poly 1963-80, external examiner Univs of Bath and Birmingham 1968-80, conslt BBC 2 series Embroidery 1980, freelance maker of embroidered panels hangings and vestments, lectr tours to USA and Canada 1973-78 and 1982; exhibitions incl: one man exhibition (Foyles Art Gallery) 1981, Twelve British Embroiderers (Osaka and Tokyo) 1985, Art 87 (Business Design Centre London) 1987, one man show (Smiths Gallery Covent Garden) 1988; listed as conslt under DTI Design Initiative; life memb Embroiderers' Guild (chm 1978-85), chm and fell Soc of Designer Craftsmen 1987-90, panel lectr V and A Museum; *Books* Canvas Embroidery (1969), Embroidery (1980), Twelve British Embroiderers (1984), Design for Embroidery (1988); *Recreations* gardening, travel; *Style*— Mrs Diana Springall; Oast Cottage, Park Lane, Kemsing, Sevenoaks, Kent TN15 6NU (☎ 0732 61501)

SPURLING, Nigel Roy; s of Geoffrey Frank Spencer Spurling, of Nuffield, Oxfordshire, and Betty, *née* Hayne; *b* 12 March 1943; *Educ* Queen Marys Sch Basingstoke; *m* 27 July 1968, Pauline Joy, da of Henry Arthur Roberson (d 1982); 1 s (Jonathan Henry Charles b 20 July 1973), 1 da (Deborah Louise b 10 July 1970); *Career* Barclays Bank plc: asst mangr Birmingham New St

1970-72, asst mangr Birmingham High St 1972-75, asst dist mangr Reading local head office 1975-79, branch mangr Ashford Kent 1979-88, business centre mangr Canterbury 1988-; memb: Kent CCC, Canterbury Industl Consultative Cncl, Canterbury Branch NFU; *Recreations* cricket, tennis, skiing, family; *Style—* Nigel Spurling, Esq; Barclays Bank plc, Barclays Business Centre, 9 St George's St, Canterbury, Kent CT1 2JX (☎ 0227 451789, fax 0227 451789)

SPURWAY, (Marcus) John; s of Marcus Humphrey Spurway, of Goudhurst, Kent, and Eva, *née* Mann (d 1980); *b* 28 Oct 1938; *Educ* Archbishop Tenison's Sch Croydon; *m* 23 Oct 1963, Christine Kate, da of Robert Charles Townshend (d 1981), of Canterbury; 2 s (Marcus b 1967, Edward b 1969); *Career* Nat Serv 4 Regt RHA; insur broker; dir Insur Brokers Div Morgan Reid & Sharman Ltd (Lloyd's Brokers, formerly B & C Aviation Insurance Brokers); specialist in aviation insur; *Style—* John Spurway, Esq; Lomeer, Common Rd, Sissinghurst, Kent; 6 Alie St, London E1 8DD (☎ 071 488 9000, fax 071 480 6914, telex 8811401 and 8954576 COMORE G)

SQUIRES, Leslie Mervyn; s of Capt Leslie Squires (d 1971), of Folkestone, Kent, and Antoinette, *née* Georgiou; *b* 8 July 1947; *Educ* Gordon Sch; *m* 5 May 1971, Jane Barkby, da of Victor Harold Pochin, of Dartford, Kent; 1 s (Jonathan b 25 May 1975), 1 da (Joanna b 1 Sept 1978); *Career* civil servant in Civil Serv 1964-67, administrative offr Lloyds Register of Shipping 1967-69, New business exec Lloyds & Scottish Ltd 1969-72, regnl Mangr Western Trust & Savings 1972-74, dir Jonathon Wren & Co Ltd 1975-79, md Jonathon Wren City 1977-79, gen mangr Financial Recruitment 1979-81, dir and fndr Anderson Squires 1981-; FInstSMM 1980, FInstD 1986, MBIM 1986; *Recreations* travel, current affairs, sport, music; *Clubs* Rugby Football, Bishopsgate Ward; *Style—* Leslie Squires, Esq

STACEY, Hon Mrs (Anne Caroline Mary); *née* Bridgeman; e da of 2 Viscount Bridgeman; *b* 30 July 1932; *Educ* Univ of Reading (BSc); *m* 1955, Rev Nicolas David Stacey, *qv*, er s of David Stacey, of Knaphill Manor, nr Woking (whose mother was Beatrice, sis of 1 Baron Brassey of Apethorpe); 1 s (David Robert b 1958), 2 da (Caroline Jill b 1956, Mary Elizabeth b 1961); *Career* ptnr English Homes and Country Tours; memb Nat Tst Regnl Ctee Kent and E Sussex 1984-90; *Style—* The Hon Mrs Stacey; The Old Vicarage, Selling, Faversham, Kent (☎ 022 785 833)

STACEY, Air Vice-Marshal John Nichol; CBE (1972), DSO (1945), DFC (1943); s of Capt Herbert Chambers Stacey (d 1966), of Rhydyfantwn, Moylegrove, nr Cardigan, S Wales, and Brittannia May, *née* Davies (d 1972); *b* 14 Sept 1920; *Educ* Whitgift Middle Sch; *m* 29 April 1950, Veronica, da of Air Vice-Marshal Harry Vivian Satterly, CB, CBE, DFC (d 1982); 2 da (Amanda (Mrs Reuter) b 1953, Caroline (Mrs Russell) b 1956); *Career* served WWII 4 operational tours incl Co 160 Liberator Sqdn Ceylon as Wing Cdr 1944-45 (despatches 3 times), asst air attaché Washington DC 1947-48, RAF Staff Coll Bracknell 1949, instructional staff Bracknell 1958-60, CO Royal Malayan AF 1960-63, CO RAF Station Laarbruch Germany 1963-66, Air Offr cmdg the ATC and Air Cadets 1968-71, AOA Air Support Cmd 1974-75, ret RAF 1975; dir Stanham Housing Assoc 1976-82; memb: Tunbridge Wells Health Authy 1981-85, RAF Housing Assoc 1982-86, Tunbridge Wells and Dist Housing Assoc 1989-; tstee: Housing Assoc Charitable Tst 1978-86, Bedgebury Sch Governing Cncl 1983-, Tunbridge Wells Cancer Help Centre 1983-; MBIM 1966-82; Johan Mangku Negara Malaya 1963; *Recreations* golf, DIY; *Clubs* RAF, Dale Hill Golf, Lamberhurst Golf; *Style—* Air Vice-Marshal John Stacey, CBE, DSO, DFC; Riseden Cottage, Riseden, Goudhurst, Kent TN17 1HJ (☎ 0580 211 239)

STACEY, Prof Kenneth Arthur; s of Arthur William Stacey, of Brighton (d 1933), and Edith Beatrice, *née* Mancktelow (d 1976); *b* 20 June 1927; *Educ* Verdean Sch Brighton, Queen Mary Coll London (BSc), Imperial Coll London (PhD); *m* 1, 1959, Josepha de Groot (d 1963); m 2, 31 Dec 1966, Rosalie Marian, da of Harold Boynton Stoddard, of Lakewood, New Jersey; 1 s (b 1961); *Career* sr res fell Univ of Sussex 1965-70, prof Univ of Kent 1970-; memb: Patrixbourne Parish Cncl 1987-, Governing Body Christ Church Coll Canterbury; FIBiol 1972; *Books* Light-Scattering in Physical Chemistry (1956); *Recreations* gardening; *Style—* Prof Kenneth Stacey; Joslet, Keepers Hill, Patrixbourne, Canterbury, Kent CT4 5BT; Biological Laboratory, University of Kent at Canterbury, Canterbury, Kent (☎ 0027 764000)

STACEY, Rev Nicolas David; s of David Henry Stacey (d 1986), and Isobel Ewem *née* Part; *b* 27 Nov 1927; *Educ* RNC Dartmouth, St Edmund Hall Oxford (BA), Cuddesdon Theol Coll Oxford; *m* 19 July 1955, Anne Caroline Mary, *qv*, eld da of 2 Viscount Bridgeman, KBE, CB, DSO, MC, JP (d 1982); 1 s (David Robert b 10 May 1958), 2 da (Caroline Jill b 28 Aug 1956, Mary Elizabeth b 15 May 1961); *Career* Midshipman RN 1945-46, Sub Lt 1946-48; asst curate St Marks Portsmouth 1953-58, domestic chaplain to Bishop of Birmingham 1958-60, rector of Woolwich 1960-68, dean London Borough of Greenwich 1965-68, dep dir Oxfam 1968-70; dir social services: London Borough of Ealing 1971-74, Kent CC 1974-85; social services conslt 1985-88, dir Aids Policy Unit 1988-89, ptnr English Homes and Country Tours, govr Reeds Sch Cobham, dir Faversham Oyster Co, patron Terrence Higgins Tst, hon sr memb Darwin Coll Univ of Kent, chm Youth Call 1981, dep chm Television South Charitable Tst 1988, six preacher Canterbury Cathedral 1984-90; int sprinter 1948-52, Br Empire Games 1949, Olympic Games 1952, pres Oxford Univ Athletic Club 1951, capt Combined Oxford and Cambridge Athletics Team 1951; *Books* Who Cares (autobiography, 1971); *Recreations* skiing, golf; *Clubs* Beefsteak, Vincents (Oxford), Royal St Georges Golf (Sandwich); *Style—* The Rev Nicolas Stacey; The Old Vicarage, Selling, Faversham, Kent (☎ 0227 752 833)

STACPOOLE, John Wentworth; s of George Wentworth Stacpoole (d 1983), of The Mount, St Leonards-on-Sea, and Mina Gascoigne Butt, *née* Furrel, of Stick Hill Edenbridge; *b* 16 June 1926; *Educ* Sedbergh, Magdalen Coll Oxford (MA); *m* 4 Sept 1954, (Sophia) Charmian, da of late John Percival Bishop; 1 s (Harold Adam (Tom)), 1 da (Miranda Jane (Min)); *Career* Army 1944-47, Lt Assam Regt (private 1944, cadet 1946, 2 Lt 1946, Lt 1947); Colonial Office 1951-68 (private sec to Sec of State 1964-65); DHSS: joined 1968, under sec 1973, dep sec 1979-82; memb Maidstone Health Authy 1982-90; Stansted and Fairseat Soc: chm 1984-86, sec 1986-; chm Maidstone Hospice Appeal 1987-; treas and sec Stansted Almshouse; *Recreations* walking, reading, sketching; *Style—* John Stacpoole, Esq; Fairseat Lodge, Fairseat, nr Sevenoaks TN15 7LU (☎ 0732 822201)

STAINER, Michael; s of Peter Stainer (agent to the Duke of Bedford's Estates 1951-67), of The Grand, Folkestone, and Gretl Ilse Emmi Ruth, *née* Gosewisch; *b* 20 Dec 1947; *Educ* Bedford Sch; *Career* CA; Touche Ross & Co 1966-73; own practice 1973-; chm and md The Grand Hotel Ltd 1976-; Freeman City of London 1983, memb Worshipful Co of CAs; *Style—* Michael Stainer, Esq; The Grand, Folkestone, Kent CT20 2LR (☎ 0303 56789)

STAINTON-JAMES, Ian Charles; s of Lionel Charles Stainton-James (d 1977), of Sydenham, and Eileen Olivia, *née* Latham; *b* 21 May 1943; *Educ* St Dunstan's Coll, Trinity Coll Dublin, Univ of London Inst of Educn; *m* 25 July 1970, Angela Margaret, da of Captain Eric Musgrove-Wethey, of The Laurels, Ladock, nr Truro, Cornwall; 1 s (Mark b 21 April 1973), 2 da (Claire b 6 August 1974, Harriet b 22 July 1983); *Career* asst master: Forest Hill Sch 1967-71, St Dunstan's Coll Catford 1971-74; dep head St Dunstan's Sch Burham-on-Sea 1974-76, dir of studies Brighton Coll Jr Sch 1976-80, headmaster Underhill Preparatory Sch 1980-; cncl memb IAPS 1990- (memb 1982-), chm Sutton Valence Hockey Club; vice pres: Old Dunstorians RFC, St Agnes RFC; *Recreations* hockey, sailing, rugby football, golf, music; *Clubs* Bewl Valley Sailing, Killiow Golf; *Style—* Ian Stainton-James, Esq; The Old Manse, St Agnes, Cornwall; Underhill Preparatory School, Chart Sutton, Maidstone, Kent ME17 3RF (☎ 0622 842117)

STALLARD, Hon Richard; o s of Baron Stallard (Life Peer); *b* 1945; *Educ* Richard Acland Sch London; *m* 1969, Carol, da of William Packman, of Swanley, Kent; 1 s, 1 da; *Style—* The Hon Richard Stallard

STANDEN, Ian Gordon; s of Gordon Standen (d 1983), of Tolehurst Farm, Cranbrook, and Beryl, *née* Dowding; *b* 8 May 1949; *Educ* St Lawrence Coll Ramsgate Kent, RAC Cirencester Glos (Dip); *m* 1, 1972 (m dis 1976), Paula; m 2, Aug 1977, Caroline, da of John Brown, of Holders Farm, Buxted, Sussex; 1 s (Jack Ian Gordon Dudley b 4 May 1987), 1 da (Melissa Polly Talbot b 5 Nov 1982); *Career* chartered surveyor; fndr: Bumbles Farm Shop 1981, Cranes 1983, Bax Standen 1989; dir GA Property Services 1986-89; memb: Ctee League of Gentlemen, Purchasers' Soc, Cncl Br Inst of Agric Conslts (fell), Weald of Kent Preservation Soc; FRICS (ARICS); *Recreations* golf, skiing, shooting, tennis; *Clubs* Rye Golf, Royal St George's Golf, Farmers; *Style—* Ian Standen, Esq; Ockley, Hawkhurst, Kent TN18 4EX (☎ 0580 752290); Bax Standen, The Estate Office, Cranbrook, Kent TN17 3HD (☎ 0580 713250, fax 0580 712339)

STANLEY, Rt Hon Sir John Paul; PC (1984), MP (C) Tonbridge and Malling Feb 1974-; s of Harry Stanley (d 1956), and Maud Stanley; *b* 19 Jan 1942; *Educ* Repton, Lincoln Coll Oxford; *m* 1968, Susan Elizabeth Giles; 2 s, 1 da; *Career* Cons Res Dept (Housing) 1967-68, res assoc IISS 1968-69, fin exec RTZ Corporation 1969-74, memb Parly Select Ctee Nationalised Industs 1974-76, PPS to Rt Hon Margaret Thatcher 1976-79, min for Housing and Construction with rank of min of state (DOE) 1979-83, min of state for the Armed Forces MOD 1983-87, min of state for NI 1987-88; kt 1988; *Recreations* music, arts, sailing; *Style—* The Rt Hon Sir John Stanley, MP; House of Commons, London SW1

STAVELEY, Adm of the Fleet Sir William Doveton Minet; GCB (1984, KCB 1981); s of Adm Cecil Minet Staveley, CB, CMG (d 1934), and Margaret Adela, *née* Sturdee (d 1960); gs of Gen Sir Charles Staveley and of Adm of the Fleet Sir Doveton Sturdee Bt, of First World War Battle of the Falkland Islands fame; *b* 10 Nov 1928; *Educ* West Downs, Winchester, RNC Dartmouth, RNC Greenwich; *m* 1954, Bettina Kirstine, da of L R A Shuter (d 1960); 1 s (Richard), 1 da (Juliet); *Career* joined RN 1942, served HM Yacht Britannia 1957, subsequently in Far East Middle East and Mediterranean, dir Naval Plans Naval Staff 1974-76, Flag Offr 2 Flotilla 1976-77, Flag Offr Carriers and Amphibious Ships and NATO Cdr Carrier Striking Gp 2 1977-78, COS to C-in-C Fleet 1978-80, Vice Chief of Naval Staff 1980-82, Allied C-in-C Channel, C-in-C Eastern Atlantic Area and C-in-C Fleet 1982-85, Chief Naval Staff and First Sea Lord 1985-89, First and Princ Naval ADC to HM The

Queen 1985-89; chm elect Royal London Hosp and Assoc Community Health Servs NHS Tst; tstee and dir: Chatham Historic Dockyard Tst, Florence Nightingale Museum; memb: Court Univ of Kent, London Advsy Ctee on English Heritage; govr Sutton Valence Sch; Freeman City of London, Liveryman Worshipful Co of Shipwrights, yr bro Trinity House; CBIM; *Recreations* gardening, shooting, riding, restoring antique furniture, fishing; *Clubs* Boodle's, RNSA; *Style*— Adm of the Fleet Sir William Staveley, GCB; c/o Lloyds Bank, 83 High St, Sevenoaks, Kent TN13 1LG

STEBLES, Andrew Gordon; s of Capt George Douglas Stebles (d 1983), and Stella Swan (d 1987); *b* 12 March 1950; *Educ* Queen Elizabeth GS Wakefield, Downing Coll Cambridge (BA, MA); *m* 20 Sept 1975, Diane Vivien, da of Gordon William Samuel Johnson of Bromely, Kent; 3 s (Paul Michael Alexander b 15 Aug 1979, Mark Christopher James b 9 July 1981, Jonathan Simon Philip b 17 Mar 1986) ; *Career* Blue Circle Industries plc: joined 1972, chief programmer 1978-80, systems assur and standards mangr 1980-83; data admin mangr 1983-85; database admin mangr Corp of Lloyds 1985-86, sr devpt mangr Lloyds Bank plc 1986; *Recreations* cycling, swimming, gardening; *Style*— Andrew Stebles, Esq

STEED, David; s of Norman Harold Steed, MBE, of Grove, Nr Canterbury, and Margaret, *née* Cloke; *b* 3 Feb 1945; *Educ* St Lawrence Coll Ramsgate, Kent Farm Inst; *m* 4 May 1986, Edwina Ruth Irene, da of Gordon Edwin Sampson (d 1988), of Ramsgate; 1 s (Piers David b 6 April 1976), 1 da (Alexandra May b 12 Sept 1972); *Career* managing ptnr N H & D Steed 1972-; Thanet Branch NFU: chm 1981-83, spokesman for Nitrate Issue; columnist The English Farmer 1984-86; memb Round Table 1972-83; pres Thanet Archaeological Soc 1985-; chm: Manston Parish Cncl 1986-, Thanet Tst for Archaeology 1988-; memb: Consultative Cncl Invicta Radio, Exec Ctee Abbeyfield; *Recreations* shooting, travel, genealogy; *Clubs* Kent and Canterbury (ctee memb 1988-), Canterbury Farmers, East Kent C of C, Wingham Wheat (chm 1989-); *Style*— David Steed, Esq

STEELE, John Roderic; CB (1978); s of Harold G Steele (d 1968), of Wakefield, and Doris, *née* Hall (d 1986); *b* 22 Feb 1929; *Educ* Queen Elizabeth GS Wakefield, Queen's Coll Oxford (MA); *m* 22 Sept 1956, (Margaret) Marie, da of Joseph Stevens (d 1963), of Ingleton, Yorks; 2 s (Richard b 1957, David b 1963), 2 da (Alison b 1959, Elisabeth b 1965); *Career* civil serv; asst princ Miny of Civil Aviation 1951-54, private sec to Parly sec 1954-57; princ: road tport div 1957-60, sea tport 1960-62, shipping policy 1962-64; asst sec shipping policy Bd of Trade 1964-67, cnsllr (shipping) Br Embassy Washington 1967-71, asst sec (civil aviation div) DTI 1971-73; under sec: (space div) 1973-74, shipping policy 1974-75; gen div Bd of Trade 1975-76 (dep sec 1976-80), dep sec Dept Indust 1980-81, DG tport Cmmn of Euro Communities 1981-86; tport conslt 1986-; FCIT; *Recreations* cricket, tennis, opera; *Clubs* United Oxford and Cambridge Univ, Philippics; *Style*— John Steele, Esq, CB; 7 Kemerton Rd, Beckenham, Kent; Sq Ambiorix 30, BTE 30, 1040 Bruxelles, Belgium; c/o Prisma Transport Consultants, 4 Rue Charles Bennet Case 269, 1211 Geneve 12, Switzerland

STEELE, Thomas (Tom); JP (1978); s of Thomas Steele (d 1948), and Elizabeth (d 1936); *b* 12 June 1935; *Educ* Whitehaven GS Cumbria, St Mary's Coll Twickenham (CertEd); *m* 3 April 1961, Janet Lesley, da of Leslie Law; 1 s (Timothy David b 18 March 1962), 1 da (Jennifer Catherine b 8 April 1965); *Career* teacher: LCC 1958-62, St Vincent's Sch Whitstable 1962-76 (dep head 1966-76); head of remedial dept Archbishop's C of E Secdy Sch Canterbury 1976-; memb: Whitstable Round Table 1969-75, Whitstable Rotary Club 1973-76; co cncllr Canterbury 1977-80 and 1983-, Sheriff of Canterbury 1984-85, Mayor of Canterbury 1988-89, First Lord Mayor of Canterbury 1988; *Recreations* rugby, country walking, real ale, family; *Style*— Tom Steele, Esq, JP; 23 River Court, Chartham, Canterbury, Kent CT4 7JN (☎ 0227 731357); Archbishop's School, St Stephen's Hill, Canterbury, Kent (☎ 0227 765805)

STEIN, George Stanley; s of Stephen Stein, and Susan Stein; *b* 23 March 1944; *Educ* Hendon Co GS, UCL (BSc), UCH (MB BS), Kingston Coll, Maudsley Hosp, MRCP, MRCPsych; *m* 27 July 1969, Suzanna Eugenie Siegliende Isabella, da of William Miller (d 1979); 2 s (Benjamin b 5 June 1979, Joseph b 3 Sept 1983); *Career* RCPsych Bronze Medal 1980, sr lectr in psychiarty KCH 1981, conslt psychiatrist Bromley AHA 1981, res centres an post natal depression, pubns on triptophan metabolism in the maternity blues; *Recreations* music; *Style*— George Stein, Esq

STEPHENS, Cedric John; s of Col James Edward Stephens (d 1974), of Truro, Cornwall, and Hilda Emily Stephens (d 1972); *b* 13 Feb 1921; *Educ* Univ of London (BSc); *Career* transmission devpt engr STC 1945-51, def researcher ADE Fort Halstead and RAE Farnborough 1951-60, dir (space) Miny of Aviation 1961-64, memb Cncl (chm Tech Ctee) Euro Launcher Devpt Orgn 1962-64, chm Tech Ctee Euro Orgn on Satellite Communications 1964, IDC 1965, dir Signals Res and Devpt Estab MOD 1966-67, chief scientist and dir gen res Home Office 1969-73 (chief scientific advsr 1967-69), memb Def Scientific Advsy Cncl, chm Civil Serv Engrg Graduate Selection Bds 1973-75, memb Electronics Divnl Bd IEE 1973, dir Exford (Highcliffe) Ltd 1987-; called to the Bar Gray's Inn 1971; memb: Forensic Sci Soc, memb Hon Soc Grays Inn; CEng, FIEE, FRAeS; *Recreations* playing viola; *Style*— Cedric Stephens, Esq; 6 Newlyn Rd, Welling, Kent DA16 3LH; 7 Exeter Court, Wharncliffe Rd, Christchurch, Dorset BH23 5DF (☎ 081 856 1750)

STEPHENS, John Lindsay; s of Rev Grosvenor Stephens, of 9 Leasingham Gardens, Bexhill on Sea, E Sussex, and Olive, *née* Voysey-Martin (d 1987); *b* 23 July 1951; *Educ* Christ's Hosp, Lanchester Poly (BA); *m* 30 Aug 1975, Nicola Elizabeth (Nikki), da of Neville Brouard, of Les Eturs, Catel, Guernsey, CI; 1 s (David b 1982), 1 da (Joanna b 1980); *Career* admitted slr 1977; ptnr Simmons and Simmons; memb: Nat Tst, Residents Action Gp WABF, Weald of Kent Preservation Soc, Law Soc; *Recreations* family, music, food and wine, photography, tennis, fitness training; *Clubs* Frittenden Tennis; *Style*— John Stephens, Esq; 14 Dominion St, London EC2M 2RJ (☎ 071 628 2020, fax 071 588 4129, telex 888562 SIMMON G)

STEPHENS, Malcolm George; s of Frank Ernest, and Annie Mary Janet, *née* Macqueen; *b* 14 July 1937; *Educ* St Michael and All Angels and Shooters Hill GS, St John's Coll Oxford (BA); *m* 5 Dec 1975, Lynette Marie, da of John Patrick Caffery (d 1972); *Career* Dip Serv: joined 1953, Ghana 1959-62, Kenya 1963-65, exports credits guarantee dept 1965-82, princ 1970, seconded to Civil Service Staff Coll as dir of economics and social admin courses 1971-72, asst sec 1974, estab offr 1977, under sec 1978, head project gp 1978-79, princ fin offr 1979-82; int fin dir Barclays Bank International 1982, export fin dir and dir Barclays Export Servs with Barclays Bank 1983-87; memb: Overseas Projects Bd 1985-87, British Overseas Trade Bd 1987; FIB, Fell Inst of Export; *Recreations* gardening, reading; *Clubs* Overseas Bankers, Travellers'; *Style*— Malcolm Stephens, Esq; 111 Woolwich Road, Bexleyheath, Kent DA7 4LP (☎ 081 303 6782); ECGD, PO Box 272, Export House, 50 Ludgate Hill, London EC4M 7AY (☎ 071 382 7004)

STEPHENSON, Geoffrey Charles; s of Edmund Charles Stephenson, and Hilda Rose, *née* Bates; *b* 19 Aug 1943; *Educ* Bromley GS; *m* 3 Sept 1966, Margaret, da of Frank Wirth (d 1989); 1 s (Alistair James b 2 May 1974), 2 da (Louise Elizabeth b 26 March 1970, Rebecca Dorothy b 8 Feb 1972); *Career* Legal and General Assurance Society Ltd 1964-72; called to the Bar Grays Inn 1971; FCII; *Recreations* sport; *Clubs* Sundridge Park Lawn Tennis and Squash Rackets (chm), British Sub-Aqua; *Style*— Geoffrey Stephenson, Esq; 8 New Square, Lincolns Inn, London WC2 (☎ 071 242 4986, fax 071 406 1166, car 0836 775 208)

STEPHENSON, Prof Geoffrey Michael; s of Maurice Stephenson (d 1958), of Kenton Harrow Middx, and Laura, *née* Sharp (d 1975); *b* 16 April 1939; *Educ* Harrow County GS, Univ of Nottingham (BA, PhD); *m* 1, 14 April 1962 (m dis 1981), Marguerite Ida, da of James Lindsay (d 1986), of Kettering; 1 s (Lawrence James b 1963), 1 da (Katherine b 1965); m 2, 9 July 1982 (m dis 1987) Gillian Sarah, da of Geoffrey Wade, of Cheadle Hulme; m 3, 10 Jan 1989, Jennifer Anne, da of Frederick Williams, of St Melton, Cardiff; 1 s (David Field William b 1989); *Career* res psychologist Balderton Hosp 1960-61, lectr in psychology Univ of Keele 1962-66, reader in psychology Univ of Nottingham 1976-78 (lectr 1966-74, sr lectr 1974-76), prof and dir of Social Psychology Res Unit Univ of Kent at Canterbury 1978- (dir Inst of Social Psychology 1986-); ed: British Journal of Social Psychology 1978-84, Social Behaviour International Journal 1986-; memb: Br Psychological Soc 1960- (chm social psychology section 1977-80), Euro Assoc of Experimental Social Psychology 1972- (pres 1984-87); chm IBA advertising advsy ctee 1988-; FBPsS 1980-; *Books* The Development of Conscience (1966), The Social Psychology of Bargaining (with Ian Morley, 1976), Industrial Relations: A Social Psychological Approach (with C J Brotherton, 1978), Progress in Applied Social Psychology Vols 1 and 2 (jtly, 1981 and 1983), Environmental Social Psychology (jt ed, 1988), Introduction to Social Psychology: A European Perspective (jt ed, 1989); *Recreations* sailing, music (violin playing), cooking; *Clubs* LSO, Kent CCC; *Style*— Prof Geoffrey Stephenson; Institute of Social and Applied Psychology, The University, Canterbury, Kent (☎ 0227 764000, telex 965449, fax 0227 763674)

STEPHENSON, (Augustus) William; s of Sir Guy Stephenson, CB (d 1930), and Gwendolen, *née* Talbot (d 1960); *b* 1 March 1909; *Educ* Harrow; *m* 1, 18 April 1939 (m dis 1952), (Mary) Gloria, da of Maj William La Touche Congreve, VC, DSO, MC (ka 1917); 3 s (Tim b 1940, Martin b 1942, Ben b 1948); m 2, 21 Sept 1962, Elizabeth, da of Arthur James Whittall (d 1971); *Career* RE (TA) 1938, WWII Capt Welsh Gds in N Africa and Italy 1943-45; mangr for Belgium Whitbread & Co 1935-38 (joined 1930), ptnr James Capel & Co 1946-74; memb London Stock Exchange; church warden St Mary Magdalene Cowden 1953-80, pres Cowden Dist Branch Royal Br Legion, vice pres Falconhurst CC; *Clubs* Army and Navy, MCC, Holtye Golf; *Style*— William Stephenson, Esq; Saxbys Mead, Cowden, Edenbridge, Kent (☎ 0342 850520)

STERNDALE, Jennifer Catherine; JP (1982); da of Bernard Francis Weston Allen (d 1976), and Esther Pauline, *née* Alcock; *b* 9 Sept 1943; *Educ* Les Oiseaux Convent Westgate on Sea, Coloma Coll of Educn (Cert Ed), Open Univ (BA); *m* 21 April 1979, Dr Harold Sterndale, s of Maurice Sterndale (d 1985); *Career* WRNS 1962-63, med discharge; asst teacher: Holy Cross Secdy Sch Broadstairs 1970-71, Abbey Jr Sch Westgate on Sea 1971-74; princ and proprietor Chartfield Prep Sch Westgate on Sea 1974-79; sec Med Res

Cncl 1979-83; memb: Canterbury and Thanet Health Authy 1985-, Nat Assoc of Decorative and Fine Arts, Victim Support Gp; friend of the Burma Star Assoc; *Recreations* horse riding, travel, golf; *Clubs* North Foreland Golf (Broadstairs); *Style—* Mrs Jennifer Sterndale, JP; 19 Seacroft Rd, Broadstairs, Kent CT10 1TL

STEVENS, Anne Eileen; da of Wilfred Willett (d 1961), and Eileen Estelle Josephine, *née* Stenhouse (d 1961); *b* 6 May 1923; *Educ* St Clair Tunbridge Wells; *m* 1, Jan 1943, Roger Finney; 1 da (Elizabeth Anne); m 2, Sept 1947, James Palmer; m 3, Jan 1978, Ronald Stevens; *Career* fndr and md Consultus Services Agency 1962-; *Recreations* gardening; *Style—* Mrs Anne Stevens; The Oast Cottage, Uckfield, E Sussex; Consultus Services Agency, 17 London Rd, Tonbridge, Kent (☎ 0732 355231)

STEVENS, Irmela Helene Dorothea Elisabeth; da of Ernst Gieseke, of Hannover, W Germany, and Anni Gieseke; *b* 10 Jan 1937; *Educ* Sophienschule GS for Girls Hannover, Univ of Göttingen, Univ of Nottingham (BA, PGCE), Univ of Leicester (MA); *m* 8 March 1958, Brian D N Stevens, s of Capt Joseph Eric Stevens, MBE (d 1959), of Reigate, Surrey; *Career* teacher and lectr: Aden 1960-61, Goethe GS Hannover 1961-63, Univ of Loughborough 1964, Leicester Poly 1964-69, E Hone Coll Lusaka Zambia 1969-72, St Michael's Ahlen Germany 1972-73, Quarrydale Comp Sch Notts 1973-78, Breezehill Sch Wellingborough 1978-81; dep head Welshpool HS 1981-84, headmistress Weald of Kent Girls' GS Tonbridge 1984-; memb: Nat Exec AMMA 1979-84, B & P Woman Welshpool 1981-84, Sch Curriculum Cncl 1982-84, Initial Undergraduate Trg Bd CNAA 1982-84; *Books* Wahlmagazin (1978); *Recreations* reading, travel, philately, classical music; *Style—* Mrs Irmela Stevens; Weald of Kent Girls' Grammar School, Tudeley Lane, Tonbridge, Kent TN9 2JP (☎ 0732 352819)

STEVENS, John Harding; s of late Wilfrid Gordon Stevens, of Great Missenden, Bucks, and Marjorie Cynthia, *née* Hadfield; *b* 9 Feb 1949; *Educ* Ottershaw Sch Chertsey Surrey, European Sch of Osteopathy Maidstone Kent (DO); *m* 28 April 1972, Valerie, da of John Edward Hands, RN, of Liverpool; 1 s (Alexander b 1983), 1 da (Leonie b 1973); *Career* Euro Sch of Osteopathy Maidstone: lectr in neuroanatomy 1976-84, lectr in clinical neurology 1976-, lectr in osteopathic technique, examiner to English and French students, sr clinical supervisor; memb of Bd of Postgraduate Studies Br Sch of Osteopathy London 1986-; MRO; *Recreations* sailing, skiing, karate, rowing; *Style—* John Stevens, Esq; The Old Rectory, Rectory Lane, Saltwood, Hythe, Kent CT21 4QA (☎ 0303 67374); The Coach House Clinic, 155 High Street, Tenterden, Kent TN30 6JS (☎ 05806 3481)

STEVENS, Mark Richard; s of Lawrence Edward John Stevens, of Milton Keynes, and Joan Elizabeth Morton, *née* Shaw; *b* 12 Dec 1960; *Educ* Leon Comp Milton Keynes, Orpington Coll of Further Educn, South Bank Poly (BA); *m* 10 Nov 1984, Shani Maureen, da of Augustine Thomas O'Toole, of Cricklewood, London; 1 s (Luke Daniel b 2 April 1988); *Career* CA; trainee Howard Tilly & Co (CAs) 1981-86, Merrill Lynch Ltd 1986-88, asst vice pres Merrill Lynch International Bank Ltd 1988-; ACA 1986; *Recreations* swimming, cinema, science fiction; *Style—* Mark R Stevens, Esq; 4 Knowle Ave, Bexleyheath, Kent DA7 5LX (☎ 081 310 4520); Merrill Lynch International Bank Ltd, Ropemaker St, London EC2Y 9AS (☎ 071 867 2725, fax 071 867 4837)

STEWART, Robin Milton; QC (1978); s of Brig Guy Milton Stewart (d 1943), and Dr Elaine Oenone Stewart, *née* Earengey; *b* 5 Aug 1938; *Educ* Winchester, New Coll Oxford (MA); *m* 8 Sept 1962, Lynda Grace, da of Arthur Thomas Albert Medhurst (d 1976); 3 s (Andrew Douglas Lorn b 1964, James Milton b 1966, Sholto Robert Douglas b 1969); *Career* called to the Bar Middle Temple 1963, Kings Inns Dublin 1975; prosecuting counsel to Inland Revenue (NE circuit) 1976-78, rec Crown Court 1978-, bencher Middle Temple 1988; former memb Hexham UDC and Tynedale DC; parly candidate (C) Newcastle upon Tyne W 1974; Freeman City of London, Liveryman Worshipful Co of Glaziers 1966; *Recreations* gardens, silver, pictures, opera, Scottish family history; *Clubs* Oriental; *Style—* R M Stewart, Esq, QC; Little Chart, 46 Oak Hill Rd, Sevenoaks, Kent TN13 1NS (☎ 0732 453475); 2 Harcourt Buildings, Temple, London EC4Y 9DB (☎ 071 353 1394, fax 071 353 4134)

STEWART-CLARK, Alexander Dudley; s and h of Sir John Stewart-Clark, 3 Bt, MEP; *b* 21 Nov 1960; *Educ* Worth Abbey; *Career* dir Douglas Timber Ltd; *Books* Hydroscopics of Oak (1987); *Recreations* rugby, tennis; *Style—* Alexander Stewart-Clark, Esq; Puckstye House, nr Cowden, Kent TN8 7ED; 28 Edgeley Road, London SW4 6ES

STIRLING, Prof (Arthur) Paul; s of Arthur Oscar Stirling (d 1957), of Exeter, and Lily Jane, *née* Folkes (d 1962); *b* 13 Oct 1920; *Educ* Whitgift Sch Croydon, Exeter Coll Oxford, Magdalen Coll Oxford (DPhil); *m* 3 April 1948, Margaret Lesley, da of The Rev E Clifford Urwin (d 1978), of Croydon, Surrey; 2 s (Nicholas Arthur b 10 Jan 1952, Simon Mark b 26 Feb 1960), 2 da (Elisabeth Hope b 8 Jan 1956, Catharine Lesley b 20 June 1958); *Career* RN 1941-45; lectr in anthropology LSE 1952-65; Univ of Kent: prof of sociology and social anthropology 1965-84, p/t teacher and res fell 1984-91, prof emeritus 1987-; visiting prof of sociology ME Tech Univ Ankara Turkey 1983-86, hon professorial res fell Modern Turkish Studies Prog SOAS 1988-92; prison visitor HM Borstal Dover, fndr chm Canterbury and Dist Mental Health Assoc, govr Farrington's Sch Chislehurst; FRAI; *Books* Turkish Village (1965); *Recreations* travel, walking, music, philosophy; *Style—* Prof Paul Stirling; 20 Canon Close, Rochester, Kent ME1 3EN (☎ 0634 843869); Eliot College, University of Kent, Canterbury, Kent CT2 7NS (☎ 0227 764000)

STOATE, Dr Howard Geoffrey Alvan; s of Alvan Charles Stoate, of Walton on Thames, and May, *née* Russell; *b* 14 April 1954; *Educ* Kingston GS, Kings Coll Univ of London (MB BS), Guys Hosp Univ of London (MSc), RCOG (Dip); *m* 22 Sept 1979, Deborah Jane, da of John Desmond Dunkerley, of Portsmouth; 2s (Thomas Henry George b 27 Sept 1984, George Timothy Charles b 18 April 1987); *Career* SHO Dartford Hosp 1978-81, princ in gen practice Bexley Heath 1982-, GP trainer 1988-, GP tutor Queen Mary's Hosp Sidcup 1989-; contrib: regular feature articles to Pulse, Financial Pulse, local newspapers and radio on issues regarding health and the environment; author of weekly page Clinical Roundup in Medical Monitor; memb Lab Pty 1970-, chm Heath Gundulf and Maypole Branch Lab Pty 1984-, parly lab candidate Old Bexley and Sidcup 1987, prospective parly lab candidate Dartford 1989-, current vice chm Dartford Lab Pty (1983-86), cncllr Littlebrook Ward Dartford Borough 1990-; chm Dartford Fabian Soc 1987- (fndr memb), sch govr Dartford 1988-89; memb: Greenwich and Bexley Local Med Ctee 1989-, GP Writers Assoc, Ethics and Res Ctee Queen Mary's Hosp Sidcup, Amnesty Int, Greenpeace, Friends of the Earth, Co-operative Pty; MRCGP; *Books* Can Health Screening Damage Your Health (1989); *Recreations* travel, sailing, reading, music; *Clubs* RCGP, BMA; *Style—* Dr Howard Stoate; 36 Heathcote Rd, Dartford, Kent DA1 2PU (☎ 0322 75661); The Albion Surgery, 6 Pincott Rd, Bexleyheath, Kent DA6 7LP (☎ 081 304 8334, fax 081 298 0408)

STOCKDALE, Malcolm Howard; s of Samuel Dorian Stockdale, of Stanwix, Cumbria, and Elsie, *née* Yarker; *b* 26 Feb 1954; *Educ* Trinity Sch Carlisle, Univ of Newcastle (BA); *Career* Marks & Spencer plc: dep mangr Kingston 1985-86, mangr Dunfermline 1986, dep gen mangr Metro Centre 1986-87, mangr Tunbridge Wells 1987-; memb: Calverley Rd Traders Assoc, C of C; *Recreations* jogging, gym work, fell walking; *Style—* Michael Stockdale, Esq; Marks & Spencer, Calverley Rd, Speldhurst, Kent (☎ 0892 44945, fax 0892 45809)

STOCKER, Ann Elizabeth; da of James Crabtree Heyworth (d 1975), of Grimsby, Lincs, and Mildred Moulton, *née* Eason (d 1977); *b* 6 Aug 1931; *Educ* Wintringham GS Grimsby, Sch of Architecture Univ of Liverpool (BArch), AA (Dipl Cons), RIBA; *m* 20 July 1962, Malcolm James Stocker, s of Charles Henry Stocker (d 1967), of Warwick; 1 s (Robert James b 1966), 1 da (Rachael Ann b 1964); *Career* asst architect: Yates Cook and Darbyshire 1955-57, Crowe and Greenwood 1957-60, Clifford Culpin and Partners 1960-63, assoc ptnr Purcell Miller and Partners 1976- (asst architect 1973-76); memb: Southwark Diocesan Advsy Ctee, Kent Building Preservation Tst Ctee; *Recreations* Kentish history, travel; *Style—* Mrs Ann Stocker; 23 Knole Way, Sevenoaks, Kent TN13 3RS (☎ 0732 453835); Purcell Miller Tritton & Partners, 9 London Rd, Sevenoaks, Kent TN13 1AH (☎ 0732 459504, fax 0732 740760)

STONE, Michael; s of Robert Stone (d 1970), of Dulwich, London, and Nancy, *née* Lorimer (d 1948); *b* 20 May 1935; *Educ* Dulwich; *m* 28 June 1958, Olive Margaret, da of Norman Eric Wilks (d 1957), of Ringmer, Sussex; 2 s (Julian Andrew b 30 July 1962, Jeremy Michael b 12 May 1965); *Career* md Beck and Pollitzer Engineering Ltd 1967- (dir 1957-67); chm Lords Taverners Kent Region 1988 (treas 1984-87); *Recreations* gardening, travel, sport, good food and wine, reading; *Clubs* Lords Taverners, Old Alleynian Sports; *Style—* Michael Stone, Esq; Rothbury, Canons Walk, Brasted Chart, Westerham, Kent TN16 1NA (☎ 0959 64494); Beck & Pollitzer Engineering Limited, Burnham Rd, Dartford, Kent DA1 5BD (☎ 0322 223494, fax 0322 91859)

STONEHAM, Martin William; s of George William David Stoneham, of Swanley, Kent, and Barbara Mary, *née* Smith; *b* 16 Feb 1946; *Educ* Malmesbury GS; *m* 24 June 1972, Elizabeth Irene, da of Lt Cdr Douglas Windsor Ernest Baker, of Chatham, Kent; 1 s (Douglas b 1978), 1 da (Helen b 1975); *Career* RE 1963-70; admin trainee SE Met Regnl Hosp Bd 1970-71, asst hosp sec Bromley Hosps 1971-73, dep hosp sec Farnborough Hosp 1973-75, supplies asst Lambeth Southward and Lewisham AHA 1975-77; dist supplies offr: Medway Health Dist 1977-81, Cantebury and Thanet Health Authy 1981-84, divnl supplies mangr SE Thames RHA NW Kent Supplies Div 1984-90; regnl purchasing mangr SE Thames RHA 1990-; memb Dept of Business and Mgmnt Advsy Ctee Mid Kent Coll of Higher and Further Educn, community advsr Sevenoaks DC, memb Radio Amateur Emergency Network; AHSM 1977, MInstPS 1977, MBIM 1980; *Recreations* motor sport, amateur radio, reading; *Style—* Martin Stoneham, Esq; Hafnia, 139 Hever Avenue, West Kingsdown, Sevenoaks, Kent TN15 6DT (☎ 0474 3014); Regional Supplies Agency, SE Thames Regional Health Authority, Thrift House, Bexhill on Sea, E Sussex TN39 3NQ (☎ 0424 730073)

STOSSEL, Clifford Alain; s of Adalbert Bela Stossel (d 1987), of London, and Esther Judith, *née* Weinstein; *b* 5 June 1938; *Educ* Univ Coll Sch

Hampstead, St Mary's Hosp Med Sch (MB BS, LRCP); *m* 28 Aug 1966, Kathleen Diana (Katie), da of Maj Osmond Gibson (d 1965), of London; 2 da (Louisa Margriet b 1968, Hilary Jeanne b 1969); *Career* conslt orthopaedic surgn Maidstone, conslt i/c Churchill Rehabilitation and Assessment Centre; dist rep Hosp Conslts and Specialists Assoc, FRCSEd; FRCS; *Recreations* swimming; *Clubs* Otter Swimming; *Style*— Clifford Stossel, Esq; Flagstones, Millbank, Headcorn, Ashford, Kent TN27 9RB (☎ 0622 890702); Somerfield Hospital, London Rd, Maidstone, Kent (☎ 0622 686581)

STRAKER, Hon Mrs (Ann Geraldine); *née* Milne; da of 2 Baron Milne; *b* 1946; *Educ* Queens Gate Sch London; *m* 1969, Ian Frederick Lawrence Straker; 1 s (Ross b 1977), 1 da (Frances b 1980); *Career* home and publishing; dir Bishopsgate Press London; Liveryman Worshipful Co of Grocers; *Recreations* tennis, skiing, gardening, art, Birman cats; *Style*— The Hon Mrs Straker; Hever Warren, Hever, Kent

STRANGE, Frederick Griffiths St Clair; s of Dr Charles Frederick Strange (d 1927), of 5 Rosslyn Hill, Hampstead, and Olive Cecilia Harrison (d 1970); *b* 22 July 1911; *Educ* Rugby, Royal London Hosp Med Coll, Univ of London; *m* 17 June 1939, Joyce Elsie, da of A Percy Kimber (d 1944), of South Croxted Rd, Dulwich; 1 s (Richard b 1942), 2 da (Diana b 1941, Angela b 1944); *Career* consltg orthopaedic surgn: Kent and Canterbury and Ramsgate Hosps 1947-48, Canterbury and Thanet HMC (later Dist) Areas 1948-75 (hon 1975-); numerous contribs to orthopaedic lit; pres Orthopaedic Section RSM 1965-66 (hon memb 1975-); vice pres: RSM 1965-66, Br Orthopaedic Assoc 1971-72; Hunterian prof RCS 1947, Nuffield travelling fell 1948; hon civilian conslt orthopaedics to the Army at The Royal Herbert Hosp 1967-76; former pres Combined Servs Orthopaedic Soc; Robert Jones Gold Medallist Br Orthopaedic Assoc 1943; FRCS (MRCS), LRCP; *Publications* The Hip (1965); *Recreations* photography, philately, travel; *Style*— F G St Clair Strange, Esq

STRANGE, Prof John Harvey; s of Harvey Albert William Strange, of Craigholme, Collington Ave, Bexhill-on-Sea, Sussex, and Ethel Frances, *née* Cottee; *b* 12 Dec 1938; *Educ* Eltham Coll, Univ of London (BSc, PhD); *m* 11 Aug 1962, Annette Conron, da of James Smith (d 1981), of Canterbury; 1 s (Nicholas John b 1966), 2 da (Alison Claire b 1965, Charlotte Elizabeth b 1969); *Career* res fell Cornell Univ USA 1963-64; Univ of Kent: lectr 1964-, sr lectr 1972-, reader in physics 1974-84, dir of physics laboratory 1982-, prof of experimental physics 1984-; author of 100 pubns in scientific jls; cncl memb Ashford Sch; FInstP, CPhys 1973; *Recreations* music; *Style*— Prof John Strange; Hillmead, Canterbury, Kent (☎ 0227 760808); The University, Physics Laboratory, Canterbury, Kent CT2 7NR (☎ 0227 764000)

STRANGE, Dr Philip Gordon; s of Gordon Wilfred Strange, of Parkstone, Dorset, and Penelope Mary, *née* Oscroft; *b* 3 March 1949; *Educ* Poole GS, Purbrook Park Co GS, Sidney Sussex Coll Cambridge (BA, MA, PhD); *m* 3 June 1978, Margaret Winsome, da of Kenneth Archer Young, of Johannesburg, SA; *Career* res fell: Univ of California at Berkeley 1973-75, Nat Inst For Med Res London 1975-76; lectr in biochemistry Univ of Nottingham Med Sch 1976-85, reader in biochemistry Univ of Kent at Canterbury 1986-; memb: Main Ctee Biochemical Soc of London 1985-, Editoriaal Bd The Biochemical Journal 1985-, Senate Univ of Kent 1986-88 and 1989-; author of over 60 scientific articles on receptors; memb: Royal Soc of Chemistry, The Biochemical Soc, Br Pharmacological Soc; *Books* Cell Surface Receptors (ed 1982); *Recreations* reading, walking, gardening, music, badminton; *Style*— Dr Philip G Strange; The Biological Laboratory, The University, Canterbury CT2 7NJ (☎ 0227 764000)

STRATTON, Nigel Morris; s of Harold Ralph Stratton (d 1971), of Fleet, Hants, and Pamela Rebecca, *née* Lintine; *b* 30 June 1955; *Educ* Salesian Coll Farnborough Hants, Univ of Birmingham (LLB); *Career* admitted slr 1979; ptnr: Vallis & Struthers Sevenoaks 1984-88, Berry & Berry (after merger with Vallis & Struthers) 1988-; chm: Sevenoaks Cons Assoc, Sevenoaks and Dist Vol Bureau, Sevenoaks Branch Nat Fedn of Self Employed and Small Businesses Ltd; govr Sevenoaks Co Primary Sch, vice-chm Sevenoaks Philharmonic Soc; hon legal advsr: Southborough and High Brooms Age Concern, Sevenoaks Mencap; *Recreations* classical music, gardening, badminton, golf; *Clubs* Wig and Pen; *Style*— Nigel Stratton, Esq; Flat 7, Ashbrook, 1 Vine Court Rd, Sevenoaks, Kent TN13 3UU (☎ 0732 458395); Messrs Berry & Berry, 11 Church Rd, Tunbridge Wells, Kent TN1 1JA (☎ 0892 26344, fax 0892 511223)

STREETER, His Hon John Stuart; DL (Kent 1986); s of Wilfrid Alberto Streeter (d 1962), of Park St, London, and Margaret Law, *née* Stuart (d 1982); *b* 20 May 1920; *Educ* Sherborne; *m* 4 Feb 1956, (Margaret) Nancy, da of Arthur Maurice Richardson (d 1980), of Nutfield, Surrey; 1 s (Graham), 2 da (Coralie, Jacqueline); *Career* WWII Capt RSF (despatches), Hon Maj ACF 1939-53; called to the Bar Gray's Inn 1947; counsel to PO SE Circuit 1959, treas counsel London Sessions 1961; Kent QS: dep chm 1963, perm 1967, chm 1971; circuit judge 1972-86, (res judge Kent 1972-85), dep circuit judge 1986; chm and tstee Sherborne House Day Centre Bermondsey, pres Old Sherbornian Soc 1990; *Style*— His Honour John Streeter, DL; Playstole, Sissinghurst, Cranbrook, Kent TN17 2JN (☎ 0580 712847); Law Courts, Barker Rd, Maidstone, Kent ME16 8EQ (☎ 0622 54966)

STRICKLAND-CONSTABLE, Frederic; s (by 2 m) and h of Sir Robert Strickland-Constable, 11 Bt; *b* 21 Oct 1943; *Educ* Westminster, CCC Cambridge (BA); *Style*— Frederic Strickland-Constable, Esq; Elm Tree Cottage, Rowdow Lane, Otford Hills, Sevenoaks TN16 6XN

STRICKLAND-CONSTABLE, Sir Robert Frederick; 11 Bt (E 1641), of Boynton, Yorkshire; s of Lt-Col Frederick Charles Strickland-Constable (d 1916) (ggs of 7 Bt), and Margaret (d 1959), da of late Rear-Adm Hon Thomas Pakenham, s of 2 Earl of Longford, KP, and bro of 3 and 4 Earls; suc bro, Sir Henry Marmaduke Strickland-Constable, 10 Bt, 1975; *b* 22 Oct 1903; *Educ* Eton, Magdalen Coll Oxford (MA, DPhil); *m* 1, 1929 (m annulled 1931), Rosalind Mary, da of Arthur Webster; m 2, 1936, Lettice, da of late Maj Frederic Strickland (d 1934), (2 s of 8 Bt), and Mary, da of late Sir John Isaac Thornycroft; 2 s (Frederick b 1944, J R F b 1949), 2 da (Miranda b 1938, Elizabeth b 1940); memb Royal Soc of Chem; *Heir* s, Frederick Strickland-Constable; *Career* Lt Cdr RNVR 1940-44; Imperial Coll London Chem Engrg Dept 1948-71 (reader 1963-71); memb Royal Soc of Chemistry; *Books* Kinetics of Crystallisation (1968), contributed to numerous scientific journals; *Recreations* mountaineering, music; *Style*— Dr Robert Strickland-Constable, Bt; c/o Barclays Bank, The Green, Westerham, Kent

STRONG, Anthony Robin; s of Ivon Michael Strong (d 1984), of 6 Gloucester Rd, Maidstone, and Joyce Mary, *née* Blight; *b* 22 Dec 1962; *Career* sole proprietor AS Services Property Maintenence Painters and Decorators; *Recreations* Latin American and ballroom dancing (Gold Star 1); *Style*— Anthony Strong, Esq; 6 Gloucester Rd, Maidstone, Kent ME15 7HR (☎ 0622 759399)

STRONG, John Clifford; CBE (1980); s of Clifford Maurice Strong (d 1967); *b* 14 Jan 1922; *Educ* Beckenham GS, Univ of London; *m* 1942, Janet Doris, *née* Browning; 3 da; *Career* Lt RNVR; HMOCS Tanzania 1946-63, Cwlth Rels Office 1963, first sec Nairobi 1964-68, FCO 1968-73, cnsllr and head Chancery Dar-es-Salaam 1973-78, govr Turks and Caicos Islands 1978-82; *Clubs* Royal Over-Seas League; *Style*— John Strong, Esq, CBE

STRONG, William George Michael; s of Ivan Michael Strong (d 1984), of Maidstone, and Joyce Margret, *née* Blight; *b* 23 May 1959; *Educ* St Simon Stock RC Secdy Sch, Westree Coll (HND); *m* 20 Aug 1982, Heather Rosemary, da of Ronald Douglas Halmer, of Staplehurst, Kent; 1 s (Michael Douglas William b 12 June 1983), 1 da (Charlotte Michell b 14 April 1985); *Career* mechanical engr Engis Ltd 1976-86, proprietor own engrg business 1986-; best young business awards in S and SE 1986 and 1988 (6th in UK 1988); chm Holy Family Playgroup 1988-89, pres Gillingham Lions Club 1990-91; memb: TA 1983-84, RAOC 1984-89; *Recreations* karate; *Style*— William Strong, Esq; R W Regrinds, Unit D, 256 Lower Twydall Lane, Gillingham, Kent ME8 6QP (☎ 0634 376150, 35124, fax 0634 35124)

STROUD, Rev Robert Owen; s of Ronald Stroud (d 1979), of Pangbourne, and Gwenllian Stroud (d 1973); *b* 22 June 1929; *Educ* Trinity GS, Kings Coll London (AKC); *m* 13 Sept 1958, (Elizabeth) Dawn Stroud; 4s (Robert, David, Andrew, Christopher), 1 da (Alison Clare); *Career* vicar: St Philip High Elswick Newcastle upon Tyne 1966-72, St Paul Whitley Bay 1972-77; rector Orlestone Ruckinge Warehorne 1977-81; rural dean: N Lympne 1977-81, Elham 1990-; team rector Holy Trinity Folkestone 1981-; memb Rotary Club 1988, pres Folkestone Childrens' Soc 1988, chm Friends of the Music Holy Trinity Folkestone; *Recreations* hill walking, reading, European travel; *Style*— The Rev Robert Stroud; Holy Trinity Rectory, Folkestone; 13 Blackfriars St, Canterbury (☎ 0303 53831)

STURT, Richard Harry Brooke; s of Horace Holford Sturt (d 1962), of Wimborne, Dorset, and Eveline Frances, *née* Brooke; *b* 14 Nov 1939; *Educ* Marlborough, Peterhouse Cambridge (BA, MA); *m* 3 March 1962, Ann Lesley, da of Brig Charles Leslie Morgan, OBE (d 1982), of Walmer, Kent; 4 s (Richard Michael Villers b 1964, (Charles) Patrick Holford b 1966, Alexander Fitzgerald Brooke b 1969, (Nicholas) Julian Holford b 1972); *Career* admitted slr 1966; sr ptnr Mowll & Mowll 1984- (ptnr 1967-84); slr: Dover Harbour Bd 1979-, Ind Schs Action Ctee 1980-82; slr and clerk to govrs King's Sch Canterbury 1979-; memb CAA 1990-; dep coroner E Kent 1972-79, HM Coroner for Kent (Canterbury and Dover Dist) 1979-, conducted inquest into Herald of Free Enterprise disaster 1987; dir: Dover & Folkstone Building Society 1978-84, Mellow 1557 Ltd 1990-, Waldershare Park farms Ltd 1990-; chm: Gateway Broadcasting Ltd 1982-84, Invicta Radio (Invicta Sound plc) 1984-; fndr and chm E Kent Holiday Music Tst 1979-; govr: Betteshanger Sch 1978-80, Northbourne Park Sch 1980-85; tstee: Keepershield Charitable Tst, All Saints Waldershare Tst, David Barlow Tst, Cicely Stockmann Meml Fund, The Invicta Radio Charity; memb: SE England Coroners' Soc (pres 1981-82), Coroners' Soc England and Wales 1972; FRSA 1990; *Books* Fishery Protection and Foreign Sea Fishing Boats (1973), Halsbury's Laws of England (contrib, 4 edn), Vaughan on The Law of the European Communities Fisheries (1986), The Collision Regulations (2 edn, 1984), The Role of the Coroner in Major Disasters (1988); *Recreations* cricket, singing, bridge, genealogy, fly-fishing; *Clubs* Athenaeum, Flyfishers; *Style*— Richard Sturt, Esq; Kent Cottage, 7 Granville Rd, Walmer, Deal, Kent CT14 7LU (☎ 0304 375057)

SUMMERFIELD, Dr Brian John; s of Eric Gordon Summerfield (d 1984), of London, and Grace Nellie, *née* Mellor; *b* 10 Oct 1948; *Educ* Alleyn's Coll Dulwich, Univ of Sheffield (MB ChB); *m* 7 July 1973, Brenda Joan, da of Norman Jack Roostan (d 1984), of Leeds, W Yorks; 2 s (David Jon b 1974, Chistopher James b 1976); *Career* house surgn Doncaster Royal Infirmary 1972-73, house physician to Prof Sir Robert Kilpatrick Wharnecliffe Hosp Sheffield; Northern Gen Hosp Sheffield: sr house offr 1973-74, med registrar 1974-75; sr house offr St John's Hosp Chelmsford 1975, princ in gen med practice Margate 1976-; author of Progressive Systemic Sclerosis With Complete Heart Block (British Heart Journal 1975); gp ldr Isle of Thanet Membs' Gp of the RSPB 1980-90, tstee Thanet Countryside Tst 1982-; memb: Br Ornithologists' Union, Br Tst for Ornithology, Kent Ornithological Soc, Kent Tst for Nature Conservation, Sandwich Bay Bird Observatory Tst; DRCOG, memb BMA 1972-; *Recreations* ornithology, photography, natural history, travel; *Style—* Dr B J Summerfield; The Limes, Hawley St, Margate, Kent CT9 1PU (☎ 0843 227567)

SUMMERFIELD, Sir John Crampton Summerfield; CBE (1966, OBE 1961), QC (Bermuda 1963); s of Arthur Frederick Summerfield (d 1941), and Lilian Winifred, *née* Staas (d 1958); *b* 20 Sept 1920; *Educ* Lucton Sch Herefordshire; *m* 11 Aug 1945, Patricia Sandra, da of John Geoffrey Musgrave (d 1926), of Salisbury, Rhodesia; 2 s (John b 1946, Michael b 1948), 2 da (Rosemary b 1955, Margaret (Mrs Goodwin) b 1960); *Career* served WWII, E Africa NFD, Ethiopia and Madagascar, Capt Royal Signals; barr Gray's Inn 1949; Tanganyika crown counsel/legal draftsman 1949-58, dep legal sec E Africa High Cmmn 1958-62, AG Bermuda 1962-72; chief justice: Bermuda 1972-77, Cayman Islands 1977-87; justice of appeal Court of Appeal Bermuda 1980-, pres Court of Appeal Belize 1981-82; memb Exec Cncl and MLC Bermuda until 1966; kt 1973; *Recreations* photography, chess; *Clubs* Royal Cwlth Soc; *Style—* Sir John Summerfield, CBE, QC; 3 The Corniche, Sandgate, Folkestone, Kent CT20 3TA (☎ 0303 49479)

SUMMERS, David Lewis; s of Maj Lewis Summers (d 1948), and Beatrice, *née* Greenaway; *b* 25 Nov 1941; *Educ* Mundella Sch Nottingham, St Edmund Hall Oxford (MA); *m* 24 Dec 1966, Veronica Yvonne Elizabeth, da of Cyril Clarence King (d 1970); 2 s (Jonathan b 1971, Benjamin b 1973); *Career* RN Lt 1963-66; Longmans 1966-69, Butterworth & Co Publishers Ltd 1969-, md Butterworth Scientific 1981-86, chief exec UK Legal Publishing 1986-, dir Reed International Books 1990; contrib various chapters to professional pubns; memb: Harvard Business Club, Soc of Bookmen, Anglo-Finnish Soc; Freeman City of London 1988, Liveryman Worshipful Co of Stationers 1989; *Recreations* tennis, squash, cross-skiing, theatre, music; *Clubs* Garrick; *Style—* David Summers, Esq; Fir Tree Farm, Golford Rd, Cranbrook, Kent TN17 3NW (☎ 0580 713377); 88 Kingsway, London WC2B 6AB (☎ 071 405 6900, fax 071 831 8110)

SUMMERS, Eric William; *b* 10 Dec 1914; *Educ* Dartford Tech Coll; *m* 1939, Janet; 2 children; *Career* CIBS; chm Courtney, Pope (Holdings) Ltd; fell Inst of Plant Engrg, companion CIBS; FRSA; *Clubs* RAC, Livery; *Style—* Eric Summers, Esq; Muskoday, 29 The Meadow, Chislehurst, Kent BR7 6AA (☎ 01 467 8047); Courtney, Pope (Holdings) Ltd, Amhurst Park Works, South Tottenham, London N15 6RB (☎ 081 800 1270)

SUMMERS, William Hamilton; LVO (1990, MVO 1974); s of Dr Maxwell Hamilton Summers, DSO, OBE (d 1989), and Evelyne Elizabeth, *née* Baird; *b* 4 Oct 1930; *Educ* King's Sch Bruton Somerset; *m* 1959, Rosemarie Jean, da of Thomas Norman Hutchison (d 1982), of Chile; 1 s (John b 1964), 2 da (Alison Jane b 1961, Catherine b 1969); *Career* jeweller; dir Garrard & Co 1972; fell Gemologists Assoc, FGA; *Recreations* walking, reading; *Style—* William Summers, Esq, LVO; National Westminster Bank, 1 New Bond St, London W1Y 0HU; Garrard & Co Ltd, 112 Regent St, London W1 2JJ (☎ 071 734 7020, fax 071 439 9197, telex 8952365 REGENT G)

SURRIDGE, Chief Supt David Alan; *b* 9 Sept 1938; *Educ* The Simon Langton GS Canterbury; *m* 3 Oct 1959, Kathleen; 2 s (Clive b 6 Aug 1960, Paul b 17 Nov 1964); *Career* RN 1954-66, submarine serv 1959-66; Kent Co Constabulary 1966-: Criminal Investigation Dept, former Detective Supt, Chief Supt (and Divnl Cdr) 1987-; chm Sittingbourne and Milton Sea Cadet Corps; *Style—* Chief Supt David Surridge; Divisional Police Headquarters, Kent County Constabulary, Old Dover Rd, Canterbury, Kent (☎ 0227 762055)

SUTTON, Mark Philip; s of Ronald Sutton, of Cobham, Surrey, and Kathleen Mary Sutton; *b* 19 Dec 1962; *Educ* Esher Co GS, Esher Coll, Poly of Central London (BA); *Career* trainee accountant Reed Int Plc 1985-87, fin controller Reed Regnl Newspaper Ltd 1988-89 (project accountant 1987-88), fin dir Mega Publishing Co Ltd 1989-; memb Round Table; memb ACMA; *Recreations* photography, motoring, reading, music; *Style—* Mark Sutton, Esq; Mega Publishing Ltd, Mega House, Crestview Drive, Petts Wood, Orpington, Kent BR5 1BT (☎ 0689 36211, fax 0689 891479)

SUTTON, Capt Oliver Peter; CBE (1978); s of Albert Bernard Sutton (d 1961), of Chile, and Joan Frith, *née* Brewster (d 1981); *b* 17 Jan 1926; *Educ* RNC Dartmouth; *m* 16 Dec 1962, Gay, da of Charles Owen (d 1949); 2 s (Matthew b 5 Feb 1964, Simon b 31 Oct 1968); *Career* RN: Cadet 1939, Cdre 1978, specialist in navigation, ret as COS to Flag Offr Plymouth; dir Br Radio and Electronic Equipment Mfrs Assoc 1978-, sec Euro Assoc of Consumer Electronics Mfrs 1987-90; FBIM; *Recreations* fishing, tennis, gardening; *Style—* Capt Oliver Sutton, CBE; British Radio and Electronic Equipment Manufacturers' Association (BREMA) Landseer House, 19 Charing Cross Rd, London WC2H 0ES (☎ 01 932 3206, fax 01 839 4613, telex 296215 BREMA G)

SUTTON, Terence Albert (Terry); s of Norman Victor Sutton (d 1986), of Dover, and Daisy, *née* Chowne (d 1983); *b* 26 March 1929; *Educ* Dover GS; *m* 1 (m dis 1966), Judy, *née* Linton; m 2, 24 Sept 1971, Danielle (Dany), da of Gaston Devillard (d 1983), of Paris; 1 da (Joséphine b 1972); *Career* journalist 1949-, dep ed Dover Express; memb Rotary Club Dover, govr Dover Girls GS, vice pres Dover Soc; *Recreations* study of local history; *Style—* Terry Sutton, Esq; Abbots Barton, 17 Bewsbury Cross Lane, Whitfield, Dover, Kent CT16 3HB (☎ 0304 820122); Dover Express, 25 High St, Dover, Kent (☎ 0304 240660, fax 0304 240455)

SWAFFIELD, Sir James Chesebrough; CBE (1971), RD (1967), DL (Greater London 1978); s of Frederick Swaffield (d 1970); *b* 1924; *Educ* Cheltenham GS, Haberdashers' Aske's Sch, Univ of London (MA, LLB); *m* 1950, Elizabeth Margaret Ellen, da of Albert Victor Maunder (d 1965); 2 s, 2 da; *Career* WWII Lt Cdr RNVR Atlantic and NW Europe; asst slr: Norwich Corporation 1949-52, Cheltenham Corporation 1952-53, Southend on Sea Corporation 1953-56; dep town clerk Blackpool 1956-61 (town clerk 1961-62); sec Assoc of Municipal Corporations 1962-72, dir-gen and clerk GLC 1973-84, clerk to ILEA 1973-84, clerk of Lieutenancy for Gtr London 1973-84; chm: BR Property Bd 1984-, Outward Bound Tst; Distinguished Service Award (Int City Mgmnt Assoc) 1984; hon fell Inst Local Govt Studies Univ of Birmingham; OStJ; FRSA; kt 1976; *Clubs* Reform, Naval; *Style—* Sir James Swaffield, CBE, RD, DL; 10 Kelsey Way, Beckenham, Kent

SWAIN, Charles De Pina Beauchamp; s of Flt Lt Claude De Pina Downs Swain, of 29 Springhead, Tunbridge Wells, Kent, and Carol Margot, *née* Beauchamp; *b* 17 Aug 1959; *Educ* Univ of Exeter (BA); *m* 2 June 1984, Caroline Kerr, da of Alexander Alfred Stuart, of Hollyhouse, Manor Lane, Gerrards Cross, Bucks; 1 s (Charles Douglas Stuart b 1988); *Career* Deloitte Hoskins & Sells: articled clerk 1981, CA 1985; Cap Gp plc 1986 (now Sema Gp plc): asst to md, conslt to main UK banks on nat EFTPOS project (electronic funds transfer at point of sale); hon treas UN Devpt Fund For Women; memb Inst of CAs 1985; *Recreations* riding, golf; *Clubs* East India; *Style—* Charles Swain, Esq; Hazeldene, Oakhill Road, Sevenoaks, Kent (☎ 0732 456692); Sema Group plc, 59 Clarenden Road, Watford, Herts (☎ 0923 55000, fax 0923 249472, telex 8955910 CAPFIN G)

SWAINE, Anthony Wells; s of Albert Victor Alexander Swaine (d 1972), of Cornwall, and Hilda May Allen (d 1983); *b* 25 Aug 1913; *Educ* Chatham House, Ramsgate; *Career* architect; in private practice specialising in historic bldgs; architectural advsr to: Faversham old town (author Faversham Conserved), Historic Churches Preservation Tst (memb panel hon conslt architects); architectural advsr historic bldgs responsible for old Margate, pt/t teacher of architecture Canterbury Coll of Art (responsible for cathedral and precincts); memb of cncl and tech panel Ancient Monuments Soc (reps the Soc on Int Cncl), patron Venice in Peril, author report on conservation Il Problema di Venezia to UNESCO, served on Int Confe for Stone Conservation Athens; memb SPAB, FRIBA, FSA; *Recreations* travelling, languages, lecturing (as memb of panel of speakers of Civic Tst), history as applied to architecture, drawing, painting, photography; *Style—* Anthony Swaine, Esq, FSA; 19 Farrier St, Deal, Kent (☎ 0304 366369); Latchmere House, Watling St, Canterbury, Kent (☎ 0277 462680)

SWAINSON, Capt (John) Anthony Rowland; OBE (1971); s of Charles John Graind'orge Swainson (d 1968), and Marion Alice Vining, *née* Rudrum (d 1966); *b* 29 Oct 1921; *Educ* St Paul's, RAF Staff Coll Bracknell; *m* 1 (m dis 1961), Crystal Alison Frances; 1 s (Adam b 16 May 1952), 1 da (Nicola b 29 Dec 1950); m 2, 26 Oct 1964 (Marie-Thérèse) Délia, da of Antoine Pintur, of Chatou, Paris, France; 1 da (Caroline b 3 Oct 1965); *Career* Nat Serv RN 1941, cmmnd Sub Lt RNVR 1943 (despatches 1944), Lt (reg cmmn) 1948, served in frigates, destroyers, cruisers, aircraft carriers, action in atlantic convoys, D Day and Suez; appointed dir The Lords Taverners 1972; non exec dir: Good Books Ltd, Dowson & Salisbury Management Consultants; memb Cricket Cncl Fund, exec memb Nat Cricket Assoc; *Books* Please Give Generously (1987); *Recreations* golf, tennis, gardening, music; *Clubs* MCC, RAF, Garrick; *Style—* Capt Anthony Swainson, OBE, RN; 48 Springhead, Tunbridge Wells, Kent TN2 3NZ (☎ 0892 30786); Lord's Taverners, 1 Chester St, London SW1X 7HP (☎ 071 245 6466, fax 071 8231479)

SWAN, Danny Stephen; s of Daniel Swan (d 1986), of Broadstairs, Kent, and Ivy Susan *née* Harvey (d 1977); *b* 10 Sept 1943; *Educ* Charles Dickens Sch Broadstairs; *m* 12 March 1964, Tanis Susan, da of Claude Muckley (d 1982), of Westgate-on-Sea, Kent; 1 s (Giles Stephen b 1981), 1 da (Michelle Susan b 1965); *Career* sr exec offr Br Civil Service (joined 1964); sec Westgate-On-Sea Residents' Assoc 1984- (treas 1978-84), cncllr Thanet Dist Cncl 1987-, elected Mayor of Margate 1990; *Recreations* golf; *Clubs* Westgate and

Birchington Golf; *Style—* Danny Swan, Esq; 17 The Broadway, Broadstairs, Kent CT10 2AD (☎ 0843 62042)

SWANN, Dr James Cyprian; s of Ven Cecil Gordon Aldersey Swann (d 1969), and Hilda, *née* McMahon (d 1978); *b* 10 July 1931; *Educ* Gosfield Sch, The London Hosp Med Coll (MB BS, DMRD); *m* 28 Jan 1961, Josephine Margaret, da of Joseph Winston Ellis (d 1975); 3 da (Rachel b 1963, Laura b 1965, Clare b 1972); *Career* 2 Lt RA; conslt radiologist: The London Hosp 1968-76, The Royal Masonic Hosp 1970-84, Bromley Health Authy 1976-; chm Bromley Health Dist CAT Scanner Appeal; FFR, memb Br Inst Radiology 1965, FRCR 1975; *Recreations* painting in oils, photography, gardening; *Clubs* BMA; *Style—* Dr James Swann; 104 Hayes Way, Beckenham, Kent BR3 2RT (☎ 081 650 3673); Department of Radiology, Farnborough Hospital, Farnborough Common, Orpington, Kent BR6 8ND (☎ 0689 53333)

SWANTON, Ernest William (Jim); OBE (1965); s of William Swanton (d 1966), of Malvern, Worcs, and Lillian Emily, *née* Walters (d 1953); *b* 11 Feb 1907; *Educ* Cranleigh Sch; *m* 11 Feb 1958, Ann Marion Carbutt, da of R H de Montmorency (d 1938), of Wentworth, Surrey; *Career* served WWII 1939-45, Actg Maj 148 FD Regt Bedfords Yeo RA (captured Singapore POW 1942-45); journalist author and bdcaster 1924-; journalist Evening Standard 1927-39, rugby corr Daily Telegraph 1984-64 (cricket corr 1946-75); played cricket for Middx 1937-38; managed own X1: W Indies 1956 and 1961, Malaya and Far East 1964; ctee memb MCC 1975-85, Kent CCC 1971-89; pres: Cricket Soc 1976-83, Sandwich Town CC 1977-, Forty Club 1983-86, The Cricketer 1988-; *Books* A History of Cricket (with HS Altham, 1938), Denis Compton a Cricket Sketch (1948), Elusive Victory (1951), Cricket and the Clock (1952), Best Cricket Stories (1953), West Indian Adventure (1954), Victory in Australia 1954/55 (1955), Reports from South Africa (1957), West Indies Revisited (1960), The Ashes in Suspense (1963), World of Cricket (ed, 1966, 1980, 1986), Cricket from All Angles (1968), Sort of a Cricket Person (1972), Swanton in Australia (1975), Follow On (1985), As I Said at the Time (anthology, 1984), Kent Cricket a Photographic History 1744-1984 (with CH Taylor, 1985), Back Page Cricket (1987); *Recreations* golf, watching cricket; *Clubs* MCC, Vincent's (Oxford), Naval and Military, 1 Zingari; *Style—* Jim Swanton, Esq, OBE; Delf House, Sandwich, Kent CT13 9HB

SWANTON, Nigel Stephen; s of Leonard James Swanton (d 1979), and Maud Lydia Charlotte Felicia Aris; *b* 4 Feb 1943; *Educ* Clarks Coll Surbiton Surrey; *m* 29 Oct 1966, Rita Mavis, da of Alfred Lesley Ashby, of Ticehurst, East Sussex; 1 s (Elliot James Russell b 1976), 2 da (Dionne Nicola b 1968, Shelley Louise b 1970); *Career* Gilco Optics Ltd: sales dir 1978-85, md and ptnr 1985; chm and ptnr Opticard Ltd 1990; fndr memb Industl Ctee Tunbridge Wells C of C; *Recreations* badminton, tennis, cookery, horse riding; *Style—* Nigel Swanton, Esq; Gilco Optics Ltd, North Farm Rd, Tunbridge Wells, Kent TN2 3DH (☎ 0892 542844, fax 0892 548847)

SWIFT, Prof Cameron Graham; s of Rev Graham Swift (d 1973), and Victoria, *née* Williamson; *b* 5 April 1946; *Educ* Lawrence Sheriff Sch Rugby, Univ of London (MB BS), Univ of Dundee (PhD); *m* Margaret Rosemary, da of Henry K Vernon; *Career* MRC Res Fell in clinical pharmacology Univ of Dundee 1977-80, conslt physician Dept of Med for the elderly N Humberside 1980-84, dir of postgraduate med educn N Humberside 1982-84, conslt physician and sr lectr Dept of Geriatric Med Univ of Wales Coll of Med 1984-86, prof of health care of the elderly Univ of London 1986-; conslt physician; Kings Coll Hosp, Dulwich Hosp 1986-; hon prof of health care Univ of Kent 1986-; chm Trg Ctee and Pharmacology and Therapeutic Section of Br Geriatric Soc; bd memb: Age Concern, King's Coll Inst of Gerontology; memb: Sub Ctee on Efficacy and Adverse Reactions, Ctee on Safety of Meds, Br Pharmacological Soc, Br Geriatrics Sco; FRCP 1988; *Books* Clinical Pharmacology in the Elderly (ed, 1987); *Recreations* music, ornithology, hill walking; *Style—* Prof Cameron Swift; Kings College School of Medicine and Dentistry, Kings College Hospital, Denmark Hill, London SE5 9RS (☎ 081 693 3377 ext 3312)

SWIFT, Jack; JP; s of Herbert Swift (d 1976), and Mable, *née* Hyde; *b* 19 Jan 1943; *Educ* Northumberland Heath Sch, Erith Tech Coll, SE London Tech Coll, NW Kent Coll of Technol, Inst of Mgmnt Servs (Dip); *m* 4 Sept 1965, Sylvia, da of Edward Knott (d 1987); 1 s (Richard b 1968), 1 da (Catherine b 1971); *Career* mechanical engr GEC/CA Parsons 1958-66, work study offr Mechanical and Electrical Div GLC 1966-70, work study engr J and E Hall Products 1970-71, mgmnt servs offr London Borough of Bromley 1971-; asst dist cmmr (scouts) Swanley 1980-; MMS 1972; *Recreations* badminton, history; *Style—* Jack Swift, Esq, JP; 11 Sermon Drive, Swanley, Kent BR8 7HS (☎ 0322 63472); London Borough of Bromley, Civic Centre, Rochester Ave, Bromley, Kent (☎ 081 464 3333)

SWINBURNE, Prof Terence Reginald; s of Reginald Swinburne, of Gravesend, Kent, and Gladys Hannah, *née* Shrusbsall; *b* 17 July 1936; *Educ* Kent Co GS for Boys Gravesend, Imp Coll of Sci and Technol Univ of London (BSc, PhD, DSc); *m* 23 Aug 1958, Valerie Mary, da of Daniel Parkes; 2 s (Julian Edward b 25 Sept 1965, Nigel David b 17 Jan 1968); *Career* reader Faculty of Agric Queens Univ of Belfast 1977 (joined 1960), sr princ sci offr Plant Pathology Res Div Dept of Agric NI 1979-80, head of Crop Protection Div E Malling Reo Station 1980-85, dir AFRC Inst of Hort Res 1985-; memb Br Mycological Soc, Assoc of Applied Biologists, Inst of Biol; FIHort; *Books* Iron, Siderophores and Plant Diseases; *Recreations* sailing; *Clubs* Farmers; *Style—* Prof Terence Swinburne; Tan House, Frog lane, West Malling, Kent (☎ 0732 846 090); AFRC Institute of Horticultural Research, Bradbourne House, East Malling, Kent (☎ 0732 843 833)

SWINGLAND, Dr Ian Richard; s of Hugh Maurice Webb Swingland, of West Chiltington and Freshwater, Isle of Wight, and Flora Mary, *née* Fernie; *b* 2 Nov 1946; *Educ* Haberdashers' Aske's, Univ of London (BSc), Univ of Edinburgh (PhD), Univ of Oxford; *m* 16 Aug 1985, Fiona Mairi Lawson, da of Henry Cant Lawson, of Andorra; 1 s (Kieran Lawson b 1987), 1 da (Anna Lawson b 1989); *Career* asst Shell Research Ltd 1969, biologist Zambian Govt 1973-74, visiting scientist Royal Soc at Aldabra Atoll Res Station 1974-76; Univ of Oxford: res assoc Animal Ecology Res Gp 1974-79, tutor in ecology Dept of Zoology 1974-79; Univ of Kent: lectr in natural scis 1979-88, chm Ecology Res Gp 1983-, sr lectr in natural scis 1985-89, dir First World Congress of Herpetology 1986-, dir Durrell Inst of Conservation and Ecology 1989-; Univ of Michigan: visiting prof in biology 1986-87, sr res fell Museum of Zoology 1986-87; res assoc Smithsonian Instn 1987-; memb: Ctee Inst of Biology (Kent, Surrey and Sussex) 1979-83, cncl Br Herpetological Soc 1980-83, Cncl Kent Tst for Nature Conservation 1980-85 (Conservation Ctee 1980-85, Professional Advsy Gp 1982-), Farming and Wildlife Advsy Gp Kent 1980-84, RSPCA 1980-, Post-Doctoral Fellowship Panel of Natural Environmental Res Cncl 1983, Scientific Advsy Ctee Jersey Wildlife Presentation Tst 1985-, Cncl Fauna and Flora Preservation Soc 1985-, Kent Adult Educn Sci Curriculum Devpt Gp 1988-89, E Kent Adult Educn Devpt Gp 1988-89; sci advsr and memb directing staff Operation Drake and Operation Raleigh 1979-84, fndr and cncl memb RURAL 1980- (memb Exec Ctee 1980-83); IUCN: founding chm Tortoise and Freshwater Turtle Gp of Species Survival Cmmn 1980-, memb UK Ctee 1983-; chm: Wild Animals Advsy Ctee RSPAC 1985-; fndr and chm The Herpetological Conservservation Tst 1988-; co fndr Int Advsy Gp of Scientists for Madagascar 1983, govr Powell Cotton Museum Kent 1984-; CBiol, MIBiol, FZS; *Style—* Dr Ian R Swingland; Clement Cottage, Wingham, Kent CT3 1AE; The Durrell Institute of Conservation and Ecology, University of Kent, Canterbury, Kent CT2 7NY (☎ 0227 746000, fax 0227 459025)

SWINGLAND, Owen Merlin Webb; QC (1974); s of Charles Swingland (d 1941), of Kent, and Maggie Eveline , *née* Webb (d 1961); family moved from Worcestershire circa 1680 to parish of St Margaret Pattens, Eastcheap, London; lived in Kent about 200 years; *b* 26 Sept 1919; *Educ* Haberdashers' Aske's, King's Coll London; *m* 1941, Kathleen Joan Eason, da of late Frederick William Parry; 1 s (Charles), 2 da (Diana, Carole); *Career* barr; bencher of Gray's Inn, gen cmmr of income tax; a church cmmr for England 1982-90; Master Worshipful Co of Haberdashers' 1987; memb Lincoln's Inn 1978; *Recreations* reading, music, theatre, gardening; *Style—* Owen Swingland, Esq, QC; Redwings House, Bayleys Hill, Weald, Sevenoaks, Kent (☎ 0732 451

SWIRE, Sir John Anthony; CBE (1977); s of John Kidston Swire (d 1983); bro of Sir Adrian Swire; *b* 1927; *Educ* Eton, Univ Coll Oxford; *m* 1961, Moira Ducharne; 2 s, 1 da; *Career* served Irish Gds (UK and Palestine) 1945-48; joined Butterfield & Swire Hong Kong 1950, chm John Swire & Sons Ltd 1966- (joined 1955); former dir: Royal Insurance Co, British Bank of the Middle East, Ocean Transport & Trading Ltd; dir James Finlay & Co plc 1976-; memb: London Advsy Ctee Hongkong and Shanghai Banking Corpn 1969-89, Euro-Asia Centre Advsy Bd 1980-, Advsy Cncl Sch of Business Stanford Univ 1981-; memb of court Univ of Kent 1989; hon fell St Antony's and Univ Colls Oxford; Hon DL Hong Kong 1989; kt 1990; *Style—* Sir John Swire, CBE; Luton House, Selling, nr Faversham, Kent; John Swire & Sons Ltd, Swire House, 59 Buckingham Gate, London SW1E 6AJ (☎ 071 834 7717)

SYDDIQUE, Eric Mahmood; JP (Kent 1978); s of Ahmed Syddique (d 1967), of Eynsford, Dartford, Kent and Calcutta, India, and Martha Sophia, *née* Schmidt; *b* 2 April 1936; *Educ* St Dunstans Coll Catford London, Univ of London (external, BSc); *Career* family business 1955-67; Electoral Reform Society: asst sec 1972-79, educn offr 1979-84, head of res and info 1984; chm Eynsford Parish Cncl 1973-76 (memb 1968-83 and 1987-), Sevenoaks DC: memb Eynsford Ward 1973-, sr Lib memb 1976-87, Alliance gp ldr (now SLD gp) 1987-; Dartford and Gravesham CHC 1974-76, various offices in Bexley and Dartford Lib Assocs 1953-70, sec Eynsford Friendship Guild 1968-73, chm Lewisham and Kent Islamic Centre 1978-87, pres Sevenoaks Lib Assoc 1985-88; *Recreations* reading; *Clubs* Nat Lib; *Style—* Eric Syddique, Esq, JP; 42 St Martin's Drive, Eynsford, Dartford, Kent DA4 0EZ (☎ 0322 863048); Electoral Reform Society, 6 Chancel St, London SE1

SYKES, (John) Keith; *b* 5 Feb 1933; *Educ* Wrekin Coll, Univ of Leeds, Grays Inn; *m* 1958, Undine, *née* Hodgetts; 1 s, 4 da; *Career* chm Keith Ceramic Materials Ltd; dir: Television South West plc, CPA Holdings Ltd, Ferro (GB) Ltd, British Ceramic Research Ltd; *Recreations* fishing; *Style—* J Keith Sykes,

Esq; Keith Ceramic Materials Ltd, Fishers Way, Crabtree Manor Way, Belvedere, Kent

SYKES, Michael James Lount; s of James Wilfred Sykes, of Crawley Down, W Sussex, and May Sykes (d 1972); *b* 11 Jan 1925; *Educ* Highgate Sch, Guy's Hosp (LDS, MRCS); *m* 5 Sept 1946, Moira, da of Jack Douglas Tomlin (d 1968), of Maidstone, Kent; 1 s (Roger b 1949), 2 da (Georgina b 1951, Josephine b 1956); *Career* Flt Lt short serv cmmn Dental Branch RAF 1947-49; dentist; sr ptnr Sykes Arnold Pilc and Ward-Davies Maidstone; former pres Rotary Club Maidstone; memb BDA; *Recreations* gardening, music, tennis, golf; *Style—* Michael Sykes, Esq; The Coach House, Sissinghurst Place, Cranbrook, Kent TN17 2JP (☎ 0580 712007); 42 College Rd, Maidstone, Kent (☎ 0622 52340)

SYKES, Roger James; s of Michael James Lount Sykes, of The Coach House, Sissinghurst Place, Cranbrook, Kent, and Moira, *née* Tomlin; *b* 19 Jan 1949; *Educ* Sutton Valence, Univ of London (LLB); *m* 17 July 1971, Sabrina Ann, da of John Ambrose Thompson Hancock, of Greystone Cottage, Southview Rd, Crowborough, E Sussex; 1 s (James b 1976), 1 da (Emily b 1974); *Career* admitted slr 1974; ptnr Whitehead Monckton 1979, appointed HM Coroner for Maidstone 1986; mgmnt ctee memb of various Maidstone charities; memb Coroners' Soc of Eng and Wales 1986; *Recreations* fine wines, swanning; *Style—* Roger Sykes, Esq; Jacksons, Leeds, nr Maidstone, Kent (☎ 0622 861856); 72 King St, Maidstone, Kent (☎ 0622 690090, fax 0622 690055)

SYMONS, Julian Gustave; s of Morris Albert Symons (d 1929), and of Minnie Louise, *née* Bull (d 1963); *b* 30 May 1912; *m* 25 Oct 1941, Kathleen, da of Sydney Hatch Clark (d 1967); 1 s (Marcus Richard Julian b 1951), 1 da (Sarah Louise b 1948 d 1976); *Career* RAC 1942-44; freelance author; chm Crime Writers Assoc 1958-59, pres The Detection Club 1976-85; grand master: Mystery Writers of America 1982, Swedish Acad 1978; Crime Writers Assoc: Golden Dagger Award 1957, Silver Dagger Award 1960; Mystery Writers of America Edgar Award (1960 and 1963), Cartier Diamond Dagger Award (1990), FRSL 1976; *Books* incl: The Colour of Murder (1957), The Progress of a Crime (1960), Bloody Murder (1972); *Recreations* walking in cities; *Clubs* Detection; *Style—* Julian Symons, Esq; Groton House, 330 Dover Rd, Walmer, Deal, Kent CT14 7NX (☎ 0304 365209)

T

TALBOT, Hon Mrs (Cynthia Edith); *née* Guest; da of 1 Viscount Wimborne, JP, and Hon Alice Grosvenor, da of 2 Baron Ebury; *b* 24 Oct 1908; *m* 1933, Capt Thomas Talbot, CB, QC, *qv*; 1 s, 3 da; *Style*— The Hon Mrs Talbot; Falconhurst, Edenbridge, Kent (☎ 034 286 641)

TALBOT, Maj-Gen Dennis Edmund Blaquière; CB (1960), CBE (Mil 1955), DSO (1945), MC (1944), DL (1964); s of Walter Blaquière Talbot (d 1953), of Hadlow, Kent, and St John, Jersey, and Ethel Louise, *née* Webb (d 1973); *b* 23 Sept 1908; *Educ* Tonbridge, RMC Sandhurst, Staff Coll Camberley, RN Staff Coll Greenwich, Jt Servs Staff Coll Latimer, IDC London; *m* 23 Sept 1939, Barbara Anne, da of Rev Richard Bevan Pyper (d 1954), Rector of Pluckley, Kent; 3 s (Richard Dennis Blaquière b 1941, Rupert Michael Blaquière b 1943, Antony John Blaquière b 1949), 2 da (Elizabeth Ann Louise b 1948, Victoria Helen (Mrs Rosner) b 1959); *Career* 2 Lt Royal W Kent Regt 1928, served India 1928-37, Co Cdr Depot Maidstone 1938-39, served WWII 1939-45 (despatches), Bde Maj 30 Inf Bde 1940, POW after fall of Calais 1940, escaped to UK and became Bde Maj 141 Inf Bde 1940, GSOII HQ1 Corps 1940-41, GSOII and I Combined Ops 1942-44, 2 i/c 5 Bn Dorset Regt 1944; CO: 7 Bn Hamps Regt during Invasion of Europe 1944-45, CO 2 Bn Royal W Kent Regt UK Belgium Germany 1945-46; GSO1 HQ Far ELF 1947-48, sr UK army liaison offr NZ 1948-51, Lt-Col 1949, AAG War Office 1951-53, Col 1952; Malayan Emergency: Cdr 18 Inf Bde Pahang and Trenganu 1953-55, Cdr 99 Gurkha Inf Bde S Johore 1955; BGS HQ BAOR 1957-58, Maj-Gen 1958, GOC E Anglian Dist and 54 Inf Div TA 1958-61, Col The Queen's Own Royal W Kent Regt 1959-61, Dep Col The Queen's Own Buffs The Royal Kent Regt 1961-65; Dep Cdr BAOR 1961-63, COS BAOR 1963-64, GOC Rhine Army Troops 1963-64, ret 1964; civil servant MOD 1964-73; memb Kent TAVR Assoc 1964-68, Hon Col 8 Bn The Queens Regt TAVR 1968-71; chm regtl ctee The Queen's Own Royal W Kent Regt Museum & Offrs' Club 1966-77, ctee chm Kent Army Benevolent Fund 1967-78, vice pres local branch Royal Br Legion, pres Barham and Dist Hort Soc; memb: The Band of Brothers, Men of Kent and Kentish Men Assoc, Friends of Canterbury Cathedral, Friends of All Saints Church Maidstone; Order of the Dannebrog of Denmark: Kt Cdr 1962, Kt Grand Cross 1965; *Recreations* formerly all round sportsman now reduced to gardening, reading, crossword puzzles, mil and regtl history; *Style*— Maj-Gen Dennis Talbot, CB, CBE, DSO, MC, DL; Oast Court, Barham, Canterbury, Kent CT4 6PG (☎ 0227 831308)

TALBOT, Thomas George; CB (1960), QC (1954); s of Rt Hon Sir George Talbot, PC (ggs of Hon John Talbot, QC, 4 s of 2 Earl Talbot, which title is now merged with Earldom of Shrewsbury), and Gertrude, *née* Cator; *b* 21 Dec 1904; *Educ* Winchester, New Coll Oxford; *m* 1933, Hon Cynthia Guest (*see* Hon Mrs Talbot); 1 s, 3 da; *Career* served WW II RE (TA) and Scots Gds; called to the Bar Inner Temple 1929; bencher 1960; asst subsequently dep parly counsel to Treasy 1944-53, counsel chm ctees House of Lords 1953-77 (asst counsel chm 1977-82); *Clubs* Brooks's; *Style*— Thomas Talbot, Esq, CB, QC; Falconhurst, Edenbridge, Kent (☎ 0342 850 641)

TANNER, Adrian Christopher; s of Alfred Charles Tanner, and Betty Margaret Tanner; *b* 13 Oct 1946; *Educ* Skinners Sch Tunbridge Wells; *m* 1969, Anna Margaret, *née* Shepherd; 2 da; *Career* marine insur broker; dir Alexander Howden Insurance Brokers Ltd 1978-81, Robert Fleming Marine Ltd 1982-; memb of Lloyd's; *Style*— Adrian Tanner Esq; Wallington House, Smarden, Kent

TAPP, Robert John; s of Col Arthur Griffin Tapp, MC, OBE, TD (d 1976), of St Nicholas At Wade, Kent, and Edith May, *née* Steed; *b* 23 May 1926; *Educ* The Leys Sch Cambridge, Univ of Cambridge (MA); *m* 31 Aug 1956, Ann Gordon, da of Frederick William Gordon Smith (d 1986); 2 s (William Robert Nicholas b 1959, Andrew John Singleton b 1959); *Career* Fleet Air Arm 1944-46; dir St Nicholas Court Farm Birchington Kent; pres Lochaber Branch NFU Scotland; *Recreations* game fishing; *Clubs* Farmer's; *Style*— Robert John Tapp, Esq; Ford House, Furley, Membury, Axminster, Devon EX13 7TU (☎ 040 488368)

TAPP, (Arthur) Rodney; s of Col Arthur Griffin Tapp, OBE, MC, TD (d 1976), and Edith May, *née* Steed; *b* 10 Jan 1933; *Educ* The Leys Sch, Gonville and Caius Coll Cambridge (BA, MA); *m* 15 Sept 1956, Mary Violet, da of Capt Aubrey Cecil Hatfeild, MBE, JP (d 1971); 1 s (Jonathan Hatfeild b 1960), 3 da (Sarah Helen b 1957, Rosalind Frances b 1963, Anne-Marie Elizabeth b 1967); *Career* farmer Wade Farm St Nicholas at Wade, ptnr Hatfeild Farms Margate, non-exec dir St Nicholas Court Farms Ltd; chm Thanet branch NFU 1968-70; pres: Drapers Mill Tst 1970-, Westgate and Birchington Rotary Club 1978-79; memb NFU; *Recreations* skiing, flying light aircraft, shooting, fishing; *Clubs* Farmers, Ski; *Style*— Rodney Tapp, Esq; Wade House, Potten St, St Nicholas-at-Wade, Birchington, Kent CT7 0ND (☎ 0843 47289)

TAPPENDEN, Chief Supt Kenneth Ernest; MBE (1988); s of Ernest Henry Tappenden, of 63 Lilac Rd, Strood, Kent, and Jenny, *née* Austen (d 1987); *b* 30 March 1938; *Educ* Temple Secdy Sch Strood, Medway Coll of Art (City & Guilds Intermediate Printing), Maidstone Coll of Art (City & Guilds Printing); *m* 7 March 1959, Pauline, da of George Samuel Elkins, of 45 Longley Rd, Rochester, Kent; 1 s (Curtis Lee b 4 May 1967), 1 da (Janita Jayne b 1 Aug 1963); *Career* Nat Serv Royal Signals 1959-61; printer with Kent Art Printers and Mackays of Chatham 1953-59; Kent Co Constabulary: joined 1961, Detective Constable Medway Canterbury and Whitstable 1963-68, Uniform Sgt Tunbridge Wells 1968-69, Detective Sgt Regnl Crime Squad 1969-72, Detective Inspr Gravesend 1972-76, Detective Chief Inspr Ashford and Folkestone 1976-78, Detective Supt Force Headquarters 1978-81, dep Divnl Cdr NW Kent 1981-85, Chief Supt ops Force Headquarters 1985-87, Divnl Cdr and Chief Supt NW Kent 1987-; memb: Br Acad of Forensic Scientists, Int Police Assoc, City of Rochester Soc, Nat Tst, Cat Assoc of GB; pres Medway Artistic Roller Dance Club, govr Chatham Boys GS; Kent Co Constabulary: chm Sports Club, sec Sr Offrs Mess; awarded Police Long Serv Medal 1986; FBIM; *Recreations* artistic roller skating, cat shows, art and antiques; *Clubs* Royal Academy Friends; *Style*— Chief Supt Kenneth Tappenden, MBE; The Old Coach House, 1 Gleanings Mews, St Margaret's St, Rochester, Kent ME1 1SS; Police Station, Windmill St, Gravesend, Kent DA12 1DB (☎ 0474 564346 ext 300, fax 0474 564346 ext 169)

TARDIF, Graham Mackenzie de Putron; s of Frederick Graham Charles Tardif (d 1972), and Mabel Marion, *née* Mackenzie (d 1987); *b* 27 June 1935; *Educ* Tonbridge; *m* 1, 9 April 1960 (m dis 1971), Judith Livock; 1 s (Simon b 1963 d 1987), 1 da (Michele b 1962); m 2, 8 Jan 1972, Lucinda, da of John Hoskyns-Abrahall; 1 s (Ben b 1972), 2 da (Kate b 1975, Lucy b 1981); *Career* Nat Serv RAF 1953-55; dir: J H Minet UK 1968, Frank B Hall UK 1970, Wigham Poland UK 1973, Frizzell Group 1976; pres and chief exec Canadian Internat Insurance Management Ltd Bermuda USA 1981, chm Soberbiew Ltd and Graham Tardif Assoc Ltd, Leslie & Godwin UK Ltd 1990; Freeman City of London 1989; *Recreations* golf, rugby football, dog-walking, cooking; *Clubs* Royal St Georges Golf, Richmond FC (pres 1989), London Rowing; *Style*— Graham Tardif, Esq; Kippen, Frinsted, Sittingbourne, Kent ME9 0SN (☎ 062 784 202); PO Box 219, 6 Braham St, London E1 8ED (☎ 071 480 7200)

TATE, Alan George; s of George Tate (d 1967), of Beckenham, Kent, and Margaret Grace, *née* Holmes (d 1988); *b* 19 Nov 1927; *Educ* Colfe's GS Lewisham, Univ of London (BSc); *m* 14 June 1952, Barbara Victoria, da of Donald Mason (d 1973), of Nottingham; 1 s (Neil), 2 da (Jill, Karen); *Career* dir G Tate and Son Ltd civil engrg contractors 1949-63, fndr ptnr A G Tate & Partners conslt civil and structural engrs 1963-; Master Worshipful Co Paviors 1990- (memb 1957-); FICE 1964, FIStructE 1961, MConsE 1967; *Recreations* photography, foreign travel; *Clubs* City Livery; *Style*— Alan Tate, Esq; 17 Orchard Rd, Bromley, Kent BR1 2PR (☎ 081 464 2830); 39-41 High St, Bromley, Kent BR1 1LE (☎ 081 464 7438)

TATTON, Brian Michael; s of Edward Tatton, of Uckfield, Sussex, and Lilian, *née* Hobart (d 1987); *b* 10 Oct 1943; *Educ* Sunbury GS Sunbury-on-Thames; *m* 1 June 1985, Sally Elizabeth, da of Capt Peter Frame, of Chester; *Career* md: The Tatton Group of Companies Ltd 1962-, Tatton Electric Co Ltd 1974-, Powerent Ltd 1979-, Puma Power Plant Ltd 1982-, Enercol Energy Systems Ltd 1989-; chm Kartret Switchgear Ltd 1985-; memb: IOD, Inst of Sales Mgmnt, Inst of Diesel and Gas Turbine Engrs; *Recreations* music, shooting, travel, classic cars; *Clubs* Wig and Pen, Tramp, Mortons; *Style*— Brian Tatton, Esq; Flint Cottage, White Horse Lane, Wingmore, Elham Valley, Kent CT4 6LR (☎ 0227 831427); Puma Power Plant Gp,

Sandwich Rd, Ash, nr Canterbury, Kent CT3 2AJ (☎ 0304 812818, fax 0304 813331)

TAYLOR, Colin Ogden; OBE (1985); s of William Ogden Taylor, OBE (d 1929), of Dorin Court, Stifford, Essex, and Edith, *née* Wright (d 1966); *b* 29 Dec 1916; *Educ* Palmers Sch Grays Essex, Harvard Univ Graduate Sch of Business Studies Cambridge Mass USA; *m* 6 March 1943, Margaret Hope, da of Frank Hartley (d 1970), of Leeds; 1 s (Andrew John b 1944); *Career* flying and staff duties with FTC and Bomber Cmd RAF 1940-45; fin admin and mktg activities Mexican Repuls 1947-84; involved with all Br expatriate orgns during later residence in Mexico, hon treasy American Br Cowdray Hosp Mexico City 1960-64; FCA 1960, fell IOD 1968; *Recreations* serious music, electronics, reading; *Clubs* RAF; *Style—* Colin O Taylor, Esq, OBE; Flat C, The Woodlands, 5 Pembury Rd, Tunbridge Wells, Kent TN2 3QY (☎ 0892 29017)

TAYLOR, Dr Deryck John Edward; s of Edward James Taylor (d 1982), of Elham, Kent, and Elsie Gladys Taylor; *b* 8 Feb 1933; *Educ* Ilford Co HS, King's Coll London, Westminster Hosp (MB BS); *m* 11 Aug 1956, Janet Mary, da of Eric Alexander Barnes (d 1965), of London; 3 da (Alison Caroline b 1965, Katherine Elizabeth b 1969, Claire Louise b 1969); *Career* conslt physician and cardiologist 1971-; pubns in med jnls on cardiology; FRCP; memb of Br and Euro Cardiac Soc; *Recreations* music, bridge, fishing; *Clubs* Canterbury; *Style—* Dr Deryck Taylor; 118 North Rd, Hythe, Kent CT21 5DY (☎ 0303 268257); Kent and Canterbury Hospital, Canterbury, Kent (☎ 0227 766877)

TAYLOR, Dr James Francis Nuttall; s of Evan Nuttall Taylor, of 34 Andorra Court, Bromley, Kent, and Margaret Susie, *née* Howes (d 1979); *b* 19 Oct 1938; *Educ* Sherborne, Queens' Coll Cambridge (MA, MD, BChir), St Thomas' Hosp Med Sch; *m* 18 Sept 1965, Ann, da of Ernest Ensor (d 1985); 4 s (Jonathan James b 30 May 1969, Andrew David b 10 Aug 1970, Richard Paul b 31 Jan 1973, Michael Christopher b 14 June 1974); *Career* res fell: Yale Univ Sch Med New Haven Conn 1971-72, Br Heart Assoc 1972-75; conslt paediatric cardiologist Hosp for Sick Children 1975-, sr lectr Inst Child Health 1975-, hon conslt paediatric cardiologist E Anglian RHA 1978-; memb Bd Govrs Hosps for Sick Children 1982-84 and 1985-90; memb: Br Paediatric Assoc 1970, Br Cardiac Soc 1971, Assoc Euro Paediatrics Cardiologists 1975; FRCP 1978, FACC 1979, FRSM 1985; Knight Order of Falcons Iceland 1981; *Recreations* music, photography, walking; *Style—* Dr James Taylor; 1 Bolton Gardens, Bromley, Kent BR1 4ES (☎ 081 464 8027); Hospital for Sick Children, Cardiac Wing, Great Ormond St, London WC1N 3JH (☎ 071 405 9200 ext 5294)

TAYLOR, Dame Jean Elizabeth; DCVO (1978); da of Capt William Taylor (ka 1917); *b* 7 Nov 1916; *Career* joined Office of Private Sec to HM The Queen 1958, chief clerk 1961-78; *Recreations* music, walking, looking at old buildings; *Style—* Dame Jean Taylor, DCVO; Church Cottage, Frittenden, Cranbrook, Kent

TAYLOR, Neil Royston; s of Leonard Bertram Taylor, and Audrey Margaret, *née* Wilson; *b* 21 July 1959; *Educ* Gray Valley Tech HS Sidcup; *m* 25 Sept 1982, Jane Claire, da of Frank Cecil Fitzearle (d 1987); 2 da (Amy Louise b 7 Nov 1985, Lauren Francesca b 21 July 1988); *Career* debut Kent CCC 1979, century on debut v Sri Lanka, played for Eng 'B' v Pakistan 1982, winner of 7 Benson and Hedges Man of the Match awards, Kent Player of the Year 1989; fielded twelth man for Eng at Oval: v India 1982, v West Indies 1988; *Recreations* golf, rugby union; *Clubs* Westcombe Park RFC; *Style—* Neil Taylor, Esq; Kent County Cricket Club, St Lawrence Ground, Canterbury, Kent (☎ 0227 456886)

TAYLOR, Neville; CB (1989); s of late Frederick Herbert Taylor, and late Lottie, *née* London; *b* 17 Nov 1930; *Educ* Sir Joseph Williamson's Mathematical Sch Rochester, Coll of Commerce Gillingham; *m* 4 Sept 1954, Margaret Ann, da of late Thomas Bainbridge Vickers; 2 s (Andrew b 1956, Martin b 1958); *Career* RCS 1948-50; journalist 1950-58; press offr Admty 1958-63, fleet info offr Far E Fleet Singapore Malaysia 1963-65, chief press offr MOD 1966-68, info advsr NEDO/NEDC London 1968-70, dep dir PR RN 1970, head of info MAFF 1971-72, dir info DOE 1974-79 (dep dir 1972), DHSS 1979-82, chief of PR MOD 1982-85, dir gen COI and head of Govt Info Serv 1985-88, princ assoc Defence Public Affairs Consultants Ltd 1989-; freelance journalist 1989-; *Recreations* fishing, bird watching; *Clubs* Castle, Rochester; *Style—* Neville Taylor, Esq, CB; Crow Lane House, Crow Lane, Rochester, Kent (☎ 0634 842 990)

TAYLOR, Dr Robert Thomas; s of George Taylor (d 1973), of Derwent Rd, Warrington, Lancs, and Marie Louise, *née* Fidler (d 1986); *b* 21 March 1933; *Educ* Boteler GS, Univ of Oxford (BA, MA, DPhil); *m* 1, 20 Aug 1954 (m dis 1965), Ina, *née* Wilson; 1 s (Timothy b 1959); m 2, 25 Sept 1965, Rosemary Janet, da of Charles Leonard Boileau, of 36 Ryders Bolt, Bexhill on Sea, Sussex; 2 s (Aubrey b 1967, Christopher 1968), 1 da (Alison b 1973); *Career* res assoc in Randall laboratory physics Univ of Michigan USA 1957-58, lectr in physics Univ of Liverpool 1959-61 (ICI res fell 1958-59); The Br Cncl: asst regnl rep Madras 1961-64, sci offr Spain 1964-69, dir staff recruitment 1969-73, regnl rep Bombay 1973-77, rep Mexico 1977-81, personnel controller London 1981-86, rep Greece 1986-90, ADG 1990-; examiner physics: Oxford Local Bd 1956-61, Oxford and Cambridge Bd 1957; chief examiner physics NUJMB 1961 (examiner 1960); *Books* Chambers Encyclopaedia (contrib, 1967); *Recreations* war games, computers, theatre; *Style—* Dr Robert T Taylor; Mark Haven, High St, Cranbrook, Kent TN17 3EW (☎ 0580 714212); The British Council, 10 Spring Gardens, London SW1A 2BN (☎ 071 389 4875, fax 071 389 4971, telex 8952201 BRICON G)

TAYLOR, Dr Roger George; *b* 26 Nov 1934; *Educ* City of London Freemens Sch, St Mary's Hosp Med Sch London (MB BS); *m* 27 Feb 1960, Pamela Violet; 1 s (Richard b 8 Sept 1966), 2 da (Melanie b 28 June 1962, Sally b 15 July 1963); *Career* Nat Serv RAMC; GP; sr ptnr Taylor McGregor Turtle Dean and Meakin (joined 1961), course organiser Isle of Thanet Vocational Trg Scheme for Gen Practice 1977-90, asst advsr in gen practice SE Thames Region 1990-; memb BMA 1958; *Recreations* golf, bridge; *Clubs* Royal St George's Golf; *Style—* Dr Roger Taylor; Fairways, Dudley Ave, Westgate-on-Sea, Kent CT8 8PT; 60 Westgate Bay Ave, Westgate-on-Sea, Kent (☎ 0843 31335)

TAYLOR, William Bernard; s of Francis Augustus Taylor (d 1956), of Swansea, and Mary Elizabeth, *née* George; *b* 13 Dec 1930; *Educ* Dynevor Sch Swansea, Univ of Kent (MA); *m* 26 April 1956, Rachel May, da of Daniel Brynmor Davies (d 1959), of Godre Rhiw, Morriston, Swansea; 1 s (Simon b 1965), 2 da (Kim b 1959, Deborah b 1961); *Career* Nat Serv 1949-51, cmmnd RNVR 1950, Sub Lt RNVR 1951-53; Dist Audit Serv 1951-61, treas Llwchwr UDC 1967-68 (dep treas 1961-67), asst educn offr fin and mgmnt Manchester Corp 1969-72, co treas Kent 1980-87 (asst co treas 1972-73, dep co treas 1973-80), specialist local authy advsr Arthur Young Management Consultants 1987-89, MIM Ltd, Lombard N Central plc, Sedgwick James (Nat) Ltd 1987-, dir Interlake DRC Ltd 1989-, non-exec memb Medway Health Authy 1990-; author of numerous articles for learned magazines; memb Exec Ctee Soc of Co Treas 1983-86, fin advsr to Social Servs Ctee of Assoc of CCs 1983-86, Lloyds Underwriter 1988-; memb: Maidstone Rotary Club, Union St Methodist Church; life memb W Kent Speakers Club, hon treas SE Eng Tst Bd 1980-87, govr Kent Inst of Art and Design (chm fin ctee 1989-); FRSA, memb IPFA; *Books* Terotechnology & The Pursuit of Life Cycle Costs (1980); *Recreations* public speaking, tennis, cricket, watching rugby; *Style—* William Taylor, Esq; Selby Shaw, Heath Rd, Boughton Monchelsea, Maidstone, Kent ME17 4JE (☎ 0622 7450 22)

TAYLOR-JONES, Thomas Henry Edward; s of Henry George Tetley Taylor-Jones (1939), and Emily Laura *née* Shorter (d 1963); *b* 6 Feb 1906; *Educ* Dulwich, Univ of London, Kings Coll Hosp (MRCS, LRCP, DCH); *m* 27 May 1931, Dorothy Amy (Peta), da of John Corbett; 1 s (William b 1936 d 1945), 1 da (Sarah b 1934); *Career* casualty offr orthopaedics Kings Coll Hosp 1929-30, sr house offr Belgrave Hosp for Children 1930-31, GP Tenterden 1931-52, med offr West View Hosp Tenterden 1952-68; patron Tenterden Tst (former pres), vice pres Tenterden Museum Assoc (former pres), pres Tenterden Age Concern, chm of govrs Homewood Comp Sch; Red Cross: med offr Kent 20 1937-53, med offr Kent Branch 1953-65, dep pres Kent Branch 1965-85, patron Kent Branch 1985-; memb BMA; *Recreations* gardening; *Clubs* The Band of Brothers; *Style—* Dr Thomas Taylor-Jones, DL; The Garden, St Michael's, Tenterden, Kent (☎ 05806 3193)

TEMPLE, Marie, Lady; Marie Wanda; da of late F C Henderson, of Bombay, India; *m* 1939, as his 2 w, Sir Richard Durand Temple, 3 Bt, DSO (d 1962); *Style—* Marie, Lady Temple

THEOBALD, Deborah; da of James Eric Yates, of Martyr Worthy, nr Winchester, Hants, and Audrey, *née* Allaway; *b* 11 May 1957; *Educ* Ashford Sch for Girls, Brighton Poly Coll of Art, Harrow Coll of Art; *m* 26 July 1986, Bernard Andrew, s of Douglas Percy Theobald (d 1978); 1 s (Rufus William Alaric b 6 March 1988); *Career* freelance illustrator and designer; chm Monks Horton Parish Meeting; *Style—* Mrs Deborah Theobald; Kite Manor, Monks Horton, nr Selinge, Kent TN25 6DW (☎ 0303 813025)

THEOBALD, Cnclr Robin Neville; s of Ronald Frederick Theobald (d 1980), of Shorne, and Dorothy Elizabeth, *née* Eves (d 1986); *b* 17 June 1944; *Educ* Gordon Sch for Boys Gravesend, Gravesend Tech Coll, NW Kent Coll, Medway and Maidstone Coll of Technol (HNC); *m* 19 Oct 1985, Juliet Ann, da of Cdr Michael William Morris, RN, of Banbury; 2 da (Lucy b 1 Oct 1986, Katy b 17 May 1989); *Career* GA Ratray Building Contractors 1960-66, J Mowlem & Co Civil Engineering Contractors 1966-68, PLA Engineering Department 1968-72, Peter Fraenkel & Partners 1972-84, Peter Fraenkel Int 1984-90, princ technician Peter Fraenkel BMT Ltd 1990-; ctee memb Local Cons Assoc 1974-; Gravesham Borough Cncl: memb 1976-, planning chm 1979-86, property and projects chm 1986-; vice chm Dickens Country Protection Soc 1988- (ctee memb 1972-), chm Shorne Parish Cncl 1988- (memb 1976-); *Recreations* music, swimming, tennis; *Style—* Cncllr R N Theobald; Silvester House, Gravesend Rd, Shorne, nr Gravesend, Kent DA12 3JH (☎ 0474 823674); Peter Fraenkel BMT Ltd, City Innovation Centre, 26-31 Whiskin St, London EC1

THIN, Dr (Robert) Nicol Traquair; s of Robert Traquair Thin (d 1990), of Bromley Kent, and Annie Dempster, *née* Snowball; *b* 21 Sept 1935; *Educ*

Loretto Sch Musselburgh Scotland, Edinburgh Univ Med Sch (MB, ChB, MD); *m* 1962, (Agnes) Ann, da of Alexander William Graham, OBE (d 1964), of Inverness; 2 s (Sandy b 1964, Iain b 1968); *Career* cmmnd into RAMC 1964: Malaya, Singapore and UK ret Maj; Maj TA 1974-76; venereologist BMH Singapore 1969-71, conslt venereologist Edinburgh Royal Infirmary 1971-73, conslt in genitourinary med St Bartholomews Hosp London 1973-81, conslt venereologist St Peters Hosps London 1975-, civilian conslt in genitourinary Med to the Army 1981-, hon sr lectr Inst of Urology and conslt in genitourinary med St Thomas Hosp London 1982-, personal conslt advsr in genitourinary med to The CMO at The Dept of Health; ed British Journal of Veneral Diseases 1975-80, contrib specialist and general textbooks, incl Lecture Notes on Sexually Transmitted Diseases; pres Med Soc of Venereal Diseases 1987-89 (memb 1968-), chm specialist advsy ctee on genitourinary medicine of the Jt Ctee on Higher Med Training 1982-83 (memb 1976-81, sec 1981-82), examiner for Dip in Genitourinary Med for The Soc of Apothecaries of London 1981-, pres Soc of Health Advsrs in Sexually Transmitted Diseases 1983-86, memb expert advsy gp on AIDS 1985-87, external examiner of Dip in Venereology for Univ of Liverpool 1987-89, memb genitourinary med sub ctee of RCP 1987-, memb Nat Tst; former: postgrad dean St Bartholomews Hosp Med Coll, pres Edinburgh Univ Boat Club; vice pres St Thomas' Hosp Boat Club; memb: BMA 1960-, Med Soc of Venereal Diseases 1968-, FRSM 1988-, FRCP, FRCPE; *Recreations* music, reading, overseas travel; *Clubs* City Volunteer Officers; *Style—* Dr Nicol Thin; Teratak, 13 Park Ave, Bromley, Kent BR1 4EF (☎ 081 464 9278); Dept of Genitourinary Medicine, St Thomas' Hospital, London SE1 7EH (☎ 071 928 9292 ext 2429, fax 071 922 8079, telex 27913 STHLDN G)

THIRD, Rt Rev Richard Henry McPhail; *see:* Dover, Bishop of

THIRLWALL, Prof Anthony Philip; s of Isaac Thirlwall (d 1960), and Ivy, *née* Ticehurst (d 1988); *b* 21 April 1941; *Educ* Clark Univ USA (MA), Univ of Leeds (BA, PhD); *m* 26 March 1966, Gianna, da of Bruno Paoletti (d 1985), of Trieste; 2 s (Lawrence b 1967, Adrian b and d 1975), 1 da (Alexandra 1974); *Career* asst lectr economics Univ of Leeds 1964, lectr economics Univ of Kent 1966, prof applied economics 1976-; econ advsr Dept of Employment 1968-70; memb: Action Aid, Royal Econ Soc 1964; *Books* Growth and Development: With Special Reference to Developing Economies (1972, 4th edn 1989), Inflation, Saving and Growth in Developing Economies (1974), Regional Growth and Unemployment in the United Kingdom (with R Dixon, 1975), Financing Economic Development (1976), Keynes and International Monetary Relations (ed, 1976), Keynes and Laissez Faire (ed, 1978), Keynes and the Bloomsbury Group (ed with D Crabtree, 1980), Balance of Payments Theory and the United Kingdom Experience (1980, 3rd ed, 1986), Keynes and Economic Development (ed, 1987), Nicholas Kaldor (1987), Collected Essays of Nicholas Kaldor Volume 9 (ed with F Targetti, 1989), The Essential Kaldor (ed with F Targetti, 1989), European Factor Mobility: Trends and Consequences (ed with I Gordon, 1989), Deindustrialisation (with S Bazen, 1989); *Recreations* athletics; *Style—* Prof Anthony Thirlwall; 14 Moorfield, Canterbury, Kent (☎ 0227 766904); Keynes College, University of Kent, Canterbury, Kent (☎ 0227 764000, fax 0227 459025, telex 965449)

THIRSK, Dr (Irene) Joan; da of the late William Henry Watkins, and Daisy, *née* Frayer (d 1955); *b* 19 June 1922; *Educ* Camden Sch for Girls London, Westfield Coll Univ of London (BA, PhD); *m* 12 Sept 1945, James Wood, s of Christian Wilkie Thirsk (d 1954); 1 s (Martin David b 1956), 1 da (Jane Freya b 1958); *Career* War Serv, ATS Intelligence Corps 1942-45; asst lectr LSE 1950-51, sr res fell Dept of English Local History Univ of Leicester 1951-65, reader in econ history Univ of Oxford 1965-83, professorial fell St Hilda's Coll Oxford; memb: Royal Cmmn on Hist Monuments of Eng 1977-86, Royal Cmmn on Hist Manuscripts 1989-; vice pres Soc for Lincolnshire History and Archaelogy 1979-; pres: Br Assoc Local History 1986-, Br Agric History Soc 1983-86, Kent Fedn of Local History Soc 1990-; cncl memb Kent Archaelogical Soc 1987-, tstee Romney Marsh Res Tst 1987-; Hon D Litt: Univ of Leicester 1985, Univ of East Anglia 1990; FBA 1974; *Books* The Agrarian History of England and Wales IV and V (ed and co author, 1967 and 1984), Economic Policy and Projects (1978), The Rural Economy of England (1984); *Recreations* sewing, machine-knitting, gardening; *Style—* Dr Joan Thirsk; 1 Hadlow Castle, Hadlow, Tonbridge, Kent TN11 0EG (☎ 0732 850708)

THOMAS, Dr Adrian Mark Kynaston; s of Prof Peter Kynaston Thomas, of Highgate, London, and Mary Truscott, *née* Cox (d 1977); *b* 1 April 1954; *Educ* Christs Coll Finchley, UCL (MB BS, BSc, MRCP); *m* 8 July 1978, Susan Margaret, da of Arthur Oliver Viney, of Amersham, Bucks; 2 s (Gareth Kynaston b 4 Dec 1985, Owen Matthew Truscott b 7 July 1990), 1 da (Charlotte b 1 Sept 1988); *Career* Radiology Dept Hammersmith Hosp: registrar 1981-84, sr registrar 1984-87; sr registrar Hillingdon Hosp 1984-87; conslt radiologist: Bromley, Beckenham, Farnborough, Sloane Hosps 1987-; vice chm Bromley Portage Steering Ctee (immediate past chm), ctee memb Bromley Learning Disabilities forum, memb Radiology History Ctee, cncl memb Charles Williams Soc; FRCR; *Books* Nuclear Medicine Self-Assessment in Radiology and Imaging (jt author, 1989); *Recreations* works of Charles Williams, John Milton; *Clubs* RSM; *Style—* Dr Adrian Thomas; 3 Cedar Copse, Bickley, Kent BR1 2NY (☎ 081 467 6808); Bromley Hospital, X-Ray Dept, 17 Cromwell Rd, Bromley, Kent BR2 9AJ (☎ 081 460 9933)

THOMAS, Air Vice-Marshal Geoffrey Percy Sansom; CB (1970), OBE (1945); s of Reginald Ernest Sansom Thomas (d 1949); *b* 24 April 1915; *Educ* King's Coll Sch Wimbledon; *m* 1940, Sally, *née* Biddle; 1 s, 1 da; *Career* cmmnd RAF 1939, served with Turkish Air Force 1950-52, served with RAAF 1960-62, Air Cdre 1965, dir of Movements 1965, Air Vice-Marshal 1969, SASO Maintenance Cmd 1969-71, ret 1971; *Style—* Air Vice-Marshal Geoffrey Thomas, CB, OBE; Elms Wood House, Elms Vale, Dover, Kent (☎ 0304 206375)

THOMAS, John Richard; s of David Edgar Thomas (d 1954), of Talog, Manor Way, Petts Wood, Kent, and Daisy Thomas (d 1949); *b* 11 Sept 1927; *Educ* Dulwich; *m* 4 July 1953, Pamela Mary, da of Owen Henry White (d 1959), of Three Chimneys, Fittleworth, West Sussex; 2 s (Mark David b 2 May 1955, Richard Jeremy b 19 Sept 1958); *Career* Royal W Kent Regt: Private 1946, cmmnd 2 Lt 1947, demobilised 1948; chm and sr ptnr Baxter Payne & Lepper Chartered Surveyors 1973-87 (ptnr 1959, conslt 1987-90); dir: South of England Building Society 1967-82, Nationwide Anglia Society 1987-, Surveyors Holdings (RICS) Ltd 1986-; dep chm Anglia Building Society 1985-87 (vice chm 1982-85); chm: Nationwide Anglia Estate Agents 1987-, Peter Ling plc (bldg contractors); chm Gtr London (SE) Scout Cncl 1973-, hon sec Bromley Literary and Music Soc 1970-85; pres Gen Practice RICS 1977-78 (memb Gen Cncl 1974-88), magistrate SE Cmmn 1975-; fndr memb Worshipful Co of Chartered Surveyors 1977-; FRICS 1954, FRSA 1973; *Books* Valuations for Loan Purposes (1981), Estate Agents Act 1979 (1982); *Recreations* golf, music, gardening; *Clubs* St Stephens, Ham Manor Golf, Sundridge Park Golf; *Style—* John Thomas, Esq; 6 Glenbyrne Lodge, Albemarle Rd, Beckenham, Kent (☎ 081 464 1181); Nationwide Anglia Building Society, Chesterfield House, Bloomsbury Way, London (☎ 071 242 8822/071 379 0101)

THOMAS, Patrick James; s of Frederick George Thomas (d 1980), of Swindon, and Ruby Ethel, *née* Bright; *b* 31 Aug 1941; *Educ* Commonweal GS Swindon, Univ of Kent at Canterbury (MA); *m* 22 Aug 1964, Patricia Mary, da of John Edward Hughes (d 1985), of Swindon; 2 da (Sara Jayne b 23 April 1965, Nicola Anne b 13 March 1967); *Career* asst exec engr Post Office Telephones 1959-61, process control supervisor Plessey Semiconductors 1961-62, jr accountant Swindon Borough Cncl 1962-65, chief programmer and systems analyst; Reading Borough Cncl 1967-69 (accountant 1965-67); Kent Co Cncl: asst computor mangr 1969-73, data processing mangr 1973-86, asst head of computing and mgmnt servs 1986-87, head technology servs 1987-; memb: Kent Assoc for The Blind, The Kent Soc, various charitable orgns; CIPFA 1966, MBIM 1986, MIAM 1986; *Recreations* squash, motoring, philately, clay pigeon shooting, golf; *Style—* Patrick Thomas, Esq; 10 Bull Orchard, Barming, Maidstone, Kent ME16 9EU (☎ 0622 726257); Computor Centre, West Malling Air Station, West Malling, Kent ME19 6QE (☎ 0622 605024, fax 0732 849312, car phone 0836 787095)

THOMAS, Stephen Outar; s of Alfred Outar Thomas (d 1979), and Sylvia Maureen, *née* Bennett; *b* 10 May 1956; *Educ* Beckenham and Penge GS, King's Coll Univ of London (LLB, AKC); *m* 3 Sept 1983, Anne, da of William Richard Covington, of 8 Princes Ave, Petts Wood, Kent; 2 da (Sarah Anne Sylvia b 4 Jan 1988, Hannah Mary Louise b 23 Oct 1989); *Career* admitted slr 1980; articled clerk Judge & Priestley & Prothero & Prothero London; ptnr Argles and Court Slrs Maidstone 1986-, admin Maidstone and W Malling Duty Slr Scheme 1986-, ptnr i/c Larkfield Office 1989-; fndr and musical dir St Francis Church Music Gp Petts Wood 1978-, supt St Peter and St Paul Jr Church 1984-89, chm Leybourne Residents Assoc 1986-87, church warden St Peter and St Paul Leybourne April 1987-; memb: Convocation Senate Univ of London, King's Coll Law Assoc; *Recreations* badminton, football, piano and organ music; *Style—* Stephen Thomas, Esq; Argles and Court Solicitors, Larkfield Chambers, 38 Larkfield Rd, Larkfield, Aylesford, Kent ME20 6BW (☎ 0732 844411, fax 0732 842542)

THOMASON, Dr Benjamin; s of David Thomason (d 1976), of Mottram, Hyde, Cheshire, and Ruby, *née* Taylor (d 1983); *b* 16 Sept 1932; *Educ* Harris Coll Preston, Univ of Bradford (MSc, PhD); *m* 1, 24 May 1952, Sylvia May (d 1985), da of Walter Furniss (d 1936), of Manchester; 1 s (Brian David b 2 Nov 1959), 3 da (Janet Susan b 22 Dec 1957, Julie Carol b 26 March 1962, Sally Marie b 16 March 1966); m 2, 21 Oct 1988, Wendy, da of Ronald Fletcher, of Dartmouth; *Career* trained as electrical engr ICI 1947-57; lectr: Gt Yarmouth Coll 1957-61, Bristol Coll 1961-68; head of dept Bradford Coll 1975-79 (lectr 1968-75), vice princ Coventry 1979-82, princ S Kent 1982-; author of various tech papers incl Sensed Reconnection of Induction Motor Supplies (1978); CEng, FIEE, FBIM, FRSA; *Recreations* sailing, music, riding; *Style—* Dr Benjamin Thomason; South Kent College, Shorncliffe Rd, Folkestone, Kent CT20 2NA (☎ 0303 850061, fax 0303 220354)

THOMPSETT, Glen David; s of Donald Stanley Thompsett, and Valerie Elizabeth, *née* Westrop; *b* 9 Aug 1959; *Educ* Chippenham High (Grammer) Wilts, The Coll Swindon Wilts; *Career* radio presenter and broadcaster, TV continuity announcer TVS and LWT, voice over artist; *Recreations* squash, skiing, driving, reading; *Style*— Glen Thompsett, Esq; Invicta Radio, 15 Station Rd East, Canterbury, Kent CT1 2RB (☎ 0227 767661); TVS, Television Centre, Northam, Southampton SO9 5HZ (☎ 0703 634211)

THOMPSON, James Craig; s of Alfred Thompson, of Newcastle upon Tyne, and Eleanor, *née* Craig; *b* 27 Oct 1933; *Educ* Meaton GS Newcastle upon Tyne, Rutherford Coll Newcastle upon Tyne; *m* 4 Sept 1957, Catherine, da of the late James Warburton; 1 s (Roderic b 1959), 1 da (Fiona b 1963); *Career* commercial exec: Belfast Telegraph, Newcastle Chronicle and Journal, Scotsman Pubns, Liverpool Post and Echo 1960-76; advertising mangr and mktg dir Kent Messenger Group 1976-79, md SE Newspapers 1975-79 (dir 1972-79); chm and md: Adverkit International Ltd 1973-89, Maidstone United FC Ltd 1970-, Harvest Publications Ltd 1983-; conslt dir Adverkit Internatoinal Ltd 1989-, dir Weekly Newspaper Advertising Bureau 1977; author numerous articles on newspaper publishing and assoc football; Distinguished Serv Award Int Classified Advertising Assoc Baltimore 1968; life govr Kent Co Agric Soc 1976, hon life memb Kent CCC 1978, pres Maidstone Catenian Assoc 1974-75, chm S Football league 1977-79 (life memb 1985); pres: E Professional Floodlight League 1976-90, Football Conf 1989-, Kent League 1984-89; chm Alliance Premier Football League 1970-89, cncl memb Football Assoc 1982-; Liveryman Worshipful Co of Stationers and Newspaper Makers, Freeman City of London; MBIM, FIOD, MCIM; *Recreations* walking, Northumbrian history; *Clubs* Wig and Pen Maidstone, MCC; *Style*— James C Thompson, Esq; Prescott House, Otham, Kent ME15 8RL (☎ 0622 861606); Maidstone United Football Club Ltd, Bowerdene House, 1 Bower Terrace, Maidstone, Kent ME16 8RY (☎ 0622 756700, fax 0622 685803)

THOMPSON, Sir John; s of Donald Thompson; *b* 16 Dec 1907; *Educ* Bellahouston Acad, Glasgow Univ, Oriel Coll Oxford; *m* 1934, Agnes, da of John Drummond, of Glasgow; 2 s; *Career* called to the Bar Middle Temple 1933; QC 1954, vice chm Gen Cncl Bar 1960-61, cmmr assize Birmingham 1961, judge High Court (Queen's Bench) 1961-82; kt 1961; *Recreations* golf; *Clubs* R & A, Sundridge Park Golf; *Style*— Sir John Thompson; 73 Sevenoaks Rd, Orpington, Kent BR6 9JN (☎ 0689 22339)

THOMPSON, Peter John; s of Henry Vernon Thompson (d 1988), of London, and Mona Irene, *née* Cook; *b* 5 Dec 1941; *Educ* Forest Hill Comp, Wandsworth Tech Coll (HNC), Sir John Cass Coll (Licentiateship of the Inst of Metallurgists); *m* 20 June 1970, Julia Susan, da of John Donald Sproston (d 1987), of Dorset; 2 s (Nicholas Andrew b 1972, Daniel Peter b 1975); *Career* Stone Foundries Ltd: technician 1959-68, technologist 1968-69, works metallurgist 1969-79, approved metallurgist 1979-84, foundry planning mangr 1984-86; tech dir Kent Aerospace Castings plc 1986-; fell Inst of Br Foundrymen 1990; *Recreations* football, angling; *Style*— Peter Thompson, Esq; Kent Aerospace Castings plc, Eurolink Way, Sittingbourne, Kent ME10 3RN (☎ 0795 476333, fax 0795 473438)

THOMPSON, Philip Richard; s of Richard Brian Thompson, and Joscelyn Hope Courtney, *née* Child; *b* 19 Oct 1945; *Educ* Marlborough House Sch, Cranbrook Sch; *m* 3 April 1971, Joanna Mary, da of Neil Arthur Campbell; 2 s (James Courtney b 24 May 1973, Charles Neil b 28 June 1976); *Career* position in Tstee Dept: National Westminster Bank 1964-69, Mann Judd and Co 1969-73, Coopers and Lybrand 1973-76; asst dir shipping insur A Bilborough and Co Ltd 1978-83, ptnr certified accountants practice Cranbrook 1983-; treas: Hawkhurst Cottage Hosp League of Friends, Weald of Kent 41 Club, Old Cranbrookians Assoc, Marlborough House Soc; memb: Cranbrook and Hawkhurst Rotary Club, Cranbrook Sch Parent Assoc, Tunbridge Wells C of C; fell Chartered Assoc of Certified Accountants; *Recreations* reading, hockey, golf, cricket, gardening; *Clubs* Marden Russets Hockey; *Style*— Philip Thompson, Esq; Thompson Partnership, 21 Stone St, Cranbrook, Kent TN17 3HF (☎ 0580 713 519, fax 0580 713178)

THOMPSON, Sir Richard Hilton Marler; 1 Bt (UK 1963), of Reculver, Co Kent; s of Richard Smith Thompson (d 1952), and Kathleen Hilda, *née* Marler (d 1916), of London and Calcutta; *b* 5 Oct 1912; *Educ* Malvern; *m* 9 Aug 1939, Anne Christabel de Vere, da of late Philip de Vere Annesley (bro of 13 Viscount Valentia); 1 s; *Heir* s, Nicholas Annesley Marler Thompson; *Career* Nat Serv RNVR 1940-46, cmmnd 1941 (despatches 1942), Lt Cdr 1944; business in India 1930-39; MP (C) Croydon West 1950-55, asst-govt whip 1952, Lord Cmmr of the Treasy 1954, MP (C) Croydon South 1955-66 and 1970-74, vice chamberlain of HM Household 1956, parly sec Miny of Health 1957-59, under-sec of state CRO 1959-60, parly sec Miny of Works 1960-62; tstee Br Museum 1951-84, memb Cncl Nat Tst 1978-84; dir: Rediffusion TV Ltd and Rediffusion Hldgs Ltd 1966-83; fndr memb and first elected pres Br Museum Soc 1970-74, chm Capital Counties Property Co Ltd 1971-77; pres Br Property Fedn 1976-77; *Recreations* gardening, country pursuits, reading; *Clubs* Carlton, Army and Navy; *Style*— Sir Richard Thompson, Bt; Rhodes House, Sellindge, Kent

THOMPSON, (Rhoderick Grahame) Timothy; s of Wellington James (Ken) Thompson, of Penryn, Cornwall, and Enid, *née* Newbold (d 1985); *b* 23 Sept 1949; *Educ* Falmouth GS, Univ of Southampton (BA), Univ of Liverpool (MCD), Mid Kent Coll (Postgrad Dip Mgmnt Studies); *m* 6 Oct 1973, Susan, da of William Radcliffe, of Woolton, Liverpool; 2 s (Simon b 1978, Adam b 1980); *Career* Tonbridge & Malling Borough Cncl: princ and chief planning offr 1976-85, dir of planning 1985-87, dir of devpt servs 1987-89, chief exec 1990-; memb Soc of Local Authy Chief Execs; MRTPI, MBIM; *Recreations* cricket, travel, family; *Style*— Timothy Thompson, Esq; 20 Haste Hill Close, Boughton Monchelsea, Maidstone, Kent ME17 4LS (☎ 0622 743394); Tonbridge & Malling Borough Council, The Air Station, West Malling, Maidstone, Kent ME19 6LZ (☎ 0732 844522, fax 0732 842170)

THOMSON, Charles Geoffrey; s of Arthur Albert Leonard Thomson, of Burwash, East Sussex, and Mary Catherine, *née* Drury; *b* 6 Feb 1953; *Educ* Brentwood Sch, Maidstone Coll of Art; *m* 25 Oct 1974 (m dis 1980), Andrea, da of Božo Mestanek, of Stanford-le-Hope, Essex; 1 s (Sebastian Ben b 1987); *Career* poet; writer in residence Borough of Bexley 1985, poet in Chaucer in Performance video 1985, res poet Invicta Radio 1987, poetry ed Kent Companion 1987-88; poet in residence: Medway Arts Centre 1988, France Hill Festival 1989; author Poet At Large feature in Kent Life 1989-; readings incl: ICA (London) 1979, Kent Lit Festival 1980-89, Cambridge Poetry Festival 1981, Nat Poetry Centre 1982, Sevenoaks Summer Festival 1984, Brighton Festival 1985, Maidstone Summer Festival 1985 and 1987, Zap Club Brighton 1985 and 1987; TV bdcasts: Getting It On (TVS) 1982, Coast to Coast (TVS) 1983, 1987 and 1989, No 73 (ITV) 1987, Late Night Late (TVS) 1988; radio bdcasts incl BBC Radio 1 and BBC Radio 4; fndr Havering Arts Lab 1969, memb Havering Arts Cncl 1970, fndr memb The Medway Poets 1979, fndr chm Maidstone Poets 1985, co-ordinator The Poetry Show 1986, hon sec Maidstone Area Arts Cncl 1986-87, artistic conslt Nat Convention Of Poets and Small Presses 1988, memb Soc of Authors 1990; *Books* The Royal Tour (1983), The End Of The Boer War (1985), The Art of Killing Chickens (1985), Lunchtime Rhymes (1988), The Manic Computer (for children, 1990); *Recreations* record collecting; *Style*— Charles Thomson, Esq; 50 Buckland Rd, Maidstone, Kent ME16 0SH (☎ 0622 752656)

THOMSON, Robert Stephen; s of Arthur Albert Leonard Thomson, of Burwash, E Sussex, and Mary Catherine, *née* Drury; *b* 18 Feb 1955; *Educ* Royal Liberty GS Romford, Univ of Leeds (BSc), Univ of Cambridge (Dip Statistics); *m* 12 June 1982, Alison Mary Thomson, da of Geoffrey Bonnett, of Barford St Martins, Salisbury, Wiltshire; 1 s (Jack Robert Bonnett b 1988); *Career* ptnr Clay & Partners 1986- (actuarial trainee 1979); FIA 1986; *Recreations* tennis, squash, golf, reading, gardening; *Clubs* Biddenden Tennis, Biddenden Squash; *Style*— Robert Thomson, Esq; Clay & Partners, 61 Brook St, London W1Y 2HN (☎ 071 408 1600, fax 071 499 0711)

THOMSON, William Chalmers; s of William Thomson (d 1968), of Glasgow, and Catherine, *née* Chalmers (d 1943); *b* 22 Feb 1929; *Educ* Royal Coll of Science and Technol Strathclyde (Dip Arch, Dip Town Planning); *m* 2 April 1955, Elizabeth Penman, da of John Sinclair (d 1972), of Glasgow; 1 s (Alan Sinclair b 1963), 1 da (Karen Jane b 1966); *Career* architect/planner East Kilbride Devpt Corp 1954-56; Cumbernauld Devpt Corp 1957-61; actg Chief Architect & Planning Offr Basingstoke Devpt Corp 1962-64; dir Colin Buchanan and Ptnrs 1964-; RIBA, Fellow Royal Town Planning Inst; *Recreations* riding, target shooting, cycling; *Style*— William C Thomson, Esq; 3 Vine House, 4 St Johns Rd, Sevenoaks, Kent TN13 3LW (☎ 0732 46024); Colin Buchanan & Ptnrs, 59 Queen Gdns, London W2 3AF (☎ 071 258 3799, telex 263802 COBPARG, fax 071 258 0299)

THORBEK, Erik; s of Kai Birch (d 1988), and Dr Agro Grete Thorbek; *b* 10 Jan 1941; *Educ* Billum Coll Denmark; *m* 6 April 1963, Susan Margaret, da of Sidney Gair (d 1977); 2 s (Alexander b 1964, Nikolas b 1973), 2 da (Francesca b 1966, Natasha b 1975); *Career* H & T Walker Group of Companies: dir 1964-72, md 1972-77, chm and chief exec 1977-; *Recreations* golf, skiing, horse racing, shooting, sailing, travel; *Clubs* Turf, Helford River Sailing, Nevill Golf; *Style*— Erik Thorbek, Esq; Maynards, Matfield, Kent TN12 7DU (☎ 0892 72 3966); Walker House, London Rd, Riverhead, Sevenoaks, Kent TN13 2DN (☎ 0732 450712, fax 0732 459288)

THORNE, Terry John; s of Ronald Ernest Stanley Thorne (d 1965), of Lower Halstow, and Joan Phyllis, *née* Hunt (d 1967); *b* 15 Aug 1939; *Educ* Sittingbourne West Secdy Sch, Mid Kent Tech Coll Chatham, Cass Elliot Coll London; *m* 25 Nov 1961, Marjorie Joan, da of Harold Edward John Ward (d 1960), of Gillingham, Kent; 3 s (David Adrian b 31 Oct 1963, Andrew Philip b 9 June 1965, Martin John b 6 March 1968), 1 da (Rachel Claire b 20 Jan 1973); *Career* apprentice panel beater and sheet metal worker A Wraight Ltd Sittingbourne 1954, transferred to Burnett & Rolfe Ltd 1957 (site installation and commissioning engr 1961-68), sales mangr APV Burnett & Rolfe 1977-86, currently gen sales mangr int APV Rosista Ltd; memb: Inst of Brewing, Br Bottlers Inst; export ctee memb Allied Brewery Traders Assoc, ctee memb Kent Export Assoc, dir Medway and Gillingham C of C; sch govr: The Oaks Infant Sittingbourne, Minterne Jr Sittingbourne, Lansdowne Primary Sittingbourne, St Thomas Special Sch Sittingbourne; *Recreations* model engineering, philately, DIY, caravanning; *Clubs* Landrover Owners, Caravan, Crews Quarters (Chatham), Nat Tst; *Style*— Terry Thorne, Esq; 48 Highsted

Rd, Sittingbourne, Kent ME10 4QH (☎ 0795 425531); APV Rosista Ltd, Whitewall Rd, Medway City Estate, Strood, Rochester, Kent ME2 4EJ (☎ 0634 717888, fax 0634 711601)

THORNTON, Lady; Agnes Margaret; *née* Masson; *m* 1927, Sir Ronald Thornton, late dir Bank of England (d 1981); 1 s, 1 da; *Style*— Lady Thornton; South Bank, Rectory Lane, Brasted, Westerham, Kent

THORNTON, Christopher Cholmondeley; s of Reginald Trelawny Thornton, MBE, MC (d 1968), and Elsie Barbara Anson, *née* Tate; *b* 28 Sept 1933; *Educ* St Andrews Sch Pangbourne, Marlborough; *m* 17 June 1961, Jennifer, da of Ernest Charles Goldsworthy (d 1986); 1 s (Philip Charles b 1965), 1 da (Julia Lucy b 1967); *Career* Nat Serv Midshipman HMS Perseus and HMS Excellent RN 1952-54; slr's articled clerk Mackrell Maton & Co 1954-60, admitted slr 1960, Stephenson Harwood Linklaters & Paines 1963-65, mangr Hill Samuel & Co Ltd 1965-68; dir: Rediffusion (West Indies) Ltd 1970-, Rediffusion plc 1984-88 (exec 1968-84), Rediffusion (Hong Kong) Ltd 1985-; chm: Telcommunications Network Ltd 1990-; chm WI Trade Advsy Gp to BOTB 1983-85, vice pres W India Ctee 1988- (chm 1985-87); cncllr Sevenoaks UDC 1967-70, chm Dartford and Gravesham DHA 1990-; Liveryman City of London Slrs Co 1967; memb Law Soc 1960, fell IOD 1987; *Recreations* fly fishing, tennis, choral singing, gardening; *Clubs* East India; *Style*— Christopher Thornton, Esq; Kettleshill House, Underriver, Sevenoaks, Kent TN15 ORX

THORPE, Richard Malin; s of Capt Bernard Thorpe (d 1987), and Hilda Mary Thorpe (d 1971); *b* 15 Oct 1926; *Educ* Cranleigh Sch, Trinity Coll Cambridge (MA); *m* 31 Dec 1948, Alice Daisy, da of Henry Samuel Adlam; 1 s (Malin b 1950); *Career* cmmnd Irish Gds 1944, demob 1947; joined family firm Bernard Thorpe & Ptnrs land agents and surveyers 1951, managing ptnr and chm Main Equity Partnership 1973, chm and sr ptnr Nat Partnership 1983, churchwarden Parish church of St Lawrence Bidborough, former co and dist cncllr Kent, vice chm Citicare St Clememts; pres: Cons Assoc Constit (Tunbridge Wells), local cons Assoc (Southborough), West Kent Hunt Supporters Club (former master Kent Hunt); former memb Westminster C of C Fin & Gen Purposes ctee; Master of Worshipful Co of Gold and Silver Wyre Drawers 1987 (Freeman and memb ct), Freeman and Liveryman Worshipful Co of Farmers 1967; FRICS 1954; *Recreations* gardening; *Clubs* Oriental; *Style*— Richard Thorpe, Esq; Home Farm, London Rd, Southborough, Tunbridge Wells, Kent TN4 0UH (☎ 0732 354744)

TIBBALDS, Francis Eric; s of late William Eric Tibbalds, of Beckenham, Kent, and Elsie Agnes, *née* Wood; *b* 16 Oct 1941; *Educ* Farnham GS, Regent St Poly (Dip Arch), Univ of London (MPhil); *m* 6 Sept 1969, Janet Grace, da of Kenneth Malcolm McDonald, of Hayes, Bromley, Kent; 2 s (Adam Dominic b 1971, Benedict Malcolm b 1973); *Career* sr architect planner Llewelyn-Davies Weeks Forestier-Walker & Bor 1969-70, princ architect planner Westminster City Cncl 1970-72, dep chief planning offr Lambeth Borough 1972-74, jt project dir Gp Five (Nigeria) 1974-75, dir of planning Llewelyn-Davies Weeks 1975-78, fndr ptnr Tibbalds Partnership 1978, Tibbalds Colbourne Karski Williams Ltd Architects and Planners 1990-; visiting prof Bartlett Sch of Architecture and Planning UCL 1989-; pres London Univ Town Planning Soc 1968, fndr Urban Design Gp (chm 1979-86), assoc memb Soc of Architect Artists, hon sec RTPI 1990- (pres 1988); memb: Cncl (and chm Environment Ctee) RSA 1989, London Advsy Ctee and Historic Areas Advsy Ctee English Heritage (The Historic Buildings and Monuments Cmmn) 1990-; Freeman City of London 1988, memb Worshipful Co of CAs; RIBA 1968, FRTPI 1970, FRSA 1980, FFB 1985; *Books* Urban Sketchbook (1988); *Recreations* sketching, choral singing, fitness training; *Style*— Francis E Tibbalds, Esq; 37 Kelsey Park Ave, Beckenham, Kent BR3 2NL (☎ 081 658 3479); Tibbalds Colbourne Karski Williams Ltd, 39 Charing Cross Rd, London WC2H 0AW (☎ 071 439 9272, fax 071 439 0323)

TICKLE, Brian Percival; CB (1985); s of William Tickle, and Lucy, *née* Percival; *b* 31 Oct 1921; *Educ* The Judd Sch Tonbridge; *m* 3 March 1945, Margaret Alice; 1 s (John b 1948), 1 da (Margaret (Mrs Schofield) b 1949); *Career* WWII RCS 1941-46; Civil Serv 1938-70; sr registrar Family Div High Court of Justice 1982-88 (registrar 1970-), ret 1988; co-chm Independent Schools Tribunal 1988-; capt Nevill Golf Club 1975 (tstee 1974-); *Books* Rees Divorce Handbook (ed 1963), Atkins Court Forms and Precedents Probate (2 edn, 1984); *Recreations* golf; *Clubs* Cwlth Tst, Nevill Golf; *Style*— B P Tickle, Esq, CB; 1A Royal Chase, Tunbridge Wells, Kent, TN4 8AX

TILL, Ven Michael Stanley; s of Maj Stanley Brierley Till (d 1985), of Sunderland, and Charlotte Mary, *née* Pearse; *b* 19 Nov 1935; *Educ* Brighton Hove and Sussex GS, Lincoln Coll Oxford (BA), Westcott House Cambridge; *m* 1965, Theresa Sybil Henriette (Tessa), da of Capt Stephen Wentworth Roskill, CBE, DSC, RN (d 1982), of Cambridge; 1 s (Tobias b 21 April 1969), 1 da (Sophie Elizabeth b 18 May 1971); *Career* Nat Serv 2 Lt RASC HQ NID 1955-57; asst curate St John's Wood Parish Church 1964-67, dean and fell King's Coll Cambridge 1970-81, (chaplain 1967-70), vicar All Saints Fulham 1981-86, rural dean Hammersmith and Fulham 1982-86, archdeacon of Canterbury 1986-; memb ACCM selector 1975-, memb General Synod 1986-, vice chm Canterbury Arts Cncl, prior of St Nicholas Hosp Harbledown; govr: The Kings Sch, St Edmund's Sch, Benenden; *Recreations* painting, walking, art and music appreciation, building; *Style*— The Ven the Archdeacon of Canterbury; Chillenden Chambers, 29 The Precincts, Canterbury, Kent CT1 2EP (☎ 0227 463036)

TIMANS, Janis Karlis; s of Otto Atis Timans (d 1963), of Alsviki, and Aline, *née* Biezais (d 1975); *b* 11 Jan 1922; *Educ* Med Faculty Univ of Riga, Univ of Bristol, RCS (LDS); *m* 1, 22 March 1956, Lilija Erika Antonija (d 1981); 1 s (Paul b 1962), 1 da (Dr Anita Timans b 1960); m 2, 2 July 1983, Pamela Ann, da of Sgt Percy Rae Cuckow; 1 s (Karl b 1984); *Career* house surgn Chest Hosp Riga 1943; asst dental surgn: Swindon 1952, Gravesend 1953; dental surgn : General Dental Services Rochester 1959, Private Practice 1972; princ of large practice 1978; actively involved in Nat Fedn of Self-Employed; memb BDA, fndr memb GDPA; *Recreations* skiing, chess; *Style*— Janis Timans, Esq; 5 London Rd, Strood, Rochester, Kent ME2 3JA (☎ 0634 718882)

TIMMS, Ven George Boorne; s of George Timms (d 1936), and Annie Elizabeth, *née* Boorne (d 1939); *b* 4 Oct 1910; *Educ* Derby Sch, St Edmund Hall Oxford (MA), Coll of the Resurrection Mirfield; *Career* clerk in Holy Orders; deacon 1935, priest 1936; curacies: St Mary Magdalen Coventry 1935-38, St Bartholomew Reading 1938-49; Oxford diocesan inspr of schs 1944-49, sacrist Southwark Cathedral 1949-52, vicar St Mary the Virgin Primrose Hill 1952-65, rural dean Hampstead 1959-65, prebendary St Paul's Cathedral 1964-71, proctor in convocation 1955-59 1965-70 and 1974-80, dir ordination trg and examining chaplain to Bishop of London 1965-81, archdeacon Hackney 1971-81 (emeritus 1981-); chm and dir The English Hymnal Co Ltd 1968-; chm Alcuin Club 1968-87, pres Sion Coll 1980-81; *Books* Dixit Cranmer (1946), The Liturgical Seasons (1965), The Cloud of Witnesses (1982), The New English Hymnal (ed, 1986); *Style*— The Ven George B Timms; Cleve Lodge, Minster-in-Thanet, Ramsgate, Kent CT12 4BA (☎ 0843 821777)

TINHAM, Alan Clement John; s of Victor Robert Sydney Tinham (d 1964), of Broadstairs, Kent, and Ethel Mabel, *née* Clements (d 1985); *b* 25 Jan 1948; *Educ* Chatham House GS Ramsgate; *m* 27 Sept 1969, Margaret Catherine, da of John Handford, of Broadstairs, Kent; 1 s (Richard b 1975), 3 da (Rebecca b 1973, Victoria b 1979, Ruth b 1987); *Career* managing ptnr Margate branch of Reeves & Neylan CAs; FCA, ATII; *Recreations* windsurfing, sea angling; *Style*— Alan Tinham, Esq; Spindrift, Marine Drive, Kingsgate, Broadstairs, Kent CT10 3LU (☎ 0843 63450); Reeves and Neylan, Cecil Sq House, Cecil Sq, Margate, Kent (☎ 0843 227937)

TOALSTER, John Raymond; s of Chief Petty Offr John Edward Toglster RNVR (ka 1944), and Adeline Enid, *née* Smith; *b* 12 March 1941; *Educ* Kingston HS Hull N Humberside, LSE (BSc); *m* 21 Sept 1963, Christine Anne, da of Edward Percival Paget (d 1970); 1 s (Quentin Simon Edward b 1966), 2 da (Rachel Jane b 1969, Bethan Claire b 1981); *Career* lectr econs Univ of Sierra Leone 1964-67, corporate planner Mobil Oil 1967-69, sr analyst (oils) stockbroking 1970-77, corporate fin mangr Kuwait Int Investmt Co 1977-81, energy specialist stockbroking 1982-; dir: Hoare Govett, Security Pacific; FInstPet 1988; private circulation to clients; *Recreations* swimming, sailing, badminton; *Style*— John Taolster, Esq; Fig St Farm, Sevenoaks, Kent (☎ 0732 453357); Hoare Govett, 4 Broadgate, London EC2N 7LE (☎ 01 601 0101, fax 01 256 8500, telex 297 801)

TODD, Ralph Ronald; s of William Alan Todd, of Ipswich, Suffolk, and Cicely Hannah, *née* Mayes; *b* 30 Oct 1950; *Educ* Tower Ramparts Sch Ipswich, W London Coll of Further Educn (ONC); *m* 19 May 1973, Brenda June, da of Rex William Frampton (d 1969), of Weymouth; *Career* joined BBC Publications 1970, admin mangr BBC World Service 1986- (joined 1981); RSPB: fndr memb and chm Bexley Memb Gp 1979-85, SE London and NW Kent hon rep 1985-, memb Nat Cncl 1988; *Recreations* birdwatching, athletics, photography/lecturing; *Style*— Ralph Todd, Esq; 9 Horsham Rd, Bexleyheath, Kent DA6 7HU (☎ 0322 528335); BBC World Service, Bush House, The Strand, London WC2B 4PH (☎ 071 257 2986)

TONBRIDGE, Archdeacon of; *see*: Mason, Ven Richard John

TONBRIDGE, Bishop of 1982-; Rt Rev David Henry Bartleet; s of Edmund Arthur Bartleet, MC, Croix de Guerre (d 1981), of Broad Eaves, Mill Lane, Broxbourne, Herts, and Helen, *née* Holford; *b* 11 April 1929; *Educ* St Edward's Sch Oxford, Architectural Assoc Sch of Architecture, St Peter's Coll Oxford (MA); *m* 1 Sept 1956, Jean Mary, da of Thomas Arthur Rees (d 1969), of Worcester; 1 s (Andrew b 31 Jan 1958), 2 da (Claire b 30 Dec 1959, Emma b 15 Jan 1963); *Career* Nat Serv Royal Signals 1947-49; curate St Mary Le Tower Ipswich 1957-60, priest i/c St Edmunds Doncaster 1960-64; vicar: Edenbridge Kent 1964-73, Bromley 1973-82; Bishop of Tonbridge 1982-; *Recreations* music, gardening, painting; *Style*— The Rt Rev the Bishop of Tonbridge; Bishop's Lodge, 48 St Botolph's Rd, Sevenoaks, Kent TN13 3AG (☎ 0732 456070)

TONG, Prof Howell; s of Kwan Tak Tong, of Bramhall, Cheshire, and Wing Ngan, *née* Li; *b* 2 Feb 1944; *Educ* Wah Yan Coll SJ Hong Kong, Barnsbury Sch for Boys London, Univ of Manchester Inst of Sci and Technol; *m* 16 July 1971, (Ann) Mary, da of Po Yan Leong, of Wembley, Middx; 1 s (Simon Sea-Yuen b 1976), 1 da (Anna Sea-Lin b 1980); *Career* lectr and sr lectr in statistics Univ of Manchester Inst of Sci and Technol 1968-82, founding prof of statistics Chinese Univ of Hong Kong 1982-86; Univ of Kent: prof and head of statistics 1986-, dir Inst of Mathematics and Statistics 1990-; former advsr to Hong Kong Govt Dept of Census and Statistics; memb res section RSS, Int Statistics Inst; assoc ed: Journal of Royal Statistical Society (series B), Statistica Sinica; *Books* Threshold Models in Nonlinear Time Series Analysis (1983), Nonlinear Time Series: a dynamical system approach (1990); *Recreations* table tennis, ancient chinese poetry, philately, reading and writing; *Style*— Prof Howell Tong; University of Kent, Inst of Mathematics and Statistics, Canterbury, Kent CT2 7NF (☎ 0227 764000 ext 3658, fax 0227 471078)

TOPLISS, John Martin; s of Alfred John Topliss (d 1986), and Edith Olive, *née* Smith; *b* 17 Oct 1946; *Educ* Wednesfield GS, Loughborough Univ of Technol (MSc); *m* 25 Aug 1971, Christine, da of Albert Edward Brown (d 1986); 1 s (Richard b 24 April 1974), 1 da (Rosalind b 6 July 1976); *Career* accounting mangr Pedigree Petfoods Ltd 1972-76, chief accountant Spillers Foods Ltd 1976-78, fin dir then sales dir Barratt Essex Ltd 1981-83, mangr of in-co devpt PA Int Mgmnt Conslts Ltd 1983-88 (strategic servs conslt 1978-81), client dir Professional Mgmnt Devpt Ltd 1988-; FCA 1969, FBIM 1983, MIMC 1987; *Recreations* modern literature; *Style*— John Topliss, Esq; 1 Brooklands Farm Close, Springhill, Fordcombe, Tunbridge Wells, Kent TN3 0SF (☎ 0892 74551)

TOPPING, Rev Francis (Frank); s of Francis Bede Topping (d 1982), of Birkenhead, and Dorothy Veronica, *née* Kelly (d 1985); *b* 30 March 1937; *Educ* St Anselm's Coll Birkenhead, The North West Sch of Speech and Drama Southport, Didsbury Coll Bristol; *m* 15 April 1958, June, da of Alfred Sydney Berry; 2 s (Simon b 1961, Mark b 1963), 1 da (Anne b 1959); *Career* Nat Serv RAF Cyprus 1955-57, temp officiating Chaplain RSME Regt 1983-84; stage mangr, electrician, asst carpenter and actor Leatherhead Repertory Co 1957-58, stage mangr and actor Wolverhampton Grand Theatre 1959-60, played Krishna in Dear Augustine (Royal Court Theatre) 1959, actor and stage mangr Touring Co 1960-; Granada TV: stage hand, TV floormangr 1960, first asst film dir 1962-64; Theological Coll 1964-67, probationer Methodist min Woodingdean Brighton and univ chaplin Univ of Sussex 1967-70, freelance bdcaster BBC Radio Brighton 1967-70, ordained Methodist min 1970, prodr BBC Radio Bristol 1970-72 (and short story ed and presenter), asst religious progs organizer for all religious progs in N Manchester BBC Network Centre 1972-73, nat ed London 1973-80; progs on BBC radio incl: Good Morning Sunday, Thought for the Day, Pause for Thought; presenter: Sunday Best (ITV), Topping on Sunday (ITV) 1982-84, The 5 Minute Show (TVS) 1989; nat chaplain Toch 1984-86 (hon chaplain 1985-), chaplain Kent Coll 1988-; with Donald Swann wrote songs and sketches for Radio and TV and Swann with Topping (Ambassadors Theatre); presented three one-man plays; *Books* Lord of the Morning (1977), Lord of the Evening (1979), Lord of my Days (1980), Working at Prayer (1981), Pause for Thought - with Frank Topping (1981), Lord of Life (1982), The Words of Christ, 40 Meditations (1983), God Bless You Spoonbill (1984), Lord of Time (1985), An Impossible God (1985), Wings of the Morning (1987), Act Your Age (1989); *Recreations* sailing, sketching, watercolours; *Clubs* Naval, Hurst Castle Sailing; *Style*— The Rev Frank Topping; Browning Lodge, Kent College, Pembury, Tumbridge Wells, Kent (☎ 0892 282 2887); 3 Springfield Cottages, Brede, Rye, E Sussex

TOWSE, Rev Anthony Norman Beresford; s of Maj Edward Beresford Towse (d 1959), of Orpington, Kent, and Nora Alice, *née* Selby (d 1988); *b* 30 April 1921; *Educ* Westminster, Lincoln Coll Oxford (MA), Westcott House Cambridge; *Career* clergyman RAFVR 1941-46; vicar: Appledore Kent 1964-90, Stone in Oxney and Ebony 1972-82, Kenardington 1975-90, Brookland and Fairfield and Brenzett with Snargate 1982-90; rural dean of South Lympne 1981-87 and 1989; contrib to pubn Archaelogia Cantiana Vol 99 (1983); TV South documentary films: appeared in Two Men in a Marsh (1987), advisor Local Human Factor (1990); chm Rye Spring Music 1975-79; govr C of E primary schs: Appledore 1964-90 (former chm), Brenzett 1981-90, Wittersham 1969-81 (former chm); chm Bd of Govrs Brookland C of E primary Sch 1981-90, tstee the Charity of the Rev Tatton Brockman 1981-90, cncl memb The Romney Marsh Historic Churches Tst; Citizen and Fishmonger of London; *Recreations* family history; *Style*— The Rev Anthony Towse; 3 Oaks Rd, Tenterden, Kent TN30 6RD (☎ 05806 6402)

TOY, Philip Henderson; s of James Ernest Henderson Toy (d 1958), of Sevenoaks, and Dora Evelyn, *née* Martin (d 1951); *b* 19 Nov 1908; *Educ* Eltham Coll, Coll of Estate Mgmnt; *m* 6 July 1935, Enid Margaret (d 1987), da of George Gibbon Whitelegg (d 1957), of Chislehurst and Knockholt; 1 da (Elizabeth Margaret b 1937); *Career* sr ptnr D R Nolans and Co chartered surveyors London and Maidstone 1943-74; memb SE Region Jt Consultative Bldg and Engrg Ctee 1948-74, RICS 1967-73; chm Kent branch RICS 1960, fndr and chm Kent branch Chartered Quantity Surveyors; chm: Hildenborough Parish Cncl 1965-81 (memb 1959-83), Tonbridge RDC 1970-72 (memb 1960-74), Kent Assoc Parish Cncls 1973-76, Local Govt Reorganisation Ctee 1973; hon alderman Tonbridge and Malling Borough Cncl 1974-; Friends of Kent Churches: hon sec 1949-68, hon chm 1968-83, vice pres 1984-; memb: Cncl of Sevenoaks Civic Soc 1948-53, Ctee for the Protection of Rural Kent 1950-76, Rochester Diocesan Dilapidations Bd 1958-63, Central Cncl of Architectural advsy panels 1967-76, Cncl of Kent Naturalist Tst 1967-78, Soc for Protection of Ancient Bldg tech panels 1975-78; chm: CPRE (Kent) 1963-80 (memb 1949-), Rochester Diocesan Advsy Ctee 1975-83 (memb 1961-83); vice pres Kent Rural Community Cncl 1983- (ctee memb 1963-); govr Hardwick Special Sch Hildenborough 1975-88; memb Worshipful Co of Gardeners 1956, Freeman City of London; FRICS; *Recreations* reading, walking, enjoyment of the countryside and ancient bldgs; *Clubs* Nat Lib; *Style*— Philip Toy, Esq; Oakhurst Manor, Bank Lane, Hildenborough, Tonbridge, Kent TN11 8NR

TOYNBEE, Simon Victor; s of Ralph Victor Toynbee (d 1970), and Bridget, *née* Monins; *b* 30 Jan 1944; *Educ* Winchester; *m* 12 Aug 1967, Antoinette Mary, da of John Walter Devonshire, of Santa Monica, California, USA; 3 da (Georgina, Elizabeth, Susannah); *Career* 2 Lt The RB 1963-65; Jessel Toynbee and Co Ltd 1966-72; dir: Investmt Dept Singer and Friedlander Ltd 1977-82 (joined 1973), Henderson Administration Ltd 1987-90 (joined 1982), Mercury Fund Managers and Mercury PTE Investors Ltd; Mercury Asset Mgmnt plc 1990-; hon investmt advsr Royal Greenjackets Funds and Church Army; *Recreations* gardening, deerstalking; *Clubs* Royal Greenjackets, MCC; *Style*— S V Toynbee, Esq; Old Tong Farm, Brenchley, Kent TN12 7HT (☎ 0892 723552); 33 King William St, London EC4R 9AS (☎ 071 280 2254, fax 071 280 2827)

TRAYLING, Dr Anthony Peter Allam; s of Thomas Benjamin Trayling (d 1977), of Bexhill on Sea, E Sussex, and Ethel Beatrice, *née* Allam (d 1981); *b* 10 May 1936; *Educ* UCL Med Sch, Guy's Med Sch; *m* 4 Nov 1967, Laurie Ann, da of Charles Edward Pierce (d 1972), of St Paul, Minnesota; 1 s (John Benjamin Edward b 21 Oct 1971), 2 da (Susannah Elizabeth b 10 Dec 1973, Catherine Victoria b 31 Oct 1978); *Career* GP Cranbrook 1966-; med offr: Cranbrook Sch, Dulwich Coll Prep Sch (Cranbrook); chm Br Standing Ctee for Sch and Univ Health and Med, hon treas Euro Union for Sch and Univ Health and Med; MRCS; *Style*— Dr Anthony Trayling; Dog Kennel Farm, Cranbrook, Kent TN17 2PT (☎ 0580 713360); 37 Stone St, Cranbrook, Kent TN17 3HF (☎ 0580 712476)

TREADWELL, Lt-Col Gerald William; OBE (1964); s of Claude Mallam Treadwell (d 1931), and Emily Dorothy, *née* Mixer (d 1911); *b* 26 Nov 1905; *Educ* Stamford, King's Coll London; *m* 25 Jan 1941 (in Jerusalem Cathedral), Margaret, da of Frederick Rogers (d 1972), of Llanusk, Usk, Mon; 1 s (John b 1950), 1 da (Ann b 1945); *Career* Lt-Col serv Middle E (1 Cav Div), Italy and Austria 1939-48, mil prosecutor, Jerusalem Mil Court 1943-44; slr; pres: City of Westminster Law Soc 1969-70, Blackheath CC 1971-76; chm Bromley Cons Assoc 1958-62; *Books* Military Courts Manual; *Clubs* Blackheath Rugby (vice pres); *Style*— Lt-Col Gerald Treadwell, OBE; Ashlawn, Bickley Rd, Bickley, Kent BR1 2ND; 1 Pall Mall East, London SW1Y 5AY

TRESS, Dr Ronald Charles; CBE (1968); s of Stephen Charles Tress (d 1953), and Emma Jane, *née* Blewitt (d 1975); *b* 11 Jan 1915; *Educ* Gillingham Co Sch, Univ Coll Southampton, Univ of London (BSc), St Deiniol's Library Hawarden, Univ of Manchester; *m* 25 July 1942, Josephine Kelly, da of Hubert James Medland (d 1968); 1 s (Thomas b 1949), 2 da (Sarah b 1944, Janet b 1946); *Career* asst lectr econs Univ Coll of SW Exeter 1938-41, econ asst War Cabinet Offices 1941-45, econ advsr Cabinet Sec 1945-47, reader in public fin Univ of London 1947-51, prof political economy Univ of Bristol 1951-68, master Birkbeck Coll London 1968-77, dir The Leverhulme Tst 1977-84; South West Econ Planning Cncl: devpt cmmr 1959-81, chm 1965-68; tstee City Parochial Fndn 1974-77 and 1979-89, govr Christ Church Coll Canterbury 1975-, cncl memb Univ of Kent Canterbury 1977-, vice pres Royal Econ Soc 1979- (sec gen 1975-79), chm Lord Chllr's Advsy Ctee on Legal Aid 1979-84, memb Mgmnt Ctee Seaside Camps for London Boys and Girls Hawkshill Deal 1986-; Hon: DSc Bristol 1968, LLD Furman S Carolina 1973, DUniv Open Univ 1974, LLD Exeter 1976, DSc Southampton 1978, DCL Univ of Kent at Canterbury 1984; *Clubs* Athenaeum; *Style*— Dr R C Tress, CBE; 22 The Beach, Walmer, Deal, Kent CT14 7HJ (☎ 0304 373254)

TRIBBLE, Norman Reginald; s of Frederick John Tribble (d 1972), of Exeter, and Alice Maud, *née* Hooper (d 1980); *b* 17 Feb 1927; *Educ* St Luke's Coll Sch Exeter, Univ of London (BSc); *m* 20 July 1946, Christine Mary, da of Stuart Allen Moore (d 1960), of Folkestone; 1 da (Hilary b 1953); *Career* Lt 1 Bn Devonshire Regt 1945-48, served Singapore 1946 and Hong Kong 1947; accountant Inst Prodn Engrs 1948-53; mgmnt accountant Shell-Mex and BP Ltd 1953-60, dir and proprietor Manchester Exchange and Investment Bank Ltd 1960-89; dir: London Advsy Bd, Bank Julius Baer & Co Ltd, Reliance Bank Ltd; life pres ACT (fndn chm 1979), chm Patrons Club Tunbridge Wells, memb Cons Assoc; churchwarden; Liveryman Worshipful Co of Musicians; FCCA 1953; *Recreations* music, sport; *Clubs* Naval and Military; *Style*— Norman Tribble, Esq; 237 Forest Rd, Tunbridge Wells, Kent TN2 5H7 (☎ 0892 20149); Manchester Exchange and Investment Bank, International House, 1 St Katherine's Way, London E1 9UN (☎ 071 488 4888, fax 071 488 3480, telex 261238)

TRICE, Cyril Leonard; s of John Thomas Trice (d 1962), of Ash, Canterbury, Kent, and Eva Frances, *née* Olive (d 1982); *b* 16 July 1931; *Educ* Army Tech Sch Chepstow (HNC), Inst of Plant Engrs; *m* 6 June 1959, Valerie, da of Joseph Robinson (d 1964), of 85 Willow Rd, Dartford, Kent; 2 s (Gary Leonard 11 April 1963, Stephen John 22 January 1968), 1 da (Deborah Lynn 12 August 1961); *Career* Sgt REME 1946-57; charge engr CEGB (ops engr 1957-87); city cncllr Rochester upon Medway 1987-, chm Cliffe Parochial Charities, vice chm Cliffe Woods Middle Sch, ctee memb Brit Assoc of Road Races, gp ldr Lib Democrats Rochester upon Medway CC; *Recreations* roadrunning, squash; *Clubs* Gravesend RR Athletics; *Style—* Cyril Trice, Esq; 54 Town Rd, Cliffe Woods, Rochester, Kent ME3 8JJ (☎ 0634 2204411)

TROUP, Donald Alexander Gordon; OBE (1988); s of Francis Gordon Troup (d 1984), of Haslemere, and Olive Mary Katharine, *née* Mosse (d 1959); *b* 20 Dec 1927; *Educ* Radley, Corpus Christi Coll Cambridge; *m* 1, 22 May 1954, Alison Joyce (d 1985), da of Dr Clement Neve (d 1939), of Croydon; 3 s (Robert James b 1955, Andrew Richard b 1957, Nigel Francis b 1960); m 2, 20 Dec 1986, Anne Hanson Barnes, wid of Brian Dearden Barnes (d 1982), da of Walter Hanson Freeman, MC, TD (d 1949); *Career* ptnr Porter & Cobb 1963-85, dir Cobbs 1985-86, exec conslt G A Property Servs 1986-; cncl memb RURAL 1984-, pres RICS 1986-87; tstee Richard Watts and City of Rochester Almhouse Charities 1969-; Freeman Worshipful Co of Chartered Surveyors 1978; FRICS 1954, FAAV 1970; *Books* Agricultural Holdings Act 1984; *Style—* Donald Troup, Esq, OBE; Lees Lodge, Yalding, Kent (☎ office: 0622 690160, home 0622 814169)

TROWELL, Oliver Burnet; s of Arnold Thomas Wilberforce Trowell (d 1966), and Eileen May, *née* Woodhead (1963); *b* 30 May 1927; *Educ* Ashford GS, Dover Sch of Art, Brighton Coll of Art (NDD, ATC); *m* 18 Aug 1961, Margaret Young, da of Robert Culbertson (d 1962); 2 s (Nicholas b 1963, David b 1965), 3 da (Angela b 1962, Marcella b 1967, Diana b 1970); *Career* teacher of art; head of Art Dept: Westminster City Sch 1960-67 and 1975-77, The King's Sch Canterbury (responsible for devpt of art dept in 13 century Blackfriars refectory) 1981-89; freelance artist 1967-75 and 1977-80; exhibitions incl: USA 1969, Nevill Gallery Canterbury 1971 and 1973, Royal Museum and Art Gallery Canterbury 1990; decorated harpsichords for Trevor Pinnock and Colin Tilney 1974; owners of work incl: Archbishop of Canterbury, Sheikh Raschid of Dubai; fndr memb Local History Soc, memb E Ashford Rural Tst (produced drawings for the For A Better Ashford exhibition at Civic Centre 1990); *Recreations* gardening, restoration of old buildings and enjoyment of music and painting; *Style—* Oliver Trowell, Esq; Coquet Lodge, East Brabourne, Ashford, Kent TN25 5LR (☎ 0303 812268)

TRUSSLER, Simon; s of John Trussler, and Joan, *née* Ovenden; *b* 11 June 1942; *Educ* UCL (BA, MA); *m* 1, 23 Aug 1966 (m dis 1984), Glenda, *née* Leeming; 1 s (Nicholas), 1 da (Anna); m 2, 29 Aug 1984, Laverne, *née* Anderson; 1 s (Jonathan), 1 da (Meryl); *Career* founding ed: Prompt 1962-64, Theatre Quarterly 1967-81, New Theatre Quarterly 1984-; ed asst Plays and Players 1964-67, co-ed Encore 1965, London theatre critic Tulane Drama Review 1965-70, theatre critic Tribune 1966-72, radio critic The Listener 1969; visiting lectr: London Prog Tufts Univ USA 1973-81, Univ of Kent 1984-86; pt/t lectr City Univ London 1980-82, ed Theatre International for the International Theatre Inst Paris 1981-83, visiting prof Drama Dept Univ of California at Santa Barbara 1983, gen ed Writer-File Series 1985-, reader in drama Goldsmiths' Coll London 1986-, series ed Swan Theatre Plays 1986-; *Books* The Plays of John Osborne (1969), Burlesque Plays of the Eighteenth Century (ed 1969), The Plays of Arnold Wesker (1971), The Plays of John Whiting (1972), The Plays of Harold Pinter (1973), A Classification for the Performing Arts (1974), New Theatre Voices of the Seventies (1981), Shakespearean Concepts (1989); *Style—* Simon Trussler, Esq; Great Robhurst, Woodchurch, Ashford, Kent TN26 3TB; Drama Dept, Goldsmiths' College, University of London, New Cross, SE14 6NW

TUBBY, Derek Bert; s of George Walter Tubby (d 1954), and Beryl Money, *née* Gibbons; *b* 29 Sept 1947; *Educ* Charlton Secdy Sch, SE London Tech Coll; *m* 30 Aug 69, Janet Linda, da of Leonard George Nourse; 1 da (Anita Lesley b 1965); *Career* sales and mktg dir Special Telephone Systems Ltd 1985-, sales and mktg dir Questel plc 1985-; *Recreations* smallholder; *Style—* Derek Tubby, Esq; Tilmans, Sandy Lane, Daniels Water, Great Chart, Kent TN26 1JN (☎ 0233 82474); Special Telephone Sytems Ltd, Sidcup Technology Centre, 3 Maidstone Rd, Sidcup, Kent DA14 5HW (☎ 081 308 1000, fax 081 308 1234)

TUCKER, Cncllr (John Martyn) Kent; s of Martyn Tucker (d 1946), of Withycombe Raleigh, Devon, and Phyllis Louise, *née* Simms (d 1947); *b* 9 July 1928; *Educ* Exmouth GS, Univ Coll Of The South West Exeter Devon (BSc); *m* Eileen Doris, da of William Thorne, of Boreham Wood; 2 s (William Martyn, Mark Andrew), 2 da (Susan Elizabeth, Anne Mary Louise); *Career* photographic chemist Dufay Chromex Ltd 1949-53, res chemist and engr Electronic Tube Ltd (subsid EMI-Cossor) 1953-1956, engr Esso Petroleum Company Ltd 1956-; Kent co cncllr 1989-; former memb Hartley Parochial Church Cncl, memb Sevenoaks and Dartford Cons Assocs; *Style—* Cncllr Kent Tucker

TUCKWELL, Dr Gareth David; s of Sir Edward Tuckwell, KCVO (d 1988), and Phyllis Courthope, *née* Regester (d 1970); *b* 3 Dec 1946; *Educ* Charterhouse, Univ of London and St Bartholomew's Hosp Med Coll (MB BS, DObstRCOG, LRCP); *m* 4 Aug 1973, (Susan) Mary, da of Dr Hugh Wilfred Sansom, OBE, of 29 Holmewood Ridge, Langton Green, Kent; 2 s (Jonathan b 1977, Paul b 1984), 1 da (Deborah b 1976), 1 adopted da (Alexandria b 1984); *Career* princ in gen practice 1974-86, clinical tutor in gen practice St Bartholomew's Hosp Med Coll 1976-86; dir Dorothy Kerin Tst 1986-, med dir of Burrswood Tunbridge Wells 1986-, vice pres Phyllis Tuckwell Memorial Hosp Farnham; memb: Working Pty on The Churches Miny of Healing in the Light of Hospice Experience, Caring Professions Concern; tstee The Burrswood Endowment Tst, Coke Hole Tst Drug Rehabilitation Centre; memb and area rep Christian Med Fellowship; editorial advsr Healing and Wholeness magazine; Freeman City of London, Liveryman Worshipful Soc of Apothecaries 1971; MRCS 1971, MRCGP; memb: Assoc of Palliative Medicine, BMA; *Recreations* photography, walking, gardening; *Style—* Dr Gareth Tuckwell; St Luke's House, Burrswood, Groombridge, Tunbridge Wells, Kent TN3 9PY (☎ 0892 864349); Burrswood, Groombridge, Tunbridge Wells, Kent TN3 9PY (☎ 0892 863637)

TURCAN, Robert David; s of Geoffrey Robert Turcan (d 1984), Orchard Farm, Upper Rodmersham, nr Sittingbourne, Kent, and Agnes, *née* Barrie; *b* 8 Nov 1949; *Educ* St Andrews Coll Boxley, Sheerness Tech HS for Boys, Mid Kent Coll of Technol Maidstone; *m* 8 Sept 1973 (m dis 1988), Joyce, da of Philip Fleur St Julian Carpenter, of Sittingbourne; 1 s (Edward b 1975), 1 da (Charlotte b 1978); *Career* TA 1983-85; mangr Bank Dept Messrs Grenfell & Colegrave 1981-83, clients servs mangr Portfolio Administration Ltd 1983-85, sr investmt mangr Canadian Imperial Bank of Commerce 1985-87, freelance investmt mgmnt conslt UK & ME 1987-, owner Orchard Farm Upper Rodmersham; memb Swale Borough Cncl 1982-86, chm Rodmersham Parish Cncl 1987 (vice chm 1982); registered rep Int Stock Exchange London 1986; *Recreations* literature, playing rugby, travel; *Clubs* Sheppey & Sittingbourne RFC; *Style—* Robert Turcan, Esq; Orchard Farm, Upper Rodmersham, nr Sittingbourne, Kent ME9 0QL (☎ 079 583 208)

TURK, Rodney Jack; s of Jack Turk, MC (d 1987), of Deal, Kent, and Winifred Agnes, *née* Tapping (d 1988); *b* 23 June 1923; *Educ* King's Sch Canterbury; *m* 1 June 1956, Joan Flora, da of Arthur Martin; 1 s (Nicholas), 2 da (Caroline, Jennifer); *Career* Capt 3 QAO Gurkha Rifles 1942-46, Lieut HAC 1950-55; PA consulting Group 1956-83: conslt 1956-62, sr conslt 1962-79, int fin controller 1979-83; self-employed mgmnt conslt 1983-, chm Brunton and Williams Ltd 1987- (fin dir 1985-88); treas PCC St Luke's Sevenoaks, cncl memb Kent Beekeepers' Assoc, hon auditor various socs; FCA 1959; *Recreations* bee-keeping, walking, gardening; *Clubs* HAC; *Style—* Rodney Turk, Esq; Hatch Cottage, Godden Green, Sevenoaks, Kent TN1S 0JR (☎ 0732 61856)

TURNBULL, Rt Rev Anthony Michael Arnold; *see*: Rochester, Bishop of

TURNBULL-WALKER, Anna (Mrs David Strang); da of Arthur Toney Walker, of Sutton Coldfield, W Midlands, and Jean, *née* Mann; *b* 11 Aug 1950; *Educ* High Clare Sch for Girls, Univ of Warwick (BA), Birmingham Sch of Law; *m* 30 Nov 1983, David Ivor Strang, s of Cecil Strang, of Glasgow; 2 s (Isaac Jacob Toney b 1984, Noah Jack b 1989), 1 da (Fay Avital b 1986); *Career* slr; articled clerk Rubenstein Callingham Gray's Inn London 1980-82, admitted 1982, ptnr Hatten Wyatt & Co 1987- (asst slr 1982); Assoc of Women Slrs, Slrs Benevolent Soc; membership sec Working Mothers Gp; memb Law Soc 1980; *Recreations* swimming, reading; *Style—* Ms Anna Turnbull-Walker; 51 Caterham Rd, London SE13 5AD; Hatten Wyatt & Co, 18-21 Wrotham Rd, Gravesend, Kent (☎ 0474 351199, fax 0474 334345)

TURNER, (Charles) Brian Godsell; s of Ernest Joseph Turner (d 1964), of Harpenden, and Bertha, *née* Harris (d 1968); *b* 26 Oct 1913; *Educ* Tottenham GS; *m* 28 June 1941, Helen, da of Cecil Robert Slowe (d 1968), of Wadhurst; 2 s (Christopher b 1943, Richard b 1946), 1 da (Sally b 1949); *Career* TA (HAC) 1930-Aug 1939, OCTU (Bulford) Aug-Oct 1939, cmmnd 2 Lt KOYLI Nov 1939, Capt 1940; served UK, Normandy, Belgium, Holland, Germany; demobbed 1945; CA; apprentice 1930-39, qualified incorporated accountant 1939, mangr 1946, qualified CA 1949, ret 1974; non exec dir Med Kent Water Co; chm: Eastbourne Water Co, Bournemouth and Dist Water Co; hon treas: Nat Assoc of Parish Cncls 1974, Local PCC; Freeman City of London, Liveryman and Asst Worshipful Co of Wheelwrights; FCA, FRSA; *Recreations* gardening, stamp collecting; *Style—* Brian Turner, Esq; Dellside, Tongswood Dr, Hawkhurst, Kent TN18 5DS (☎ 05805 3145)

TURNER, Brian William; s of William Edward Turner (d 1949), of Surbiton, Surrey, and Caroline Rose, *née* Camp (d 1958); *b* 21 Sept 1936; *Educ* Royal Masonic Sch; *Career* admitted slr 1959; sr ptnr Messrs Gill Turner & Tucker Slrs Maidstone; hon slr Age Concern Kent; memb Law Soc; *Style—* Brian Turner, Esq; Byne Cottage, Chart Sutton, Maidstone, Kent; Colman House, King St, Maidstone, Kent ME14 1JE (☎ 0622 590 51, fax 0622 621 92, telex 965343)

TURNER, Rev Canon Edward Robert; s of Robert Turner, of Sutton-at-Hone, Kent, and Florence, *née* Shipman (d 1960); *b* 29 Sept 1937; *Educ*

Dartford GS, Emmanuel Coll Cambridge (MA), Westcott House Cambridge; *m* 3 Aug 1968, Anne Mary, da of Edgar Bracher (d 1962), of London; *Career* in commerce and indust with: Br India SN Co Ltd London, Seager Evans & Co Ltd London; ordained curate St Philip with St Stephen Salford 1966-69, chaplain Tonbridge Sch 1969-81, dir of educn for the diocese of Rochester 1981, advsr for in-serv training 1981-89, vice dean Rochester Cathedral 1988- (residentiary canon 1981-); memb: Bexley Educn Ctee 1981-84, Bromley Educn Ctee 1981-, Kent CC Educn Ctee 1981-, governing body Christ Church Coll Canterbury, farmington scholar Manchester Coll Oxford 1990; *Recreations* walking, opera, literature; *Clubs* Athenaeum; *Style*— The Rev Canon Edward Turner; 1 King's Orchard, The Precinct, Rochester, Kent ME1 1TG (☎ 0634 42756); St Nicholas Church, Rochester, Kent ME1 1SL (☎ 0634 830333, fax 0634 829463)

TURNER, Gordon Hamilton; s of Benjamin Archibald Hamilton Turner (d 1945), of Ashford, and Alice Ruth, *née* Elgar (d 1988); *b* 25 April 1928; *Educ* Ashford North Secdy Sch; *m* 6 June 1953, Betty Helen Jane, da of Leonard Henry Watlins (d 1939), of Chatham; 1 s (Howard Hamilton b 1958); *Career* mktg; Liverpool Victoria Insur 1952-65, Fitch Lovell Gp 1974-81, local newspaper (Ind and EMAP) 1986-89, proprietor Coffilta Coffee Services E Kent 1989-; ctee memb: Ashford Lib Democrats, Ashford Civic Soc; signatory Charter 88; memb: Ashford Museum Soc, Kent Men of the Trees; elected memb: Ashford Borough Cncl S Willesborough Ward 1973- (Ashford Urban Dist Cncl 1961-64 and 1972-74); *Books* Ashford - The Coming of the Railway (1984), Ashford - A Saxon Phoenix (1990); *Recreations* steam railways, local history, environment; *Style*— Gordon Turner, Esq; 6 Glebe Way, Kennington, Ashford, Kent TN24 9AU (☎ 0233 620352); The Enterprise Centre, Newton Rd, Ashford, Kent TN23 OPN (☎ 0233 631500)

TURNER, John Frayn; s of late George Francis Turner, and late Daisy Louise, *née* Frayn; *b* 9 Aug 1923; *Educ* Royal GS Guildford; *m* 9 Aug 1945, Joyce Isabelle, da of late Wilfred Ernest Howson; 1 da (Francesca Lynn b 1947); *Career* served Admty and RN 1941-47; journalist; writer and ed 1948-63, responsible for RAF publicity MOD 1963-73, sr ed pubns COI 1973-83; managing ed 1984-85: Art and Artists, Dance and Dancers, Films and Filming, Music and Musicians, Plays and Players; *Books* Service Most Silent (1955), VCs of the Royal Navy (1956), Prisoner at Large (1957), Hovering Angels (1957), Periscope Patrol (1958), Invasion '44 (1959), VCs of the Air (1960), Battle Stations (1960), Highly Explosive (1961), The Blinding Flash (1962), VCs of the Army (1962), A Girl Called Johnnie (1963), Famous Air Battles (1963), Fight for the Sky (with Douglas Bader, 1973), Destination Berchtesgaden (1975), British Aircraft of World War 2 (1975), Famous Flights (1978), The Bader Wing (1981), The Yanks Are Coming (1983), Frank Sinatra (1983), The Bader Tapes (1986), The Good Spy Guide (1988), Rupert Brooke - The Splendour and the Pain (1990); *Recreations* music, theatre, films, art; *Style*— John Frayn Turner, Esq; Apartment 302, The Metropole, Folkestone, Kent (☎ 0303 50144)

TURNER, Martin William; s of William Alexander Turner (d 1972), of 24 Marshall Rd, Rainham, Kent, and Enine Felicity, *née* McCabe; *b* 3 Oct 1940; *Educ* Gravesend Tech Sch, Medway Coll of Art (Nat Dip in Design); *Career* artist; mural painting cmmnd by: MOD 1971, GEC Ltd 1976, Rochester upon Medway Civic Centre 1987; series of paintings and limited edition prints based on the Medway Towns and exhibited regularly at Royal Acad 1960-; chm local youth club 1957-65; memb ROI 1975; *Recreations* photography, walking, model making; *Style*— Martin Turner, Esq; 24 Marshall Rd, Rainham, Kent (☎ 0634 319 94)

TURNER, Stephen George; s of George Turner, of Dewsbury, West Yorkshire, and Margaret, *née* Shelton; *b* 25 March 1954; *Educ* Univ of Leeds (BA), Univ of Regina Saskatchewan Canada (MFA); *m* 12 Aug 1978, Julie Anne, da of Dennis Curtis, of Esher, Surrey; *Career* artist; artist in residence Blackfriars Arts Centre Boston 1979-80, fellowship in painting Exeter Coll of Art & Design 1980-82; head of art and craft: Gillingham Adult Educn Centre 1984-86, N Kent Area Adult Educn Serv 1987, p/t exhibitions and events offr Common Ground 1990- (full time 1987-89); organiser of various exhibitions incl: Medway Artists '84, Maritime Medway, Open View, A Private View (nat touring exhibition by Kent Opera's artist in residence Jane Lewis) 1987; memb exec Visual Arts Panel Metropole Arts Centre Folkestone 1987-90; created community arts newsletter Medway Artlink 1984; memb: Gen Arts Panel SE Arts 1985-88, Mgmnt Ctee Arts In Medway 1986-; fndr West End Studios 1987; advsr and selector for exhibitions: Tree of Life (South Bank and Common Ground), Out of the Wood (Crafts Council and Common Ground) 1989; *Recreations* local conservation, archaeology; *Style*— Stephen Turner, Esq; 234 Old Rd West, Gravesend, Kent DA11 0LY (☎ 0474 332249); Common Ground, 45 Shelton St, London WC2H 9HJ (☎ 071 379 3109)

TURNPENNY, John Harvey; JP (1967); s of Sidney Bertie Turnpenny (d 1975), and Lilian Valentine, *née* Vass; *b* 21 March 1923; *Educ* Dover Coll; *Career* dir Turnpenny Bros Ltd Dover; pres Dover C of C 1954-55 and 1962-63; chm Bd of Visitors HM Borstal Dover 1976-80 (memb 1959-81); tstee: Royal Cinque Ports Yacht Club 1976-, Dubris Tst Dover; chm: Dover Coll 1987- (govr 1972-), Dover and E Kent Magistrates 1988-; memb St Alphege Tst Dover; *Recreations* golf, bridge, going to France; *Clubs* Royal Cinque Ports Golf, Royal Cinque Ports Yacht, Walmer and Kingsdown Golf; *Style*— John Turnpenny, Esq, JP; Deepdene, 14 Park Ave, Dover, Kent CT16 1HE (☎ 0304 206905)

TURVEY, Garry; s of Henry Oxley Turvey (d 1981), and Annie Maude, *née* Braley; *b* 11 Oct 1934; *Educ* Morecambe GS, Manchester Business Sch; *m* 11 June 1960, Hilary Margaret, da of Walter Saines; 3 s (Ian Michael b 1961, Peter Geoffrey b 1964, David Mark b 1965); *Career* Nat Serv RAF 1954-56; sec Traders Rd Tport Assoc 1966-68 (asst sec 1960-66); Freight Tport Assoc: sec 1969-74, dep dir gen 1974-83, dir gen 1984-; FCIS 1959, FCIT 1983, FILDM 1988; *Recreations* cricket, gardening; *Clubs* RAC; *Style*— Garry Turvey, Esq; 139 Imberhorne Lane, E Grinstead, W Sussex RH19 1RD (☎ 0342 325829); Freight Transport Association Ltd, Hermes House, St Johns Rd, Tunbridge Wells, Kent (☎ 0892 26171, fax 0892 34989, telex 957158, car tel 0836 591581)

TWISTON DAVIES, David James; s of Mervyn Peter Twiston Davies, of Somerset, and Isabel Anne, *née* Fox; *b* 23 March 1945; *Educ* Downside; *m* 10 June 1970, Margaret Anne (Rita), da of Francis Gerard Montgomery (d 1978); 3 s (Benedict, James, Huw), 1 da (Bess); *Career* journalist; East Anglian Daily Times 1966-68, Winnipeg Free Press 1968-70; The Daily Telegraph: news sub ed 1970-77, asst literary ed 1977-86, dep obituaries ed 1986-88, ed Peterborough column 1988-89, letters ed 1989-; Freeman City of London; *Recreations* defending reputation of the British Empire; *Clubs* Travellers'; *Style*— David Twiston Davies, Esq; 20 Warwick Park, Tunbridge Wells, Kent (☎ 0892 30341); The Daily Telegraph, 181 Marsh Wall, London E14 (☎ 071 538 6458, fax 071 538 6455)

TYLER, John William; s of Joseph Thomas Tyler (d 1975), of Newark, Notts, and Clara Gertrude, *née* Martin (d 1979); *b* 21 Nov 1931; *Educ* The Magnus Sch Newark Notts, Univ of Nottingham (BA), Coll of Law; *m* 8 Jan 1955, Patricia, da of John Reginald Neal (d 1966), of Hove, E Sussex; 2 s (Timothy John Neal b 30 Oct 1957 d 1978, Gavin Thomas b 6 Dec 1960), 1 da (Nicola Patricia (Mrs Hulm) b 3 March 1965); *Career* Flt Lt Adjs Branch RAF 1952-58; dir and co sec Atcost gp of co's 1958-69; admitted slr 1973; ptnr Cripps Harries Hall 1974- (joined 1970); NP; chm Jones Clifton gp of co's 1985 (dir 1975-); chm Local Advsy Ctee Nuffield Hosp Tunbridge Wells, dir Heathlands House Ltd (private charity for severely disabled young people); Freeman City of London, Liveryman Worshipful Co of Carmen 1977; memb Law Soc; *Recreations* golf, skiing, gardening; *Style*— John Tyler, Esq; 14 Blatchington Rd, Tunbridge Wells, Kent TN2 5EG (☎ 0892 27822); Cripps Harries Hall, 84 Calverley Rd, Tunbridge Wells, Kent TN1 2UP (☎ 0892 515121, fax 0892 515444)

TYLER-WHITTLE, Rev Michael Sidney; s of Ven John Tyler-Whittle (d 1969), former Archdeacon of Macclesfield and Canon of Chester, and Florence Emily Wilbraham, *née* Bowler (d 1960); *b* 8 Feb 1927; *Educ* Denstone, Peterhouse and Fitzwilliam House Cambridge (MA), Wells Theol Coll; *m* 2 Oct 1970, Bridget Joanna, da of Gp Capt Frank Hastings Tyson (d 1980), of Diss, Norfolk; 1 s (Jack b 9 April 1976), 2 da (Magdalen b 18 Aug 1972, Richeldis b 16 March 1974); *Career* Royal Marines 1944-47, Actg Capt Gen List TA Scottish Cmd Edinburgh 1950-53; made deacon 1955, curate of Wymondham Abbey 1955-58, ordained priest Norwich Diocese 1956, hon chaplain to Bishop of Norwich 1957-59, perpetual curate of Old Buckenham 1958-69, chaplain Univ of East Anglia 1965-67, hon coll bursar and asst at Shrine of Our Lady of Walsingham 1968-70, licensed to officiate Norwich and Gibraltar Dioceses 1969-80, non stipendiary chaplain of the Costiera Divina of Amalfi Italy 1972-80, priest i/c Rectory of Forton and Norbury in the diocese of Lichfield 1980-83; Rector: Mereworth with West Peckham in Kent 1983-85, Penshurst and Fordcombe 1985-; writer of fiction and non-fiction, reviewer and literary critic, regular free-lance broadcaster of talks and feature progs for BBC radio and Br Italian and German TV 1954-; FRSL 1971, FLS 1977; *Books* as Tyler Whittle incl: Spades and Feathers (1954), Castle Lizard (1956), The Last Plantagenet (1970), The Plant Hunters (1971), The Last Kaiser (1977), Victoria and Albert At Home (1980), Solid Joys and Lasting Treasures (1985); as Mark Oliver incl: A Roll of Thunder (1960), Feet of Bronze (1962), Fire Spinning Tops of Naples (1964); *Recreations* all forms of hunting, national hunt racing, sailing, fishing, reading, collecting and cultivating ferns; *Clubs* Athenaeum; *Style*— The Rev Michael Tyler-Whittle; Penshurst Rectory, Tonbridge, Kent TN11 8BN (☎ 0892 870316); Curtis Brown Ltd, 162-168 Regent St, London W1R 5TA (☎ 071 872 0331, fax 071 872 0332, telex 920379, Cables Browncourt, London W1)

TYRER, Michael Richard (Mike); s of Thomas Tyrer (d 1970), of 92 Town Court Crescent, Petts Wood, Orpington, Kent, and Mary Kathleen, *née* Moran; *b* 7 Aug 1943; *Educ* St Joseph's Coll London; *m* 16 Jan 1971, Hilary Mary, da of Lt Cdr R A H Panter, RN, of Colyton, Devon; 2 s (Paul Anthony, Richard Thomas), 1 da (Emily Suzanne); *Career* fin dir and co sec Freshbake Foods Ltd 1970-73; BT: dep corp fin accountant 1981-86, regulatory accountant 1986-88, gp chief internal auditor 1988-; chm Hartley Churches Assoc; FCA; *Recreations* gardening, walking, DIY, travel; *Style*— Mike Tyrer, Esq; Belsfield, 83 Fant Rd, Tunbridge Wells, Kent TN2 5LP (☎

0892 39091); British Telecom, BT Centre, Newgate St, London EC1A 7AJ (☎ 071 356 4862, fax 071 356 6251, car tel 0860 530 889)

TYSON, John Vernon; s of Gilbert John Gilbanks Tyson (d 1942), and Caroline, *née* Smith (d 1985); *b* 16 Feb 1937; *Educ* Keswick Sch Cumbria, Fitzwilliam Coll Cambridge (MA, CertEd); *m* 30 July 1966, Nigella Jane, da of Frederick John Sewry (d 1978); 1 s (Robin Timothy Gilbanks b 1971), 2 da (Rachel Caroline b 1969, Helen Mary b 1976); *Career* asst master Abingdon Sch Oxon 1960-66, head of mathematics and headmaster's admin asst Bradfield Coll Berks 1966-78, headmaster St Edmund's Canterbury 1978-; chm: Canterbury Cathedral Old Choristers' Assoc, Ellis Ctee Mathematics Panel 1980-84; cncl memb ISCO 1989-; *Books* School Mathematics Project (jtly), Individualised Mathematics (jtly); *Recreations* music, chess, DIY; *Style*— John Tyson, Esq; Pontigny, St Edmunds School, Canterbury, Kent CT2 8HU (☎ 0227 454575; 0227 464496, fax 0227 471083)

U

UNDERWOOD, Derek Leslie; MBE (1981); s of Leslie Frank Underwood (d 1978), of Kent, and Evelyn Ann, *née* Wells; *b* 8 June 1945; *Educ* Dulwich Coll Prep Sch, Beckenham and Penge GS; *m* 1973, Dawn, da of Gerald Daniel Sullivan, of Surrey; 2 da (Heather b 1977, Fiona b 1977); *Career* cricketer; joined Kent 1962, County Cap 1964, England debut 1966, left-arm spin bowler, 86 Test matches - 297 test wickets; yst player ever to take 100 wickets in debut season, ret from first class cricket 1987; working for Club Surfaces (artificial sports surfaces co); pres Met Dist Assoc of Kent CCs; *Style*— Derek Underwood, MBE; Kent County Cricket Club, St Lawrence Ground, Canterbury, Kent (☎ 0227 456886)

UNDERWOOD, Grahame John Taylor; s of Wing Cdr Shirley Taylor Underwood, OBE, of Elstone, nr Newark, and Joyce Mary, *née* Smith; *b* 1 July 1944; *Educ* Ashby De La Zouch GS, Poly of N London (Dip Arch); *m* 4 May 1968, Christine Elva, da of Sqdn Ldr Cecil Reginald Long, MBE, DSM (d 1972); 2 s (Christopher Taylor b 1971, Toby Grahame b 1972), 1 da (Lucy Jane b 1974); *Career* Watkins Gray Int: architect and planner 1969-72, assoc 1972-83, ptnr 1983, dir 1983-; dir: Watkins Gray Peter Jones 1983-, Watkins Gray Int Ltd, Watkins Gray Ho & Ptnrs; princ designs incl: Royal Masonic Hosp, Nat Heart and Chest Hosps London and Baghdad, Dammam and Unayzah Hosps Saudi Arabia; chm Edgbaston Round Table 1984; memb: BSI Tech Ctee, RIBA 1973; *Books* Architects Jl Handbook of Ironmongery (1979), The Security of Buildings (1984), num tech articles; *Recreations* gliding (holder int silver cert); *Clubs* Midland Gliding; *Style*— Grahame Underwood, Esq; Watkins Gray Int, Alexander House, Spur Rd, Orpington, Kent BR6 0QR (☎ 0689 70521, fax 0689 35151)

UNGERSON, Dr Clare Elizabeth Jordan; da of Bernard Ungerson, CBE, of Oxshott, Surrey, and Annelis Lore Grete, *née* Gumbel; *b* 8 Feb 1944; *Educ* St Paul's Girls' Sch, Birkenhead HS, St Hugh's Coll Oxford (BA), LSE (MSc), Univ of Kent (PhD); *m* 20 Jan 1979, William Archer, s of Lt-Col William Grenville Irvine-Fortescue (d 1980); *Career* res offr: Inst of Race Rels 1969-71, Centre for Environmental Studies 1971-73; Univ of Kent 1973-: lectr in social policy, sr lectr, reader; memb Canterbury Constituency Lab Pty; *Books* incl: Women and Social Policy - a reader (1985), Policy is Personal: sex, gender and informal care (1987); *Recreations* playing early music, swimming, watching soap operas; *Clubs* Univ Women's; *Style*— Dr Clare Ungerson; Darwin College, The University, Canterbury, Kent CT2 7NY (☎ 0227 764000, fax 0227 459025)

UNWIN, David Charles; s of Peter Charles Unwin, and Rosemary Gwendolen Winifred, *née* Locket; *b* 12 May 1947; *Educ* Clifton Coll, Trinity Coll Oxford (BA); *m* 16 Aug 1969, Lorna, da of Richard Frank Bullivant; 1 s (James b 1978), 1 da (Catherine b 1974); *Career* called to the Bar Lincoln's Inn 1971, treasy jr counsel in charity matters 1987-; *Recreations* music, mountaineering, sailing; *Style*— David Unwin, Esq; 7 Stone Bldgs, Lincoln's Inn, London WC2 (☎ 071 405 3886, fax 071 242 8502)

UREN, (John) Michael Leal; s of Arthur Claude Uren (d 1977), of Rickmansworth, Herts, and Doris May, *née* Leal (d 1983); *b* 1 Sept 1923; *Educ* Sherborne, Imperial Coll London (BSc); *m* 26 Nov 1955, Serena Anne, da of Edward Raymond Peal, of Salisbury; 2 s (David Richard b 1960, (Robert) Mark b 1962); *Career* RN 1943-46: cmmnd Sub-Lt RNVR, air engr offr Fleet Air Arm; chartered civil engr; Sir Alexander Gibb and Partners Persia 1946-51, The Cementation Company Hydro Electric Scotland 1951-53; Holland and Hannen & Cubitts 1953-58: construction of Hydro Electric Roxburgh NZ, industl complex Swindon Wilts, British European Airways Base Heathrow; Civil and Marine Ltd: fndr, dir 1955-, chm 1982-; md Dowsett Engineering Construction 1961-65 (dir 1958-61); currently chm: Camey SA Dunkirk, Germain D'Hoore NV Brugges, Purfleet Aggregates Ltd Essex; currently dir: Evered plc, Blackwall Aggregates Ltd London; chm Royal London Soc for the Blind 1981- (cncllr 1974-); Freeman City of London 1958; Worshipful Co of Cordwainers: Liveryman 1958, Sr Warden 1989, Master 1990; CEng, MIWEM, MICE, MIStructE, ACGI, FRICS; *Recreations* 15th and 16th century timber framed buildings, country pursuits, farming (pedigree flock Romney sheep, cereals and linseed); *Clubs* Naval and Military; *Style*— Michael Uren, Esq; Priory Farm, Appledore Rd, Tenterden, Kent TN30 7DD (☎ 05806 4161); Civil & Marine Ltd, Johnsons Wharf, King Edward Road, Greenhithe, Kent DA9 9AD (☎ 0322 844646, fax 0322 847211)

V

VADASZ, Dr Imre Mihall; s of Imre Vadasz (d 1944), of Budapest, Hungary, and Renee, *née* Rasko; *b* 8 March 1938; *Educ* Guys' Hosp Med Sch, Univ of London (MB BS, MRCP); *m* 22 April 1989, Bridget Christine, da of Raymond Joseph Mannion (d 1974); *Career* sr registrar Guys Hosp 1967-70, conslt physician and rheumatologist Dartford and Gravesend Hosps 1970-, clinical tutor Univ of London 1973-81; cncl memb Nat Assoc of Clinical Tutors 1977-81; FRCP 1972; *Recreations* sailing, flying; *Clubs* Royal Ocean Racing; *Style*— Dr Imre Vadasz; Legge Lodge, Legge Lane, Briling, nr Maidstone, Kent ME18 5JH (☎ 0634 240213)

VAILE, (Philip) Bryn; MBE (1989); s of Philip Edward Burdock Vaile, of Lymington, Hants, and Florence, *née* Hughes (d 1983); *b* 16 Aug 1956; *Educ* Belfairs HS, Singapore Int Sch, Thames Poly, Portsmouth Poly; *m* 4 Feb 1989, Erika, da of Erik Lessmann, of São Paulo, Brazil; *Career* Mobil Oil Co Ltd: retail mktg 1978-, credit controller 1982-, liquid petroleum gas mktg admin 1986-; sales mangr Mondosport Ltd 1989, mktg exec PNTA 1990; asst dist sec Int Star Class Solent Fleet 1990; *Recreations* yacht racing, golf, photography, music, walking; *Clubs* Royal Lymington Yacht; *Style*— Bryn Vaile, Esq, MBE; 22 Terrington Hill, Marlow, Bucks SL7 2RF (☎ 0628 476082); 94a High St, Sevenoaks, Kent TN13 1LP (☎ 0962 741742, fax 0962 741141)

VAILE, Dr Michael Steel Berkeley; s of Dr J D B Vaile (d 1987), and Audrey, *née* Girling; *b* 25 July 1937; *Educ* Kings Sch Bruton, St Thomas' Hosp (MB BS, MRCGP); *m* 17 Dec 1967, Caroline Mary Esmé, da of Michael Hayward, of Winchelsea; 2 s (Damian John Berkeley b 9 May 1969, Quentin Michael Berkeley b 24 May 1971); *Career* various posts in Nigeria, Malawi and S Arabia, GP Whitstable 1967-76, currently dir of pub health Maidstone Health Authy (pub health 1978-); memb: Med Advsy Ctee, Women's Nat Cancer Control Campaign, Royal Cwlth Soc; memb BMA, FFPHM; *Books* Health and Health Services (with J R Butler); *Recreations* travelling, yachting, music, drama; *Style*— Dr Michael Vaile; 63 Joy Lane, Whitstable, Kent CT5 4DD; Maidstone Health Authority, Preston Hall, Maidstone, Kent ME20 7NJ (☎ 0622 710161)

VANCE, Charles Ivan; s of E Goldblatt; *b* 1929; *Educ* Royal Sch Dungannon, Queen's Univ Belfast; *m* 1966, Hon Imogen Moynihan; 1 da (Jacqueline); *Career* actor and theatrical dir/prodr/publisher and ed; dep chm Festival of Br Theatre 1974- (vice chm 1975), chm Standing Advsy Ctee on Local Authy and the Theatre 1983-; chm Charles Vance Ltd and Beck Theatre Prodns Ltd, pres Theatrical Mgmnt Assoc 1971-76; vice chm: Theatres Advy Cncl 1974; dir: Empire Theatre York 1987-, Top Hat Catering 1986-; chm Platform Publications Ltd; FRSA, FInstD; *Books* Amateur Stage (ed), Br Theatre Directory (1971-75), Br Theatre Review (1973), Stage Adaption: Jane Eyre and Wuthering Heights; *Recreations* travel, cooking, sailing (in 1956 single handed crossing Atlantic), dog breeding; *Clubs* RAC, Kennel, Hurlingham, Tenterden GC, Wig and Pen; *Style*— Charles Vance, Esq; Quince Cottage, Bilsington, nr Ashford, Kent

VASSAR-SMITH, John Rathborne; s and h of Sir Richard Vassar-Smith, 3 Bt, TD, *qv*; *b* 23 July 1936; *Educ* Eton; *m* 1971, Roberta Elaine, da of Wing Cdr Norman Williamson; 2 s (Richard b 1975, David b 1978); *Career* runs St Ronans Prep Sch with father; *Style*— John Vassar-Smith, Esq; St Ronans, Hawkhurst, Kent

VASSAR-SMITH, Sir Richard Rathborne; 3 Bt (UK 1917), of Charlton Park, Charlton Kings, TD (1950); s of late Maj Charles Martin Vassar-Smith (2 s of 1 Bt); suc unc, Sir John George Lawley Vassar-Smith (d 1942); *b* 24 Nov 1909; *Educ* Lancing, Pembroke Coll Cambridge; *m* 1932, Dawn Mary, da of Sir Raymond Wybrow Woods, CBE (d 1943); 1 s, 1 da (and 1 child decd); *Heir* s, John Rathborne Vassar-Smith, *qv*; *Career* Maj RA 1939-45; St Ronans Prep Sch: ptnr 1946-57, ptnr with son John Vassar-Smith, *qv* 1957-, headmaster 1957-; *Recreations* golf; *Clubs* Hawks (Cambridge), Rye Golf; *Style*— Sir Richard Vassar-Smith, Bt, TD; Orchard House, St Ronans, Hawkhurst, Kent (☎ 058 05 2300)

VERNON, Richard Wallace; s of Herbert Wallace Vernon (d 1974), of Aldeburgh, Suffolk, and Gertrude Mary, *née* Jackson (d 1959); *b* 18 Oct 1927; *Educ* Loretto, Univ of Cambridge (MA); *m* 8 Jan 1955, Pamela Violet, da of Lt-Col Alexander George William Grierson (d 1951), of Walmer, Kent; 2 s (David Grierson b 1956, Simon Richard b 1958), 2 da (Sally Pamela Clare Daniell b 1960, Joanna Caroline Bennett b 1963); *Career* Lt RA 1945-48; dir: R K Harrison J I Jacobs (Insurance) Ltd 1967-82, R K Harrison & Co 1975-82, Harrison Horncastle (Insurance) Ltd 1982-84; conslt Towry Law (International) Ltd 1988- (md 1984-88); Freeman City of London; *Recreations* sailing; *Clubs* Aldeburgh Yacht, Lloyds Yacht, Haven Ports Yacht, Little Ship; *Style*— Richard Vernon, Esq; Scotch Corner, Wildernesse Ave, Sevenoaks, Kent TN15 0EA (☎ 0732 61 567)

VERRILL, Paul David; s of Dennis Charles Verrill, and Joyce, *née* Button; *b* 21 April 1957; *Educ* Astor Secdy Sch Dover; *m* 27 May 1978, Susan, da of William Gatehouse; 1 s (Jonathan David b 20 Dec 1979), 2 da (Melony Anne b 30 March 1978, Susanna Judith b 3 April 1988); *Career* coalminer Snowdown Colliery; Shelter 1986-; chm (Nat) Anti Black-list Campaign; memb: One World, Friends of John McCarthy; formerly with Band Aid and Sport Aid; *Recreations* most sports; *Style*— Paul Verrill, Esq; 28 Crabble Rd, Dover, Kent CT17 OQE (☎ 0304 213621)

VICK, His Hon Judge (Arnold Oughtred) Russell Vick; QC (1980); yr s of His Hon Judge Sir Godfrey Russell Vick, QC (d 1958), of Seal, and Lady Marjorie Vick, JP, *née* Compston (d 1985); *b* 14 Sept 1933; *Educ* The Leys Sch, Jesus Coll Cambridge (MA); *m* 5 Sept 1959, Zinnia Mary, da of Thomas Brown Yates (d 1968), of Godalming; 2 s (Philip Godfrey Russell b 1960, Mark Thomas b 1964), 1 da (Tessa Louise b 1963); *Career* Nat Serv RAFVR Flying Offr 1952-54; called to the Bar Inner Temple 1958; practised SE Circuit 1958-82: jr 1962-65, prosecuting counsel to PO 1964-69, rec 1978-80, dep rec Rochester City QS 1971, rec Crown Court 1972-82; circuit judge Kent 1982-, princ civil judge Ken 1990-; govr New Beacon Sch; Master Worshipful Co of Curriers' 1976-77; *Books* A Hundred Years of Golf at Wildernesse 1890-1990; *Recreations* golf, cricket, bridge, gardening; *Clubs* MCC, Hawks (Cambridge), Wildernesse Golf (capt 1978), Band of Brothers, Royal Worlington and Newmarket Golf, Bromley Hockey; *Style*— His Hon Judge Russell Vick, QC; The Law Courts, Barker Rd, Maidstone, Kent ME16 8EW (☎ 0622 754966, fax 0622 685428)

VICKERMAN, Prof Roger William; s of William Vickerman (d 1964), of Blackpool, Lancs, and G Ethel, *née* Passingham; *b* 31 Aug 1947; *Educ* Ecclesbourne Sch Duffield Derbyshire, Clare Coll Cambridge (MA), Univ of Sussex (DPhil); *m* 28 July 1973, Christine Ann, da of John Alma Wragg (d 1988), of Hull, Yorks; 2 s (Stephen Roger b 1979, Thomas John b 1986), 2 da (Jennifer Ann b 1979, Karen Elizabeth b 1984); *Career* res fell Univ of Sussex 1972, lectr in econs Univ of Hull 1972-76; Univ of Kent at Canterbury: lectr in econs 1977-79, sr lectr 1979-87, reader 1987-89, prof of regnl and tport econs 1989-; dir Channel Tunnel Res Unit 1986-; concurrent posts held at Univs of: Muenster, Germany (1980), Guelph, Ontario, Canada (1984); memb: Royal Econ Soc, Regnl Sci Assoc (ctee memb Br Section 1986-), Regnl Studies Assoc; FRSA; *Books* The Economics of Leisure and Recreation (1975), Spatial Economic Behaviour (1980), Urban Economics: Analysis and Policy (1984); *Recreations* travel and transport, music; *Style*— Prof Roger Vickerman; Peacock Cottage, Tyler Hill Rd, Blean, Canterbury, Kent CT2 9HT (☎ 0227 47134); University of Kent, Cornwallis Building, Canterbury, Kent CT2 7NF (☎ 0227 764000 ext 3495, fax 0227 459025)

VIGAR, John Edwin; s of Edwin Peter Vigar, of Maidstone, Kent, and Alice Ethel, *née* Miles; *b* 10 May 1960; *Educ* Maidstone; *Career* historian and freelance lectr 1975- (gave 5000th lectr in 1990), reg contrib local and nat jls, travels widely researching and speaking, frequent bdcasting local and nat TV and radio; former chm The Aylesford Soc, former memb Exec Ctee Heart of Kent Tourist Assoc, active memb local and nat hist orgns, fndr and dir Hist Appreciation Soc 1986-, hon historian to The Theatre Royal Conservationists (Chatham), life memb Friends of Friendless Churches, supporter Redundant Churches Fund; *Books* Curious Kent (1984), Exploring Kent Churches (1985), Exploring Sussex Churches (1986), Shire County Guide Kent (1988); *Recreations* cinema architecture, swimming, visiting the seaside, watching television; *Style*— John Vigar, Esq; The White House, Rochester Rd, Aylesford, Maidstone, Kent ME20 7BL (☎ 0622 718118)

VOS, Michael Scott (Mike); s of Wing Cdr Clifford Scott Vos (d 1988), of Chorley Wood, Herts, and Jane Alison Caroline, *née* Firbank; *b* 7 June 1952;

Educ Stamford Sch Lincs, Framlingham Coll Suffolk, LSE (BSc); *m* 16 Aug 1980, Alison Judy, da of Maurice Edgar Howes, of Tunbridge Wells; 1 da (Holly Elizabeth b Dec 1989); *Career* slr and ptnr: Glanvilles Wells and Way Newport IOW 1981-86, Simmonds Church Smiles and Co Holborn London 1987-88, Cripps Harries Hall Crowborough E Sussex 1988-; vice chm Royal Tunbridge Wells Round Table; *Recreations* rugby, sailing, riding; *Clubs* Royal Tunbridge Wells, Round Table, Tunbridge Wells Rugby, Bewl Valley Sailing, Wig and Pen; *Style—* Michael Vos, Esq; Cripps Harries Hall, Croham House, Croham Rd, Crowborough, E Sussex TN6 2RL (☎ 0892 662233, fax 0892 652067)

VOYSEY, Dr Margaret Mary; da of Richard Alan Elison Voysey (d 1968), of Eye, Suffolk, and Nancy, *née* Rowbotham (d 1989); *b* 7 Sept 1925; *Educ* Dr Williams Sch Dolgelly N Wales, St Bartholemew's Hosp Sch of Med (MB BS, FFARCS); *Career* WAAF 1944-47; jr doctor 1954-62, conslt anaesthetist Canterbury and Thanet 1962-86, gen mangr Thanet Unit 1986-90; memb BMA; *Recreations* gardening, travel; *Style—* Dr Margaret Voysey; 9 Reading St Rd, Broadstairs, Kent CT10 3EA (☎ 0843 63019); Thanet District General Hospital, St Peter's Rd, Margate, Kent CT9 4AN (☎ 0843 225544)

W

WADDAMS, (Austen) Lawrence; s of Capt C T Waddams (d 1958), of Shepherds Bush, London, and Alice Edith, *née* King (d 1958); *b* 2 April 1917; *Educ* Latymer Upper Sch Hammersmith, Imperial Coll London (BSc, DIC); *m* 1, 23 March 1940, Elizabeth Irene, *née* Lyon (d 1988); 4 da (Joan Lesley b 1942, Elizabeth Janet b 1944, Alison Sheila b 1949, Christine Mary b 1961); m 2, 10 March 1990, Mollie Emily Laura, da of Douglas Cozens Baker (d 1976), of Bournemouth; *Career* wartime managerial appts: Rowntrees, Procter and Gamble, Royal Ordnance Factory Irvine; various mgmnt functions in UK and Australia Shell Group 1945-62 and BP Group 1962-77, conslt on petrochemicals SRI (Stanford Research Institute) 1977-87; industl mktg res on petrochemicals 1945-77, fndr and chm Euro Chem Mktg Res Assoc 1966-71, chm Industl Mktg Res Assoc 1974-76, sec gen Euro Assoc for Industl Mktg Res 1976-90; CEng, ARCS, MIChemE; American Chem Mktg Res Assoc Distinguished Serv Award 1977 (only non American recipient to date), Euro Chem Mktg Res Assoc created a similar award 1985 (the Lawrie Waddams Award); author item on petrochemicals Encyclopaedia Britannia 1974; *Books* Chemicals From Petroleum (1 edn 1962, 4 edn 1978), The Petroleum Chemicals Industry (with R F Goldstein, 1965); *Style—* Lawrence Waddams, Esq; 4 The Terrace, Church St, Shoreham, Sevenoaks, Kent TN14 7SN (☎ 09592 2970)

WADE, David Anthony; s of Col Harold Wade (d 1945), and Olive, *née* Baldwin (d 1961); *b* 22 Dec 1925; *Educ* Stonyhurst; *m* 1, 1 Dec 1949, Nancy (d 1965), da of Col R Stalker; 4 da (Linda b 9 Oct 1950, Louise b 2 June 1952 d 1953, Judith b 6 Jan 1955, Annabel b 6 June 1957); m 2, 29 April 1968, Amy Kathrine, da of Thomas Culley (d 1982), of Nova Friburgo, Brazil; 2 s (Mark b 13 March 1969, Sebastian b 3 Feb 1970), 1 da (Alexandra b 21 May 1971); *Career* served WWII Queens Regt 1943, cmmnd 2 KEO Gurkha Rifles, served Assam and Burma 1944-47; FO Singapore Burma and Germany 1947-50; called to the Bar Inner Temple 1959; gen mangr: Synthetic Fibres Div Courtaulds Group 1961-65 (joined 1951), Wm Brandts Sons & Co Ltd 1965-66; gp md Alfred Dunhill Ltd 1967-69, md Australasian Assets Ltd 1969-72, chm Camel Investments Ltd 1975-; *Books* Disaster (1987); *Recreations* skiing, sailing; *Clubs* Reform; *Style—* David Wade, Esq; Roman Way, Benenden, Kent TN17 4ES (☎ 0580 240873); 2 Mitre Court Buildings, Temple, London EC4Y 7BZ (☎ 071 353 1353, fax 071 353 8188)

WADE, Robert Edward; s of Edward William Wade, of Southend House, Footscray Rd, Eltham, and Rosina Alice, *née* Gill; *b* 29 Dec 1949; *m* 26 April 1975, Monica Jane, da of Alex Rennie, of Gerrard House, Norwich, Norfolk; 1 da (Joanne Lisa b 7 May 1980); *Career* dir: Bisgood Bishop 1984-86, County Bisgood 1986, Citicorp Scrimgeour Vickers 1986-88, Robert Fleming Secs 1988-; memb Stock Exchange 1975; *Recreations* golf; *Clubs* Royal Blackheath Golf; *Style—* Robert Wade, Esq; Glebe House, Chislehurst Rd, Bickley, Bromley, Kent BR1 2NS (☎ 081 467 8964); Robert Fleming & Co, 25 Copthall Ave, London EC2 (☎ 081 588 9452)

WAIN, Prof (Ralph) Louis; CBE (1967); s of George Wain (d 1943), of Hyde, Cheshire, and Eliza, *née* Hardy (d 1947); *b* 29 May 1911; *Educ* Co GS Hyde Cheshire, Univ of Sheffield (BSc, MSc, PhD), Univ of London (DSc); *m* 24 Aug 1940, Joan, da of Thomas Bowker (d 1947), of Denton, Lancs; 1 s (Michael Louis b 10 March 1948), 1 da (Rosemary Joan b 21 March 1944); *Career* res Univ of Manchester 1935-37, Univ of Bristol 1939-45; Wye Coll Univ of London: lectr 1937-39, head Chemistry Dept 1945-50, prof of agric chemistry 1950-78, dir Agric Res Cncl Unit 1953-78; hon prof chemistry Univ of Kent 1978-; vice pres RSC 1961-64 and 1975-78, UK rep E African Natural Resources Res Cncl 1963-, mangr Royal Inst 1971-74, chm Wain Fellowships Ctee 1976-; Hon DSc: Univs of Ghent, Sheffield, Lausanne, Kent; Pruthivi Gold Medal 1957, RAS Res Medal 1960, John Scott Medal (USA) 1963, Flintoff Medal of RSC 1969, Int Res Medal (USA) 1972, John Jeyes Gold Medal of RSC 1976, Royal Instn Actonian Award 1977, Mullard Medal of Royal Soc 1988; memb Internationale Academie de Lutée (1980), fell Wye Coll (1981); FRS 1960; *Books* Plant Growth Substances (co-ed F Wightman, 1956); *Recreations* painting, travel; *Clubs* Royal Soc Dining; *Style—* Prof Louis Wain, CBE, FRS; Crown Point, Scotton St, Wye, Kent TN25 5BZ (☎ 0233 812157); Dept of Chemistry, University of Kent, Canterbury, Kent CT2 7NH (☎ 0227 764000)

WAINMAN, Allison Joan; da of John Hopkin (d 1942), and Estelle Marguerite, *née* Pine (d 1966); *b* 30 July 1940; *Educ* Priory Sch Jamaica WI; *m* 1 May 1965, David Peter Wainman, s of Phillip Richard Wainman (d 1948); 1 s (William Slingsby b 1968), 1 da (Susanna Jane b 1966); *Career* trainee journalist 1957-59, journalist 1959-64, printer and publisher 1978-, ed Kent Seen; memb Lib Pty 1972-; chm Bicknor Parish 1973-, memb Maidstone Health Authy 1981-89; Kent CC rep for Maidstone West: Lib candidate 1981, SLD candidate 1985 and 1988, elected ldr SLD Pty 1985; fndr memb and tstee Kent Gdns Tst, former dir and vice chm Voice (Employers Orgn Swale); *Recreations* gardening, photography, swimming; *Style—* Mrs Allison Wainman; Placketts Hole, Bicknor, Sittingbourne, Kent ME9 8BA (☎ 062784 258); Centre 2000, St Michael's Rd, Sittingbourne, Kent ME10 3DZ (☎ 0795 420314, fax 0795 422633)

WAKEFIELD, Cncllr (Trevor) Ian Marsden; s of Trevor Marsden Wakefield, of Devoran, Cornwall, and Dorothy Nan, *née* Laidlaw; *b* 30 June 1947; *Educ* Sevenoaks, Imperial Coll London (BSc); *m* 20 June 1970, Faith Mary Barbara, da of Maj Richard Burrows, of Tunbridge Wells; 2 da (Emma Mary b 3 April 1973, Louise Claire b 8 March 1975); *Career* chief prodn engr Henry Balfour & Co 1973-76, prodn mangr APV Kestner 1976-78, nat accounts mangr local authorities Amoco UK Ltd 1978-90, account mangr Business Development MPSI Ltd 1990-; memb: Meopham Parish Cncl 1984-85, Gravesham Borough Cncl 1985-; chm Gravesham Cons Assoc 1988-; ACGI, MIProdE, MInstPet, CEng; *Clubs* ESU; *Style—* Cncllr Ian Wakefield; 81 Timberbank, Vigo Village, Meopham, Kent DA13 0SN (☎ 0732 823404); MPSI Systems Ltd, Castlemead, Lower Castle St, Bristol BS1 3AG (☎ 0272 279653, fax 0272 292056)

WAKELEY, Dr Richard Michael; s of Sir Cecil Wakeley (d 1979), and Dr Elizabeth Muriel Wakeley, *née* Nicholson-Smith (d 1985); *b* 21 Jan 1933; *Educ* Winchester, King's Coll London (MB BS); *Career* house surgn King's Coll Hosp 1958; actor 1960-66; literary agent 1968-; Freeman City of London 1956; memb: City Co of Barber Surgns, Worshipful Soc of Apothecaries; *Recreations* music, tennis; *Style—* Dr Richard Wakeley; 1 Wordsworth Mansions, Queens Club Gardens, London W14 9TE (☎ 071 385 0908); Coves Cottage, St Peter's, Broadstairs, Kent CT10 2TH; Peters Fraser & Dunlop, 5th Floor, The Chambers, Chelsea Harbour, Lots Rd, London SW10 0XF (☎ 071 376 7676, fax 071 352 7356)

WALDRON, Lady Olivia Elsie June; *née* Taylour; da of 5 Marquess of Headfort, TD (d 1960), and Elsie Faith (formerly w of Sir Rupert Clarke, Bt); *b* 20 June 1929; *Educ* St Catherine's Melbourne Aust, St Mary's Convent Ascot; *m* 1955, Victor Echevarri Waldron, s of Ernest Victor Echevarri; 2 da; *Career* dir The Hunger Project Ltd (UK) 1980-84, tstee The Hunger Project Tst 1984-89, chm Waldron Properties Ltd, memb Exec Cncl UK chapter Soc for Int Devpt, chm Advsy Cncl The Hunger Project 1989-; *Style—* The Lady Olivia Waldron; Idleigh Cottage, nr Meopham, Kent (☎ 0474 872363)

WALEY, His Hon Judge (Andrew) Felix; VRD (1962, clasp 1972), QC (1973); s of Guy Felix Waley (d 1959), of Askerswell, Dorset, and Anne Elizabeth, *née* Dickson (d 1959); *b* 14 April 1926; *Educ* Charterhouse, Worcester Coll Oxford (MA); *m* 3 Sept 1955, Petica Mary, da of Sir Philip Humphrey Vere Rose, 3 Bt (d 1980); 1 s (Simon b 9 Sept 1964), 4 da (Sarah b 17 Feb 1958, Jane b 27 Feb 1959, Juliet b 10 Feb 1960, Victoria b 21 Jan 1961 d 1962); *Career* RN 1944-48, pilot offr RAFVR 1948-51, RNVR and RNR 1951-72 (promoted to Cdr RNR 1965); called to the Bar Middle Temple 1953; recorder of the Crown Court 1974-81, bencher Middle Temple 1981, circuit judge 1982, resident judge Co of Kent 1985, Judge Advocate of the Fleet 1986; cncllr Paddington Borough Cncl 1956-59, parly candidate (C) Dagenham 1959, chm London Flotilla 1980-86; *Recreations* gardens, boats, birds; *Clubs* Garrick, Naval, RNSA; *Style—* His Hon Judge Waley, VRD, QC; The Law Courts, Barker Rd, Maidstone, Kent ME16 8EQ (☎ 0622 754966)

WALKER, Christopher John; s of John Samuel Walker, of E Preston, W Sussex, and Joan Isabel, *née* Taylor; *b* 10 Aug 1942; *Educ* Ardingly Coll Sussex, St Mary's Hosp Med Sch Univ of London (MB BS); *m* 9 Oct 1982, Janet Louise, da of Peter Jeffery Maurice Golston, of 31 Beatty St, Balgowlah, Sydney, NSW, Australia; 1 s (Thomas Edward Walker b 13 Feb 1984), 1 da (Sally Margaret Isabel Walker b 28 Aug 1985); *Career* GP

Brighton 1968-71, sr orthopaedic registrar in rotation St Mary's Hosp London 1974-79, conslt orthopaedic surgn Maidstone Dist 1979-; Liveryman Worshipful Soc of Apothecaries; FRCS; *Recreations* cricket, golf, wine; *Clubs* MCC, Marden Cricket and Hockey, Cranbrook Golf; *Style*— Christopher Walker, Esq; Chittenden House, Lovehurst Lane, Staplehurst, Tonbridge, Kent TN12 0EX (☎ 0580 891989); Maidstone Hospital, Hermitage Lane, Barming, Maidstone, Kent ME16 9QQ (☎ 0622 729000)

WALKER, Ian Hugh; s of John Walker, and Joan, *née* Crowther; *b* 3 Jan 1950; *Educ* Huntley's Tunbridge Wells; *m* 15 July 1975, Lorraine, da of George Armstrong; 2 s (Matthew James Hugh b 1979, Robert George b 1982); *Career* estate agent; ptnr Page & Wells Maidstone, dir Page & Wells Financial Services Ltd; chm Bearsted Round Table 1989-; FNAEA; *Recreations* golf, squash, running, skiing; *Clubs* Tudor Park, Mote Squash, Bearsted; *Style*— Ian Walker, Esq; 132 Ashford Rd, Bearsted, Maidstone, Kent (☎ 0622 39574)

WALKER, Dr Ian Robert; s of Robert Douglas Walker, of Ballina, NSW, Australia, and Rhoda Ruby, *née* Faunce; *b* 21 July 1951; *Educ* Sydney Boy's HS, Melbourne Coll of Divinity (LTh), Univ of Bristol (BA), Univ of Wales (PhD); *m* 8 Dec 1973, Kerrie Jane, da of Allan Hilary Nugent, of Sydney, Australia; 1 s (Timothy Angus b 1983), 1 da (Hilary Louise b 1987); *Career* asst master Dulwich 1979-86, headmaster King's Sch Rochester 1986-; author of various articles in philosophical jls and reviews; involved with Headmasters' Conf, memb Admiralty Interview Bd 1987-; FCP, assoc Bankers' Inst of Australasia; *Books* Plato's Euthyphro (1984), Christ in the Community (ed, 1990); *Recreations* oil painting, classical music, cello, rugby; *Clubs* Athenaeum, E India; *Style*— Dr Ian Walker; King's School Rochester, Satis House, Boley Hill, Rochester, Kent ME1 1TE (☎ 0634 843913, fax 0634 832493)

WALKER, Capt Leonard; s of Joseph Walker (d 1967), of Dover, and Helen Lydia Violet, *née* Johnson (d 1969); *b* 17 May 1927; *Educ* Dover GS, Coll of St Mark and St John; *m* 6 Aug 1955, (Ena) Elaine, da of Charles Walter Hawkins (d 1969), of Dover; 3 da (Anne b 1958, Elizabeth b 1959, Sarah b 1964); *Career* RE 1945-47, offr i/c Rhine Army Sch of Preliminary Educn RAEC 1948-49, Capt RARO 1949-82; tutor i/c Dover Prison Borstal 1953-58; headmaster: Bluntisham C of E Sch Huntingdon 1964-67, Salmestone Sch Margate 1967-90; reader C of E, churchwarden Parish of Birchington with Acol and Minnis Bay, govr and sec Crispe Charity, former pres and sec Rotary Club Westgate and Birchington; ACP 1967; *Recreations* history, gardening, travel, reading; *Style*— Capt Leonard Walker; 49 Dane Rd, Birchington, Kent (☎ 0843 42660)

WALKER, Peter Frank; s of Wilfrid Herbert Hornsey Walker (d 1965), and Mildred Sheila, *née* Caddell (d 1984); *b* 27 June 1937; *Educ* Oundle, King's Coll London (BSc); *m* 27 March 1965, Susan Margaret, da of Geoffrey Hugh Sharp, of Leicester; 1 s (Richard b 1972), 2 da (Fiona b 1967, Julia b 1969); *Career* Nat Serv 2 Lt RE 1955-57; CChem; chm Usher-Walker plc 1985- (md 1974-); pres Soc of Br Printing Ink Mfrs 1985-86 (cncl memb 1973-76 1979-82 and 1983-87); MRIC, MIOP; *Recreations* racing, antiques, bridge; *Clubs* RAC; *Style*— Peter Walker, Esq; Usher-Walker plc, Chancery House, Chancery Lane, London WC2A 1SA (☎ 071 405 3642, fax 071 831 9921, telex 261293)

WALKLEY, John Michael; s of John Walkley, and Lily, *née* Horn; *b* 9 Dec 1941; *Educ* New Coll Sch Oxford, King's Sch Ely, Univ of London (LLB), Cranfield Inst of Technol (MSc); *m* 23 July 1960, Anne, da of George Ditton, of Lincs; 1 s (John Ditton b 1964), 3 da (Sally Anne b 1961, Penny b 1962, Mandy b 1966); *Career* Lincs Constabulary: Constable 1960-83, Detective Chief Inspr 1983-85; Kent Constabulary: Supt 1985-90, Chief Supt head of mgmnt servs 1990-; past memb Amherst Rotary Club Sevenoaks; *Books* Police Interrogation: A Handbook for Investigators (1987); *Style*— John Walkley, Esq; Kent County Constabulary, Police Headquarters, Sutton Rd, Maidstone, Kent ME15 9BZ (☎ 0622 690690, fax 0622 690511)

WALLACE, Hon Michael George; o s of Baron Wallace of Coslany (Life Peer), *qv*; *b* 1944; *m* 1974, Susan, da of Henry William Price, of Orpington, Kent; *Recreations* gardening, amateur radio; *Style*— The Hon Michael Wallace; 17 Leamington Ave, Orpington, Kent

WALLACE OF COSLANY, Baron (Life Peer UK 1974), of Coslany, City of Norwich; George Douglas Wallace; s of George Wallace, of Cheltenham, Glos; *b* 18 April 1906; *Educ* Central Sch Cheltenham; *m* 1932, Vera, da of William Joseph Randall, of Guildford, Surrey; 1 s (Hon Michael George, *qv*, b 1944), 1 da (Hon Elizabeth Anne b 1933); *Career* sits as Lab Peer in House of Lords; MP (Lab): Chislehurst 1945-50, Norwich N 1964-74; govt whip 1947-50, lord in waiting 1977-79, oppn whip 1979-84, oppn spokesman (Lords) Health 1983-84; memb: Chislehurst and Sidcup UDC 1937-46, Kent CC 1948-53; pres: Radio Soc GB 1977, London Soc of Recreational Gardeners, League of Friends Queen Mary's Hosp Sidcup; *Recreations* gardening, amateur radio; *Style*— The Rt Hon the Lord Wallace of Coslany; 44 Shuttle Close, Sidcup, Kent (☎ 081 300 3634)

WALLBANK, Cncllr Mark Andrew; s of Leslie James Wallbank, of 45 Alexandra Ave, Gillingham, and Rosemary Betty, *née* Barlow; *b* 22 April 1963; *Educ* Gillingham GS, Howard Grammer Modern, Mid Kent Coll, Medway Coll of Design (Dip); *Career* Lloyds of London 1988-89, Minets Insurance Brokers Leman St London 1990-; past chm NUS Kent Area 1984, past pres Medway Coll of Design Students' Union 1984-85, memb Lib Democrats, Gillingham borough cncllr Priestfield Ward 1986- (yst elected cncllr), Kent co cncllr Gillingham NE 1989- (yst elected cncllr); *Style*— Cncllr Mark Wallbank; 3 Garfield Rd, Gillingham, Kent ME7 1QB; J H Minet & Co Ltd, 100 Leman St, London E1 8HG (☎ 071 481 0707 ext 3255, fax 071 488 9786)

WALLIS, David Anthony; s of George Arthur Wallis (d 1950), and Marjorie Jane, *née* Faulkner (d 1940); *b* 24 Nov 1932; *Educ* Victoria Sch Watford, Goldsmiths Coll New Cross (City and Guilds); *m* 11 Aug 1956, Edna, da of Thomas Harold Harrison (d 1977), of Croydon; *Career* Nat Serv RAF 1950-52, instrument specialist; apprentice instrument maker Charles Baker and Sons Ltd Holborn, salesman of wholesale optical prods CS Pyser Ltd of Holborn 1952-56; ptnrship with Pyser family formed Survey and General Instrument Co Ltd (md 1956-86), chm of Bd Pyser (Holdings) plc 1986; cncl memb Drawing Office Material Mfrs and Dealers Assoc, past pres Photogrammetric Soc, memb UK Nat Ctee Photogrammetry and Remote Sensing; judge for Kent Exporters of the Year contest 1990-91; Freeman: City of London 1977, Worshipful Co of Scientific Instrument Makers 1977 (memb of Court); FRGS 1981, FCIM 1986, ARICS 1988; *Recreations* golf, sea fishing; *Clubs* Shortlands Golf, City Livery, United Wards; *Style*— David A Wallis, Esq; Pyser (Holdings) plc, Fircroft Way, Edenbridge, Kent TN8 6HA (☎ 0732 864111, fax 0732 865544, car tel 0860 391113, telex 95527 OPTSLS G)

WALLIS, Pamela June; da of Henry Charles Wallis (d 1954), and Annie, *née* Duffield (d 1976); *b* 27 May 1932; *Educ* St Bernards Convent Slough Berks, AA London (AADip); *Career* chartered architect in private practice; memb AA 1957, ARIBA 1959; *Recreations* architecture, china painting, gardening, walking, water colours; *Style*— Miss Pamela Wallis; 69 Harvest Bank Rd, West Wickham, Kent BR4 9DP (☎ 081 462 4801)

WALMSLEY, Kevin; s of James Walmsley, and Evelyn Grace, *née* Bunnett; *b* 20 Aug 1959; *Educ* Runshaw Coll Lancs, Univ of Liverpool; *Career* cncllr Dartford Borough Cncl 1983-: ctee memb Fin and Personnel (later chm), ctee memb Policy, Planning, Contracts, Resources and Housing; *Recreations* travel, walking, current affairs, reading; *Style*— Kevin Walmsley, Esq; Fairhaven, 28 Miskin Rd, Dartford, Kent DA1 2LS (☎ 0322 27398); King & Co Chartered Accountants, 12 Fife Rd, Kingston-upon-Thames, Surrey KT1 1S2 (☎ 081 546 7562, fax 081 541 1387)

WALTER, Edwin Frederick (Ted); s of Frederick Edwin Walter (d 1946), of Swanley, and Edith Bessie, *née* Coppins (1977); *b* 20 Nov 1933; *Educ* Beckenham Tech Sch; *m* 15 June 1957, Hazel Doreen, da of Edward George Bean (d 1981), of Swanley; 2 s (Stephen David b 1960, Timothy John b 1962); *Career* Constable Met Police 1955-80, highways inspr Sevenoaks Dist Cncl 1980-90, freelance writer as Willing Words 1989-, pt/t highway admin 1990; adult educn tutor in Writing for Pleasure: WEA 1976-, local educn Bromley 1978-, bdcast two series of Writing For Pleasure (Radio Kent) 1979; writer in schs 1981-, on Lit Panel SE Arts 1987-91; memb: Nat Poetry Soc, Ed Panel Envoi Poetry Wales, Greenpeace, Rain Forest Fndn, Woodland Tst, Nat Tst, Kent Tst For Nature Conservation; involved in Sevenoaks AEC Adult Literacy 1990, arranges and tutors writing weekends around the world, poet in schs in the WH Smith Poetry Soc Scheme; *Books* Kindling (Poems, 1979), Choosing Yellow (Poems, 1986); *Recreations* theatre going, listening to music, reading; *Style*— Ted Walter, Esq; Highfield, 29 Crown Rd, Chelsfield, Orpington, Kent BR6 6JN (☎ 0689 58639); Willing Words, 29 Crown Rd, Chelsfield, Orpington, Kent BR6 6JN (☎ 0689 58639)

WARD, Dr Adam Anthony; s of Dennis Harold Ward, of Avening, Mark Cross, Crowborough, East Sussex, and Margaret Maud, *née* Record; *b* 15 June 1947; *Educ* Tonbridge, Springhill Sch, King's Coll London, Westminster Med Sch, Univ of London (MB BS), LSHTM (MSc), Hotel Dieu Univ of Paris (DipOrthMed); *Career* ed Broadway Magazine 1970; lectr and hon sr registrar (epidemiology) Westminster Med Sch 1978-79; physician: Dept of Orthopaedic Med Hotel Dieu Paris 1982-83, Royal London Homoeopathic Hosp 1983-; specialist in complimentary med; clinician; broadcaster; memb: Cncl The Faculty of Homoeopathy London, Medical Homoeopathic Res Gp London; *Recreations* walking in Rupert Bear country; *Style*— Dr Adam A Ward; 41 Frankfield Rise, Tunbridge Wells, Kent TN2 5LF (☎ 0892 25799)

WARD, Sir Alan Hylton; s of Stanley Victor Ward (d 1974), and Mary, *née* Whittingham; *b* 15 Feb 1938; *Educ* Christian Bros Coll Pretoria, Univ of Pretoria (BA, LLB), Univ of Cambridge (MA, LLB); *m* 1, 22 June 1963 (m dis 1982); 1 s (Mark b 1968), 2 da (Wendy b 1965, Emma b 1966); m 2, Helen Madeleine, da of Keith Gilbert, of Berkswell, Warwicks; 2 da (Amelia b 1984, Katharine (twin) b 1984); *Career* attorney Supreme Court SA 1959-61, called to the Bar Gray's Inn 1964; QC (1984), Justice of the High Court assigned to the Family Div 1988; kt 1988; *Recreations* knocking balls about; *Clubs* MCC; *Style*— The Hon Sir Alan Ward; Royal Courts of Justice, The Strand, London WC2A 2LL (☎ 071 936 6000)

WARD, Clive Richard; s of William Herbert Ward (d 1982), and Muriel, *née* Wright; *b* 30 July 1945; *Educ* Sevenoaks Sch, Univ of Cambridge (MA); *m* 9 Sept 1972, Catherine Angela, da of Lt Cdr Godfrey Joseph Hines, of Droxford, Hants; 3 da (Joanna b 1975, Diana b 1977, Emily b 1979); *Career* CA 1971, asst sec Take Over Panel 1975-77, ptnr Ernst and Young 1979-90, head corp fin London 1987, corp devpt dir Shardwick plc 1990; Freeman Worshipful Co of Barbers 1985, Worshipful Co of Tobacco Pipe Makers and Tobacco Blenders 1975; FCA 1979; *Books* Guide to Company Flotation (1989); *Recreations* fishing, music, gardening; *Style*— Clive Ward, Esq; Market Heath House, Brenchley, Tonbridge, Kent TN12 7PA (☎ 089272 2172); Shadwick plc, 61 Grosvenor St, London W1X 9DA (☎ 071 408 2232, fax 071 493 8246)

WARD, Denis John; s of George Hartwell Ward (d 1978), of Rainham, Kent, and Enid Joyce, *née* Randall (d 1982); *b* 3 Dec 1923; *Educ* King's Sch Rochester; *m* 10 Oct 1959, (Mary) Rosina, da of Cdr Harry Marshall (d 1943), of Hartlip, Kent; 1 s (Timothy b 1964 d 1987), 1 da (Claire b 1961); *Career* Br Army 1943-46: bomb disposal SE Eng, W African Frontier Force in Nigeria, served in Burma; chm and md: Ward Holdings plc, Wards Construction (Medway) Ltd; dir: Wards Construction (Industrial) Ltd, Ward Homes (South East) Ltd, Ward Homes (Anglia) Ltd, Ward Bros (Gillingham) Ltd, Wards Construction (London) Ltd; chm White Seal Stairways Ltd; *Recreations* tennis, squash; *Clubs* Gore Court Cricket, Teynham Squash, Tudor Park Squash; *Style*— Denis Ward, Esq; Ward Holdings plc, 2 Ashtree Lane, Chatham, Kent ME5 7BZ (☎ 0634 55111)

WARD, John Stanton; CBE; s of Russell Stanton Ward, and Jessie Elizabeth, *née* Watson; *b* 10 Oct 1917; *Educ* St Owen's Sch Hereford, Hereford Art Sch, RCA; *m* 18 April 1950, Alison Christine Mary; 4 s (William, George, Jack, Toby), 2 da (Celia, Charlotte); *Career* RE 1939-46; painter and illustrator; books incl: Cider with Rosie by Laurie Lee, The Little Kingdom by Richard Church, Stateley as a Galleon and George Don't Do That by Joyce Grenfell, Autobiography by H E Bates; portraits incl HRH Princess Royal in The National Portrait Gallery; tstee Royal Acad of Arts, pres Ashford Art Soc; Hon DLitt Univ of Kent; ARA 1956, RA 1966, RWS, RP; *Clubs* Athenaeum; *Style*— John Ward, Esq, CBE; Bilting Court, Ashford, Kent

WARDE, John St Andrew; s of Maj John Roberts O'Brien Warde, TD, DL (d 1975), of Squerryes Court, Westerham, Kent, and Millicent Anne Warde, CBE, *née* Cook (d 1982); *b* 8 March 1940; *Educ* Eton, Trinity Coll Cambridge (MA); *m* 10 April 1973, Anthea, da of Anthony Francis Holland, MC (d 1982), of Lullings, Balcombe, Sussex; 2 s (Charles Anthony b 1974, Henry John b 1976), 2 da (Anne Charlotte b 1982); *Career* farmer and landowner 1963-; served with Kent and Sharpshooters Yeo 1960-68; chm Sevenoaks DC 1980 (memb 1976-87), High Sheriff of Kent 1990-91; former chm: CLA Kent, HHA South East; dep chm Timber Growers UK; *Recreations* shooting, fishing; *Clubs* Cavalry and Guards; *Style*— John Warde, Esq; Squerryes Court, Westerham, Kent TN16 1ST (☎ 0959 63118)

WARLAND, Philip John; s of Ernest Alfred Henry Warland, of Christchurch, and Winifred Mary, *née* Poyntz-Owen; *b* 25 Dec 1945; *Educ* KCS; *m* 19 Sept 1970, Sandra, da of Jack Cross (d 1987); 3 s (David b 1972, Richard b 1973, John b 1978); *Career* head Info Div Bank of England 1985-89, gp personnel resources mangr Standard Chartered Bank 1989-; *Recreations* squash, golf, cricket, walking; *Style*— Philip Warland, Esq; Standard Chartered Bank, 38 Bishopsgate, London EC2N 4DE (☎ 071 280 7700)

WARREN, Kenneth Robin; MP (C) Hastings and Rye 1983-; s of Edward Charles Warren (d 1987), of St Leonards on Sea, East Sussex; *b* 15 Aug 1926; *Educ* Midsomer Norton, Aldenham, De Havilland Aeronautical Tech Sch, Univ of London; *m* 1962, Elizabeth Anne, da of Russell Chamberlain; *Career* aero and electronics engr; De Havilland Aircraft 1947-51, BOAC 1951-57, Smith Industries Ltd 1957-60, Elliott Automation Ltd 1960-69; chm Warren Woodfield Assocs; dir: Datapoint (UK) Ltd, Gulf Guaranty Bank Ltd, Loral International; memb Paddington Borough Cncl 19653-65, contested (C) St Pancras North 1964, MP (C) Hastings 1970-1983; chm: Parly Ctee on Offshore Technol 1974-75, Cons Parly Aviation Ctee 1974-76, Western European Univ Sci, Technol and Aerospace Ctee 1977-80; memb Select Ctee on Sci and Technol, PPS to Rt Hon Sir Keith Joseph, Bt, MP, Sec of State Industry 1979-81 (educn and sci 1981-83); chm: Select Ctee on Trade and Indust 1983-, Br-Soviet Party Gp 1986; Freeman City of London; Liveryman: Worshipful Co Coachmaker's and Harness Maker's, Worshipful Co Air Pilots and Navigaters; CEng, FRAeS, FCIT FRSA; *Clubs* Special Forces; *Style*— Kenneth Warren, Esq, MP; Woodfield House, Goudhurst, Kent (☎ 0580 211 590)

WARREN, Prof Michael Donald; s of Charles Warren (d 1966), of Brook Vale, Rattlesden, Bury St Edmunds, Suffolk, and Dorothy Gladys Thornton, *née* Reeks (d 1979); *b* 19 Dec 1923; *Educ* Bedford Sch, Guy's Hosp Med Sch (MB BS), LSHTM (MD, DPH, DIH); *m* 8 March 1946, Joan Lavina, da of Robert Horace Peacock (d 1955), of Green Acre, New Farm Rd, Abridge, Romford, Essex; 1 s (David b 1947), 2 da (Dorothy b 1948, Penelope b 1958); *Career* RAF Med Branch 1947-51, Sqdn Ldr 1948-51; dep med offr of health Hampstead 1952-54, asst princ med offr London CC 1954-58, sr lectr in social and preventive med Royal Free Sch of Med and LSHTM 1958-64, hon conslt in social and rehabilitation med Royal Free Hosp 1958-64, reader in pub health Univ of London 1964-71, prof of social med and dir Health Servs Res Unit Univ of Kent Canterbury 1971-83 (emeritus prof of social med 1984); academic registrar faculty of community med RCP 1971-77; memb: Cncl for Postgrad Med Educn 1972-76, Regnl Res Ctee SE Thames Regnl Health Authy 1974-83, Exec Cncl Kent Postgrad Med Centre Canterbury 1974-88; chm Soc for Social Med 1982-83, FFCM 1972, FRCP 1975; *Books* Public Health and Social Services (3 edn 1965), Physically Disabled People Living at Home (1978), Recalling the Medical Officer of Health (1987); *Recreations* reading, genealogy, light gardening; *Clubs* RSM, Kent CCC; *Style*— Prof Michael Warren; 2 Bridge Down, Bridge, Canterbury, Kent CT4 5AZ (☎ 0227 830 233)

WARREN, Ven Norman Leonard; s of Arthur Henry Warren (d 1987), and Gwendoline Catharine, *née* Hallett; *b* 19 July 1934; *Educ* Dulwich, Corpus Christi Coll Cambridge (MA); *m* 15 April 1961, Yvonne; 3 s (Andrew Mark b 12 March 1962, Philip James b 11 July 1965, David John Chi Hank b 1 Jan 1970), 2 da (Ruth Elizabeth b 21 Dec 1963, Sarah Rachel b 10 Jan 1968); *Career* vicar St Pauls Leamington Spa 1963-77, rector of Morden 1977-89, archdeacon of Rochester 1989-; memb: Gen Ctee Royal Sch of Church Music, Gen Synod C of E 1974-77; pres Music in Worship Tst; *Books* Journey Into Life (1963), Directions (1966), Signposts (1974), What's The Point (1986), A Certain Faith (1988), The Path of Peace (1988); *Recreations* music, walking; *Style*— The Ven the Archdeacon of Rochester; The Archdeaconry, Rochester, Kent ME1 1SX (☎ 0634 842527)

WASTELL, Prof Christopher; s of Edgar Barker Wastell (d 1963), and Doris Emmeline, *née* Pett (d 1965); *b* 13 Oct 1932; *Educ* Drax GS; Guy's Hosp Med Sch (MB BS), Univ of London Med Sch (MS); *m* 2 April 1958, Margaret Anne, da of Joseph Fletcher (d 1976); 1 s (Giles Richard b 1965), 2 da (Jacqueline Anne b 1961, Vivien Clare b 1963); *Career* house physician Joyce Green, house surgn Franborough Kent, sr house offr Bristol Royal Infirmary, house surgn Great Ormond St, registrar Westminster Hosp, lectr Westminster Med Sch 1964-67, C and H J Gaisman Res Fell Mount Sinai Hosp NY USA 1965-66, sr lectr and hon conslt surgn Westminster Med Sch and Hosp 1968-73 (rdr 1973-82), prof and hon conslt surgn Charing Cross and Westminster Med Sch London Univ at Westminster Hosp 1983-, conslt to accident and emergency Westminster Hosp 1971-; FRCS; *Books* Chronic Duodenal Ulcer (1972), Westminster Hospital Symposium on Chronic Duodenal Ulcer (1974), Surgery for Nurses (with Ellis, 1976), Surgery of the Stomach and Duodenum (with Nyhus, 1977 and 1986), Cimetidine, The Westminster Hospital Symposium (1978); *Recreations* sailing, gardening, walking; *Clubs* Wilsonian Sailing, RSM; *Style*— Prof Christopher Wastell; 7 Manor Way, Beckenham, Kent BR3 3LH; 3 North Rd, Kingsdown, Deal, Kent CT14 8AG (☎ 081 650 5882); Surgical Unit, Westminster Hospital, Page St Wing, London SW1P 2AP (☎ 081 746 8000/081 746 8466, fax 081 746 8111, telex 919263 RHIVA G)

WATERS, Keith Stuart; s of Thomas Charles Waters, and Elsie Lillian, *née* Addison; *b* 18 March 1951; *Educ* Leigh GS, Wigan Tech Coll, Univ of Newcastle upon Tyne (BA); *m* 10 April 1976, (Elizabeth) Jane, da of James Weeks; 1 s (James b 1981), 2 da (Amanda b 1979, Kate b 1987); *Career* CA; Deloitte Haskins & Sells Manchester 1973-77, CA 1976, Peat Marwick Mitchell Kingston Jamaica 1978; Price Waterhouse: Miami Florida USA 1978-80, Melbourne Australia 1980-82, London 1982-85; Guinness plc London 1985-87; govr Balgowan Primary Sch Beckenham Kent; Asst Clerk Worshipful Co of Fishmongers 1987-; FCA 1981; *Recreations* golf, fishing, squash, tennis, sailing; *Style*— Keith Waters, Esq; 63 Kings Hall Rd, Beckenham, Kent BR3 1LR (☎ 081 659 0245); Fishmongers' Co, Fishmongers' Hall, London Bridge, London EC4R 9EL (☎ 071 626 3531, fax 071 929 1389)

WATKINS, Cncllr Paul Alexander; s of Alexander Charles Watkins, of Deal, Kent, and Margaret Eileen, *née* Kennedy; *b* 25 Feb 1947; *Educ* Archers Court Dover, Dover Sch of Nursing (SRN), Kent Community Nurse Trg Centre (Nat Dist Nurse Cert); *m* 21 Oct 1972, Christine Carolyn, da of Reginald Cyril Joy (d 1985), of Deal, Kent; 2 da (Claire Elizabeth b 26 May 1973, Emma Jane b 28 sept 1976); *Career* SRN in Kent hosps and community 1973-85, dist nurse in Kent hosps and community 1976-85, latterly community and hosp sr nurse Canterbury and Thanet DHA; involved in private residential and nursing care 1979-; proprietor The Carleton Nursing Home in Deal and other properties; chm Dover DC 1989- (memb 1983, ldr 1986-89); memb: Kent CC (rep Deal E), Kent Educn Ctee; govr: Walmer Sch (chm), S Kent Tech Coll, Court Univ of Kent; memb Royal Coll of Nursing; *Recreations* golf, cricket, reading; *Clubs* Kent CCC; *Style*— Cncllr Paul Watkins; 71 London Rd, Deal, Kent CT14 9TG (☎ 0304 368662)

WATKINS-PITCHFORD, Dr John; CB (1968); s of Wilfred Watkins-Pitchford (d 1952), and Olive Mary, *née* Beynon Nicholl (d 1960); *b* 20 April 1912; *Educ* Shrewsbury, St Thomas's Hosp (MB BS, MD, DPH, DIH, MRCS, LRCP); *m* 14 Aug 1945, (Elizabeth) Patricia, da of Hubert Wright (d 1959), of Guernsey; 1 s (Michael); *Career* Sqdn Ldr RAF 1939-46; chief med offr Miny Social Security, chief med advsr in Social Security Miny of Health;

memb: Industl Injuries Advsy Cncl 1975-84, Cncl Chest Heart and Stroke Assoc; Queens Hon Physician 1971; *Recreations* gardening; *Style*— Dr John Watkins-Pitchford, CB; Hill House, Farley Lane, Westerham, Kent TN16 1UD (☎ 0959 64448)

WATMORE, Leslie John; s of Arthur Watmore (d 1962), of London, and Edith Alice, *née* Giles (d 1986); *b* 8 May 1929; *Educ* St Olave's GS, Keble Coll Oxford (MA); *m* 19 Dec 1953, Iris Daphne, da of Charles William Enever (d 1981), of London; 2 s (Stephen Charles b 26 Nov 1954, David Anthony b 22 Oct 1960); *Career* admitted slr 1957; ptnr L Bingham and Co 1959-76, sr ptnr L Watmore and Co 1976-; chm Legal Aid Area 1981-84; former capt and chm W Kent GC; Freeman City of London, Liveryman Worshipful Co of Slrs 1966; memb Law Soc; *Recreations* golf, hill walking; *Clubs* RAC, City Livery, Cordwainer Ward, West Kent Golf; *Style*— Leslie Watmore, Esq; Tudor Cottage, 10 Downs Hill, Beckenham, Kent (☎ 081 650 4807); L Watmore and Co, Chancery House, 53/66 Chancery Lane, London WC2A 1QU (☎ 071 430 1512, fax 071 405 7382)

WATSON, Rev Canon Alan; *b* 15 March 1934; *Educ* Maidstone GS, UCL (LLB), Lincoln Theological Coll; *m* 1 July 1961, Rosemary; 2 da (Caroline b 7 May 1962, Elizabeth b 8 April 1964); *Career* curate: All Saints Spring Park 1960-63, Holy Trinity Sheerness 1963-68; rector of Allington 1968-, hon canon Canterbury Cathedral 1985-, rural dean of Sutton 1986-; *Style*— The Rev Canon Alan Watson; Allington Rectory, 35 Poplar Grove, Maidstone, Kent ME16 0DE (☎ 0622 58704)

WATSON, Andrew Stewart; s of Leslie Donald Watson, of Malvern, Worcestershire, and Joan Beatrice, *née* Everton; *b* 29 March 1950; *Educ* King's Sch Worcester, St John's Coll Oxford; *m* 11 Dec 1976, Lea Karin, da of Eino Arvid Nordberg (d 1963); *Career* admitted slr 1975; Thomson Snell and Passmore: articled clerk 1973, ptnr 1981, head Litigation Dept 1986; memb: Legal Aid Area Ctee 1986, Local Advsy Ctee Headway Gp, Law Soc; *Recreations* running, reading, music, cooking; *Clubs* Tunbridge Wells Runners (chm); *Style*— Andrew Watson, Esq; 3 Lonsdale Gardens, Tunbridge Wells, Kent TN1 1NX (☎ 0892 510000)

WATSON, Brig Bruce Edmeston; s of Prof Herbert Edmeston Watson (d 1980), and Margaret Kathleen, *née* Rowson (d 1952); *b* 5 April 1918; *Educ* Marlborough, UCL; *m* 1941, Joan Elizabeth, da of William Moore (d 1950); 1 s (Andrew), 2 da (Susan, Gillian); *Career* served RA 1939-73; dep dir Inspectorate of Armaments 1967-70, dir Heavy Weapons Projects 1970-73, dir FN(Eng) Ltd 1973-85; tstee Keston Village Hall 1974-; FBIM 1980 (MBIM 1969); *Recreations* photography, gardening; *Style*— Brig B E Watson; Chestnut Cottage, 12 Longdon Wood, Keston Park, Kent BR2 6EW (☎ 0689 852619)

WATSON, Edward Howsley; CB (1968); s of Ernest Watson (d 1945); *b* 16 June 1910; *Educ* Harrogate GS, Univ of Leeds (LLB); *m* 1951, Alice Mary, *née* Atkinson; 1 s; *Career* WWII Serv RA Maj; joined Miny of Health 1946; slr and legal advsr: Miny of Health 1965-68, Miny of Housing and Local Govt 1965-70; *Style*— Edward Watson, Esq, CB; 10 The Terrace, Hales Place, Canterbury, Kent CT2 7AJ (☎ 0227 450 978)

WATSON, Ian Robert; s of Dr Geoffrey Herbert Watson, of Manchester, and Dr Marjorie Watson; *b* 31 Oct 1955; *Educ* Manchester GS, King's Coll Cambridge (MA); *m* 6 July 1985, Eileen Watson, da of Frederick Charles Gleadle, of Sheerness, Kent; 2 da (Victoria Louise b 21 Jan 1988, Katherine Rose b 6 Nov 1989); *Career* res offr MOD Intelligence Servs 1976-78; chm and jt md 1978-: Queenborough Rolling Mill Ltd, Shipbreaking (Queenborough) Ltd, Senorvic Ltd, various other cos (The Q Gp); *Recreations* chess (several times Kent champion), bridge, piano playing, obscure plants; *Style*— Ian Watson, Esq; Chrismill Manor, Chrismill Lane, Bearsted, Maidstone, Kent ME14 4NT (☎ 0622 37246); Queenborough Rolling Mill Co Ltd, Rushenden Rd, Queenborough, Kent ME11 5HS (☎ 0795 580880, fax 0795 580165)

WATSON, James; s of James Watson (d 1954), of Darwen, Lancs, and Miriam, *née* Arnold (d 1982); *b* 8 Nov 1936; *Educ* Darwen GS, Univ of Nottingham (BA), Univ of Sussex (MA); *m* 6 July 1963, Kitty, da of Michael Downey (d 1979), of Middlesborough; 3 da (Rosalind b 1964, Miranda b 1966, Francesca b 1970); *Career* former journalist, sr lectr in communication media and educn West Kent Coll, author of novels for young readers and radio plays; memb: Amnesty International, Greenpeace, NATFHE, Trinity Arts Assoc Tunbridge Wells, Tunbridge Wells Labour Pty; *Books* for young readers: Sign of the Swallow (1967), The Bull Leapers (1970), Legion of the White Tiger (1973), The Freedom Tree (1976), Talking in Whispers (1983), Where Nobody Sees (1987), Make Your Move (short stories, 1988); academic books: Liberal Studies in Further Education (1973), The Loneliness of a Long Distance Innovation (1980), Censorship: Six Assignments for Amnesty (1983), A Dictionary of Communication & Media Studies (1984), What is Communication Studies? (1985); *Recreations* swimming, recorder playing, art, architecture and gardens, film; *Style*— James Watson, Esq; 9 Farmcombe Close, Tunbridge Wells, Kent TN2 5DG; Creative and Media Studies Division, West Kent College, Brook St, Tonbridge, Kent (☎ 0732 358101)

WEALE, Felix Ernest; s of Dr Frederick Julius Weale (d 1981), of Barnet, Herts, and Mary Weale; *b* 15 Feb 1925; *Educ* Kingston GS, Univ of London (MB BS, MS, MRCS, LRCP, PhD); *m* 17 May 1951, Audrey, da of Harold Elliott (d 1973), of Wiveliscombe; 2 s (Peter b 1957, Adrian b 1963); *Career* Nat Serv Sqdn Ldr RAF Egypt and Iraq 1949-51; house surgn: Westminster Hosp 1947, Ipswich Hosp 1948; casualty offr Middx Hosp 1948-49, sr house offr Hosp for Sick Children 1952, pathological registrar Westminster Hosp 1953, surgical registrar St Stephens Hosp 1953-55, lectr in physiology RCS 1955-57, cardiac res fell Guy's Hosp 1957-59, sr lectr in surgery and asst dir St Bart's Hosp 1959-69, conslt gen and vascular surgn Dartford and Gravesend 1969-90, ret 1990; memb Br Exec Servs Overseas; FRCS 1954; *Books* Irreversible Shock (1959), Arterial Stenoses (1966), An Introduction to Surgical Haemodynamics (1966); contrib: The Heart (1963), Current Operative Surgery (1985), Surgical Management of Vascular Diseases (1990); *Recreations* music, gardening, painting; *Clubs* Peripheral Vascular; *Style*— Felix Weale, Esq; Top Corner, 9 Warren View, Shorne, Kent DA12 3EJ

WEBB, Anthony Michael Francis; CMG (1963), QC (1961), JP (1966); s of Sir Ambrose Henry Webb, QC (d 1964), and Agnes Ellen, *née* Gunn (d 1969); *b* 27 Dec 1914; *Educ* Ampleforth, Magdalen Coll Oxford (MA); *m* 1948, Diana Mary, da of Capt Graham Farley (d 1942); 1 s (Simon), 1 da (Amanda); *Career* 2 Lt Queen's Bays 1940, SOE ME and Europe 1941-46, Maj; called to the Bar Gray's Inn 1939; Colonial Legal Serv: Malaya 1947-55, Kenya 1955-64 (AG and min for legal affrs); Lord Chllrs Office 1964-78 (dep sec of commns and head of court business); chm Indust Tbnls 1978-87; *Clubs* Special Forces; *Style*— Anthony Webb, Esq, CMG, QC, JP; Yew Tree Cottage, Speldhurst Rd, Langton Green, Tunbridge Wells, Kent TN3 0JH

WEBB, Anthony Ronald; s of Ronald Alfred Webb, of East Sutton, Kent, and Muriel Dorothy, *née* Empleton; *b* 17 July 1947; *Educ* Chislehurst and Sidcup GS, Univ of Bristol (LLB); *m* 29 Sept 1979, Sarah Lynette, da of Denzil Edward Kieft, of Lagos, Portugal; 1 da (Camilla); *Career* called to Bar Inner Temple 1970; *Recreations* equestrian, travel, gardening; *Clubs* Kent CCC; *Style*— Anthony Webb, Esq; Capel Cross, Grovehurst Lane, Horsmonden, Tonbridge, Kent TN12 8BB (☎ 0892 72 3973); Farrar's Building, Temple, London EC4Y 7BD (☎ 071 583 9241, fax 071 583 0090)

WEBB, Rodney Anson John; s of Ernest Herbert Webb (d 1983), of Norwich, and Irene Maud, *née* Gotts; *b* 24 April 1944; *Educ* Bracondale Sch Norwich; *m* 8 Nov 1969, Angela Delys, da of Frederick Lukies (d 1982); 3 da (Alison Harriet Louise b 27 Feb 1971, Victoria Felicity Alexandra b 28 Aug 1977, Hannah Fiona Eleanor b 20 Sept 1986); *Career* md: Crest Packaging Ltd, Crest Flexible Packaging Ltd, Crest Cartons Ltd; ctee memb Br Carton Assoc 1980-81, pres Flexible Packaging Assoc 1983-84, vice pres European Flexible Packaging Assoc 1984-86, UK spokesman European Aluminium Foil Assoc 1988-; FCA 1965; *Recreations* golf, tennis; *Clubs* Bearsted Golf; *Style*— Rodney Webb, Esq; Spitzbrook House, Collier St, Tonbridge, Kent TN12 9RH (☎ 089 273 241); Crest Packaging Ltd, Gillingham, Kent ME8 0RX (☎ 0634 34444, fax 0634 362473)

WEBSTER, John Dudley; *b* 13 Nov 1939; *Educ* Merchant Taylors', UCL (BSc); *m* 1967, Barbara Joan; 1 da (Katherine b 1969); *Career* dir and sec Sun Life Assurance Society plc, md Sun Life Asset Management Ltd, dir Sapphire Petroleum plc 1981-88; dir: Group Investors plc 1984-86, Save and Prosper Return of Assets Investment Trust plc 1984-; chm Br Insur Assoc Investmt Protection Ctee 1982-84, lay memb Cncl of Stock Exchange 1985-86 and 1988-, ind dir Securities Assoc 1986-90, tstee The Charties Official Investmt Fund 1988-; FIA; *Style*— John Webster, Esq; c/o Sun Life Assurance Society plc, 107 Cheapside London, EC2V 6DU (☎ 071 606 7788); 10 Merrydown Way, Chislehurst, Kent BR7 5RS

WEBSTER, Richard Joseph; s of Peter Joseph Webster, of Dulwich, London; *b* 7 July 1953; *Educ* William Penn Dulwich; *m* 1980, Patricia Catherine, da of Gerald Stanley Edwards (former Chief Supt Sussex Police), of East Grinstead; 1 s (James Joseph b April 1985), 1 da (Victoria Catherine b Sept 1983); *Career* Lloyd's insur broker; dir: Howden Cross Ltd 1977-82, Alexander Howden insur Brokers Ltd 1978-82, Hogg Robinson & Gardner Mountain (reinsurance and non marine) Ltd 1982-87, Hogg Robinson (London) Ltd 1983-87, Hogg Robinson Ltd 1986-87, Hispano American Reinsurance Brokers Ltd 1984-87, J Besso & Co Ltd 1987-; chm: R J Webster Insurance Brokers Ltd 1987-, Besso Int Ltd 1989-; *Recreations* family, riding, swimming, watching rugby; *Clubs* Lloyd's of London; *Style*— Richard Webster, Esq; 23a The Glen, Farnborough Park, Locksbotton, Kent BR6 8LP; 57 Mansell St, London E1 8AN (☎ 071 265 0797, fax 071 480 7725, telex 938046 BESS G)

WEEKES, Rt Rev Ambrose Walter Marcus; s of Lt Cdr William Charles Tinnoth Weekes (d 1958); *b* 25 April 1919; *Educ* Rochester Cathedral Choir Sch, Sir Joseph Williamson's Rochester, King's Coll London, AKC 1941, FKC 1970, Scholoe Cancellarii Lincoln; *Career* deacon 1942, priest 1943, Chaplain RN 1944-72, Chaplain of the Fleet 1969-72; QHC 1969, Dean of Gibraltar 1973-78; asst bishop of Gibraltar 1978; suffragan bishop of Gibraltar in Europe 1980-86; Dean, Pro-Cathedral of the Holy Trinity, Brussels 1980-86; Hon Asst Bishop of Rochester 1986-88; *Recreations* music, yachting; *Clubs* RAC; *Style*— The Rt Rev Ambrose Weekes; Deanery Lodge, Kings Orchard, The

Precinct, Rochester, Kent (☎ 0634 44165); St John's House, Avenue de Chillon 92, CH-1820 Territet (Montreux), Switzerland

WEIGHT, Richard James; step s of Henry George Richman, of Selsey Sussex, and Ellan Rebecca, *née* Williams; *b* 17 June 1944; *Educ* Sir Joseph Williamson's Mathematical Sch Rochester Kent; *m* 23 March 1968, Pamela, da of Leonard James Wilkinson (d 1955), of Gillingham, Kent; 1 s (David b 27 June 1973), 1 da (Jennifer b 18 Jan 1977); *Career* trooper The Life Gds 1962-65; TA & VR: Lt 2 Bn Wessex Regt (V) 1976, Capt 4 Bn The Royal Regt of Wales (V) 1978, Capt Intelligence Corps (V) 1984; computer mangr The Mettoy Co Swansea, computer services mangr London Regional Transport, vice-pres Citibank NA, currently dir info technol Security Pacific Hoare Govett (Holdings); *Recreations* private pilot, sailing; *Style*— Richard Weight, Esq; 5 South Lea, Kingsnorth, nr Ashford, Kent TN23 3EH (☎ 0233 642137); 4 Broadgate, London EC2M 7LE (☎ 071 374 7309, telex 887887, fax 071 256 8500, car phone 0836 242729)

WEINBERG, Arthur Maurice; s of Abram Weinberg (d 1971), and Betty, *née* Feinstein (d 1982); *b* 21 Dec 1932; *Educ* Univ of The Witwatersrand Johannesburg (BArch); *m* 25 July 1963, Marion June, da of Victor Brand; 2 s (Timothy b 2 July 1964, Robert b 31 Oct 1965); *Career* qualified teacher i/c of backward children: Faversham Remedial Advsy Centre 1969-76, Canterbury Remedial Advsy Centre 1976-88; reading conslt; lectr on Education and Peace Issues; sec Canterbury Baha'i Community 1961-, memb UNA, representative of Canterbury Baha'i Community and UNA at Canterbury Link Group of Peace Organisations; *Books* The Refuge and The Cave (1982), The City and The Heart (1989); *Recreations* writing children's materials, music; *Style*— Arthur Weinberg, Esq; 5 Rhodaus Close, Canterbury CT1 2RE (☎ 0227 68458)

WELLESLEY, Robin Alfred; s of Quintin Gilbey (d 1979), of London; step s of Gerald Wellesley (d 1961), of Withyham, Sussex; *b* 23 July 1928; *Educ* Eton; *m* 1953, Marianne, da of John McDonald, of Chicago; 1 s (Gerald), 2 da (Diana, Laura); *Career* dir: Prestige Group 1965-82, Aust Br C of C 1984-, NZ UK C of C and Indust 1984-; *Recreations* gardening, cricket, travel; *Clubs* Buck's; *Style*— Robin Wellesley, Esq; Shingle Barn, Dwelly Lane, Edenbridge, Kent (☎ 0732 862251); 36 Edge St, London W8 (☎ 071 727 4503); Suite 615, 162-168 Regent St, London W1R 5TB

WELLS, (William Arthur) Andrew; TD (1984); s of Sir John Wells, *qv*; *b* 14 June 1949; *Educ* Eton, Univ of Birmingham, N London Poly; *m* 19 Oct 1974, Tessa Margaret, da of Lt-Col Jocelyn Eustace Gurney, DSO, MC, DL (d 1973), of Tacolneston Hall, and Sprowston, Norfolk; 2 s (William b 1980, Frederick b 1982), 1 da (Augusta b 1984); *Career* TA: cmmnd 1971, extra lectr Jr Div Staff Coll 1978-79, Maj Royal Green Jackets 1981-90, RARO 1990; publisher 1969-81; chief exec and co sec Minories Holdings Ltd 1981-; landowner Mereworth Kent; memb: Kent Cobnuts Assoc, Exec Ctee Friends of Kent Churches; pres N Battersea Cons Assoc 1981-83 (div chm 1977-80), div chm Tooting Cons Assoc 1983-86; Liveryman Stationers' Co 1977, Clerk 1986-; *Recreations* country interests, gardening, architectural history; *Clubs* City Univ; *Style*— Andrew Wells, Esq, TD; Mere House, Mereworth, Maidstone, Kent ME18 5NB; 47 Streathbourne Rd, London SW17 8QZ

WELLS, Sir John Julius; o s of Rev (Arthur) Reginald Kemble Wells (d 1964), and Margaret Evelyn, *née* Hodgson; ggg nephew of John Wells, JP, DL, MP for Maidstone 1820-30; *b* 30 March 1925; *Educ* Eton, CCC Oxford (MA); *m* 31 July 1948, Lucinda Mary Helen Francis, eldest da of Francis Ralph Meath Baker, JP, of Hasfield Court, Glos; 2 s ((William Arthur) Andrew *qv*, Oliver Reginald b 5 Nov 1955), 2 da (Julia Jane b 1 Feb 1951, Henrietta Frances b 27 Feb 1952); *Career* served WWII in HM Submarines; contested (C) Smethwick 1955, MP (C) Maidstone 1959-87; chm: Cons Pty Horticultural Ctee 1965-71 and 1973-87, Horticulture sub ctee of Agric Select Ctee 1968, Parly Waterways Gp 1974-80; vice chm Cons Agric Ctee 1970; memb Mr Speaker's Panel of Chairmen 1974-87; pres Nat Inst of Fresh Produce 1984-; Master Worshipful Co of Fruiterers 1977, Hon Freeman of Maidstone 1979; Kt Cdr Order of Civil Merit (Spain) 1972, Cdr Order of Lion (Finland) 1984; kt 1984; *Clubs* Army and Navy; *Style*— Sir John Wells; Mere House, Mereworth, Kent

WELLS, Meher Derek; da of Burzorji Behmanshah Mehta (d 1981), of Hyderabad AP, India, and Nergis Pastakia (d 1979); *b* 22 Feb 1937; *Educ* Most Holy Rosary Convent HS Hyderabad AP India, Osmania Med Coll Hyderabad (MB BS), Univ of London (MD); *m* 1, widowed 1973; m 2, 21 March 1977, Derek Geoffrey Wells, s of Henry William Sparks Wells (d 1964); 2 step s (Henry Tagore, Alexander Derek); *Career* sr house offr ENT: Queen Elizabeth Hosp Birmingham 1963, Royal Nat Throat Nose and Ear Hosp London 1966 (locum registrar 1966-67); registrar ENT Hosp for Sick Children Gt Ormond St London 1967-68, sr registrar ENT UCH 1970-74 (acting conslt 1973); conslt: SE Kent Health Dist, Canterbury and Thanet Health Dist 1974-; res fell Pathology Dept Inst of Laryngology and Otology, recognised teacher Univ of London; author of numerous articles on clinico-pathological aspects of deafness; FRCS, FRCSI; *Books* Pathology of the Ear (with L Michaels), chapter in Audiology and Audiological Medicine (vol 3 1981, ed H A Beagley); *Recreations* cooking, embroidery, drawing; *Style*— Mrs Meher Wells; Ty-Fry Cottage, Cliff Rd, Hythe, Kent CT21 5XL (☎ 0303 266469); William Harvey Hospital, Ashford, Kent (☎ 0233 633331); Kent and Canterbury Hosp, Canterbury, Kent (☎ 0227 766877); Buckland Hosp, Dover, Kent

WELSBY, Rev Dr Paul Antony; *b* 18 Aug 1920; *Educ* Alcester GS, Univ of Durham (MA), Lincoln Theol Coll, Univ of Sheffield (PhD); *m* 1948, Cynthia Mary Hosmer; 1 da (Rosamund); *Career* curate: Boxley Kent 1944-47, St Mary Le Tower Ipswich 1947-52; rector Copdock with Washbrook Suffolk 1952-66, rural dean Samford 1964-66, canon residentiary of Rochester Cathedral 1966-88, dir post-ordination training for diocese of Rochester 1966-88, examining chaplain to Bishop of Rochester 1966-88, canon emeritus Rochester Cathedral 1988-, personal chaplain to Bishop of Rochester 1988-; memb: Church Assembly 1964-70, Gen Synod 1970-80; chm House of Clergy of Gen Synod, prolocutor of Convocation of Canterbury 1974-80; chaplain to HM The Queen 1980-; former chm City of Rochester Soc; *Books* A Modern Catechism (1956), Lancelot Andrewes (1958), The Unwanted Archbishop: Life of George Abbot (1962), The Bond of Church and State (1962), Sermons and Society (1970), A History of the Church of England 1945-80 (1984), How the Church of England Works (1985); *Recreations* reading detective fiction, genealogy; *Style*— The Rev Dr Paul Welsby; 20 Knights Ridge, Pembury, Tunbridge Wells, Kent TN2 4HP (☎ 089 282 3053)

WEST, Prof David Richard Frederick; s of Sydney West, and Frederica May, *née* Horsman (d 1986); *b* 7 March 1926; *Educ* Bromley County Sch, Univ Coll Cardiff (BSc), Imperial Coll London (PhD, DIC, DSc); *m* 23 June 1951, Phyllis Edith, da of Robert Wade (d 1956), of Bromley, Kent; 2 s (Peter Robert b 1954, Michael John b 1964), 1 da (Elisabeth Susan b 1957); *Career* scientific offr MOS 1949-50; Imperial Coll: lectr 1950-63, sr lectr 1963-70, reader 1970-86, sr tutor metallurgy and materials 1966-, memb governing body 1981-89, prof physical metallurgy 1986; vice pres Inst of Metals (memb cncl, chm Materials Sci Div); memb Rochester Diocesan Synod; FIM 1978, CEng 1978; *Books* Ternary Equilibrium Diagrams (1982); *Recreations* music, reading; *Style*— Prof David West

WESTPHAL, William Henry (Bob); OBE (1972), DFC (1944); s of William Mathias Westphal (d 1950), of Sydney, Aust, and Madeline May, *née* Pepper (d 1962); *b* 5 Nov 1921; *Educ* North Sydney HS, Univ of Sydney (LLB); *m* 23 July 1945, Daphne Meta Astrid; 3 s (John b 1947, Michael b 1949, David b 1954), 1 da (Pamela b 1951); *Career* WWII RAAF Sqdn Ldr 83 Pathfinder Sqdn Europe; dir Rentokil Group plc 1956-87 (chm 1981-87); FRSA; *Recreations* golf, travel; *Clubs* Pathfinder; *Style*— W H Westphal, Esq, OBE, DFC; The Grove, Penshurst, Kent (☎ 0892 870 504); Penshurst Vineyards, Penshurst, Kent (☎ 0892 870255)

WETHERELL, John Michael Hugh Paxton; s of Paxton Wetherell, MBE (d 1978), of Whitstable, Kent, and Catherine Wilson, *née* Collins; *b* 24 Oct 1942; *Educ* Ampleforth; *m* 2 May 1964, Elizabeth Ann, da of Harold Thompson (d 1988), of Broadstairs, Kent; 1 s (Joseph b 1979), 5 da (Laura b 1966, Kate b 1968, Beatrice b 1972, Gabrielle b 1974, Jessica b 1978); *Career* Lloyd's underwriter Janson Green/Bolton Ingham Non-marine syndicate 1983; dir: Bolton Ingham Agency Ltd 1983-88, Janson Green Management Ltd 1986; memb Lloyd's 1973; *Recreations* reading, music, racing; *Clubs* City University; *Style*— John Wetherell, Esq; Claremont House, Claremont Rd, Tunbridge Wells, Kent (☎ 0892 36481); Lloyd's, Lime St, London EC3 (☎ 071 623 5190)

WHARTON, Dr Christopher Frederick Percy; s of John Christopher Wharton, of Banbury, Oxon, and Gertrude Margaret, *née* Dingwall; *b* 19 Feb 1937; *Educ* Shrewsbury, Worcester Coll Oxford (BM, BCh, MA, DM), (MRCS, MRCP, LRCP); *m* 10 Aug 1963 (m dis 1980), Andrea Mary Puckle, da of (Andrew) Gordon Leslie Puckle (d 1988), of Loxwood, W Sussex; 2 da (Antonia Helen Jane b 30 May 1969, (Virginia Phillippa Gertrude) Rose b 29 Oct 1972); m 2, 23 May 1980, Pamela Mary, da of Sqdn Ldr William Henry Deane, of Pretoria, SA; *Career* house offr and registrar cardiology gen med Guy's 1963-73, conslt physician med and cardiology Bromley Dist Hosps 1963-, hon tutor Guy's Med Sch 1979-, teacher Univ of London 1986- (clinical tutor 1974-84), dist tutor RCP; memb Mgmnt Bd Bromley DHA, chm Bromley Hosps Med Exec Ctee; memb Mgmnt Ctee Chipstead Lake Cheshire Home; Freeman City of London 1982, Liveryman Worshipful Co of Gunmakers; FRCP 1980; memb: British Cardiac Soc 1982, BMA; *Books* Cardiological Problems in Practice (1981), Management of Common Disease in Practice Cardiology (with A R Archer, 1986); *Publications* various pubns on echocardiography (1967-72), Myocardial Infarct-Management and Rehabilitation article in Cardiac Update (1987), A Case of Angina-Dual Pathology (1989), Silent Ischaemia - What Implications (1989); *Recreations* shooting, golf, tennis, skiing, Chelsea football, travel, wine and food; *Clubs* Athenaeum; *Style*— Dr Christopher Wharton; 24-26 High St, Chipstead, nr Sevenoaks, Kent (☎ 0732 452906); The Medical Unit, Farnborough Hospital, Farnborough Common, Orpington, Kent (☎ 0689 53333)

WHEATLEY, Alan Edward; s of Edward Wheatley, of 135 Upney Lane, Barking, Essex, and Margaret Rosina Turner; *b* 23 May 1938; *Educ* Ilford GS; *m* 30 June 1962, Marion Frances, da of John Douglas Wilson (d 1968); 1 da (Susan b 1966), 2 s (Michael b 1968, Jonathan b 1974); *Career* Price

Waterhouse 1960- (sr ptnr London Office 1985-), non-exec dir EBS Investments Ltd (Bank of England subsid) 1977-, non-exec dep chm Cable & Wireless plc 1984-85 (govt dir 1981-84), non-exec bd memb British Steel Corporation 1984-; bd memb Industl Devpt Advsy Bd 1985-; govr Solefield Sch; FCA; *Recreations* golf, tennis, badminton, music, bridge; *Clubs* Wildernesse Golf; *Style*— Alan E Wheatley, Esq; Price Waterhouse, Southwark Towers, 32 London Bridge St, London SE1 (☎ 071 939 3000, fax 071 378 0647, telex 884 657/8)

WHEELER, Dr Patrick Clive Gage; s of Cdr Leonard Gage Wheeler, of Alresford, Hants, and Nancy Dorothea, *née* Cross; *b* 6 Oct 1943; *Educ* St Edward's Sch Oxford, Ch Ch Oxford (MA, DM, BM BCh), St Thomas Hosp London (MRCP); *m* 7 June 1975, Diana Lilian, da of Cdr Edward Stanley, of Waldringfield, Suffolk; 3 da (Anna b 1976, Kate b 1978, Gemma b 1981); *Career* med registrar St Thomas Hosp 1971-75, sr med registrar Kings Coll Hosp 1975-80, conslt physician and gastroenterologist SE Kent Health Authy 1980-; author of various articles in scientific pubns; FRCP 1987; *Recreations* fly fishing, music; *Style*— Dr Patrick Wheeler; Elham Manor, Elham, Canterbury, Kent CT4 6UL

WHETNALL, Paul Edward; s of Robert Frederick William Stonnel Whetnall (d 1965), of Birmingham, and Constance Georgina, *née* Bryan; *b* 19 Feb 1947; *Educ* Handsworth New Road Secdy; *m* 30 March 1968, Susan Dorothy, *qv*, da of Edward George Pound (decd); 1 s (Andrew Edward b 18 Oct 1977), 1 da (Claire Rebecca b 15 July 1979); *Career* badminton player; represented England 36 times; Eng Nat mens singles champion: 1969-70, 1975, 1976; mixed doubles champion 1979; nat coach Canadian Badminton Assoc 1976-79, coach to Int Teams and dir Squads Devpt 1980-85, Eng Team mangr Badminton Assoc of Eng 1986-90 (staff coach 1985-86; Cwlth World Games Eng Badminton Assoc: coach Edinburgh 1986, mangr Auckland 1990; gold memb Br Inst of Sports Coaches; *Books* Badminton (with Sue Whetnall), Badminton (with Leahy); *Recreations* cricket, football, home; *Style*— Paul Whetnall, Esq

WHETNALL, Susan Dorothy; da of Edward George Pound (d 1988), and Mabel Olive, *née* Lockwood (d 1989); *b* 11 Dec 1942; *Educ* Bexley Tech Sch, Chelsea Coll of Physical Educn; *m* 30 March 1968, Paul Edward Whetnall, *qv*, s of Robert Frederick Whetnall (d 1965); 1 s (Andrew Edward b 18 Oct 1977), 1 da (Claire Rebecca b 15 July 1979); *Career* teacher: Midfield Secdy Sch 1964-74, Walsingham Sch 1974-76; England int badminton player, 5 times winner All England Badminton Championships; Euro Championships successes: Gold medallist Ladies Doubles and Mixed Doubles 1968, Gold medallist Ladies and Mixed 1970, Silver medallist Ladies and Mixed 1974, Gold medallist Ladies 1976; Cwlth Games successes: Gold medallist Ladies Doubles and Bronze medallist Mixed Doubles 1970, Silver medallist Ladies Doubles and Bronze medallist Mixed Doubles 1974; player rep Badminton Assoc of England Cncl, hon life vice pres Kent Co Badminton Assoc, fndr memb and current working memb Kent Badminton Supporters Assoc, memb Exec Ctee Christians in Sport, currently i/c 4 keep fit classes; *Books* Paul and Sue Whetnall: Badminton (1975); *Recreations* badminton playing and coaching; *Style*— Mrs Susan Whetnall

WHITBOURN, Dr Philip Robin; s of Edwin Arthur Whitbourn (d 1953), of Badgers Mount, Sevenoaks, Kent, and Kathleen, *née* Sykes; *b* 10 March 1932; *Educ* Sevenoaks Sch Kent, UCL (PhD); *m* 10 Jan 1959, Anne Pearce, da of Peter Melrose Marks (d 1938), of Glasgow; 1 s (James b 1963), 1 da (Katherine b 1960); *Career* architect; Sir Edwin Cooper RA and Partners 1955-58, Stewart Hendry and Smith 1958-60, Fitzroy Robinson Partnership 1960-66, Historic Bldgs Div GLC 1966-86, divnl architect London Div English Heritage 1988 (joined 1986); chm Royal Tunbridge Wells Civic Soc 1969-70 1972-73 1978-80 and 1990-91; FRIBA 1968, FRTPI 1983, FSA 1984; *Style*— Dr Philip Whitbourn, FSA; Rosaville Lodge, 40 Beulah Rd, Tunbridge Wells, Kent TN1 2NR (☎ 0892 23026)

WHITE, John Charles; s of John William White, and Irene Winifred Blanche, *née* Ife; *b* 23 July 1951; *Educ* Downer GS, NELP (BSc); *m* 10 March 1978, Gillian, da of Capt Denys Herbert Rumble, of Hatch End, Middx; 2 da (Laura b 1980, Karen b 1983); *Career* overseas devpt admin: Lesotho Guyana and Seychelles 1973-76, Zambia 1978-79; MOD Mapping and Charting Estab 1976-78, sr surveyor Sir Owen Williams & Partners 1979-81, in private practice as land surveyor 1981-; presented paper on boundary disputes to RICS 1988; ARICS 1977; *Recreations* squash, running, walking, photography; *Style*— John White, Esq; Cedar Lodge, Woolpack Hill, Smeeth, Ashford, Kent TN25 6QJ (☎ 0303 812508); The Old Barn, Evegate Farm, Smeeth, Ashford, Kent TN25 6SX (☎ 0303 812763)

WHITE, Capt Richard Taylor; DSO (1940, and bars 1941 and 1942); s of Sir Archibald Woolaston White, 4 Bt (d 1954), and hp of bro, 5 Bt; *b* 29 Jan 1908; *Educ* RNC Dartmouth; *m* 1936, Gabrielle Ursula, yr da of Capt Robert Style, JP (n of Sir William Style, 9 Bt); 3 s, 2 da; *Career* WWII RN served Atlantic Med and Far E; Capt RNC Dartmouth 1951-53; *Style*— Capt Richard White, DSO, RN; Tilts House, Boughton Monchelsea, Maidstone, Kent ME17 4JE (☎ 0622 743465)

WHITE, Stephen John; s of George Edward White, and Doreen Ivy White; *b* 23 July 1948; *Educ* St Olaves GS; *m* 24 April 1971; 2 da (Claire Louise b 1975, Victoria Emily b 1978); *Career* dir WCRS Gp plc, dep chm WCRS-Mathews Marcantonio; MAA, MIPA, MCAM; *Recreations* tennis, swimming, boating, vintage cars; *Clubs* RAC, Vanderbilt; *Style*— Stephen White, Esq; c/o Lloyds Bank, 9 High Street, Bromley, Kent; WCRS Group plc, 41/44 Gt Queen St, London WC2B 5AR

WHITE-THOMSON, Very Rev Ian Hugh; s of Rt Rev Leonard Jauncey White-Thomson, Bishop of Ely (d 1933), and Margaret Adela Hepburn Stuart Forbes Trefusis (d 1939); *b* 18 Dec 1904; *Educ* Harrow, Univ of Oxford; *m* 1954, Wendy Ernesta, da of Gp Capt Frank Hawker Woolliams (d 1980); 2 s (Stephen Jauncey b 1955, John Harvey b 1963), 2 da (Lucy Margaret b 1957, Morwenna Anne b 1958); *Career* ordained 1929, curate of St Marys Ashford 1929-34, rector St Martin with St Paul Canterbury 1934-39, chaplain to Archbishops of Canterbury (Lang, Temple, and Fisher) 1939-47, vicar of Folkestone 1947-55; chaplain to: HM King George VI 1947-52, HM The Queen 1952-63; archdeacon of Northumberland 1955-63, dean of Canterbury 1963-76; Freeman City of Canterbury 1976; Hon DCL Univ of Kent at Canterbury 1971; *Recreations* painting; *Style*— The Very Rev Ian White-Thomson; Camphill, Wye, Kent (☎ 0233 812210)

WHITEHEAD, Frank Ernest; s of Ernest Whitehead, (d 1963), of Walmer, and Isabel, *née* Leslie (d 1978); *b* 21 Jan 1930; *Educ* Leyton Co HS, LSE (BSe); *m* 7 Jan 1961, Anne Gillian, da of James Clifford Marston (d 1979), of Silverdale, Lancs; 3 s (David Clifford b 1962, (Edward) Peter b 1964, Michael Frank 1968); *Career* Nat SeN LAC RAF 1948-49; Rio Tinto Co 1952-54, professional offr in Statistics Fedn of Rhodesia and Nyasaland 1955-64, statistician Gen Register Office 1964-68, chief statistician Miny of Social Security (later DHSS) 1968-77, dep sir Office of Population Census and Surveys 1982-89 (head of social survey div 1977-82), author of various articles in statistical jls; memb C of E; vice pres RSS 1988-89 (fell 1966, cncl memb 1987); *Recreations* family history, gardening; *Style*— Frank Whitehead, Esq; Queensmead, Pilgrims Way, Kemsing, Kent TN15 6XA (☎ 0732 61787)

WHITEHOUSE, Martin Henry Leigh; s of William Henry Whitehouse (d 1963), of Four Elms, and Constance Mary, *née* Hucklesbury (d 1945); *b* 13 March 1921; *Educ* Rugby, Peterhouse Cambridge (MA), Univ of London (BSc); *m* 8 Sept 1956, Angela Rica, da of Edward Meadows Penman (d 1980), of Four Elms; 2 s (Timothy Martin Henry b 1958, Christopher William b 1960), 1 da (Melanie Rose b 1964); *Career* Sqdn Ldr RAF 1941-46; SWS Electricity Supply Co 1946-48, Br Mechanical Engrg Fedn 1949-68; sheep farmer 1966- ; sec Br Mechanical Engrg Confedn 1968-76, conslt Process Plant Assoc 1976-78, conslt Econ Policy Dept CBI 1976-81; memb Valve Productivity Team Mission to USA 1949; Organisme de Liaison des Industries Métalliques Européenes: fairs and exhibitions working gp memb 1955-65, trade policy working gp memb 1962-76, chm Statistics Working Group 1974-76 (memb 1969); UK advsr UN Atoms for Peace Conf 1958, memb Bd of Trade Advsy Ctee on Overseas Construction 1962-66, memb Br Engrg Mission to Sweden 1962, memb Exec Bd BSI 1975-76; ldr Sevenoaks DC 1988- (cncllr 1983-); CEng, MIMechE, MIEE; *Books* Sources and Availability of Statistics (1973); *Recreations* gardening, fishing, travel; *Style*— Martin Whitehouse, Esq; Sevenoaks District Council, Argayle Rd, Sevenoaks, Kent TN13 1HG (☎ 0732 741222, fax 0732 740693)

WHITER, John Lindsay Pearce; s of Nugent Whiter (d 1966), and Jean Dorothy, *née* Pearce; *b* 10 May 1950; *Educ* Eastbourne GS; *m* 5 July 1975, Janet Dulcie Sarah, da of Dr Kenneth Oswald Albert Vickery, of Eastbourne; 2 s (Timothy b 1976, William b 1989), 1 da (Nancy b 1979); *Career* articled clerk and audit sr Honey Barrett & Co Eastbourne 1968-72, mangr Brebner Allen & Trapp 1973-74, managing ptnr Neville Russell 1988- (ptnr 1977-88); Freeman City of London; FCA 1973; *Recreations* golf, tennis, the arts; *Clubs* The Nat, City of London; *Style*— John Whiter, Esq; Twowayes, 29 Dry Hill Rd, Tonbridge, Kent TN9 1LU (☎ 0732 355088); Neville Russell, 246 Bishopsgate, London EC2M 4PB (☎ 071 377 1000, fax 071 377 8931)

WHITING, Cncllr Michael John; s of Leonard Frederick Whiting (d 1970), of Isle of Sheppey, and Rose Evelyn, *née* Hopper (now Mrs Richard Alfred Moreton); *b* 24 March 1959; *Educ* The Sheppey Sch; *m* 22 Sept 1984, Susan Karen, da of John Kevin Ashton, of Isle of Sheppey; 1 s (Luke Michael John b 18 Sept 1989), 1 da (Amy Charlotte Whiting b 7 July 1987); *Career* photographer: Croydon Advertiser 1979-88, Kent Evening Post 1988-; chm Queenborough and Halfway Branch Faversham Cons Assoc, memb Swale Borough Cncl 1987-, spokesman for health and the environment Swale Borogh Cncl Cons Gp 1988-, vice chm Environment Ctee Swale Borough Cncl 1989-; *Recreations* playing and listening to music; *Style*— Cncllr Michael Whiting; 32 Queens Rd, Minster, Isle of Sheppey, Kent (☎ 0795 873217); The Kent Evening Post, High St, Chatham, Kent (☎ 0634 830999)

WHITMORE, Ellis, Lady; Ellis Christense; *née* Johnsen; da of Herr Direktor Knud Christian Johnsen (d 1945), of Bergen, Norway, and Thora Heltberg, *née* Lampe (d 1978); *b* 29 Aug 1904; *Educ* U Phils Coll Bergen Norway; *m* 1 Oct 1931, as his 2 w, Sir Francis Henry Douglas Charlton Whitmore, 1 Bt, KCB, CMG, DSO, TD (d 1962); 1 s (Sir John Henry Douglas, 2 Bt, *qv*), 1 da (Anne Catherine (Mrs D J E O'Connell) b 1933);

Career DStJ; *Recreations* gardening, canvas embroidery; *Style*— Ellis, Lady Whitmore; c/o Barclays Bank, 155 Beehive Lane, Chelmsford, Essex CM29 9SG

WHITMORE, Sir John Henry Douglas; 2 Bt (UK 1954), of Orsett, Co Essex; s of Col Sir Francis Henry Douglas Charlton Whitmore, 1 Bt, KCB, CMG, DSO, TD (d 1962, maternal gs of Sir William Cradock-Hartopp, 3 Bt, while his paternal grandmother was Lady Louisa Douglas, eldest da of 5 Marquess of Queensberry); *b* 16 Oct 1937; *Educ* Eton; *m* 1, 1962, Ella Gunilla, (m dis 1969), da of Sven A Hansson, of Danderyd, Sweden; 1 da; m 2, 1977, Diana Elaine, da of Fred A Becchetti, of California USA; 1 s; *Heir* s, Jason Whitmore b 26 Jan 1983; *Career* sports psychologist, also concerned with psychology of int relations; dep dir Centre for Int Peacebuilding; author of books on the mental aspects of sport life and work; *Recreations* squash, skiing, motor racing; *Clubs* British Racing Drivers; *Style*— Sir John Whitmore, Bt; Southfield, Leigh, nr Tonbridge, Kent TN11 8PJ, (☎ 0732 454490)

WHITWORTH, John Vincer; s of Hugh Hope Aston Whitworth, MBE, of Twickenham, Middlesex, and Elizabeth, *née* Boyes (d 1960) ; *b* 11 Dec 1945; *Educ* Royal High Sch Edinburgh, Merton Coll Oxford (MA, BPhil); *m* Doreen Anne, *née* Roberts; 2 da (Eleanor Ruth b 1984, Catherine Rebecca b 1987); *Career* writer; winner of numerous literary prizes incl: Alice Hunt Bartlett Prize from Poetry Soc 1980, SE Arts Lit Prize 1980, The Barbara Campion Meml Prize 1983, Nat Poetry Competition Prize 1985, Cholmondeley Award 1988; teacher and lectr on Eng poetry and creative writing at Sch of Continuing Educn Univ of Kent; reviewer for Poetry Review and The Spectator; *Books* Unhistorial Fragments (1980), Poor Butterflies (1982), Lovely Day for a Wedding (1985), Tennis and Sex and Death (1989), Faber Book of Blue Verse (ed, 1990); *Recreations* cooking, playing with the children; *Style*— John Whitworth, Esq; 20 Lovell Rd, Rough Common, Canterbury, Kent CT2 9DG (☎ 0227 462400)

WIBBERLEY, Prof Gerald Percy; CBE (1972); s of Percy Wibberley (d 1915), of Abergavenny, Gwent, and Ellen Mary, *née* Jackson (d 1962); *b* 15 April 1915; *Educ* King Henry V111 GS Abergavenny, Univ Coll of Wales Aberystwyth (BSc,PhD), Univ of Oxford, Univ of Illinois USA (MSc); *m* 1, 18 Sept 1943, Helen Cecilia (d 1964), da of John Youmans (d 1967), of Newport, Indiana, USA; 1 da (Jane b 1945); m 2, Sept 1972, Peggy, *née* Samways; *Career* E Sussex Agric Exec Ctee 1941, chief res offr Land Use Miny of Agric 1948 (asst 1945), head Econs Dept Wye Coll Univ of London 1954; UCL: personal chair in rural economy 1963, personal chair in countryside planning; conslt to Kent CC on rural planning; cncl memb: Ctee for Small Industs in Rural Areas 1960-86, Nature Conservancy 1972-80; memb Kent Educn Ctee 1982-89, vice chm Wye Parish Cncl 1984-; hon memb Royal Town Planning Inst 1949; Hon DSc Univ of Bradford 1984; memb: Br Agric Econ Soc 1939- (pres 1975), Int Assoc of Agric Econs; Order of Merit Univ of Padua Italy 1982; *Books* Agriculture and Urban Growth (1959), Planning and The Rural Environment (with J Davidson, 1977); *Recreations* choral music; *Clubs* Farmers; *Style*— Prof Gerald Wibberley, CBE; Vicarage Cottage, 7 Upper Bridge St, Wye, nr Ashford, Kent TN25 5AN (☎ 0233 812 377)

WICKENDEN, Robin James; s of Henry A Wickenden (d 1977), of Otford, and Amelia Jane Wickenden; *b* 19 Sept 1943; *Educ* Wilderness Boys Sch Sevenoaks; *m* 21 Sept 1978, Janet, da of E Buck (d 1956), of Farnborough, Kent; 1 s (Daniel James b 14 May 1974); *Career* mgmnt servs asst: British Gas Corporation 1964-66, London Boroughs Mgmnt Unit 1966-72; head of Mgmnt Servs Dartford RDC 1972-74, econ tourism and euro liaison devpt offr Dartford Borough Cncl 1974-; local govt offr 1966-, vice pres Sevenoaks Branch Kent Referees Assoc (former chm); memb: Sevenoaks and Dist Football League Cncl, Homesdale CC Ctee; MBIM 1974, MMS 1978; *Recreations* cricket, golf, football referee, music; *Style*— Robin Wickenden, Esq; 9 Orchard Way, Kemsing, Sevenoaks Kent (☎ 0732 62478); Civic Centre, Home Gardens, Dartford, Kent (☎ 0322 343434, fax 0322 343422)

WICKHAM, Robert Oliver Lawrence; s of Humphrey Robert Wickham (d 1973), of Sevenoaks, and Dr Mary Wickham, *née* Ormiston (d 1975); *b* 14 March 1946; *Educ* Sevenoaks Sch, Sidney Sussex Coll Cambridge (Trevelyan scholar, BA, MA), Univ of London (M Phil); *m* 1 Aug 1981, Jennifer Kathleen, da of Bernard Brown, of Cambridge; 1 s (James Charles b 9 March 1983), 1 da (Sarah Elizabeth b 21 Dec 1986); *Career* chartered surveyor and chartered town planner; Ibbett Mosely: asst planner 1967-69, planning ptnr 1972-74, jt sr ptnr 1974-; planning offr London Borough of Haringey 1970-72, jt sr ptnr Howard Sharp & Partners (chartered surveyors and town planning conslts) 1974-; memb Centre for Policy Studies; ARICS (prizeman of RICS), MRTPI; *Recreations* family, travel, Alvis cars, 19th century history, hill walking; *Clubs* Royal Cwlth Soc; *Style*— Robert Wickham, Esq; 22 Wildernesse Mount, Sevenoaks, Kent TN13 3QS (☎ 0732 454042); Howard Sharp & Partners, 79 Great Peter St, Westminster, London SW1P 2EZ (☎ 071 222 4402); Howard Sharp & Partners, 125 High St, Sevenoaks, Kent TN13 1UT (☎ 0732 456888)

WIDDECOMBE, Ann Noreen; MP (C) Maidstone 1987-; da of James Murray Widdecombe, CB, OBE, of Haslemere, Surrey, and Rita Noreen, *née* Plummer; *b* 4 Oct 1947; *Educ* Royal Naval Sch Singapore, La Sainte Union Convent Bath, Univ of Birmingham (BA), Lady Margaret Hall Oxford (MA); *Career* sr admin Univ of London 1975-87; former vice chm: Nat Assoc Cons Graduates, Women and Families For Defence; vice pres Maidstone Mencap; pres: Maidstone Guide Dogs For the Blind, Maidstone River Users Assoc, Maidstone Civil Def; nat patron life; *Books* Layman's Guide to Defence (1984); *Recreations* reading, researching Charles II's escape; *Style*— Miss Anne Widdecombe, MP; 9 Tamar House, Kennington Lane, London SE11 4XA (☎ 071 735 5192); House of Commons, Westminster, London SW1 (☎ 071 219 5091, fax 071 219 6840)

WIGAN, Michael Christian; s of Maj John Derek Wigan (d 1985), and Anne Geraldine Wigan; *b* 3 Nov 1945; *Educ* Eton; *m* 14 Oct 1971, Eugenie Mary Felicity, da of Peter Egbert Cadbury, of Armsworth Hill, Old Alresford, Hants; 3 s (Charlie Christian b 1976, James Patrick Cameron b 1978, Rollo Richard b 1980); *Career* chm and dir: Wigan Richardson Int Ltd, Hop Developments Ltd, Fanfire Ltd, Wild Neame Gasgain Ltd, Interhop Ltd, Hopair Ltd; sr ptnr Wigan Richardson and Co; memb Lloyd's; *Clubs* White's; *Style*— Michael Wigan, Esq; Bighton House, nr Alresford, Hants; c/o Wigan Richardson & Co, Church Rd, Paddock Wood, Tonbridge, Kent TN12 6EP (☎ 089283 2235, fax 089283 6008)

WIGGINS, Linda Margaret; da of Frederick John Coe, of 58 Park Lane, Snettisham, King's Lynn, Norfolk, and Edna May, *née* Winner; *b* 21 Dec 1949; *Educ* W Norfolk King's Lynn HS for Girls, Univ of Essex (BA); *m* 12 Feb 1972, Derek Ernest Wiggins, s of Frank Wiggins, of 33 Fourth Cross Rd, Twickenham (d 1976); *Career* CA 1975-; ptnr in local firm 1978-84, started own pratice Wiggins & Co 1984; *Recreations* riding, embroidery; *Style*— Mrs Linda Wiggins; 5 Granada House, Gabriel's Hill, Maidstone, Kent ME15 6JP (☎ 0622 688 189)

WILDING, Thomas Henry (Tom); s of Jack Wilding (d 1985), and Ivy, *née* Spicer (d 1963); *b* 29 March 1930; *m* 27 Feb 1954, Ruby Edna, da of Charles William Wix (d 1954); 3 s (Andrew b 1958, Gavin b 1960, Mark b 1961), 1 da (Julia b 1967); *Career* chief chemist St Andrews Paper Mill 1950-57; mill mangr: Bowater Scott Walthamstow 1960-62 (dep 1957), Bowaters 1965 (mill dir 1968); dir: Kemsley Mill 1968-71, Southern Mills 1971, Independent Sea Terminals Ltd, Bowaters UK Paper Co Ltd 1971, Thames Mill 1973, Paper and Bd Div 1973 (and gen mangr); md: Paper and Bd Div 1977, Bowaters UK Paper Co Ltd 1978 (chm and md 1981); exec dir Bowaters Industries plc 1984, chief exec UK Paper plc 1988; bd memb Wilding Office Equipment Ltd; pres: CEPAC, Euro Paper Indust Fndn; bd memb Clares Equipment Holdings Ltd; appeals pres Nat Playing Fields Assoc; *Recreations* golf, skiing; *Clubs* Tudor Park Golf and Country; *Style*— Tom Wilding, Esq; Garden Lodge, Boxley, Maidstone, Kent ME14 3CX; UK Paper plc, UK Paper House, Kemsley, Sittingbourne, Kent ME10 2SG (☎ 0795 24488, telex 96102, fax 0795 78038)

WILKINSON, Alan Richard; s of Rev Richard Brindle Wilkinson, OBE (d 1966), and Mary, *née* Bretherton (d 1970); *b* 19 July 1923; *Educ* Culford Sch Bury St Edmunds; *m* 9 May 1953, Margaret Ruth, da of Dr Cuthwin Eagleston Donaldson (d 1988); 2 s (Andrew b 1956, Richard b 1962), 1 da (Jane b 1959); *Career* RE: sapper 1942, 2 Lt Trg Unit 1944; Lt 1 Para Sqdn RE 1944-45, Lt First Airborne Div, Burma Engrs Field Co 1946, Capt and Adj Depot Burma Engrgs 1946-47; design engr: Lewis & Duvivier, Coode & Partners (consltg engrs) 1947-54; Coode & Partners (later Coode Blizard): asst res engr Baghdad 1954-57, res engr Mombasa Port Kenya 1957-60, engr London 1960-62, res engr Mailsi Siphon Pakistan 1962-65, res chief engr Indus Basin Barrages Pakistan 1965-68, ptnr 1969, sr ptnr and md 1985-89; FICE 1964 (MICE 1956), MConsE 1969; *Recreations* wood carving, sculpture, swimming, gardening; *Style*— Alan Wilkinson, Esq; Spinneys, Kippington Rd, Sevenoaks, Kent TN13 2LN

WILKINSON, Lt-Col Sir Peter Allix; KCMG (1970, CMG 1960), DSO (1944), OBE (1944); s of Capt Osborn Cecil Wilkinson (ka 1915), by his w Esmé Barbara, da of Sir Alexander Wilson; *b* 15 April 1914; *Educ* Rugby, Corpus Christi Coll Cambridge; *m* 1945, Mary Theresa (d 1984), da of Algernon Hyde Villiers (ka 1917, 3 s of Rt Hon Sir Francis Hyde Villiers, GCMG, GCVO, CB, sometime ambass Brussels, 4 s of 4 Earl of Clarendon) by his w Beatrix (who subsequently m (1919) 4 Baron Aldenham and (2 Baron) Hunsdon, by whom she was mother of 5 Baron Aldenham); 2 da (Virginia b 1947, m 1971, Daniel Worsley; 1 s, 1 da; Alexandra b 1953; 1 s, 2 da); *Career* cmmnd 2 Bn Royal Fusiliers 1935, served WWII (Poland, France, Balkans, Central Europe, Italy) Lt-Col, ret 1947; joined Dip Serv 1947; 1 sec: Vienna 1947, Washington 1952; cnsllr Bonn 1955-60, under sec Cabinet Office 1963-64, sr civilian instr IDC 1964-66, ambass Vietnam 1966-67, asst under sec FO 1967-68, dep under sec and chief admin Dip Serv 1968-70, ambass Vienna 1970-71, ret 1972; re-employed as dep sec Cabinet Office 1972-73; Polish Cross of Valour 1940, Czech Order of White Lion 1945, Order of Yugoslav Banner (hon) 1984; *Recreations* reading, trout fishing; *Clubs* White's, Army and Navy; *Style*— Lt-Col Sir Peter Wilkinson, KCMG, DSO, OBE; 18 High St, Charing, Kent (☎ 023 371 2306)

WILKS, Stanley David (Jim); CB (1979); *b* 1 Aug 1920; *Educ* Polytechnic

Sch London; *m* 1947, Dorothy Irene, *née* Adamthwaite; 1 s (Howard John b 1965), 1 da (Penelope Jane b 1968); *Career* RAC 1939-46, served with 48 Bn RTR, 3 Carabiniers (Imphal 1944); Home Office 1946-50, BOT (later DTI) 1950-80: 1 sec Br Embassy Washington 1950-53, GATT non-ferrous metals, ECGD, airports policy; chief exec BOTB 1980-85; dir: Matthew Hall Business Development Ltd 1981-89, Hadson Petroleum International plc 1981-, Hadson Corporation (USA) 1985-, Associated Gas Supplies Ltd 1987-90; regnl dir James Hallam Ltd 1984-, chm Export Network Ltd 1985-89; dep chm: Technology Transfer Group 1986-89 (formerly DG 1981-86), Strategy International Ltd 1987- (conslt dir 1981-87); MIEx 1980; *Recreations* sailing, water skiing; *Clubs* Royal Over-Seas League, Medway Yacht, Lloyds Yacht, Tamesis; *Style*— Jim Wilks, Esq, CB; 6 Foxgrove Avenue, Beckenham, Kent BR3 2BA

WILLACY, Michael James Ormerod; CBE 1989; s of James Willacy (d 1977), of Plymouth, Devon, and Majorie Winifred, *née* Sanders; *b* 7 June 1933; *Educ* Taunton Sch Somerset; *m* 1, 25 Nov 1961, Merle Louise, da of Johannes Schrier, of Denia, Spain; 2 s (Richard b 1962, Peter b 1969), 1 da (Jennifer b 1963); m 2, Victoria Stuart, da of Cecil Stuart John, of Mobberley, Cheshire; 2 s (James b 1985, Michael b 1986, David b 1990), 1 da (Elizabeth b 1988); *Career* dir HM Govt Central Unit on Purchasing 1985-, gen mangr Shell UK Materials Services 1983-85; chm Macclesfield C of C 1981-83; fndr chm Macclesfield Business Ventures 1982-83, gen sec Old Tauntonian Assoc 1978- (pres 1988-89); FInstPS; *Recreations* golf, travel, gardening; *Clubs* Royal Cwlth Soc; *Style*— Michael Willacy, Esq, CBE; Lower Barn, Coarsewell, Ugborough, Ivybridge, Devon PL21 OHP (☎ 054 882 536)

WILLIAMS, Barry James; s of Harry George Williams, of Dover, and Patricia Eileen, *née* Redman; *b* 5 March 1955; *Educ* Astor Secdy Sch Dover; *m* 24 Nov 1979, Helen Margaret, da of Henry Dyer, of Dover; 1 s (Laurence James b 1986); *Career* chm: Dover Young Conservatives 1978-81, Dover Cons Political Ctee 1981-84; Dover DC: elected 1983, re-elected 1987, vice chm Fin Ctee 1986, vice chm Tourism Ctee 1987, chm Tech Servs 1989 (vice chm 1988); *Clubs* Dover Cons; *Style*— Barry Williams, Esq; 144 Buckland Ave, Dover, Kent CT16 2NN (☎ 0304 207680); General Portfolio FPS Ltd, Kent House, Station Rd, Ashford, Kent TN23 1PP (☎ 0233 640388, fax 0233 640377)

WILLIAMS, Christopher Hywel; s of Aubrey Howell Williams (ka 1943), of Pembroke Dock, and Patricia Florence, *née* Coombes; *Educ* Gillingham GS, UCL (BA); *m* 4 Oct 1980, Caroline Rose, da of John William Macey White, of Llantwit Major, S Wales; 1 da (Rebecca Siân Williams b 22 Oct 1983); *Career* accountant; Br Olivetti 1971-79, ind consultancy 1980-85; Tack Organisation 1985- (md Tack Research, assoc dir Tack Training International); Cons cncllr Riverside Ward Gillingham Borough Cncl, appeals speaker Survive, memb Inst Mktg; *Recreations* amateur dramatics; *Clubs* Wig and Pen; *Style*— Christopher Williams, Esq; Llahdaot, 11 Mayfield Close, Rainham, Kent ME8 7DP (☎ 0634 366740); Tack Organisation, 1-5 Longmore St, London SW1V 1JJ (☎ 071 834 5001, fax 071 828 8434)

WILLIAMS, Cncllr Frank Thomas Bosley; s of Ronald Arthur Williams, of Symonds Yat West, Herefordshire, and Winifred Elizabeth, *née* Bosley; *b* 19 Sept 1950; *Educ* St Albans Sch, Univ of Birmingham (BSoc Sci), Univ of London (PGCE); *m* 13 Sept 1975, Kay Elisabeth, da of Richard George Edmund Kenwood, of Harpenden, Herts; 1 da (Kim b 1968); *Career* National Westminster Bank 1973-75; teacher: St George's Sch Harpenden 1975-79, St George's Coll Weybridge 1979-81, Bennett Meml Girls Sch Tunbridge Wells 1981-; cncllr St John's Ward Tunbridge Wells 1986-; memb: Age Concern, Sports Advsy Cncl; *Recreations* politics, taking my daughter to the park; *Style*— Cncllr Frank Williams; 3 Sandhurst Park, Tunbridge Wells, Kent TN2 3SU (☎ 0892 25720); Bennett Memorial Sch, Culverden Down, Tunbridge Wells, Kent (☎ 0892 21595)

WILLIAMS, Air Vice-Marshal Graham Charles; AFC (1971, and bar 1975); s of Charles Francis Williams (d 1968), and Molly, *née* Chapman (d 1988); *b* 4 June 1937; *Educ* Marlborough, RAF Coll Cranwell; *m* 3 March 1962, Judy Teresa Ann, da of Reginald Walker (d 1972); 1 s (Mark b 1963), 1 da (Kim b 1966); *Career* Pilot 54 Sqdn Odiham 1958-60, instr 229 OCU Chivenor 1961-63, Flt-Cdr 8 Sqdn Khormaskar 1964-65, Empire Test Pilot's Sch 1966, 'A' Sqdn (fighter test) A and AEE Boscombe Down 1967-70, RAF Staff Coll Bracknell 1971, OC 3 (F) Sqdn Wildenrath 1972-74, jr directing staff RCDS 1975-77, Stn Cdr RAF Bruggen 1978-79, Gp Capt Ops HQ RAF Germany 1980-82, CO Experimental Flying RAF Farnborough 1983, Cmdt A and AEE Boscombe Down 1984-85, DOR (Air) MOD 1986, asst chief of def staff Operational Requirements (Air) 1987-; FRAeS 1984; Harmon Trophy USA 1970; *Recreations* squash, golf; *Clubs* RAF; *Style*— Air Vice-Marshal Graham Williams; 3 The Ramparts, Knightrider St, Sandwich, Kent CT13 9ER (☎ 0304 613030); 31 Chester Way, London SE11; MOD, Whitehall, London SW1A 2HB (☎ 01 218 7221)

WILLIAMS, Dr (Daniel) Gwyn; s of Rev Daviel James Williams (d 1967), of Cardiff, and Elizabeth Beatrice Mary Walters (d 1974); *b* 7 March 1940; *Educ* Cardiff HS, Univ Coll Cardiff (MB, BCh), Welsh Nat Sch of Med (MD); *m* 21 Jan 1967, Angela Mary, da of John Edwin Davies (d 1974), of Petts Wood, Kent; 4 da (Rachel b 1968, Sian b 1970, Hannah b 1972, Leah b 1976); *Career* jr hosp appts at Cardiff Royal Infirmary and The Radcliffe Infirmary Oxford, sr registrar in med Radcliffe Infirmary, res fell and asst lectr Royal Postgrad Medical Sch London, conslt physician and sr lectr in med United Medical and Dental Schs of Guy's and St Thomas's Hosp Univ of London; MRS, The Renal Assoc; FRCP 1978; *Books* The Oxford Textbook of Medicine (contrib, 1987), The Oxford Textbook of Clinical Nephrology (contrib, 1990); *Style*— Dr Gwyn Williams; The Renal Unit, Guy's Hospital, St Thomas's St, London SE1 9RT (☎ 071 955 4306, fax 071 407 6689)

WILLIAMS, Dr John Desmond; s of Jack Williams (d 1969), of Dover, Kent, and Frances Alice Elizabeth, *née* Carey (d 1979); *b* 23 Nov 1925; *Educ* Dover GS, Imperial Coll London, Guy's Hosp Med Sch (MB BS); *m* 2 April 1960, Lesley Peto, da of Harold Lennox Garner Hornby (d 1974), of Northampton; 2 s (David John Carey b 1965, Richard Charles Peto b 1970), 2 da (Fiona Helen b 1962, Louisa Jane b 1967); *Career* conslt physician: Bromley Health Dist 1961-90, Bexley Health Dist 1961-90; FRCP 1973; *Recreations* cricket, golf; *Clubs* MCC, Chislehurst Golf, Rye Golf; *Style*— Dr John Williams; Stable House, Wilderness Rd, Chislehurst, Kent BR7 5EY (☎ 081 467 3896)

WILLIAMS, Mair; da of William Joseph Thomas (d 1966), of Bridgend, Glamorgan, and Elvira, *née* Hopkins (d 1987); *b* 12 July 1930; *Educ* Bridgend GS for Girls; *m* 12 July 1951, Raymond Samuel Williams, s of Harold Stanley Williams (d 1974); 1 s (Richard b 1955), 1 da (Ceri b 1952); *Career* lab technician 1947-51, occupational therapy aid 1968-82; Gillingham Age Concern: memb 1967-, fund raising chm 1973-79, chm 1979-; tstee: Houses for the Aged Charity 1986-, Gillingham Day Care Centre, Dobbies Pop in Gillingham, Charity Shop Rainham, Charity Shop Gillingham; memb: Gillingham Ladies Circle 1964-68, Radio Medway Advsy Cncl, Medway DHA 1982-87, Kent FPC 1983-90; *Recreations* dressmaking, handicrafts, gardening, cooking, travelling; *Style*— Mrs Mair Williams; 12 Kingsway, Chatham, Kent ME5 7HT (☎ 0634 52065)

WILLIAMS, Col William Trevor (Bill); s of Francis Harold Williams (d 1951), and Ethel Mabel, *née* Gwyther (d 1964); *b* 16 Oct 1925; *Educ* Whitchurch GS, Univ of Kent (MA); *m* 6 Feb 1951, Elizabeth, da of Brig A H Goldie (d 1967); 2 s (Stephen b 15 May 1952, Richard b 16 Nov 1961), 2 da (Amanda b 11 June 1957, Mary b 13 April 1967); *Career* enlisted Grenadier Gds 1943, cmmnd Black Watch, served with Royal Scots RCT, GS to 1977, served Malaysia, South America, Ethiopia, Libya, Germany and Singapore, ret as full Col; dir SATRA (GB) 1978-79, dir gen EIA 1980-; TECs SATROs, FBIM 1965, FCIS 1979, MCIT 1980; *Recreations* golf, photography; *Clubs* IOD; *Style*— Col Bill Williams; 15 Mill Lane, Lower Harbledown, Canterbury, Kent CT2 8NE (☎ 0227 768170); Engineering Industries Association, 16 Dartmouth St, London SW1H 9BL (☎ 071 222 2367, fax 071 222 2782)

WILLIAMSON, (Alicia) Ann; JP; da of Andrew James Bligh (d 1981), and Dorothy Irene, *née* Carter; *b* 7 June 1938; *Educ* Talbot Heath Sch, Whiteland Tech Coll (Dip), Univ of London (BSc); *m* 11 Aug 1961, John Bryan Williamson, s of William Williamson (d 1964); 1 da (Clare Ann b 14 July 1970); *Career* asst mistress: S Croydon Secdy Modern 1958-61, Bexley GS 1961-71; head of year Highfield Comp Letchworth 1972-74, headmistress Stratford House 1974-; SHA: cncl memb 1982-, chm Area 2 1984-85, exec memb 1986-, chm Pub and Parly Affrs 1989; chm NW Kent Assoc of Univ Women 1988-89, vice chm Bromley Young Enterprise Bd; memb: Employment Ctee IOD, GSA, ISA, BFUW, AFA; *Recreations* singing, drama, fencing, bridge, rugby, knitting and sleeping; *Style*— Mrs Ann Williamson, JP; Stratford House School, 8-10 Southborough Rd, Bickley, Bromley, Kent BR1 2EB (☎ 081 467 3580)

WILLIAMSON, Ann Mary; da of Maj John Williamson, RA (d 1949), of Wiltshire, and Jean Isobel, *née* McDonald (d 1975); *b* 8 March 1929; *Educ* Godolphin Sch Salisbury, Univ of Edinburgh (MA); *Career* Andry Montgomery Ltd (exhibition organisers) 1957-69, conference organiser Northwood Conferences and Seminars (subsid of Thomson Organisation and Seminars) 1969-79, headmaster's sec Caterham Sch 1979-89, currently freelance journalist proofreader and indexer; ed of Roundabout (Brenchley and Matfield Village Magazine), vice pres Matfield Womens Inst; sec: Brenchley and Matfield Local History Soc, sec Over Sixties; memb: Brenchley Drama, Horticultural Soc, The Soc of Indexers; *Recreations* gardening, reading, visiting historical buildings and sites; *Style*— Miss Ann Williamson; 5 Whitethorn Cottages, Brenchley Rd, Matfield, Kent TN12 7PR (☎ 089272 2174)

WILLIAMSON, David Francis; CB (1984); s of Samuel Charles Wathen Williamson, of Bath, and late Marie Eileen Williamson; *b* 8 May 1934; *Educ* Tonbridge, Exeter Coll Oxford (MA); *m* 1961, Patricia Margaret, da of Eric Cade Smith, of Broadclyst, Exeter; 2 s; *Career* civil servant; MAFF 1958-65 and 1967-77, seconded to HM Dip Serv for Kennedy Round Trade Negotiations 1965-67, dep dir Gen Agric European Cmmn Brussels 1977-83, dep sec Cabinet Office 1983-87, sec gen Euro Cmmn Brussels 1987-; *Style*— David Williamson, Esq, CB; European Commission, 200 Rue de la Loi, 1049 Brussels, Belgium

WILLIAMSON, Cncllr Heather Cecilia Mary; da of Campbell Mackessaack (d 1956), of London, and Florence Leah, *née* Smith (d 1981); *b* 4 Sept 1928; *Educ* Elgin Acad Moray Grampian, Royal Infirmary Edinburgh (RGN Orthopaedic Cert); *m* 28 March 1953, Bill Graham Hurst Williamson, of Edinburgh; 2 s (Graham Mackessack b 22 March 1956, Donald Currie b 28 Nov 1957), 1 da (Sheila Ann b 8 July 1954); *Career* relief matron Day and Residential Nurseries The City of Edinburgh, staff nurse Canterbury and Margate Hosps; memb: LDP, Broadstairs and St Peters Town Cncl, Thanet DC 1983 and 1987, Canterbury and Thanet Health Authy, Kent Mayors Assoc, Mayor Broadstairs and St Peters 1958-86; chm Thanet DC Gen Purposes Ctee 1987-90, memb local div Oxfam, pres Thanet Div Multiple Sclerosis Soc, formerly dep organiser Canterbury WRVS, chm Broadstairs Open Bowls Tournament; *Recreations* walking, travel, DIY; *Clubs* Royal Overseas League, Pfizer Retirement; *Style*— Cncllr Heather Williamson; Tait Cottage, 2 Lanthorne Rd, Broadstairs, Kent CT10 3NH (☎ 0843 64802)

WILLIAMSON, Nigel; s of Neville Albert Williamson, of Arizona, and Ann Maureen Kitson; *b* 4 July 1954; *Educ* Chislehurst and Sidcup GS, UCL; *m* 1976, Magali Patricia; 2 s (Adam b 1977, Piers b 1978); *Career* ed: Tribune 1984-87, Labour Party News 1987-89, New Socialist 1987-89; diary ed The Times 1990- (political corr and columnist 1989-90); *Books* The SDP (1982), The New Right (1984); *Recreations* cricket, opera, gardening; *Clubs* Skyliners Cricket; *Style*— Nigel Williamson, Esq; High Beeches, 60 Sutherland Ave, Biggin Hill, Westerham, Kent TN16 3HA (☎ 0959 71127); c/o The Times, 1 Pennington St, London E1 (☎ 071 782 5753)

WILLIAMSON, Cnclr William Graham Hurst (Bill); s of William Currie Williamson (d 1961), of Edinburgh, and Jane Adeline Leadbetter, *née* Hurst (d 1985); *b* 21 March 1927; *Educ* Boroughmuir Edinburgh, Univ of Edinburgh (BSc); *m* 28 March 1953, Heather Cecilia Mary, da of Campbell Mackessack (d 1959), of Assam; 2 s (Graham Mackessack b 1956, Donald Currie b 1957), 1 da (Sheila Ann b 1954); *Career* regnl sales dir Chem Div of Pfizer Ltd Sandwich Kent (area covered incl UK I Scandinavia Nigeria Central Africa SA), ret 1989; vice pres Thanet MENCAP Soc; memb: Kent CC, S Thanet Lib Dem Assoc; *Recreations* travel, reading, gardening; *Clubs* The Royal Overseas, Pfizer Retirement; *Style*— Cncllr Bill Williamson; Kent County Council, Members Lounge, County Hall, Maidstone, Kent ME14 1XX (☎ 0622 671411, fax 0622 59905)

WILLIS, Lady Audrey Mary; JP (Bromley); da of Alfred Hale (d 1984), and Ethel May Hale (d 1981); *b* 19 July 1924; *Educ* Tottenham Poly; *m* 12 Aug 1944, Lord Willis of Chislehurst, *qv*, s of Alfred John Willis (d 1973); 1 s (John b 4 April 1948), 1 da (Sally b 8 Jan 1951); *Career* memb: SE Thames RHA 1974-90, Special Health Authy Royal Bethlem and Mandsley Hosps 1974-90, bd London Provincial Nursing Serv 1984-; pres Stone House Hosp League of Friends; *Recreations* theatre and soccer fan; *Style*— Lady Willis, JP

WILLIS, Baron (Life Peer UK 1963), of Chislehurst, Co Kent; Edward Henry Willis (Ted); s of Alfred John Willis, of Tottenham, London, and Maria Harriet Willis; *b* 13 Jan 1918; *Educ* Downhills Central Sch Tottenham; *m* 12 Aug 1944, Audrey Mary, *qv*, da of Alfred Hale, of Enfield, Middx; 1 s (Hon John Edward b 4 April 1946), 1 da (Hon Sally Ann Hale (Hon Mrs Murray) b 8 Jan 1951); *Career* served WWII Royal Fus; sits as Lab Peer in House of Lords; playwright and writer; dir: World Wide Pictures 1967-, Vitalcall Ltd 1983-, Netherburn Ltd 1989-; pres Authors' Lending and Copyright Soc; life pres Writers Guild of GB; FRTS, FRSA; *Books Incl:* Whatever Happened to Tom Mix? (auto-biography 1970), The Churchill Commando (1977), The Naked Sun (1980), Spring at the Winged Horse (1983), The Green Leaves of Summer (1988), The Bells of Autumn (1990), A Problem for Mother Christmas (1988); *Plays include* Hot Summer Night, New (1957), A Slow Roll of Drums (1964), Mr Polly (1977), Stardust (1983), Battle at Lavender Lodge (1985), Tommy Boy (1988), Intent to Kill (1989), Doctor on the Boil (1989); *Films include* Woman in a Dressing Gown (1958, later also a play), A Long Way to Shiloh (1969), Mrs Harris Goes to Monte Carlo (1986), Spy on Ice (1987), The Valley of the Dream (1987), Mrs Harris Goes to Moscow (1988), Mrs Harris Goes to Majorca (1989); *TV scripts include* Dixon of Dock Green, Crime of Passion, Black Beauty, Valley of Kings, Sergeant Cork, A Home for Animals, Racecourse; *Clubs* Garrick, Wig and Pen; *Style*— The Rt Hon the Lord Willis; 5 Shepherds Green, Chislehurst, Kent

WILLIS FLEMING, Hon Mrs (Elizabeth Sarah); *née* James; da of 4 Baron Northbourne; *b* 1933; *m* 1960, Michael Edward Willis Fleming; 1 s, 1 da; *Style*— The Hon Mrs Willis Fleming; Updown Farm, Betteshanger Deal, Kent

WILLMOT, Mark Andrew; s of Graham Frederick Willmot, and Pamela, *née* Braine; *b* 1 June 1954; *Educ* Gravesend Tech HS, Hadlow Agric Coll, Purdue Univ Indiana, USA, London Business Sch; *m* 28 Aug 1976, Karen Valerie, da of Dennis Briggs, of Withernsea, N Humberside; 1 s (Daniel Christopher b 1979), 1 da (Victoria Louise b 1982); *Career* C & G Willmot (AMC) Ltd: sales rep 1976, sales mangr 1981, dir 1983, dir responsible for fin and admin 1986; dir Willmot Industs Ltd (hldg co of Willmot gp) 1989; purchased farm in Scot Borders; *Clubs* IOD; *Style*— Mark Willmot, Esq; West Yoke Farm, Ash, Sevenoaks, Kent TN15 7HU (☎ 0474 872395, fax 0474 874876)

WILLS, Peter Gordon Bethune; TD (1967); s of Lionel Wills (d 1967), of Trieste, Italy, and Sita, *née* Stapleton (d 1982); *b* 25 Oct 1931; *Educ* Malvern, Corps Christi Coll Cambridge; *m* 1, 1957, Linda Hutton; 2 s, 1 da; m 2, 1982, Faith Hines; *Career* served Royal Inniskilling Fusiliers in NI and Korea 1950-52, London Irish Rifles (TA) 1952-67; memb Stock Exchange 1960, ptnr Sheppards and Chase (Stockbrokers) 1960-85 (joined 1955); memb Cncl of Stock Exchange 1973-86 (dep chm 1979-82); chm: Security Settlements Options Ltd 1979-, Sheppards Moneybrokers Ltd 1985-89; dir: The Securities Assoc 1986-89, London Clear Ltd 1987-89, BAII Holding Ltd 1986-89; *Style*— Peter Wills, Esq, TD; 54 Frant Rd, Tunbridge Wells, Kent (☎ 0892 26705)

WILMSHURST, John; s of Alfred William Wilmshurst, and Frances May, *née* Handy; *b* 30 Jan 1926; *Educ* Maidstone GS, Univ Coll Oxford (MA); *m* 31 March 1951, Patricia Edith, da of R John W Hollis, MBE; 1 s (Jonathon 1968), 3 da (Letitia 1953, Felicity 1955, Priscilla 1960); *Career* Lt RASC 1945-48; patents offr Glaxo Laboratories Ltd 1950-52, gp advertising mangr Reed International Ltd 1952-59, dir Roles & Parker Ltd 1959-67, md Stuart Advertising Ltd 1967-71, chm and chief exec John Wilmshurst Marketing Consultants Ltd 1971-; memb: Gen Cncl Church Missionary Soc 1970-78, Kent Playing Fields Assoc, SE Publicity Club, Ctee Oxford Soc; chm Kent Branch Chartered Inst of Mktg 1972, church warden Farleigh Parish Church 1979-82, Freeman City of London, Liveryman asst Worshipful Co of Carmen; FCIM 1986, FCAM 1982; *Books* The Fundamentals and Practice of Marketing (1978), The Fundamentals of Advertising (1985); *Recreations* birdwatching, horse-racing, theatre, music, collecting first editions; *Clubs* City Livery; *Style*— John Wilmshurst, Esq; The Stable Cottage, East Farleigh, Kent (☎ 0622 728241)

WILSKI, Dr Andrew; s of Ingénieur Boguslaw Jaloszynski, of Piotrówek, Warsaw, Poland, and Janina Zofia, *née* Zalewska; *b* 2 April 1947; *Educ* Med Acad Warsaw (DM), Univ of London (DPM), Royal Coll of Psychiatrists (MRCPsych); *m* 2 April 1982, Phillippa, da of Patrick Green, of Freshfields, Harpenden, Herts; 3 s (Alexis b 1983, Nicholas b 1984, Piers b 1986), 1 da (Francesca Marya b 1989); *Career* sr registrar Westminster Hosp London 1976-83, conslt psychotherapist Univ of Essex and community psychiatrist Mental Health Centre London 1984-88, lectr Herts Coll of Art 1986-87, conslt psychiatrist Tunbridge Wells Health Authy 1988-; memb Assoc of Christian Psychiatrists; *Books* Health in Towns (contrib, 1985); *Recreations* travel, reading, arts, photography; *Style*— Dr Andrew Wilski; 4 Berkeley Rd, Mount Sion, Royal Tunbridge Wells, Kent TN1 1YR (☎ 0892 27304); Sevenoaks Hospital, Hospital Rd, Sevenoaks, Kent TN13 3PG (☎ 0732 455155)

WILSON, Brig Alexander David Robin Graham; CBE (Mil 1971, MBE (Mil) 1945); s of Lt-Col Alexander Robert Graham Wilson, DSO (d 1963), and Violet Alice, (d 1976), da of Lt-Col Henry Morland, and Lady Alice Morland; *b* 10 Aug 1916; *Educ* Wellington, RMC Sandhurst; *m* 1, 9 July 1945, Sylvia Marianna (d 1971), da of Lionel Oliver Brian Russell; m 2, Alison Mary (formerly Mrs Clapham), da of Spencer Bernau Wilks (d 1972); 1 s (Alexander James Graham b Jan 1954), 1 da (Margaret Jane b March 1948); *Career* cmmnd A & SH, served NW Frontier, Malaya, Burma, Palestine, Korea, cmd 1st Bn 1946-47, 8 Bn (Argyllshire) 1958-61, MA to FM Montgomery (SHAPE) 1957, cmd 125 Bde (W Lancs) 1962-65, Chief BRIXMIS 1965-67, cmd Commonwealth Liaison Mission and rep UNCMAC KOREA 1968-70; borough cncllr Lamberhurst Ward Tunbridge Wells 1984-; memb: Ex Servs Mental Warfare Soc, W Kent War Pensions Ctee, SSAFA Kent, Tunbridge Wells Community Health Cncl; *Recreations* fishing, sailing, model making; *Clubs* Army and Navy, Band of Brothers, Bluemantles; *Style*— Brig Alexander Wilson, CBE; Flat 5, Court Lodge, Lamberhurst, Kent TN3 8DU (☎ 0892 890913)

WILSON, David; s of Frederick Charles Wilson, of Ashtead, Surrey, and Phyllis Cissie, *née* Brooks; *b* 3 Nov 1944; *Educ* Ottershaw Sch, City of London Poly; *m* 21 Oct 1971 (m dis 1988), Elizabeth Margaret, da of Maj Arthur Bartram Savage, OBE, MVO (ret), of Wendover, Bucks; 3 da (Emma Louise b 1975, Charlotte Elizabeth b 1977, Rebecca Jane b 1981); *Career* co sec Industl and Mfrg Div Trafalgar House Investments plc 1964-71, sec Tender Construction Div Bovis P & O Group plc 1971-75, div dir and gp sec The British Land Co plc 1975-86, gp sec Eurotunnel Plc/SA 1986-89; former dir: Br Land Developments Ltd, Euston Centre plc, City Wall Hldgs Ltd, Jarvis Builders Ltd; currently: admin dir Eurotunnel Plc/SA, dir and gen mangr Eurotunnel Developements Ltd, dir Eurotunnel Developements SA, Eurotunnel Services Ltd, Eurotunnel Servs GiE; Freeman City of London, Liveryman Worshipful Co of Secretaries, former memb Co Secs Panel Chartered Inst of Secs, memb Kent Econ Devpt Bd Developers Gp; FCIS, FCT, FBIM, fell Chartered Inst of Administrators; *Recreations* shooting, opera; *Clubs* MCC, Harlequin RUFC, RAC; *Style*— David Wilson, Esq; Victoria Plaza, 111 Buckingham Palace Rd, London SW1W 0ST (☎ 071 326 7226, fax 071 821 5242)

WILSON, Jeremy Paul; s of Charles Paul Wilson, CVO (d 1972), of Much Hadham, and Margaret, *née* Fraser Cameron; *b* 27 Jan 1932; *Educ* Bryanston, Downing Coll Cambridge, Middx Hosp Med Sch (MA, MB BChir); *m* 1, 24 Feb 1962 (m dis 1986), (Margaret) Clare, da of Rev Gordon Addenbrooke, of Lympstone, Devon; 1 s (James b 1965), 1 da (Harriett b 1967); *Career* conslt surgn Queen Mary's Hosp Sidcup 1974-, hon clinical lectr St Thomas' Hosp London 1975-; memb advsy cncl: Paintings in Hospitals 1976-, Dartington Int Summer Sch 1981-; cncl memb Section of Coloproctology RSM 1982-; princ bassoon and vice chm Sidcup Symphony Orchestra; memb: BMA 1965, Br Soc Gastroenterology 1974; FRCS 1963, FRSM 1965; *Recreations* playing bassoon, walking, philandering; *Style*— Jeremy Wilson, Esq; 2 Montpelier Row, Blackheath, London SE3 0RL (☎ 081 463 9111); Queen Mary's Hospital, Sidcup, Kent (☎ 081 302 2678)

WILSON, Sir (Mathew) Martin; 5 Bt (UK 1874), of Eshton Hall, Co York; s of Sir Mathew Richard Henry Wilson, 4 Bt, CSI, DSO (d 1958), by his w Hon Barbara Lister (da of 4 & last Baron Ribblesdale); bro of Peter; *b* 2 July 1906; *Educ* Eton; *Heir* n, Mathew Wilson, MBE, MC, *qv*; *Career* patron of four livings; *Style*— Sir Martin Wilson, Bt; 1 Sandgate Esplanade, Folkestone, Kent

WILSON, Col Timothy John Michael; s of Lt-Col AC Wilson (d 1975), of Kent and Devon, and Margaret Beverley, *née* Iliffe; *b* 23 March 1932; *Educ* Cranbrook Sch Kent, Canadian Army Staff Coll, Nat Defence Coll, Indian Nat Defence Coll; *m* 23 Sept 1961, Kitty Maxine, da of Maj Seymour Norton-Taylor, of Poole, Dorset; 2 da (Vanessa b 1963, Jennifer b 1965); *Career* 2 Lt and Lt 1950-53, Lt 2 i/c RM Detachment HMS Gambia 1953-55 (memb earthquake relief team Zante Ionian Islands 1953), Troop Subaltern 40 Commando RM 1955-57 served Cyprus, Near East (severely wounded at Port Said landings 1956, despatches), housemaster RM Sch of Music 1957-59, motor tport course 1959-60, local Capt ADC to C-in-C Near East HQ Near East Cyprus 1960-61, Capt Motor Tport Offr RM Poole 1961-63, staff course Canadian Army Staff Coll 1963-65, Adj 40 Commando RM (subsequently Maj) 1965-68 (served Malaysia 1965-67), Maj GSO 2 (instr) Jr Div Army Staff Coll Warminster 1968-70, Bde Maj UK Commandos GSO 2 Ops and Planning HQ Commando Forces RM 1970-72, staff course Nat Def Coll 1972-73, Lt-Col Royal Marines Rep USMC Devpt and Educn Cmd 1973-75, CO 42 Commando RM 1975-78 (served N Ireland 1976), Col Dir drafting and records RM HMS Centurion 1978-79, staff course Indian Nat Def Coll New Delhi 1979-80, Asst Adj Gen to Cmdt Gen RM MOD London 1980-83, ADC to HM The Queen 1982-83; Ptnrship sec Radcliffes & Co Slrs Westminster; Working volunteer memb Kent and E Sussex Steam Railway, memb HM Bodyguard of the Hon Corps of Gentlemen of Arms 1984; hon MSc (def studies) Allahabad 1980; FBIM 1980, MInstAM 1982; *Recreations* beagling, golf, tennis, travel; *Clubs* Army and Navy; *Style*— Col Timothy Wilson

WILSON-SHARP, Philip; s of Cecil Dereck Wilson-Sharp, of Bridlington, and Marjorie Elaine Elliott, *née* Jenkins; *b* 8 March 1949; *Educ* Colchester Royal GS, Downing Coll Cambridge (MA); *m* 16 Aug 1975, Janet Christine Elisabeth, da of Sidney Herbert Boor, of Peterborough; 1 s (Mark b 1980 and d 1980) 3 da (Janet Ruth b 1978, Alice Claire b 1981, Kathryn Emma b 1984); *Career* admitted slr 1974, asst slr Joynson-Hicks & Co 1974-75, princ slr Peterborough City Cncl 1975-83, ptnr Buckle Mellows 1984-89, head Legal Dept Canterbury City Cncl 1989-; vice chm Home Counties Branch Assoc Dist Secs; memb: Law Soc, St Andrew's URC; *Recreations* walking, gardening, scrabble; *Style*— Philip Wilson-Sharp, Esq; Chief Solicitor, Canterbury City Council, Military Rd, Canterbury, Kent CT1 1YW (☎ 0227 763763, fax 0227 763727)

WINCKLESS, Frederick Charles (Fred); s of Charles Frederick Winckless (d 1951), of Goodmayes, Essex, and Daisy, *née* Hicks (d 1933); *b* 18 March 1925; *Educ* Pitmans Coll Univ of London (dip sociology, cert criminology), Univ of Kent (dip theology); *m* Doreen Elsie, da of Richard Cantwell (d 1970), of Ilford, Essex; 1 s (Antony Charles b 2 May 1953), 1 da (Sharon b 10 Oct 1957); *Career* prison welfare offr Nat Assoc for Discharged Prisoners Aid Soc 1959, probation offr Kent Probation Serv 1966, sr lectr in soc work Kent Educn Authy 1977 (lectr 1972); fndr memb SDP in Maidstone; memb: Green Democrats, Cncl for Social Democracy 1981-87; parly candidate Lib-SDP Alliance Medway 1983, elected Lib-SDP cncllr Langley and Otham 1984, reelected 1987, resigned Lib-Democrat Whip to sit as Ind Lib Maidstone Borough Cncl 1989; govr St Michael's C of E Sch Maidstone; *Style*— Fred Winckless, Esq; 30 Royston Rd, Bearsted, Maidstone, Kent ME15 8NS (☎ 0622 39400)

WINNIFRITH, Charles Boniface; s of Sir (Alfred) John Digby Winnifrith, KCB, *qv*, and Lesbia Margaret, *née* Cochrane (d 1981); *b* 12 May 1936; *Educ* Tonbridge, ChCh Oxford (MA); *m* 21 April 1962, Josephine Joy Winnifrith, MBE, da of Roger Spencer Poile (d 1974), of Kingston, Kent; 1 s (John b 1964), 2 da (Charlotte b 1966, Laura b 1968); *Career* Nat Serv 2 Lt RAEC 1958-68; Dept of the Clerk of House of Commons 1960-, second clerk of Select Ctees 1983-87, clerk of Select Ctees 1987-89, princ clerk of Table Office 1989-; memb Gen Synod of the C of E 1970-90, chm House of Laity Canterbury Diocesan Synod 1979-; govr Ashford Sch Kent 1973; *Recreations* cricket, American soap opera; *Clubs* MCC; *Style*— Charles Winnifrith, Esq; Cliffe Cottage, St Margaret's at Cliffe, Kent CT15 6BJ (☎ 0304 853280); House of Commons, London SW1 (☎ 071 219 3312)

WINNIFRITH, Sir (Alfred) John Digby; KCB (1959, CB 1950); s of Rev Bertram Thomas Winnifrith, Rector of Ightham, Kent; *b* 16 Oct 1908; *Educ* Westminster, ChCh Oxford; *m* 1935, Lesbia Margaret (d 1981), eld da of Sir Arthur Cochrane, KCVO, sometime Clarenceux King of Arms; 2 s, 1 da; *Career* civil servant 1932-67: BOT to 1934, transfd to Treasy 1934, asst sec War Cabinet and civil sec Combined Ops HQ 1942-44, 3 sec Treasy 1951-59, perm sec MAFF 1959-67; tstee Nat History Section Br Museum 1967-72, dir gen Nat Tst 1968-70 (chm Regnl Ctee for Kent and E Sussex 1971-78), memb Cwlth War Graves Cmmn 1969-83; *Style*— Sir John Winnifrith, KCB; Hallhouse Farm, Appledore, Ashford, Kent (☎ 023 383 264)

WINNIFRITH, Josephine Joy; MBE, JP; da of Roger Spencer Poile (1974), of Kingston, Kent, and Alice Irene, *née* Harris (d 1985); *b* 8 June 1934; *Educ* Ashford Sch, Sch of Radiography KCH London; *m* 21 April 1962, Charles Boniface Winnifrith, s of Sir (Alfred) John Digby Winnifrith, KCB, of Appledore, Kent; 1 s (John b 1964), 2 da (Charlotte b 1966, Laura b 1968); *Career* various radiography posts in London and overseas 1955-62; pt/t fundraiser Winged Fellowship Tst 1985-88, chm Consumers Ctee SE Region Office of Electricity Regulation 1990-, non-exec dir SE Kent Health Authy 1990- (memb 1981-90); organiser Ashford WRVS Centre 1963-76; Ashford borough cncllr (Ind) 1973-87 (Mayor of Ashford 1983-84); magistrate: Ashford and Tenterden Bench 1976-88, Dover and E Kent Bench 1988-; chm SE Kent Community Health Cncl 1979-81 (memb 1973-81), memb Bd of Visitors HM Prison Aldington (formerly Aldington Detention Centre) 1981-90, dep chm SE Electricity Consultative Cncl 1986-90 (memb 1976-90); *Recreations* travel, talking; *Clubs* New Cavendish; *Style*— Mrs Josephine Winnifrith, MBE, JP; Cliffe Cottage, St Margaret's-At-Cliffe, Kent CT15 6BJ (☎ 0304 853280); Office of Electricity Regulation, 1-4 Lamberts Yard, Tonbridge, Kent TN9 1ER (☎ 0732 351356, fax 0732 355388)

WISEMAN, Dr Martin Jeremy; s of Leslie Wiseman, of Faversham, Kent, and Sonia Wiseman, *née* Linder; *b* 18 April 1953; *Educ* King's Sch Canterbury, Guy's Hosp Med Sch; *m* 5 May 1979, Jane Carol, da of Dennis Bannister, of Bournemouth, Dorset; 1 s (Daniel b 1987), 2 da (Jessica b 1982, Anna b 1985); *Career* res fell metabolic unit Guys Hosp 1981-86, head of Nutrition Unit Dept of Health 1986-; author of publications on diabetes nutrition and kidney disease; memb: Br Diabetic Assoc, Nutrition Soc; MRCP 1977; *Recreations* gastronomy, travel, family, Times crossword; *Style*— Dr Martin Wiseman; Department of Health, London SE1 (☎ 071 407 5522)

WISEMAN, Thomas Alan; s of Thomas Edward Wiseman (d 1959, 5 in descent from Sir Thomas Wiseman, 6 Bt), and Anna Louisa, *née* Allen; hp to fifth cous, Sir John Wiseman, 11 Bt; *b* 8 July 1921; *Educ* Gravesend Co Sch for Boys; *m* 11 Dec 1946, Hildemarie, da of Gustav Domnik, of Allenstein, formerly E Prussia; 1 s (Thomas b 1947), 1 da (Susan b 1949); *Career* Army 1941-46, Staff Quartermaster Sgt RAOC 1946-48; English corr and Eng/German interpreter in Brussels 1949-75, Ships Agent 1975-86, admin offr Forest Prods Terminal Northfleet Terminal Ltd, ret WEF 1986; *Style*— Thomas Wiseman, Esq; 14 Havisham Rd, Chalk, Gravesend, Kent DA12 4UN (☎ 0474 361575)

WITNEY, Kenneth Percy; CVO (1976); s of Rev Thomas Charles Witney (d 1952), of Church of South India Theological Coll, Nazareth, Tamil Nadu, India, and Dr Myfanwy Dyfed, *née* Rees (d 1951); *b* 19 March 1916; *Educ* Eltham Coll Mottingham London, Wadham Coll Oxford (BA, MA); *m* 3 April 1947, Joan Agnes, da of Harold Tait, of 76 Simonside Terr, Newcastle-on-Tyne; 1 s (Nicholas b 1949), 1 da (Jane (Mrs Witney-Smith) b 1948); *Career* private sec to Parly Under-Sec Miny of Home Security 1942-44 (admin asst 1940-42), asst private sec to Home Sec 1945-47; princ: Home Off 1945-47, Colonial Off (police div) 1955-57; asst under-sec of state Home Off 1969-76 (asst sec 1957-69), ret 1976; special advsr to Royal Cmmn on Gambling 1976-78; memb: Tonbridge Civic Soc, Romney Marsh Res Tst; chm Kent Fedn of Amenity Socs 1982-84; fell Royal Archaeological Inst; *Books* The Jutish Forest (1976), The Kingdom of Kent (1982); *Recreations* historical research (dark age and earlly mediaeval); *Style*— Kenneth Witney, Esq, CVO

WOLFSON, (Geoffrey) Mark; MP (C) Sevenoaks 1979-; s of Capt Vladimir Wolfson, RNVR (d 1954); *b* 7 April 1934; *Educ* Eton, Pembroke Coll Cambridge; *m* 1965, Edna Webb, *née* Hardman; 2 s; *Career* warden Brathay Hall Centre Cumbria 1962-65, head Youth Services Industrial Society 1965-69 (head of personnel 1969), dir Hambros Bank 1973-88 (head of personnel 1969); PPS: to Adam Butler as Min State NI 1983-84, as Min for Def Procurement 1984-85, to Ian Stewart as Min for the Armed Servs 1987-88; *Style*— Mark Wolfson, Esq, MP; House of Commons, London SW1A 0AA

WOOD, (Harold) Eric; s of Edwin Wood, of Maidstone, Kent, and Sophia Harriet, *née* Ward; *b* 12 Jan 1918; *Educ* Maidstone Boy's GS; *m* 17 Aug 1941, Dorothy Ellen, da of William Stevens (d 1952), of The George, Mill Hall, Aylesford; 1 s (Christopher Alan b 21 Dec 1944), 2 da (Jennifer Lesley b 5 April 1948, Deborah Anne b 17 Sept 1952); *Career* serv RN 1939-46 (despatches), cmmnd 1941, currently Lt Cdr RNR; local govt serv Kent CC 1946-80 (princ admin offr Co Estates and Valuation Dept 1950-59); fndr memb Chatham Naval Offrs Assoc; St Nicholas PCC Maidstone: sec 1946, sidesman 1946-, churchwarden 1960-69; treas Sutton Deanery Synod Canterbury Diocese; memb: Fin Sub Ctee Canterbury Diocesan Cncl, Cncl for Social Responsibility, Devpt Ctee Maidstone Dist Scout Cncl; former chm Maidstone

Cncl of Churches, clerk Boxley Parish Cncl 1963-; Kent Assoc of Parish Cncls: sec Maidstone Area Ctee 1981-, vice chm 1986-89, chm 1989-; treas Kent Youth Community Voluntary Serv Cncl, exec memb Kent Rural Community Cncl; former memb: Kent Area Manpower Bd, Co Scout Cncl; former memb of Parent Teacher Assoc Ctee: Brunswick House Co Primary Sch Maidstone, Maidstone Boys' GS, Maidstone Girls' GS (sec); pres Maidstone Mid-Kent Div Guides 1982-; chm: Naval Offrs Assoc, Maidstone Sea Cadets, Maidstone Churches' Housing Assoc, Maidstone Scout Gang Show Bd, Age Concern Maidstone 1987- (memb exec ctee 1985-); active in masonic orgns; *Style*— Eric Wood, Esq

WOOD, Col (Basil) Reginald; OBE (mil 1962, MBE mil 1956), TD (1948 and three clasps), DL (Bromley 1967-); s of Capt Basil Harry Wood (d 1947), of Chiswick, London, and Winifred, *née* Blore (d 1976); *b* 18 Dec 1916; *Educ* St Paul's; *m* 8 Aug 1945, Marjory Dorothae, da of Ernest George Webb (d 1949), of Croydon; *Career* cmmnd Princess Louise's Kensington Regt (TA) 1938, served France and Europe 1940-45, Lt-Col cmdg Princess Louise's Kensington Regt 1957-62, Col and Cdr 2 Signal Gp (TA) 1962-67, chm Gtr London TA & VRA 1971-76, Hon Col 31 Signal Regt 1967-77; gen mangr and sec C Hoare & Co Bankers 1972-82 (joined 1934); pres: Princess Louise's Kensington Regimental Assoc 1967-, St John Ambulance London Dist SE Area 1980-87, Bromley Dist Scout Cncl 1984-, SSAFA/FHS London SE 1988-, memb: FANY Advsy Cncl 1976-90, Bromley FPC 1981-85, Mgmnt Ctee Servite Houses 1982-90; chm: Bromley CAB 1981-86 (later pres), Mgmnt Ctee Burrows House Penge for frail elderly and confused elderly) 1981-87; patron: S Bromley Hospice Care, Bromley Y (youth counselling serv), Ravensbourne Light Operatic Soc; Freeman City of London 1975, Hon Freeman Bromley 1989; SBStJ 1983; *Books* The Kensingtons Second World War (co-author, 1951); *Recreations* reading history, watching rugger, tennis, ice skating, athletics; *Clubs* Army and Navy, Wig and Pen; *Style*— Col Reginald Wood, OBE, TD, DL

WOODFORD, Jeremy Patrick; s of John Francis Woodford (d 1978), and Mary Elizabeth Hamilton, *née* Twyford; *b* 16 March 1956; *Educ* Skinners GS Tunbridge Wells, Coll of Law Guildford; *m* 6 March 1982, Sandra Anne, da of Basil Beach; *Career* admitted slr 1981; slr Blok Woodford 1981-85 (articled clerk 1976-81); slr and ptnr: Freeboroughs 1985-87, Bailey & Cogger 1987-; memb Law Soc; *Recreations* cricket, squash; *Clubs* Lamberhurst Cricket; *Style*— Jeremy Woodford, Esq; Elmore Cottage, The Down, Lamberhurst, Kent TN3 8HA (☎ 0892 890563); Bailey & Cogger, 139 High St, Tonbridge, Kent TN9 1DH (☎ 0732 35305, fax 0732 359678)

WOODWARD, Raymond Charles George; s of Philip William Lewis Woodward (d 1968), and Violet Margaret, *née* Carter; *b* 31 March 1916; *Educ* Colfe's GS Lewisham, Northern Poly, Hammersmith Coll of Art; *m* 15 Sept 1962, Marion Rose Ethel, da of The Rev Ben Edward Grigsby (d 1944); 3 s (Simon Philip b 10 Nov 1967, Lee Alexander b 11 March 1971, André Nicol b 2 Aug 1973); *Career* Architects' Dept CWS London 1956-58; architect: Eley and Rickcord London 1958-61, Met Borough of Greenwich 1961-63, Croydon Corp 1963-68; princ RC Woodward and Assocs 1968-, sr ptnr Kennedy Woodward Ptnrship 1986-, ptnr Kennedy and Ptnrs; treas Westerham Men's Club, chm Brasted Boys Football Club; memb RIBA; *Recreations* golf, squash, travelling; *Clubs* Addington Palace golf, Limpsfield Chart Golf; *Style*— Raymond Woodward, Esq; 17 Marwell, Westerham, Kent TN16 1SB (☎ 0959 62880); Millwood, 95 High St, Westerham, Kent TN16 1RE (☎ 0959 62616, fax 0959 65180, car 0860 521428)

WOODWARD, Ronald Charles (Ron); s of Frederick Ronald Woodward (d 1981), of Herne Bay, and Ruth Muriel, *née* Hawkins (d 1984); *b* 24 April 1939; *Educ* Kent Coll Canterbury; *m* 5 Sept 1959 (m dis 1985), Pamela, da of Edward Charles Laws (d 1986); 1 s (Robin Edward b 20 Oct 1965), 2 da (Joanna Mary b 7 Sept 1963, Catherine Gay b 17 Nov 1968); *Career* dir and chm Pharos Insurance Brokers (Herne Bay) Ltd (now Pharos Insurance Brokers Ltd) 1964-; dir: Pharos Insurance Brokers (Life and Pensions) Ltd, Pharos Investment Management Ltd, Pharos Property Sales Ltd; ACII 1964, first recipient Francis Perkins Award 1980, elected Chartered Insur Practitioner 1989; chm BIBA Kent and E Sussex 1981, pres Canterbury and E Kent Insur Inst 1982-83 and 1984-85; memb: PR Ctee BIBA 1981-87, Insur Indust Trg Cncl and Trg Devpt Ctee 1984-, CII Cncl 1985-; patron and tstee local CC, Roller Hockey Club, Speedskating Club; *Recreations* watercolour painting and cartoons, jazz musician (double bass), restoring old cars; *Style*— Ron Woodward, Esq; 17 Beacon Hill, The Downs, Herne Bay, Kent CT6 6AY (☎ 0227 369147); Pharos Goup of Companies, 45-47 William St, Herne Bay, Kent CT6 6NR (☎ 0227 369876, fax 0227 740847)

WOOLDRIDGE, Frank Douglas; s of Frank Wooldridge (d 1956), of London, and Mary Margaret, *née* Douglas (d 1962); *b* 2 March 1916; *Educ* Colfes' Sch London, Coll of Estate Mgmnt; *m* 15 Nov 1941, Elizabeth Julia, da of Engr Capt John Edmund Moloney, CIE (d 1972), of Falmouth, Cornwall; 1 s (John b 1943), 1 da (Anne b 1947); *Career* joined TA 1938, WWII 1939-46, Maj RE served India (SO Grade II Command HQ Agra 1942-45); princ in private practice joined by s 1968; memb Common Cncl City of London 1988-; Freeman City of London 1965, Liveryman Worshipful Co of Cutlers 1966; FRICS 1949 (ARICS 1939); *Recreations* sailing, appreciation of music; *Clubs* City Livery (asst hon sec), Farringdon Ward (past pres), United Wards (memb Governing Body), Royal Soc of St George (cncl memb City of London Branch), REYC, Medway Yacht; *Style*— Frank Wooldridge, Esq; 3 Harton Close, Bromley, Kent (☎ 081 290 1466)

WOOLFORD, Alfred John (Jack); s of Alfred James Woolford (d 1935), of Hartlepool, and Elizabeth, *née* Townley (d 1974); *b* 12 June 1917; *Educ* Henry Smith Sch Hartlepool, Christ's Coll Cambridge (MA), Wadham Coll Oxford (MA); *m* 10 Nov 1945, Mabel Angela, da of Peter O'Hara (d 1933), of Co Cavan; 1 s (John b 31 Oct 1946), 2 da (Elizabeth Ann b 27 Feb 1949, Cynthia Ruth b 17 Aug 1956); *Career* RA 1939-46, Hon Capt RA; staff tutor in history Univ of Oxford Extra-Mural Delegacy 1946-75, lectr in history Sch of Continuing Educn Univ of Kent at Canterbury 1975-78; author of: various reviews published in Scrutiny 1945-46, various articles published by Nat Inst Adult Educn; chm and sec New Dover Gp 1965-76, sec Assoc of Tutors in Adult Educn 1966-68, fndr and organiser of annual confs of amenity socs and local govt 1972-90, treas Canterbury Branch Assoc of Univ Teachers 1976-78, chm Kent Fedn of Amenity Socs 1976-90; *Recreations* music, photography, DIY (baking, brewing, gardening); *Style*— Jack Woolford, Esq; 1066 Green Lane, Temple Ewell, Dover, Kent CT16 3AR (☎ 0304 822871)

WOOTTON, David Hugh; s of James Wootton, and Muriel Wootton; *b* 21 July 1950; *Educ* Bradford GS, Jesus Coll Cambridge; *m* 23 April 1977, Elizabeth Rosemary, da of Peter Knox; 2 s (James b 1979, Christopher b 1985), 2 da (Alexandra b 1978, Sophie b 1981); *Career* currently ptnr Allen & Overy; memb Law Soc 1975; *Clubs* Leander; *Style*— David Wootton, Esq; Allen & Overy, 9 Cheapside, London EC2V 6AD (☎ 071 248 9898, fax 071 236 2192, telex 8812801)

WORBOYS, Annette Isobel (Anne); d of Thomas Edwardes Eyre (d 1963), of New Zealand, and Agnes Hellen, *née* Blair (d 1981); *b* 30 June 1920; *Educ* New Zealand; *m* 20 Sept 1946, Walter Brindy, s of Walter Worboys (d 1966), of IOW; 2 da (Carolyn Lee b 1949, Robin Jillian b 1950); *Career* romantic novelist; author of 18 novels as Annette Eyre, 5 under pseudonym Vicky Maxwell and 6 as Anne Worboys; *books incl:* A Kingdom for the Bold 1986, The Lion of Delos 1974, Every Man a King 1977 (best romantic novel of the year Romantic Novelists Assoc); memb: Soc of Authors, Soc of Women Writers and Journalists, Crimewriters Assoc, Romantic Novelists Assoc (memb ctee), Tunbridge Wells and Dist Writers Circle (fndr memb and past chm), Tonbridge Theatre and Arts Club, Leigh Cons Assoc (former memb ctee); *Recreations* theatre, gardening, travel; *Style*— Mrs Anne Worboys; The White House, Leigh, Tonbridge, Kent TN11 8RH (☎ 0732 83 3355)

WORSDALE, Desmond Slinn (Des); s of Robert Worsdale (d 1952), of Grantham, and Kate Maud, *née* Slinn (d 1949); *b* 22 July 1915; *Educ* Grantham Central Selective, Shenstone Teacher Trg Coll Kidderminster; *m* 5 April 1952, Margaret Joyce, da of Morgan Hopkin Evans (d 1987), of Ammanford; 1 s (Stephen John Morgan b 1958), 1 da (Claire Suzanne b 1963); *Career* army: vol entry 1940, Middle E and Malta 1940, commissioned Haifa 1942, released 1946; Grantham Gas Co 1930-35, Bridlington Gas Co 1935-40, Lt RA 1942-46, dep headmaster comprehensive sch 1963-79 (actg headmaster 1968-69); art gallery exhibition 1989; chm: local scouting troop 1963-73, Cons Party local branch 1974-88, parish cncl 1979-80, Kent Assoc parish cncls Medway 1987-89 (memb 1986-89); parish cncllr 1976-; *Books* Peninsula Round (1982), Parish History (1983), Hoo Saint Werburgh in Old Picture Postcards (1984), Hoo Hundred in Old Postcards (1989); *Recreations* painting, drawing, walking; *Clubs* Strood Cons; *Style*— Des Worsdale, Esq; 18 Elm Ave, Chattenden, Rochester, Kent ME3 8LY (☎ 0634 250843)

WRIGHT, Adela Lucia Lyndon; da of Maj Frederick Edward Gordon Stanford (d 1958), of Carshalton, Surrey, and Peggy Lucy, *née* Chivers (d 1955); *b* 23 Jan 1924; *Educ* St Michaels Sch, Regent St Poly (Dip Arch), Dip Conservation 1980; *m* 2 July 1949, George Broughton Wright, s of Joseph William Wright (d 1960), of Carshalton, Surrey; 1 s (Timothy Lyndon b 1951), 2 da (Hilary Teresa b 1954, Antonia Sophie b 1962); *Career* architectural asst: Historic Bldgs Div Miny of Works 1946-48, Architects Div Oxford CC 1948-49, Hulme Chadwick 1949-52; private practice 1952-75; tech advsr Soc for the Protection of Ancient Bldgs 1980; memb Worshipful Co of Gardeners; ARIBA 1947; *Books* Craft Techniques for Traditional Buildings (1990); *Recreations* archaeology, travelling; *Style*— Mrs Adela Wright; The Walled Garden, 118 Kippington Rd, Sevenoaks, Kent TN13 2LN

WRIGHT, Barbara Janet; da of John Sutherland, of Bredhurst, nr Gillingham, Kent, and Betty Dorothy Gladys, *née* Durrant; *b* 16 March 1955; *Educ* Romford Co HS for Girls, Univ of Sheffield, Chester Coll of Law; *m* 23 Oct 1982, Lynton Wright, s of John Wright (Jack), of Stockport, Cheshire; *Career* admitted slr 1979; slr: Gill Turner and Tucker Maidstone 1977-80, Cripps Harries Hall & Co Tunbridge Wells 1980-82, Cripps Harries Hall & Co Crowborough 1982-84; ptnr: Walkers Tunbridge Wells 1986-87 (slr 1984-86), Thomson Snell & Passmore Tunbridge Wells 1987-; memb Panel Arbitrators of Tunbridge Wells Equitable Friendly Soc 1987-; memb: Tunbridge Wells and Dist Law Soc, Law Soc; *Style*— Mrs Barbara Wright; Thomson Snell & Passmore Solicitors, 3 Lonsdale Gardens, Tunbridge Wells, Kent (☎ 0892

510000, fax 0892 49884, telex 95194)

WRIGHT, David William; s of William Richard Douglas Wright, of Whitstable, Kent, and Doris Jane, *née* Arnold; *b* 2 May 1942; *Educ* Kent Coll Canterbury, Univ of Edinburgh (MA); *m* 23 Sept 1967, Barbara Rita, da of Gerald Gardner (d 1973); 1 s (Oliver b 1971), 2 da (Annabel b 1973, Eleanor b 1978); *Career* called to the Bar Lincolns Inn; posts in various cos 1968-76; co sec Coates Bros plc 1979-84, First Leisure Corp plc 1984-; vice pres Royal Tunbridge Wells Civic Soc; Freeman City of London 1983, Liveryman Worshipful Co of Spectaclemakers 1983; FCIS 1977; *Recreations* squash, tennis, theatre; *Style—* David Wright, Esq; Hollin House, Court Rd, Tunbridge Wells, Kent TN4 8EF (☎ 0892 32 943); 7 Soho St, London W1V 5FA (☎ 071 437 9727, fax 071 439 0088)

WRIGHT, Gerald; s of William Arthur Reginald Wright (d 1967), of Bexleyheath, Kent, and Olive Annie Neal Wright; *b* 9 Sept 1935; *Educ* Monmouth Sch, Queens' Coll Cambridge (MA); *m* 1959, Elizabeth Ann, da of Dr William Edward Harris (d 1974), of Llandaff; 3 s (Jeremy, Mathew, William); *Career* Nat Serv 2 Lt Welch Regt 1954-56; dir: Lintas London 1972-73, chm Lintas Scandinavia 1973-74, dep chm and md Lintas London 1974-80, md Thresher and Co Ltd 1980-81, mktg dir (UK) Whitbread & Co 1981-82 (chm Nat Sales Div) 1982-83; chm and chief exec Lintas London 1983-89, regnl dir Germany Austria and Switzerland Lintas Worldwide 1989-; *Recreations* reading, opera, walking, jogging, rugby, cricket; *Clubs* Reform, Solus; *Style—* Gerald Wright, Esq; 25 Crown Lane, Chislehurst, Kent (☎ 081 467 7918); Lintas Worldwide, 84 Eccleston Square, London SW1; Lintas Worldwide Frankfurt, Zeppellin Allee 77, Frankfurt am Main, Germany

WRIGHT, Hugh Ronald; s of Ronald Claude Wright (d 1970), of Beckenham, Kent, and Ellen Emma, *née* Lewis (d 1987); *b* 24 Dec 1943; *Educ* Dulwich, ChCh Oxford (MA); *m* 16 Aug 1965, Beryl Frances, da of John Norman Samuel Burnby (d 1959), of W Wickham, Kent; 2 s (Howard b 1969, Harvey b 1972), 1 da (Virginia b 1975); *Career* ptnr Brookes and Martin Chartered Patent Agents of London Tunbridge Wells and Munich; Tunbridge Wells Borough Cncl: cncllr 1983-, chm Tourism Gp, vice chm Cleaner Borough Sub Ctee; govr Girls GS Tunbridge Wells; fell: Chartered Inst of Patent Agents 1969, Euro Inst of Patent Attornies 1978; *Recreations* architecture, classic British sports cars, organic vegetable growing; *Style—* Hugh Wright, Esq; Pippin House, 36 Earl's Rd, Tunbridge Wells, Kent TN4 8EE (☎ 0892 538864); 1 Boyne Park, Tunbridge Wells, Kent TN4 8EL (☎ 0892 510600, fax 0892 510666, telex 957078)

WRIGHT, John Harold; s of Cyril Walter Wright, and Emily Mary, *née* Laming; *b* 23 Oct 1943; *Educ* Canterbury Tech Sch, Univ of Kent (BA); *m* 11 April 1963, Julia Diane, da of George Foster Cook (d 1973), of Broadstairs, Kent; 1 s (Phillip John b 1965), 2 da (Jacqueline Ann b 1963, Joanna Kate b 1972); *Career* police cadet Kent Police 1959-62; Kent Constabulary: Police Constable Dover 1962-67, Sgt Rochester Traffic 1967-71, Inspr Chatham and Ramsgate 1971-73, memb of directing staff; Univ Bramshill Staff Coll 1979-81 (scholarship 1973-76); Supt Police Cdr: Canterbury 1986-89, Margate 1989-; author of various articles on police incl implications of membership of EEC and implications of Euro Convention on Human Rights; chm Int Police Assoc Thanet Branch, vice chm Kent Police Supt's Assoc; *Recreations* travelling, reading, golf; *Clubs* North Ireland Golf; *Style—* John Wright, Esq; Wyndrush, Dumpton Gap Rd, Broadstairs, Kent CT10 1SA (☎ 0843 69975); Police Station, Margate, Kent (☎ 0843 225566)

WRIGHT, John Keith; JP (Dover and E Kent 1983); s of James Henry Wright (d 1965), and Elsie May Willis (d 1984); *b* 30 May 1928; *Educ* Tiffins, King's Coll Cambridge, Yale Univ; *m* 1958, Thérèse Marie Claire, da of René Aubenas (d 1977), of Paris; *Career* OEEC (Paris) 1951-56, UKAEA 1956-61, MOD 1961-66, FCO 1966-71, under sec ODA FCO 1971-84; econ and fin conslt; dir Sadler's Wells (Trading) 1983-; cncl memb: Queen Elizabeth Coll London 1982-85, King's Coll London 1984-; tstee Thomson Fndn 1986-, memb Bd of Visitors Canterbury Prison 1987-; *Recreations* econ and mil history, music, amateur radio; *Clubs* Athenaeum, Beefsteak; *Style—* John Wright, Esq, JP; Laurie House, Airlie Gardens, London W8 7AW; Bowling Corner, Sandwich, Kent

WRIGHT, Miles Francis Melville; s of Montague Francis Melville Wright (d 1968), and Marjorie Isobel, *née* Brook (d 1968); *b* 3 Dec 1943; *Educ* Ampleforth, ChCh Oxford (MA); *Career* dir American International Underwriters (UK) Ltd 1982-84 (asst md 1984-87), md Polwring Underwriting Agency at Lloyds 1988-, Active Underwriter Syndicate 1098 Lloyds 1988-; Freeman: Worshipful Co of Glaziers, Worshipful Co of Insurers; *Recreations* cricket, tennis, shooting, gardening; *Clubs* Naval and Military, MCC, I Zingari; *Style—* Miles Wright, Esq; The Barracks, Cranbrook, Kent TN17 2LG (☎ 0580 712209); 10 Philpot Lane, London EC3M 8AA; Lloyds, 1 Lime St, London EC3 (☎ 071 626 8201/623 7100 ext 3634, fax 071 283 2381, telex 9419440)

WRIGHT, Neville Clarkson; s of Percival Albert Wright, of Petts Wood, Kent (d 1965), and Phyllis Marjorie, *née* Clarkson (d 1984); *b* 21 Feb 1929; *Educ* Aldenham, Queens' Coll Cambridge (MA); *m* 18 April 1959, Jennifer Margaret, da of Geoffrey William Tookey, QC, of Beckenham, Kent (d 1976); 1 s (Andrew b 1962), 2 da (Jane b 1960, Victoria b 1964); *Career* 2 Lt RA; slr in private practice; ptnr Clarkson Wright and Jakes (Orpington), dir Loxleys KJ Holdings Ltd; NP; former pres Petts Wood Operatic Soc; memb: The Law Soc, The Prov Notaries Soc; *Clubs* Hawks (Cambridge), West Kent Golf, Bromley Hockey (former pres); *Style—* Neville C Wright, Esq; Vine Cottage, Hollybush Lane, Sevenoaks, Kent TN13 3UJ; Villa San Miguel, Binisafua, Menorca; Clarkson Wright and Jakes, Valiant House, 12 Knoll Rise, Orpington, Kent BR6 0PG (☎ 0689 871621, fax 0689 878537)

WRIGHT, Cncllr (Mary) Patricia; da of Sir Roy Matthews, CBE (d 1981), of Wadhurst, E Sussex, and Violet Mary, *née* Wilkinson (d 1982); *b* 10 May 1932; *Educ* Queenswood Sch Hatfield Herts, Univ of London (BA); *m* 25 April 1959, Richard Mounsteven Wright, s of Richard Oliver Wright (d 1947); 2 da (Katherine Mary b 1960, Penelope Diana b 1962); *Career* articled and asst agent to Lord Abergavenny's Eridge Estate 1954-56, asst surveyor and land agent Hughes & Wilbraham Exeter 1956-58, negotiator and surveyor Allsop & Co London 1958-59, teacher of history and econs Tunbridge Wells GS 1967-79; author of 15 published books and winner of a literary prize, contrib to History Today; co cncllr E Sussex 1981- (chm Property Environment Libraries and Social Serv Ctees), dist cncllr Wealden DC 1983-89; memb: Dungeness Nuclear Local Liaison Ctee, E Sussex Drugs Advsy Ctee; vice chm Conservators of Ashdown Forest; involved in other local orgns incl: Sussex Police Authy, High Weald, Hastings Urban Conservation Project; ARICS 1955, QALAS 1956; *Books* Conflict on the Nile (1959), Womans's Estate (1959), Space of the Heart (1977), Journey into Fire (1978), Shadow of the Rock (1979), Blind Chance (1980), Storm Harvest (1980), This My City (1981), Forbidden Places (1981), State of Fear (1986), While Paris Danced (1987), I Am England (1987), That Near and Distant Place (1988), Heartsearch (1989), Powers of Darkness (1990); *Recreations* badminton, reading, prairie bashing in the churchyard; *Style—* Cncllr Patricia Wright; Whitehill House, Frant, nr Tunbridge Wells, Kent TN3 9DX (☎ 089 275312)

WRIGHT, Thomas William John; s of John William Richard Wright (d 1977), of Canterbury, Kent, and Jane Elizabeth, *née* Nash (d 1978); *b* 5 Aug 1928; *Educ* Kent Coll, Simon Langton Sch Canterbury, Wye Coll London (BSc); *m* 4 Jan 1956, Shirley Evelyn, da of Henry Parkinson (d 1943), of Beckenham, Kent; 2 da (Geraldine b 1959, Jane b 1962); *Career* garden estate mgmnt conslt and int lectr; tea plantation mangr Kenya and govt horticultural res offr UK 1953-58, mangr Nursery and Landscape Co Devon 1956-60; lectr Pershore Coll 1962-68, sr lectr in landscape horticulture Wye Coll London 1968-90; visiting prof Univs of Beijing and Shanghai China, main lectr Univ of Kent's Summer Acad on Kent's Historic Gdns; Veitch Memorial Medal (RHS) 1989; tstee: Landscape Design Tst, Kent Gardens Tst, Cobham Hall Heritage Tst, Fortescue Gardens Tst; memb: Gdns Ctee HHA, Gdns Panel Nat Tst, Shows Ctee RHS; ALI 1978, FIHort 1986; *Books* The Gardens of Kent, Sussex and Surrey (No 4 in Batsford Series, 1978), Large Gardens and Parks, Management and Design (1982); *Recreations* travel, natural history, gardening, music; *Style—* Thomas Wright, Esq; Cumberland House, Chilham, Canterbury, Kent (☎ 0227 730 246)

WYATT, Arthur Powell; s of Dr Henry George Wyatt (ka 1938), and Edith Maud, *née* Holden (d 1972); *b* 14 Oct 1932; *Educ* Taunton Sch, Eltham Coll, Bart's Med Sch (MB BS); *m* 20 Aug 1955, Margaret Helen, da of Rev W H Cox (d 1988); 4 s (John b 1958, Robert b 1961, David b and d 1964, Andrew b 1966); *Career* lectr in surgery Bart's 1961-63, sr registrar in surgery KCH 1964-67, post graduate res surgn Univ of California San Francisco 1965-66, conslt surgn Greenwich Health Dist 1967-; pres: RSM Surgery Section 1989-90, Eltham Combined Div St Johns Ambulance; memb Court of Examiners RCS, past pres W Kent Medico Chirurgical Soc; memb: BMA, Vascular Surgery Soc, Br Soc Gastroenterol; fell Assoc of Surgns of GB and I, FRCS, FICS; *Recreations* orchid growing, travel, skiing; *Clubs* Woolwich Rotary, Huntarian Society; *Style—* Arthur Wyatt, Esq; The Cottage, 72 Camden Park Rd, Chislehurst, Kent BR7 5HF (☎ 081 467 9477); The Blackheath AMI Hospital, 40-42 Lee Terrace, Blackheath, London SE3 9UD (☎ 081 318 7722)

WYNESS, James Alexander Davidson; s of Dr James Alexander Davidson Wyness (d 1984), of Dyce, Aberdeen, and Millicent Margaret, *née* Beaton; *b* 27 Aug 1937; *Educ* Stockport GS, Emmanuel Coll Cambridge (MA, LLB); *m* 18 June 1966, Josephine Margaret, da of Lt-Col Edward Stow Willard Worsdell, MBE, TD, of Eynsford, Kent; 3 da (Rachel b 28 July 1968, Emily b 3 Feb 1971, Jeannie b 27 Aug 1974); *Career* Nat Serv 2 Lt RA; slr; articled clerk AF & RW Tweedie 1964-66; Linklaters & Paines 1966-: ptnr 1970-87, managing ptnr 1987-; non exec dir Bowthorpe Holdings plc 1979-; vice pres and memb Gen Ctee Saracens FC RFU (Capt Middx and London Div) 1962-65); memb Worshipful Co of City of London Slrs; memb Law Soc; *Recreations* visiting France, growing vegetables, rugby football, reading; *Style—* James Wyness, Esq; Linklaters & Paines, Barrington House, 59-67 Gresham St, London EC2V 7JA (☎ 071 606 7080)

WYNN, Carol Frances; da of William Henry Nugent, of Ludlow, Shrops, and Renée Mabel, *née* Simons; *b* 4 Aug 1949; *Educ* Ludlow Girls' HS; *m* 11 Aug 1973, Sqdn Ldr David Ian Wynn, s of Douglas Ralph Wynn, of Gloucester; 1 s

(Rhys David b 22 Sept 1981), 2 da (Kerri Jane b 7 April 1976, Rhiann Gayle b 22 Dec 1977 d 1980); *Career* offr RAF 1968-75, served Cyprus 1970-72 and 1977-80, served Belize CA 1985-87; professional appeals mangr Barnardo's W Kent 1988-; travelled extensively with rep sport incl Combined Servs; grade 2 official track and field Amateur Athletics Assoc; *Recreations* playing and watching sport; *Clubs* Cambridge Harriers; *Style—* Mrs Carol Wynn; 10 Mouchotte Close, Biggin Hill, Westerham, Kent TN16 3ES (☎ 0959 76282)

Y, Z

YATES, Nicholas; s of Peter Yates, of 4 Downs Bridge Rd, Beckenham, Kent, and Ellen, *née* McDermott; *b* 23 May 1931; *Educ* Langley Park Sch for Boys; *Career* badminton player; singles winner Dutch and Canadian Open 1981, singles winner German Open 1985, singles bronze and team gold winner Cwlth Games 1986 (singles silver and doubles silver winner 1982), singles winner Japan Open 1988, former Eng no 1, holder of 107 caps; *Recreations* golf, computers; *Clubs* Park Langley Badminton, Sundridge Park Golf; *Style*— Nicholas Yates, Esq

YEABSLEY, Lady; Hilda Maude; da of Wilmot C M Willson; *m* 1923, Sir Richard Ernest Yeabsley, CBE (d 1983); 1 da; *Style*— Lady Yeabsley; Ingles Court Hotel, Ingles Rd, Folkestone, Kent CT20 2SN

YEANDLE, Geoffrey Ernest Lascelles; s of Rev Walter Harold Yeandle (d 1952), of Bearsted Vicarage, Maidstone, Kent, and Irene Mary, *née* Snow (d 1972); *b* 12 Oct 1931; *Educ* Maidstone GS; *m* 14 Sept 1957, June Pamela, da of Nathaniel Mendess (d 1957); 2 s (Mark b 1962, Simon b 1966); *Career* Nat Serv 1950-52, cmmnd RA Lt, TA 1952-58, cmmnd Capt Kent Yeo; sales dir Warner Fabrics plc 1972-, chm West End Furnishing Fabrics Assoc 1980-84; vice chm Borden Parish Cncl 1981-; Freeman City of London 1980, Liveryman Worshipful Co of Weavers 1980; MIEK, FBIM, FRSA; *Recreations* shooting, cricket, photography; *Style*— Geoffrey Yeandle, Esq; The Thatched Cottage, Chestnut Wood, Borden, Sittingbourne, Kent (☎ 0795 842343); Warner Fabrics plc, 7-11 Noel St, London W1V 4AL (☎ 071 439 2411)

YERBURGH, Lt-Col John Rochfort; s of Canon Oswald Rochfort Yerburgh (d 1966), and Cicely Joan, *née* Savile (d 1981); *b* 14 Sept 1931; *Educ* Marlborough, RMA Sandhurst, RMCS Shrivenham; *m* 17 Aug 1963, Gillian Elizabeth, da of Derek Plint Clifford, of Hartlip Place, Sittingbourne, Kent; 1 s (Toby b 9 Oct 1965), 1 da (Sophia b 8 Jan 1967); *Career* cmmnd RE 1952 C RE NI 1972-74, ret 1983; High Sheriff of Kent 1988-89; memb for Swale Central Kent CC 1984, vice chm Gillingham Cons Assoc 1987; Freeman City of London 1989; *Recreations* travel, tennis; *Clubs* Turf; *Style*— Lt-Col John Yerburgh; Hartlip Place, Sittingbourne, Kent ME9 7TR (☎ 0795 842 583); West Heath, Ashgrove Rd, Sevenoaks, Kent (☎ 0732 452 541)

YOUNG, Charles Frederick James; s of James Charles Frederick Young (d 1917), of Richmond, Surrey, and Eleanor Elizabeth, *née* Evans; *b* 5 Sept 1912; *m* 26 Dec 1936, Rose Elizabeth, da of Arthur George Walton; 4 da (Margaret Rose b 1938, Eleanor Ann b 1939, Patricia Ann b 1941, Wendy Elizabeth 1942); *Career* co sec and dir 1943-51; chm: Area Cncl Nat Fedn of Retirement Pensions Assoc, Lab Gp Kent CC; co cncllr 1981-, dist cncllr 1983-87; memb Fabian Soc; *Style*— Charles Young, Esq; 26 Marlborough Rd, Margate, Kent CT9 5SU (☎ 0843 226182); Members Suite, County Hall, Maidstone, Kent

YOUNG, Hon Mrs (Gillian Margaret); *née* Campbell; da of late 2 Baron Colgrain; *b* 1925; *m* 1951, Peter Scott Young (d 1988); 2 s, 2 da; *Style*— The Hon Mrs Young; Orchard House, Broom Lane, Langton Green, Tunbridge Wells, Kent TN3 0RA

YOUNG, John Adrian Emile; s of John Archibald Campbell Young (d 1979), of Plaxtol, Kent, and Irene Eugenie, *née* Bouvier (d 1976); *b* 28 July 1934; *Educ* Cranbrook Sch Kent, Univ of London (LLB); *m* 20 June 1959, Yvonne Lalage Elizabeth, da of John Digby Hyde Bankes (d 1976), of Twitton House, Otford, Kent; 3 s (Charles b 1961, Paul b 1962, Simon b 1965), 1 da (Anna b 1963); *Career* ptnr Cameron Markby Hewitt Slrs 1965-; nat chm Young Slrs Gp 1965-66, pres Association Internationale des Jeunes Avocats 1968-69, cncl memb Int Bar Assoc 1983-; choirmaster/organist of local church; Master City of London Slrs Co 1989-90 (Freeman 1967); memb Law Soc 1958 (asst sec 1958-64, cncl memb 1971-); *Recreations* music, gardening, foreign travel; *Style*— John Young, Esq; Stonewold House, Plaxtol, Kent (☎ 0732 810 289); Cameron Markby Hewitt, Sceptre Court, 40 Tower Hill, London EC3N 4BB (☎ 071 702 2345, fax 071 702 2303, telex 925779)

YOUNG, Sir John Kenyon Roe; 6 Bt (UK 1821), of Bailieborough Castle, Co Cavan; s of Sir John William Roe Young, 5 Bt (d 1981), by his 1 w, Joan Minnie Agnes, *née* Aldous (d 1958); *b* 23 April 1947; *Educ* Hurn Court Sch, Christchurch, Napier Coll; *m* 1977, Frances Elise, only da of W R Thompson; 1 s, 1 da (Tamara Elizabeth Eve b 9 Nov 1986); *Heir* s, Richard Christopher Roe Young, b 14 July 1983; *Career* former hydrographic surveyor; sr buyer; *Recreations* golf; *Style*— Sir John Young, Bt; Bolingey, 159 Chatham Rd, Maidstone, Kent ME14 2ND

YOUNG, (Roderic) Neil; JP; s of Frederick Hugh Young, OBE (d 1969), of The Gables, Woodhurst Lane, Oxted, Surrey, and Stella Mary, *née* Robinson; *b* 29 May 1933; *Educ* Eton, Trinity Coll Cambridge (MA); *m* 16 June 1962, Gillian Margaret, da of Col William Alexander Salmon, OBE, of Balcombe Place, Balcombe, W Sussex; 2 s (Peter b 1964, Rupert b 1969), 1 da (Jennifer b 1966); *Career* 2 Lt Queens Own Royal W Kent Regt 1952; dir: Murray Johnstone Ltd 1969-70, Kleinwort Benson Ltd 1972-86, Globe Investment Trust plc 1973-, Brunner Investment Trust plc 1975-, Merchants Trust plc 1975-85, Kleinwort Grievson Investment Management Ltd 1986-88, Aberdeen Petroleum plc 1988-; dep chm Assoc of Investmt Tst Cos 1987-; memb Advsy Ctee Greenwich Hosp, almoner Christ's Hosp; alderman and JP City of London; Liveryman and memb of Court Worshipful Co of Gunmakers, Liveryman Worshipful Co of CAs; FCA 1969 (ACA 1959); *Recreations* shooting, gardening, DIY, golf, tennis; *Style*— Neil Young, Esq, JP; Pembury Hall, Pembury, Kent TN2 4AT (☎ 089 282 2971)

YOUNG, Philip Martin; y s of Bertram Allen (Bay) Young (d 1989), of Sevenoaks, and Betty, *née* Mostyn Hoops; *b* 23 Jan 1945; *Educ* Tonbridge, Guy's Hosp Med Sch; *Career* Peat Marwick Mitchell London and Geneva 1965-77, Twinlock Group plc 1977-78, commercial and fin dir and acting md Carson Office Firniture Ltd 1977-78; co sec and commercial mangr: Hayward Bros (wines) Ltd 1978-80, Tunnel Avebe Starches Ltd 1982-; commercial and fin dir Invicta House Chips Ltd 1980-81; chm West Malling Parish Cncl 1984-88; *Recreations* work; *Style*— Philip Young, Esq; 114 St Leonards St, West Malling, Kent ME19 6PD; Avebe House, Otterham Quay, Upchurch, Kent ME8 7UU (☎ 0634 373551, fax 0634 378542, telex 965005 TUNAVB G)

ZAMOYSKI, Count Zdzisz; s of late Count (Stefan) Zamoyski, *chef de famille* in UK; er bro of Count Adam Zamoyski, *qv*; *Style*— Count Zdzisz Zamoyski; Ashfield House, The Horns, Hawkhurst, Kent

ABBREVIATIONS

A

AA Automobile Association; Anti-Aircraft; Architectural Association
AAAS American Association for the Advancement of Science
AACCA Associate of Association of Certified & Corporate Accountants
AACI Accredited Appraiser, Canadian Institute
AADipl Diploma, Architectural Association
A&AEE Aeroplane and Armament Experimental Association
AAF Auxiliary Air Force
AAFCE Allied Air Forces Central Europe
AAG Assistant Adjutant-General
AAGBI Associate, Anaesthetists of GB and Ireland
AAI Association of Chartered Auctioneers' and Estate Agents' Institute
AALPA Associate of Incorporated Auctioneers & Landed Property Agents
AAM Association of Assistant Mistresses in Secondary Schools
AAMC Australian Army Medical Corps
AA&QMG Assistant Adjutant & Quarter-Master-General
AASA Associate of Australian Society of Accountants
AASC Australian Army Service Corps
AASF Advanced Air Striking Force
AB Bachelor of Arts (USA); Able-bodied Seaman
ABA Associate of British Archaeological Association; Antiquarian Booksellers' Association; Amateur Boxing Association
ABIBA Associate of the British Institute of Brokers Association
ABIM Associate of British Institute of Management
ABOD Advance Base Ordnance Depot
ABPS Associate of the British Psychological Society
ABRC Advisory Board of Research Councils
ABTA Association of British Travel Agents
AC Companion of the Order of Australia
ACA Associate of the Institute of Chartered Accountants
Acad Academy
ACARD Advisory Council for Applied Research and Development
ACAS Advisory, Conciliation and Arbitration Service
ACBSI Associate, Chartered Building Societies Institute
ACC Association of County Councils
ACCA Associate, Association of Certified Accountants
ACCM Advisory Council for the Church's Ministry
ACCS Associate of the Corporation of Secretaries
AcDipEd Academic Diploma in Education
ACDS Assistant Chief of Defence Staff
ACE Association of Consulting Engineers; Member, Association of Conference Executives
ACF Army Cadet Force
ACG Assistant Chaplain General
ACGI Associate of City & Guilds of London Institute
ACGS Assistant Chief of General Staff
ACIArb Associate, Chartered Institute of Arbitrators
ACIB Associate, Chartered Institute of Bankers
ACII Associate of Chartered Insurance Institute
ACIS Associate of Chartered Institute of Secretaries
ACMA Associate, Institute of Cost and Management Accountants
ACNS Assistant Chief of Naval Staff
ACommA Associate, Society of Commercial Accountants
ACORD Advisory Committee on Research and Development
ACOS Assistant Chief of Staff
ACOST Advisory Council on Science and Technology
ACP Association of Clinical Pathologists; Associate, College of Preceptors
ACPO Association of Chief of Police Officers
ACRE Action with Rural Communities in England
ACS American Chemical Society
ACSEA Allied Command SE Asia
ACT Australian Capital Territory; Australian College of Theology; Association of Corporate Treasurers
Actg Acting
ACTT Association of Cinematograph, Television and Allied Technicians
ACVO Assistant Chief Veterinary Officer
ACWA Associate of Institute of Cost and Works Accountants
AD Corps Army Dental Corps
ADAS Agricultural Development and Advisory Service (MAFF)
ADC Aide-de-Camp
ADC(P) Personal Aide-de-Camp to HM The Queen
ADGB Air Defence of Great Britain
ADGMS Assistant Director-General of Medical Services
Adj Adjutant
Adj-Gen Adjutant-General
Adm Admiral
Admin Administration; Administrative; Administrator
ADMS Assistant Director of Medical Services
Admty Admiralty
ADNI Assistant Director of Naval Intelligence
ADOS Assistant Director of Ordnance Service
ADP Automatic Data Processing
ADPR Assistant Director Public Relations
ADS&T Assistant Director of Supplies and Transport
Adv-Gen Advocate-General
Advsr Adviser
Advsy Advisory
ADVS Assistant Director of Veterinary Services
AE Air Efficiency Award (see AEA)
AEA Air Efficiency Award; Atomic Energy Authority
AEAF Allied Expeditionary Air Force
AEC Army Educational Corps (Now RAEC); Agricultural Executive Committee
AED Air Efficiency Decoration
AEF Amalgamated Union of Engineering and Foundry Workers
AEM Air Efficiency Medal
AER Army Emergency Reserve
AERE Atomic Energy Research Establishment
AEU Amalgamated Engineering Union
AF Air Force
AFAIM Associate Fellow of the Australian Institute of Management
AFC Air Force Cross; Association Football Club
AFCENT Allied Forces Central Europe
Affrs Affairs
AFHQ Allied Force Headquarters
AFI Associate of the Faculty of Insurance
AFIMA Associate Fellow, Institute of Mathematics and its applications
AFM Air Force Medal
AFOM Associate, Faculty of Occupational Medicine
AFRAeS Associate Fellow of the Royal Aeronautical Society
AFRC Agricultural and Food Research Council

AFS	Auxiliary Fire Service
AFV	Armoured Fighting Vehicles
AG	Attorney-General
Agent-Gen	Agent-General
AGI	Artistes Graphiques Internationales
AGRA	Association of Genealogists and Record Agents
Agric	Agriculture, Agricultural
AHA	Area Health Authority
AHQ	Army Head Quarters
AHSM	Associate, Institute of Health Services Management
AIA	American Institute of Architects; Associate, Institute of Actuaries: Association of International Artists
AIAA	Associate of the Institute of Administrative Accountants
AIAC	Associate of the Institute of Company Accountants
AIB	Associate of Institute of Bankers
AIBD	Associate, Institute of British Decorators
AICA	Associate Member Commonwealth Institute of Accountants
AICE	Associate, Institute of Civil Engineers
AIChor	Associate of the Institute of Choreography
AICS	Associate of the Institute of Chartered Shipbuilders
AICTA	Associate, Imperial College of Tropical Medicine
AIEE	Associate of the Institution of Electrical Engineers
AIF	Australian Imperial Forces
AIG	Adjutant-Inspector-General
AIIA	Associate of the Institute of Industrial Administration
AIL	Associate, Institute of Linguists
AIM	Associate of the Institution of Metallurgists
AIMarE	Associate of the Institute of Marine Engineers
AIMSW	Associate, Institute of Medical Social Workers
AINA	Associate of the Institute of Naval Architects
AInstM	Associate Member of the Institute of Marketing
AInstP	Associate of the Institute of Physics
AInstT	Associate, Institute of Taxation
AIPM	Associate of the Institute of Personnel Management
AIPR	Associate, Institute of Public Relations
Air Cdre	Air Commodore
AIT	Associate, Institute of Taxation
AIYL	Association of International Young Lawyers
aka	Also known as
AKC	Associate, King's College London
ALA	Associate, Library Association
ALAS	Associate Member of Chartered Land Agents' Society
ALFSEA	Allied Land Forces South East Asia
ALI	Argyll Light Infantry; Associate, Landscape Institute
ALLC	Association for Literary and Linguistic Computing
Alta	Alberta (Canada)
AM	Member of the Order of Australia; Albert Medal; Master of the Arts (USA); Alpes Maritimes
AMA	Associate, Museum Association; Association of Metropolitan Authorities
Ambass	Ambassador
AMBIM	Associate Member of the British Institute of Management
AMCT	Associate, Manchester College of Technology
AMDEA	Associate of Manufacturers of Domestic and Electrical Appliances
AMEC	Association of Management Education for Clinicians
AMEME	Association of Mining Electrical and Mechanical Engineers
AMF	Australian Military Forces
AMGOT	Allied Military Government Occupied Territory
AMIBE	Associate Member of the Institution of British Engineers
AMICE	Associate Member of the Institution of Civil Engineers
AMIChemE	Associate Member of the Institution of Chemical Engineers
AMIED	Associate Member of the Institution of Engineering Designers
AMIEE	Associate Member of the Institution of Electrical Engineers
AMIMechE	Associate Member of the Institution of Mechanical Engineers
AMIMinE	Associate Member of the Institution of Mining Engineers
AMInstNA	Associate Member of the Institution of Naval Architects
AMIPE	Associate Member of the Institution of Production Engineers
AMIStructE	Associate Member, Institute of Structural Engineers
AMP	Air Ministry Personnel; (Harvard Business School) Advanced Management Programme
AMPC	Auxiliary Military Pioneer Corps
AMRAes	Associate Member, Royal Aeronautical Society
AMS	Army Medical Service; Assistant Military Secretary
AMSIA	Associate Member, Society of Investment Analysts
AMTPI	Associate of the Town Planning Institution
ANU	Australian National University
AO	Air Officer; Officer of the Order of Australia
AOA	Air Officer in Charge in Administration
AOC	Air Officer Commanding
AOC-in-C	Air Officer Commanding-in-Chief
AOD	Army Ordnance Department
AOEng	Air Officer Engineering
AOER	Army Officers' Emergency Reserve
AOM	Air Officer Maintenance
APA	American Psychiatric Association
APEX	Association of Professional, Executive, Clerical and Computer Staffs
APM	Assistant Provost Marshal
Appt	Appointment
APRA	Association of Political Risks Analysts
APS	American Physical Society
AQ	Administration and Quartering
AQMG	Assistant Quarter-Master General
ARA	Associate of the Royal Academy of the Arts
ARAD	Associate, Royal Academy of Dancing
ARAeS	Associate of the Royal Aeronautical Society
ARAM	Associate of the Royal Academy of Music
ARBA	Associate of the Royal Society of British Artists
ARBS	Associate of the Royal Society of British Sculptors
ARC	Agricultural Research Council
ARCA	Associate of Royal College of Art
ARCA (Lond)	Associate of the Royal Academy of Arts
ARCM	Associate of the Royal College of Music
ARCO	Associate of the Royal College of Organists
ARCS	Associate, Royal College of Science
ARCST	Associate, Royal College of Science and Technology
ARCUK	Architects' Registration Council of the UK
ARCVS	Associate of the Royal College of Veterinary Surgeons
ARE	Associate, Royal Society of Painters-Etchers and Engravers
ARELS	Association of Recognised English Language Schools
ARIAS	Associate, Royal Incorporation of Architects in Scotland
ARIBA	Associate of the Royal Institute of British Architects

ARIC	Associate of the Royal Institute of Chemistry
ARICS	Associate of the Royal Institution of Chartered Surveyors
ARINA	Associate of the Royal Institution of Naval Architects
ARMCM	Associate, Royal Manchester College of Music
Armd	Armoured
ARP	Air Raid Precautions
ARPS	Associate of the Royal Photographic Society
ARRC	Associate of the Royal Red Cross
ARSA	Associate of the Royal Scottish Academy
ARSM	Associate of the Royal School of Mines
ARTC	Associate of the Royal Technical College
ARWS	Associate of the Royal Society of Painters in Water Colours
ASA	Associate Member of the Society of Actuaries; Australian Society of Accountants; Army Sailing Association
ASAA	Associate of the Society of Incorporated Accountants and Auditors
ASC	Army Service Corps
ASCAP	American Society of Composers, Authors and Publishers
ASD	Armament Supply Department
ASF	Associate of the Institute of Shipping and Forwarding Agents
A&SH	Argyll and Sutherland Highlanders
ASIA	Associate, Society of Investment Analysts
ASIAD	Associate, Society of Industrial Artists and Designers
ASLEF	Associated Society of Locomotive Engineers and Fireman
ASLIB	Association of Special Libraries and Information Bureaux
ASME	American Society of Mechanical Engineers; Association for Study of Medical Education
ASO	Air Staff Officer
assas	assassinated
Assoc	Association; Associate; Associated
Assoc InstT	Associate of the Institute of Transport
Asst	Assistant
Assur	Assurance
ASTMS	Association of Scientific, Technical and Managerial Staff
ASVO	Association of State Veterinary Officers
ATA	Air Transport Auxiliary
ATAF	Allied Tactical Air Force
ATC	Air Training Corps
ATD	Art Teachers' Diploma
ATI	Associate, Textile Institute
ATII	Associate Member, Institute of Taxation
ATO	Ammunitions Technical Officer
ATS	Auxiliary Territorial Service
AUEW	Amalgamated Union of Engineering Workers
Aust	Australian, Australia
AUT	Association of University Teachers
Authy	Authority
Aux	Auxiliary
Ave	Avenue
AVR	Army Volunteer Reserve
AWRE	Atomic Weapons Research Establishment
AWS	Graduate of Air Warfare Course

B

b	Born
BA	Bachelor of Arts; British Airways
BAAL	British Association for Applied Linguistics
BAAS	British Association for the Advancement of Science
BAC	British Aircraft Corporation
BADA	British Antique Dealers Association
BAFO	British Air Forces Occupation
BAFSEA	British Air Forces South East Asia
BAFTA	British Academy of Film and Television Arts
BAI	Baccalarius in Arte Ingeniaria
BAIE	British Association of Industrial Editors
BALPA	British Airline Pilots Association
BAO	Bachelor of Obstetrics
BAOMS	British Association of Oral and Maxillo-Facial Surgeons
BAOR	British Army of the Rhine
BARC	British Automobile Racing Club
BArch	Bachelor of Architecture
Barr	Barrister
Bart's	St Bartholomew's Hospital
BAS	Bachelor in Agricultural Science
BASc	Bachelor of Applied Science
Batty	Battery
BAUA	Business Aviation Users Association
BBA	British Banker's Association; Bachelor of Business Administration
BBC	British Broadcasting Corporation
BBS	Bachelor of Business Studies
BC	British Columbia
BCE	Bachelor of Civil Engineering
BCh or BChir	Bachelor of Surgery
BCL	Bachelor in Civil Law
BCOF	British Commonwealth Occupation Force in Japan
BCom	Bachelor of Commerce
BCS	British Computer Society; Bengal Civil Service
BCU	British Canoe Union
BD	Bachelor in Divinity
Bd	Board
BDA	British Dental Association
Bdcast(ing)	Broadcast(ing)
Bde	Brigade
BDS	Bachelor of Dental Surgery
BE	Bachelor of Engineering
BEA	British European Airways
BEAMA	Federation of British Electrotechnical and Allied Manufacturers Association
BEcon	Bachelor of Economics
BEd	Bachelor of Education
BEE	Bachelor of Electrical Engineering
BEF	British Expeditionary Force
BEM	British Empire Medal
BEng	Bachelor of Engineering
BETRO	British Export Trade Organisation
BFI	British Film Institute
BFME	British Forces Middle East
BFPO	British Forces Post Office
BFSS	British Field Sports Society
BGGS	Brigadier-General, General Staff
BGS	Brigadier, General Staff
BHS	British Horse Society
BHy	Bachelor of Hygiene
BIBA	British Insurance Brokers Association
BICC	British Insulated Callender's Cables
BIEE	British Institute of Energy Economics
BIM	British Institute of Management
BIR	British Institute of Radiology
BJSM	British Joint Service Mission
BL	Bachelor of Law; British Leyland
BLA	British Army of Liberation
Bldgs	Buildings
BLESMA	British Limbless Ex-servicemens' Association
BLitt	Bachelor of Letters
BM	Bachelor of Medicine (Oxford); Brigade Major
BMA	British Medical Association
BMet	Bachelor of Metallurgy
BMH	British Military Hospital
BMus	Bachelor of Music
Bn	Battalion

BNAF	British North Africa Force
BNC	Brasenose (College)
BNEC	British National Export Council
BNES	British Nuclear Energy Society
BNF	British Nuclear Fuels
BNFL	British Nuclear Fuels Ltd
BNSC	British National Space Centre
BNurs	Bachelor of Nursing
BOA	British Olympic Association
BOAC	British Overseas Airways Corporation
BOT	Board of Trade
BOTB	British Overseas Trade Board
BP	British Petroleum
BPA	British Paediatric Association
BPharm	Bachelor of Pharmacy
BPIF	British Printing Industries Federation
Br	British
BR	British Railways
BRA	British Rheumatism and Arthiritis Association
BRCS	British Red Cross Society
BRDC	British Racing Drivers' Club
Brig	Brigadier
bro	brother
BS	Bachelor of Surgery
BSAC	British Sub Aqua Club
BSc	Bachelor of Science
BSC	British Steel Corporation; British Society of Cinematographers
BSI	British Standards Institution
BSS	Bachelor of Social Sciences (USA)
Bt	Baronet
BT	British Telecom
BTA	British Troops in Austria; British Tourist Authority
Bt-Col	Brevet-Colonel
Btcy	Baronetcy
BTEC	Business and Technicians Education Council
Btss	Baronetess
BUPA	British United Provident Association
BVA	British Veterinary Association
BVMS	Bachelor of Veterinary Medicine and Surgery
BWI	British West Indies
BWM	British War Medal
BWS	Member of the British Watercolour Society

C

c	children
ca	circa
C	Conservative
C of C	Chamber of Commerce
C of E	Church of England
CA	Chartered Accountant; County Alderman
CAA	Civil Aviation Authority
CAB	Citizens Advice Bureau
CACTM	Central Advisory Council of Training for the Ministry
CAMC	Canadian Army Medical Corps
CAMRA	Campaign for Real Ale
Cantab	Of Cambridge University
Capt	Captain
CARE	Cottage and Rural Enterprises
CAS	Chief of Air Staff
CB	Companion of the Order of the Bath
CBA	Council for British Archaeology
CBC	County Borough Council
CBE	Commander of the Order of the British Empire
CBI	Confederation of British Industry
CBIM	Companion, British Institute of Management
CBiol	Chartered Biologist
CBIREE	Companion, British Institute of Radio and Electronic Engineers
CC	County Council: Companion of the Order of Canada; Cricket Club
CCA	County Councils' Association
CCAB	Consultative Committee of Accounting Bodies
CCBE	Consultative Council of European Bars and Law Societies (Commission Consultative des Barreaux de la Communant Européene)
CCC	Corpus Christi College; County Cricket Club
CCF	Combined Cadet Force
CCG(BE)	Control Commission, Germany (British Element)
CChem	Chartered Chemist
CCHMS	Central Committee for Hospital and Medical Services
CCIBS	Companion, Chartered Institute of Building Services
CCncllr	County Councillor
CCO	Conservative Central Office
CCPR	Central Council of Physical Recreation
CCRE	Commander Corps of Royal Engineers
CCRA	Commander Corps, Royal Artillery
CCRSigs	Commander Corps of Royal Signals
CCS	Casualty Clearing Station
CCSC	Central Consultants and Specialists Committee
CD	Canadian Forces Decoration
CDipAF	Certified Diploma in Accounting and Finance
Cdr	Commander
Cdre	Commodore
CDS	Chief of Defence Staff
CE	Chief Engineer
CEDEP	Centre Européen d'Education Permanente
CEFIC	Counseil Européen des Federations de L'Industrie Chimique
CEGB	Central Electricity Generating Board
CEI	Council of Engineering Institutions
CEng	Chartered Engineer
CERN	Conseil (now Organisation) Européenne pour la Recherche Nucléaire
CertEd	Certificate of Education
CF	Chaplain to the Forces
CFM	Canadian Forces Medal
CFS	Central Flying School
CGA	Country Gentleman's Association
CGIA	City and Guilds of London Insignia Awards Association
CGLI	City and Guilds of the London Institute
CGS	Chief of the General Staff
CH	Companion of Honour
ChB	Bachelor of Surgery
CHC	Community Health Council
ChCh	Christ Church (Oxford)
Chem	Chemical
Chev	Chevalier
Chllr	Chancellor
Chm	Chairman
ChM	Mastery of Surgery
ChStJ	Chaplain of the Order of St John of Jerusalem
CI	Order of the Crown of India; Channel Islands
CIArb	Chartered Institute of Arbitrators
CIBS	Chartered Institute of Building Services
CIBSE	Chartered Institution of Building Services Engineers
CICeram	Companion, Institute of Ceramics
CICHE	Committee for International Co-operation in Higher Education
CID	Criminal Investigation Department
CIE	Companion of the Order of the Indian Empire
CIEE	Companion, Institution of Electrical Engineers
CIGS	Chief of the Imperial General Staff
CII	Chartered Insurance Institute
CIMarE	Companion of the Institute of Marine Engineers
CIMechE	Companion of the Institution of Mechanical Engineers

C-in-C Commander-in-Chief
CIPFA Chartered Institute of Public Finance and Accountancy
CIPM Companion, Institute of Personnel Managers
CIRIA Construction Industry Research and Information Association
CIT Chartered Institute of Transport
CLA Country Landowners' Association
CLitt Companion of the Royal Society of Literature
CLP Constituency Labour Party
CM Member of the Order of Canada; Master of Surgery
CMA Cost and Management Accountant (New Zealand)
Cmd Commanded; command
Cmdg Commanding
Cmdt Commandant
CMF Commonwealth Military Forces; Central Mediterranean Force
CMG Companion of the Order of St Michael and St George
Cmmn Commission
cmmnd Commissioned
Cmmr Commissioner
CMO Chief Medical Officer
CMP Corps of Military Police
CMS Church Missionary Society
CNAA Council for National Academic Awards
Cncl Council
CND Campaign for Nuclear Disarmament
CNRS Centre Nationale du Recherche Scientifique
Cnsllr Counsellor
CO Commanding Officer
Co Company; County
Co L Coalition Liberal
COD Communications and Operations Department (FO)
C of C Chamber of Commerce
C of E Church of England
COGS Chief of General Staff
COI Central Office of Information
Col Colonel
Coll College
COMMET Council of Mechanical and Metal Trade Associations
Comp Comprehensive
CompIEE Companion to the Institute of Electrical Engineers
Conf Conference
Confedn Confederation
Conn Connecticut
Cons Conservative
Conslt Consultant
consltg consulting
contrib Contributor, contributed, contribution
Co-op Co-Operative
COPA Committee of Agricultural Organisations in the European Community
Corp Corporation, corporate
Corpl Corporal
Corr Correspondent
COS Chief of Staff
COSIRA Council for Smaller Industries in Rural Areas
cous cousin
CP County Primary
CPA Commonwealth Parliamentary Association
CPC Conservative Political Centre
CPhys Chartered Physicist
CPM Colonial Police Medal
CPRE Council for the Protection of Rural England
CPRS Central Policy Review Staff
CPS Canadian Pacific Steamships
CPU Commonwealth Press Union
cr created
CRA Commander Royal Artillery
CRAC Careers Research and Advisory Council
CRAeS Companion, Royal Aeronautical Society
CRC Community Relations Commission
CRD Conservative Research Department
CRE Commanding Royal Engineers
CRMP Corps of Royal Military Police
CRO Commonwealth Relations Office
CS Clerk to the Signet
CSA Commonwealth Society of Artists; Chair Schools Association
CSD Chartered Society of Designers
CSERB Computer Systems and Electronics Requirements Board
CSI Companion of the Order of the Star of India; Council for the Securities Industries
CSIR Council for Scientific and Industrial Research
CSIRO Commonwealth Scientific and Industrial Research Organisation
CSO Chief Signal Officer; Chief Staff Officer; Chief Scientific Officer
CStJ Commander of the Order of St John of Jerusalem
CSTI Council of Science and Technology Institutes
CSV Community Service Volunteers
Ct Court
Ctee Committee
CText Chartered Textile Technologist
CUF Common Universities Fund
CUP Cambridge University Press
CVCP Committee of Vice-Chancellors and Principals of the UK
CVO Commander of the Royal Victorian Order
CWA Crime Writers' Association
Cwlth Commonwealth
CWCC Conservative Women's Constituency Committee

D

d Died, death
da Daughter
DA Diploma in Anaesthetics; Diploma in Art
DA & QMG Deputy-Adjutant and Quartermaster-General
DAA & QMG Deputy Assistant-Adjutant and Quartermaster-General
DAAG Deputy-Assistant-Adjutant-General
D & ADA Designers & Art Directors' Association
DACG Deputy Assistant Chaplain General
DADGMS Deputy Assistant Director General of Medical Services
DADMS Deputy Assistant Director Medical Services
DADR Deputy Assistant Director of Remounts
DAD Deputy-Assistant Director
DADST Deputy Assistant Director of Supplies and Transport
DAG Deputy-Adjutant-General
DAMS Deputy-Assistant Military Secretary
DAPM Deputy Assistant Provost Marshall
DAPS Director of Army Postal Services
DAQMG Deputy-Assistant-Quartermaster-General
DBA Doctor of Business Administration
DBE Dame Commander of the British Empire
DC District Council
DCAS Deputy Chief of Air Staff
DCB Dame Commander Order of the Bath
DCGS Deputy Chief of General Staff

DCH Diploma in Child Health
DCL Doctor of Civil Law
DCLI Duke of Cornwall's Light Infantry
DCM Distinguished Conduct Medal
DCMG Dame Commander Order of St Michael and St George
DCMS Deputy Commissioner Medical Services
DCSO Deputy Chief Scientific Officer
DCVO Dame Commander Royal Victorian Order
DD Doctor in Divinity
DDDS Deputy Director of Dental Services
DDME Deputy Director Mechanical Engineering
DDMS Deputy Director of Medical Services
DDO Diploma in Dental Orthopaedics
DDOS Deputy Director of Ordnance Services
DDPH Diploma in Dental Public Health
DDPS Deputy Director of Personal Services
DDR Deputy Director of Remounts
DDS Doctor of Dental Surgery; Director of Dental Services
DDS & T Deputy Director Supplies and Transport
DDSD Deputy Director of Staff Duties
DDVS Deputy-Director of Veterinary Services
DDWE & M Deputy Director of Works, Electrical and Mechanical
decd deceased
DEd Doctor of Education
Def Defence
Del Delegate
Delgn Delegation
DEM Diploma in Education Management
DEME Director of Electrical and Mechanical Engineering
DEng Doctor of Engineering
Dep Deputy
Dep-Adv-Gen Deputy-Advocate-General
Dep-Sec Deputy Secretary
Dept Department
DES Department of Education and Science
DèsL Docteur ès Lettres
DesRCA Designer of the Royal College of Art
Devpt Development
DFA Doctor of Fine Arts
DFC Distinguished Flying Cross
DFH Diploma of the Faraday House
DG Director General
DGAMS Director-General of Army Medical Services
DGCStJ Dame Grand Cross of the Order of St John of Jerusalem
DGMS Director-General of Medical Services
DGStJ Dame of Grace of the Order of St John of Jerusalem
DH Doctor of Humanities
DHA District Health Authority
DHMSA Diploma in the History of Medicine (Society of Apothecaries)
DHQ District Headquarters
DHSS Department of Health and Social Security
DHy Doctor of Hygiene
DIC Diploma of the Imperial College
DIH Diploma in Industrial Health
Dio Diocese
Dip Diploma; Diplomatic
DipAD Diploma in Arts and Design
DipAg Diploma in Agriculture
Dip Arch Diploma in Architecture
DipBA Diploma in Business Administration
DipCAM Diploma in Communication, Advertising and Marketing of the CAM Foundation
DipCD Diploma in Civic Design
DipEd Diploma in Education
DipHA Diploma in Hospital Administration
DipOrthMed Diploma in Orthopaedic Medicine
DipTP Diploma in Town Planning
Dir Director
dis dissolved (marriage)
Dist District
Div Division
Divnl Divisional
DJAG Deputy Judge Advocate General
DJStJ Dame of Justice of the Order of St John of Jerusalem
DL Deputy-Lieutenant for the County of
DLC Diploma Loughborough College
DLI Durham Light Infantry
DLitt Doctor of Letters
DLit Doctor of Literature
DLO Diploma in Larynology and Otology
DM Doctor of Medicine
DMD Doctor in Dental Medicine
DME Director of Mechanical Engineering
DMGO Divisional Machine Gun Officer
DMI Director Military Intelligence
DMJ Diploma in Medical Jurisprudence
DMO & I Director Military Operations and Intelligence
DMRD Diploma in Medical Radiological Diagnosis
DMRE Diploma in Medical Radiology and Electrology
DMRT Diploma in Medical Radiotherapy
DMS Director of Medical Services; Diploma in Management Studies
DMSI Director of Management and Support Intelligence
DMT Director of Military Training
DMus Doctor of Music (Oxford)
DNI Director of Naval Intelligence
DNO Director of Naval Ordnance
DO Diploma in Ophthalmology; Divisional Officer
DOAE Defence Operational Analysis Establishment
DObstRCOG Diploma Royal College of Obstetricians and Gynaecologists
DOC District Officer Commanding
DOE Department of Environment
DOI Department of Industry
DOMS Diploma in Ophthalmic Medicine
DOR Director of Operational Requirements
DOS Director of Ordnance Services
DPA Diploma in Public Administration
DPH Diploma in Public Health
DPhil Doctor of Philosophy
DPL Director of Pioneers and Labour
DPM Diploma in Psychological Medicine
DPMO Deputy Principal Medical Officer
DPR Director of Public Relations
DPS Director of Personal Services
DQMG Deputy Quartermaster-General
DRC Diploma of the Royal College of Science and Technology, Glasgow
DRVO Deputy Regional Veterinary Officer
DS Directing Staff
DS & T Director of Supplies and Transport
DSAC Defence Scientific Advisory Committee
DSAO Diplomatic Service Administration Office
DSC Distinguished Service Cross
DSc Doctor of Science
DSD Director of Staff Duties
DSIR Department of Scientific and Industrial Research
DSM Distinguished Service Medal (United States of America)
DSO Companion of the Distinguished Service Order
dsp *decessit sine prole* (died without issue)
DSP Docteur en Sciences Politiques (Montreal)
DSSC Doctor of Social Science
DStJ Dame of Grace of the Order of St John of Jerusalem
DS & T Director of Supplies and Transport
DTech Doctor of Technology
DTh Doctor of Theology
DTI Dept of Trade and Industry

DTM & H Diploma in Tropical Medicine and Hygiene
DUniv Doctor of the University
DVFS Director, Veterinary Field Services
DVM Doctor of Veterinary Medicine
DVO Divisional Veterinary Officer
DVS Director of Veterinary Services
DVSM Diploma of Veterinary State Medicine

E

E East; Earl; England
EASA Ecclesiastical Architects and Surveyors Association
EBU European Broadcasting Union
EC European Commission
ECGD Export Credit Guarantee Department
Econ Economic
Ed Editor; edited
ED Efficiency Decoration; European Democratic (Group)
EDC Economic Development Committee
EDG European Democratic Group (UK Conservative Group, European Parliament)
edn edition
educnl educational
Educn education
EETPU Electrical, Electronic, Telecommunication and Plumbing Union
EFTA European Free Trade Association
EIU Economist Intelligence Unit
eld eldest
EMS Emergency Medical Service
Eng English; England
Engr Engineer
Engrg Engineering
ENO English National Opera
ENSA Entertainments National Services Association
ENT Ear, Nose and Throat
er elder
ERD Emergency Reserve Decoration
ESRC Economic and Social Research Council
ESRO European Space Research Organisation
Estab Established; establishment
ESU English-Speaking Union
Eur Ing European Engineer
Euro European
Exec Executive
Expdn Expedition
Ext Extinct; extension

F

f father
FA Football Association
FAA Fellow of the Australian Academy of Science
FAAAS Fellow, American Academy of Arts & Sciences
FAAP Fellow, American Academy of Paediatrics
FAAV Fellow, Central Association of Agricultural Valuers
FACC Fellow, American College of Cardiology
FACCA Fellow of the Association of Certified and Corporate Accountants
FACD Fellow, American College of Dentristry
FACE Fellow, Australian College of Education
FACOG Fellow, American College of Obstetricians and Gynaecologists
FACP Fellow, American College of Physicians
FACS Fellow, American College of Surgeons
FACVT Fellow, American College of Veterinary Toxicology
FAES Fellow of the Audio Engineering Society
FAI Fellow of the Chartered Auctioneers' and Estate Agents' Institute
FAIA Fellow, American Institute of Architects
FAIM Fellow of the Australian Institute of Management
FAIP Fellow, of the Australian Institute of Physics
FAIRE Fellow of the Australian Institute of Radio Engineers
FALPA Fellow of the Incorporated Auctioneers and Land Property Agents
FAMEME Fellow, Association of Mining, Electrical and Mechanical Engineers
FAMI Fellow of the Australian Marketing Institute
FAMS Fellow of the Ancient Monuments Society
FANY First Aid Nursing Yeomanry
FAO Food and Agricultural Organisation
FAPM Fellow of the Association of Project Managers
FARELF Far East Land Forces
FAS Fellow, Antiquarian Society
FASA Fellow of the Australian Society of Accountants
FASCE Fellow of the American Society of Civil Engineers
FBA Fellow of the British Academy
FBCO Fellow of British College of Opticians
FBCS Fellow, British Computer Society
FBHI Fellow of the British Horological Institute
FBI Federation of British Industries
FBIBA Fellow of the British Insurance Brokers Association
FBIEE Fellow of the British Institute of Energy Economists
FBIM Fellow of the British Institute of Management
FBIPP Fellow of the British Institute of Professional Photographers
FBIS Fellow of the British Interplanetary Society
FBKSTS Fellow, British Kinematograph, Sound and Television Society
FBOA Fellow of the British Optical Association; Fellow, British Orthopaedic Association
FBPsS Fellow, British Psychological Society
FBSI Fellow of the Boot and Shoe Industry
FC Football Club
FCA Fellow of the Institute of Chartered Accountants
FCAI Fellow of the Canadian Aeronautical Institute
FCAM Fellow, Communications Advertising & Marketing Educational Foundation
FCBSI Fellow of the Chartered Building Societies Institute
FCCA Fellow of the Association of Certified and Corporate Accountants
FCCS Fellow of the Corporation of Certified Secretaries
FCDA Fellow of the Company Directors Association of Australia
FCEC Federation of Civil Engineering Contractors
FCFA Fellow of the Cookery and Food Association
FCGI Fellow, City and Guilds of London Institute
FCIA Fellow, Corporation of Insurance Agents
FCIArb Fellow, Chartered Institute of Arbitrators
FCIB Fellow of the Corporation of Insurance Brokers; Fellow, Chartered Institute of Bankers
FCIBS Fellow, Chartered Institution of Building Services
FCIBSE Fellow, Chartered Institution of Building Service Engineers

FCII Fellow of the Chartered Insurance Institute
FCIM Fellow, Chartered Institute of Marketing
FCIOB Fellow, Chartered Institute of Building
FCIS Fellow of the Chartered Institute of Secretaries
FCIT Fellow of the Chartered Institute of Transport
FCMA Fellow, Institute of Cost and Management Accountants
FCO Foreign and Commonwealth Office
FCOG Fellow of the College of Obstetrics and Gynaecology
FCommA Fellow of the Society of Commercial Accountants
FCP Fellow, College of Preceptors
FCPS Fellow of the College of Physicians and Surgeons
FCS Fellow of the Chemical Society
FCSD Fellow, Chartered Society of Designers
FCT Fellow of the Institute of Corporate Treasurers
FCWA Fellow of the Institute of Cost and Works Accountants
FDI Féderation Dentaire Internationale
FDR Federalische Deutsche Republik
FDS Fellow in Dental Surgery
FDSRCS Fellow in Dental Surgery Royal College of Surgeons of England
FEAF Far East Air Force
Fed Federal
Fedn Federation
FEIS Fellow of the Educational Institute of Scotland
Fell Fellow
FEng Fellow, Fellowship of Engineering
FES Fellow of the Entomological Society
FFA Fellow of the Faculty of Actuaries (Scotland)
FFARACS Fellow, Faculty of Anaesthetists Royal Australian College of Surgeons
FFARCS Fellow of the Faculty of Anaesthetists, Royal College of Surgeons
FFARCSI Fellow, Faculty of Anaesthetists Royal College of Surgeons of Ireland
FFAS Fellow of the Faculty of Architects and Surveyors
FFB Fellow of the Faculty of Building
FFCM Fellow, Faculty of Community Medicine (now FFPHM)
FFDRCSI Fellow, Faculty of Dentistry, Royal College of Surgeons in Ireland
FFHom Fellow, Faculty of Homeopathy
FFOM Fellow, Faculty of Occupational Medicine
FFPHM Fellow, Faculty of Public Health Medicine
FFR Fellow of the Faculty of Radiologists
FGA Fellow of the Gemmological Association
FGS Fellow of the Geological Society
FGSM Fellow, Guildhall School of Music
FHA Fellow, Institute of Health Service Administrators
FHCIMA Fellow of the Hotel Catering and Institutional Management Association
FHKIE Fellow, Hong Kong Institute of Engineers
FHSM Fellow, Institute of Health Service Managers
FIA Fellow, Institute of Actuaries; Fédération Internationale de L'Automobile
FIAAS Fellow Architect Member of the Incorporated Association of Architects and Surveyors
FIAC Fellow, Institute of Company Accountants
FIAeS Fellow of the Institute of Aeronautical Sciences
FIAgrE Fellow, Institution of Agricultural Engineers
FIAL Fellow, International Institute of Arts and Letters
FIAM Fellow, International Academy of Management
FIArb Fellow of the Institute of Arbitration
FIAS Fellow, Institute of Aeronautical Sciences (US)
FIB Fellow of the Institute of Bankers (now FCIB)
FIBC Fellow, Institute of Business Counsellors
FIBiol Fellow, Institute of Biology
FIBM Fellow, Institute of Builders' Merchants
FIBScot Fellow of the Institute of Bankers in Scotland
FICA Fellow of the Institute of Chartered Accountants in England and Wales (now FCA)
FICAS Fellow, Institute of Chartered Accountants in Scotland
FICD Fellow of the Institute of Civil Defence
FICE Fellow of the Institution of Civil Engineers
FICeram Fellow, Institute of Ceramics
FICFor Fellow, Institute of Chartered Foresters
FIChemE Fellow of the Institution of Chemical Engineers
FICM Fellow, Institute of Credit Management
FICMA Fellow, Institute of Cost and Management Accountants
FICS Fellow of the Institute of Chartered Shipbrokers
FICSA Fellow of the Institute of Chartered Secretaries and Administrators
FID Fellow of the Institute of Directors
FIE(Aust) Fellow, Institution of Engineers, Australia
FIEE Fellow of the Institution of Electrical Engineers
FIEEE Fellow, Institution of Electrical and Electronics Engineers (New York)
FIERE Fellow of the Institution of Electronics and Radio Engineers
FIEx Fellow, Institute of Export
FIFM Fellow, Institute of Fisheries Management
FIFor Fellow, Institute of Forestry
FIFST Fellow of Food Science and Technology
FIGD Fellow, Institute of Grocery Distribution
FIGE Fellow, Institute of Gas Engineers
FIGeol Fellow, Institute of Geology
FIH Fellow, Institute of Housing
FIHE Fellow, Institute of Health Education
FIHort Fellow of the Institute of Horticulture
FIHospE Fellow, Institute of Hospital Engineering
FIHT Fellow, Institute of Highways and Transportation
FIHVE Fellow, Institution of Heating and Ventilating Engineers
FIIM Fellow, Institute of Industrial Managers
FIInfSc Fellow, Institute of Information Scientists
FIInst Fellow of the Imperial Institute
FIL Fellow of the Institute of Linguists
FILA Fellow of the Institute of Landscape Architects
FILDM Fellow, Institute of Logistics and Distribution Management
FilDr Doctor of Philosophy
FIM Fellow, Institute of Metals (formerly Institution of Metallurgists)
FIMA Fellow of the Institute of Mathematics and its Applications
FIMarE Fellow, Institute of Marine Engineers
FIMBRA Financial Intermediaries, Managers and Brokers Regulatory Association
FIMC Fellow, Institute of Management Consultants
FIM&C Fellow of the Institute of Measurement and Control
FIMechE Fellow of the Institution of Mechanical Engineers
FIMFT Fellow, Institute of Maxillo-Facial Technology
FIMH Fellow, Institute of Materials Handling; Fellow, Institute of Military History
FIMI Fellow, Institute of Motor Industry
FIMinE Fellow, Institute of Mining Engineers
FIMIT Fellow, Institute of Musical Instrument Technology
FIMLS Fellow, Institute of Medical and Laboratory Sciences
FIMM Fellow, Institution of Mining and Metallurgy
FIMT Fellow of the Institute of the Motor Trade
FIMTA Fellow of the Institute of Municipal Treasurers & Accountants
Fin Finance; financial

FInstAA Fellow of the Institute of Administrative Accountants
FInstAM Fellow, Institute of Administrative Management
FInstCES Fellow of the Institution of Civil Engineering Surveyors
FInstCS Fellow, Institute of Chartered Secretaries
FInstD Fellow, Institute of Directors
FInstF Fellow of Institute of Fuel
FinstFF Fellow, Institute of Freight Forwarders
FInst GasE Fellow, Institution of Gas Engineers
FInstGeol Fellow Institute of Geologists
FInstHE Fellow, Institution of Highway Engineers
FInstLEx Fellow, Institute of Legal Executives
FInstM Fellow, Institute of Marketing (now FCIM)
FInstMC Fellow, Institute of Measurement and Control
FInstMSM Fellow of the Institute of Marketing and Sales Management
FInstP Fellow of the Institute of Physics
FInstPet Fellow of the Institute of Petroleum
FInstPI Fellow, Institute Patentees (Incorporated)
FInstPS Fellow, Institute of Purchasing and Supply
FInstSMM Fellow, Institute of Sales and Marketing Management
FINucE Fellow of the Institute of Nuclear Engineers
FIOA Fellow, Institute of Acoustics
FIOB Fellow, Institute of Building
FIOP Fellow of the Institute of Printing
FIOSc Fellow of the Institute of Optical Science
FIP Fellow, Australian Institute of Petroleum
FIPA Fellow of the Institute of Public Administration; Fellow of the Institute of Practitioners in Advertising
FIPHE Fellow of the Institution of Public Health Engineers
FIPI Fellow, Institute of Professional Investigators
FIPlantE Fellow, Institute of Plant Engineers
FIPM Fellow, Institute of Personnel Management
FIPR Fellow of the Institute of Public Relations
FIProdE Fellow of the Institute of Production Engineers
FIPS Fellow, Institute of Purchasing and Supply
FIQ Fellow, Institute of Quarrying
FIRE Fellow of the Institution of Radio Engineers
FIRI Fellow of the Institution of the Rubber Industry
FIS Fellow, Institute of Stationers
FISE Fellow of the Institute of Sanitary Engineers
FISTD Fellow, Imperial Society of Teachers of Dancing
FIStructE Fellow, Institution of Structural Engineers
FITA Fellow, International Archery Federation
FITD Fellow, Institute of Training and Development
FIWEM Fellow, Institution of Water and Environmental Management
FIWES Fellow, Institute of Water Engineers and Scientists
FIWSc Fellow, Institute of Wood Science
FJI Fellow, Institute of Journalists
FKC Fellow, King's College London
FLA Fellow, Library Association
FLAS Fellow, Land Agents Society
FLCM Fellow, London College of Music
FLI Fellow, Landscape Institute
FLIA Fellow, Life Assurance Association
FLS Fellow, Linnean Society
Flt Flight
Flt Lt Flight Lieutenant
FMA Fellow of the Museums' Association
FMS Fellow, Institute of Management Services; Fellow, Institute of Medical Society; Fellow, Manorial Society
FNAEA Fellow, National Association of Estate Agents
Fndn Foundation
Fndr Founder
FNI Fellow, Nautical Institute
FNIAB Fellow, National Institute of Agricultural Botany
FO Foreign Office
FOR Fellowship of Operational Research
FPC Family Practitioner Committee
FPCA Fellow of Practising and Commercial Accountants
FPEA Fellow, Physical Education Association
FPhS(Eng) Fellow, Philosophical Society of England
FPMI Fellow, Pensions Management Institute
FPRI Fellow, Plastics and Rubber Institute
FPS Fellow of Philological Society of Great Britain
FRACDS Fellow, Royal Australian College of Dental Surgeons
FRACP Fellow of the Royal Australasian College of Physicians
FRACS Fellow of the Royal Australasian College of Surgeons
FRAeS Fellow, Royal Aeronautical Society
FRAgS Fellow, Royal Agricultural Societies
FRAI Fellow of the Royal Anthropological Institute
FRAIC Fellow, Royal Architectural Institute of Canada
FRAM Fellow of the Royal Academy of Music
FRAS Fellow of the Royal Astronomical Society; Fellow, Royal Asiatic Society
FRBS Fellow of the Royal Botanic Society; Fellow of the Royal Society of British Sculptors
FRCAA Fellow of the Royal Cambrian Academy of Art
FRCGP Fellow, Royal College of General Practitioners
FRCM Fellow of the Royal College of Music
FRCN Fellow, Royal College of Nursing
FRCO Fellow of the Royal College of Organists
FRCOG Fellow of the Royal College of Obstetricians and Gynaecologists
FRCP Fellow of the Royal College of Physicians
FRCPA Fellow, Royal College of Pathologists of Australia
FRCPath Fellow, Royal College of Pathologists
FRCPE Fellow of the Royal College of Physicians of Edinburgh
FRCPG Fellow, Royal College of Physicians, Glasgow
FRCPI Fellow, Royal College of Physicians in Ireland
FRCPS Fellow of the Royal College of Physicians and Surgeons (Glasgow)
FRCPsych Fellow, Royal College of Psychiatrists
FRCR Fellow, Royal College of Radiologists
FRCS Fellow of the Royal College of Surgeons; Fellow of the Royal C'wlth Society (formerly Royal Empire Soc)
FRCSEd Fellow, Royal College of Surgeons Edinburgh
FRCSGlas Fellow, Royal College of Surgeons, Glasgow
FRCSI Fellow, Royal College of Surgeons in Ireland
FRCVS Fellow, Royal College of Veterinary Surgeons
FREconS Fellow of the Royal Economic Society
FREntS Fellow of the Royal Entomological Society
FRG Federal Republic of Germany
FRGS Fellow of the Royal Geographical Society
FRHistS Fellow of the Royal Historical Society
FRHS Fellow of the Royal Horticultural Society
FRIA Fellow, Royal Institute of Arbitrators
FRIAS Fellow of the Royal Incorporation of Architects in Scotland
FRIBA Fellow of the Royal Institute of British Architects
FRIC Fellow of the Royal Institute of Chemistry
FRICS Fellow of the Royal Institution of Chartered Surveyors
FRIN Fellow of the Royal Institute of Navigation
FRINA Fellow of the Royal Institution of Naval Architects
FRIPH Fellow of the Royal Institute of Public Health
FRMetS Fellow of the Royal Meteorological Society
FRMIA Fellow of the Retail Management Institute of Australia
FRMS Fellow of the Royal Microscopical Society
FRNCM Fellow, Royal Northern College of Music

FRNS Fellow of the Royal Numismatic Society
FRPharmS Fellow, Royal Pharmaceutical Society
FRPI Fellow, Institute of Rubber and Plastics Industry
FRPS Fellow of the Royal Photographic Society
FRPSL Fellow of the Royal Philatelic Society, London
FRS Fellow of the Royal Society
FRSA Fellow of the Royal Society of Arts
FRSAIre Fellow of the Royal Society of Antiquaries of Ireland
FRSAMD Fellow Royal Scottish Academy of Music and Drama
FRSC Fellow of the Royal Society of Canada; Fellow, Royal Society of Chemistry
FRSCM Fellow, Royal School of Church Music
FRSE Fellow of the Royal Society of Edinburgh
FRSGS Fellow of the Royal Scottish Geographical Society
FRSH Fellow of the Royal Society of Health
FRSL Fellow of the Royal Society of Literature
FRSM Fellow of the Royal Society of Medicine
FRSNZ Fellow, Royal Society of New Zealand
FRSTM & H Fellow, Royal Society of Tropical Medicine and Health
FRTPI Fellow, Royal Town Planning Institute
FRTS Fellow, Royal Television Society
FRVA Fellow of the Rating and Valuation Association
FRZS Scot Fellow of the Royal Zoological Society of Scotland
FSA Fellow of the Society of Antiquaries
FSAA Fellow of the Society of Incorporated Accountants and Auditors
FSAE Fellow, Society of Arts Education
FSAS Fellow, Society of Antiquaries of Scotland
FSCA Fellow, Society of Company and Commercial Artists
FSE Fellow of Society of Engineers
FSF Fellow of the Institute of Shipping and Forwarding Agents
FSG Fellow of the Society of Genealogists
FSI Fellow, Royal Institution of Chartered Surveyors (*see also* FRICS)
FSIA Fellow of the Society of Industrial Artists
FSIAD Fellow, Society of Industrial Artists and Designers
FSLAET Fellow, Society of Licensed Aircraft Engineers and Technologists
FSLGD Fellow, Society for Landscape and Garden Designs
FSS Fellow of the Royal Statistical Society
FSScA Fellow of the Society of Science and Art, of London
FSTD Fellow, Society of Typographic Designers
FSUT Fellow, Society for Underwater Technology
FSVA Fellow, Incorporated Society of Valuers and Auctioneers
FTC Flying Training Command
FTCL Fellow of Trinity College of Music, London
FTI Fellow of the Textile Institute
FTII Fellow, Institute of Taxation
FTS Fellow of the Tourism Society
FUMIST Fellow, University of Manchester Institute of Science and Technology
Fus Fusiliers
FVI Fellow, Valuers Institution
FWA Fellow, World Academy of Arts and Sciences
FZS Fellow of the Zoological Society

G

g great
Ga Georgia (USA)
GA Geologists' Association
GAA Gaelic Athletic Association
GAMTA General Aviation Manufacturers' Association
GATT General Agreement on Tariffs and Trade
G&MWU General and Municipal Workers' Union
GB Great Britain
GBA Governing Bodies Association
GBE Knight of the Grand Cross of the British Empire
GBSM Graduate, Birmingham and Midland Institute School of Music
GC George Cross; Grand Cross
GCB Knight Grand Cross of the Bath
GCBS General Council of British Shipping
GCH Knight Grand Cross of Hanover
GCHQ Government Communications Headquarters
GCIE Knight/Dame Grand Commander of the Indian Empire
GCMG Knight/Dame Grand Cross of St Michael and St George
GCON Grand Cross, Order of the Niger
GCSE General Certificate in Secondary Education
GCSI Knight Grand Commander of the Star of India
GCStJ Bailiff or Dame Grand Cross of the Order of St John of Jerusalem
GCVO Knight or Dame of the Grand Cross of the Royal Victorian Order
gda granddaughter
gdns gardens
GDR German Democratic Republic
Gds Guards
Gen General
Ger Germany
gf grandfather
ggda great granddaughter (and so forth)
ggs great grandson (and so forth)
GHQ General Headquarters
GIMechE Graduate Institution of Mechanical Engineers
GLC Greater London Council
GM George Medal
gm grandmother
GMB Great Master of the Bath
GMBATU General Municipal Boilermakers and Allied Trade Unions
GMC General Medical Council
GMIE Grand Master of the Indian Empire
GMMG Grand Master of St Michael and St George
GMSI Grand Master of the Star of India
GMWU General Municipal Workers Union
gn great nephew; great niece
GO Grand Officier (de la Légion d'Honneur)
GOC-in-C General Officer Commanding- in-Chief
Govr Governor
Govt Government
GP General Practitioner
Gp Group
Gp Capt Group Captain
GPDST Girls' Public Day School Trust
GPO General Post Office
GRCM Graduate of the Royal College of Music
GRSM Graduate of the Royal Schools of Music
GS General Staff; Grammar School
gs grandson
GSA Girls' School Association
GSM General Service Medal; Guildhall School of Music and Drama
GSO General Staff Officer
Gt Great
Gtr Greater
Guy's Guy's Hospital
GWR Great Western Railway

H

h	heir
ha	heir apparent
HA	Historical Association
HAA	Heavy Anti-Aircraft
HAC	Honourable Artillery Company
HBM	His/Her Britannic Majesty
hc	honoris causa
HCF	Hon Chaplain to the Forces
HCITB	Hotel and Catering Industry Training Board
HDip in Ed	Honorary Diploma in Education
HE	His Excellency
HG	Homeguard
HESIN	Higher Education Support for Industry in the North
HG	Homeguard
HH	His/Her Highness
HHA	Historic Houses Association
HHD	Doctor of Humanities (US)
High Cmmr	High Commissioner
HIH	His/Her Imperial Highness
HIllH	His/Her Illustrious Highness
HIM	His/Her Imperial Majesty
Hist	Historical
HKIA	Member, Hong Kong Institute of Architects
Hldgs	Holdings
HLI	Highland Light Infantry
HMC	Headmasters' Conference; Hospital Management Committee
HMEH	His Most Emminent Highness
HMHS	Her Majesty's Hospital Ship
HMOCS	Her Majesty's Overseas Civil Service
HMS	Her Majesty's Ship
HMSO	Her Majesty's Stationery Office
HNC	Higher National Certificate
HND	Higher National Diploma
Hon	Honourable; Honour (Judges); Honorary
Hons	Honours
Hort	Horticultural
Hosp	Hospital
hp	heir presumptive
HQ	headquarters
HRE	Holy Roman Empire
HRH	His/Her Royal Highness
HRI	Hon Member of the Royal Institute of Painters in Water Colours
HRSA	Hon Member Royal Scottish Academy
HS	High School
HSE	Health and Safety Executive
HSH	His/Her Serene Highness
husb	husband
HVCert	Health Visitors Certificate

I

I	Ireland
IA	Indian Army
IAAF	International Amateur Athletics Federation
IACP	International Association of Chiefs of Police (USA)
IADR	International Association for Dental Research
IAEA	International Atomic Energy Agency
IAF	Indian Air Force; Indian Auxiliary Force
IAMC	Indian Army Medical Corps
IAOC	Indian Army Ordnance Corps
IAOMS	International Association of Oral and Maxillo-Facial Surgeons
IAP	Institute of Analysts and Programmers
IAPS	Incorporated Association of Preparatory Schools
IARO	Indian Army Reserve of Officers
IAS	Indian Administrative Service
IASC	Indian Army Service Corps
IATA	International Air Transport Association
IATEFL	International Association of Teachers of English as a Foreign Language
IBA	Independent Broadcasting Authority
IBPA	International Bridge Players Association
IBRC	Insurance Brokers' Registration Council
IBRD	International Bank for Reconstruction and Devpt (World Bank)
IBRO	International Brain Research Organisation
i/c	in charge of
ICA	Institute of Contemporary Arts
ICE	Institute of Civil Engineers; In Car Entertainment
ICAEW	Institute of Chartered Accountants of England and Wales
ICF	International Canoe Federation
ICFC	Industrial and Commercial Finance Corporation
ICI	Imperial Chemical Industries
ICL	International Computers Ltd
ICOM	International Council of Museums
ICS	Indian Civil Service
ICSA	Institute of Chartered Secretaries and Administrators
ICSID	International Council of Societies of Industrial Design
idc	has completed a course at, or served for a year on the staff, of The Imperial Defence Coll
IDC	Imperial Defence College
IDS	Institute of Development Studies
IEE	Institution of Electrical Engineers
IEF	Indian Expeditionary Force
IFC	International Finance Corporation
IFLA	International Federation of Library Associations
IFPA	Industrial Fire Protection Association
IG	Instructor in Gunnery
IIEP	International Institute for Educational Planning
IIM	Institution of Industrial Managers
IISS	International Institute of Strategic Studies
ILEA	Inner London Education Authority
ILO	International Labour Office
ILP	Independent Labour Party
IMA	International Music Association
IMCB	International Management Centre Buckingham
IMRO	Investment Management Regulatory Organisation
IMS	Indian Medical Service; International Military Services
IMechE	Institution of of Mechanical Engineers
IMF	International Monetary Fund
Imp	Imperial
Inc	Incorporated
incl	include; including
Ind	Independent
Indust	Industry
Industl	Industrial
Industs	Industries
Inf	Infantry
Info	Information
INSEAD	Institut Européen d'Administration des Affaires
Inspr	Inspector
Inst	Institute
Instn	Institution
Instr	Instructor
Insur	Insurance
Int	International
Investmt	Investment

IOD Institute of Directors
IOM Isle of Man
IOW Isle of Wight
IPA Institute of Practitioners in Advertising
IPCS Institution of Professional Civil Servants
IPFA Chartered Institute of Public Finance and Accountancy
IPHE Institution of Public Health Engineers
IPI Institute of Patentees and Inventors
IPM Institute of Personnel Management
IPPA Independent Programme Producers' Association
IProdE Institute of Production Engineers
IPS Indian Political Service
Ir Irish
IRA Irish Republican Army
IRC Industrial Re-organisation Corporation
IRE Indian Corps of Royal Engineers
IRN Independant Radio News
Is Island(s)
ISBA Incorporated Society of British Advertisers
ISC Indian Staff Corps; Imperial Service College
ISCO Independent Schools Careers Organisation
ISI International Statistical Institute
ISID International Society of Interior Design
ISIS Independent Schools Information Service
ISM Imperial Service Medal; Incorporated Society of Musicians (member/associate)
ISO Imperial Service Order
ISOCARP International Society of City and Regional Planning
ISPP International Society of Political Psychology
IStructE Institution of Structural Engineers
ITA Independent Television Authority
ITCA Independent Television Companies Association
ITN Independent TV News
ITV Independent Television
IUCN International Union for the Conservation of Nature and Natural Resources
IUPAC International Union of Pure and Applied Chemistry
IY Imperial Yeomanry

J

JAG Judge Advocate General
JCD Doctor of Canon Law (Juris Canonici Doctor)
Jcl Licentiate of Canon Law
JD Doctor of Jurisprudence
JDipMA Joint Diploma in Management Accounting Services
jl/s journal/s
JP Justice of the Peace
jr junior
JSM Johan Seita Mahkota (Malaysia)
jssc Qualified at Joint Services Staff College
Jt Joint
jtly jointly

K

k killed
ka killed in action
KAR King's African Rifles
KASG Knightly Association of St George the Martyr
KBE Knight Commander of the Order of the British Empire
KC King's Counsel
KCB Knight Commander of the Order of the Bath
KCH King's College Hospital
KCIE Knight Commander of the Order of the Indian Empire
KCMG Knight Commander of the Order of St Michael and St George
KCS King's College School
KCSG Knight Commander of St Gregory
KCSI Knight Commander of the Star of India
KCVO Knight Commander of the Royal Victorian Order
KDG King's Dragoon Guards
KEH King Edward's Horse Regiment
KEO King Edward's Own
KG Knight of the Order of the Garter
KGStJ Knight of Grace, Order of St John of Jerusalem (*see also* KSEJ)
KGVO King George V's Own
KHC Honorary Chaplain to the King
KHDS Honorary Dental Surgeon to the King
KHP Honorary Physician to the King
KHS Honorary Surgeon to the King
K-i-H Kaisar-i-Hind
KJStJ Knight of Justice, Order of St John of Jerusalem
KMN Kesatria Mangku Negara (Malaysian Decoration)
KORR King's Own Royal Regiment
KOSB King's Own Scottish Borderers
KOYLI King's Own Yorkshire Light Infantry
KP Knight of the Order of St Patrick
KPFSM King's Police and Fire Service Medal
KPM King's Police Medal
KRI King's Royal Irish
KRRC King's Royal Rifle Corps
KSG Knight of St Gregory
KSLI King's Shropshire Light Infantry
KStJ Knight of the Order of St John of Jerusalem
KT Knight of the Order of the Thistle
kt knighted (Knight Bachelor)

L

L Labour
LA Los Angeles
La Louisiana
LAA Light Anti-Aircraft
Lab Labour
LAC Leading Aircraftsman
LACOTS Local Authorities Co-ordination of Trading Standards Committee
LACSAB Local Authorities' Conditions of Service Advisory Board
LAH Licentiate of Apothecaries Hall, Dublin
LAMDA London Academy of Music and Dramatic Art
LBC London Broadcasting Co
LCC London County Council
LCDS London Contemporary Dance Studio
LCDT London Contemporary Dance Theatre
LCJ Lord Chief Justice
LCP Licentiate of the College of Preceptors
Ldr Leader
LDS Licentiate in Dental Surgery
LDV Local Defence Volunteers
LEA Local Education Authority
LEB London Electricity Board
lectr lecturer
LesL Licenciees Lettres
LF Land Forces
LG Life Guards
LGSM Licentiate, Guildhall School of Music and Drama
LH Light Horse
LI Light Infantry

Lib Liberal
LIBC Lloyd's Insurance Brokers' Committee
Lieut Lieutenant
LIFFE London International Financial Futures Exchange
Lit Literature
LittD Doctor of Letters (Cambridge & Dublin)
LLA Lady Literate in Arts
LLB Bachelor of Laws
LLCM Licentiate London College of Music
LLD Doctor of Laws
LLM Master of Laws
LM Licentiate in Midwifery
LMCC Licentiate of Medical Council of Canada
LMSSA Licentiate in Medicine and Surgery, Society of Apothecaries
LMTPI Legal Member of the Town Planning Institute
LNER London and North East Railway
LPTB London Passenger Transport Board
LRAM Licentiate of the Royal Academy of Music
LRCP Licentiate of the Royal College of Physicians
LRCPE Licentiate, Royal College of Physicians Edinburgh
LRCSE Licentiate, Royal College of Surgeons Edinburgh
LRFPS Licentiate of the Royal Faculty of Physicians and Surgeons (Glasgow)
LRIBA Licentiate of the Royal Institute of British Architects
LSA Licentiate of the Society of Apothecaries
LSCA London Society of Chartered Accountants
LSE London School of Economics
LSHTM London School of Hygiene and Tropical Medicine
LSO London Symphony Orchestra
LTA Lawn Tennis Association
LTCL Licentiate, Trinity College of Music, London
Lt-Col Lieutenant-Colonel
Ltcy Lieutenancy
Lt-Gen Lieutenant-General
LTh Licentiate in Theology
LU Liberal Unionist
LVO Lieutenant of the Royal Victorian Order
LWT London Weekend Television

M

m married, marriage
m dis marriage dissolved
MA Master of Arts; Military Assistant
MAAEM Member, American Association of Electrodiagnostic Medicine
MAAF Mediterranean Allied Air Forces
MACE Member, Association of Conference Executives
MAFF Ministry of Agriculture, Fisheries and Food
MAI Master of Engineering
MAIAA Member, American Institute of Aeronautics and Astronautics
Maj Major
Maj-Gen Major-General
mangr manager
Mans Mansions
MAOT Member of the Association of Occupational Therapists
MAP Ministry of Aircraft Production
MArch Master of Architecture
Marq Marquess
MASAE Member, American Society of Agricultural Engineers
MASCE Member, American Society of Civil Engineers
Mass Massachusetts (US)
MB Bachelor of Medicine
MBA Master of Business Administration
MBAE Member, British Academy of Experts
MBCS Member, British Computer Society
MBCHA Member, British Chiropody Association
MBE Member of the Order of the British Empire
MBEDA Member, Bureau of European Designers
MBHI Member of the British Horological Institute
MBII Member of the British Institute of Innkeeping
MBIM Member of the British Institute of Management
MBKS Member, British Kinematograph Society
MBOU Member, British Ornithologists' Union
MBSG Member British Society of Gastroenterology
MC Military Cross
MCAM Member, Institute of Communications, Advertising and Marketing
MCB Master of Clinical Biochemistry
MCC Marylebone Cricket Club; Metropolitan County Council
MCD Master of Civic Design
MCFA Member of the Cookery and Food Association
MChir Master in Surgery
MChOrth Master of Orthopaedic Surgery
MCIA Member, Chartered Institute of Arbitrators
MCIOB Member Chartered Institute of Building
MCIT Member of the Chartered Institute of Transport
MCom Master of Commerce
MConsE Member Association of Consulting Engineers
MCOphth Member, College of Ophthalmologists (formerly Faculty of Ophthalmologists, FacOpth, and Ophthalmic Society of UK, OSUK)
MCP Member of Colonial Parliament
MCPath Member of the College of Pathologists
MCPS Member, College of Physicians and Surgeons
MCSD Member Chartered Society of Designers
MCSP Member of the Chartered Society of Physiotherapy
MCT Member, Association of Corporate Treasurers
MD Doctor of Medicine
md managing director
MDC Metropolitan District Council
MDes Master of Design
MDS Master of Dental Surgery
ME Middle East
MEAF Middle East Air Force
MEC Member, Executive Council
MECAS Middle East Centre for Arab Studies
MECI Member, Institute of Employment Consultants
MEd Master of Education
Med Medical; medicine; Mediterranean
MEF Mediterranean Expeditionary Force
MEIC Member of the Engineering Institute of Canada
MELF Middle East Land Forces
memb member
Meml Memorial
MEP Member of the European Parliament
Met Metropolitan
MFARCS Member of the Faculty of Anaesthetists, Royal College of Surgeons
MFCM Member, Faculty of Community Medicine
MFH Master of Fox Hounds
MFHom Member, Faculty of Homeopathy
MFOM Member, Faculty of Occupational Medicine
mfr/mfrg manufacturer/manufacturing
MGC Machine Gun Corps
MGDS RCS Member in General Dental Surgery, Royal College of Surgeons
MGGS Major-General General Staff
Mgmnt Management
MGO Master General of the Ordnance
Mgr Monsignor
MGRA Major-General Royal Artillery
MGT Mine's a Gin and Tonic
MH Military Hospital

MHCIMA Member, Hotel Catering and Institutional Management Association
MHK Member of the House of Keys (IOM)
MHR Member of the House of Representatives
MI Military Intelligence
MIAeE Member, Institute of Aeronautical Engineers
MIBE Member of the Institution of British Engineers
MIBG Member, Institute of British Geographers
MIBiol Member, Institute of Biology
MICAS Member of the Institute of Chartered Accountants of Scotland
MICE Member, Institution of Civil Engineers
MICEI Member, Institution of Civil Engineers of Ireland
MICFM Member of the Institute of Charity Fund-Raising Managers
MIChemE Member of the Institution of Chemical Engineers
MIConsE Member Institute of Consulting Engineers
MIEA Member of the Institution of Engineers, Australia
MIED Member, Institution of Engineering Design
MIEE Member of the Institution of Electrical Engineers
MIEEE Member, Institute of Electrical and Electronics Engineers (NY)
MIEI Member of the Institute of Engineering Inspection
MIERE Member of the Institution of Electronic and Radio Engineers
MIES Member of the Institution of Engineers and Shipbuilders in Scotland
MIEx Member of the Institute of Export
MIFA Member, Institute of Field Archaeologists
MIH Member of the Institute of Housing
MIHT Member, Institute of Highways and Transportation
MIInfSc Member, Institute of Information Sciences
MIL Member, Institute of Linguists
Mil Military
MILE Member of the Institution of Locomotive Engineers
MIM Member, Institution of Metallurgists
MIMarE Member of the Institute of Marine Engineers
MIMC Member of the Institute of Management Consultants; Corporate Member of the Institute of Measurement and Control
MIMCE Member of the Institute of Municipal and County Engineers
MIME,MInstME Member of the Institution of Mining Engineers
MIMechE Member of the Institution of Mechanical Engineers
MIMI Member of the Institute of the Motor Industry
MIMM Member of the Institution of Mining & Metallurgy
Min Minister
MIngF Member, Danish Engineers' Association
Miny Ministry
MInstD Member of the Institute of Directors
MInstE Member, Institute of Energy
MInstGasE Member of the Institution of Gas Engineers
MInstHE Member of the Institution of Highway Engineers
MInstM Member of the Institute of Marketing
MInstMC Member, Institute of Measurement and Control
MInstMet Member of the Institute of Metals
MInstP Member of the Institute of Physics
MInst Pet Member of the Institute of Petroleum
MInst Pkg Member of the Institute of Packaging
MInstPS Member, Institute of Purchasing and Supply
MInstW Member of the Institution of Welding
MINucE Member of the Institution of Nuclear Engineers
MIOB Member of the Institute of Building
MIPA Member of the Institution of Practitioners in Advertising
MIPharmM Member, Institute of Pharmacy Management
MIPHE Member of the Institute of Public Health Engineers
MIPlantE Member of the Institute of Plant Engineers
MIPM Member of the Institute of Personnel Management
MIPR Member of the Institute of Public Relations
MIProdE Member of the Institution of Production Engineers
MIQ Member, Institute of Quarrying
MIRE Member of the Institution of Royal Engineers
MIS Member of the Institute of Statisticians
MISA Member, Institute of South African Architects
MISI Member of the Iron and Steel Institute
Miss Mississipi (USA)
MIStructE Member of the Institution of Structural Engineers
MIT Massachusetts Institute of Technology (USA)
MITD Member, Institute of Training and Development
MIWE Member of the Institution of Water Engineers
MJI Member of the Institute of Journalists
MJInstE Member of the Junior Engineers Institute
Mktg Marketing
ML Master of Laws
MLA Member, Legislative Assembly; Modern Language Association; Master in Landscape Architecture
MLC Member of the Legislative Council
MLitt Master of Literature
MLO Military Liaison Officer
MM Military Medal
MMC Monopolies and Mergers Commission
MMechE Master of Mechanical Engineering
MMet Master of Metallurgy
MMIM Member, Malaysian Institute of Management
MMS Member of the Institute of Management Services
MN Merchant Navy
MNECInst Member, North East Coast Institution of Engineers and Shipbuilders
MNI Member, Nautical Institute
MNYAS Member, New York Academy of Sciences
MNZIE Member of the New Zealand Institution of Engineers
Mo Missouri (USA)
MO Medical Officer
MOD Ministry of Defence
MOH Medical Officer of Health
MOI Ministry of Information
MOP Ministry of Power
MOS Ministry of Supply
MP Member of Parliament
MPBW Ministry of Public Building and Works
MPhil Master of Philosophy
MPO Management and Personnel Office
MPRISA Member of the Public Relations Institute of South Africa
MPS Member of the Pharmaceutical Society of Great Britain
MR Master of the Rolls
MRAC Member of the Royal Agricultural College
MRAD Member of the Royal Academy of Dancing
MRAeS Member, Royal Aeronautical Society
MRAS Member of the Royal Asiatic Society
MRC Medical Research Council
MRCGP Member, Royal College of General Practitioners
MRCOG Member of the Royal College of Obstetricians and Gynaecologists
MRCP Member of the Royal College of Physicians
MRCPath Member, Royal College of Pathologists
MRCPI Member, Royal College of Physicians in Ireland
MRCPsych Member, Royal College of Psychiatrists

MRCR Member, Royal College of Radiologists
MRCS Member of the Royal College of Surgeons
MRCVS Member of the Royal College of Veterinary Surgeons
MRI Member Royal Institution
MRIA Member of the Royal Irish Academy
MRIBA Member of the Royal Institute of British Architects
MRIC Member, Royal Institute of Chemistry
MRICS Member of the Royal Institution of Chartered Surveyors
MRIN Member of the Royal Institute of Navigation
MRINA Member of the Royal Institution of Naval Architects
MRO Member of the Register of Osteopaths
MRPharmS Member, Royal Pharmaceutical Society
MRS Market Research Society
MRSH Member of the Royal Society of Health
MRST Member of the Royal Society of Teachers
MRTPI Member of the Royal Town Planning Institute
MRUSI Member of the Royal United Service Institution
MRVA Member, Rating and Valuation Association
MS Master of Surgery; Manuscript; Master of Science (US)
MSAE Member Society of Automotive Engineers (US)
MSC Manpower Services Commission
MSc Master of Science
MScD Master of Dental Science
MScL Member, Society of Construction Law
MSE Member of the Society of Engineers
MSIA Member of the Society of Industrial Artists
MSIAD Member of the Society of Industrial Artists and Designers
MSM Meritorious Service Medal
MSocC Master of Social Sciences
MSSCh Member, School of Surgical Chiropody
MSST Member of the Society of Surveying Technicians
MTB Motor Torpedo Boat
MTG Member of the Translators' Guild
MTh Master of Theology
MTPI Member, Town Planning Institute
MTTA Machine Tool Trades Association
MusB Bachelor of Music
MusD Doctor of Music (Cambridge and Durham)
MusM Master of Music
MV Motor Vessel
MVO Member, Royal Victorian Order
MW Master of Wine
MWB Metropolitan Water Board
MWeldI Member, Welding Institute
MY Motor Yacht

N

N Nationalist; North
n nephew
NAAFI Navy, Army and Air Force Institutes
NABC National Association of Boys' Clubs
NAC National Agriculture Centre
NADFAS National Association of Decorative and Fine Arts Societies
NAG Northern Army Group
NAHT National Association of Head Teachers
NALGO National and Local Government Officers' Association
NAMH National Association for Mental Health
NAO National Audit Office
NAPM National Association of Paper Merchants
Nat National
Nat Lib National Liberal
NATCS National Air Traffic Control Services
NATFHE National Association of Teachers in Further and Higher Education
NATO North Atlantic Treaty Organisation
NBL National Book League
NBPI National Board for Prices and Incomes
NC Nautical College
NCA National Certificate of Agriculture
NCB National Coal Board
NCCI National Committee for Commonwealth Immigrants
NCCL National Council for Civil Liberties
NCLC National Council of Labour Colleges
NCO Non-commissioned officer
NCVO National Council for Voluntary Organisation
NDA National Diploma in Agriculture
NDC National Defence College
NDD National Diploma in Dairying; National Diploma in Design
NEAC New English Art Club
NEAF Near East Air Force
NEC National Executive Committee
NEDC National Economic Development Council
NEDO National Economic Development Office
NERC Natural Environment Research Council
NFL National Football League
NFS National Fire Service
NFU National Farmers' Union
NFWI National Federation of Women's Institutes
NHS National Health Service
NI Northern Ireland
NICG Nationalised Industries Chairmen's Group
NICS Northern Ireland Civil Service
NID Naval Intelligence Department
NIESR National Institute of Economic and Social Research
NILP Northern Ireland Labour Party
NJ New Jersey (USA)
NLF National Liberal Federation
NMCU National Metrological Coordinating Unit Committee
NP Notary Public
NRA National Rifle Association
NRDC National Research Development Corporation
ns Graduate of the Royal Naval Staff College, Greenwich
NS Nova Scotia
NSocIs Member Societé des Ingenieurs et Scientifiques de France
NSW New South Wales
NT National Theatre
NTDA National Trade Development Association
NUGMW National Union of General and Municipal Workers
NUI National University of Ireland
NUJ National Union of Journalists
NUM National Union of Mineworkers
NUPE National Union of Public Employees
NUR National Union of Railwaymen
NUS National Union of Students
NUT National Union of Teachers
NWFP North West Frontier Province
NY New York
NYBG New York Botanical Garden
NYC New York City
NZ New Zealand
NZEF New Zealand Expeditionary Force

O

o	only
O & O	Oriental and Occidental Steamship Co
OA	Officier d'Académie
OB	Order of Barbados
OBE	Officer of the Order of the British Empire
OC	Officer Commanding; Officer of the Order of Canada
OCF	Officiating Chaplain to the Forces
OCS	Officer Cadet School
OCTU	Officer Cadet Training Unit
ODA	Overseas Development Administration
ODI	Overseas Development Institute
ODM	Ministry of Overseas Development
OECD	Organisation for Economic Co-operation and Development
OEEC	Organisation for European Economic Co-operation
OER	Officers' Emergency Reserve
Offr	Officer
OFMCap	Order of Friars Minor Capuchin (Franciscan)
OFS	Orange Free State
OFT	Office of Fair Trading
OIC	Officer in Charge
OJ	Order of Jamaica
OM	Order of Merit
O & M	Organisation and Method
OMC	Oxford Military College
ON	Order of the Nation (Jamaica)
OND	Ordinary National Diploma
Oppn	Opposition
Ops	Operations
OR	Order of Roraima (Guyana)
Orch	Orchestra
Orgn	Organisation
ORS	Operational Research Society
OSB	Order of St Benedict
OSC	Graduate of Overseas Staff College
OSNC	Orient Steam Navigation Company
OSRD	Office of Scientific Research and Development
OStJ	Officer of the Order of St John of Jerusalem
OTC	Officers' Training Corps
OUBC	Oxford University Boat Club
OUDS	Oxford University Dramatic Society
OUP	Oxford University Press

P

pa	per annum
Pa	Pennsylvania (USA)
PA	Personal Assistant
pac	Passed final exam of advanced class Military College of Science
Paiforce	Palestine and Iraq Force
PAO	Prince Albert's Own
Parl	Parliament
Parly	Parliamentary
PBWS	President, British Watercolour Society
PC	Privy Councillor; Peace Commissioner (Ireland)
PCC	Parochial Church Council
PDSA	People's Dispensary for Sick Animals
PDTC	Professional Dancers' Teaching College
PE	Procurement Executive
PEI	Prince Edward Island
PEN	Poets, Playwrights, Editors, Essayists, Novelists Club
PEng	Registered Professional Engineer (Canada)
PEP	Political and Economic Planning
Perm	Permanent
PGA	Professional Golf Association
PGCE	Post Graduate Certificate of Education
PHAB	Physically Handicapped and Able Bodied
PhD	Doctor of Philosophy
PhL	Licentiate of Philosophy
PID	Political Intelligence Department
PIRA	Paper Industries Research Association
PLA	Port of London Authority
PLC, plc	Public Limited Company
Plen	Plenipotentiary
PLP	Parliamentary Labour Party
PM	Prime Minister
PMG	Postmaster-General
PMN	Pangilma Mangku Negara (Malaysia)
PMO	Principal Medical Officer
Pmr	Paymaster
PMRAFNS	Princess Mary's Royal Air Force Nursing Service
PNEU	Parents' National Educational Union
PNG	Papua New Guinea
PO	Pilot Officer; Post Office
POD	Personnel Operations Department
POEU	Post Office Engineering Union
Poly	Polytechnic
P & OSNCo	Peninsular and Oriental Steam Navigation Company
post grad	post graduate
POUNC	Post Office Users' National Council
POW	Prisoner of War
PPE	Philosophy, Politics and Economics (Oxford University)
PPRA	Past President of the Royal Academy
PPS	Parliamentary Private Secretary
PR	Public Relations
PRA	President of the Royal Academy
PRE	President of the Royal Society of Painters, Etchers and Engravers
Preb	Prebendary
Prep	Preparatory
Pres	President
prev	previously
Princ	Principal
PRO	Public Relations Officer; Public Records Office
Prodn	Production
Prodr	Producer
Prods	Products
Prof	Professor
prog/s	programme/s
Prov	Provost; Provincial
PRS	President of Royal Society
psa	Graduate of RAF Staff College
PSA	President of the Society of Antiquaries; Property Services Agency
psc	Staff College Graduate
PSD	Petty Session Division
psm	Certificate of the Royal Military School of Music
PSM	President of the Society of Miniaturists
PSNC	Pacific Steam Navigation Society
PSO	Principal Staff Officer
pt	part
PT	Physical Training
PTE	Passenger Transport Executive
ptnr	partner
pt/t	part time
Pty	Proprietary; Party
Pub	Public

Pubns Publications
PWD Public Works Department
PWO Prince of Wales's Own

Q

QAIMNS Queen Alexandra's Imperial Military Nursing Service
QALAS Qualified Associate of Land Agents' Society
QARANC Queen Alexandra's Royal Army Nursing Corps
QARNNS Queen Alexandra's Royal Naval Nursing Service
QC Queen's Counsel
QFSM Queen's Fire Service Medal for Distinguished Service
QGM Queens Gallantry Medal
QHC Honorary Chaplain to The Queen
QHDS Honorary Dental Surgeon to The Queen
QHNS Honorary Nursing Sister to The Queen
QHP Honorary Physician to The Queen
QHS Honorary Surgeon to The Queen
Qld Queensland
QMAAC Queen Mary's Army Auxiliary Corps
QMG Quartermaster-General
QO Qualified Officer
QOH Queen's Own Hussars
QPM Queen's Police Medal
qqv Qua Vide (which see-plural)
QRIH Queen's Royal Irish Hussars
QS Quarter Sessions
QSM Queen's Service Medal (NZ)
QSO Queen's Service Order (NZ)
qv Quod Vide (which see)

R

(R) Reserve
R & A Royal and Ancient (St Andrews) Club
R & D Research and Development
R of O Reserve of Officers
RA Royal Artillery; Royal Academician
RAAF Royal Australian Air Force
RAAMC Royal Australian Army Medical Corps
RAC Royal Armoured Corps; Royal Automobile Club; Royal Agricultural College
RACGP Royal Australian College of General Practitioners
RACP Royal Australasian College of Physicians
RACS Royal Australasian College of Surgeons
RADA Royal Academy of Dramatic Art
RADC Royal Army Dental Corps
RAE Royal Australian Engineers; Royal Aircraft Establishment
RAEC Royal Army Educational Corps
RAeS Royal Aeronautical Society
RAF Royal Air Force
RAFA Royal Air Force Association
RAFO Reserve of Air Force Officers
RAFRO Royal Air Force Reserve of Officers
RAFVR Royal Air Force Volunteer Reserve
RAI Royal Anthropological Institute
RAIA Royal Australian Institute of Architects
RAIC Royal Architectural Institute of Canada
RAM (member of) Royal Academy of Music
RAMC Royal Army Medical Corps
RAN Royal Australian Navy
RANR Royal Australian Naval Reserve
RANVR Royal Australian Naval Volunteer Reserve
RAOC Royal Army Ordnance Corps
RAPC Royal Army Pay Corps
RARO Regular Army Reserve of Officers
RAS Royal Agricultural Society; Royal Astronomical Society; Royal Asiatic Society
RASC Royal Army Service Corps (now RCT)
RASE Royal Agricultural Society of England
RAuxAF Royal Auxiliary Air Force
RAVC Royal Army Veterinary Corps
RB Rifle Brigade
RBA Royal Society of British Artists
RBC Royal British Colonial Society of Artists
RBK & C Royal Borough of Kensington and Chelsea
RBS Royal Society of British Sculptors
RC Roman Catholic
RCA Royal College of Art
RCAC Royal Canadian Armoured Corps
RCAF Royal Canadian Air Force
RCAMC Royal Canadian Army Medical Corps
RCDS Royal College of Defence Studies
RCGP Royal College of General Practitioners
RCHA Royal Canadian Horse Artillery
RCM Royal College of Music
RCN Royal Canadian Navy
RCNC Royal Corps of Naval Constructors
RCNR Royal Canadian Naval Reserve
RCNVR Royal Canadian Naval Volunteer Reserve
RCO Royal College of Organists
RCOG Royal College of Obstetricians and Gynaecologists
RCP Royal College of Physicians, London
RCPath Royal College of Pathologists
RCPE(d) Royal College of Physicians, Edinburgh
RCPSGlas Royal College of Physicians and Surgeons, Glasgow
RCPI Royal College of Physicians in Ireland
RCPsych Royal College of Psychiatrists
RCR Royal College of Radiologists
RCS Royal College of Surgeons of England; Royal Corps of Signals; Royal College of Science
RCSE(d) Royal College of Surgeons of Edinburgh
RCSI Royal College of Surgeons in Ireland
RCT Royal Corps of Transport
RCVS Royal College of Veterinary Surgeons
Rd Road
RD Royal Naval Reserve Officers' Decoration
RDA Royal Defence Academy
RDC Rural District Council
RDF Royal Dublin Fusiliers
RDI Royal Designer for Industry (RSA)
RE Royal Engineers; Fellow, Royal Society of Painter-Etchers and Engravers
Rear-Adm Rear-Admiral
Rec Recorder
Reg Regular
Regnl Regional
Regt Regiment
Regtl Regimental
Rels Relations
REME Royal Electrical and Mechanical Engineers
REngDes Registered Engineering Designer
Rep Representative
Repub Republic(an)
RERO Royal Engineers Reserve of Officers
Res Reserve; Research; Resident
RES Royal Empire Soc (Now Royal Commonwealth Soc)
ret retired
Rev Reverend
RFA Royal Field Artillery
RFC Royal Flying Corps; Rugby Football Club
RFU Rugby Football Union

RGA	Royal Garrison Artillery
RGI	Royal Glasgow Institute of Fine Arts
RGS	Royal Geographic Society
RHA	Royal Horse Artillery; Royal Hibernian Academy; Regional Health Authority
RHB	Regional Hospital Board
RHF	Royal Highland Fusiliers
RHG	Royal Horse Guards
RHR	Royal Highland Regiment
RHS	Royal Horticultural Society
RI	Royal Institute of Painters in Water Colours; Rhode Island
RIAI	Royal Institute of Architects of Ireland
RIAS	Royal Incorporation of Architects in Scotland
RIASC	Royal Indian Army Service Corps
RIBA	Royal Institute of British Architects
RIC	Royal Irish Constabulary
RICS	Royal Institute of Chartered Surveyors
RIF	Royal Irish Fusiliers
RIIA	Royal Institute of International Affairs
RIM	Royal Indian Marine
RIN	Royal Indian Navy
RINA	Royal Institute of Naval Architects
RINVR	Royal Indian Navy Volunteer Reserve
RIOP	Royal Institute of Oil Painters
RIPA	Royal Institute of Public Administration
RIPH & H	Royal Institute of Public Health and Hygiene
RIrR	Royal Irish Rifles
RL	Retired List
RLSS	Royal Life Saving Society
RM	Royal Marines
RMA	Royal Military Academy; Royal Marine Artillery
RMC	Royal Military College, Sandhurst (now Royal Military Academy)
RMCS	Royal Military College of Science
RMFVR	Royal Marine Forces Volunteer Reserve
RMLI	Royal Marine Light Infantry
RMO	Resident Medical Officer
RMP	Royal Military Police
RMR	Royal Marine Reserve
RMS	Royal Meterological Society
RN	Royal Navy
RNAS	Royal Naval Air Service
RNC	Royal Nautical College; Royal Naval College
RNCM	(Member of) Royal Northern College of Music
RND	Royal Naval Division
RNEC	Royal Naval Engineering College
RNIB	Royal National Institute for the Blind
RNID	Royal National Institute for the Deaf
RNLI	Royal National Lifeboat Institution
RNR	Royal Naval Reserve
RNSA	Royal Naval Sailing Association
RNSD	Royal Naval Store Depot
RNVR	Royal Naval Volunteer Reserve
RNVSR	Royal Naval Volunteer Supplementary Reserve
RNZADC	Royal New Zealand Army Dental Corps
RNZAF	Royal New Zealand Air Force
RNZN	Royal New Zealand Navy
RNZNVR	Royal New Zealand Naval Volunteer Reserve
ROC	Royal Observer Corps
ROI	Royal Institute of Painters in Oils
ROSPA	Royal Society for the Prevention of Accidents
R of O	Reserve of Officers
RP	Member of the Royal Society of Portrait Painters
RPC	Royal Pioneer Corps
RPMS	Royal Postgraduate Medical School
RPO	Royal Philharmonic Orchestra
RPS	Royal Photographic Society
RR	Royal Regiment
RRAF	Royal Rhodesian Air Force
RRC	Royal Red Cross
RRF	Royal Regiment of Fusiliers
RSA	Royal Scottish Academician; Royal Society of Arts
RSAA	Royal Society for Asian Affairs
RSAC	Royal Scottish Automobile Club
RSAMD	Royal Scottish Academy of Music and Drama (Diploma of)
RSBA	Royal Society of British Artists
RSC	Royal Shakespeare Co; Royal Society of Canada; Royal Society of Chemistry
RSE	Royal Society of Edinburgh
RSF	Royal Scots Fusiliers
RSL	Royal Society of Literature; Returned Services League of Australia
RSM	Royal Society of Medicine; Regimental Sergeant Major
RSMA	Royal Society of Marine Artists
RSME	Royal School of Military Engineers
RSPB	Royal Society for the Protection of Birds
RSPCA	Royal Society for the Prevention of Cruelty to Animals
RSPP	Royal Society of Portrait Painters
RSRE	Royal Signals and Radar Establishment
RSS	Royal Statistical Society
RSSPCC	Royal Scottish Society for the Prevention of Cruelty to Children
RSW	Royal Scottish Water Colours Society
Rt Hon	Right Honourable
Rt Rev	Right Reverend
RTC	Royal Tank Corps
RTE	Radio Telefis Eireann
RTO	Railway Transport Officer
RTPI	Royal Town Planning Institute
RTR	Royal Tank Regiment
RTS	Royal TV Society
RUC	Royal Ulster Constabulary
RUFC	Rugby Union Football Club
RUI	Royal University of Ireland
RUKBA	Royal United Kingdom Beneficent Association
RUR	Royal Ulster Regiment
RUSI	Royal United Services Institute
RVC	Royal Veterinary College
RVO	Regional Veterinary Officer
RWA	Member, Royal West of England Academy
RWAFF	Royal West African Frontier Force
RWAR	Royal West African Regiment
RWF	Royal Welch Fusiliers
RWS	Member, Royal Society of Painters in Water Colours
RYA	Royal Yachting Association
RYS	Royal Yacht Squadron
RZS	Royal Zoological Society

S

s	son
S	South; Scotland/Scottish (Peerages)
SA	South Africa; South Australia; Société Anonyme
SAAF	South African Air Force
sac	Qualified at Small Arms Technical Long Course
SAC	Senior Aircraftsman
SACEUR	Supreme Allied Commander Europe
SACLANT	Supreme Allied Commander Atlantic
SACSEA	Supreme Allied Commander, S E Asia
SADG	Societé des Architectes Diplomés par le Gouvernement
Salop	(now) Shropshire
SAS	Special Air Service
Sask	Saskatchewan
SASO	Senior Air Staff Officer
SAT	Senior Member, Association of Accounting Technicians
SATRO	Science & Technology Regional Organisation
SBAC	Society of British Aircraft Constructors, now Society of British Aerospace Companies

SBNO	Senior British Naval Officer
SBStJ	Serving Brother of the Order of St John of Jerusalem
ScD	Doctor of Science (Cambridge and Dublin)
SCF	Senior Chaplain to the Forces
SCGB	Ski Club of Great Britain
Sch	School
Sci	Science
SCI	Society of Chemical Engineering
SCL	Student in Civil Law
SCM	State Certified Midwife
SCONUL	Standing Conference of National and University Libraries
Scot	Scottish; Scotland
SCUA	Scottish Conservative Unionist Association
SDP	Social Democratic Party
SDLP	Social Democratic and Labour Party
SEAC	South East Asia Command
SEATAG	South East Asia Trade Advisory Group
Sec	Secretary
Secdy	Secondary
Sec-Gen	Secretary-General
Sen	Senator
SEN	State Enrolled Nurse
sep	separated
SERC	Science and Engineering Research Council
SERT	Society of Electronic and Radio Technicians
Serv	Service
SFInstE	Senior Fellow Institute of Energy
SFTA	Society of Film and Television Arts
SG	Solicitor-General
SGM	Sea Gallantry Medal
Sgt	Sergeant
SHA	Secondary Heads Association; Special Health Authority
SHAEF	Supreme Headquarters, Allied Expeditionary Force
SHAPE	Supreme Headquarters, Allied Powers Europe
SHHD	Scottish Home and Health Department
SIAD	Society of Industrial Artists and Designers
sis	sister
SJ	Society of Jesus (Jesuits)
SLD	Social and Liberal Democrats
SLDP	Social, Liberal and Democratic Party
slr	solicitor
SM	Service Medal of the Order of Canada; Master of Science (USA); Member, Society of Miniaturists
SME	School of Military Engineering
SMMT	Society of Motor Manufacturers and Traders
SMN	Seri Maharaja Mangku Negara (Malaysia)
SMO	Senior Medical Officer; Sovereign Military Order
SMOM	Sovereign Military Order of Malta
SNO	Senior Naval Officer
SNP	Scottish Nationalist Party
SNTS	Society for New Testament Studies
SO	Scottish Office; Staff Officer
SOAS	School of Oriental and African Studies
Soc	Society
SOE	Special Operations Executive
SOGAT	Society of Graphical and Allied Trades
Som	Somerset
SOTS	Society for Old Testament Studies
Sov	Sovereign
sp	sine prole (without issue)
SPCK	Society for Promoting Christian Knowledge
SPG	Society for the Propagation of the Gospel
SPNM	Society for the Promotion of New Music
SPSO	Senior Personnel Staff Officer
SPTL	Society of Public Teaching of Law
Sq	Square
Sqdn	Squadron
Sqdn Ldr	Squadron Leader
sr	senior
SR	Special Reserve; Southern Railway; Southern Region
SRC	Science Research Council
SRHE	Society for Research in Higher Education
SRN	State Registered Nurse
SRO	Supplementary Reserve of Officers
SSA	Society of Scottish Artists
SSAFA	Soldiers', Sailors', and Airmen's Families' Association
SSC	Solicitor, Supreme Court (Scotland); Short Service Commission
SSEES	School of Slavonic and East European Studies
SSO	Senior Supply Officer
SSRC	Social Science Research Council
SSStJ	Serving Sister of the Order of St John of Jerusalem
STA	Society of Technical Analysts
STC	Senior Training Corps
STD	Doctor of Sacred Theology
STh	Scholar in Theology
STL	Licenciate of Sacred Theology
STM	Master of Sacred Theology
STSO	Senior Technical Staff Officer
Subalt	Subaltern
Subs	Submarines (RN)
Subsid	Subsidiary
Subst	Substitute
suc	succeeded
Sup	Supérieure
Supp	Supplementary
Supt	Superintendent
Surgn	Surgeon
Survg	Surviving
SWB	South Wales Borderers
SWET	Society of West End Theatres

T

TA	Territorial Army
TA & VR	Territorial Army and Volunteer Reserve
TA & VRA	Territorial Army and Volunteer Reserve Association
TAA	Territorial Army Association; Tropical Agriculture Association
TAF	Tactical Air Force
T&AFA	Territorial and Auxiliary Forces Association
TANS	Territorial Army Nursing Service
TARO	Territorial Army Reserve of Officers
Tas	Tasmania
Tbnl	Tribunal
TC	Order of Trinity Cross (Trinidad and Tobago)
TCCB	Test and County Cricket Board
TD	Territorial Officers' Decoration; Teachta Dala (member of the Dail Parliament of Eire)
Tech	Technical
Technol	Technology; Technological
TEM	Territorial Efficiency Medal
Temp	Temporary
TEng	Technician Engineer
TES	Times Educational Supplement
TF	Territorial Force
TGWU	Transport and General Workers' Union
Theol	Theological
ThM	Master of Theology
TLS	Times Literary Supplement
TMA	Theatre Managers Association
Tport	Transport
Transfd	Transferred
TRE	Telecommunications Research Establishment
Treasy	Treasury
Treas	Treasurer
Trg	Training

TRH Their Royal Highnesses
Tst Trust
Tstee Trustee
TUC Trades Union Congress
TV Television
TVEI Technical and Vocational Educational Initiative

U

U Unionist
UAE United Arab Emirates
UAR United Arab Republic
UC University College
UCCA Universities Central Council on Admissions
UCH University College Hospital
UCL University College London
UCLA University of California at Los Angeles
UCNS Universities' Council for Non-Academic Staff
UCNW University College of North Wales
UCS University College School
UCW University College of Wales
UDC Urban District Council
UDF Union Defence Force; Ulster Defence Force
UDR Ulster Defence Regiment
UDS United Drapery Stores
UDUP Ulster Democratic Unionist Party
UEA University of East Anglia
UFC Universities Funding Council
UFO Unidentified Flying Object
UGC University Grants Committee
UHS University High School
UK United Kingdom
UKAEA United Kingdom Atomic Energy Authority
UKLF United Kingdom Land Forces
UMDS United Medical and Dental Schools
UMIST University of Manchester Institute of Science and Technology
UN United Nations
UNA United Nations Association
unc uncle
UNCTAD United Nations Commission for Trade and Development
UNDP United Nations Development Programme
UNESCO United Nations Educational, Scientific and Cultural Organisation
UNFAO United Nations Food and Agricultural Organisation
UNICE Union des Industries de la Communauté Européenne
UNICEF United Nations International Children's Emergency Fund
UNIDROIT Institut International pour l'Unification du Droit Privé
Univ University
UNO United Nations Organisation
UNRRA United Nations Relief and Rehabilitation Administration
UP Uttar Pradesh; United Provinces; United Presbyterian
UPNI Unionist Party of Northern Ireland
URCC United Kingdom Central Council for Nurses, Midwives and Health Visitors
URSI Union Radio-Scientifique Internationale
US United States
USA United States of America
USAF United States Air Force
USDAW Union of Shop, Distributive and Allied Workers
USM Unlisted Securities Market
USMC United States Military College
USN United States Navy
USNR United States Naval Reserve
USSR Union of Soviet Socialist Republics
UTC University Training Corps
UWIST University of Wales Institute of Science and Technology

V

v versus (against)
V & A Victoria and Albert (Museum)
VA Lady of the Order of Victoria and Albert
Va Virginia
VAD Voluntary Aid Detachment
VAT Value Added Tax
VBF Veterinary Benevolent Fund
VC Victoria Cross
VCAS Vice-Chief of the Air Staff
VCC Vintage Car Club
VD Volunteer Officers' Decoration (now VRD)
VDC Volunteer Defence Corps
Ven Venerable
Very Rev Very Reverend
Vet Veterinary
Visc Viscount
VM Victory Medal
VMH Victoria Medal of Honour (Royal Horticultural Society)
VO Veterinary Officer
Vol Volunteer
VRD Volunteer Reserve Officers' Decoration
VSCC Vintage Sports Car Club
VSO Voluntary Service Overseas

W

w wife
W West
WA Western Australia
WAAF Women's Auxiliary Air Force (now WRAF)
WEA Worker's Educational Association
WEU Western European Union
WFN World Fund for Nature, see World Wildlife Fund
WFTU World Federation of Trade Unions
WHO World Health Organisation
WI West Indies
wid widow
WIPO World Intellectual Property Organisation
Wm William
WNO Welsh National Opera
WNSM Welsh National School of Medicine
WO War Office
WRAC Women's Royal Army Corps
WRAF Women's Royal Air Force
WRNR Women's Royal Naval Reserve
WRNS Women's Royal Naval Service
WRVS Women's Royal Voluntary Service (formerly WVS)
WS Writer to the Signet
WVS Women's Voluntary Service
WWI First World War
WWII Second World War
WWF World Wildlife Fund

Y

Yeo Yeomanry
YHA Youth Hostels' Association
YMCA Young Men's Christian Association
yr younger
yst youngest
YWCA Young Women's Christian Association

PROFESSIONAL AND COMMERCIAL LISTINGS

Accountancy And Property Management

ACCOUNTANCY AND PROPERTY MANAGEMENT SERVICES
2 Westbourne Place, Hove
East Sussex BN8 4GN
Tel: 0278 27160

Accountants

ALLENDALE HARVEY & CO AND CONRADI AND MORRISON AND CO
Chartered Accountants
33 London Road
Southborough, Tunbridge Wells
Kent TN4 0PB
Tel: 0892 39267/543374 *Fax*: 0892 510174

BAKER TILLY
Chartered Accountants
2 Newman Road
Bromley, Kent BR1 1RJ
Tel: 081 290 5522 *Fax*: 081 460 9156

CLARK WHITEHILL
Chartered Accountants
10 Palace Avenue, Maidstone
Kent ME15 6NF
Tel: 0622 692122 *Fax*: 0622 691399

NORMAN COX AND ASHBY
Grosvenor Lodge, 72 Grosvenor Road
Tunbridge Wells, Kent TN1 2AZ
Tel: 0892 22551

DAVID EAST AND CO
Chartered Accountants
95 High Street, Beckenham, Kent
Tel: 081 650 1044

FINN-KELCEY AND CHAPMAN
Ashford House, The Tufton Centre
Ashford, Kent TN23 1YB
Tel: 0233 629255 *Fax*: 0233 43901

DANIEL KHAN AND CO
Certified Accountants
Ibis House, 14 Canterbury Street
Gillingham, Kent ME7 5TX
Tel: 0634 574639 *Fax*: 0634 31992

GEOFFREY KNIGHTS AND CO
11 Kingsgate, 111 The Drive
Hove, East Sussex BN3 6FU
Tel: 0273 737109 *Fax*: 0273 737109

LEGG AND CO
12 Dover Street, Canterbury
Kent CT1 3HD
Tel: 0227 462211 *Fax*: 0227 762213

LEGG AND CO
St Georges House
103 Tonbridge Road
Maidstone, Kent ME16 8JN
Tel: 0622 671717 *Fax*: 0622 691434

MACADIE AND CO
Chartered Accountants
Suite 5
Talland Parade, High Street
Seaford, East Sussex BN25 1PJ
Tel: 0323 892122 *Fax*: 0323 898268

E G McDONALD AND CO
Holden House, Biddenden
Kent TN27 8EX
Tel: 0580 291799

NORRIE STOKES AND PERRETT
Chartered Accountants
Wharf House
Medway Wharf Road, Tonbridge
Kent TN9 1RE
Tel: 0732 771567 *Fax*: 0732 359418

B S ROBINSON AND CO
27A London Road, Sevenoaks
Kent TN13 1AR
Tel: 0732 460513

GARY SARGEANT AND COMPANY
Chislehurst Business Centre
1 Bromley Lane
Chislehurst
Kent
Tel: 081 295 1360 *Fax*: 081 467 0950

SCOTT ELLISON
35 Watling Street
Canterbury, Kent CT1 2UH
Tel: 0227 763500 *Fax*: 0227 762365

THOMPSON AND HUNTER
43-45 High Street
Sevenoaks, Kent TN13 1JF
Tel: 0732 740575 *Fax*: 0732 740804

Advertising Agencies

ADLAB PARTNERSHIP
The Cutting Rooms
Durgates, Wadhurst
East Sussex TN5 6DF
Tel: 0892 884455 *Fax*: 0892 882880

BUNGEY PARKES ADVERTISING
8-10 Neals Yard, Covent Garden
London WC2
Tel: 071 836 6845 *Fax*: 071 831 1348

CONCEPT DESIGN AND MEDIA LIMITED
32 King Edward Road
Maidstone, Kent
Tel: 0622 692762 *Fax*: 0622 672816

QUINTETE LIMITED
Mill House, 42 Mill Place
Chislehurst, Kent
Tel: 081 467 1195 *Fax*: 081 467 0855

Air Charter

BIGGIN HILL EXECUTIVE AVIATION LIMITED
Building 509, Biggin Hill Airport
Westerham, Kent TN16 3BN
Tel: 0959 76137

Antiquarian Bookshop

FOXED AND BOUND BOOKSHOP
8 West Street, West Malling
Kent ME19 6QZ
Tel: 0732 847886

Antique Dealers

ABBYBILLE
10 Northwold Road
London N16
Tel: 071 923 1053

COTTAGE STYLE ANTIQUES
24 Bill Street
Rochester, Kent
Tel: 0634 717623

DAVID BOWDENS ANTIQUES
Stand 303, Gray's Antique Market
58 Davies Street
London W1Y 1LB
Tel: 071 495 1773 *Fax*: 071 495 8599

DICKENS OLD CURIOSITY SHOP
London's Oldest Shop Built in 1567
13-14 Portsmouth Street
London WC2A 2ES
Tel: 071 405 9891

GROSVENOR PRINTS
28-32 Shelton Street
Covent Garden
London WC2H 9HP
Tel: 071 836 1979

KEITH SKEEL ANTIQUES
94-98 Islington High Street
London N1 8EG
Tel: 071 226 7012 *Fax*: 071 226 0935

MEI LENG COLLECTION
124 New Bond Street
London W1
Tel: 071 373 1069

PENNY LAMPARD
31-33 High Street
Headcorn, Kent
TN27 9SE
Tel: 0622 890682

RON'S EMPORIUM
98 Church Lane
Sholden, Deal
Kent CT24 9OL
Tel: 0304 374784

SQUIRES ANTIQUES
Jacob Yard, Preston Street
Faversham, Kent
Tel: 0795 531503

TAYLOR-SMITH ANTIQUES
4 The Grange, High Street
Westerham, Kent TN6 1AH
Tel: 0959 63100

THE IMPERIAL LEATHER AND SWORD CO LIMITED
Chenil Galleries
181-183 Kings Road
London SW3
Tel: 071 351 5903

TIME AND CHIMES
10A North Street, Strood
Kent ME2 4SH
Tel: 0634 715574

TRADITIONAL PINE FURNITURE
248 Seabrook Road, Seabrook
Hythe, Kent CT21 5RQ
Tel: 0303 239931

Antique Furniture Restoration

AVENUE ANTIQUES
39 Littlestone Road
New Romney
Kent TN28 8LN
Tel: 0679 62720

MICHAEL LAMB ANTIQUES AND RESTORATION
The White Horse
2 Church Street
Minster, Ramsgate
Kent CT12 4BX
Tel: 0843 821666

NEOCLASSIC
No 16 Old Surrenden Manor
Bethersden, Kent TN26 3DL
Tel: 023382 502

Antique Jewellers

FRANÇOISE BROWN
329-330 Gray's Antique Market
London W1
Tel: 071 355 1109

JOHN JOSEPH – ANTIQUE JEWELLERS
Antique Edwardian and Deco
John's Antiques
Gray's Antique Centre
Stand 346, 58 Davies Street, London W1
Tel: 071 629 1140 *Fax*: 071 491 8599

PAYNE AND SON (SILVERSMITHS) LIMITED
37 High Street, Tunbridge Wells
Kent TN1 1XL
Tel: 0892 25874

Antique Restoration

BENEDICT RESTORATIONS
(Rear of 20) Camden Road
Tunbridge Wells, Kent
Tel: 0892 548095

FENS RESTORATION
46 Lots Road, London SW10
Tel: 071 352 9883

Antique Valuers

RICHARD F MOY
SPREAD EAGLE ANTIQUES
No 9 Nevada Street, London SE10 9JL
Tel: 081 305 1666

Architects

CHAPMAN AND HANSON
Chartered Architects & Interior Designers
29 Widmore Road, Bromley, Kent BR1 1RT
Tel: 081 460 8834 *Fax*: 081 460 8838

KEITH DAY PARTNERSHIP LIMITED
6 Ambley Green
Gillingham Business Park
Gillingham, Kent ME8 0NJ
Tel: 0634 379982

PHILLIP THOMAS ASSOCIATES
Chartered Architects
105 St Johns Hill
Sevenoaks, Kent TN13 3PE
Tel: 0732 457600 *Fax*: 0732 740149

JULIUS A WEEKS
Chartered Architects
Durlaston, Western Road
Crowborough, East Sussex TN6 3EH
Tel: 0892 655615 *Fax*: 0892 667760

Artists and Galleries

BOURNE FINE ART
English and Scottish Prints 1800–1990
14 Mason's Yard, Duke Street
St James's, London SW1 6BN
Tel: 071 930 4215/6 *Fax*: 071 839 8307

BRIAN LEWIS
Royal Star Arcade
Maidstone, Kent ME14 1JL
Tel: 0622 764811/0732 841419

BROMLEY GALLERIES LIMITED
37 East Street, Bromley
Kent BR1 1QW
Tel: 081 466 6682

198 GALLERY
Contemporary Art by Black Artists
198 Railton Road, Herne Hill
London SE24 0LU
Tel: 071 978 8309 *Fax*: 071 738 7018

DOUWES FINE ART LIMITED
38 Duke Street, St James's
London SW1Y 6DF
Tel: 071 839 5795/071 839 5904

GABRIS ARTS
16 Weavers Lane, Sevenoaks
Kent TN14 5BT
Tel: 0732 456527

JUST PAINTINGS
11 Maritime Close
Medway City Estate, Frindsbury
Rochester, Kent ME2 4DJ
Tel: 0634 290792

PEARTREE STUDIOS
Fine Arts, Paintings and Etchings
Harwich Street, Whitstable
Kent CT5 4HU
Tel: 0227 770875 *Fax*: 0227 264062

SLOMAN AND PETTITT ART CENTRE
33 High Street, Maidstone
Kent ME14 1JF
Tel: 0622 757908

Asset Management

MIDLAND PERSONAL ASSET MANAGEMENT
Royal Victoria House
51-55 The Pantiles
Tunbridge Wells, Kent TN5 2TE
Tel: 0703 229929

Auctioneers

F L PETTMAN
Bonhams of Knightsbridge Kent Agent
48–52 Athelstan Road
Margate, Kent CT9 2BH
Tel: 0843 220234 *Fax*: 0843 293085

MID KENT SPORTS AUCTIONS
Forge Armoury, Lenham Heath
Nr Maidstone, Kent ME17 2BP
Tel: 0622 859165

PHILLIPS FINE ART AUCTIONEERS
11 Bayle Parade, Folkestone
Kent
Tel: 0303 45555

ROSEBERY'S
The Old Railway Booking Hall
Crystal Palace Station Road
London SE19 2AZ
Tel: 081 778 4024

Bakers/Confectioners

WEEKS OF GOUDHURST LIMITED
High Street, Goudhurst
Cranbrook, Kent TN17 1AG
Tel: 0580 211380 *Fax*: 0580 212121

Boat Hire/Charter

LIVETT'S LAUNCHES
PO Box 288, Chislehurst, Kent BR7 5SP
Tel: 081 468 7201

THAMES LEISURE
Highwood, Mead Road
Chislehurst, Kent BR7 6AD
Tel: 081 467 6314 *Fax*: 081 467 2060

Booksellers

JOHN ADAMS BOOKS
10 Angel Walk, Tonbridge, Kent TN9 1TJ
Tel: 0732 353519

THE OLD GALLERY BOOKSHOP
125 High Street, Hythe, Kent
Tel: 0303 269339

Car Hire (Chauffeur Driven)

AA EXECUTIVE (Estab 1977)
Kent and Westminster
8 Luddesdon Road
Erith, Kent DA8 1NG
Tel: 081 303 5815

ABACUS CHAUFFEUR SERVICE
29 Prospect Road, Southborough
Tunbridge Wells, Kent TN4 0EN
Tel: 0892 26581

BETJEMANN CHAUFFEUR SERVICES LIMITED
137 Julien Court, Regency Walk
Shirley, Croydon CR0 7UU
Tel: 081 776 0263

BROMLEY TRAVELWAYS
76 Palace Road, Bromley
Kent BR1 3JX
Tel: 081 313 1222/081 460 6473

ELBA PRIVATE CAR HIRE
40 Winchester Road, Hawkhurst
Kent TN18 4DE
Tel: 0580 752934

EXECUTIVE LIMOUSINES UK
PO Box 112, West Malling
Kent ME19 5DZ
Tel: 0732 870539 *Fax*: 0732 846398

FAIRWAY CHAUFFEURS SERVICE
Room 9, Camden House
North Farm Road
Tunbridge Wells, Kent TN2 3DH
Tel: 0892 511913

PRE-FLIGHT TRAVEL
(See advertisement)
The Airport Transfer Company
Chauffeur and Airport Services
3 Willow Grove, Chislehurst
Kent BR7 5BN
Tel: 081 295 1705 *Fax*: 081 295 1012

RYEWOOD CHAUFFEUR DRIVE
15 Ryewood Cottage
Rye Lane, Dunton Green
Sevenoaks, Kent
Tel: 0732 462386

Car Showrooms

ASHWAL GARAGE LIMITED
Wilsley Pound, Cranbrook
Kent TN17 2HR
Tel: 0580 713262 *Fax*: 0580 713312

BOURNE ROAD MAIDSTONE MAZDA
92-100 Upper Stone Street
Maidstone, Kent ME15 6HF
Tel: 0622 753096

GRAYSTONE GROUP (Sevenoaks)
128 Seal Road, Sevenoaks
Kent TN14 5AY
Tel: 0732 451337 *Fax*: 0732 452506

JOHN FOWLER
SAAB GARAGES LIMITED
195 Linton Road, Loose
Maidstone, Kent ME15 0AS
Tel: 0622 746629 *Fax*: 0622 744448

Catering Specialists

JANET SAMPSON
Hollands Farm, Chart Sutton
Nr Maidstone, Kent ME17 3ET
Tel: 0622 842127

Charities

CHEST HEART AND STROKE ASSOCIATION
C H S A House, Whitecross Street
London EC1Y 8JJ
Tel: 071 490 7999 *Fax*: 071 490 2686

MALCOLM SARGENT CANCER FUND
FOR CHILDREN
Dept DP, 14 Abingdon Road
London W8 6AF
Tel: 071 937 4548 *Fax*: 071 376 1193

THE CARE FOUNDATION LIMITED
Hospice at Home
Michael Tetley Hall, Sandhurst Road
Tunbridge Wells, Kent TN2 3JS
Tel: 0892 544877

THE LILIAN FAITHFULL HOMES
Northcroft House
Malvern Road
Cheltenham GL50 2NR
Tel: 0242 512935

Clubs

LONDON FLIGHT CENTRE
(HEADCORN) LIMITED
Headcorn Airfield, Headcorn
Ashford, Kent TN27 9HX
Tel: 0622 890997 *Fax*: 0622 890876

Computer and Business Consultancies

THE L M R COMPUTER CONSULTANCY
19 South Walk, West Wickham
Kent BR4 9JA
Tel: 081 462 7740 *Fax*: 081 462 7739

Corporate Images

ANDERSEN DISTRIBUTION LIMITED
Lodge Cottage, Court Lodge, Harrietsham
Nr Maidstone, Kent ME17 1AS
Tel: 0622 850249

Curtain Makers and Designers

PAMELA BURGESS
22A Market Street, Sandwich, Kent
Tel: 0304 613517 *Fax*: 0304 613517

FARNBOROUGH INTERIORS LIMITED
Blind and Curtain Makers
Piells Yard, Bourne Road
Bromley, Kent BR2 9NT
Tel: 081 313 0888 *Fax*: 081 313 0891

FINBAR SOFT FURNISHINGS
Bay 8, Constellation Works
153 Hamilton Road, London SE27 9SE
Tel: 081 670 5642

CURTAIN DESIGN BY MARGARET SHARPE
73 Culverley Road, Catford
London SE6 2LD
Tel: 081 698 1307

Dental Surgeons

P M BARNARD
71 Station Road, Birchington
Kent CT7 9RE
Tel: 0843 42153

DAVIES AND ROBERTSON
The Dental Health Centre
7 South Street
Lydd, Romney Marsh
Kent TN29 9DQ
Tel: 0679 20826

A C MURCH AND L R D GREEN
71 Broad Street, Canterbury, Kent CT1 2LS
Tel: 0227 768368

N AND MRS P A PATSIAS LDS RCS AND ASSOCIATES
14 Bromley Road, Beckenham
Kent BR3 2JE
Tel: 081 650 1209

M J L SYKES, D J ARWOLD, B L PILC, A WARD DAVIES
42 College Road, Maidstone
Kent ME15 6YF
Tel: 0622 752340

H H TOH AND MISS J HOGAN
Dental Surgery
3 Priory Road, Dover, Kent CT17 9RQ
Tel: 0304 206558

Design Consultants

PENTAD DESIGN CONSULTANTS
108-110 High Street, Rainham
Kent ME8 8AR
Tel: 0634 377271 *Fax*: 0634 388445

Design Consultants/PR

PEARSON PR LIMITED
Graphic House, Unit 2
Thayers Farm Road, Beckenham
Kent BR3 4LZ
Tel: 081 663 3504

Detective Agencies

PRIVATE INTELLIGENCE SERVICES
330 Kilburn Lane, London W9 3EF
Tel: 081 968 0227 *Fax*: 081 968 0194

A P RICH AND PARTNERS
Ex CID New Scotland Yard
Tunbridge Wells, Kent TN3 0NT
Tel: 0892 862973 *Mobile*: 0860 213996

Electronics

LAWTRONICS LIMITED
Unit 4, Block 3, Enterprise Way
Edenbridge, Kent TN8 6HF
Tel: 0732 865191

Engineering Services

ENGINEERS

KETLON (UK) LIMITED
Dana Estate, Paddock Wood
Tonbridge, Kent TN12 6UU
Tel: 0892 8355555

CONSULTING ENGINEERS

MERVYN HAYES ASSOCIATES
Chartered Building Services
Consulting Engineers
1 Bradford Street, Tonbridge
Kent TN9 1DU
Tel: 0732 770748 *Fax*: 0732 770910

JOHN HEMSLEY ASSOCIATES LIMITED
5 Clanricarde Gardens, Tunbridge Wells
Kent TN1 1PG
Tel: 0892 515500 *Fax*: 0892 515501

CONSULTING STRUCTURAL ENGINEERS

COLIN TOMS AND PARTNERS
Watermill House, Chipstead
Sevenoaks, Kent TN13 2RY
Tel: 0732 740195 *Fax*: 0732 740649

Engravers

ENGRAVASALES
27 James Street, Maidstone
Kent ME14 2UP
Tel: 0622 677056/7

MR RODNEY JAMES RIGBY
(See advertisement)
Heathleigh House, Maidstone Road
Horsmonden, Kent TN12 8JJ
Tel: 0892 72 3075

Estate Agents

FITZ HOFFMAN AND CO
130 Rye Lane, London SE15 4RE
Tel: 071 639 4144 *Fax*: 071 277 7351

FOX AND SONS
27 Mount Pleasant, Tunbridge Wells
Kent TN1 1NP
Tel: 0892 515252 *Fax*: 0892 515868

LINAYS COMMERCIAL
269A High Street, Orpington
Kent BR6 0NW
Tel: 0689 875511 *Fax*: 0689 31416

PARK COOPER (OVERSEAS) LIMITED
120 Croydon Road, Beckenham
Kent BR3 4DF
Tel: 081 650 9429 *Fax*: 081 663 3929

VILLAGE PROPERTIES
Independent Estate Agents
78 Church Street, Cliffe Village
Nr Rochester, Kent ME3 7PP
Tel: 0634 220426

WOOD AND PILCHER
23 High Street, Tunbridge Wells
Kent TN1 1UT
Tel: 0892 511211 *Fax*: 0892 515906

Financial Advisors

ADVISORY AND BROKERAGE SERVICES LIMITED
35 Watling Street, Canterbury
Kent CT1 2UH
Tel: 0227 762380 *Fax*: 0227 762365

ALLIED ANGLO FINANCIAL SERVICES LIMITED
11 Albion Place, Maidstone
Kent ME14 5DY
Tel: 0622 765005 *Fax*: 0622 687926

BLACKMORE HEATH LIMITED
6-8 Park Road, Sittingbourne
Kent ME10 1DR
Tel: 0795 421844 *Fax*: 0795 420684

NEWMAN HOUGHTON AND CO
Regency House, 25 High Street
Tunbridge Wells, Kent TN1 1UT
Tel: 0892 548255

PROGRESSIVE MANAGEMENT
A FIMBRA Member
33 Station Road, Rainham, Kent ME8 7RS
Tel: 0634 373757 *Fax*: 0634 364556

Financial Consultants

CHANNEL FINANCIAL SERVICES
Shalom, Queensdown Road
Kingsdown, Deal
Kent CT14 8EF
Tel: 0304 362700 *Fax*: 0304 360039

CHARTWELL FINANCE
44 High Street, Seal, Nr Sevenoaks
Kent TN15 0AP
Tel: 0732 62994 *Fax*: 0732 63626

DIAMOND FINANCIAL CONSULTANTS
Nightingale Cottage, Stone Cross
Bilsington, Kent TN25 7JN
Tel: 0233 732281 *Fax*: 0233 733172

F AND M ASSOCIATES
68 Franklin Road, Gillingham
Kent ME7 4DF
Tel: 0634 280775/6 *Fax*: 0634 281011

R AND S ASSOCIATES
1 Middleton Buildings, Langham Street
London W1P 7PF
Tel: 071 323 2824 *Fax*: 071 636 8359

Financial Services

LADY HELEN C KENNEDY
VAN BERGEN FINANCIAL SERVICES
49 Windsor Drive, Chelsfield
Nr Sevenoaks, Kent
Tel: 0689 62769/0732 770679

Firework Manufacturers

THEATRICAL PYROTECHNICS (FIREWORKS) LIMITED
The Loop, Manston Airport
Ramsgate, Kent CT12 5DE
Tel: 0843 823545 *Fax*: 0843 822655

Florists

BLOOMS (OF KENT) FLORISTS
3 Twydall Green, Gillingham, Kent ME8 6JY
Tel: 0634 33505 *Fax*: 0634 31902

C DRURY FLORIST
118 Maidstone Road, Rochester
Kent ME1 3DT
Tel: 0634 843024

Food

FRIDAY'S (CRANBROOK) LIMITED
Chequer Tree Farm, Benenden Road
Cranbrook, Kent TN17 3PN
Tel: 0580 714014

Food Importers and Distributors

H AND T WALKER LIMITED
Walker House, London Road, Riverhead
Sevenoaks, Kent TN13
Tel: 0732 450712 *Fax*: 0732 459288

Funeral Directors

LEWIS SOLOMON FUNERAL SERVICE
19 Darnley Road, Gravesend
Kent DA11 0RZ
Tel: 0474 352261

Furniture Storage and Overseas Removal

KIDDS SERVICES (YORKSHIRE)
Head Office, Bessingby Industrial Estate
Bridlington YO16 4SJ
Tel: 0262 672842 *Fax*: 0262 603312
Telex: 527249

Garden Services

SOUTH EAST WATER GARDENS
Bellers Bush (A256), Sandwich
Kent CT13 0DG
Tel: 0304 614963

Genealogists

ACHIEVEMENTS LIMITED
80-82 North Gate, Canterbury, Kent CT1 1BA
Tel: 0227 462618 *Fax*: 0227 765617

Gold and Silversmiths

MARTIN WILDE
Mill Yard Craft Centre, Mill Yard
Swan Street, West Malling, Kent
Tel: 0732 870665

Golf and Country Clubs

BROOME PARK GOLF AND COUNTRY CLUB
Broome Park, Nr Canterbury, Kent CT4 6QX
Tel: 0227 831701 *Fax*: 0227 831973

Hospices

THE CARE FOUNDATION LIMITED
Hospice at Home
Michael Tetley Hall, Sandhurst Road
Tunbridge Wells, Kent TN2 3JS
Tel: 0892 544877

Hotels

BRIDGE HOTEL
13-15 St Mildred's Road, Westgate on Sea
Thanet, Kent CP8 8RE
Tel: 0843 31023

BUCKHURST PLACE HOTEL
Buckhurst Lane, Wadhurst
East Sussex TN5 6JY
Tel: 0892 883181

COODEN RESORT HOTEL
Cooden Beach, Bexhill
East Sussex TN39 4TT
Tel: 04243 2281 *Fax*: 04243 6142

DANEHURST
41 Lower Green Road
Rusthall, Tunbridge Wells
Kent TN4 8TW
Tel: 0892 27739

DOVER MOAT HOUSE
Townwall Street, Dover
Kent CT16 1SZ
Tel: 0304 203270 *Fax*: 0304 213230

EASTWELL MANOR
Eastwell Park, Boughton Lees
Ashford, Kent TN25 4HR
Tel: 0233 635751 *Fax*: 0233 635530

THE MIDDLE HOUSE HOTEL
High Street, Mayfield
East Sussex TN20 6AB
Tel: 0435 872146

THE ROYAL OAK
Main Street, Beckley
East Sussex TN31 6RJ
Tel: 0797 26312

RUSSELL HOTEL
136 Boxley Road, Maidstone
Kent ME14 2AE
Tel: 0622 692221 *Fax*: 0622 762084

RUSSELL HOTEL
80 London Road
Tunbridge Wells
Kent TN1 1DZ
Tel: 0892 544833 *Fax*: 0892 515846

THE SPA HOTEL
Mount Ephraim, Royal Tunbridge Wells
Kent TN4 8XJ
Tel: 0892 20331 *Fax*: 0892 510575

WATERINGBURY HOTEL
Tonbridge Road, Wateringbury
Nr Maidstone, Kent ME18 5NS
Tel: 0622 812632 *Fax*: 0622 812720

WHITE LION HOTEL
High Street, Tenterden
Kent TN3 6BD
Tel: 05806 5077

Insurance Brokers

BLACKMORE HEATH LIMITED
6-8 Park Road, Sittingbourne
Kent ME10 1DR
Tel: 0795 421844 *Fax*: 0795 420686

D B INSURANCE BROKERS LIMITED
84 King Street, Maidstone
Kent ME14 1BH
Tel: 0622 676113 *Fax*: 0622 677887

E C PARKER AND CO LIMITED
34 St Georges Place, Canterbury
Kent CT1 1XB
Tel: 0227 451133 *Fax*: 0227 766027

HATCH BATTEN
42 High Street, West Malling
Kent
Tel: 0732 844111

LAWRENCE INSURANCE GROUP
43-45 High Street, Sevenoaks
Kent TN13 1JF
Tel: 0732 740777 *Fax*: 0732 740804

P T MARTIN AND CO
101 High Street, Rochester
Kent ME1 1OA
Tel: 0634 842365 *Fax*: 0634 826573
Telex: 0634 965937

OSMOND DAVIS AND CO LIMITED
Minerva House, Bordyke
Tonbridge, Kent
Tel: 0732 366611 *Fax*: 0732 770972

SHORTER AND CO
5 Walderslade Centre, Walderslade Road
Chatham, Kent
Tel: 0634 861578 *Fax*: 0634 864532

TUFTON AND FARMER LIMITED
29 High Street, Maidstone
Kent ME14 1JF
Tel: 0622 679351 *Fax*: 0622 678644

Insurance Consultants

THANET INSURANCE SERVICES LIMITED
85 Station Road, Birchington
Kent CT7 9RE
Tel: 0843 43244 *Fax*: 0843 47571

Insurance Loss Assessors

INSURANCE CLAIMS NEGOTIATORS
27 Montague Place, Brighton BN2 1JE
Tel: 0273 689199 *Fax*: 0273 571850

Interior Design and Soft Furnishings

JOHNSON AND BAKER
Interior Designers and
Specialist Soft Furnishers
3 Lyndhurst Square, London SE15 5AR
Tel: 071 708 1035

Kennels

CUCKOOWOOD BREEDING AND BOARDING KENNELS
Cold Harbour Road, Otterden
Nr Lenham, Maidstone, Kent ME17 2EA
Tel: 0233 712050

WOODLANDS (KENNELS AND ANIMAL PSYCHOLOGIST)
Grays Road, Westerham Hill
Westerham, Kent TN16 2HU
Tel: 0959 72201

Landscape Specialists

C D BROWN (LANDSCAPING) LIMITED
Sole Suppliers – Willow Wall Sound
Barrier System
Udimore Farm, Chapel Lane, Ightham
Sevenoaks, Kent TN15 9AQ
Tel: 0732 884286 *Fax*: 0732 886102

DAVID STEAD
1 Park Hill Road, Otford
Sevenoaks, Kent TN14 5QH
Tel: 09592 4267

Legal Services

BARRIER LEGAL SERVICES
PO Box 612, London SE7 8AW
Tel: 081 858 4909

VENETIA CARPENTER
Company Law
Wanshurst Green Farm, Marden, Tonbridge
Tel: 0622 832280

Leisure Complexes

CHALLENGE OUTDOOR PURSUITS CENTRE
Court Lodge Down, Hawkenbury Road
Bells Yew Green, Tunbridge Wells, Kent
Tel: 0892 35432 *Fax*: 081 688 7041

LARKFIELD LEISURE CENTRE
New Hythe Lane, Larkfield
Kent ME20 6RH
Tel: 0622 719345 *Fax*: 0622 710822

Marketing and Communications

JOHNSON NORGATE RANSON
Marketing Consultants
27 Gabriels Hill, Maidstone
Kent ME15 6HX
Tel: 0622 690334 *Fax*: 0622 671976

L C F AND PARTNERS
Droveway House, 1-3 The Droveway
St Margaret's Bay, Kent
Tel: 0304 853102

Marquee Hire

FOUR JAYS MARQUEES
Barling Farm, East Sutton
Maidstone, Kent ME17 3DX
Tel: 0622 843135 *Fax*: 0622 842218

KENT MARQUEES
Marquee and Associated Equipment Hire
Grazings, Perry Wood, Selling
Faversham, Kent ME13 9SF
Tel and Fax: 0227 750620

MANOR MARQUEE HIRE
22 Ragstone Road, Bearsted
Maidstone, Kent ME15 8PA
Tel: 0622 38973

ROYAL EVENT MARQUEES
Hartmere, Hartfield, East Sussex TN7 4DJ
Tel: 0892 770864 *Fax*: 0892 770848

Medical Services

CONSULTANT DERMATOLOGISTS

DOCTOR W A D GRIFFITHS, MA
MD (Cantab), FRCP
6 Harley Street, London W1N 1AA
Tel: 071 631 3459

DOCTOR PETER ARTHUR JOHN SMITH
MB, FRCP
82 Harley Street, London W1N 1AE
Tel: 071 935 9727

CONSULTANT PHYSICIANS

DOCTOR ANDREW STRIGNER
MBBS, MFhom.
17 Harley Street, London W1N 1DA
Tel: 071 935 4543

CONSULTANT PSYCHIATRISTS

DOCTOR GRAHAM PETER SHEPPARD
Ticehurst House Hospital
Ticehurst, East Sussex TN5 7HU
and
152 Harley Street, London
Tel: 0580 200391

CONSULTANT UROLOGISTS

MR O'DONOGHUE
99 Harley Street, London W1N 1DF
Tel: 071 935 6200 *Fax*: 071 224 6177

CONSULTANT SKIN PHYSICIANS AND SURGEONS

DOCTOR J D EVERALL, FRCP (N.O.N.D)
122 Harley Street, London W1N 1AG
Tel: 071 935 3468

CONSULTANT SURGEONS AND ONCOLOGISTS

MR R D ROSIN, MS, FRCS, FRCS(ED)
6 Harley Street, London W1N 1AA
Tel: 071 631 3447

COSMETIC SURGEONS

MR J R SCHETRUMPF
17 Harley Street, London W1
Tel: 071 637 5005 *Fax*: 071 323 5314

NUTRITION AND DIETETIC CONSULTANTS

DOCTOR A R LEEDS
Nutrition and Dietetic
97 Harley Street, London W1N 1DF
Tel: 071 487 3740

OPHTHALMIC SURGEONS

MR E W GEOFFREY DAVIES, FRCS, FCOphth
Consultant Ophthalmic Surgeon
127 Harley Street, London W1N 1DJ
Tel: 071 580 1631

MEDICAL HERBALISTS

CANTERBURY CLINIC OF
HERBAL MEDICINE
15 Ethelbert Road, Canterbury
Kent CT1 3ND
Tel: 0227 766797

MEDICAL PRACTITIONERS

DOCTOR C R AYLING, MB BS, FRCOG
Corner House, 30 Limes Road
Folkestone, Kent CT19 4AU
Tel: 0303 275500

DOCTOR K E BURTON WEST
127 Harley Street
London W1N 1DJ
Tel: 071 935 8570

DOCTOR MALCOLM CARRUTHERS, MD FRCPath, MRCGP
Positive Health Centre
101 Harley Street
London W1N 1DF
Tel: 071 935 1811 *Fax*: 071 935 6659

DOCTOR RONALD D'SILVA
130 Harley Street
London SW1
Tel: 071 580 1336

DOCTOR LOUIS FREEDMAN
D/21 Devonshire Place
London W1
Tel: 071 935 7665

DOCTOR M M HENRY
106 Harley Street
London W1N 1AF
Tel: 071 935 3889

DOCTOR LOUIS HUGHES
99 Harley Street
London W1
Tel: 071 935 9004

DOCTOR I KASHI
55 Harley Street
London W1N 1DD
Tel: 071 636 0942

DOCTOR ANTHONY RICHARD LEEDS MB BS, MSC
97 Harley Street
London W1N 1DF
Tel: 071 487 3740

DOCTORS GEORGE LEWITH JULIAN KENYON AND DAVID DOWSON
The Centre for the Study of
Complementary Medicine
6 Upper Harley Street
London W1N 4PS
Tel: 071 935 7848

DOCTOR P J O'CONNOR
Saint Benedict
Bacombe Lane
Wendover HP22 6EQ
Tel: 071 935 8033

DOCTOR SISIR RAY
74 Harley Street
London W1N 1AE
Tel: 071 580 1444

MR MICHAEL PATRICK STEARNS
97 Harley Street
London W1N 1DF
Tel: 071 487 4695

MR THOMAS GORDON WADSWORTH
152 Harley Street
London W1N 1HH
Tel: 071 723 5785/071 935 1858

MR HARVEY WAGMAN
40 Harley Street
London W1N 1AB
Tel: 071 580 9944

MR KENNETH JOHN WATERS
42 Harley Street
London W1N 1AB
Tel: 071 255 1308

DOCTOR ADRIAN WHITESON
58A Wimpole Street
London W1M 7DE
Tel: 071 935 3351/071 580 3637

DOCTOR DONALD WINSTOCK
Middlesex Hospital
Mortimer Street
London W1N 8AA
Tel: 071 380 9022

PHYSICIANS

ALTERNATIVE HEALTH RETREAT
Little Pitchford Manor
Dean Street, East Farleigh
Kent ME15 0PS
Tel: 0622 729011

DOCTOR M F A BROOK, MB.FRC.pysc.DPM
79 Harley Street, London W1N 1DE
Tel: 071 935 3000

DOCTOR C B CROFT
55 Harley Street, London W1N 1DD
Tel: 071 580 2426

DOCTOR RICHARD LANCASTER
54 Wimpole Street, London W1M 7DE
Tel: 071 486 7797

DOCTOR Y SOLIMAN
21 Wimpole Street, London W1M 7AD
Tel: 071 637 1565

ORTHOPAEDIC PHYSICIAN

DOCTOR BERNARD WATKIN
62 Wimpole Street, London W1M 7DE
Tel: 071 486 8684

Opticians

KEITH BROWN
23-27 Swan Street, West Malling, Kent
Tel: 0732 848384

Osteopaths

COACH HOUSE CLINIC
115 High Street
Tenterden, Kent TN30 6SN
Tel: 0580 63481/0303 267374

BRIAN COOK OSTEOPATH
49 Shooters Hill, London SE18 3RL
Tel: 081 319 2410

DAVID R GALE, DO, MRO
Registered Osteopath
Hall House, King Street
Sandwich, Kent CT13 9BY
Tel: 0304 612141

GILLINGHAM CLINIC OF COMPLEMENTARY MEDICINE
50 Watling Street, Gillingham
Kent ME7 2YN
Tel: 0634 576292

KORTH FLEMMING AND ASSOCIATES
Registered Osteopaths
159 St Johns Road, Tunbridge Wells
Kent TN4 9UP
Tel: 0892 21134

COLLIN J WINER
31 Weymouth Street, London W1N 3FJ
Tel: 071 580 6939

Physiotherapists

THE ANDREWS PHYSIOTHERAPY CLINIC
High Street, Horam, Heathfield
East Sussex TN21 0EY
Tel: 04353 2429

ASHFORD PHYSIOTHERAPY CLINIC
49 Albert Road, Ashford
Kent TN24 8NU
Tel: 0233 622575

MS ANN DOHERTY
FOLKESTONE PHYSIOTHERAPY AND SPORTS INJURY CLINIC
Chartered Physiotherapists
11A Earls Avenue, Folkestone
Kent CT20 2HW
Tel: 0303 43727

HYTHE PHYSIOTHERAPY CENTRE
6 Scrape Street, Hythe, Kent
Tel: 0303 266470

MRS J W KENNEDY, MCSP, SRP
Ivy Court Surgery, Tenterden, Kent
Tel: 0580 63666

JEANNE T ROGERS
1 Clanricarde Gardens
Tunbridge Wells, Kent
Tel: 0892 39802

Office Products

FACIT LIMITED
Computers, Printers, Typewriters
and Calculators
Maidstone Road
Rochester, Kent ME1 3QN
Tel: 0634 830008 *Fax*: 0634 841825

Outfitters

DEAKIN AND SONS (Estab 1856)
School Outfitters, Menswear and
Protective Clothing
1-2 and 18 Sun Street
17/18 Guildhall Street
Canterbury, Kent CT1 2HX
Tel: 0227 462116

SIMMONDS AND SONS
64 Calverly Road, Tunbridge Wells
Kent TN1 2UG
Tel: 0892 510123 *Fax*: 0892 512123

Packaging

GARD PLASTICASES LIMITED
Unit 12
Branbridges Industrial Estate
East Peckham, Tonbridge
Kent TN12 5HF
Tel: 0622 871887 *Fax*: 0622 871895
Telex: 96374

Paper Conservation

CASTLE FINE ART STUDIO
26 Castle Street, Dover
Kent CT16 1PW
Tel: 0304 206360

Photographers

MARIA BUCKINGHAM, BSc, LMPA
Portrait and Weddings
Photography By Maria Studios
224A High Street, Bromley
Kent BR1 1PQ
Tel: 081 313 0235

STEPHEN CURTIS PHOTOGRAPHY
16 The Avenue, Eastbourne
East Sussex BN21 3YA
Tel: 0323 24888

DELAINE STUDIOS
39 Rushey Green
London SE6 4AS
Tel: 081 698 3111

MARK HOWELLS, LBIPP, LMPA
Level Gold Photos
7 The Broadway Centre
Maidstone, Kent ME16 8PS
Tel: 0622 690616

DAVID J JACOBS
2 Falcon Avenue, Bickley
Kent
Tel: 081 460 3194

MALLING PHOTOGRAPHIC
14-16 Swan Street
West Malling
Kent ME19 6LP
Tel: 0732 870474

THOMAS NEILE PHOTOGRAPHERS
Commercial and Industrial
South Street Industrial Estate
Whitstable, Kent
Tel: 0227 272650 *Fax*: 0227 770233

POSITIVE IMAGE PHOTOGRAPHERS
124 Woolwich High Street, London SE18
Tel: 081 854 5294

GEOFFREY SHAW. Case MPA
ITS/Lido Photographics
Lido, Ethelbert Terrace
Margate, Kent CT9 1RX
Tel: 0843 290653/34892

MELVIN STILLCOCK PHOTOGRAPHY
41 Park Road, Sittingbourne
Kent ME10 1DX
Tel: 0795 426856

SWEATMAN HEDGELAND LIMITED
Commercial and Industrial
Unit 6, Bircholt Road
Parkwood Industrial Estate
Maidstone, Kent ME15 9XP
Tel: 0622 754142 *Fax*: 0622 753950

Photographic Studios

IMPTON STUDIOS
319 Boxley Road, Penenden Heath
Maidstone, Kent ME14 2HN
Tel: 0622 758897

Piano Manufacturers, Restorers and Tuners

JOHN BROADWOOD AND SONS LIMITED
45A High Street, Stony Stratford
Milton Keynes MK11 1AA
Tel: 0908 561927/560520

JAMES CROUCH
Piano Tuners and Repairers
The Retreat, Plaxtol Lane, Plaxtol
Nr Sevenoaks, Kent TN15 0PZ
Tel: 0732 810207

OAST PIANOS
Tuners and Repairers
Forsham Oast, Rolvenden, Kent TN17 4PP
Tel: 0580 241245

Picture and Photograph Framers

ANTHONY DAWSON FINE ART
SRAD Gallery
65 Sheen Lane, East Sheen
London SW14 8AD
Tel: 081 878 8800 *Fax*: 081 878 8744

THE ROWLEY GALLERY
115 Kensington Church Street
London W8 7LN
Tel: 071 727 6495

JOHN SPEER
The Old Town Picture Framer
Salters, 11 High Street
Hastings TN34 3EY
Tel: 0424 422332

VILLA FRAMING
8 Windmill Street, London W1P 1HS
Tel: 071 323 5347

Picture Cleaners and Restorers

ROBERT MITCHELL OIL PAINTING CONSERVATION
The Studio, 114 Station Road
Chertsey, Surrey KT16 8BT
Tel: 0932 567874

SOUTH EAST CONSERVATION CENTRE
5 North Street
St Leonards on Sea TN38 0EY
Tel: 0424 431157 *Fax*: 0424 431807

TRADE PICTURE SERVICES LIMITED
Neckinger Mills
162-164 Abbey Street, London SE1 2AN
Tel: 071 237 4388

Printers

PATERSON PRINTING LIMITED
21 Chapman Way, Tunbridge Wells
Kent TN2 3EF
Tel: 0892 511212 *Fax*: 0892 28224

ROBERT STACE LIMITED
Longfield Road, Tunbridge Wells
Kent TN2 3ET
Tel: 0892 24225

Property Management Residential Lettings

A AND E SERVICES (BROMLEY) LIMITED
106 Beckenham Lane, Shortlands
Bromley, Kent BR2 0DW
Tel: 081 290 0148 *Fax*: 081 313 0808

Public Relations

B D PUBLIC RELATIONS
Tollgate House, Biddenden
Kent TN27 8JN
Tel: 0580 291560 *Fax*: 0580 292080

QUINTETE LIMITED
Mill House, 42 Mill Place
Chislehurst, Kent
Tel: 081 467 1195 *Fax*: 081 467 0855

Residential and Retirement Homes

BEULAH LODGE
1 Beulah Road, Tunbridge Wells
Kent TN1 2NP
Tel: 0892 549448

CLARENCE NURSING HOME
3-4 Clarence Road, Tunbridge Wells
Kent TN1 1HD
Tel: 0892 25794

DARENTH GRANGE
Darenth Hill, Darenth
Nr Dartford, Kent DA2 7QR
Tel: 0322 224423

COLIN N V GILLIGAN, BSc, MSc
Proprietor
Eversleigh Residential Home
13 Sundridge Avenue, Bromley
Kent BR1 2PU
Tel: 081 464 2998

HARPWOOD RESIDENTIAL REST HOME
Seven Mile Lane
Wrotham Heath
Kent TN15 7RY
Tel: 0732 882282

HASLINGTON RESIDENTIAL HOME
Cobham Terrace
Bean Road
Greenhithe
Kent DA9 9JB
Tel: 0322 843229

HOLYWELL PARK
Hodsoll Street
Ash Cum Ridley
Nr Sevenoaks, Kent
Tel: 0732 822215

KENT RESIDENTIAL CARE HOMES ASSOCIATION
68 Sidney Road
Borstal
Rochester
Kent ME1 3HQ
Tel: 0634 409360

LAVENDERS
Lavenders Road
West Malling
Nr Maidstone
Kent ME19 6HP
Tel: 0732 844744

THE OLD DOWNS RESIDENTIAL HOME
Castle Hill, Hartley
Longfield
Kent DA3 7AA
Tel: 04747 2146

WAINFYLDE HOUSE
51 Madeira Park
Tunbridge Wells
Kent TN2 5SY
Tel: 0892 30404

THE WHITE HOUSE
95 Maidstone Road
Chatham
Kent ME4 6HY
Tel: 0634 848547

Restaurants

AKASH TANDOORI RESTAURANT
24 Crowborough Hill
Jarvis Brook
Crowborough
East Sussex
Tel: 0892 661881/664647

ALCASH TANDOORI
42 High Street
Chatham
Kent ME4 4DS
Tel: 0634 846742

BEVERLEY'S RESTAURANT
60 Central Parade
Herne Bay
Kent CT6 5JG
Tel: 0227 374115

THE DEVIL'S KNEADING TROUGH RESTAURANT
Wye Downs, Hastingleigh
Ashford, Kent TN25 5HE
Tel: 0233 813212

THE FOUR LANTERNS
6 Market Place
Margate
Kent CT9 1EN
Tel: 0843 293034

GREENMAN RESTAURANT
Longfield Hill
Longfield
Nr Dartford
Kent DA3 7AS
Tel: 04747 2234

L'ESCARGOT
22 High Street
Herne Bay
Kent CT6 5LH
Tel: 0227 372876

LIGHT OF INDIA
Burlton House Complex
Townwall Street, Dover
Kent CT16 1JR
Tel: 0304 210666

MARCHESI BROTHERS RESTAURANT
18 Albion Street
Broadstairs
Kent CT10 1LU
Tel: 0843 62481 *Fax*: 0843 61509
Telex: 967561

THE MARY ROSE
40-50 High Street
St Mary Cray, Kent
Tel: 0689 871917

THE OAST RESTAURANT
Shoreham Road
Otford, Kent
Tel: 0959 23335

REIDS RESTAURANT
Specialising in French Cuisine
4 Church Street
St Pauls
Canterbury
Kent CT1 1NH
Tel: 0227 456655

THACKERAY'S HOUSE
85 London Road
TunbridgeWells
Kent TN1 1EA
Tel: 0892 511921

TUDOR TAVERN
11-12 Burgate
Canterbury
Kent CT2 2HG
Tel: 0227 462163

THE WEAVERS RESTAURANT
London Road
Southborough
Kent TN4 0PU
Tel: 0892 29896

YE MAYDES RESTAURANT
15 High Street
Biddenden
Ashford
Kent TN27 8AL
Tel: 0580 291306

Riding Schools and Stables

PLUM PUDDING EQUESTRIAN CENTRE
Plum Pudding Island
Dane Road
Birchington, Kent
Tel: 0843 47142

WESTERHAM RIDING CENTRE LIMITED
Grays Road
Westerham Hill, Westerham
Kent TN16 2HB
Tel: 0959 72241

Saddlers and Gunsmiths

THE SADDLERY AND GUN ROOM
368 Main Road, Biggin Hill
Kent TN16 2HN
Tel: 0959 63100

School Outfitters

FORSTERS OUTFITTERS
17-19 East Street, Sittingbourne
Kent ME10 4VQ
Tel: 0795 472947 *Fax*: 0795 428898

FORSTERS OUTFITTERS
77 Preston Street, Faversham
Kent
Tel: 0795 537044

FORSTERS OUTFITTERS
62 Pudding Lane, Maidstone
Kent
Tel: 0795 753900

FOR YOUNGSTERS
16 High Street, Sheerness, Kent
Tel: 0795 660765

Schools

ARCHBISHOP MICHAEL RAMSEY C E SCHOOL
Farmers Road, London SE5 0UB
Tel: 071 701 4166 *Fax*: 071 701 8461

ASHGROVE SCHOOL
116 Widmore Road
Bromley, Kent BR1 3BE
Tel: 081 460 4143

BISHOP CHALLONER SCHOOL
Boys Senior Public School
Bromley Road, Shortlands
Kent BR2 0BZ
Tel: 081 460 3546

CRANBROOK SCHOOL
Co-Ed Voluntary School
Waterloo Road, Cranbrook
Kent TN17 3JD
Tel: 0580 712163

MAYFIELD COLLEGE
Mayfield, East Sussex TN20 6PL
Tel: 0435 872041

ST AUGUSTINE'S COLLEGE
Independent School
Canterbury Road
Westgate on Sea
Kent CT8 8NL
Tel: 0843 32441 *Fax*: 0843 35579

Shooting Schools

BARBURY SHOOTING
65 Windsor Road, Swindon SN3 1JU
Tel: 0793 530564/0836 282312
Fax: 0793 481448

Sign Makers

ACRYNEON LIMITED
Leigh Road Haine Industrial Estate
Ramsgate, Kent CT12 5EU
Tel: 0843 597555

Silver Plating

C J PLATING
42 Manor Road
Hastings, East Sussex TN34 3LL
Tel: 0424 437595

Solicitors

BAILEY AND COGGER
139 High Street, Tonbridge
Kent TN10 1DH
Tel: 0732 353305 *Fax*: 0732 359678

BASSETTS SOLICITORS
156 High Street, Rochester
Kent ME1 1ET
Tel: 0634 400161 *Fax*: 0634 408251

NICHOLAS BENNETT AND CO
21 Market Street, Sandwich
Kent CT13 9DA
Tel: 0304 617988 *Fax*: 0304 612464

DAKERS GREEN BRETT
125 High Street, Strood
Kent ME2 4TJ
Tel: 0634 290929 *Fax*: 0634 290398

GIRLINGS SOLICITORS
Head Office
3-6 Dane John, Canterbury
Kent CT1 2UG
Tel: 0227 768374 *Fax*: 0227 450498

HARRIS CHRISTOPHER AND CO
202 High Street, Sheerness
Kent ME12 1UQ
Tel: 0795 661521 *Fax*: 0795 661487

LEE BOLTON AND LEE
8-9 The Precincts, Canterbury
Kent CT1 2EE
Tel: 0227 761261 *Fax*: 0227 762232

MARSLAND AND BARBER
51 Hawley Square, Margate
Kent CT9 1NY
Tel: 0843 221466 *Fax*: 0843 290283

SKINGLEY AND CO
161 High Street, Tonbridge
Kent TN9 1BX
Tel: 0732 770760 *Fax*: 0732 770425

Stamps and Coins

LING OF LONDON
52 King Street, Ramsgate, Kent CT11 8NT
Tel: 0843 593562

THE STAMP CENTRE
Stamp Dealers
8 Mark Lane, Eastbourne
East Sussex BN21 4RJ
Tel: 0323 645418

Stockbrokers

COBBOLD ROACH LIMITED
5 York Road, Tunbridge Wells
Kent TN1 1JX
Tel: 0892 515156 *Fax*: 0892 543121
DX 3956

Surveyors

BUILDING & VALUATION SURVEYORS & PROPERTY MANAGEMENT SURVEYORS

W J STEVENS AND ASSOCIATES
521-523 Upper Elmers End Road
Beckenham, Kent BR3 3DE
Tel: 081 650 9157 *Fax*: 081 633 3717

CHARTERED SURVEYORS

SHEFFORD'S
Chartered Surveyors and Estate Agents
13 London Road, Sevenoaks
Kent TN13 1AH
Tel: 0732 450866

Swimming Pools

FOUR JAYS (COURTS AND POOLS) LIMITED
Barling Farm, East Sutton
Maidstone, Kent ME17 3DX
Tel: 0622 843996 *Fax*: 0622 842218

Tailors

ALTERATION TAILORS OF KENT
25 Turner Road, Tonbridge, Kent TN10 4AG
Tel: 0732 353603

GEES EXCLUSIVE
155 Lee High, Lewisham, London SE13
Tel: 081 318 9887

SUSSEX COUNTRYMAN
68 High Street, Steyning
West Sussex BN44 3RD
Tel: 0903 812261

Telecommunications

T.C.S.I. LIMITED
Independent Communications
Consultants and Installers
Brooklands House, Willow Grove
Chislehurst, Kent BR7 5BU
Tel: 081 467 0909 *Fax*: 081 295 1094

Toastmasters

LESLIE HILL
National Association of Toastmasters
St Mawgan, 12 Chipstead Park, Chipstead
Sevenoaks, Kent TN13 2SN
Tel: 0732 455739

Travel Agents

JETLIFE HOLIDAYS
33 Swanley Centre, Swanley, Kent BR8 7TL
Tel: 0322 614801 *Fax*: 0322 615172
Telex: 24187

B G TRAVEL
Handley House, 62 High Street
West Malling, Kent ME19 6LU
Tel: 0732 840361 *Fax*: 0732 842029

Tree Surgeons

J A DOLWIN, B.Sc.(For.), F.Abor.A., M.I.C.For.
DOLWIN AND GRAY
Alpha House, Crowborough Hill
Crowborough, East Sussex TN6 2EG
Tel: 0892 664612 *Fax*: 0892 663636

MR D W G DRURY
12 The Green, Sevenoaks, Kent TN13 3RH
Tel: 0732 454392

KENT AND SUSSEX TREE SURGEONS
Coldbath Farm, Tea Garden Lane
High Rocks, Tunbridge Wells
Kent TN3 9JH
Tel: 0892 515400

Warehouses

LEIANE'S SECONDHAND WAREHOUSE
The Old Mill, London Road
Dover, Kent
Tel: 0304 203961

Welding Equipment and Consumables

GAUGE AND WELDING EQUIPMENT REPAIRS LIMITED
8-14 St Vincents Road, Dartford
Kent DA1 1YA
Tel: 0322 270036

Wine Merchants

BRAMLEY FERRY SUPPLIES LIMITED
Wine and Spirit Merchants (Wholesale)
Duke of Clarence Trading Centre
Sheerness, Kent ME12 1RN
Tel: 0795 580001 *Fax*: 0795 580002
Telex: 966203 *LEBRAM*

KENNETH A BROWN
86 Ennersdale Road, London SE13
Tel: 081 852 5518

STAPYLTON FLETCHER LIMITED
Wine Merchants and Shippers
3 Haslemere, Sutton Road
Maidstone, Kent ME15 9NE
Tel: 0622 691188 *Fax*: 0622 763863

Woodland Management

WOODLAND PLUS
Dibgate Farm, Chevening Road
Sundridge, Sevenoaks, Kent
Tel: 0959 65483